ILLUSTRATED ENCYCLOPEDIA OF ESSENTIAL KNOWLEDGE

ILLUSTRATED ENCYCLOPEDIA OF ESSENTIAL KNOWLEDGE
was edited and designed by The Reader's Digest Association (Pty) Limited, Cape Town.

ISBN 1-874912-40-8

READER'S DIGEST

ILLUSTRATED ENCYCLOPEDIA OF ESSENTIAL KNOWLEDGE

Published by The Reader's Digest Association (Pty) Limited, Cape Town

WHAT EVERYONE NEEDS TO KNOW

The *Illustrated Encyclopedia of Essential Knowledge* is the perfect antidote to dry works of reference – it contains the kind of information that people feel they ought to know, selecting nuggets of essential knowledge from the morass of information with which we seem to be bombarded daily. Reflecting the culture of today, the book provides a diverse and lively guide to all those disparate subjects which well-informed people want to understand and discuss – from Leonardo da Vinci to junk bonds. The range of the book is vast; the academic gravitas of Aristotle or quantum mechanics is balanced by the fun of James Bond or *The Pink Panther.* It travels lightly through the arts, business, food and drink, geography, history, music, philosophy, politics, science and sport. Its 23 thematic chapters contain some 6 000 clear, concise entries brought to life by more than 800 colour photographs, pictures and diagrams that capture key moments and explain essential facts.

The *Illustrated Encyclopedia of Essential Knowledge* does not contain obscure or highly technical information; its editors have also rejected subjects which were considered too obvious or too well known. The choices of entries may well be considered contro-

versial; inevitably, people will argue about inclusions and omissions, echoing the many debates between editors, experts and laypeople as the book evolved. The simple aim has been to create a reference book that is as entertaining as it is useful – a compendium of general knowledge spiced with intriguing facts.

HOW TO USE THE BOOK

Within each of the 23 sections, entries have been compiled in alphabetical order. The pronunciation of difficult words is explained clearly, without resort to accents or strange symbols. Cross-references to other entries in the same section appear in SMALL CAPITAL LETTERS; if precededby a ▹ symbol, they appear in a different section and should be looked up in the comprehensive index. The index also lists a host of subsidiary subjects which are referred to in the course of main entries. A ❖ symbol at the end of an entry prefaces an offbeat, sometimes amusing sidelight on a subject – that French fashion designer Coco Chanel made the sun tan fashionable, for example, or that Namibia's world-rated sprinter, Frankie Fredericks, had a street in Windhoek named after him in 1993.

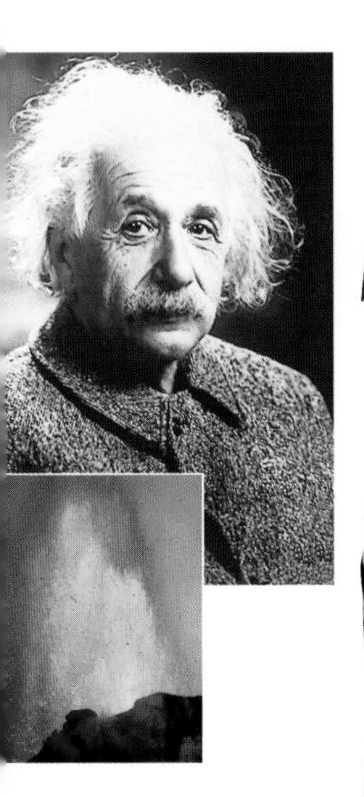

CONTENTS

Editors Alasdair McWhirter, Dougie Oakes, Alfie Steyn
Art Editor Christabel Hardacre
Chief Researcher Frances le Roux
Researchers Rose-Ann Myers, Yana Jardine
Project Coordinator Carol Adams
Assistant Project Coordinators Tania Johnson, Grant Moore
Indexer Ethleen Lastovica

CONTRIBUTORS

Writers

Margaret Allen, Norman Barrett, Nigel Cawthorne, Peter Davies, Miki Flockemann, Alison Freegard, Rob Gaylard, Derek Hall, Tim Healey, Edwin Hees, Merle Huntley, Brian Johnson Barker, Robin Kerrod, John Ellison Khan, Keith Lye, Andrew Panos, Gillian Peele, Hedley Pocock, Hugh Roberton, Shirley Robinson, Fiona Ross, Christopher Saunders, John Sharp, Ronelle Scheffer, Robert Sneddon, Helen Spence, Keith Spence, Stephen Williams

Consultants and Checkers

Pat Alburey, Sally Bamber, John Bentin, The Board of Deputies of British Jews, Nicola Boyne, Michael Bright, A J Brook, Leon J Clarke, Lucinda A Cooke, Jim Cox, Celia Dearling, Robert Dearling, Gavin Drewy, Eve Dunnell, Alison Felstead, C J Fuller, Lesley Glasser, Andrew Goudie, Stan Freenberg, Phyllis Hands, Richard Hift, Larry Johnston, K J A Larkin, Luke McKernan, Norris D McWhirter, Venetia J Newall, Peter Nicholl, Malcolm Rees, Regional Tourist Boards (UK), Monique Riccardi-Cubitt, Jane Ridley, Valerie Sanders, M B Skinner, Terry Staunton, R L A Tames, Christopher Thurling, Hannes van der Merwe, Richard Walker, David Wells, Douglas Wood, Arnold Zuboff

Artists

Dick Bonson, Colin Emberson, Kevin Jones Associates, Malcolm McGregor, Sheila Nowers, Precision Illustration, Dave Snook

WORDS, PHRASES AND LANGUAGE

The ability to use language defines us as human and forms the basis of all our relationships. Not only is it the principal means we have for expressing our feelings and exchanging ideas, but it is also a fascinating subject in its own right – a complex structure of sounds and symbols, rules of grammar, new words and dying words as well as phrases and proverbs with layers of significance much deeper than their literal meaning.

abbreviation Shortened form of a word or phrase, used mainly in writing, and often having full stops to indicate missing letters. *Adj.* is the abbreviation of adjective, *SA* of South Africa, and *kg* of kilogram. (Compare ACRONYM; CONTRACTION; INITIALISM.)

abstract noun NOUN referring to an idea or a quality rather than to an actual thing. *Happiness, parenthood* and *cause* are examples of abstract nouns.

accent Way in which words are pronounced in a particular region or by a particular social group. It also refers to DIACRITICAL MARKS such as the ACUTE ACCENT and GRAVE ACCENT, which adjust the way letters are pronounced in some languages. The word can also refer to the emphasis or stress placed on a particular SYLLABLE in a word. For example, *inflammable* is pronounced with an accent on its second syllable.

acid test Any crucial or decisive test. The phrase derives from the practice of checking the amount of gold in a sample of metal by testing it with acid that will dissolve base metals but not gold.

acronym Word formed by combining the initial letters or syllables of a name or phrase, and pronouncing it as if it were an ordinary word. Examples include the word AIDS, from *A*cquired *I*mmune *D*eficiency *S*yndrome, and radar, from *ra*dio *d*etecting *a*nd *r*anging. (Compare INITIALISM.)

active VOICE, or verb form, indicating that the SUBJECT of the sentence performs the action of the VERB. For example, the sentence *The choir sang the hymn* is active (or 'in the active voice'). The counterpart of active is PASSIVE, as in the sentence *The hymn was sung by the choir.*

acute accent Mark (´) placed above a vowel, either to adjust the way it is pronounced, as in *glacé* or *flambé*, or to indicate that it should be stressed, as in *Márquez.* (Compare CIRCUMFLEX; GRAVE ACCENT.)

AD Abbreviation used to indicate a specific year after the birth of Jesus Christ. In formal writing, AD precedes the year, as in *He was born in AD 371.* It stands for *anno Domini*, a Latin phrase meaning 'in the year of the Lord'. Instead of AD, non-Christians sometimes use CE, which stands for 'Common Era'. (Compare BC.)

adage Short saying or PROVERB, especially a traditional and very old one. An example is *He who laughs last laughs longest.*

ad hoc An arbitrary arrangement, action, decision or committee that deals with an irregular or a one-off situation: *The government appointed an ad hoc committee to coordinate flood relief.* The phrase is Latin in origin, meaning literally 'towards this'.

adjective Word that modifies a NOUN or NOUN PHRASE. In the sentence *She is a beautiful woman* the word *beautiful* is an adjective. (See COMPARATIVE; SUPERLATIVE; DETERMINER.)

ad lib Freely, undirected, without restrictions: *Experienced jazz musicians are often at their best when playing ad lib.* As a verb, ad-lib means to improvise: *I left my speech at home and had to ad-lib.* The term is short for the Latin *ad libitum*, meaning 'as desired'.

ad nauseam To a tedious extreme, to a sickening extent: *He spoke ad nauseam about his hobby.* The phrase comes from Latin, and means 'to the point of nausea'.

adverb Word that modifies a VERB, an ADJECTIVE or another adverb, as *delightfully* does in these three sentences: *She dances delightfully; Her dancing is delightfully innocent; She dances delightfully slowly.* Although adverbs often end in *-ly*, as in *quickly, immediately* or *extremely*, they do not always do so: *fast, soon* and *very* are adverbs too. Adverbs typically answer such questions as *How? Where? When?* (See COMPARATIVE; SUPERLATIVE.)

Afrikaans Language originally developed from Dutch at the Cape and now an official, standardized language spoken by ▷AFRIKANERS and most coloured South Africans. Its first grammar was written in 1876 by S J du Toit, an ▷AFRIKAANS LANGUAGE MOVEMENT campaigner who founded the *Genootskap van Regte Afrikaners* (Society of Real Afrikaners) and the first Afrikaans newspaper, 'Die Afrikaanse Patriot'.

Afrikanerism Language usage that has been transferred from AFRIKAANS to English. In the sentence *I forgot my jersey* the use of *forgot* for *left behind* is an Afrikanerism and is considered incorrect. (Compare LOAN WORD.)

agreement See CONCORD.

alliteration The repetition of the beginning sounds of words, for example in *Peter Piper picked a peck of pickled peppers* and *the fickle finger of fate.*

allusion Indirect reference to someone or something without specifically identifying it, as in *He made an allusion to his time in prison when he said he had been out of circulation for several years*; or *The headmaster's speech was full of classical allusions, most of which were lost on his pupils.*

alma mater School, college or university that one attended as a student. The Latin phrase means 'a cherishing mother'.

ambiguity The quality of having more than one possible interpretation. Both these sentences are ambiguous: *The peasants are revolting; Visiting aunts can be a bore.*

ampersand The sign (&) representing the word *and*, as in *Gross & Co.*

anachronism Placing a person or event in the incorrect historical time. The sentence *Some dinosaurs were man-eaters* is anachronistic, as dinosaurs became extinct before human beings evolved. (Compare ARCHAISM.)

anagram Word or phrase formed by reordering the letters of another word or phrase. The words *pots, tops, spot, stop* and *opts* are all anagrams of one another, and *one hug* is an anagram of *enough.*

analogy Similarity or comparison made between otherwise dissimilar things: *The lecturer drew an analogy between his daughter's make-up and the courtship displays of the animal kingdom.* The term also describes the extension of an existing pattern or model. For example, young children sometimes say *teached* rather than *taught*, by analogy with the word *reached.*

Anglo- A COMBINING FORM, derived from the Latin 'Anglus', meaning English or England, as in *Anglo-Zulu War* and *Anglophone.*

REAL AFRIKANER *S J du Toit, politician and language campaigner, vowed to 'champion our language, our nation and our country'.*

anonymous By a person whose name is unknown or withheld, or of unknown origin. In attributions, it is often abbreviated to 'Anon'.

ante- PREFIX, from Latin, meaning 'before', as in *antenatal, antediluvian* or *anteroom.* (Compare POST-; PRE-.)

anti- PREFIX, from Greek, meaning 'against', 'opposed to', 'opposite to' or 'inhibiting', as in *anti-Communist, anticlockwise, antihero* and *antihistamine.* (Compare PRO-.)

antithesis The juxtaposition of sharply contrasting ideas, using a careful balance of words or phrasing; as in *More haste, less speed.* The word also refers to a direct opposite, as in *Despair is the antithesis of hope.*

antonym Word having the opposite sense from another word. *Hot* is the antonym of *cold*, and *slowly* is the antonym of *quickly* or *fast.* (Compare SYNONYM.)

aphorism Brief, pithy statement expressing a truth or an opinion: *Time is money*; or *Blood is thicker than water.*

apostrophe Punctuation mark ('), used to indicate possession in a noun – *a teacher's pet, the miners' strike* – or to indicate a missing letter or letters in a CONTRACTION – *isn't, we'll, fish 'n chips.*
❖ Apostrophes are often used incorrectly to create plurals: *Potato's R10 a pocket; Have your photo's developed here.*

apposition NOUN or NOUN PHRASE positioned directly after another to help to explain it. For example, in the sentence *Mandela, the South African president, spoke to the crowd,* the noun phrase *the South African president* is in apposition to the noun *Mandela.* When in apposition, the nouns or noun phrases should always be interchangeable.

apropos (A-pro-POH) Term derived from French, meaning 'with reference to' or 'concerning'. It is sometimes used with the preposition *of*, but can also stand without it, as in the sentence *Apropos your suggestion, I think we should wait and see what happens before making a final decision.*

aqua- PREFIX, derived from Latin, meaning 'water', as in the words *aquarium, aqualung, aquasports* and *Aquarius.* HYDRO- is a similar prefix meaning 'water', but originating from the Greek.

arch- PREFIX, derived from Greek, meaning 'first' or 'main', as in *archangel, archbishop* and *archetypal.*

archaism Word or expression widely used in earlier times which now sounds very old-fashioned, such as *doth, perchance, yonder* and *wench.* (Compare ANACHRONISM.)

-archy SUFFIX, from Greek, meaning 'form of government', as in the words *monarchy, oligarchy* and *patriarchy.*

argot (AR-go) Special and often secret vocabulary used by a particular group, class or profession. Prison gangs, for example, often use a kind of secret slang, and some members of the Mafia still use their own argot. (Compare JARGON; SLANG.)
❖ Examples of the names given to township argot in South Africa include *tsotsi-taal, town talk, fly taal, scamto, mensetaal* and *gamtaal.*

article Word used before a NOUN to indicate how widely it applies. *A* and *an* are indefinite articles and do not define a specific thing: *Pass me a chair,* for example, refers to any chair. *The* is the definite article and is used to specify a particular object: *Pass me the chair.* (See DETERMINER.)

***au fait* (OH FAY)** Fully informed, skilled or familiar: *Are you* au fait *with the rules of cricket?* The phrase is French in origin.

auto- PREFIX, from Greek, meaning 'self', used in words such as *automatic, autobiography* and *autopilot.*

auxiliary verb VERB that helps (or 'modulates') the main verb in a sentence. *May, could* and *did* are auxiliary verbs in the sentences *He may run faster; He could run faster;* and *Did he run faster?*

avant-garde (AV-on-gard) The group considered most modern in a given field, especially among musicians, artists or writers. The term is also used as an ADJECTIVE, which usually implies a sense of being daring or radical: *The avant-garde poetry of the 1960s seems curiously tame today.* The term is French in origin, and refers to the vanguard or front troops of the army.

back formation Word created accidentally, on the mistaken assumption that it is an earlier and more basic form of an existing word. For example, the words *burgle* and *laze* are back formations of *burglar* and *lazy.*

Bantu languages Term linguists use for the group of languages of central, eastern and southern Africa, belonging to the larger Niger-Congo family. Most tongues spoken by black people in southern Africa (including the NGUNI and SOTHO-TSWANA languages) fall in this group, with the notable exception of those that belong to the KHOISAN group.

BC Abbreviation for 'before Christ', written after a date to indicate that the year is being counted backwards from the birth of Jesus Christ: *Aristotle was born in 384 BC and died in 322 BC.* Non-Christians sometimes use BCE instead, standing for 'before the Common Era'. (Compare AD.)

bene- PREFIX, from Latin, meaning 'well', 'good' or 'kind', as in *benefit, benevolent* and *benediction.* The prefix with the opposite meaning is MALE-.

***bête noire* (BETT NWAAR)** Person or thing that one particularly dislikes or avoids: *She is my best friend but her husband is my* bête noire. The plural is *bêtes noires*, which is pronounced in the same way as the singular. The term is French in origin, meaning literally 'black beast'.

beyond the pale Totally unacceptable, unreasonable or unbearable: *Simon's behaviour last night was really beyond the pale.* The original Pale was an area surrounding Dublin which was under English control from the 12th to the 16th centuries. People living outside the area were considered to be dangerous and uncivilized.

biblio- PREFIX, derived from the Greek *biblion*, meaning 'book', as in the words *bibliography* and *bibliophile.*

bibliography A list of the written sources of information on a subject. Bibliographies generally appear at the end of a book or an article, and may show which works the author consulted, or list works on the subject that a reader might find useful.

bilingual Capable of speaking two languages fluently, or something that involves two languages: *She is bilingual in Zulu and English; a bilingual Bible.*
❖ When English and Afrikaans were the only two official languages of South Africa, bilingualism was often used to describe proficiency in both.

bio- PREFIX, from the Greek for 'life', as in *biography, biology* and *biodegradable.*

blend See PORTMANTEAU WORD.

bona fides (BOH-na FYE-deez) Good faith, or honest intention: *We stupidly accepted the bona fides of the man who sold us a Caribbean holiday for R2 000.* When used as an ADJECTIVE, without the 's', the phrase also means authentic: *It is a bona fide Van Gogh.* The term is Latin for 'good faith'.

brackets See PARENTHESES; SQUARE BRACKETS.

brei (also bry) A burr in speech, with a GUTTURAL pronunciation of the letter 'r', particularly in Afrikaans. The speech pattern, common in the Malmesbury district in the Western Cape, is also called a *Malmesbury brei* or a *rolling 'r'*.

burn one's boats (or burn one's bridges) To commit oneself to a course of action that will be impossible to back out of later. The idea behind the phrase is drawn from ancient warfare: by burning its boats, an invading army would be destroying its own means of retreat, and would fight more bravely in the knowledge that safety lay only in victory.

capital letters See UPPER CASE.

caret Mark used by editors in the shape of an upside-down V or Y, placed in the text to indicate to the typist or printer where new material is to be inserted. The name comes from Latin and means literally 'there is lacking'.

carte blanche Unlimited power or permission to act as one thinks best: *The department store gave me carte blanche to choose any coat I liked, after I was stuck in one of their lifts all night.* The term is French in origin, meaning literally 'white card' or 'blank paper' – that is, a document allowing the bearer to write in whatever terms or conditions he wishes.

case The category of a NOUN or PRONOUN that shows its relationship to other words in a sentence. In English, nouns are either in the basic case (*James, dog, babies*) or the POSSESSIVE (*James's hat, dog's bone, babies' clothes*). Pronouns can be in the subjective, objective or possessive case. In the sentence *He admitted that his conscience was troubling him*, the pronoun *He*, as SUBJECT of the VERB, is in the subjective case; *his* is in the possessive case; and *him*, as the OBJECT of the verb, is in the objective case.

catch-22 Situation in which your apparent options tend to cancel each other out, leaving you the loser no matter which way you turn: *Starting a career in PR is a catch-22 situation – they won't offer you a job unless you have experience, but you can't get experience until you have a job.* The term comes from Joseph Heller's novel ▷CATCH-22.

cause célèbre (sil-LEB'R) Interesting public matter, such as a trial or scandal, arousing much discussion and taking of sides: *The minister's habitual visits to the casino became a nationwide cause célèbre only when his debts were revealed.* The plural is causes célèbres, which is pronounced in the same way as the singular. The phrase is French for 'famous case'.

cedilla (si-DILL-uh) Mark (¸) shaped rather like a comma, placed beneath a letter in some languages to adjust the way it is pronounced. For example, a cedilla placed beneath the letter 'c' in French words indicates that it should be pronounced as 's', as in *garçon*.

centi- PREFIX, from Latin, meaning 'hundred' or 'hundredth', as in *centipede* (an insect which was traditionally thought to have a hundred feet) and *centimetre* (a hundredth of a metre). Similarly, milli- is a prefix meaning 'thousand' or 'thousandth'. (See DECI-.)

cf ABBREVIATION of the Latin word *confer*, which directs the reader to compare the item under discussion with a related item, as in *For another example of Dickens's delight in children's parties cf p37.*

Chilapalapa (chil-LAH-pa-LAH-pa) A Zimbabwean equivalent of FANAKALO.

chrono-, -chron- PREFIX or COMBINING FORM, from Greek, meaning 'time', as in *chronology, chronometer* and *synchronize*.

circum- PREFIX, from Latin, meaning 'around', or 'on all sides', as in *circumnavigate* and *circumstance*.

circumflex Mark (ˆ) placed above a vowel in certain languages to adjust the way it is pronounced, for example, in the French word *château* and the Afrikaans word *môre*. In Afrikaans a circumflex is called a *kappie*.

circumlocution Use of long-winded and roundabout language, often as a means of avoiding spelling out an unwelcome piece of information. (See also EUPHEMISM.)

clause Group of words containing both a SUBJECT and a PREDICATE, and typically forming part of a COMPLEX SENTENCE or COMPOUND SENTENCE. The sentence *I will come if I can* contains two clauses: *I will come* (MAIN CLAUSE) and *if I can* (SUBORDINATE CLAUSE). (Compare PHRASE.)

cliché Expression that is used so often and so automatically that it has lost its freshness and descriptive power, and sounds boring or insincere. *Green as grass, shining example* and *bright as a button* are all clichés.

COLLECTIVE NOUNS

A collective noun refers to a group of people, animals or things regarded as a unit, such as a *family*, an *assembly*, a *team* or an *orchestra*. Over the centuries, writers have delighted in coining witty, apt or colourful collective nouns; for example *a parliament of rooks* or *an exultation of larks*, though not all of them are in standard current use.

BENCH OF BISHOPS
CHARM OF GOLDFINCHES
CHOIR OF ANGELS
CLUTCH OF EGGS
DIGEST OF LAWS
DREY OF SQUIRRELS
GAGGLE OF GEESE
KINDLE OF KITTENS
LODGE OF BEAVERS
MURDER OF CROWS
MURMURATION OF STARLINGS
MUSTER OF PEACOCKS
NEST OF HORNETS
PLUMP OF WATERFOWL
POD OF WHALES
PRIDE OF LIONS
SCHOOL OF PORPOISES
SHOWER OF BLESSINGS
SKULK OF FOXES
UNKINDNESS OF RAVENS
WISP OF SNIPE

cloud-cuckoo-land An idealized fantasy world: *Stop living in cloud-cuckoo-land for once, and be realistic.* The term is a translation of the name for an imaginary city, floating in the air, in the play *The Birds* by the ancient Greek dramatist ▷ARISTOPHANES.

colloquialism Informal word or expression typical of speech rather than writing, as in *Who does he think he is?* and *She should get her act together.* (Compare SLANG.)

colon Punctuation mark (:) used to introduce a list, an explanation or an example, as in *Here's what you will need to bring: a tent, a sleeping bag, a compass, a camping stove and five days' rations.*

combining form Word or part of a word used to form new words by combining with others. For example, in *multipurpose*, 'multi-' is a combining form; in *psychology*, 'psycho-' and '-logy' are both combining forms. (See PREFIX; SUFFIX.)

comma Punctuation mark (,) used to separate ideas or elements within a sentence, as in *If you hurry, you should be in time to meet the deadline* and *Your rations should include apples, powdered milk and sliced bread.*

common noun NOUN referring to a member of a class of things, rather than to a named individual: *dog, book* and *planet* are examples of common nouns. (Compare ABSTRACT NOUN; PROPER NOUN.)

comparative Form of an ADJECTIVE or ADVERB indicating a greater or more intense degree of the quality, for example the use of 'taller' in the sentence *Simon is the taller of the two brothers.* (Compare SUPERLATIVE.)

complement The part of a sentence that 'completes' a VERB such as 'to be', 'to seem', 'to become' or 'to feel', usually in the form of an ADJECTIVE or NOUN PHRASE. In the following sentences, the adjective 'drunk' and the noun phrase 'managing director' are known as complements: *George is drunk; The company decided to appoint Gillian managing director.* (Compare PREDICATE; OBJECT.)

complex sentence SENTENCE that has at least one SUBORDINATE CLAUSE in addition to its MAIN CLAUSE, such as *There I met an old man* (main clause) *who wouldn't say his prayers* (subordinate clause). (Compare COMPOUND SENTENCE; SIMPLE SENTENCE.)

compos mentis Sane, of sound mind: *The psychiatrist testified that the accused was* compos mentis, *and therefore fit to stand trial.* The phrase is Latin in origin, meaning 'having control of one's own mind'. The opposite is *non compos mentis.*

compound sentence SENTENCE that has at least two MAIN CLAUSES, often joined by a CONJUNCTION such as *and* or *or.* For example, *So I took him by the left leg and threw him down the stairs.* (Compare COMPLEX SENTENCE; SIMPLE SENTENCE.)

concord (also agreement) Compatibility of GENDER, NUMBER, CASE and PERSON among words in a sentence or clause. In the sentence *She is still in her twenties,* the subject pronoun *she* is feminine, singular and third person, and is in concord with the verb *is* (third-person singular), and the possessive adjective *her* (feminine and third-person singular). Sometimes, concord is disregarded, as when a plural noun is seen as a single quantity, as in *Ten miles is a long walk.*

❖ In BANTU LANGUAGES, the verb in a sentence requires a specific PREFIX, which is determined by the class of the subject, to achieve concord. Such a prefix is also called a concord or a subject (or subjectival) concord.

concordance Index listing every occasion on which individual words are used in a particular text, such as the Bible or the works of Shakespeare.

conjunction 'Joining' word or PART OF SPEECH that connects other words, phrases or sentences. There are three main types: coordinating conjunctions such as *and, but* and *so* which join two or more similar elements; correlative conjunctions such as *either . . . or* which are used in pairs; and subordinating conjunctions such as *when, if* and *before* which link a SUBORDINATE CLAUSE to the remainder of the sentence.

connotation Sense of a word or an expression, apart from its literal meaning and including its emotional suggestions and personal associations. For example, the word *bitch* means a female dog, but has unflattering connotations when applied to a woman. (Compare DENOTATION.)

consonant Letter of the alphabet or speech sound that – unlike a VOWEL – is made by obstructing the air stream with the tongue, teeth, throat or lips.

continuous (also progressive) Kind of TENSE form known as an 'aspect' which indicates that an action or a process is continuing. In English, it consists of a form of *be* and the *-ing* form of the verb, as in *She will be giving a recital* and *The cat is sleeping on the chair.* (Compare PERFECT.)

contra- PREFIX, from Latin, meaning 'against', 'opposite' or 'counter-', as in *contravene, contradict* and *contraflow.*

contraction Shortened form of a word or phrase, formed by leaving out or fusing some of the sounds or letters, such as *we'd* for *we would, shan't* for *shall not, flu* for *influenza,* and *pram* for *perambulator.* The omitted letters are sometimes replaced by APOSTROPHES. Contractions are often, although not always, informal in use. (Compare ABBREVIATION; ACRONYM; ELLIPSIS.)

copyright The legal protection given to published works, forbidding anyone but the author from publishing or selling them. An author can transfer the copyright to another person or business, such as a publisher.

❖ The symbol for copyright is ©.

❖ When a writer duplicates another writer's language or ideas and then calls the work his or her own, the act is called plagiarism.

corollary Conclusion or inference drawn from a previously proven idea, but not actually proved itself, such as *He did not know about the robbery, so as a corollary he could not have been the person who reported it to the police.*

cosmo- PREFIX, from the Greek, meaning 'universe' or 'world', for example in *cosmology, cosmonaut* and *cosmopolitan.*

count noun (also countable noun) NOUN that can occur in the plural or be preceded by a number or by *a* or *an*: *dog* and *child* are count nouns. Many words can be either count nouns or MASS NOUNS (uncountable nouns), depending on the way they are used in a sentence: compare the use of the noun *fear* in the sentences *A fear of the dark is only one of my many irrational fears* (count noun) and *She seems devoid of fear when she steps into the ring* (mass noun).

coup de grâce **(KOO duh GRASS)** Final blow or finishing stroke, either literally (as when killing a fatally wounded person or animal to prevent further suffering) or figuratively, as in *The financial scandal delivered the* coup de grâce *to the politician's declining career.* The term is French in origin, meaning literally 'stroke of mercy'.

creole In linguistics, a mixed tongue developed from two other languages, usually because of conquest or colonization – especially combinations of English, French and Portuguese with African languages. Creoles keep the grammar of the local language but add the vocabulary of the foreign one, eventually forming their local mother tongue. (Compare PIDGIN.)

❖ Creole also refers to the language and culture of French descendants in Louisiana and other southern states of America.

cross-reference Indication in one part of a book, an index or other text, directing the reader to consult another part which contains related information, as in *The entry on Wordsworth contains a cross-reference to the Lake Poets.* In this book, cross-references are indicated by small capital letters.

cross the Rubicon To take a step or make a decision on which there is no going back, and which marks the start of a chain of events: *By rejecting the offered compromise, my ex-partner has crossed the Rubicon, and our differences will now be settled in court.* The Rubicon is the ancient name of a river in northern Italy, believed to be the present-day Fiumicino, which Julius Caesar was prohibited from crossing. In 49 BC, however, he

TRUE HUMILITY *The phrase 'curate's egg' derives from this cartoon of 1895 – Bishop: 'I'm afraid you've got a bad egg, Mr Jones!' Curate: 'Oh no, my Lord, I assure you! Parts of it are excellent!'*

forded the river with his army, thus effectively declaring war on Rome.

cuneiform (KEW-ni-form) Writing system used in the ancient Middle East, consisting of wedge-shaped symbols or letters drawn with a sharpened reed on a soft clay tablet. The tablet was baked in a kiln to harden it. Originally derived from PICTOGRAMS, the symbols were later used to represent words, syllables and phonetic elements. Earliest examples were written from top to bottom, but around 3000 BC scribes found that they could write better by turning the tablets and writing from left to right in horizontal rows.

curate's egg Something that is bad although claimed by some – out of sensitivity or some other reason – to have both good and bad parts. The phrase derives from a 'Punch' cartoon in which a nervous young curate at a bishop's table is given what is obviously a bad boiled egg but, fearful of giving offence, tells his host that 'parts of it are excellent'.
❖ This term is often misused. It correctly refers to something which is completely bad or which cannot be redeemed, and does not mean something which has both good and bad qualities.

curriculum vitae (CV) Résumé or short account of one's education, work experience, achievements and interests, as compiled and submitted when applying for a job. The phrase is Latin in origin, meaning 'the course of one's life'. CVs should be concise – one side of paper should usually be enough. They should also be relevant to the job being applied for. Any previous work experience should be listed in reverse chronological order, since a prospective employer will be most interested in recent jobs.

cut the Gordian knot To solve a problem by taking prompt and extremely bold or unconventional action, as in *Faced with intolerable financial difficulties, the directors cut the Gordian knot by declaring the company bankrupt.* The phrase is based on a supposed incident that occurred in ancient history. The Gordian knot was an enormous and intricate knot tied with rope made of bark by King Gordius of Phrygia in the 4th century BC. According to an ▷ORACLE, whoever could undo the knot was destined to reign over a large empire in Asia Minor. ▷ALEXANDER THE GREAT apparently took up the challenge by simply hacking through the knot with his sword in 334 BC. He went on to extend Greek civilization as far east as India.

dangling participle Form of MISRELATED CONSTRUCTION in which a PARTICIPLE, especially a PRESENT PARTICIPLE, is linked not to the word intended but to some empty word such as *it* or *there*, as in the sentence *Having no umbrella, there was nothing to do but take shelter from the rain.* A better version would be *Having no umbrella, we had to take shelter from the rain,* where the participle *having* is linked to the subject *we* instead of simply being left 'dangling'.

dark horse Unfamiliar competitor or quiet newcomer whose abilities remain unknown or untested. *Although he was a dark horse during the opening rounds of his first Wimbledon, McEnroe was a household name by the time he reached the semifinals.* The phrase derives from horse racing: the betting public might be 'in the dark' regarding the speed, stamina or jumping ability of an unfamiliar runner – a dark horse – and therefore uncertain about the odds.

dash Punctuation mark (–) used to indicate a break in thought, to introduce a summing up or to mark off a PARENTHESIS, as in *Then she hit me – what for? Demand and supply – there you have economics in a nutshell. Very few of the football players – three, to be exact – were reselected by the coach.* The dash can also serve some of the functions of a COLON, such as introducing an explanation: *She went to college with one clear intention – to find a husband.*

CYRILLIC ALPHABET

The Cyrillic alphabet is used for writing various eastern European languages, such as Russian and Bulgarian. Its name is derived from its supposed inventor, St Cyril, who was a 9th-century Macedonian theologian and missionary.

АБВГДЕ
ЖЗИКЛМ
НОПРСТ
УФХЦЧЩ
ЪЫЭЮЯ

SLAVIC SCRIPT *The alphabet known as Cyrillic developed out of Greek.*

dead language A language that is no longer spoken. Some dead languages, such as Latin and Sanskrit, may nevertheless be studied by large numbers of people because of their literary, religious or historical importance.

deci- PREFIX, from Latin, meaning 'a tenth', as in the words *decibel, decimal* and *decilitre*. (Compare CENTI-.)

declarative sentence SENTENCE that 'declares' something or makes a statement; the most common form of sentence. *He is making a speedy recovery* and *We leave at midnight* are declarative sentences. (See INDICATIVE; compare IMPERATIVE; INTERROGATIVE.)

deelteken Afrikaans for DIAERESIS.

de facto (day FAC-toe) Phrase referring to a state of affairs that exists but is not officially recognized. *The administrator was supposedly in charge of the township, but the street committees were the de facto governors.* The phrase is Latin in origin, meaning literally 'from the fact'. (Compare DE JURE.)

defining clause (also restrictive clause) RELATIVE CLAUSE, often introduced by *that* rather than *which*, that defines or specifies the NOUN it modifies, and is a crucial part of the meaning of the sentence. In the sentence *The family that prays together stays together*, the clause *that prays together* is called a defining clause. (Compare NONDEFINING CLAUSE.)

definite article The word *the*. Unlike the INDEFINITE ARTICLE *a*, it indicates that a particular item is being referred to by the NOUN or NOUN PHRASE that follows it.

déjà vu The strange feeling of 'I've been here before' when it is impossible for this to be the case. It is French for 'already seen'.

de jure (day JOOR-ay) By legal right, in keeping with the law, officially: *The de jure government was overthrown in a coup, and the country is now run by the military.* The phrase is Latin in origin, meaning literally 'according to the law'. (Compare DE FACTO.)

demi- PREFIX, from French, meaning 'half' or 'less than full status', as in *demigod*. (Compare SEMI-.)

demonstrative pronoun PRONOUN that specifies or points out the person(s) or thing(s) referred to; specifically, *this, that, these* and *those* when used independently, rather than directly before a noun, as in the sentence *He likes those, but she prefers these.* In the following sentences, the words *this* and *these* are demonstrative ADJECTIVES: *He sits in this chair; She likes these fabrics.*

denotation The literal sense or basic dictionary meaning of a word or an expression, without its CONNOTATIONS. The denotation of the word *modern* is 'belonging to or characteristic of recent times'. While the denotation stays the same, the connotations will be positive for some people and negative for others.

dependent clause See SUBORDINATE CLAUSE.

de rigueur **(duh-ri-GERR)** Socially compulsory, required by custom or fashion: *It is no longer* de rigueur *to wear a suit and tie to the opera.* It is a French phrase, and means literally 'of strictness'.

derivative Word formed by adding a PREFIX or SUFFIX to another word. *Importation*, for example, is a derivative of *import*. Derivative also refers to a word's origin and historical development, or ETYMOLOGY.

determiner Word placed in front of a NOUN or NOUN PHRASE in order to limit its meaning. *The, all, that* and *their* are determiners in these examples: *the brilliant, award-winning biologist; all things bright and beautiful; that interesting new magazine; their computer operator.* (Compare ADJECTIVE; ARTICLE.)

devil to pay An IDIOM used to warn that trouble is on the way: *There'll be the devil to pay when father finds out what you've done.* The original version shows how its meaning has changed: *the devil to pay and no pitch hot* suggests a lack of preparation for an important task – that is, the sailors' task of sealing with tar (pitch) the seam (known as 'the devil') between the planks of a wooden ship.

Dewey Decimal System A system used in libraries for the classification of books and other publications. It uses the numbers 000 to 999 to cover the general fields of knowledge, and subdivides each field by the use of decimals. It was named after its American inventor, Melvil Dewey.

diacritical marks Marks used in writing and printing to adjust the way in which a letter is pronounced, such as the marks in the French words *tête* and *garçon*. (See also ACUTE ACCENT; CEDILLA; CIRCUMFLEX; DIAERESIS; GRAVE ACCENT; TILDE; UMLAUT.)

diaeresis Mark (¨) placed over a VOWEL to indicate that it should be independently pronounced, as in the words naïve, Noël, and Brontë. In Afrikaans it is called a *deelteken* (division sign). (Compare UMLAUT.)

Dictionary of South African English Compiled by Dr Jean Branford while she was with the Rhodes University Dictionary Unit, this reference work was first published in 1978. It includes 5 000 entries, covering LOAN WORDS, as well as words that have particular CONNOTATIONS in South Africa or were coined locally. (See SOUTH AFRICAN ENGLISH panel, p 27.)
❖ The Rhodes Dictionary Unit's own scholarly, 800-page *Dictionary of South African English on Historical Principles* was due to be published in 1996 after 25 years in preparation. Its earliest examples of South African English date from the late 1500s.

diminutive SUFFIX or word conveying the idea of small size, youthfulness, unimportance, or else of affection. The words *piglet* and *kitchenette* are diminutives, and so are their suffixes *-let* and *-ette*.

diphthong (DIF-thong) Complex speech sound beginning with one vowel sound and moving to another within a single syllable; for example the sound *oy* in *boy*, which involves a shift between the two sounds *aw* and *ee*. Diphthong also refers to the fused letters æ and œ (also called ligatures), as in the old-fashioned spelling of *amœba*.

direct object Person, thing or set of circumstances directly affected by the action of a VERB. In English, the direct object almost always follows the verb. It may consist of a simple NOUN or PRONOUN, a PHRASE or a CLAUSE. In the sentence *I cannot understand her*, the direct object is the pronoun *her*. In the sentence *I cannot understand why she gave me so many roses*, the direct object is the entire clause *why she gave me so many roses*. (Compare INDIRECT OBJECT.)

direct speech Speech or writing quoted exactly in its original words. When written, direct speech is usually enclosed in quotation marks, as in *The suspect declared: 'I swear it wasn't me!'* (Compare INDIRECT SPEECH.)

Don't look a gift horse in the mouth PROVERB advising that one should accept gifts without inspecting them too closely, let alone criticizing them. It refers to the practice of inspecting a horse's teeth to find out its age – the shorter the teeth, the older the horse, since chewing wears the teeth down. Someone buying a horse would obviously inspect its mouth – this is the origin of the expression 'from the horse's mouth' as an assurance of reliable information.

double entendre (DOOB'L on-TOND-ruh) Word or expression having two different meanings, especially when one of them is indelicate or bawdy, as in many saucy jokes and funny headlines: *Cricket captain bowls a maiden over; Rival nudist clubs meet to air their differences.* In French, the phrase means 'double understanding', though the French no longer use the term.

double negative Use of two negative or near-negative expressions, such as *not* or *barely*, in a sentence. When used correctly it conveys a positive sense, as in *He's hardly unenthusiastic; She's not unintelligent.* Double negatives intended to convey a negative meaning – as in *I'm so drunk I can't hardly stand up* or *You don't know nothing about it* – are considered wrong in modern English, though not in all other languages (for example Afrikaans) or earlier English.

dys- PREFIX, from Greek, meaning 'bad', as in *dysentery, dyslexia* and *dysfunctional.*

eat humble pie To admit one's mistakes, or apologize for them, often in humiliating circumstances: *The boastful physicist was forced to eat humble pie when a student pointed out a simple error in his calculations.* The phrase is based on a clever play on words. A humble pie was formerly one made from the internal organs or offal of a deer – its 'humbles', 'umbles' or 'numbles' in earlier English. Since this was the cheapest and least desirable meat, it would be eaten mainly by poor or humble people, though the two words spelt 'humble' are unrelated in origin.

eg ABBREVIATION of the Latin phrase *exempli gratia*, meaning 'for example' and used to introduce an example or a list of examples: *With this new diet, your breakfast is restricted to tropical fruit – eg mangoes, pineapples, guavas and papayas.* (Compare IE.)

ego- PREFIX, from Latin, meaning 'I' or 'myself', as in *egotism, egomania* or *ego trip.* (Compare AUTO-.)

ellipsis Omission from a sentence of a word or phrase that is implied by the context, as in *Know what I mean?* for *Do you know what I mean?* or *Alan cannot and Beryl will not play bridge* for *Alan cannot play bridge and Beryl will not play bridge.* Faulty ellipsis is a common error of GRAMMAR or STYLE, as in *Alan has never and Beryl will never play bridge.* The correct form is *Alan has never played and Beryl will never play bridge.*
❖ Ellipsis also refers to the 'dot-dot-dot' punctuation mark (. . .) used to indicate that something is missing from a quoted passage: *Macmillan described the growth of African nationalism as a 'wind of change . . . blowing through this continent'.*

***enfant terrible* (on-FON teh-REEB'L)** Person of unconventional ideas or behaviour who causes dismay to the established members of his group or profession: *Ken Russell used to be the* enfant terrible *of the British film industry, but he seems to have mellowed.* The plural is *enfants terribles*, pronounced in the same way as the singular. The term comes from the French for 'terrible child'.

epigram Brief, pithy statement or striking observation, often with a witty twist, such as Oscar Wilde's remark: *Work is the curse of the drinking classes.*

epitaph Inscription on a tombstone or monument in memory of the person or people buried there.

epithet ADJECTIVE or PHRASE used to characterize a person or thing, or as a nickname or substitute title. *Lionheart*, for example, was an epithet for Richard I.

eponymous Referring to the person after whom something such as a book or a city is named: *The eponymous hero of the film 'Ben Hur' was played by Charlton Heston.*

ersatz German word used to refer to an imitation or a substitute, particularly an inferior one, as in *ersatz coffee.*

Esperanto Artificial language invented in 1887 by the Polish linguist Dr Ludwig Lazarus Zamenhof, and intended as an international language. It is based on words familiar in many European languages, and its grammar is very regular.

esprit de corps (ess-PREE duh KOR) Spirit of fellowship, or feeling of mutual support or team spirit among the members of a group: *During their training the army recruits developed a strong esprit de corps.* The phrase is French in origin, meaning literally 'spirit of body' or 'platoon spirit'.

ethno- PREFIX, from Greek, meaning 'people', 'race' or 'ethnic', as in *ethnology, ethnography* and *ethnocentric.*

etymology The origin and historical development of a word, or the study of word origins, as in *You can trace the etymology of the word 'scrupulous' back to the Latin word for a rough stone.*

eu- PREFIX, from Greek, meaning 'good', as in *euphemism, euphonious* and *eulogy.*

euphemism Bland or neutral expression used in place of one that might give offence: *pass away* and *expire* are both euphemisms for *die* and *ethnic cleansing* is a euphemism for *genocide.* (See CIRCUMLOCUTION.)

exclamation mark Punctuation mark (!) used after a command, an exclamation of surprise, an INTERJECTION or an abrupt and emphatic statement, such as *Ouch!* or *Life discovered on Mars!*

ex gratia (eks GRA-shia) Given purely as a favour, without any legal necessity, as in *an ex gratia payment.* The phrase is Latin for 'from kindness' or 'as a favour'.

expletive Any exclamation, swearword or oath, especially one considered to be blasphemous or obscene, whether currently or formerly, such as *Damn!* or *Heavens above!* Nowadays, any obscene word can be loosely referred to as an expletive.

***fait accompli* (FET a-COM-plee)** Established fact or performed action that cannot be reversed: *The publication of the rumour is a* fait accompli *– all we can do now is to issue a denial and try to limit the damage.* The plural is *faits accomplis*, pronounced in the same way as the singular. The term is French, meaning literally 'accomplished fact'.

Fanakalo (also Fanagalo) PIDGIN language, based on a simplified version of NGUNI LANGUAGES plus English and AFRIKAANS, sometimes used as a LINGUA FRANCA on South African mines. The word comes from Zulu for 'to be like this'.

faux pas (FOH PAA) Social blunder, mistake of etiquette or failure of tact, as in *She committed the faux pas of mistaking the duchess for her maid.* The plural is also *faux pas*, and is pronounced in the same way as the singular. The term is French in origin, meaning literally 'false step'.

feet of clay Phrase used of a highly regarded person revealed to have a character weakness or flaw: *The priest's arrest for burglary revealed him to have feet of clay.* It probably comes from a passage in the Book of Daniel in the Bible. King Nebuchadnezzar had dreams of a huge statue with a gold head, silver arms, and so on, down to feet of iron and clay. Daniel interpreted the dream to mean that a future kingdom would be divided, and that it would eventually crumble like the clay that supported the statue.

figure of speech Expression in which the words are used for emphasis or dramatic effect rather than their literal meaning. LITOTES, SIMILES and HYPERBOLES are figures of speech, as are METAPHORS such as *the last flickering flames of consciousness before sleep.*

flash in the pan Something that suddenly seems to have great interest, appeal or promise, but that soon loses it and returns to obscurity, as in *His dramatic improvement in last term's exams turned out to be a flash in the pan – this term, he almost failed.* The original flash in the pan occurred in the old flintlock gun. The loose gunpowder, carefully measured and placed in the gun's 'flashpan', was meant to be ignited by a spark from the flint. If the gunpowder was damp or insufficient, however, it would fizzle or flash rather than explode effectively.

fly taal See ARGOT.

Fourth Estate Term referring to journalism or to journalists generally, regarded as a power in the land. In France before the French Revolution, the three 'Estates of the Realm' were the Church, the nobility and the people. The reference to a Fourth Estate was supposedly first made by the British writer and politician Edmund Burke (1729-97) in the late 18th century, as a joking comment on the power of the press.

full stop (or a period, in American English) Punctuation mark (.) used to end a DECLARATIVE SENTENCE and sometimes – but now less commonly – to indicate an ABBREVIATION.

future perfect See PERFECT.

future tense See TENSE.

gender Classification of NOUNS, PRONOUNS and sometimes ADJECTIVES, as 'masculine', 'feminine' or 'neuter', as in the pronouns *he, she* and *it.* In English, nouns referring to male and female creatures are of the obvious gender, and inanimate objects are normally neuter. Countries, ships and other vehicles may be feminine.

generalization Sweeping statement or broad conclusion about an entire group of people or things, that may be true of many of the items but is probably not true of all of them, such as *The Swedes are extraordinarily good at playing tennis* and *The more trees a Johannesburg neighbourhood has, the wealthier its residents are.*

geo- PREFIX, from Greek, meaning 'the Earth', as in *geology* and *geography.*

Germanic languages Subfamily of the INDO-EUROPEAN group, including English, Dutch, German and Swedish.

GRAPHOLOGY: WHAT HANDWRITING REVEALS

Graphology is the study of handwriting and is sometimes used to analyse personality. Graphologists believe that handwriting is a form of 'brain-writing', in which the unconscious mind is conveyed to the fingers and reveals itself on paper.

SIZE

have your an

Large writing This usually denotes ambition or 'thinking big'. People in show business often have large writing.

My present handwriting is the

Small writing This indicates modesty or a feeling of inferiority; alternatively, the writer may be objective and scientific.

WIDTH

The waves war and whirl.

Narrow writing People with narrow writing are often disciplined and inhibited. They may be mean and restricted in view.

Broad writing Those with broad writing tend to be uninhibited, and to like to travel. They may also be rash and uncontrolled.

SLANT

The probability

Left slant A left-hand slant is typical of people who are shy and retiring. They tend to stay in their shell, hide their emotions and adopt a passive attitude.

Now is the time

Right slant Writing that leans to the right suggests an outgoing personality – an ability to mix with other people.

SPACING

convinced at this

Wide spacing People who leave large spaces between words are often ill-at-ease in company, and can be stand-offish.

Your children are not your

Narrow spacing Small spaces between words can indicate a gregarious personality. But they also suggest that the writer chooses friends discriminatingly.

gerund Form of a VERB, ending in '-ing' in English, that functions as a NOUN in a sentence. For example, the word *walking* is a gerund in the sentence *Walking in the woods alone can be dangerous at night.* The POSSESSIVE case is linked with the gerund in sentences such as *Jane's talking in class was annoying.* (Compare PRESENT PARTICIPLE.)

gild the lily To try to improve something that is already beautiful or perfect: *Dyeing her naturally blonde hair would just be gilding the lily.* The phrase is often taken to be a quotation from Shakespeare, but the words he actually used in *King John* were: 'To gild refined gold, to paint the lily . . . is wasteful and ridiculous excess.'

glossary List of words with accompanying definitions, rather like a short, specialized dictionary. A glossary is often included at the end of a textbook to explain the difficult or technical terms used throughout the work. (Compare LEXICON.)

gobbledegook (also officialese) Needlessly complicated and unclear speech or writing, as used by some officials. An example is the use of the word *dwelling unit* instead of *house.* It often includes an excessive use of bureaucratic or technical JARGON.

-gram SUFFIX, from Latin and Greek, meaning 'writing', as in the words *diagram, anagram* and *telegram.*

grammar Analysis and classification of the elements of a language, such as the pronunciation and meaning of words, and the system of rules for using it.

-graph- COMBINING FORM, from Greek, meaning 'draw' or 'write', as in *biography, autograph* and *geography.*

grave accent (GRAAV) Mark (`) placed above a vowel, either to adjust the way it is pronounced, as in *Sèvres*, or to indicate that it needs to be sounded out, as in the poetic use of *agèd.* (Compare ACUTE ACCENT.)

grist to the mill Something that can be turned to one's advantage, or something that should prove useful even though it may not appear particularly promising at first: *As a comedy writer, he almost welcomes life's setbacks* *since they are all grist to the mill.* The image is of an old grain mill, such as a water mill, which treats anything presented to it as grist or grain, and grinds it regardless.

guttural Sound that is produced in the throat or in the back of the mouth, for example the guttural CONSONANTS 'k' and 'g' in the words *keg* and *gawky*. (See also BREI.)

haemo-, haem- PREFIX, from the Greek for 'blood', as in *haemorrhage* and *haemophilia*.

hetero- PREFIX, from Greek, meaning 'different', as in *heterogeneous, heterodoxy* and *heterosexual*. (Compare HOMO-.)

hide one's light under a bushel To be excessively modest about one's talents or unadventurous in developing them: *She's a fine actress, but she hides her light under a bushel, always keeping in the background and never auditioning for major roles.* The phrase is an allusion to the call by Jesus, in the Sermon on the Mount, for open practice of one's faith: *'Neither do men light a candle, and put it under a bushel, but on a candlestick'* (Matthew 5:15). The bushel was a vessel used to measure out corn.

hieroglyphs Characters used in the writing system of ancient ▷EGYPT, in which pictures of people or things were used for words or sounds. (See also IDEOGRAM; PICTOGRAM.)

Hobson's choice Apparent choice in which all options turn out to be the same: *Henry Ford offered his customers a Hobson's choice by telling them they could have any colour of car they liked, as long as it was black.* The original Hobson's choice was offered in the time of Shakespeare by a Cambridge stablekeeper called Hobson. He hired out his horses in strict rotation, forcing clients to take the one next in line.

hocus-pocus Nonsense words uttered by a magician when performing a trick, or pompous phrases used by officials to avoid giving a straight answer. A likely origin for the term is mimicking, perhaps by mocking Protestants, of the Roman Catholic Mass, in which the phrase *Hoc est corpus* occurs, meaning 'This is the body'.

hoi polloi The common people, the masses. The words are used dismissively by those who consider themselves superior: *If hoi polloi keep picnicking on the beach, we'll have to introduce admission control.* The phrase is usually preceded in English by 'the', although this is not strictly correct as it is Greek for 'the many'.

hoist with one's own petard Caught out by one's own scheming, or being the victim of one's own cleverness: *To avoid speaking to her fellow traveller, Mary pretended to speak only German. She was hoist with her own petard when he broke into perfect German.* The expression means literally 'blown up by one's own small bomb'.

homo- PREFIX, from Latin and Greek, meaning 'same' or 'equal', as in *homogenize* and *homosexual*. (Compare HETERO-.)

homograph Word that has the same spelling as another, but a different meaning and origin, such as *sewer* (a drain) and *sewer* (a person who sews) or *lead* (to show the way) and *lead* (the metal). Some homographs have the same pronunciation as each other, in which case they may also be called HOMONYMS.

homonym Word that has the same pronunciation and spelling as another word, but a quite different meaning and origin; for example, *row* (a line) and *row* (to use oars); and *bill* (an invoice) and *bill* (a duck's beak).

homophone Word having the same pronunciation as another, but a different meaning and origin, and usually a different spelling. *Pear* and *pair* are homophones.

hydro-, hydr- COMBINING FORM, often a PREFIX, from the Greek for 'water', as in *hydroelectric* and *dehydrate*. (Compare AQUA-.)

hyper- PREFIX, from Greek, meaning 'too much' or 'excessive', as in *hyperactive* and *hypersensitive*. (Compare HYPO-.)

hyperbole (hye-PER-ba-lee) FIGURE OF SPEECH consisting of an exaggerated expression, such as *I could sleep for weeks* or *This book weighs a ton*. (Compare LITOTES.)

hyphen Punctuation mark (-) used to link associated words into a compound, as in *self-love* or *mother-in-law*, and to split a word that runs over at the end of a line.

hypno- PREFIX, from Greek, meaning 'sleep', as in *hypnosis* and *hypnotherapy*.

hypo- PREFIX, from Greek, meaning 'under' or 'below', as in *hypodermic* (under the skin) and *hypothermia* (below normal body temperature). (Compare HYPER-.)

ibid (also ib) ABBREVIATION of the Latin word *ibidem*, meaning 'in the same place'. It is used in footnotes to refer to the book, chapter, article or page cited just before. (Compare IDEM; LOC CIT.)

idem Latin term meaning 'the same', used in footnotes to indicate a reference previously mentioned. Sometimes the abbreviation *id* is used. (Compare IBID; LOC CIT.)

ideogram (or ideograph) Sign or symbol used in Chinese and some Japanese writing to represent an idea or object without indicating pronunciation; also, any symbol used in writing, other than letters of the alphabet and punctuation marks, such as %, £, $, @. (Compare PICTOGRAM.)

idiolect The unique speech or language patterns of an individual person.

idiom Common phrase or traditional expression, often informal, whose meaning cannot be derived from the literal meanings of the individual words. *Under the weather* (feeling poorly) and *round the bend* (mad) are examples of idioms.

ie ABBREVIATION of the Latin phrase *id est*, meaning 'that is', used to specify or explain the term preceding it: *As from tomorrow the new rules apply, ie no going out during the week, and no staying out after 10 o'clock on weekends.* (Compare EG.)

illiteracy Inability to read or write. Functional illiteracy means an inability to write and read well enough for most employment or tasks of urban life.

imperative Grammatical form or MOOD of a VERB used in expressing commands or requests. In the following sentences, the verbs *save, leave* and *be* are imperative (or 'in the imperative'): *Save me from such an indignity! Leave that equipment alone! Be ready by midnight.* (Compare DECLARATIVE SENTENCE; INDICATIVE; SUBJUNCTIVE.)

impersonal verb A VERB that expresses an action or state without ascribing it to a particular subject, as in *It snowed.* Some verbs can be used either personally or impersonally, such as *looks* or *seems* in *Joseph looks/seems ill* (personal) and *It looks/seems as if Joseph is ill* (impersonal).

in camera In private or in secret; specifically, behind closed doors rather than in an open court: *The Gerhardt trial was held in camera, since it involved issues of state security.* The phrase is Latin in origin, and means 'in the chamber'.

indefinite article The word *a* or *an*, the article that introduces a NOUN or NOUN PHRASE without specifying the particular individual referred to, as in the phrases *a jar, an urn.*

The choice of *a* or *an* is determined by the sound rather than by the letter following it: hence *an hourglass*, but *a unicorn*. (Compare DEFINITE ARTICLE.)

indefinite pronoun PRONOUN that stands in for an undefined or unidentified person or thing, as in *anyone, some, nobody*.

independent clause See MAIN CLAUSE.

indicative Grammatical form or MOOD of a VERB which indicates that the action or condition mentioned is factual or probable, in contrast to the SUBJUNCTIVE, where it is only supposed. In the following sentences, the verb *was* in the first is indicative (or 'in the indicative'), whereas the verb *were* in the second is subjunctive (or 'in the subjunctive'): *Mary was delayed and missed her train. If Mary were delayed, she would have telephoned to say that she'd missed her train.* (Compare IMPERATIVE.)

indirect object Object indirectly affected by the action of a TRANSITIVE VERB, usually as if one had placed the word *to* or *for* in front of it. In the sentence *She gave me a withering look*, the pronoun *me* is the indirect object, whereas the phrase *a withering look* is the DIRECT OBJECT.

indirect speech (or reported speech) Speech or writing reported in different words from those originally used. It is typically introduced by a verb such as *say* or *tell*, and sometimes by *that*, and involves changes in PERSON or TENSE, as in *The suspect then swore that he had not committed the crime.* (Compare DIRECT SPEECH.)

Indo-European Family of languages that includes most European tongues (notably excluding the Uralic languages Finnish and Hungarian), as well as many languages of India and Iran. Two of the many subfamilies are the GERMANIC and ROMANCE LANGUAGES.

in extremis On the verge of death, or in very serious difficulties: *The victim lay* in extremis, *trapped in no-man's-land;* or *The company is* in extremis, *and will go under unless the bank agrees to a further loan.* The phrase is Latin, meaning literally 'in the last'.

infinitive Basic form of a VERB, as it appears in a dictionary, without any INFLECTION to indicate TENSE, NUMBER, MOOD or the like. The forms *walk, fly* and *be* are infinitive (or 'infinitives' or 'in the infinitive'), unlike *walking, flew* and *were*. In English, the word *to* often marks a verb as an infinitive, for example: *to walk, to fly, to be.*

in flagrante delicto In the very act of committing an offence; red-handed: *The police caught the forger in flagrante delicto as he sat operating his printing press.* The phrase is Latin in origin, meaning 'with the crime still blazing'. It is often used of people found in the act of having adulterous sex.

inflection Changes in the form of a word according to its different grammatical functions within a sentence, such as PERSON, GENDER, NUMBER, CASE, TENSE, VOICE and MOOD. English has only a few inflections left, notably those indicating the past tense of VERBS by means of a different ending, as in *walked* or *walking*; those indicating the plural (*-s* or *-es*) and possessive (*-'s* or *-s'*) of NOUNS, as in *his girlfriend's parents*; those affecting PRONOUNS, as in *he, him, his*; and those in IRREGULAR VERBS and nouns, such as *shrink, shrank, shrunk*, and *mouse, mice.*

infra dig Informal CONTRACTION of the Latin phrase *infra dignitatem*, meaning 'beneath one's dignity', as in the following sentence *The dean considers it infra dig to say hello to any student.*

initialism ABBREVIATION of a phrase formed by the initial letters of each word, but not pronounced as a single word. Examples include SABC for *South African Broadcasting Corporation* and OTT for *over the top*. (Compare ACRONYM.)

in loco parentis Acting in the role of parents, or having the responsibilities or duties of a parent: *The housemaster at a boarding school acts* in loco parentis. The phrase is Latin for 'in a parent's place'.

innuendo An indirect suggestion, often intended as a veiled insult or accusation, as in the remark *Not everyone would be able to believe your story.*

inter- PREFIX, from Latin, meaning 'between', 'among' or 'together with', as in *intercity, interval, interbreed* and *interdependent.* (Compare INTRA-.)

inter alia Among other things: *Several European currencies,* inter alia *the guilder and the French franc, surged as a result of the announcement.* The term is Latin in origin. It is often used to mean 'among other people' as well, although strictly speaking that should be *inter alios.*

interjection An exclamation. Interjections are often single words or brief phrases that can stand alone as complete utterances, such as *Oh! Gosh! Never!*

interrogative Word, construction or sentence asking a question, for example: *How are you feeling? Where were you born?* or *Will we be leaving before dawn?* (Compare DECLARATIVE SENTENCE; IMPERATIVE.)

in the doldrums Gloomy, down in the dumps, feeling depressed and lazy: *I'm always in the doldrums in winter, when nature seems fast asleep.* It can also be used of economic conditions: *The housing market will remain in the doldrums until interest rates come down.* The phrase originated as a reference to equatorial seas, where ships were often becalmed.

in toto As a whole, totally, completely: *The repairs will cost an estimated R2 300,* in toto *– that includes parts, labour and VAT.* The phrase is Latin, meaning 'as a whole'.

intra- PREFIX, from Latin, meaning 'inside' or 'within', as in *intravenous, intramural* and *intrauterine.* (Compare INTER-.)

intransitive verb VERB that does not take a DIRECT OBJECT. The verbs *wonder* and *die* are intransitive, as is *despair*: *My teachers despair (of me).* Many verbs can be transitive or intransitive, depending on how they are used in a sentence; compare the verb *argue* in the sentences *My teachers always argue their case energetically* (transitive) and *You always argue!* (intransitive). An intransitive verb cannot occur in the PASSIVE voice.

inverted commas Another term for QUOTATION MARKS.

in vino veritas Latin phrase or PROVERB, suggesting that people speak the truth when they are drunk. The literal meaning is 'in wine there is truth'.

ipso facto By the very fact or deed; as a logical result of the fact itself; by definition: *A 10-year-old is, ipso facto, unable to vote.* The phrase is Latin for 'by the fact itself'.

irony Use of words to convey a meaning opposite to that of their literal or surface meaning: *Their love affair is one of the great secrets of Hollywood.* Irony is a major ingredient of sarcasm, a biting kind of ridicule: *Thank you for all your support – your silence was a great help!*

irregular verb (or strong verb) VERB that changes its whole form, rather than simply adding *-ed* or *-d*, when forming the past TENSE and PAST PARTICIPLE: *I drew, I have drawn* and *I went, I have gone.* (Compare REGULAR VERB.)

italics Slanted typeface, as in *This example is printed in italics*, in contrast to the ordinary upright (Roman) typeface of the rest of this sentence. Italics have many uses – to give emphasis or stress to certain words, to indicate words in a foreign language, or to mark the titles of books, works of art or films.
❖ In typing and handwriting, underlining usually takes the place of italics.

ivory tower Institution or way of life secluded from reality and often devoted to abstract intellectual concerns rather than practical everyday matters: *The professor lived in an ivory tower and had no idea of what was going on in the outside world.*

jargon Specialized or technical language used by a particular group, often by members of a profession, such as lawyers, stockbrokers or doctors. For those who use it, jargon may be an efficient shorthand for communicating complex ideas. To outsiders, however, it often seems incomprehensible, elitist and manipulative. An objectionable use of jargon would occur, for example, if a doctor warned a patient that his diet may cause 'epidermal seborrhoea' – actually referring to nothing more than an oily skin. (See also SLANG; VOGUE WORD.)

***je ne sais quoi* (zhuhn-say-KWAA)** Quality that one notices clearly but cannot define or identify properly: *She has a certain* je ne sais quoi *that always attracts attention.* The phrase is French and means literally 'I do not know what'.

***joie de vivre* (JWAH-de-VEEV'R)** High spirits, zestfulness, carefree enjoyment of life: *His* joie de vivre *makes him the life and soul of the party.* The phrase is French in origin, meaning literally 'joy of living'.

kappie Afrikaans word for CIRCUMFLEX.

Khoisan (or Khoesan) languages Collective name for the languages spoken by ▷KHOIKHOI and San people of southern Africa, as well as in parts of Tanzania. Examples include Khoekhoegowab (previously Nama/Damara) and several San varieties spoken by small groups in Botswana, Namibia, Angola and South Africa. They are distinct from the BANTU LANGUAGES spoken by the majority of blacks in southern Africa.

laconic Using few words, terse: *The cowboy's laconic style developed during long periods of isolation from other people.* The term is derived from the ancient Greek name for the Spartans or Laconians, who were famous for their brevity of speech.

lexicon Dictionary, especially of an ancient language such as Latin; also a specialized vocabulary used by a particular profession or interest-group, as in *Computer experts use a lexicon which is completely incomprehensible to outsiders.* (Compare GLOSSARY.)

ligature See DIPHTHONG.

lingua franca Language adopted as a means of communication between people who speak different mother tongues: *English is increasingly the lingua franca of those associated with the international art world.*
❖ Lingua Franca was what the Italians called the French language of the Crusaders. Later it referred to the medieval PIDGIN – composed of a mixture of Italian, French and other tongues – that was used by traders in Mediterranean ports.

linguistics The science or study of language and its structure, including PHONETICS, SEMANTICS and SYNTAX.

litho-, -lith- COMBINING FORM, sometimes used as a PREFIX, from Greek, meaning 'stone', as in *lithograph* and *Neolithic.*

litotes (lye-TOH-teez) FIGURE OF SPEECH consisting of a deliberate UNDERSTATEMENT, typically by denying the opposite, for example: *We weren't exactly sweet-smelling after our three-day hike.* (Compare HYPERBOLE.)

loan word Word adopted, with or without being changed, from another language. The words *veld, donga* and *kloof* are loan words from Afrikaans, while *boma* (enclosure) is a loan word from Swahili. (See SOUTH AFRICAN ENGLISH panel, p 27.)

loc cit ABBREVIATION of the Latin phrase *loco citato*, meaning 'in the place mentioned'. It is used in footnotes to refer to a book, article or page previously cited. (Compare IBID; IDEM.)

logo (or logotype) Symbol or name used to identify a company, magazine or product. The symbol of Pegasus, the flying horse, is the logo of Reader's Digest.

lower case Small letters, the common form of the letters of the alphabet, as opposed to capital letters. (Compare UPPER CASE.)

macro- PREFIX, from Greek, meaning 'large', as in the words *macroeconomics* and *macrocosm.* (Compare MICRO-.)

magnum opus Masterpiece or great work, especially the single greatest work of a writer, an artist or a composer, as in: *Beethoven's 9th Symphony is the composer's magnum opus.* The term is Latin for 'great work'.

main clause (or independent clause) CLAUSE – particularly in a COMPLEX SENTENCE – that can stand alone as a full sentence and has one VERB. In the sentence *When snow falls, children often rush out to play*, the main clause is *children often rush out to play.* (Compare SUBORDINATE CLAUSE.)

malapropism Humorous misuse of a word that sounds similar to the intended word: *an allegory on the banks of the Nile* in place of *an alligator* is an example from Mrs Malaprop in Richard Brinsley ▷SHERIDAN's play *The Rivals.*

male-, mal- PREFIX, from Latin, meaning 'bad' or 'badly', as in *maladroit, maladministration* and *malediction.* (Compare BENE-.)

mass noun (also uncountable noun or noncountable noun) NOUN referring to an object or a substance that has no clear limits. It cannot usually occur in the plural or be preceded by *a* or *an. Milk* and *information* are mass nouns. Many words can be either mass nouns or COUNT NOUNS, depending on the way they are used, as with *wine* in the sentences *Have a glass of wine* (mass noun) and *We stock two thousand different wines* (count noun).

maxim Brief summing-up of some general truth, guiding principle or rule of conduct, such as *Do as you would be done by* or *It ain't necessarily so.* (See MOTTO.)

mega- PREFIX, from Greek, meaning 'million' or 'very large', as in *megaton, megawatt* and *megaphone.*

metaphor Figure of speech in which one thing is compared to another, without the use of *like* or *as* to make the comparison obvious. The effect can vary greatly from the extremely evocative, as in *The road through the village was a ribbon of moonlight*, to the overused cliché, as in *He is in the twilight of his life.* (Compare SIMILE.)

metonymy Figure of speech in which an idea is referred to by a related, and usually more specific, term, such as *the Bench* to refer to judges collectively or *treading the boards* for acting. (Compare SYNECDOCHE.)

-metry SUFFIX, from Greek, meaning 'measuring', as in *geometry* and *symmetry.*

micro- PREFIX, from Greek, meaning 'small', as in *microbe, microdot* and *microscopic.* (Compare MACRO-.)

Middle English Form of English written and spoken from *c*1150 to 1500. Its basis was the Germanic language OLD ENGLISH – also called Anglo-Saxon – with the addition after the ▷NORMAN CONQUEST of England in 1066 of a large number of Norman French words. There were five main dialects in Middle English: East Midland, West Midland, South Eastern, South Western and Northern. Much literature of the time was written in the two Midlands dialects, and it was a London version of East Midlands that later developed into modern English.
❖ There was no standard system of spelling in Middle English, and even in the same text a word may be spelled in several different ways. Some of the literature – as, for instance, Geoffrey Chaucer's The ▷CANTERBURY TALES – can be appreciated by modern readers, but authentic pronunciation of the language needs special training.

misnomer Incorrect or unsuitable term for a person or thing: *It would be a misnomer to call her beautiful – 'pretty' might be a more appropriate word.*

misrelated construction VERB or PHRASE linked by the SYNTAX of the sentence to a NOUN other than the one intended. For example, *While strolling along the pavement, a loose flagstone sent her sprawling,* which suggests that a flagstone was strolling along. In *As prime minister, I would like to ask you about your cabinet reshuffle* it sounds as if the speaker is the prime minister. Correct wording would be *While strolling along the pavement, she was sent sprawling by a loose flagstone* and *I would like to ask you, as prime minister, about your cabinet reshuffle.* (See also DANGLING PARTICIPLE.)

mixed metaphor Sequence of METAPHORS or SIMILES drawn from clashing fields of comparison and producing a ridiculous effect, as in the sentences *By sitting on the fence you are just burying your head in the sand* and, from Shakespeare's ▷HAMLET, *to take up arms against a sea of troubles.*

mnemonic (neh-MONN-ick) Rhyme, formula or device used as an aid to memory. For example, the colours of the rainbow can be recalled by the sentence *Richard of York gave battle in vain.* The initial letters of the words in the sentence prompt the names of the colours in their correct order: red, orange, yellow, green, blue, indigo, violet.

modifier (or qualifier) Word, PHRASE or CLAUSE that describes or defines the sense of another word or phrase. The modifier of a NOUN is an ADJECTIVE – for example, *green* in *the green door.* An ADVERB modifies a VERB, adjective, or another adverb, for example *desperately* in *desperately seeking Susan.*

modus operandi Manner in which a thing operates or a person works: *The company's modus operandi was to poach customers from its rivals*; or *The artist's modus operandi is to make sketches of buildings abroad and then come home to paint.* The phrase is Latin for 'way of working'.

modus vivendi Living arrangement or practical compromise between people or groups with different interests or habits: *She's not the housemate I'd have chosen, but we've found a modus vivendi*; *The Republicans' modus vivendi with the Nationalists could not last, and the coalition government collapsed.* The phrase is Latin for 'way of living'.

monkey's wedding South African English term for the weather phenomenon when it rains and the sun shines at the same time. The phrase is a direct translation from similar expressions in NGUNI LANGUAGES.

mono- PREFIX, from Latin, meaning 'one', as in *monorail, monopoly* and *monotonous.*

mood Form of a VERB indicating the speaker's attitude towards either the utterance or the person being addressed, such as whether the action mentioned is true or doubtful, and whether the listener is meant to react (as to a command) or simply absorb information (as from a statement). In English, the INDICATIVE mood is used for statements of fact (*The fence is blue*), the SUBJUNCTIVE is used for wishes and doubts (*If the fence were blue*), the IMPERATIVE is used for commands (*Paint the fence blue*), and the INTERROGATIVE is used for questions (*Is the fence blue?*).

-morph- COMBINING FORM, from Greek, meaning 'shape', as in *morphology, endomorph* and *amorphous.*

morpheme Another word for STEM.

motto Word, phrase or short sentence, typically expressing some belief or ideal and sometimes accompanying a coat of arms, as in *Ex unitate vires* (Unity is strength) – the motto South Africa adopted after ▷UNION. The word also refers to a MAXIM adopted as a guide to conduct, such as *give and take* or *If a thing is worth doing, it's worth doing well.*

Mrs Grundy (or Mother Grundy) Prudish and narrow-minded person, always ready to criticize the morals and behaviour of others. The original Mrs Grundy was a character mentioned (though not appearing) in Thomas Morton's play *Speed the Plough* (1798).

multi- PREFIX, derived from Latin, meaning 'many' or 'much', as in *multinational* and *multifaceted.* (Compare POLY-.)

Murphy's Law The principle humorously adopted by engineers and scientists, stating 'If anything can go wrong, it will'.

nail one's colours to the mast To state one's policy openly, or make a clear commitment to pursue a particular goal: *The third candidate nailed his colours firmly to the mast, and announced that he would raise taxes if elected.* The phrase is of nautical origin. The 'colours' of a ship are its flags, which in battle would be lowered to surrender. By nailing the colours to the mast, the captain would make surrender impossible, and so announce his intention to fight to the death. (Compare SAIL UNDER FALSE COLOURS.)

NB ABBREVIATION of the Latin phrase *nota bene,* meaning 'note well', used to emphasize or draw attention to an important point.

neo- PREFIX, originating from the Greek for 'new' or 'revived', as in *Neolithic* and *Neo-Nazi.* (Compare PALAEO-.)

neologism Newly coined word or phrase, or a familiar word used in a new sense. Recent neologisms include *greenhouse effect, yuppie* and *toy boy.*

newspeak Language that is full of ambiguities, JARGON and propaganda, especially as used by bureaucrats and politicians. The original newspeak was a bureaucratic language invented by George Orwell in his novel ▷NINETEEN EIGHTY-FOUR.

Nguni languages Subfamily of BANTU LANGUAGES including Zulu, Xhosa, Swazi and Ndebele.

nom de plume False name or pseudonym adopted by an author. Mark Twain was the nom de plume of the American writer Samuel Langhorne Clemens, and the thriller-writer Ruth Rendell also writes under the nom de plume Barbara Vine. The term means 'pen name' in French, although the French themselves now prefer the phrase *nom de guerre* (war name).

noncountable noun See MASS NOUN.

nondefining clause (or nonrestrictive clause) RELATIVE CLAUSE that gives some extra information about the NOUN it refers to, but does not define it or crucially limit it. Nondefining clauses can be left out without drastically affecting the meaning of the sentence. They are often introduced by *which* or *who* and are usually placed between commas in the sentence, as in *The family, which is the basic unit of society, is gradually losing its appeal*; or *Mr Jones, who lives next door to my parents, is emigrating to New Zealand.* (Compare DEFINING CLAUSE.)

non sequitur Irrelevant remark lacking a logical connection with what has just been said, or a false deduction incorrectly derived from given information, as in the sentence *Born in Glasgow, he was fascinated by aeroplanes from an early age.* The Latin phrase means literally 'it does not follow'.

noun PART OF SPEECH that refers to a person, place, thing or idea. Nouns may be COMMON NOUNS (referring to things), such as *dog* or *child*; or PROPER NOUNS (names), such as *Mary, Beethoven* or *Scotland*; or ABSTRACT NOUNS (referring to qualities or ideas), such as *happiness, beauty* or *cause.* They may be SINGULAR, as in *dog, fly* and *child*; PLURAL, as in *dogs, flies* and *children*; or MASS NOUNS (uncountable nouns), as in *jealousy* and *milk.* Within sentences, nouns may function as SUBJECTS, OBJECTS or COMPLEMENTS. (See also COLLECTIVE NOUNS panel; GERUND; COUNT NOUN; POSSESSIVE.)

noun phrase Phrase that functions as a NOUN in a sentence. In the sentence *The whole family, including the dog, sat down and watched the video of our holiday,* there are two noun phrases: *The whole family, including the dog* and *the video of our holiday.*

nouveau riche Person who has recently become rich. The expression often carries the CONNOTATION of an upstart lacking in taste or social graces. The plural is *nouveaux riches,* pronounced in the same way as the singular: *The nouveaux riches are moving into our area in droves, with their flashy cars and their ridiculously expensive and pretentious parties.* The term is French for 'new rich'.

nuance Subtle variation of meaning. For example, the verbs *to prevaricate* and *to dissemble* have a nuance that distinguishes them from the blunter verb *to lie.*

number Way in which a word varies according to whether it refers to one thing or to many (that is, whether it is in the SINGULAR or PLURAL). In English, NOUNS, VERBS and PRONOUNS may vary in number: *ox, has* and *it* are singular; *oxen, have* and *them* are plural. (See also CONCORD; PERSON.)

object Part of a sentence or CLAUSE that receives or is affected by the action of a VERB, often answering the questions 'Whom?' or 'What?' after the verb. In the sentence *She gave me roses,* the NOUN *roses* is the DIRECT OBJECT, directly affected by the action, and the PRONOUN *me* is the INDIRECT OBJECT, being indirectly on the receiving end of the action. An object may consist of a single noun or pronoun, or of a phrase or clause such as *three gifts, including a necklace* in the sentence *On my twenty-first birthday, my mother gave me three gifts, including a necklace.* (Compare COMPLEMENT; PREDICATE; SUBJECT.)

Old English GERMANIC LANGUAGE with genders and cases, also called Anglo-Saxon, which was spoken and written from 700 AD to *c*1150. At least four dialects were used – Northumbrian, Mercian, Kentish and West Saxon. The best-known Old English poetry, including ▷BEOWULF, is contained in four manuscripts from the late 10th and early 11th centuries. The earliest known work is the *Hymn of Creation,* which was composed in the late 7th century by Caedmon, a Northumbrian cowherd.

omni- PREFIX, from Latin, meaning 'all' or 'totally', as in *omnivorous* and *omnipotent.*

onomatopoeia (ON-a-MAT-a-PEE-a) Words whose sounds suggest their meaning, for example *buzz, crackle, whoosh* and *squelch.* Poets often use onomatopoeic words to great effect, to evoke a particular sound or association with a noise.

on tenterhooks Anxious, in suspense, waiting uneasily for news: *We were on tenterhooks until the doctor phoned to assure us that the operation had been a success.* In weaving or clothmaking, a tenter was a frame over which new cloth would be stretched taut and held in place by hooked nails, or tenterhooks. By association, tense people were said to be on tenterhooks.

Oxford English Dictionary Standard work of reference for the English language. The first edition was completed in 1928 after 70 years in preparation. The current version was published in 1989 in 29 volumes and contains almost half a million entries and two million quotations giving the earliest uses of each meaning of a word.

oxymoron FIGURE OF SPEECH in which a dramatic effect is achieved by using two contradictory words together, such as *sweet sorrow, a militant pacifist, a cheerful pessimist, a profoundly superficial answer.* The term is Greek and means 'pointedly foolish'.

palaeo-, paleo- PREFIX, from Greek, meaning 'old' or 'ancient', as in *palaeontology* and *Palaeolithic.* (Compare NEO-.)

palindrome Word or expression that reads the same backwards and forwards, for example the words *reviver* and *Otto,* and the sentences *Evil rats on no star live* and *Able was I ere I saw Elba.*

pan- PREFIX, from the Greek, meaning 'all' or 'everywhere', as in *pantheism, panacea* and *Pan-Africanist.*

paradox Statement that seems absurd or self-contradictory but turns out to have a striking truth or wisdom about it, such as *You have to be cruel to be kind* and *non-conformists tend to think alike.*

paragraph Division of written text, usually marking a change of theme or topic. A paragraph may consist of a single sentence, but usually contains several sentences that develop the central idea into a fairly self-contained unit. Each paragraph is marked off by beginning on a separate line, which is often indented from the margin.

paraphrase Different and often shorter version of a spoken text or written passage, expressing the same ideas but using more easily understood words to clarify the meaning. For example, the sentence *Her intellectual faculties are exceptional* could be paraphrased as *She is very bright.*

parentheses (or brackets) The punctuation marks ( ), used to mark off secondary material in a sentence, such as a phrase that explains or qualifies something without altering the grammatical structure of the sentence, as in the sentence *Grandma Margaret (she is actually my great-aunt) still rides a motorbike.* The singular is parenthesis. (See also PARENTHESIS; SQUARE BRACKETS; DASH.)

parenthesis Phrase or clause within a sentence, typically marked off by dashes or PARENTHESES, that qualifies or explains something without affecting the grammatical structure of the rest of the sentence. The words between the dashes or brackets form a parenthesis within the sentence *This is the best wine – and I've tried thousands – that I've ever tasted.*

par excellence To the highest degree, supremely, serving as an outstanding example of its kind, as in the sentence *The show house is an example of energy efficiency* par excellence. The term is French in origin, meaning literally 'by way of excellence'.

parsing The analysing of a SENTENCE into its various PARTS OF SPEECH, with an explanation of their forms, functions and relationships.

participle Form of a VERB that combines with an AUXILIARY VERB to indicate a certain TENSE, to indicate the PASSIVE VOICE, or to form an ADJECTIVE. In the following sentences, *affecting* is the present participle, and *affected* is the past participle of the verb *affect*: *The noise was affecting my concentration. My concentration was affected by the noise. He is an affected young man, but he can certainly write an affecting love story.* (See DANGLING PARTICIPLE; MISRELATED CONSTRUCTION.)

parting shot (also Parthian shot) Final sneer or cutting remark at the close of an argument. The phrase is an allusion to the battlefield tactics of the ancient Parthians, an Asian people, whose warriors would turn in the saddle while retreating and shoot a volley of arrows at the pursuing enemy.

part of speech Category or type of word, classified according to its function within a sentence and its relations to other words. The main traditional parts of speech are ADJECTIVE, ADVERB, ARTICLE, CONJUNCTION, INTERJECTION, NOUN, PREPOSITION, PRONOUN and VERB. (See PARSING.)

passé Out of date, no longer in fashion, as in *His views on women not working outside the home are passé.* The term is French in origin, and means literally 'past' or 'passed'.

passim Term used in footnotes and indexes to indicate that the word or subject under discussion is found very often within the reference cited. For example, the footnote *For his striking use of similes, see the story 'Mrs Harris', pp13-18* passim, means that similes occur throughout pages 13 to 18. The term is Latin for 'throughout'.

passive VOICE, or VERB form, indicating that the action of the verb is done to (rather than by) the SUBJECT. For example, the sentence *The hymn was then sung by the cantor* is passive, or 'in the passive', since the subject (the hymn) undergoes rather than performs the action of the verb (the singing). The counterpart of the passive is the ACTIVE, as in the sentence *The cantor then sang the hymn.* The passive is often used when the person or thing responsible for an action is unknown: *My car was stolen* or in official notices such as *Trespassers will be prosecuted.*

past participle PARTICIPLE used to indicate a past or completed action, or the PASSIVE voice, and usually ending in *-ed* or *-d*: *The curfew was lifted; The storm has broken.* (Compare PRESENT PARTICIPLE.)

past perfect See PERFECT.

past tense See TENSE.

patois (PAT-wa) JARGON belonging to a particular group, especially a gang or an underclass; a regional dialect; or Jamaican English, CREOLE or any other mixed language. (Compare ARGOT.)

pecking order Hierarchy of power or importance in any group or organization: *The scriptwriter ranks very low in the Hollywood pecking order.* The phrase comes from the behaviour of chickens, where weaker or less aggressive individuals submit meekly to the pecking of stronger ones.

per capita Per person: *In some countries the per capita income is less than US$100 a year.* The phrase is Latin, meaning 'by heads'.

perfect Kind of TENSE form known as an 'aspect' used to indicate that an action has been completed. In English, perfect tenses always include a form of the VERB *to have* along with the PAST PARTICIPLE. *They have finished* is in the 'present perfect'; while *They had finished* is in the 'past perfect', or 'pluperfect'; and *They will have finished* is in the 'future perfect'. (Compare CONTINUOUS; PRETERITE.)

periodic sentence COMPLEX SENTENCE in which the MAIN CLAUSE or main point appears at the end, producing the effect of a climax after a build-up; for example, *Even though they needed our help, instead of welcoming us they resented our arrival.*

per se In itself, as such, through its own nature: *I've nothing against the proposal per se – it's just that the details need thinking through.* The phrase is Latin in origin, meaning literally 'by itself'.

person Form of a PRONOUN or VERB that distinguishes the speaker ('first person'), the person addressed ('second person'), and the person or thing spoken about ('third person'). In combination with NUMBER (singular or plural), person determines the word's INFLECTION. For example, for personal pronouns and the present-tense verb *to be*, the first person singular is *I am*, and the third person plural is *they are*.

personal pronoun PRONOUN that indicates the person or people, thing or things, performing an action, involved in an action or being spoken about. Its form depends on PERSON, NUMBER, GENDER and CASE. For example, *she* is first person, singular, feminine, subject; and *them* is third person, plural, any gender, object. The other personal pronouns include *I, you, he, it* and *us* and are sometimes considered to include POSSESSIVE PRONOUNS such as *his, hers, ours, yours, mine, its* and *theirs*.

persona non grata Unwelcome or unacceptable person, especially a diplomat whose presence is no longer acceptable in a foreign country: *The cultural attaché was accused of spying and declared* persona non grata. *I'm* persona non grata *at the Winthorpes, after criticizing their daughter's poetry in public.* The phrase is Latin in origin and means literally 'unacceptable person'.

petro-, petr- PREFIX, from Greek, meaning 'stone' or 'rock', as in *petroleum, petrology* and *petrify*.

-phil- COMBINING FORM, from Greek, meaning 'love' or 'tendency towards', as in *Anglophile, philharmonic* and *haemophilia*.

-phobe, -phobia SUFFIX, from Greek, meaning 'fear' or 'irrational hatred', as in *Francophobe, claustrophobia* and *hydrophobia*.

-phon- COMBINING FORM, from Greek, meaning 'sound' or 'speaking', as in *stereophonic, telephone* and *Anglophone*.

phonetic alphabet Set of letters and symbols used to represent the sounds of speech in writing. The term also refers to letters of the alphabet by words such as Foxtrot for 'f', Oscar for 'o' and Tango for 't'.

phonetics Science or study of speech sounds, including the way in which they are produced by the voice.

phrase Group of connected words within a sentence, typically having a SUBJECT or a PREDICATE, but not both. In the sentence *A litter of piglets trotted towards the fence*, the words *a litter of piglets* is a NOUN PHRASE, and *towards the fence* is an ADVERB phrase.

pictogram (also pictograph) Picture used to represent a word or an idea, as in HIEROGLYPHS. Pictograms are the oldest form of writing known. (Compare IDEOGRAM.)

pidgin Simplified language based on two or more other tongues, and generally developed in colonial times as a means of communication between foreigners and indigenous people. Pidgin often sounds comical to speakers of one of the original languages – for example, when an English-speaker hears Prince

Philip described as *number one fellah bilong Missis Queen.* (Compare CREOLE; FANAKALO.)
❖ Pidgin English was originally a form of Anglo-Chinese used by 17th-century traders; curiously, 'pidgin' is believed to have been a Chinese corruption of the word 'business'.

pig in a poke A purchase made sight unseen. The phrase goes back to the old market custom of selling live piglets in a sack or 'poke'. A dishonest trader might sneak a stray cat or dog into the sack, and the unwary buyer might be 'sold a pup'; the buyer who opened the sack to check its contents might 'let the cat out of the bag'.

pleonasm REDUNDANCY through the use of more words than necessary, as in *ancient old man.* (Compare also TAUTOLOGY.)

pluperfect See PERFECT.

plural A word that indicates that more than one object or person is being spoken about is said to be plural (or 'a plural' or 'in the plural'). In English, NOUNS, PRONOUNS and VERBS may be plural; for example, each of the words in the sentence *Doctors cure themselves* is plural. Most nouns in English form the plural by adding *-s* or *-es*: *cows, cats, potatoes;* others have irregular plurals such as *oxen, fungi* and *geese*; others are always plural (*cattle*) or the same in the singular and in the plural (*deer, sheep*). (Compare SINGULAR; see also NUMBER; CONCORD.)

poly- PREFIX, from Greek, meaning 'many' or 'much', as in *polygamy, polyglot* and *polygon.* (Compare MULTI-.)

portmanteau word (also blend) Word formed by fusing the sounds and meanings of two different words, such as *Chunnel* (from *Channel* and *tunnel*) and *chortle* (*chuckle* and *snort*). The second example was coined by Lewis ▷CARROLL, who was also responsible for the term 'portmanteau word'. In *Through the Looking-Glass,* Humpty Dumpty describes such blends as 'like a portmanteau – there are two meanings packed up into one word' – just as a portmanteau bag consists of two thinner cases hinged together at the back.

possessive CASE, or form, of a NOUN or PRONOUN indicating possession or association. Nouns usually form the possessive by adding an apostrophe if plural, or *'s* if singular or an irregular plural: *It is to the students' credit rather than the teacher's; the children's toys.*

possessive pronoun PRONOUN indicating possession; specifically the pronouns *mine, hers, his, its, ours, yours, theirs* and *whose.* The adjectival forms – *my, her, his, its, our, your* and *their* – are called possessive adjectives. (Compare PERSONAL PRONOUN.)

post- PREFIX, derived from Latin, meaning 'after' or 'behind', as in *postgraduate* and *posterior.* (Compare ANTE-; PRE-.)

pre- PREFIX, derived from Latin, meaning 'before', as in *prefix, pre-date* and *pre-Victorian.* (Compare ANTE-; POST-.)

predicate Part of a sentence that indicates something about the SUBJECT. The predicate includes the main VERB as well as all its MODIFIERS. In the following sentence, only the first word is the subject, and all the rest is the predicate: *You can hardly expect me to dance with delight at the news.* (Compare COMPLEMENT; OBJECT.)

prefix Letter or letters attached to the beginning of a word to modify the meaning, such as 'dis-', 'pro-' and 're-' in the examples *disallow, pronoun* and *regroup.* Most prefixes are COMBINING FORMS – that is, they can be combined with other words or other combining forms to create new words. (Compare SUFFIX.)

preposition PART OF SPEECH indicating the relationship of a NOUN or PRONOUN to another word or words nearby. Common English prepositions are *to, for, in, on, with, at, by* and *from,* as in *We spoke to the guard* and *Could you run an errand for me?* An old schoolroom rule used to forbid the use of prepositions at the end of a sentence. However, this rule is often ignored if the alternative leads to a clumsy sentence. Except in very formal contexts, it is just as correct to say *That is the guard we spoke to* as it is to say *That is the guard to whom we spoke.*
❖ When British prime minister Sir Winston ▷CHURCHILL's secretary changed a sentence of his to ensure it did not end with a preposition, Churchill is said to have written beside it: 'This is the kind of English up with which I will not put!'

present participle PARTICIPLE consisting of the *-ing* form of the VERB, typically indicating a present or continuing action: *The drought in the Karoo is ravaging the veld.* (Compare PAST PARTICIPLE; GERUND.)

present perfect See PERFECT.

present tense See TENSE.

preterite (PRETT-er-it) The past TENSE, or a VERB in the past form, indicating a completed action or condition. In the sentence *Tom stole a pig,* the verb *stole* is in the preterite.

prima facie (PREE-mah FAY-see) At first sight; on the face of it; before a more detailed inspection: *It seems prima facie that she died of a heart attack; There is prima-facie evidence of insider trading.* The phrase is Latin, meaning 'on first appearance'.

pro- PREFIX, taken from Latin and having many meanings, including 'in favour of', as in *pro-American,* and 'serving in place of', as in *pronoun.* (Compare ANTI-.)

proactive Taking actions in advance so as to try to determine a course of events, rather than waiting for something to happen and then merely reacting to it.

progressive See CONTINUOUS.

pronoun Word that serves in place of a NOUN or NOUN PHRASE that has been mentioned before or that can be understood from the context. For example, by substituting the pronouns *she, it* and *mine* for the various noun phrases, the sentence *The princess modelled her story on my story* could become *She modelled it on mine.* (See DEMONSTRATIVE PRONOUN; INDEFINITE PRONOUN; PERSONAL PRONOUN; POSSESSIVE PRONOUN; REFLEXIVE PRONOUN; RELATIVE PRONOUN.)

proper noun (also proper name) NOUN referring by name to an individual person, animal, country or book, etc, and typically spelt with a capital first letter. *Mary, Zimbabwe* and *Mars* are examples of proper nouns. (Compare COMMON NOUN.)

pro rata In proportion: *The liquidator distributed all remaining assets pro rata to the creditors.* The term is a shortened version of the Latin phrase *pro rata parte,* meaning 'according to the calculated share'.

proverb Short, memorable, widely known saying that expresses a traditional piece of wisdom or advice, such as *More haste, less speed; A bird in the hand is worth two in the bush;* or *Spare the rod and spoil the child.* Sometimes, several proverbs convey a single idea in their different ways, as in *Beauty is only skin deep* and *Don't judge a book by its cover.* Sometimes one proverb appears to contradict another, as in *Too many cooks spoil the broth* and *Many hands make light work;* or *Look before you leap* and *He who hesitates is lost.* But they do not invalidate each other; they are both true of human experience in different contexts.

pseudo- PREFIX, taken from the Greek, meaning 'false', as in the words *pseudonym* and *pseudointellectual.*

pseudonym False or adopted name, especially the 'pen name' or NOM DE PLUME of an author. 'George Eliot', for example, was the pseudonym of the English novelist Mary Ann Evans (1819-80) and the Danish writer Karen Blixen (1885-1962) wrote under several, including Isak Dinesen.

pull out all the stops To put all one's energies into pursuing a goal. The phrase is based on organ playing, and refers to the effort and dexterity needed to manipulate the many stops (knobs) while playing.

pun Play on words, based either on juggling different senses of the same word or on substituting one word for another that sounds similar: *My moustache makes it quite a strain to drink soup.* Many newspaper headlines and advertisements rely on the use of puns to create a comic effect: *Cemetery in grave financial difficulties.*

purple passage (also purple prose) Passage of speech or writing that is full of flowery language and uses long sentences and extravagant METAPHORS.

Pyrrhic victory Victory that involves such great losses for the victor as to be almost as bad as defeat. The phrase is based on a supposed remark by Pyrrhus, a Greek king of the 3rd century BC. After defeating the Roman army in a battle, but suffering severe losses to his own army, he is believed to have said: 'We cannot afford another victory like that.'

QED ABBREVIATION of the Latin phrase *quod erat demonstrandum*, meaning 'which was to be demonstrated'. It is used when a conclusion has been reached that cannot be doubted or questioned, as well as at the end of a geometry theorem.

qualifier See MODIFIER.

quasi- PREFIX, from Latin, meaning either 'almost', as in *quasi-scientific*, or 'resembling but not really the same as', as in *quasi-intellectual.*

question mark Punctuation mark (?) used after a direct question: *How are you feeling? Has the meeting started yet?* (See also INTERROGATIVE; RHETORICAL QUESTION.)

quid pro quo Something given in exchange, compensation, in return or received, as in *He never does anyone a favour without calculating what he can expect as a quid pro quo.* The plural is *quid pro quos.* The phrase is Latin in origin, meaning literally 'something for something'.

IN THE WARS *Pyrrhus, King of Epirus, wins the battle at Asculum in 279 BC. However, he suffered such heavy losses in his 'victory' that he was unable to avert eventual defeat by the Romans.*

quixotic (kwik-SOT-ik) ADJECTIVE meaning enthusiastic and well-meaning, but given to unreachable ideals. The word derives from the hero of Cervantes's novel ▷DON QUIXOTE, who was a romantic idealist, and is often misused to mean 'gallant but absurd' or 'dangerously foolish'.

quotation marks (also inverted commas) Punctuation marks (') and (') used to mark the beginning and end of dialogue, quoted words, definitions and titles. When quoted material appears within a quotation, the quotation marks switch from single to double, or vice versa: *She told the typist, 'Every time I write "salt" you type "slat".'*

qv ABBREVIATION of the Latin phrase *quod vide*, meaning 'which see'. It is used to refer the reader to the item mentioned, which is discussed under its own heading elsewhere, as in *Headaches can sometimes be caused by tension (qv) in the neck.*

raison d'être **(RAY-zon DETT'R)** The central purpose of a person or object's existence; the point of living or being: *Wine-tasting seems to be his entire* raison d'être, *so it's no wonder he feels suicidal when he has a cold*; *She was devastated when the company made her redundant, as work was her* raison d'être. The term is French in origin, meaning literally 'reason to be'.

rat race Term meaning the struggle for power, promotion or survival in urban society, and often used in the context of work or earning a living. It may have originated from experiments into animal behaviour in which rats try to find their way out of a maze, or run or walk continuously on a treadmill.

red herring False clue or trail; a distraction; something that draws attention away from more important matters. The original phrase was *to draw a red herring across the path.* In the past foxhunting hounds were trained to ignore distracting scent trails – or to avoid being 'thrown off the scent' – by having a smoked herring (reddish in colour) dragged across the countryside.

redundancy In grammar, unnecessary repetition or excessive wordiness in speech or writing. The phrases *freedom and liberty* and *brotherhood and fraternity* display redundancy. (Compare PLEONASM; TAUTOLOGY.)

reflexive pronoun PRONOUN, typically ending in *-self*, that refers to a previously mentioned NOUN or pronoun, as in *I hurt myself*; *The candidates voted for themselves*; *The cat licked itself clean.*

regular verb (also weak verb) VERB that follows the standard pattern of INFLECTION when forming its past TENSE and PAST PARTICIPLE, by simply adding *-ed* or *-d*, as in, for example, *talk* and *hope*, which become *I talked, I have talked* and *I hoped, I have hoped.* (Compare IRREGULAR VERB.)

relative clause SUBORDINATE CLAUSE that functions like an ADJECTIVE to describe the NOUN it follows. The clause beginning *who* is a relative clause in the sentence *Bianca is the woman who lives in the tower in the middle of the forest.*

relative pronoun PRONOUN that relates one part of a sentence to another, such as *who, whom, whose* and *which*. In *He was the famous stuntman who climbed the tower which belongs to a life assurance company, who* and *which* are relative pronouns.

reported speech Another term for INDIRECT SPEECH.

rest on one's laurels To rely on one's past achievements instead of maintaining one's efforts: *If the champion rests on his laurels and doesn't train properly, he will be beaten by his young opponent.* The opposite is *look to one's laurels*, which means to protect one's reputation or leading position by taking care not to underestimate the task ahead or the competition facing one: *He'd better look to his laurels, because his young opponent seems very sharp.* The original laurels were wreaths presented as marks of honour in antiquity. The tradition of giving champions laurel wreaths was carried on until quite recently in motor racing.

restrictive clause Another name for DEFINING CLAUSE.

rhetoric The study or use of style in literature and public speaking, especially to persuade or influence listeners. It can also refer to high-flown but empty or insincere language, as sometimes used by politicians.

rhetorical question Question that is posed in order to make a point rather than to elicit an answer: *You don't really expect me to accept that story, do you?* or *Where have good manners gone?*

rhyming slang Humorous and often complicated form of SLANG, associated with Cockneys and other Londoners. A word is replaced by another word or phrase that rhymes with it – as, for example, *brown bread* for *dead, mince pies* for *eyes, trouble and strife* for *wife*. Sometimes only the first word of the phrase is used, as in *china* for *friend* (from *china plate* for *mate*) or else the phrase is modified, as in *titfer* (from *tit for tat*) meaning *hat*.

risqué (RISS-kay) Slightly rude, mildly indecent or improper, saucy: *None of your risqué jokes tonight, please – Aunt Myrna will be present.* The term is French in origin, meaning literally 'risked'.

Roman alphabet The letters A-Z used for writing most western European languages (including English). The alphabet was developed by the ancient Romans for the purpose of writing Latin. (Compare CYRILLIC ALPHABET panel, p 14; see also ITALICS.)

Romance languages Group of INDO-EUROPEAN tongues descended from Latin which include French, Spanish and Italian.

root Word or word-element, often Latin or Greek, which forms the core or basis of other words. For example, the element *nov* (from the Latin *novus*, 'new') is the root of such words as *novelty, novice* and *renovate*; and the form *soph* (from the Greek *sophia*, 'wisdom') is the root of such words as *sophisticated* and *philosophy*. The word 'root' can also be used to refer to a STEM.

RSVP ABBREVIATION of the French phrase *répondez s'il vous plaît*, which literally means 'please reply'. It is written or printed at the end of formal letters and invitations, and demands a response.

runes The letters of an ancient alphabet used in northern Europe before the ROMAN ALPHABET took over in the Middle Ages.
❖ Each letter was thought to have magical properties, and runes were used for charms. *Rūn* is an Old English word meaning 'secret'.

run-on sentence Sentence, considered faulty in standard grammar, in which two or more independent MAIN CLAUSES are linked without an appropriate CONJUNCTION or punctuation mark, as in the sentence *The fog was thick he could not drive home.* Inserting *and* or a SEMICOLON after *thick* would remedy things, but a COMMA would be insufficient.

run the gamut To cover the entire range of something: *She accused me of running the gamut of deadly sins, from sloth to gluttony.* The original gamut was the entire series of musical notes, a contraction of the medieval Latin *gamma* and *ut*, the names of the highest and lowest notes of the scale.

run the gauntlet To face criticism or disgrace: *After another home defeat, Rangers have yet again had to run the gauntlet of their fans.* The phrase comes from a military punishment in which the victim had to run between two lines of men who hit him with sticks or ropes. The word *gauntlet* comes from the Swedish for 'passageway'. The spelling was influenced by the word *gauntlet*, meaning 'a glove', as in THROW DOWN THE GAUNTLET, but the phrase is otherwise unrelated to it.

sacred cow Person, object, institution or idea held in such high regard as to be above criticism: *The theory of monetarism became a sacred cow in our department in the 1980s.* The phrase probably comes from the sacred status of the cow in Hindu society.

sail under false colours To take on a false name or identity, or pretend to believe in a policy, in order to hide one's real purpose: *A private investigator often has to sail under false colours in order to gain information.* The phrase harks back to the days of sailing ships, when a pirate ship or a warship might fly a false flag, or 'false colours', to trick an approaching vessel. Similarly, revealing one's true colours, or showing oneself in one's true colours, means revealing one's real nature or purpose at last – in the same way as the pirate ship or warship might hoist its real flag at the last moment, just before attacking. (Compare NAIL ONE'S COLOURS TO THE MAST.)

sang-froid (SAHN-FRWAA) Well-controlled feelings, calm behaviour, self-control, self-possession: *She showed admirable sang-froid when her ex-husband tried to gatecrash the wedding ceremony.* The term is French in origin, meaning literally 'cold blood'.

sarcasm See IRONY.

savoir-faire Ability to say or do the correct thing in any given situation, particularly in social terms: *For a teenager he has great savoir-faire.* The term is French in origin, meaning literally 'knowing to do'.

scapegoat See WHIPPING BOY.

sell down the river To cheat, betray or desert, as in *He promised to keep quiet about the accident, but when the police arrived we realized that we'd been sold down the river.* The phrase comes from the days of slavery in North America. The further south a slave was sent, the harsher the conditions became.

semantics The study or science of word meaning, including changes of meaning over time and the way that words or sentences convey sense.
❖ The word is often used to mean a difference in the meaning of words, particularly in an argument: *You're talking about a gut reaction and I'm talking about instinct – it all comes down to semantics.*

semi- PREFIX, from Latin, meaning 'half', as in *semitone, semidetached* and *semifinals.* (Compare DEMI-.)

semicolon Punctuation mark (;) used to separate two MAIN CLAUSES in a sentence, such as *Human effort arranges the pieces on the board; blind fate decides the outcome.* A COMMA would be insufficient, since the two clauses are grammatically independent (see RUN-ON SENTENCE). A full stop would be possible but less satisfactory, since the ideas within the two clauses are closely linked.

sentence A complete and independent unit of expression, consisting of a group of words or occasionally a single word, and typically containing a SUBJECT and a PREDICATE. The three expressions *Help!* and *How are you?* and *Rumour has it that the chairman will resign tomorrow* are all sentences. (See also COMPLEX SENTENCE; COMPOUND SENTENCE; DECLARATIVE SENTENCE; SIMPLE SENTENCE.)

shibboleth Word or phrase used by members of a group as a sign of solidarity, such as a SLOGAN or catchphrase that excludes outsiders. It is also used of a traditional belief or policy accepted unquestioningly by a group, as in *By getting rid of some of its old apartheid shibboleths, the National Party widened its electoral appeal.* The word is Hebrew in origin, meaning 'an ear of corn', and was a password used by the Gileadites to identify enemy Ephraimites, who always pronounced the 'sh' sound as 's'.

short shrift Brief and unsympathetic treatment, or abrupt dismissal: *The management gave short shrift to the strikers' demands.* The word *shrift* is a term previously used for confession in church, and short shrift originally referred to the brief time in which a condemned prisoner could make his confession before being executed.

sibilant Hissing sound in speech, specifically the English CONSONANT sounds 'sh', 's', 'z' and 'zh', as in the sentence *She sells leisurewear.*

sic Latin word meaning 'thus' which is used in a quoted passage of writing to indicate that an odd or incorrect word, spelling, phrase or statement has been accurately quoted, as in *Her diary refers to 'the storm of 31 November (sic) last year'.* 'Sic' often appears in ITALICS, either in PARENTHESES or in SQUARE BRACKETS.

simile (SIM-i-lee) FIGURE OF SPEECH in which one thing is compared to another by the use of words such as *like, as* or *similar to.* The effect is sometimes vivid, as in *He squatted there like an unexploded bomb, glaring at me.* However, a simile can degenerate into cliché: *My mother's bright as a button during the day, and sleeps like a log at night.* (Compare METAPHOR.)

simple sentence Sentence that has only one MAIN CLAUSE and no SUBORDINATE CLAUSES, such as *She gave them some soup without*

SOUTH AFRICAN ENGLISH

Politics, geography and a diversity of cultures have given South African English a flavour – and many words – of its own. Some, such as donga, veld, krans (or krantz), impi, trek and commandeer, became part of world English a long time ago. Others, such as apartheid, Bantustans and black-on-black violence, gained a wider currency more recently as local political events made world news. Here are some examples, gleaned from thousands of words that have been 'borrowed' from other languages or invented locally. (See also DICTIONARY OF SOUTH AFRICAN ENGLISH.)

aikona	emphatic no, never! (Nguni *hayikhona*, 'no')
boep	pot belly (Afrikaans *boepens*, 'paunch')
bonsella/basella	gift; gratuity (Zulu *ibhanselo*, 'a gift'; Xhosa *ukubasele*, 'to give')
brinjal	aubergine, egg plant (Portuguese *berinjela*, 'egg fruit')
cocopan	wagon used on narrow rails in mines (may be from Nguni, *nqukumbana*, 'Scotch cart')
dagga	cannabis, marijuana (thought to be from Khoi)
fundi	expert (Nguni *umfundisi*, 'teacher')
ghoen	marble used for shooting other marbles, hopscotch marker (Malay or Khoi)
hamba	go away (Nguni *ukuhamba*)
indaba	conference, meeting (Nguni *indaba*); concern, affair
larney	posh; boss; rich (or white) person (unknown)
lekker	pleasant, superb; good-tasting (Afrikaans)
muti	medicine (Zulu *umuthi*, 'medicine' or 'plant')
naartjie	tangerine (Afrikaans from Tamil *nartei*)
putu	stiff porridge made from mealie meal (Zulu *-phutu*, 'stiff porridge')
rondavel	circular building with a cone roof (may be from Dutch *rond*, 'round', and Malay *de wala*, 'wall')
shebeener	someone who lives off running a shebeen – an illegal/informal bar (from shebeen, from Gaelic *síbín*, 'bad ale')
spoor	track, footprint (Afrikaans)
stokvel	mutual support club whose members pool money at their social gatherings (unknown)
takkies	canvas shoes; motor car tyres (unknown)
toyi-toyi	dance/style of marching often seen during protests and pickets (unknown)
tsotsi	criminal, especially a gang member (unknown, but possibly a *fly taal* word)
ubuntu	traditional African values of humanity, goodness (Nguni)
voetsek	be off! get lost! (Afrikaans, from Dutch *voort*, 'away', *seg ik*, 'say I')

any bread. (Compare COMPLEX SENTENCE; COMPOUND SENTENCE.)

***sine qua non* (SEE-nay kwaa NON)** Essential condition or element: *An outgoing personality is a* sine qua non *for success in public relations.* The plural would be *sine qua nons.* The phrase is Latin in origin, meaning literally 'without which not'.

singular A word that indicates that a single person or thing is being spoken about is said to be singular (or 'a singular' or 'in the singular'). Each of the words in the sentence *She is a surgeon* is singular. (Compare PLURAL; see NUMBER; CONCORD.)

slang Casual or informal language used among people familiar with one another or from a similar group. Slang is considered to be inappropriate for conventional speech or writing. It is often colourful and fairly short-lived. The words *hassles* and *hang-ups* are slang terms that communicate meaning more directly than formal wording such as *pressing demands* and *personal anxieties.* (Compare COLLOQUIALISM; see ARGOT; JARGON; RHYMING SLANG.)

slogan Short phrase, typically expressing some principle, purpose or boast, as used in political or advertising campaigns, such as *Peace, jobs, security* and *Everything keeps going right.* (Compare MOTTO.)

solecism (SOHL-a-sizm) Error or unconventional use of grammar, such as the failure of CONCORD in the following sentence: *The delivery of letters and parcels have been delayed by the flooding.*

Sotho-Tswana languages Subfamily of BANTU LANGUAGES spoken in southern Africa, including Sotho, Tswana and Shona.

sotto voce (SOT-oh VO-chay) Very softly, as if to avoid being overheard: *She warned me, sotto voce, not to mention our hosts' imminent divorce.* The phrase is Italian in origin, meaning literally 'under the voice'.

split infinitive Phrase in which the INFINITIVE form of a VERB (for example 'to go' or 'to fix') is split by another word or words, usually an ADVERB, as in *to boldly go* or *to quickly and easily fix.* To split an infinitive is still widely regarded as poor style, but can sometimes add vividness.

square brackets (also brackets) Punctuation marks [ ] used within PARENTHESES for a second stage of subordinate information: *Follow the dirt road to the parking area (about 10 km [6 miles] from the tarred road).* They are also used within quotations to surround material that is not part of the original, as in *The mayor's promise was to 'aid [us] if necessary and compensate [us] if possible'.*

status quo Existing state of affairs or present condition. The term is Latin in origin, meaning literally 'state in which'.
❖ *Status quo ante* means 'in the previous state of affairs', and *in status quo* means 'in the same state (as before)'.

steal someone's thunder To gain the praise or profits that really belong to someone else, by claiming his efforts, idea or invention as one's own, as in *I did most of the research, but the project director stole my thunder by publishing the report under his own name.* The phrase apparently goes back to the 18th century, when an English playwright, John Dennis, invented a machine to make the noise of thunder during a storm scene in a play. A similar machine was later used in a performance of Shakespeare's ▷MACBETH, and Dennis complained that the management had 'stolen his thunder'.

stem Main, unchanging part of a word to which a PREFIX or SUFFIX may be added. For example, the stem of the verb *raise* is *rais-*, allowing for the words *raising, raised* and *raises.* (Compare ROOT.)

stet Word written in the margin, often by an editor, to indicate to the typist or printer that a correction made to the text should be ignored. The word is usually accompanied by a line of dots under the word or phrase referred to. It comes from Latin, and means literally 'let it stand'.

strong verb An IRREGULAR VERB.

style A manner of expression characteristic of a nation, a period of time, a school of artists, or an individual.

sub- PREFIX, from Latin, meaning 'under', as in *subnormal, subzero* and *submarine.*

subject Part of a SENTENCE or CLAUSE that indicates what it is about. The subject may be a NOUN, PRONOUN, NOUN PHRASE, or clause, and usually introduces the VERB. In the sentence *We resent your suspicions,* the pronoun *we* is the subject. Sometimes the subject is only implied, as *you* is in the sentence *Go and fetch your coat.* (Compare COMPLEMENT; OBJECT; PREDICATE.)

subjunctive Grammatical form or MOOD of a VERB expressing a wish or a doubt. In the following sentences, the verbs *save, be* and *were* are in the subjunctive: *God save the Queen; Far be it from me to tell you what to do. If I were you, I'd resign immediately; I wish I were dead.* The subjunctive mood is now used less frequently in English. (Compare IMPERATIVE; INDICATIVE.)

subordinate clause (also dependent clause) CLAUSE that cannot stand alone as a full sentence, but instead forms part of a COMPLEX SENTENCE, functioning in the same way as a NOUN, an ADVERB or an ADJECTIVE. For example, in the sentence *When the wind blows, the cradle will rock,* the clause *When the wind blows* is a subordinate clause. (Compare MAIN CLAUSE; see also RELATIVE CLAUSE.)

substantive NOUN, PRONOUN, word or group of words acting as a noun.

SPOONERISMS

William Spooner (1844-1930), who was warden of New College, Oxford, from 1903 to 1924, was well known for transposing the initial sounds of words when speaking, often with bizarre results. He is said to have once described the Lord as a 'shoving leopard', and to have announced a hymn as 'Kingquering kongs their titles take'. Some colourful 'spoonerisms' are, however, probably apocryphal. These include the claim that he said 'There's nothing to beat a ride on a well-boiled icicle', and rebuked an undergraduate with the words: 'You have hissed my mystery lectures and tasted a whole worm. You were fighting a liar in the quadrangle, and you will leave Oxford immediately by the town drain.'

PUZZLING DON *During a speech, Spooner supposedly asked: 'Which of us has not felt in his bosom a half-warmed fish?'*

suffix Letter or set of letters attached to the end of a word or STEM that modifies the meaning. In the words *feverishness* and *raising*, *-ish* and *-ness* are suffixes to the word *fever*, and *-ing* is a suffix to the stem *rais-*. (Compare PREFIX; COMBINING FORM.)

superlative Form of an ADJECTIVE or ADVERB indicating the greatest or most intense degree of the quality concerned. *Greatest, best* and *most intense* are the superlative forms of *great, good* and *intense*.
❖ When only two items are being compared, the COMPARATIVE should be used and not the superlative: *He is the taller of the twins*, not *He is the tallest of the two.*

sword of Damocles An ever-present danger, a constantly worrying threat of disaster: *Until the company announces who will be retrenched, we are all under the sword of Damocles.* The phrase goes back to an ancient legend in which an envious court flatterer called Damocles was invited to a feast by the ruler of Syracuse. Damocles was seated beneath a deadly sword which was suspended from the roof by a single horsehair – a symbol of the ever-present uncertainty and danger involved in the life that he coveted.
❖ The phrase *hanging by a thread*, as in *The victim's life is still hanging by a thread*, probably alludes to the same story.

syllable Basic unit of the sound of a word, usually containing one vowel sound and one or more consonants. The word *basic* has two syllables (ba-sic), and the word *containing* has three (con-tai-ning). A person who is curt could be described as *monosyllabic*, suggesting that he speaks in words of one syllable.

sym-, syn- PREFIX, from Greek, meaning 'together', 'with' or 'same', as in *symphony, sympathy* and *syndicate.*

synecdoche (si-NEK-da-kee) A FIGURE OF SPEECH in which a part of a person or an object is used to refer to the whole, or vice versa. For example, in the phrase *All hands on deck*, sailors are referred to by means of only their hands. (Compare METONYMY.)

synonym Word having a meaning identical or very similar to that of another in the same language. The noun *container* is a synonym of *receptacle*, and the verbs *mix, blend* and *mingle* are roughly synonymous. The opposite is ANTONYM.

synopsis Brief or condensed review of a subject or text; a summary: *I haven't time to read the whole report, but if you prepare a synopsis, I'll read that.* (See also PARAPHRASE.)

syntax The way in which words are arranged to form phrases and sentences, and the system of rules for acceptable sentence structure. In English, word order is very important (*Jack loves Jill* does not mean the same as *Jill loves Jack*), but in Latin, for example, different word endings indicate meaning, therefore allowing a more flexible sentence structure. (Compare GRAMMAR.)

tautology Superfluous or unnecessary repetition of an idea or thought through the use of different words or phrases. For example, *Both species share the same ancestor in common* is tautological several times over. *Advance planning* also involves a tautology, as planning is necessarily done in advance. (Compare PLEONASM; REDUNDANCY.)

telegraphese Abbreviated style of writing developed to save money on telegrams charged by the word. Evelyn ▷WAUGH's novel *Scoop* contains such extreme examples as *News exyou unreceived.*

tense Form of a VERB ('past', 'present' or 'future') indicating the time the sentence is uttered in relation to the action or condition described in the sentence. The present simple tense is used for permanent truths, such as *The Earth is round*, and for regular actions or a skill, occupation, and so on, for example *I bake cakes.* The past tense refers to something that has already happened, as in *I baked a cake*, and the future tense refers to something yet to occur, as in *I shall bake a cake.* Tense also includes the 'aspect' of the verb – that is, whether the action is considered complete (PERFECT) or continuing (CONTINUOUS or progressive). Aspect allows for the formation of compound tenses such as the present continuous, which is used for actions taking place now (*I am baking a cake*), and the future perfect (*I shall have baked a cake*). (See also PRETERITE.)

terra firma Solid ground or dry land: *A round-the-world yachtsman must feel very relieved to get back on terra firma.* The phrase is Latin for 'firm ground'.

tête-à-tête A private conversation between two people: *His arrival interrupted the twins' tête-à-tête.* The term is French in origin, meaning literally 'head to head'.

thesaurus Book of SYNONYMS systematically arranged for easy use as a word finder. The first serious English thesaurus, compiled by the physician Peter Mark Roget (1779-1869) after he retired from medical practice, was published in 1852, and modern editions of it are still published today.

throw down the gauntlet To issue a challenge: *By rejecting the offered pay rise, the trade union members threw down the gauntlet to the management.* The original challenge involved was to a duel. The gauntlet was the protective glove worn as part of a soldier's armour in the Middle Ages. Throwing one's gauntlet at the feet of a rival knight was a standard way of challenging him to one-to-one combat. (Compare RUN THE GAUNTLET.)

tilde (TIL-da) DIACRITICAL MARK (˜) placed above a letter to adjust the way in which it is pronounced. A tilde is often placed above the letter 'n' in Spanish to indicate that it should be pronounced nasally (something like the 'ny' in the English word *canyon)*, as in *mañana* or *señorita.*

topic sentence Main sentence in a PARAGRAPH, often the first sentence, conveying the central idea of the paragraph.

tour de force Brilliant display of strength or skill; an outstanding or impressive deed, work of art or performance: *His paintings are all wonderful, but 'Aunt Myrna in Tears' strikes me as a* tour de force *that surpasses everything else in the exhibition.* The term is French in origin, meaning 'turn of strength' or 'feat of skill'.

ENDURING SYMBOL *Francis Barraud's painting of a terrier called 'Nipper', entitled* His Master's Voice, *provided the name for the famous record label as well as its trademark.*

trademark Name or symbol used to identify a product. Trademarks are officially registered and legally restricted so that only the owner or manufacturer may use them. For example, the names *Reader's Digest* and *The Digest*, and the LOGO of Pegasus, the flying horse, are registered trademarks of The Reader's Digest Association, Inc.

trans- PREFIX, from Latin, meaning 'across' or 'beyond', as in the words *translate, transplant* and *Transvaal.* A prefix with the opposite meaning is *cis-*, from the Latin for 'this side' or 'on the near side'.

transitive verb VERB that needs a DIRECT OBJECT to complete its meaning, or that can occur in the PASSIVE voice. The verbs *solve* and *use* are transitive, as is *betray*: *He betrayed his country*; *His country was betrayed by him.* Many verbs can be either transitive or intransitive, depending on the way they are used in a sentence: compare the use of *yell* in the sentences *My teachers regularly yell abuse at me* (transitive) and *My teachers regularly yell at me* (intransitive). (Compare INTRANSITIVE VERB.)

transliteration Conversion of one alphabet into another in order to represent a foreign language: *A better transliteration of the Chinese name 'Peking' would be 'Beijing'.*

tsotsi-taal See ARGOT.

ultra- PREFIX, from Latin, which means 'beyond' or 'extremely', as in *ultraviolet, ultraconservative* and *ultramodern.*

umlaut Mark (¨) used particularly in German. It is placed over the vowels 'a', 'o' and 'u' to lengthen and flatten the sound. In English, an umlaut is often replaced by an 'e' written after the vowel, as when *Göring* is written *Goering.* (Compare DIAERESIS.)

uncountable noun See MASS NOUN.

understatement Restrained speech or writing in which claims are given less importance than they deserve: *He was quite pleased when he inherited two million dollars.* It can be used as a sort of reverse emphasis: *Compared with his peers, Einstein was quite bright.* (Compare EUPHEMISM; see LITOTES.)

upper case Capital letters, the larger and less common form of the letters of the alphabet, as used at the start of sentences or proper names. The 'M' and 'C' are upper case in the sentence *My dog bit Charlotte's leg.* (Compare LOWER CASE.)

❖ The terms 'upper case' and 'lower case' come from the early days of the printing industry when type was stored in a case, with capital letters at the top and small letters at the bottom.

verb PART OF SPEECH that represents an action or existence of a state of being. The words *run, raise, think, be* and *become* are all verbs. The form that a verb takes is determined by such factors as NUMBER, PERSON, TENSE, MOOD and VOICE. (See AUXILIARY VERB; GERUND; IMPERATIVE; IMPERSONAL VERB; INFINITIVE; INFLECTION; INTRANSITIVE VERB; IRREGULAR VERB; PARTICIPLE; REGULAR VERB; SUBJUNCTIVE; TRANSITIVE VERB.)

verbatim Using exactly the same words, word-for-word: *a verbatim report of her speech.* The term comes from the Latin *verbum*, meaning literally 'word'.

vernacular Ordinary language of the people of a region. It refers to informal everyday speech rather than strictly correct or formal written language.

vice versa With the reverse order or meaning, conversely: *Teachers gossip about pupils and vice versa.* The phrase is Latin in origin, meaning roughly 'the position being changed'.

vis-à-vis (VEEZ-a-VEE) In relation to, or regarding: *Could we have a quick talk vis-à-vis your holiday plans?* The term is French in origin, meaning literally 'face to face'.

viz ABBREVIATION of the Latin word *videlicet*, meaning 'it is permitted to see' or 'plainly', used to introduce an item or a list of items previously referred to, as in the sentence *The novelist derived little benefit from the three most noted teachers of the day, viz Leavis, Holloway and Hough.*

vogue word Word that rises quickly into fashion, appearing in newspapers, on radio and television and in the conversation of people trying to sound up-to-date. Vogue words may be old terms used in a new sense, such as *syndrome* and *parameter*, or new words such as *interface* and *clone.* (Compare JARGON.)

SACRED BEAST *White elephants were treated with awe as long ago as the 6th century. An illustration shows Abraha, viceroy of Yemen, whispering his grandson's name into the animal's ear to bring the child luck.*

voice Form of a VERB indicating the relationship between the SUBJECT of a sentence and the action expressed by the verb. In the sentence *The liquidators auctioned the stock*, the verb *auctioned* is in the ACTIVE voice, whereas in the sentence *The stock was auctioned by the liquidators*, the verb is in the PASSIVE voice.

volte-face (VOLT-FASS) Turn-around, reversal, U-turn or complete change in policy or belief: *In yet another volte-face, the government has bowed to pressure and raised the price of fuel.* The plural can be either *volte-face* or *volte-faces*, and is pronounced in the same way as the singular. The word came into English from French, which adopted it from an Italian term meaning 'turn-face'.

vowel Speech sound produced by a relatively unobstructed air stream and made with an open or partially open mouth, or a letter of the alphabet representing such a sound: 'a', 'e', 'i' ,'o', 'u' and sometimes 'y' as in *rhythm.* (Compare CONSONANT.)

weak verb See REGULAR VERB.

whipping boy Person who gets blamed for the mistakes of others, especially those more powerful: *Poor Henry is always the whipping boy when the financial manager has to explain his own bungling.* The phrase goes back to an old practice of transferring the punishment for wrongdoing by a young prince or nobleman to an innocent fellow pupil.

❖ A person who carries the blame for others is also termed a *scapegoat.* This term comes from the Israelite practice of confessing sins over the head of a goat which was then released into the wilderness to carry them away – literally an (e)scape(d) goat.

white elephant Large or impressive possession that costs more to maintain than it is worth, or an expensive project that turns out to be a failure: *This new heating system is a white elephant as it has already cost more in repairs than we can ever save in fuel costs.* In ancient Siam (now Thailand), elephants with a pale hide were highly valued and their owners were required to pamper them. According to tradition, such an elephant might be presented by a king to a courtier who had offended him. What appeared a generous gift turned out to be a harsh punishment, given the cost of feeding and housing the animal.

zeugma (also syllepsis) FIGURE OF SPEECH in which a single word is used to apply to two others either wrongly or in different ways: *She left in high dudgeon and a taxi.*

SOUTHERN AFRICAN LITERATURE

Somehow the heroes, villains, victims and oppressors who have spanned the pages of southern African literary history over the past two hundred years or so often seem far more real than their counterparts in other parts of the world. And it seldom seems to matter that their backgrounds are usually the opposite of the people who read about them. Thus, residents of city suburbs have come out rooting for Dalene Matthee's woodcutters of the lonely Knysna forest, the simple Afrikaner tenant farmers of Pauline Smith's Little Karoo, the raucous shebeen patrons of Can Themba's Soweto, and even for the gutsy Poppie Nongena ....

Abrahams, Lionel (1928-) Johannesburg-born poet, editor, publisher and man of letters. Abrahams has edited the stories of Herman Charles BOSMAN, published the work of the black poets of the 1970s such as MTSHALI and SEROTE and founded the literary magazine 'The Purple Renoster'. He is the author of several collections of poetry and a sequence of stories entitled *The Celibacy of Felix Greenspan* (1977). His poetry reflects the Johannesburg urban scene and represents the values of South African liberal humanism at its best. Abrahams has twice won the Thomas PRINGLE Prize for Poetry (1977 and 1987) and is also a recipient of the Olive SCHREINER Prize (1986).

Abrahams, Peter (1919-) Born in Vrededorp, Johannesburg, of mixed parentage, Abrahams is best known for his autobiography *Tell Freedom* (1954) and his novel *Mine Boy* (1946). The novel tells the story of a black miner, Xuma, who comes to Johannesburg and stays with Leah, a shebeen queen in Malay Camp. Abrahams' work helped put black South African writing on the literary map. He left South Africa for Britain in 1939; in 1995 he was living in Jamaica.

African-language literature Literature in the various African languages of South Africa includes the oral as well as the written form. The best-known oral form is the praise poem (in Zulu, *isibongo*) recited by a praise-singer, or *imbongi*. Written literature begins with the missionaries and their mission presses, and with early black newspapers such as 'Imvo Zabantsundu', which was established in 1884. Major writers include: in Sesotho, Thomas MOFOLO; in Xhosa, S E K Mqayi and A C Jordan; and in Zulu, R R R Dhlomo and B W Vilakazi. The finest novel is A C Jordan's *Ingqumbo Yeminyanya* (1940), published in English as *The Wrath of the Ancestors* (1980). During the apartheid years many writers found themselves restricted to producing the kind of works that would be approved for use in schools.

Afrikaans literature Although Afrikaans became one of South Africa's official languages only in 1925, the struggle for recognition of the language in the face of British imperialism dates back at least to the 1870s. By the early years of the 20th century several major writers were being published; Eugène MARAIS's poem 'Winternag' ('Winter Night') (1905) is usually regarded as a kind of watershed. There were major creative periods by the 'Dertigers' in the 1930s (notably N P van Wyk LOUW, Uys KRIGE, Elisabeth EYBERS), which marked a decisive break with more conventional rural themes, and by the 'Sestigers' of the 1960s such as Etienne LEROUX, André P BRINK, and Breyten BREYTENBACH, expressing a new sexual and political freedom.

Altman, Phyllis Best known for her novel *The Law of Vultures* (1952) and her work as a trade unionist and political activist both in South Africa and abroad. She left the country on an exit permit in 1965. Her novel interweaves the stories of Thaele, who comes to Johannesburg to educate himself and find work, Nkosi, a World War II veteran, and Dhlamini, a trade unionist. It is unusual for its multiple treatment of the 'JIM COMES TO JOBURG' experience and its insight into black oppositional politics.

Aucamp, Hennie (1934-) Writer of Afrikaans short stories and cabaret texts. While the short stories are characterized by finely observed details, delicacy of tone and an intimate atmosphere, the cabaret pieces, which have been widely performed, are more sharply satirical about the Afrikaners' political and sexual norms.

Barnard, Lady Anne (Lindsay) (1750-1825) Born in Scotland, she became 'first lady' of the Cape when her husband was appointed colonial secretary to the governor in 1797. Her perceptive account of colonial life is recorded in her letters and journals, first published in 1849.

Beadle, The Novel by Pauline SMITH, first published in 1926. Set in the Little Karoo around 1920, it describes the seduction of the innocent Andrina by a visiting Englishman, and explores the dilemma of the beadle (a minor church official), Aalst Vlokman, who is in fact her father. The novel examines in simple, but moving terms the crippling effect of the stern ▷CALVINISM by which the Afrikaans farmers lived, but ends on a note of hope and reconciliation.

CAPE DIARIST *Lady Anne Barnard left a perceptive record in her letters and journals of colonial life at the end of the 18th century.*

Becker, Jillian (1932-) Johannesburg-born novelist who emigrated to the United Kingdom in 1961. *The Virgins* (1976), the third of a trilogy, describes the experiences of a young white woman growing up in suburban Johannesburg during the 1970s.

Black, Stephen (*c*1880-1931) Journalist and playwright whose first and best-known play, *Love and the Hyphen*, appeared in 1908. Later plays include *Helena's Hope, Ltd.* (1910), *The Uitlanders* (1911), *A Boer's Honour* (1912), *Van Kalabas Does His Bit* (1916); his novel *The Dorp* was published in 1920. Black was a keen and witty observer of local manners and he deliberately gave his plays a distinctively South African flavour. He remained active as a somewhat provocative journalist throughout his life.

black theatre This term now refers primarily to the various forms of protest theatre performed by anti-apartheid activists in South Africa, especially during the 1970s and 1980s as a response to the ▷BLACK CONSCIOUSNESS MOVEMENT. H I E DHLOMO had published *The Girl Who Killed to Save: Nongquase the Liberator* as early as 1936, but what makes the protest plays distinctive is their desire to address, empower and mobilize black audiences by making them aware – often in their own languages – of their oppression. An example is *Woza Albert!*, devised by Barney Simon, Percy Mtwa and Mbongeni Ngema.

Blackburn, Douglas (1857-1929) English-born journalist and novelist, regarded as one of the founders of the genre of South African novels in English. Initially based on the Reef, he spent some years in Natal before returning to England in 1908. *A Burger Quixote* (1903, reissued 1984) describes the South African War exploits of Sarel Erasmus; *Leaven* (1908) is an early treatment of the 'JIM COMES TO JOBURG' story and a satirical indictment of colonial prejudices in Natal.

Bloom, Harry (1913-81) A lawyer, best known for *Transvaal Episode*, which was first published in 1955 but immediately banned. The novel graphically describes the racial violence which engulfs a small town in the north of South Africa and is unusual for its insight into the needs and feelings of the black township dwellers. Bloom also collaborated on the lyrics of the musical *King Kong* (1961).

Boesman and Lena Play by Athol FUGARD, first performed in 1969. The play describes one night in the lives of two 'coloured' outcasts, during which they redefine their relationship. Lena, usually the submissive partner, successfully defies the more hardened and callous Boesman. The arrival and death of an anonymous black man at their makeshift shelter precipitates their existential crisis. The play has strong political overtones as their condition is explored largely in terms of the consequences of apartheid policies. It was made into a film in 1973, starring Yvonne Bryceland and Athol Fugard.

Bosman, Herman Charles (1905-51) Perhaps South Africa's best-known storyteller. His short stories are mostly set in the Marico district of the North West, where he worked as a schoolteacher. *Mafeking Road* (1947) was an instant success. Subsequent collections were published posthumously and confirmed his place in South Africa's literature. Through his narrator, Oom Schalk Lourens, Bosman exploits the device of the limited, half-ironic narrator. Initially sentenced to death for the murder of his stepbrother, he was released after four years in prison. This experience is the subject of *Cold Stone Jug* (1949).

❖ Oom Schalk has become widely known through actor Patrick Mynhardt's dramatizations of Bosman's stories.

Breytenbach, Breyten (1939-) Afrikaans poet, novelist, painter and political commentator. His marriage to a Vietnamese woman in France meant he could not live in ▷APARTHEID South Africa. When he returned in disguise in 1975, he was arrested, tried and jailed for attempted subversion; an account of this appears in *The True Confessions of an Albino Terrorist* (1984). His first published poems (1964) introduced surrealistic imagery into Afrikaans poetry.

Brink, André P (1935-) Afrikaans novelist and academic. His early works, often drawing their inspiration from contemporary French writers, appeared in the late 1950s and the 1960s and established him as a leading figure of the 'Sestiger' movement, which challenged the literary and political establishment. Brink writes extensively in English; many of his Afrikaans works have been translated into English. His novel *A Dry White Season* (1979) was written in English and Afrikaans by Brink himself, and filmed in 1979.

Brutus, Dennis Vincent (1924-) Poet and anti-apartheid activist born in Harare, Zimbabwe. A schoolteacher in Port Elizabeth, Brutus was sentenced to 18 months on ▷ROBBEN ISLAND in 1963. He left South Africa as a political exile in 1966. *Letters to Martha and Other Poems* (1968) is a poignant account of his prison experience. He continued to write poetry in exile and, with Arthur NORTJÉ, won the Mbari poetry prize in 1962.

SENTENCED TO DEATH

BOSMAN FOUND GUILTY

"DELIBERATE ACT"

ACCUSED'S VERSION OF TRAGEDY

Herman Charles Bosman, a young school teacher, who was charged at the Rand Criminal Sessions with the murder of his stepbrother, David Russell, by shooting him with a rifle at the house of deceased's father at Bellevue East, Johannesburg, on July 18 last, was to-day found guilty and sentenced to death.

Mr. Justice Gey van Pittius and two assessors, Messrs. James Young and Hull, magistrates of the city, were on the Bench.

"SAD AND PATHETIC."

In a packed court at 2.30 his lordship dealt with the facts of the case, which he said was "a sad and pathetic one."

TALES OF PRISON *Storyteller Herman Charles Bosman spent four years in prison after his death sentence was commuted.*

Butler, Guy (1918-) Leading poet, playwright, editor and critic, whose efforts have helped to popularize the exploits and legacy of the 1820 settlers. Born in Cradock, he served in World War II and made his reputation as a poet with *Stranger to Europe* (1952). A series of autobiographies, beginning with *Karoo Morning* (1977), gained him a wide audience.

❖ Butler's central theme is the 'complex encounter' between Europe and Africa – a theme captured specifically in the lines: 'In all of us two continents contend;/ Two skies of stars confuse us.'

Campbell, Roy (1901-57) South Africa's best-known English poet, Campbell burst onto the English literary scene with *The Flaming Terrapin* (1924). He returned to South Africa from England in 1924, and briefly edited the literary journal 'Voorslag' with Sir Laurens VAN DER POST and William PLOMER. His reputation now rests mainly on the poems in *Adamastor* (1930), of which 'The Zulu Girl' and 'The Serf' are the best known. His views on colonial Natal society are expressed in the satirical poem *The Wayzgoose* (1928). Campbell left South Africa in 1927, and settled first in Spain, then in Portugal. His pro-Franco sentiments made him a controversial figure at the time of the ▷SPANISH CIVIL WAR.

❖ The title of the *Adamastor* collection was taken from the mythical character said to inhabit the 'Cape of Storms'. (See ▷ADAMASTOR in 'Myths and legends'.)

Cloete, Stuart (1897-1976) Popular novelist and short-story writer. Cloete was born in Paris, served in World War I, and came to South Africa in 1927. He is perhaps best known for his novel about the Great Trek, *Turning Wheels* (1937), which was initially banned. Other novels include *The Hill of Doves* (1942) and *Rags of Glory* (1963).

Clouts, Sydney (1926-82) Cape Town-born poet whose reputation was established by *One Life* (1966). His poetry is characterized by its highly personal vision and condensed style. After qualifying as a librarian in London he spent the last 20 years of his life there.

CNA Literary Award Awarded annually since 1961 to both English and Afrikaans writers for work over a wide range of categories. Winners of this award include Sir Laurens VAN DER POST (1963), Alan PATON (1964), Jack COPE (1971), Guy BUTLER (1975), and J M COETZEE and Nadine GORDIMER, who both received it more than once.

Coetzee, J M (1940-) Currently South Africa's most highly regarded novelist and the recipient of various prestigious awards, including the Booker prize in 1983 for *Life and Times of Michael K.* He first attracted attention with *Dusklands* (1974). WAITING FOR THE BARBARIANS (1980) is a key text. Coetzee's particular preoccupation is the ordeal of the colonizer, and the seemingly futile attempt of his narrators to transcend or escape the limits of their condition. His work marks a break from the conventions of realism and assumes a sophisticated reader. He has also published extensively as an academic; his writings on southern African letters have been collected as *White Writing* (1988).

colonial fiction A wide category that includes the ▷ROMANCE and the adventure story, and is associated with the colonial stereotype of Africa as exotic, wild and savage. It celebrates the 'masculine' virtues of toughness, independence and self-reliance associated with the frontier. Its most notable exponents are Rider HAGGARD, Edgar Wallace, John ▷BUCHAN and Percy FITZPATRICK, all of whom wrote in the late 19th and early 20th centuries. Harriet Ward, who wrote a series of novels in the 1850s based on her experience of the eastern frontier, was a significant forerunner. The mode survives in the writing of popular authors such as Stuart CLOETE and Wilbur SMITH.

Cope, Jack (1913-91) Prolific novelist and short-story writer, and for many years editor of the literary magazine 'Contrast', founded in 1961. Cope was born and educated in Natal, worked overseas and in South Africa as a journalist, and made an important contribution to South African literature as a writer and editor. Although best known for his short stories, his novel *The Rain Maker* (1971) won the CNA LITERARY AWARD.
❖ Cope wrote about South African writers during the apartheid era: 'They come from every nationality, race, belief, outlook. Many are banned, exiled. But they form a republic of talent rising about the jargon and propaganda, throwing shadows ahead.'

Cronin, Jeremy (1949-) Poet, critic and political activist. He served a seven-year sentence after being convicted under the Terrorism Act in 1976. His first collection of poems, *Inside* (1983), dealt with his prison experience and is unusual for its fusion of the personal and the political. Cronin is a leading member of the ▷SOUTH AFRICAN COMMUNIST PARTY.

Cry, the Beloved Country Novel by Alan PATON, which attracted international attention to South Africa when first published in 1948. It tells the story of the Reverend Stephen Kumalo, an elderly African priest who leaves his home in rural Natal to travel to Johannesburg in search of his son Absolom. He finds tragedy and suffering, and undergoes a crisis of faith. Parallel to his story is that of the white farmer Jarvis, whose son has been murdered by Absolom. The novel is characterized by lyrical description, biblical cadences, and a yearning for a lost innocence and wholeness. It was turned into a Broadway musical in 1949 and has been the subject of two films (1952 and 1995).

Cullinan, Patrick (1932-) South African-born poet, educated in Magdalen College, Oxford, who has also used the pen-name Patrick Roland. He was cofounder of Bateleur Press in 1974 and edited the literary journal 'The Bloody Horse' (1980-1). He has published four collections of poetry and an illustrated biography of the Dutch soldier and explorer Robert Jacob Gordon (1743-95). The title poem of *White Hail in the Orchard* (1984) captures the grace and control of his best work: 'To have love and then lose it:/ the white hail in the orchard/ lying with leaves it has stripped/ and the storm moving away.' His *Selected Poems 1961-1994* includes translations of Italian poet Eugenio Montale.
❖ He has been awarded the Thomas Pringle Prize for Poetry (twice) and was the recipient, with Christopher van Wyk (1957-) of the Olive Schreiner Prize in 1980.

Delius, Anthony (1916-89) Poet and journalist who was born in Simon's Town but later moved to London. One of the generation of South African war poets, he wrote a satirical long poem *The Last Division* (1959) and was awarded the CNA LITERARY AWARD for his novel *Border* (1976).

Dhlomo, Herbert Isaac Ernest (1903-56) Journalist, essayist and playwright. His involvement in the 1930s with the Bantu Dramatic Society at the Bantu Men's Social Centre in Johannesburg prompted a number of critical essays and plays, the best known of which is *The Girl Who Killed to Save: Nongquase the Liberator* (1936). The play describes the ▷CATTLE-KILLING in 1856, in which the Xhosa people slaughtered their cattle and stopped planting crops on the basis of a girl's prophecy that this would lead to a national revival. His *Collected Works* was published in 1985.
❖ His brother, R R R Dhlomo (1901-71), wrote a number of historical novels in Zulu. *An African Tragedy* (1928) was the first fictional work in English by a black South African novelist to be published.

Driver, Jonty (1939-) Cape Town-born poet, novelist and teacher, who left South Africa in 1964 after a spell in detention. His first novel, *Elegy for a Revolutionary* (1969), deals with the political and moral issues facing a group of young white people trying to bring about change in South Africa.

'Drum' writers A new generation of urbanized black South Africans who worked for 'Drum' magazine in the 1950s and lived in Sophiatown. This talented group of individuals forged a new, racy township idiom, and their work signalled a renaissance in black writing. Outstanding figures were Can THEMBA, Es'kia MPHAHLELE, Bloke Modisane, Todd Matshikiza, Nat Nakasa and Casey Motsisi. They wrote mainly short stories, for which 'Drum' provided an outlet, and often went on to write autobiographies. The political repression that came after the ▷SHARPEVILLE SHOOTINGS brought this era to an abrupt end.

GROUNDBREAKER *Twice filmed, Alan Paton's* Cry, the Beloved Country *starred James Earl Jones (left) as the Rev Stephen Kumalo in the 1995 version. It also became a Broadway musical.*

Essop, Ahmed (1931-) Novelist and short-story writer who came to South Africa from India in 1934. *The Hajji and other Stories* (1978), deals with the cross-cultural encounters in the 'mixed' Fordsburg-Vrededorp area of Johannesburg. He has published two novels, *The Visitation* (1980) and *The Emperor* (1984), and a second collection of stories.

exile literature Term commonly used to describe the literature of writers driven into exile as a result of their opposition to apartheid. The first wave of departures was prompted by the ▷SHARPEVILLE SHOOTINGS and the repression of the 1960s. Writers such as Alex LA GUMA, Can THEMBA, Dennis BRUTUS, Es'kia MPHAHLELE, Lewis Nkosi and Bloke Modisane all left at this time, mostly on one-way exit permits. While articulating their political commitment, their writing is often informed by a sense of alienation and homesickness. Many writers died in exile, though some, such as Mphahlele and SEROTE, have returned. Different responses to exile can be seen in the work of writers as diverse as Arthur NORTJÉ, Bessie HEAD, Zoë Wicomb, Farida Karodia and, among whites, David WRIGHT, Dan JACOBSON and Christopher HOPE.

Eybers, Elisabeth (1915-) Afrikaans poet who moved in 1961 to the Netherlands, where she continued to write in Afrikaans. Her first works appeared in the 1930s. She writes with great sensitivity about the experiences of women, but an ironic tone enters the later poetry about art, exile and growing old.

FitzPatrick, Sir James Percy (1862-1931) Popular novelist, and author of South Africa's most famous children's book, JOCK OF THE BUSHVELD (1907). Born in King William's Town, FitzPatrick worked as a transport rider, digger and journalist. A friend of Cecil Rhodes, he was briefly imprisoned after the ▷JAMESON RAID. He was knighted in 1902.

Fugard, Athol Harold Lannigan (1932-) Prolific English South African playwright. He was introduced to the theatre by his wife, Sheila, and together they worked on the fringes of the theatrical establishment of the late 1950s and early 1960s to explore the condition of the South African dispossessed (black people, 'poor whites') in a way that challenged both liberal complacency and segregated theatre practices. Fugard's greatest international exposure came with BOESMAN AND LENA (1969) and he has subsequently worked extensively abroad. He employs a wide range of styles, from the naturalism of *The Blood Knot* (1961), *People Are Living There* (1969) and *Master Harold and the Boys* (1983) to the highly symbolic abstractions of *Dimetos* (1975) and the politically explicit workshopped plays such as *Sizwe Bansi Is Dead* (1972), *The Island* (1973) and *My Children! My Africa!* (1989). His *Road to Mecca (1984),* based on the life of Helen Martins, the eccentric sculptress of ▷NIEU BETHESDA, became a successful film (1992).

❖ Sheila Fugard (1932-) is a prize-winning novelist and poet. Her novels include *The Castaways* (1972), *Rite of Passage* (1976) and *A Revolutionary Woman* (1983).

Gordimer, Nadine (1923-) Springs-born writer whose output of fiction represents an imaginative record of the last half-century of South African life. A conscious stylist with a eye for detail, she has shown an unflinching honesty and integrity in exploring the difficulties of life under apartheid. As a result, several of her works were banned on publication. Her most accomplished novel is probably *The Conservationist* (1974). *A World of Strangers* (1958) is an excellent introduction to the era of the 1950s, while *July's People* (1981) examines survival in an imagined post-apartheid South Africa. She was awarded the Nobel Prize for literature in 1991.

Gray, Stephen (1941-) Poet, novelist, academic, literary critic and editor, Gray has played an important role in the retrieval of literary texts and the promotion of South African literature. His novels include *Caltrop's Desire* (1980), in which his customary satire is tempered by an underlying seriousness. Set in 1948, the novel links the narrator's approaching demise with the demise of liberal hopes for South Africa.

Gwala, Mafika Pascal (1946-) Poet and cultural critic from Natal, Gwala played an active role in promoting the ideals of black consciousness in the 1970s. He is best known as one of the SOWETO POETS for whom 'Black is struggle'. His poetry is characterized by a fusion of the traditional vernacular forms with the rhythms of contemporary jazz. His first volume of poetry was *Jol'iinkomo* (1977).

Haggard, Sir Henry Rider (1856-1925) Popular novelist. An Englishman, Haggard spent some years in South Africa as a young man. His sagas of heroic adventure set in an exotic Africa are outstanding examples of the quest ▷ROMANCE. His most popular works are *King Solomon's Mines* (1885) and *She* (1887), both of which have been made into films.

Head, Bessie (1937-86) One of most important women writers to come out of South Africa, and Africa. Head was born in Pietermaritzburg of mixed parentage and died in self-imposed exile in Botswana. Questions of personal and cultural identity are explored in semi-autobiographical novels – *Maru* (1971) and the powerful and disturbing *A Question of Power* (1973). Her stories in *The Collector of Treasures* (1977), based on interviews with neighbours in her rural village, reflect her search for what she has called 'a sense of historical continuity, a sense of roots.'

INTERNATIONAL SUCCESS *South Africa's dispossessed are vividly portrayed in Athol Fugard's* Boesman and Lena, *characters played here by Fugard and Yvonne Bryceland.*

Hope, Christopher (1944-) Novelist, poet and critic who left South Africa in 1974. He is a fine satirist of South African life. His first novel, *A Separate Development* (1980), is remarkable for its comic treatment of the absurdities generated by apartheid. It was, ironically, banned on publication. He describes his autobiographical novel *White Boy Running* (1988) as being about 'the horrifying comedy of the place'. He has published several collections of poetry and short stories, and has worked for radio and television.

Jacobson, Dan (1929-) South African-born novelist and journalist who left for England in 1954. He has published several collections of short stories, based partly on his experience of growing up in Kimberley. His best-known South African work is his novella *A Dance in the Sun* (1956), which explores familial and racial conflict in a small Karoo town. He is an example of a writer who has successfully made the transition to England; his recent work does not rely on South Africa for either its themes or its setting.

Jenkins, Geoffrey (1920-) Best-selling novelist. He made his name with popular novels of adventure set along the Skeleton coast, such as *A Twist of Sand* (1959), which was filmed in 1968.

'Jim Comes to Joburg' A recurring theme in South African fiction. The typical narrative traces the experience of an unsophisticated rural person encountering the city for the first time. Early examples are Douglas BLACKBURN's *Leaven* (1908) and R R R Dhlomo's *An African Tragedy* (1928). Alan Paton's CRY, THE BELOVED COUNTRY (1948) is the most famous instance, while Phyllis ALTMAN's *Law of Vultures* (1952) is a more comprehensive treatment. A more recent reworking of the theme is to be found in Mbulelo MZAMANE's *Mzala* (1980), a collection of short stories.

***Jock of the Bushveld* (1907)** South Africa's best-loved children's book, written by Percy FITZPATRICK. Based on his own experience as a transport rider in the Eastern Transvaal (present-day ▷MPUMALANGA), it describes the bond that develops between a boy and his pup as they grow to maturity. It is also a fine evocation of a frontier lifestyle. The book, which has been reprinted many times, was made into a film in 1986 and again in 1995.

Jonker, Ingrid (1934-65) Afrikaans poet who committed suicide and whose work focuses on the disillusionments of youth. Nelson Mandela selected an English translation of one of her poems – on the death of a black child during police operations – to open the first session of parliament over which he presided as South Africa's president in 1994.
❖ The Ingrid Jonker prize for poetry (English and Afrikaans) was instituted in 1965.

Kente, Gibson (1932-) Popular black dramatist and theatrical entrepreneur who saw the need to cater for African township audiences without the intervention of white organizations. He produced popular musical melodramas, starting with *Manana, The Jazz Prophet* (1963). He initially tended to avoid explicit political themes in his works, but *How Long* (1973) is regarded as anticipating the 1976 uprisings in black communities. He helped to found the Federated Union of Black Arts.

Krige, Uys (1910-87) Afrikaans poet, critic and writer of short stories. His first book in English was *The Way Out* (1946), based on his escape from an Italian prisoner of war camp. He lived for some years in Spain and France while preparing his first volume of Afrikaans poetry. Works in English include the play *The Two Lamps* (1964) and a collection of autobiographical sketches. He also translated works from Spanish, French and English – including some of Shakespeare's plays – into Afrikaans. He co-edited the *Penguin Book of South African Verse* (1968).

La Guma, Alex (1925-85) The outstanding exponent of 'District Six writing'. Best known for his short stories and his novella *A Walk in*

LEGENDARY PET *Percy FitzPatrick's famous companion, depicted by E Caldwell, who illustrated editions of* Jock of the Bushveld.

the Night (1962), he wrote with conviction of the lives of the poor and the marginalized. *The Stone Country* (1967) vividly describes prison conditions. La Guma, a member of the ▷SOUTH AFRICAN COMMUNIST PARTY and an accused in the ▷TREASON TRIAL, suffered detention and house arrest. He left South Africa in 1966 and died in Havana in 1985.

Leroux, Etienne (1922-89) Controversial Afrikaans novelist and a leader of the 'Sestigers', a group of progressive Afrikaner intellectuals. His works are characterized by a complex interweaving of symbol and myth, though set within a local context. He is best known for his *Welgevonden* trilogy of novels, translated into English as *To a Dubious Salvation* (1962). His satirical novel *Magersfontein, O Magersfontein!* (1979), which was originally banned, was nevertheless awarded the prestigious Hertzog Prize.
❖ Leroux was a friend of the British novelist Graham ▷GREENE and his writings were strongly influenced by the ideas of the Swiss psychologist C G ▷JUNG.

Lessing, Doris May (1919-) Internationally known novelist and short-story writer. Lessing was born in Iran but grew up in the former Rhodesia. This experience is reflected in her early short stories and in the first novels of the *Children of Violence* (1952-69) sequence, *Martha Quest* and *A Proper Marriage* (1965). She has lived in England for most of her adult life and is a prolific writer whose work has earned her a considerable following. She has also turned to science fiction in a series of novels entitled *Canopus in Argos: Archives* (1971-81).

Lindsay, Kathleen Mary (1903-73) South African writer named in the *Guiness Book of Records* as the world's most prolific novelist. She wrote over 400 novels ranging from romances to thrillers, using 10 different pen names. No fewer than 117 novels were published under the name 'Mary Richmond'. She also published two collections of poetry.

Livingstone, Douglas (1932-) One of South Africa's foremost poets, a marine bacteriologist by profession. Livingstone was born in Malaya, spent some time in the former Rhodesia, and settled in South Africa. *Sjambok and Other Poems from Africa* (1964) established him as an important new voice. A meticulous craftsman whose poems have a distinctively 'modern' feel, his work embraces a wide range of themes and styles. He has received various poetry awards, including the CNA LITERARY AWARD for his *Selected Poems* in 1984.

Louw, N P van Wyk (1906-70) Regarded by many as one of the finest Afrikaans poets, he wrote a number of plays as well as essays on literature and on the cultural condition of the Afrikaner. He came to prominence in the 1930s as one of the 'Dertigers' bringing what was virtually a new urban and profoundly philosphical idiom into Afrikaans poetry.

Marais, Eugène (1871-1936) Afrikaans writer and highly influential poet even though he wrote only a few poems. His interests, which were wide-ranging, included law, medicine and the natural world. Two well-known studies are *Die Siel van die Mier* (1934) (*The Soul of the White Ant*) and *Burgers van die Berge* (1939) (*My Friends the Baboons*).
❖ The Suid-Afrikaanse Akademie vir Wetenskap en Kuns instituted the Eugène Marais Prize for first published works in 1961.

Marechera, Dambudzo (1952-87) Controversial Zimbabwean writer. Expelled from both the University of Rhodesia and from New College, Oxford, Marechera was a nonconformist all his life. He won the Guardian newspaper fiction prize for his first novella, *House of Hunger* (1978), a powerful indictment of conditions in racist Rhodesia. He returned to Zimbabwe in 1982 and his later work deals with the predicament of the 'internal exile'. Shortly before his death he said: 'My whole life has been an attempt to make myself the skeleton in my own cupboard.' He died in 1987.
❖ The Dambudzo Marechera Trust was

founded in 1988 to collect his unpublished works and encourage other young writers.

Matthee, Dalene (1938-) Best-selling Afrikaans novelist whose work has helped to focus attention on the Knysna forest. Her Knysna trilogy, beginning with *Kringe in die Bos* (1984) (*Circles in a Forest*), captured the popular imagination. Her works deal with the problems faced by small communities (the woodcutters) whose identity and way of life are threatened. All three novels won the ATKV (Afrikaanse Taal- en Kultuurvereniging) prize. *Fiela se Kind* (1985) was successfully dramatized by CAPAB in 1987; her novels have also been filmed. She was the first South African to receive a prestigious Swiss cultural award in 1992. She translates her work into English herself.

Mda, Zakes (1948-) Black South African dramatist whose best-known play is *We Shall Sing for the Fatherland*, which was first performed in 1979. The play is set in the aftermath of a liberation struggle. In the same year Mda won the Amstel Playwright of the Year award for his play *The Hill* about migrant workers.

Mhlophe, Gcina (1958-) Poet, playwright, theatre director, actress, and storyteller. Mhlophe was born in Hammarsdale near Durban, and grew up in the Transkei. She was the first black woman to be appointed artistic director of the Market Theatre in Johannesburg, and has received international recognition for her autobiographical play *Have You Seen Zandile* (1986). Her stories and poems appear in several anthologies, and she has travelled widely to encourage the art of storytelling.
❖ In 1993 she received an honorary doctorate from the Open University for her contribution to South African literature.

Millin, Sarah Gertrude (1889-1968) Leading early 20th-century novelist. Millin was born in Lithuania, came to South Africa as a young child and grew up near the Vaal River diamond diggings. A prolific writer, she became well known as a result of *God's Stepchildren* (1924), a novel which deals with miscegenation and is characterized by what would now be regarded as racist stereotyping. She published 17 novels in all, as well as short stories, biographies of ▷RHODES (1933) and ▷SMUTS (1936) and two autobiographies.

Mofolo, Thomas (1876-1948) Pioneering Sesotho writer whose work was published by the Morija Mission Press in Lesotho. *Chaka*, published in 1925 but written earlier, is a fictional recreation of the life of the founder of the Zulu kingdom. It shows the consequences of Shaka's pact with Isanusi (a sorcerer) and his final descent into madness. Translated into several European languages, it is regarded as the first novel by an African writer.
❖ The Mofolo-Plomer Prize, initiated in 1976 by Nadine GORDIMER in conjunction with South African publishers, was awarded annually to the best unpublished work of fiction. It was discontinued after 1984.

FORGOTTEN FORESTER *A Knysna woodcutter is caught in a typically wary pose in the screen version of Dalene Mathee's* Kringe in die Bos.

Mphahlele, Es'kia (1919-) Doyen of black South African writers. His childhood in ▷MPUMALANGA province and Marabastad was the subject of his well-known autobiography, *Down Second Avenue* (1959). Before leaving the country on an exit permit in 1957, he worked as a teacher and then as a journalist on 'Drum' magazine. He pursued an academic career in Africa and the USA before returning in 1978 to become professor of comparative and African literature at the University of the Witwatersrand. His critical work, *The African Image* (1962), helped to put African writing on the map. A selection of his essays and short stories have been collected in *The Unbroken Song* (1981) and a second volume of autobiography, *Africa My Music*, was published in 1984.

Mtshali, Mbuyiseni Oswald (1940-) One of the best known SOWETO POETS. Born in Natal, Mtshali's first volume of poetry, *Sounds of a Cowhide Drum* (1971), was a commercial and critical success and established him as one of the leading black poets of the 1970s. It won the Olive SCHREINER Prize in 1975. His poetry deals with the harsh realities of township life and employs vivid imagery and precise diction: 'The wintry air nipped their navels/ as a calf would suck the nipple' (from 'A Brazier in the Street'). His second collection, *Fireflies* (1980), was banned on publication.

Mungoshi, Charles (1947-) Zimbabwean novelist, poet and short-story writer. His first collection of stories, *Coming of the Dry Season* (1972), was originally banned. He has written a novel, *Waiting for the Rain* (1975), as well as poems, a play and two novels in Shona. His *Some Kinds of Wounds and Other Stories* was published in 1980. In the early 1990s he was the writer-in-residence at the University of Zimbabwe.

Mzamane, Mbulelo (1948-) Best known as a short-story writer, Mzamane is professor of English and rector of the University of Fort Hare. His collection of stories *Mzala* (1980) represents the humour and variety of township life. It was reissued as *My Cousin Comes to Jo'burg and Other Stories* in 1981.

Ndebele, Njabulo (1948-) Writer and academic, and author of the award-winning *Fools and Other Stories* (1983). His stories examine the tensions of growing up in a black township – in his case at Charterston, Nigel – with insight and sensitivity. His critical essays have made an important contribution to South Africa's literary culture and are collected as *Rediscovery of the Ordinary* (1991). He is principal of the University of the North and chairman of the Congress of South African Writers.

Ngcobo, Lauretta (1932-) South African novelist who left in the 1960s and is now based in London. Her first novel, *Cross of Gold* (1981), was banned in South Africa. *And They Didn't Die* (1990) tells of the struggle of a young woman who is caught between restrictive traditions and racial oppression.

Nortjé, Arthur (1942-70) Gifted poet who died in exile. Nortjé was born in Oudtshoorn, educated at the University of the Western Cape and left South Africa on a scholarship to Oxford in 1965. His poems explore the effects of exile and his alienation as a 'coloured' South African: 'Origins trouble the voyager much, those roots/ that have sipped the waters of another continent.' *Dead Roots* and *Lonely Against the Light* (both 1973) were published posthumously.

Opperman, D J (1914-85) Afrikaans poet whose first collection of poetry appeared in 1945. He produced an astonishingly varied selection of highly acclaimed works, including criticism and three historical dramas, and has influenced many younger writers as poet and university lecturer.

Paton, Alan (1903-88) Famous both as the author of CRY, THE BELOVED COUNTRY (1948) and as a lifelong opponent of apartheid. The success of his first novel has tended to overshadow his other literary achievements. *Too Late the Phalarope* (1953) explores the agony of a young Afrikaner policeman and rugby hero who is found guilty of an offence under the ▷IMMORALITY ACT. Paton also wrote notable biographies of the gifted scholar and politician Jan Hendrik Hofmeyr and of the staunch apartheid critic Archbishop Geoffrey Hare Clayton, as well as two autobiographical volumes. He was leader of the ▷LIBERAL PARTY until its dissolution in 1968.
❖ The Sunday Times/Alan Paton Prize is given annually for nonfiction writing.

Plaatje, Sol T (1875-1932) A remarkable man, Plaatje was the first black South African to write a novel in English. *Mhudi*, published in 1930 but written by 1920, is a historical romance that explores the human and historical impact of events in the northwest of South Africa in the 1830s. Its central event is the defeat of ▷MZILIKAZI by a combined force of Boers, Barolong and Griquas. Plaatje was also a leader of the then South African Native National Congress (later the ANC), a journalist and newspaper editor, a linguist and translator of Shakespeare into Setswana. He also wrote *Native Life in South Africa* (1916), which documents the effects of the Land Act of 1913. Plaatje was present at the Siege of ▷MAFEKING and his diary was later discovered and published in 1973.

MABOLELO A GA TSIKINYA-CHAKA
(The Sayings of William Shakespeare)

DIPHOSHO-PHOSHO
(Comedy of Errors)

A fetoleçoe mo puong oa Secoana
ke
SOL. T. PLAATJE
Morulaganyi oa "Diane tsa Secoana le Maele a Sekgoa."
(Sechuana Proverbs and European Equivalents)
P.O. Box 143, Kimberley, South Africa.

MABOLELO a maŋoe a ga TSIKINYA-CHAKA
MASHOABI-SHOABI,
MATSAPA-TSAPA A LEFELA,
DINCHO-NCHO TSA BO JULIUS KESARA,
Le Buka tse diŋoe gape.

MORIJA PRINTING WORKS.

NOVELIST AND LINGUIST *Sol T Plaatje, the first black South African to write a novel, also translated Shakespeare into Setswana.*

Plomer, William (1903-73) South African-born writer and man of letters. Plomer is best known for *Turbott Wolfe* (1925), the novel he wrote as a young man of 20 in Natal. Its sympathetic presentation of an interracial love affair provoked outraged responses when first published. He left the country in 1926 after briefly co-editing 'Voorslag' (with CAMPBELL and VAN DER POST) and settled in England, where he continued to write poetry and prose of distinction.
❖ His well-known poem 'The Scorpion' presents the Europe-Africa encounter in emblematic terms: 'That was the Africa we knew,/ Where, wandering alone,/ We saw, heraldic in the heat,/ A scorpion on a stone.'

Poppie Nongena *Poppie* (1980), a book originally written in Afrikaans by Elsa Joubert, (*Die Swerfjare van Poppie Nongena*, 1978), is the harrowing story of a black domestic worker and her attempt to survive the dislocations forced on her by apartheid. The book became a best-seller and helped to open people's eyes to the effects of the pass laws. Poppie was also successfully dramatized.
❖ Joubert says of her collaboration with 'Poppie': 'Her need to talk was as great as my need to listen. And that was how we started working on the book. I knew at once: no travelogue, no allegory, but the stark truth, the story of this woman's life.'

popular literature A mode that originates in the ▷ROMANCE and adventure stories of writers such as Rider HAGGARD, John ▷BUCHAN, Percy FITZPATRICK and Bertram Mitford. Modern publishing and its attendant publicity have produced the best seller, and among South Africa's best-selling authors are Wilbur SMITH, Geoffrey JENKINS, Alan Scholefield, John Gordon Davis and, from an earlier era, Stuart CLOETE, Lawrence G Green and Francis Brett YOUNG. Many of the 'DRUM' WRITERS produced crime stories or romances, often influenced by American models.
❖ Popular literature should be distinguished from 'people's literature', a term sometimes used to describe the politically orientated writing produced by black writers in the 1970s and 1980s.

Pringle, Thomas (1789-1834) South African poetry in English begins with Pringle, the Scottish-born leader of a party of 1820 settlers. His *Poems Illustrative of South Africa*, published together with his *Narrative of a Residence in South Africa* (1834), register the impact of the South African landscape on a young man schooled in the traditions of English pastoral poetry. Pringle struck the first blow for press freedom in South Africa when his 'South African Journal' ran foul of Lord Charles Somerset and ceased publication. On his return to England in 1826 he became secretary to the Anti-Slavery Society.
❖ The Thomas Pringle Prize for Poetry has been presented by the English Academy since 1963 for work in various categories.

prison literature A genre of South African writing that emerged as a result of the efforts of the apartheid regime to stifle dissent through detention, imprisonment and banning. Many of these writers later went into exile (see EXILE LITERATURE). Since the release of Nelson Mandela, prison literature has received renewed attention. His autobiography, *Long Walk to Freedom* (1994), on release seemed set to break all sales records for works in this category. Other notable works include Ruth First's *117 Days* (1965), Albie Sachs's *Jail Diary* (1966), Dennis BRUTUS's *Letters to Martha* (1968), Jeremy CRONIN's *Inside* (1983), and Breyten BREYTENBACH's *The True Confessions of an Albino Terrorist* (1984). An early example of the genre is Herman Charles BOSMAN's *Cold Stone Jug* (1949).

protest literature A term originally used to describe the work of young black writers in the 1950s, also including some of the 'DRUM' WRITERS. They were well educated, had middle-class aspirations and hoped that, by drawing attention to grievances, they would bring about their redress. Examples are short stories by Richard RIVE ('The Bench') and James Matthews ('The Park'), and the early poetry of Oswald MTSHALI. Sharpeville exposed the futility of these hopes, and the 1970s saw the development of a new, more militant literature, which was often strongly influenced by black consciousness, and directed towards a black audience. It affirms 'black values', invokes black solidarity, sees poetry as a 'weapon of the struggle', and often takes the form of public performance. The work of the SOWETO POETS, the poems of Mafika GWALA and the stories of Mtutuzeli Matshoba are obvious examples.

Renault, Mary (1905-83) English-born novelist who emigrated to South Africa in 1948. She is best known for her novels based on life in Ancient Greece. She achieved popular success with *The Charioteer* (1953), *The Last of the Wine (1956), The King Must Die* (1958), *The Bull from the Sea* (1962) and her trilogy of novels based on the life of Alexander the Great. She served as president of the South African PEN Club (PEN is an acronym for the International Association of Poets, Playwrights, Editors, Essayists and Novelists).

Rive, Richard (1931-89) Scholar, teacher and writer whose work was strongly informed by

WORDSMITHS *For more than 30 years Wilbur Smith has remained one of the world's top-selling adventure-story writers. His wife has written two books under the name Danielle Thomas.*

his experience of growing up in ▷DISTRICT SIX. He received a doctorate from Oxford University for a thesis on Olive SCHREINER. His first collection of short stories, *African Songs* (1963), was followed by a novel, *Emergency* (1964), which was banned. At the time of his brutal murder in Cape Town he was working on the production of a play based on his novel *Buckingham Palace, District Six* (1986). His extensive travels overseas and his efforts to promote African and South African writing are related in his autobiographical *Writing Black* (1981).

❖ In 1972 Rive won the African Theatre Competition sponsored by the BBC with the radio play *Make Like Slaves.*

Schreiner, Olive (1855-1920) Author of *The* STORY OF AN AFRICAN FARM (1883). The daughter of Wesleyan missionaries, she wrote the first draft of *Story* while working as a governess near Cradock. Its publication in England made her a celebrity. On her return to South Africa she became a prolific essayist and pamphleteer. *Woman and Labour* (1911) clearly demonstrates her preoccupation with 'the woman question', while in *Thoughts on South Africa*, published posthumously in 1923, she examines South Africa's political and racial problems. Her pro-Boer sympathies made her a controversial figure during the South African War. She spent the last seven years of her life in England and returned to Cape Town only a few months before her death.

❖ Since 1961 the Olive Schreiner Prize has been awarded to new and promising writers by the English Academy of Southern Africa. Recent recipients include Ivan Vladislavic and Tatamkulu Afrika.

Sepamla, Sipho (1932-) Poet, novelist, editor and teacher, born in Krugersdorp. One of the SOWETO POETS, his work was first published in the 1970s and poetry collections include *The Blues is You in Me* (1976). His poetry is concerned with black urban life and ranges from stinging attacks on the injustices of apartheid to attempts at capturing the multilingual flavour of township expression. He has also written plays, short stories and two novels. *A Ride on the Whirlwind* (1981) deals with the ▷SOWETO REVOLT.

❖ In 1977 he was corecipient, with Lionel ABRAHAMS, of the Thomas Pringle Prize for Poetry.

Serote, Mongane Wally (1944-) Poet and novelist who was born in ▷SOPHIATOWN and lived in Alexandra. He went into exile, first in Botswana, and then England, before returning to South Africa after the release of Nelson Mandela. He was one of the first poets to develop a black consciousness aesthetic, as illustrated in his epic poem, *No Baby Must Weep* (1975). His novel *To Every Birth its Blood* (1981) was formally innovative and explored the developing responses of a group of young black people to the situation in their country. He is now a member of parliament.

❖ Serote won the Noma Award in 1993 for *Third World Express.*

Slabolepszy, Paul (1948-) Prolific English South African playwright and actor whose best-known play is *Saturday Night at the Palace* (1982). It deals with two callow young men who terrorize a black waiter at a roadhouse ('The Palace'); they express their personal dilemmas and prejudices by taking out their frustrations on the waiter. The escalating levels of tension and violence carry strong political overtones.

Slater, Francis Carey (1876-1958) Poet from the Eastern Cape. Collections such as *The Karoo and Other Poems* (1924) capture both the landscape and the rural way of life. He edited the first important anthology of South African poetry, *The Centenary Book of South African Verse (1820-1925)*, and helped to foster an interest in South Africa's own literature. His epic poem *The Trek* (1938), coinciding with the centenary celebrations of that year, views the achievements of the ▷VOORTREKKERS in heroic terms.

Small, Adam (1936-) A 'coloured' Afrikaans poet whose first collection appeared in 1957; it introduced strikingly and seriously the distinctive Afrikaans idiom of the coloured people, an idiom that had until then been used almost exclusively for social comedy. A collection of English poems, *Black Bronze Beautiful*, appeared in 1975. His play *Kanna Hy Kô Hystoe* (translated as *Kanna He Is Coming Home*) deals with the social tensions that arise when a 'coloured' man who has been successful in the 'white' world returns to his community.

Smith, Pauline (1882-1959) One of South Africa's finest early writers, noted for her sympathetic treatment of the rural Afrikaner. Smith grew up in Oudtshoorn, where her father was a doctor. *Platkop's Children* (1935) was based on her childhood recollections. The English novelist Arnold Bennet encouraged her literary efforts and recognized what he called her 'strange, austere, tender and ruthless talent'. She is best known for her volume of short stories, *The Little Karoo* (1925) and her novel, *The* BEADLE (1926). The last part of her life was spent living with her sister in Dorset, England.

Smith, Wilbur (1933-) South African best-selling novelist, whose reputation was established with his first novel, *Where the Lion Feeds* (1964). His racy narratives are packed with action and adventure in an African setting and have to date sold 65 million copies worldwide. Ancient Egypt is the setting of his most recent novels, *River God* and *The Seventh Scroll.* Several of his novels have been made into Hollywood films.

❖ Smith describes his writing as 'pretty old-fashioned' and says: 'I believe in the triumph of good over evil and that love conquers all'.

Soweto poets Name given to the work of a new post-Sharpeville generation of black poets who started publishing in the early 1970s. Their work addressed itself to what

MTSHALI calls 'the harsh realities that are part and parcel of black man's life'. SEPAMLA's 'To Whom it May Concern,' Mtshali's 'An Abandoned Bundle' and SEROTE's 'Joburg City' are representative examples. These poets often find an identity and solidarity as blacks; in this they were strongly influenced by the ▷BLACK CONSCIOUSNESS MOVEMENT with its slogan, 'Black man, you're on your own.' Their idiom was direct and colloquial, energized by the rhythms of jazz and township music or the rhetoric of public performance. The first poet to make his mark was Mtshali with *Sounds of a Cowhide Drum* (1971) – an unexpected best seller. In the late 1970s the magazine 'Staffrider' was an important outlet for this group of writers.

Story of an African Farm, The English fiction takes root in South Africa with this novel by Olive SCHREINER, published in 1883. Set in the Karoo, it describes the attempts of Lyndall and Waldo, who appear as children in Part One, to find fulfilment or meaning in life. Lyndall, who becomes at times a vehicle for the author's feminist views, dies after giving birth to an illegitimate child. Schreiner's most remarkable achievement is her ability to assimilate the ideas of Spencer, Darwin and Emerson (whom she read while serving as a governess in the eastern Cape) to the realities of life on a Karoo farm.

Themba, Can (1924-68) Perhaps the most talented of the 'DRUM' WRITERS, Themba embodied the hard-living, hard-drinking lifestyle associated with 'Drum' magazine and the shebeen culture of his beloved Sophiatown. He never fulfilled his literary promise; what remains apart from the journalism are a few short stories and one or two penetrating autobiographical pieces. His work was published posthumously in *The Will to Die* (1972) and *The World of Can Themba* (1985).

Tlali, Miriam (1933-) One of the first black women writers in South Africa to have her work published, Tlali has written sketches, short stories and novels. *Muriel at Metropolitan* (1975) is partly autobiographical and describes the experiences of a black woman employed by an insurance company in Johannesburg. *Amandla* (1980) deals with the ▷SOWETO REVOLT and was originally banned. Stories and interviews were published in 'Staffrider' magazine, and subsequently collected in *Mihloti* (1984) and *Soweto Stories* (1989). These describe the domestic and political realities of township life and their effect on women in particular.

Uys, Pieter-Dirk (1945-) Satirist, entertainer and dramatist, equally at home in English and Afrikaans. His most enduring creation has been Evita Bezuidenhout, a character he played with relish in satirizing the Afrikaner establishment which ran the country before the 1994 election. His plays have been innovative in their approach to language and subject matter. Published plays include *Paradise is Closing Down* (1978) and *God's Forgotten* (1981). His political satires in the revue format include *Adapt or Dye, Total Onslaught* (1984) and *A Part Hate, A Part Love: A Biography of Evita Bezuidenhout* (1990).

van der Post, Sir Laurens (1906-) Writer and journalist with an affinity for wilderness and the San (Bushmen) of the Kalahari. Born in Philippolis in the Free State, Van der Post settled in England in 1928. He is known for travelogues and romances such as *Venture into the Interior* (1952), *The Lost World of the Kalahari* (1958) and *A Story Like the Wind* (1972). Strongly influenced by the psychology of C G ▷JUNG, whom he knew personally, he takes a somewhat romantic view of Africa's landscape and indigenous peoples. ❖ He has been something of a mentor to Prince Charles, and was knighted in 1981.

***Waiting for the Barbarians* (1980)** Probably the most memorable of J M COETZEE's novels. The narrator is a magistrate who presides over an obscure oasis town on the frontier of an (unnamed) empire. The arrival of Colonel Joll, a specialist in torture, precipitates the central action of the novel. The magistrate has to play host and witness to crimes committed in the name of civilization. Eventually he is himself arrested and tortured. The novel is a profound examination of the nature of imperial (or colonial) rule and the position of the colonizer who dissents.

Wright, David (1920-94) Poet, editor and scholar who left South Africa in 1934, although he made several return visits. His publications include *Poems* (1949), and *Monologue of a Deaf Man* (1958). Wright was born deaf. He won several awards, including the Atlantic Award for literature in 1950 and the Guiness Poetry Prize (in 1958 and 1960).

Young, Francis Brett (1884-1954) Popular novelist born in Worcestershire and a doctor by profession. A visit to South Africa in 1922 inspired his first novel, *Pilgrim's Rest* (1922). A prolific writer, he is best known for *A City of Gold* (1939), which tells the story of the Grafton family against the background of dramatic events in South African history. The novel includes portraits of Kruger, Rhodes and Jameson. Young settled in South Africa in 1945 and died in Cape Town.

LITERARY GROUP *Writer Can Themba (left) holds court in a Sophiatown shebeen, 'The House of Truth'. Themba joined 'Drum' after winning a short-story competition run by the magazine.*

ENGLISH AND WORLD LITERATURE

The literature of the English-speaking world is a treasure house of stories, plays and poems. The works of Chaucer and Shakespeare, of Keats and Dickens, mould us and mark us; in the 19th century, American writers such as Edgar Allan Poe and Mark Twain began to add their contribution. In modern times, writers from Australia, other parts of Africa, Asia and the Caribbean have enriched our literature still further. The passionate Anna Karenina is not just Russian; she is an archetypal tragic heroine. The name Don Juan is synonymous with cruel seduction everywhere. In our children's imagination, fictional characters from many nations – Cinderella, Hansel and Gretel, The Ugly Duckling – jostle for attention.

INSTANT SUCCESS *Nigerian Chinua Achebe's first novel,* Things Fall Apart *(1958), dealing with the Ibo people in the late 19th century, has been translated into 40 languages.*

Achebe, Chinua (1930-) Nigerian novelist and academic who writes about the effects of colonialism on African society, and the conflict between modern and traditional values. His first novel *Things Fall Apart* (1958), which depicts a tribal society's first contact with Europeans, attracted considerable attention. Achebe won the Nobel prize for literature in 1989.

Aeschylus (EES-ki-luss) (c525-c456 BC) Classical Greek dramatist who is believed to have introduced dialogue into Greek tragedy and is known for the grand style of his works. Only seven of his estimated 90 plays survive, including the *Oresteia*, a sequence of three plays recounting the tragic tale of ▷AGAMEMNON and his family.

Aesop's *Fables* Collection of animal tales with a strong moral point, such as *The Boy Who Cried Wolf* and *The Fox and the Grapes*. The fables are attributed to 'Aesop', a legendary Greek storyteller of the 6th century BC.

aesthetes (or aesthetic movement) Writers and artists of the late 19th century who devoted themselves to beauty and style above all else. They were influenced by the ▷PRE-RAPHAELITES and adopted the motto 'Art for art's sake'. The aesthetes included Oscar WILDE, W B YEATS in his younger days, and the French writer Villiers de l'Isle-Adam, who once said: 'Live? Our servants will do that for us.'

Alcott, Louisa May (1832-88) American author known for *Little Women, Little Men* and other books for and about children. She began writing when young – to help support her family – and later became a campaigner for women's votes.

Alice's Adventures in Wonderland Children's book by Lewis CARROLL, published in 1865 and written for Alice Liddell, the daughter of a friend. Alice enters Wonderland by following the White Rabbit down his hole, and has many strange adventures there. She meets the Mad Hatter and the March Hare, the grinning Cheshire cat (which tends to disappear, leaving only its smile hanging in the air) and the Queen of Hearts, who shouts 'Off with her head!' when Alice makes a mistake at croquet. The book was highly successful and was followed in 1872 by *Through the Looking-Glass*, in which Alice meets the equally bizarre characters Tweedledum and Tweedledee, Humpty-Dumpty and the red and white queens.

❖ The tales about Alice have been interpreted in many different ways, from being a SATIRE on the court of Queen Victoria or academic pedantry at Oxford, to mocking the legal system or exploring the unconscious mind.

allegory Use in literature or art of apparently realistic characters, objects or events to stand for abstract qualities or ideas. An allegory can also be any work with such a double meaning. John Bunyan's *The* PILGRIM'S PROGRESS, for example, uses a physical journey to represent the spiritual search of a man as he travels through life.

All Quiet on the Western Front Novel, published in 1929 by the German author Erich Maria Remarque, about the horrors of World War I. In an understated style it describes the experiences of soldiers who seem to have no life beyond the trenches.

Amis, Sir Kingsley (1922-) British novelist and poet who achieved fame with the publication of the satirical novel *Lucky Jim* in 1954 and has written prolifically ever since. The hero of *Lucky Jim* is Jim Dixon, a university lecturer who takes an uncompromising stand against all forms of pretension. Amis, hailed as one of the writers known as the Angry Young Men in the 1950s, has written in a variety of styles, but his comic novels are the best known of his works. His later writings reflect an increasingly pessimistic attitude to the world. His son Martin Amis (1949-) is also a writer.

Andersen, Hans Christian (1805-75) Danish writer known for collections of fairy tales such as *The Emperor's New Clothes* and *The Ugly Duckling*. The tales are based on Danish folklore, but also clearly bear the stamp of Andersen's own personality and sometimes rather morbid outlook.

CHESHIRE CAT *John Tenniel's line drawings created the popular view of Alice and of other Lewis Carroll characters. He never drew from life, saying that he remembered his observations.*

Angelou, Maya (1928-) American writer, former musical star and activist whose best-known work is *I Know Why the Caged Bird Sings* (1970), the first of several volumes of an autobiography. The book is a poignant account of growing up as a black girl in the rural South. She has also published several volumes of poetry.

Anna Karenina Tragic novel by Leo TOLSTOY, written between 1873 and 1877. Anna, a beautiful woman trapped in an unhappy marriage, falls passionately in love with a young army officer, Vronsky. She leaves her husband, who forbids her ever to see her son again. In the end, her life becomes intolerable and she throws herself under a train.

❖ The book begins with one of the most celebrated sentences in literature: 'All happy families are like one another; each unhappy family is unhappy in its own way.'

Antony and Cleopatra TRAGEDY by William SHAKESPEARE, thought to have been written in 1606-7. It dramatizes the ill-fated love of the Roman general Mark Antony for Cleopatra, queen of Egypt, and his ensuing struggle between duty and desire.

***Arabian Nights, The* (or *The Thousand and One Nights*)** Collection of folk tales from Indian, Persian and Arabian sources. One of the best-known versions is the translation

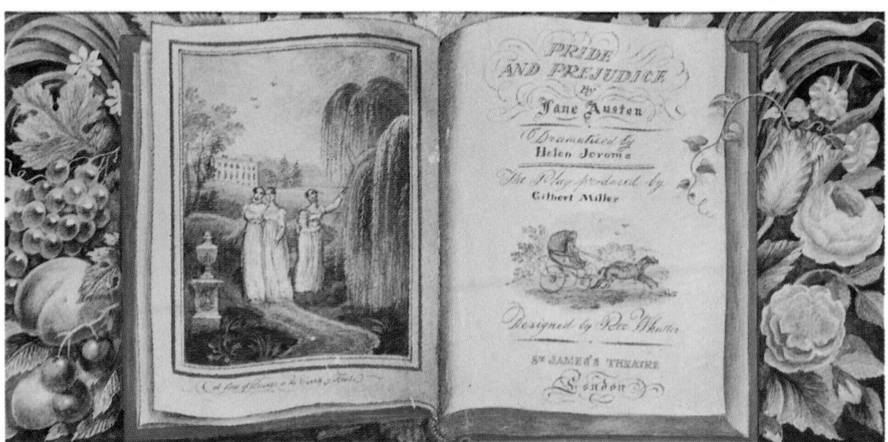

SCENE CHANGE Pride and Prejudice – *one of Jane Austen's best-loved novels – was adapted for the stage in 1936. The English artist Rex Whistler designed the sets, including this drop curtain.*

into English made by the explorer Sir Richard Burton between 1885 and 1888. The tales purport to be those told by Scheherazade to her husband – a king who habitually executed his wives after a single night because his first wife had been unfaithful. Each night Scheherazade would begin a tale so riveting that the king would spare her one more night in order to hear the end – but then she would begin the next tale, so delaying her fate.

Archer, Jeffrey (1940-) Popular novelist and former British MP who wrote his first bestseller, *Not a Penny More, Not a Penny Less*, after losing a fortune in a bad investment. Later works include *Kane and Abel* and the play *Beyond Reasonable Doubt*.

Aristophanes (*c*448-*c*380 BC) Classical Greek dramatist whose satirical comedies dealt with issues of Athenian life. His 11 surviving plays include *The Birds*, *The Clouds*, *The Frogs* and *Lysistrata*.

Asimov, Isaac (1920-) Russian-born American scientist and prolific science fiction writer who, with his contemporary Ray Bradbury, first made the genre respectable. He won fame with early works such as *I, Robot* (1950) and the *Foundation* trilogy (1951-3), and coined the term 'robotics'.

Atwood, Margaret (1939-) Canadian poet, critic and novelist whose witty and accessible works often explore complex female themes. Her novels include *The Edible Woman* (1969), *Life Before Man* (1979), *Bodily Harm* (1981), *The Handmaid's Tale* (1986) and *Cat's Eye* (1989).

Auden, W H (1907-73) British-born poet who wrote prolifically in a wide range of styles. His use of ordinary speech rather than high-flown 'poetic' language influenced many other poets in the English-speaking world. Auden was the leading figure among the radical writers of the 1930s and went to Spain to support the Republicans during the ▷SPANISH CIVIL WAR. In 1939 he emigrated to the USA with Christopher ISHERWOOD, but eventually returned to Britain to become professor of poetry at Oxford University. His later poetry became increasingly Christian.

Austen, Jane (1775-1817) One of the finest English novelists, known for her witty and sensitive portrayal of middle-class social life and relationships of the late 18th and early 19th centuries. Her works include PRIDE AND PREJUDICE, *Emma* and *Northanger Abbey*. Austen, who never married, shows deep insight into the character of her heroines, who come to recognize and eventually marry the right suitor.

Baldwin, James (1924-87) American writer and activist, born in Harlem, New York, who wrote about the condition of black Americans in works such as *Go Tell it on the Mountain* (1953) and *Another Country* (1962).

WANDERER *James Baldwin spent a decade in Europe before returning to the United States as a civil rights activist in 1957.*

ballad Traditional poem or song – originally an accompaniment to a dance – which tells the story of an event from history or legend. Examples include the Scottish ballads 'Sir Patrick Spens' and 'Barbara Allen'. Most ballads have short rhyming verses with a repeated REFRAIN.

Balzac, Honoré de (1799-1850) French novelist, author of a series of 91 books and stories known as *La Comédie Humaine* (*The Human Comedy*) that give a wide-ranging picture of contemporary French society and earned Balzac a reputation as one of the world's greatest novelists.

Barrie, Sir J M (1860-1937) Scottish novelist and playwright, best known for the play *Peter Pan*, which was first performed in 1904. The title character is a boy who lives in Never Never Land, where children never grow up.

Baudelaire, Charles Pierre (1821-67) French poet best known for the collection *Les Fleurs du Mal (The Flowers of Evil)* in which he employs exquisite IMAGERY and compelling rhythms to describe evil, decadence and the quest for love and beauty.

Beauvoir, Simone de (1908-86) French feminist, writer and long-time partner of the philosopher Jean-Paul ▷SARTRE. Her books include *The Second Sex*, *The Mandarins* and several volumes of autobiography.

Beckett, Samuel (1906-89) Irish novelist, poet, dramatist and critic with a despairing yet humorous outlook on life. He settled in Paris during the 1930s and consequently wrote many of his works in both French and English. In the 1950s he became a leading figure in the THEATRE OF THE ABSURD following the success of his play WAITING FOR GODOT. Beckett was awarded the Nobel prize for literature in 1969.

Beggar's Opera, The Satirical lowlife opera in BALLAD form by the 18th-century English playwright John Gay. It tells the story of the highwayman Macheath who marries Polly Peachum, the daughter of one of his criminal clients. Mr Peachum, furious at the bad match, informs on Macheath, who is arrested and taken to Newgate prison, where he falls for the warder's daughter Lucy.

❖ In the 1920s the German playwright Bertold BRECHT and composer Kurt Weill collaborated on a modern version called *The Threepenny Opera*.

Bellow, Saul (1915-) American novelist born in Canada of Jewish emigrants from Russia. His novels include *The Adventures of Augie*

March, the story of a boy growing up and moving from the USA to Paris, and *Herzog*, about an intellectual whose wife leaves him and who then becomes obsessed with communicating his thoughts in letters to the living and the dead. Bellow received the Nobel prize for literature in 1976.

Beowulf **(BAY-uh-wolf)** EPIC poem in ▷OLD ENGLISH; the earliest long work of literature in English. *Beowulf* survives in a 10th-century manuscript, but may be much older. It tells how the hero Beowulf slays the monster Grendel and Grendel's mother, and of Beowulf's battle with a dragon, in which he is mortally wounded.

Biggles Hero of a series of children's books written in the 1930s-70s by Captain W E Johns. Biggles – short for Major James Bigglesworth, DSO, MC – is a daring British airman who flies adventurous missions with his two companions Algy and Ginger. Some of the earlier Biggles books have been criticized for jingoism and insulting references to foreigners.

biography A literary work about a real person's life. An autobiography deals with the writer's own life.

Black Beauty Children's classic written by English novelist Anna Sewell, and popular since its publication in 1877. It describes the experiences of a black mare which suffers at the hands of several cruel masters before eventually finding a kind owner.

black comedy Type of cynical humour developed in the 20th century, particularly in the THEATRE OF THE ABSURD. It represents a view of life in which human striving is futile, beliefs and values are arbitrary, and events are governed by chance. Samuel Beckett's WAITING FOR GODOT and Joe ORTON's *Loot* are black comedies.

Blake, William (1757-1827) Visionary English poet and one of the most important early figures in ROMANTICISM. An engraver by trade, Blake illustrated and printed most of his works himself. They brought little financial reward during his lifetime, but he is now considered one of Britain's greatest poets. Many of Blake's works contain ALLEGORY and symbolism that make them difficult to understand, but verses such as 'The Lamb', 'The Tyger' and 'Jerusalem', which opens 'And did those feet in ancient time/ Walk upon England's mountains green?', are widely known and loved.

CREATIVE ENERGY *Blake's engraving* The Ancient of Days *(1794) was the frontispiece to his poem 'Europe'. It shows God measuring the Universe with a pair of compasses.*

blank verse Unrhyming VERSE, usually with five stresses per line, which is very close to the natural rhythm of speech. It is the commonest form of English dramatic verse, perfected in the works of William SHAKESPEARE and his contemporaries.

Blixen, Karen (1885-1962) Danish writer, known for her short stories and for *Out of Africa* – an autobiographical account of a coffee-farming venture in Kenya which ended in failure. Blixen wrote under various ▷PSEUDONYMS, including Isak Dinesen.
❖ In 1985 *Out of Africa* was made into a film starring Meryl Streep as Karen Blixen and Robert Redford as the Oxford-educated flying pioneer Denys Finch-Hatton, with whom Blixen had an affair.

Bloomsbury Group Influential group of British writers, artists and intellectuals who met at the Bloomsbury home of the novelist Virginia WOOLF and her artist sister Vanessa Bell during the early years of the century. The members included the writers E M FORSTER and Lytton Strachey, the economist John Maynard ▷KEYNES, the painter Duncan Grant and the art critic Roger Fry. They were devoted to friendship, conversation, art, and the rejection of Victorian standards of morality.

Blyton, Enid (1897-1968) Best-selling English children's author, known for her 'Noddy', 'Famous Five' and 'Secret Seven' series.
❖ Enid Blyton's books have been accused of racism and sexism; new versions exclude such characters as the 'naughty Golliwog'.

Boccaccio, Giovanni (bo-KACH-io) (1313-75) Italian writer and humanist of the Middle Ages. His best-known work – a collection of 100 tales encompassing both comedy and tragedy called *The Decameron* – influenced

AT HOME IN AFRICA *Karen Blixen, outside her farmhouse in Kenya, holds the son of her servant Farah (left). Bankruptcy and personal tragedy eventually forced her to return to Denmark, where she made her name as a writer.*

Geoffrey CHAUCER and William SHAKESPEARE and inspired Italian literature for centuries.
❖ Chaucer used some of Boccaccio's stories in his CANTERBURY TALES.

Booker prize Name by which Britain's oldest major literary award – the Booker McConnell Prize for Fiction – is known. Founded in 1969, the prize is awarded annually to a novel in English. Well-known winners include V S NAIPAUL, Iris MURDOCH, William GOLDING, Salman RUSHDIE and the South African writer J M ▷COETZEE.

Borges, Jorge Luis (BOR-khez) (1899-1986) Argentinian writer of poems, short stories and essays, including the collections *Fictions* (1944), *The Aleph* (1949) and *Labyrinths* (1953), which brought him fame. His works are concerned with theoretical and philosophical issues, and often mix reality and imagination. Borges was an exponent of MAGIC REALISM.

Boswell, James (1740-95) Scottish lawyer and writer, best known for his biography of his friend Samuel JOHNSON, which was published in 1791.
❖ 'Boswell' has become a general term for a biographer, as in 'James Joyce found his Boswell in Richard Ellmann'. Sometimes it can also mean simply a devoted admirer.

bowdlerize To amend a book by removing passages and words deemed obscene or objectionable. The name comes from Thomas Bowdler's 1818 edition of the plays of William SHAKESPEARE, which was amended so that it could 'be read aloud in the family'.

Brave New World Futuristic novel by the British author Aldous Huxley (1894-63), published in 1932. It is set in a time when society is governed by science, and solutions have supposedly been found to all human problems. The main character is an intellectual, Bernard Marx, who in his travels encounters 'Savages' who still lead lives of unscientific disorder. Marx returns to London accompanied by a Savage, and the book ends with a debate on human freedom versus scientific ▷DETERMINISM.
❖ The book's title comes from William SHAKESPEARE's play *The Tempest* in which Miranda, brought up alone on an island, catches her first glimpse of a man other than her father. 'O brave new world,' she exclaims, 'that has such people in it.'

Brecht, Bertolt (1898-1956) Experimental German writer known for plays with a ▷MARXIST message, including *Mother Courage*, set in the ▷THIRTY YEARS' WAR, and *The Threepenny Opera*, an adaptation of the English 17th-century *The* BEGGAR'S OPERA.

Brontë, Charlotte, Emily and Anne Three daughters of a Yorkshire clergyman who were all novelists. They lost their mother in early childhood but, with their brother Branwell (1817-48), lived a rich imaginative life, inventing fantasy worlds, writing stories and poems, and producing their own miniature magazine. In later life Charlotte (1816-55) became a teacher and governess, and went on to write novels, including the romantic tale JANE EYRE. Emily (1818-48), who also worked as a governess, is known both for her poems and for WUTHERING HEIGHTS. Anne (1820-49) was the author of two novels – *Agnes Grey* and *The Tenant of Wildfell Hall*. Branwell, who showed great early promise as both a writer and a painter, became an alcoholic and an opium addict. Tragically, he, Emily and Anne died of tuberculosis during 1848-9.

Brookner, Anita (1928-) English novelist and art historian who began writing fiction in middle age. Her heroines are innocent romantics who find to their cost that in life – unlike in literature – there are few happy endings. Her novel *Hôtel du Lac* won the 1984 Booker prize.

Brothers Karamazov, The Novel by Fyodor DOSTOYEVSKY, published in 1880 and generally considered his finest work. It deals with the complex psychological and ethical issues involved in the trial of one of four brothers for the murder of their father.

Browning, Robert (1812-89) English Romantic poet whose many works include 'The Pied Piper of Hamelin' and 'My Last Duchess'. In 1846 Browning eloped with the poet Elizabeth Barrett, who is known for her works *Aurora Leigh* and *Sonnets from the Portuguese*, one of which begins 'How do I love thee? Let me count the ways.'
❖ The Brownings' romantic courtship inspired the play *The Barretts of Wimpole Street* by Rudolf Besier.

Buchan, John (1875-1940) Scottish author of action stories such as *The Thirty-Nine Steps* and *Greenmantle*, featuring Richard Hannay and other similar heroes. His books contain vivid descriptions of landscapes, from the Cotswolds and Scotland to Canada and South Africa – all of which he knew from first-hand experience. One of his early novels, *Prester John*, is a strongly pro-imperialist adventure story set in the Soutpansberg of the then northern Transvaal (now Northern Province).
❖ Buchan, who worked in the British foreign service, came to South Africa in 1901 as part of Lord ▷MILNER's 'Kindergarten'. He later became governor-general of Canada.

Burgess, Anthony (1917-93) Prolific novelist born and brought up in Manchester, England (as John Anthony Burgess Wilson), but later lived in Italy, Monaco and Switzerland. Burgess began writing in middle age after a period of colonial service in Malaysia and Borneo. His best-known novel is *A Clockwork Orange* (1962), which deals with man's capacity to choose evil of his own free will, and which was made into a film by Stanley Kubrick in 1971. Burgess's other works include *The Malayan Trilogy*, first published in the 1950s, and three humorous novels about a minor poet called Enderby.

GREAT SCOT *Robert Burns is credited with rescuing and reviving – and occasionally embellishing – the Scottish folk tradition with which his poetry so strongly identified.*

Burns, Robert (1759-96) Poet who rose from a poor farming background to become one of Scotland's greatest writers of verse, known particularly for poems in the Scottish dialect such as 'To a Mouse', 'A Red, Red Rose', 'John Anderson, my Jo' and the well-known 'Auld Lang Syne'.
❖ Some of Burns's lines have become proverbial, such as 'The best-laid schemes o' mice an' men/ Gang aft a-gley' (often go astray).
❖ His birthday, 25 January (Burns Night), is celebrated with whisky and haggis by Scots the world over.

Byron, Lord George Gordon (1788-1824) English poet known for his sexual exploits and rebelliousness as well as for his verse. He was one of the leading figures in ROMANTICISM, although both his life and his works were attacked for immorality – particularly his long satirical poem *Don Juan*. Byron had a deep love of Greece and in 1824 joined the Greek struggle against the occupying Turks. Before he saw active combat, however, he died from a fever.

❖ The epithet 'Mad, bad, and dangerous to know' was applied to Byron by the novelist and socialite Lady Caroline Lamb, who had a passionate affair with him.

Camus, Albert (kaa-MOO) (1913-60) French existentialist writer born in Algeria. His works, which include the two highly acclaimed novels *The Plague* and *The Outsider*, explore the dark, irrational side of human nature. He received the Nobel prize for literature in 1957.

Canterbury Tales, The Greatest work of the medieval English poet Geoffrey CHAUCER. Written in the late 14th century in ▷MIDDLE ENGLISH, the 17 000-line poem is made up of a series of tales told by a group of pilgrims as they travel from London to Canterbury. The tales have many different styles, reflecting the different personalities and occupations of the pilgrims; for instance, some are notoriously bawdy while others are at least superficially pious. Some of the best known are *The Knight's Tale*, *The Miller's Tale* and *The Wife of Bath's Tale*.

Capote, Truman (1924-84) American novelist whose works include *Breakfast at Tiffany's* and the 'non-fiction novel' *In Cold Blood*, based on a multiple murder in Kansas.

❖ *Breakfast at Tiffany's* was made into a popular 1961 film, starring Audrey Hepburn as Holly Golightly.

Carroll, Lewis ▷PSEUDONYM of the English writer, mathematician and Oxford don Charles Lutwidge Dodgson (1832-98), author of the children's classics ALICE'S ADVENTURES IN WONDERLAND, *Through the Looking-Glass* and the mock-heroic nonsense poem 'The Hunting of the Snark'.

TELLERS OF TALES *Chaucer's pilgrims prepare for the ride to Canterbury, in a detail from an engraving by William Blake. At the centre are the jovial Host and the Prioress.*

Cartland, Barbara (1901-) One of the most prolific authors, with some 600 romantic novels to her name and a worldwide readership of more than 650 million. She is known for her professional approach, dictating her novels into a tape recorder at the rate of approximately 23 a year.

Catch-22 Satirical war novel by American author Joseph Heller, published in 1961. 'Catch-22' is a provision in army regulations that stipulates that a soldier's request to be relieved from active duty can be accepted only if he is mentally unfit to fight. Any soldier, however, who has the sense to ask to be spared the horrors of warfare is obviously mentally sound, and therefore must stay on to fight.

❖ A 'catch-22 [situation]' means a predicament in which the alternatives are equally undesirable with no means of escape.

Catcher in the Rye, The Novel by the American author J D SALINGER, published in 1951. It relates the experiences of Holden Caulfield, a sensitive and idealistic but sceptical youth who runs away from boarding school to New York, and attacks the phoniness of the adult world.

catharsis Term used by ▷ARISTOTLE to describe the purifying effect of releasing the emotions of pity and terror which he believed was the purpose of TRAGEDY.

Catullus, Gaius Valerius (*c*84-*c*54 BC) Roman poet known for love lyrics addressed to 'Lesbia', a married society woman whose real name was Clodia.

Chandler, Raymond (1888-1959) American writer of detective fiction, who began writing only at the age of 44. He is known for his dry, ironic style and for creating Philip Marlowe – a tough, witty and eccentric private detective. Chandler's most successful books include *The Big Sleep*, *Farewell, My Lovely* and *The Long Goodbye*, all of which have been filmed.

character A person represented in a literary work, play or film, for example Ebenezer Scrooge is a character in Charles Dickens's *A* CHRISTMAS CAROL.

Chaucer, Geoffrey (*c*1345-1400) One of the greatest English poets and the most renowned of those who wrote in ▷MIDDLE ENGLISH. He came from a middle-class background, the son of a wine merchant, and married into the aristocracy. He held several positions in the service of the Crown and at the court of John of Gaunt, where his literary talents were highly appreciated. As a diplomat Chaucer travelled to France and Italy, and his work was much influenced by Italian literature, particularly the works of DANTE and BOCCACCIO. Some of Boccaccio's stories are retold in Chaucer's best-known work, *The* CANTERBURY TALES.

CLASSIC CHEKHOV Three Sisters *by Anton Chekhov is one of the masterpieces of the Russian stage and is regularly performed all over the world. This 1902 edition of the play is housed in Moscow's Chekhov Museum.*

Chekhov, Anton Pavlovich (1860-1904) Russian dramatist and short-story writer best known for his plays *The Seagull*, *Uncle Vanya*, *The Cherry Orchard* and *Three Sisters* – a comedy about three women brought up in the countryside and their longing for Moscow. Chekhov first wrote comedy sketches while studying medicine in Moscow from 1879 to 1884. Although humorous, his later work often depicts characters whose lives are frustrated or empty, and who take refuge in dreams, memories or illusions.

Chesterton, G K (1874-1936) English journalist, poet, novelist and playwright. His best-known works include *The Man Who Was Thursday* and the Father Brown detective stories, such as *The Innocence of Father Brown*, which tell of an unassuming Catholic priest with remarkable powers of deduction.

Christie, Dame Agatha (1890-1976) British writer of thrillers and detective fiction, and creator of Hercule Poirot, a precious and plump Belgian detective who relies on his 'little grey cells', and Miss Marple, an elderly spinster with a flair for solving mysterious crimes. Christie wrote nearly 70 detective novels, many of which have been filmed, including *Murder on the Orient Express* and *Death on the Nile*.

❖ Christie's play *The Mousetrap* is the world's longest-running show, having played in London continuously since 1952.

❖ In 1926, Christie created her own personal mystery: she prompted nationwide concern in Britain when she disappeared for ten days after hearing of her husband's love affair.

Christmas Carol, A Novel by Charles DICKENS, published in 1843, about the spiritual conversion of the miser Ebenezer Scrooge. After the appearance of the ghosts of Jacob Marley and of the Christmases Past, Present and Future, Scrooge becomes a reformed character. He gives money to the poor and delights the young family of his ill-used clerk Bob Cratchit by sending a Christmas turkey to his home.

Cicero, Marcus Tullius (106-43 BC) Orator, writer and statesman of ancient Rome. His speeches to the Senate are renowned for their ornate style and his letters provide a picture of Roman life at the time.

❖ His prose has yielded Latin tags such as *O tempora! O mores!* ('What times! What customs!') and *cui bono?* ('to whose profit?').

Cinderella One of the world's most popular fairy tales, loved for its rags-to-riches optimism and for the magical transformations that enable Cinderella to go to the ball despite the meanness of her stepmother and ugly stepsisters. More than 600 variations of the tale have been identified by scholars, including a Chinese story of the 9th century – hundreds of years before the first Western versions appeared.

❖ *Cinderella* has inspired numerous works of art, including a sparkling opera by Rossini and a much-loved ballet by Prokofiev.

classicism In literature, any style of writing based on the principles and forms used by classical Greek and Roman authors, such as those laid down by ▷ARISTOTLE in his *Poetics*. It is sometimes contrasted with ROMANTICISM, which concentrates on imagination and feeling rather than form and style. Classicism flourished during the 17th and 18th centuries when writers such as VOLTAIRE and MOLIÈRE in French, SWIFT and JOHNSON in English, and GOETHE and SCHILLER in German all based their work on classical models.

ALL MY OWN WORK *Agatha Christie is shown here at her home in Berkshire in 1950, surrounded by her novels. In all, she published 82 books in a literary career spanning half a century.*

Coleridge, Samuel Taylor (1772-1834) Poet, philosopher and critic regarded as a leader of English ROMANTICISM. During the 1790s Coleridge became a close friend of the poet William WORDSWORTH and his sister Dorothy. For a while they lived close together in Somerset, where Coleridge wrote some of his greatest poems, including 'Kubla Khan' and *The* RIME OF THE ANCIENT MARINER. For much of his life he suffered from ill health and opium addiction. In his later years he turned increasingly to writing criticism.

Colette, Sidonie Gabrielle (1873-1954) French novelist known for her sensitive handling of nature and childhood. Her novel *Gigi* – a version of the PYGMALION theme – was turned into a prize-winning musical film in 1958 starring Leslie Caron.

comedy Type of literature that treats its subject matter humorously and usually has a happy ending. The plot is often unbelievable and the characters are usually ordinary people rather than the kings and heroes of TRAGEDY. Western comedy grew out of ancient Greek fertility rituals in which well-known people were publicly ridiculed. Later it became unacceptable to mock individuals and instead stock characters or 'types' were used. In modern times, SATIRE, BLACK COMEDY, FARCE and THEATRE OF THE ABSURD have tended to dominate the comic form.

Conrad, Joseph (1857-1924) Novelist and short-story writer, born in the Ukraine to Polish parents and whose real name was Teodor Jozef Konrad Nalecz Korzeniowski. He later became a British citizen. Both his parents died when he was young, and at the age of 14 he began a seafaring career. His experiences at sea and in southeast Asia and the Belgian Congo (now Zaire) inspired much of his writing. English was Conrad's third language, but novels such as *Chance* and *Lord Jim*, and the novella HEART OF DARKNESS, have established him as a 20th-century master. His works deal with human weakness and the devastating effects of corrupted idealism.

Cookson, Catherine (1906-) One of Britain's most popular novelists. She has written more than 80 books and sold more than 85 million copies worldwide. They are frequently set in northeastern England, where she was born, and concentrate on unglamorous working-class family life and historical adventures.

❖ Catherine Cookson has also written under the ▷PSEUDONYM Catherine Marchant.

Corneille, Pierre (1606-84) French dramatist who has been described as the father of the French tragedy as well as the French comedy. His best-known work, *Le Cid*, took Paris by storm when it was first performed in 1636. In later life Corneille lost popularity to RACINE.

couplet Pair of lines of VERSE that RHYME and usually have the same METRE. Some poems, such as the early 19th-century *The Night Before Christmas* by the American writer Clement C Moore, are written entirely in couplets. The poem contains the lines:

'Twas the night before Christmas, when all through the house
Not a creature was stirring, not even a mouse;
The stockings were hung by the chimney with care
In hopes that St Nicholas soon would be there.

courtly love Idealised form of love in medieval ROMANCE literature, supposed to exist between a knight and the lady whom he served. The essence of courtly love was an almost religious devotion which uplifted and ennobled the knight and inspired him to great deeds. In theory the love was spiritual and unfulfilled.

❖ There is still much debate as to whether courtly love existed in real life or whether it was just a convention of the poets.

Crime and Punishment Novel by the 19th-century Russian author Fyodor DOSTOYEVSKY, published in 1866. A poor young student, Raskolnikov, kills an elderly pawnbroker for money. Afterwards, his conscience begins to torment him so that he eventually confesses and then begins the slow path to repentance and atonement. The book was Dostoyevsky's first great novel.

cummings, e e (1894-1962) American poet who spurned the use of many conventions of standard written English, including capital letters. His poetry is often ironic in tone, and covers subjects as disparate as love and public institutions.

Cyrano de Bergerac Comic swashbuckling play by the French dramatist Edmond Rostand (1868-1918), nominally based on the life of a 17th-century soldier and writer. Cyrano is cursed with a long nose which makes him unattractive to women. However, his literary gifts succeed in wooing a beautiful woman on behalf of a handsome but inarticulate friend.

❖ The story has been been filmed in the USA and France, most recently in 1990 with Gérard Depardieu in the leading role.

LITERARY LOVER *José Ferrer gave an excellent performance as the long-nosed, lovelorn Cyrano de Bergerac in the 1950 film version of Edmond Rostand's romantic play.*

Dahl, Roald (1916-90) British writer who became known in the 1960s for collections of macabre short stories such as *Kiss, Kiss*, and for children's tales of fantasy such as *Charlie and the Chocolate Factory* (1964) – a world bestseller which tells the story of a boy who wins a tour around a bizarre sweet-making plant – and its sequel *Charlie and the Great Glass Elevator* (1972).

❖ Some adults consider Dahl's books gruesome, but his brand of surreal, naive horror appeals to children.

Dante Alighieri (1265-1321) Greatest and most influential Italian writer of the Middle Ages. His early life was spent in Florence, where as a child he fell in love with 'Beatrice', who figures in his writing. She was also a child, and appears to have done no more than acknowledge him from time to time. For Dante, however, the experience was a spiritual revelation that affected him for the rest of his life. When Beatrice died in 1290, Dante was devastated and turned to philosophy and writing for consolation. Between 1290 and 1294 he wrote his first great work *La Vita Nuova* (*The New Life*) – about his love for Beatrice. Later, he was forced to take up a life of wandering because of political intrigue in Florence. He died in Ravenna, soon after finishing *The* DIVINE COMEDY.

David Copperfield Novel by Charles DICKENS, published in instalments during 1849 and 1850, and largely based on events in Dickens's own life. The story begins with the birth of David Copperfield and follows his experiences as he is sent away to school and then to work while still very young. Gradually David grows to manhood, eventually achieving fame as an author and marrying first a child-bride Dora and then, after her death, the loyal and good Agnes.

❖ Part of Dickens's purpose in writing his grim account of David's boyhood was to expose the cruel conditions of child labour he had witnessed in Britain.

Defoe, Daniel (*c*1660-1731) Writer of a large number of political and religious tracts, and also books including *A Journal of the Plague Year*, *Moll Flanders* and ROBINSON CRUSOE, which combine factual detail with highly imaginative writing. Because of his mastery of sustained story-telling in prose, Defoe is often called the first true English novelist.

denouement (day-NOO-mon) Point at the end of a book or play when all the intricacies of the PLOT are untangled for the reader or audience. It usually occurs during or soon after the climax.

❖ Denouement is a French word that means 'untying' or 'unknotting'.

Dickens, Charles (1812-70) One of Britain's greatest novelists, and author of such works as *A* CHRISTMAS CAROL, DAVID COPPERFIELD, GREAT EXPECTATIONS, *The* PICKWICK PAPERS and OLIVER TWIST. Dickens wrote 20 novels, many as serials in magazines which became very popular as a result. His writing combines humour, warmth, sentiment and often pathos to paint a detailed picture of life in Victorian times, including suffering and injustice, which he worked hard to expose. His novels are notable for their memorable characters such as Uriah Heep, Scrooge and Mr Micawber. (See panel opposite.)

Dickinson, Emily (1830-86) American writer whose short, evocative, and often mystical poems had a strong influence on modern poetry. Some of the best-known first lines of her more than 1 000 poems are: 'There is no frigate like a book', 'Because I could not stop for Death/ He kindly stopped for me' and 'I'm nobody! Who are you?'

❖ Only two of her poems were printed in her lifetime – and those without her permission.

Divine Comedy, The Finest work of the medieval Italian writer DANTE ALIGHIERI, completed soon before his death in 1321. There are three sections, Hell (*Inferno*), Purgatory (*Purgatorio*) and Heaven (*Paradiso*), each dealing with a vision of a different supernatural realm. In the first two sections Dante, guided by the Roman poet VIRGIL, meets the souls of pagans and sinners. At the end of Purgatory he enters the Earthly Paradise

CHARLES DICKENS: CREATOR OF CHARACTERS

Dickens had a great gift for bringing to life the characters of his novels. Few were based directly on real people (although the novelist himself provided the model for David Copperfield), but readers have always responded as if they were reading about flesh and blood people. The plight of Little Nell in the instalments of *The Old Curiosity Shop* aroused such public emotion that Dickens was flooded with letters begging him to let her live, and he admitted that the story was breaking his own heart.

'God bless us every one!'
Tiny Tim
A Christmas Carol

'It's always best on these occasions to do what the mob do.'
'But suppose there are two mobs?' suggested Mr Snodgrass.
'Shout with the largest,' replied Mr Pickwick.
The Pickwick Papers

'Bah! . . . Humbug!'
Ebenezer Scrooge
A Christmas Carol

In came little Bob the father . . . his threadbare clothes darned up and brushed to look seasonable; and Tiny Tim upon his shoulder.
Bob Cratchit
A Christmas Carol

The solemn presence . . . on every side, of Death – filled her with deep and thoughtful feelings, but with none of terror or alarm.
Little Nell
The Old Curiosity Shop

Uriah, with his long hands slowly twining over one another, made a ghastly writhe from the waist upwards.
Uriah Heep
David Copperfield

'Oliver Twist has asked for more!'
Mr Bumble
Oliver Twist

where he finds his beloved Beatrice, who becomes his guide to Heaven, which Virgil, a pagan, cannot enter. The poem, noted for its symbolism and ALLEGORY, influenced writers such as MILTON, BYRON and T S ELIOT.

❖ In the Middle Ages, any work that started off badly but ended well could be called a comedy. Thus *The Divine Comedy*, although a serious work, is a comedy because it begins in hell and ends in heaven.

Don Juan (DON HWAAN) Cruel aristocratic Spanish seducer who features in some 200 literary works, including a satirical poem by BYRON, and Mozart's opera *Don Giovanni* (his name in Italian). In the basic version of the story, the Don kills an elderly man after attempting to rape his daughter. Later, a memorial statue is erected to the old man, and Don Juan mockingly invites the statue to dinner. The invitation is accepted, and the tale ends with the old man returning from the dead to drag the unrepentant libertine off to hell.

Don Quixote **(DON kee-HOH-tee)** Satirical novel by the Spanish writer Miguel de Cervantes, published in two parts in 1605 and 1615. The title character is a poor country gentleman whose mind becomes deranged by reading too many knightly ROMANCES. Obsessed with the idea of reviving the age of chivalry, he climbs into a rusty suit of armour, mounts his old horse Rosinante and sets off with his fat friend Sancho Panza as his squire. Together they have a series of absurd adventures, including an incident where Don Quixote attacks windmills, believing they are giants.

❖ The expression 'tilting at windmills' means taking on an imaginary enemy.

❖ A 'quixotic' person is enthusiastic and well-meaning, but given to unreachable ideals. The word is often misused to mean 'gallant but absurd' or 'dangerously foolish'.

Donne, John (DUN) (1572-1631) English poet and Dean of St Paul's Cathedral in London. Donne is known for witty and passionate love poetry, for sermons and holy poems, and for his use of intricate ▷METAPHORS, as in 'A Valediction Forbidding Mourning', where the souls of two lovers are compared with the legs of mathematical compasses. (See METAPHYSICAL POETS.)

Dostoyevsky, Fyodor Mikhailovich (1821-81) One of the greatest Russian novelists and short-story writers of the 19th century. As a young man he was arrested for belonging to a socialist group and underwent a mock execution in which he was reprieved at the last minute. While in prison, Dostoyevsky experienced a religious conversion, and his earlier

ROMANTIC SETTING *Daphne du Maurier wrote much of* Rebecca *at Menabilly, her house in Cornwall, which she used as the model for the fictional Manderley.*

political views were replaced by an outlook based on spiritual and humanitarian values. His books, including CRIME AND PUNISHMENT and *The* BROTHERS KARAMAZOV, are known for their insight into human psychology and for their philosophical depth.

Drabble, Margaret (1939-) Novelist known for books mainly about the lives of middle-class women. Her works include *A Summer Birdcage* and *The Radiant Way.*

Dracula Classic vampire tale from the late 19th century by the Irish writer Bram (Abraham) Stoker (1847-1912). The book has inspired several ▷DRACULA FILMS. (See also DRACULA in 'Myths and legends'.)

dramatis personae List of the CHARACTERS appearing in a play (as opposed to a cast list, which gives the actors' names). Literally, 'the persons of the drama'.

Dr Jekyll and Mr Hyde Novel by Robert Louis STEVENSON, published in 1886. The well-intentioned experiments of the scientist Dr Jekyll periodically turn him into the sadistic Mr Hyde.

❖ Dr Jekyll and Mr Hyde is used as a symbol of the good and evil side of an individual.

Dryden, John (1631-1700) English poet, dramatist and critic known for his biting satire and works on public, political and religious topics. These include the tragedy *All For Love* (1677) and the comedy *Marriage à la Mode* (1673), which are still performed, and the poem *Absalom and Achitophel.* Much of Dryden's work was inspired by several Classical authors, and he made many translations from Greek and Latin. In 1668 he became poet laureate.

Dumas, Alexandre (doo-MAH) (1802-70) French novelist and playwright best known for the historical adventure tales *The Count of Monte Cristo* and *The Three Musketeers* – the exploits of Athos, Porthos, Aramis and their friend D'Artagnan.

❖ Dumas's son Alexandre (1824-95) was also a writer. His play *La Dame aux Camélias* inspired Verdi's opera *La Traviata* and a 1937 film, *Camille,* starring Greta Garbo.

du Maurier, Dame Daphne (1907-89) English writer of historical romances and novels concerned with family history and mysteries about the past. Her books include *Jamaica Inn, Frenchman's Creek* and *Rebecca* – a 20th-century GOTHIC NOVEL about a young woman whose husband, Max de Winter, is obsessed by memories of his dead first wife, Rebecca. It is largely set in the house they shared, hauntingly beautiful Manderley.

❖ The film of *Rebecca* (1940), which starred Laurence Olivier, was film maker Alfred Hitchcock's first Hollywood production.

elegy Reflective poem, particularly one mourning someone's death or a sad event. MILTON's *Lycidas* and GRAY'S ELEGY are well-known examples. In Classical times, an elegy was any poem written in alternating lines of six stresses and then five stresses – a form used for love poetry and comic verse as well as serious subjects.

Eliot, George ▷PSEUDONYM of Mary Ann Evans (1819-80), author of *The Mill on the Floss, Silas Marner, Adam Bede, Middlemarch* and other books, and generally regarded as one of the greatest English novelists. Her works deal with moral issues in human relationships – often between incompatible individuals – and the conflict between duty and social convention on the one hand and personal feelings on the other.

❖ George Eliot lived for many years with the writer G H Lewes, but was never able to marry him because he could not obtain a divorce from his estranged wife.

Eliot, T S (1888-1965) American-born author who settled in Britain in 1914. Eliot wrote poems, plays and essays, and urged the use of ordinary language and images from everyday life in poetry. He was much concerned with the emptiness of modern life and the need for a revitalization of religion. Among his best-known works are the poems 'The Love Song of J Alfred Prufrock', *The* WASTE LAND and *Four Quartets,* and the play *Murder in the Cathedral,* about the death of 12th-century English churchman Thomas Becket. Eliot won the Nobel prize for literature in 1948.

❖ In 1981 a collection of Eliot's comic poems *Old Possum's Book of Practical Cats* was turned into the musical *Cats* by Andrew Lloyd Webber.

Emerson, Ralph Waldo (1803-82) American lecturer, Unitarian minister and writer who, in his poetry and essays such as 'Self-Reliance', espoused transcendentalism, a belief in the importance of the individual and that people should follow their own conscience in secular and religious life.

epic Long poem about the larger-than-life achievements of a great hero from history or legend, such as Achilles in Homer's ILIAD, and Aeneas in VIRGIL's *Aeneid.* The stories told in epics are often part of a people's culture, but they can deal with the destiny of all humanity, as in MILTON's *Paradise Lost.*

❖ 'Epic' can also be used to refer to any work on a grand scale, such as Cecil B De Mille's film *The Ten Commandments* or Tolstoy's novel WAR AND PEACE.

eulogy Formal written or spoken tribute to someone's accomplishments or character; particularly a speech made to honour a person who has recently died – for example, Mark Antony's speech in honour of Brutus, 'This was the noblest Roman of them all . . .', from JULIUS CAESAR.

❖ To praise something extravagantly and at length is to eulogize it.

Euripides (*c*480-406 BC) Greek tragic playwright known for the splendour of his verse, his interest in extreme states of mind such as madness and passionate love, as well as his sympathetic portrayal of women and everyday people. His plays appear to question the Greek myths and even the existence of the gods, and were disapproved of by more conventional members of Greek society. *The Bacchae, Electra* and *Medea* are among Euripides' 18 surviving plays.

Everyman Morality play of the 15th century. As death approaches, Everyman finds himself deserted by old associates Fellowship, Kindred, Cousin and Goods, and therefore reliant on Good Deeds and Knowledge, who speaks the lines:

Everyman, I will go with thee and be thy guide,
In thy most need to go by thy side.

Falstaff Endearing, fat rogue who appears in several of the plays of William SHAKESPEARE, notably *The Merry Wives of Windsor* and *Henry IV*. Falstaff is a lover of wine, women and song. Although he is a coward, he often tells tales of his supposed bravery.

Fanny Hill Sexually explicit novel by English author John Cleland (1709-89), originally published with the title *Memoirs of a Woman of Pleasure*. It enjoyed great success, and although Cleland was summonsed for indecency, he was discharged.

farce Type of low COMEDY based on ridiculous situations, exaggerated characters and over-the-top buffoonery. The French playwright Georges Feydeau (1862-1921) was among the best-known writers of farce.
❖ The word comes from the Latin *farcire* meaning 'to stuff', because originally farces were inserted as brief comic interludes in otherwise serious dramas.

Faulkner, William (1897-1962) American author of powerful, symbolic novels, mostly set in the southern states of the USA. His books include *As I Lay Dying*, which he wrote in six weeks, *Absalom, Absalom!* and *The Sound and the Fury*. He won the Nobel prize for literature in 1949.

Fielding, Henry (1707-54) English lawyer and author with a witty writing style and a humane, tolerant outlook. Among Fielding's best-known books are the comic novel *Joseph Andrews* and the adventure tale TOM JONES. His work helped to establish the position of the novel in English literature and paved the way for later writers such as Charles DICKENS and William Makepeace THACKERAY.

fin de siècle French for 'end of the century'. Spirit of effete refinement that affected late 19th-century writers such as the AESTHETES and SYMBOLISTS.

Fitzgerald, F Scott (1896-1940) American writer of novels and short stories about fashionable life in the Jazz Age of the 1920s, such as *This Side of Paradise* and *The Diamond as Big as the Ritz*. His best-known work is *The Great Gatsby*, about the destructive passion of the millionaire Jay Gatsby for his former mistress Daisy Buchanan. During the 1920s Fitzgerald was one of several American authors, including Ernest Hemingway, to live in Paris.

Flaubert, Gustave (floh-BAIR) (1821-80) French novelist and story writer known for his careful style, precise choice of words and exact descriptions. His best-known work is the novel *Madame Bovary*, published in 1857. The main character, Emma Bovary, is obsessed with dreams of passion and romance which remain unfulfilled in her loveless marriage. She has two unhappy affairs and then falls deeply into debt. When her creditors threaten to tell her husband, she commits suicide.

Fleming, Ian (1908-64) English journalist and author who worked in Naval Intelligence during World War II, and afterwards wrote thrillers featuring the suave, sophisticated British secret agent James ▷BOND. The first of 12 Bond novels, *Casino Royale*, was published in 1953. Fleming is also remembered for his *Chitty-Chitty-Bang-Bang* series of children's stories.

Forster, E M (1879-1970) English novelist, short-story writer, critic and member of the BLOOMSBURY GROUP. In his novels, Forster considered plots to be somewhat incidental; he was more interested in characterization and themes. He championed the values of individualism, imagination and sincerity against narrow-mindedness and prejudice of all forms. Several successful films have been made from Forster's novels, including *A Passage to India*, *A Room with a View* and *Howards End*.

Forsyth, Frederick (1938-) Best-selling British author of suspense thrillers, including *The Day of the Jackal* and *The Odessa File*. His books are known for the accuracy of their research, down to the smallest detail, and their meticulous and compelling plots.

'for whom the bell tolls' Phrase from a sermon by John DONNE, in which he expresses a view of human fellowship: 'Any man's death diminishes me, because I am involved in

EASTERN EPIC *David Lean's lavish 1985 film version of* A Passage to India *followed Forster's novel closely. When the book was published, in 1924, the author was accused of anti-British bias.*

mankind; and therefore never send to know for whom the bell tolls; it tolls for thee.' The sermon begins with the words 'No man is an island'.
❖ Ernest HEMINGWAY used the words 'for whom the bell tolls' as the title of a novel set during the ▷SPANISH CIVIL WAR.

Fowles, John (1926-) Schoolteacher who turned to writing in the 1960s and made his name with disturbing psychological novels such as *The Collector* and *The Magus*. One of his most experimental works, *The French Lieutenant's Woman*, offers two different endings; a film version (1981) starred Meryl Streep and Jeremy Irons.

Frankenstein GOTHIC NOVEL by English writer Mary Shelley, wife of the poet Percy Bysshe SHELLEY, published in 1818. The title character, Dr Victor Frankenstein, makes a manlike monster from parts of corpses, and brings it to life by electricity. Horrible to look at but capable of human emotion, the creature is eaten up by loneliness and begs for a mate. When Frankenstein refuses, it unleashes vengeance.
❖ The monster itself is often incorrectly referred to as Frankenstein.

free verse VERSE without METRE or RHYME.

Frost, Robert (1874-1963) American nature poet known for such works as 'Mending Wall', 'The Road not Taken' and 'Stopping by Woods on a Snowy Evening', which contains the lines:

The woods are lovely, dark and deep.
But I have promises to keep,
And miles to go before I sleep.

Genji, The Tale of Early 11th-century novel generally regarded as one of the greatest works of Japanese literature. It was written by the novelist and diarist Murasaki Shikibu, probably to entertain the Empress Akiko, whom she served. Its 54 chapters chronicle the romances of the fictional Prince Genji and provide fascinating insights into Japanese court life.

genre Class or category of literature with a specific form, such as the NOVEL or SHORT STORY. In Classical times, the three great genres were EPIC, LYRIC and dramatic poetry (the last divided into TRAGEDY and COMEDY), and the rules for each were very strict. Until the 18th century genres were sharply distinguished, but later writers have produced more mixed works.

Gide, André (JEED) (1869-1951) French writer of novels and journals about the inner conflict between his Protestant upbringing and his intense longing for personal freedom. His homosexuality and communist politics made him a highly controversial writer. His novels include *The Immoralist* (1902) and *Strait is the Gate* (1909). He won the Nobel prize for literature in 1947.

HIGH GOTHIC *Quasimodo climbs the bell-tower in the 1939 film version of the great Gothic novel* The Hunchback of Notre Dame. *Charles Laughton played the monster with a heart of gold.*

Goethe, Johann Wolfgang von (GER-tuh) (1749-1832) German writer, scholar and statesman whose works include the autobiographical novel *The Sorrows of Young Werther* and the two-part drama *Faust* – a philosophical treatment of the ▷FAUST legend, which ends with Faust's redemption. His early writing was Romantic in style but, after a visit to Italy in the 1780s, he drew on Classical models in his later works. Goethe wrote outstanding LYRIC poetry, spoke six languages and was knowledgeable about a wide range of subjects, including the theatre, science, philosophy and even the occult.

Golding, Sir William (1911-93) English writer who made his name in the 1950s with LORD OF THE FLIES, a novel about a group of boys stranded on a deserted island, where the law of the jungle quickly asserts itself. Many of Golding's other novels, such as *Pincher Martin*, also deal with people in isolated or extreme positions who battle to survive without the normal supports of civilization. His novel *Rites of Passage* won the Booker prize in 1980, and Golding won the Nobel prize for literature in 1983.

Gorky, Maxim (1868-1936) (Real name Alexei Maxsimovich Peshkov) Russian writer best known for his three autobiographical books, *Childhood, In the World* and *My Universities*. He supported the ▷RUSSIAN REVOLUTION, and in 1934 became the first president of the Soviet Writers' Union. He protected persecuted writers, which may have led to his death – said to have been engineered by his political enemies.

Gothic novel Work of fiction concerned with supernatural, macabre or grotesque events, often set in a wild, haunted or isolated location. The genre became established in the 18th century and was closely associated with ROMANTICISM. It acquired the name 'Gothic' because originally such novels were set in medieval times, but by the beginning of the 19th century the historical element had become less important than the extraordinary.
❖ Gothic novels include *The* HUNCHBACK OF NOTRE DAME and FRANKENSTEIN.

Grass, Günter (1927-) German novelist, poet and playwright whose striking first novel *The Tin Drum*, written in 1959, established his literary reputation as the voice of his generation. The book is a colourful exaggeration of his experiences of creeping prewar Nazification, the war and postwar years. Serious moral and socialist convictions underlie the fantasy of this and later works, such as the novella *Cat and Mouse* and his epic novel *Dog Years*.

Graves, Robert (1895-1985) British poet, novelist and critic. His books include an autobiography of his early life and experiences in World War I, *Goodbye to All That*; a collection of poems, *Over the Brazier*; two novels set in ancient Rome, *I, Claudius* and *Claudius the God*; and works about mythology, including *The White Goddess* and *Greek Myths*.

Gray's Elegy Popular name for the poem *Elegy Written in a Country Churchyard* by English poet Thomas Gray (1716-71). The poem begins by considering the lives of those who lie buried in the village churchyard and then turns into a meditation on death. It contains many well-known lines, such as:

Full many a flower is born to blush unseen,
And waste its sweetness on the desert air.

Great Expectations Novel by Charles DICKENS, published in monthly instalments from 1860 to 1861. The story concerns a young man, Pip, who develops grandiose ambitions when he falls in love with the beautiful Estella, who has been brought up by Miss Havisham to break men's hearts. An anonymous benefactor enables Pip to leave home and embark on a new life as a gentleman in London. However, when he discovers that the source of his money is the ex-convict Abel Magwitch, whom Pip helped many years before, Pip learns the folly of his great expectations.

Greene, Graham (1904-91) One of the greatest British novelists of the 20th century, also known for his short stories, essays, plays and other writings. Greene joined the Roman Catholic Church in 1926 and elements of Catholic doctrine – such as sin, damnation and redemption – are central to many of his novels. He wrote a large number of novels, including *Stamboul Train*, a thriller which takes place on the Orient Express, *The Honorary Consul*, which is set in South America, and *The Heart of the Matter*, whose main character, a police officer in West Africa, is driven to dishonesty and eventual suicide by a combination of good motives and treacherous circumstances. Greene classed some of his works as 'entertainments', including one of his best-known novels, *Brighton Rock* – a story set against the background of gang warfare in Brighton. Greene's other books include *The Quiet American*, *Our Man in Havana*, *The Comedians* and *Travels with my Aunt*.

❖ Greene's novel *The Third Man* was originally written as a screenplay. It was filmed in 1949 and starred Orson Welles.

MORAL NARRATIVE *A convert to Roman Catholicism, Graham Greene dealt with good and evil in his novels.* Brighton Rock *(1948 film still, background) is a stark portrayal of human brutality.*

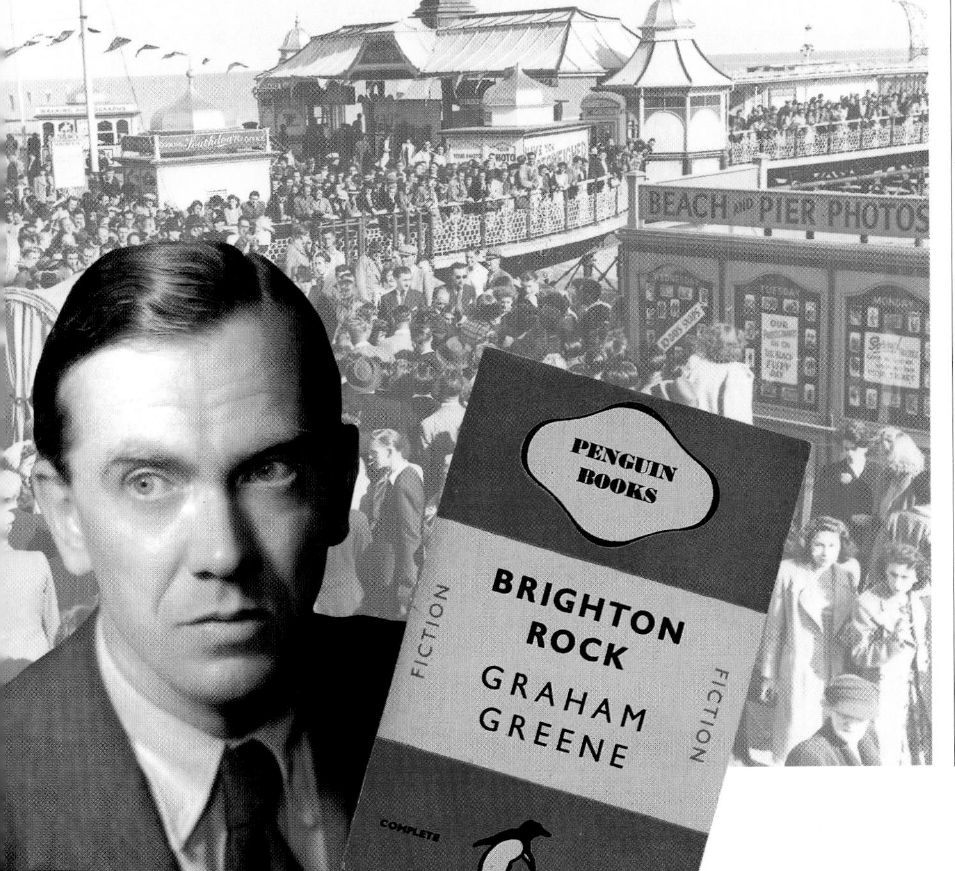

Grimm, The Brothers Two German linguists and scholars, Jakob (1785-1863) and Wilhelm (1786-1859) Grimm, who collected popular German folk tales. Their three-volume work *Grimm's Fairy Tales* contains more than 200 traditional stories, including such favourites as 'Hansel and Gretel', 'Snow White and the Seven Dwarfs' and 'Rumpelstiltskin'.

Gulliver's Travels SATIRE on human folly by Jonathan SWIFT, published in 1726. Lemuel Gulliver is shipwrecked on the island of Lilliput, where the inhabitants are just 15 centimetres tall but take themselves and their petty squabbles very seriously – a satire on contemporary English politics and self-importance. Gulliver then travels to Brobdingnag, a land of giants, and to Laputa, where the professors are so involved with projects such as extracting sunshine from cucumbers that practical matters are quite forgotten. His last encounters are with noble, intelligent horses called Houyhnhnms and brutish, degraded men called Yahoos. Gulliver finally returns home and finds himself unable to tolerate even his own family.

Gutenberg Bible (*c*1455) Named after its German printer Johann Gutenberg (*c*1400-68), this Bible is thought to be the first book in the West printed with 'movable type'. Gutenberg is credited with introducing the technique, where each letter is on a separate block and can be reused after a page has been printed.

Hamlet TRAGEDY by William SHAKESPEARE, written around 1599-1601. Before the play opens, the king of Denmark has been murdered by his brother, Claudius, who has taken the throne and married the queen, Gertrude. The ghost of the dead king visits his son, Prince Hamlet, and urges him to avenge the murder. Hamlet, tormented by this revelation, appears to be mad and cruelly rejects Ophelia, whom he loved. Using a troupe of visiting players to act out his father's death, the prince is able to prompt Claudius to expose his guilt. Hamlet then kills Ophelia's father Polonius, mistaking him for Claudius, and Claudius tries, but fails, to have Hamlet killed. Ophelia drowns herself in grief, and her brother Laertes fights a duel with Hamlet. The play ends with the death by poison of the main characters and the arrival of Fortinbras, prince of Norway, who assumes control.

❖ *Hamlet* contains several fine examples of SOLILOQUY, such as Hamlet's speech lamenting his mother's hasty remarriage and Claudius's reign, which opens 'O! that this too too solid flesh would melt', and 'TO BE OR NOT TO BE'. Much-quoted lines include 'Neither a borrower nor a lender be', 'Something is rotten in the state of Denmark',

ALAS, POOR YORICK *Laurence Olivier as the prince laments an old friend in one of the most moving scenes from* Hamlet. *Olivier also directed this 1947 film version of Shakespeare's tragedy.*

'Brevity is the soul of wit', 'To sleep: perchance to dream: ay, there's the rub;' 'The lady doth protest too much, methinks,' and 'Alas, poor Yorick'.

Hardy, Thomas (1840-1928) British writer of novels, short stories and poems, many set in the West Country – 'Wessex'. His best-known works are the novels *Far from the Madding Crowd, Jude the Obscure, The Mayor of Casterbridge* and *Tess of the D'Urbervilles.* Hardy's main theme is the struggle of the individual against the impersonal, and sometimes hostile, forces of nature and fate that determine events. Although their endings are often tragic, Hardy's books are full of humour and human sympathy. He wrote more than 900 poems dealing with deeply personal subjects, including reminiscences of his first wife, Emma.

Hawthorne, Nathaniel (1804-64) American author best known for *The Scarlet Letter*, a novel about the brutal treatment meted out to an adulterous wife in 17th-century Boston. His children's stories, such as *Tanglewood Tales*, are also well known.

Heart of Darkness NOVELLA by Joseph CONRAD, published in 1902. The narrator Marlow tells of a journey upriver in Africa to find a successful ivory dealer called Mr Kurtz, who is ill. When he finds Kurtz, Marlow discovers that hideous barbarism and corruption underlie the dealer's achievements. At the end, in bitter self-recrimination, Kurtz dies uttering the words 'The horror! The horror!'

❖ The novel's theme inspired the Vietnam war film epic ▷APOCALYPSE NOW.

Hemingway, Ernest (1899-1961) American novelist and short-story writer known for tough, masculine subjects and an economical prose style. In such books as *A Farewell to Arms, The Sun Also Rises, Death in the Afternoon, For Whom the Bell Tolls* and *The Old Man and the Sea* he glorified heroic male exploits such as bullfighting, boxing, soldiering, safari hunting and game fishing – many of which he took part in himself. Hemingway also wrote collections of short stories such as *Men without Women*, and worked as a war correspondent. He won the Nobel prize for literature in 1954. In 1961 he shot himself after a long illness.

Henry V Historical play by SHAKESPEARE, written in 1599. The new king, Henry V, is advised that he has a claim to the French throne and wages war on France. After his rousing and patriotic speech – designed to increase his soldiers' comradeship, and which includes the line 'We few, we happy few, we band of brothers' – the English win a great victory at Agincourt. The play ends with peace re-established and Henry courting Katherine of France.

❖ Films of *Henry V* include a 1944 version starring Laurence Olivier, and a 1989 version directed by Kenneth Branagh in which he also played the title role.

Hesse, Hermann (1877-1962) German novelist and poet. His books include *Steppenwolf* (1927), which explores the split personality of an artist, and *The Glass Bead Game* (1943), which envisages a future Utopia. He won the Nobel prize for literature in 1946.

Holmes, Sherlock Fictional English detective created by the writer Sir Arthur Conan Doyle (1859-1930). Holmes's extraordinary powers of memory, observation and deduction enable him to solve the most baffling crimes from minute pieces of evidence. Holmes smokes a pipe, wears a deerstalker hat and cloak, takes opium and cocaine, and plays the violin. His archenemy is Professor James Moriarty. His companion and foil is Dr John Watson, with whom he shares rooms at 221b Baker Street, London. Watson records Holmes's accomplishments but can hardly keep pace with his brilliant mind.

❖ Sherlock Holmes is said to be based on Dr Joseph Bell, an eminent Edinburgh surgeon under whom Doyle, who practised medicine for some years, had studied.

❖ The expression, 'Elementary, my dear Watson' has become associated with Sherlock Holmes, but in fact these exact words never appear in any of Doyle's stories.

Homer Greek EPIC poet who wrote in the 8th century BC and is traditionally assumed to have composed the ILIAD and the ODYSSEY – although this is disputed by many scholars. Almost nothing is known about Homer's life, except that he probably lived in Ionia in Asia Minor and may have come from a poor family. According to legend, he was blind. The poems attributed to him were clearly put together from a wide variety of sources and were probably not written down until about the 6th century BC. The surviving versions date from the 5th to 4th centuries BC, and almost certainly contain substantial alterations from the originals. In antiquity, Homer was considered the greatest of all poets, and his influence ever since has been immense.

Hopkins, Gerard Manley (1844-89) English poet and Jesuit priest who used inventive and beautiful language to express the divinity he saw in humanity and nature. Two of Hopkins's best-known poems are 'The Windhover', which compares the mastery of a falcon riding the wind with the majesty of Christ, and 'Pied Beauty', which begins 'Glory be to God for dappled things'.

Horace (65-8 BC) (Full name Quintus Horatius Flaccus) Latin poet, the son of a freed slave, and one of the most frequently quoted Classical authors. He is known for his vivid portrayal of Roman society and for his humane point of view.

❖ The expression *carpe diem*, meaning 'seize the day', comes from Horace, as does the line *Dulce et decorum est pro patria mori* ('It is sweet and fitting to die for one's country') – used ironically in a poem about World War I by Wilfred OWEN.

Hughes, Ted (1930-) British poet known for works – such as the poem sequence *Crow* – which deal with the darker, more violent side of nature, including the human unconscious. Hughes was married to the writer and poet Sylvia PLATH, who committed suicide a year after their separation. He was appointed poet laureate in 1984.

Hugo, Victor (1802-85) French novelist, poet, dramatist and the leading figure in French ROMANTICISM. He was also involved in politics, and was a keen upholder of republican ideals. Hugo is best remembered for his poetry and for the novels *Notre Dame de Paris* (published in English as *The* HUNCHBACK OF NOTRE DAME) and *Les Misérables*, on which the long-running musical of 1980 was based.

Hunchback of Notre Dame, The GOTHIC NOVEL by the French writer Victor HUGO, published in 1831. It is set in the Middle Ages and tells the story of Quasimodo, a deformed bell-ringer at Notre Dame Cathedral in Paris, who falls in love with a beautiful gypsy girl, Esmeralda.

Ibsen, Henrik (1828-1906) Norwegian dramatist and poet, considered to be the founder of modern drama. He wrote many powerful plays concerned with social, political and psychological themes. *A Doll's House*, *Ghosts* and *Hedda Gabler*, for example, have become modern classics.

Iliad EPIC Greek poem attributed to HOMER but possibly the work of many hands. It survives on papyrus fragments dating from the 5th and 4th centuries BC, from which the modern version is taken. It tells the story of the ▷TROJAN WAR – Ilios was the Greek name for Troy. Homer's ODYSSEY takes up where the *Iliad* left off.

imagery Figurative language used to convey a mental picture of an object or to represent some aspect of it. HOMER's expression 'the wine-dark sea' is an example of visual imagery because it creates an impression of the water's colour. In the Bible the image of 'the Lamb' is used in reference to Christ in order to express the abstract ideas of mildness and sacrifice. Imagery often makes use of ▷METAPHORS, ▷SIMILES and other ▷FIGURES OF SPEECH.

Ionesco, Eugène (1912-94) Romanian-born French playwright who was influential in establishing the THEATRE OF THE ABSURD. His works are known for their bizarre comedy and use of symbolism. They include *The Bald Prima Donna* – an often farcical study of an empty marriage – and *Rhinoceros*, a play about prejudice which was based on Ionesco's own experience of Nazism.

Isherwood, Christopher (1904-86) British novelist best known for his books *Mr Norris Changes Trains* and *Goodbye to Berlin*, which are largely based on his own experiences of living in Berlin in the early 1930s. He was an intimate friend and associate of the poet W H AUDEN.

James, Henry (1843-1916) American writer who moved to Europe in his early thirties and eventually settled in Britain, where many of his best-known books were written. His novels include *Washington Square* and *The Bostonians*, both of which deal with the position of women in society, and *The Portrait of a Lady* and *The Ambassadors*, which are about Americans living in Europe. James's other works include *What Maisie Knew*, which describes adult corruption from a child's point of view, and the ghost story *The Turn of the Screw*, in which a governess becomes convinced that evil powers are threatening her young charges. The latter was made into a spine-chilling opera by the composer Benjamin Britten in 1954.

❖ James's prose is known for long, convoluted sentences and occasional obscurity.

James, P D (1920-) Crime writer who created the superior and poetic detective Adam

PLAY OF PASSIONS *More than a century after it was written, the violent emotions of* Hedda Gabler *can still disturb a modern audience. Theatregoers of the 1890s were shocked and outraged by Ibsen's forthright portrayal of destructive human relationships and suffering in marriage.*

LITERARY SISTERS *This portrait of Charlotte, Emily and Anne Brontë was painted by their brother Branwell. A ghostly smudge marks the place where he humbly erased himself from the scene.*

Dalgleish in books such as *A Taste for Death* (1986). At one time, earlier in her career, James worked for the forensic science department at the British Home Office.

Jane Eyre Romantic novel by Charlotte BRONTË, published in 1847. It describes how Jane, an orphan, becomes governess at Thornfield Hall and eventually marries its intense, brooding master, Mr Rochester.

Jerome, Jerome K (1859-1927) English humorist remembered for writing *Three Men in a Boat*, a whimsical account of three friends' chaotic progress along the Thames between Kingston and Oxford.
❖ Jerome's initial 'K' stands for 'Klapka'.

Johnson, Samuel (1709-84) English writer, wit, critic and lexicographer, best known for his *Dictionary of the English Language*, published in 1755. In it, Johnson defines more than 40 000 words and includes more than 100 000 quotations illustrating their usage. The book remained the standard reference work until publication of the ▷OXFORD ENGLISH DICTIONARY began in 1884.
❖ A few of Johnson's entries contain his own eccentric definitions, as for *lexicographer*, 'a writer of dictionaries, a harmless drudge'.

Jonson, Ben (1572-1637) English dramatist and poet who was a contemporary of William SHAKESPEARE. His first success came with the comedy *Every Man in his Humour*, performed in 1598, and based on the medieval theory that certain humours, or liquids in the body, determined a person's dominant temperament. This was followed the next year by *Every Man out of his Humour* and by a series of other comedies and satires. The best known are *Volpone* – about a wealthy man who exploits his relatives through feigning illness – and *The Alchemist*, which deals with the comings and goings of lowlife thieves and tricksters.

Joyce, James (1882-1941) Dublin-born author who left Ireland as a young man to escape what he saw as the narrowness of Irish society and the overwhelming influence of the Roman Catholic Church. Joyce lived in Paris, Trieste and Zürich, but the works for which he is known are all set in Ireland. His early books include the short-story collection *Dubliners* and the autobiographical novel *A Portrait of the Artist as a Young Man*, which chronicles the struggle of young Stephen Dedalus to establish himself as a poet. Stephen also appears in Joyce's best-known book, the controversial ULYSSES, which presents the events of a single day in Dublin. Both *Ulysses* and Joyce's other mature novel, *Finnegans Wake*, are known for their passages of STREAM OF CONSCIOUSNESS writing.

Julius Caesar TRAGEDY by William SHAKESPEARE, probably written in 1599. It deals with the assassination of Julius Caesar and its aftermath, and is largely based on historical fact. The assassination is the work of a group of influential Romans – including Cassius and Brutus – who mistrust Caesar's ambitions. After the murder, an army is raised against them, Brutus's wife commits suicide, and Brutus and Cassius kill themselves after defeat at Philippi.

Jungle Book, The Collection of short stories for children by Rudyard KIPLING, published in 1894 and followed by *The Second Jungle Book*. Many of the stories feature Mowgli, a boy who is brought up by wolves and educated in the ways of the jungle by animals such as Baloo, the brown bear, and Bagheera, the black panther.
❖ Mowgli and his friends are now, perhaps, best known to thousands of youngsters through Walt Disney's delightful animated film version of *The Jungle Book* (1967).
❖ *The Jungle Book* was the inspiration behind the Wolf Cubs, the junior division of the Boy Scouts, founded in 1916.

Juvenal (*c*60-*c*140) (Decimus Junius Juvenalis) Latin poet known for his 16 brilliant satires attacking the affectation, greed and corruption of Roman society. His work has had a strong influence on satirists ever since.
❖ The expression *Mens sana in corpore sano* ('A sound mind in a sound body') comes from one of Juvenal's satires.

Kafka, Franz (1883-1924) Czech novelist and short-story writer. His writing – in German – depicts the terrors and frustrations of modern life in terms of surreal, nightmarish events afflicting characters who are lonely, tormented or victimized. Kafka's works include *The Trial*, a novel in which a man unaccountably finds himself under arrest, and the short story 'The Metamorphosis', a tale of psychological terror in which the main character, Gregor Samsa, suddenly finds himself transformed into a giant insect.

Kazantzakis, Nikos (1885-1957) Greek writer best known for the colourful novels *Zorba the Greek* and *The Last Temptation of Christ*. The latter caused an uproar when it was filmed in 1988 because it contains a scene in which Christ is tempted, as he is dying on the Cross, by a vision of life as an ordinary man.

Keats, John (1795-1821) English poet who was one of the leading literary figures of ROMANTICISM. Keats died of tuberculosis in Rome at the age of just 25, by which time he had written a number of great poems inspired by nature, art and mythology, and dealing with themes such as artistic creation and the relationship between art and life. The best known include 'Ode on a Grecian Urn', 'Ode to a Nightingale', 'To Autumn', 'Hyperion', and *Endymion*, which contains the line 'A thing of beauty is a joy for ever'. His work is known for its beauty and sensuousness. Keats is also remembered for his doomed love affair with Fanny Brawne, and for his many letters.

Keneally, Thomas Michael (1935-) Prolific Australian novelist whose book *Schindler's Ark* (1982), based on a true account of Polish Jews saved by a German industrialist during World War II, won the Booker prize. The director Steven Spielberg turned it into a powerful film, *Schindler's List* (1993).

King Lear TRAGEDY by William SHAKESPEARE, written in about 1605. It is based on a legendary British king who in old age unwisely hands over his kingdom to his two elder daughters, Goneril and Regan. The daughters turn on him, reducing him to poverty and, eventually, to madness. Lear's youngest daughter Cordelia, whom the king at first spurned, remains faithful to him and helps to raise an army against his enemies. She and Lear are captured, however, and she is hanged. Lear dies with her in his arms.

❖ Many familiar lines come from *King Lear*, including: 'Nothing will come of nothing'; 'As flies to wanton boys, are we to the gods;/ They kill us for their sport'; and 'How sharper than a serpent's tooth it is/ To have a thankless child'.

Kipling, Rudyard (1865-1936) British author of poems, short stories and novels, many dealing with the British Empire, particularly the Indian Raj. Kipling was born in India, where he returned as an adult and worked as a journalist. He also travelled to the USA, and to South Africa during the South African War. In 1907 he became the first English writer to receive the Nobel prize for literature. Kipling's best-known works are the children's books *Just So Stories*, *The* JUNGLE BOOK and *Kim*, and poems such as 'Mandalay', 'If' and 'Gunga Din'.

❖ Kipling spent several summers in Cape Town, staying at the Woolsack, a lavish summer 'cottage' commissioned by Cecil John ▷RHODES to attract poets and artists to the beauty of the Cape. Kipling later wrote Rhodes's obituary and the poem quoted on Rhodes Memorial in Cape Town.

❖ The University of Cape Town has a noted Kipling Collection.

Lady Chatterley's Lover Novel by D H LAWRENCE, written in the 1920s but not published in full in Britain until 1960 because of its explicit sexual descriptions and strong language. It concerns a passionate love affair between Lady Chatterley, the wife of an intellectual but invalid landowner, and the gamekeeper Oliver Mellors. Lady Chatterley becomes pregnant with Mellors's child and, despite the scandal, she turns her back on respectable society rather than deny her love.

❖ In 1960 Penguin Books were prosecuted for publishing *Lady Chatterley's Lover.* They were acquitted, after which ▷CENSORSHIP laws were relaxed in Britain.

❖ The book was also banned in South Africa until 1980.

La Fontaine, Jean de (1621-95) French poet known for his elegant *Fables*, adapted from AESOP'S FABLES and other sources. His moral tales, told in verse, remain popular because of his colourful characterizations of humanity, beasts and nature.

THE MIGHTY FALLEN *The great tiger Shere Khan is slain by Mowgli in* The Jungle Book *story 'Tiger! Tiger!'. Rudyard Kipling began writing the tales in 1892 when he was living in the USA. They were based on his childhood memories of India and experiences he had there as a journalist in the 1880s.*

Lake poets Group of 19th-century Romantic poets whose work is associated with the Lake District of Britain. They include Samuel Taylor COLERIDGE, Robert Southey and William WORDSWORTH.

Larkin, Philip (1922-85) English writer of complex satirical and melancholic poems about modern life, incorporating themes such as old age and death. Larkin delighted in breaking taboos, but his writing can also be sincere and moving.

Last of the Mohicans, The Novel by American writer James Fenimore Cooper (1789-1851). Part of *The Leatherstocking Tales*, the book tells the story of a noble Native American who helps a family of British settlers during the American phase of the ▷SEVEN YEARS' WAR.

Lawrence, D H (1885-1930) English poet, novelist and short-story writer much concerned with human passions and sexuality, and the stultifying effects of social convention. He began writing poems and short stories at an early age, and made his name with the semi-autobiographical novel *Sons and Lovers* (1913) while in his twenties. At about this time, he eloped with a married woman, Frieda Weekley. In 1914 she obtained a divorce and they were married. Years of travel followed, in Europe, Ceylon (Sri Lanka), Australia, the USA and Mexico. Despite the disruption of travel, poor health and a difficult relationship with Frieda, Lawrence wrote many novels now considered classics, including *The Rainbow*, *Women in Love* and LADY CHATTERLEY'S LOVER.

Lear, Edward (1812-88) English writer of humorous and nonsense verse for children, including 'The Owl and the Pussycat', 'The Jumblies', 'The Pobble Who Has No Toes' and 'The Dong with a Luminous Nose'. His *Book of Nonsense* (1846) popularized the LIMERICK. Lear was also a talented artist, and illustrated many of his own rhymes.

Le Carré, John ▷PSEUDONYM of the writer David Cornwell (1931-), the author of thrillers and spy novels such as *The Spy Who Came in from the Cold*; *The Honourable Schoolboy*; *Tinker, Tailor, Soldier, Spy*; *Smiley's People* and *The Little Drummer Girl.* Le Carré is known for the intricacy of his plots and for creating the intellectual British spy master George Smiley, who features in many of his books.

limerick Humorous nonsense jingle, usually consisting of two long rhyming lines followed by two short rhyming lines and a longer final line that rhymes with the first two or, more strictly, ends on the same word as the first line. Limericks often begin, 'There was a . . . ', as in this one by Edward LEAR:

There was an Old Man with a beard,
Who said, 'It is just as I feared! –
Two owls and a hen,
Four larks and a wren,
Have all built their nests in my beard!'

Lolita Novel by the Russian-born writer Vladimir Nabokov (1899-1977), published in 1955. It tells the story of a middle-aged professor of English, Humbert Humbert, and his sexual obsession with Lolita, his precocious adolescent stepdaughter.

❖ Nabokov, also a poet and literary critic, wrote his early books in Russian under the name of V Sirin. He left Russia in 1919 and lived the rest of his life in the West. After 1940 all his novels, including *Pale Fire*, were written in English, using original storytelling techniques and inventive language.

Longfellow, Henry Wadsworth (1807-82) American poet whose popular works include 'The Song of Hiawatha', 'The Village Blacksmith' and 'The Wreck of the Hesperus'.

Lorca, Federico Garcia (1898-1936) One of Spain's greatest modern dramatists and poets, and one of the few writers in any language to produce outstanding verse tragedy in this century. His best-known plays are *Blood Wedding* and *The House of Bernarda Alba*, which deal with passion, violence and emotional repression in Andalusian culture. Lorca was shot by Nationalist partisans at the outbreak of the ▷SPANISH CIVIL WAR.

Lord of the Flies Novel by William GOLDING, published in 1954. It tells the story of a group of schoolboys who are stranded on an island after a plane crash. Two of the boys, Ralph and Piggy, try to get the group to cooperate in establishing a rational, ordered society. However, their authority is soon challenged and a reign of terror begins under a boy called Jack. Piggy and another boy are killed before the boys are finally rescued.

❖ William Golding wrote the *Lord of the Flies* in response to *The Coral Island*, a novel by R M Ballantyne in which three shipwrecked children have a series of exciting but innocent adventures.

❖ Beelzebub, derived from the Hebrew for 'lord of flies', is a name for the devil.

Lord of the Rings, The Fantasy novel by J R R TOLKIEN, published in three volumes between 1954 and 1955. It is a sequel to his earlier novel *The Hobbit*, published in 1937. Four Hobbits, Frodo, Sam, Merry and Pippin, set out on a dangerous mission to prevent the evil Sauron from obtaining a golden ring which will give him power to control the world. The Hobbits' mission is aided by the Elves and by the good wizard Gandalf, but on several occasions they almost lose their lives doing battle with the fearsome Orcs, Ringwraiths and other agents of Sauron. Eventually the ring is destroyed, Sauron falls and a benevolent human ruler is established in his place.

❖ Tolkien's Hobbits, a race of small people with large, furry feet, are home-loving and peaceable, and live underground in the fictional world of Middle Earth.

lyric Type of POETRY which is written to express the subjective thoughts, feelings or impressions of a single speaker. It is distinguished from EPIC and NARRATIVE verse, which tells a story, and from dramatic verse, which has parts for different speakers.

❖ In ancient Greece such poems were usually sung to the lyre, which is why the words of songs are often referred to as lyrics.

Macbeth TRAGEDY by William SHAKESPEARE, dating from about 1606 and based on historical events of the 11th century. The Scottish nobleman Macbeth, encouraged by the prophecy of three witches and by his ambitious wife, murders the king, Duncan, and usurps the throne. To maintain his ill-gotten position, Macbeth is driven to increasingly desperate measures, and arranges the murders of his friend Banquo and the family of his enemy Macduff. At the end, Lady Macbeth loses her mind and dies, and Macbeth is killed in battle by Macduff.

❖ Many lines from *Macbeth* have become familiar expressions: 'the milk of human kindness'; 'Is this a dagger which I see before me?'; the witches' chant 'Double, double, toil and trouble'; 'Out, damned spot!'; and 'Lay on, Macduff' – Macbeth's challenge to his rival to fight to the death, often misquoted as 'Lead on, Macduff'.

❖ Within theatrical circles, superstition precludes any mention of the title 'Macbeth'; it is always called 'The Scottish Play'.

Maclean, Alistair (1922-87) Best-selling Scottish author of adventure tales and thrillers set in exotic locations. His books include *The Guns of Navarone*, *Ice Station Zebra*, the Western *Breakheart Pass* and *Where Eagles Dare*. Many of his novels have been made into films.

magic realism Term applied to works written in a realistic style about events that include

PERILOUS ROUTE *Rivendell was the last of the 'homely houses' in* The Lord of the Rings, *on Frodo's route through Mordor, land of darkness and evil. The illustration is by Tolkien himself.*

imaginary and fantastic elements alongside the credible and everyday. Exponents of magic realism include Salman RUSHDIE, Jorge Luis BORGES and Gabriel García MÁRQUEZ.

Mailer, Norman (1923-) American novelist and journalist regarded as a leading writer of his generation. His many works, often highly critical of modern American norms and mores, include the 1948 antiwar novel *The Naked and the Dead.* He was a prominent protester during the 1960s, during which he wrote *Why Are We in Vietnam?* and *Armies of the Night,* for which he won the Pulitzer prize. Later works include *The Executioner's Song,* an account of the events leading to the execution of murderer Gary Gilmore.

Malamud, Bernard (1914-86) One of America's leading contemporary writers, best known for his novels *The Assistant* and *The Fixer,* a bleak but powerfully written tale set in tsarist Russia. He won the Pulitzer prize for literature in 1967.

Mallarmé, Stéphane (1842-98) French SYMBOLIST poet who tried to describe a world of abstract ideals lying beyond physical reality. His works include *L'Après-midi d'un Faune* (*The Afternoon of a Faun*) which inspired a tone poem by the composer ▷DEBUSSY and a ballet by ▷NIJINSKY.

Man for All Seasons, A Play by the British dramatist Robert Bolt (1924-95), about Sir Thomas More, who was beheaded in 1535 for refusing to recognize King Henry VIII instead of the pope as the head of the Church in England.

Mann, Thomas (1875-1955) German novelist and short-story writer whose books deal with artistic creation and the moral and intellectual struggles of individuals trying to come to terms with the world around them. His masterpieces include *The Magic Mountain* and *Death in Venice.* He won the Nobel prize for literature in 1929. Mann opposed the Nazi regime and became a US citizen in 1940.

Mansfield, Katherine (1888-1923) New Zealand author known for her fine short-story writing and her original and experimental style. She settled in London in 1908 and her stories first appeared in several weekly magazines. She published various collections, notably *In a German Pension*; *Bliss, and Other Stories*; and *The Garden Party, and Other Stories.* Her reputation grew as her health deteriorated; she died from tuberculosis. Several works were published after her death, including her poetry and many of her letters.

Marlowe, Christopher (1564-93) English poet and playwright whose style of blank verse influenced William SHAKESPEARE's early plays. Marlowe was quick-tempered, irreligious and apparently involved in crime. He died after a brawl in a tavern while awaiting trial for blasphemy; it has been suggested that he was murdered by his criminal accomplices who were afraid of exposure in Marlowe's evidence. Marlowe's best-known works are tragedies such as *Tamburlaine the Great, The Jew of Malta* and *Dr Faustus,* in which bold, ruthless individuals take on the fates, eventually bringing about their own destruction. However, Marlowe was also capable of sensuous love poetry such as 'The Passionate Shepherd to his Love', which begins 'Come live with me and be my love'.

Márquez, Gabriel García (1928-) Colombian writer known for books and short stories that combine realistic characters and details with mysterious and magical events. His works include the fine novel *One Hundred Years of Solitude,* about the Buendía family, and *Love in the Time of Cholera.* In 1982 he received the Nobel prize for literature.

masque (or mask) Lavish courtly entertainment of the 16th and 17th centuries, popular in Italy, France and England. It usually took the form of a procession or pageant, with costumed amateurs acting out a dramatic poem or ALLEGORY to the accompaniment of music and dancing.

Maugham, (William) Somerset (1874-1965) British short-story writer, novelist and playwright. Many of Maugham's works are based on the writer's travels in China, the Pacific Islands, India, southeast Asia and Mexico. 'Rain', one of his best-known short stories, deals with an encounter between a prostitute and a missionary on the island of Samoa. Maugham's novels include *The Moon and Sixpence,* based on the life of the artist Paul Gauguin in Tahiti; *Cakes and Ale,* whose main character is the cheerful wife of a distinguished writer; and the autobiographical novel *Of Human Bondage.*

Maupassant, Guy de (1850-93) French short-story writer and novelist. He was encouraged to write by FLAUBERT and ZOLA and produced some 300 stories on subjects ranging from peasant life to high society.

melodrama A play or film in which the PLOT is often sensational, and the CHARACTERS may display exaggerated emotion.

Merchant of Venice, The Play by William SHAKESPEARE, written between 1596 and 1598. A Venetian merchant, Antonio, borrows money from Shylock, a Jew, to help his friend Bassanio to woo Portia. If Antonio fails to repay the money on time, he is to forfeit a pound of his flesh. Bassanio marries Portia, but Antonio's ships are wrecked and he cannot repay the debt. Portia, disguised as a lawyer, appeals to Shylock to have mercy on Antonio, but he refuses. She concedes the moneylender's right to Antonio's flesh but points out that the agreement does not permit him to spill a single drop of blood. Outwitted, Shylock gives up the case and, as punishment for conspiring against the life of a Venetian, he is required to become a Christian and leave his money to his runaway daughter Jessica.

❖ Although the play reflects the anti-Semitic attitudes of the time, it also contains a moving speech in which Shylock asserts his common humanity: 'I am a Jew,' he says. 'Hath not a Jew hands, organs, dimensions, senses, affections, passions?'

Metaphysical poets Group of English poets of the 17th century, including John DONNE and Andrew Marvell. Their work often uses intricate scholarly arguments and elaborate comparisons to make its point.

❖ ▷METAPHYSICS is a speculative branch of philosophy that examines such issues as life and death, reality, knowledge, time and space, and the interplay between them.

metre The rhythmic pattern of POETRY created by the mixing of stressed and unstressed syllables in a single line. The unit of poetic metre is known as a 'foot' and can have various forms such as the *iamb* (an unstressed syllable followed by a stressed one, as in to-DAY), the *trochee* (a stressed syllable followed by an unstressed one, as in NEV-er) or the *dactyl* (a stressed syllable followed by two unstressed ones, as in YES-ter-day). Poetry with one foot per line is known as monometer; with two feet per line as dimeter; with three feet per line as trimeter; and so on. One of the best-known forms of metre is iambic pentameter, which has five iambs in every line – the metre used in the plays of William SHAKESPEARE. Until the 19th century strict metrical rules were generally applied to Classical literature and to European poetry. Romantic and modern poets have adopted a freer approach.

Midsummer Night's Dream, A COMEDY by William SHAKESPEARE, written around 1595. Four lovers spend a night in a wood outside Athens, where the fairy king and queen, Oberon and Titania, have had an argument. To punish Titania, Oberon gets the sprite Puck to drop the juice of a magic herb on her

eyes while she sleeps so that she will fall in love with the first thing she sees when she wakes. This turns out to be the weaver Bottom wearing an ass's head mask for a play rehearsal. Puck also uses the herb on the human lovers who unfortunately set eyes on the wrong partners first. When Titania and Oberon are reconciled, Oberon releases the human lovers from the spell.
❖ Well-known lines from the play include 'Ill met by moonlight, proud Titania', and 'Lord, what fools these mortals be!'

Miller, Arthur (1915-) American dramatist known for realistic and often tragic plays about modern life. His works include *Death of a Salesman*, about an ordinary man's inability to face up to what he sees as his own failure, *All My Sons*, which deals with the emotional effects of war, and *The Crucible*, which deals with the 17th-century Salem witch trials, but refers by implication to the anti-Communist witch-hunts of the McCarthy era in the USA.
❖ Arthur Miller was the third husband of the film actress Marilyn Monroe.

Milne, A A (1882-1956) British author known for his 1920s children's books *Winnie the Pooh* and *The House at Pooh Corner* which feature the little boy Christopher Robin – modelled on Milne's own son – and toy animals such as the bear Winnie the Pooh, the donkey Eeyore, Rabbit, Piglet, Owl, Tigger, Kanga and Roo. Milne also wrote two books of children's verse, *When We Were Very Young* and *Now We Are Six*.

MAKING TRACKS *The familiar outlines of Pooh and Piglet. The Pooh books made the illustrator E H Shepard almost as well known as the author A A Milne (left).*

Milton, John (1608-74) English poet considered to be one of the greatest ever to write in English along with Geoffrey CHAUCER and William SHAKESPEARE. Milton's best-known poem is *Paradise Lost*, which he dictated after he went blind. It describes in EPIC form the events of the Book of Genesis surrounding the Fall of Man. Milton later wrote a sequel, *Paradise Regained*, about Christ's triumph over Satan's temptation in the wilderness. His other well-known works include *Lycidas* – an elegy on the death of a friend – and *Samson Agonistes*, which describes the last days of Samson after he had been taken prisoner. Milton supported Parliament in the ▷ENGLISH CIVIL WAR and became Oliver Cromwell's Latin secretary. He was an outspoken campaigner for liberty and justice, writing many tracts on subjects ranging from divorce to the freedom of the press and of religion.

Mitty, Walter Title character in the 1930s short story 'The Secret Life of Walter Mitty' written by the American humorist James THURBER. Walter Mitty is a repressed and henpecked man who takes refuge in romantic or fantastic daydreams.
❖ A Walter Mitty character is someone who lives in a fantasy world.

Moby Dick Symbolic novel by the American writer Herman Melville, published in 1851. The central character, Captain Ahab, sets off on an obsessive quest for revenge on the great white whale Moby Dick, which had cost him a leg on an earlier encounter. The story is narrated by the young sailor Ishmael, who begins the book with the much-quoted sentence 'Call me Ishmael'. For both men, the voyage, on the ship *Pequod*, becomes as much a journey of self-discovery as a whaling expedition. While Ishmael discovers compassion and love, Ahab becomes enveloped by the dark, destructive forces represented by the whale.
❖ In this book, as well as in *Billy Budd* – about the sentencing and execution of a young sailor after he accidentally kills one of the crew – Melville drew on several adventurous years at sea, including time spent on a whaling ship.

mock-heroic Work that satirizes the conventions of the heroic or EPIC style of writing by using it to describe trivial events or lowlife characters. Alexander POPE's poem *The Rape of the Lock* is an example.

modernism Literary movement associated with writers of the first half of the 20th century such as Marcel PROUST, Ezra POUND, Virginia WOOLF and James JOYCE. Its main features were experimentation, rejection of 19th-century attitudes and values, and an interest in the unconscious processes of the mind, inspired in part by the theories of Sigmund ▷FREUD. One of modernism's most important contributions was the STREAM OF CONSCIOUSNESS technique, where a character's inner thoughts are told within the story.

Molière Pen name of the French playwright, actor and director Jean-Baptiste Poquelin (1622-73), known for social satires such as *The Misanthrope* and *Tartuffe*. Molière began his theatrical career at the age of 21 by forming an acting troupe called L'Illustre Theatre. He won acclaim as an actor and playwright, writing 30 comedies, all showing his profound understanding of human nature and French society of the time.

Morrison, Toni (1931-) American novelist whose richly detailed novels explore life among rural blacks in the deep South. They include *Song of Solomon* (1977), *Tar Baby* (1981) and *Beloved* (1987) – a factually based account of infanticide which won the 1988 Pulitzer prize. She also won the Nobel prize for literature in 1993.

Morte d'Arthur, Le Series of stories about the legendary King ▷ARTHUR and the Knights of the Round Table, by Sir Thomas Malory, published in 1485. The book brought together a diverse assortment of French and English legends, turning them into the great tales of quests, chivalry and romance that still colour the popular view of the Middle Ages.
❖ *Le Morte d'Arthur* has inspired many other works, including poems by TENNYSON, paintings by the ▷PRE-RAPHAELITE BROTHERHOOD, the children's book *The Sword in the Stone*, the film *Excalibur* and the musical *Camelot*.

Murdoch, Iris (1919-) Irish novelist, playwright and philosopher known for novels concerned with the inner lives of individuals and with complex moral and psychological issues such as good and evil, religious belief and sexuality. Her best-known books include *Under the Net* and *The Black Prince* (both narrated by a male in the first-person); *The Bell*, which is set in a lay religious community; *A Severed Head*, about marriage and infidelity; and *The Sea, the Sea*, a love story, which won the Booker prize in 1978.

TALENT TO AMUSE *Admired by theatregoers of all classes, Molière single-handedly created a new style of 17th-century French comedy.*

mystery plays Cycles of dramas enacting events from the Bible, performed annually by members of craftsmen's guilds in many parts of Europe from medieval times until as late as the 17th century. Mystery plays developed out of dramatized Bible stories presented in church at Christmas, Easter and other festivals, and were one of the earliest forms of popular theatre. The Oberammergau Passion Play performed every ten years in Bavaria is a mystery play.

Naipaul, Sir V S (1932-) Novelist and travel writer born in Trinidad and resident in Britain since 1950. Naipaul's early books were comedies about Trinidadian life, but his later works take a deeper view, probing issues of personal and national identity, politics and alienation. His best-known novels are *A House for Mr Biswas*, whose main character was modelled on Naipaul's father, and *A Bend in the River*, set in the turbulent times that follow independence in an imaginary African state. *A Bend in the River* won the Booker prize in 1979.

narrative Writing which tells a story or describes a sequence of events. The word can also be used as an adjective to refer to the quality of telling a story. Narrative poetry, for example, includes medieval ROMANCES about King Arthur and his knights, and VIRGIL's *Aeneid*, which tells of the founding of Rome.

narrator The 'speaker' in a poem, NOVEL or SHORT STORY. Sometimes he is named and it is clear that the work is written from his point of view, as in Herman Melville's MOBY DICK, where the speaker is identified in the first sentence: 'Call me Ishmael.' Often there appears to be no narrator, but even then it cannot be assumed that the author is speaking directly to the reader; instead there is said to be an 'implied narrator'. In a play, the narrator speaks directly to the audience.

Nash, Ogden (1902-71) American poet known for outrageous rhymes such as 'A bit of talcum/ Is always walcum' and 'Candy/ Is dandy/ But liquor/ Is quicker'.

***Nibelungenlied* (*The Song of the Nibelungs*)** Medieval German epic written around 1200 but based on much older sources. The first part deals with the hero Siegfried's wooing of the Burgundian (Nibelung) princess Kriemhild, his subduing of the warrior-queen Brunhild (or Brünnhilde), and his murder by the Burgundians. In the second section Kriemhild marries Attila the Hun and with his help wreaks vengeance on her own people for Siegfried's death – a historical event that has been dated to the 5th century. Scandinavian SAGAS relate similar legends.
❖ Richard Wagner's opera cycle *The Ring of the Nibelung* is based on the *Nibelungenlied* and the Scandinavian sagas.

Nineteen Eighty-Four Novel by George ORWELL, published in 1949. The book is set in the imaginary totalitarian state of Oceania, whose population is controlled in word, deed and thought by the Party, the menacing but unseen Big Brother, the Thought Police and all-pervading propaganda. The main character, Winston Smith, tries to stand up for truth and humanity, but is broken by the system. Orwell wrote the book as a general warning against totalitarianism and the loss of individual freedom, but it has also been interpreted by some as referring specifically to Josef Stalin's USSR.
❖ The terms ▷'NEWSPEAK' and 'Doublespeak' were coined in the novel to refer to types of propaganda. Doublespeak, for example, uses slogans such as 'Freedom is Slavery' and 'War is Peace'.
❖ The term 'Big Brother' is used to refer to any ruler or government seen as invading the privacy of individuals.

Noma Top award for writing and publishing in Africa, named after its founder, Japanese publisher Shoichi Noma. It has been given annually since 1980 to a writer or scholar from Africa, whose work was published in Africa during the previous year. Winners have included South Africans Njabulo S ▷NDEBELE and Mongane Wally ▷SEROTE.

nonsense verse Humorous POETRY which is absurd or illogical, or based on comic made-up words. These lines from Lewis CARROLL's poem *The Walrus and the Carpenter* are a typical example:

'The time has come,' the Walrus said,
'To talk of many things:
Of shoes – and ships – and sealing-wax –
Of cabbages – and kings –
Of why the sea is boiling hot –
And whether pigs have wings.'

novel Extended work of PROSE fiction. Its early roots are found in ancient Egyptian literature from around 1200 BC, and in Latin writing from the first and second centuries AD. There is also a long history of storytelling in Arabic and Japanese literature from the 11th century. The modern novel, however, developed in the 18th century out of the work of English writers such as Daniel DEFOE, Henry FIELDING and Samuel Richardson (1689-1761). Since then the novel has become the most prominent form of literature, with dozens of specialist categories such as SCIENCE FICTION, crime, fantasy and ROMANCE.

novella Compact story which hinges on a single episode or event and which has an unexpected, but logical, twist at the end – such as the tales in BOCCACCIO's *Decameron* or Joseph Conrad's HEART OF DARKNESS. The term is also loosely used to refer to any short NOVEL or long SHORT STORY.

O'Casey, Sean (1880-1964) Irish playwright who wrote tragicomedies about the dangers and beliefs behind Irish patriotism, the comedy of everyday life and the realities of poverty. His best-known plays are *Juno and the Paycock* and *The Plough and the Stars*.

ode Formal poem expressing lofty thoughts or profound emotions. Public odes, such as those by the ancient Greek poet Pindar, have a stately, ceremonial tone and were written for important occasions. Private odes, such as those of the Latin poet HORACE and the Englishman John KEATS, deal with personal emotion and intense inner experience.

Odyssey Ancient Greek EPIC attributed to HOMER, and considered one of the greatest works of literature ever constructed. It follows on from the ILIAD and tells of the Greek king Odysseus' ten-year voyage home to Ithaca after the ▷TROJAN WAR. His many strange adventures on the way include encounters with a one-eyed Cyclops called Polyphemus, the enchantress Circe and the goddess Calypso, who keeps him as her lover for eight years. Eventually, Odysseus arrives back in Ithaca where his wife Penelope is faithful despite her many suitors. With the help of his son Telemachus, Odysseus slays the suitors and resumes his kingship.
❖ Figuratively, an odyssey is any long, difficult journey.

Oliver Twist Novel by Charles DICKENS, published in instalments during 1837 and 1838. Oliver is born in a workhouse, where his mother soon dies, leaving no clue to his identity. At the workhouse, the children are treated cruelly, and Oliver runs away to London, where he falls in with a group of thieves led by Fagin. The members of the band – which includes a young pickpocket known as the 'Artful Dodger' and the burglar Bill Sikes – try to force Oliver to join them, but after a disastrous expedition he is taken in by the kindly Mrs Maylie. However, an evil man called Monks continues to pursue him. The plot becomes more violent and several deaths occur. Eventually Monks's motives are revealed, the evil characters are punished, Oliver is adopted by a benefactor and, in the process, the identity of his parents is revealed.

❖ A film of *Oliver Twist* was made in 1948, and a musical, ▷OLIVER!, was first produced in 1960 and filmed in 1968.

Omar Khayyám (*c*1048-*c*1123) Persian poet and mathematician, who is credited with writing the *Rubaiyat*, a collection of four-line verses, or *ruba'is*, that became enormously popular in the 19th century when they were first translated into English by Edward Fitzgerald. This translation – which is poetic rather than strictly accurate – is still the best-known form of the *Rubaiyat*, opening with the celebrated lines, 'Awake! for Morning in the Bowl of Night/ Has flung the Stone that puts the Stars to Flight'.

A FLASK OF WINE, A BOOK OF VERSE – AND THOU *Edmund Dulac captured the sensuality and romance of the East in his illustrations for a 1909 edition of Omar Khayyám's* Rubaiyat.

O'Neill, Eugene (1888-1953) American playwright known for dramas such as his great trilogy *Mourning Becomes Electra, The Iceman Cometh*, about a group of hopeless alcoholics and their fantasies, and *A Long Day's Journey into Night*, a domestic tragedy partially based on O'Neill's own family background. O'Neill won the Nobel prize for literature in 1936.

Orton, Joe (1933-67) British dramatist known for black comedies such as *Entertaining Mr Sloane, What the Butler Saw* and *Loot* – a grotesque farce involving stolen money hidden in the coffin of the hero's mother.

❖ Orton's death was as macabre as one of his plots: he was murdered by his homosexual lover, who then committed suicide.

Orwell, George ▷PSEUDONYM of the writer Eric Blair (1903-50). Orwell was interested in political and social issues, and in his writings he defended the liberty of the individual against all forms of oppression. Identifying with the working classes, he took various lowly jobs – experiences which he drew on in writing *Down and Out in Paris and London* and in *Keep the Aspidistra Flying.* After a journey in 1936 he wrote a heartfelt account of poverty and hardship in the north of England, entitled *The Road to Wigan Pier.* He fought for the Republicans in the ▷SPANISH CIVIL WAR and afterwards wrote an account of it in *Homage to Catalonia.* The best known of all his works are the 1940s satirical novels *Animal Farm* and NINETEEN EIGHTY-FOUR, both of which deal with political oppression and the evils of totalitarianism.

Osborne, John (1929-94) British dramatist associated with the group of writers in the 1950s known as the Angry Young Men. His plays are realistic portrayals of ordinary life, often containing impassioned social criticism. His best-known work, *Look Back in Anger*, was written in 1956 and inspired a trend for social REALISM in British drama. The play concerns the lives of an ill-matched couple, Jimmy and Alison Porter, the conflicts that tear them apart, and their eventual imperfect reconciliation.

Othello TRAGEDY by William SHAKESPEARE, probably written between 1602 and 1604. Othello, a Moor, has command of the Venetian forces in Cyprus. However, the villain Iago cunningly convinces Othello that Desdemona, his beautiful and faithful wife, has committed adultery with Cassio, a lieutenant. Consumed by jealousy, Othello murders Desdemona by smothering her while she is in bed. When he realizes his error and Iago's malice, Othello kills himself.

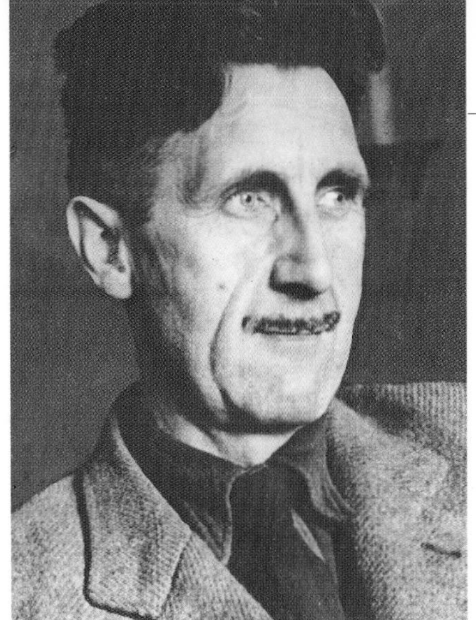

FREE THINKER *George Orwell reacted against his public-school education by championing the individual against the establishment.*

Ovid (43 BC-*c*AD 17) One of the wittiest and most accomplished Roman poets, known for his compilation of myths, the *Metamorphoses*, and for poems about love, including the *Ars Amatoria* ('Art of Love') and *Remedia Amoris* ('Remedy for Love'). The erotic *Ars Amatoria* helped to bring about his exile to Tomi on the Black Sea.

Owen, Wilfred (1893-1918) British poet who served in World War I. His verses describe the suffering of soldiers in the trenches; among his most famous poems is 'Anthem for Doomed Youth'. Owen was killed a week before the armistice. His poems were not popular at the time, but he has now come to be highly regarded as a war poet.

Parker, Dorothy (1893-1967) American satirist and acid wit who wrote poems, short stories, film scripts and reviews. She once said of the actress, the late Katharine Hepburn in a Broadway play 'She ran the whole gamut of the emotions from A to B.' Other well-known lines include 'Men seldom make passes/ At girls who wear glasses.'

parody In literature, a work that mimics or exaggerates another work or a style of writing in such a way as to make it appear ridiculous. ARISTOPHANES used parody in *The Frogs*, mimicking the style of AESCHYLUS and EURIPIDES. Cervantes parodied the medieval chivalric style in DON QUIXOTE.

Pasternak, Boris (1890-1960) Russian writer known for his poems and for the novel *Doctor Zhivago*, which was banned in the Soviet Union for almost 40 years. He initially supported the Russian revolutionary movement, but became increasingly critical of its inhumanity under Stalin. In 1958 he was expelled from the Soviet Writers' Union and forced to turn down a Nobel prize for literature.

pastoral Work or passage that portrays scenes of rural life, usually in an idealized manner. Many of the shorter poems of the Latin poet VIRGIL fall into this category, as does William SHAKESPEARE's *As You Like It.*

ANGRY YOUNG MEN *Jimmy Porter (Allan Bates, centre) chafes at the restraints of marriage in the original production of John Osborne's* Look Back in Anger *at the Royal Court Theatre (1956).*

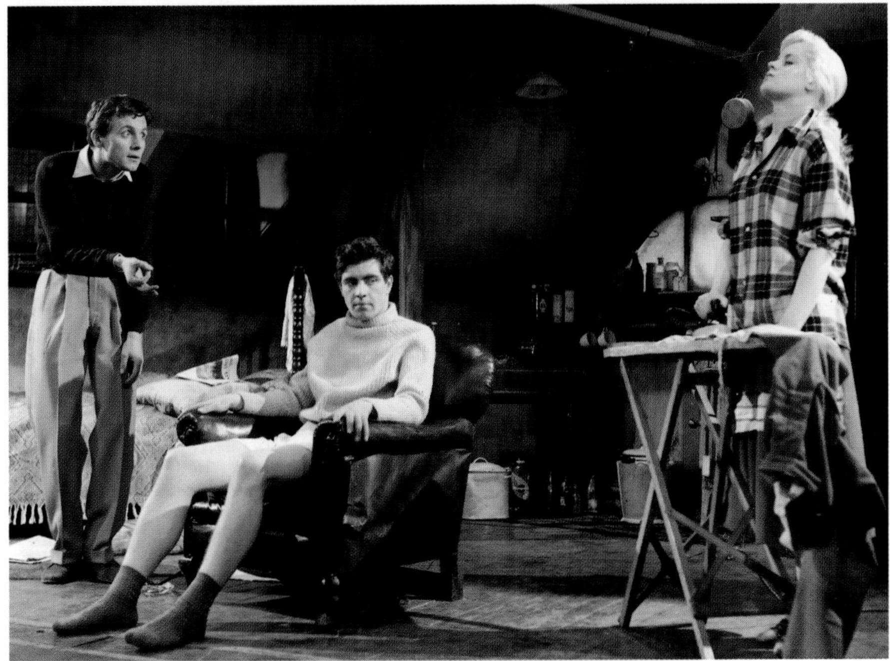

Pepys, Samuel (1633-1703) English civil servant who kept a diary from 1 January 1660 to 31 May 1669, in which he recorded such events as the Great Fire of London, the Restoration and the Great Plague, as well as giving an extraordinarily frank account of his private and social life. The diary was written in a shorthand code and was not published until 1825. A complete, 11-volume version appeared in the 1970s and 1980s.

personification Embodiment of an abstract quality or idea as a CHARACTER in a drama, poem or novel, such as EVERYMAN in the 15th century morality play; or the attribution of human qualities to an inanimate object. It is a common technique found in many languages and periods.

Petrarch (1304-74) (Full name Francesco Petrarca) Italian Renaissance poet who combined Classical scholarship with Christian and humanist beliefs. He is known for his love poems to 'Laura', written in the SONNET form which takes his name. Petrarch inspired many English imitators.

picaresque Literary term used to describe a satirical novel with a rogue hero, such as Henry Fielding's TOM JONES. The form originated in 16th-century Spain; *pícaro* is Spanish for 'rogue'.

Pickwick Papers, The Novel by Charles DICKENS, published in 1836-7. It has a loose plot and purports to be a record of the proceedings of the Pickwick Club – a group of eccentrics who use words in unusual ways and entertain one another with tales of their adventures. The main characters are Mr Pickwick, the club chairman, and his cheerful servant Sam Weller.

Piers Plowman One of the greatest poems in ▷MIDDLE ENGLISH, written by William Langland between the 1360s and 1380s. Three different versions exist, all telling of a series of visions which the narrator has while asleep. The visions concern various virtues and vices at large in the world, and the search for spiritual truth and redemption from sin through Christ.

❖ Langland's poem contains serious criticism of the medieval Church and other institutions of the time.

Pilgrim's Progress, The Spiritual ALLEGORY by the English author and preacher John Bunyan (1628-88), published in two parts in 1678 and 1684. In Part I the author sees in a dream the character Christian carrying a burden and reading a book which tells him of the imminent destruction of the city in which he lives. Christian sets off on a pilgrimage, passing through the Slough of Despond, the Valley of Humiliation and other treacherous regions until he comes at last to the Celestial City. Part II deals with a similar pilgrimage made by Christian's wife, Christiana, and their children, who had at first refused to go with him.

❖ *The Pilgrim's Progress* was among the first books to be printed in Xhosa and Sotho. The Xhosa translation of Part I by the priest Tiyo Soga (*c*1829-1871) was published in 1867. His son John Henderson Soga completed the translation of Part II.

Pinter, Harold (1930-) British dramatist known for plays in which inconsequential small talk between the characters gradually builds up an atmosphere of tension and menace. His works include *The Birthday Party*, about the mysterious persecution of an unemployed pianist by two characters who arrive from nowhere, and *The Caretaker*, which follows the shifting relationships and balance of power between two brothers and a tramp who accompanies them home. Pinter has also written scripts for films such as *The Servant* and *The French Lieutenant's Woman*, which was adapted from John FOWLES's novel. Pinter's 1993 play *Moonlight* deals with a dying man who wants to see his sons – but they refuse to visit him.

❖ Harold Pinter is married to the writer Antonia Fraser, who is known for her historical biographies and detective stories.

Pirandello, Luigi (1867-1936) Italian writer known chiefly for his two plays, *Henry IV* and *Six Characters in Search of an Author*, which deal with the nature of madness and identity. He won the Nobel prize for literature in 1934.

Plath, Sylvia (1932-63) American writer known for poems dealing with troubled states of mind such as depression and despair, from which she suffered herself. She also wrote one novel, *The Bell Jar*, an autobiographical account of a young woman's life after she leaves university, including a description of her mental breakdown and recovery. Sylvia Plath's death was the result of a suicide attempt – one of several she made – which some associates believe was never intended to succeed.

❖ Sylvia Plath was the wife of the current poet laureate, Ted HUGHES.

plot The organization of events in a work of fiction.

Poe, Edgar Allan (1809-49) American writer of stories and poems dealing with the macabre and mysterious. His best-known works are the story *The Fall of the House of Usher* and the poem 'The Raven', in which a man mourning his lost lover is visited by a raven that tells him he will see her 'nevermore'.

poet laureate Title conferred for life on a British poet who is appointed the official poet of the royal household. The poet laureate is expected to compose verses for such occasions as royal birthdays, coronations and military victories. The first official laureateship was conferred in 1668 on John DRYDEN. Other major poets who have held the position include William WORDSWORTH and Alfred, Lord TENNYSON. Ted HUGHES received the title in 1984.

❖ Since 1985 a poet laureate has also been appointed in the USA.

poetry Literature that is distinct from PROSE, usually with a rhythmic structure, or METRE. Poetry is often divided into regular STANZAS with a set pattern of rhymes. As well as RHYME, it may make use of ▷ALLITERATION and ▷ONOMATOPOEIA. Poetry often employs IMAGERY or imaginative language in order to convey its meaning. It can be LYRIC, EPIC or NARRATIVE. Some form of poetry exists in almost every language and culture. (See VERSE.)

Pope, Alexander (1688-1744) British poet who tried to introduce the forms of classical Latin verse into English. Pope's best-known works include the mock-heroic poem *The Rape of the Lock*, based on a real incident in which the playful theft of a snippet of hair from a young lady set two families at odds, and the more serious philosophical poems *An Essay on Man* and *An Essay on Criticism*. The latter contains many familiar lines including 'A little learning is a dang'rous thing', 'To err is human, to forgive, divine' and 'Hope springs eternal in the human breast'.

Portnoy's Complaint Novel by prolific American writer Philip Roth (1933-) that takes the form of a confession by the NARRATOR, Alexander Portnoy, to his psychiatrist. The book's explicit descriptions of adolescent sexual fantasies created much controversy at the time of its publication in 1969.

Potok, Chaim (1929-) American rabbi and writer of novels and short stories. His works are a sensitive exploration of Jewish culture and history, and of the relationship between God and the individual in contemporary life.

COUNTRY CHARM *Beatrix Potter grew up in London but always loved the English countryside which she came to know during childhood holidays. Her later life was spent farming and writing at Sawrey in the Lake District.*

His first novel, *The Chosen* (1967), which deals with a family of Hassidic Jews living in Brooklyn, New York, was made into a film in 1981 starring Rod Steiger as Reb Saunders and Robbie Benson as his son. Potok's later novels include *The Promise, My Name is Asher Lev* and *In the Beginning.*

Potter, Beatrix (1866-1943) English author and illustrator of small-format children's books about human and animal characters such as the mischievous Peter Rabbit, his adversary Mr McGregor, the hedgehog-washerwoman Mrs Tiggywinkle, and the rivals Mr Tod the fox and Mr Brock the badger. The books are set in England's Lake District, where Potter eventually settled. Many of her characters were based on real people.

Pound, Ezra (1885-1972) American poet who went to Europe and helped to establish MODERNISM. He had a flair for languages and his verses, particularly his *Cantos*, reflect influences from many cultures. During World War II, he supported Mussolini and was later accused of treason by the USA. The charge was dropped when Pound was judged insane; he spent the next 14 years in an asylum.
❖ Pound helped T S Eliot to edit his poem *The* WASTE LAND.

Pride and Prejudice Novel by Jane AUSTEN, published in 1813. The story concerns an upper-middle-class family in Hertfordshire, in southern England, consisting of the foolish Mrs Bennet, her wryly humorous husband and their five daughters. After a complex succession of proposals, refusals, engagements and even an elopement, three of the daughters end up happily married.
❖ The book's opening sentence is well known: 'It is a truth universally acknowledged, that a single man in possession of a good fortune, must be in want of a wife.'

prose Ordinary writing, which – unlike POETRY – is written without METRE or RHYME. There are many forms of literary prose, including the NOVEL, NOVELLA, SHORT STORY, essay and newspaper editorial.
❖ The word 'prosaic' is used to describe someone or something as dull.

protagonist Principal CHARACTER in a literary work.

Proust, Marcel (1871-1922) French novelist best-known for his 12-volume masterpiece *À la Recherche du Temps Perdu*, which was first translated into English as *Remembrance of Things Past.* Proust was one of the important figures in literary MODERNISM, particularly in his exploration of the workings of human memory and the influence of the past on experience in the present.

Pulitzer prize One of the prizes awarded annually for excellence in American journalism, literature and music. The prizes were established from a bequest by Hungarian-born Joseph Pulitzer (1847-1911), who emigrated to the USA and became a successful newspaper publisher.

Pushkin, Alexandr (1799-1837) Russian poet, novelist and playwright, regarded as one of the founders of Russian literature. His works include *Eugene Onegin*, a novel in verse, which was turned into an opera by the Russian composer Tchaikovsky. His historical drama *Boris Godunov* was also made into an opera, by the Russian composer Mussorgsky. Pushkin was exiled from Moscow in 1820 for his political verse. He returned six years later, but was still subject to censorship. He was fatally wounded in a duel over his wife in 1837.

Pygmalion Play by George Bernard SHAW, first performed in 1913. To win a bet, Professor Henry Higgins – a specialist in English phonetics – trains an ill-spoken Cockney flower girl, Eliza Doolittle, to speak and behave like a lady. Eventually her training is complete and Eliza successfully mixes in high society without giving away her origins. Higgins wins his bet, but Eliza eventually rebels and asserts her right to control her own life. In Classical mythology ▷PYGMALION was a Cypriot king who fell in love with a sculpture he created.
❖ The 1957 musical ▷MY FAIR LADY was based on Shaw's play; however, it emphasizes a romantic attraction between Eliza and Higgins that Shaw only hints at.

Rabelais, François (*c*1494-*c*1553) French satirist known for his humanitarian outlook and earthy humour. He was a former monk with a deep religious faith but he delighted in all forms of comedy, including obscenity and bawdy farce. His masterpieces, *Gargantua* and *Pantagruel* – named after two giants who are the main characters – provide a scathing portrait of French Renaissance society.

Racine, Jean Baptiste (1639-99) French poet and dramatist, who is regarded as the master of tragic pathos. His plays include *Andromaque, Bérénice, Iphigénie* and *Phèdre.*

Rattigan, Sir Terence (1911-77) English dramatist known for well-crafted plays about emotional suffering and troubled human relationships, such as *The Winslow Boy, The Browning Version, Separate Tables* and *The Deep Blue Sea.* He was knighted in 1971.
❖ *The Browning Version* has been filmed twice: in 1951 starring Michael Redgrave and in 1994 with Albert Finney.

realism Broad term for literature that attempts to give a close impression of real life by means of accurate descriptions, believable events and characters with understandable motives. In particular, it is applied to 19th-century novels by writers such as Émile ZOLA, Charles DICKENS and Leo TOLSTOY.

refrain In some pieces of VERSE, a set of words repeated at the end of each STANZA. In music the word refers to a regularly recurring melody.

Restoration comedy Style of comic drama developed in England around the time of the restoration of the monarchy in 1660. The humour was bawdy, the plots complex and the morals questionable or nonexistent.

revenge tragedy Type of TRAGEDY popular in late Elizabethan and Jacobean England. It deals with a quest for vengeance or retribution in return for a wrong – usually murder. Well-known revenge tragedies include *The Spanish Tragedy* by Thomas Kyd, Christopher MARLOWE's *The Jew of Malta* and John WEBSTER's *The Duchess of Malfi.* The greatest of all, however, is William Shakespeare's HAMLET, which contains many typical elements of revenge tragedy – such as ghosts, madness, graveyard scenes, poisoning and a conclusion in which the main characters come to an unpleasant end.

rhyme Use in POETRY of words that echo one another's sounds for two main purposes: to create a musical effect and to structure the verse by marking line endings and emphasizing rhythm. Rhyme helps to stress the meaning of verse and makes it easier to remember and recite accurately.

Richard III Historical drama by William SHAKESPEARE, written around 1591. It portrays the end of the Wars of the Roses between the houses of York and Lancaster. As the Yorkist king, Edward IV, is dying, his brother, Richard of Gloucester, has their other brother, Clarence, murdered. Richard cynically woos and marries the widow of the Lancastrian Prince of Wales. When Edward dies, Richard seizes the throne, imprisoning and then murdering his nephews, the Princes, in the Tower. Richard's excesses in eliminating all rivals unites opposition under the Lancastrian Henry Tudor, who defeats and kills Richard at Bosworth and becomes Henry VII.
❖ Among the most memorable lines from

KING ON CRUTCHES *The actor Anthony Sher created a menacing Richard III in the Royal Shakespeare Company's 1984-5 production of the play. Sher exaggerated Richard's hunched back to symbolize his moral deformity, and played him as a cripple, dragging himself about on crutches. The costume enhanced the spidery silhouette.* Richard III *completes the series of plays, beginning with* Richard II, *that gives a vivid account of 85 turbulent years of English history.*

Richard III are: 'My horse, my horse, my kingdom for a horse!' and 'Now is the winter of our discontent/ Made glorious summer by this sun of York.'

❖ The Richard III Society was set up in 1924 to try to restore the king's reputation which the members maintain Shakespeare had distorted and unfairly destroyed.

Rime of the Ancient Mariner, The Supernatural poem by Samuel Taylor COLERIDGE, published in 1798. An old sailor stops a stranger and tells him of a voyage during which he shot an albatross. A curse fell upon the ship, which was becalmed, and the rest of the crew were struck dead. The mariner drifted alone until he caught sight of some water snakes and spontaneously 'blessed them unaware', breaking the spell. The mariner now wanders about telling his story and teaching reverence for life. Some of the poem's best-known lines are 'Water, water, everywhere/ Nor any drop to drink'.

❖ Albatrosses are known for accompanying ships at sea, and an old superstition holds that killing one brings a lifetime of bad luck.

❖ The expression an 'albatross round one's neck' refers to any problem or burden that has to be borne.

Rip Van Winkle Story by American author Washington Irving in which the title character goes to sleep after a game of bowling and much drinking in the mountains with a band of dwarfs. He awakens 20 years later, an old man. Back home, Rip finds that all has changed: his wife is dead; his daughter has married; and the ▷AMERICAN WAR OF INDEPENDENCE has taken place.

Robbins, Harold (1916-) Best-selling American novelist known for books such as *Never Love a Stranger* and *The Carpetbaggers* (which has sold more than 6 million copies).

Robinson Crusoe Adventure tale written by Daniel DEFOE, published in 1719 as a true story. It is based on the real-life experience of the sailor Alexander Selkirk, who spent five years alone on an island before being rescued in 1709. Defoe's novel vividly describes how Crusoe is shipwrecked, but ingeniously clothes himself, cultivates crops, domesticates wild animals and builds a house and a boat. Eventually he acquires a companion and servant, Friday, whom he saves from cannibals. After 28 years, Crusoe is finally rescued by a passing English ship. Defoe wrote a sequel to the book, *The Farther Adventures of Robinson Crusoe.*

❖ *Robinson Crusoe* was an instant success and inspired many works, including the *Swiss Family Robinson* by a Swiss pastor, Johann David Wyss, published in 1812-13. The book tells how a shipwrecked family – very like Wyss's own – survives and even prospers on an uninhabited island.

roman à clef (roh-MAHN ah KLAY) NOVEL in which real people and places are disguised as fictional characters. *Roman à clef* is French for 'novel with a key'.

romance Courtly adventure tale about great deeds of chivalry or love, of a type popular in the Middle Ages; alternatively, a love story. Literature of the first type frequently involves magical or mystical events, such as a sighting of the ▷HOLY GRAIL or encounters with mythical beasts.

❖ Shakespeare's plays *The Tempest* and *The Winter's Tale* are called romances because they involve strange adventures culminating in a fantastical happy ending.

romanticism Revolutionary artistic movement beginning in the late 18th and early 19th centuries. It stressed the value of personal emotion and imagination, and freedom from the strict rules of form that dominated 18th-century literature. It also expressed a new view of nature, seen as being spiritually connected with humanity and a source of inspiration. Romantic writers include WORDSWORTH and BLAKE (English), SCHILLER and GOETHE (German), and Victor HUGO (French).

Romeo and Juliet Romantic TRAGEDY by William SHAKESPEARE, written around 1595. The action is set in Verona, where bitter hatred divides the powerful Montague and Capulet families. Romeo (a young Montague) and Juliet (a Capulet) fall in love and are secretly married. However, Romeo is banished for duelling and he and Juliet have just one night together. Juliet's parents are meanwhile planning her marriage to Count Paris. In desperation she consults the friar who married her to Romeo. She arranges to take a potion which makes her appear dead while the friar sends a message to Romeo. It fails to reach him; he hears only that Juliet is dead. He returns and drinks poison at her side. She wakes and, finding him dead, kills herself with his dagger. When the two families realize what has happened, they vow to end their tragic feud.

❖ When Juliet utters the well-known exclamation 'Romeo, Romeo! Wherefore art thou Romeo?' she is lamenting Romeo's name because it ties him to the Montague family. 'Wherefore' means 'why'.

❖ The 1957 musical *West Side Story* transferred the tale of Romeo and Juliet onto the streets of New York.

Rushdie, Salman (1947-) English novelist born in India of Muslim parents. He won the Booker prize in 1981 for *Midnight's Children*, which deals with the independence of India and its separation from Pakistan at midnight on 14 August 1947. Rushdie's MAGIC REALISM – his technique of mingling fact, fiction and fantasy – had serious consequences when he applied it to Muslim beliefs in his 1988 novel *The Satanic Verses*. Rushdie's alleged blasphemy outraged Muslim fundamentalists and a death sentence – or ▷FATWAH – was declared on him by the Iranian leader Ayatollah Khomeini. As a result, Rushdie went into hiding and could make only irregular, unannounced appearances in public.

Sackville-West, Vita (Victoria) (1892-1962) English writer and friend of the novelist Virginia WOOLF. She married the diplomat Harold Nicolson in 1913 and, though both partners had homosexual love affairs, the marriage survived. The main character of Virginia Woolf's novel *Orlando: A Biography* – a beautiful youth who lives for 400 years as both man and woman – was modelled on Vita Sackville-West.

❖ Vita Sackville-West was also an accomplished gardener. The grounds she created at Sissinghurst in Kent attract thousands of visitors every year.

sagas Ancient EPICS from Scandinavia and Iceland, composed in the Dark Ages but not written down until around the 12th and 13th centuries. They are a mixture of history and legend, and recount the deeds of heroes, kings, great families and characters from pagan ▷NORSE MYTHOLOGY. Many of the tales are brutal, painting a picture of a fierce, warrior society dominated by superstition and long, bitter feuds.

Salinger, J D (1919-) American novelist and short-story writer best known for his classic novel about the turmoil of adolescence, *The* CATCHER IN THE RYE, published in 1951. In other works, such as *Franny and Zooey*, *Raise High the Roof Beam, Carpenters* and *Seymour: an Introduction*, Salinger describes the experiences of various members of the eccentric Glass family.

Sand, George (SAH'N) (1804-76) Pen name of the French writer Amandine-Aurore Lucie Dupin. She separated from her husband Baron Dudevant in 1831, adopted a man's name, wore trousers and began a literary career in Paris. Her works, which include *Indiana* (1832), *The Devil's Pool* (1846) and *The Little Fairy* (1848), were popular and dealt with themes ranging from romance to women's emancipation and idealized country life. She had an affair with the poet Alfred de Musset and a lengthy relationship with the composer ▷CHOPIN.

Sappho (*c*612-*c*580 BC) Greek poet known for passionate love poems written for her female followers on the island of Lesbos. Only fragments of her work have survived, but it was greatly revered in the ancient world.

❖ Sappho's admirers on Lesbos gave rise to the words 'lesbian' and 'sapphism'. Popular but discredited legend has it that she drowned herself because her love for the boatman Phaon remained unrequited.

satire Work or type of writing that ridicules human vice and folly, particularly among the rich and powerful. Two early satirists were the Latin poets JUVENAL and HORACE, who used their verses to criticize Roman society. The 17th and 18th centuries in France and England were a great age of satirical writing and produced such masterpieces as VOLTAIRE's *Candide* and Jonathan Swift's GULLIVER'S TRAVELS.

HERO OF THE YOUNG *Dr Seuss's mischievous, rhyming feline makes several appearances in books, beginning with* The Cat in the Hat.

Satyricon Novel-like account of lowlife society in ancient Rome by the first-century Latin author Petronius, who was probably a close friend of the emperor Nero. Manuscripts of the work were often hidden as it was considered pornographic, and only small sections have survived.

Schiller, Friedrich von (1759-1805) German poet and playwright, influential in German ROMANTICISM. His works are concerned with the issue of human freedom.

❖ Schiller's best-known work is his ode *To Joy*, which the composer Beethoven set to music in the last movement of his Ninth Symphony.

science fiction Works of fiction that use scientific discoveries or advanced technology – either real or imaginary – as part of their PLOT. Jules VERNE and H G WELLS were early writers of science fiction. More recent ones are Isaac ASIMOV and Ray Bradbury.

Scott, Sir Walter (1771-1832) Scottish author of historical novels, ballads and romantic poetry based mainly on tales and legends of the Scottish border region. His works include *The Lay of the Last Minstrel*, a love story in verse, and the adventure tales *Waverley* and *Rob Roy*, both set during the Jacobite rebellions in Scotland. *Ivanhoe* is set in medieval England. Scott is considered to be the inventor of the historical novel and also, by some, of the short story.

❖ Scott's tragic novel *The Bride of Lammermoor* – in which the heroine is driven mad and provoked to commit murder by the appalling cruelty of her family – provided the inspiration for Gaetano Donizetti's opera *Lucia di Lammermoor*.

Seneca (*c*4 BC-AD 65) (Full name Lucius Annaeus Seneca; also known as Seneca the Younger) Roman writer of Latin tragedies based on Greek myths, such as *Oedipus*, *Medea* and *Agamemnon*, and for philosophical works advocating the beliefs of the ▷STOICS. Seneca was an adviser to the emperor Nero but was forced to commit suicide after being accused of conspiring to assassinate him.

Seuss, Dr ▷PSEUDONYM of the American children's author and illustrator Theodor Seuss Giesel (1904-91). Initially Giesel worked as a cartoonist and then as a film animator in Hollywood, but in the 1930s he began to produce children's picture books with comic rhymes. His best-known books are an illustrated series for young readers, beginning with *The Cat in the Hat*.

sex-and-shopping novels Popular works of fiction, generally written for and by women, in which glamorous characters indulge in steamy romantic affairs and spend vast sums of money. Typical examples include Judith Krantz's novel *Princess Daisy*, Shirley Conran's *Lace* and Jackie Collins's *Hollywood Wives*. An earlier example is Jacqueline Susann's 1968 novel *The Valley of the Dolls*, which sold more than 28 million copies.

Shaffer, Peter (1926-) British playwright. His works include *The Royal Hunt of the Sun*, which deals with the conquest of Peru, and *Equus*, a play about the relationship between a youth obsessed with horses and a psychiatrist who tries to help him. In *Amadeus* Schaffer dramatized – and exaggerated – the rivalry between the composer Mozart and his contemporary Salieri.

❖ An Oscar-winning film of ▷AMADEUS was released in 1984.

Shakespeare, William (1564-1616) English poet and dramatist, generally considered the greatest writer in the English language for his insights into human nature and for his poetic brilliance. Shakespeare was born in Stratford-upon-Avon, and was the eldest son of the glove seller John Shakespeare and his wife Mary Arden. In 1582 he married Anne Hathaway, who was eight years his senior and already pregnant. A daughter, Susannah, was born in 1583 and twins, Hamnet and Judith, two years later. Some time in the late 1580s or early 1590s Shakespeare became established as an actor and playwright in London. In 1594 he became a partner in a group of actors called Lord Chamberlain's Men, and from that time on almost all his work was written for that company. From 1599, Shakespeare and his colleagues occupied the Globe Theatre in Southwark, London. They soon became London's leading theatrical company and in 1603 received royal patronage, after which they were known as the King's Men. Shakespeare's success eventually enabled him to buy a large house and retire to Stratford, where he died. His earliest known works date from the late 1580s and early 1590s and include the three *Henry VI* plays, RICHARD III, *The Taming of the Shrew* and the narrative poems *Venus and Adonis* and *The Rape of Lucrece*. These were followed between the mid-1590s and about 1600 by comedies such as *A* MIDSUMMER NIGHT'S DREAM, *The* MERCHANT OF VENICE, *Much Ado About Nothing* and TWELFTH NIGHT; the tragedies ROMEO AND JULIET and JULIUS CAESAR; the historical plays *Richard II*, HENRY V and *Henry IV, Parts 1 and 2*; and a sequence of more than 150 sonnets. Between 1600 and 1607 Shakespeare produced the great tragedies HAMLET, OTHELLO, KING LEAR and ANTONY AND CLEOPATRA, and the 'problem plays' *Troilus and Cressida* and *Measure for Measure*. In the last years of his life Shakespeare wrote the romances *Cymbeline*, *The Winter's Tale* and *The Tempest*, and is thought to have collaborated with other authors on *Pericles* and *Henry VIII*.

❖ It has been argued that Shakespeare's plays could have been written by a group of Elizabethan authors or by other, individual authors such as Francis Bacon or Christopher MARLOWE. However, few experts take these theories seriously.

Shaw, George Bernard (1856-1950) Irish dramatist and critic. Shaw moved to London as a young man and became an influential member of the socialist Fabian Society and a renowned public speaker. He wrote novels, criticism, political tracts and more than 50 plays, including *Arms and the Man, Man and Superman, Major Barbara, Heartbreak House, Saint Joan* and PYGMALION. Shaw's plays are known for their wit and for their social and moral concerns, which he often spelled out in lengthy prefaces. His other works include *The Intelligent Woman's Guide to Socialism and Capitalism* and *The Perfect Wagnerite* – a political interpretation of the operas of Richard Wagner. Shaw won the Nobel prize for literature in 1925.

❖ Shaw and the British prime minister Winston Churchill disliked each other but enjoyed exchanging insults. On one occasion Shaw sent the statesman two tickets for the first night of his new play with a note saying, 'Bring a friend – if you have one.' Churchill returned the tickets, asking instead for tickets for the second night – 'if there is one'.

PRECIOUS RELICS *Modern editions of Shakespeare's plays are largely based on the First Folio, which was brought out in 1623 and contains probably the only authentic portrait of the bard. Earlier printings of the plays – such as the 1597* Romeo and Juliet – *were often less accurate.*

Shelley, Percy Bysshe (1792-1822) English poet and a leading figure in ROMANTICISM. Shelley held radical views and fought all his life for causes such as vegetarianism, republicanism and free love. As a student, he was expelled from Oxford for publishing an atheistic pamphlet, and he later lost custody of his children because of his antireligious views. In 1818 Shelley went to live in Italy, where he composed many of his best-known works. Four years later he was drowned in a boating accident off the Italian coast on his way home from visiting his friend Lord BYRON, who was also living in Italy. Shelley's best-known poems include the political fables *Queen Mab, Prometheus Unbound* and *The Mask of Anarchy*; an elegy on the death of John KEATS entitled *Adonais*; and the lyrical poems 'Ode to the West Wind' and 'To a Skylark'. One of his most popular poems is the sonnet 'Ozymandias', in which he describes a magnificent statue from antiquity, lying shattered but bearing the still-legible inscription:

> 'My name is Ozymandias, king of kings:
> Look on my works, ye Mighty, and despair!'

❖ Shelley's private life was as unconventional as his beliefs. He eloped with his first wife, Harriet Westbrook, when she was just 16. Despite having two children, he left her within a few years for Mary Wollstonecraft Godwin, another 16-year-old and daughter of the philosopher William Godwin. For some years Shelley and Mary lived as a *ménage à trois* with Mary's stepsister Claire, who was also Byron's lover. When Harriet drowned herself in 1816, Shelley married Mary, who wrote FRANKENSTEIN.

Sheridan, Richard Brinsley (1751-1816) English playwright born in Dublin. He wrote light social comedies such as *The Rivals* – known for the delightful character Mrs Malaprop who habitually uses the wrong word, so creating a ▷MALAPROPISM; at one point she exclaims, 'If I reprehend any thing in this world, it is the use of my oracular

WITTY AND WISE *George Bernard Shaw's public writing began in 1875 with a letter to the press – an outlet for his political and philosophical views that he continued to enjoy.*

tongue, and a nice derangement of epitaphs!' Sheridan's other comedies include *The School for Scandal* and *The Critic.*

short story Tale that aims to convey a single impression of emotion or focuses on a single event. The author Edgar Allan POE is generally regarded as the father of the modern short story and was one of the first to set out its principles. After him the form was developed in Russia and France by writers such as Gogol, TURGENEV, CHEKHOV, FLAUBERT and MAUPASSANT.

Simenon, Georges (1903-89) Prolific Belgian writer who created the celebrated detective Maigret in a series of crime novels which achieved international acclaim.

Singer, Isaac Bashevis (1904-91) Polish-born author of novels and short stories in both Yiddish and English. He emigrated to the USA as a young man, but in works such as *The Magician of Lublin* and *The Spinoza of Market Street* he recorded the colourful, lively way of life of Polish Jews before the ▷HOLOCAUST. He won the Nobel prize for literature in 1978.

soliloquy Speech in which a character in a play reveals his thoughts while alone on the stage, as in Hamlet's much-quoted 'TO BE, OR NOT TO BE' speech.

Solzhenitsyn, Alexandr (1918-) Russian writer and dissident. He was exiled to Siberia during the 1940s and 1950s for criticizing Stalin. Works such as *One Day in the Life of Ivan Denisovich* and *The Gulag Archipelago* draw on that experience. He received the Nobel prize for literature in 1970. Four years later, Solzhenitsyn was expelled from the Soviet Union and settled in the United States. He regained his Russian citizenship in 1990 and moved back to Russia in 1994.

sonnet Poem of 14 lines, divided either into one section of eight lines and one of six – the form favoured by PETRARCH – or into three sets of four lines and one of two – as used by William SHAKESPEARE. The poem often airs a proposition – commonly on the subject of love – which is developed to a logical or witty conclusion. The earliest sonnets were written in the Middle Ages by poets such as Petrarch and DANTE. MILTON and WORDSWORTH and the French poet Ronsard also used the form.

Sophocles (*c*496-406 BC) Classical Greek dramatist, known for his theatrical innovations, his range of styles and his ability to create rounded characters in tragedies such as *Antigone, Electra* and *Oedipus Rex.* He wrote more than 120 dramas, of which only seven have survived.

Soyinka, Wole (1934-) Nigerian writer whose plays, poetry and novels are evocative explorations of the conflict between African traditions and modern life. His best-known play, *The Lion and the Jewel*, is a ribald comedy about Sidi (the Jewel), a 'village belle', Baroka (the Lion), a traditionalist, and Lakunle, a young teacher who espouses modern ways. Soyinka's first novel, *The Interpreters*, appeared in 1970 and was described as 'the first really modern African novel'. He was awarded the Nobel prize for literature in 1986. He went into exile in 1994.

Spark, Muriel (1918-) Scottish author known primarily as a novelist, although she also wrote poems, plays and criticism. Many of her books contain elements of fantasy, the macabre or the supernatural. Spark's best-known book is *The Prime of Miss Jean Brodie*, a novel about a schoolmistress who leads her teenage protégés onto dangerous moral ground. It was filmed in 1969 with Maggie Smith in the leading role.

Spenser, Edmund (*c*1552-99) English poet, considered one of the greatest of the Elizabethan age. His first important work was a series of seasonal verses, *The Shepheardes Calendar*, which was dedicated to his contemporary Sir Philip Sidney, the English poet, sportsman, soldier and courtier. This was followed by the poem for which Spenser is best known, a long moral and political ALLEGORY entitled *The Faerie Queene.* It was published in six books between 1590 and 1596, and glorified the reign of Elizabeth I. His other works include *Amoretti*, in which he wooed his second wife, and *Epithalamion*, which celebrated their marriage.

❖ In *The Faerie Queene* Spenser developed a new form of poetic STANZA that became known as the Spenserian stanza.

stanza Group of lines of VERSE, usually set off from other groups by a space. The stanzas of a poem often have the same internal pattern of RHYMES.

Steinbeck, John (1902-68) American author of novels and short stories mainly about the lives of the rural working class in the western

THE JERO PLAYS *Nkosinathi Gqotso and Aziwe Magida perform in a UCT student production of two plays by Wole Soyinka about a self-proclaimed prophet called Brother Jero.*

USA. His books include *Of Mice and Men*, a study of the relationship between two travelling labourers, *Cannery Row* and *East of Eden*, a family saga about the conflict between good and evil. The best known is *The Grapes of Wrath* – the tale of a family from the American Dust Bowl who, displaced by drought and bankruptcy, set off for California in search of a better life. Steinbeck received the Nobel prize for literature in 1962.

Stendhal ▷PSEUDONYM of the French novelist Henri Beyle (1783-1842). His work was an important influence on the development of the novel in France and is known for combining romance and passion with deep psychological analysis, as in *Le Rouge et le Noir* (*The Red and the Black*).

Sterne, Laurence (1713-68) Innovative Irish-born author who became famous after writing the eccentric comedy *Tristram Shandy*, which is often seen as a precursor of STREAM OF CONSCIOUSNESS writing. Sterne also wrote sermons and a chronicle of his travels abroad entitled *A Sentimental Journey*. His witty, original books are highly regarded for their humane outlook, tolerance and warmth.

Stevenson, Robert Louis (1850-94) Scottish novelist and essayist who wrote some of the best-known tales of adventure and romance in the English language, including TREASURE ISLAND, *Kidnapped* and DR JEKYLL AND MR HYDE, as well as the well-known *A Child's Garden of Verses*. Many of Stevenson's most memorable characters are complex mixtures of good and evil, and his books often leave the reader uncertain about the distinction between right and wrong.

❖ Stevenson's life was colourful: he married an American woman ten years his senior and they eventually settled in Samoa. His last book, *Weir of Hermiston*, was left unfinished when he died.

Stoppard, Tom (1937-) English dramatist born in Czechoslovakia. His plays are comedies which satirize social and theatrical conventions at the same time as tackling moral issues. The best known include *Rosencrantz and Guildenstern are Dead*, a fantasy woven around a scene from HAMLET; *Jumpers*, a satire on academic philosophy; and *Travesties*, a farce bringing together James Joyce, Lenin and Tristan Tzara, the founder of ▷DADA art, in Zürich during World War I. In his play *Arcadia*, a female historian and a male academic visit a country estate and uncover a 180-year-old dangerous liaison.

stream of consciousness A NARRATIVE technique that gives an impression of the way thoughts, perceptions and emotions flow through the mind of a character. Virginia WOOLF is one exponent; parts of James JOYCE's novel *Ulysses* and all of his book *Finnegans Wake* are also examples.

BOLD WRITER *August Strindberg formed his own theatre companies so that he could stage his unconventional, visionary plays.*

Strindberg, August (1849-1912) Swedish playwright and novelist, known for pioneering psychological REALISM in the theatre. He had an unhappy childhood and three disastrous marriages, leading to a passionate dislike of women which influenced some of his best-known plays, including *Miss Julie* and *The Father*.

***Sturm und Drang* ('Storm and Stress')** Late 18th-century movement in German literature and music, associated with the beginning of ROMANTICISM. The movement rejected conventional ideas about literary form and structure and emphasized the passionate, heroic side of human nature.

Swift, Jonathan (1667-1745) Anglo-Irish satirist, poet and Anglican cleric, who used his sharp wit to attack ignorance, vice and folly wherever he found it – particularly in high places. His books include *A Tale of a Tub* – a satire on religious extremism – and GULLIVER'S TRAVELS, which ridicules many aspects of life from politics to science, philosophy and, in the end, humanity itself. Swift also wrote on issues that aroused his indignation, such as the British treatment of Ireland. In the satirical pamphlet *A Modest Proposal* (1729) – written in outrage at government policies and the plight of the peasants in Ireland – he suggests the eating of children as a way of solving the country's social problems. Although never well-off, he gave a third of his income to charity and another third towards the founding of a Dublin hospital for the insane. The last years of his life were dogged by ill health, probably caused by an inner-ear disorder.

❖ Swift's personal life is still something of a mystery. For many years he was close to Esther Johnson – addressed as 'Stella' in his journals and letters – and, although it seems their relationship was not sexual, they may have married secretly. He was also pursued by Esther Vanhomrigh – 'Vanessa' – until her jealousy of Stella led Swift to break off all contact with her.

❖ Swift is sometimes referred to as 'Dean Swift', in reference to his position as Dean of St Patrick's in Dublin from 1713.

symbolists Group of late 19th-century French poets, including MALLARMÉ, Verlaine and Rimbaud, who rejected realism in favour of abstraction and attempts to portray spiritual and philosophical truths symbolically. They were influenced by ▷MYSTICISM as well as by musical techniques such as Richard Wagner's *leitmotifs*.

Synge, John Millington (SING) (1871-1909) Irish dramatist best known for plays about peasant life, including the tragedy *Riders to the Sea* (1904), about a mother's loss of her six sons, and *The Playboy of the Western World* (1907), in which a young stranger arrives in a village and talks his way into the affections of the local women.

❖ Synge's forthright language – in particular his use of the word 'shift' (meaning petticoat) – caused a riot when *The Playboy of the Western World* was first performed in Dublin in 1907.

Tennyson, Alfred, Lord (1809-92) The most renowned English poet of the Victorian age, known for his lyrical, musical poems on subjects ranging from mythology and religion to personal relationships and contemporary events. He was named poet laureate in 1850 and received a peerage in 1884. Tennyson's best-known works include 'The Lady of Shalott'; 'The Charge of the Light Brigade'; *In Memoriam*, a sequence of verses mourning the death of his friend Arthur Hallam; and *Idylls of the King*, a retelling of the legend of King Arthur. Tennyson's last poem, 'Crossing the Bar', symbolizes death as a sea voyage that begins by crossing the harbour bar:

Sunset and evening star,
And one clear call for me!

And may there be no moaning of the bar,
When I put out to sea.

Thackeray, William Makepeace (1811-63) English writer born in India. He wrote essays, articles and novels, including *Vanity Fair* – a social satire about the lives of two women, Becky Sharp and Amelia Sedley, at the time of the Napoleonic wars of the late 18th and early 19th centuries.

theatre of the absurd Type of drama developed in the 1950s and 1960s by writers such as Samuel BECKETT, Eugène IONESCO and Harold PINTER. By 'absurdity' they meant a view of life that was contradictory, meaningless, and ruled by chance or by forces too mysterious to understand. Some of the best absurdist plays are comedies, such as Beckett's WAITING FOR GODOT.

theme Central idea in a piece of writing or other work of art. For example, the theme of personal responsibility is found throughout the works of Ralph Waldo EMERSON.

Thomas, Dylan (1914-53) Welsh writer of poetry and prose about the country life of his youth and his own experiences. His work is known for verbal inventiveness and vivid portraits of landscapes and people. Thomas was a meticulous craftsman and revised his work to fit strict poetic forms. His writings include the poems 'Fern Hill', 'And Death Shall Have No Dominion' and 'Poem in October', and the 1954 drama *Under Milk Wood*, a dramatic evocation of a Welsh seaside town, peopled by such characters as the church organist Organ Morgan, the old sea-dog Captain Cat and the twice-widowed Mrs Ogmore-Pritchard. It was later adapted for the stage.
❖ Thomas's heavy drinking probably contributed to his early death during a lecture tour of the USA.

DIVINE INTERVENTION *Leo Tolstoy spent the second half of his life obsessed by evangelism. He condemned his great works as worthless and lived the life of a peasant.*

PORTRAIT OF THE ARTIST *Augustus John painted Dylan Thomas as a young man. The poet's flamboyant personality and brilliance as a speaker later won him a large following.*

Thurber, James (1894-1961) American humorist whose stories and essays, many of which appeared in *The New Yorker*, often explore the dilemma of a naive hero in trendy society. He created the character Walter MITTY, and was also known for his charming sketches of lugubrious dogs.

'To be, or not to be' Opening line of one of the most celebrated speeches in English literature. It comes from William Shakespeare's play HAMLET, and occurs in a SOLILOQUY in which the prince considers suicide as a way out of his dilemma. Ultimately, he rejects it because of fears about 'what dreams may come' – that is, the possibility of damnation and eternal torment – and concludes: 'Thus conscience doth make cowards of us all.'

Tolkien, J R R (1892-1973) English scholar and critic, born in Bloemfontein in the Free State and sent back to England at an early age. He wrote the fantasy novels *The Hobbit* and *The* LORD OF THE RINGS trilogy. He attracted a cult following in the 1960s, having created complete mythologies of his own, influenced by a knowledge and love of ▷OLD ENGLISH literature and ▷NORSE MYTHOLOGY.

Tolstoy, Count Leo (1828-1910) Russian writer, regarded as one of the world's finest novelists for his epic masterpieces WAR AND PEACE and ANNA KARENINA. His works paint a vivid portrait of 19th-century Russian society, covering a vast sweep of characters and events. Tolstoy inherited a large estate, where he worked hard to improve the lot of the peasants. After a spiritual crisis in middle age, however, he concentrated on religious works such as the short story *The Death of Ivan Ilyich*.

Tom Jones PICARESQUE novel by Henry FIELDING, published in 1749 and generally considered Fielding's greatest work. It follows the adventures of the title character from the time that he is found abandoned as a tiny baby, through childhood and youth, and into manhood and the discovery of his true identity. While upholding the values of innocence and kindness, the book ignores conventional morality (which Fielding saw as hypocritical), as, for example, by openly describing Tom's sexual encounters.
❖ *Tom Jones* was one of the first novels to be written in English and its style had a major influence on the development of fiction.

Tom Sawyer, The Adventures of Children's book by Mark TWAIN, published in 1876. The hero is a wily, independent boy who engages in a series of anarchic escapades. In one episode, Tom tricks his friends into whitewashing a fence for him by pretending it is a great privilege and making them pay to take over the job. On another occasion, Tom and his friends disappear for so long that they are presumed dead, finally returning to find their own funeral in progress.
❖ Tom's best friend is Huckleberry Finn, a character who reappears as the hero of *The Adventures of Huckleberry Finn*.

tragedy Drama dealing with the death or downfall of a noble character, usually as the result of some error of judgment or crime against the natural order, as when Oedipus kills his father and marries his mother. Tragedy is considered the most elevated form of drama. Ancient Greek dramatists believed it should provoke CATHARSIS.
❖ The word 'tragedy' comes from the Greek for 'goat song' as the form developed from choral songs which accompanied goat sacrifices to the god Dionysus.

tragi-comedy Drama that combines elements of both TRAGEDY and COMEDY. In the most common form an essentially tragic plot is given a happy – or at least not fatal – ending, as in William SHAKESPEARE's *Measure for Measure*. Alternatively, the wit and lightness of a comedy may be overshadowed by unexpectedly serious developments, as in Shakespeare's *Much Ado About Nothing*.

Treasure Island Adventure tale by Robert Louis STEVENSON, originally published as a magazine serial (1881-2). A young boy, Jim Hawkins, lives with his mother, who keeps the Admiral Benbow inn. An old pirate comes to stay at the inn but drops down dead when he receives the dreaded 'black spot' – a sign that his enemies are closing in. Among the old pirate's papers Jim finds a map of buried treasure and sets off with two associates on the schooner *Hispaniola* to look for the hoard. However, among the ship's crew are the villainous pirate and his men who are after the hoard for themselves. With great daring, and the help of his friends, Jim foils their plans and gains the treasure.

Turgenev, Ivan (1818-83) Russian novelist whose works include the play *A Month in the Country*, and the great novel *Fathers and Sons*, which deals with revolutionary aspirations and nihilist philosophy. He spent his later life in Western Europe, where his work was admired for its poetic REALISM and fine characterization.

Twain, Mark ▷PSEUDONYM of the American writer Samuel Langhorne Clemens (1835-1910). Twain won acclaim in 1869 with *The Innocents Abroad*, an account of a voyage to the Mediterranean which satirizes both European and American pretensions. His best-known books are the children's novels *The Adventures of* TOM SAWYER and *The Adventures of Huckleberry Finn*. In later works such as *A Connecticut Yankee in King Arthur's Court* Twain's satire became increasingly biting.

❖ As a young man Twain worked on a Mississippi steamboat. His pen name comes from a call used in taking river soundings meaning 'two fathoms deep'.

❖ Twain is well known for witty sayings, such as 'The report of my death was an exaggeration' and 'A classic is something that everybody wants to have read and nobody wants to read'.

Twelfth Night COMEDY written by William SHAKESPEARE around 1601. The twins Sebastian and Viola are separated in a foreign land after a shipwreck. Viola disguises herself as a young man and is employed in the service of Duke Orsino, a bitter man who has been rejected by his beloved Olivia. Olivia falls for the disguised Viola, Sebastian returns, and one confusion follows another before, finally, Sebastian marries Olivia and the duke marries Viola.

❖ Much of the humour in the play is provided by lesser characters such as the pompous steward Malvolio and Olivia's uncle Sir Toby Belch.

Ulysses Controversial novel, experimental in form, written by the Irish author James JOYCE and published in Paris in 1922, although not in England until 1936 because of obscenity laws. *Ulysses* deals with the experiences of a small number of Dublin characters as they go about their business on 16 June 1904 – a date now known as Bloomsday. In themselves the events are ordinary, everyday occurrences, but Joyce describes them in terms of episodes from Homer's ODYSSEY. The main characters are a middle-aged Jewish advertisement salesman Leopold Bloom (representing Homer's hero Odysseus), a young poet Stephen Dedalus – to whom Bloom acts as a father-figure – and Leopold's wife Molly.

❖ *Ulysses* introduced STREAM OF CONSCIOUSNESS into English writing and greatly influenced the modern novel.

Uncle Tom's Cabin Novel by the American author and antislavery campaigner Harriet Beecher Stowe (1811-96), describing the grim realities of slave life in the Southern states. It was serialized in 1851-2 and was considered by some people – including American statesman Abraham Lincoln – to have contributed to the ▷AMERICAN CIVIL WAR by arousing antislavery sentiment in the North. The title character is a pious, loyal slave who is eventually beaten to death by the cruel overseer of the plantation.

❖ An 'Uncle Tom' is a disparaging reference to a black person who is seen as being servile or overly tolerant towards a white oppressor.

UP, UP AND AWAY *A poster advertises the 1956 film* Around the World in Eighty Days, *starring David Niven as Phileas Fogg and the comic Cantinflas as his valet Passepartout.*

Verne, Jules (1828-1905) French author of adventure tales including *Around the World in Eighty Days*, and science fiction such as *Journey to the Centre of the Earth* and *Twenty Thousand Leagues Under the Sea*. His books were based more on imagination than on scientific knowledge, but some of them anticipated inventions such as space travel and television.

verse POETRY, usually employing devices such as METRE and RHYME, although not always (see FREE VERSE and BLANK VERSE). Verse is also another word for STANZA.

Vidal, Gore (1925-) American novelist, essayist and satirist, best known for *Myra Breckinridge* (1968) and historical fiction, including *Burr* (1973) and *Lincoln* (1984).

Virgil (70-19 BC) (Full name Publius Vergilius Maro) Greatest poet of classical Rome, known for his epic *Aeneid*, which tells how the Trojan hero ▷AENEAS founded Rome after the war with the Greeks. Virgil also wrote lyric pastoral poems known as the *Eclogues* and *Georgics*.

Voltaire ▷PSEUDONYM of the French writer, philosopher and wit François Marie Arouet (1694-1778). His works express the spirit of the Age of Enlightenment and uphold the values of reason, toleration and justice. Voltaire's best-known books include the satire *Candide*, which makes fun of the optimistic philosophy of ▷LEIBNIZ, and the *Philosophical Dictionary*, in which he expressed his views on morality, faith, art, science and justice.

Waiting for Godot Play by Samuel BECKETT, produced in French in 1953 and in English two years later. Two tramps, Vladimir and Estragon, spend the entire play waiting for a mysterious character called Godot, who never appears. *Waiting for Godot* was a milestone in the development of THEATRE OF THE ABSURD.

Walcott, Derek (1930-) West Indian poet and playwright, born in St Lucia, whose works combine elements such as Creole vocabulary and classical mythology. His best-known poem is *Omeros* (1990), based on Homer's ODYSSEY. Walcott won the Nobel prize for literature in 1992.

Walker, Alice (1944-) American novelist and poet whose best-known work, the novel *The Color Purple*, won her the 1983 Pulitzer prize

for literature. The book, which describes the lives of two sisters living in the racist American South before World War II, was made into a 1985 film starring American actress Whoopi Goldberg.
❖ At the time of its release Alice Walker refused permission for the film to be screened in South Africa, because of the country's policy of ▷APARTHEID.

War and Peace Sweeping novel by the Russian writer Leo TOLSTOY, published in 1869 and considered by many to be the greatest novel ever written. It recounts the histories of several Russian families during the ▷NAPOLEONIC WARS.

Waste Land, The Poem by T S ELIOT, published in 1922 and considered one of the major works associated with MODERNISM. The poem deals despairingly with the state of post-World War I society, which Eliot saw as sterile and decadent. Numerous references to religious imagery, mythology and literature of the past are used ironically to point out the comparative emptiness of Eliot's time. The poem begins:

April is the cruellest month, breeding
Lilacs out of the dead land, mixing
Memory and desire, stirring
Dull roots with spring rain.

Waugh, Evelyn (1903-66) English novelist known for his social satire and black humour. Waugh's first novel *Decline and Fall*, based on his unhappy experiences as an assistant schoolmaster, was an immediate success. It was followed by several other comic works, including *A Handful of Dust*, *Scoop* (a hilarious account of the attempts of an incompetent journalist to cover a civil war in Africa) and *The Loved One*, a grotesque satire on California-style death. In 1930 Waugh converted to Roman Catholicism. More serious works include *Brideshead Revisited* – the saga of a decadent family, turned into a popular television series in 1981 – and *The Ordeal of Gilbert Pinfold*, which deals with faith, redemption and madness. Waugh also wrote travel books and about his experiences in the Balkans and Crete during World War II – in the 'Sword of Honour' trilogy.
❖ Waugh's satirical style has been continued by his son, the journalist Auberon.

Webster, John (*c*1580-1634) English playwright generally considered, after Shakespeare, to be the greatest of the Jacobean period. His dark, bloodthirsty REVENGE TRAGEDIES *The White Devil* (*c*1612) and *The Duchess of Malfi* (*c*1613-14) are still performed today.

Wells, H G (1866-1946) Prolific English author, and one of the first to write science fiction. His first book, *The Time Machine*, is partly set in a distant future age when the human race is divided into the subterranean workers, the Morlocks, and the decadent class of the Eloi. Wells's other fantasies include *The Island of Doctor Moreau*, *The Invisible Man* and *The War of the Worlds* – a tale about Martians invading the Earth which caused panic when an adaptation by American actor and director Orson Welles was broadcast by radio in the USA in 1938. H G Wells wrote more than 100 books in all, including works on politics and history, and comic novels such as *The History of Mr Polly*, in which a shopkeeper plots a daring escape from his dreary existence.

DOUBLE TAKE *The Color Purple* won wide acclaim for author Alice Walker (below) as well as for actress Whoopi Goldberg (right) for her portrayal of Celie in the 1985 film version.

White, Patrick (1912-1990) Australian writer of poems, novels and short stories, who first made an international name for himself with the novel *The Tree of Man* (1954), which portrays life in a small Australian community. His long, involved novels, which deal with the nature of human existence, include *Voss*, *Riders in the Chariot*, *The Solid Mandala* and *The Twyborn Affair*. He received the Nobel prize for literature in 1973.

Whitman, Walt (1819-92) American poet best known for his collection *Leaves of Grass*, in which he tried to express the young, independent spirit of the USA. He revised the book continually throughout his lifetime and it eventually grew from 12 poems to more than 150. Like all Whitman's work, it celebrates nature and upholds the values of individualism, freedom and brotherhood.

Who's Afraid of Virginia Woolf? Tragi-comic play by the American dramatist Edward Albee (1928-), first produced in 1962. It concerns the events of a single, tense evening during which an alcoholic academic couple play a series of mutually destructive games while supposedly entertaining their guests.
❖ The 1966 film of the play starred Richard Burton and Elizabeth Taylor.
❖ The title is a literary play on words sung by the 'heroine' to the tune of 'Who's Afraid of the Big, Bad Wolf'.

Wilde, Oscar (1854-1900) Irish writer known for his wit, brilliant conversation and extreme aestheticism – the view that art should be judged solely by standards of beauty and that issues such as morality are irrelevant. Wilde wrote poems, fairy tales such as *The Happy Prince*, and a single novel, *The Picture of Dorian Gray*. His best-known works are comic plays such as *Lady Windermere's Fan*, *An Ideal Husband* and *The Importance of Being Earnest*. Wilde also wrote a tragedy, *Salome*, which was later turned into an opera by the composer Richard Strauss. Wilde led a flamboyant life and made enemies among the establishment. In 1895 he was bankrupted by a lawsuit and imprisoned for homosexuality. He later described his experience of prison in *The Ballad of Reading Gaol*. After his release in 1897, Wilde went to live in Paris, where he remained until his death.
❖ His witty lines are legion; he defined the

STUDIED POSE *Oscar Wilde's sharp wit was renowned in London's literary salons. 'The man who can dominate a London dinner-table can dominate the world,' he claimed.*

cynic as 'A man who knows the price of everything and the value of nothing' and fox-hunting as 'the unspeakable in full pursuit of the uneatable'.

Williams, Tennessee (1911-83) American playwright known for psychological dramas such as *The Glass Menagerie*, *A Streetcar Named Desire* and *Cat on a Hot Tin Roof*. His plays deal with small groups of characters who battle against the odds, handicapped by their personal inadequacies and desperate circumstances. Undercurrents of violence and sexual tension are usually never far below the surface.

Wilson, Sir Angus (1913-91) English writer of social satires in which middle-class life is disrupted by unforeseen and, occasionally, bizarre events. His books include *Hemlock and After* and *Anglo-Saxon Attitudes*, in which mysteries from the past come back to haunt a middle-aged historian.

Wind in the Willows, The Animal story for children by British author Kenneth Grahame (1859-1932), published in 1908. The book started out as a series of tales told to Grahame's son, featuring the highly strung, conceited and irresponsible Toad and his riverside companions Rattie, Mole and Badger – characters partly based on friends of Grahame's and partly on the rural gentry.

❖ A musical, *Toad of Toad Hall*, was adapted from the book by A A MILNE in 1930.

Wodehouse, Sir P G (1881-1975) Comic writer known for novels and short stories about the foppish, helpless aristocrat Bertie Wooster and his manservant Jeeves, a master of British understatement and reserve. He also wrote humorous school stories about an extremely dignified youth, Rupert Psmith.

Woolf, Virginia (1882-1941) English novelist, and a leading figure in MODERNISM. She came from a well-known intellectual family and with her brothers and her sister – the artist Vanessa Bell – she held meetings of friends at her home in Bloomsbury, from which the BLOOMSBURY GROUP was born. In 1912 she married the writer and left-wing political thinker Leonard Woolf and together they set up the Hogarth Press. Virginia Woolf's principal novels were *Mrs Dalloway*, *To the Lighthouse* and *The Waves* – all of which use experimental techniques such as STREAM OF CONSCIOUSNESS writing to give expression to the inner lives of characters. Woolf was also an outstanding journalist and critic, and her witty feminist essay *A Room of One's Own* is particularly well known. She suffered from recurrent periods of depression and mental illness, and finally drowned herself.

❖ Woolf dedicated *Orlando: A Biography*, her most commercially successful work, to her friend Vita SACKVILLE-WEST. It was made into a 1993 film starring Tilda Swinton.

Wordsworth, William (1770-1850) English poet whose work played a major role in the development of ROMANTICISM in English literature. His writing expresses a mystical view of life in which nature and the human spirit are closely connected. Wordsworth grew up in Cumbria, and the Lake District countryside inspired many of his poems, such as 'The Prelude', 'Intimations of Immortality' and 'Resolution and Independence'. He was a close friend of the poet Samuel Taylor COLERIDGE, and in 1798 they published a joint volume, *Lyrical Ballads*, which included such poems as *The* RIME OF THE ANCIENT MARINER and *Tintern Abbey*. He was made poet laureate in 1843.

Wuthering Heights Romantic novel by Emily BRONTË, published in 1847. It tells the story of the passionate but troubled relationship between Catherine Earnshaw and the brooding Heathcliff, a homeless youth taken in by her family. Heathcliff overhears Catherine say that it would degrade her to marry him, and he leaves the house in a fury. Three years later, Heathcliff returns, seeking vengeance. A series of disasters ensues; most notably, Catherine – now married to the feeble Edward Linton – dies in childbirth. The story ends with Heathcliff's death – which he sees as a reunion with his beloved Catherine.

❖ Wuthering Heights is the name of the Earnshaws' home on the Yorkshire moors.

Yeats, William Butler (1865-1939) Irish poet and playwright influential in the revival of Irish literature in the late 19th and early 20th centuries, and in the founding of an Irish national theatre. His early works were romantic and based on Irish history and legend. Later on, however, Yeats's style became starker and his mature poems – such as 'Sailing to Byzantium', 'The Tower' and 'The Second Coming' – are dominated by themes of historical change, old age and death. He was a senator of the Irish Free State from 1922 to 1928, and won the Nobel prize for literature in 1923.

❖ Yeats died in the south of France, but his body was taken back to Ireland in 1948. His epitaph comes from one of his poems:

Cast a cold eye
On life, on death.
Horseman, pass by!

Zola, Émile (1840-1902) French novelist whose principal work *Les Rougon-Macquart* comprises 20 novels written between 1871 and 1893. The books deal with two branches of the same family – the Rougons and the Macquarts – and paint a vivid picture of middle-class and working-class life in France in the 19th century. Zola is also remembered for his open letter *J'accuse* ('I accuse'), a heavy criticism of the French government over the Dreyfus Affair.

POWER OF THE PEN *Édouard Manet's painting of Émile Zola, whose letter* J'accuse *helped to secure justice for Alfred Dreyfus, a Jewish army officer falsely accused of treason.*

MYTHS AND LEGENDS

At the edge of our knowledge of the Universe lies the shadowy realm of myth and legend. It embraces narratives of gods and people set in the remote past, earthly heroes whose exploits have captured the popular imagination, as well as spells and stories passed down from one generation to the next in the form of folklore. In every culture, this is the world of the human imagination, of tales and symbols, many of which reflect and represent fundamental truths and mysteries of life.

ABOMINABLE ENCOUNTER *Peering from the pages of a 1950s Italian magazine, a fanciful Yeti watches two unsuspecting explorers.*

Abominable Snowman Shaggy man-beast, also known as the Yeti, said to live in the Himalayas. According to local folklore, the Yetis were the offspring of a monkey king who married an ogress. In spite of reported sightings and discoveries of extraordinary tracks, there is still no firm evidence of the existence of the Abominable Snowman or its Western counterpart, Bigfoot, which has been reported in various locations throughout America.

Achilles Greatest Greek warrior in the TROJAN WAR, and the hero of Homer's ▷ILIAD. When he was an infant, his mother Thetis tried to protect Achilles by bathing him in the magical River STYX to make him immortal, but the heel by which she held him remained vulnerable. During the siege of Troy, Achilles quarrelled with Agamemnon and withdrew his army, but he eventually returned to slay the Trojan hero Hector, whose corpse he then dragged in the dust behind his chariot. Later, Achilles was fatally wounded in the heel by an arrow fired from the bow of Hector's brother Paris.
❖ The phrase 'Achilles heel' is sometimes used to describe a person's one significant weakness.

Adamastor Giant of Classical mythology. The early Portuguese explorers believed the stormy seas off the Cape of Good Hope were inhabited by the vengeful spirit of Adamastor, who sought to overthrow the gods and was turned into a mountain at Cape Point. In the *Lusiad* (1572) of the Portuguese poet Luis de Camões the spirit makes a dramatic appearance to Vasco da Gama at sea, predicting the vengeance he would wreak on mariners such as Bartolomeu Dias and others shipwrecked on the South African coast.
❖ *Adamastor* is also the title of a poetry volume (1930) by the South African poet Roy Campbell.

Adonis In Greek mythology, a beautiful youth who was loved by APHRODITE. He was killed by a wild boar when hunting, but allowed to return from the underworld for six months every year so that he and Aphrodite could be reunited.
❖ A young man considered as handsome as a Greek god may be called an Adonis.

Aeneas (ee-NEE-uss) Trojan warrior in Greek mythology. A son of the goddess APHRODITE and the hero of ▷VIRGIL's *Aeneid*. After the fall of Troy, Aeneas fled with his father and son and was shipwrecked at Carthage in northern Africa. Dido, the queen of Carthage, fell in love with him, and burned herself to death on a funeral pyre when he left her. After many trials, Aeneas arrived in what is now Italy. Rome was believed to have been founded by his descendants.
❖ Because he carried his father Anchises out of the ruins of defeated Troy, Aeneas represents filial devotion.

Agamemnon King of Mycenae who led the Greeks against Troy in the TROJAN WAR. While he was away, his wife Clytemnestra took a lover called Aegisthus, and they murdered Agamemnon when he returned home. The guilty pair were killed by Agamemnon's son Orestes, encouraged by his sister Electra.
❖ The psychoanalyst Sigmund Freud described the early romantic attraction he believed girls have towards their fathers as an 'Electra complex'.

GODDESS OF LOVE AND BEAUTY *A bronze head of Aphrodite, from 100-200 BC, portrays the Greek ideal of feminine beauty.*

alchemy A combination of magic and scientific experiment that was widely practised during the Middle Ages, and the forerunner of modern chemistry. Alchemy arose from the search for the 'philosopher's stone' that would turn base metals such as lead into gold, and for the 'elixir of life' that would bring eternal youth. However, the alchemists' true goal lay beyond the material world; they believed that perfecting metals would provide the key to perfecting the human spirit too. Alchemy is thought to have originated in Egypt during the 2nd century BC, but it did not reach its height in Europe until the Middle Ages. For reasons of secrecy, alchemical formulae were usually written in code.

Amazons In Greek mythology, a group of female warriors who lived near the Black Sea. They had their right breasts burnt off in order to use a bow and arrow more efficiently in war. The legendary hero THESEUS took captive an Amazon named Hippolyta, and they had a son called Hippolytus.
❖ A strong, aggressive woman is sometimes called an Amazon.

ambrosia Food of the gods in Greek mythology. Those who ate it were said to become immortal.
❖ Particularly delicious food is sometimes referred to as ambrosia.

Antigone (an-TIG-o-nee) In Theban legend, the daughter of King OEDIPUS. After the abdication of Oedipus, Antigone's two brothers, Polynices and Eteocles, became joint sovereigns of Thebes and agreed to govern in alternate years. After his first year, Eteocles refused to give up the throne, and the two brothers fought and killed each other. Although burial of the dead was a religious obligation among the Greeks, the new Theban king, Creon, forbade the burial of Polynices because he was considered to be a traitor. Because Antigone buried him, she was ordered to be buried alive, but she committed suicide.
❖ Antigone is the heroine of the tragedy of the same name by ▷SOPHOCLES.

Aphrodite (AFF-rer-DYE-tee) (Roman name Venus) Greek goddess of love and beauty, the mother of EROS and AENEAS. In the Judgment of PARIS, Paris chose Aphrodite as the most beautiful goddess. Aphrodite was believed to have been born out of the foam of the sea, and is often pictured rising from the water, notably in the painting *Birth of Venus* by the Italian artist Sandro ▷BOTTICELLI.

Apollo Greek and Roman god of music, prophecy, medicine and the Sun. Apollo represents order and civilization, and is sometimes contrasted with Dionysus (or BACCHUS), who represents the relaxation of inhibitions. Apollo was worshipped at the Delphic ORACLE, where a priestess gave forth his predictions. ZEUS was his father, and ARTEMIS was his sister.

Argonauts In Greek mythology, the companions of JASON in the quest for the Golden Fleece. Their ship was the *Argo*.
❖ *Naut* means 'sailor' in Greek, and is the root of the word nautical.

Artemis (Roman name Diana) Greek virgin goddess of hunting and the Moon; daughter of Zeus and twin sister of Apollo.

Arthur, King Legendary English king who was born out of wedlock and raised by the wizard MERLIN. When he was only a boy, Arthur gained the throne by withdrawing the magic sword Excalibur from a stone, after many men had tried and failed. According to another version of the legend, he received the sword from the Lady of the Lake, who lived in the middle of a lake. Arthur established his court at Camelot, where he gathered around him the knights of the ROUND TABLE. Other characters associated with the legends of Arthur are his wife Queen GUINEVERE and his treacherous nephew Modred. When a love affair between Guinevere and Sir LANCELOT was discovered, Modred exploited the scandal to start a civil war, and caused Arthur's downfall at the Battle of Camlann. Mortally wounded, Arthur sailed to the mysterious isle of Avalon, promising to return whenever his people needed him. The tales of Arthur may have been based on a 6th-century Celtic chieftain of the same name, who united the squabbling, regional kings of Britain and led them to victory against the Saxons. In Somerset, Cadbury Castle has been identified with Camelot, and GLASTONBURY has often been associated with the isle of Avalon where Arthur is said to be buried.

astral body In occult belief, an exact – though nonmaterial – copy of the physical body. It is capable of separating itself, and remains attached to the physical body by a seemingly endless cord. At death the cord is severed and the astral body is freed from the limitations of the flesh.

astral projection Experience of seeming to leave one's body and observing it from outside. Occultists believe that this occurs when the ASTRAL BODY leaves the physical body. People who claim to have had an 'out-of-body experience' have talked of a sense of well-being, vitality and buoyancy. This experience usually occurs involuntarily, and can happen whether the subject is conscious or unconscious. The natural habitat of the astral body is said to be a kind of 'fourth dimension' called the astral plane, and its experiences there may sometimes be remembered as dreams.

ARTHURIAN LEGEND *The Round Table was said to have been designed to promote equality by avoiding disputes over which of King Arthur's knights should preside at its head.*

astrology Study of the relative position of the planets and stars, in order to predict their supposed influence on human actions. The principles were laid down by Babylonian priests around 3000 BC. Having observed that the Sun, Moon and five known planets seemed to move around the Earth along a track passing through 12 constellations, they divided the track into 12 segments, or signs of the ZODIAC. Each month, as the Earth moves in its annual orbit, the Sun appears to rise in a different segment. To cast a horoscope, an astrologer must know the date, time and place of a person's birth. The sign in which the Sun was rising, as well as the positions of the planets, are considered in reading the horoscope. Astrology became discredited with the discoveries of astronomers such as ▷GALILEO, but many still believe that there is some truth in it.

Athena (Roman name Minerva) Greek goddess of war, wisdom and the arts. At birth she sprang fully grown and fully armed out of the forehead of her father Zeus. Athena was one of the goddesses slighted by the Judgment of PARIS; as Paris was a Trojan prince, Athena gave her help to the Greeks in the TROJAN WAR. Athena was the patron goddess of Athens, which was named after her. The greatest of her temples was the ▷PARTHENON.

Atlantis Lost continent first described by the Greek philosopher ▷PLATO more than 2 000 years ago. Atlantis was said to have been a marvel of prosperity and advanced engineering, enjoyed by a just and peaceful society, until it became corrupted by its wealth. The gods then directed earthquakes and floods against Atlantis until it was swallowed up by the sea. This legend may simply have been a moral fable invented by Plato, but historians still argue about the continent's possible existence and geographical position. Some scientists think it may have been based on the Minoan civilization of Crete, destroyed around 1500 BC by a series of natural disasters. Archaeological discoveries suggest that the island of Santorini, 112 km north of Crete, may have been Atlantis.

Atlas In Greek mythology, son of one of the TITANS, famous for his strength. He refused hospitality to PERSEUS, who, using the head of

MEDUSA, turned him into stone. He became the Atlas mountains, forced to support the heavens for ever.

❖ Since the 16th century, pictures of Atlas and his burden have been used as decoration on maps. Accordingly, the word atlas is used for a book of maps.

Bacchus (Greek name Dionysus) Roman god of wine, ecstasy and fertility, whose followers were called bacchants (priests) and bacchantes (priestesses). In the 2nd century BC the worship of Bacchus was banned in Rome, but it was readmitted as a mystery cult under the empire.

❖ In art, Bacchus is often depicted eating a bunch of grapes, surrounded by SATYRS.

❖ A 'bacchanalian' party or feast is marked by unrestrained drunkenness. The name recalls the Roman festivals called Bacchanalia, held in honour of Bacchus, which usually culminated in drunken orgies.

Bermuda Triangle Area of the north Atlantic Ocean lying between Florida, Bermuda and Puerto Rico. Numerous aircraft and ships and their crews and passengers are said to have vanished here. Most experts now believe that many of the so-called unexplained disappearances either never occurred or can be explained rationally.

Blarney Stone Block of rough limestone set high in the battlements of 15th-century Blarney Castle in County Cork, Ireland. According to an Irish legend, those who kiss the Blarney Stone receive a gift of eloquence that enables them to obtain anything they want through persuasion. Visitors have to lie on their backs, leaning out over a sheer drop, in order to kiss it.

❖ Blarney can be used as an expression to describe flattery designed to gain a favour.

Bluebeard Villain of European folk tales, who murdered his wives and kept their bodies in a locked room in his castle. The legend may have been based on Comorre the Cursed, a 6th-century Breton chief, but it also became interwoven with that of the mass-murderer Gilles de Rais, who was executed at Nantes in 1440. Bluebeard appears in Charles Perrault's *Histoires ou Contes du temps passé* of 1697.

Book of the Dead Ancient Egyptian texts concerned with the guidance of the soul in the afterlife. Containing spells, incantations and rituals, they were placed in the tombs of the dead to help them rise again, pass safely through the dangers of the underworld, and achieve eternal happiness in the next life. They were adapted from Pyramid Texts (*c*2350-2175 BC) written by priests for dead pharaohs, and Coffin Texts (*c*2160-1580 BC) written for nobles. Simple versions were available to the poor, while the wealthy bought elaborate, illustrated versions. The use of these texts continued into the 1st century BC.

Brünnhilde (broon-HILL-der) VALKYRIE in NORSE MYTHOLOGY who loved the hero Sigurd (or Siegfried). When he deceived her, she had him killed and then committed suicide.

❖ The characters of Brünnhilde and Siegfried appear in Wagner's *The Ring of the Nibelung*, a cycle of four operas based on a German poem written in the 12th century.

Brutus In British mythology, the founder and first king of Britain. According to Geoffrey of Monmouth's 12th-century *History of the Kings of Britain*, Brutus and his Trojan settlers killed the last remaining GIANTS who lived on the island, after which Britain was named after Brutus.

Cassandra In Greek mythology, daughter of Priam, king of Troy. To win Cassandra's love, APOLLO gave her the gift of prophecy; however, when she rejected his advances, he ordained that nobody would believe her predictions.

❖ A Cassandra is a prophet of doom, especially one whose prophecies go unheeded.

centaur Creature in Greek mythology with the upper part of a human being and the lower body and legs of a horse, representing animal desires and barbarism. Centaurs were often depicted being ridden by Eros, the Greek god of love – an allusion to their lustful nature.

Ceres (SEER-eez) Roman name for DEMETER, the goddess of agriculture.

chimera Fire-breathing she-monster in Greek mythology, usually represented with the head of a lion, the body of a goat and the tail of a serpent.

Circe (SUR-see) Sorceress in Greek mythology, who turned the followers of ODYSSEUS into swine. With the help of a magic herb,

EGYPTIAN RITUAL *A papyrus from a Book of the Dead of 1310 BC depicts the ritual of 'Opening the Mouth', designed to restore the faculties of the embalmed body and help it into the afterlife.*

Odysseus resisted Circe's magic and forced her to restore his men. Enamoured of Odysseus, Circe persuaded him to stay for a year on her island, before giving him directions to his home in Ithaca.

clairvoyance Supposed psychic ability of 'second sight', which enables someone to see or know things that are out of the natural range of human perception, such as ghosts, objects that are far away, and events that have passed or are yet to happen.

Classical mythology Collection of myths about the origin and history of the Greeks and Romans. The Romans adopted a vast part of their mythology, such as the system of gods, from the Greeks, but gave the gods Roman names. Works recounting these myths include the *Aeneid* by the Roman poet ▷VIRGIL, and the *Iliad* and the *Odyssey* by the Greek author ▷HOMER.

corn circles Circular formations that began to materialize in British cornfields in the 1980s. The crops are flattened into precise circles and patterns. Theories regarding their creation range from UFOs to rampaging hedgehogs, but in September 1991, two artists called Doug Bower and Dave Chorley admitted that they had made many of the more elaborate circles. Some scientists believe that others may be caused by electrically charged whirlwinds.

Cupid Roman name of Eros, the beautiful, young god of love who inspired physical desire. When his mother Venus grew jealous of PSYCHE's beauty, she ordered Cupid to make Psyche fall in love with the ugliest of men, but instead he fell in love with her himself.
❖ Cupid is often depicted as a cherub shooting an arrow at someone to make them fall in love – a favourite device of Victorian valentine cards and rococo art.
❖ The term 'Cupid's bow' refers to the top of the upper lip, because it resembles the shape of Cupid's double-curved bow.

Cyclopes Savage one-eyed giants in Greek mythology. Their leader Polyphemus, son of POSEIDON, imprisoned ODYSSEUS in his cave and ate some of his men. The survivors, using a red-hot poker, blinded Polyphemus in his drunken sleep and escaped by clinging to the bellies of his sheep when they were let out of his cave to graze. Odysseus thus incurred the undying hatred of Poseidon, who burdened his journey home with difficulties.

Daedalus Legendary Greek inventor who built the LABYRINTH at Knossos in which the MINOTAUR was kept. He was later imprisoned in it by Minos, king of Crete, for revealing the secret of the Labyrinth. Daedalus escaped with his son Icarus by making artificial wings. Icarus, however, flew too close to the Sun; the wax that held his wings together melted and he fell to Earth.

Damocles, sword of Subject of a story about a sycophantic but envious courtier called Damocles and a Greek ruler called Dionysus the Elder. To show Damocles what it felt like to be a king, Dionysus held a magnificent banquet and seated Damocles under a sword that was suspended from the ceiling by a single hair.
❖ Figuratively speaking, a sword of Damocles is an impending danger that may strike at any moment, causing much anxiety.

Demeter (Roman name Ceres) Greek goddess of corn, agriculture and fruitfulness. Persephone, her daughter by Zeus, was taken to the underworld by HADES to be his bride. Demeter was so forlorn that she neglected the crops and brought about the first winter. Zeus arranged for Persephone to be returned to her mother, but she had to spend some part of every year underground, when winter would begin again.

Devil Supreme embodiment of evil and the archenemy of God, also known as Beelzebub, Lucifer, Old Nick, Satan and the Prince of Darkness. Satan has been depicted in many ways: as a man with horns, goat hoofs and a pitchfork, and as an angel with large bat wings. In the early books of the Old Testament, it was God who inflicted punishment on men, while one of his officials – known as 'the satan', Hebrew for 'adversary' – acted as a prosecutor. In the New Testament and in later times, the image of Satan grew increasingly monstrous, until he was eventually blamed for all sin and evil. The story of the fall from heaven of Lucifer is told in the Book of Isaiah, in the Old Testament. Belief in the Devil was largely abandoned among theologians as a result of the ▷ENLIGHTENMENT.
❖ John Milton's epic poem *Paradise Lost* tells of the rebellion and punishment of Lucifer, a proud, arrogant and tragic figure who believes that it is 'better to reign in hell than serve in heaven'.

Diana Roman name of Artemis, goddess of hunting, wild animals, childbirth, fertility and the Moon.

Dionysus Greek name for BACCHUS, the god of wine and revelry.

divination Art of predicting future events and giving supernatural guidance, with the use of intuition or occult techniques such as ASTROLOGY, CLAIRVOYANCE, palmistry, ▷RUNES and TAROT CARDS, as well as the techniques of ▷PRIEST DIVINERS. The ancient Greeks regularly consulted ORACLES.

Dracula, Count Bloodthirsty nobleman of the Middle Ages who was born in Transylvania (now a part of Romania) in about 1430. Dracula was nicknamed Vlad the Impaler because he skewered his victims on stakes. Dracula was the inspiration for a novel by English author Bram Stoker, published in 1897, as well as for many ▷DRACULA FILMS. In Stoker's novel a VAMPIRE remained 'un-dead' until laid to rest by having a wooden stake driven through its heart – the eventual fate of Count Dracula.
❖ Crucifixes, garlic and holy water supposedly help to keep vampires at bay.

dragon Imaginary fire-breathing beast that figures in mythology and tales of chivalry, usually as a winged serpent with glaring eyes, flared nostrils, sharp teeth and talons. To Christians in the past the dragon was a symbol of the DEVIL, and slaying the beast symbolized the triumph of Christ over evil. Many saints were depicted as dragon slayers, including ST GEORGE. In heraldry the dragon symbolizes strength, and in Chinese mythology it is a benevolent beast.

THE FALL OF THE BONES *Objects, or 'bones', are widely used by Zulu priest-diviners, along with other techniques of divination.*

Druids Priesthood of pre-Roman Celtic religion in Gaul and Britain, whose rites are said to have involved human sacrifice. They seem to have had knowledge of astronomy, and claimed to have prophetic powers. They believed the soul was immortal. It was once thought that the Druids had built STONEHENGE and other stone circles as their temples. However, although the Druids may have used Stonehenge, archaeology shows that the circle was finished around 1550 BC – some 1 200 years before the earliest-known Druids.
❖ The name Druid means 'knowing the oak tree' and may refer to their rituals, which took place in sacred oak groves.

Eldorado Mythical 'Golden Land' in South America said to belong to El Dorado, a 'Golden Man' who covered himself with gold dust. The Golden Land was thought to exist in the area of the Orinoco and Amazon rivers, but centuries of exploration, including two expeditions led by Sir Walter ▷RALEIGH, failed to locate it.
❖ Figuratively, Eldorado is a place of fabulous wealth, or an opportunity to obtain it.

Elysian Fields In Greek mythology, the place where the souls of the righteous go after death. According to ▷HOMER, it is a beautiful region at the end of the Earth.
❖ Figuratively, the Elysian Fields are a place or condition of ideal happiness.
❖ The French translation of Elysian Fields, 'Champs Élysées', is the name of the principal boulevard in Paris.

Eros (EAR-os) (Roman name Cupid) Greek and Roman god of love, associated with all beautiful things. Eros was both playful and cruel, and he fired arrows that produced physical desire in his victims.

ESP Abbreviation for extrasensory perception, the supposed reception of information through other means than the five senses of seeing, hearing, smelling, tasting and touching. It is often referred to as the 'sixth sense'. Types of ESP include CLAIRVOYANCE and telepathy.

fairies Supernatural beings found in the folklore of many countries; often mischievous, they are capable of assisting or harassing human beings. Hundreds of kinds of fairies have been described, varying in size, character and magical powers. They are said to covet human babies, and cradle-snatching is their chief vice. In place of the stolen baby they leave a changeling – a fairy child or a piece of wood carved to look like a child. The Christian Church once thought that fairies were fallen angels, or the souls of babies who had died before they had been baptized.
❖ Oberon and Titania were introduced by Shakespeare as the King and Queen of Fairyland in *A* ▷MIDSUMMER NIGHT'S DREAM.

Fates, The Three Greek and Roman goddesses who governed human fate. They are Clotho, the spinner of man's destiny; Lachesis, the weaver of chance; and Atropos, who cuts the thread of life with her scissors when death comes.

Faust Legendary scholar, magician and practitioner of astrology, who sold his soul to the Devil in exchange for youth, knowledge and power. A 'real' Faust lived in 16th-century Germany – a charlatan who boasted that he could perform miracles because he was in league with the Devil. The writers Christopher ▷MARLOWE and Johann Wolfgang von ▷GOETHE wrote plays about Faust. In Marlowe's *Dr Faustus*, Faust ends up being dragged to hell to face an eternity of torment; in Goethe's version, however, Faust is finally redeemed.
❖ A 'Faustian' bargain is one in which a person sells his soul for huge material gain.

Fisher King King in Arthurian legend who presided over the Grail castle where the HOLY GRAIL was kept; he is also known as the Grail King. The Fisher King had been severely wounded yet was incapable of dying. His land was in desolation and the crops would not grow. According to a prophecy, he could be healed only when an innocent fool arrived in the court and asked him why he was ill. An innocent knight called PARSIFAL found the castle, and eventually asked the necessary question.

Flying Dutchman Dutch phantom ship which, according to legend, was doomed to roam the seas until the ▷DAY OF JUDGMENT. Old records show that a real ship of that name set sail from Amsterdam in 1680, but was caught in a gale near the ▷CAPE OF GOOD HOPE. Because the captain defied God by persisting in his attempt to round the Cape, he was condemned to roam the seas forever and to lure other ships to their destruction. Many supposed sightings of a ship fitting the *Flying Dutchman's* description have been dismissed as mirages, but the similarity of detail given by witnesses cannot be explained.
❖ The *Flying Dutchman* legend inspired Wagner to write his opera *Der Fliegende Holländer.* He wrote it after a rough North Sea crossing in 1839, which took three weeks instead of the expected eight days.

Furies, The (Greek name Erinyes) Three hideous female goddesses in Classical mythology – winged monsters called Tisiphone, Alecto and Megaera, with snakes in their hair. They pursued evildoers, and their main duty was to destroy those who had murdered their own kin. When the Titan KRONOS castrated his father (Heaven), his father's blood fell upon the Earth and she conceived and bore The Furies.

Gaia The 'earth goddess' of Greek mythology. The daughter of Chaos, she was both mother and wife of Uranus, by whom she produced the CYCLOPES and TITANS. (See ▷GAIA HYPOTHESIS in 'The Earth and the environment'.)

Galahad, Sir Young knight in the tales of King ARTHUR. The son of Sir LANCELOT and the model of a perfect Christian knight, Galahad marked the end of the worldly values of chivalry and the beginning of the spiritual quest for the HOLY GRAIL. His exceptional purity enabled him to have a vision of Heaven in which he found the Grail, after which he died in ecstasy.
❖ A 'Sir Galahad' refers, figuratively, to a noble or chivalrous person.

Gawain, Sir A knight of the ROUND TABLE famous for his courage and courtesy, and a

FOUL AVENGERS
The three Furies shriek for the blood of Orestes because he killed his mother Clytemnestra. It was his tragic duty to kill her after she had murdered his father Agamemnon.

HEROES AND VILLAINS OF AFRICAN FOLK TALES

Legend and myth in the oral tradition of southern Africa resemble much in Classical mythology. In African legend the gods and spirits, heroes and institutions, and natural phenomena have a distinctly ordinary, human side in addition to their superhuman and mysterious qualities. The fables and tales are less dominated by the moral element than in Europe – some are art for art's sake while others are more didactic and moralizing. The tales generally are told for delight rather than for mere instruction and the dramatic style of the reciters is critical to the audiences' enjoyment. Animals are favoured characters, and many are common to the tales of several cultures of the region.

lightning A lightning-bird is used to explain this weather phenomenon, but the description varies from group to group. Various taboos are associated with lightning – the Zulu will not eat an animal struck dead, unless it has been doctored in the correct manner; traditionalists will not use firewood from a tree that has been struck by lightning.

elephant and lion Both are regarded as king of the jungle.

birds Among the Xhosa, the hammerkop (associated with rain and lightning) and the hornbill (bringer of rain) are seen as sacred. The bateleur eagle delivers omens of various kinds.

Hlakanyana A small creature associated with the weasel and seen to be cunning. Many Zulu stories feature the hlakanyana instead of the hare or jackal.

Zim The wicked Zim, or cannibal, features in many African tales. At birth the Zim has two legs, one sweet, which is soon eaten by its parents, and one bitter. Nevertheless, the fearsome Zim can hop at a great speed.

chameleon and lizard Used to explain how death came into the world. When people first appeared, the animals consulted on their fate. The lizard wished all people would die, the chameleon that they would live forever. They ran a race which the lizard won, sealing the fate of humanity. Several variations of the story are told, with the San (Bushman) tales featuring the hare as well.

mantis The mantis was a powerful figure in the mythology of the southern San people, who saw it as the founder of all creation. Some believed it could transform itself into various animal forms, as well as foretell the future. If killed, it always came to life again. It was sometimes also depicted as mischievous or foolish. Prayers were offered by the Cape San to the Moon, said to have been created by the mantis.

jackal A clever creature who outwits his enemies. Many of the hare's exploits become those of the jackal in the Khoikhoi (Hottentot) tales.

snake A common belief is that the spirits of the dead come back in the form of snakes, making them an important link with the ancestors.

hare The hare is often wise and helpful, figuring prominently in African tales. The San attribute the origin of death to an incorrect message given to people by the hare. He is sent by the Moon to give people the instruction, 'As I die and return again, so shall man die and return again.' The hare distorts the message and the Moon curses him with a cleft lip.

tortoise The tortoise, together with the hare, is seen as wise and wily. The slow, patient wisdom of the tortoise enables him to overcome his enemies. In one story, he even proves too smart for the hare.

nephew of King ARTHUR. Gawain failed in his quest for the HOLY GRAIL but he proved his honour, as recounted in the 14th-century poem *Sir Gawain and the Green Knight.*

giants Colossal beings who feature in myths, legends and folk tales around the world. Because ancient peoples found dinosaur bones, massive Stone Age monuments and strangely shaped rocks, they believed that a race of giants once existed. In folklore, these giants were often slow-witted, and were easily defeated by heroes such as ODYSSEUS – who escaped from Polyphemus, leader of the CYCLOPES – and BRUTUS, who killed GOG AND MAGOG. In Greek mythology, the Giants' War was a revolt against ZEUS that was easily quashed with the help of HERCULES. The giants of Scandinavian myths were more formidable; dubbed 'the voracious ones', they represented the unbridled forces of nature and were ascribed superhuman powers.

Glastonbury Town in Somerset, England, and traditional site of King ARTHUR's isle of Avalon. Bones discovered in the graveyard of Glastonbury Abbey in 1191 are said to be those of Arthur and Guinevere. According to legend, Christ visited Glastonbury as a boy, and later so did Joseph of Arimathea, who brought with him the HOLY GRAIL and began the conversion of Britain to Christianity. The Grail is said to rest below the spring on Glastonbury Tor. Because of its mystical past, Glastonbury has become a focus for hippie and New Age culture.

Godiva, Lady Heroic English noblewoman of the 11th century. While Godiva was virtuous and charitable, her husband – Earl Leofric of Mercia – was a tyrant who imposed severe taxes on his people. According to legend, Leofric agreed to change his ways if his modest wife would ride naked through Coventry on market day. She accepted the challenge. One account says that Godiva covered her nakedness with her long hair; a later version says that the people of Coventry stayed indoors and that only one man, later known as Peeping Tom, looked into the streets, and was struck blind.

Gog and Magog Two mythical giants in British legend said to be the last survivors of a race of British giants conquered by BRUTUS and his Trojan warriors.

Golden Fleece In Greek mythology, the fleece of the winged ram Chrysomallus. It hung on a sacred oak tree at Colchis, south of the Caucasus mountains, and was guarded by a dragon. It was stolen by JASON and his companions, the ARGONAUTS.

GRIM REAPER *Depictions of death in the form of a walking skeleton, here seen coming to claim three victims, were common in medieval times, especially during the great plague epidemics.*

Gorgons Three frightful sisters in Greek mythology – Stheno, Euryale and MEDUSA. They had glaring eyes, huge teeth, and snakes for hair, and anyone who looked at them was turned to stone by their gaze. The Gorgons figure chiefly in the story of PERSEUS, who looked only at Medusa's reflection in a polished shield while he cut off her head.

Graces Three goddesses in Greek mythology who personified and bestowed the qualities of grace, charm and beauty. The daughters of Zeus, they were named Aglaia (the radiant), Thalia (the flowering) and Euphrosyne (joy).

Green Man Woodland spirit, also known as Jack-in-the-Green, who was an important figure in springtime festivities throughout Europe. Dressed from head to foot in green branches, he represented new life in plants and trees. The Green Man is depicted in medieval churches as a sinister mixture of man and tree and can still be seen on some English-style pub signs.

gremlins Mischievous spirits in the lore of British and American airmen. Gremlins were blamed for causing mechanical problems in military aircraft during World War II. They supposedly drank petrol, and were said to have the ability to raise and lower airfields beneath novice pilots as they came in to land.

Grim Reaper Figure used to represent death, and taking the form either of a cloaked skeleton or of Father Time wielding his scythe.

Guinevere Wife of King ARTHUR. In some versions of the legends of Arthur, she had a love affair with Sir LANCELOT. Arthur's treacherous nephew Modred used this affair to start a civil war, which led to the end of Arthur's reign and of the fellowship of the ROUND TABLE.

Hades (Roman name Pluto) Greek name for both the god of death and the gloomy underworld which he ruled. Charon (KAAR-on), the ferryman, carried the souls of the dead across the River STYX into Hades, where a three-headed dog called Cerberus guarded the entrance. When souls drank from the River Lethe, they forgot their former lives. Persephone spent each winter with the god Hades as his queen.

❖ Hades later became associated with the ▷HELL of Christianity.

Halloween The eve of All Saints' Day on October 31, which used to be called Samhain Eve in the Celtic calendar. The Celts believed that the dead walked the Earth on that night, and could only be placated by gifts of food from the living. The Christian Church incorporated Samhain into its own calendar by calling it All Saints' Day, but pre-Christian beliefs remained, and the living dead were joined by witches and demons. In some Western countries Halloween has since become the night of 'trick or treat', when children in fancy dress go from door to door demanding gifts.

Harpies Vicious monsters in Greek mythology, often depicted as birds of prey with women's faces and breasts. In the story of JASON, the Harpies were sent by the gods to punish the blind King Phineus, by stealing his food at every meal.

❖ Figuratively, a harpy is a fierce, grasping hag or a merciless sponger.

Hector A prince of Troy in Greek mythology – eldest son of Priam, and the bravest of the Trojan warriors. At the end of the TROJAN WAR, Achilles killed Hector, tied him to his chariot and dragged him over the battlefield.

Helen of Troy In Greek mythology, the most beautiful woman in the world. She was daughter of the mortal Leda and the god Zeus. She married Menelaus, king of Sparta, and her abduction by Paris led to the TROJAN WAR. The playwright Christopher ▷MARLOWE described Helen's face as 'the face that launch'd a thousand ships', referring to the fact that the entire Greek army sailed to Troy to recover her.

Hephaestus (heh-FYE-stus) (Roman name Vulcan) Greek god of fire and blacksmith of the gods. He was lamed by being flung out of OLYMPUS after interfering in a quarrel between his parents Hera and Zeus. According to some stories, Hephaestus was married to APHRODITE, in others to one of the three GRACES. According to the account in Homer's ▷ODYSSEY, when Aphrodite was unfaithful, Hephaestus trapped her and her lover Ares in an invisible net, and the gods came to laugh at them.

Hera (Roman name Juno) Greek goddess who protected women and marriage, and was the wife of Zeus. Hera is best known for her jealousy and animosity towards the many mortal women with whom her husband fell in love.

Hercules (Greek name Heracles) One of the greatest heroes of Classical mythology – a son of ZEUS and supposedly the strongest man on Earth. To atone for slaughtering his family in a fit of madness – inflicted on him by Hera – he was set 12 seemingly impossible tasks by Eurystheus, the ruler of Tiryns. Called the Labours of Hercules, the 12 tasks were: to kill the Nemean Lion; to kill the many-headed HYDRA; to catch the Arcadian stag; to kill the Erymanthian boar; to clean the Augean stables; to kill the vicious flock of Stymphalian birds; to catch the Cretan bull given to Minos by POSEIDON; to round up the man-eating horses of Thrace; to seize the girdle of the queen of the AMAZONS; to catch the cattle of the monster Geryon; to obtain the golden apples of the Hesperides nymphs; and to fetch the three-headed dog Cerberus who guarded the entrance to HADES. After successfully completing his labours and surviving many other adventures, Hercules was rewarded with immortality.

❖ Any extraordinary effort or task can be described as 'herculean'.

Hermes (Roman name Mercury) Messenger of the gods who flew with great speed aided by the wings he wore on his sandals and cap. He was a son of Zeus and the father of Pan.

❖ The wand of Hermes – a caduceus – is the symbol of physicians, with wings at the top and serpents twined about the staff.

Holy Grail Sacred cup said to have been used by Jesus at the Last Supper. It became an object of quest for the knights of the ROUND TABLE, including Sir GALAHAD and PARSIFAL. In one story, it was kept in the Grail castle of the crippled FISHER KING. According to legend, the Grail is said to rest beneath the spring on Glastonbury Tor.

❖ A grail can be any esteemed object which people strive at length to attain.

Hydra In Greek mythology, a many-headed water snake that lived in the marshy plain of Lerna in new Argos. As one of his 12 Labours, HERCULES was sent to kill the Hydra, but as soon as he cut off one of its heads two grew in its place. His charioteer had to help by burning the roots of each head.

Icarus Son of DAEDALUS in Greek mythology, who melted the wax of his wings by flying too near the Sun.

Jason Greek hero and leader of the ARGONAUTS. Jason was heir to a kingdom in Greece, but his uncle Pelias had seized the throne and would only let it go in return for the magical GOLDEN FLEECE at Colchis. Jason set sail and obtained the fleece with the help of Medea – a Colchian princess as well as a sorceress – who fell in love with him. Medea helped Jason to escape from her father, the king, by killing and cutting up her brother and throwing his body into the sea. While the distraught king was gathering up the remains of his son for burial, Jason and Medea fled. The couple returned to Greece and successfully toppled the usurper, King Pelias. They married and raised a family, but Jason later decided to divorce Medea and marry another princess. Enraged, Medea killed their children and the princess. Jason was crushed to death when the stern of his ship, the *Argo*, fell on him.

Juno Roman goddess who is usually associated with HERA.

Jupiter Roman name of ZEUS.

Kronos In Greek mythology, chief of the TITANS – the gods who were children of Heaven and Earth, and who ruled before the Olympians. Because Heaven kept his offspring imprisoned within the body of Earth, who groaned with the burden, Kronos castrated his father with a sickle to separate Heaven from Earth and free himself and his siblings. Kronos married his sister Rhea, who had six children: Hestia, DEMETER, HADES, HERA, POSEIDON and ZEUS. Because of a prophecy that one of his children would overthrow him, Kronos tried to swallow them as they were born. They survived, however, and his son Zeus eventually dethroned him and became chief of the gods. The Romans identified Kronos with their god SATURN.

Kruger millions Fortune in gold rumoured to have been in the possession of Transvaal president Paul ▷KRUGER on his retreat from Pretoria to Lourenço Marques (now Maputo). The legend that he had buried it somewhere in the Transvaal originated at the end of the South African War, and persists despite more than 50 unsuccessful expeditions to find it. Supreme Court documents relating to the Kruger estate and accounts in the Transvaal Archives discount the possibility that the 'Kruger millions' could have come from the pockets of either Kruger or his government.

Labyrinth Vast maze which, according to Greek mythology, was built at Knossos by the craftsman DAEDALUS, on the orders of King Minos of Crete, to hide the monstrous MINOTAUR. The Athenean hero Theseus killed the Minotaur, and used a thread which he played out to retrace his route out of the maze. Daedalus escaped from the labyrinth with his son Icarus by making artificial wings and flying over the walls.

❖ Figuratively, a labyrinth can be any intricate construction or problem.

Lancelot, Sir Greatest and most tragic of the heroes of the knights of the ROUND TABLE. Lancelot was torn between his loyalty to King Arthur and his love for Arthur's wife, Queen Guinevere. When their affair was openly denounced it led to civil war, and Arthur was fatally wounded at the Battle of Camlann. Heavy with grief, Lancelot became a hermit and eventually died of a broken heart.

❖ Lancelot is a prominent character in Malory's *Le* ▷MORTE D'ARTHUR, where the knight's tragic love for his queen prevents him finding the HOLY GRAIL.

Leda and the swan Story from Greek mythology about the rape of Leda, a queen of Sparta, by Zeus, who had taken the form of a swan. As a result of the rape, HELEN OF TROY hatched from a white egg.

❖ The rape of Leda has often been portrayed in art, and W B ▷YEATS wrote a poem entitled *Leda and the Swan*.

leprechauns Fairy shoemakers of Irish folklore who resemble elves and bury hoards of gold. If caught, a leprechaun can be forced to reveal his hidden treasure.

Loch Ness Monster Large aquatic creature, nicknamed Nessie, said to live in Scotland's Loch Ness. The first sighting was made in AD 565 by St Columba, but only after a newspaper article in 1933 did the creature become world famous. In 1934, a London gynaecologist, R K Wilson, supposedly took a photograph of Nessie's swanlike neck, which resembled that of an extinct marine reptile known as a plesiosaur. This has since been exposed as an elaborate hoax mounted by Marmaduke Wetherell, a film producer and big game hunter. Large, unidentified shapes in the lake have been picked up on sonar

MONSTER HOAX *The 'surgeon's photograph' of the Loch Ness Monster fooled experts for 60 years until it was revealed in 1994 that the serpentlike neck was a plastic model of a toy submarine.*

equipment, but there is still no undisputed proof of Nessie's existence.

mandrake Narcotic plant with purple flowers from the family *Solanaceae*, once used as an anaesthetic and as an aphrodisiac. Dogs were often used to uproot the plant because the long, forked root was said to embody a demon, and pulling it from the ground would make the demon shriek so horribly that anyone hearing it would die.

Mars Roman name for the Greek god Ares, the god of war, farmers and herdsmen. He was the son of ZEUS and HERA, and the lover of the beautiful APHRODITE.

❖ The fourth planet from the Sun is named Mars, probably because of its reddish tinge.

May Day Festival of rebirth and renewal once held on the first day of May throughout Europe. May Day has its origins in the Celtic festival of Beltane, when the return of summer was celebrated.

Medea Sorceress who fell in love with JASON and used magic to help him and the Argonauts obtain the Golden Fleece.

Medusa In Greek mythology, the best known of three GORGONS whose gaze turned people to stone. The hero PERSEUS killed her with the aid of Athena. While fighting Medusa, he avoided her stare by looking only at her reflection in his polished shield. From the blood of the slain Medusa sprang the winged horse PEGASUS.

DUGONG AHOY *The source of the legends of mermaids may be sailors' accounts of marine mammals called dugongs or sea cows.*

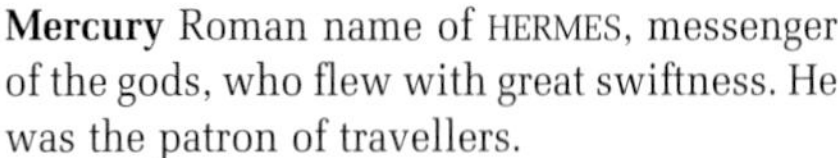

Mercury Roman name of HERMES, messenger of the gods, who flew with great swiftness. He was the patron of travellers.

❖ The planet nearest the Sun is named Mercury because of its swift motion.

Merlin Wizard who acted as adviser to King ARTHUR, said to have been fathered by a demon. He may have been founded upon a real-life Celtic bard and seer – named Myrddin – who lived in the land of the northern Welsh in the 5th or 6th century AD. There are many legends about Merlin; one tells how he used magic to transport STONEHENGE from Ireland to England.

❖ The legend of Merlin was the inspiration for T H White's *The Once and Future King*, on which the film *The Sword in the Stone* was based.

mermaid Mythical sea creature with a woman's body and a fish's tail. Mermaid legends are very old, and are remarkably similar whatever their country of origin. Mermaids are seductive SIRENS, personifying the beauty and treachery of the sea. They are said to lull sailors to sleep with their sweet singing and then carry them away beneath the waves. Belief in the existence of a race of merfolk was widespread among seamen until the late 19th century. To see a mermaid was considered a portent of danger and disaster.

Midas King of Phrygia in Greek mythology, who was granted one wish by the god Dionysus – that everything he touched would turn to gold. He regretted his request when his food became inedible metal and he turned his daughter into a golden statue. On the instruction of Dionysus, he bathed in the river Pactolus to rid himself of his golden touch.

❖ A person who easily acquires riches is sometimes said to have the 'Midas touch'.

Midsummer Eve Night of 23 June when in Celtic times in the Northern Hemisphere great sacrificial bonfires were lit in honour of the Sun. Even in recent centuries, rural folk lit bonfires and men and beasts passed through the embers to ward off disease and bad luck. It was also a time when witches and evil creatures were believed to be active, and when girls practised simple magic to discover the identity of their future husbands.

Minerva Roman name of ATHENA, goddess of war, wisdom and the arts.

Minotaur Monster in Greek mythology with a human body and a bull's head. It was born to Pasiphae, the queen of Crete, after she mated with a sacred bull. King Minos ordered DAEDALUS to construct the LABYRINTH in which to keep the monster, and every year seven young men and seven maidens were sent from Athens to be its prey. To stop the slaughter, the Athenean hero Theseus volunteered to fight the Minotaur. As he went through the maze he unwound a ball of thread and, after killing the Minotaur, used the thread to find his way out.

Monomotapa European name for the precolonial empire of Mwene Mutapa, reputed to be as rich and prosperous as the legendary ELDORADO. The Monomotapa legends were based on a real kingdom in the south of Zimbabwe, which boasted argricultural achievements, had a flourishing mining industry in copper, gold and iron, and built unique stone walls around their settlements, the largest of which was ▷GREAT ZIMBABWE. The Portuguese exploitation of the gold of the region hastened the disintegration of the empire in the 15th century. Mwene Mutapa means 'master of the plundered lands'.
❖ Modjadji, the rain goddess and queen of the Lobedu people in Northern Province, is said to have descended from royal refugees of the Mwene Mutapa empire who fled south with the rain 'medicine'.

Morpheus God of sleep and dreams in Greek and Roman mythology.
❖ Someone who is 'in the arms of Morpheus' is asleep.
❖ The narcotic morphine was named after the god Morpheus.

Muses Nine goddesses in Greek mythology, all daughters of Zeus. Each Muse presided over a different art or science: Calliope (epic poetry), Clio (history), Erato (love poetry), Euterpe (lyric poetry), Melpomene (tragedy), Polyhymnia (hymns), Terpsichore (dance), Thalia (comedy), and Urania (astronomy).
❖ To this day, writers, artists and musicians often speak of their muse as a source of inspiration. By analogy, a muse can also be a real person, such as Beatrice Portinari, who inspired the Italian poet ▷DANTE.

Narcissus Beautiful youth in Greek mythology who fell in love with his own reflection. Because he was unable to tear himself away from the image, he wasted away and turned into the narcissus flower.
❖ In psychology narcissism is the excessive admiration of oneself.

Nemesis Greek goddess of retribution who punished the wicked as well as anyone she deemed to be too fortunate.
❖ Anything that brings about a person's downfall is described as their nemesis.

FABLED KINGDOM *The kingdom of 'Monomotapa' appears on an 18th-century map of Africa. Both the position of the region and the wealth of its gold deposits were miscalculated.*

Neptune Roman god of fresh water, who became a sea god when the Romans identified him with the Greek god Poseidon. He is portrayed as a bearded giant, holding a three-pronged spear, or trident.
❖ The planet Neptune, cold and dimly lit, is the eighth planet from the Sun.

Norse mythology The mythology of Scandinavia, which also became widespread in Germany and Britain until the establishment of Christianity. People and places in Norse mythology include: BRÜNNHILDE, ODIN, THOR, TROLLS, Valhalla and the VALKYRIES.

Nostradamus (1503-66) Latinised name of Michel de Nôtredam, a French astrologer and physician who wrote a strange collection of obscure rhymed prophecies. The first edition was published in 1555, and the ambiguity of the verses has fired the imaginations of Nostradamus enthusiasts ever since. In recent times his followers have credited Nostradamus with foretelling the outbreak of World War II, as well as many other significant events.

nymphs Young and beautiful female spirits of nature in Classical mythology who lived in forests, caves, seas, rivers and springs. They liked dancing and music, and were companions of the SATYRS.
❖ Any young, beautiful or seductive woman may be referred to as a nymph.

Odin Father and leader of the gods in NORSE MYTHOLOGY. Odin sacrificed one of his eyes to obtain wisdom, hung himself upon the World Tree (the tree of life and knowledge), and acquired a magic drink called the Mead of Inspiration, in order to bestow the gifts of wisdom and poetry upon humanity. He was the god of battle and of the dead. His messengers, the VALKYRIES, were responsible for escorting the souls of heroic slain warriors to his realm of Valhalla, where there was eternal joy and feasting.
❖ Wednesday is named after Odin's Germanic name, Woden.

Odysseus (oh-DISS-ee-uhs) (Roman name Ulysses) King of Ithaca and a Greek leader in the TROJAN WAR. He helped bring about the fall of Troy by conceiving the ruse of the TROJAN HORSE. He is also the central character of the ▷ODYSSEY, in which the Greek epic poet Homer recounts the adventures of Odysseus involving CIRCE, the CYCLOPES, SCYLLA AND CHARYBDIS, and the SIRENS. Odysseus returned home after an absence of 20 years, and killed the suitors who were pressing his wife PENELOPE to marry again. The character of Odysseus may have been based on a real

ENCHANTING SEAS *A Greek vase from the 5th century BC shows how Odysseus was lashed to the mast of his ship, so that he could listen to the song of the sirens without falling under their spell.*

chieftain around whom legends gathered.
❖ The novel ▷ULYSSES by James Joyce is based on the legend of Odysseus.

Oedipus (EE-di-puhs) Tragic king in Greek mythology who unknowingly killed his father and married his mother. Warned by APOLLO that his son would kill him, King Laius of Thebes left his newborn son on a mountainside, but the infant was found and raised by the king and queen of Corinth. Ignorant of his true ancestry, Oedipus left Corinth when the Delphic ORACLE predicted that he would kill his father and marry his mother. He killed Laius in a chance encounter on the way to Thebes and also vanquished a SPHINX that had been troubling the city, and was made the new king of Thebes. Oedipus married his mother Jocasta, not knowing her true identity; when he learned the truth he blinded himself and Jocasta hanged herself.
❖ In psychology, an ▷OEDIPUS COMPLEX is a boy's sexual desire for his mother.

Olympus, Mount Legendary home of the gods, and an actual mountain in Greece on the borders of Thessaly and Macedonia. The Greek gods were known as Olympians.

oracle Greek shrine at which a deity was consulted about the future. An oracle was also the priest through whom the prophecy was given, as well as the prophecy itself. The Delphic Oracle was the most influential, the shrine at which APOLLO answered questions about the future. The Temple of Apollo at Delphi was built over a volcanic chasm on Mount PARNASSUS, where a priestess inhaled the sulphurous fumes, entered into a trance and acted as the medium for Apollo's prophetic messages. These messages were so ambiguous that a priest had to interpret them.

Orpheus and Eurydice (yoo-RID-i-see) Orpheus was a great poet and musician in Greek mythology, and Eurydice was his wife. Orpheus sang so beautifully to the accompaniment of his lyre that he attracted wild animals, trees and even stones. When Eurydice was killed by a snake, Orpheus went to the underworld and begged HADES to let Eurydice return to Earth. Hades agreed on one condition – that Orpheus should go on ahead of her and not look back until they had reached the Earth again. Orpheus could not resist looking, and so he lost her for ever.

Pan Shepherd god of the Greek countryside who had the legs, ears and horns of a goat, and was the son of Hermes. He wandered through woodland glades playing his reed panpipes and was believed to be the source of frightening noises in the wilderness at night, which could cause fear among herds and men – the origin of the word *panic.*

Pandora In Greek mythology, the first mortal woman, created by HEPHAESTUS. To punish humanity for PROMETHEUS's theft of fire, Zeus sent Pandora to Earth with a box containing a few blessings, but many more evils, such as war and sickness. When she opened the box the evils flew out, to plague humanity; only hope remained.
❖ The phrase 'a Pandora's box' means any source of great suffering or trouble, often unsuspected at first.

Paris In Greek mythology, the son of Priam, king of Troy, whose actions led to the TROJAN WAR. When the goddess Discord threw the Apple of Discord marked 'For the Fairest' among the gods, it was claimed by Aphrodite, Athena and Hera. Zeus asked Paris to decide which goddess was the most beautiful and each of them tried to bribe him: Athena with military power, Hera with political power, and Aphrodite with the most beautiful woman in the world. In the Judgment of Paris, he gave the apple to Aphrodite, who as his reward led him to HELEN OF TROY. She was already the wife of the Greek king of Sparta, but Paris abducted her. The Greeks, helped by the slighted Hera and Athena, waged war on Troy to recover Helen. After Achilles killed Paris's brother Hector, Paris killed Achilles by piercing his heel with an arrow.

Parnassus Mountain in Greece, north of the Gulf of Corinth. One of its peaks was revered as the abode of APOLLO and the MUSES, while the other belonged to Bacchus. The Delphic Oracle lived on its south side. Because of its link with the Muses, Parnassus is known as the mythological home of poetry and music.

Parsifal A simple country boy who became a knight in King ARTHUR's court. When he left home his mentor Gurnemanz instructed him never to ask any questions. He searched for the castle of the wounded FISHER KING where the HOLY GRAIL was kept, and when he found it, obediently refrained from asking the Fisher King why he was ill. This question would have healed the Fisher King, and Parsifal would have become his successor as the new Grail King. Only after many years did Parsifal return to the castle to ask the vital question.

Pegasus Winged horse in Greek mythology, that sprang from the blood of the dying MEDUSA. The hero Bellerophon mounted Pegasus and tried to fly to heaven, but was thrown off. Pegasus created Hippocrene, the fountain of the MUSES, when he struck his hoof on Mount Helicon.
❖ Pegasus is the logo of Reader's Digest.

Penelope Wife of ODYSSEUS in Greek mythology. Penelope remained true to her husband while he was away fighting in the TROJAN WAR, even though she was harassed by suitors pressing her to remarry. To stall for time, she promised to choose someone after she had finished the weaving of a robe for her father-in-law, but she unravelled her work every night. When her trick was discovered, she agreed to give herself to whoever could bend Odysseus's mighty bow – a bow which only he could string. When a man she did not recognize managed the task, Penelope knew that her husband had returned, in disguise.

Perseus Greek hero and a son of Zeus, who killed the Gorgon MEDUSA. Anyone who looked at a Gorgon was turned to stone, but Hermes and Athena helped Perseus by giving him winged shoes, a magical sword, and a polished shield. He swooped down on Medusa from the air and used the shield as a mirror so that he could cut off her head without looking at it directly.

phoenix A mythical bird that lived in Arabia and burned itself to death every 500 years. The roots of this story first appeared in Greek literature, in an account of Egypt given by ▷HERODOTUS around 430 BC. When the phoenix was nearing death, it built a nest of sweet spices and sang while the sun ignited it. A worm arose from the ashes and grew into the new phoenix.

❖ A phoenix can also be a person or thing that has been restored to a new existence from destruction, downfall or ruin.

Pied Piper of Hamelin German folk tale from the Middle Ages about a town that was infested with rats until a mysterious piper lured them into a river with his music. When the townspeople refused to pay the piper his fee, he used his strange music to lure their children away. The legend may be based on a folk memory of a medieval epidemic of ergotism, caused by a hallucinogenic fungus that grows on grain, which apparently caused crowds of people to dance from town to town until they were exhausted. However, a more likely basis for the legend is the children's ▷CRUSADE of the 13th century.

Pluto Roman name of HADES, god of the underworld and ruler of the dead.

❖ The planet Pluto is the ninth and normally the farthest known true planet from the Sun. However, because of its elliptical orbit, Pluto will be closer to the Sun than Neptune until the year 2000.

poltergeist Mischievous household spirit that manifests itself by moving objects and making noises, named from the German *polter* meaning noise, and *geist* meaning spirit. In many cases a particular person is said to be the focus of the disturbances, often an adolescent with emotional troubles. Some parapsychologists believe that the disturbances may be caused by an involuntary form of psychokinesis – the supposed ability to move objects using psychic powers.

Poseidon Greek name for NEPTUNE, the god of the sea. Poseidon could command the waves, provoke storms and cause springs to flow. He was the brother of Zeus, Hades and Hera.

SHADOW DANCE *A sinister figure sets the pace on the cover of this 1934 edition of the Robert Browning poem 'The Pied Piper of Hamelin'.*

Prester John Legendary Christian monarch of the Middle Ages, believed to rule a kingdom in central Asia. His name means 'Priest John', and he is thought to be descended from the Magi. In the Middle Ages many journeys were made to try to find his country in the hope that he would help Europe's kings to fight against Islam. From the mid-14th century the search was focused on Ethiopia, a Christian country cut off from Europe.

Priam Aged king of TROY at the time of the TROJAN WAR. He was the father of 50 children, including Cassandra, Hector and Paris. When the Greeks sacked the city, Priam was killed by Neoptolemus, son of Achilles.

Prometheus One of the TITANS in Greek mythology. When Zeus denied people the use of fire, Prometheus stole fire from HEPHAESTUS and brought it to Earth to save humanity. Zeus punished humanity by sending PANDORA to Earth with a box of evils. He also ordered Prometheus to be chained to a rock while an eagle preyed upon his liver. Every day his liver grew back and was eaten again by the eagle. Prometheus was eventually rescued by HERCULES.

❖ ▷AESCHYLUS wrote a play called *Prometheus Bound*, and ▷SHELLEY wrote a long poem entitled *Prometheus Unbound*.

❖ Prometheus has become a symbol of lonely and valiant resistance to authority.

Psyche Beautiful girl in Roman mythology. Venus was so jealous of her beauty that she ordered her son Cupid to make Psyche fall in love with someone ugly. But Cupid himself fell in love with Psyche; he visited her every night in the dark and ordered her never to try to see him. One night Psyche lit a lamp to look at Cupid while he was asleep, but he awoke and fled. While Psyche searched for him, Venus treated her cruelly and set her many harsh tasks. Eventually Jupiter made Psyche immortal, and she and Cupid were married.

Pygmalion Legendary king of Cyprus who fell in love with a statue he had made of his ideal woman. APHRODITE brought it to life so that he could marry her. George Bernard Shaw's play ▷PYGMALION adapts this theme.

Robin Hood Folk hero of English ballads, who stole from the rich and gave to the poor. His 'merry men' included Friar Tuck and Little John; his sweetheart was Maid Marian. The first known literary reference to Robin is in William Langland's *The Vision of Piers Plowman* (1377), in which a chaplain boasts that he can recite ballads about 'Robyn Hode' – ballads with which he expected his audience to be familiar. The first collection of such ballads was published at the end of the 15th century and titled *A Lytell Geste of Robyn Hode*. The legends of Robin Hood vary, but they all stress his skill as an archer. Some say that he was born Robert Fitz-Ooth, Earl of Huntingdon, in Locksley, Nottinghamshire, in 1160. He was outlawed for some unknown offence, and his haunts were said to be Sherwood Forest in Nottinghamshire and Barnsdale Forest in Yorkshire. There is no firm evidence that Robin existed; he may have been an idealized figure created by the peasants.

❖ Robin Hood's grave is said to be in the park of Kirklees Hall, Yorkshire. Legend has it that Robin was killed by a prioress when he sought refuge at a nunnery.

Romulus and Remus Twin brothers in Roman legend and founders of the city of Rome. They were sons of the god Mars and a VESTAL VIRGIN called Rhea Sylvia. Because Rhea had been violated by Mars, her sons were set adrift in a boat and left to die. They drifted ashore and were suckled by a she-wolf. Romulus killed Remus in a quarrel over the site for the city of Rome. Romulus ruled for 40 years, then vanished in a storm and became a god.

Round Table, Knights of the Fellowship of the knights of King ARTHUR, who included Sir GALAHAD, Sir GAWAIN, Sir LANCELOT and

CHRISTMAS HAMPER *A card from the early 1900s shows a jovial Santa. A generous saint has become a symbol of Christmas.*

PARSIFAL. Among their adventures was the quest for the HOLY GRAIL. The Round Table was first described in 1155 by the poet Robert Wace, who held that Arthur devised the table to promote equality among the knights.
❖ A table said to be the Round Table hangs in the Castle Hall in Winchester in southern England, but this dates from only the 13th century.

St George Saint of the Christian Church, who may have been a high-ranking officer in the army of the Roman Empire in Asia Minor in about AD 300. In early Christian belief, the legendary slaying by St George of a DRAGON symbolized the triumph of Jesus Christ over the Devil.
❖ St George is the patron saint of England and Portugal. It seems likely that Edward III made him patron saint when he founded the Order of the Garter in St George's name in the mid-14th century.

Santa Claus Legendary character based on St Nicholas – patron saint of children – whose gifts of gold to poor children led to the European custom of exchanging presents on 5 December, the eve of his feast day. Early Dutch settlers in America took this custom with them; Santa Claus is an American corruption of *Sinter Klaes*, the Dutch form of St Nicholas. The old custom is still maintained in Germany and the Netherlands, but elsewhere Santa Claus has become a central figure in Christmas celebrations. By the 1890s, the English Father Christmas, originally a character in village folk plays, had become firmly linked to Santa Claus, and now the two figures are thought of as being one and the same.
❖ The first association of a reindeer with St Nicholas was in 1821 in an American publication called *The Children's Friend*.

Saturn Roman god of agriculture, identified with the Greek Titan called KRONOS. He established a Golden Age, in which all people were equal and harvests were plentiful. Saturn's festival – the Roman Saturnalia – took place in December and was a time of merrymaking and debauchery.
❖ Saturday is named after Saturn, and the sixth planet from the Sun bears his name.

satyrs Forest gods or demons in Greek mythology who were part-human and part-goat, with horns, pointed ears and the tail of a horse. They were called fauns by the Romans. Satyrs were pleasure-loving, fond of wine and joined in wild dances with the NYMPHS. They were companions of Dionysus, the god of wine and revelry.

Scylla and Charybdis (SILL-er; ka-RIB-dis) In Greek mythology, Scylla was a six-headed sea monster who lived on a rock on one side of a narrow strait, while Charybdis was a whirlpool on the other side. When ships passed close to Scylla's rock to avoid Charybdis, she would seize and devour their sailors.
❖ Someone 'caught between Scylla and Charybdis' is forced to choose between two equally unpleasant options.

sirens Evil sea nymphs in Greek mythology who, by their sweet singing, lured sailors to destruction on the rocks surrounding their island. When ODYSSEUS encountered the sirens, he ordered his crew to plug their ears with wax and to bind him to the mast of his ship, so that he could listen to their song without peril.
❖ A siren is a dangerous or alluring woman; a 'siren song' is an irresistible distraction.

Sisyphus In Greek mythology, king of Corinth. He offended Zeus, the chief of the gods, who condemned him to push a huge boulder up a steep hill eternally.

Sphinx Monster of Greek and Egyptian mythology. In Greek mythology, the Sphinx had the head and breasts of a woman, the body of a lion, and the wings of a bird. In the story of OEDIPUS it waylaid travellers on the roads near the city of Thebes, carrying away and devouring anyone who could not answer its riddle: 'What creatures walk on four legs in the morning, on two legs at noon, and on three legs in the evening?' Oedipus finally gave the correct answer: human beings, who crawl on all fours as infants, walk upright in maturity, and use a walking stick in old age. The Egyptian sphinx was usually portrayed as a lion with a pharaoh's head, like the huge stone statue at Giza in Egypt.

Stonehenge Great circle of stones standing on England's Salisbury Plain, and the focus of several romantic legends. The 12th-century chronicler Geoffrey of Monmouth wrote that the massive stones were brought from Africa to Ireland by a race of giants, then moved to Wiltshire in the 6th century by the wizard MERLIN. The 17th-century antiquary John Aubrey suggested that the DRUIDS built Stonehenge as a temple. Although the Druids may have used Stonehenge for ceremonies, archaeology shows that it was built some 1 200 years before the Druids had established themselves in Britain. Stonehenge was constructed in three stages by many generations of prehistoric people between about 3000 and 1550 BC, using bluestones from the Prescelly Mountains in southwest Wales and sarsen stones from the Marlborough Downs. Set in upright pairs and arranged in concentric circles, some pairs were topped by lintels. Opinion differs as to whether Stonehenge served as a temple, a royal palace, or an observatory – used to study the Sun and Moon, predict eclipses and create a seasonal calendar for harvests and festivals.

Styx In Greek mythology, the river that flowed seven times around the underworld of HADES, and across which Charon ferried the souls of the dead. Its waters were thought to be poisonous.

Tantalus King in Greek mythology who offended the gods by divulging their secrets to mortals. They punished him with everlasting thirst and hunger. He stood up to his chin in a river in HADES, but each time he bent to quench his thirst the water receded. Similarly the boughs above him, heavy with fruit, were always just out of reach.
❖ The ordeal of Tantalus is the origin of the word 'tantalize', meaning to tease or torment by exciting a hope and then disappointing it, or to keep out of reach something that is much desired.

Tarot cards Elaborately decorated cards of unknown origin that are used for fortune-telling or DIVINATION. There are 78 cards in the pack – 56 divided into four suits and 22 trump cards with symbolic pictures. There is no standard design for Tarot symbols, and there are many ways of interpreting them.

Tell, William Legendary 14th-century hero of Switzerland, famous for his skill as an archer. Because he refused to salute Gessler, the steward of a tyrannical Austrian ruler, Tell was sentenced to shoot with his crossbow and arrow an apple resting on his son's head. After accomplishing this, Tell killed Gessler and led an uprising that established the independence of Switzerland. The first written account of the legend dates from 1474.

Theseus Legendary hero of Athens who killed the MINOTAUR.

Thor God of thunder and lightning in NORSE MYTHOLOGY who had three magic weapons: a hammer which returned to him after it was thrown, iron gloves which helped him to throw the hammer, and a belt which increased his size and strength.
❖ Thursday is named after Thor.

Titans Greek gods of enormous size and strength who were the children of Heaven and Earth. The youngest Titan, KRONOS, overthrew his father and became king of the gods, until he in turn was overthrown by his own son ZEUS. Other Titans included ATLAS and PROMETHEUS.
❖ The terms titan and titanic are used to describe a powerful person or thing.

Tristan and Iseult (Iz-OOLT) Two tragic lovers in the medieval legends of England, Ireland and Germany (where Iseult is called Isolde). After being wounded by a poisoned spear, Tristan was nursed back to health by Iseult the Fair – the king of Ireland's beautiful daughter. Tristan brought her back to England to be the bride of his uncle, King Mark of Cornwall, but on the journey home, the two accidentally drank a love potion which had been prepared for Mark and Iseult on their wedding night. They fell deeply in love, and although Iseult married King Mark, the lovers were discovered and fled into the forest where they lived happily for four years, until Iseult decided to return to Mark, who banished Tristan. Many years later, Tristan was wounded in battle and sent for Iseult to heal him – telling his messenger to hoist a white sail on the returning ship if Iseult was on board, a black sail if not. As the ship approached, Tristan's jealous wife lied and told him it had a black sail, whereupon Tristan died of grief. Iseult, on hearing the news, died soon afterwards.

Trojan horse In Greek mythology, a large, hollow horse made from wood and used by the Greeks to win the TROJAN WAR. Greek soldiers hid inside the horse, which was left outside the gates of Troy, masquerading as a harmless offering to the gods. The Trojans ignored a priest called Laocoon, who warned against bringing the horse into the city, saying that he was 'wary of Greeks even when they are bringing gifts'. The soldiers emerged at night to open the city gates to their awaiting army.

Trojan War Great war fought between the Greeks and the Trojans, the story of which is told in Homer's ▷ILIAD. According to the legend, the ten-year siege of Troy was brought on by an incident known as the Judgment of PARIS, which led to HELEN – the beautiful wife of a Greek king – being abducted by Paris, a Trojan prince. The Greeks sailed to Troy to recover her, under the leadership of their legendary king AGAMEMNON. Their greatest warrior, ACHILLES, killed the Trojan warrior HECTOR. The Greeks achieved a final victory through the device of the TROJAN HORSE and burned Troy to the ground. The *Iliad* was not based purely on legend and imagination; an actual war did take place around 1200 BC, 400 years before the poem was written.

TAROT SPREAD *A selection of Tarot cards depicting the Knight of Wands, Death, The Magician, The Sun and the Four of Pentacles. The four suits of Swords, Cups, Wands and Pentacles tell of everyday issues concerning conflicts, emotions and prosperity. The symbolic trump cards contain a wealth of occult lore.*

trolls In NORSE MYTHOLOGY, mischievous dwarfs or giant ogres who lived in caves and mountains. They were skilled at working metals and notorious for stealing.

Troy Ancient city inhabited by the Trojans, and site of the TROJAN WAR. Troy was believed to be a mythical city until the 19th-century German archaeologist Heinrich Schliemann used clues from Homer's epic poem, the ▷ILIAD, to find the lost city. Its Roman name was Ilium and its ruins can still be seen in the western part of Turkey.

UFOs Abbreviation for 'Unidentified Flying Objects' – a modern phenomenon that was first reported in 1947 when Kenneth Arnold in the American state of Washington saw from his private aircraft some silvery disc-like objects. He described them as looking like 'pie plates'. The term 'flying saucers' was coined in headlines the next day, and hundreds of sightings poured in from around the world. Some people thought that UFOs were interplanetary space vehicles and that the world's governments were involved in a cover-up; 'men in black' were said to turn up after sightings to intimidate witnesses and destroy evidence. Most scientists still dismiss UFOs as illusions caused by natural phenomena.

Ulysses Roman name of the Greek hero ODYSSEUS, king of Ithaca.

unicorn Mythical and heraldic animal resembling a small white horse with one spiralled horn growing out of its forehead. According to medieval writing, the horn represented the Gospel of Truth. The unicorn was an untameable beast that could only be captured by a young virgin. It supports the British royal coat of arms, along with its traditional enemy, the lion.
❖ The source of the unicorn legends may be unusual whales called narwhals; the male of the species has a single spiralled tusk.

urban legends Modern mythology of the urban environment. The same stories, always credible and often amusing, are passed on in different variations worldwide. A typical tale is that of the hitchhiker who is given a ride in the back of a truck which has an empty coffin in it. Chilled by the wind, he decides to take a nap in the coffin. The driver picks up a second hitchhiker who settles himself near the coffin. When the hiker in the coffin wakes up and lifts the coffin lid, his fellow passenger takes fright and leaps off the moving truck – never to be seen again.

Valkyries In NORSE MYTHOLOGY, fierce battle-maids of the god ODIN. They rode into battle and selected those who were destined to die, then conducted the souls of these heroes to Valhalla, the hall of the slain.

vampires Living corpses who, according to legend, leave their coffins at night to feed on human blood. Their appearance in central European folklore in the Middle Ages may have originated when graves left empty by grave-robbers led people to believe that the dead could rise at night. The most notorious vampire is Count DRACULA.
❖ Vampire bats in South America feed on the blood of living mammals at night.

Van Hunks and the Devil The two adversaries whose legendary smoking contest is connected with the 'tablecloth' of cloud on Table Mountain at Cape Town. Jan van Hunks, a retired pirate in the early 18th century, spent his days sitting on the mountain, smoking his mixture of rum-soaked tobacco. One day a stranger challenged him to a smoking contest which lasted for days. When Van Hunks finally defeated the stranger, who turned out to be the Devil, both of them vanished in a puff of smoke. The cloud of tobacco smoke became the white cloud pouring over the mountain when the southeast wind blows, and the 1 000 m peak in that area became known as Devil's Peak. Another ending of the tale is that the contest continues throughout the summer months when the southeaster blows – in winter Van Hunks's rheumatism prevents him from climbing the mountain. There is some doubt about the origins of this legend. A similar tale of a contest, set in Holland, is told in Dante Gabriel Rossetti's poem 'The ballad of Jan van Hunks'. It is believed to be based on another story, Henkerwyssel's 'Challenge', which appears in *Tales of Chivalry*.

Venus Roman name of APHRODITE, goddess of love and beauty.
❖ The second planet from the Sun is named Venus, possibly because it is one of the most beautiful sights in the night sky.

Vestal Virgins Six maidens who tended the sacred flame of Vesta, the Roman goddess of the hearth and home.

Vulcan (Greek name Hephaestus) Roman god of metalworking and fire, and the blacksmith of the gods. His forge was believed to be the source of rumblings of volcanoes.

THE SIGNS OF THE ZODIAC

Astrologers believe that the most important clue to people's characters is in their birth sign – the sign of the Zodiac in which the Sun was rising when they were born. For a full character analysis, the exact positions of the Moon and planets at the moment of birth are also taken into account when casting a person's horoscope.

ARIES *22 Mar-20 April*; TAURUS *21 April-21 May*; GEMINI *22 May-22 June*; CANCER *23 June-23 July*

LEO *24 July-23 Aug*; VIRGO *24 Aug-23 Sept*; LIBRA *24 Sept-23 Oct*; SCORPIO *24 Oct-22 Nov*

SAGITTARIUS *23 Nov-22 Dec*; CAPRICORN *23 Dec-19 Jan*; AQUARIUS *20 Jan-19 Feb*; PISCES *20 Feb-21 Mar*

werewolves Men who, according to ancient superstition, could assume the form and characteristics of a wolf. The term lycanthropy (from the Greek *lukos* meaning wolf and *anthropos* meaning man) is used to describe both this supernatural ability and the insanity afflicting a person who imagines himself to be some kind of animal.

will-o'-the-wisps English fairies that played tricks on people crossing the marshes at night. Their lights flickered alluringly above the water, inviting wayfarers to follow them to certain death in the deep bogs. The lights were in fact caused by burning marsh gas (methane) given off by rotting vegetation.
❖ The phrase will-o'-the-wisp is used to describe any illusory human hope or aim.

witchcraft Practices of a witch. The European image of a witch is a person who practises magic and occult pursuits. While some modern authorities believe that European witchcraft was a figment of medieval imagination, others argue that it can be traced back to pagan religions. Superstitious belief in the Devil in Europe led to the torture and execution of around 200 000 people accused of witchcraft, most of them solitary old women. In Africa the witch is the embodiment of evil, and witchcraft has considerable social significance; witchcraft accusations are legitimate channels for expressing fear and jealousy, and are also commonly used to make someone a scapegoat. (See also ▷WITCHES in 'Ideas, beliefs and religion'.)

Zeus (Roman name Jupiter) Chief of the Greek gods, and father and ruler of the human race. Zeus defeated the TITANS and dethroned his father KRONOS to become ruler of the Universe. He lived on Mount OLYMPUS and ruled by power rather than righteousness. He fathered many children, both by goddesses and by mortal women, including APOLLO, HELEN OF TROY and HERCULES.

Zodiac A band of the sky along which the Sun, Moon and principal planets appear to move. In ASTROLOGY this band is divided into 12 segments, or signs of the Zodiac, which are named after constellations.

IDEAS, BELIEFS AND RELIGION

Belief in some power beyond the world we inhabit is as old as the human race. Different religions have given this belief enduring substance, and spawned a rich diversity of ritual and ceremony. While theologians debate religious truths, great philosophers attempt to understand our physical world, grappling with logic in their search for knowledge and certainty.

Abraham According to the Book of Genesis, the founder of the Hebrew nation. Around 1800 BC he settled with his wife Sarah in Canaan, where God told them they would become members of a mighty race. God tested Abraham's faith by asking him to sacrifice his son Isaac. However, as Abraham raised a knife to kill the boy, an angel appeared and told him to spare Isaac: Abraham's obedience had proved the strength of his faith.
❖ Abraham is also honoured in Islam as one of the great prophets.

absolution Forgiveness of sins when the penitent has made a full confession and truly repents. In the Roman Catholic and Orthodox churches, it is performed by an ordained priest in the sacrament of PENANCE; in the Protestant and Anglican churches it is included in the Eucharist or Holy COMMUNION.

Adam and Eve According to the Bible, the first man and woman, ancestors of all humanity. The Book of Genesis tells how God created Adam by breathing life into 'the dust of the ground', and later created Eve from Adam's rib. God intended them to live in the Garden of Eden, but they were tempted by SATAN in the form of the serpent to eat the forbidden fruit of the Tree of Knowledge of Good and Evil, and expelled. This was the Fall of Man which most Christians believe was the beginning of ORIGINAL SIN, which all humanity inherits. Muslims believe IBLIS (the DEVIL) was responsible for their disobedience.

African Independent churches Indigenous Christian churches in South Africa, formed since 1880 independently of European mission churches and white control. Now having about 5 000 denominations and eight million followers, they reflect a vast range of religious, ritual, faith-healing and prophetic expression. The main groups are the ETHIOPIAN, ZIONIST and Apostolic churches.
❖ The first significant churches were the Thembu Church, founded by Nehemiah Tile in 1884, and the Ethiopian Church of Mangena Mokone in 1892

agnosticism Claim that it is impossible to know something, particularly whether or not God exists. The word was coined by the 19th-century British philosopher Thomas Huxley from the Greek word *gnosis*, 'knowledge', and the prefix *a*, meaning 'not'.
❖ It is logically possible for an agnostic to believe in God, if he accepts that his belief is a matter of faith and not of knowledge.

Allah Muslim name for God. (See ISLAM.)

Amish North American Protestant sect which migrated from Switzerland, France and Germany in the 18th and 19th centuries. The Amish adhere strictly to the word of the Bible, and are known for their austere way of life, which uses no modern machinery, cars, phones or electric lights.

Anabaptists Radical Protestant group that arose out of the REFORMATION, and later gave rise to the BAPTIST CHURCHES. The name Anabaptist means 'rebaptizer' and refers to the sect's insistence that a convert baptized in infancy must be baptized again as an adult. The Anabaptists advocated strict adherence to the Bible, and the separation of Church and State, maintaining that true Christians should not hold government office or bear arms.

ancestor religion Traditional African belief systems include a vague belief in a supreme creator, but emphasize the role of the ancestors who take a close interest in the affairs of their descendants and have some influence over their welfare. They communicate with the living through dreams, messages passed through a PRIEST DIVINER, or omens. The ancestors must be appeased by means of sacrifices and offerings and are invoked in all important domestic rituals.

Anglican churches Churches that share a religious tradition stemming from the English REFORMATION in the 16th century. They also claim a Catholic heritage of faith and order from the ancient, undivided church. An autonomous Church of the Province of Southern Africa, established in 1870, is the major Anglican Church in the region today. It operates independently from the much smaller Church of England in South Africa.
❖ In 1986 Nobel peace prize winner Archbishop Desmond Tutu became the first black person to become primate of the Anglican Church in South Africa.

Anglican Communion Family of churches with the same doctrine as the Church of England, and accepting each other's sacraments and ministry. Every ten years, its archbishops meet at the Lambeth Conference in London.

animism Belief that spirits are active in nature and that animals, plants and even rocks have souls. Celtic religion was animistic, as are many African traditions, although in a limited way. Two important nature spirits are the Corn Goddess of the

OUTSPOKEN PRIEST *Archbishop Desmond Tutu was one of the most feared critics of the apartheid regime during the 1980s and was often scorned for supporting sanctions.*

SIMPLE LIVING *The Amish of Pennsylvania live frugally, and dress plainly and alike. Men wear black hats in winter and straw hats in summer, and a beard without a moustache.*

Zulu (*Nomkubulwana*) and the River People (*Abantubamlambo*) of the Xhosa, the former a personification of spring, the latter a symbol of spiritual life.

Antichrist In Christianity, a false messiah who will appear shortly before the end of the world. According to the First Epistle of John, he will attract followers but will eventually be vanquished by Jesus.

apocalypse Type of Jewish and Christian writing which claims to reveal secrets, especially concerning the future, and which generally gives hope to persecuted groups. The best known of these is St John's Book of Revelation in the New Testament, which prophesies the end of the world. The word comes from the Greek for 'unveiling'.
❖ Figuratively, an apocalypse is any cataclysmic event marked by violence and destruction, as in the title of the Vietnam War film *Apocalypse Now.*

Apocrypha Writings accepted by some churches, but not all, as part of the BIBLE. Roman Catholics, for example, include some 14 more books in the Old Testament than those recognized by Jews and Protestants. Various early Christian writings have also been proposed as additions to the New Testament but have not so far been accepted by any of the Christian churches.

a posteriori Statement whose truth or falsity would have to be discovered by observation – *the Earth is round*; *unicorns do not exist* – or an argument based on INDUCTIVE REASONING. By contrast, *A PRIORI* statements and arguments are independent of observation.

apostles Twelve men chosen by Jesus Christ to follow him and spread his teachings after his death. They included PETER, James, John, Thomas, Matthew and Judas Iscariot, who betrayed Jesus to the authorities. PAUL, although not one of the original 12, is often also considered an apostle because of his crucial role in the spread of Christianity among all, not only the Jews.

Apostolic succession Belief that there is an unbroken line of successive consecrations of bishops from the time of Jesus and the APOSTLES to present-day bishops of the CATHOLIC churches. The apostles founded the first churches at sites such as Alexandria, Jerusalem and Rome and these churches claimed primacy over all churches that were established afterwards. Rome later claimed authority over all the others, based on its link with St PETER, whom Roman Catholics consider to have been the first pope.

appearance and reality Since at least the 6th century BC, thinkers have puzzled about the nature of reality and how – or if – we can know it, given that every one of our five senses can deceive us. One response to the problem is IDEALISM, which claims that nothing exists except in the mind, while SCEPTICISM argues that nothing can be known for sure. The question of how we gain our knowledge of the external world is one of the major concerns of EPISTEMOLOGY.

a priori Statement that is necessarily true, requiring no verification by experience. It is true or false by virtue of the meaning of the words or the laws of logic, such as: *All kittens are cats* or *Three is greater than two*, or alternatively, any argument which is based on DEDUCTIVE REASONING.

SAINTLY THOUGHTS *Thomas Aquinas, philosopher and saint, is depicted by Fra Bartolommeo in the habit of a Dominican friar.*

Aquinas, St Thomas (*c*1225-74) Medieval philosopher and theologian who compiled a comprehensive summary of all the important ideas of his day. Aquinas was influenced by ARISTOTLE, whose theories he adapted to Christian theology, arguing that reason and faith are compatible. He is known especially for his *Summa Theologica*, a summary of theology. In 1879 his works were recognized as the basis of Catholic theology

Arianism Doctrine based on the views of Bishop Arius, a 4th-century theologian who held that Christ, although divine, is subordinate in status to God the Father, having been created by him. The Arians were persecuted by the orthodox Church, and Arianism had largely died out by the 6th century.

Aristotle (384-322 BC) Ancient Greek philosopher. He was a pupil of PLATO, but developed his ideas in a more methodical and scientific way. Aristotle devised a comprehensive system of thought embracing logic, ethics, aesthetics, metaphysics, politics and science, much of which is still studied and taught today. His method was analytical and systematic, questioning everything and always looking for the essential principles in every area of knowledge. His ideas dominated European thought at least until the ▷RENAISSANCE. (See also ▷ARISTOTLE in 'Science, space and mathematics'.)
❖ Aristotle was tutor to Alexander the Great and acquired considerable political prestige in the Greek world.

Ark of the Covenant Portable wooden chest constructed by the Israelites in the time of Moses to house the TEN COMMANDMENTS. It was thought to provide protection and divine guidance for the Jewish nation, and was sometimes taken into battle. Eventually the Ark was placed in the Temple of Jerusalem, but it is now lost.
❖ Every Jewish synagogue contains a cabinet known as an Ark, which holds the TORAH, or Jewish religious teachings, and other important writings. The scrolls are considered sacred and a symbol of divine presence.

Armageddon In the Book of Revelation of the BIBLE, the site of the final battle between good and evil, which will herald the end of the world and the DAY OF JUDGMENT, a basic belief held by both Christians and Muslims.

asceticism Spiritual discipline practised in many religions, including Christianity and Hinduism, which attempts to conquer the desires of the body so that the spirit can be freed and purified. It often involves fasting, self-inflicted pain (such as flagellation), self-imposed discomfort (such as sleeping on cold floors or not washing), and nearly always the avoidance of sex.

atheism Non-belief in, or denial of the existence of a god or gods. Reasons for atheism range from the view that the world is so full of injustice and suffering that it cannot be governed by a benevolent deity to scientific arguments that the idea of a creator does not help to explain the existence of the universe. Many Greek philosophers were atheists, although this could be dangerous; SOCRATES was forced to take poison because he argued against belief in the Grecian gods. The Roman pagans accused the early Christians of atheism, since they denied the traditional gods. Atheism was long suppressed in Christian Europe and North America.

Augustine, St (354-430) One of the most influential bishops of the early Christian Church, born in North Africa to a pagan father and a Christian mother. Augustine originally followed the Manichean religion which accorded God and Satan equal power, but converted to Christianity after a series of dramatic spiritual crises. He was a powerful thinker, and developed the doctrines of the Fall of Man, ORIGINAL SIN and predestination – which scholars have claimed still show some Manichean influence. As Bishop of Hippo, near Carthage, he became known for his vigorous defence of the teachings of the orthodox Church against the many rival beliefs of the time.

❖ Augustine described his spiritual journey in his *Confessions*, which contains the prayer, 'O Lord, give me chastity and continence . . . but not yet.'

ayatollah Learned leader and teacher among SHIAH Muslims, and the nearest Islamic equivalent to a Christian priest. In 1979 the revolution in Iran overthrew the Shah and replaced him with a religious regime, headed by the Ayatollah ▷KHOMEINI.

Ayer, Sir Alfred Jules (1910-89) English philosopher known for his book *Language, Truth and Logic* (1936) which set out the principles of LOGICAL POSITIVISM. He argued that, as METAPHYSICS is meaningless, philosophy should concentrate on criticism and analysis. He was knighted in 1970.

Baal Powerful warrior-god in the biblical land of Canaan, and a rival of the Israelite God YAHWEH (Jehovah). The first commandment given to Moses, 'thou shalt have no other gods before me', was particularly aimed at discouraging Baal-worship.

❖ The Baal cult was taken to Carthage in North Africa by the Phoenicians. Many Carthaginian names, such as Hannibal, take 'bal' as the last syllable in honour of the god.

Bahaism Religious movement that developed out of Islam in the late 19th century. It preaches the oneness of God, reconciliation among different faiths, and the unity of humanity. Prejudice of any type is strongly opposed, and social justice is stressed alongside spiritual development.

baptism (or christening) Rite or SACRAMENT that initiates a person into the Christian community. Baptism usually occurs soon after birth, although in some denominations such as the BAPTIST CHURCHES it is reserved for adult converts and involves complete bodily immersion. In the early Church it was often administered shortly before death to absolve

JESUS BAPTIZED *John baptizes Jesus in the River Jordan, as depicted by Piero della Francesca – in an Italian landscape.*

the person's sins. The first Christian emperor, Constantine, was accused by pagan enemies of choosing Christianity because baptism offered the chance to wash away the guilt of executing several members of his family.

Baptist churches Group of evangelical Protestant churches which baptize by immersion, but only those old enough to make a personal confession of faith. They adhere strictly to a literal understanding of the Bible, and each congregation governs itself, although there is a Baptist World Alliance with more than 20 million associated members.

❖ Baptist churches are strong in the USA, especially among black communities.

Bar Mitzvah Jewish ceremony marking an adolescent boy's coming of age at 13, after which he is considered a full member of the congregation. A Bat Mitzvah is performed for girls at the age of 12 in some synagogues. The words are Hebrew for 'son of the Commandment' and 'daughter of the Commandment'.

belief Opinion or point of view which is based on varying degrees of evidence. One extreme of belief is FAITH, which is not based on evidence and may even contradict the evidence. The other is KNOWLEDGE, which is often defined as justified, true belief. Religious belief generally involves strong personal and moral commitments. Belief that the sun will rise tomorrow morning, however, requires only a generalization based on reasonable expectations from past experience.

Benedict, St (*c*480-*c*547) Italian monk and founder of Christian monasticism in the West. He studied in Rome but as a young man went to live in a cave as a hermit. After three years he emerged to do good works. He soon gathered a devoted following and began to found small religious communities, culminating in the establishment of the first Benedictine monastery at Monte Cassino near Naples. His book *The Rule of St Benedict* established the basic principles of European monasticism, stressing manual labour, scholarship and teaching. In 1964 Pope Paul VI declared St Benedict patron saint of all Europe.

❖ The Benedictines became one of the most prosperous monastic orders, contrasting with the austerity of the Franciscans, who taught that monks should be poor.

Bentham, Jeremy (1748-1832) English political thinker and philosopher. He established the foundations of UTILITARIANISM, which presented the theory that society should try to provide the greatest happiness for the greatest number. Bentham's work was further developed by John Stuart MILL.

Berkeley, George (1685-1753) Irish bishop and empiricist philosopher who shocked conventional opinion by arguing that material objects exist only in our perceptions of them – in Berkeley's words 'to be is to be perceived'. To get round the problem of appearing to claim that ordinary objects stopped existing the moment no one was looking at them, he argued that God was always there to perceive them.

***Bhagavad Gita* (Song of the Lord)** Sanskrit poem, dating from around 300 BC, expressing some of the basic ideas of Hinduism, and forming part of the epic *Mahabharata*. It takes the form of a dialogue between Lord Krishna and the prince Arjuna. Krishna, in the shape of Arjuna's charioteer, describes the cycle of reincarnation and the many paths to NIRVANA or spiritual liberation.

Bible Sacred text of the Christian religion. It comprises the Old Testament, a collection of Hebrew and Aramaic scriptures written up to about the 2nd century BC, and the New Testament, written within about a century of Jesus' death. The books of the Old Testament record the history of the Jewish people and their relationship with God. The New Testament includes the four Gospels relating the life of Jesus, the Acts of the Apostles, the letters of St Paul, and the Book of Revelation. The best-known versions of the Bible include the Latin Vulgate, which is the oldest surviving translation of the complete Bible, and the English King James Bible, sometimes referred to as the 'Authorized Version'.

❖ There are also some editions with notorious misprints, such as the 'Wicked Bible' of 1631 in which the seventh commandment

BUDDHA'S WAY *The Wheel of Becoming shows the six states of existence into which Buddhists believe humans are continually reborn. Monks such as those at Mandalay seek to break free from the cycle of reincarnation by meditation – as Buddha teaches.*

was printed 'Thou shalt commit adultery'.

❖ The sacred scriptures of Judaism correspond roughly to the Old Testament of the Christian Bible and are sometimes referred to as the Hebrew Bible.

Book of Common Prayer Service book of the Church of England, introduced by its main author Thomas Cranmer in 1549. It has been revised many times, and was suppressed by the Catholic Queen Mary I (1553-8) and by English statesman Oliver Cromwell (1649-60). The English Act of Uniformity (1662) enforced its use in all Anglican churches. A modern alternative was introduced in 1980.

❖ The Church of the Province of South Africa published revised service books in 1954, 1975 and 1989, including changes required by local circumstances. The Church of England in South Africa also has its own liturgy.

Brahma One of the three central personifications of divinity in HINDUISM, the others being Shiva and Vishnu. Brahma is considered to be the creator of the cosmos.

Brahman Supreme power or eternal spirit of the universe in Hinduism, from which everything originates and to which it all, eventually, returns again.

❖ Members of the traditional priestly caste, the highest in Hindu society, are known as Brahmans or Brahmins. In everyday usage, a Brahman can also mean anyone belonging to an elite group in society.

Buddha Name meaning 'Enlightened One', applied to the Indian prince and mystic Gautama Siddhartha (*c*563-*c*483 BC), the founder of BUDDHISM. He was born in northern India in a region that is now part of Nepal, and at about 30 – after seeing the suffering of the people outside his father's palace for the first time – gave up all worldly possessions and ambitions to live a life of contemplation and spiritual devotion. He is said to have achieved ENLIGHTENMENT while sitting under a bodhi tree – or holy fig tree – after which he spent the rest of his life travelling and teaching a philosophy of compassion and spiritual insight, but rejecting ASCETICISM.

❖ Many other Buddhas are also revered in Buddhism. Mahayana Buddhism also venerates *bodhisattvas* – those who have reached enlightenment but who forgo NIRVANA and choose to continue living in the world to work for the good of all beings.

Buddhism Religion based on the teachings of Gautama Siddhartha, or the BUDDHA. It teaches that suffering is part of existence, but that spiritual liberation can be achieved through overcoming all desires. It has many similarities to Hinduism, but offers the hope of NIRVANA and freedom from the cycle of death and rebirth to all, rather than a select few. It is a peaceable religion, advocating meditation, compassion and good works. There is no worship of a supreme god. It has several branches – including Mahayana, Theravada and ZEN. There are more than 300 million Buddhists worldwide, mainly in central and Southeast Asia, Tibet and Japan.

Calvinism Christian doctrine based on the views of the 16th-century Protestant reformer John ▷CALVIN. It emphasizes obedience to God, strict adherence to the Bible, the importance of faith and the doctrine of predestination, according to which some people are born destined for salvation, the remainder for damnation. Dutch settlers of the late 17th and 18th centuries in South Africa subscribed to these beliefs, which included the concept of a 'chosen people'. This influenced white race attitudes in South Africa, and ▷AFRIKANER NATIONALISM later advocated a strong link between the church and the state. The work of Karl Barth sparked a Neo-Calvinist revival in the 20th century.

Cathars Members of a medieval Christian sect who believed that the material world was evil, and that spiritual salvation required the giving up of all physical pleasures. They included the Albigensians of southern France. They were considered heretical by the Church, and were brutally suppressed during the 13th century.

Catholic Church Shorter name for the Roman Catholic Church. The term is also sometimes used for any Church which is governed by bishops, such as the CHURCH OF ENGLAND, which combines Catholic and Protestant elements, or the Greek Orthodox Churches.

cause and effect An apparently simple idea which has caused philosophers much difficulty ever since David HUME pointed out that there is no logical connection between events and the things that are supposed to cause them. The assertion that a spark 'causes' gunpowder to explode is based merely on the fact that one event has always followed the other in the past. Immanuel KANT, however, later contended that cause and effect is a fundamental principle of human thought.

Chanukkah (or Hanukkah) Eight-day Jewish festival beginning on the 25th day of the month of Kislev, which falls in December (or sometimes November), also called the Feast of Lights or Feast of Dedication. It commemorates the rededication of the Temple of Jerusalem after the Jewish defeat of the Syrians in the 2nd century BC. A range of candles are lit in the home each day and presents are given to children.

charismatic movement See PENTECOSTAL MOVEMENT.

Christ Saviour or MESSIAH prophesied in the Old Testament. Christians believe that he was Jesus; Jews, that he has not yet appeared on Earth. Muslims do not believe in a messiah, but only in prophets, including Jesus.

Christianity Worldwide religion based on the teachings and example of JESUS CHRIST. It developed out of Judaism, retaining many of the Hebrew scriptures and beliefs, but differing in that it acknowledges Jesus as the Christ or MESSIAH and accepts the law of love and compassion that he taught. The central doctrines of Christianity are: that God is a Trinity expressed as God the Father, God the Son and God the Holy Spirit; that the path to salvation is through Jesus Christ; and that at the end of the world Jesus will return to judge both the living and the dead. After Christ's death, the religion was spread by his APOSTLES and their followers, and rapidly developed in the Roman and Greek worlds. In 315 it was declared the official religion of the Roman Empire by the Emperor ▷CONSTANTINE. After a period of decline during the Dark Ages, it revived spectacularly in later medieval times and has remained the major European religion ever since. Christianity's three principal branches are the ROMAN CATHOLIC and ORTHODOX churches and PROTESTANTISM. Although differences in doctrine have led to many splits and disputes, Christianity in its various forms is practised by more than 1 300 million people throughout the world. During the 19th century MISSIONARIES contributed to the growth of Christianity in southern Africa.
❖ The first place of Christian worship in South Africa was a small chapel erected in 1501 at Mossel Bay, where the explorer Vasco da Gama and his shipmates celebrated mass in 1498 and 1499.

Christian Science Movement devoted to spiritual healing, founded as the Church of Christ, Scientist by Mary Baker Eddy in Boston in 1879. Its basis is that sickness only seems real and that sin and disease can be healed through prayer to God. Followers generally reject orthodox medical treatment, relying on prayer instead. The Christian Science movement operates worldwide, and publishes the *Christian Science Monitor,* a daily newspaper of international repute.

Christmas Central Christian festival held on 25 December to celebrate the birth of Jesus Christ. The date was probably agreed to as a compromise with pagan cults which also had festivals around the same time, marking the winter solstice and anticipating the return of the sun. Non-Christian midwinter celebrations are still evident in traditions such as the decorated tree, the evergreen holly and ivy, feasting, partying and giving presents.
❖ Christmas is also sometimes called 'Yule', from the Old English word *geol,* a time of traditional midwinter feasting.

church Place of Christian worship, and – usually with a capital 'C' – the name for the community of Christians. From early on the Church had a hierarchy of bishops, priests and other officials and was based in areas such as the cities and provinces of the Roman Empire. The Orthodox, Roman Catholic and Anglican churches retain this basic structure, but others such as the Baptist, Congregationalist and Presbyterian churches are less hierarchical and give more power of decision to individual congregations.

Church of England The established Church in England, formed in the 16th century after Henry VIII broke away from the Roman Catholic Church and denied the authority of the pope. It combines both Catholic and Protestant elements and is headed by the British monarch as a temporal leader. Under the monarch come the archbishops of Canterbury and York, and under them 44 bishops, each of whom presides over a diocese containing a number of local parishes. The Church of England's doctrines and practices, known as Anglicanism, are very broad and encompass both 'high' and 'low' versions. High Anglicanism – or Anglo-Catholicism – is much closer to Rome and retains many rituals of Catholicism, while low Anglicanism keeps ceremony to a minimum and emphasizes the importance of scripture. The Church of England is the leading member of the worldwide ANGLICAN COMMUNION.

Communion, Holy Central SACRAMENT in the Christian religion, also known as the MASS, the Eucharist or Lord's Supper. It re-enacts the Last Supper in which Jesus blessed the bread and wine before giving them to his disciples, saying, 'This is my body; this is my blood.' Unlike Protestants, Roman Catholic and Orthodox Christians believe that by a repeated miracle 'the substance of bread and wine' actually become the body and blood of Christ (transubstantiation). Lutherans believe that Jesus is present in the Spirit but not in the flesh (consubstantiation) – and members of the REFORMED CHURCHES accept his presence in a symbolic way only.

confession Public or private admission of sin, required before PENANCE occurs and ABSOLUTION can be administered in the Roman Catholic and Orthodox churches. In the Anglican and Protestant churches, it is a regular part of the Eucharist or Holy COMMUNION.

confirmation Christian service marking the admission of the baptized to full membership of a Church. It is usually celebrated about the time of adolescence, although adult confirmation is becoming popular.

Confucianism Ancient Chinese philosophy based on the teachings of the sage Confucius (551-479 BC). It emphasizes social order and responsibility; respect for parents, elders and authorities; and the veneration of ancestors. Confucius was chief minister of the state of Lu (now Shandong Province) and was deeply concerned with ethics, piety, duty and the

SAYINGS OF THE SAGE

The Chinese sage Confucius was more concerned with the management of society than with religion. A collection of his sayings called the *Analects* includes the words of advice: 'If you would divine the future, study the past'; 'What you do not want done to yourself, do not do to others'; and 'Repay injury with justice, and kindness with kindness'.

LASTING IDEAS *Confucian thought still influences many societies, even those that are under Communist rule.*

stability of the state. In his philosophy, ethics and politics were inseparable. He sought to relieve the suffering of the poor through government reform, and drew up a code of behaviour for the honourable civil servant (or 'mandarin') which has been influential in China ever since. Religious concepts such as God and heaven were viewed by Confucius only as a way of inspiring correct behaviour.
❖ Chinese leader Mao Zedong said: 'I have hated Confucius since I was eight.'

Congregationalism Christian movement that rejects the hierarchy of the Anglican and Catholic churches, allowing each church to be independent and to elect its own minister. It began in England in the 16th century, but persecution drove many followers to Holland and America. The Congregational Church was established in southern Africa when the interdenominational ▷LONDON MISSIONARY SOCIETY began its work in the country in 1799. The United Congregational Church of Southern Africa was formed in 1967.

Coptic Church Main Christian Church of Egypt and the Sudan, which refused to convert to Islam after the Arab conquest. It separated from the ORTHODOX CHURCH in the 5th century and holds the belief that Jesus was wholly divine and not both fully human and fully divine – the 'Monophysite' doctrine.

Counter Reformation Reforms made by the Roman Catholic Church in response to the REFORMATION. Some of the beliefs criticized by reformers, such as veneration of the saints and acceptance of the authority of the pope, were reaffirmed, but others were rejected. The JESUITS emerged as leaders of the Counter Reformation, which culminated in a general redefinition of Roman Catholic doctrine at the Council of Trent (1545-63) and extended into the 17th century. (See also ▷COUNTER REFORMATION in 'World history'.)

crucifixion Common and cruel form of execution for non-citizens in the Roman Empire. The victim was bound or nailed to a wooden cross, often after a beating, then left to die. In particular, the Crucifixion refers to the death of JESUS CHRIST on the cross at Calvary *c*AD 30. The cross has become the central symbol of Christianity.

Dalai Lama Traditional ruler and Buddhist spiritual leader in Tibet and Mongolia, believed by his followers to be the reborn *bodhisattva* Avalokitshvara (see BUDDHA). After the death of a Dalai Lama, the search begins for a new incumbent who shows signs of being the same spirit reborn.
❖ The current Dalai Lama, forced into exile in India after the Chinese suppression of Tibetan nationalism in 1959, continues to work for the freedom of Tibet.

AGONY ON THE CROSS *For six hours Jesus hung crucified, a crown of thorns mocking the kingship claimed for him by his followers. Christ's ordeal is vividly portrayed by Diego Velásquez.*

damnation Condemnation of the souls of the wicked to torment in HELL, which Christians saw as the place of eternal punishment. The precise grounds for damnation have been the subject of much debate in Christianity, but traditionally anyone who dies in a state of SIN is considered to be damned.

Day of Judgment Most Christians believe that at the end of the world Christ will return in glory, and the dead will rise up and be miraculously reunited with their bodies for final judgment to be passed on them. The good will be separated from the evil, and taken up into heaven to live with God.
❖ The Day of Judgment is also one of Islam's most basic beliefs, and Jews look forward to the Day of YAHWEH which will inaugurate the Kingdom of God.

SCROLLS OF MYSTERY *For 1 000 years, caves in the arid cliffs above the Dead Sea were the hiding place of scrolls apparently made by the Essenes, a sect who followed a monastic type of Judaism. Discovered in 1947, the scrolls have cast new light on the relations between Judaism and early Christianity.*

Dead Sea Scrolls Ancient texts discovered by chance by a shepherd at Qumran, near the Dead Sea, in 1947. Some are copies of Old Testament books dating back 1 000 years earlier than previously known versions. They are believed to be the scriptures of the Essenes, a Jewish sect living an ascetic, communal way of life in desert locations.

deductive reasoning Logical and indisputable derivation of a conclusion from a PREMISE, as in: *If Sue is older than Tom and Tom is older than James, then Sue must be older than James.* Mathematics is based on deductive reasoning, but most ordinary thinking and much of science relies on less certain INDUCTIVE REASONING.

deism Belief that God or a supreme being exists but does not actively intervene in the universe or in human affairs. It was at its strongest in Britain in the 17th and 18th centuries, when scientifically minded thinkers sought to establish reasonable grounds for belief in God, without falling back on the idea of divine revelation. It contrasts with THEISM – belief in a personal God directly involved with creation.

Derrida, Jacques (1930-) French philosopher associated with the theory of 'deconstruction' – the attempt to take apart an idea or system to show what has been excluded. He argues that language creates our idea of reality and refers to itself rather than to anything in the real world. Instead of searching vainly for truth, Derrida says philosophy should 'deconstruct' the way meaning is created in words. His views are controversial because they suggest that distinctions between fact and fiction, good and evil, and truth and falsity are no more than semantic differences or games with words.

Descartes, René (1596-1650) French philosopher, mathematician and a founder of RATIONALISM – a school of thought which tries to explain how knowledge can be derived from reasoning alone. Descartes wanted to discover which aspects of human knowledge are absolutely certain and cannot be doubted. To do this, he began by imagining that an evil demon was deliberately trying to mislead him and that he had to doubt everything. But the one thing he could not doubt was the fact that he was thinking and, consequently, that he existed to be able to do the thinking. This led to his celebrated conclusion, *Cogito, ergo sum* – 'I think, therefore I am', on which he built a systematic philosophy with several proofs of the existence of God. He believed the entire material universe could be explained in terms of mathematical physics. (See also ▷DESCARTES in 'Science, space and mathematics'.)

determinism Belief that the way events occur is fixed in advance, either by some supernatural plan of God or by the laws of nature. The concept appears to undermine ideas such as FREE WILL, morality, justice and responsibility. Many philosophers, however, have tried to find ways of reconciling human freedom with the belief that there are causes for our behaviour. The problem is difficult for religious believers who maintain that God knows everything, including the future, since this implies that the future is fixed. On the other hand, these thinkers also believe that people are responsible for their actions and are free to choose between good and evil.

❖ Modern physics ceased to be deterministic in the early part of the 20th century, with the development of the theories of ▷QUANTUM MECHANICS, which suggests that, at the most fundamental level, the behaviour of matter cannot be predicted with any certainty.

devil Malevolent spirit or supernatural being responsible for causing suffering and for tempting people to commit evil acts. The idea is common to many religions, including Islam, Hinduism, Buddhism, Judaism and Christianity. The concept of the Devil as the embodiment of evil and the archenemy of God is also found in many faiths. The Devil is called SATAN by Jews and Christians, IBLIS by Muslims and Mara by Buddhists. (See also ▷DEVIL in 'Myths and legends'.)

dialectic Term used in philosophy to describe theories or methods based on dialogue or competition between opposing points of view. It is mainly applied to SOCRATES' method of arriving at knowledge by a process of questioning, and to HEGEL's view of the way ideas develop through contradiction between thesis and antithesis, resulting in a synthesis. MARX applied the process to the material world; his theory of class conflict that results in the overthrow of capitalism has been called 'dialectical materialism'.

Diaspora The dispersal of the Jewish people from Jerusalem and Judaea, after the Assyrian conquest of 722 BC, the Babylonian conquest of 586 BC and the disastrous revolts of AD 70 and 135 against the Roman rulers. These led to the destruction of the TEMPLE OF JERUSALEM and finally to the expulsion of Jews from their holy city. From the Middle East, the Jews spread over other areas such as North Africa and Europe, but maintained their religion and identity despite opposition and persecution, especially from Christians.

❖ The term Diaspora is used to refer to all Jews now living outside Israel, or the dispersion of any once homogenous people.

Diderot, Denis (1713-84) French philosopher and writer who edited the *Encyclopédie*, a se-

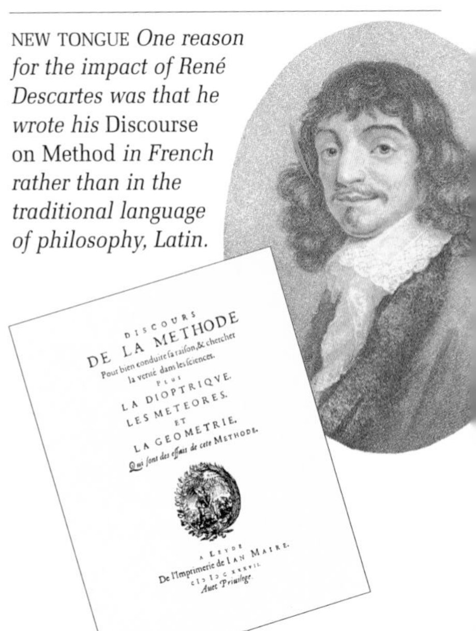

NEW TONGUE *One reason for the impact of René Descartes was that he wrote his* Discourse on Method *in French rather than in the traditional language of philosophy, Latin.*

ries of books which were a major expression of the ENLIGHTENMENT movement. Diderot's belief in the supremacy of reason over religious faith often brought him into conflict with the Church. Contributors to the *Encyclopédie* included philosophers and thinkers such as ROUSSEAU and ▷VOLTAIRE, who became known as the Encyclopaedists.

Diwali (or Deepavali) The HINDU Festival of Lights which is the major annual commemoration of the faith and regarded by some as the start of the new year. It celebrates the conquest of evil by good and also honours Lakshmi, goddess of beauty, wealth and pleasure. Presents and sweetmeats are exchanged, lamps are lit and fireworks set off.

dogma Unproved, and often unprovable, theory or doctrine which has to be accepted as true without question. The term is often applied to the teachings of the Roman Catholic Church, which are pronounced on by the pope and which all Catholics are bound to accept and follow.

Druse Faith that broke away from mainstream ISLAM in the 10th and 11th centuries to become a new religion in Jordan, Syria and Lebanon. Followers reject many traditional Islamic teachings, accept the idea of reincarnation, and await the return of the Muslim religious leader al-Hakim, who died in 1021.
❖ The Druse militia, which showed equal hostility to Christians and Muslims, was one of the factions in the Lebanese civil war during the 1980s.

dualism System of thought which, in some manner, divides everything into two categories, or which has as a basic principle an important opposition, such as 'the world as it exists' as opposed to 'the world as it is perceived'. In philosophy, it usually refers to the idea that a person has both a physical body and a non-material mind or soul. In religion, dualism refers to faiths that place good and evil, spirit and matter, or God and the Devil in absolute opposition. (Compare MONISM.)

Dutch Reformed churches The once politically powerful Afrikaans-speaking REFORMED CHURCHES in South Africa and their racially separate mission churches, known as the Nederduitse Gereformeerde family of churches. It is the largest of the established Church groups in the country. The Reformed Church was the official Church in the ▷CAPE COLONY during Dutch rule, but broke with the mother Church in Holland after the second British occupation (1806). Three separate churches (Nederduitse Gereformeerde Kerk, Hervormde Kerk and Gereformeerde Kerk) were subsequently formed. Mission churches for coloured, African and Indian members followed after 1857 when the Cape DRC authorized the separation of congregations. ▷APARTHEID was rejected as unbiblical in October 1986 by the DRC's general synod, which also opened membership to all races.

Easter Christian festival commemorating the resurrection of Jesus after his Crucifixion. On Maundy Thursday the Last Supper is recalled; Good Friday commemorates the Crucifixion; and the festival ends with Easter Sunday. The penitential season of Lent is a preparation for Easter. Palm Sunday, the Sunday before Easter, commemorates Jesus' entry into Jerusalem, when people laid palm leaves in his path as a sign of homage.
❖ Easter Sunday is the first Sunday after the full moon on or after March 21. In the ORTHODOX CHURCH it falls slightly later.

ecumenism Movement that promotes cooperation and understanding among Christian churches and their eventual reunification. Its main achievements in recent years have been the establishment of the World Council of Churches (WCC) in 1948 and the encouragement of closer ties and joint services between similar denominations.
❖ The South African Council of Churches, formed in 1968 from the Christian Council of South Africa, is an affiliate of the WCC.

empiricism Philosophical view that knowledge arises from experience and observation rather than from pure reason or innate ideas, as RATIONALISM claims. It adopts a sceptical attitude, refusing to take anything for granted or to rely on conventional authorities, such as the Bible or popular belief. Empiricism became a powerful force in the 17th and 18th centuries as a result of the work of philosophers such as BERKELEY, HUME and LOCKE, and was closely related to the development of experimental science.

Engels, Friedrich (1820-95) Revolutionary German political thinker. He collaborated with Karl MARX on *The Communist Manifesto* of 1848, and wrote a number of other works influential in developing the political theories of ▷COMMUNISM.

enlightenment In Eastern religions such as HINDUISM and BUDDHISM, a state of spiritual insight that brings liberation from the unending cycle of reincarnation. It is closely tied to the concept of NIRVANA.

Enlightenment Intellectual movement of the 18th century which promoted rational scientific enquiry and advocated religious toleration, social reform, progress and the elimination of tyranny. Major figures of the Enlightenment included Diderot, Hume, Kant, Locke, Rousseau and ▷VOLTAIRE.

episcopacy System of Church government based on bishops, as in the Roman Catholic, Anglican, Orthodox and Lutheran traditions, as well as several AFRICAN INDEPENDENT CHURCHES. The word comes from the Latin *episcopus* 'bishop', which in turn comes from the Greek word for an overseer.
❖ Churches other than the Church of England belonging to the ANGLICAN COMMUNION, particularly in North America, are known as the Episcopal or the Episcopalian churches.

epistemology Branch of philosophy concerned with knowledge and where it comes from. Traditionally, the two main positions on the issue were RATIONALISM, which claimed that knowledge is somehow 'built in' to the human mind, and EMPIRICISM, which maintained that it is a result of experience. Since KANT, however, this distinction has broken down, and many modern philosophers such as WITTGENSTEIN have concentrated more on analysing the meaning of statements rather than deciding whether they constitute knowledge.

Erasmus, Desiderius (*c*1466-1536) Dutch priest and Renaissance scholar who encouraged a form of HUMANISM which laid stress on free will and taught that people should think for themselves in spiritual matters. Erasmus urged reforms to make the Roman Catholic Church less worldly. He was, however, repelled by the violence that accompanied the REFORMATION when it came.

ethics Branch of philosophy that deals with morality. It attempts to define the difference between good and evil in the world, right and wrong in human actions, and virtue and wickedness in people.

Ethiopian churches AFRICAN INDEPENDENT CHURCHES movement which started towards the end of the 19th century in South Africa and asserted black religious autonomy as a response to racial inequality within the Church. The first Ethiopian church, which also bore that name, was established by Mangena Mokone in Pretoria in 1892. Ethiopian churches have generally retained the practices and methods of worship of the main Christian churches.
❖ The ancient Church of Ethiopia – not a product of Western missionary effort – provided the inspiration for the movement.

Eucharist See COMMUNION, HOLY

evangelist Preacher or missionary (usually Protestant) who spreads the Christian message. Matthew, Mark, Luke and John, the writers of the GOSPELS, are sometimes referred to as the four Evangelists.

evil Force or power working against humanity, God or the gods. In ancient Greek thought and in Buddhism there is little concern for the origin of evil, which is generally seen as the result of human ignorance and error. In Christianity, Judaism and Islam, however, the DEVIL, SATAN or IBLIS is widely perceived to be a central, intelligent source of evil.

excommunication Exclusion from membership of a Church because of a serious challenge to its teaching or authority. In Roman Catholic tradition this means DAMNATION unless it is later revoked. In medieval times the threat of excommunication was often used by the pope for political reasons.

existentialism Movement in 20th-century philosophy, theology and literature, based on the view that people are entirely free and therefore responsible for what they make of themselves. With this responsibility comes anguish or dread. One of the most influential existentialist philosophers was the French thinker and writer Jean-Paul SARTRE, who summed up his views in the maxim, 'Existence precedes essence' – that is, human beings spring up in the world undefined and without a fixed nature or 'essence'. There is no divine plan, nor any fixed values by which they can guide themselves; they are 'condemned to be free'. An important forerunner of Sartre was Søren KIERKEGAARD.

Exodus Journey of MOSES and the ancient Israelites out of slavery in Egypt in about 1200 BC, as told in Exodus, the second book of the Bible. According to the Bible, the Red Sea parted to let the Israelites cross, after which they wandered in the desert for 40 years before reaching Canaan, the land they believed was promised to them by God.

exorcism The casting out of demons or evil spirits believed to have 'possessed' a person or place. Among the ancient Israelites, mental conditions such as schizophrenia and epilepsy were often considered to be a sign of demonic possession and were treated by ritual exorcism. Jesus Christ performed many exorcisms, and in the early Church there was a standard office of Exorcist. Exorcisms are still occasionally performed by Roman Catholic and some Protestant churches.

faith Belief that is not based on scientific evidence. It is one of the three great virtues – together with hope and charity (or love) – listed by St PAUL in the New Testament.
❖ Faith is not always possible, even for the devout. Doubting Thomas believed Jesus had risen from the dead only when he saw him and touched his wounds.

fatwah Edict issued by a Muslim religious leader. The term came to prominence in 1989 when the Ayatollah ▷KHOMEINI of Iran issued a fatwah offering a huge cash reward to any Muslim who assassinated the writer Salman ▷RUSHDIE, after the publication of his novel *The Satanic Verses*, which was deemed to have grossly insulted the Islamic faith. In 1995, in response to the threat of international sanctions, the Iranian government declared the fatwah illegal.

first principles Underlying assumptions or basic ideas on which a theory or system of thought is founded. Modern science, for example, is based on the belief that nature obeys regular laws, and theology assumes, or rests on, a belief in God.

Francis of Assisi, St (*c*1181-1226) Italian monk and founder of the Franciscan Order. He was born Giovannidi Bernardone, into a wealthy family. After a serious sickness and a religious dream, he gave away all his property and devoted himself to helping the poor. He took the name Francis from the nickname of his youth 'Il Francesco' – 'The Little Frenchman' – given to him because he spoke French. Francis's simplicity, goodness and love of all living things soon won him a band of devoted followers. Franciscans still live by his rules, taking vows of chastity, poverty, obedience, and giving up personal property.

DEVOUT FLOCK *A love of nature led St Francis to preach to the birds. He is the patron saint of animals and the ecology movement.*

RICH SYMBOLISM *A ladder – which represents levels of consciousness to Freemasons – rises among many other masonic symbols, including Classical columns and the mason's tools.*

Freemasons Secret men's society that developed out of the medieval stonemasons' ▷GUILD. Members are now men who meet together in 'lodges' to practise rituals and ceremonies said to date back centuries, and to work for charity. The movement is non-religious, requiring only a belief in some form of supreme being.
❖ The Masons' secrecy has led to accusations that they favour one another in business and professional life.

free will Human capacity to choose, think and act voluntarily. Christians, Jews and Muslims believe that God has given the human race free will to choose between good and evil. (Compare DETERMINISM.)

fundamentalism Conservative and often zealous religious movement seeking to preserve and strengthen the basic doctrines of a faith, and stressing their literal truth. In Christianity, it usually takes the form of reaffirming beliefs such as the Virgin Birth and the Resurrection of Jesus. Islamic fundamentalists desire the religious organization of society and the state.

fuzzy logic New branch of thought that rejects conventional 'black or white' logic in favour of a flexible approach that can accommodate shades of grey, ambiguity and contradictions, making it more akin to Far Eastern philosophies. Its chief exponent, American academic Bart Kosko, claims that binary logic, which demands that things be right or wrong, 1 or 0, sacrifices accuracy for convenience, as many of the greatest mathematicians and philosophers of the 20th century have proved that almost nothing is certain, including long-established laws of logic and science. Fuzzy logic enables computers to reason more like humans.

Genesis First book of the Bible, describing the creation of the world, the expulsion of ADAM AND EVE from the Garden of Eden, the story of Noah and the Flood, and the founding of the Hebrew nation under ABRAHAM.
❖ Genesis is Greek for 'beginning' or 'origin'.

Gnostics Members of a variety of sects in the early Christian era who claimed their doctrines were based on knowledge *(gnosis)* rather than faith. Some also claimed that they possessed secret teachings transmitted orally from the time of Jesus. They were considered heretical by the Church and most of their writings were eventually destroyed.

God In religions with one god, such as Christianity, Judaism and Islam, God is the supreme being or power, and creator of the universe. Even in systems with many gods, there is usually one primary deity more powerful than the rest, such as BRAHMA in Hinduism, ▷ZEUS in Classical Greek belief and Jupiter in ancient Rome. Many different views of God exist, generally based on attributes such as goodness, wisdom, perfection, power, justice, completeness and love. Since Classical times various unsuccessful attempts have been made to use logic to prove or disprove the existence of God or the gods

Good Friday The most sacred day of the Christian calendar, known as Great Friday in the ORTHODOX CHURCH. It falls on the Friday before EASTER Sunday and commemorates the Crucifixion of Jesus.
❖ Hot cross buns, marked with a cross, are traditionally eaten on Good Friday.

Gospels Biblical message of Christian salvation, in particular the four books of the New Testament, which record the life, teachings and miracles of Jesus Christ. Their authorship is unknown, but they are traditionally attributed to the four Evangelists – Matthew, Mark, Luke and John – and were probably put together from the spoken tradition of the apostles within a century of Jesus' death. Together with the letters of St Paul, they form the central Christian scriptures.
❖ The word 'gospel' derives from the Anglo-Saxon *god-spell*, which literally meant 'good news' or 'good tidings'.

grace In Christianity, love, protection and favour bestowed by God as an unmerited gift which leads to salvation. According to the New Testament, it is freely given to those who have faith. Whether grace could be increased by doing good works or purchasing an INDULGENCE was one of the major issues of the REFORMATION. Martin Luther argued, against the Roman Catholic Church, that salvation was by faith alone. However, there is now little difference between the churches, most Christians accepting that faith without deeds is empty.
❖ 'Grace' is also a short blessing or prayer said before a meal.

DECISION FOR CHRIST *Himself converted at a revival meeting at the age of 16, Baptist preacher Billy Graham's worldwide 'crusades' are credited with bringing millions to Christianity.*

Graham, Billy (1918-) American Baptist EVANGELIST noted for the charismatic eloquence of his preaching and mass rallies held in the course of his worldwide tours. His preaching, writing and radio and television broadcasts have made him well known to millions, and he became the friend of several presidents of the United States.

guru Hindu religious teacher who gives personal instruction to a disciple and is greatly revered. Sikhs also have gurus, whom they consider semi-divine and directly inspired by God. The word comes from the Sanskrit *guruh*, meaning 'venerable'.
❖ In general usage, a guru can be any leader or sage who inspires some sort of following.

Hare Krishna movement Common name for the International Society for Krishna Consciousness, a Hindu movement founded in the United States in 1953, to spread the message that human happiness can be found only through greater love of God or KRISHNA. Disciples wear saffron robes, chant a mantra, or sacred phrase, while processing through city streets, and shave their heads except for a topknot – which they believe Krishna will use to pluck them up to heaven.
❖ The Hare Krishna Temple of Understanding at Chatsworth, Durban, was built in the 1980s after the movement's spiritual leader in the West visited the country.

Hegel, Georg Wilhelm Friedrich (1770-1831) German philosopher who argued that mind or spirit, rather than matter, is the basic reality. History, according to Hegel, shows a gradual unfolding of the universal Mind (or World Spirit), and proceeds by means of a DIALECTIC. By this he meant that every idea or state of affairs (which he called a 'thesis') is sooner or later confronted by its opposite (or 'antithesis'). Eventually, a combination (or 'synthesis') of the two arises, which then becomes a new thesis, giving rise to a new antithesis and so on. The task of philosophy, according to Hegel, is to demonstrate the rationality of what exists. Hegel's philosophy was an important influence on many other thinkers, including Karl MARX.

hell In Christianity, the place where the souls of the damned are sent after judgment. It was traditionally thought of as a place of eternal punishment, but in modern theology hell is

more generally regarded as the state of separation from God.
❖ The Jewish hell is called Gehenna and the Islamic hell Johannam.

heresy Belief or doctrine opposed to orthodox teaching, especially of a religion. Religions or beliefs considered heretical by the Christian Church have included the ANABAPTISTS, the GNOSTICS and ARIANISM. Although many heretics have been savagely persecuted, tortured and burnt at the stake by the Church in the past – particularly by the ▷INQUISITION – the strongest punishment used today is EXCOMMUNICATION. In Islam, the penalty for heresy is still death.

Hinduism Indian religion that aims at liberating the spirit from the material world through the purification of desires and the surpassing of personal identity. Hindu writings go back to around 1200 BC, but there is no single founder, sacred text or set of doctrines. Instead, emphasis is placed on right living, or *dharma*, and spiritual development throughout life. Although some Hindus believe in one God and some in none, most worship a number of deities, of whom the most important are BRAHMA, SHIVA and VISHNU. All Hindus, however, share a belief in KARMA and reincarnation. There are about 500 million Hindus in the world. Traditionally, Hinduism was linked to the Indian ▷CASTE SYSTEM, a rigid social hierarchy with some 3 000 subdivisions which governs every aspect of an individual's life, from birth to death.

Hobbes, Thomas (1588-1679) English political philosopher known for his book *Leviathan*, which advocates absolute government as the only means of achieving order; otherwise, he said, life is 'solitary, poor, nasty, brutish, and short'. He proposed a social contract under which the ruled agree to obey the ruler if he in turn provides social peace.

holism View that whole systems – such as living beings or societies – are more than the sum of their parts and cannot be explained simply by examining and evaluating their components. Holists believe that people and events can be understood only within a social or historical context.
❖ Holistic medicine, such as ▷HOMEOPATHY, aims to treat the 'whole person' – the body, mind and spirit.
❖ South African Prime Minister Jan Smuts put forward his views on the operation of holism in history in his philosophical work *Holism and Evolution* (1926).

Holy Spirit (or Holy Ghost) Third person of the divine TRINITY believed in by most Christians. The Holy Spirit is often described as the creative power or breath of God, responsible for miracles such as the conception of Jesus by the Virgin MARY.
❖ Christian missionary work and experiences such as speaking in tongues and prophecy are said to be inspired by the Holy Spirit.
❖ The Holy Spirit is occasionally described in the Bible as descending in the form of a dove, and is often represented this way in art.

JUNGLE TEMPLE *The 12th-century temple at Angkor Wat in the Cambodian jungle was dedicated to Vishnu – one of Hinduism's principal gods, together with Shiva (bottom) and Brahma.*

humanism Cultural movement of the ▷RENAISSANCE, inspired by the rediscovery of Classical authors and an optimistic belief in the glory and accomplishments of the human race. Humanism is also a 20th-century philosophy which rejects religious belief, claiming that people are capable of achieving happiness and behaving morally without any divine guidance.

Hume, David (1711-76) Scottish philosopher whose *Treatise of Human Nature* (1740) is a central text of British EMPIRICISM. His ideas were based on the work of BERKELEY and LOCKE, but went much further. Starting from a sceptical point of view, he questioned all claims to knowledge, including the idea of CAUSE AND EFFECT, which he argued lacked logical justification. He concluded that all knowledge had to be based either on perceptions of the senses or on logical relationships between ideas.

hypothesis Any PROPOSITION that has yet to be proved or disproved. In logic, hypotheses form the basis for argument and reasoning. In science, they give rise to predictions that can be tested in experiments before being put forward as a theory.

Iblis The devil in ISLAM. Like SATAN, he is said to have rebelled against God and to have been banished from heaven. In Muslim belief, Iblis is responsible for the disobedience of ADAM AND EVE in the Garden of Eden, and so there is no doctrine of ORIGINAL SIN. The KORAN suggests that, even in hell, Iblis remains the servant of God and that he will eventually be saved.

***I Ching* (Book of Changes)** Chinese book of wisdom dating in its original form from about 1000 BC or earlier. It was later elaborated on the basis of Taoist and Confucianist principles. It attempts to explain nature and human fortune as a constant cycle of change, and can be used as an oracle to give advice.

iconoclasm Rejection or destruction of religious images, often on the grounds that they are forbidden by the second commandment ('thou shalt not make unto thee any graven image'). In the 8th and 9th centuries many images and icons were destroyed with the blessing of the pope. However, during the REFORMATION, the Roman Catholic Church itself became a victim of iconoclasm, and lost

many religious images of great artistic value.
❖ The word 'iconoclasm' comes from Greek words for 'image breaking'.

idealism In philosophy, any view that the material world is in some way dependent on the mind that perceives it. Idealist thinkers do not necessarily deny that material objects exist, but claim that they cannot be known to exist independently of the human mind. BERKELEY, HEGEL and KANT were all idealist thinkers. Idealism is contested by proponents of REALISM and MATERIALISM.

idolatry Worship of images or idols as if they were divine. The term has often been misapplied to people who merely make use of sacred images as symbols in order to worship some unseen power.
❖ The Islamic faith forbids the representation of living creatures in art because of the danger of idolatry – hence the rich abstract designs found in mosques.

imam In Islam, either a prayer leader in a mosque or an important Muslim scholar. Although it is not a priestly office, among SHIAH Muslims imams are religious leaders believed to have been appointed by God and to have special spiritual powers.

inductive reasoning Type of reasoning that uses individual observations to build up general rules – for example: *If every raven that has ever been seen is black, it is reasonable to conclude that all ravens are probably black.* The result is not absolutely certain and could be disproved by a single observation of a white raven. However, it is a reasonable assumption at the time. Modern science is based on this type of thinking. (Compare DEDUCTIVE REASONING.)

indulgence In the Roman Catholic Church, forgiveness of sin granted after repentance, which is believed to reduce the amount of time to be spent in PURGATORY after death. The idea was abused in medieval times when spiritual merit was openly bought and sold for money. Disgust at this system was a principal factor leading to LUTHER's break with Rome and the beginning of the REFORMATION.

infallibility Roman Catholic doctrine that the Church is assisted by the HOLY SPIRIT and cannot be mistaken when teaching on matters of faith and morals. At a Vatican Council in 1869-70 this authority was partly extended to the pope himself. Protestants deny that any human pronouncement is infallible.

Islam Religion founded in the 7th century by the prophet MUHAMMAD, and based on the teachings of the KORAN. It acknowledges one God – the same as that worshipped by Jews and Christians – called Allah in Arabic. Islam means 'submission to the will of God', and followers are known as MUSLIMS. In Islam, there is no distinction between spiritual and secular life, and believers are expected to obey sharia – the religious law, as laid down in the Koran and the sayings of Muhammad, supplemented by agreements among Muslims over the centuries. Religious observances centre on the 'Five Pillars of the Faith': reciting the creed ('There is no God but God, and Muhammad is His prophet'), praying five times a day facing MECCA, giving alms to the poor, fasting during RAMADAN, and making a pilgrimage to Mecca at least once. The public place of worship is the MOSQUE. There are around 700 million Muslims in the world. Islam is the dominant faith in the Arab nations, in some countries of central Asia and southeast Europe, as well as in Malaysia and Indonesia. From the 10th century, Islam spread south of the Sahara. In many Muslim countries Islamic FUNDAMENTALISM is a powerful political force.
❖ Sheikh ▷YUSSUF, an influential religious figure in western Java, was banished to the Cape by the Dutch East India Company in 1694 and is considered the pioneer of the religion in South Africa. Fellow Muslims erected a *kramat* (holy place) in his honour at Faure near Cape Town.

Jainism Indian religion which dates back to the 6th century BC, and shares many elements with HINDUISM and BUDDHISM. The religion has no deity and is monastic, like Buddhism. Jains believe in reincarnation and aim at spiritual development as the way to liberation from the cycle of birth and death. They are strict vegetarians and strive to follow a practice of nonviolence towards all living creatures.

Jehovah The name of God as translated by 15th and 16th-century Western scholars from the consonants YHWH – the written Hebrew form. The Hebrews, who spoke of him as *Adonai* 'Lord', considered his proper name too holy to be pronounced. Modern scholars prefer to use YAHWEH.

Jehovah's Witnesses Group founded as the International Bible Students' Association in 1872 by the American Charles Taze Russell (1852-1916), who believed that the SECOND COMING of Jesus and the MILLENNIUM were imminent. They insist on using Jehovah as a name for God, reject the doctrine of the TRINITY and consider Jesus as God's agent who will come to establish a divine kingdom on Earth. There are nearly 5 million members worldwide who refuse to bear arms or obey any law that goes against the Bible. There are no clergy.
❖ Jehovah's Witnesses are known for vigorous door-to-door missionary work, during which they distribute copies of their magazine *The Watchtower.*

Jesuits Members of the Society of Jesus (SJ), the largest and most influential Roman Catholic religious organization, founded by St Ignatius of Loyola in 1534 and approved by the Pope in 1540. They spearheaded the COUNTER REFORMATION and have a long tradition of missionary and scholarly work. In recent years they have been influential in modernizing the Roman Catholic Church.

Jesus Christ (*c*6 BC-*c*AD 30) Prophet believed by Christians to be the Son of God, the second person of the Holy TRINITY and the Christ or MESSIAH sent by God to save the world. According to the New Testament, Jesus was conceived by the Virgin MARY through the power of the Holy Spirit, making him both human and divine. He was born in Bethlehem but raised in Nazareth by Mary and her husband Joseph. After baptism by John the Baptist in the River Jordan, he chose 12 disciples with whom he travelled throughout Palestine, preaching the coming of the kingdom of God, teaching a gospel of love and compassion, healing the sick and performing miracles. He attracted many followers but also made enemies by failing to observe Jewish laws and for turning the moneylenders out of the Temple. Jesus was betrayed by Judas Iscariot, condemned by the Roman governor Pontius Pilate at the insistence of the Jewish hierarchy and crucified at Calvary. Christians believe that he rose again from the dead and that he will return to Earth at the SECOND COMING to save those who believe in him.
❖ Muslims consider Jesus a great prophet, second only to MUHAMMAD, and in Judaism he is generally acknowledged as a religious teacher, or rabbi.

Judaism Traditional religion of the Jews, based on the teachings of the Hebrew Scriptures (roughly the same as the Christian OLD TESTAMENT), the TALMUD and other religious commentaries. It involves belief in one God, creator of the world and liberator of his chosen people, the Jews, whom he delivered from slavery in the EXODUS from Egypt. ABRAHAM is considered the founder of Judaism, around 1800 BC, and MOSES, with whom God renewed his covenant in about 1200 BC, is one of its major prophets. Followers believe that a MESSIAH will appear in the future to gather all the Jews together again in the Promised Land, and to rebuild the great

HOLY WALL *Judaism's holiest site, the Western Wall in Jerusalem, is a remnant of Herod's Temple. The Jews' lamentation over its ruin and their long exile earned it the name of 'Wailing Wall'.*

TEMPLE OF JERUSALEM. The faith is taught by the RABBI and through family life, which is central to Jewish culture and religion. Jewish law – or TORAH – lays down strict ritual observances in many areas of life, particularly regarding the SABBATH and the preparation of kosher food. In recent times, the Reform and Liberal movements in Judaism have relaxed some of the rules observed by Conservative or Orthodox Jews.

❖ Jews have their own calendar based on the lunar cycle. Some of their festivals include Chanukkah, Passover, Rosh Hashanah (New Year) and Yom Kippur (Day of Atonement).

Kant, Immanuel (1724-1804) German philosopher who, in *The Critique of Pure Reason* and other works, sets out views which attempted to bridge the gap between EMPIRICISM and RATIONALISM. Kant was concerned that conventional METAPHYSICS had failed to resolve issues such as the existence of God, the immortality of the soul and the operation of FREE WILL. He maintained that the first step to answering such questions was to investigate the limits of human understanding and reasoning – a type of investigation he called a 'critique'. In the end, Kant concluded that we cannot ever know a 'thing-in-itself', but only as it appears to the human mind. Kant also argued that 'right action' could not be based on intuition or desire but must conform to a law of reason, the Categorical Imperative, which urges people to behave as they would wish everyone else to.

❖ Kant led a simple life, never leaving his home town of Königsberg in Prussia. The townspeople were said to be able to set their clocks by his punctual afternoon walks.

karma In Eastern religions such as HINDUISM and BUDDHISM, the principle that all good and bad actions have consequences that will affect one throughout life, and even in future lives. Karma is Sanskrit for 'fate'.

❖ By extension, 'karma' is sometimes loosely used to mean fate or destiny.

Kierkegaard, Søren (1813-55) Danish philosopher and religious writer who defended Christianity. His work concentrates on the emotions of fear and loneliness which he believed to be part of true religion.

❖ Kierkegaard was a forerunner of existentialist thinkers such as Jean-Paul SARTRE.

knowledge Something which has been defined as justified true BELIEF, and which is studied in the branch of philosophy known as EPISTEMOLOGY. Because knowledge is clearly different from 'feeling sure' about what exists or about the course of events, most philosophical debate on the subject centres on the nature of TRUTH and on what counts as appropriate evidence for claiming to know something.

Koran (or Qur'an) Islamic sacred book, held by believers to be the word of God as revealed to MUHAMMAD by the archangel Gabriel. Its central message is belief in one God, the obedience due to him, and his involvement in history from the creation to the Last Judgment. It also lays down religious principles that form the basis of Islamic law, or sharia.

❖ The Koran contains many parallels with the Old Testament. It also venerates Jesus as a prophet, or messenger of God, but maintains that God saved him from dying on the cross.

Krishna In HINDUISM, an incarnation of the god VISHNU in human form. He was supposedly a great ruler and was known for amorous encounters with milkmaids. He plays a leading role in the BHAGAVAD GITA.

Lao-Tzu (also Lao Zi or Lao Tan) Ancient Chinese philosopher of the 6th century BC – but possibly a legendary figure. His thought is said to have provided the inspiration for TAOISM and for the *Tao te Ching* (*The Way of Power*) – a series of philosophical meditations compiled some 300 years after his supposed lifetime. Much of Lao-Tzu's teaching appears to complement the ideas and precepts of CONFUCIANISM.

Leibniz, Gottfried von (1646-1716) German RATIONALIST philosopher, mathematician and optimist who, like SPINOZA, developed an entire system of philosophy by deduction from FIRST PRINCIPLES. According to Leibniz, the universe consists of an infinite number of independent units ('monads') which God has placed in harmony with one another in 'the best of all possible worlds'.

❖ Leibniz is satirized in ▷VOLTAIRE's book *Candide* as Dr Pangloss.

liberation theology Belief that Christ's message was one of liberation and preferential treatment for the poor, and that the Church should campaign for worldwide economic and political justice. It originated in the 1960s within a radical branch of the Roman Catholic Church in Latin America. In the 1980s Pope John Paul II accused its followers of wrongly supporting violent revolution and marxist class-struggle.

Locke, John (1632-1704) English philosopher, regarded as one of the founders of EMPIRICISM. Locke rejected the view of RATIONALISM – that some ideas are innate in the human mind – and insisted that knowledge is based on experience alone. A newborn baby's mind, he said, is a *tabula rasa*, or 'blank slate', until experience begins to 'write' on it. As a political philosopher, Locke opposed the ▷DIVINE RIGHT OF KINGS and maintained that the legitimacy of governments should depend on the consent of the governed, and that the role of government is only to safeguard the liberty and rights of the individual.

❖ Locke's views were influential in the

▷FRENCH REVOLUTION and in the drawing up of the American Constitution.

logic Branch of philosophy dealing with the principles of reasoning. Classical logic, as developed in ancient Greece, particularly by ARISTOTLE, is concerned with the rules for deriving valid conclusions from a set of propositions (DEDUCTIVE REASONING). Logic today has become more abstract and mathematical. (See also FUZZY LOGIC and SYLLOGISM.)

logical positivism Philosophical movement of the first half of the 20th century, influenced by the early works of AYER, RUSSELL and WITTGENSTEIN. It insisted that a statement is meaningful only if it can be logically or experimentally tested. Statements such as 'God exists' are meaningless as there is no way to test them. 'The Moon is made of green cheese' is meaningful (although false) because it can be tested.

Luther, Martin (1483-1546) German priest whose criticism of the Roman Catholic Church initiated the REFORMATION, which led to the rise of PROTESTANTISM. As professor of Biblical Exegesis at the University of Wittenburg he compiled a list of Ninety-Five Theses which attacked the Church for selling indulgences, and argued that faith alone is sufficient for salvation. He denied the authority of the pope and other aspects of Catholic doctrine and wrote many books and pamphlets.

Lutheran Church Protestant denomination that accepts the teachings of Martin LUTHER and stresses the importance of 'justification' (being made righteous) by God's grace, which is received through faith alone. The Church is non-hierarchical and grants autonomy to each individual congregation. The Lutheran churches in southern Africa grew mainly out of the work of MISSIONARIES from Germany, Scandinavia and America. Nearly half of the population of Namibia is Lutheran.

❖ Lutherans are known for their choral and organ music. J S ▷BACH wrote much of his music for Lutheran worship.

HOLY SCRIPTURE *Islamic tradition forbids the representation of human and animal figures, so manuscripts like this 15th-century Koran are adorned with geometric shapes and plant motifs.*

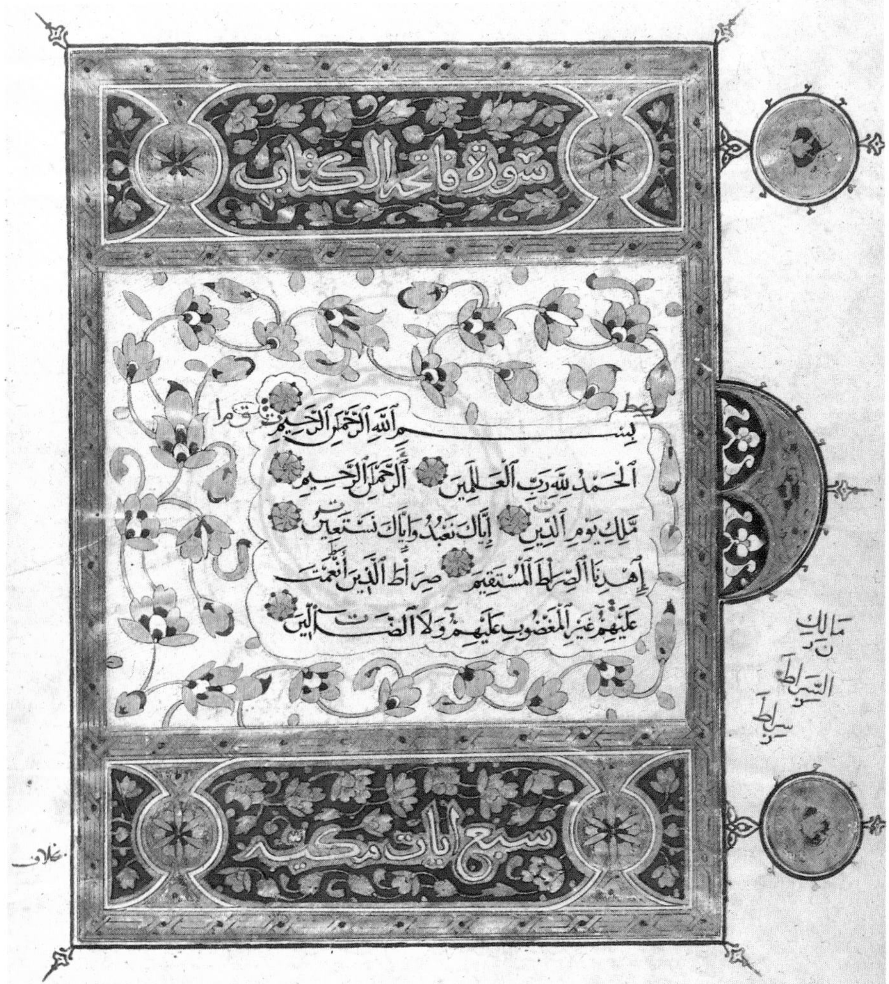

Machiavelli, Niccolò (1469-1527) Italian statesman and political philosopher whose name is synomous with cunning statecraft. In *The Prince* (1532) he argues that to win and maintain power, rulers should not be constrained by Christian morality – that a noble end can justify ruthless means. Critics called him a dangerous cynic, admirers claimed he was a pragmatic realist. He was the first to base his political thought on the study of human nature, observed during 23 years on the council of the Florentine republic.

Marcuse, Herbert (1898-1979) Radical German-born American philosopher whose Marxist writings were influenced by Hegel and Freud. He believed that Western societies are not free, and that the masses are only kept docile by the technology that permits widespread possession of material goods.

Marx, Karl (1818-83) German thinker concerned with theories of economics and history. His views were based on the philosophy of HEGEL, but replaced Hegel's IDEALISM with a form of MATERIALISM. His systematic study of class struggles and belief in the DIALECTICS of the development of history have been enormously influential. Marx is best known for the theory that violent proletarian revolution will eventually topple capitalism and bring about a just and classless society. (See also ▷MARX in 'Business and economics'.)

❖ Marx's *Das Kapital* and *The Communist Manifesto* – the latter written in collaboration with ENGELS – were highly influential in the development of ▷SOCIALISM and ▷COMMUNISM. However, many political systems going by the name ▷MARXISM bear little relationship to Marx's own ideas.

Mary (or Virgin Mary) Mother of Jesus. According to the New Testament, she miraculously conceived while still a virgin and betrothed to Joseph, after the HOLY SPIRIT had visited her. She is revered throughout Christianity for her humility and maternal love, particularly by Roman Catholics who believe strongly in her mercy and her power to plead on their behalf with God. The Roman Catholic Church also teaches the doctrine of the Immaculate Conception – that Mary herself was different in that she was born free from all stain of ORIGINAL SIN.

❖ One of the most familiar Roman Catholic prayers – known as the 'Hail Mary' – begins 'Hail Mary, full of grace, the Lord is with thee, Blessed art thou among women . . . '

Mass Central liturgical rite in the Roman Catholic, Orthodox and some Anglican churches; also known as the Eucharist or Holy COMMUNION. It commemorates Christ's sharing bread and wine with his disciples at the Last Supper.

❖ The word 'Mass' comes from the Latin *missa*, used in dismissing communicants after the service.

materialism In philosophy, the position that nothing exists except physical objects and forces that are perceptible and measurable. Materialists deny the existence of spirit, soul or mind as a separate type of reality, and they look for physical explanations of all phenomena – for example, by explaining thoughts, emotions or impulses in terms of chemical reactions in the brain.

❖ ▷MARXISM is a form of materialism in which almost every aspect of culture is seen in terms of economic forces.

Mecca Birthplace in present-day Saudi Arabia of MUHAMMAD in about AD 570. It is revered as Islam's holiest place. Forced in 622 to flee from Mecca to Medina, Muhammad returned to the city in triumph a few years later. The Koran decrees that every Muslim, whose health and means permit them to, should make a pilgrimage, or *hadj*, to Mecca once in their lifetime, after which they can take the title *Hadji*.

Messiah The 'anointed one', the promised saviour, or 'Christ', foretold by the Old Testament prophets. Christians believe that JESUS CHRIST was the Messiah, although he never explicitly claimed the title. In Judaism, the Messiah has yet to appear. When he does, Jews believe he will gather them all together in the Holy Land, after which the dead will be resurrected for the DAY OF JUDGMENT.

metaphysics Branch of philosophy dealing with the ultimate nature of reality and the fundamental principles on which other systems of thought are based – such as the assumption in science that nature obeys regular laws, or in theology that God exists. Metaphysics has often been criticized for its hypothetical nature and for dealing in theories that can be neither supported nor disproved by any form of evidence. Some views, such as LOGICAL POSITIVISM, have argued that metaphysical statements are totally meaningless.

Methodist (or Wesleyan) Church Protestant Church begun by the breakaway Anglican preacher John WESLEY and his brother Charles in the 18th century. It appeals directly to the Gospels and stresses the freely given grace of God which leads to salvation. The Church is regulated by an annual Conference, and emphasizes the social and individual responsibility of Christians. The Methodists are the third largest church grouping in South Africa. Wesleyan missions established throughout southern Africa in the 19th century made a significant contribution to black education and social advancement. Their missionaries produced the first Xhosa grammar textbook (1834) and Xhosa Bible (1859).

Mill, John Stuart (1806-73) English philosopher and economist, who refined the idea of UTILITARIANISM – the pursuit of 'the greatest happiness of the greatest number' – by arguing that some types of pleasure were of a higher order than others. His book *On Liberty* is a classic endorsement of liberal government, stressing freedom of belief, speech and behaviour; arguing for individual responsibility; and advocating a severe restriction on the powers of the state.

❖ Mill was reputedly learning Greek by the age of three; by eight he was reading Plato.

millennium According to some Christian groups, including SEVENTH-DAY ADVENTISTS and JEHOVAH'S WITNESSES, a period of 1 000 years during which Jesus and his followers will reign over the Earth after the battle of ARMAGEDDON between good and evil. The doctrine is based on the Book of Revelation, but it has never been adopted by any of the more traditional Christian churches.

missionaries During the 18th and 19th centuries Christianity was advanced worldwide by missionaries who converted indigenous populations and sought to uplift them by introducing Western medicine, schooling and modern agriculture and commerce. At the Cape, a Moravian missionary, George Schmidt, did the first missionary work among the Khoikhoi at Baviaanskloof (now ▷GENADENDAL) in 1737. Missionaries from the ▷LONDON MISSIONARY SOCIETY arrived in 1799, followed by Lutheran missions, the Wesleyans (Methodists), Scottish Presbyterians and Roman Catholics. The Dutch Reformed Church and the Baptists also conducted missionary work.

❖ London Missionary Society pioneers J T van der Kemp and Dr John Philip campaigned for the extension of equality and political rights to black people.

Mithraism Cult in the Roman Empire during the first centuries of the Christian era, and found as far afield as Germany and Britain. It was based on worship of the Persian god Mithras, who was believed to have come from the Sun and to have slain a bull whose blood fertilized the Earth. The cult was particularly popular in the Roman armies, and in the 3rd century AD was one of the main rivals to Christianity.

monasticism Devotion of one's life entirely to God and to spiritual development. It usually involves separation from the world and residence in a monastery or convent. In Christianity, it is practised by monks and nuns in the Roman Catholic, Orthodox and some Anglican churches. Followers take vows of poverty, chastity and obedience, for example, and are committed to a rigorous regime of

ISLAM'S SACRED SHRINE *Every year some 2 million Muslims flock to Mecca to make seven circuits of the Kaaba, which holds the black stone reputedly given to Abraham by the archangel Gabriel.*

PIONEER MISSIONARY *Dr John Philip ministered to the Cape's indigenous people for 30 years and took up their cause in London.*

prayer and work. Some orders are extremely strict, such as the silent Trappists; others, such as the Benedictines, do teaching and missionary work. Some other faiths, such as BUDDHISM, also have versions of monasticism.

monism View that reality consists of only one basic substance, generally either mind (thoughts, emotions, perceptions, intuitions and all other inner experiences) or matter (physical objects and forces). MATERIALISM and IDEALISM are both monist theories. Monism is opposed by DUALISM, which maintains that there are two basic substances, and by PLURALISM, which maintains that there are many ultimate substances.

Montesquieu (Charles de Secondat) (1689-1755) French political philosopher of the ENLIGHTENMENT. His major work, *The Spirit of Laws*, sets out the theory that states should have separate legislative, executive and judicial powers. Montesquieu influenced the Founding Fathers of the United States and many countries' constitutions.

Moonies Common name for members of the Unification Church, founded in 1954 by the Korean religious leader Sun Myung Moon. Moon offers a new interpretation of the Bible and claims to have had direct revelations from God. Church members live in strictly disciplined communal groups and some revere Moon as a MESSIAH.

❖ The Unification Church has been accused of brainwashing and splitting up families. Meanwhile, followers accuse their opponents of kidnapping members and indoctrinating them against the movement.

Mormons Members of the Church of Jesus Christ of Latter-Day Saints, founded in 1830 by the American religious leader Joseph Smith. Smith claimed that a new book of the Bible, the *Book of Mormon*, was revealed to him by an angel and that Jesus would return to America to build a New Jerusalem. After Smith's death, the Mormons moved west under the leadership of Brigham Young and founded a new capital at Salt Lake City in Utah. They have distinctive religious practices such as marriages for eternity and baptism of the deceased. Today, there are some 6 million members worldwide.

❖ In the past the Mormons were controversial for practising polygamy, but this is no longer officially sanctioned by their Church.

Mosaic law In JUDAISM, the law – or TORAH – believed to have been passed down to the Israelites through God's revelation to Moses. It offers spiritual guidance and includes the TEN COMMANDMENTS.

Moses Prophet and leader of the ancient Israelites. According to the Bible, Moses was born in the 13th century BC in Egypt, where the Israelites were living as slaves. While he was still an infant, the ruling pharaoh ordered all male Hebrew children to be slain. Moses' mother placed him in a basket of rushes and hid him in a marsh, where he was found and adopted by the pharaoh's daughter. As a man, Moses was commanded by God to bring the Israelites out of bondage, and he led his people out of Egypt on the journey that became known as the EXODUS. Moses received the TEN COMMANDMENTS from God on Mount Sinai, after which he and his people wandered in the wilderness for 40 years. Just as they came in sight of the 'Promised Land' of Canaan, Moses died – according to tradition – at the age of 120.

mosque Islamic place of worship, prayer and meeting. In many mosques, the faithful are called to prayer by a *muezzin*, or crier, from the top of a minaret. Although Muslims believe that daily prayers can be said anywhere, most try to attend the communal service at their mosque at noon on Fridays. (See also ▷MOSQUE in 'Architecture and engineering.')

❖ The tradition in many Islamic countries of fine, decorated carpets comes from the use of prayer mats in mosques.

Muhammad (or Mohammed) (cAD 570-632) Founder and chief prophet of ISLAM. He was born in MECCA, where he became familiar with both Judaism and Christianity. Initially a wealthy merchant, he was convinced by religious revelations that he was the last great prophet in the line of MOSES and JESUS, and that he had been chosen to spread the divine message in its final form. As a result of persecution he fled Mecca in 622 with a few followers – a journey known as the Hegira. They settled at Yathrib, renaming it Medina ('city of the prophet'), and set up a form of religious rule. A few years later Muhammad reconquered Mecca and began to spread Islam across the Arab world. His teachings are recorded in the KORAN, which Muslims believe was dictated to him by the archangel Gabriel in a series of visions.

mullah Title given to a learned and devout Islamic scholar, or one who executes Islamic law. The word is a corruption of the Arabic word for 'master'.

❖ In fundamentalist Islamic states such as Iran, mullahs often have considerable political influence.

Muslim Follower of ISLAM – literally one who has 'surrendered' to God. The majority of Muslims belong to the orthodox SUNNI branch or to the more fundamentalist SHIAH (or Shiite) group, but there are many smaller branches, including SUFISM.

mystery religions Ancient Greek and Roman religious cults which grew up around various pagan gods and goddesses. Initiation was by secret rites, and held out the promise of life after death. One of the best-known cults was that of the fertility goddess ▷DEMETER at Eleusis in Greece, where initiation rituals were enacted annually for more than 1 000 years.

mysticism Religious belief based on personal spiritual experience or union with God, or with some other divine being or principle.

SACRED SITE *Muslims revere the site of the Dome of the Rock in Jerusalem, which is the place from where they believe Muhammad, who died in AD 632, rose to heaven.*

Most of the world's great religions have mystical traditions, in which direct contact with the supernatural is said to be achieved by practices such as meditation, rhythmic chanting, fasting or going into trances.

naturalism Philosophical view that there is no need to go beyond the natural world in explaining anything – that, for example, society can be studied in a similar way to the climate. Instead of seeing life as part of a divine plan, naturalists argue that it is the result of certain physical and chemical conditions. Similarly, they see ethics and morality as codes developed to ensure survival by means of social cooperation.

natural theology Attempt to base religious thought on a rational foundation; the belief that knowledge of God and the divine order can be based on observation of the natural world, without the need for revelation. One example is the so-called 'argument from design', according to which the natural world shows such intricate and beautiful design that it could not have arisen accidentally but must have been created.

New Testament Second section of the Christian BIBLE, dealing with the life of JESUS CHRIST and its aftermath. It contains the four GOSPELS of Matthew, Mark, Luke and John; the Acts of the APOSTLES; the Epistles of St PAUL and others; and the Book of Revelation.

Nicene Creed Fundamental statement of belief recited in the Roman Catholic and Orthodox churches, as well as in many Protestant churches, beginning: 'I believe in One God, the Father Almighty, Creator of Heaven and Earth . . .' It was the outcome of a council of bishops called in AD 325 by Emperor Constantine at Nicaea (now in Turkey), to settle disagreements over Christian doctrine.

Nietzsche, Friedrich (1844-1900) Radical German philosopher and linguist. He vigorously rejected all philosophy since SOCRATES, appealing instead to early Greek thought and its dual view of human nature, embodied in the distinction between ▷APOLLO (representative of reason) and ▷DIONYSUS (representative of emotion and instinct). Nietzsche rejected the accepted moral values of Christianity and condemned it as a religion suitable only for the weak. In place of its 'slave morality' he advocated the assertion of the self and the idea of the Superman (*Übermensch*) – an ideal superior being, free from conventional notions of right and wrong, who would be supremely creative. He had a major influence on many schools of 20th century thought.

ROLE MODEL *Nazis corrupted the 'Superman' ideal proposed by Friedrich Nietzsche (right) – and chose to ignore that Nietzsche condemned nationalism and praised Jews.*

nihilism Radical type of MATERIALISM which rejects all moral values in the name of science and popular revolution. It arose in Russia, inspired by Bazarov, the hero of Ivan ▷TURGENEV's masterpiece, the novel *Fathers and Sons* (1862). Philosophers have generally rejected nihilism.

nirvana In Buddhism and other Indian religions, the highest state of blessedness, in which the individual is freed from all desires and attachments, as well as from the cycle of reincarnation. After his ENLIGHTENMENT, the BUDDHA is said to have attained partial nirvana – complete nirvana not being possible until after death.

❖ 'Nirvana' is sometimes used inaccurately to refer to heaven, paradise or simply bliss.

Nonconformists Protestant groups – also known as Free churches or Dissenters – who broke away from the Church of England in the 17th century, rejecting the authority of bishops and the influence of Roman Catholic forms of worship. Today the term is applied to any Protestant denomination which dissents from established Churches such as the Roman Catholic and Anglican churches.

Ockham (or Occam), William of (*c*1285-*c*1349) English philosopher and theologian who wrote extensively on logic and politics. He was excommunicated in 1328 and exiled to Bavaria after supporting the Franciscans on the issue of monastic poverty, which the pope opposed.

❖ Ockham is remembered for the philosophical principle – 'Ockham's razor' – that the simplest explanation is the best one; in his own words, 'a plurality is not to be posited without necessity'.

Old Testament Christian term for the first part of the Bible. It consists of 39 books (which correspond to the 24 books in the Hebrew scriptures) or 51 including the APOCRYPHA recognized by the Roman Catholic Church. It records the history of the Jews, their relationship with God and their prophets' sayings. Christians believe its prophecies were fulfilled by JESUS CHRIST, as told in the NEW TESTAMENT.

Opus Dei International Roman Catholic society founded in Spain in 1928 and approved by the Holy See in 1950, to promote Christian ideals in modern life. It has sometimes been controversial for its secrecy and political involvement, especially in Spain, where it was used to bolster the fascist regime of ▷FRANCO.

ordination Admission into the Christian priesthood. In the Roman Catholic, Anglican and Orthodox Churches it is a solemn sacrament that is considered to confer priestly powers such as the power to celebrate COMMUNION or give ABSOLUTION.

PARADISE LOST *The serpent tempts Adam and Eve to eat the forbidden fruit of the Tree of Knowledge of Good and Evil – which led to their expulsion from the Garden of Eden.*

original sin The corruption of ADAM AND EVE as a result of their tasting the forbidden fruit of the Tree of Knowledge of Good and Evil. This was 'the Fall', which led to the concept of innate sinfulness inherited by all human beings. Christians believe that Jesus atoned for original sin and that those who believe in him and accept BAPTISM are redeemed from it. Muslims reject the doctrine of original sin; they believe the Devil, Iblis, was responsible for Adam and Eve's disobedience

Orthodox Church (or Eastern Orthodox Church) Group of churches forming one of the three main branches of Christianity, together with Protestantism and Roman Catholicism. They include the Russian and Greek Orthodox churches and other smaller churches of eastern Europe and the Balkans

HOLY ICON *In Eastern, or Orthodox, Christianity, icons or paintings on wood were revered as taking on the sacredness of their subjects, such as the Madonna and Child.*

recognizing the supremacy of the patriarch of Constantinople. They broke away from the Roman Catholic Church in 1054, after centuries of disagreement over ritual and doctrine, particularly on the relation between the three persons of the Holy TRINITY. Orthodox worship centres on the celebration of the Eucharist, or Holy COMMUNION, although six other SACRAMENTS (or 'mysteries') are also recognized – baptism, confirmation, penance, last rites, ordination and marriage. Clergy below the rank of bishop are allowed to marry. There are 130 million adherents.
❖ The word 'orthodox' comes from the Greek words meaning 'correct belief'.

Oxford Movement Theological tendency within the Church of England which urged closer ties with the Roman Catholic Church and the restoration of Catholic ceremonies and rituals in Anglican services. It was begun in 1833 by John Newman – who later became a Roman Catholic cardinal – and other theologians associated with Oxford University. Although the movement itself was short-lived, its influence remains in the Anglican High Church, or Anglo-Catholicism.

paganism Term first used by early Christians to describe the beliefs of all non-Christians. The word comes from the Latin for 'country-dweller'. These days it is usually applied to religious beliefs that are not part of a world religion such as Christianity, Judaism, Buddhism or Islam.

Paine, Thomas (1737-1809) Radical English political philosopher known for his pamphlet *Common Sense*, which argued for American independence, and for *The Rights of Man* – a defence of the French Revolution and of democracy and republicanism, which prompted a charge of treason and his escape to France. He wrote *The Age of Reason* as a defence of DEISM, but it led to accusations of atheism because of its attack on Christianity. He died in poverty in New York.

pantheism Belief that God and the natural world are identical, as found in HINDUISM, some forms of BUDDHISM and the philosophy of the Greek STOICS, HEGEL and SPINOZA. It also refers to belief in the worship of all gods.

paradigm Prevailing framework of theories on which scientists base their work. If a fundamental theory is proved wrong, this may cause a scientific revolution; for example, Einstein transformed Newtonian physics.

paradise Place or state of pure happiness. In Christianity, paradise has been identified with both heaven and the Garden of Eden, which is sometimes called the 'earthly paradise'. The Islamic paradise is concerned with sensual pleasures.
❖ The word 'paradise' comes from an ancient Persian term for a walled garden.

Parsees Followers of the Persian religion of ZOROASTRIANISM, who settled in India in the 10th century. They now live mainly in the area around Bombay, and since the 19th century have modernized and reformed the faith, mainly as a result of Western education and missionary influence.

Passover (or Pesach) Jewish festival at the beginning of spring (or autumn in the southern hemisphere), commemorating the deliverance of the first-born on the eve of the EXODUS of the ancient Israelites from Egypt. During Passover – which lasts for eight days, except for Reform Jews and in Israel where it is seven days – unleavened bread called *matzo* and other kosher foods are eaten.
❖ Jesus was crucified at Passover.

Paul, St (*c*3-*c*67) Early Christian theologian and apostle to the non-Jewish communities of the Mediterranean and Near East. Paul (formerly Saul) was a Jew from Tarsus (now in Turkey) who had trained as a rabbi and was an opponent of the early Christians until around AD 35, when he had a vision on the road to Damascus. He later became an energetic Christian leader who preached Christianity to all, not only the Jews.

penance Repenting for one's sins, or acts performed to make up for them. After CONFESSION in the Roman Catholic and Orthodox churches, penance usually involves being asked to say so many 'Hail Marys' or 'Our Fathers'. Today, fasting, pilgrimage and good works such as giving alms are also sometimes regarded as penance.

Pentecost In Judaism, the feast of Shavuot held in May or June to commemorate Moses receiving the TEN COMMANDMENTS. Christians celebrate Pentecost seven Sundays after EASTER in remembrance of the descent of the HOLY SPIRIT on Jesus' disciples at the time of the Jewish feast, bringing them the ability to 'speak in tongues'.

Pentecostal movement Breakaway Christian group – now also known as the charismatic movement – started in the United States in 1901, in reaction to what was considered the rigidity of traditional services. Worship is seen as a joyful occasion, involving singing, chanting and invoking the HOLY SPIRIT in activities such as healing, prophesying and speaking in tongues. Pentecostalists take the Bible literally and are zealous missionaries.
❖ The Apostolic Faith Mission (1908), the Full Gospel Church and the Assemblies of God were the first Pentecostal churches in South Africa, and many of the AFRICAN INDEPENDENT CHURCHES have been influenced by Pentecostalism. The Rhema Church has in recent years attracted members from the established denominations.

Peter, St Foremost of Christ's APOSTLES, originally a fisherman called Simon, but renamed Peter (meaning 'rock') by Jesus. Just before the Crucifixion, Peter denied being a follower of Jesus three times, as Jesus had predicted he would. He became the leader of the early Christians, so beginning the APOSTOLIC SUCCESSION and fulfilling another of Christ's prophecies – 'Upon this rock I will build my Church'. Peter died at the foot of the Vatican Hill, in Rome, near the site of ▷ST PETER'S BASILICA, named after him.
❖ Peter is often depicted holding the keys to the kingdom of heaven. In Roman Catholic tradition, he was the first POPE.

phenomenology Philosophical approach that studies concrete personal experiences as subjectively described without making judgments about whether this reflects 'reality'. It was developed by the German thinker Edmund Husserl in the early 20th century, and became a major force in modern European philosophy and psychology.

Plato (*c*428-*c*348 BC) Ancient Greek philosopher, considered one of the most important figures in Western philosophy. He was a pupil of SOCRATES and became the teacher of ARISTOTLE. Plato's writings take the form of dialogues in which Socrates conducts discussions with other thinkers on subjects such as politics, ETHICS, KNOWLEDGE and METAPHYSICS. Plato is best known for his theory (which probably did not originate with Socrates) that abstractions such as truth or the good – which he called 'forms' or 'ideas' – exist in a realm beyond the physical world. Unlike individual material objects which are perceived with the senses, forms can be grasped only by reason – which is why philosophy is so important. In his *Republic*, Plato suggested that the ideal state would be one ruled by the 'philosopher-king'.

pluralism Theory that reality is composed of many different basic types of substance; the opposite of MONISM.

polytheism Belief in more than one god. Ancient Greek and Roman religion was polytheistic, as are some forms of HINDUISM. Usually the various gods govern particular places or aspects of life; in Greece, ▷ATHENA protected Athens and was the goddess of wisdom, while ▷APHRODITE ruled love and ▷PLUTO the underworld. Monotheism is belief in one God.

pope Bishop of Rome and head of the Roman Catholic Church, also known as the Holy Father, Vicar of Christ or Roman Pontiff. According to Roman Catholic doctrine, all popes are direct successors of the apostle St PETER through APOSTOLIC SUCCESSION. In the past, popes have had extensive political power and influence. Today, however, their authority is mainly restricted to spiritual and administrative matters.

❖ New popes are chosen by a conclave – a meeting of cardinals in the Sistine Chapel. Crowds wait for white smoke from the chimney, signalling a successful ballot.

Popper, Sir Karl (1902-94) British philosopher, born in Austria. He argues that it is impossible to prove a theory, since however many observations support it, a vital exception may have been overlooked. However, finding a single exception is enough to disprove – or falsify – a theory. Scientists must therefore look for contradictions and exceptions. If they find them, they must revise their theories; if they do not find them, their theories gain validity. Popper contends that science progresses in an orderly, logical manner as theories are exposed to the possibility of refutation. He is also known for his criticism of ▷MARXISM and other totalitarian systems of government (which he traces back to Plato).

positivism Philosophical view that the only genuine knowledge is that based on science and factual observation. It rejects the attempts of theology and metaphysics to understand things – such as the purpose of life – that lie beyond the physical world. LOGICAL POSITIVISM was popular in academic circles in the first half of the 20th century.

DIVINERS' WISDOM *Most* izangoma *(Zulu for priest diviner) are women who are 'called' to service by the ancestors; they can be recognised by their elaborate headgear and distinctive garments.*

premise In logic, a PROPOSITION forming the basis of an argument or from which a conclusion is drawn. The classical SYLLOGISM has a major premise and a minor premise. Logic is not concerned with the truth or falsity of premises, only with the logical relationship between them.

Presbyterianism Previously called the Church of Scotland, and a version of CALVINISM found in English-speaking Reformed churches, which refers essentially to a form of Church government. Ministers are democratically elected and a system of Church courts oversees the conduct of the congregation. The Presbyterian Church is the established Church in Scotland and is also a powerful influence in Northern Ireland. There are some 250 Presbyterian congregations in South Africa, where the first gatherings of the church took place in Cape Town in 1806.

❖ Among the educational institutions the Presbyterians started were the Lovedale Institute and the University of Fort Hare, famous places of learning in South Africa. They also founded three training centres in Zimbabwe.

priest diviner Sacred specialist central to the healing rituals of traditional African belief systems. The diviner (*sangoma* in Zulu; *igqira* in Xhosa) is usually called to his or her profession by the ancestors, who transfer supernatural knowledge in dreams or through induced states of semi-trance. Other techniques of ▷DIVINATION include the use of bones, sticks and dice.

❖ Western medicine now believes that the *sangoma* or *igqira* has an important role as the psychiatrist of traditional medicine.

prophet Person who brings a message from God to the people. Old Testament prophets such as Isaiah preached virtuous living, true worship of God and the future coming of an ideal ruler. They were often unpopular for condemning immorality and idol worship.

proposition In philosophy, an assertion, supposition or any idea that can be expressed, whether true, false or still hypothetical. After a proposition has been put forward it is scrutinized and, if found to be true, it may give rise to a new theory. Propositions are the building blocks of LOGIC and science.

Protestantism One of the three branches of Christianity, the others being the Roman Catholic Church and the Eastern Orthodox Church. Although foreshadowed by earlier developments, it arose in the 16th century as part of the REFORMATION initiated by Martin LUTHER as a reaction against the Roman Catholic Church. The Protestants viewed Catholicism as corrupt, riddled with superstition and more concerned with wealth and power than with spirituality. They rejected the authority of the pope and urged a return to the teachings of the Bible and the spirit of the early Church. In many groups more democratic forms of Church government were established. Protestant churches stress prayer, conscience, the performance of good works and personal commitment to God rather than ritual and reliance on priests.

❖ Protestant churches range from those of the ANGLICAN COMMUNION, which have hierarchies of priests and bishops and administer the same sacraments as the Roman Catholic Church, to extreme Puritan sects such as the QUAKERS, who have no formal structure, do not have to acknowledge the Scriptures and take none of the sacraments. Between these are denominations such as the Baptists, Congregationalists, Dutch Reformed churches, Lutherans, Methodists and Presbyterians.

purgatory In Roman Catholic belief, a place of suffering and punishment where the souls of the dead are purified before being admitted to heaven, where they are united with God.

❖ Purgatory, which is vividly described in Dante's ▷*DIVINE COMEDY*, is not mentioned anywhere in the Bible, but Catholics argue that praying for the dead is an ancient Christian practice, and one which implies that their souls must somehow be suffering.

Puritanism Extreme form of PROTESTANTISM, originating in England in the 16th century. Its followers believed that the Church of England had not gone far enough in rejecting Roman Catholic dogma and ritual. The movement included the Presbyterian movement and other NONCONFORMISTS. Persecution drove many Puritans to the Netherlands and the United States in the early 17th century.

❖ Among the Puritans were the Pilgrim Fathers who travelled to America on the ▷MAYFLOWER and who founded the first settlements in New England.

Quakers Unofficial name – originally derogatory – for the Society of Friends, a Protestant sect founded in the mid-17th century by the English religious leader George Fox. They have no priesthood or formal structure and do not take sacraments. Instead, they practise simplicity of life and worship, and stress the importance of the inner voice of the spirit. Worship, which takes place in meeting houses that are open to all, is conducted in silence until someone is moved by the spirit to speak. The movement is strongly pacifist.

rabbi In JUDAISM, a teacher and leader of a congregation, usually associated with a particular synagogue. Rabbis are responsible for the religious education and welfare of the community, and may also conduct religious services. In some synagogues women can become rabbis, and there are also some rabbis who officiate on a part-time basis.

Rama An incarnation of the Hindu god VISHNU, and hero of the epic Sanskrit poem *Ramayana*, which tells of Rama's triumph over the demon Ravana who had abducted Rama's wife Sita. Episodes from the poem are often depicted in Hindu art.

Ramadan Holy ninth month in the Islamic calendar, corresponding roughly to the Christian season of Lent. It includes a commemoration of the Night of Power, when it is believed MUHAMMAD received his revelation from the archangel Gabriel. During Ramadan, Muslims fast from dawn to dusk as a form of purification. Eid-ul-Fitr marks the end of Ramadan and involves a festive meal and the exchange of gifts.

Rastafarianism West Indian religious movement. It developed out of the views of Marcus Garvey (1887-1940), who urged black people to return to Africa to escape oppression. Rastafarians recognize ▷HAILE SELASSIE, who became Emperor of Ethiopia in 1930, as their Messiah, and view Ethiopia as their 'promised land'. They follow a distinctive way of life involving strict dietary rules, smoking dagga, wearing distinctive knitted hats called 'toms' and styling their hair in long 'dreadlocks'.

rationalism Philosophical movement of the 17th and 18th centuries, according to which pure reasoning, rather than observation, is the source of knowledge. DESCARTES, LEIBNIZ and SPINOZA were all rationalist thinkers. They were opposed by EMPIRICISM, which stressed the importance of discovering truth through experience.

realism In modern philosophy, the view that opposes IDEALISM in maintaining that material objects exist independently of human observers. Applied to medieval philosophy, realism is the belief that abstractions such as truth and beauty have an independent existence rather than simply being qualities of individual objects.

reductionism View that entities of one kind are combinations of entities of a simpler kind and can be explained in terms of the simpler entities. For example, if society is no more than a collection of individuals, psychology can explain it, and sociology is irrelevant.

Reformation Movement against the corruption and worldliness of the 16th-century

SILENT WORSHIP *The simple oak panelling and benches at Brigflatts in Cumbria are typical of the meeting houses in which George Fox told his followers to 'tremble at the word of the Lord' – the phrase which gave Quakers their name.*

REVOLT FROM ROME *Statues and other ornaments of the Roman Catholic Church were targets of the zealots of the Reformation, who attacked and condemned them as objects of superstition.*

ROMAN CATHOLIC CHURCH, foreshadowed by events from the 12th century onwards, but set in motion by Martin LUTHER in the early 16th century. It spread rapidly to many countries, and resulted in the establishment of PROTESTANTISM and numerous new churches which rejected the authority of the pope. (See also ▷REFORMATION in 'World history'.)

Reformed churches The churches of PROTESTANTISM and especially CALVINISM.

reincarnation Belief that after death some part of a person's identity – usually the soul – is reborn in a new human or animal body. It is one of the basic teachings of BUDDHISM and HINDUISM, and also appears in many esoteric Western belief systems.

Roman Catholic Church Worldwide body of Christians who recognize the spiritual authority of the POPE, which is often referred to simply as the Catholic Church. It emphasizes the authority of the pope and bishops to teach on matters of faith and morality, and recognizes seven sacraments: BAPTISM, CONFIRMATION, Eucharist or Holy COMMUNION, confession, marriage, ORDINATION and the anointing of the sick. Roman Catholics venerate saints and the Virgin MARY, to whom they pray. The largest Christian denomination in the world, it has more than 900 million members.

❖ The Roman Catholic stance on birth control is controversial, persistently opposing abortion and any form of artificial contraception.

❖ The Dutch and the British forbade public practice of Roman Catholicism at the Cape for a time and its mission work among blacks was delayed until the late 19th century.

Rosh Hashanah Two-day Jewish New Year festival. It takes place at the first new moon after the autumnal equinox (spring equinox in the southern hemisphere), in late September or early October, and marks the start of a period of evaluation and prayer concluding eight days later with the observance of YOM KIPPUR, the Day of Atonement.

Rousseau, Jean Jacques (1712-78) French philosopher, and a leading figure of the ENLIGHTENMENT. He believed that people are naturally good but are corrupted by society's false values. He also developed the idea of the general will, and argued that conformity with it had to be the guiding principle of government. Essentially concerned with the notion of freedom, Rousseau began his masterpiece *The Social Contract* (1762) with the words 'Man is born free, and everywhere he is in chains'.

❖ Rousseau's ideas were an important influence on ▷ROMANTICISM and on the leaders of the ▷FRENCH REVOLUTION.

Russell, Bertrand (1872-1970) British philosopher and mathematician, known for his work in logic and the theory of knowledge. His *Principia Mathematica* (written with A N Whitehead) set out to show how mathematics is based on LOGIC. Russell tutored WITTGENSTEIN at Cambridge University, although they later disagreed. In 1950 Russell was awarded the Nobel prize for literature, mainly in tribute to his *History of Western Philosophy*. Russell was critical of religion, which he believed had hindered human progress.

Sabbath Seventh day of the week, reserved in Judaism for rest and worship. It recognizes the seventh day of creation when, according to GENESIS, God rested, and also the fourth of the TEN COMMANDMENTS, which says: 'Six days shalt thou labour . . . But the seventh day is the sabbath . . . in it thou shalt not do any work.' Jews observe the Sabbath (or Sabbat, from the Hebrew word for 'rest') from nightfall on Friday until nightfall on Saturday. Most Christians do not observe the Sabbath but regard Sunday as 'the Lord's Day' or day of rest and worship. However, some so-called 'Sabbatarian' Christian sects such as the SEVENTH-DAY ADVENTISTS observe the Sabbath as their day of worship. In ISLAM Friday is regarded as the holy day, although it is not a day of rest.

sacrament Christian ritual considered as an outward sign of inner grace. There are seven sacraments in the Catholic and Orthodox churches: BAPTISM, CONFIRMATION, Eucharist or Holy COMMUNION, confession, marriage, ORDINATION and the anointing of the sick. Many Protestant faiths acknowledge only

PIPE OF PEACE *A prominent pacifist in both world wars, the philosopher Bertrand Russell became a leading figure in the Campaign for Nuclear Disarmament (CND) in the 1960s.*

baptism and Communion as sacraments, and some – such as the QUAKERS – not even these.

saint In the Roman Catholic and Orthodox churches, saints are venerated and invoked to intercede with God on behalf of those who pray to them. Other Christian churches recognize saints but do not permit veneration or invocation. Buddhism and Islam also acknowledge many saints to whom devotees address their prayers.

salvation In Christianity, a state of union or closeness to God, and deliverance from evil – the reverse of DAMNATION. Jesus promised salvation to all who followed him, but this has not prevented disagreements among Christians as to who was saved, and whether salvation has to do with good works on Earth or only with faith. The idea of salvation is also found in some form in other faiths, including ISLAM and BUDDHISM.

Salvation Army Christian mission, originally the Christian Revival Association, founded by William Booth in 1865 to minister to the poor of London, and now one of the biggest voluntary social work agencies in the world. The Salvation Army is organized in military fashion and is renowned for its work with the destitute and homeless, its rousing brass bands, and its collections in pubs.

Sartre, Jean-Paul (1905-80) French philosopher, novelist and a leading proponent of EXISTENTIALISM, as outlined in his philosophical essay *Being and Nothingness* (1943). His main concern was the nature of human existence and the freedom of human beings to create their own destiny.

Satan In Jewish and Christian belief, a fallen angel who opposes God and tempts people to commit evil – also identified as Lucifer or the DEVIL. In the early books of the Old Testament, Satan is simply an opponent or adversary. In later books and in the New Testament he is increasingly identified as the personification of evil and the archenemy of Christ.

scepticism Philosophical approach of rigorously doubting and questioning what others claim to know. It was used by DESCARTES, who hoped that if he was as critical as possible about everything people normally claimed to know, he would eventually discover something that could not be doubted. Sceptics, however, say there is no such thing as certain knowledge.

Scientology Movement founded in the 1950s by the American philosopher and science-fiction writer L Ron Hubbard, which claims to increase spiritual awareness. Its use of dianetics, a form of psychotherapy, has been denounced as unscientific, and the sect has been criticized for seeking to influence vulnerable young people.

Second Coming According to the New Testament, the future return of Jesus to Earth to judge the living and the dead and to bring about the final triumph of good over evil. The APOSTLES appeared to believe this would occur soon after their own time. Since then, many religious groups have propounded the imminence of Christ's appearance, including the JEHOVAH'S WITNESSES, the SEVENTH-DAY ADVENTISTS and various ephemeral cults.

Seventh-Day Adventists Christian denomination founded in 1863 in the United States. Adventists worship on Saturdays, abstain from alcohol and tobacco, and practise adult baptism by total immersion. They believe that the SECOND COMING is imminent.

Shakers Members of the United Society for Believers in Christ's Second Appearing, which stemmed from a group of radical English QUAKERS. In 1744 the English visionary Ann Lee and eight followers emigrated to America, where they and a number of converts won respect for their orderly and prosperous communities and for their simple but beautiful artefacts, especially their furniture.
❖ The name 'Shaker' refers to dancing designed to induce visionary experience.

Shiah Second-largest branch of the Islamic faith, influential mainly in Iran, Iraq and the Indian subcontinent. Adherents are known as 'Shiites' and follow the teachings of MUHAMMAD's cousin Ali. Shiah Islam has its own system of law and theology, and emphasizes FUNDAMENTALISM and the political role of Islam more than the main SUNNI branch.

Shinto Religion of Japan. It goes back to ancient times but has little established theology. Instead, it stresses the forces of nature, which are seen as divine gifts to humanity. Natural objects are believed to symbolize gods, and the purpose of worship is seen as purification. Followers prefer to pray and place shrines in natural surroundings. The religion is officially recognized but has not been state-supported since it was disestablished after World War II.
❖ Most Japanese follow both Shinto (which is concerned with the here and now) and Buddhism (for the afterlife).

Shiva (or Siva) One of the three major gods of HINDUISM, along with Brahma and Vishnu. He rules over creation and destruction, and symbolizes fertility, often being represented by a phallic symbol, or lingam. Shiva is called the Lord of the Dance and is often depicted also as a dancing figure with four arms.

Sikhism Indian religion founded by the religious teacher Guru Nanak (1469-*c*1539). The name 'Sikh' means disciple. Sikh belief

HELPING THE POOR *William Booth, founder and first general of the Salvation Army, tirelessly campaigned for the poor and homeless. 'Sally Army' trademarks remain its military titles, brass bands and its journal* – The War Cry.

is a combination of Hinduism and Islam, but rejects ritual in favour of meditation and simple devotion. The religion recognizes a single god or creator of the universe, and it is felt that closeness to God comes only through grace. There is considerable tension between Sikhs and Muslims, particularly in the Punjab region of India. Sikhism is professed by some 14 million Indians, and it is strongly opposed to caste divisions.
❖ All Sikhs take the surname Singh (Sanskrit for 'lion') and the men do not cut their hair.

sin Evil that stems from actions that offend a deity. In Christianity, humanity is believed to inherit the ORIGINAL SIN of Adam and Eve, redemption from which can come only through faith and the grace of God. Roman Catholicism distinguishes between mortal sin (such as murder, suicide, bestiality and crimes against the HOLY SPIRIT), which leads to damnation; and venial sin, which is a lesser misdemeanour and punished in PURGATORY. In the Anglican, Roman Catholic and Orthodox churches, sin is atoned for in collective or individual CONFESSION, but in the Reformed churches it is considered purely a matter between the conscience of the individual and God.

Socrates (*c*469-399 BC) Philosopher in Ancient Greece, generally considered the father of Western philosophy and one of its greatest minds. He conducted his speculations by means of question-and-answer discussion (DIALECTIC), and had a devoted following of wealthy young men. Socrates wrote nothing himself, but his teachings are recorded in the early dialogues of PLATO, his pupil. Socrates was primarily concerned with ETHICS and KNOWLEDGE, arguing that virtue is the same as knowledge and vice the result of ignorance. He was also an outspoken opponent of political tyranny.

Solomon Jewish king and lawgiver of the 10th century BC. He was the son of David and built the first TEMPLE OF JERUSALEM. He is credited with vast wisdom and wealth, and many wives.
❖ The 'Judgment of Solomon' involved two women claiming to be the mother of a baby. Solomon decreed that the child be cut in half. When one woman said that she would rather it be given to the other, he knew that she was the real mother.

sophists Group of Greek philosophers and teachers of public speaking in the 5th century BC. They felt that genuine knowledge was impossible to achieve, and were accused by SOCRATES and PLATO of being more interested in winning arguments than in pursuing truth.
❖ The term 'sophistry' refers to the use of devious or cunning argument.

DEADLY SINS *The sins incurring damnation in the Middle Ages, as depicted by Hieronymus Bosch, were (clockwise from top) gluttony, sloth, lust, pride, anger, envy and covetousness.*

Spinoza, Baruch de (1632-77) Dutch philosopher who developed a notoriously difficult system of thought set out like a series of mathematical proofs. It was founded on a form of PANTHEISM which identified God with nature, but denied the immortality of the soul and the personal nature of God. Spinoza argued that good and evil are relative terms. He also rejected FREE WILL, arguing that 'self-determination' – acting in accordance with one's nature – is the only true freedom.

Stoics Ancient philosophers who advocated calm acceptance of the natural order, including death, and the overcoming of all passions, both pleasurable and painful. Stoicism was started by the Greek philosopher Zeno around 308 BC, but was later taken up in ancient Rome, notably by the writer and philosopher ▷SENECA.
❖ The word 'stoic' comes from the Greek *stoa*, meaning a portico, after the porch of a building in Athens where Zeno taught.

Sufism Mystical sect in ISLAM, dating from the 8th century AD, which developed chiefly in Iran. Sufis live in religious communities and devote themselves to spiritual development and the search for God – often by means of chanting, music, dancing and controlled breathing. They also do charitable and educational work.

Sunni Larger of the two main branches of ISLAM, the second being SHIAH. Members recognize the first four caliphs, or leaders, as the true successors of Muhammad, and base their teachings on the KORAN and traditional Muslim law (Sunna).

syllogism Formal logical argument composed of two statements – the major PREMISE and minor premise – and a conclusion derived from them by DEDUCTIVE REASONING. A classic example is: *All men are mortal* (major premise); *Socrates is a man* (minor premise); therefore *Socrates is mortal* (conclusion).

synagogue Building for Jewish religious services and instruction. The term is also applied to a Jewish congregation.
❖ The first South African Hebrew congregation was founded in Cape Town in 1841 by 17 colonists. The oldest remaining synagogue in the country – the Old Shul in Government Avenue in Cape Town – was built in 1863 and

DEATH OF A PHILOSOPHER *Condemned to death for 'corrupting' the youth of Athens by his teaching, Socrates calmly drinks the deadly hemlock and dies, philosophically consoling his friends.*

now houses the Jewish Museum. Next to it is the Great Synagogue, built in 1905.

Talmud Compilation of Jewish traditions, law and commentary. The rules of the Talmud are strictly followed by Orthodox Jews, but more freely interpreted in Reform and Liberal synagogues.

Taoism Ancient Chinese school of thought dating from around the 3rd century BC. It is based on the idea of *Tao*, or 'the Way' – an indefinable principle believed to govern the universe – and emphasizes the need for harmonious interaction with the environment. Taoists aim at personal tranquillity and detachment, and at living in harmony with *Tao*. One of the main Taoist texts is the *Tao te Ching* attributed to LAO-TZU.

Temple of Jerusalem Place of worship built by King SOLOMON in the 10th century BC for the ancient Israelites. It housed the ARK OF THE COVENANT containing the TEN COMMANDMENTS, but was destroyed in 587 BC by Nebuchadnezzar. A later temple built on the same site was also destroyed. The Western Wall in Jerusalem (also known as the Wailing Wall) was part of the second Temple, destroyed by the Romans in AD 70. Jews believe the Temple will be rebuilt when their Messiah comes.

Ten Commandments (or Decalogue) Fundamental laws of JUDAISM, which are said to have been handed down by God to Moses on Mount Sinai. Slightly different commandments are given in the Books of Exodus and Deuteronomy, but the ten are usually accepted as being: I. I am the Lord thy God; thou shalt have no other gods before me. II. Thou shalt not make unto thee any graven image. III. Thou shalt not take the name of the Lord thy God in vain. IV. Remember the Sabbath day, to keep it holy. V. Honour thy father and thy mother. VI. Thou shalt not kill. VII. Thou shalt not commit adultery. VIII. Thou shalt not steal. IX. Thou shalt not bear false witness against thy neighbour. X. Thou shalt not covet thy neighbour's house. Thou shalt not covet thy neighbour's wife, nor his manservant, nor his maidservant, nor his ox, nor his ass, nor anything that is thy neighbour's.

theism Belief in the existence of God or the gods, particularly in a personal, all-powerful, all-knowing creator. Theism is the basic foundation of such faiths as Christianity, Islam and Judaism.

Theosophical Society Esoteric religious movement founded in 1875 by the Russian-born psychic and voluminous metaphysical writer Madame H P Blavatsky (1831-91). Her ideas were based on Eastern religion, but she developed them into a complex system of her own. Two years after its founding the Society moved to India, where its headquarters remain. After the death of Madame Blavatsky, Annie Besant took over the leadership.

torah Term which can embrace all Jewish literature, laws, customs, ceremonies and religious teachings. In a more limited sense Torah refers only to the Pentateuch (the first five books of the Old Testament); the whole Jewish Bible is normally called the Tanakh or sometimes the Miqra.

Trinity, Holy Central Christian doctrine that God, although one, exists in the form of three 'persons': Father, Son and Holy Spirit. Disputes about the exact relationship of the three to one another caused the split between the Orthodox and Roman Catholic Churches in the 11th century.

truth One of the most basic philosophical concepts, but without a simple, agreed definition. The commonsense view that truth somehow corresponds with reality (the correspondence theory) raises problems about the nature of reality and what constitutes KNOWLEDGE. The coherence theory is equally problematic, maintaining that only complete understanding can provide truth – everything else is merely an approximation. Another approach is the 'pragmatic' theory, according to which truth is simply the point of view that is most useful in the long run.

Unitarians Christian sect that grew out of PROTESTANTISM. It rejects the central Christian doctrines of the TRINITY and the divinity of Christ, but recognizes the importance of Jesus as a religious teacher.

utilitarianism Theory of ethics developed by the British philosopher Jeremy BENTHAM in the 18th century and further refined by John Stuart MILL. Its basis is the principle that actions are morally good in so far as they promote human happiness, and bad in so far as they promote pain or suffering. Versions of utilitarianism are still highly influential in moral philosophy.

Virgin Birth Christian belief that JESUS CHRIST did not have a human father, but was conceived by the Virgin MARY through the power of the HOLY SPIRIT. The Roman Catholic doctrine of the IMMACULATE CONCEPTION, according to which the Virgin Mary was conceived and born without sin, was a matter of dispute for centuries but established as DOGMA in 1854. It is rejected by both Protestants and the Orthodox Church because it is not supported by the Bible.

❖ Mary's virginal conception of Jesus is sometimes mistakenly referred to as the Immaculate Conception.

Vishnu Hindu god known as the 'Preserver', and considered the embodiment of goodness and mercy. He is said to have appeared several times on Earth, including incarnations as KRISHNA and RAMA.

Voodoo Folk religion of Haiti and some other Caribbean islands, as well as some parts of Africa. It arose in the 17th century on slave plantations and contains both Roman Catholic elements and West African beliefs. Voodoo rituals involve animal sacrifice and the conjuring of spirits.
❖ Legends of zombies – mindless human beings who can be controlled by witchcraft and kept as slaves – are part of Voodoo belief.

Wesley, John (1703-91) English clergyman and founder of the METHODIST CHURCH. He travelled around on horseback, preaching in the open air. He made many converts, particularly among labourers, miners and factory workers at public meetings of up to 30 000 people. He insisted that his followers should stay within the Church of England, but they broke away four years after his death.

witches In traditional African religion the spells and evil workings of witches and their 'familiars' or assistants are seen as the usual causes of misfortune. Sorcerers rely more on medicines and are associated with *muti* killings. Notorious witches' familiars are the dwarf-like *thokoloshe* and the zombie. It is the task of the PRIEST DIVINER to identify and destroy the witch. (See also ▷WITCHCRAFT in 'Myths and legends'.)

Wittgenstein, Ludwig (1889-1951) One of the most influential philosophers of the 20th century. He was born into a wealthy Austrian family, but spent much of his life in Britain. He studied under Bertrand Russell at Cambridge, where he later became professor of philosophy. Wittgenstein's early work attempted to apply strict logical criteria to language and was a major influence on LOGICAL POSITIVISM. Later he became interested in the variety and flexibility of language, and its power to shape our view of reality.
❖ In the 1920s, 'to avoid having friends for the sake of . . . money' Wittgenstein gave away all his inheritance.

Yahweh Hebrew name of God deduced by modern scholars from the four consonants YHWH (the 'Tetragrammaton') which are written in Judaism but considered too sacred to be spoken. (See also JEHOVAH.)

yin and yang In Chinese and Japanese thought, two principles or qualities eternally in opposition. Yin represents femininity, darkness, coldness, passivity and the Earth; while yang represents masculinity, light, heat, activity and heaven. Each contains a tiny fragment of the other and everything in nature is in a constant state of flux between the two polar opposites.

DIVIDED WORLD *At the heart of the circle, a curved line separates yin and yang, the two complementary and opposing forces of the universe. In China, the lacquer board was hung on a door to deter the entry of devils.*

yoga Technique used in Indian religious traditions to achieve mental tranquillity and detachment from worldly concerns. The type most frequently practised in the West is hatha yoga, based on physical postures and breathing. Other forms of yoga focus on meditation and supernormal states of consciousness.

Yom Kippur (or Day of Atonement) Most solemn holy day in the Jewish year, which occurs ten days after the beginning of ROSH HASHANAH. It commemorates the creation of the world, and the bond between God and the Jewish people. It is traditionally observed by fasting, prayer, repentance and silent reflection in a synagogue.

Zen Buddhism School of BUDDHISM taken to Japan from China in the 12th century. The goal of Zen is a state of deep insight known as *satori*. This is said to be achieved by a combination of meditation, study with a Zen master and, in some schools, the contemplation of riddles, or *koans*, such as 'What is the sound of one hand clapping?' Precise skills such as calligraphy and archery are also taught as a path to spiritual insight.
❖ As an aid to meditation followers of Zen have constructed gardens of great simplicity and beauty – often consisting simply of raked gravel, a few rocks and some moss.

Zionist churches The largest grouping among the AFRICAN INDEPENDENT CHURCHES in South Africa and inspired by the American faith-healing and pentecostal movements of the early 20th century. Zionist leaders and prophets rely less on the Scriptures and practise faith-healing techniques. They advocate personal morality, hard work and abstinence from alcohol and tobacco. After World War II, Zionist churches flourished among impoverished urban blacks. The largest church is the Zion Christian Church (ZCC), founded by Ignatius Lekganyane around 1910. At Easter its annual assemblage attracts hundreds of thousands of worshippers to Moria, its spiritual centre in Northern Province.

Zoroastrianism Persian religion founded by the prophet Zoroaster (or Zarathustra), who lived around the 7th or 6th century BC. It teaches that the world is the site of a cosmic battle, in which the good god Ahura Mazda will eventually defeat the powers of evil.
❖ The Magi who came from the East to present gifts of gold, frankincense and myrrh to the infant Jesus in Bethlehem may have been Zoroastrian priests.

ZION FAITHFUL *Zion Christian Church followers gather at Moria for the annual Easter pilgrimage which attracts up to two million worshippers to the church's Northern Province base.*

ART AND DESIGN

Art is the visual expression of civilization: every age is remembered for its artistic legacy. Painters and sculptors inspire awe and delight in their quest to express themselves and reflect the human condition. Photographers chronicle social change as they capture moods and moments. Designers shape and colour our everyday world, influencing the clothes we wear and the homes we live in. Without them all our lives would be dull and grey.

SIMPLE STYLE *This sketch design by Giorgio Armani shows his concern with comfort as well as elegance and his unstructured, understated tailoring.*

abstract art Painting and sculpture that explores form and colour, conveying an emotion or idea without using recognizable images. Vasily KANDINSKY's *Blue Rider* (1911) was one of the first abstract paintings.

abstract expressionism American painting style of the 1940s and 1950s, which had its roots in the early abstract works of KANDINSKY, and in SURREALISM. It emerged in New York with the migration of many European artists during World War II. The opening of Peggy Guggenheim's gallery, Art of This Century, exposed American artists to European modernism. Major figures were Jackson POLLOCK, Mark ROTHKO, Willem de Kooning, and Adolph Gottlieb.

acrylic Water-soluble synthetic paint which can be used thickly or thinly and allows an artist to combine the techniques of oil and watercolour paintings.

Adams, Ansel (1902-84) American photographer known for his black-and-white landscapes of America's western states, and especially for his pictures of the Yosemite National Park. Adams accentuated the tonal contrast in his photographs, giving them more depth and drama.

Ainslie, Bill (1934-89) South African artist of works executed in the manner of the abstract expressionists, with paint dripped and poured on to a canvas laid flat on the floor. An influential and committed art educator, whose own art school led to the establishment of the Johannesburg Art Foundation in 1982, he was a founder figure in the Federated Union of Black Artists (FUBA) and the Alexandra Art Centre.

Anreith, Anton (1754-1822) German-born sculptor who came to Cape Town in 1777 with the Dutch East India Company. He collaborated with the French architect, Louis-Michel Thibault, and German master builder Hermann Schutte on Cape BAROQUE buildings. Among his major works in Cape Town are the RELIEF plaster sculptures on the pediment of the wine cellar at Groot Constantia and the carved wooden pulpit of the Lutheran Church in Strand Street.

Armani, Giorgio (1935-) Italian fashion designer who has had enormous success with his modern but classic collections for men and women. He has shops in most of the world's major cities.

BOLD MOVES *This 1925 headscarf shows the strong geometric forms of Art Deco, which discarded the gentle curves of Art Nouveau.*

Art Deco Style of architecture, decoration and design popular in the late 1920s and the 1930s. Unlike the flowing forms of the earlier ART NOUVEAU movement, Art Deco used bold geometric shapes and manufactured materials such as steel, glass and plastic. Art Deco designers were strongly influenced by CUBISM. (See also ▷ART DECO in 'Architecture and engineering'.)

❖ Art Deco's name was derived from the first major exhibition of decorative arts after World War I – the *Exposition Internationale des Arts Décoratifs*, held in Paris in 1925.

NATURAL GRACE *Alfonse Mucha's* Poster of a Girl *(1899) shows the flowering lines and sinuous forms which typify Art Nouveau.*

Art Nouveau Style of design and architecture popular during the 1890s which often incorporated stylized plants and the sinuous, flowing lines of the human body. It formed part of the late 19th-century reaction against the decline of craftsmanship after the Industrial Revolution and attempted to create a new form of art that broke free from tradition and history. Art Nouveau was largely inspired by the ARTS AND CRAFTS MOVEMENT and especially the work of William MORRIS. Among its principal exponents were Aubrey BEARDSLEY, Charles Rennie MACKINTOSH, and René LALIQUE. (See also ▷ART NOUVEAU in 'Architecture and engineering'.)

Arts and Crafts Movement Social and aesthetic movement in England during the late 19th century, inspired by John RUSKIN and the architect Augustus ▷PUGIN, which sought to reassert the value of handmade objects in the

face of ever-increasing mass production. William MORRIS and Charles Voysey led the movement, which aimed to produce objects that were individual, functional and decorative. The Arts and Crafts Movement influenced the development of ART NOUVEAU and eventually the BAUHAUS, particularly in the USA and Canada, where the movement flourished until the outbreak of World War I. (See also ▷ARTS AND CRAFTS MOVEMENT in 'Architecture and engineering'.)
❖ Previously rigid divisions between art and craft are now being questioned. A more inclusive attitude is being adopted, particularly in Africa, where a central issue in the debate is the often negative perception of so-called 'women's work'.

Ashley, Laura (1925-85) British designer who originally made furnishing materials in the 1950s. She later expanded into clothing design and manufacture in the 1960s. The Laura Ashley style is characterized by romantic English designs – often with a 19th-century rural feel – and the use of natural fabrics.

Bacon, Francis (1909-92) Self-taught Irish-born artist, widely regarded as one of the foremost postwar British painters. His best-known work includes the grotesque *Three Studies for Figures at the Base of a Crucifixion* (1944) and dramatic portraits of screaming, tortured popes, which convey a sense of unease and alarm.

Badsha, Omar (1945-) South African photographer, founding member of Afrapix, a collective which attempted to promote change in South Africa using cameras instead of guns. He edited *South Africa: the Cordoned Heart* (1986) and co-edited *Beyond the Barricades* (1989), which contained images of everyday life in South Africa highlighting social injustices and the plight of those oppressed under the apartheid regime.

Baines, Thomas (1820-75) English explorer and self-taught artist who spent most of his adult life in southern Africa and has left a record of a vanished world. He travelled extensively in South Africa, Zimbabwe and Namibia, as well as northern Australia, avidly painting the people, plants, mammals and birdlife he encountered in his travels.

baroque Dramatic and decorative style of art and architecture that originated in Italy in the late 16th century. It spread to France, and then to Germany and Austria, where it lasted into the 18th century. Its curved lines, ornate decoration and flamboyant compositions create a theatrical effect, as seen in the works of RUBENS and BERNINI. The works of POUSSIN

AFRICAN ADORNMENT Amakosa Woman Returning from Work *is one of the many records of the past left by Thomas Baines.*

and CARRACCI show how the baroque also drew on the Classical tradition. It is typified by the LOUIS QUATORZE style and the work of LE BRUN. The baroque period succeeded MANNERISM and was followed by the ROCOCO style of art. (See also ▷BAROQUE in 'Architecture and engineering'.)

Battiss, Walter (1906-1982) Versatile, inventive South African artist, art teacher and educator, who left a legacy of art as adventure. He held the chair of fine arts at Unisa, where he founded the academic journal *de Arte*. He had an absorbing interest in ROCK ART, which influenced his own work, and was co-creator, with Norman Catherine (1949-), of the mythical Fook Island, for which they devised its own passport, currency, postage stamps, fauna and flora.

Bauhaus (bow-howss) Probably the most influential school of design and architecture of the 20th century. It was founded at Weimar, in Germany, in 1919 by the architect Walter ▷GROPIUS; the school sought to mix modern technology with architecture and the decorative arts. Bauhaus designers attempted to produce functional and well-made designs – carrying on some of the earlier ideals upheld by the ARTS AND CRAFTS MOVEMENT – that could be successfully mass-produced. In 1933 the school was shut down by the Nazis, but its ideas continued to be influential, especially in the USA. (See also ▷BAUHAUS in 'Architecture and engineering'.)

beadwork An art form which plays an important role in the social and political life of many of southern Africa's cultural groups, where beaded objects, including clothing, ornaments and dolls, are in daily use or reserved for festive occasions. Beaded clothing can be a signifier of social status, and of certain milestones, such as puberty and marriage. Cross-cultural influences, from the Victorian fashions to contemporary styles, are evident in much southern African beadwork.

Beardsley, Aubrey (1872-98) British illustrator whose stylized black-and-white ART NOUVEAU drawings reflect the decadence of the times. He belonged to an aesthetic movement which included the writer Oscar ▷WILDE and the painter James WHISTLER.

Beaton, Sir Cecil (1904-80) British photographer and designer known for his distinctive portraits of politicians, royalty and other famous people. He designed many film and stage shows, including Oscar-winning sets and costumes for films such as *Gigi* (1958) and *My Fair Lady* (1964).

Bellini, Giovanni (*c*1430-1516) Venetian artist whose early use of Flemish oil glazing techniques and the introduction of naturalistic landscape backgrounds had a strong influence on Venetian painting. His style and use of colour were further developed by his pupils, TITIAN and Giorgione (*c*1478-1511). His brother-in-law was the artist MANTEGNA.

Bernini, Giovanni Lorenzo (1598-1680) Italian sculptor, painter and architect who was the leading exponent of BAROQUE art. In sculpture, his skill in portraying gesture, facial expression and movement in draperies was unequalled. (See also ▷BERNINI in 'Architecture and Engineering'.)

Bhengu, Gerard (1910-92) One of the pioneers of black art in South Africa. He painted naturalistic landscapes and small-scale, intimate human studies, mainly in SEPIA, which provide a valuable and accurate record of the traditional clothing, hairstyles and ornamentation of the Zulu people. He also worked as a book illustrator.

Biedermeier (BEE-der-my-er) Style of decoration and solid, comfortable-looking furniture which flourished in Austria, Scandinavia and Germany from the 1820s until the 1840s. It was the Continental equivalent of REGENCY, its functional pieces resembling many of those inspired by the French Empire style.

Bosch, Hieronymus (*c*1450-1516) Flemish artist widely regarded as among the world's greatest painters of fantasy. His obsessive and often horrific work, full of bizarre imagery, as

in *The Garden of Earthly Delights* (*c*1500-10), is often considered to be a precursor of SURREALISM. It was also the first convincing visual depiction of evil and of human fears.

Botticelli, Sandro (BOT-ti-CHEL-lee) (*c*1445-1510) Italian artist whose flowing draughtsmanship and religious and mythological paintings influenced the RENAISSANCE art of Florence. He was supported by the ruling Medici family, who probably commissioned his *Birth of Venus* (*c*1478). He also painted frescoes in the Sistine Chapel in the Vatican.

Bowler, Thomas (1812-69) British-born artist who settled in Cape Town in 1833. He worked mainly in watercolours. His landscapes of town and countryside are a rather romanticized visual record of 19th-century South Africa. Lithographs and engravings were made of many of his works, including the *Great Anti-Convict Meeting* held in Cape Town in 1849 in protest against the Cape being used as a penal colony.

Brancusi, Constantin (1876-1957) Romanian sculptor who settled in Paris in the early 1900s. He was a major figure in 20th-century sculpture. His elegantly simple works remain figurative, although he reduced forms to their essence, refining and reworking concepts. Recurrent themes are creation, birth, life and death. Among his most famous works is *Sleeping Muse* (1909-10), a highly polished marble head, resting on its side.

Braque, Georges (1882-1963) French painter whose collaboration with PICASSO in the development of CUBISM was crucial to the evolution of modern art. He worked briefly in the bright colours of the Fauves (see FAUVISM), but was strongly influenced by CÉZANNE's structural compositions. He met Picasso in 1907 when he first saw the painting, *Les Demoiselles d'Avignon*, and worked closely with him until 1914. After World War I, during which he was badly wounded, he developed a style of his own. His late paintings are harmonious and calm, a bird in flight being a recurrent motif.

Brown, David (1951-) South African sculptor whose powerful works, combining bronze, wood and steel, are influenced by the political and social milieu in which he lives. He often works in series, such as in his *Procession* (1985) and *Voyage* (1988), where ships, chariots and carts become vehicles of horror.

UNEARTHLY VISION *The depiction of hell in Bosch's masterpiece* The Garden of Earthly Delights *brims over with grotesque images.*

The strange, puppetlike human and animal creatures he depicts seem caught between the routine of everyday life and a descent into brutal insanity.

Brueghel, Pieter ('the Elder') (BROY-gul) (*c*1530-69) Flemish painter known for his amusing but sensitive pictures of peasant life, which often show scenes of drunkenness, gluttony and lechery but also include a moral message. His best-known works include *Hunters in the Snow* (1565), *The Wedding Banquet* and *The Peasant Dance* (both *c*1568). His sons, Jan and Pieter the Younger, were also painters.

Byzantine Style of painting and design developed in the ▷BYZANTINE EMPIRE from 330 to 1453. As the ▷ORTHODOX CHURCH imposed strict constraints on art, paintings of the period depicted religious scenes in formal and often two-dimensional designs, with simple, stylized figures, or in icons using rich colour and gold leaf. (See also ▷BYZANTINE in 'Architecture and engineering'.)

Calder, Alexander (1898-1976) American artist best known for his hanging sculptural mobiles and towering stabiles (abstract works, usually of sheet metal, with no moving parts). Trained as an engineer, he worked as an illustrator. His hanging mobiles of the 1930s gave way to standing mobiles in the 1940s and 1950s and stabiles in the 1960s.

Canaletto, Giovanni Antonio (1697-1768) Italian painter and printmaker, famous for his picturesque scenes of the canals and grand architecture of Venice. His works were in great demand by English visitors on the Grand Tour (the extended educational tour of Continental Europe fashionable during the 18th century, particularly among the British). He is a forerunner of the 19th-century landscape tradition.

Caravaggio, Michelangelo Merisi da (1573-1610) Tempestuous Italian painter, one of the forerunners of the BAROQUE style. He rejected RENAISSANCE idealism and portrayed subjects in a naturalistic manner in works of great pictorial drama. The emotional impact is intensified by the use of CHIAROSCURO. A controversial figure, Caravaggio was protected by influential patrons, but fled Rome after killing a companion in 1606. He spent his last years in Naples, Malta and Sicily.

caricature Comic picture of a person with at least one feature exaggerated, but not to the extent that the likeness is lost. The first great artist to use caricature was Annibale CARRACCI in *c*1600. William HOGARTH popularized caricatures in the 1730s, after which James Gillray in England (1757-1815) and Honoré Daumier (1808-79) in France used them as a political weapon in satirical cartoons.

Caro, Sir Anthony (1924-) English sculptor, who initially studied engineering. His large constructions, assembled from steel girders or flat sheets of steel, are generally brightly painted or varnished. His late modernist philosophy influenced the work of several South African artists whom he taught in London.

Carracci (ka-RAA-chee) Family of Bolognese painters, including Ludovico (1555-1619) and his cousins Agostino (1557-1602) and Annibale (1560-1609) – the greatest of the Carraccis. The family revived the Renaissance style of RAPHAEL and set up a widely celebrated teaching academy. Annibale's most renowned work is the set of mythological paintings he produced for the Farnese Gallery in Rome.

Cartier-Bresson, Henri (1908-) French pioneer of photojournalism who took great care in composing and framing his photographs of people at a 'decisive moment'. He said: 'To me, photography is the simultaneous recognition, in a fraction of a second, of the significance of an event as well as a precise organization of forms which give the event proper expression.'

cartoon In fine art, a cartoon is a preparatory sketch, usually the same size as the painting to be made from it; LEONARDO DA VINCI's cartoons are well-known examples.

Cassatt, Mary (1845-1926) American painter known for her pictures of mothers with their children, as in *The Bath* (1892). She worked mainly in France with the impressionists and befriended Edgar DEGAS.

Cellini, Benvenuto (1500-71) Italian sculptor and goldsmith, born in Florence. His bronze figure *Perseus* (1545-54) is one of the finest pieces of Mannerist sculpture. He wrote a detailed autobiography.

ceramic art An art form in which clay is used as an art material in its own right, rather than as a vehicle for metal casting, or in the making of functional objects such as pottery. In South Africa notable ceramic artists include Fee Halsted Berning, Esias Bosch, Noria MABASA, Bonnie Ntshalintshali, Hylton Nel and Ephraim Ziqubu.

Cézanne, Paul (1839-1906) French post-impressionist painter, of seminal importance in the evolution of modern art. He worked briefly in the impressionist style, and had a long association with PISSARRO, but devoted himself to a structural analysis of nature, painting the same landscapes – particularly

PAINTING BY PLANES The Lake at Annecy, *painted in the summer of 1896, reflects Cézanne's study of the interlocking forms which make a picture, and displays his skilful use of colour.*

Mont St Victoire – countless times. His work was the major influence on BRAQUE and PICASSO's development of CUBISM. His late landscapes demonstrate a vast range of tones.

Chagall, Marc (1887-1985) Russian artist who settled in France and is best known for his lyrical fantasy works and floating figures. Prolific and versatile, he designed the sets and costumes for the Stravinsky ballet *Firebird* in 1945, painted the ceiling of the Paris Opera House, and left a great legacy of stained glass windows and murals.

Chanel, Gabrielle (Coco) (1883-1971) French designer who revolutionized women's fashion in the 1920s and 1930s. She was noted for designing the 'little black dress', classic tailored ladies' suits and perfumes – especially *Chanel No 5*. She began a vogue for costume jewellery, which she also designed.
❖ It was Coco Chanel who first made a suntan fashionable, after a holiday on the Duke of Westminster's yacht in 1927.

Chardin, Jean-Baptiste (1699-1779) French painter of genre scenes and still lifes. His compositions of everyday middle-class life are direct and intimate, but never sentimental. His use of reflected or silhouetted light was influenced by VERMEER, and his works strongly influenced the 19th-century realists, in particular MANET.

chiaroscuro (ki-a-re-SKEW-ro) Use of strong contrasts of light and shade for dramatic effect. REMBRANDT and CARAVAGGIO were the most accomplished masters of chiaroscuro.

Chippendale, Thomas (1718-79) English cabinet-maker whose book of furniture designs, *The Gentleman and Cabinet Maker's Director* (1754), made him a household name. His elaborate, ornate work was usually in the ROCOCO style. Designs by Chippendale incorporating Chinese motifs are often called 'Chinese Chippendale'.

Chirico, Giorgio de (1888-1974) Italian painter, born in Greece, and the founder of the Metaphysical School of painting. He was influenced by the writings of the philosophers ▷NIETZSCHE and Schopenhauer. His enigmatic townscapes, with strange perspectives, peopled by isolated figures and menacing shadows, have a haunting quality. His works influenced the surrealists.

Cimabue, Giovanni (Cenni de Peppi) (*c*1240-1302) Italian painter, contemporary of the poet ▷DANTE. Only the mosaic figure of St John in the apse of the Pisa cathedral can be conclusively attributed to him, although he is believed to have painted the altarpiece of the enthroned Madonna, now in the Uffizi Gallery, and the frescoes in the upper and lower churches at Assisi. He began the shift away from the rigid conventions of the BYZANTINE style.

Classicism Style based on the culture and art of the Classical period in ancient Greece, around the 5th century BC, and the art of ancient Rome. The importance of proportion, balance and clarity of form was emphasized. Exemplified in the art of the RENAISSANCE, it is again manifest in the work of POUSSIN and DAVID in France in the 17th and 18th centuries, mainly as a reaction to the frivolity of the ROCOCO style.

Claude Lorrain (1600-82) French artist who studied under the Italian landscape painter Agostino Tassi. By the end of the 1630s

ENGLISH IDYLL *With bold strokes and fresh colours, Constable depicted unspoiled landscapes. Much of his work, such as* The Hay Wain *(1821), was done in his native Suffolk.*

Claude Lorrain's vast atmospheric and contrived Classical landscapes, seascapes and port scenes had become extremely popular. Although often compared with his contemporary POUSSIN, he was more inspired by the work of late Mannerist landscape artists – and in turn his work influenced TURNER.

Cole, Ernest (1940-90) South African photographer, on the staff of *Drum* magazine, who went into exile in 1966. His book, *House of Bondage* (1967), which was a searing indictment of South Africa in the 1950s and 1960s and was banned in South Africa at the time, influenced the young photographers who had access to it. He died destitute in New York.

community arts projects The concept of the community arts centres reflects an increasing political awareness, particularly from the 1970s onwards. Associated with socialist politics, they are multicultural and serve the needs of the people at grassroots level, exposing them to a range of art forms. Major projects include CAP (Community Arts Project) in Cape Town, AIA (African Institute of Arts), FUNDA and the Alexandra Arts Centre in Johannesburg, and the African Art Centre in Durban. These centres have played a major role in the tuition of black artists, in marketing their work, and in training participants to go back into their communities as teachers.

❖ Many rural, self-help projects have emerged, mainly run by women. Examples are the Weya appliqués of the Mukute Cooperative in Zimbabwe, the alternative beadwork of the Zulu women at Mdukutshani, and the Ardmore Project, initiated by Fee Halsted Berning.

Constable, John (1776-1837) Leading English Romantic painter whose natural and fresh-looking views of the British countryside and rural landmarks are among the most familiar of all landscape paintings. Constable's paintings appear to be spontaneous likenesses of the scene, but are in fact skilfully contrived. His style greatly influenced DELACROIX and other French Romantic painters. About 40 of Constable's works are in the National and Tate galleries in London.

❖ Some paintings previously attributed to Constable are now known to have been painted by his son Lionel (1828-87).

constructivism A Russian movement influenced by FUTURISM and cubist constructions. Leading figures were Naum Gabo, his brother Antoine Pevsner and Vladimir Tatlin, whose model for the *Monument to the Third International* (1919-20) demonstrated their support for the 1917 October Revolution. Tatlin and Alexander Rodchenko insisted that art must serve the revolution, and only 'practical' art, such as design, photography and architecture was tolerated. Gabo and Pevsner left Russia in the 1920s.

UNPOSED SCENE The Rehearsal *(1875) demonstrates Degas's interest in movement, space and the effect of light and shade on the human form – supplied here, as so often, by ballet dancers.*

Corot, Jean Baptiste Camille (KORR-oh) (1796-1875) French landscape painter who enjoyed enormous success in the latter half of his career, when he softened his Classical pictures with an evocative, slightly fuzzy style using soft grey-green tones. Corot's work had great influence on the impressionists.

cubism Art movement which analysed the geometry and structure of objects rather than their ordinary appearance. It developed out of African art, FAUVISM and Paul CÉZANNE's earlier attempts to replace IMPRESSIONISM with a less aesthetic and more intellectual approach to form and colour. The creators of cubism were PICASSO and BRAQUE. Their first exhibition was held in 1907 in Paris. After 1912 Picasso and Braque were joined by artists such as GRIS, Robert Delaunay and Fernand Lèger, who took Cézanne's ideas much further by trying to express the concept of an object – often by superimposing several different views of it in one picture. Cubism opened the way for ABSTRACT ART.

Dada A movement which began in 1916 in Zürich, where artist exiles from World War I assembled. A mad humour pervaded all their performances and poetry readings, causing public outrage. Their aim was to re-examine the traditions of logic, coherence and order, which they believed had brought nothing but chaos and disorder. New York Dada began in 1915 under the influence of Marcel DUCHAMP and Francis Picabia (1879-1953), and merged with its European counterpart when Picabia moved to Switzerland.

❖ 'Dada' is a French word for a child's hobbyhorse, and was chosen at random.

Dali, Salvador (1904-89) Spanish surrealist painter. Influenced by psychoanalytic theories of the unconscious, he painted dream-like visions in a meticulous, photographic style. Among his best-known images are limp pocket-watches and oversized ants in harshly lit landscapes.

❖ Dali's eccentricities included shaving off half his waxed moustache and calling his autobiography *Diary of a Genius* (1964).

David, Jacques Louis (da-VEED) (1748-1825) French painter who was a leading exponent of NEO-CLASSICISM. During the ▷FRENCH REVOLUTION he dominated French art and created powerful propaganda for the revolutionaries. His best-known paintings are the *Death of Marat* (1793), and the huge *Coronation of the Emperor Napoleon* (1805-7).

Degas, Edgar (DAY-gah) (1834-1917) French painter and sculptor who was one of the first members of the impressionist movement. His favourite subjects included ballet dancers, young women bathing and café scenes. He was chiefly concerned with depicting movement and often used pastels to create fluid and lively drawings.

Delacroix, Eugène (dell-a-KRWAH) (1798-1863) Leading Romantic painter in France. His brilliant use of colour, freedom of style and contemporary subject matter influenced many artists, including the impressionists, and persuaded others to turn to ROMANTICISM from NEO-CLASSICISM.
❖ Delacroix's great rival was INGRES.

Dior, Christian (1905-57) French fashion designer who introduced a glamorous era for women in Europe and North America with his 'New Look' in 1947: dresses and outfits with narrow shoulders and long, flared skirts.

Donatello (1386-1466) Florentine sculptor, one of the most important figures in 15th-century Italian art. His dramatic shift from the International Gothic style to a more naturalistic style, influenced by the Classical works excavated in Rome, changed the course of Italian sculpture. His relief sculptures were masterly both in their command of dramatic narrative and their accurate illusion of perspective.

Duccio di Buoninsegna (*c*1260-*c*1319) Siennese painter who was an early master of dramatic pictorial narrative with a superb sense of colour. The *Maestà* (1311), an altarpiece painted for the Siena cathedral, is his most famous work. He began the shift away from stylized BYZANTINE conventions of the time to more lively, realistic compositions.

Duchamp, Marcel (1887-1968) French artist who moved to New York in 1913, and was the co-leader of New York DADA. An artist who delighted in paradox, Duchamp created some of the most intriguing and perplexing art works of the 20th century. In 1913, he initiated the use of the ready-made or found object. The most notorious of these were the urinal titled *Fountain* (1917), and the reproduction of Leonardo's *Mona Lisa* in 1919, to which he had added a moustache and goatee.

Dumile Feni (1942-91) Figurative artist who left South Africa as an exile in 1968. He lived first in London, then in New York. He is best known for his compelling drawings in conté-crayon or charcoal on paper. In his twenties he lived in Johannesburg, where he actively identified with the black consciousness poets of Soweto. His apocalyptic work *African Guernica* powerfully reflects the violence and anxiety of his social milieu.

Dürer, Albrecht (DOO-rur) (1471-1528) German painter, designer and engraver who created expressive and extremely detailed woodcuts and copper engravings. Dürer was greatly influenced by the Italian Renaissance and was responsible for introducing many of its ideas to his fellow artists in northern Europe. In turn, the northern realism of his work had an influence on Italian art.

Egyptian art Because of the ancient Egyptians' belief in an afterlife, which dominated their religion, their art is found in tombs, temples and on monuments. Both painting and sculpture were governed by strict conventions. On temple walls and papyri associated with the ▷BOOK OF THE DEAD, the human figure was almost invariably painted with the faces, legs and feet in profile but eyes, torsos and arms seen frontally. The clear line and idealized forms greatly influenced ancient Greek art.

Elgin Marbles Ancient friezes taken from the ▷PARTHENON in Athens by the 7th Earl of Elgin, a British diplomat and art connoisseur, between 1801 and 1803. Elgin's action has been strongly criticized, but he claimed that he was saving important works of art from destruction by the Ottoman Turks. In 1816 the marbles were bought for the British nation, and are now in the British Museum.
❖ In 1983 the Greek government asked for the marbles to be returned. The British Museum refused on the grounds that they were the marbles' legal custodians.

El Greco (1541-1614) One of the greatest artists of the Spanish school, best known for his religious paintings. His real name was Domenicos Theotocopoulos, 'El Greco' being Spanish for 'the Greek'. He was born in Crete, but he moved to Italy, and then settled in Spain in 1577. Although he was supposedly the last pupil of TITIAN, his work is much more obviously influenced by TINTORETTO, RAPHAEL, DÜRER, MICHELANGELO and by Mannerists such as Francesco Parmigianino (1503-40). His ecstatic and passionate style was highly individual: he painted elongated figures in a BYZANTINE manner. *The Burial of Count Orgaz* (1586) shows how El Greco's use of livid blues, greens, yellows and pinks gives his work an eerie appearance.

HAPPY EASTER *Tsar Nicholas II presented this Fabergé egg to the Empress Alexandra Feodorovna in 1897. The coach fits inside it.*

Elizabethan style Term applied to any decorative object or piece of furniture made in England during the reign of Elizabeth I (1558-1603). Furniture, usually made from oak, tended to be massive, squat and richly carved with a mix of ▷GOTHIC and RENAISSANCE motifs. Pottery and metalwork designs were usually very simple.

engraving Art of making a design on a printing block or plate. Strictly speaking, engraving refers only to designs cut into metal plates, usually made from copper, zinc, pewter or steel. This type of engraving is called 'intaglio' (Italian for 'cut into'). Mezzotints and aquatints are both types of intaglio. Engraving is also used as a generic term that covers etchings, woodcuts, linocuts and even potato cuts.

Ernst, Max (1891-1976) German painter and sculptor of the surrealist school, and co-founder of the DADA movement. He was also one of the leading exponents of collage and photomontage.

expressionism Two dominant styles described as expressionist emerged in Germany in the early 20th century. The *Brücke* (Bridge) began in Dresden around 1905, with KIRCHNER, NOLDE and Max Pechstein as leading figures. Their works are characterized by bold forms, jagged lines and strong colour. The *Blaue Reiter* (Blue Rider) group was formed in Berlin in 1911, with KANDINSKY the dominant figure. Their concerns were more with the spiritual element of art and the harmony of colour and form. Fauve colour almost certainly influenced them, as did the art of VAN GOGH and MUNCH.

Fabergé, Peter Carl (1846-1920) Russian goldsmith and jeweller who made a range of exquisite decorative objects such as tea services, cigarette cases and statuettes. Most famous of all are his gold and enamel eggs, encrusted with precious stones and containing miniature figures or trinkets.

Fauvism The first of a succession of revolutionary 20th-century art movements. The major figures in the group were MATISSE, André Derain and Maurice de Vlaminck, and their common interest was the use of pure, brilliant colour. The word *fauves*, or wild beasts, was used by a critic, shocked at the

AT EASE *Gainsborough's picture of* Mr and Mrs Andrews *combines skilful portraiture set against the reassuring background of a peaceful country estate.*

works on show at the Salon d'Automne of 1905. The use of colour applied without regard to natural appearance is well illustrated in Matisse's work *The Green Stripe (Madam Matisse)* painted that year.

❖ The *Brücke* group, which was active in Dresden, Germany, from 1905 to 1913, grew out of EXPRESSIONISM and had many similarities to Fauvism.

Fragonard, Jean Honoré (1732-1806) French ROCOCO artist who painted decorative romantic and gallant scenes in clear, pastel colours. Like his teacher Francois Boucher, he painted in what was then considered an erotic style – in *The Swing* (1769), one of his best-known works, he shows the legs and underclothes of a young woman as she swings exuberantly through the air.

Frankenthaler, Helen (1928-) American painter, transitional figure between ABSTRACT EXPRESSIONISM and colour-field painting in which paint was applied in thin washes directly on to the raw canvas. No sense of paint texture or brushwork distract from her sensitively coloured, abstract images.

fresco Picture painted on to a freshly plastered wall or ceiling. *Buon fresco* – painting on to damp plaster – has proved to be one of the most durable forms of decoration. Painting on to dry plaster, known as *fresco secco*, was normally reserved for repairing an existing fresco. The great era of *buon fresco* began in Italy with GIOTTO at the end of the 13th century and ended in 1770 with the death of TIEPOLO, famed for his ROCOCO style.

Freud, Lucian (1922-) British painter and grandson of the psychoanalyst Sigmund Freud. His early work is remarkably intense and expressive, his nudes are often unsettling, and his portraits, including those of his friend Francis BACON, are either painted close-up or set in barren interiors.

Friedrich, Caspar David (1774-1840) A major figure in the German romantic movement. His landscapes, such as *The Wanderer above the Mists* (*c*1818), capture the romantic sentiment of humanity set against the vastness of nature. ▷GOTHIC ruins, snow-covered peaks and melancholy foggy plains are among the images typical of his paintings.

futurism A strongly politicized art movement, founded in Milan in 1909, reflecting enthralment with the machine age, revolution, and speed. The major figures were Giacomo Balla and Umberto Boccioni. Balla's *Dynamism of a Dog on a Leash* (1912) captures the blurred movements of a dog in motion. Robert Delaunay and DUCHAMP were influenced by the futurists.

Gainsborough, Thomas (1727-88) English landscape artist and portraitist who was patronized by the royal family and the wealthy. His personal preference was for landscapes, and in many of his paintings, for example *Mr and Mrs Andrews* (1748), he was able to combine the two styles by portraying the figures against an expansive landscape.

❖ The open-sided upholstered armchairs seen in many Gainsborough paintings became known as 'Gainsborough chairs'.

Gauguin, Paul (GO-gan) (1848-1903) French post-impressionist painter who, with VAN GOGH and CÉZANNE, had a great influence on the development of modern art. Gauguin abandoned his family and his respectable job in a Paris bank to paint. He spent most of the 1890s in Tahiti, where he developed his own style of imaginative symbolism, using very bright colours and simple, flat, rather distorted forms. Gauguin's rejection of NATURALISM and IMPRESSIONISM and his attention to the expressive power of African art inspired many artists, including the NABIS.

❖ Gauguin's life has been the subject of several novels, most notably Somerset Maugham's *The Moon and Sixpence*.

ART GALLERIES AND MUSEUMS OF THE WORLD

Guggenheim Museum	New York City	European and American post-impressionist and modern art, with a major Kandinsky collection, housed in a building designed by Frank Lloyd Wright.
Hermitage	St Petersburg	Largest collection of art in the world – mainly 16th to 19th-century European and Russian works.
Louvre	Paris	14th to 19th-century European art, including Leonardo's *Mona Lisa*, and Egyptian, Oriental, Roman and Greek antiquities, including the *Venus de Milo*.
Metropolitan Museum of Art	New York City	Wide range of European and American paintings, furniture and decorative objects, including period-room reconstructions.
Musée d'Orsay	Paris	Former railway station housing 19th and early 20th-century art, including works of Manet, the impressionists, Van Gogh and Rodin.
Museum of Modern Art (MOMA)	New York City	Art from 1880 onwards, including Van Gogh's masterpiece *Starry Night*.
National Gallery	London	Collections of 14th to 20th-century British and European paintings, including works by Leonardo, Van Dyck, Constable and Turner.
National Gallery of Art	Washington	West Wing houses works of all periods and nationalities, including a comprehensive Cézanne collection. East Wing houses modern art, including paintings, sculptures and prints, and many of Matisse's collages.
Prado	Madrid	12th to 19th-century Spanish and European art, including the largest collection of paintings by Velasquez and Bosch, and Picasso's *Guernica*.
Rijksmuseum	Amsterdam	15th to 19th-century Dutch and European paintings, with the world's finest collection of Rembrandts, including *The Night Watch*.
Tate Gallery	London	British paintings from 1500 onwards, including several rooms devoted to Turner; a large international collection of modern art, including Rodin's *The Kiss* and sculptures by Henry Moore.
Uffizi	Florence	13th to 18th-century Italian and European art, and the world's greatest collection of Renaissance paintings, with rooms devoted to Botticelli, Leonardo, Raphael, Michelangelo and Rubens.

Gaultier, Jean-Paul (1952-) Innovative designer whose witty creations often mix the traditional with the strikingly new. He formed his own company in 1976 and became the *enfant terrible* of French fashion, designing costumes for pop star Madonna and creating skirts for men.

genre painting Paintings in which the subject matter deals with the lives of ordinary people in everyday situations. It is typified by much 17th-century Dutch art, particularly that of VERMEER and Pieter de Hooch. The term does not, however, apply to narrative or allegorical art, nor to portraiture.

Georgian A variety of decorative styles popular in Britain from 1714 to about 1800. Early Georgian styles were extravagant and ornate, influenced by the BAROQUE. Around 1730, the French ROCOCO style became popular, with its elaborate ornamentation, furniture and fabrics. CHIPPENDALE was the major cabinet-maker of this period. The influence of CLASSICISM is reflected in Late Georgian, epitomized by the elegant line and fine craftsmanship of HEPPLEWHITE and Thomas Sheraton.

Ghiberti, Lorenzo (1378-1455) Italian sculptor, goldsmith, writer, architect and designer who was a major figure in the transition between ▷GOTHIC and RENAISSANCE art. He is best remembered for his bronze sculpted doors of the baptistery in Florence Cathedral which depict scenes from the Old and New Testaments. UCCELLO and DONATELLO both trained in Ghiberti's workshop .

❖ Ghiberti's *Commentaries* – incomplete and written throughout his life – give a fascinating account of his own career and of Italian art history.

SPANISH BEAUTY *The clarity and strength of Goya's style shines out in this lively portrait of the beautiful Dona Isabel de Porcel.*

Giacometti, Alberto (1901-66) Swiss artist known mainly for his elongated, skeletal sculptures. His works of the 1920s and 1930s are among the masterpieces of surrealist sculpture. By the mid 1940s, the figures had become thinner and more isolated, and stood rigid on large, heavy bases. Even in groups the figures seem isolated.

Giotto (di Bondone) (*c*1267-1337) Florentine artist whose paintings are early masterpieces of dramatic narrative. His figures are no longer static and positioned frontally as they had been in BYZANTINE art. Instead they occupy space and express real emotions. His most famous work is the FRESCO cycle in Arena Chapel, Padua, in which three tiers of paintings detail the lives of the Virgin and Christ.

Glaser, Milton (1929-) American graphic designer whose work uses a great diversity of styles and has covered everything from labels and packaging to corporate identity, shopfittings and magazine design. His new designs for *Paris Match* and *Esquire* magazines, among others, gained him international recognition.

❖ Glaser's best-known design is I ❤ NY.

Goldblatt, David (1930-) South African photographer whose penetrating vision depicts the hardships of the underprivileged. Like the French painter and caricaturist Honoré Daumier, he sees beyond the mundaneness of scenes to capture cameos of great poignancy. His books include *On the Mines* (1973) and *Lifetimes under Apartheid* (1986) with text by Nadine ▷GORDIMER.

Gorky, Arshile (1904-48) Pivotal figure in the development of ABSTRACT EXPRESSIONISM in America. Born in Armenia, he emigrated to America in 1920 and played a major role in bridging the gap between the sophisticated modernism of Europe and the emerging style of abstract expressionism.

Goya, Francisco de (1746-1828) Spanish artist considered one of the world's greatest portrait painters. He gave an extraordinary insight into the character of his sitters and had an unusual freedom of style inspired by VELASQUEZ. Goya was also an outstanding draughtsman, and his etchings record the political, social and religious climate of his time with intense realism – as in the *Disasters of War* series (1810-20), which records the horrors of the Napoleonic wars. His work has had a profound influence on many 19th and 20th-century painters, especially DELACROIX, PICASSO and MANET.

❖ In his later years, Goya, who after 1792 became increasingly deaf, produced the so-called 'Black Paintings' – dark, grim visions of human fear and cruelty.

graphic arts Term that applies to any form of drawing or engraving, or any piece of art that depends more on line than on colour for its overall effect.

Gris, Juan (GREES) (1887-1927) Spanish artist who turned to CUBISM under the influence of another Spaniard, PICASSO. He helped define the style and developed a personal version where each work began as 'flat coloured architecture'. He also designed costumes and stage sets for ▷DIAGHILEV.

Grundlingh, Geoffrey (1954-) South African fine-art photographer who works mainly in a studio, where he creates his own environments with selected objects and artefacts. He deals with formal, conceptual issues and manipulates the medium, breaking down expected notions of photography.

Guardi, Francesco (1712-93) Best-known member of a family of artists who worked in Venice. Guardi is usually remembered for his views of Venice which, unlike the minutely detailed studies of his contemporary CANALETTO, capture the atmosphere of the city in a free and evocative style. Guardi's brother Giovanni and his brother-in-law TIEPOLO were also important painters.

Hals, Frans (c1580-1666) Dutch portrait painter whose lively domestic scenes and portraits, such as the much-reproduced *The Laughing Cavalier* (1624), show genius in catching a subject's fleeting expression. Hals often painted *alla prima* – painting on to canvas without preliminary drawing or underpainting. Hals's formal commissioned civic group portraits, which he painted later in his life, are more reflective and show greater insight than he demonstrated in his earlier, more showy style.

❖ *Portrait of a Woman* (1644) by Frans Hals is the centrepiece of the Michaelis Collection of 17th-century Dutch and Flemish paintings in the Old Town House in Cape Town.

TOP TABLE
Hepplewhite's 18th-century design for a pier table marries an ornamental style with functionality.

Hepplewhite, George (-1786) English cabinet-maker who became well known two years after his death when his book of designs for furniture, *Cabinet-Maker and Upholsterer's Guide*, was published. The neo-Classical designs combine elegance with utility. However, little is known of Hepplewhite's life, and no piece of furniture can definitely be ascribed to him.

Hepworth, Dame Barbara (1903-75) One of the first British abstract sculptors. Like Henry MOORE, she made no preliminary models and carved directly into wood and stone. Hepworth also used bronze towards the end of her life. She belonged to a group of English artists living at St Ives in Cornwall, and married the abstract painter Ben NICHOLSON. She died in a fire at her studio.

Hlungwani, Jackson (1923-) South African sculptor, graphic artist and Christian mystic. His roughly worked figures in wood capture the essence of the images he creates, from the monumental *Adam* to a humorous depiction of *Christ Playing Football* (1983). The fish, as a Christian symbol, is an oft-repeated motif in his works. In his home village of Mbhokota in Northern Province, he has erected a series of sculptural sanctuaries.

Hockney, David (1937-) Painter, etcher, set-designer and film-maker who became the

ART GALLERIES OF SOUTHERN AFRICA

Durban Art Gallery	Durban	Victorian paintings and South African art, in particular sculpture, beadwork, basketry, ceramics and glass of the KwaZulu-Natal region.
Johannesburg Art Gallery	Johannesburg	South African art, 17th-century Dutch and 19th and 20th-century French and English works. Collections of lace, fans, furniture, prints and oriental ceramics.
King George VI Art Gallery	Port Elizabeth	South African art mainly of the Eastern Cape, from Thomas Baines to the present day. Collections of Indian miniatures and late 20th-century British works.
National Gallery of Zimbabwe	Harare	Mainly contemporary Zimbabwean art, with emphasis on stone sculpture.
Pretoria Art Museum	Pretoria	South African paintings, sculpture, graphics, tapestries, photographs and ceramics; also 17th-century Dutch paintings.
South African National Gallery	Cape Town	South African paintings, sculptures and beadwork; 18th and 19th-century English art, including the Abe Bailey collection of sporting paintings; also prints and drawings.
Tatham Art Gallery	Pietermaritzburg	South African art past and present, British and French art and *objets d'art*, including a Lalique collection.
William Humphreys Art Gallery	Kimberley	South African art, rock engravings and ceramics; 16th and 17th-century Dutch, Flemish, British and French paintings, and a collection of antique furniture.

most prominent British artist of his generation. Hockney, later resident in California, USA, usually uses acrylic paint in strong, light colours in his portraits and paintings. His early work, which had a flat, naive style incorporating bold, simple forms, was associated with POP ART. Many of his paintings explore the effect of light on reflecting objects, such as water and glass, and some have a frank homosexual content. Among his best-known works are *A Bigger Splash* (1967) and *The Rake's Progress* (1961-3). Hockney has also designed costumes and sets for opera productions and experimented with photomontage. He has even created art works with fax machines.

Hodgins, Robert (1920-) English-born artist who settled in South Africa in 1953. He paints satirical works and social commentary using a deliberately crude style reminiscent of the art of George Grosz, who was associated with the German Dadaists. He draws extensively from art and literary sources. There is a preoccupation with disorder in his works, and vanity, corruption, greed and brutality are recurrent themes.

Hogarth, William (1697-1764) One of Britain's most original and influential painters and engravers. He began painting small portrait

BIG HEAT, COOL WATER *The sunshine and swimming pools of California inspired David Hockney to paint* A Bigger Splash *(1967).*

groups, called conversation pieces. He then invented the genre for which he is best remembered – moral narrative – using paintings to tell a story and expose the follies of the age, as in *A Rake's Progress* (1733-5).

Holbein, Hans, (the Younger) (*c*1497-1543) German artist and one of the greatest north European portrait painters. He originally worked in the workshop of his father – Hans Holbein the Elder (*c*1465-1524). Holbein the Younger's pictures were remarkable for their realism; he painted his subjects' faces or costumes in minute detail, and captured their characters with relentless accuracy. Holbein gained an international reputation, and in 1532 he settled in London, where he became court painter to ▷HENRY VIII.

icon A devotional painting or mosaic of Christ, the Virgin Mary or other holy personage. The word is derived from the Greek word *eikon* or image. In the Greek and Russian Orthodox churches icons are used as a means of contact between the worshipper and the holy figure to whom he or she prays.
❖ ▷ICONOCLASM led to the mass destruction of paintings, mosaics and frescoes.

impressionism Movement in 19th-century painting from which modern art evolved. The impressionists abandoned traditional methods of composition, drawing and perspective in favour of painting more spontaneously to capture a particular moment. The artists aimed to achieve greater naturalism, and preferred to paint outdoors – where they were fascinated by changing colour and light. They often used primary colours and small brush strokes to simulate reflected light. The artists who exhibited in the eight impressionist exhibitions from 1874 to 1886 were MONET, DEGAS, PISSARRO, MORISOT, RENOIR and SISLEY.
❖ The movement's name was coined by a critic – in a derisive sense – from the title of Monet's work *Impression: Sunrise* (1872).
❖ A key factor in the development of impressionism was the manufacture of paint in tubes, which enabled artists to leave their studios and work outdoors.

Ingres, Jean Auguste Dominique (1780-1867) French painter and champion of the classical tradition, who studied in the studio of DAVID. His mastery of draughtsmanship and fine brushwork are evident in the sumptuous clothing and rich drapery of his portrait compositions, but he showed little interest in facial characteristics or colour. His nudes, such as the *Grande Odalisque* (1814), have a fleshy sensuality which is restrained in comparison with the robust colour and romantic vision of DELACROIX, whose paintings he detested.

STARS AND STRIPES *Jasper Johns'* Three Flags *(1958), a three-dimensional work made from encaustic (coloured wax fixed with heat) on canvas, was sold for US$1 million in 1980.*

Islamic art Islamic art is a religious art form, mainly nonfigurative and highly decorative. Its dominant form, the arabesque, is created by a variety of swirling, stylized plant shapes. It appears carved or moulded into stucco or stone, in the patterning of tiles and woven into carpets. It also appears on the pages of manuscripts, combined with calligraphy, or stylized decorative writing.

John, Augustus (1878-1961) British painter, remembered as much for his rebellious and passionate character as for his bold and colourful portraits and drawings of gypsies.
❖ John's sister Gwen (1876-1939), an artist and artist's model, was RODIN's mistress.

Johns, Jasper (1930-) American artist often regarded as the father of POP ART, and one of the outstanding figures of post-World War II art. In his bold, flat paintings and sculptures Johns uses collage, metal, plastic, plaster casts and bronze as well as paint. His themes include flags, targets, numbers and letters, and he casts everyday objects such as light bulbs and beer cans in bronze.

Kandinsky, Vasily (1866-1944) Russian-born painter, one of the most influential figures in 20th-century art. He was a founder member of the *Blaue Reiter* (Blue Rider) group, part of the expressionist movement in Germany. In 1911, he painted what is considered to have been the first ABSTRACT ART work. He was concerned with the harmony of colour and form and the relationships between art and music. In 1914 he returned to Moscow and here, influenced by the constructivists, his art became more hard-edged and geometric, a trend which was to continue during his ten years of teaching at the BAUHAUS.

Karsh, Yousouf (1908-) Armenian-born photographer whose sharp and extraordinarily detailed portraits appear to give great insight into the characters of subjects such as Winston ▷CHURCHILL, ▷NEHRU and PICASSO.

Kentridge, William (1955-) South African artist, whose satirical works are a sensitive, educated comment on contemporary South African life. His fluent drawings in charcoal, ink and pastel use literary and historical sources as the point of departure for incisive local parodies.

Kibel, Wolf (1903-38) Polish-born artist who settled in South Africa in 1929. He was influenced by European modernism, in particular by MATISSE, CHAGALL and KOKOSCHKA. In his intimate, controlled paintings and monotypes, Kibel uses expressive brushwork and texture and exaggerated perspectives to evoke mood or tension. His early death was due to tuberculosis.

kinetic art Painting and sculpture that incorporates real or apparent movement, often using an optical illusion, artificial lighting or a motor. Alexander CALDER's mobiles are an example of kinetic art.

Kirchner, Ernst Ludwig (1880-1938) German expressionist painter and founder member of the *Brücke* (Bridge) group formed in Dresden around 1905. Influenced by the emotional subject matter, style and graphic techniques of German GOTHIC art, his works are characterized by jagged, angular forms. One of the many artists labelled 'degenerate' by the Nazis, Kirchner suffered severe bouts of depression and committed suicide.

Klee, Paul (CLAY) (1879-1940) Swiss painter and etcher, associated with the *Blaue Reiter* (Blue Rider) group. He was one of the 20th century's most original artists. His style is characterized by precise draughtsmanship combined with free fantasy. Klee described some of his small, exquisitely painted abstract pictures as 'taking a line for a walk'. His wit, inspired use of colour and complete lack of pretentiousness make some of his works appear almost childlike.

Klein, Calvin (1942-) American fashion designer best known for his figure-hugging underwear ranges (with his name printed on the waistbands) and for his 'designer' jeans and casual sportswear.

Klimt, Gustav (1862-1918) Austrian decorator and painter known for his sensuous pictures of women painted against brilliant, bejewelled backgrounds and for his mosaics and murals. His best-known work is *The Kiss* (1908), which shows a couple embracing amid a riot of colours and gold. His work influenced Egon Schiele and KOKOSCHKA. Klimt was a founder of the Vienna Sezession – the Austrian equivalent of ART NOUVEAU.

FARMYARD VIGNETTE Ducks *(1968) by South African artist Maggie Laubser typifies her bold style, with bright colours and simplified outlines. She favoured such tranquil, countryside scenes.*

Kokoschka, Oskar (1886-1980) Austrian artist and writer and leading expressionist painter with an imaginative and vivid style. He is best known for his brightly coloured and rather restless portraits, allegorical pictures and urban landscapes often painted from a curiously high viewpoint.

SLEEPING BEAUTIES The Young Girl *(1912-13) is classic Klimt: a languid, erotic scene rendered in rich, jewel-like colours. His decadent life and paintings scandalized Austria's art establishment.*

Kollwitz, Käthe (1867-1945) German graphic artist and sculptor. She was intensely concerned with social issues, in particular with the plight of women. Poignant studies of women and children dominate her work, in which she captures the essence of suffering, despair and courage. She was expelled by the Nazi regime from the Prussian Academy and her art was suppressed.

Koloane, David (1938-) South African painter of expressive, increasingly abstract works. He trained with Bill AINSLIE in Johannesburg, and later in America. He was the head of fine art at FUBA (Federated Union of Black Artists) in 1982-3, and later curator of the FUBA gallery. In his works colour is at times subtle and at other times dark and sombre; his paintwork is tactile and layered.

Kumalo, Sydney (1935-88) South African figurative sculptor, mainly of bronzes. He began his studies at POLLY STREET ART CENTRE, where VILLA and SKOTNES were important early influences. His abstracted depictions of human beings, animals and mythical creatures are imaginative and often extremely powerful and his work has been a model for many young South African artists.

Lagerfeld, Karl (1938-) One of the most prolific and successful modern fashion designers. He was born in Germany, but has spent most of his working life in France and Italy. His best-known work has been for the CHANEL fashion house, whose classic designs he has wittily updated.

Lalique, René (1860-1945) French jeweller and glassmaker who was one of the leading exponents of ART NOUVEAU and ART DECO. He began designing perfume bottles for Coty in 1907 and from 1910 concentrated on glassware, creating a huge range of figurines and vases decorated with relief figures, animals and flowers.

Laubser, Maggie (1886-1973) South African painter and major figure in South African art, who was strongly influenced by the German expressionists. Her work features simplified and boldly coloured figures and landscapes. Vividly responsive to her surroundings, she painted tranquil pastoral scenes, farmyard animals, still lifes and portraits.

DECAYED MASTERPIECE *Leonardo's mural of* The Last Supper *has been badly damaged, partly by several attempts at restoration.*

Lauren, Ralph (1939-) American clothing designer whose Polo label ranges from classic semi-formal 'Ivy-League' styles to native American designs.

Leach, Bernard (1887-1979) Generally considered the greatest and most influential British potter. Leach studied ceramics in Japan for 12 years and on his return to Britain in 1920 established a pottery in St Ives, Cornwall. His work always has a simple, almost austere, practical quality.

Le Brun, Charles (1619-90) Chief designer of the LOUIS QUATORZE style. He ran the Gobelins factory, the European centre of tapestry-making, from 1663 and was director of the French Academy. Le Brun's elegant and decorative CLASSICISM influenced French art for generations. He oversaw the interior decoration of the Palace of ▷VERSAILLES and designed several rooms, including the *Galerie des Glaces* (Hall of Mirrors) (1679-84).

Legae, Ezrom (1938-) South African sculptor of bronzes and accomplished graphic artist. He has produced several series of sensitively drawn works, including *Jail Series* (exhibited in 1978) in memory of Steve ▷BIKO. His sculptures are stylized and abstract and sometimes show a quirky sense of humour.

Leonardo da Vinci (1452-1519) Italian RENAISSANCE artist of extraordinary ability and versatility. His talents and interests extended into the applied and natural sciences, which led to his discovery of aerial perspective. A restless artist with a prodigious intellect, he filled his notebooks with drawings of flying machines, plants, birds, anatomy, clouds and studies of water. His output of paintings was small but exquisite. His *Mona Lisa* (1503-6) is probably the world's most famous art work. Most of his works were painted in Milan or Florence, including two versions of *The Virgin of the Rocks* (*c*1508) and the *Last Supper* (1495-7), a FRESCO in the refectory of the

monastery of San Maria delle Grazie. His late works, in particular *The Virgin and St Anne* (*c*1500), like many of Michelangelo's works, show a shift from the high Renaissance style towards MANNERISM.

❖ The fresco of the *Last Supper*, in which Leonardo experimented with oil paint, soon showed signs of deterioration. Despite its far from perfect condition, the work remains one of the great masterpieces of the Renaissance. It survived the bombing of the church in 1943, when one wall of the refectory was badly damaged.

Liberty, Sir Arthur Lasenby (1843-1917) Promoter of ART NOUVEAU and founder of Liberty's store in London's Regent Street, a large department store which pioneered the importing of foreign decorative goods. The store commissioned many lasting designs, especially of textiles, which came to be known as 'Liberty prints'.

Lichtenstein, Roy (1923-) American artist who became one of the leading exponents of POP ART in the 1960s. He is best known for his large pictures based on advertising imagery and strip cartoons. Many of his paintings duplicate in enlarged form the dot patterns found in newspaper reproductions.

Lipshitz, Lippy (1903-80) Lithuanian-born figurative sculptor and graphic artist, who settled in South Africa in 1908. He was a founder member of the NEW GROUP and an associate professor at the Michaelis School of Fine Art in Cape Town. His works, mainly in wood or stone, are expressive, rough-hewn and rugged. He produced many woodcuts and, like KIBEL, was fascinated by monotypes.

Louis Quatorze (ka-TORZ) French style of furniture and decoration popular in France from the 1640s to about 1715. It closely mirrored the taste of King Louis XIV and his finance minister, Jean-Baptiste Colbert, and tempered richness with Classical restraint. It was a grand, masculine, militaristic style, taking many motifs from ancient Rome – such as shields, eagles and palms. Sumptuously gilded furniture made in the BAROQUE style was created in the royal workshops to adorn many palaces, including ▷VERSAILLES.

Louis Quinze (KANZ) Main style of interior design and furnishings in France from about 1720 to 1750, named after Louis XV. It was an elegant, light-hearted and feminine style, using nature's curves – a reaction to the ostentatious LOUIS QUATORZE style. However, it encompassed the elaborate ROCOCO style which, during the mid-18th century, spread through Europe.

Louis Seize (SEHZ) French style of design and decoration profoundly influenced by the renewed interest in CLASSICISM prompted by the discovery of the ancient cities of ▷POMPEII and Herculaneum. It began in the 1750s, some 20 years before Louis XVI came to the throne, and lasted until the outbreak of the French Revolution in 1789. It rejected ROCOCO excesses, using Classical motifs such as key patterns and caryatids, and straighter, more elegant lines. It coincided with the late GEORGIAN period in Britain.

Lowry, (Laurence) Stephen (1887-1976) English artist known for his highly original paintings of antlike figures in almost monochromatic industrial, urban landscapes. The earliest date from the 1920s and most are set in and around his home town of Salford in Lancashire, where he spent most of his life.

Mabasa, Noria (1938-) South African figurative sculptor who worked initially in clay, later in wood. Her clay figurines portray a wide range of characters, including police, clergy and politicians. Her apocalyptic wooden sculptures, *Natal Flood Disaster* (*c*1985) and *Carnage II* (1988), reflect the destructive forces of nature.

Mackintosh, Charles Rennie (1868-1928) Scottish designer and architect who was one of the most notable exponents of ART NOUVEAU. Mackintosh combined the languid curves of Art Nouveau with the crisp rectangular forms that were to characterize the work of many 20th-century architects. He is known for his modern interiors and rectilinear, often inlaid, furniture – especially high-backed chairs. He had little influence in Britain, but he was highly regarded in Austria, Germany and Italy, where artists were abandoning Art Nouveau for a clearer style. Some of his designs are still made.

Magritte, René (1898-1967) Belgian surrealist painter of paradox and magic realism, influenced by CHIRICO. His paintings tend to shock because of the unexpected juxtaposition of the strange, the erotic and the ordinary, like the bowler-hatted men who appear frequently in his works. The image of a pipe, with the inscription, 'This is not a pipe', typifies his fascination with the theme of reality as opposed to illusion.

Mancoba, Ernest (1904-) South African artist whose early sculptures were naturalistic and idealized, influenced by his mission school training. The rough-hewn forms in the work *Faith* (1936), shows the influence of Lippy LIPSHITZ and Mancoba's growing interest in the indigenous art of Africa. He settled in Paris in 1938, where he married a Danish artist Sonja Ferlov. They moved to Denmark after World War II, and were members of the short-lived CoBrA group, which encouraged free and spontaneous expression. From the early 1950s, Mancoba concentrated on painting rather than sculpture. Retrospective exhibitions were held in 1994-5 to celebrate his return to South Africa.

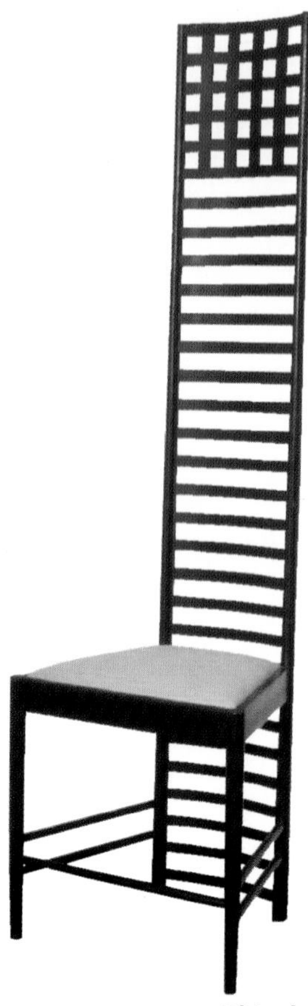

STRAIGHT AND NARROW *This ladder-back chair by Mackintosh is on view in Hill House, Helensburgh, of which he was the architect.*

Manet, Édouard (1832-83) French realist painter whose works scandalized the establishment because of their forthright modernity. *Olympia* (1863-5) and *Le Déjeuner sur l'herbe* (1863) drew on RAPHAEL and TITIAN as source material. Manet's naked women stare unselfconsciously at the viewer, bridging the gap between the real and the painted world. From 1870 Manet began to work out of doors and was influenced by the technique and palette of the impressionists.

mannerism The style of art which occurred between the High RENAISSANCE and the BAROQUE in Italy. The harmony and restraint of the High Renaissance was replaced by contrived, asymmetrical compositions, where colour became heightened or unnatural, and figures were often elongated or in exaggerated poses. The most important mannerist painters were Francesco Parmigianino (1503-40), Jacopo da Pontormo, Agnolo Bronzino and Rosso Fiorentino, while the sculptor CELLINI and the architect and painter Giulio Romano epitomize the virtuosity and capriciousness of the style.

Mantegna, Andrea (man-TAIN-ya) (*c*1431-1506) Italian early RENAISSANCE artist who was greatly influenced by DONATELLO. His study of Greek and Roman archaeology – he built up a large collection of ancient statuary – is reflected in his use of Classical architecture and sculptural forms. Mantegna was the first artist to paint a *sotto in su* (Italian for 'from below upwards') – an illusion achieved by dramatic foreshortening in which the ceiling appears to be open to a sky where figures seem to float above the viewer. This technique later became popular in BAROQUE decoration. Mantegna was one of the first Italian artists to experiment with ENGRAVING.

Marc, Franz (1880-1916) German expressionist painter, co-founder of the *Blaue Reiter* (Blue Rider) group. His figurative works are painted in non-naturalistic tones, which show a preoccupation with colour, its expressive properties, and the states of mind it evokes. His last works became more sombre and the forms more abstracted. Shortly before he was killed in action in World War I, he painted an apocalyptic vision in black and red of abstract fighting forms.

Martini, Simone (*c*1284-1344) Pupil of the Sienese painter DUCCIO. Martini's graceful use of outline and the decorative richness of his religious and courtly paintings influenced many Italian artists. The grand and elegant style of his best-known work, the *Annunciation* (1333), is reminiscent of BYZANTINE and French GOTHIC art.

Masaccio (ma-SACH-ee-oh) (1401-*c*1428) Florentine artist whose understanding of light, form and realistic perspective built on the art of GIOTTO. His innovations gave his work a much greater degree of realism, in keeping with the intellectual approach developed by his contemporaries – ▷BRUNELLESCHI (in architecture) and DONATELLO (in sculpture). Masaccio's frescoes in the church of Santa Maria del Carmine in Florence were an inspiration to many artists, including MICHELANGELO, who emulated their grand, realistic and heroic style in his ceiling frescoes in the Sistine Chapel in the Vatican.

Mason, Judith (1938-) South African artist of exceptionally skilled drawings and paintings. There is an enigmatic quality in her delicately drawn shells, skulls, embryos and wings. Her paintings range from the pathos of *She-wolf* (1965) to the raw power of *Leopard's Breath* (1970). Many of her later works are multimedia assemblages. Her work has influenced many young South African artists.

MOULD-BREAKER *Manet's depiction of naked women with fully clothed men in* Le Déjeuner sur l'herbe *(1863) flouted convention and shocked the critics, but led to the birth of impressionism.*

Maswanganyi, Johannes (1948-) Self-taught South African sculptor, who carves indigenous wood, which he often paints. His lively, innovative and wry imagery is drawn from a wide variety of sources, such as imaginative animal figures, pop stars and smartly dressed city dwellers.

Matisse, Henri (1869-1954) French painter and sculptor, one of the most influential figures in 20th-century art. Influenced by CÉZANNE and the post-impressionists, he was the leading exponent of FAUVISM. Colour remained the most important element in his paintings throughout his life, while draughtsmanship ranged from the crude simplicity of *Dance* (1909) to the sensuous *Odalisques* of the 1920s. Extreme simplification characterized the late works, in particular his coloured paper cutouts, which led to the ultimate linear refinement of the decorations in the chapel at Vence (1949-51).

❖ In his autobiographical *Notes of a Painter* (1908), Matisse wrote: 'What I dream of is an art of balance, purity and serenity . . . something like a good armchair in which to rest from physical fatigue.'

Mbatha, Azaria (1941-) South African-born artist, trained at RORKE'S DRIFT in Natal. He is best known for his intricate linocuts, mainly of religious subjects, with imagery such as tribal huts and cattle drawn from his environment. His early works are narrative, often with a medieval quality. In 1966 he was awarded a scholarship to study in Sweden, and settled here in 1969.

medium Term for the method and materials used in art. For example, painting is a different medium from sculpture, and acrylic paint is a different medium from oil paint. A work of art using more than one medium – collage and paint, for example – is described as mixed media. The term can also refer to water, oil, turpentine or varnish added to paint for an effect.

Michelangelo Buonarroti (1475-1564) RENAISSANCE painter, sculptor, architect and poet, born and trained in Florence. With LEONARDO DA VINCI, he radically changed the status of the artist. His first major work was his PIETÀ (*c*1500) for St Peter's in Rome. This was followed by the famous marble of *David* (1504) in Florence, after which he began work on the tomb of Pope Julius II, a project which was to occupy him intermittently for 40 years. The tomb was never completed and only the marble *Moses* and two unfinished *Slaves* remain. From 1508 to 1512 he painted the frescoes on the Sistine Chapel ceiling in the Vatican, one of the great masterpieces of pictorial art. The figures on the wall tombs of the Medici in Florence, as well as his design for the vestibule of the Laurentian Library, are considered early exmples of MANNERISM. In 1534 he returned to Rome to paint his apocalyptic *Last Judgement* on the altar wall of the Sistine Chapel. Among his later projects was the design for the dome of St Peter's.

❖ Michelangelo took four years to paint the Sistine Chapel ceiling. Restoring the work took 14 years – from 1980 to 1994.

Millet, Jean François (mill-AY) (1814-75) French artist whose paintings of rustic peasant life such as *The Winnower* (1846) and *The Sower* (1850) are grimly realistic. But he achieved immense popular success with his more sentimental pictures, such as *The Angelus* (1857-9) – in which two peasants stand in a field, praying in the evening light.

Miró, Joán (mee-ROH) (1893-1983) One of the leading Spanish surrealist painters, with Salvador DALI. His paintings tended towards abstract art; his best-known pictures have brightly coloured amoebalike forms in apparent movement against a dark background.

IN HIS OWN IMAGE The Creation of Adam, *one of Michelangelo's ceiling frescoes in the Sistine Chapel, is one of the best-known and most memorable images of the Renaissance.*

Miró also worked in ceramics, and used the medium to create enormous wall decorations for Harvard University (1950) in the USA and the UNESCO building in Paris (1955-8).

Miyake, Issey (1939-) Japanese fashion designer who spent six years working in Paris and New York fashion houses in the 1960s before opening the Miyake Design Studio in Tokyo in 1971. The cut of his clothes is inspired by traditional Japanese forms, but it is the richness and subtlety of his fabrics that set his designs apart.

Modigliani, Amedeo (1884-1920) Italian-born painter and sculptor who spent most of his career in Paris. He is best known for his dramatic nudes and portraits, which often depict dark, almond-eyed women with elongated oval faces. Modigliani took a great interest in African sculpture. Although he was well known in bohemian circles in Paris, he gained wider recognition only after his early death from tuberculosis.

❖ The handsome Modigliani was also known for his dissolute and amorous life style and his addiction to alcohol and drugs.

Mohl, John Koenakeefe (*c*1903-85) Born in South Africa, Mohl studied painting in Windhoek before returning to Sophiatown, where he became involved in art education and training. He painted landscapes as well as images of township life, capturing the long shadows of dawn or dusk, and the atmospheric effects of mist or rain.

Mondrian, Piet (1872-1944) Dutch artist who was one of the most important purely abstract painters. He was greatly influenced by CUBISM and he sought what he described as

'pure reality' – a harmonized sense of order without expression. His paintings became increasingly geometric – many of them consisted of rectangles of flat, primary colour framed by black lines. During the last four years of his life he lived in New York, where his work found a more lively rhythm, influenced by his love of jazz – shown in works such as *Broadway Boogie-Woogie* (1942-3).

Monet, Claude (1840-1926) French impressionist painter whose works are concerned with light and its changing effect on nature. He was influenced by Eugène Boudin and Johann Jongkind, as well as TURNER, whose works he encountered in London. He began the first of a series, in which he painted the same subject in different light and atmospheric conditions, at the railway station of St Lazare (1876), followed by his *Haystacks* and *Poplars* (1890-2), and the *Rouen Cathedral* series (1891-5). An interest in oriental art is shown in his water-lily garden, created at Giverny in 1883, which became the subject of many of his late paintings. His works became increasingly abstracted as he reduced detail and concentrated on colour and the richness of surface textures.

❖ Monet presented a series of vast water-lily canvases to the State in 1926; these are now installed in the Musée de l'Orangerie in Paris.

CALM REFLECTIONS *As Monet's* Water Lilies *series (1895-1926) progressed, the shapes and colours gradually became less defined. Some regard these paintings as the starting point of abstract work, while others think of them as the ultimate impressionist works – pure and spontaneous visual impressions.*

STRANGE FIGURE *Henry Moore returned to the theme of* Reclining Figure *again and again. This example, from 1939, shows the daring way he hollowed out solid forms to create internal shapes.*

monochrome Any painting, drawing or print executed in a range of tones of only one colour. Works that are executed only in neutral shades of grey are termed grisaille.

montage Picture made by combining ready-made images – often by sticking one over another. Montage differs from collage in that each element is chosen for its subject matter, whereas in collage material is used simply for its overall visual effect, as in MATISSE's 'cutouts'. From about 1911 montage was used by cubists, who included newspaper clippings and menus in their pictures; ERNST produced haunting surrealist montages using engravings from cheap illustrated novels and from catalogues. Photomontage – using cut-out photographic images, often mixed with other media – is now a widespread form of montage and has made a considerable impact on commercial art since the 1920s.

Moore, Henry (1898-1986) Widely regarded as one of Britain's greatest sculptors, known for his simple, hollowed out or pierced human forms. Works such as the famous *Reclining Figure* (1939) display his interest in the relationship between the human form and the landscape. Like Barbara HEPWORTH, Moore favoured direct carving into blocks of wood or stone – without making preparatory models. He was greatly influenced by the simplicity of form in African and Mexican art, and his own work became so simplified that it was sometimes considered to be ABSTRACT ART. In 1940 he was appointed an official war artist, after his drawings of figures sheltering from air raids became popular.

Moreau, Gustave (1826-98) French artist and leading symbolist painter. He created fabulous mythological and biblical scenes in a detailed style, often layering on bright oil colours to give an encrusted, bejewelled appearance, as in *The Unicorns* (*c*1855). In contrast, his watercolours, which were often swiftly executed, can appear almost abstract. During the last six years of his life, he taught at the Ecôle des Beaux Arts in Paris, where he influenced students such as MATISSE.

Morisot, Berthe (1841-95) French artist and the first woman impressionist, known for her paintings of quiet scenes of women and children. She was influenced by her early teacher COROT, but in 1868 she met MANET, who became her mentor and whose brother, Eugène, she married. She in turn encouraged Manet to abandon his use of black paint and to adopt the bright primary colours used by the emerging band of impressionists; the result directly inspired and shaped IMPRESSIONISM. From about 1885 onwards her work was strongly influenced by RENOIR.

Morris, William (1834-96) English craftsman, painter, designer, poet and left-wing political activist who was one of the great Victorian reformers. He first made his name as a painter linked to the PRE-RAPHAELITE BROTHERHOOD and as the driving force behind the ARTS AND CRAFTS MOVEMENT. In 1861 he set up a decorating company that produced only handmade goods, to combat the new phenomenon of mass-production in the wake of the ▷INDUSTRIAL REVOLUTION. The carpets, tapestries, carvings, textiles, wallpaper, stained glass and furniture he designed, with his friend Edward Burne-Jones (1833-98), are some of the finest examples of 19th-century decorative art. In 1890 he founded the Kelmscott Press, with the aim of improving book design and printing. He designed ornamental borders for his books and created several new typefaces. Many of Morris's fabric and wallpaper designs are still reproduced today.

❖ Morris summed up his aesthetic philosophy in the following way: 'Have nothing in your home that you do not know to be useful or believe to be beautiful.'

mosaic Design made by setting small pieces of marble, glass or ceramic into cement or plaster. The small pieces are known as tesserae (from the Latin for 'squares'), and are often irregular in shape. Mosaic is one of the oldest known forms of decoration; the earliest known example is Sumerian, from around 3000 BC. Most early mosaics were used to cover floors, but with the rise of Christianity mosaics were widely used for murals to decorate the walls of BYZANTINE churches. After the 13th century, mosaics were largely superseded by frescoes, although a few artists such as Paolo UCCELLO continued the tradition.

PATTERN WITH A PURPOSE *The handmade products of William Morris's south London company, such as this* Wey *cotton textile print, combined decorative beauty with traditional craftsmanship.*

Motswai, Tommy (1963-) South African artist specializing in joyous, colourful scenes of everyday life. He works mainly in pastels in a disarmingly naive manner. His lively works are closely observed records of life in contemporary South Africa, ranging from humorous interactions on the highways and streets of the cities to jolly tea parties and weddings.

Muafangejo, John (1943-87) Angolan-born graphic artist who was educated in Anglican missions in Namibia. He studied art at RORKE'S DRIFT in Natal, before returning to Namibia. His densely packed linocuts are accompanied by large tracts of text, often explaining events from everyday life in great detail. A religious theme runs through much of his work, an example being *New Archbishop Desmond Tutu* (1986).

Muir, Jean (1933-95) British fashion designer known for her classic and supremely simple dresses and women's suits. Her restrained clothes are usually made in brown, grey, dark blue or black fabrics.

Mukhuba, Nelson (1925-87) South African sculptor, who worked mainly in wood. A figurative artist, his subject matter ranged from religious imagery to colonial curiosities, such as *Drunk Boer*, depicted with a wry sense of humour. His monumental *Nebuchadnezzar* (*c*1979) is reminiscent of the visionary works of the English poet William ▷BLAKE.

SCENE OF SLAUGHTER *In the linocut* Battle of Rorke's Drift *Namibian artist John Muafangejo depicts in abstract style the Voortrekkers' laager surrounded by attacking and slain Zulus.*

CRY FOR HELP *Munch painted* The Scream *(1893) after a moment of personal crisis in which he became aware of a 'great cry' in nature. It has come to symbolize the loneliness of modern life.*

Munch, Edvard (1863-1944) Norwegian painter and graphic artist best known for his 1893 work *The Scream.* He studied in Europe and was influenced by the symbolists GAUGUIN and VAN GOGH. His own work influenced the German expressionists. An intense emotionalism characterizes all his work, in which there is an obsessive preoccupation with sexuality, violence and death.

mural art A traditional form of decorative art in South Africa, which is rapidly vanishing as rural communities are drawn to the cities. Wall painting is the domain of women, foremost among whom is Esther Mahlangu. In Ndebele art, brightly coloured geometric designs decorate all the outer surfaces of the dwellings, including the courtyard walls.

❖ In many urban areas mural art involving the participation of the community has been encouraged as a deterrent to graffiti artists.

❖ A famous exponent of mural art was the Mexican Diego Rivera (1886-1957), who was influenced by Aztec art.

Nabis (nah-BEE) Small group of French artists founded by the post-impressionist Pierre Bonnard (1867-1947) and Édouard Vuillard (1868-1940) which was active during the 1890s. The group was influenced by the vogue for Japanese art, with its simplified forms and unusual perspectives, and by GAUGUIN's advice to paint in pure, flat colours. The Nabis believed that painting should go further than imitating reality and should stress the artist's subjective perceptions. They produced work for theatre design, posters, book illustrations and stained glass.

❖ The name of the group is derived from the Hebrew word *nābhi*, meaning 'prophet'.

naive art A term applied to many art works that have disarming charm and an absence of sophistication. A childlike quality is often deliberately feigned by highly skilled artists, such as KLEE and CHAGALL, while others, such as ROUSSEAU, lack formal training. Naive art often shows an innocent, visionary wisdom, manifest in South Africa in the sculptures of Jackson HLUNGWANI, the paintings of Gladys Mgudlandlu, and the linocuts of Azaria MBATHA and John MUAFANGEJO.

❖ Among the leading exponents of the genre was the American painter Grandma Moses (1860-1961).

Nash, Paul (1889-1946) British painter, designer and book illustrator, known for his beautiful and lyrical pictures of the English landscape. As an official war artist during both world wars, he often used SURREALISM to create a sense of mystery and threat, as in *Totes Meer* (*Dead Sea*, 1940-1) in which the waves are the wings of crashed aircraft.

naturalism Style which attempts to make an accurate copy of nature without stylizing it in any way. The meaning is often confused with that of REALISM.

Naudé, Hugo (1869-1941) South African painter best known for his richly coloured, sun-drenched Cape landscapes, and his somewhat more formal portraits. He studied in London and Europe, and was influenced by the impressionists, although his work is intuitive and individual, not adhering strictly to the impressionists' style.

Nel, Karel (1955-) South African painter of complex pastels and graphic works with layers of meanings and interpretations. He draws from many branches of knowledge sources, including nuclear physics, literature and the major religions, using universal symbols from all these sources.

neo-Classicism Movement that dominated European art and architecture in the late 18th and early 19th centuries. It was a reaction to the heaviness of BAROQUE and the frivolity of ROCOCO. It was also inspired by the rediscoveries of Herculaneum (1709) and ▷POMPEII (1748). Neo-Classicism sought to revive the simplicity and grandeur of ancient Greek and Roman CLASSICISM and deliberately imitated Roman and Greek art. It was a philosophical and intellectual movement which affected all European countries, but had especially strong associations with the ▷FRENCH REVOLUTION. Among the great neo-Classical artists were the French painters INGRES and DAVID, the German painter Anton Mengs (1728-79) and the British architect Robert ▷ADAM. As the 19th century progressed, neo-Classicism was replaced by ROMANTICISM, which moved away from the rigid rules and limitations of the Classical tradition towards more subjective experience. (See also ▷NEO-CLASSICISM in 'Architecture and engineering'.)

New Group Formed in 1937 by a group of progressive young South African artists working in the modern styles current in Europe. They played a major role in raising the standards and status of art in South Africa. Among the almost 50 members were Gregoire Boonzaier (1909-), BATTISS, LIPSHITZ, PRELLER and NAUDÉ. The New Group played a major role in introducing art to a wider public, beyond the main art centres. The last exhibition of the group was held in 1953.

Nicholson, Ben (1894-1982) British abstract artist who produced geometric paintings inspired by MONDRIAN and CUBISM. He is best known for his carved white plaster abstract reliefs, in which rounded and rectangular shapes give a sense of space. Nicholson was married to the sculptor Barbara HEPWORTH.

GEOMETRIC TENSION *Ben Nicholson's elegant linking of rectangular forms, as seen in his* Painting *(1937), depends on a carefully worked out balance of shape, line and colour.*

Nolde, Emil (1867-1956) German expressionist painter and printmaker, initially a member of the *Brücke* group. He was influenced by folk art, VAN GOGH, MUNCH and the Belgian artist James Sidney Ensor, and painted many religious scenes. His bold use of colour and dense, crowded compositions are powerful and exuberant. The pagan abandon of *Dance around the Golden Calf* (1910) has as its antithesis the poignancy of *Christ Among the Children* (1910). He also produced many etchings, lithographs and woodcuts.

O'Keeffe, Georgia (1887-1986) American watercolourist best known for her paintings of natural objects and landscapes. O'Keeffe's typically stark paintings of bleached bones, plants and the desert show her strong sense of design, although they are almost abstract.

op art Paintings or sculptures which use optical illusion to create visual sensations. Many op art works are in black and white, with swirling or geometric patterns which appear to move and change shape. The Hungarian Victor VASARELY was a leading figure in the field, and one of its most skilled practitioners was the British artist Bridget Riley.

Orphism An art form that extended the analytical cubist fragmentation of form into the field of colour. Main figures in the movement were the French artist Robert Delaunay (1885-1941) and his Russian-born wife, Sonia, and the Czech Frank Kupka. Delaunay's *Windows* series (*c*1910), inspired by Paris, is a riot of colour.

Parkinson, Norman (1913-90) British photographer known for his glamorous and lively fashion shots and his elegant and attractive celebrity portraits. He was also a competent reportage photographer, and worked for many magazines, including *Vogue*, *Life* and *Harper's Bazaar*.

pastels Soft-coloured sticks made of dried pigment and chalk bound by gum and used to make sharp, vivid lines or areas of soft, bright colour. Pastel was a favourite medium of 18th and 19th-century French artists, and was often used, with particular flair, by DEGAS, TOULOUSE-LAUTREC and Odilon Redon. Different colours can be easily merged or built up in layers to create a rich and varied effect. Pastels tend to smudge unless they are treated with a fixative.

❖ In everyday usage, 'pastel colours' are soft shades of blue, pink, green and yellow.

pastiche Unashamed, often witty imitation or use of another's work. Some artists may also create a pastiche by copying and combining parts of other works of art in an original way.

patina Surface colour and finish which builds up on furniture or metal through a combination of age, usage and polishing. On metals such as bronze or copper, the greenish or brown colour on the surface is the result of oxidization. On bronze sculpture the effect is usually created artificially.

Pemba, George (1912-) One of the early black social realists of South African art. An accomplished portraitist, he has also painted narrative group scenes, townscapes and interiors, in which the emphasis is placed particularly on the interaction between people in his own social environment.

perspective A system developed during the RENAISSANCE where an illusion of three-dimensionality or pictorial space is created on a flat or relief surface. Linear perspective is based on the theory that objects appear smaller the further they are from the viewer, and that lines appear to converge as they recede into the distance. Aerial perspective, developed by LEONARDO DA VINCI, uses differences in tone, lighting and clarity to make objects seem nearer or more distant. In a landscape, for example, warm reds and browns would be used in the foreground, greens in the middle distance and cool blues and purples in the background.

Picasso, Pablo (1881-1973) Spanish painter, sculptor, graphic artist and designer, who became the most renowned artist of the 20th century. Picasso was a child prodigy, producing exquisite Classical drawings by the age of ten. He lived in Barcelona, where he developed his 'Blue period' (1901-4), which reflects the influence of TOULOUSE-LAUTREC in its colour and form as well as its subject matter – the poor and down-and-outs. In 1904 he moved to Paris, where he lived until 1945. The 'Rose period', which lasted less than a year, is warmer but more enigmatic than the Blue. Influenced by the work of CÉZANNE and West African and ancient Iberian art, Picasso painted *Les Demoiselles d'Avignon* (1907) a work which greatly impressed BRAQUE and led to their collaboration in the development of CUBISM. Picasso's output was prolific and he experimented with many ideas – from using more decorative elements to producing works of almost Classical poise and weight. He also produced collage and sculpture, often incorporating discarded everyday objects, such as pieces of string, wire and newspaper. *Guernica* (1937), one of his most famous works, was painted in response to the Spanish Civil War; it is a devastating attack on human cruelty and folly. Picasso's creativity and a quirky playfulness in his approach gave a freedom to 20th-century art which is still apparent among contemporary artists.

❖ When the Johannesburg Art Gallery acquired Picasso's *Tête d'arlequin II* (1971) in 1974 it created a rumpus in the city, but the interest it aroused doubled the gallery's annual attendance figures at the time.

Pierneef, J(acob) H(endrik) (1886-1957) South African artist who was committed to the cause of Afrikaner culture and whose expansive landscapes, stylized umbrella trees and huge cloud formations are instantly recognizable. He studied in Holland during the South African War. In 1929 he was commissioned to paint 32 mural panels for the Johannesburg railway station. An accomplished draughtsman, he produced many woodcuts, linoprints and drawings.

Piero della Francesca (*c*1420-92) Italian painter who, with his contemporary MASACCIO, was a pioneer of linear PERSPECTIVE. He was a mathematician as well as a painter, uniting science and art in keeping with RENAISSANCE ideals. The solemn grandeur and monumental, simplified forms of his religious and secular scenes have influenced many artists and art movements.

pietà Italian word meaning 'pity', generally applied to paintings or sculptures of the Virgin Mary holding the dead Jesus on her lap. The best-known example is MICHELANGELO's marble pietà in St Peter's, Rome.

Pissarro, Camille (1830-1903) One of the leading French impressionists, who exhibited at all eight of the impressionist exhibitions. Born in the West Indies, he moved to Paris, where he studied with COROT and met MONET. He painted atmospheric views of Montmartre in Paris, and of Norwood in London, where he lived from 1870 to 1872 and where he studied the work of TURNER and CONSTABLE. Pissarro often adapted the art of his contemporaries into his own paintings, such as the POINTILLISM of SEURAT. As the teacher of CÉZANNE and GAUGUIN, he was an important influence on 20th-century art.

pointillism Technique of painting with small dots of pure colour which, observed from a distance, are intended to fuse without losing the intensity of colour. The two neo-impressionists SEURAT and SIGNAC were its chief exponents, but they called the technique 'divisionism'.

Pollock, Jackson (1912-56) American artist, central figure in ABSTRACT EXPRESSIONISM. His drip paintings, or 'action paintings', were poured directly from a paint tin, or from a paint-soaked stick, onto large canvases laid out on the floor. The apparently random network of lines, splashes and drips exude a raw energy, and introduced a new mode of painting to the repertoire of modern art.

Polly Street Art Centre Established in 1952 in Johannesburg under the guidance of Cecil SKOTNES, the centre was the first important training school for black artists in South Africa, among whom were Sydney KUMALO, Lucas SITHOLE, Ezrom LEGAE and DUMILE FENI. It was closed in 1960 because of apartheid policies and the art group moved to the Jubilee Social Centre.

ANGUISH OF WAR *Picasso's* Guernica *(1937) was inspired by the vicious aerial bombing of that town during the Spanish Civil War.*

ACTION ART *For Jackson Pollock, the process of painting was more important than the result – huge abstract canvasses without formal composition such as* Guardians of the Secret *(1943).*

CHEEKY COUTURE
Mary Quant (centre), in 1967, shows off some of the bold designs that revolutionized fashion for young women.

pop art Movement which began in the mid-1950s and reached its peak in the 1960s in both Britain and the USA, although it is still quite active today. It mocks 'serious' art and takes its images from the media, advertising, popular culture and everyday life – as in the work of the British painter Peter Blake and American Roy LICHTENSTEIN. Ordinary consumer objects, such as in Andy WARHOL's *100 Campbell's Soup Cans* (1962), are also popular subject matter. JOHNS was a major figure in the movement.

post-impressionism A term coined by the artist and critic Roger Fry (1866-1934) to describe the works on a London exhibition in 1910. The major artists of the period, VAN GOGH, CÉZANNE, GAUGUIN and SEURAT, were concerned with the importance of form as opposed to the more spontaneous subject matter and brushstrokes of the impressionists. Most modern art derives to some degree from the works of the post-impressionists.

Poussin, Nicolas (1594-1665) French painter who worked mainly in Italy but who profoundly affected French Classical painting. He was also a philosopher, and his highly disciplined work was based on his theory that the moral content of a painting should be enhanced by its intellectual content. He also thought that colour should be subservient to the overall vision. Poussin often sought to convey the innocence and dignity of the past. His emphasis on formal values and draughtsmanship strongly influenced LE BRUN. Among his many mythological and biblical works is *The Adoration of the Golden Calf* (*c*1630).

Preller, Alexis (1911-75) South African artist of highly stylized, figurative paintings. He was a member of the NEW GROUP. A recurrent source of imagery in his paintings was the Ndebele people, their colourful blankets, beaded clothing, brass necklets and architecture. He treats the subject with an aura of exoticism. Three paintings of *The Grand Mapogga* (*c*1957) portray figures with tiny heads perched on huge, elongated bodies, in almost surreal surroundings.

Pre-Raphaelite Brotherhood Group formed in 1848 by several English writers and painters, notably Dante Gabriel Rossetti, Sir John Everett Millais and William Holman Hunt. They wanted to return to the purity of art before RAPHAEL, whose work they considered overpraised and insincere. The group used bright colours, complex symbolism and elaborate detail. Their realistic treatment of religious subjects caused great indignation and the group's motives were attacked by critics. However, in 1851 they became widely acclaimed after John RUSKIN defended them, praising their aims and efforts. The group broke up in 1853, but Rossetti founded a second partnership in the late 1850s, with MORRIS and Sir Edward Burne-Jones.

❖ The writing style of the group was deliberately literary and archaic, harking back to the spirit of the Middle Ages.

protest art Art has always been a vehicle for protest against political systems, religious abuses and social injustice. Among the pioneers of protest art were GOYA, the DADA movement, KOLLWITZ, PICASSO, HOGARTH and the German-born American artist George Grosz. In South Africa the apartheid policy generated a wealth of protest art, much of it direct and blunt, some of it subtle, poignant and shaming.

Quant, Mary (1934-) British fashion designer whose name is synonymous with the 'Swinging Sixties'. She made cheap and cheerful geometric designs in bright colours and is best known for her revolutionary innovation – the miniskirt.

quattrocento (KWAT-tro-CHEN-toh) Italian word for 400. It refers to the 1400s (the 15th century) – which marked the start of the RENAISSANCE. Major quattrocento artists were PIERO DELLA FRANCESCA, UCCELLO, MANTEGNA and BOTTICELLI.

Raphael (1483-1520) The youngest of the three great Italian painters of the High RENAISSANCE – he was 31 years younger than LEONARDO DA VINCI and eight years younger than MICHELANGELO. Raphael was a pupil of Pietro Perugino (*c*1445-1523) and in 1504 went to Florence to study the work of Leonardo and Michelangelo. He moved in 1508 to Rome where he worked relentlessly to emulate the two great masters. He painted a FRESCO cycle, including *The School of Athens* (*c*1511), in the Pope's chambers in the Vatican, which epitomizes the High Renaissance ideal of beauty, serenity and harmony. In 1514 he was appointed architect in charge of St Peter's, as well as of Rome's town planning. Raphael's later style was simpler and more monumental, but retained the vitality and warmth of his earlier work. His depiction of feminine beauty was particularly influential in NEO-CLASSICISM.

❖ Raphael was the first artist to become a

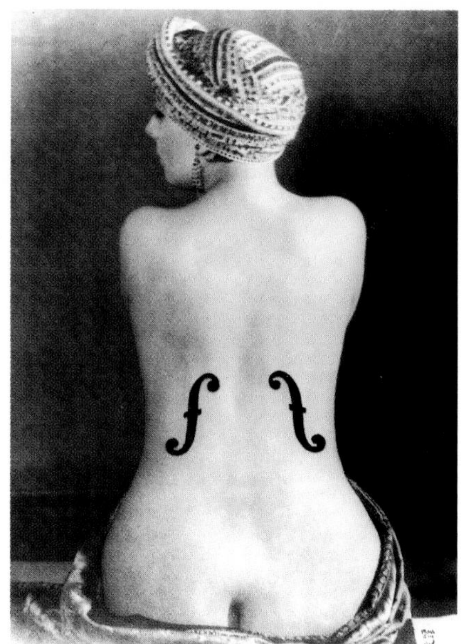

SEEING THINGS *Man Ray explored many photographic techniques to create surreal images such as* Le Violon d'Ingres *(1924).*

A LIFE IN PICTURES *Rembrandt painted a series of searchingly honest self-portraits over a period of 40 years. This one, from* c*1665, reveals his sadness as a despairing, bankrupt, lonely old man.*

close friend of princes and cardinals; he was buried in the ▷PANTHEON in Rome at the request of Pope Leo X.

Ray, Man (1890-1976) American painter, photographer, sculptor and film-maker who was one of the leading figures in the New York DADA movement. He is best known for his black-and-white art photography and for his imaginative SURREALIST work.

realism Nineteenth-century French art movement dedicated to depicting life as it really is, and was therefore close to NATURALISM – copying nature without stylizing it. Realist painters, such as MILLET, Gustave Courbet and Honoré Daumier, rebelled against the idealized images of formal art and produced uncompromisingly honest pictures. These artists painted candid scenes of everyday life, inspired by contemporary writers such as the French novelists Gustave ▷FLAUBERT and Honoré de ▷BALZAC.

Regency Period in Britain from 1800 to 1830, typified by elegant, lavish and exotic furnishings, fashion and architecture. It takes its name from the flamboyant Prince of Wales who became King George IV in 1820. A great patron of the arts, he acted as Regent from 1811 because of George III's bouts of mental illness. (See also ▷REGENCY in 'Architecture and engineering'.)

relief A term that applies both to sculpture and to certain print media, including linocuts and woodcuts. The background plane is cut away, leaving a raised foreground image. In relief prints, when paper is pressed on to an inked block, only the foreground image is reproduced. Relief sculpture, including moulded bronzes, is a combination of two and three-dimensional art, where some degree of illusionism is used.

Rembrandt van Rijn (1606-69) Dutch artist, draughtsman and etcher regarded as one of the greatest artists of all time. His prodigious output included at least 600 paintings, 300 etchings and 1 500 ink and wash drawings. His reputation was established in 1632 with *The Anatomy Lesson of Dr Tulp*, a group portrait of the Amsterdam Guild of Surgeons. His most celebrated work, *The Night Watch*, a group portrait of volunteer militia, was painted in 1642. Just as his fortunes changed, his wealthy wife Saskia died, and his finances collapsed. Although he painted landscapes and biblical, mythological and historical pictures, as well as scenes from everyday life, Rembrandt is mainly remembered as a remarkably sensitive portrait painter who endowed his sitters with great inner dignity, but at the same time provided an uncanny insight into their character.

Renaissance French term meaning 'rebirth' which refers to the renewal of Classical ideals in literature, art and architecture that took place from the late 14th to the end of the 16th century. One of the early Renaissance masters was MASACCIO, who was followed by the artists of the QUATTROCENTO. The High Renaissance, which lasted from 1500 to about 1527, was dominated by LEONARDO DA VINCI, MICHELANGELO and RAPHAEL, whose mastery of technique, faithfulness to nature and elimination of all superfluous detail produced paintings of such serenity and harmony that they still have the power to inspire awe. The High Renaissance gave way to greater expressiveness – which was already inherent in the work of Michelangelo and Leonardo – in the form of MANNERISM.

❖ The blossoming of the arts that occurred during the Renaissance was based on the rediscovery of the art and literature of ancient Greece and Rome. The Renaissance is seen as marking the transition from the ▷MIDDLE AGES to modern times.

Renoir, Pierre Auguste (1841-1919) French artist who trained as a porcelain painter and became one of the leading impressionists. Renoir's sensuous use of light and colour, the voluptuous nudes in his later works and the vitality and warmth of his style make him one of the best-loved of all the impressionists. His early paintings typically depict bright, sun-filled scenes with light glinting on water and people by the river or at festivities. He almost always painted outside, or away from his studio, and often worked with MONET. Renoir gradually came to use lighter tones and his paintings were increasingly made up of patches of light and shadow. In paintings such as *The Umbrellas* (*c*1881-4) and *The Bathers* (*c*1884-7) he began to concentrate more on form and on the pinks and reds of flesh tones. Other well-known works include *The Theatre Box* (1874) and *Le Moulin de la Galette* (1876). Renoir produced almost 6 000 paintings, and continued to work right up to his death, even though he was crippled with arthritis.

Restoration Style of English furnishing from *c*1660-1700, inspired by the French fashions brought back to England when Charles II was restored to the throne in 1660. Furniture was lighter and more elegant, fashioned after that at ▷VERSAILLES. The style became widespread in the refurbishing of thousands of homes destroyed in the Great Fire of London in 1666.

Reynolds, Sir Joshua (1723-92) British painter who, unlike most artists of the time, came from an educated background; his friends included such figures as the writer Samuel ▷JOHNSON, the poet Oliver Goldsmith, the statesman and philosopher Edmund Burke and the actor and dramatist David Garrick. An extraordinarily prolific and versatile painter, Reynolds was inspired by the Old Masters, especially VAN DYCK and REMBRANDT. He combined Classical allusion with competent painting, especially in his portraits. His learned writings, particularly his *Fifteen Discourses on the Rules of Art* (1769-90), his enthusiasm and his social standing made a major contribution to raising the status of art and the artist in Britain.

rock art Southern Africa is endowed with an abundance of rock paintings, which are among the oldest of the world's art forms. While most of the rock paintings in Europe occur in caves, southern African works are

HAPPY CROWD *Renoir captures the exuberant, relaxed mood of Parisians at play in the sun in his picture* Le Moulin de la Galette *(1876).*

DEEP IN THOUGHT *This 1880 sculpture, one of several that Rodin made of* The Thinker, *shows his skill at modelling the human form.*

often in open areas, on exposed rock faces or overhangs. Rock art is not simply narrative but integral to the culture, social system and religious beliefs of the societies that made it. Most works are believed to have been painted by shamans (or ▷PRIESTLY DIVINERS) and may have been associated with trance states.

❖ Two important discoveries have recently been made of rock art sites in Europe, one in northern Portugal, the other in France.

❖ Vandalism is a serious problem in the preservation of rock art. Hundreds of sites have been damaged or destroyed by graffiti, or by the removal of pieces of rock. In an attempt to prevent this, books on the subject seldom disclose the exact locations.

rococo Decorative, light and frivolous style of painting and decoration which developed in early 18th-century France as a reaction to the heavier style of the BAROQUE and LOUIS QUATORZE period. The main exponents of rococo painting were François Boucher, FRAGONARD and WATTEAU. The rococo style was fashionable throughout Europe until about 1760, when it was succeeded by NEO-CLASSICISM, but it remained popular in Germany, where it mingled with the baroque style in churches and palaces. Rococo designs are characterized by scrolls, asymmetrical curves and motifs taken from nature, such as rocks, shells and flowers. (See also ▷ROCOCO in 'Architecture and engineering'.)

❖ The term 'rococo' derives from the French *rocaille*, which means 'rockwork' and *coquillage*, which means 'shellwork'.

Rodin, Auguste (1840-1917) French sculptor whose name is synonymous with *The Kiss* (1886) and the various versions of *The Thinker* (1880-1900). These sculptures, and many other large works, had their origins in his designs for the *Gates of Hell* (1880-1917), inspired by GHIBERTI's *Gates of Paradise*. He worked on 186 figures for these bronze doors, but the project was never completed. The dignity of the common person is captured in the moving *The Burghers of Calais* (1884-6), and in his monumental *Balzac* (1898) Rodin reduces detail and presents instead the essence of the personality.

❖ By far the largest collection of Rodin's work is at the Musée Rodin in Paris.

romanticism Movement in late 18th and early 19th-century art, literature and music which arose in reaction to the ▷INDUSTRIAL REVOLUTION and to the previously unquestioned adherence to reason and tradition. Romanticism strove to express humanity's feelings, innate powers of creativity, spontaneity and relationship with the natural world. In the visual arts, TURNER, CONSTABLE, ▷BLAKE and DELACROIX were among its best-known exponents.

Rorke's Drift Established by Swedish missionaries Peder and Ulla Gowenius in 1962, the Evangelical Lutheran Church Art and Craft Centre moved in 1963 to Rorke's Drift in Natal and became known by that name. It is one of the pioneer art and craft centres in southern Africa, having produced many of South Africa's leading art educators. Women play a significant role, mainly in the execution of tapestries and in the ceramic workshop, while men generally design the tapestries and work in the ceramic and print workshops. Azaria MBATHA, John MUAFANGEJO and the weaver Allina Ndebele are among the artists trained at Rorke's Drift.

Rothko, Mark (1903-70) Latvian-born American abstract painter who portrayed soft-edged rectangles of intense, almost luminous colour which seem to float on a solid background of harmonizing or contrasting deep hues. His very large canvases were meant to create a sense of awe.

Rousseau, Henri (1844-1910) French part-time painter known for his meticulous and often fanciful works of NAIVE ART that verge on SURREALISM. These large, detailed pictures of exotic subjects and fantastic landscapes, painted in a precise but unsophisticated manner have a haunting, dreamlike quality. He is best known for jungle scenes in which wild animals prowl sedately through lush fo-

PRIMITIVE DREAM *Rousseau's untutored style, as seen in* The Jungle – Tiger Attacking a Buffalo *(1908), was very influential. His dreamlike clarity of vision prefigured the surrealist movement.*

LEGENDARY TRIO *The term 'Rubenesque' – for plump, sensuous women – stems from paintings such as* The Three Graces *(1639).*

EVERYDAY LIFE *Pioneer black South African artist Gerard Sekoto's* Street Scene *(1939) uses vivid colours and an impressionistic technique to capture a fleeting moment in a shantytown.*

liage. His portraits are in a similar style.
❖ Rousseau's job as a goods inspector in the Paris customs-house earned him the nickname of *Le Douanier* (the customs officer).

Rubens, Sir Peter Paul (1577-1640) Flemish artist, scholar, linguist and diplomat, one of the great figures in BAROQUE art and one of the most influential artists of his age. He studied in Italy, where he was influenced by the art of MICHELANGELO, TITIAN and TINTORETTO. As court artist to the Spanish regent in Antwerp, he painted for most of Europe's royalty. He was a devout Catholic and many of his major commissions were for the Church, among them the vast altarpiece *The Elevation of the Cross* (1610-11) in Antwerp Cathedral. Rubens's chalk and pen drawings are as masterly as his preparatory oil sketches, or his finished paintings, which drew from mythological, historical, secular and religious subjects. His works are imbued with exuberant life and vitality, vibrant colour and expressive brushwork.

Ruskin, John (1819-1900) English writer and eminent art critic who was himself a talented draughtsman and watercolourist. Ruskin was a celebrated figure during his lifetime, and his criticism and writings on the philosophy of art were highly influential. A champion of the underprivileged, he viewed art as an expression of morality, and believed that social problems could be solved through art. His highly spirited defence of the PRE-RAPHAELITE BROTHERHOOD single-handedly secured its success, and his praise of TURNER rescued the artist from obscurity and established him as the leading landscape painter of the day.
❖ In 1877 Ruskin made an astounding and vitiolic attack on the artist WHISTLER, who sued him for damages.

Saint Laurent, Yves (1936-) French designer of glamorous and well-cut clothes. He became head designer at the major fashion house Christian Dior at the age of 21. Five years later, he opened his own couture house and designed the 1960s 'rich hippy' look, which was strongly influenced by gypsy and North African motifs. By the 1970s Yves St Laurent had become a household name, selling perfumes and ready-to-wear clothes as well as *haute couture.*

Sargent, John Singer (1856-1925) American portrait painter who studied in Paris, where he developed his 'loaded brush' technique, involving long, fluent brush strokes of pure colour. In 1884, his 'erotic' painting of *Madame Gautreau* caused such a scandal that he moved to London. There he became the most celebrated portrait painter of Edwardian society, sometimes ironically conveying his sitters' sense of their own grandeur. He was an official war artist during World War I.

Schadeberg, Jürgen (1931-) German-born photographer, who trained in Berlin and emigrated to South Africa in 1950. An influential figure in the development of South African photographic art who trained many young photographers, he was one of the first staff members of the magazine *Drum*. *The Fifties People* (1987) and *The Finest Photographs from the Old Drum* (1987) are among the books edited by Schadeberg, drawing from the *Drum* archives.

Schwitters, Kurt (1887-1948) German abstract painter, poet and sculptor, and a leading member of the DADA group. He developed a type of collage art he called *Merz*: pictures and sculptures made with everyday materials, such as bus tickets, newspapers, lino and wire. Schwitters also created three *Merzbau*, structures the size of a house made from the same material.

Sekoto, Gerard (1913-93) A pioneer of black South African art. His most productive years were in the township of Sophiatown where he painted scenes of everyday life – portraits, landscapes and indoor cameos. He moved to Paris in 1947. Except for a short spell in Senegal, he never returned to Africa. African imagery remained dominant in his paintings, which in later years became idealized.

sepia Brown pigment made from the inklike secretions of cuttlefish which was sometimes applied to early photographs. The term can refer to any brown ink or wash.

Seurat, Georges (1859-91) Leading French neo-impressionist painter who invented POINTILLISM – a technique in which pictures are composed of small dots of pure colour

SHIMMERING DOTS *Seurat's mastery of pointillism, as in* Déjeuner à la Grande-Jatte *(1886), produced stunning effects of light and shade.*

which merge together when viewed from a distance. Among his most famous paintings are *Bathers at Asnieres* (1884), *Dejeune à la Grande-Jatte* (1886), *Les Poseuses* (1887-8) and the unfinished *The Circus (1891).*

❖ The life and work of Seurat is the subject of Stephen Sondheim's 1984 musical *Sunday in the Park with George.*

sfumato Italian term, meaning 'smoky', that refers to a subtle blending of tones which makes the transition from light to dark imperceptible. LEONARDO DA VINCI invented the technique, which was one of the distinctive innovations of the RENAISSANCE. He said that light and shade should blend 'without borders or lines, in the manner of smoke'.

Sibiya, Lucky (1942-) South African artist, best known for his graphic works and coloured, incised woodcut panels. He studied under Cecil SKOTNES. His increasingly stylized subject matter is drawn from African history, images of rural life and the decorative mural of the Ndebele.

Signac, Paul (1863-1935) French painter, a neo-impressionist who became the leading exponent of POINTILLISM after the death of SEURAT in 1891; but he used patches of pure colour rather than small dots.

Siopis, Penny (1953-) South African painter of complex still lifes and figurative works. Much of her subject matter is drawn from the classics and from historical painting. Feminist perspectives are often apparent in her works, such as *Patience on a Monument* (1988), in which tiny, collaged images of soldiers and battles are overwhelmed by the huge seated figure of a black woman.

Sisley, Alfred (1839-99) Painter of the impressionist school, born in France of English parents. The influence of his friendship with MONET and RENOIR shows in his carefully composed landscapes, painted with delicate, patchlike brushwork. Sisley lived in France, but during visits to England he painted at Hampton Court and in London. His paintings did not sell well during his lifetime.

DECADENT DISPLAY Still life with Watermelon and Other Things *(1986) by South African artist Penny Siopis is a feast of colour.*

BRIGHT AND BOLD *Vigorous brushwork and strong, thickly applied oil colours are characteristic of the works of leading South African artist Irma Stern, as in this still life,* Redgums *(1938).*

Sithole, Lucas (1931-) South African figurative sculptor in bronze, stone and mainly wood. He trained at the POLLY STREET ART CENTRE, where he was influenced by the work of SKOTNES and KUMALO and their synthesis of African and Western traditions. His often poignant works are generally elongated, with expressive distortions.

Skotnes, Cecil (1926-) South African artist and art educator whose leadership of the POLLY STREET ART CENTRE in Johannesburg was of seminal importance in the emergence of the urban black artistic movement. He works in a neo-African style, mainly with coloured, engraved wood panels and printed woodcuts as well as abstract paintings.

Smith, David (1906-65) American sculptor and pioneer in the field of metal sculpture. After working in a car factory, he began to experiment with constructed sculpture, influenced by Picasso's welded steel works of the late 1920s. His early works have a surrealist quality, but he gradually moved towards linear and increasingly abstracted forms.

Stern, Irma (1894-1966) Prolific South African artist whose formative years were spent in Germany, where she was influenced by the expressionists, in particular Max Pechstein (1881-1955). Her first exhibition in Cape Town (1920) shocked the locals, but drew big attendances. Her figure studies and still lifes exude colour and vitality. Her intrepid spirit and bold style helped to liberate South African painting.

Stieglitz, Alfred (1864-1946) American photographer and New York gallery owner who played a key role in establishing photography as an art form and in promoting modern art to the American public. He mounted major exhibitions of works by artists, including MATISSE, RODIN, and PICASSO. He was married to the American painter Georgia O'KEEFFE.

still life A term that derives from the Dutch *stil-leven* for an art form made popular in the Netherlands in the 17th century. Still-life paintings are generally of inanimate objects such as fruit, flowers, platters of food and decorative objects. One of the great masters of the still life was CÉZANNE, whose works inspired the still lifes of the FAUVISM and CUBISM movements.

Stubbs, George (1724-1806) British painter and engraver, best known for his studies of horses. Stubbs had no formal training as an artist, but began to paint portraits in order to earn a living while studying anatomy. His work is remarkable not only for its beauty, but also for its accuracy. *Mares and Foals in River Landscape* (1763-8) and *Horse Attacked by a Lion* (1770) are among his best-known works.

❖ The South African National Gallery has an important collection of Stubbs's paintings.

surrealism An art and literary movement which began in France in 1924, inspired partly by Freudian psychology. Major figures were ERNST, MAGRITTE, DALI and MIRÓ. Dream imagery, association, instinct, the subconscious are all part of the surrealists' attempts to achieve absolute or 'super' reality. There was no unified style, but most surrealist work has a disturbing quality. Real objects are distorted and robbed of their function or appear in strange settings, such as Dali's folded clocks in *The Persistence of Memory* (1931) or Magritte's train emerging from a fireplace.

Sutherland, Graham (1903-80) British official war artist whose etchings and paintings of World War II show disturbing scenes of desolation. After the war Sutherland created some important religious paintings and designs, notably a *Crucifixion* (1946) for St Matthew's church, Northampton, and a huge tapestry, *Christ in Majesty* (1962), for Coventry Cathedral. He was also a leading portrait painter, whose sitters included Somerset Maugham, Lord Beaverbrook and Sir Winston Churchill – who hated the painting so much that Lady Churchill eventually burned it.

symbolism A European literary and visual arts movement which began in *c*1885. It was a reaction against the objective art of the realists and impressionists and moved instead towards a more symbolic or poetic expression of ideas. Among the most important figures in the movement were MOREAU, Puvis de Chavannes and Odilon Redon.

❖ In a more general sense, symbolism is the visual representation of an idea, such as a lamb being used to represent the holiness of Christ, or a dog implying fidelity.

tapestry Handwoven fabric with a non-repetitive pattern woven in silk or wool. The Aubusson factories near Limoges, France, began making tapestries in the early 16th century and are best known for weaving scenes of La Fontaine's fables. The Gobelins factory near Paris was unrivalled in the 17th and 18th centuries, when it produced BAROQUE tapestries for Louis XIV, designed by Charles LE BRUN. Both centres remain active.

❖ Several South African tapestries have been woven at the famous Aubusson factory in

France, including the 13 m by 4 m *Orpheus* in the Nico Malan Opera House in Cape Town, designed by the South African Eleanor Esmonde-White (1914-).
❖ The term 'tapestry' is often incorrectly used in reference to embroidery or upholstery.

tempera Medium used in painting made from ground pigment bound with egg and water. Tempera gives a quick-drying, bright result that can be worked over with oil glazes to enhance its colour and sheen. It was often used on wooden panels prepared with gesso – a thin layer of plaster of Paris.

Tiepolo (1696-1770) Last and greatest in the line of Venetian decorative artists which included Veronese and TINTORETTO. Tiepolo became renowned as a decorator in ROCOCO style of palaces and churches throughout Europe. An example of his celebrated frescoes of skies filled with floating figures painted in clear pastel colours, full of movement and energy, can be seen on the ceilings of the Archbishop's Palace at Würzburg, Germany.

Tiffany, Louis Comfort (1848-1933) American ART NOUVEAU designer and interior decorator. Inspired by William MORRIS, Tiffany decorated many public buildings, including several rooms in the White House in Washington, DC, in a curious mixture of Moorish, BYZANTINE and ▷ROMANESQUE styles. His hallmark was his handmade, iridescent glass, which he called favrile. He also made lampshades from leaded mosaics of opaque, tinted glass and produced goblets and glasses in flowing shapes resembling plants and flowers.
❖ Tiffany's father founded the New York jewellers Tiffany & Co, featured in the film *Breakfast at Tiffany's* (1961).

LIGHT WORK *A 'Wisteria' leaded glass and bronze table lamp, designed by Tiffany in 1902.*

Tintoretto (Jacopo Robusti) (1518-94) Prodigiously talented Venetian painter, a student of TITIAN. A master of narrative, he painted mainly religious subjects. His paintings throb with tempestuous action, theatrical lighting and dramatic perspective. His crowning achievement was the cycle of paintings for the Scuola di San Rocco in Venice (1575-7). One of the most mysterious and mystical of his works was *The Last Supper* (1592-4) in San Giorgio Maggiore in Venice. He was a major influence on the art of EL GRECO.
❖ The name 'Tintoretto' came from his father's profession as a dye-maker (*tintore*).

Titian (Tiziano Vecellio) (*c*1487-1576) Italian artist and dominant figure in 16th-century Venetian art. Titian's reputation in his day was as great as MICHELANGELO's. He trained with BELLINI and Giorgione, whose poetic style is reflected in his *Venus of Urbino* (1538). His output was vast, encompassing religious, mythological and historical subjects, as well as the most celebrated portraits of his time. His works are renowned for their rich, varied colour. His influence on later artists was profound.
❖ 'Titian hair' is golden red or auburn. The term derives from the fact that Titian often gave his subjects auburn hair.

tone Although the hue of a colour may remain the same, the tone can be changed so as to make it darker or lighter by adding either black or white pigment. Any shade of grey or any other colour that is not pure, or 'solid', can be called a half-tone.

Toulouse-Lautrec, Henri de (1864-1901) French painter and graphic artist best known for his paintings of Parisian low-life and his bold designs for posters. He did not belong to a particular art movement, but was strongly influenced by DEGAS and the contemporary vogue for Japanese prints. His subject matter reflects his life style: he painted prostitutes, their clients, dancers and café scenes with great insight and detachment. He was less interested in light or colour than in form and the depiction of movement, which he captured with bold lines and large, flat areas of colour. His style and technique – using oil paints thinned with spirit on cardboard – influenced the new arts of lithography and postermaking.
❖ Toulouse-Lautrec suffered two accidents in his childhood which stunted the growth of his legs.

township art A term used to describe the works of black artists living in South Africa's 'townships' – settlements on the outskirts of towns and cities. The term has been criticized on the grounds that it is derogatory and reinforces racial prejudice and stereotypes. It applies almost exclusively to figurative art; the work of black abstract artists is generally excluded. The subject matter includes everyday scenes in the townships – in the streets as well as cameos of indoor life. Social commentary and images of hardship and oppression become more overt from the 1970s with the rise of ▷BLACK CONSCIOUSNESS.

triptych Painting, usually a religious altarpiece, consisting of three hinged panels. The subject matter varies, but triptychs often portray the Madonna or the Crucifixion in the centre panel and patron saints on the side panels. Some triptychs were owned privately and show the owner's coat of arms when the side panels are folded shut. A painting with only two panels is called a diptych and one with more than three panels a polyptych.

PUBLICITY WITH PANACHE *Toulouse-Lautrec designed this bold image for Aristide Bruant, a satirical nightclub singer.*

trompe l'oeil (tromp-LEUYEE) French term for something that 'deceives the eye'. It is used to describe a painting which creates a three-dimensional illusion on a flat surface by using perspective – such as a false window with views painted on a solid wall. It is also used to refer to a depiction so realistic that the viewer is tricked into believing that the object is real, such as a fly on a frame.

Turner, Joseph Mallord William (1775-1851) One of the greatest and most original of British landscape painters, who first exhibited in the Royal Academy at the age of 15. After a visit to Italy and Switzerland, he produced oil paintings suffused with pale, brilliant light which Constable described as 'tinted steam'. Critics either loved or hated Turner's work. His reputation was secured only after he gained the support of John RUSKIN. In paintings such as *The Fighting Temeraire* (1838) and *Rain, Steam and Speed* (1844) Turner took ROMANTICISM to its height as he used nature to express human emotions. In these works his representations of the effects of light and air count for more than the subject matter itself. Turner was strongly influenced by Dutch seascapes and particulalry by the contrived Classical landscapes of CLAUDE LORRAIN. His work in turn influenced the impressionists.

❖ When Turner died, he left 300 paintings and 20 000 watercolours and drawings to the British nation on the condition that they were kept and displayed together. His wishes were ignored for more than a century until 1987, when the Clore Gallery was opened at the Tate Gallery, London, to house a permanent exhibition of Turner's work.

DRAMATIC TURMOIL *Turner was fascinated by water, moody skies and rapid movement, as seen in* Rain, Steam and Speed *(1844).*

Uccello, Paolo (*c*1397-1475) Italian painter of the Florentine school who had a decorative, elegant and courtly style, and used brilliant colours and sinuous lines. Under the influence of DONATELLO, he developed a fascination for perspective which is particularly apparent in *The Flood* (*c*1445) and his masterpiece, *The Battle of San Romano* (*c*1455).

Van Dyck, Sir Anthony (1599-1641) Flemish artist renowned for his portrait paintings. He originally worked as an assistant to RUBENS, but quickly became independent – displaying a less robust and more introspective style than his master. Van Dyck was most popular in England, where he became court painter to Charles I, whose portrait he painted several times and who awarded him a knighthood. The portraits Van Dyck painted during the period he lived in England – from 1632 until his death – convey his extraordinary sensitivity to the individuality of each sitter. His work influenced many other British portrait painters for several generations.

Van Eyck, Jan (*c*1390-1441) Flemish painter whose NATURALISM and extraordinary attention to detail has possibly never been matched. He had an enormous influence on 15th-century art in northern Europe. Among

EXHILARATING COLOURS *Van Gogh used free brush strokes and brilliant tones to express his turbulent emotions. This is one of several still lifes of sunflowers which he painted in 1888.*

his best-known masterpieces are the *Portrait of Giovanni Arnolfini and Giovanna Cenami* (1434) (popularly known as the *Arnolfini Marriage*) and the *Adoration of the Lamb* (1432). The second is one of 20 panels forming the altarpiece in the cathedral of Ghent, Brussels (which bear the name also of Van Eyck's brother Hubert).

❖ For many years Van Eyck was incorrectly credited with the invention of oil painting. In fact, he simply refined existing techniques with remarkable skill.

Van Gogh, Vincent (1853-90) Dutch post-impressionist painter who was one of the greatest and most influential artists of the 19th century. He began to paint only in 1880 after being dismissed from the mission where he preached in Belgium. He lived in poverty and was largely self-taught, although he was influenced by the flat, colourful designs of Japanese prints, which were then gaining popularity in Europe. After meeting DEGAS, GAUGUIN, SEURAT and TOULOUSE-LAUTREC in Paris in 1886, Van Gogh began to use vivid colours and experiment with different brush strokes. In 1888 he moved to Arles, in southern France, where he painted some of his greatest pictures, including *Sunflowers* (1888), *Bedroom at Arles* (1888-9) and *Starry Night* (1889). In letters to his brother Theo, Van Gogh conveyed the thrill and struggle of using paint to express exactly what he felt. He suffered from loneliness and depression and after a quarrel with Gauguin, he cut off part of one ear. Soon afterwards he went into an asylum where, during lucid periods, his paintings became even more intense. Van Gogh shot himself on 27 July 1890, and died two days later. His work had an immense influence on FAUVISM, EXPRESSIONISM and SURREALISM, and he was a pivotal figure in the evolution of modern art.

❖ Van Gogh is believed to have sold only two paintings during his lifetime, including one to his brother. In 1990, however, his *Dr Gachet* (1890) sold for a record US$82,5 million (then nearly R300 million).

Van Wouw, Anton (1862-1945) Major South African naturalistic sculptor. Born and educated in Holland, he settled in South Africa in 1890. He produced a great many small-scale bronzes, considered to be his most sensitive works. His large-scale works include the poignant *Women's Monument* in Bloemfontein (1914), in which a group of two women and a dying child commemorate the lives lost in concentration camps in the South African War.

Vasarely, Victor (1908-) Hungarian-born French painter and sculptor who pioneered OP ART. His paintings combine variations of circles, squares and triangles, sometimes with gradations of pure colour, to create undulating abstract images.

Vasari, Giorgio (1511-74) Italian painter and architect best known as a critic and biographer. His book *Lives of the Most Eminent Italian Painters, Sculptors and Architects* (1550) is still an essential work for art scholars of the RENAISSANCE period. His most successful architectural achievement was the Uffizi Palace in Florence, now a major art museum.

Velasquez, Diego (1599-1660) Spanish artist who became court painter to King Philip IV of Spain and raised the art of portraiture to new levels of unflattering realism and avoidance of embellishment. He was much affected by two visits to Italy, where he painted a portrait of the pope as well as his only known female nude, the *Toilet of Venus* (*c*1650). On his return to Spain, he produced even more vivid paintings of a richness and brilliance not seen before. In his celebrated group portrait *Las Meniñas* (*The Maids of Honour*) (1656), a fleeting moment at court is captured with an almost photographic quality. Velasquez was greatly influenced by TITIAN and RUBENS and in his turn led the way for GOYA.

Venus de Milo Statue of the Greek goddess Aphrodite (Venus was the Roman equivalent), found on a beach on the Greek island of Milos in 1820 and now in the Louvre, Paris. Probably dating from *c*100 BC, it embodied the Greek ideal of female beauty – feminine and elegant yet sturdy. Although the arms are missing, the soft appearance of the flesh and the heavy texture of the falling drapery contribute to the statue's enduring beauty.

Vermeer, Jan (1632-75) Dutch painter born in Delft, where he spent most of his time dealing in art. Virtually forgotten for two centuries, Vermeer is now regarded as one of the greatest of the Dutch masters. He often painted quiet domestic scenes, such as people absorbed in sewing or reading, with the aid of a camera obscura – a darkened chamber in which a clear image of the scene outside is received through a small opening or through a lens and mirrors. Although precise, Vermeer's paintings seem almost mellow and often have a cool silvery light, created by using subtle tones of yellow and blue. Among his best-known works are *The Maid with the Milk Jug* (*c*1658), *View of Delft* (*c*1662), *A Lady at the Virginals with a Gentleman* (*c*1662) and *The Lacemaker* (*c*1665).

Versace, Gianni (1946-) Italian fashion designer whose clothes are among the most expensive and exclusive in the world. Versace is known for combining incongruous fabrics such as leather and silk and for his skill in cutting material on the bias, or diagonally across the weave.

Victorian style Term applied to several different styles of architecture, furniture and furnishings in Britain and its empire during the reign of Queen Victoria (1837-1901). At the beginning of the period, the lingering designs of the Regency (post-GEORGIAN) style became more elaborate, curved and detailed, taking on a ROCOCO feel. However, it was the onset of mass production and the new prosperity of the middle classes, caused by the Industrial Revolution, that really determined the style of the mid-Victorian era. Houses were filled with increasingly ornate and heavy furniture, covered with an array of bric-a-brac and framed photographs. At the Great Exhibition of 1851 more interest was shown in technical advances than in design. In the late Victorian period, under the influence of MORRIS and the ARTS AND CRAFTS MOVEMENT, decoration became much more restrained. (See also ▷VICTORIAN in 'Architecture and engineering'.)

Villa, Eduardo (1920-) Italian-born sculptor who came to South Africa in 1940 as a prisoner of war. An important figure in South African art, he played a major role in sculpture at the POLLY STREET ART CENTRE and influenced many young artists, in particular KUMALO and SITHOLE. Although initially controversial, his works such as *The Knot* (1981), a brightly coloured, abstract work in front of the Civic Centre in Cape Town, have now become familiar landmarks.

CONTORTED TUBING The Knot *by sculptor Eduardo Villa was greeted by some with incredulity when it was unveiled in 1981. Now it is an accepted landmark on the Foreshore, Cape Town.*

Warhol, Andy (Andrew Warhola) (1928-87) Controversial American artist and film-maker of Czech origin best known for his contribution to POP ART. Warhol often used stencils to create outsized depictions of everyday objects, such as dollar bills and Coca-Cola bottles. He also made multiple images printed by the silk-screen process – using the faces of celebrities such as Marilyn Monroe or everyday objects, as in *100 Campbell's Soup Cans* (1962), varying only the colours and adding no other detail. Production of these series was handled by 'The Factory', a group of admirers who also starred in Warhol's avant-garde films. These included *Sleep* (1963), which shows a man sleeping for six hours; *The Chelsea Girls* (1966), set in New York's Chelsea Hotel; and *Empire* (1964), a static view of the Empire State Building which lasts for eight hours.

❖ Warhol is also known for declaring: 'In the future, everybody will be famous for 15 minutes' – a recognition of the increasing power of the mass media.

Watteau, (Jean) Antoine (1684-1721) French artist whose style of painting was so innovative that the French Academy created a new category for his work: *fêtes galantes* (countryside parties). His wistful and dreamlike paintings created a fantasy world where love was supreme. He was influenced by Rubens, and his own work and ideals had a significant effect on the development of ROCOCO art.

POP ICON *The repetition and false colours of Andy Warhol's silk-screened* Marilyn Monroe *(1967) are deliberately dehumanizing.*

weaving The term is used rather loosely to encompass a wide variety of woven works, including TAPESTRY. Two main weaving techniques are applied in southern Africa – the Flemish technique, used by the RORKE'S DRIFT art centre weavers, and the Gobelin technique, practised at Aubusson in France. Among those using the latter is Marguerite Stephens, who has translated the works of many South African painters into woven wall hangings. One of the most creative weavers is Allina Ndebele, a pioneer at RORKE'S DRIFT, who was trained in Sweden. Many of her works are colourful interpretations of traditional myths and legends.

Wedgwood, Josiah (1730-95) British master potter, inventor, philanthropist and industrialist. He emulated antique models and is best known for his invention of jasper ware – a dense hard stoneware which could be matt-finished and tinted (especially with 'Wedgwood blue') and decorated with white figures in relief – and Queen's ware – a strong, cream-coloured pottery used for plates and other tableware. Wedgwood's shrewd business sense led him to pioneer sales catalogues for the public, and with instantly recognizable colours and styles his name soon became a trademark. Many of his original designs are still in production.

Weinberg, Eli (1908-81) South African photographer, born in Latvia. He emigrated to South Africa in 1929, but was denied South African citizenship because of his trade-union and communist affiliations. He compiled a major photographic documentary of the ▷CONGRESS ALLIANCE before it was banned in 1960. In 1964 he was arrested with fellow anti-apartheid activist Braam Fischer and, in 1976, after a period of house arrest, fled South Africa for Tanzania. A collection of his photographs, published shortly before his death, was banned in South Africa and most of his negatives have been lost.

Westwood, Vivienne (1941-) Unconventional British fashion designer who has based her collections on themes such as fetishes, pirates and folk dress. Many of her designs, such as see-through dresses and enormously high platform shoes, were derided at first, but quickly appeared in department stores in less extreme guises.

Whistler, James Abbott McNeill (1834-1903) American-born painter who, after failing the exams for entry into West Point military academy, studied art in Paris. Here he was influenced by the simplicity of Japanese prints, then gaining popularity in Europe. After moving to London he became a celebrated portraitist. He also painted innovative landscapes dominated by one or two colours.

❖ Whistler's *Nocturne in Black and Gold: The Falling Rocket* (1877) so disgusted John RUSKIN that he accused the artist of 'flinging a pot of paint in the public's face'. Whistler successfully sued him, but won damages of only a farthing; the cost of the action forced Whistler to move to Venice, where he sold his etchings to earn a living.

❖ Whistler was an argumentative conversationalist but quite as witty as his friend Oscar ▷WILDE. Admiring one of Whistler's remarks, Wilde said: 'I wish I had said that!' to which Whistler retorted: 'You will, Oscar, you will!'

GRACE AND REFINEMENT Three Women Seen in a Mirror *reflects the mastery of the art of the coloured woodcut achieved by Japanese painter and engraver Kitigawa Utamaro (1753-1806).*

woodcut Print made by gouging out sections from a flat block of wood, leaving untouched parts raised. These are inked, so that paper pressed against the block picks up the design in reverse. A similar technique in which the design itself is cut away – so that they appear white against a black background – is known as wood engraving.

❖ Among the greatest exponents of woodcutting was DÜRER.

ARCHITECTURE AND ENGINEERING

The basic human need for shelter and the desire to honour deities have given rise to a rich diversity of buildings, ranging from private homes and office blocks to cathedrals and palaces. Buildings reflect the lives and culture of the people who build and use them. The skills of the engineer underpin the architect's vision, bringing about a marriage of function and beauty.

Aalto, Alvar (1898-1976) Finnish architect and designer, celebrated for his simple and elegant bent-plywood furniture. One of his finest buildings is the Finlandia concert hall in Helsinki (1962-75).

acropolis Highest part of a fortified Greek city or citadel which comprises its principal temples and public buildings. The Acropolis at Athens, which is crowned by the remains of the PARTHENON, is the supreme example.

Adam, Robert (1728-92) First architect to design and execute buildings and contents as a unit, from the structure down to the fireplaces, door handles and furniture. Adam worked with his two brothers to create a style that has become associated with their name. His delicate interpretation of NEO-CLASSICISM aimed 'to transfuse the beautiful spirit of antiquity with novelty and variety'. One of his best-known buildings is Kenwood House on Hampstead Heath, London.

Akashi-Kaikyo Bridge Steel bridge under construction since 1988 between Honshu and Shikoku islands in Japan. When complete, it will be 4 km long – by far the world's longest suspension bridge. Its six-lane highway is scheduled to open in 1998.

Alberti, Leon Battista (1404-72) Italian RENAISSANCE architect whose treatise *De Re Aedificatoria* (*On Building Matters*, 1485) was the first printed book on architecture. The only buildings Alberti designed in their entirety are the churches of San Sebastiano (1460 onwards) and San Andrea (1470) in Mantua, Italy.

Alhambra, The Citadel-palace built in Granada by the Muslim rulers of Spain between 1238 and 1391. Set on a dramatic ridge, The Alhambra is one of the most celebrated architectural achievements of Muslim Spain. Part of it is a castle, and the whole area is enclosed by high walls. It was created as an evocation of the paradise the ▷KORAN describes, with water flowing in channels and small fountains through buildings, gardens and terraces, collecting in many basins and pools.

amphitheatre Round or oval arena, open to the sky and surrounded by tiered seating on all sides. Amphitheatres, built in ancient Rome, were adapted from Greek theatres, to make them suitable for holding gladiatorial combats, wild animal hunts, sports events and other public entertainments. They could even be filled with water to stage sea battles. The largest to have survived is the Colosseum in Rome, which was built in about AD 80 and held 50 000 spectators.

Angkor Ruined city in Cambodia, centred on a vast complex of Hindu and Buddhist temples dating from the 9th century AD. The main building, Angkor Wat – a stepped pyramid with five ornate towers, set in a large moated rectangle – was built by King Suryavarman II in the 12th century. Reliefs covering its walls depict scenes from the mythology of ▷HINDUISM. The city covers 190 km^2.
❖ Angkor was abandoned in the 15th century. It was unknown to the West until 1860, when a French naturalist was led through the Cambodian jungle to the city.

aqueduct Stone or brick channel with elevated sections designed to move water from one place to another – usually a city. Aqueducts were a Roman invention; 11 major aqueducts were in use in Rome alone. However, the longest was in Carthage, which stretched over a distance of about 140 km. One of the best-preserved aqueducts is the Pont du Gard in Provence, France.

arch Curved structure which redistributes the pressure and weight of the material above it to its supports at either end. The two main forms are the ROMANESQUE arch, which is rounded, and the GOTHIC, which is pointed. During construction, arches are supported by wooden frameworks. Triumphal arches, which celebrate great victories, were first built in Roman times; more recent examples include the Arc de Triomphe in Paris and Marble Arch in London.

Art Deco Style that influenced architecture during the 1920s and 1930s, using straight lines and regular curves as a modern return to Classical styles and as a reaction to the organic curves of ART NOUVEAU. Some cinemas provide good examples, with their slabs of bright, flat colours, shiny metals and strong geometric patterns. In the USA development of the style led to the design of skyscrapers such as the Chrysler Building in New York. (See also ▷ART DECO in 'Art and design'.)
❖ Many examples of architecture with Art Deco features still exist in South Africa's major towns and cities. One of Johannesburg's Art Deco landmarks, the Colosseum Theatre (1933), was demolished in 1985 in spite of strenuous efforts to preserve it.

Art Nouveau Decorative style which used swirling lines and writhing plant forms that was popular in Europe between 1890 and 1914. Well-known examples are the ornate entrances to many Parisian Metro stations. Charles Rennie ▷MACKINTOSH and Antonio GAUDÍ were among the leading architectural exponents of the style. (See also ▷ART NOUVEAU in 'Art and design'.)

Arts and Crafts Movement British movement originating in the late 19th century whose

WATER CARRIER *The Pont du Gard – a three-tiered Roman aqueduct built in AD 19 – transported water from a source in Uzès to Nîmes in Provence, France. It was engineered with extraordinary precision: over a distance of 50 km the water dropped only 17 m.*

POINT OF STYLE *The distinctive Art Deco form of the Chrysler Building, completed in 1930, soars 319 m above New York.*

members – most notably William ▷MORRIS – advocated a return to functional designs and individual craftsmanship in the face of increasing mass production. Its influence can be seen in the work of Norman Shaw (1831-1912), Charles Voysey (1857-1941) and Edwin LUTYENS, especially in their domestic architecture. (See also ▷ARTS AND CRAFTS in 'Art and design'.)

Arup, Sir Ove (1895-1988) British engineer who pioneered the imaginative use of REINFORCED CONCRETE. As a consultant he collaborated closely with the architects of important buildings such as the SYDNEY OPERA HOUSE – for which he also designed the roof shells – and the POMPIDOU CENTRE in Paris.

❖ One of Arup's largest overseas practices is Ove Arup Incorporated, a consulting engineering firm with its headquarters in Johannesburg. Apart from its road, water and sewerage reticulation systems, the company has constructed many sports arenas, including the Johannesburg's FNB Stadium (1989), the Centenary and Unity Stands at the Wanderers cricket stadium (1991-2) and the Johannesburg Athletics Stadium (designed by Arup Associates in London).

atrium Large open space inside a building, usually topped by a glass roof to provide light. An atrium was originally the open inner court of a Roman house.

❖ Atriums are a feature of many contemporary South African buildings, particularly in central business districts, where plants feature prominently and provide welcome relief from the surrounding city environment. An impressive example is in the Sandton Sun in Johannesburg.

DECORATIVE WELCOME *Hector Guimard's Art Nouveau designs for some of the Paris Metro stations featured cast-iron supports with 'organic' forms and curvaceous, top-heavy calligraphy.*

Bain, Andrew Geddes (1797-1864) Road engineer, geologist, writer, artist, poet, soldier, explorer, trader and farmer. Scottish-born Bain arrived at the Cape in 1816. A combination of boredom and mishap set him on varied careers, the most well known being as a mountain pass builder, geologist and writer. He is also believed to be the first European to have travelled as far north as Botswana. Among the passes he constructed are Michell's Pass near Ceres, Bain's Kloof Pass near Wellington and the Katberg Pass near Fort Beaufort. He was also acclaimed for his ground-breaking book *The Geology of South Africa* (1851) and tried his hand at fiction – his character Kaatjie Kekkelbek is part of South African tradition.

Baker, Sir Herbert (1862-1946) English architect whose first assignment in South Africa was the renovation, after its destruction in a fire, of Groote Schuur (1892), then the official residence of the prime minister of the Cape, Cecil John Rhodes. He drew from a variety of sources in his designs for houses, churches, schools and civic buildings. A study tour of Egypt, Greece and Italy, sponsored by Rhodes, inspired the classicism of the UNION BUILDINGS in Pretoria and Rhodes Memorial in Cape Town. Baker's use of natural materials in the stonework of Northwards in Johannesburg (now the offices of the Parktown Heritage Committee), and the local stones, wood and floor and roof tiles for the Union Buildings was influenced by the ARTS AND CRAFTS MOVEMENT.

❖ At the invitation of Sir Edwin LUTYENS, a lifelong friend and colleague, Baker left South Africa in 1912 for India, where the two architects collaborated on the government buildings in New Delhi.

baroque Grand, flamboyant style that originated in Rome in the early 17th century and spread through Europe over the next 100 years. Its fusion of architecture, painting and sculpture created ostentatious, lavishly decorated buildings of theatrical grandeur. Its direct appeal to the emotions was exploited by Church and State, and can be seen in BERNINI's churches and fountains in Rome, the interiors of VERSAILLES, and WREN's St Paul's Cathedral in London. It was succeeded by the rococo style, which used elegant and fanciful forms inspired by nature. (See also ▷BAROQUE in 'Art and design'.)

basilica Roman assembly hall, usually rectangular with rows of columns on each side of the central nave and two or more aisles at the sides. This plan was adopted by early Christian churches, and was recently revived in Africa's largest church, the Basilica of Our

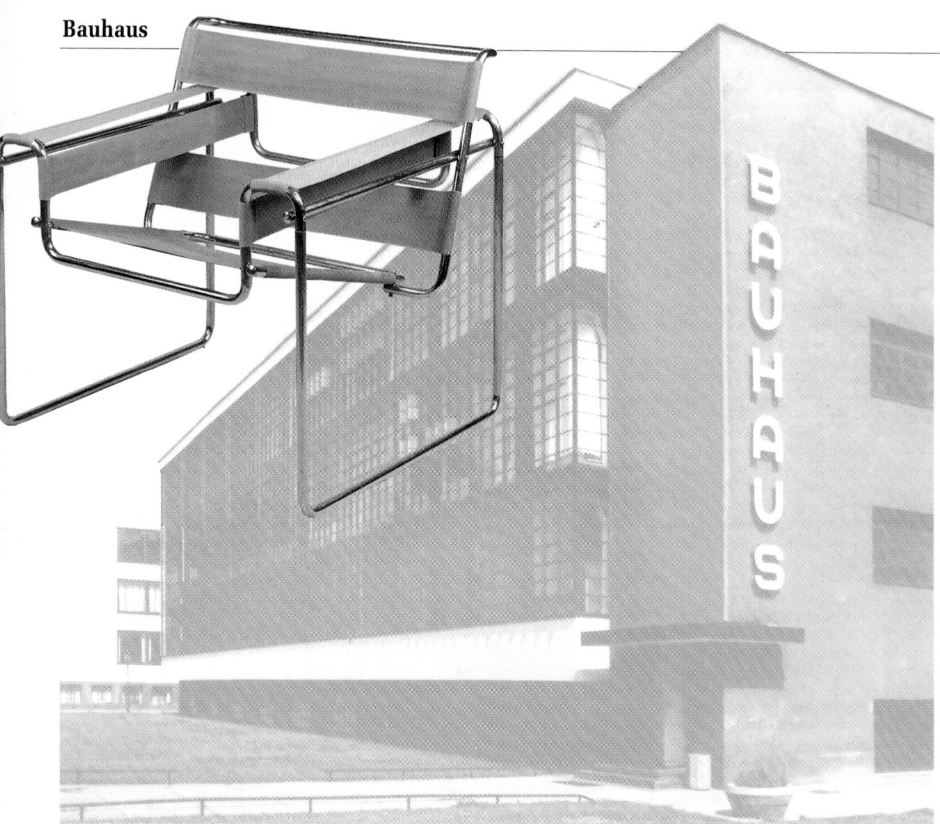

SEAT OF DESIGN *Walter Gropius's building for the Bauhaus school of design was a monument to its philosophy: its furniture, such as this 'Wassily' chair, by Marcel Breuer, was created here.*

Lady of Peace at Yamoussoukro, in Côte d'Ivoire, which was modelled on St Peter's Basilica in Rome.

Bauhaus School of architecture and applied arts founded in Weimar, Germany, in 1919 by the architect Walter GROPIUS. Its purpose was to create a closer relationship between design, craft and industry. Its influence spread worldwide before it was closed down by the Nazis in 1933. (See also INTERNATIONAL STYLE, and ▷BAUHAUS in 'Art and design'.)

beehive VERNACULAR style of circular dwellings found mainly in the southeastern parts of southern Africa. They are constructed from a circular base of saplings, drawn together in a series of arches. These are bound together into a hemispherical framework and covered with thatch, made from grass matting, thatching grass or reeds.
❖ The Nama in southern Namibia, whose beehive dwellings were originally covered with reed-matting, have replaced this with hessian, which is more durable and easily transported.

Bernini, Giovanni Lorenzo (1598-1680) Italian architect, sculptor and exponent of the BAROQUE. He designed the piazza in front of ST PETER'S BASILICA, Rome, and many of the city's churches and fountains. (See also ▷BERNINI in 'Art and design'.)

bridge There are five main designs of bridge: (i) A beam bridge is a simple slab of reinforced concrete or a steel girder supported at each end. (ii) An arch bridge spans a river or gorge from side to side in a curve, so that the weight pushes down and outwards to its supports. The world's longest single spans are those of (iii) suspension bridges, in which the bulk of the load is carried by cables supported by giant towers and anchored to the ground on each bank. (iv) Cantilever bridges have two projecting arms which meet or are joined together by a central span, and are supported on piers and anchored by counterbalancing posts. (v) Bascule bridges, such as London's Tower Bridge, have hinged sections which can be raised to let tall vessels pass.
❖ One of South Africa's most spectacular arch bridges crosses the Bloukrans River in the Tsitsikamma area of the Garden Route, one of five similar bridges in the area. Its length is 451 m, the span of the arch 272 m and the height above water 216 m. The first of these great bridges was the Paul Sauer Bridge, across the mouth of the Storms River (1956); it is 191 m long and 130 m above the river.

Brunel, Sir Marc Isambard (1769-1849) French-born British architect and engineer who in 1818 invented the tunnelling shield, which made it practicable to build TUNNELS under water or in soft earth. The earliest use of the shield – a giant iron casing that could be pushed along to protect workers at the tunnelling face – was to build the first tunnel under the River Thames (1825-43).
❖ Sir Marc's son, Isambard Kingdom Brunel (1806-59), also an engineer, revolutionized steam travel in 1838 with the ocean-going paddle steamer *Great Western*. His *Great Britain*, launched in 1843, was the first iron-built, ocean-going ship with a screw propeller and his *Great Eastern* (1858) was the world's largest.

Brunelleschi, Filippo (1377-1446) Florentine architect who was one of the leading exponents of RENAISSANCE architecture. He drew on Classical models for their methods of construction as well as for aesthetic reasons. His masterpiece is the enormous yet elegant dome of Florence Cathedral (1420-36), which has a unique structure of an inner and an outer shell.

buttress Brick or stone structure which projects from, or is built against, an external wall to give it extra strength, or in order to counteract the outward thrust of a roof, vault or arch. Flying buttresses, which elegantly arch away from the wall they support, are a feature of GOTHIC cathedrals and enabled their architects to build wide, soaring VAULTS.
❖ In southern African church architecture based on medieval styles, buttressing is often decorative rather than structural. Although doors and windows have pointed arches, typical of the Gothic style, their buttressing is in ROMANESQUE style.

HISTORIC LINKS *Isambard Kingdom Brunel stands before the enormous launching chains of the* Great Eastern *– the largest and most sophisticated liner of its time.*

Byzantine Early Christian style of architecture which developed after AD 330 in Constantinople. Byzantine churches have round arches, massive domes, intricate spires and minarets; inside ▷MOSAIC is often used extensively. The masterpiece of Byzantine architecture is the HAGIA SOFIA in Istanbul. (See also ▷BYZANTINE in 'Art and design' and ▷BYZANTINE EMPIRE in 'World history'.)

canals The earliest canals are thought to have been built around 4000 BC in Iraq. Work on the GRAND CANAL in China, the world's oldest artificial waterway still in use, was begun in AD 540.

❖ The great breakthrough in canal building came with the invention of the lock on China's Grand Canal in AD 984. By flooding or draining a section of water between two watertight gates, vessels can move from one level to another, allowing them to climb or descend gradients.

Cape Dutch The style of VERNACULAR architecture inspired by the Dutch, Flemish and Huguenot settlers at the Cape in the 17th to early 19th centuries. Characteristic features were the pitched roof with a decorative GABLE above the front door and end gables. The buildings were rectangular and symmetrical, generally in the shape of an 'I', 'T', 'H' or 'U'. Roofs were thatched with local reeds, and the thick outer walls were whitewashed.

cast iron Made from pig iron, melted down and cast in moulds. It was particularly popular in late VICTORIAN architecture. One of the major international suppliers of prefabricated, mass-produced cast iron was Macfarlane's Foundry in Glasgow, Scotland, whose catalogue of 2 000 pages included decorative balconies, balustrades, and the filigree edging on veranda roofs, so characteristic of the late Victorian style.

❖ The CRYSTAL PALACE was one of the earliest large-scale cast iron constructions.

castle There have been fortified buildings or settlements from prehistoric times, but the first true castles were built in Europe during the Middle Ages. Early castles consisted of a fortified timber stockade, or 'keep', raised on a circular mound called a 'motte', encircled by a ditch. Inside the castle a courtyard or 'bailey' was enclosed by a wall with battlements on top. The entrance was guarded by a 'barbican', or gatehouse. By the end of the Middle Ages, artillery had been invented which was capable of breaking down the walls and castles lost their defensive role. By the end of the 15th century the European castle had evolved into the French chateau and the German *Schloss*, designed more as an impressive dwelling place than as a stronghold against enemy attack.

❖ The Castle in Cape Town, designed on a pentagonal plan, was built as a military fortress to house the Dutch garrison, military supplies and administrators. Begun in 1665, it was completed in 1680 under the governorship of Simon van der Stel. The Castle replaced the Fort de Goede Hoop, overlooking Table Bay, which was built immediately after Jan van Riebeeck's arrival in 1652 and was, with the POSTHUYS, a watch-house on False Bay, among the earliest buildings at the Cape. It has been extensively restored and has become a tourist attraction.

❖ The Castle's five bastions were named after the titles of the Prince of Orange: Leerdam, Oranje, Nassau, Buren and Katzenellenbogen

cathedral Main church of a diocese, in which the *cathedra*, the bishop's chair or throne, is placed. Some cathedrals are known as minsters – from the Old English term *mynster* meaning 'monastery church'. Westminster Abbey, in London, is a famous example.

Channel Tunnel Anglo-French project linking Britain with continental Europe by a tunnel under the English Channel between Cheriton, near Folkestone, and Sangatte, near Calais. Work, which took longer than planned, began in 1987 and was completed in 1994. There are three tunnels: two 7,6 m diameter single-track railway tunnels – one for each direction – and a central service tunnel. The tunnels are 50 km long, and lie 40 m beneath the seabed.

❖ The first serious proposal for a Channel tunnel was made to Napoleon Bonaparte in 1802 by his chief engineer Albert Mathieu. Work was started, but soon abandoned for lack of funds.

church Early churches in Europe were built on the BASILICA plan, with a nave, aisles and a high altar in the apse at the east end, so that the congregation faced in the direction of the land of Jesus's birth and crucifixion. The Greek cross plan has four arms of equal length, and was the model used for BYZANTINE churches. In northern Europe, the Latin cross design, with one arm longer than the others, was used from the 11th century onwards. The nave occupied the longer arm and a dome or spire was commonly placed over the intersection.

Classical Architectural style based on the buildings of ancient Greece and Rome. Classical architecture emphasizes simplicity of form and proportion, following several distinct 'orders', and makes extensive use of columns with decoration, especially 'fluting', or vertical grooves. The great Classical revival of the RENAISSANCE was partly inspired by rediscovery of a book by Vitruvius, who

COLUMNS AND THE CLASSICAL ORDERS

Classical architects designed buildings according to three main styles, or 'orders', each of which had its own mathematical rules for harmony and balance. The Doric order was the simplest; Ionic columns were slimmer, with scrolled capitals and ornate bases; the Corinthian order had a motif based on acanthus leaves.

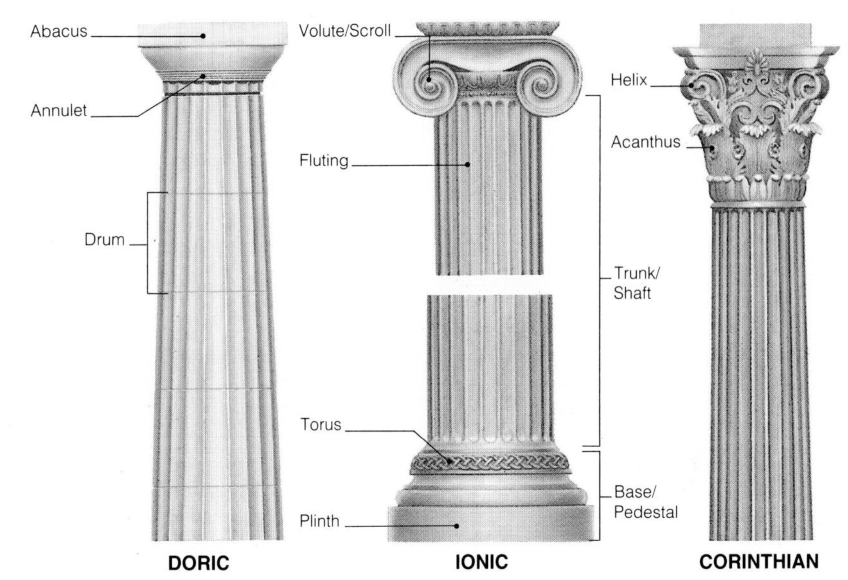

READY MADE *This pot lid depicts the Crystal Palace – the first prefabricated building, assembled from factory-made parts in 1850-1.*

was a Roman architect in the 1st century BC. Entitled *De Architectura* (*On Architecture*), it is the only Classical treatise on the subject to have survived. (See also ▷CLASSICISM in 'Art and design'.)

concrete Cement mortar mixed with broken brick, shingle, gravel or stones to make a strong building material. In and around Rome, the Romans added *pozzolana* (a volcanic ash) to make an extremely strong – and lasting – form of concrete. The use of concrete declined after the fall of the Roman Empire, although it was still used throughout Europe in the building of durable castle walls and for the foundations of cathedrals and churches. It gained popularity again after it was 'rediscovered' in the 18th century and ever since then has been extensively used. (See also REINFORCED CONCRETE.)

STAGE BY STAGE *The Eiffel Tower, which took 18 months to erect, was the world's tallest building when it was completed in 1889.*

10 Août 1887 — 8 Octobre 1887 — 15 Mars 1888 — 10 Juillet 1888

Coode, Sir John (1816-1892) British engineer responsible for the planning and construction of the first modern harbours in South Africa. He was appointed by the British Government to build a breakwater in Table Bay, and later returned to Cape Town to reclaim land from the sea and enlarge the dock area. He was also engaged in the construction of harbours in East London and Port Elizabeth, and was a consultant for the Durban harbour.

corbelled houses VERNACULAR style of building with layers of overlapping stones, each layer being placed slightly inwards and culminating in a domed roof. The earliest corbelled constructions in southern Africa were small stone huts used as shelter for herders or livestock. These simple buildings occur on the southern highveld and in parts of Lesotho. Larger corbelled houses seen in the Karoo were built by ▷TREKBOERS who used stone in the absence of building timber. Many of these buildings had vertical walls with small windows and corbelled roofs.

corrugated iron A form of iron sheeting, usually galvanized, introduced in England in the late 1830s and widely exported to colonial territories. It was used extensively in southern Africa in the building of low-cost houses.

Crystal Palace World's first major prefabricated building of iron and glass, built for the Great Exhibition of 1851 in Hyde Park, London. It was designed by Sir Joseph Paxton and it took only six months to build. The Crystal Palace covered 7,7 ha and its 300 000 panes of glass were held up by thousands of iron columns and girders. After the Great Exhibition the palace was re-erected at Sydenham, in south London, but it was destroyed by fire in 1936.

curtain wall A feature of modern architecture in which the outer wall of a building becomes a 'skin' of glass, metal or masonry. Pioneered by, among others, Walter GROPIUS, it developed as a result of framed building construction which served to free walls from their load-bearing function.

dams There are two basic types of dam: gravity dams and arch dams. Both can be used to hold back a body of water and so prevent floods and provide irrigation or water for human consumption, or to generate hydroelectric power. Gravity dams are simply earth or concrete embankments which depend on their own weight to resist the force of the water. Arch dams curve towards the body of water which they contain, resisting and redistributing the pressure of the water against each bank, in much the same way as an ARCH does in a building. Some dams are hybrid structures, combining both types. The earliest known dams, uncovered in Jerusalem and Jordan, date from about 3200 BC.

❖ The most important dam in South Africa is the Vaal Dam, the cornerstone of the vast Vaal River System. It supplies water to about 77 per cent of the country's mines, 58 per cent of industry, to areas supplying 42 per cent of the agricultural production, and to the most densely populated region in South Africa, with a projected population of around 13 million people by the year 2010.

deconstructivism Term based on the literary and philosophical theories of Jacques ▷DERRIDA, which 'deconstruct' literary texts in search of contradictory or hidden meanings. Deconstructivist architecture attempts to find new solutions without the constraints of structural, functional and thematic hierarchies. The result is often fantastic and seemingly disjointed, exemplified by the *Parc de la Villette* (1982) in Paris, designed by Bernard Tschumi (1944-).

drostdy Name given to the residence of the landdrost, or regional magistrate, during the Dutch colonial period in South Africa. Most of the early drostdys were built in the simple, VERNACULAR style, but during the periods of French, and later, British influence, buildings became more elaborate. Many drostdy buildings also incorporated Classical elements in their façades.

❖ One of the features of the Drostdy at Swellendam is the kitchen floor, made of peach pips laid in a bed of clay.

dykes Embankments used to reclaim land from the sea or to prevent flooding. A dyke along a river bank may be called a levee.

eclecticism Architecture (and art) that borrows from a variety of past styles. It was particularly prevalent in early 20th-century domestic architecture in southern Africa, where many styles were combined indiscriminately in one building.

Edwardian The Edwardian period, which refers to the first decade of the 20th century – when King Edward VII reigned in Britain – coincided with South Africa's gold boom. The use of new building materials and technology followed developments in Chicago, particularly in the use of framed construction. But the styles of financial and educational buildings remained grand and weighty, and essentially classicist. The Rand Club (1904), Corner House (1903-5) in Johannesburg, and the Old Archives in Cape Town (1906), epitomize the style. In domestic architecture, the style became ordered and dignified, discarding the decorative fussiness of the VICTORIAN style.

Eiffel Tower Paris's most prominent landmark was built as a temporary structure in 1887-9 for the Paris Exhibition by the French engineer Gustave Eiffel (1832-1923). Made of wrought iron sections bolted together, it is 300 m high. It was the world's tallest building and remained so until the Empire State Building was completed in 1931.

Empire State Building The most celebrated skyscraper in New York City, which opened in 1931. A popular vantage point for tourists, it is 381 m high, has 102 floors, and took just under 14 months to build. The top of the building sways about 1 m in high winds; it is crowned by a 68 m television aerial.

Foreshore, The Area of 221 ha of land between Table Bay and the city of Cape Town reclaimed from the sea between 1880 and 1934. The reclamations expanded the harbour and its facilities, enabling it to dock larger vessels, and made possible the extension of the overcrowded central business district. The Foreshore changed the character of the city, with the erection of skyscrapers such as the Sanlam Centre (1957), the tallest build-

ing in South Africa at the time, followed by a succession of high-rise buildings, a new railway station and a sprawling Civic Centre, incorporating the Nico Malan Opera House.

Fuller, Richard Buckminster (1895-1983) American inventor, engineer and architect. Among his many inventions was the geodesic dome – a lightweight hemispherical structure composed of interlocking tetrahedrons (four-faced sections) which at little cost covers a large area.

gable Upper, triangular part of a wall at the end of a pitched, or sloping, roof or above the entrance door. Among the several types of decorative gables are 'crowstepped' gables with stepped sides, and the more common Dutch gables with curved sides. One of the most characteristic features of the CAPE DUTCH style is the decorative central gable, placed above the front doorway. The style had become popular by the mid-1700s, and was a feature of most Cape Dutch homesteads. Later, the gable was to become popular even on flat-roofed town houses. The variety of gables was endless, from simple curvilinear mouldings to ornate baroque, or elegant neo-Classical.

STRANGE DESIGN *Antonio Gaudí's peculiar openwork spires (1903-26) at the Sagrada Familia church in Barcelona are part of one of the most eccentric creations of Art Nouveau.*

Gaudí, Antonio (1852-1926) Spain's greatest architect and leading exponent of ART NOUVEAU. His most celebrated work is the church of the Sagrada Familia, or Holy Family, in Barcelona, which had already been started when Gaudí took over in 1883. He transformed it from a NEO-GOTHIC structure to an imaginative vision of fantastic forms and twisted shapes, decorated with fragments of multicoloured ceramics. Its extraordinary bell towers are known as the Gaudí towers. Gaudí left the church unfinished and it is still under construction. He also designed many eye-catching houses in Barcelona, including the Casa Batlló (1904-6) and the Casa Milá (1905-10), with their undulating stonework, intricate balconies, and walls studded with fragments of coloured glass.

Georgian Style of British architecture during the reigns of George I, II and III, from 1714 to about 1800. It is sometimes taken to include the REGENCY period, from about 1800 to 1830. Georgian architecture is usually restrained, with an emphasis on elegance, scale and proportion rather than decoration. The classic example of Georgian style is the terraced town house, with large sash windows divided into small panes, which lends dignity to many of Britain's cities, especially ▷BATH.

German colonial Dominant architectural style of the colonial period in Namibia. A strong GOTHIC element runs through much of the architecture, epitomized by the three castles in Windhoek and the Lutheran Church, Windhoek, with its wavy gable and tall Gothic spire. BAROQUE and neo-Classical elements also appear in many of the colonial buildings. Domestic architecture is characterized by pitched roofs and pointed gables, trimmed with decorative woodwork. Hohenzollern House and Woermann House in Swakopmund are well-preserved buildings that exemplify features of the period.

Golden Gate Bridge Suspension bridge that crosses the strait connecting San Francisco Bay with the Pacific Ocean. Fast-running tides, fogs and storms hampered the building of the bridge – which was rammed by a cargo boat while half-completed. It was opened in 1937, and had the world's longest span (1 280 m) until the 1 298 m Verrazano Narrows Bridge in New York opened in 1964.

golden section (golden mean) Particular proportion considered to be pleasing to the eye. It is based on a division of a line into two unequal parts in which the ratio of the smaller part to the larger is the same as that of the larger part to the whole; the proportions are 1:1,618. The concept goes back at least as far as the ancient Greek mathematician ▷EUCLID, and greatly influenced RENAISSANCE architects and artists.

Gothic Style of architecture which flourished in Europe from the 12th to the 15th century. It is characterized by pointed arches, ribbed VAULTS, flying BUTTRESSES and lofty cathedrals with huge windows, such as NOTRE DAME in Paris.

❖ The style takes its name from the Goths who invaded Italy from the north in the 4th and 5th centuries AD, but has no real connection with them. The term was initially used by Renaissance artists to describe medieval arts and ornamentation in general.

PERIOD PIECE *The wavy gables of this house in Swakopmund, Namibia, are a feature of the German colonial style.*

Grand Canal Waterway in China begun in the 6th century AD as a series of short sections linked to stretches of navigable rivers. By 1327 a canal 1 781 km long had been created. More than 5 million labourers worked on the project, and about 2 million of them died of exhaustion or through accidents. The canal, the world's longest, is still in use.

Great Wall of China Wall intended to keep out nomadic invaders from the north. It was first built in about 217 BC, but most of the present wall dates from the Ming Dynasty (1368-1644). The wall winds from Shanhaiguan, on the Yellow Sea near Beijing, to Jiayuguan, 2 400 km to the west in central northern China, and covers 6 400 km at an average height of 7 m.

Great Zimbabwe Ruins of massive stone buildings believed to have been occupied by the Shana-Karanga civilization (*c*1200-1450). It is thought to have been the capital of an extensive area on the Zimbabwe plateau. At

SNAKING BARRIER *The building of the Great Wall of China was begun by Qin Shi Huangdi, the first emperor of China – whose tomb is guarded by an army of some 7 000 life-sized terracotta soldiers and clay horses.*

least 50 sites with similar stone constructions have been identified. (See also ▷GREAT ZIMBABWE in 'Southern African history'.)

Gropius, Walter (1883-1969) German-born architect who founded the BAUHAUS school in 1919. He was influenced by ▷EXPRESSIONISM and the work of William ▷MORRIS, and felt that the Bauhaus should be a meeting place of all arts and crafts teaching. Gropius moved to the USA before World War II and founded his own firm, The Architects' Collaborative (TAC), a cooperative which created clean, elegant and functional designs. His work has had a lasting effect on designers in Europe and North America.

Hagia Sofia BYZANTINE church in Istanbul built between AD 532 and 537. It was formerly used as a mosque but is now a museum. Its monumental, richly decorated interior is crowned by a colossal dome 33 m in diameter. Hagia Sofia is the outstanding architectural achievement of the ▷BYZANTINE EMPIRE.

hartbeeshuis A temporary dwelling built in southern Africa until the turn of the century both by local inhabitants and white settlers. Also known as *hardebieshuis*, it was made of thick stiff reeds, called *hardebiesies.* These were placed close together in the ground in two parallel lines and bent over to join at the top, forming a Gothic arch. The reeds were then woven together by thonging and sometimes covered with dried mud; the roof was thatched with grass. The only light to come into the structure came from the entrance.

high tech Style of architecture which uses steel and glass and shows off functional elements such as ventilation ducts and lifts, in celebration of modern technology. An example is the POMPIDOU CENTRE in Paris.

Hindu temples South Africa's Indian community has built a wealth of Hindu temples throughout the country in both the main styles of India, the Nagara (north), and the Dravidian (south), as well as a hybrid style which has evolved in South Africa as the communities have merged.

International Style (Modern Movement) Architectural style developed in the first part of the 20th century by Walter GROPIUS and the BAUHAUS movement, Frank Lloyd WRIGHT and, later, Ludwig MIES VAN DER ROHE. It was adopted internationally by the late 1920s. It is typified by its smooth lines, cubic forms, large windows, often in horizontal bands, and an absence of decorative elements.
❖ The most influential figure in the development of the style in South Africa was Rex Martienssen (1905-42), who was trained at and later became a lecturer at the University of the Witwatersrand.

Islamic architecture Style which developed from BYZANTINE and early Greek architecture in Islamic countries of the present-day Middle East from the 7th to the 16th century. Its features include horseshoe arches, tunnel vaults, domed spaces, courtyards and dazzling decoration using stone carving, ▷MOSAIC, glazed tiles and painting. The earliest surviving example of Islamic architecture is the Dome of the Rock MOSQUE (685-705) in Jerusalem. One of the most impressive is the ALHAMBRA palace in Granada, Spain.

Johnson, Philip (1906-) American architect whose early work was influenced by the work of MIES VAN DER ROHE. His Late Modernist work is less austere, although it retains its elegant line. Among his main buildings are the New York State Theatre in the Lincoln Center (1964), museums and art galleries in New York, Washington and Texas, and the sculpture garden and New Building for the Museum of Modern Art in New York (1964).
❖ Johnson coined the term INTERNATIONAL STYLE in a catalogue essay for a New York exhibition in 1932.

kapstylhuisie VERNACULAR style of temporary dwelling used widely in southern Africa by indigenous peoples and white settlers until the turn of the century. These were longitudinal A-frame constructions. Their underlying framework of wooden trusses was bound together in a series of inverted Vs, strengthened with tie beams and thatched with reeds. The roofs usually reached the ground but the structure sometimes had low walls.

Kremlin Citadel in Moscow, enclosing a complex of princely residences and churches fortified in the 15th century, and now Russia's seat of government. Tsar ▷IVAN THE GREAT brought Italian architects to Russia to rebuild the Kremlin in the 15th century. Its architecture is a mixture of styles, dominated by BYZANTINE and RENAISSANCE buildings. Churches with traditional medieval onion-shaped domes surmounting Renaissance façades, show the composite style at its best.
❖ 'Kremlin' is the Russian word for 'citadel'.

Late Modernism Not to be confused with post-modernism, Late Modernism uses the language and logic of the INTERNATIONAL STYLE, often taking them to extremes of technical ingenuity and virtuosity. The SEARS TOWER building in Chicago (1974-6), the world's tallest building, is an example. Often the mechanical workings of a building become a feature, as in the POMPIDOU CENTRE in Paris (1971-7). The sweeping lines of Frank Lloyd WRIGHT's Guggenheim Museum in New York (1943-59) and the dramatic SYDNEY OPERA HOUSE are other striking examples of the style. The Johannesburg Sun Hotel and Towers (1986) and 11 Diagonal Street, Johannesburg, are excellent local examples.

Leaning Tower of Pisa Celebrated Italian bell tower, or campanile, begun in 1174, which started to lean before it was even finished as a result of weak foundations and subsidence. The 55 m high tower has been tilting ever since and the top now leans about 5 m to one side. In 1993, for the first time in 800 years, the bells were silenced because of fears that vibration would topple the tower. In the same year the tilt reversed by a few millimetres, after lead weights were placed on the ground floor of the tower. Early in 1995 workmen froze the ground on which it stands with liquid nitrogen as part of an ambitious project to stabilize the tower. A huge ring of cement was to be placed underground around the foundations of the tower and tilted by cables linked to firm layers of earth 50 m below it.

Le Corbusier (1887-1965) (real name Charles Édouard Jeanneret) Swiss-born French architect who influenced 20th-century buildings with his philosophy that a house should be a 'machine for living in' and that architecture was the 'magnificent play of masses brought together in light'. Inspired by ▷CUBISM, Le Corbusier devised an innovative system of calculating proportions to design individual buildings and entire cities. He advocated the use of concrete, standardized building elements and prefabrication. The name that he assumed for his professional life was derived from *corbeau*, French for a crow – which he supposedly resembled when wearing glasses.

CROWNING GLORY *Le Corbusier's Chapel of Notre Dame, which dominates the crest of a hill in Ronchamp, France, is often cited as one of the most important buildings of the 20th century.*

INSIDE OUT *Richard Rogers's use of external pipes and ducts at the Lloyd's building, in the City of London, is intended to reduce the maintenance and servicing costs.*

Lloyd's building In London, a major work of British architect Sir Richard Rogers (1933-) and an outstanding example of HIGH TECH style. Completed in 1986, it won him critical acclaim as well as scorn for its unconventionality. It has heating and ventilation pipework on the exterior, creating a complex maze of polished aluminium, stainless steel and smooth grey concrete.

Lutyens, Sir Edwin Landseer (1869-1944) British architect whose traditional approach made him the Edwardian establishment's favourite builder. Early in his career he was heavily influenced by the ARTS AND CRAFTS MOVEMENT and specialized in designing romantic country houses for the wealthy. He also designed a number of public buildings, his masterpiece being the plan for New Delhi, which included the Viceroy's House, now Presidential Palace (1912-31).
❖ Lutyens' only South African work of note is the original part of the Johannesburg Art Gallery (1911-15).

McAdam, John Loudon (1756-1836) Scottish engineer who devised a durable road surface composed of stones and gravel laid down to form a dense, firm base. Later, engineers added tar to bind the stones together and called the resultant surface 'tarmacadam' or 'tarmac' after him.

Mies van der Rohe, Ludwig (1886-1969) German-born architect who, with LE CORBUSIER and Frank Lloyd WRIGHT, was one of the key figures of modern architecture. In 1938 Mies van der Rohe left Germany, where, among other things, he had been a director of the BAUHAUS school, for the USA. He produced simple, clean-cut designs, and was a pioneer of the use of steel and glass in skyscrapers remarkable for their elegant proportions.

mosque Early examples of Muslim places of worship include the Holy Mosque in Mecca (built around the Kaaba, which houses a sacred stone) and the Dome of the Rock in Jerusalem. Most large mosques are built around a large courtyard containing a fountain for ritual washing. The *mihrab*, a special niche in the wall facing Mecca, shows Muslims which way to face when praying. A mosque usually has a minaret, or tower, from which the *muezzin*, or crier, calls Muslims to prayer. Minarets may be square or cylindrical in shape, and some have a series of projecting balconies. Many mosques are richly decorated with calligraphic designs, which turn quotations from the ▹KORAN into dazzling abstract patterns. (See also ▹MOSQUE in 'Ideas, beliefs and religion'.)

National Monuments Council A statutory organization established in 1969 to advise the South African Government on the preservation and protection of South Africa's natural and constructed historical and cultural heritage. Included in the country's more than 4 000 national monuments are Table Mountain, numerous rock-art sites, engineering works, historic buildings, shipwrecks, war graves and other sites of widely ranging cultural and geographical significance.

neo-Classicism Revival of the CLASSICAL style in Europe from the late 18th century to the early 19th century. It was inspired by the rediscoveries of the Roman cities of Herculaneum (1738) and ▹POMPEII (1748), and employed the simpler ideals and forms of the ancient Greeks and Romans in reaction to the highly ornate style of the ▹ROCOCO period. At the start of the revival, buildings were solid and severe, with restrained decoration and massive spaces and forms. By the end of the period, however, the design had become much more attractive, with more elaborate decoration and less austere forms. (See also ▹NEO-CLASSICISM in 'Art and design'.)

neo-Gothic (Gothic Revival) Reawakening of interest in GOTHIC architecture in the mid-19th century, based on the fashionable romantic nostalgia for medieval Europe. The decoration of Britain's Houses of Parliament (1844-52) by Augustus PUGIN and the Albert Memorial (1863-72) in London by Sir George Gilbert Scott are among the best examples of the style.

❖ In southern Africa the Gothic revival appeared again in churches, but Gothic characteristics, such as towers and high-pitched gables, were a feature also of domestic architecture and public buildings. The style was particularly prevalent in Namibia during the colonial period. In South Africa, a fine example of Gothic revivalism is the Pacaltsdorp Mission Church (1822-5) near George.

Notre Dame Name given to many French cathedrals, but particularly associated with the cathedral of Paris, which is one of France's most distinguished examples of GOTHIC architecture. It was built between 1163 and 1345 on the Île de la Cité, an island in the River Seine. The cathedral – 130 m long, 47 m wide and 35 m high – can accommodate up to 9 000 worshippers. It is supported by enormous flying BUTTRESSES, and has sunk several feet under its own weight since it was built.

obelisk Tall, four-sided shaft of stone that tapers to a point. The first obelisks were built by the Egyptians to flank the entrances of tombs and temples.

Orange-Fish River Scheme The first major multipurpose, intercatchment water project in South Africa. Its two dams, the Gariep (previously the H F Verwoerd Dam) and the Vanderkloof (previously the P K le Roux Dam), are the largest storage reservoirs in the country. The 82 km-long Orange-Fish Tunnel, the longest continuous water tunnel in the world, transfers water from the Gariep Dam to the Great Fish and Sundays River valleys. Underground hydroelectric power stations at both dams operate during periods of peak power demand, when water is released for irrigation. Construction of the dams began in 1966 and was completed in 1971.

Palladian Classically inspired architecture in the manner of the Italian architect Andrea Palladio (1508-80), whose extensive study of antique design, *The Four Books of Architecture* (1570), influenced architecture throughout Europe. In the 17th century Inigo Jones (1573-1652) took the style to Britain, where it was the precursor of NEO-CLASSICISM. The Palladian formula for the ideal villa, with Classical PORTICOS and airy colonnades, was a major influence on international architecture and many homes in southern Africa embody Palladian features.

GOTHIC GRANDEUR *Notre Dame, standing on an island in the Seine, is one of the oldest French Gothic cathedrals, dating from 1163.*

Panama Canal Link between the Atlantic and Pacific oceans across the Isthmus of ▹PANAMA, opened in 1914. The 82 km canal, which saves ships the long journey round the southern tip of South America, took 33 years to build. The canal was planned by Ferdinand de Lesseps, who also built the SUEZ CANAL.

Pantheon Circular domed temple to all the gods, rebuilt in Rome by Emperor Hadrian in AD 120-4 from an earlier building of *c*27 BC. The diameter of the building, 43 m, is the same as its height, and its entrance is through an impressive PORTICO with Corinthian columns. The monumental dome inspired a great deal of RENAISSANCE architecture, in particular BRUNELLESCHI's dome for Florence cathedral. The Pantheon, now a Roman Catholic church, contains many tombs, including that of the artist ▹RAPHAEL.

Parthenon Temple dedicated to the goddess Athena, built on the ACROPOLIS in Athens between 447 and 438 BC. It was seen by the Greeks as the architectural ideal, with its perfect combination of austerity and grace. The temple is 69,5 m long and 31 m wide. The Parthenon later served as a Christian church then an Islamic mosque before being used as an ammunition store by Turkish occupiers in the 17th century. It was badly damaged by an explosion in 1687, when it was bombarded by Venetian forces. Many friezes and sculptures, including the ▹ELGIN MARBLES were taken from the building in the 19th century.

HISTORIC WATCH HOUSE *Built in 1673, the Posthuys in Muizenberg is believed to be South Africa's oldest European house. It was used as a lookout post by the Dutch garrison defending the Cape.*

pediment In Classical architecture, a low-pitched GABLE on the façade which is placed above a PORTICO, door or window.

Pei, I M (1917-) American architect, born in China, trained at the Massachusetts Institute of Technology and at Harvard. Among his most important buildings are the J F Kennedy Library (1964-79) at Harvard University in Boston, the East Wing of the National Gallery in Washington (1968-78) and his famous, and initially highly controversial, design for the Grand Louvre Project in Paris. Inaugurated in 1989, this major undertaking links the three wings of the Louvre under a huge glass pyramid, facilitating easy access throughout the galleries and doubling the exhibition space.

Pompidou Centre HIGH TECH building constructed in Paris during 1971-7 which houses a modern art gallery as well as a centre for industrial design. British architect Sir Richard Rogers and the Italian architect Renzo Piano created the controversial six-storey structure by 'turning the building inside out'. Functional services such as staircases and escalators are visible from outside, to increase the amount of display space. The building is also referred to as the Centre Beauborg, the name of the square which it overlooks. LLOYD'S BUILDING in London, designed by Rogers, is constructed on similar lines.

❖ The centre is named after Georges Pompidou, president of France from 1969 to 1974.

portico Roofed entrance, usually in the centre of the façade of a church, house or temple. It may be open or partly enclosed, and often has columns and a PEDIMENT.

Portuguese colonial Style resulting from the influence of metropolitan Portugal on architecture in Mozambique and Angola, which continued into the 1970s. Landscapes of red tiled rooftops are as much a characteristic of the cities of the former colonies as they are of Portugal. The palaces and civic buildings of the governors of the colonies, with their elegant colonnaded porticoes, pediments and decorative wrought-iron balconies, are based on the RENAISSANCE and BAROQUE styles of architecture in Portugal. In place of the colourful, textured tiles of Portugal, colonial buildings were often painted in bold colours, mainly deep green or terracotta.

Posthuys Watch house built in 1673 on the shores of False Bay – in what is today Muizenberg – by the Dutch, who were then at war with the French and English. Constructed as a fort with thick stone walls, it was completed a year before the Castle and is reputed to be the oldest house in South Africa built by Europeans.

post-modernism Mid 20th-century stylistic shift away from the INTERNATIONAL STYLE and late-Modernist buildings. Post-modernism harks back to past architectural styles, from which it draws design elements such as columns, pediments and arcades, often applied simply as decorative pastiche.

prefabrication System in which standardized sections of a building are mass-produced in a factory and assembled on site. The CRYSTAL PALACE was an early example. After World War II European countries relied heavily on prefabricated housing to replace buildings destroyed by bombing raids, and even up to the 1980s the system was extensively used in industrialized countries. A large proportion of one-family homes in Germany, for example, are prefabricated. In South Africa the need has not been great, since labour has been abundant, but much research has been done into the viability of using factory-produced parts for housing.

pressed steel A popular style of patterned ceiling in the VICTORIAN houses of southern Africa. With the advent of industrial machinery, it became possible to mass-produce patterned pressed steel sheets, which were lightweight and easy to transport and assemble. Most pressed steel ceilings in southern Africa were imported from foundries in Scotland and the English Midlands.

prestressed concrete Extremely strong form of REINFORCED CONCRETE made by pouring CONCRETE over stretched steel cables within a mould. When the concrete has set, it stops the cables from returning to their normal length after the mould has been removed. The tension created compresses the concrete and enables it to resist enormous stresses. Prestressed concrete is often used to make slender bridges.

Pugin, Augustus (1812-52) British architect who became an ardent medievalist after converting to Roman Catholicism in 1834. He studied GOTHIC architecture and wrote several influential books promoting its virtues. He is most noted for the exterior and interior NEO-GOTHIC decoration of the Houses of Parliament on the Thames embankment in London, built between 1844 and 1852.

pyramids Colossal monuments built by the ancient Egyptians to house their ▷PHARAOHS' tombs. Pyramids date from around 2660 BC. The shape of the pyramid is thought to symbolize a staircase to the sun, so that the king could climb to heaven.

❖ The Great Pyramid of King Cheops, at Giza, near Cairo, rises 137 m above the ground. It is built from 2,3 million blocks of stone weighing an average of 2,5 tons each, and was originally covered with polished limestone slabs. The pyramids at Giza are the only one of the Seven Wonders of the Ancient World that have survived to the present day.

❖ The term 'pyramid' is also applied to hills with flat tops built by the ancient peoples of South America.

railways The world's first permanent public railway using steam traction was a 16 km stretch from Darlington to Stockton-on-Tees in northeast England opened in 1825. The first railway in subequatorial Africa was a 3,2 km line between Durban and the Point, followed by 87 km of line between Cape Town and Wellington, both opened in 1857. The Cape Town to Kimberley line was completed in 1885, connecting with Johannesburg in 1892, fanning out to include Port Elizabeth, East London, Lourenço Marques (now Maputo) and Durban by 1895.

❖ Many of the old station buildings are being put to new use. Renovations to the old Durban station workshops began in 1985, resulting in The Workshop which was completed in 1986. This was the first thematic shopping centre in South Africa.

Regency Early 19th-century style of British architecture and design which marks the concluding phase of the GEORGIAN period. Named after the fashionable Prince Regent, later King George IV, the Regency style is one of unostentatious lavishness combined with elegance – a kind of NEO-CLASSICISM with added flourishes such as exterior STUCCO work and wrought iron roofed balconies. (See also ▷REGENCY in 'Art and design'.)

regionalism An architectural movement which emerged between 1945 and 1960 as a reaction to international styles of architecture and to socialist trends in society. Major figures in the movement were Frank Lloyd WRIGHT and Alvar AALTO, who were concerned with the harmony of architecture and its environment, and a greater understanding of the basic needs and traditions of individuals and local communities.

❖ In South Africa, Norman Eaton (1902-66) was a champion of regionalism.

reinforced concrete Strong and versatile building material made from a mesh of thin steel rods embedded in CONCRETE. It can support very heavy loads – a property exploited to the full in the construction of domes, bridges and foundations. PRESTRESSED CONCRETE is even stronger.

Renaissance Renewal of CLASSICAL ideals in architecture, literature and art which took place in Europe from the late 14th century to the end of the 16th century with the rediscovery of ancient Greek art and literature. Renaissance buildings have arches borne on slender columns, graceful decoration and layers of massive stone blocks with accentuated, deeply indented joints. In architecture the style is typified by the work of Filippo BRUNELLESCHI and Leon Battista ALBERTI, and the term generally refers to the Italian Renaissance style – even though its influence spread from Italy throughout Europe. (See also ▷RENAISSANCE in 'Art and design'.)

Romanesque Style of architecture common in western Europe from the 11th century to about the mid-12th century, named after the Roman architecture from which it is derived. Romanesque buildings typically have CLASSICAL columns, round arches, tunnel vaulting and fantastical decoration. In England, the Romanesque style is called Norman. It was followed by the GOTHIC style.

Roman roads The Romans built roads that sliced across the terrain in a series of straight lines. These roads were so well constructed – with an earth base, then a layer of small stones in mortar, topped by a layer of solid material covered by stone slabs – that some, such as the Appian Way from Rome to Capua, are still in use 2 300 years later.

❖ By the end of the 3rd century AD the total distance covered by roads built in many parts of Europe by the Romans was 85 000 km – more than twice the Earth's circumference.

rondavel Circular one-roomed hut with conical thatched roof, also known as a cone-on-cylinder hut, indigenous to southern Africa. Today, similar huts are used as holiday cottages, offices and storerooms and can be bought in prefabricated kits.

St Peter's Basilica Europe's largest church, in the ▷VATICAN CITY. A BASILICA built on the site in AD 324 was demolished in 1505 to make way for the present building, which was built in the RENAISSANCE and BAROQUE styles between 1506 and 1624. Twenty popes and ten architects, including the aged ▷MICHELANGELO, worked on the building. BERNINI added the monumental entrance piazza flanked by colonnades in the 17th century. St Peter's dome, which was designed by Michelangelo and finished by his assistants, is 137 m high.

Sears Tower World's tallest office building, completed in Chicago in 1976. It has 110 storeys and is 443 m high.

Stephenson, George (1781-1848) Britain's first railway engineer, who was put in charge of the Stockton to Darlington railway which opened in 1825 with Stephenson's *Locomotion* engine pulling the first passenger train. Stephenson then built the Liverpool to Manchester railway, which opened in 1830 and incorporated 73 bridges and the first deep railway cutting. His son Robert (1803-59) was also a noted engineer who contributed to the development of railways in Britain and abroad. (See also George ▷STEPHENSON in 'Technology and invention'.)

❖ In 1829 George Stephenson's engine *The Rocket* won a prize for maintaining an average speed of 46 km/h.

stoeps and verandas The two words are used fairly interchangeably in South Africa. A stoep is the platform or paving at the entrance to a house or building which need not be covered or enclosed. Verandas are open galleries

KAROO VERANDA *Typical of innumerable houses on South African farms and in country towns, the home of a resident of Graaff-Reinet has a roofed veranda with ornate railings.*

or balconies attached to a house or building, usually covered or partly covered by a roof. Stoeps became part of settler architecture in South Africa almost immediately. The first stoep recorded was that of the POSTHUYS.

stucco Durable smooth finish for exterior walls made from a mixture of cement, sand and lime. The term also describes the REGENCY vogue for using plaster to imitate exterior stonework.

Suez Canal Waterway stretching 162 km across Egypt linking Port Said on the Mediterranean Sea to Suez on the Red Sea, saving ships the long journey around the Cape of Good Hope. It was planned by the French engineer and diplomat Ferdinand de Lesseps (1805-94) – who also planned the PANAMA CANAL – and opened in 1869. The canal was financed by an Egyptian company, and the British Government subsequently bought a major share in its ownership.
❖ The Egyptian Government nationalized the canal in 1956, sparking the ▷SUEZ CRISIS. It was closed by Egypt during the ▷SIX-DAY WAR in 1967 – sending many ships around the Cape and bringing a boom in business for South Africa's harbours – and reopened only in 1975. More than 20 000 vessels now pass through the canal every year.

AUSTRALIAN LANDMARKS *The reflected arch of Sydney Harbour Bridge frames the famous Sydney Opera House, whose ten concrete 'shells' proved to be a builder's nightmare.*

Sullivan, Louis (1856-1924) American architect, attracted to Chicago by the opportunities to rebuild the city after a great fire destroyed parts of it in 1871. Sullivan's were among the early skyscrapers. The rich ornamentation of the lower floors of his Carson Pirie Scott department store (1898-1903) in Chicago is considered a manifestation of ART NOUVEAU.

Sydney Harbour Bridge World's widest and heaviest steel arch bridge, which was opened in 1932, having taken eight years to build. The bridge's arch spans 503 m and carries two railway tracks, an eight-lane road, a footpath and a cycleway on a deck 49 m wide.

Sydney Opera House Australia's most renowned building, set on a promontory in Sydney Harbour. It houses five halls – for music, drama and exhibitions – three restaurants and six bars in its ten concrete 'shells'. The ambitious design, by Danish architect Jørn Utzon (1918-), won a competition in 1957 but proved impossible to carry out. Ove ARUP solved the problems, and the building was eventually completed in a much-altered form in 1973. The roof, covered by more than 1 million tiles, weighs more than 20 000 tons.

Taj Mahal Mausoleum at Agra, in northern India, widely regarded as one of the world's most beautiful buildings. It was completed in 1653 by the Mogul emperor Shah Jahan in memory of his favourite wife, Mumtaz Mahal. A large onion-shaped dome is flanked by four smaller domes and four minarets. An ornamental pool reflects the entire composition, which is a superb melding of Islamic and Hindu styles in white marble.
❖ The mausoleum's marble façade is inlaid with semiprecious stones but hides a structure built out of common rubble.

Thibault, Louis-Michel (1750-1815) French architect who came to the Cape as a military engineer with a French regiment in 1783, and dominated architecture in the city around the turn of the century. He introduced a classical simplicity and elegance to the buildings of the Cape. Many of his buildings have been demolished, but those remaining include the Good Hope Masonic Lodge (1803) in Stal Plein, Cape Town, the Tulbagh Drostdy (1806), and the South African Cultural History Museum, which was converted by Thibault from the old Dutch East India Company slave quarters. He collaborated frequently with the sculptor Anton ▷ANREITH and the builder Herman Schutte.

town planning System for developing towns and cities according to an orderly plan, taking into account the social, environmental, aesthetic and economic needs of a community. One of the greatest town-planning exercises was the 1852-70 transformation of Paris by Baron Haussmann, with the Arc de Triomphe the central pivot of the city. The Green Belt Act of 1939, to protect the natural countryside around London, is a more recent and a more sympathetic response to the needs of the people. Town planning is an integral part of the development of South Africa. Urgent town-planning needs have arisen as a result

MONUMENTAL LOVE *The Taj Mahal, one of India's most-visited sites, is a stunning memorial to a Mogul emperor's wife. An army of 20 000 workers took more than 12 years to complete it.*

of the rise of informal settlements with the influx of people to urban areas since the scrapping of ▷INFLUX CONTROL.

tracery Ornamental stonework in the upper part of a window or arch first used in the GOTHIC windows of Rheims Cathedral in France at the beginning of the 13th century. The dividing ribs are known as mullions (vertical) and transoms (horizontal).

Trans-Siberian Railway Longest railway line in the world. It was built largely between 1891 and 1904, and runs from Moscow to Nakhodka on the Sea of Japan – a distance of 9 436 km. Another branch goes through Mongolia and across China to the capital, Beijing.

Tudor, mock A style based on the whitewashed walls and exposed timbers of Elizabethan domestic architecture, which became popular in English and South African homes in the 1920s and 1930s. A superb South African example of the style is the Natal Playhouse in Durban, built as a cinema in 1935 and restored in 1983 to encompass several theatres and a 1 300-seat opera house.

❖ The style should not be confused with the Tudor style of the 15th and 16th centuries in England, characterized by imposing gatehouses, battlemented parapets and ornate chimneys, all built from red brick.

tunnels Shallow tunnels can be built by the 'cut and cover' method of digging a deep trench which is then covered over. Deeper tunnels have to be made by tunnelling underground, using picks and shovels or mechanical drills. The tunnelling shield invented by Marc Isambard BRUNEL was a major technical advance, enabling tunnels to be driven through soft soil as well as under rivers or the sea-bed. The shield protects the tunnellers, and prevents the tunnel walls collapsing. After it has been pushed along, support rings are installed. Modern tunnels, such as the CHANNEL TUNNEL, are excavated by enormous tunnelling machines called 'moles', which incorporate a boring mechanism and protective shield.

❖ The horseshoe-shaped Huguenot Tunnel (or Du Toitskloof Tunnel), opened in 1988, is bored a distance of 3 913 m through the mountains between Wellington and Worcester in the Western Cape. It has two traffic lanes with a vertical clearance of 5 m.

Tuynhuys Now the office of the South African president in Government Avenue, Cape Town, Tuynhuys was built in 1682 by the Dutch governor Simon van der Stel as a lodge for foreign visitors. Originally a garden pavilion, later a summer residence for the governor of the Cape, Tuynhuys has been altered many times in its three-century history. Extensive renovations to the house and garden, restoring them to their 18th-century state, were completed in 1971.

underground railways The first underground rail link was London's Metropolitan Railway from Farringdon Street to Paddington, which opened in 1863. Steam trains carried more than 9 million passengers during its first year – despite the sulphurous fumes. London's first 'tube' line, deep enough to avoid the foundations of buildings, opened in 1890. Budapest opened an underground line in 1896, Boston in 1897, Paris in 1900, New York in 1904 and Moscow in 1935. The first fully automated system, the Bay Area Rapid Transit (BART), was completed in San Francisco in 1974. London's underground network is the largest of any city.

Union Buildings Administrative seat of government in Pretoria. Designed by Sir Herbert BAKER, the sandstone buildings, with their two domed towers and linking amphitheatre, commemorate the Act of ▷UNION of 1910.

vault Arched roof used for spanning large spaces. It was employed extensively by the Romans in aqueducts, amphitheatres, warehouses and public baths. The basic 'barrel' or 'tunnel' vault, springing from a series of rounded arches, was much used in ROMANESQUE architecture. The use of the pointed arch in GOTHIC architecture from the 12th century onwards led to the 'ribbed vault', a fine skeleton of stone ribs forming the arches, with the spaces between the ribs filled in by thin stonework. Vaulting reached a peak of sophistication with the 'fan vault', the supreme example of which is at King's College Chapel, Cambridge (1446-1515), where the stone looks almost as intricate and delicate as lacework.

vernacular Style of building that evolves locally in response to people's needs and the availability of materials. The term generally applies to domestic architecture. In southern Africa it includes the traditional thatched beehive huts of the Zulu, mostly replaced by thatched cone-on-cylinder constructions (RONDAVELS) similar to those of the Xhosa, Tswana and Sotho-speaking peoples. The Cape Dutch style, and Highveld or lean-to dwellings, popular in contemporary Sotho and Ndebele architecture, are also forms of vernacular architecture.

❖ Most of the dwellings in urban squatter communities make imaginative use of found materials, which include wood, corrugated iron and plastic. They are usually adaptations of the Highveld dwelling. which is a simple, flat-roofed house, constructed on a rectangular plan, covered by a lean-to roof raised in the front of the building and sloping downwards at the back.

Versailles Spectacular palace and gardens built largely by King Louis XIV of France near Paris. Work on the building started in 1668, and the royal court moved here in 1682. The magnificent BAROQUE apartments include the

73 m long *Galerie des Glaces*, or Hall of Mirrors, where the Treaty of Versailles which ended World War I was signed in 1919.

Victorian Period during the reign of Queen Victoria (1837-1901) which saw the revival of many architectural styles, such as the CLASSICAL, ▷ROCOCO and, in particular, the GOTHIC style. Victorian building design often exaggerated the styles it revived, as with the NEO-GOTHIC work of Sir George Gilbert Scott (1811-78) and PUGIN. Buildings were massive and the ornamentation often flamboyant. Designs were also influenced by the ▷INDUSTRIAL REVOLUTION and advances in engineering which allowed many parts to be factory-made, as in the vast range of CAST IRON. In southern Africa Victorian architecture scarcely differed from that of other areas colonized by Britain because of the mass export of these standardized components. Numerous Victorian buildings still exist in the region.
❖ One of the best-preserved examples of Victoriana is Matjiesfontein, in the Karoo, developed as an elite health resort in the late 19th century, and restored in the mid-1970s. It is a major tourist attraction on the rail or road route inland from the Cape.

wattle-and-daub Popular method of building walls in the Middle Ages: a timber framework was covered with interlaced twigs, or wattles, and daubed with a mixture of clay reinforced with cow dung and horsehair, before being roughly plastered. In Africa the same method is still used in this style of construction of simple family dwellings and shelters.

WREN'S MASTERPIECE *St Paul's Cathedral, widely regarded as one of London's finest buildings, houses memorials to national heroes Kitchener, Wellington and Nelson.*

FITTING IN WITH NATURE *Frank Lloyd Wright's Fallingwater in Pennsylvania was designed to echo the natural contours of the land, making the house become part of the surrounding landscape.*

Westminster Abbey Earliest example of ROMANESQUE or Norman architecture, started under King Edward the Confessor around 1048. His original church has all but disappeared under a series of later alterations. The existing abbey was finished in about 1740.
❖ Most of England's kings and queens have been crowned at Westminster Abbey.

Wierda, Sytze (1839-1911) Dutch architect who was appointed by President Kruger to head his public works department in 1887. One of a group of youthful engineers and architects, known as 'Kruger's Hollanders', he was imported to enhance the image of the young Transvaal Republic. He designed most of the Transvaal government buildings of the 1890s, many of which still survive. These include two buildings on Church Square in Pretoria, the Palace of Justice (1896-1900), and the slightly later Raadsaal, which was derived from the 17th-century BAROQUE buildings of Amsterdam.

World Trade Centre Tallest office block in New York, its twin rectangular towers dominating the southern tip of Manhattan. Designed by the architect Minoru Yamasaki (1912-87), it was built between 1962 and 1976. The towers are 411 m high.
❖ When the Carlton Centre in Johannesburg, South Africa's first major hotel, office and shopping complex, was opened in 1973, it was the second largest commercial building development in the world after the World Trade Centre. When the site was excavated, the hole was large enough to enclose the entire cubic area of the Empire State Building.

Wren, Sir Christopher (1632-1723) English architect whose masterpiece is St Paul's Cathedral, London (1675-1710). He built 52 other churches in the City of London alone. Wren also devised a plan for the radical replanning of London after the Great Fire of 1666, but it was not adopted.

Wright, Frank Lloyd (1867-1959) American architect and one of the most influential figures in 20th-century architecture. Wright built houses in what he called an 'organic style' – that is, appearing to grow from the ground rather than just sitting on it. His most celebrated house, Fallingwater, Pennsylvania (1936-9), was built over a waterfall. He also designed New York's Guggenheim Museum (1943-59), in the form of a continuous corkscrew.

ziggurat Ancient Assyrian or Babylonian temple shaped like a stepped pyramid with the top sliced off to allow space for a shrine, with ramps giving access to each level. The earliest ziggurats were built by the Sumerians around 3000 BC.
❖ The fabled Tower of Babel was a giant ziggurat designed to reach the heavens.

HUMAN SOCIETY

A brain that evolved far beyond the instinctive responses of other animals enabled our ancestors to create complex languages and organize themselves into settled communities. Societies across the globe have developed in diverse ways according to their history and culture, but all have an elaborate web of family ties and distinctive rituals that mark an individual's progress through life.

Aborigines First human inhabitants of Australia, some 750 000 of whom were living there when European settlers arrived in 1788. The term can also refer to the earliest known inhabitants of any region. Australia's Aborigines were nomadic HUNTER-GATHERERS who migrated from southern Asia at least 50 000-60 000 years ago. Although most Aborigines now live in cities or towns, a few, mostly in the Northern Territory, strive to lead a life close to that before European contact. Land rights remain a dominant issue; Aborigines own 12 per cent of Australia but have claimed more.

❖ Australian Aborigines have a rich spiritual life based on 'Dreamtime', or 'Dreaming', a golden age at the beginning of creation, when plants, animals and human beings came into existence. Although about 600 languages were once spoken (two-thirds of which are now extinct) and there are wide cultural differences, the 265 000 Australian Aborigines have a strong sense of unity.

affirmative action Equal opportunities programme or policy that actively promotes equality between the sexes and racial categories, particularly in employment. Affirmative action, also sometimes known as 'positive discrimination', has been implemented by many organizations throughout southern Africa to try to redress the inequalities that resulted from historical practices of discrimination. The policy has been criticized for 'tokenism', an accusation that appointments lack commitment to the real objectives of affirmative action. Effective affirmative action, or 'capacity building', ensures that candidates receive appropriate training and support. After many years of affirmative action, major corporations and institutions in the USA are increasingly questioning its usefulness.

Afrikaners Descendants of Dutch, German and French settlers in South Africa. Their forebears arrived at the Cape in the 17th century and were known as ▷BOERS. They make up about 60 per cent of South Africa's white population and speak Afrikaans, a creole language derived from Dutch, French and Malay. The category Afrikaner dates only from the 19th century, particularly with the propagation of Afrikaans as a unique language. Afrikaners do not form a homogeneous group, and responded differently to southern Africa's changing politics. Like any IDENTITY, that of the Afrikaner is influenced by social factors and it therefore reflects a range of interpretations and is contested. (See also ▷AFRIKAANS LANGUAGE MOVEMENT in 'Southern African history' and ▷AFRIKANER NATIONALISM in 'Politics, government and the law'.)

INSTRUMENT MAKERS *Aborigines in northern Australia put the finishing touches to a didgeridoo – the traditional long, hollowed-out wooden tube which produces a deep note when blown.*

age of consent Minimum age below which it is a criminal offence to have sexual intercourse. In most developed countries this ranges between 15 to 18. South African law is complex as regards the age of consent in that, legally, boys and girls may marry at age 14 and 12 respectively, but it is a statutory offence to have sex with a woman under the age of 16 years. Under the same statute, homosexual sex is an offence, which means that men may not have consensual sex with each other. Although 16-year-olds may have consensual sex, they require the permission of their parents or legal guardians to marry if under the age of 21 years.

alienation Feeling of separation or isolation from other people, or from society as a whole. Karl Marx used the term to describe the effects of capitalism, which he believed dehumanized people and deprived them of creative and fulfilling work. More recently, the term has been used by psychologists to refer to feelings of powerlessness and lack of purpose in modern society, which is a theme taken up in many acclaimed films.

American Indian Term applied to the indigenous peoples of North and South America by European explorers in the 15th century who mistakenly believed they had reached India when they encountered people of Asian appearance. Many American, or 'Red', Indians now prefer to be called NATIVE AMERICANS.

androgyny Having both male and female characteristics, in appearance and behaviour. The word is a compound of the Greek *andros* ('man') and *gyne* ('woman'). Entertainers have sometimes deliberately cultivated androgynous images; among them are the rock musicians David Bowie and Boy George. Androgyny is not usually connected to hermaphroditism – the condition of having both male and female sexual characteristics.

animal rights Campaigning issue which holds that animals have the right to protection from cruel or unnatural treatment. Most groups, such as the SPCA (Society for the Prevention of Cruelty to Animals), lobby peacefully against the abuse of animals in a range of areas such as drug trials, cosmetic tests, battery farming, hunting, the fur trade and zoos. Elsewhere in the world animal rights activists have been prosecuted for vandalizing laboratories and intimidating scientists.

anthropology Study of the origin and development of humankind and, increasingly, of social interaction and societies. It has several different branches, such as social, cultural, linguistic and physical anthropology. Cultural and social anthropology, now the most important areas of anthropology, have a distinctive method which requires researchers to spend extended periods in the field, observing and participating. The aim of this is to document behaviour and beliefs of the participants in cultures, societies and organizations in their own terms.

antisemitism Persecution, discrimination or prejudice against JEWS and their religion. Hostility against Jews has existed in Europe since the days of the Roman Empire, but became particularly strong in the Middle Ages. Many countries expelled Jews or barred them from certain professions, so forcing them to make a living by money-lending, banking and trade. From the time of the ▷CRUSADES, Jewish communities in Europe suffered massacres known as pogroms, but the most extreme form of antisemitism was the Nazi ▷HOLOCAUST of 1933-45, in which approximately six million Jews were systematically murdered. Antisemitism remains a feature of many extreme right-wing groups throughout the world. In South Africa, antisemitism was never formally legislated, but negative stereotyping, especially in the 1930s and 1940s, was prevalent, and tightened immigration laws controlled the movement of Jews into the country. In this period, right-wing Afrikaner movements used antisemitic rhetoric as a political tool to unite Afrikaners. After World War II there was a decrease in antisemitism, although stereotyping persisted, especially among the poorer sections of the population. The creation of Israel and the ▷ARAB-ISRAELI CONFLICT have, however, given rise to an increase in opposition to ▷ZIONISM.

antisocial personality Term applied to a person who appears to have no conscience or concern for others, and who habitually resorts to lying, stealing and violence. Antisocial behaviour, which was previously known as psychopathy, begins in childhood or adolescence, and often leads to a life of delinquency, addiction and crime.
❖ People who dislike social gatherings should be referred to as 'asocial', 'unsocial' or 'unsociable', rather than 'antisocial'.

aptitude test Test designed to measure someone's potential for achievement, rather than what they already know or can do. General aptitude tests – such as intelligence tests – measure a broad range of abilities, while special aptitude tests can measure just one type of ability, such as eye-hand coordination or mathematical skill. They are mostly used in career guidance. It is widely questioned whether aptitude tests measure innate potential or the extent to which people tested have learnt the norms of the culture in which the test is standardized.

Arabs Group of Arabic-speaking SEMITIC PEOPLES who started to migrate from the Arabian peninsula in *c*3500 BC, and are now spread throughout the Middle East and North Africa. Most Arabs are ethnically CAUCASOID in origin, but in some areas they have intermarried with local populations. Some Arab tribes, known as Bedouins, are nomads, but the majority live more settled lives. About 95 per cent of the world's Arabs are ▷MUSLIMS.
❖ Arab rulers conquered Spain in the 8th century AD and were expelled in the 15th century. They left behind masterpieces of architecture such as the ▷ALHAMBRA.

arranged marriage Union in which the MARRIAGE partner is selected by parents, relatives or a professional matchmaker, rather than by the couple themselves. The union is frequently seen as an alliance of families based on property and social status. Arranged marriages are argued to be stronger and more successful than many 'love' marriages because they carry the sanction and protection of the social group. The responsibility for the success or failure of the marriage therefore does not lie solely with the married couple. Although the custom is widespread in the East, for example among Hindus, arranged marriages were commonplace in the West among the aristocracy and royalty until World War I.

assimilation Process of being absorbed into a culture, as when settlers or refugees take on the customs and traditions of their host country. The notion that the USA is a 'melting pot' referred to the official intention, in the past, to assimilate diverse political groups. In South Africa, German and French settlers who arrived here in the 18th century were assimilated into the Dutch culture.

Azania The word used by many black people to describe South Africa. The term is thought to have originated in the Azanian civilization of east and southeast Africa, which emerged at the same time as the Zimbabwean civilization. Those who use it as an alternative for South Africa tend to reject a name associated with white minority rule and colonization. The term is widely used but it is politicized and contested.

baby boom Sudden increase in the birth rate, as happened in Britain and the USA after World War II and again during the 1960s, following a period of sustained prosperity. People born during a baby boom are sometimes called 'baby boomers'.

behaviourism School of psychology based on the study of observable behaviour. It ignores subjective experiences, such as feelings and thoughts, because they cannot be observed directly or assessed scientifically. Behaviourism developed just before World War I through the American psychologist J B Watson, who was influenced by Ivan Pavlov's discoveries about animal CONDITIONING. The theory was refined by B F SKINNER, who said that most behaviour was shaped by learning how to win rewards and avoid punishment.
❖ Behaviour therapy involves learning new patterns of behaviour in order to confront and overcome problems such as phobias, compulsions and habits such as smoking.

betrothal Engagement or promise to be married. In many Western countries it is often an informal event. In other cultures a handfasting ceremony, at which the engaged couple join hands, counts as official permission for them to sleep together. In southern Africa engagement constitutes a legal promise of MARRIAGE, and broken engagements carry legal penalties if the parties concerned wish to enforce such penalties.

BLACK LEADER *Malcolm X addresses a 1961 rally in the USA. He moved from total rejection of white culture to a more multiracial stance which led to his murder by radical Black Muslims.*

black consciousness Movement begun in the USA in the 1950s to give black people living in a white-dominated society a sense of pride in their culture and history. Black consciousness campaigners promoted important aspects of black identity, from history to music and literature. The leading figure associated with the movement in the USA was a Baptist preacher, the Rev Martin Luther ▷KING. In South Africa, the ▷BLACK CONSCIOUSNESS MOVEMENT developed as a political movement under the leadership of Steve ▷BIKO in the 1960s and 1970s. The movement was influential in opposing the racist ideologies and practices of the ▷APARTHEID state.

blue-collar Term applied to manual jobs or labourers, as opposed to WHITE-COLLAR office workers. It refers to the blue overalls and shirts traditionally worn by mechanics, factory labourers and other people who work with their hands.

body language Non-verbal communication by means of subconscious gestures, movements and physical attitudes. People's body language may contradict their spoken message, confusing the observer or betraying their true feelings. People may sound friendly, but convey hostility by standing with their hands on their hips, or liars may give themselves away by covering their mouths with their hands, as they speak. Such behaviour owes much to our animal origins, as zoologist Desmond Morris claims in his popular 'man watching' books and TV series.
❖ One sign of guilt that officials look for as travellers go through customs is licking the lips – said to be a response to inner tension.

bonding Forming of close emotional relationships – in particular, that between a mother and baby, which normally starts to happen during the first hours of life. For this reason, newborn infants are immediately given to their mothers whenever possible.
❖ Activities which have high levels of male participation, such as playing football or spending evenings in the pub, are sometimes jokingly called 'male bonding'.

brainwashing Indoctrination aimed at fundamentally altering a person's attitudes and beliefs so that he or she unquestioningly accepts a particular political or religious point of view. Techniques such as isolation, deprivation of food or sleep, hypnosis, constant repetition and even physical torture may be used to break down resistance and increase dependence on the brainwasher.

bride price Money or goods given by a bridegroom or his family to the bride's family. Bride price is most common in cultures with extended families, where the bride becomes part of her husband's family. In South Africa, the practice is most commonly referred to by the Nguni word *lobolo* or the Sotho-Tswana word *bohadi*. Controversy exists about the reasons for the payment of bride price. Early ideas saw it as payment for the bride, but this is now widely rejected. Instead, bride price is considered to be compensation to the family of the bride for the loss of her labour and reproductive capacities. It is also seen as a formal mechanism by which the bridegroom acknowledges and takes responsibility for children born in the marriage, securing their rights in the family. In southern Africa the payment of *lobolo* or *bohadi* is a process that extends through time, and failure to pay may result in a marriage being declared dissolved – even after the birth of children. In such cases the rights of children could potentially be in jeopardy.
❖ In some traditions, the bride's family pays a dowry to the groom to defray the cost of supporting her. This is probably the origin of the modern Western custom that the bride's parents pay for the wedding.

caste system Rigid social framework in which the status of a person's family determines almost every aspect of life, from permitted diet and dress to education and choice of marriage partner. It is impossible to improve one's standing by effort or by marriage. The world's most elaborate caste system is found in India, where hereditary social divisions are based on the precepts of ▷HINDUISM. *Brahmans* (priests) are holy men with the highest status. Below them are *kshatriyas* (landowners and warriors), *vaisyas* (farmers and merchants) and *sudras* (labourers). In addition there is a vast underclass of *harijans* (previously called 'untouchables') who are allowed to make a living only by performing menial tasks – collecting the rubbish or cleaning the streets, for example.

caucasoid Term devised in 1751 by Carl Linnaeus to describe one of the three great 'races' of humankind. Linnaeus' other races were NEGROID and MONGOLOID. The term 'caucasoid' was selected because Linnaeus believed they originated in the Caucasus region of eastern Europe. It is commonly used as a synonym for 'white' and to describe large population groups in Europe, North Africa, North America, southwest Asia and the Indian subcontinent. Linnaeus and other scholars of the 18th-century believed that the three 'races' were biologically and culturally homogeneous and fundamentally different from one another. Contemporary research does not support these propositions.

censorship Restriction of the free expression or exchange of ideas and information. While authoritarian regimes censor unfavourable news to suppress dissent, most democracies generally censor only to suppress extremely violent, obscene or racially abusive material, or to protect military secrets and state security. The ▷APARTHEID regime in South Africa made widespread use of censorship to achieve its political objectives, starting with

DIRTY WORK *India has long had a strict caste system. This woman, carrying dried cow dung to sell as fuel, belongs to the lowest rank, whose members were once called 'untouchables'.*

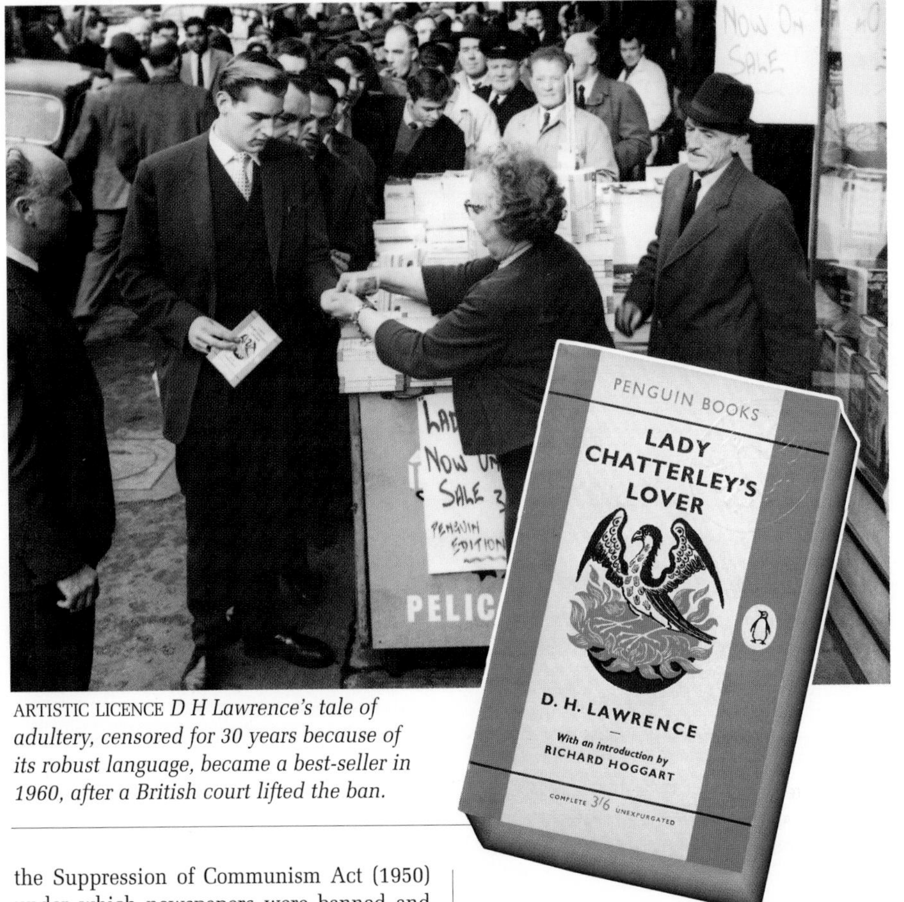

ARTISTIC LICENCE *D H Lawrence's tale of adultery, censored for 30 years because of its robust language, became a best-seller in 1960, after a British court lifted the ban.*

the Suppression of Communism Act (1950) under which newspapers were banned and banned people prohibited from being quoted or their work published. The Publications Control Board (1963) and its successor, the Directorate of Publications (1974), had wide powers to ban publications and films considered offensive or harmful to public morals or prejudicial to state security or good order. In this way the possession or distribution of thousands of publications was banned. Newspapers practised self-censorship to prevent the imposition of further control measures. In 1985, the government prohibited journalists from areas affected by a state of emergency, effectively causing a total news blackout of events in the townships. Censorship decreased considerably after the unbanning of political organizations in 1990, but restrictive legislation remained in place for some time after the first democratic election of April 1994.

❖ Early attempts at censorship in South Africa were made in the 1820s by Lord Charles Somerset, then governor of the Cape, who tried to stop publication of a newspaper and a journal.

❖ Modern technology has made censorship increasingly difficult. Electronic communications such as computer modems, satellite telephones and television stations can easily bypass the censors. Even if there is no free press in a country, photocopiers and fax machines make it possible to produce alternative news sheets.

census Population survey carried out by governments at regular intervals to obtain the statistical data they need for efficient governing. It has evolved from being simple headcount to providing detailed information about the age, occupation, lifestyle and ethnic origin of the population. Data collection and analysis is a complex and contested issue, and there are frequently large discrepancies between the official census statistics and those gathered by independent organizations. The last census in South Africa was conducted in 1991.

❖ The New Testament relates how Joseph and a heavily preganant Mary had to travel to Bethlehem in order to register for a census ordered by the Roman Emperor Augustus. As a result, Jesus was born in a manger instead of at their home in Nazareth.

chiefdom The area and the people under the authority of a chief. Membership was less by KINSHIP or 'blood' than by living in the area controlled by, and by pledging allegiance to, a particular chief. In precolonial times, chiefdoms were significant political groupings across southern Africa. Individual chiefdoms were often autonomous, but during the 19th century several chiefs, such as ▷SHAKA, ▷MOSHOESHOE and ▷MZILIKAZI, rose to prominence and brought numbers of chiefs under their authority, creating the Zulu, Basotho and Ndebele kingdoms respectively. Chiefs remain important political figures today, especially in rural areas, although their role is contested in South Africa, largely because many were used, in the ▷RESERVES and ▷BANTUSTANS, to enforce unpopular policies of segregation and apartheid.

Chomsky, Noam (1928-) American linguist whose analysis of the structure and grammar of language has produced revolutionary theories. He proposed that humanity shares a single fundamental grammar which is 'transformed' by a series of rules into all the different languages of the world. Noting the remarkable speed with which infants grasp the abstract rules of sentence construction, Chomsky suggested that humans have an instinctive, genetically programmed ability to learn languages. The existence of a universal grammar which is common to all human tongues appears to support this theory.

❖ Chomsky campaigned vigorously against US involvement in the Vietnam War, and is a well-known voice of the American left and leading critic of US imperialist tendencies.

clan Grouping of people who are ostensibly linked to one another through common ancestry or KINSHIP. The descent links may not be clear, but belief in some common relationship forms the basis of this grouping. Examples of clans include those of Africa and Scotland. Members of clans frequently do not live in a common area and a clan's significance is not felt in daily life. However, people who claim common origins are expected to be mutally supportive and clans become important for ritual reasons. Moreover, political rivalry between clans is often cited as a reason for violence. In the political language of colonial and white-minority rulers in South Africa, clan, like TRIBE, was used erroneously to imply backwardness and a failure to adapt to modern ideas and technologies.

class Denotes status or rank in industrial society based on income, occupation, education and place of residence. In a marxist sense, class refers to a grouping of people with a common relationship to the means of production. In South Africa class boundaries have been crosscut by racial categories as a result of ▷SEGREGATION legislation, including apartheid. As a result, the present class lines fall broadly along the racial classifications defined in the former Population Registration

Act, so that the working class in South Africa tends also to be people defined as black.

collective unconscious Memories and mental patterns that are shared by members of a single culture, or, more broadly, by all human beings. The psychologist Carl JUNG proposed the theory to explain recurring delusions in patients with different backgrounds, common themes in dreams, and the existence of universal ideas (or 'archetypes') which appear as similar myths in disparate cultures.

college of education Educational institution training teachers for primary and secondary schools in South Africa, also known as a teachers' training college. Cooperation between colleges and certain universities have resulted in some colleges offering primary education degrees that are conferred by the universities as well as a system of joint teacher certification that gives students degree credits for certain courses included in their diploma programmes.

coloured In South Africa, a term describing those people who, under the former Population Registration Act, were classified neither black nor white. The Act identified seven subgroups – 'Cape Coloured', 'Malay', 'Griqua', 'Indian', 'Chinese', 'Other Asiatic' and 'Other Coloured'. The term 'coloured' has been used for the offspring of 'mixed marriages', based on a notion which erroneously presumes the existence of pure races and unmixed marriages. So-called coloured people have long contested the term; some argue that it has been imposed by the State, although coloured people clearly have a range of political identities and religious affiliations, and speak different languages. During the 1980s many people who took this view identified themselves as black. However, at the beginning of the 1990s a number of people began to assert a separate coloured identity, stressing that as descendants of the Khoikhoi (Hottentots), they have a unique position as people indigenous to the Western Cape.

Comte, Auguste (1798-1857) French philosopher who founded the science of SOCIOLOGY – a term he invented. Comte believed that human society obeyed laws in much the same way as the natural world, and so could be studied scientifically, which was the goal of his philosophy of ▷POSITIVISM.

conditioning Process by which a person or animal comes to associate a certain object, sight, sound or state of affairs (known as the 'stimulus') with a pleasant or painful experience (the 'reinforcer'), so producing a particular response whenever the stimulus is present. In so-called classical conditioning, the response is usually involuntary, as when the Russian scientist, Ivan Pavlov (1849-1936), taught dogs to salivate at the sound of a bell they had learned to associate with food. In 'operant' conditioning, as it was developed by B F SKINNER, the response takes the form of voluntary behaviour; it aims at obtaining a reward or avoiding a punishment. For example, a mouse may be trained to press a lever to obtain food or avoid an electric shock.

❖ Conditioning is sometimes used to modify human behaviour. Alcoholics may be given a drug that induces nausea whenever they drink. Eventually they associate the taste of alcohol with being sick, and so find it easier to give up drinking.

cult Organization that focuses on ritual, magic or other religious observances. Many African and Oceanic peoples, for example, have ancestor cults, in which the living express respect for their dead forebears and invoke their assistance. A cult is also a religious group held together by a dominant individual. The term is often used derogatorily by members of mainstream faiths to refer to fringe groups.

❖ Religious cults in the West have often caused controversy. For example, members of the Unification Church – popularly known as ▷MOONIES – have been accused of brainwashing and extorting money from adherents.

❖ In 1978 more than 900 cult followers of the Reverend Jim Jones committed mass suicide in Guyana, and in 1993 members of David Koresh's Branch Davidian sect set fire to their compound at Waco, Texas, rather than surrender to US Government agents after complaints about the group's activities. Eighty bodies were recovered from the ruins and the government faced accusations of negligence.

❖ Millennialist groups have become popular as the end of the century approaches; Shoko Asahara's Aum Shinrikyo (Supreme Truth) sect's involvement in the 1995 poison gas attacks on Tokyo subway commuters is an example. The sect stockpiled a nerve poison, sarin, to be used in 'the final world war'.

culture Attitudes, beliefs, values and knowledge acquired through socialization. People are not born with culture, but with a capacity to acquire it through learning. The acquisition of culture – of the means to attribute meaning to human existence – is a lifelong process. Cultures are often wrongly thought of as comprising groups of people with identical attitudes, beliefs and values. This view overlooks the variability of individual experience, and often rests on the presumption that culture is inherited (like physical appearance). 'Afrikaner culture' or 'Zulu culture' is a useful generalization but does not imply that all Afrikaners or all Zulus always think and behave in the same way.

❖ Culture shock is a form of stress affecting people who have to adapt suddenly to an unfamiliar society. It is often experienced by refugees and immigrants.

defence mechanism Unconscious response which protects someone from a worrying or unpleasant experience or memory. Anger or violence could be a defensive response to fear, upset or embarrassment. Similarly, a person who feels guilty about something may produce reasons to justify his or her behaviour or blame someone else.

degree Academic award conferred by a UNIVERSITY, technikon or college on successful completion of a course or as an honorary distinction. The various faculties within a university offer undergraduate bachelor's degrees (for example BA, BCom), usually of three years' duration, and postgraduate honours (for example, BSc Hons, BEd Hons) and master's degrees (for example, MSc Eng, MSocSc) that are taken over at least one year. A doctoral degree (for example, DLitt, DArch) is the highest academic degree in any field of knowledge.

❖ A Doctor of Philosophy, PhD, is a doctoral degree awarded for original research in any subject except law, medicine or theology.

discrimination The process of differentiating between people in such a way that one is elevated over another, and is able to benefit from it. Discrimination on the grounds of 'race' was a key element in colonization, segregation and apartheid in southern Africa. SEXISM has not received as much attention as racial discrimination but is a widespread problem. Discrimination between people on the basis of skin colour, sex or creed is now unconstitutional in South Africa.

distance education Teaching system that caters for students who live in different geographical areas or who are unable to attend classes. Video, audio and written material is used in distance education; it is commonly available at secondary and tertiary level and is also popular for vocational training. In South Africa, distance education is offered by correspondence colleges, which are regulated by legislation, at least two universities – Unisa and Medunsa – one technikon and one technical college.

divorce Legal termination of marriage. In South Africa, divorce is granted when a marriage is considered to have broken down irretrievably. The grounds for divorce are adultery, desertion, insanity, sex change, 'irretrievable breakdown' and malicious desertion or withholding of conjugal rights. Other grounds sometimes recognized include prolonged unconsciousness and some forms of mental illness.

❖ South Africa's divorce rate is extremely high; it is estimated that two in five marriages end in divorce.

Durkheim, Émile (1858-1917) French social scientist and one of the first to develop SOCIOLOGY. He argued that the beliefs, attitudes and behaviour of individuals in any society are shaped by a 'collective conscience' – ideas and values shared by all of its members, and often expressed in the form of religion. His writings, including a classic work, *Suicide* (1897), are still widely studied.

ego (Latin for 'I') The 'self' or centre of a person's conscious identity and experience. The Austrian psychoanalyst Sigmund FREUD believed that there are three regions of the human mind: the unconscious ID, the rational ego and the moral SUPEREGO. In this theory the ego's task is to mediate between three contending forces – the demands of the outside world, the instinctual desires of the pleasure-seeking id and the moral strictures of the superego. It also has to control functions such as memory and problem solving.

❖ In common usage, ego means someone's self-importance or sense of superiority. For example: 'His ego is enormous – he is convinced that he is a genius at everything.'

elitism Power and privilege being held by a small group of people, or the belief in such a minority's superiority and right to dominate society. Several socio-political theories are based on the concept of elitism – some claim it is a beneficial way of organizing society, others that it is inevitable for some groups to rise to the top. Elitist theories often conflict with the ideals of equality and democracy.

empty-nest syndrome Sense of loss and purposelessness experienced by many parents when their children have grown up and leave home. Mothers without careers, who have devoted their lives exclusively to raising a family, tend to suffer most.

endogamy Marriage within specified groups, such as putative races or castes. Traditional Hindus, for example, should marry within their own CASTE. Some clans practise endogamy, insisting that members marry within the group. The purpose of this is to concentrate power and wealth within the group. Marriage outside a designated group – EXOGAMY – is much more common.

MAN, THE HUNTER *The gun strikes the only modern note in a timeless scene: dressed in a warm suit of caribou skin, this Inuit man is ready to set off in search of walrus and seal.*

equality In democratic society, equality – fair treatment, irrespective of race, sex or religion – takes several forms, including equal rights to justice and a fair trial (equality before the law), the right to be considered for a job purely on the grounds of ability and qualifications (equality of opportunity), and equal rights to vote and to stand for public office (political equality). In South Africa the debate about equality of opportunity has centred on redressing inequalities which are a result of historic discrimination. These inequalities have led to arguments in favour of programmes of AFFIRMATIVE ACTION.

Eskimo A name given to one of the ethnic categories of native peoples of Alaska, Canada, Greenland and Siberia. Eskimos are more correctly known as Inuit. Although previously HUNTER-GATHERERS, skilled in the use of their comparatively limited environmental resources, this way of life has become largely defunct, and many Eskimo people now are in regular employment as labourers in industry and trapping organizations.

ethnic cleansing Euphemism for driving ethnic minorities out of an area, either by physically removing them or by killing them. The term was often used in the early 1990s to refer to the Serbian Government's policy of creating exclusively Serb areas in the former ▷YUGOSLAVIA, which led to many atrocities.

ethnicity The notion that common origins and shared culture bind people together and has given them an identity as a group. Ethnicity can take many forms, ranging from an occasional expression of collective pride in symbols of group identity (as in ethnic festivals, cuisine and arts) to an all-encompassing sense of group loyalty. Ethnically defined groups can be mobilized for political purposes which may be positive (to resist oppression) or negative (to dominate others). The Kurds and Basques are two of the many highly politicized ethnic groups struggling to become nations in their own states. An ethnic group's members rarely have common origins: the conviction that they do, and that they possess an age-old culture, is implanted during the process of political mobilization.

ethnocentrism Understanding and judging another culture or society in terms of one's own. It usually implies that one's own culture or moral viewpoint is superior to that of the culture being judged, and one of its effects are rigid boundaries between 'us' and 'them'. Ethnocentrism is often manifested as prejudice, DISCRIMINATION or RACISM. Social anthropologists use the concept of cultural relativism – analysing behaviour and beliefs in the light of the people's own understandings – to try to reduce the possibility of making ethnocentric judgments.

euthanasia Controversial act of inducing painless death at the request of someone who is terminally ill or critically injured in order to prevent further needless suffering. In South Africa, as in many other parts of the world, active euthanasia is illegal. Passive euthanasia – refusal to prolong life artificially – is legal if the person is in a condition to make the decision, or else at the discretion of the family or doctor.

❖ In South Africa a 'living will' is a legal document which stipulates a formal refusal to be kept alive under specified conditions.

❖ In 1995 Australia's Northern Territory passed a law allowing voluntary euthanasia; it allows terminally ill patients to end their lives with the help of a doctor, after they have been diagnosed as terminally ill by two doctors and after a short 'cooling off' period (a period in which to reflect on the decision).

evolution Popular theory to describe and account for the origins of life on earth. ▷DARWIN's theory of evolution through 'the survival of the fittest' implied that only the strongest in a species usually endured and reproduced, which accounted for adaptation and diversification. Evolutionist theories were also applied in the social sciences and have frequently also been used to justify racism. As a theory of origins, evolution is strongly contested by some religious groups, including the Creationist branches of Christianity who believe God created all things.

exogamy Social requirement to marry outside of a particular group or category of people. Almost all social groups are exogamous to some extent, in that MARRIAGE to close relatives is usually TABOO. Rules of exogamy are particularly important in societies in which clans and lineages are the basis of political organization. Such rules facilitate exchanges and social alliances. ENDOGAMY, which requires choice of partner from a particular group, is less common.

extrovert Someone whose motives and actions are directed outward – towards other people or the outside world, rather than being concerned with their own inner life. Extroverts are said to have a sociable, outgoing and expressive personality, while INTROVERTS are considered to be quieter, more contemplative and reserved.

feminism Social and political movement aimed at securing equal rights for women in all spheres of life. It follows the tradition of the ▷SUFFRAGETTES, who campaigned for votes for women in the early 20th century. The many forms of current feminism range from straightforward campaigning for sexual equality to outright and often strident rejection of the male and all aspects of language and society that reflect male domination. 'Women's Lib', as it was popularly termed, was at its zenith in the early 1970s and provoked a postfeminist backlash. However, feminist approaches to literary criticism, the social sciences, history and theology are well established in those disciplines.

❖ Among the more popular and influential feminist writers world wide have been Simone de Beauvoir (*The Second Sex*), Germaine Greer (*The Female Eunuch*), Betty Friedan (*The Feminine Mystique*) and Kate Millet (*Sexual Politics*).

free association Psychological technique of exploring a person's UNCONSCIOUS mind or investigating thought processes. Words are read out one by one to a person, who is asked to say the first thing that comes to mind. A psychiatrist or psychoanalyst then interprets the responses as a way of understanding the person's thought patterns. The INKBLOT TEST is similar, but it makes use of visual rather than verbal stimuli.

DOCTOR OF THE MIND *At the age of 80, Sigmund Freud boards an aircraft for the first time. The house in Hampstead, London, where he spent his last years, is now a museum, with displays including the celebrated rug-draped couch where his patients lay for consultations.*

Freud, Sigmund (1856-1939) Influential Viennese neurologist and founder of PSYCHOANALYSIS. After training as a doctor, he became interested in mental health and investigated the subconscious mind through hypnosis, dream analysis, childhood memories and FREE ASSOCIATION. According to Freudian theories of psychoanalysis, human beings are driven by the LIBIDO – a mixture of their sex drive and survival instinct. Freud said that the human personality has three parts: the primitive, unconscious ID, the rational EGO and the SUPEREGO, or conscience. He also proposed an elaborate theory of human sexual development. Newborn infants go through an 'oral phase', in which they gain physical gratification as well as nutrition from their mouths. As toddlers, they enter the 'anal phase', in which they derive pleasure from controlling their bowel movements. Next comes a period of latent or hidden sexuality, which later gives way to the 'phallic phase' – the discovery of, and preoccupation with, the genitals. The final 'genital' stage should bring mature, loving relationships with other people. Freud's theories, especially his view that all men wrestle with the OEDIPUS COMPLEX – a combination of sexual desire for their mothers and jealousy of their fathers – were revolutionary. A Jew, Freud fled the Nazis in 1938 and settled in London. Although many of his theories are now questioned, he remains one of the most influential figures of the 20th century.

❖ A 'Freudian slip' is a verbal mistake or memory lapse which reveals an unconscious thought or emotion. For example, calling one's boss 'darling' or forgetting a dentist's appointment could signify emotional frustration or fear of the dentist.

future shock Sense of insecurity and disorientation felt by people whose societies are undergoing rapid change. The term comes from the title of a book by American author Alvin Toffler, describing the devastating effects of social and technological change in Western industrialized society, which he likened to the 'culture shock' sometimes felt by international travellers.

gay rights Movement that lobbies for recognition of the rights and social acceptance of homosexuals, both gay men and lesbian women. In South Africa the gay rights movement is relatively unknown to the general population, but its profile has improved with public processions similar to the annual 'gay pride' march in London. In Zimbabwe it has been harshly criticized by President Robert Mugabe. The general rights of homosexual people are guaranteed under the South African Constitution, but South African statutory law still makes homosexual sex an offence. In the West, gay rights movements have considerable support in some areas such as San Francisco, and are able to wield political power.

GAY RIGHTS *Displays of solidarity marked South Africa's first 'gay pride' march in October 1990 when many heterosexuals took to the streets of Johannesburg along with gays.*

gender roles Social, behavioural and cultural aspects of masculinity and femininity, as opposed to biological differences. Gender roles are continually reinforced by many aspects of social life and expectations of how each sex should behave. In many cultures, men are expected to be independent, active, ambitious and able to control their emotions; women to be dependent, sensitive, more emotional and supportive. These attitudes may have had their origins in the early human HUNTER-GATHERER lifestyle, in which males, supposedly, led an active, hunting life while females managed the demands of child rearing.

❖ Gender roles are blurring: FEMINISM has helped women to be independent, while today's 'new man' is encouraged to show his emotions, take an active part in child rearing, cook and do housework.

genocide Extermination of an entire national, racial or ethnic group, as attempted by the Nazi ▷HOLOCAUST. The Australian ABORIGINES and the San (Bushmen) of southern Africa were nearly wiped out when European settlers arrived, partly as a result of deliberate persecution, and partly because the settlers unwittingly carried diseases to which the natives had no resistance. The Ache Indians of Paraguay, the islanders of East Timor, the Kurds and the Tibetans have all suffered from genocidal oppression in recent decades.

❖ In the 1990s, Iraqi persecution of marsh-dwelling Arabs amounted to genocide: as well as taking military action against them, the authorities drained the marshes and so destroyed their habitat, forcing them to abandon their way of life and move to the towns. The Bosnian Serbs in the former Yugoslavia and the Hutus in Rwanda stand accused of genocide. Mass burials and other atrocities in these countries have shocked the world.

gestalt (German for 'form') Approach in psychology which studies responses to whole events, instead of breaking them down into constituent parts. Just as the effect of music lies in melody, tempo and orchestration rather than in the individual notes, gestalt PSYCHOTHERAPY considers the patient's overall health and analyses immediate problems, as opposed to the Freudian approach of delving into dreams and childhood memories.

ghetto Densely populated and often run-down area inhabited by poorer people. In the West ghettos are usually occupied by members of minority categories and in South Africa the term is popularly used by residents of informal and squatter settlements to refer to their substandard residential areas. Ghettos originated in the Middle Ages, when Jews were compelled to live in prescribed areas of some European cities, and the practice was revived by the Nazis in the 1930s.

❖ The term is thought to have originated from Venice's Ghetto – an iron-founding area where many Jews lived.

globalization Term for the effect that the dramatic advances in the flow of capital, people and information worldwide have on the way people see and understand the world. One example of globalization is the way in which computer-based modern technology enables people from different places of the world who have never met to communicate with one another. These flows play a significant part in altering a range of seemingly fixed IDENTITIES: national identities may be undermined by globalization, whereas other identities, such as ethnic, gender and class identities, may be strengthened.

❖ The term 'global village' was coined by the Canadian sociologist Marshall McLuhan (1911-80) to express his view that the progress and increased speed of modern communications had effectively reduced the whole world to the dimensions of a village.

'great man theory' View that human progress takes place because of the efforts of outstanding individuals – such as Mozart, Leonardo da Vinci, Napoleon and Jesus Christ. Thomas Carlyle, the 19th-century historian and the theory's creator, argued that 'the history of the world is but the biography of great men'. By contrast, the ZEITGEIST theory emhasizes the spirit of the time rather than any one person's abilities. Most historians and social scientists believe that the truth lies somewhere in between the two theories.

group therapy Form of PSYCHOTHERAPY conducted in small groups, usually supervised by a trained therapist. By sharing experiences, group members develop insight into their emotional and interpersonal problems and realize that other people have similar problems as their own.

❖ Many self-help groups, such as Alcoholics Anonymous, use group therapy techniques.

Gypsies Nomadic people found all over the world but especially in southern Europe. The origins of European Gypsies are a mystery, but their language, Romany, is related to Hindi and suggests an Indian background. Traditionally, they travelled in painted horse-drawn carriages and earned money by selling flowers and lace and telling fortunes; now, most Gypsies have motorized transport and also deal in goods and livestock. In Scotland and Ireland they are often called tinkers.

❖ The name 'Gypsy' comes from the word 'Egyptian', from a discredited theory about their origins. Gypsies usually refer to themselves as Rom or Roma (from the Romany language) or simply as 'travellers'.

hara-kiri Japanese ritual suicide by disembowelling, practised to avoid humiliation or loss of face. Many Japanese soldiers committed hara-kiri rather than surrender during World War II.

❖ In Puccini's opera *Madame Butterfly*, the main character commits hara-kiri when the American naval officer whom she believes to be her husband returns with his bride.

hippies Nonconformists drawn together in the 1960s by their rejection of standard political and social values and by their vague ideals of peace, freedom and love. The fashion began in San Francisco in the USA, fuelled by opposition to the Vietnam War, but rapidly caught on in other countries. Eastern religions such as Zen Buddhism, unkempt appearance, communal living, 'ethnic' dressing, free love and taking drugs all played a part in hippie culture, as did outdoor rock concerts such as Woodstock (1969), 'love-ins' and the declared aims of peace and 'flower power'. Hippies faded in the 1970s, but some of their ideals live on in Green parties and NEW AGE movements.

homosexuality Sexual and emotional attraction for a partner of the same sex. It may be a genetic trait, although social factors and upbringing are also thought to play a role. Homosexuality is not a medical or psychiatric disorder, but it is still regarded as immoral or abnormal by many.

❖ The GAY RIGHTS movement demands equal treatment for lesbians and gay men. Gays are not allowed in the armies of some countries.

humours Fluids in the human body whose balance, according to an ancient theory, determine a person's character and health. The four humours were seen as blood, phlegm, choler (or yellow bile) and melancholy (or black bile). The theory represented an early attempt to classify personality types.

❖ The theory of humours is reflected to this day in words describing moods, such as 'phlegmatic' (calm), 'choleric' (irascible) and 'melancholic' (gloomy, from Greek *melas*, black, and *khole*, bile).

HONOURS AND DECORATIONS

In South Africa, the president recognizes outstanding public service by citizens and foreigners with the award of national honours. An advisory body nominates the recipients of these decorations, which are usually awarded twice a year.

Order for Meritorious Service Recognizes outstanding merit and distinguished public service and is awarded in gold or silver. It was introduced in 1973 and was known as the Decoration for Meritorious Service until 1986. Recipients may use the title OMSG or OMSS after their names.

Order of the Southern Cross For achievement of a high standard which has served the national interest. The award is made in gold or silver. Established in 1986, it carries the title of OSG or OSS.

Order of the Star of South Africa (military) Awarded in gold or silver to officers of the South African National Defence Force who distinguish themselves by meritorious service of military significance. This award carrries the title of SSAG or SSAS.

Order of the Star of South Africa (non-military) Awarded for exceptionally meritorious service of military, security or national importance by civilians and civil servants, with the exception of members of the South African National Defence Force. The award is made in five classes and recipients may use the title of SSA or SSAS.

Woltemade Decoration of Bravery The highest civilian decoration for bravery in South Africa. It is awarded, in silver or gold, to citizens and foreigners in recognition of gallantry displayed in conditions of extreme danger to save or to protect the lives of South African citizens or property, or to try to do so. The medal bears a representation of the act of heroism performed by Wolraad Woltemade in 1773 when, on horseback, he rescued shipwrecked people in Table Bay. The titles used are WD or WDS.

MILITARY HONOURS

The South African National Defence Force recognizes outstanding service within its ranks with over 20 different awards which includes several decorations for bravery.

Castle of Good Hope Decoration The defence force's highest distinction for bravery which is awarded for conspicuous heroism in the field. It recognizes gallantry, single acts of valour, a daring act of self-sacrifice or extreme devotion to duty in the presence of an enemy. The award carries the title of CGH. It was instituted in 1952

Honoris Crux Diamond

Honoris Crux (all classes) Recognizing individuals from all ranks for deeds of bravery while in danger. The Honoris Crux award introduced in 1952 was extended in 1975 with the addition of diamond, gold and silver medals to distinguish different levels of bravery. Recipients of the award may use the titles HC, HCD, HCG or HCS.

hunter-gatherers Term used to describe peoples living on food and game foraged from the wild. Up to about 12 000 years ago, humans are believed to have been hunter-gatherers, living in small, usually nomadic, bands. Crop cultivation is thought to have been the first impetus to permanent settlement. Today the hunter-gatherer lifestyle is largely unviable, owing to laws controlling population movements and to the need for money. As a result, there are very few people who still practise it as a permanent lifestyle, although some PYGMIES, Australian ABORIGINES and KHOISAN may do so. (See also ▷HUNTER-GATHERERS in 'Southern African history'.)

id Primitive, instinctual, unconscious part of the human mind. Freudian psychologists believe that it is present from birth, and is the source of LIBIDO, or psychological energy, which it directs at fulfilling the basic biological needs of hunger, thirst and sex. In its efforts to satisfy the 'pleasure principle' – a strong drive to enhance pleasure and avoid pain – the *id* comes into conflict with the restraining EGO, or rational mind, and the SUPEREGO, or conscience.

identity A term denoting simultaneously the 'difference' and 'sameness' of a person. An identity document, for instance, defines its holder both as an individual and as a member of a category of people with the same identity documents. In sociological terms, individuals comprise bundles of identities, with constituent identities (woman, mother, factory worker) being more or less relevant in different contexts (at home, at work). In psychology, identity formation refers to the development, through socialization, of a balanced, integrated individual. Failure to achieve such development, or the experience of sudden disorientation, is often described as an identity crisis.

incest Sexual intercourse with a close relative, the prohibition of which is a feature of all modern human societies. In some cultures, the restrictions apply only to immediate family (parents, children and siblings); in others, aunts, uncles, cousins and in-laws are included. Incest taboos reduce the risk of genetic abnormalities arising from 'inbreeding', but scholars still dispute why they are so universal. One theory is that they protect families from the disruptive and damaging effects of sexual rivalry; another is that the rules against incest help to prepare children and adolescents for adulthood by training them to restrain their sexual desires. The anthropologist Claude LEVI-STRAUSS proposed that the incest taboo is the foundation of human culture and commerce because it forced early people to make contact with other groups and establish alliances based on exchange of both spouses and goods.

❖ Sigmund FREUD argued that the universal

MOMENT OF MANHOOD *A group of* abakwetha *(Xhosa initiates), their bodies characteristically painted white, share a meal at their isolated circumcision hut in the Eastern Cape.*

taboo against incest evolved as a result of society's desire to repress the OEDIPUS COMPLEX.

initiation Ritual marking the entry of a new member into a group; in particular the term may refer to the RITES OF PASSAGE marking the transition from childhood to adulthood. In some societies adolescents are circumcised, tatooed or scarred as part of a lengthy process, which often includes instruction in the customs and rules of adult life. Initiation is frequently an important marker of status, and applies to both females and males, although initiation ceremonies tend to be more common for males. There are widespread concerns with the health and safety aspects of some initiation practices such as male circumcision and female cliterodectomy. Other kinds of initiation practices are widespread, occurring among school children, university students, religious orders and gangs.

inkblot test Psychological assessment based on a person's responses to a standard series of abstract patterns of ink on paper. The most common method of inkblot testing is that devised by the Swiss psychiatrist Hermann Rorschach (1884-1922). The tests have been used to diagnose mental illness and even to assess creativity.

introvert Person whose interests and actions are mostly directed inward, and who usually prefers quiet, solitary contemplation to the company of others – unlike more outgoing EXTROVERTS. In practice, most people tend to display a mixture of both introvert and extrovert qualities.

IQ (intelligence quotient) Index number designed to indicate a person's intelligence. It was originally obtained by testing the subject's mental age, dividing the score by his chronological age and multiplying the result by 100. Therefore, someone whose mental age and actual age are the same has an IQ of 100. Now, more sophisticated statistical techniques are incorporated into the tests. An IQ of between 90 and 110 is considered average; most university entrants have an IQ of 120 or above. Intelligence tests have been criticized for measuring only the ability of people to pass intelligence tests, and for failing to take account of their more general skills or to allow for cultural differences.

❖ The French psychologist Alfred Binet (1857-1911) introduced the first intelligence tests in 1905.

Jews People of the Jewish faith who claim to be descended from ▷ABRAHAM, the founder of Judaism. Jews are widely dispersed in the world as a result of the ▷DIASPORA, which also produced different national and ethnic identities among them. According to Biblical references, they settled in Canaan – considered by Jews to be the present state of Israel – some 1 800 years before Christ was born. Their early history, including the migration into and flight from Egypt, is recorded in the Old Testament. After AD 70, when the Romans destroyed the second Temple, the Jews dispersed throughout Europe and the Middle East, where they were received with varying degrees of tolerance, and were often barred from certain professions. Growing ANTI-SEMITISM during the 19th century inspired the doctrine of ▷ZIONISM, which urged Jews to return to Palestine. At the turn of the 20th century, many eastern European Jews relocated to the USA and other Western countries. The sufferings during the ▷HOLOCAUST gave impetus to the founding of the state of Israel

HISTORIC SYNAGOGUE *The oldest remaining synagogue in South Africa, in St Johns Street, Cape Town, is still in use. The first service took place on Yom Kippur in 1863.*

SWISS MYSTIC *By analysing his own dreams and those of his patients, Carl Jung was able to uncover deep truths about human psychology and mythology.*

in 1948. There are about 13 million Jews today and they are a minority population in all states except Israel. South Africa's small but dynamic Jewish population is concentrated in urban centres.

Jung, Carl Gustav (1875-1961) Swiss psychologist who broke with his associate Sigmund FREUD to develop his own theories. Jung rejected Freud's emphasis on sexuality as the fundamental human drive, attempting instead to understand the unconscious mind by analysing the deep symbolism of religious experiences, myths and dreams. Many of these symbols stem from humanity's COLLECTIVE UNCONSCIOUS, which he believed was the repository of 'archetypes' – inherited, unconscious ideas and values. In studying personality, Jung coined the terms EXTROVERT and INTROVERT, and identified the existence of a feminine aspect (the *anima*) in men and a masculine aspect (the *animus*) in women.

❖ Jungian psychotherapy, a strand of which attempts to instil a sense of harmony between the patient and the human race, has influenced many NEW AGE groups.

Kamasutra Hindu classic on etiquette, home-making, marriage and the art of seduction and making love, dating from the 4th century AD. The *Kamasutra* teaches that without sensual pleasure life is incomplete, but it also advises moderation and stresses proper social behaviour. The title is Sanskrit for 'book on love'.

Khoisan Early inhabitants of southern Africa, whom European observers saw as divided into two distinct RACES. 'Hottentots', as the Khoikhoi were known by colonists, were ostensibly cattle herders, whereas the San (Bushmen) were thought to be HUNTER-GATHERERS. It now seems quite likely that this neat distinction was overstated as hunter-gatherers and cattle-herders were already living in close proximity by the time they were encountered by the Europeans, and any boundaries between them were not absolute. Seminomadic pastoralism has long since ceased to be viable, but in the Northern Cape and Namibia some people assert a Khoikhoi IDENTITY. Groups of hunter-gatherers are found in the Kalahari, but many of the descendants of Bushmen are farm labourers.

kibbutz (plural kibbutzim) Communal farm and settlement in Israel. The first kibbutz was founded by Zionist settlers in 1909, partly as an experiment in socialist living. Responsibilities such as farming, laundry, cooking and child care are shared by the residents, who work for the benefit of the community rather than for personal gain. Kibbutzim became an important part of the Israeli economy in the 1950s, supplying more than one-third of Israel's agricultural output and often growing crops from exceedingly poor soil and dry land; most settlements now run factories as well as farms.

BOOK OF LOVE *An 18th-century Indian bride feeds her husband sweetmeats, as recommended by the* Kamasutra, *whose advice on married life ranges from gardening to sex.*

Kinsey, Alfred (1894-1956) American zoologist and social scientist who investigated sexual behaviour. His findings, published in 1948 and 1953 in two books, popularly known as the 'Kinsey Reports', shattered existing conceptions of the nature and extent of American sexual practices. For example, his studies revealed that more than half of all American men were unfaithful to their wives. Kinsey's interviewing and statistical methods have been criticized, but his reports have had an enormous impact.

❖ By showing that many sexual practices considered perversions were in fact quite common, Kinsey's work is said to have hastened the arrival of the PERMISSIVE SOCIETY.

kinship Social relationship based on ties through ancestry and associations such as marriage and adoption. In some communities kinship is a major factor in social structure, involving everyone in a complex network of rights and obligations. This is particularly true of impoverished areas or where there is frequent face-to-face contact. Kinship is also often the determining factor in inheritance and social rights and obligations, especially as the latter affect children.

Laing, R D (Ronald David) (1927-89) Controversial Scottish psychiatrist who became well known in the 1960s for his criticism of conventional ▷PSYCHIATRY, which inspired a radical movement known as 'antipsychiatry'. Laing believed that conditions such as ▷SCHIZOPHRENIA could be understood as a form of desperate retreat from the stress of dealing with other people, especially the patient's immediate family. He advocated GROUP THERAPY and other forms of PSYCHOTHERAPY instead of the use of drugs.

language Although many animals use signs, sounds and gestures to communicate, true language belongs exclusively to human beings. Unlike the fixed patterns and set messages of birdsong and whale calls, our languages can convey an infinite number of different meanings once their vocabularies and grammars have been learned. Language enables humankind to transmit culture, to store and communicate information, and, according to many philosophers, even to think. It is not known how and when speech was first set down; the earliest traces of writing – ▷CUNEIFORM script from ancient Sumeria –

date from *c*5000 BC. Languages are divided into several main families and dozens of subfamilies, according to their origins, which are traced by similarities in grammar and vocabulary. One of the largest groups is the ▷INDO-EUROPEAN family, which includes languages as varied as English, Greek and Hindi. The dominant group in southern Africa is the ▷BANTU LANGUAGES.

Leakey, Louis (1903-72) British archaeologist and anthropologist known for his discoveries of early human fossil remains at Olduvai Gorge in Tanzania. Working with his wife Mary and his son Richard, both of whom have made their own important finds, Leakey found traces of human ancestors dating back more than 3 750 000 years, and showed that humankind probably evolved in Africa.

Levi-Strauss, Claude (1908-) French social anthropologist who applied STRUCTURALISM – defining cultural and social phenomena as parts of an overall system – to analyse and explain subjects such as kinship, marriage, ritual and language. Levi-Strauss concluded that apparently dissimilar beliefs and practices often had the same underlying structures.

libido Fundamental energy which motivates every human being, according to Sigmund FREUD. In Freudian psychology, the libido expresses the ID's basic biological drives of sex and hunger; through sublimation it is redirected to become the basis of all human enterprise and culture.

'Lucy' Nickname given to the most complete skeleton ever found of the early human ancestor *Australopithecus*. She was discovered in Ethiopia in 1974. About one metre tall, Lucy lived some three million years ago, walked upright, and suffered from arthritis – even though she was only 40 years old when she died. Remnants of the skeletons of human ancestors who lived 4 400 000 years ago were found nearby in 1994.

❖ The first *Australopithecus* skull, known as the 'Taung child' after the region in the Northern Cape where it was found, was identified in the 1920s by University of the Witwatersrand anatomist Raymond ▷DART.

OUT OF LUCK *New York Mafia boss Charles 'Lucky' Luciano (second from right) is led away from court in 1936, after he was sentenced to 30 to 50 years in jail for pimping and extortion.*

Mafia International crime syndicate, based in Sicily, which makes money from protection rackets, gambling, prostitution and other illegal activities. Until the 1980s, brutal intimidation and family loyalties had kept most of the *mafiosi* out of court.

❖ The activities of the American Mafia were the subject of the ▷GODFATHER films directed by Francis Ford Coppola, based on books written by Mario Puzo.

Malinowski, Bronislaw (1884-1942) Polish anthropologist known for his theory of functionalism, which asserted that social institutions develop in response to people's needs. His painstaking studies of the Pacific Trobriand islanders established new standards of accuracy and observation.

mankind Members of the family *Hominidae*, of which human beings (*Homo sapiens*) are the only surviving example. Humans are thought to share a common ancestor with chimpanzees and apes, but they developed larger brains than other ▷PRIMATES and started walking upright. The use of language, tools and the ability to think in abstract terms also distinguishes humankind – a more inclusive term – from other primates.

Maori Polynesian people who were the first inhabitants of New Zealand. They are thought to have migrated there, some perhaps from Tahiti, in *c*AD 900. The Maori people have rich traditions, especially in carving,

EVOLUTION OF HUMANKIND

Australopithecus 4,8-1,1 million years ago	Africa	Early human-like apes, closely related to chimpanzees and gorillas. They varied in height from 0,9 m to nearly 1,8 m, had a brain one-third the size of ours, and walked upright.
Homo habilis 2,3-1,4 million years ago	East Africa	Long-armed scavenger-hunters, 1,2-1,5 m tall, with protruding jaws and brains half the size of ours. They lived in organized social groups, used crude tools and probably communicated with basic speech.
Homo erectus (Java man, Peking man) 1,9 million- 300 000 years ago	Africa, Europe, Asia	Thick-set, muscular species 1,5-1,8 m tall, with sloping forehead, receding jaw and large brain (60-80 per cent of the average today). They had fire, huts, some sort of speech, specialized tools, crude rituals and advanced hunting techniques.
Homo sapiens (Neanderthal Man, modern man) 300 000 years ago to present	Worldwide	Large-brained, adaptable species with wide regional differences. They had complex social organizations, advanced speech and tool-making skills. Modern humans (subspecies *Homo sapiens sapiens*) emerged about 120 000 years ago, and displaced all rivals to colonize the world.

MASAI DANCE *Dressed in traditional robes, young* moran *(warriors) sing and take turns to make spectacular jumps into the air.*

dance, storytelling and the skills of seafaring. In the 19th century the Maori lost much of their land and culture under British rule. However, recent policies have started to undo the damage: Maori became an official language in New Zealand in 1987, and public information is now often published in both Maori and English.

❖ Before contact with Europeans, the Maori had elaborate tattoos that reflected their social status – a custom now being revived.

marriage The official union of a man and a woman is common in every society and helps to ensure children's rights to kinship and care. Monogamy – marriage to one person at a time – is the general rule, but there are many variations. Polygamy allows more than one spouse: polygyny is the practice of taking more than one wife, while polyandry, which is less common but still exists in Tibet, allows a woman to take several husbands simultaneously. In southern African customary law polygynous marriages were permitted, although conventional law did not recognize the legal status of more than one wife. In some countries, such as Britain, homosexual marriages are legal. ARRANGED MARRIAGES are still common in some cultures. In South Africa, girls may marry from age 12, and boys from age 14, with the consent of their legal guardians and the Minister of Home Affairs.

Masai East African peoples, most of whom live as nomadic cattle-herders. They have an unusual social hierarchy based on age groups: people born at the same time progress en masse through the stages of INITIATION and adult life to become elders.

matriarchy Society in which power is held by women. Many 19th-century anthropologists believed that the earliest societies were matriarchies, and that male domination, or PATRIARCHY, developed much later.

Mead, Margaret (1901-78) American anthropologist whose book *Coming of Age in Western Samoa* (1928) raised public awareness of cultural anthropology. She rejected the idea that adolescence was inevitably stressful, and identified important links between culture and personality. Mead's assertion that culture was more important than biology in determining GENDER ROLES had a powerful influence on feminism. She also studied the American Omaha Indians and Pacific tribal peoples, notably in Papua New Guinea.

migrancy Usually associated with the movement of men between a rural base and an urban workplace, although women are also migrants. Migration in southern Africa has had a devastating effect on family life; often women and children are left to cope in impoverished rural areas while men are away for long periods. The tensions generated between migrants and other urban residents, and among migrant workers themselves, have been associated with violence in hostels; migrancy is also implicated in rural feuds. (See also ▷MIGRANT LABOUR in 'Southern African history'.)

modern era The historical period marked by colonialism and the initial thrust for independence of the colonies. In this period society was understood and described largely by theories of structural-functionalism, which characterized it as a structure comprising other structures, all functioning together to create social order and balance. Such philosophies did not take account of change or conflict and tended to depict society as static and homogeneous – aspects criticized in postmodern discourses. (See also ▷MODERNISM in 'English and world literature'.)

modernism Idea that rose to prominence in the modern era – the age of industrialization and expansion of capitalism around the world. Modernist philosophies entailed the idea of the inevitable progress and perfectability of social and cultural arrangements. It often led to social engineering on a vast scale, such as communism in Europe. Apartheid in South Africa can be seen as another version of the modernist ideal. The authority of modernist philosophies is criticized in postmodern discourses.

mongoloid In an early attempt at classification of humankind, this term, alongside CAUCASOID and NEGROID, was used to describe the largest population division which included Chinese, Japanese, Malayan, Mongolian and ESKIMO people. The categorization was made on the basis of phenotype (physical appearance), and Mongoloid people were thought to have little body hair, prominent cheekbones, and dark eyes with an 'epicanthic' fold, which ostensibly provided protection against cold or stopped sand from blowing into the eyes. Its use is widely rejected outside of biological research.

Montessori, Maria (1870-1952) Italian educationalist who developed the Montessori method of teaching preschool children using an informal approach of constructive play in a stimulating environment to encourage a child to want to learn.

multiculturalism The championing of cultural diversity. Advocates of multiculturalism believe that in a multiethnic society equal weight should be given to the different traditions of its members, instead of imposing a homogeneous dominant culture on all. In South Africa, where it is commonly assumed that several different, distinct and homogeneous cultures exist, the question of how to acknowledge difference – while at the same time not allowing the recognition of difference to destroy attempts at nation-building – is a matter of ongoing debate.

Native Americans Descendants of the first inhabitants of North and South America, commonly called American Indians or, incorrectly, Red Indians. They originally came from Asia, and are thought to have crossed to North America between 40 000 and 12 000 years ago, when the two continents were joined by a land bridge at what is now the Bering Strait. In the 15th century, when Christopher ▷COLUMBUS reached the Americas, there were about two million Native Americans in the north, living in about 200 different groups and speaking nearly as many languages. While North America was dominated by warrior groups such as the Iroquois, Apache and Sioux, the great ▷MAYA, ▷AZTEC and ▷INCA civilizations flourished in Central and South America. European settlement brought bloody land wars and the

TRADITIONAL DRESS *Men of the Montana-based Crow tribe of Native Americans show off their feathered headdresses and beads.*

collapse of Native American cultures, apart from a few remote groups such as the Amazonian Indians of Brazil. In the 19th century, Native Americans in Canada and the USA were driven into restricted areas or reservations. Since the 1960s, they have campaigned to establish their land rights and increase their civil rights.

❖ The traditional image of the Native American, with headdress and bow and arrow, is based on the Plains Indian groups such as the Sioux, Cheyenne and Crow.

nature-nurture debate Long-standing controversy about whether genetic or environmental factors have a greater influence on personality and abilities. It has led to violent disagreements over sensitive issues: for example, some might argue that criminals are born delinquent, while others believe that a bad environment or upbringing is largely to blame for criminal behaviour.

negroid Category derived from early classifications of humankind by RACE, and based on appearance – as, for example, CAUCASOID and MONGOLOID. It was used as a synonym for 'black' people and to describe most of the indigenous African people south of the Sahara, and their descendants now living in many other parts of the world. So-called negroid populations living in the USA, Brazil and the West Indies are the descendants of slaves brought across from Africa by slave traders between the 16th and 19th centuries to work on plantations. In the West, particularly in the USA, the term Negro was used as a rallying point in order to protest against racial discrimination, but it is being replaced by 'African American'.

New Age Term for a wide range of activities and ideas united by a common aim to replace modern materialism with new spiritual values. The New Age 'movement' is a loose alliance of groups interested in subjects such as Eastern religion, environmental issues, the psychology of Carl JUNG, astrology, alternative medicine and the occult. Some New Agers reject conventional religion in favour of ancient pagan beliefs. The name 'New Age' comes from the astrological theory that the Earth is now entering the 'Age of Aquarius' – supposedly heralding a period of world harmony and a heightened spiritual consciousness in most people.

❖ So-called 'New Age travellers' lead a nomadic HIPPIE life, touring the countryside in battered vans and buses, occasionally converging for festivals, such as at Glastonbury in Somerset, England.

NGO Nongovernmental organization funded from sources outside of government. These organizations are frequently involved in attempts to democratize local structures and their work is often characterized by a 'bottom-up' as opposed to a 'top-down' approach. NGOs' role in human rights monitoring has been important all over the world, but increasingly their work is shifting from welfare to development. In South Africa this shift has been complicated by the political role NGOs played in 'the struggle' for democratic rule. The status of NGOs in relation to the State has become unclear, particularly as donors are now able to give direct financial assistance to a government which is perceived as legitimate. Donors therefore no longer need NGOs to the same extent for development projects.

nuclear family Family group consisting of a mother, father and children living together, as opposed to the larger extended family, which would include grandparents, cousins, uncles and aunts as well. Today many believe that the nuclear family, supposedly standard in Western societies, is endangered by a high divorce rate and a growing number of ONE-PARENT FAMILIES. Increasingly, however, it is being recognized that nuclear families are not necessarily the norm or even the most appropriate or effective in rearing children.

Oedipus complex According to Freudian theory, the unconscious desire of every young boy to have sexual intercourse with his mother and destroy his father – the rival for her love. Sigmund FREUD said that the complex (which appears in girls as the 'Electra complex' – sexual desire for the father and rivalry with the mother) develops between the ages of three and five, but is repressed, only to be resolved in an adult relationship with someone who 'reawakens' the doomed love for the unattainable parent. Freud claimed that these Oedipal feelings were at the root of many neuroses, but modern psychoanalysis regards them as one factor among many, and some practitioners ignore them.

❖ The complex is named after the mythical Greek king ▷OEDIPUS, who unwittingly killed his father and married his mother.

one-parent family Families in which one adult raises children alone. In southern Africa single-parent families are common among poorer sections of the population. Its two major causes are high rates of illegitimate births, usually associated with developing countries, and migrant labour practices which attract men to urban areas while leaving women and children behind in rural areas. One-parent families are also caused by soaring divorce rates in the developed world, where the stigma attached to single-parenting is declining.

oral tradition Aspects of culture passed on by word of mouth. In literate societies it is generally associated with folklore, but in cultures without writing it occupies a much more prominent position as the only way of recording history, myth and literature. The indigenous people of southern Africa and Australian Aborigines, for example, have outstanding oral traditions.

❖ The Bible and Homer's epics the ▷ILIAD and the ▷ODYSSEY were part of ancient Greek oral tradition for centuries before they were written down, though at different stages.

ostracism Banishment or isolation from society or from a particular group, used as a form of punishment. In its most extreme form, the person is treated as if dead, as in observant Jewish families, where parents may actually hold a funeral for a child who marries outside the faith.

❖ The word comes from the Greek *ostraka* – fragments of broken pottery on which ancient Athenians wrote the names of those they wished to have exiled from the city.

paternalism Fatherly style of management or rule where those in authority provide for people's needs but without allowing those people to have full rights or responsibilities. It is the basis of political systems such as ▷IMPERIALISM and ▷TOTALITARIANISM, and is sometimes an aspect of a company's staff policy: works outings and corporate private health schemes are paternalistic in character.

patriarchy Society in which men wield most of the power. This may mean simply that political decisions and public discussions are dominated by males, or that men hold absolute power over women and children in both public and domestic arenas. Some feminists argue that patriarchy is deeply rooted in religion, language and social structures, and is continually reinforced by popular culture.

peerage The six tiers of British nobility. These are royal duke, duke, marquess, earl, viscount and baron or baroness. Since 1958, nonhereditary life peers have also been created. All peers are entitled to sit in the British House of Lords, providing they are over 21 years of age, have British nationality and are not felons, bankrupts or lunatics. Archbishops rank between royal dukes and dukes, and bishops rank between viscounts and barons.

permissive society Term popularly used to describe the relative sexual and moral freedom that has prevailed in Western societies since the 1960s.

Piaget, Jean (1896-1980) Swiss psychologist known for his work on mental development in childhood. By careful observation, he concluded that intellectual development took place in set stages that could not be artificially altered or speeded up: for example, he argued that until the age of about seven children cannot think logically or fully accept that other people have opinions. Piaget's work has influenced primary school teaching methods throughout the world.

political correctness Policy of avoiding anything that may be offensive to certain people or categories of people, such as racist or sexist language and imagery. Political correctness is most apparent in its attempt to change people's vocabulary, for example replacing words such as 'mentally retarded', 'physically disabled' or 'short' with 'learning disabled', 'differently abled' and 'vertically challenged'. There is concern that political correctness involves a monolithic set of 'correct' attitudes which are often imposed in an inflexible manner.

population Assessing the increase, composition and distribution of the world's people is an important task at both national and international levels. The rapid growth of world population this century, from 2,5 billion people in 1925 to nearly 5,66 billion in 1994, has caused great concern; it is forecast that it will be 8,3 billion by the year 2025. This trend defied the prediction of the British economist Thomas ▷MALTHUS in 1801 that population growth would inevitably be checked by war, famine, disease or natural disaster. According to some estimates, more people are alive today than the total number of those who have died since humankind evolved.

postmodernism The current historical period of disenchantment with MODERNISM. Postmodernism provides a critique of the monolithic and hegemonic theories of Modernism. It argues strongly that human experience is neither unified nor discrete, but much more complex, frequently conflictual and fragmented. It tries to reveal the absent 'voices' in analyses and as such its philosophy is closely identified with the women's liberation movement and other ideological organizations of this ilk. (See also ▷POSTMODERNISM in 'Architecture and engineering'.)

poverty datum line (minimum living level) A statistical assessment, previously known as 'the breadline', of the minimum income presumed to be sufficient to sustain a family, maintain acceptable standards of health and hygiene and to provide for sufficient clothing needs. It is calculated biannually according to the size, gender composition, age structure and geographical location of family units. A large proportion of southern Africa's population, particularly those in rural areas, lives below the poverty datum line.

psychoanalysis Form of PSYCHOTHERAPY developed by Sigmund FREUD, based on the theory that mental and emotional problems are rooted deep in the UNCONSCIOUS mind. Psychoanalysis uses skilful questioning, FREE ASSOCIATION, dream analysis, and other methods to help to discover the causes of personal difficulties, which are often traced back to early childhood traumas. Insight into these can take several years to achieve, but once attained, it is claimed that it can resolve mental disorders completely.

psychology Study of human and animal behaviour and all its processes. Psychologists study emotions, perception, memory, development, intelligence, behaviour, personality, mental illness and the relationship between mind and body. Psychology encompasses dozens of schools and divisions, but the lack of a unified approach and difficulty in definitely proving anything, means that it is not always considered a mainstream science.
❖ Unlike ▷PSYCHIATRY, which is concerned with curing mental disorders, psychology is not a branch of medicine.

psychotherapy Generic term for all forms of nonmedical treatment for mental, emotional or behavioural problems. It includes counselling, PSYCHOANALYSIS and GROUP THERAPY, and aims at helping people to achieve personal insight and self-development.

purdah Tradition in some Hindu and Muslim cultures of barring women from public life and male society. Today it is rarely practised by Hindus, but it remains part of Muslim tradition, although many Muslims disapprove.
❖ The word 'purdah' is derived from the Hindi *pardā* – the screen or veil used to section off the women's quarter from the men's quarter in the home.

Pygmies Small-built people found in parts of central Africa, most of whom are under 1,5 m tall. A few groups still follow a traditional HUNTER-GATHERER way of life in the forests of the Congo basin.

race Scientific term used to divide human populations on the basis of appearance, particularly skin colour. It is widely used and frequently confounded with assumptions about culture. However, race has little analytic value in that variations within these populations tend to be greater than that which occurs between them. The United Nations has rejected the use of the term, but RACISM is a widespread phenomenon.
❖ Three terms that are frequently confused are antiracialism, multiracialism and nonracialism. Antiracialism recognizes that people hold stereotypes about one another based on physical appearance, but rejects such racialism. Multiracialism holds that race exists as a form of social categorization and that differences resulting from race should be accepted and acknowledged. Nonracialism rejects any notion of racial difference as a basis for ordering society.

racism The practice of reviling certain categories of people on the basis of their appearance, especially skin colour. Racist ideology, combined with the needs of capitalism in southern Africa, defined the basis of discriminatory laws which culminated in ▷APARTHEID policies. Complex interactions between racism and economics also underpinned the slave trade, the genocide of indigenous peoples, and the persecution of JEWS and other minorities.

refugees In 1995 there were an estimated 45 million displaced people in the world, with the number of refugees having grown steadily since 1945. By the early 1990s almost 5 million people had fled conflict in the former ▷YUGOSLAVIA. The war in Afghanistan during the 1980s displaced 6 million people, and a similar number (including 1,7 million Mozambicans, and 1,5 million Rwandans who fled the violence that flared after President

Juvénal Habyarimana was killed in 1994) have suffered as a result of wars and persecution in Africa. Hopes for the resolution of the most enduring refugee problem since 1945, that of Palestinians who fled Israel after its foundation in 1948, were raised following Israel's peace accord with the ▷PLO in 1993 and with ▷JORDAN in 1994.

rites of passage Ceremonies that mark important transitions in a person's life, such as birth, puberty, marriage, having children, and death. Rites of passage usually involve rituals designed to single out certain individuals, mark their transition or INITIATION, and then reincorporate them back into society.

self-determination Demand for freedom from external domination, as by nations within empires and colonized peoples under imperial control. Ethnic self-determination involves peoples, often minorities, who have been subsumed in modern nation states. Examples of such demands are those of some Welsh and Basques. The ▷APARTHEID regime in South Africa adopted self-determination in its policy of developing separate homelands for different ethnic groups. Conservative groups in the country have also used the notion of self-determination to question the transition to a democracy based on universal adult franchise. Self-determination in a ▷VOLKSTAAT has increasingly become the rallying call of right-wing Afrikaners.

Semitic peoples Ancient CAUCASOID peoples of the Middle East, including the Babylonians, Phoenicians, Assyrians and Egyptians. The term is now used to refer to the JEWS and ARABS, who are supposedly descended from Shem, the son of Noah.
❖ Hebrew, Arabic and other Semitic languages have a system of writing whose characters represent consonants only. Vowels are indicated by marks above and below the text, or are simply left to the reader to infer.

serial killer Multiple murderer whose crimes take place over a period of time. One of the first serial killers was Jack the Ripper, who murdered at least five London prostitutes in the 1880s. More recently in Britain, Frederick West was charged in 1994 with the murders of 12 women at and around his Gloucester homes; his wife Rosemary was charged with nine. Peter Sutcliffe (1946-), the 'Yorkshire Ripper', killed 13 women between 1975 and 1981, and Dennis Nilsen (1945-) confessed to strangling 15 men. In the USA, Jeffrey Dahmer (1960-) killed 17 people before being arrested, and Ted Bundy (1946-89) killed 23 women in a six-year spree of rape and murder. Several suspected serial killings have occurred in South Africa but have rarely been proved in court. The 'Station Strangler' intercepted schoolboys at Cape Town's railway stations during the 1980s and 1990s before he raped and killed them. The Cleveland killer and the Atteridgeville killer who operated on the Reef in the 1990s preyed on women.

SEA OF SHANTIES *Crossroads, one of South Africa's best-known squatter settlements, stretches as far as the eye can see on the Cape Flats in the Western Cape.*

sexism Sexual prejudice is underpinned by long-standing assumptions about what constitutes 'natural' or 'normal' behaviour for both men and women. Some argue that the sexes behave differently for cultural, rather than biological, reasons, and that, given equal opportunities, men and women can achieve equal distinction in almost every field. Others believe that physical differences – especially women's ability to give birth – and innate psychological differences create fundamental dissimilarities between the sexes which should be recognized.

Skinner, B F (1904-90) American psychologist who concluded that most behaviour, both human and animal, is learnt by trial and error. Skinner's theory of 'operant CONDITIONING' argued that people and animals repeated actions that brought rewards – 'positive reinforcement' – and avoided actions that brought punishment – 'negative reinforcement'. He suggested that these methods could be used to modify behaviour and, controversially, to solve social and political problems.

Slavs Central and east European peoples with a shared cultural and linguistic background. They include the Russians, Ukrainians, Byelorussians, Poles, Slovaks, Czechs, Serbians, Bulgarians and Croats. In the 3rd or 2nd millennium BC, Slavs migrated from Asia to remote parts of Russia, from where they spread in the 5th century, eventually becoming Christian by contact with the ▷BYZANTINE EMPIRE.
❖ The Slavs have a long history of persecution at the hands of other Europeans. During World War II, many millions died at the hands of the Nazis, who condemned them as subhuman *Untermenschen*, fit only for slave labour and slaughter.
❖ The word 'slave' is derived from 'slav'.

sociology Study of human society, often with the aim of identifying the causes of social change. The term was coined by the 19th-century French philosopher Auguste COMTE, who suggested that human behaviour and institutions could be studied using scientific methods. There are many different areas of study, ranging from social interaction in a family to the sociology of entire countries. Approaches to the subject range from the individualism of Max WEBER to Émile DURKHEIM's view that society has a separate existence of its own.

squatters Popular term for people living in housing which does not meet the requirements of municipal bylaws. 'Squatter' generally means a person occupying land illegally, while shanty towns which have legal status are more correctly known as informal settlements. In South Africa, the term usually refers to Africans living either on white-owned rural land or in informal or irregular settlements in towns. For much of the 20th century, attempts were made to remove rural squatters, the most effective measures being taken by the ▷APARTHEID regime. The shacks of urban squatters were frequently bulldozed in the 1970s, but in the 1980s the government began tolerating squatting in limited areas.

Steiner, Rudolf (1861-1925) Austrian philosopher whose name is associated with the international Waldorf School movement that provides holistic education tailored to the psychological make-up of each child, also catering specifically for so-called maladjusted children. Steiner believed human capacity for spiritual perception had become dulled by the material preoccupations of the modern world. Waldorf schools emphasize art, movement and drama.

structuralism Philosophical movement of the 20th-century which studies the structures and systems behind observable social and cultural phenomena. It developed out of the work of the Swiss linguist Ferdinand de Saussure (1857-1913), who saw language as a superficial system of signs cloaking deep underlying principles. The French anthropologist Claude LEVI-STRAUSS took a similar approach to anthropology, and proposed, among other things, that the regulations of KINSHIP are based on universal rules of communication and exchange, and that myths reflect the structure or workings of the unconscious mind. Structuralism also influenced literary criticism.

superego In Freudian psychology, the conscience, or part of the mind that acts as a rational, inner check on behaviour. As such, it is often in conflict with the ID.

taboo Symbolic or ritual ban on a person, object, action or word. The concept has now been extended to anything regarded with dread. Every culture has a taboo against INCEST. For Jews and Muslims, the eating of pork is taboo.
❖ The word 'taboo' comes from *tabu*, a Polynesian word for 'sacred', applied to objects reserved for religious use only.

technical college Institution specializing in vocational education that prepares students for the work situation. In South Africa technical colleges' study programmes are assessed for approval by the South African Certification Council. Some colleges have accreditation agreements with TECHNIKONS which help students to pursue their studies at the technikons. Technical colleges also offer nonformal education such as enrichment, language and literacy courses.

technikon Institution providing tertiary education for middle and high-level human resources in technology. Technikons in South Africa provide diploma courses that are approved by the Certification Council for Technikon Education; they may also provide degree studies and confer technikon degrees.

tribe People assumed to have a shared lineage, origin, language and customs, such as the three divisions of ancient Roman society and the 12 tribes of Israel. Colonial authorities applied the term to CHIEFDOMS in areas such as Africa and New Guinea, either to facilitate administration or in the mistaken belief that the political groupings were made up of people with family ties who came from the same region and shared a unique language and customs. The idea that tribes are intrinsic to Africa, and that membership of a tribe marks a person's basic IDENTITY, has become controversial and the concept has been rejected as racist.

tribalism Based on the idea that members owe loyalty to a TRIBE, the concept of tribalism has been used by politicians to mobilize followers on the grounds of their assumed common origin and shared CULTURE. Tribalism has often been more pronounced in urban rather than rural areas, since cities bring together people from diverse localities and cooperation with people from the same area is useful as a means of informal organization in new surroundings. The term is often perceived as insulting, in that it is reserved for the 'third world', whereas the same political or social mobilization in the 'first world' would be termed 'ethnic' or 'nationalist'.

tsotsis Name given to gangsters resident in densely populated urban areas of South Africa. Distinctive in their mode of dress, such gangsters also speak a unique street language, *tsotsitaal,* which is a mixture of African languages with Afrikaans and English phrases. Tsotsis are renowned as criminals and perpetrators of violence.

ubuntu A Bantu word roughly translated as 'humanity'. It expresses the philosophical idea that people are constituted as human through their relationships with one another rather than through their personal attributes. Personhood is therefore understood within the context of social interaction. From this perspective, *ubuntu* defines the core of what it is to be a social and moral human being. *Ubuntu* is claimed as a traditional value of African people and cultures.

unconscious Part of the mind whose thoughts and processes are hidden from the conscious mind. In the psychology of Sigmund FREUD, the unconscious contains the deep primitive impulses of the ID, together with repressed memories and desires. These can be retrieved only by PSYCHOANALYSIS, but can be expressed also in dreams and imagination. Carl JUNG believed there also was a deeper COLLECTIVE UNCONSCIOUS.

university An institution for tertiary education, usually with research facilities, which awards bachelor's and more advanced DEGREES. South Africa's universities are controlled by their own councils and administer their own affairs and admission policies.

Victoria Cross The highest decoration for bravery in the face of the enemy, awarded to citizens of Britain and the ▷COMMONWEALTH. The award is named after Queen Victoria who instituted it in 1858.

Weber, Max (1864-1920) German sociologist especially known for his work on political leadership, bureaucracy and capitalism. He said political change was often attributable to exceptional leaders such as Charlemagne or Napoleon who had 'charisma' – a term, meaning 'divine gift', that he borrowed from Christian theology. He also linked ▷PROTESTANTISM with the rise of ▷CAPITALISM: he believed that Protestant ideals of hard work, frugal living and self-control were responsible for capital being available for investment.

white-collar Colloquial description of non-manual workers such as office and shop staff, who are expected to dress more formally than BLUE-COLLAR, or manual, labourers. Although they generally receive monthly salaries rather than weekly wages, many are members of trade unions; some still consider themselves working class.

Xhosa Group of Bantu-speaking peoples, the majority of whose members live in the Eastern Cape province of South Africa. Xhosa is one of the most widely spoken African languages in the country.

yuppie Journalistic nickname, and in part an acronym, for 'Young Urban (or Upwardly mobile) Professional', meaning a career-orientated, hard-headed young adult who flaunts his or her prosperity. Yuppies appeared during the 1980s, but in the slump of the 1990s many lost fortunes made in the money markets and property.

Zeitgeist German word meaning 'spirit of the time', embodying the view that human achievements reflect or develop from the essential character of an era. The opposite point of view, that history is made by the actions of a few exceptional individuals, is known as the 'GREAT MAN THEORY'.

Zulu Group of Bantu-speaking peoples, the majority of whose members live in KwaZulu-Natal. They were wielded into a kingdom by the early 19th century chief Shaka, a military genius.

SOUTHERN AFRICAN HISTORY

For hundreds of years African chiefdoms were the only inhabitants of southern Africa. Then, from the late 1400s the first white people – European sailors searching for a sea route to India – started visiting the shores of the southern part of the continent. In 1652 the Dutch set up a refreshment station at the Cape and soon the first settlers began arriving. In South Africa, white permanency sparked a struggle with the African people that lasted for almost 340 years – and resulted in a settlement and the start of a new order that confounded all predictions.

MONUMENT TO A YOUNG LANGUAGE *Soaring upwards on Paarl Rock, the three columns of the Taalmonument, unveiled in 1975, symbolize the varied influences that shaped Afrikaans.*

Abdurahman, Dr Abdullah (1872-1940) Physician and politician who was the first coloured person to be elected a member of the Cape Town City Council and the Cape Provincial Council. As president of the AFRICAN PEOPLE'S ORGANIZATION from 1905 until his death, Abdurahman was throughout that period the most prominent coloured political figure in the country.

❖ His daughter, Cissie Gool (1897-1963), was a powerful fighter against SEGREGATION, and served for many years as a member of the Cape Town City Council.

African Mineworkers' Union Formed in 1941 to campaign against the MIGRANT LABOUR system in South Africa and to fight for better conditions for African miners, it grew rapidly in strength, although initially its officials were banned from entering African housing compounds. In 1946 it led its members into a strike, crushed violently by the UNITED PARTY Government.

African People's Organization For 40 years after its founding in Cape Town in 1902, this was the leading coloured political organization. Its goal was equality with whites for its members. Associated closely with its president, Abdullah ABDURAHMAN, and with the newspaper he edited, the 'APO', it declined in importance in the late 1930s as a more radical generation challenged its conservatism and formed the NATIONAL LIBERATION LEAGUE.

Afrikaans language movement Muslims in Cape Town who spoke Arabic were the first to write down ▷AFRIKAANS, but the campaign for its official recognition was taken up from the 1870s by protagonists such as S J DU TOIT and other whites who advocated its use as an alternative to Dutch. After the SOUTH AFRICAN WAR, in response to attempts at ANGLICISATION, the language was again forcefully promoted, and in 1925 it was recognized as the country's second official language in place of Dutch. By then it was becoming closely identified with ▷AFRIKANER NATIONALISM, and the AFRIKANER BROEDERBOND formed an Afrikaanse Taal- en Kultuurvereniging (ATKV) to help advance the use of the language. Although this associated the language with whites, a majority of coloured people continued to have Afrikaans as their first language.

Afrikaner Bond ('League of Afrikaners') The first and most important political party in the Cape before UNION, established by S J DU TOIT in 1880 to further the commercial interests of Afrikaner white farmers in the southwestern Cape. It entered into a pragmatic alliance with Cecil RHODES which lasted until the JAMESON RAID. In spite of attempts to broaden its base, the Bond never had more than a few African and coloured supporters. It was dissolved in 1911.

Afrikaner Broederbond (League of Afrikaner Brothers) Highly influential Afrikaner secret society formed in 1918. It worked to secure Afrikaner control in government, the economy and culture, and did much to promote the cause of ▷AFRIKANER NATIONALISM and of the NATIONAL PARTY.

Afrikaner Rebellion (1914) Revolt by right-wing Afrikaners in the Orange Free State and the Transvaal against the Union Government's decision, after entering ▷WORLD WAR I, to do Britain's bidding and seize SOUTH WEST AFRICA from the Germans. The rebels hoped to seize power and regain the lost independence of the BOER republics, but government troops put down the uprising. The rebels were treated leniently, but the execution of one of them, Jopie Fourie, turned him into a martyr, and many Afrikaners never forgave prime minister Louis BOTHA and his right-hand man, Jan SMUTS, for their role in suppressing the rebellion.

All-African Convention Organization of Africans established in 1935 to try to halt the passage of legislation to remove Cape African voters from the common voters' roll. After the legislation was passed in 1936, the convention remained in existence and moved towards alliances with coloured and Indian people. It lacked cohesion, however, and, although it was affiliated to the NON-EUROPEAN UNITY MOVEMENT and gained some support in the Transkei, it failed to challenge the predominant position of the ANC as the leading African political organization.

ANC (African National Congress) Founded by Africans in 1912, as the South African Native National Congress, to protest against racial SEGREGATION, it changed its name in 1923. Moderate in its early years, it became more radical in the 1940s under pressure from its YOUTH LEAGUE and in response to popular mass campaigns. In the 1950s it

FIRST BROEDERBONDERS *Leading force behind the founding of the Afrikaner Broederbond was Henning Klopper (seated, second from left), seen here with other early members.*

launched the DEFIANCE CAMPAIGN and took the lead in the CONGRESS ALLIANCE and the moves to draw up a Freedom Charter. BANNED in 1960 (along with the PAC), it reluctantly turned to armed struggle through its military wing, UMKHONTO WE SIZWE (MK). After the imprisonment of its leading members at the RIVONIA TRIAL in 1964, the ANC was led in exile by Oliver TAMBO. It capitalized on the SOWETO REVOLT of 1976, after which MK was increasingly active, and encouraged internal and external opposition to APARTHEID. Unbanned in 1990, the ANC entered formal negotiations in 1991 at CODESA on a new constitution providing for a democratic order. Under the leadership of Nelson ▷MANDELA, it successfully made the transition from liberation movement to political party, and won the 1994 election. (See also ▷ANC in 'Politics, government and the law'.)

❖ Many leading members of the ANC were also members of the ▷SOUTH AFRICAN COMMUNIST PARTY, with which it worked closely in a tripartite alliance that included the Congress of South African Trade Unions.

❖ The ANC inspired an organization of the same name in Rhodesia, founded in 1934 as a moderate pressure group. After 1957, when it amalgamated with the more radical African National Youth League, it gained wider support with its campaign for African rights. It was banned in 1959 and nearly 500 of its leaders were arrested, but in 1960 the National Democratic Party was formed to replace it, with Joshua ▷NKOMO and Robert ▷MUGABE among its leaders.

anglicization Literally, making or becoming more English. In the 1820s, the British Governor of the Cape, Lord Charles Somerset, unsuccessfully tried to promote the anglicization of the Dutch-speaking population of the colony. The attempt backfired, for it provoked some to leave the colony on the GREAT TREK. A more thorough-going attempt at anglicization was made by Lord MILNER in the aftermath of the SOUTH AFRICAN WAR, but his attempt, too, succeeded only in arousing strong opposition and boosting support for the AFRIKAANS LANGUAGE MOVEMENT.

Anglo-Boer War First, see ANGLO-TRANSVAAL WAR; Second, see SOUTH AFRICAN WAR.

Anglo-Transvaal War (1880-1) Also First Anglo-Boer War or Transvaal War of Independence. Sparked by Sir Theophilus SHEPSTONE's annexation of the TRANSVAAL in 1877, it was fought to recover Transvaal independence after three years of peaceful protest had failed to do so. The Boers won a number of confrontations, and their victory at MAJUBA became the most famous battle of the war.

REMNANTS OF BATTLE *Troops and contractors return to remove the debris at Isandlwana, scene of the first battle of the Anglo-Zulu war in 1879 when the Zulus achieved a decisive victory.*

The war ended with the British revoking their annexation (in the Pretoria Convention), but the Transvaal remained under British suzerainty (a form of government control by another state), with its foreign relations under British control.

Anglo-Zulu War (1879) Sir Bartle FRERE, the British High Commissioner, seeking to effect CONFEDERATION, was determined to overthrow the powerful ZULU KINGDOM, and he took steps which led to the outbreak of war in January 1879. The British forces that invaded Zululand met defeat at ISANDLWANA, but fought off the Zulu at RORKE'S DRIFT and went on to capture the Zulu capital and CETSHWAYO, the Zulu king. After the war, the British imposed a settlement that divided Zululand into 13 ministates. This sparked a bitter Zulu civil war, which completed the destruction of the old Zulu kingdom.

anti-Pass campaigns For much of the first half of the 20th century, South Africa's PASS LAWS were the main target of African protest. In one of the earliest anti-Pass campaigns in 1913, women in the Orange Free State successfully resisted the imposition of Passes. Another followed in 1944 when Pass controls were reimposed after a brief period in which they had been relaxed. The FEDERATION OF SOUTH AFRICAN WOMEN organized a massive anti-Pass protest in 1956. When the PAC launched its anti-Pass campaign in 1960, the result was the SHARPEVILLE SHOOTINGS.

apartheid While often used loosely to include all forms of racial SEGREGATION, apartheid (Afrikaans for 'separateness') was the name of a policy that the NATIONAL PARTY adopted in the early 1940s and put into practice after its election victory in 1948, to extend existing segregation. It was carried to its extreme under prime minister Hendrik VERWOERD, who became widely described as its architect. The BANTUSTAN system lay at the core of what was sometimes called 'grand' apartheid, but the policy also involved applying various forms of segregation to Indian and coloured people. At its most developed form in the 1960s, apartheid meant racial discrimination in almost all areas of life and brought extreme hardships to millions of its victims. It was enormously damaging psychologically, and produced such iniquities as the FORCED REMOVALS of large numbers of people. Police-state measures were used against all opponents of the system. From the late 1970s apartheid began to break down, partly as a result of resistance from within the country and internationally, and in part because it was clearly creating ever more violent conflict in the country and so gravely harming the economy. Relatively minor aspects (what was termed 'petty' apartheid) began to be eased from the late 1970s; it was not until the early 1990s that the central pillars of the policy were abandoned.

APLA (Azanian People's Liberation Army) Armed wing of the PAC formed in 1968 to suc-

SHORT-LIVED REVOLT *White settlers confront blacks with the imposition of a new tax in Natal that set off an uprising led by Bambatha, a Zulu chief. The chief's head was severed (inset) as a trophy after colonial forces massacred 500 warriors.*

ceed Poqo (Xhosa for 'standing alone'), formed in 1961 when the PAC decided to resort to armed struggle after it was banned. Both armies gained notoriety for random acts of terror often aimed at civilians. APLA, which was particularly heavily criticized for several attacks on civilians in the early 1990s during the MULTIPARTY NEGOTIATIONS, officially abandoned its armed struggle in 1993.

arms embargo Prohibition on the export of arms to a particular state. Arms sales were covered by the SANCTIONS imposed on the Rhodesian Government of Ian ▷SMITH in the mid-1960s. In 1963, in the aftermath of the SHARPEVILLE SHOOTINGS, the ▷UNITED NATIONS Security Council imposed a non-mandatory arms embargo on South Africa. In 1977, after the SOWETO REVOLT and the death in detention of Steve BIKO, it became illegal for any member of the United Nations to supply South Africa with arms. The embargo was lifted in 1994.

❖ South Africa responded by developing its own arms industry through ▷ARMSCOR, which grew until it not only met most local requirements but was able to export weapons embodying advanced technology.

Autshumao (Harry the Strandloper) (?-1663) KHOIKHOI man appointed 'postmaster' for passing English ships at the Cape in the 1640s. He later became the chief intermediary between his people and the Dutch under Jan VAN RIEBEECK at Table Bay – until he fell out with both sides and was banished by the Dutch to ▷ROBBEN ISLAND.

Bailey, Sir Abe (1864-1940) Mine magnate, soldier and politician. He made a fortune on the Witwatersrand goldfields and as a result of other investments, including in land and mining property in South Africa and RHODESIA. He worked to promote British interests in southern Africa, and became a leading philanthropist, within South Africa and abroad.

Ballinger, Margaret (1894-1980) Politician. From 1937 to 1960 she represented African voters in the South African Parliament and used that forum to protest against APARTHEID. She was a founder member of the LIBERAL PARTY in 1953.

Bambatha Rebellion (1906) Last armed uprising against white rule in South Africa led by a traditional leader. Bambatha (*c*1865-1906) was a minor chief in Natal, and the rebellion was primarily against the imposition in 1905 of a £1 poll tax designed to push more Africans into wage labour. The revolt was short-lived: it was put down after six weeks with much violence. Bambatha himself was among the more than 500 rebels killed.

banned Prohibited or restricted. The APARTHEID regime used various forms of banning as one of its main methods of dealing with political opposition: individuals were restricted to their homes, or forbidden to meet more than one other person at a time; thousands of books were banned; and organizations and newspapers were proscribed. The COMMUNIST PARTY OF SOUTH AFRICA was the first organization to be banned by the National Party Government (under the Suppression of Communism Act) in 1950, and was followed by many others, including the ANC and PAC in 1960, and several BLACK CONSCIOUSNESS MOVEMENT organizations in 1977.

Bantu Education Separate educational system introduced in 1953 by the APARTHEID regime for Africans, who were said by Hendrik VERWOERD to need only an inferior form of education. The legislation removed the education of African children from churches and missionaries, and centralized it in the hands of the state. Far less was spent on black children than white, and the standard of education was abysmal. While ever more Africans went to school, resistance to Bantu Education grew and exploded in 1976 in the SOWETO REVOLT. For much of the 1980s little learning of value took place in the Bantu Education system.

❖ The post-apartheid regime introduced a single educational system for all in 1995.

Bantu-speaking people Linguists and archaeologists believe that the ancestors of the people of southern Africa who speak ▷BANTU LANGUAGES moved south from central Africa about 2 000 years ago, and began settling in Mozambique, ▷MPUMALANGA (formerly Eastern Transvaal), KwaZulu-Natal and Eastern Cape from the 4th century AD. That settlement was associated with the spread of iron and of mixed farming. (See also IRON AGE; MAPUNGUBWE; GREAT ZIMBABWE.)

Bantustan One of the ten 'homelands' or 'self-governing territories' into which Africans were divided, according to their language group, under 'grand' APARTHEID in an attempt to create a white South Africa free of African citizens. Central to the Bantustan policy, introduced from the 1950s by Hendrik VERWOERD, was the idea that Africans had their own pockets of land, on which they had lived before white conquest and in which they could be given self-government and even independence. In 1976 TRANSKEI became the first of the Bantustans to be given 'independence' (recognized only by the South African Government). It was followed by BOPHUTHATSWANA, CISKEI and Venda. Other Bantustans obtained self-government but not nominal independence. All the Bantustans could survive only on handouts from the South African Government, and in all

CHARISMATIC LEADER *Steve Biko's death in detention provoked worldwide outrage at the cruelties and injustices of apartheid.*

there was vast corruption, while superfluous bureaucracies were created at great expense. With the advent of a new political order in 1994 all the various Bantustans were reincorporated into the nine provinces of South Africa. (See also FORCED REMOVALS.)

❖ The six non-'independent' Bantustans were: Gazankulu, KaNgwane, KwaNdebele, KwaZulu, Lebowa and QwaQwa.

Basutoland Now the kingdom of Lesotho, the state was the creation of MOSHOESHOE, who in the 1830s and 1840s gathered together Sotho-speaking people in the fertile lands west of the Drakensberg. He resisted encroachment by Boers from the ORANGE FREE STATE, but by 1868 had lost considerable tracts and accepted British rule to enable his people to keep what remained of their land. Basutoland came under Cape rule in 1871, but the Sotho took up arms against this arrangement in the early 1880s. As a result, Basutoland reverted to British control as a HIGH COMMISSION territory in 1884. It became independent in 1965.

Batavian Republic Name of the government in the Netherlands that ruled the CAPE Colony from 1803 until 1806. In that brief period, the Batavians introduced a number of reforms to the corrupt and inefficient way in which the DUTCH EAST INDIA COMPANY had run the colony. Their rule was ended by the Battle of BLAAUWBERG, after which the Cape fell under British rule again.

Bechuanaland Tswana settlement annexed in 1885 by Britain, which divided it into a northern portion (the British HIGH COMMISSION territory known as the Bechuanaland Protectorate) and a southern portion (British Bechuanaland, which was incorporated into the northern Cape in 1895). The history of the territory is closely associated with the family of the Khamas, one of whom – Sir Seretse KHAMA – led the Bechuanaland Protectorate to independence as Botswana in 1966.

Biko, Steve (1946-77) Founder of the BLACK CONSCIOUSNESS MOVEMENT who became a charismatic leader and a martyr. A student leader in the late 1960s, the highly talented Biko promoted black awareness through his writings and speeches, but from 1973 he suffered increasing harassment at the hands of the APARTHEID security system. In 1977 he died while being held in police custody under appalling conditions.

❖ The Minister responsible, Jimmy Kruger, said that Biko's death 'left him cold', but it led to worldwide protests and was followed by the imposition of a mandatory ARMS EMBARGO against South Africa imposed by the United Nations.

Blaauwberg, Battle of (1806) Fought just north of Cape Town between the Dutch defenders of the CAPE colony and the invading British forces. The latter's victory resulted in the re-establishment of British rule at the Cape, which lasted into the 20th century.

Black Consciousness Movement Political movement that emerged in the late 1960s under the leadership of Steve BIKO. It sought to promote black assertion and self-esteem, and rejected dependence on whites. In the aftermath of Biko's death in detention in 1977, the various Black Consciousness Movement organizations were BANNED, but the ideas did not die, and were stressed particularly by ▷AZAPO (the Azanian People's Organization).

black spots When whites took over land from blacks in the 19th century, small areas in the midst of white-owned land were sometimes left in African hands. These became known as black spots by the APARTHEID regime, which took steps, especially in the 1960s and 1970s, to clear them and consolidate all such land in white hands. In 1994 a Restitution of Land Rights Act was passed to provide for mechanisms for the return of such land, or for compensation to be given to those groups who had lost land.

Blood River, Battle of (1838) Fought between some 10 000 followers of the Zulu king DINGANE and a commando of VOORTREKKERS under the leadership of Andries Pretorius in what is now KwaZulu-Natal, it was a bid by the Boers to avenge the death of Piet RETIEF. Thanks to their guns, the whites were victorious, and the outcome enabled them to establish the Republic of NATALIA.

❖ The anniversary of the battle, 16 December, was celebrated in later years as the 'Day of the Vow (or Covenant)' by Afrikaner nationalists, who interpreted the victory as a sign of divine favour for their cause. The holiday was renamed the 'Day of Reconciliation' by the postapartheid government.

DAY THE RIVER RAN RED *Full-scale replicas of the ox-wagons forming the Boers' kraal commemorate their historic victory in the Battle of Blood River when they routed 10 000 Zulu warriors.*

Boer Meaning literally 'farmer' in Dutch and Afrikaans, the term has been applied in South Africa variously to early white farmers of Dutch descent, TREKBOERS, VOORTREKKERS, Afrikaners in general, and in particular the Afrikaners living in the Boer republics of the ORANGE FREE STATE and TRANSVAAL. Later it was also sometimes used in a derogatory way to refer to racist whites.

Boomplaats, Battle of (1848) Fought between British forces and Boers opposed to the proclamation of the ORANGE RIVER SOVEREIGNTY, which established British rule north of the Orange River. After their defeat, the Boers under their leader Andries Pretorius retreated from British rule into the TRANSVAAL.

Bophuthatswana BANTUSTAN created as a state for Tswana-speakers in the former Transvaal and Northern Cape, with one enclave in the Free State. After being led to self-government it was eventually recognized as 'independent' by the South African Government in 1977. Thanks to its platinum mines and the revenue it obtained from the Sun City casino complex, it was potentially the most economically viable of the Bantustans. Ruled in a highly autocratic fashion by president Lucas Mangope, it collapsed ignominiously in March 1994 when Mangope tried to stay out of the election to be held the following month. Along with the other Bantustans, it was then reincorporated into South Africa.

Border War Colloquial term for the military campaign of the SOUTH AFRICAN DEFENCE FORCE against ▷SWAPO and the ▷MPLA in northern Namibia and southern Angola from 1974 until 1989. The conflict, part of the National Party's TOTAL STRATEGY, ended in military stalemate. (See CUITO CUANAVALE.)

BOSS (Bureau for State Security) Created by prime minister John VORSTER in 1969, it engaged in intelligence and DIRTY TRICKS operations in support of APARTHEID. It was discredited in the INFORMATION SCANDAL of 1978 and was then disbanded and replaced by the National Intelligence Service.

Botha, Louis (1862-1919) A leading BOER general in the SOUTH AFRICAN WAR, he led the Het Volk party in the Transvaal and in 1907 became prime minister there, promoting the idea of reconciliation with the British. He was the first prime minister of the UNION in 1910, a post he held until his death.

Brand, Sir Johannes Henricus (1823-88) President of the ORANGE FREE STATE from 1864 until his death. His forces challenged the Sotho under MOSHOESHOE for their fertile lands along the Caledon River, until what remained of the Sotho territory was taken over by the British in 1868. Africans living in the Boer republic were treated harshly, but the Boer population praised Brand as a model leader and attributed their relative prosperity to his leadership.

ANCIENT ANCESTOR *Robert Broom (right), discoverer of* Plesianthropus transvaalensis, *examines 'Mrs Ples's' 2,5 million-years-old fossilized skull. With him is fellow researcher J T Robinson.*

British Kaffraria Name given to the land between the Keiskamma and Kei rivers, on the Cape's EASTERN FRONTIER, which was annexed by the British in 1847 at the end of the frontier conflict known as the War of the Axe. Ruled separately as a HIGH COMMISSION territory until 1866, it was then incorporated in the Cape Colony. It more recent times it came to be known as the CISKEI.

WAR HEROES *Louis Botha (seated, right), first prime minister of the Union of South Africa, later fell out with his fellow Boer generals Christiaan de Wet (left) and Koos de la Rey.*

British South Africa Company (Chartered Company) Mercantile company founded in 1889 by Cecil RHODES to open up the land north of the Limpopo River for trade, mining and settlement. In 1890 the company sent a party of whites, known as the Pioneer Column, into what eventually became Southern RHODESIA. Company troops defeated LOBENGULA's Ndebele and put down further uprisings by the resident Ndebele and Shona in the 1890s. In 1923-4 the company transferred control of its territories south and north of the Zambezi to Britain, but retained major commercial interests in those countries.

❖ Olive ▷SCHREINER's novel *Trooper Peter Halket of Mashonaland*, published in 1897, was a thinly disguised attack on Rhodes and sought to expose the excesses of his company's troops against the African inhabitants of the territory.

❖ The Pioneer Column was led by big-game hunter and scout Frederick Courtney Selous (1851-1917), who chronicled his exploration in Africa in such books as *A Hunter's Wanderings in Africa*. A man of action to the end, he was killed while serving in World War I. His name was given to the Selous Scouts, Rhodesian commandos in the guerrilla war.

Broom, Robert (1866-1951) Palaeontologist at the Transvaal Museum who discovered a number of important fossils, including the first adult skull of an *Australopithecus africanus*, which he found in 1947 in the ▷STERKFONTEIN CAVES. The discovery confirmed the earlier findings of Raymond DART about early hominids (humanlike species).
❖ The specimen was first classified as *Plesianthropus transvaalensis*, and Broom nicknamed it Mrs Ples.

Bulhoek Massacre (1921) Incident in which police killed 163 members of the Israelites, an African religious sect that was squatting in a 'refuge from oppression' on land near Queenstown in the Eastern Cape. The government of Jan SMUTS resorted to force when the Israelites refused to move.

Buller, Sir Redvers Henry (1839-1908) British soldier who was appointed Commander-in-Chief of the British forces in South Africa in 1899. When the SOUTH AFRICAN WAR went badly for the British, Buller was replaced by Field Marshall Lord Roberts.
❖ His retreat from Colenso in Natal, during an abortive effort to lift the Siege of Ladysmith, earned him the nickname 'Reverse' Buller from the British Press.

Bushmen See HUNTER-GATHERERS.

Cape (Cape Colony) Name given to the settlement of Europeans that was begun by the DUTCH EAST INDIA COMPANY in 1652 at what is now Cape Town. It was ruled by the Dutch until the British occupation in 1795 during the ▷NAPOLEONIC WARS. In 1803 the colony was handed over to the BATAVIAN REPUBLIC in terms of a treaty between Britain and France, but when war resumed in Europe the British once again seized the Cape from the Dutch in 1806 at the Battle of BLAAUWBERG. In the general peace settlement of 1814-15 at the end of the ▷NAPOLEONIC WARS, the Dutch permanently ceded the Cape to Britain. The British expanded the colony to the Orange River in the north and along its EASTERN FRONTIER as far as the border of NATAL. Responsible Government was introduced in 1872. It became the Cape Province at UNION in 1910, and was divided into the provinces of the Western, Eastern and Northern Cape in 1994.

Cape sea route This route from Europe to the east, around the southernmost part of Africa, was discovered in the 15th century by Bartolomeu ▷DIAS. It was to establish a refreshment station at the Cape on that route that the DUTCH EAST INDIA COMPANY founded a settlement at Table Bay (in what is now Cape Town) in 1652. Other countries whose ships used the route became concerned that control of the Cape by another power would be to their strategic disadvantage. Britain became so concerned that in 1795 it ousted the Dutch from the Cape. The sea route around South Africa remained a major reason for British involvement in the sub-continent throughout the 19th century. Once the Boers had moved into the interior on the GREAT TREK, the British tried to prevent them gaining access to the sea, fearing they might link up with a foreign power and threaten British control of the sea route. In the Cold War era, by which time a large proportion of the world's oil was transported around the Cape, the strategic and economic significance of the Cape sea route was cited as a reason why the West should retain good relations with the South African Government.

STRATEGIC HARBOUR *A Dutch fleet plying the route to the East led by the* Afrika *enters Table Bay in 1679. In later centuries the Dutch, French and English fought for control of the Cape.*

Carnarvon, Henry Howard Molyneux Herbert, Fourth Earl of (1831-90) As British Colonial Secretary between 1874 and 1878, Carnarvon is most noted in southern Africa for his policy of CONFEDERATION.

Cattle-killing, The (1856-7) A large number of ▷XHOSA people whose cattle had begun to die from lung-sickness, heeded the prophecies of a young girl called Nongqawuse and, on the advice of their chiefs, slaughtered their cattle. They believed that their ancestors would return to earth, and a new era would dawn as a result. A reaction to a long process of colonization, the Cattle-killing proved disastrous for the Xhosa people, tens of thousands of whom died of starvation. These events gave Sir George GREY, Governor of the Cape, the opportunity to carry forward the subjugation of the other indigenous people to white rule.

Central African Federation (Federation of Southern Rhodesia, Northern Rhodesia and Nyasaland) Federal state that came into being in 1953 as a multiracial response by the British Government to APARTHEID in South Africa. It joined together the Rhodesias and Nyasaland, with Salisbury (now Harare) as the federal capital. African nationalist opposition to the federation surfaced predominantly in Nyasaland, and within a decade it fell apart in spite of repeated conferences called by the British Government to keep it together. The three components then went their own way, with Nyasaland becoming the independent Malawi under Kamuzu ▷BANDA, Northern Rhodesia becoming independent as Zambia under Kenneth ▷KAUNDA, and the Southern Rhodesian Government unilaterally declaring independence (UDI) in 1965.

Cetshwayo (*c*1826-84) Son of Mpande, he was a dominant figure in the ZULU KINGDOM from 1856, and eventually succeeded his father as Zulu ruler in 1872. He rejected an ultimatum presented to him by Sir Bartle FRERE which demanded in effect that he disband his army; as a result, his country was invaded by British forces in 1879. With the defeat of his armies in the ANGLO-ZULU WAR, he was captured and imprisoned at the Castle in Cape Town, from where he was taken to see Queen ▷VICTORIA in England. He was then allowed to return to a portion of his former kingdom,

TAKEN CAPTIVE *Defeated in the Anglo-Zulu War, Cetshwayo was jailed in the Castle.*

but he was soon attacked by a rival faction during the Zulu civil war and it was as a refugee that he died soon after.

Christian National Education System of education – devised in the 1870s in the BOER republics – which laid stress on Christian and national values and opposed any form of liberalism. Closely linked with ▷AFRIKANER NATIONALISM, it flourished in the TRANSVAAL in response to Lord Milner's attempt at ANGLICIZATION. The system was taken over by the UNION educational structures and later became NATIONAL PARTY policy.

Church Street bombing (1983) Explosion in the centre of Pretoria, outside the building housing the headquarters of the South African Air Force, which caused more than a dozen civilian deaths. The work of UMKHONTO WE SIZWE, the blast shocked the National Party Government and its supporters, as well as the jailed ANC leader Nelson ▷MANDELA.
❖ In retaliation, the SOUTH AFRICAN DEFENCE FORCE launched an air attack on what were alleged to be ANC bases in Maputo, Mozambique, which in turn killed six civilians.

Ciskei Literally, the land this side of (ie west of) the Kei River. Traditionally the home of the western ▷XHOSA, the territory became known as BRITISH KAFFRARIA in the mid-19th century when annexed by Sir Harry SMITH. From the 1970s, a smaller area, consisting of the land under African occupation, was known as the Ciskei BANTUSTAN, which had its capital at Bisho. This was led to nominal 'independence' in 1982. For more than a decade Ciskei was ruled in a repressive and corrupt way by a succession of Bantustan politicians, the last the military ruler Brigadier Oupa Gqozo. With the advent of democratic rule in South Africa in 1994, Ciskei was reincorporated into the country as part of Eastern Cape province.

Civil Cooperation Bureau (CCB) Covert organization within the South African Defence Force which was formed in the mid-1980s to disrupt those considered to be enemies of the state, including anti-APARTHEID organizations such as the ANC and its allies, as well as ▷SWAPO. The CCB was involved in many DIRTY TRICKS, including assassinations. When news of some of its activities leaked out in 1990, the government announced that the CCB would be disbanded, but some of its projects continued and as late as 1995 much about its activities remained under wraps.

CODESA (Convention for a Democratic South Africa) A multiparty negotiating forum held in December 1991 at Kempton Park, Johannesburg, to draw up a constitution for a post-APARTHEID South Africa. The main participants were the South African Government, the NATIONAL PARTY, the ANC and ▷INKATHA. A second meeting, in May 1992, broke up in disarray when the government and the ANC could not agree on procedure. When MULTIPARTY NEGOTIATIONS resumed in 1993, the name CODESA was rejected because of the failure of the earlier talks.

Colenso, Bishop John William (1814-83) Controversial Bishop of the Church of England, biblical scholar and defender of the Zulu. He agreed with his Zulu pupils that much of the Old Testmanent was mythical. When he put forward his progressive ideas in print, he was accused of heresy. Deposed by Archbishop Robert Gray of Cape Town, he appealed to London and was able to remain Bishop of Natal. From 1873 Colenso became an arch foe of Sir Theophilus SHEPSTONE over his African policy in Natal and particularly the LANGALIBALELE affair. He was highly critical of Sir Bartle FRERE for provoking the ANGLO-ZULU WAR and was a champion of the cause of CETSHWAYO, the Zulu ruler.
❖ Colenso wrote the first Zulu grammar and translated the New Testament and parts of the Old Testament into Zulu.

coloured labour preference policy Official policy that ensured that jobs in the western Cape went to coloured people rather than to Africans. Its origins lay with the Cape Town City Council in the 1920s, but in 1954 it was adopted as National Party Government policy and was subsequently used as part of INFLUX CONTROL measures. It fell away in the 1980s, by which time the number of Africans in the western Cape had greatly increased.

Coloured Persons Representative Council (CRC) Statutory body established in 1968 by the National Party Government in an attempt to delegate certain powers to coloured people. The majority of eligible coloured voters boycotted the elections for it. The strategy of the LABOUR PARTY, however, was to participate in it in order to destroy it. The party gained control of the CRC in 1975, then succeeded in making it unworkable, and the council was disbanded in 1980.

Communist Party of South Africa Founded in 1921, it was the first political organization

LAUNCHING THE FUTURE *All smiles at the first phase of multi-party negotiations for a new South Africa were ANC delegates Cyril Ramaphosa (left), Nelson Mandela and Jacob Zuma.*

in South Africa to have a significant multiracial membership. It was, however, decimated in the late 1920s and early 1930s as a result of directives from Moscow for changes in policy (particularly that its goal should be a Native Republic under black rule) and of internal purges. A number of its members held influential positions in the ANC. After being BANNED in 1950, the party changed its name to the ▷SOUTH AFRICAN COMMUNIST PARTY and went underground.

compounds Enclosures used as living quarters for African MIGRANT LABOUR, particularly on mines. They had their origin at the Kimberley diamond mines, where they involved total seclusion of the workers for the duration of their contracts. On the Witwatersrand gold mines and elsewhere, compounds were open and the labourers could come and go with relative freedom, but living conditions were often harsh. The compounds eventually became known as single-sex hostels.

concentration camps Device developed by the British under Lord KITCHENER in an effort to bring the SOUTH AFRICAN WAR to an end. Afrikaners and Africans, especially women and children, in the former BOER republics were herded into more than 100 concentration camps. Conditions in the camps, which were appalling, were exposed by Emily HOBHOUSE. Almost 28 000 Afrikaners died, more than 22 000 of whom were children, and more than 14 000 Africans. While the policy helped to bring the Boers to the negotiation table, the concentration camps remained a lasting source of grievance among Afrikaners against the British. (See also ▷CONCENTRATION CAMPS in 'World history'.)

Confederation In the 1870s Lord Carnarvon, the British Colonial Secretary, worked actively for a confederation of the white-ruled states in South Africa, and sent out Sir Bartle FRERE to effect it. The idea failed because of strong resistance within South Africa. But the actions taken to bring about confederation – which led to both the ANGLO-ZULU WAR and the ANGLO-TRANSVAAL WAR – helped transform the sub-continent, most notably by tilting the balance of power decisively in favour of the white communities. The goal was ultimately reached – in another form – with the creation of the UNION in 1910.

Congress Alliance Joint front against the NATIONAL PARTY Government, formed after the DEFIANCE CAMPAIGN of 1952. The ANC was the leading member; another was the South African INDIAN CONGRESS. The alliance was responsible for the Congress of the People held in 1955, which approved the FREEDOM CHARTER. Many of its leading figures were charged with high treason in the TREASON TRIAL of 1956, but were later acquitted.

QUEUEING FOR SURVIVAL *Thousands of Boers – most of them women and children – and Africans died in the appalling conditions of British concentration camps during the South African War.*

Cuito Cuanavale, Battle of (1987-8) Large conventional battle around the town of Cuito Cuanavale in southern Angola, in which SOUTH AFRICAN DEFENCE FORCE and ▷UNITA troops faced the Angolan army, backed by elite Cuban forces and ▷SWAPO soldiers. The resulting battle was a stalemate, although the Cubans claimed it as a defeat for the South Africans. The stalemate did, however, encourage the withdrawal of the SADF from Angola and Namibia, and South Africa's participation in the 1988 negotiations with Cuba and Angola, which led eventually to the decision to implement RESOLUTION 435 and bring Namibia to independence.

Dadoo, Yusuf (1909-83) A committed member of the COMMUNIST PARTY OF SOUTH AFRICA, Dadoo headed the South African INDIAN CONGRESS and in 1946 led its PASSIVE RESISTANCE CAMPAIGN against anti-Indian legislation. He was banned in 1952 and went into exile in 1961 but remained active in anti-APARTHEID work in London until his death.

Dart, Raymond (1893-1988) Anatomist at the University of the Witwatersrand who in the 1920s identified the 'Taung child', the fossil of a skull belonging to a species that he named *Australopithecus africanus* (the southern ape of Africa). He suggested the species was the link between primates and humans, and it was later established that it was the earliest known hominid (human-like species), thus confirming the theory that humankind originated in in Africa.

❖ When palaeontologist Robert BROOM first saw the Taung fossil, he knelt down to have a closer look, quipping: 'I am kneeling in adoration of our ancestor.' His subsequent discoveries supported Dart's findings.

Defiance Campaign ▷CIVIL DISOBEDIENCE campaign launched in 1952 by the ANC and South African INDIAN CONGRESS against APARTHEID legislation, including Pass laws and the Group Areas Act. Volunteers deliberately courted arrest, but when harsh punishments were introduced the campaign petered out. Its main significance was that it mobilized support for the ANC.

❖ Another defiance campaign in early 1989 helped persuade president F W ▷DE KLERK to embark on a course of reform.

Delagoa Bay Natural harbour, which is today the site of Maputo (formerly Lourenço Marques) in Mozambique. Britain disputed ownership of the bay with Portugal; the French president arbitrated and awarded it to Portugal in 1875. The government of the TRANSVAAL, in a bid to avoid traffic of gold through the British-controlled territories, backed the construction of a railway from the Witwatersrand to the bay. Completed in 1895, the line was later used to transport MIGRANT LABOUR to the Rand.

De la Rey, Jacobus Hercules (1847-1914) BOER general and politician. He was famous for his military skill during the SOUTH AFRICAN WAR and after entering politics in the TRANSVAAL was elected to the first UNION Senate. In 1914 he planned an uprising to restore republican independence, and was shot dead by the police when he failed to stop at a roadblock.

destabilization Part of P W Botha's TOTAL STRATEGY of the 1970s and 1980s, it involved the use of South African power to prevent its black-ruled neighbours from assisting the ANC. This was done in many ways, from massive military incursions into Angola, to DIRTY TRICKS, support for opposition movements (such as ▷UNITA and ▷RENAMO), and subtle interference with cross-border trade. After Namibia's achievement of independence and with changing politics in South Africa, destabilization was abandoned.

détente Generally, the relaxing of tension between nations. In South Africa it referred to the policy of prime minister John VORSTER of trying to improve relations with some black states in Africa in a bid to take the pressure off APARTHEID. It led to meetings with a number of heads of state, but little more. With South Africa's invasion of Angola in 1975 during the BORDER WAR, hope of effective détente collapsed.

detention without trial Introduced after the SHARPEVILLE SHOOTINGS as part of the ordinary law of the land, this draconian measure was used widely against political opponents by the APARTHEID regime. The time-limit to such detention was first 12 days, then 90 days, then 180 days, before the limits were removed entirely. Many detained without trial alleged they had been tortured, and scores died in detention.

De Wet, Christiaan Rudolph (1854-1922) A BOER commander in the western Orange Free State during the SOUTH AFRICAN WAR and a reluctant signatory of the Treaty of Vereeniging which ended the war in 1902. In 1914 he helped J B M Hertzog form the NATIONAL PARTY and then led the AFRIKANER REBELLION against South Africa's ▷WORLD WAR I policy. He was imprisoned, but released in an amnesty in 1915.

Dingane (*c*1795-1840) Zulu king, who assumed power after murdering SHAKA, his half-brother, in 1828. When the Voortrekker leader Piet RETIEF entered his country, Dingane first promised him land, then had Retief and his party murdered in February 1838. The trekkers regrouped and defeated Dingane's army at BLOOD RIVER. Ousted by his half-brother Mpande in the aftermath of that defeat, he fled and was murdered.

dirty tricks Phrase used for undercover activities, including assassinations, used in the 1980s and 1990s by organs of the South African State such as the CIVIL COOPERATION BUREAU, against its opponents. The GOLDSTONE COMMISSION was appointed in 1991 to help investigate dirty tricks, but much remained murky and in 1994 the new government proposed a ▷TRUTH AND RECONCILIATION COMMISSION to bring these activities to light.

Dube, John Langalibalele (1871-1946) First president-general (1912-17) of the South African Native National Congress, which later became the ANC, Dube launched Natal's first black newspaper, 'Ilanga lase Natal', in 1903 and remained an influential political figure in that province after his term as national leader. In later years he was increasingly viewed as a conservative by a younger generation of ANC members.

Dutch East India Company English name of the Vereenigde Oost-Indische Compagnie (VOC), a company founded in 1602 and given a monopoly on Dutch trade east of the ▷CAPE OF GOOD HOPE. In 1652 it established a refreshment station for its ships in Table Bay, the site of Cape Town, to provide fresh food to ships en route between Holland and the company's ports in the East Indies, the most important of which was Batavia on the island of Java. The company ruled the CAPE until it was ousted by the British in 1795. By then the company was in decline, and in 1804 its charter lapsed and it disappeared.

Du Toit, Stephanus Johannes (1847-1911) Politician and campaigner in the first AFRIKAANS LANGUAGE MOVEMENT. He founded the Genootskap van Regte Afrikaners (Society of True Afrikaners) in 1875, and the first Afrikaans newspaper, 'Die Afrikaanse Patriot' (1876). He also wrote the first ▷AFRIKAANS grammar and formed the AFRIKANER BOND.

eastern frontier Term applied to the region straddling the CAPE's eastern border. In the late 18th century, the Dutch declared the Great Fish River the eastern boundary of its territory, and this frontier moved in stages – by proclamation and annexation of territories such as BRITISH KAFFRARIA and TRANSKEI – until it eventually coincided with the southern boundary of Natal. Between the 1770s and the 1870s some nine wars were fought between the colonial forces and different groups of Xhosa-speaking people, who were gradually forced out of much of their lands. With the annexation of Pondoland to the Cape in 1894, the eastern frontier can be said to have been closed.

End Conscription Campaign (ECC) Founded in 1983 to campaign against compulsory military service, most of its members were young men eligible for conscription. It was increasingly vocal in demanding that South African forces withdraw from Angola and Namibia, and in its opposition to troops being deployed in African townships. In 1989 it was BANNED, but with the end of the BORDER WAR, and State president F W ▷DE KLERK's liberal-

ZULU STRONGHOLD *Dingane's headquarters at Mgundgundlovu (Place of the great elephant) was the scene of the killing of Voortrekkers led by Piet Retief who had come to negotiate for land.*

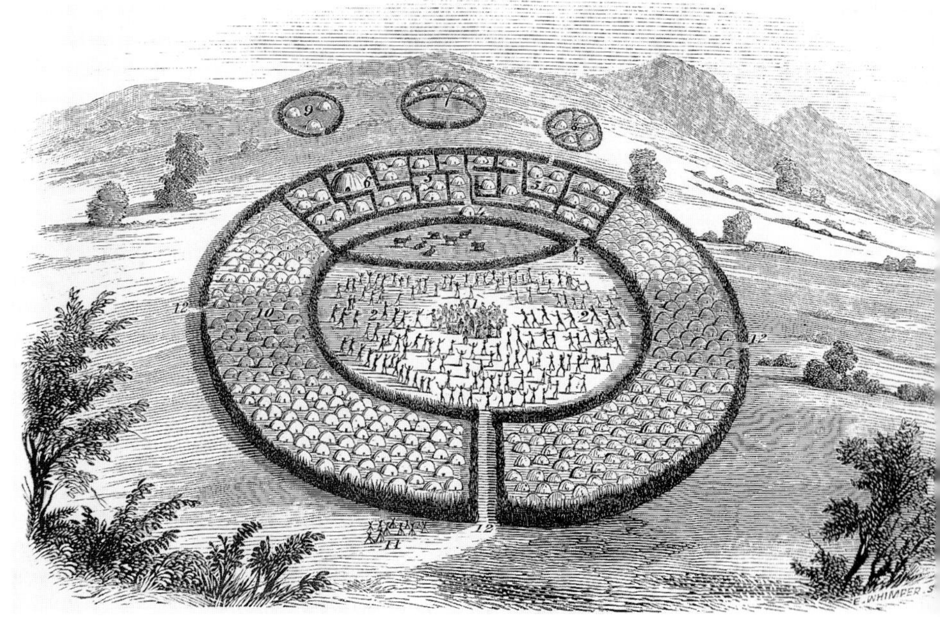

PRESS PIONEER *John Fairbairn, founder of the first commercial newspaper at the Cape, was a leader in the battle for press freedom.*

ization, the prohibition on its activities was lifted. The scrapping of conscription in 1994 removed the rationale for its existence.
❖ An associated organization in England, the Committee of South African War Resistors, helped those who fled South Africa to escape military service.

Fairbairn, John (1794-1864) Newspaper editor and Cape parliamentarian. He founded the 'South African Commercial Advertiser', the first nongovernment commercial newspaper in South Africa, in 1824, and was influential in the establishment of freedom of the press a few years later. In 1849 he was one of the leaders in the agitation against the introduction of convicts to the Cape.

Federation of South African Women Nonracial organization founded in 1954 to campaign for women's rights. It organized a march by 20 000 women to the Union Buildings in Pretoria in 1956 to protest against the PASS LAWS being extended to women. Along with fellow organizations in the CONGRESS ALLIANCE, it then suffered from repression and many of its leading figures were charged in the TREASON TRIAL or BANNED.
❖ The anniversary of the federation's anti-Pass march, 9 August, is celebrated as South African Women's Day.

Flu Epidemic The worldwide outbreak of Spanish influenza in 1918-19, more correctly called a ▷PANDEMIC, is thought to have killed perhaps a quarter of a million people in South Africa. It spread throughout the country, but hit particular areas much harder than others, and the majority of its victims were Africans. It constitutes the greatest single natural catastrophe in South Africa's history.

forced removals Term used for the relocation of black people against their will. There were many examples of forced removals from before the 20th century, but it was especially after 1950 that, as a result of APARTHEID policies, forced removals became common. In the 40 years after 1948 some 3,5 million people are said to have been moved – mostly in terms of racial laws such as the GROUP AREAS ACT and those maintaining the BANTUSTAN and INFLUX CONTROL policies. Others were also moved in terms of measures to counter the growth of squatter settlements
❖ Among the most publicized forced removals were the destruction of an entire African community in ▷SOPHIATOWN, near Johannesburg, in 1955 and a coloured community in District Six, Cape Town, from 1966.

Fox Street siege (1975) Hostage drama at the Israeli Consulate in Johannesburg in which a security guard was killed and about 45 people injured. Arab terrorists were at first thought to be responsible, but after the 17-hour siege a lone gunman, security guard David Protter, surrendered to police. Described by his trial judge as a psychopath, Protter was sentenced to 25 years in prison, but was freed in 1991 under a general remission for first offenders.

franchise The right to vote. While in the CAPE there was an effective non-racial male franchise in the late 19th century, tied to a property qualification, elsewhere in the country blacks did not have the vote. This remained the situation after UNION, but gradually the Cape's African and coloured people lost their common-roll vote, so that by 1956 only whites had the vote (white women having gained the franchise in 1930). In terms of South Africa's 1984 constitution, coloured and Indian people were given the vote for separate Houses in the TRICAMERAL PARLIAMENT, and it was not until the April 1994 general election that all people in the country enjoyed the same franchise rights.

free blacks Term used in the DUTCH EAST INDIA COMPANY period for freed slaves and other blacks from outside the country who were not slaves. They were never significant numerically, but like the slaves and indigenous black people, they were discriminated against on the grounds of colour, which indicates the crucial importance of the colour bar in the country's early history.

free burghers Employees of the DUTCH EAST INDIA COMPANY who were freed of their duties and allowed to farm on their own. The first began to do so in 1657. In the company period, the term was often applied generally to white settlers at the Cape.

Freedom Charter Central document of the CONGRESS ALLIANCE, it was adopted – after extensive grassroots consultation – by a Congress of the People held at Kliptown outside Johannesburg in 1955. Though open to different interpretations in respect of the extent to which it looked forward to a socialist future, it held out a clear vision of a multiracial, democratic society. Those members of the ANC who rejected such a vision left in 1958 and formed the PAC, which rejected the charter.
❖ The preamble to the charter reads in part: 'We, the people of South Africa, declare for all our country and the world to know: That South Africa belongs to all who live in it, black and white, and that no government can justly claim authority unless it is based on the will of the people . . . '

Frere, Sir Henry Bartle (1815-84) Governor of the Cape and High Commissioner, appointed

FORCED TO MOVE *A photograph taken by Jürgen Schadeberg in 1959 depicts the plight of African families, whose homes were demolished under apartheid legislation.*

HARDY SOUL *Here Mahatma Gandhi is dressed in the clothing he often wore, even in the coldest weather.*

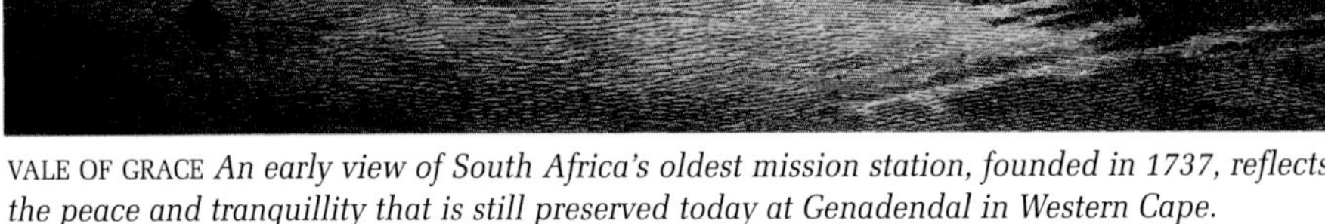

VALE OF GRACE *An early view of South Africa's oldest mission station, founded in 1737, reflects the peace and tranquillity that is still preserved today at Genadendal in Western Cape.*

in 1877 by Lord CARNARVON to bring about a CONFEDERATION of the South African states. Frere believed it was necessary for Britain to conquer the ZULU KINGDOM as a step towards that goal, but after the British defeat at the hands of the Zulu at ISANDLWANA (1879) hopes for confederation faded, and the following year Frere was recalled to London.

Frontier Wars Name given to wars fought in the century from 1779 to 1878 in the region of the EASTERN FRONTIER of the Cape. They have also been called the 'Wars of Dispossession'.

Fusion Name of the coalition in 1934 between prime minister J B M HERTZOG's National Party and the South African Party of Jan SMUTS, which fused into a new UNITED PARTY. This was in response to a crisis in the PACT GOVERNMENT precipitated by the ▷DEPRESSION and Hertzog's refusal to come off the gold standard. The Fusion Government split in 1939 over whether South Africa should enter ▷WORLD WAR II, with Smuts taking the country into the war.

Gandhi, Mahatma (Mohandas Karamchand) (1869-1948) Indian leader. Trained as a lawyer in England, Gandhi came to South Africa in 1893 and was shocked by the racial discrimination he encountered. He formed the Natal INDIAN CONGRESS in 1894 to promote the cause of Indians, and later expanded his activities to the Transvaal. In his two decades in South Africa he developed his ideas about *satyagraha* (passive resistance) – using non-violent tactics such as marches and civil disobedience to challenge the government. He was jailed several times, and won only minor victories before returning to India in 1914. There he campaigned for the uplift of poverty-stricken rural communities and led the fight for independence from Britain, which was eventually won the year before he was assassinated by a Hindu fanatic. (See also Mahatma ▷GANDHI in 'World history'.)

❖ Gandhi was famous for his ascetic style of life. His title Mahatma means 'great soul'.

❖ An event Gandhi described as directing his future political life was his eviction from a train at Pietermaritzburg station after a white passenger had objected to sharing the first class carriage with a 'coolie'.

Genadendal Previously Baviaanskloof, the earliest mission station in South Africa. It was founded among the KHOIKHOI by the Moravian Missionary Society in 1737 close to what became the town of Caledon in the Cape. After being re-established in 1792, it retained its importance as a mission station into the 20th century.

Gerhardt, Dieter (1936-) Naval commander exposed as a Soviet spy in 1983. He rose through the ranks of the navy until he was commander of the South African naval base at Simon's Town, which monitored all shipping on the CAPE SEA ROUTE. After his trial and life imprisonment for treason, he was released in August 1992 under the government's indemnity programme. He was deported to Switzerland and later professed to have been working against the APARTHEID regime rather than for the Soviet Union.

❖ His wife Ruth was sentenced to 10 years' jail for helping him, but was released in 1990.

Glen Grey Act (1894) Legislation that embodied Cecil RHODES's plan for African administration. It replaced communal land tenure with individual lots, imposed a tax on males to force them into employment, and introduced a system of district councils. It was applied in limited areas of the CISKEI and TRANSKEI and did not have the significance Rhodes intended.

Goldstone Commission Judicial commision of inquiry appointed by the F W ▷DE KLERK Government in 1991 under Judge Richard Goldstone to investigate incidences and allegations of public violence and intimidation. It began to uncover details of DIRTY TRICKS used by the APARTHEID state against its opponents, but when it ceased operations in 1994 many of its investigations were incomplete.

❖ Judge Goldstone was also appointed in 1993 to an international tribunal on war crimes committed since 1991 in the conflict between former Yugoslavian states.

Great Trek Mass migration of about 15 000 Afrikaners and roughly an equal number of their servants from the Cape's EASTERN FRONTIER in the late 1830s. Those who went on the trek sought to break with British rule. Known as VOORTREKKERS, to distinguish them from other individual TREKBOERS, they divided once in the interior. Those under Piet RETIEF entered Natal, while others moved into the the territory that became the Transvaal. The end result of the trek was the establishment in the interior of the Boer republics of the ORANGE FREE STATE and TRANSVAAL.

❖ In the 20th century the Great Trek became mythologized as the epic journey that had created ▷AFRIKANER NATIONALISM.

Great Zimbabwe Capital of the early Shona-Karanga empire of Zimbabwe that flourished from the 13th to the 15th century and engaged in extensive trade in gold with the east African coast. Impressive ruins of the largest stone edifice to have been built in pre-colonial sub-Saharan Africa remain and are today a major tourist attraction in the country of Zimbabwe. For long, whites believed erroneously that the stone buildings could not have been the work of indigenous people. Today stylized carvings of birds taken from the ruins appear on Zimbabwe's national coat of arms, its currency and insignia of various national organizations.
❖ Zimbabwe is the Shona word for stone dwelling. There are several ruins known by this word in present-day Zimbabwe.
❖ The extent of the gold deposits in the kingdom – particularly in the area Europeans called ▷MONOMOTAPA fuelled many legends of vast wealth.

Grey, Sir George (1812-98) Appointed Governor of the Cape and HIGH COMMISSIONER in 1854. An energetic administrator, extremely popular among the whites in the colony, he inaugurated representative government there. When The CATTLE-KILLING occurred, he was quick to take advantage of it, and with great ruthlessness completed the subjugation of the western ▷XHOSA. Unable to persuade the British Government of the advantages of federating the various white-ruled states in South Africa, he was recalled, then was briefly reinstated by a new government. He left the Cape in 1861 to become Governor of New Zealand.
❖ Grey's unique collection of books and manuscripts is in the South African Library.

Griqua People of mixed descent who originated in the northern Cape and who in the early 19th century formed their own small states beyond the Cape frontier, north of the Orange River, in what became known as Griqualand West. A group of Griqua under Adam Kok (*c*1710-*c*1795) settled in the southern ORANGE FREE STATE and there came under pressure from white farmers. In 1861, under Adam KOK III, they left to settle east of the Drakensberg in what they knew as 'Nomansland', later renamed Griqualand East. In both Griqualands there was armed resistance in 1878 against the imposition of colonial rule, but it was easily suppressed. Griqualand East was incorporated into the Cape in 1879, and Griqualand West (then led by Nicolaas WATERBOER) followed in 1880 after diamonds were discovered there.

Groote Schuur Minute Document agreed to at a meeting between the ANC and the NATIONAL PARTY Government at Groote Schuur, the presidential residence in Cape Town, in May 1990. It sought to clear obstacles in the way of MULTIPARTY NEGOTIATIONS, in particular relating to the release of political prisoners. In August 1990 a Pretoria Minute continued the process and provided for the suspension of the ANC's armed struggle. The talks, known initially as CODESA, began in December 1991.

TOUGH GOING *Thomas Baines's 1848 painting of an ox-wagon with its wheels chained descending Mackay's Nek in the eastern Cape typifies the hazards negotiated by the early trekkers.*

Group Areas Act (1950) A central pillar of APARTHEID, it provided for residential segregation on the basis of race in urban areas. Mainly coloured and Indian people were subjected to FORCED REMOVALS in terms of the Act, and relocated to places usually much further from their work. (Africans were removed under different legislation.) Immense bitterness was caused by the Act before it was repealed in 1991. By then it had drastically changed the social geography of most South African cities and towns.
❖ One of the most notorious proclamations under the Act provided in 1966 that Cape Town's District Six, mainly inhabited by coloured people, was to be for whites only. The buildings were demolished, and the people who had lived there were forcibly removed to the Cape Flats, a considerable distance away from the city centre.

Hani, Chris (Martin Thembisile) (1942-93) Militant, charismatic political leader and martyr. He joined the ANC's UMKHONTO WE SIZWE in 1962, left the country the following year to undergo military training and later worked actively against the APARTHEID regime. Returning to the country in 1990, he became general secretary of the ▷SOUTH AFRICAN COMMUNIST PARTY. His assassination by a Polish immigrant, at the instigation of a leading member of the right-wing ▷CONSERVATIVE PARTY, produced a great out-pouring of grief and anger, which for a time threatened the MULTIPARTY NEGOTIATIONS.

Herero Rebellion (1904-05) Uprising by the Herero of central SOUTH WEST AFRICA, under Samuel MAHERERO, against German settlers who had encroached on their land. They were later joined in the revolt by the Nama of the south under Hendrik WITBOOI. The Germans drove the Herero into the Omaheke desert, where tens of thousands died in what was virtual genocide.
❖ Of the 60 000 to 80 000 Herero population, about 16 000 survived the rebellion – of whom 14 000 were in concentration camps. The Nama lost 15 000 to 20 000 people.

Hertzog, James Barry Munnik (1866-1942) BOER general and politician. Leader of the Orangia-Unie party in the ORANGE FREE STATE before UNION, Hertzog broke with Louis BOTHA in 1912 and formed the NATIONAL PARTY in 1914. He became prime minister of the PACT GOVERNMENT with the aid of the white Labour Party in 1924, but in 1933 was forced into FUSION with the South African Party of Jan SMUTS. From 1934 he headed a new UNITED PARTY Government, losing office in 1939 when he opposed South Africa's entry into ▷WORLD WAR II. He was a strong believer in putting South African interests first, and in equal rights for Afrikaners. However, he was also an ardent segregationist, and engineered, among other legislation, the so-called Hertzog Bills, which removed Africans from the common voters' roll and established the NATIVES' REPRESENTATIVE COUNCIL in 1936.

High Commission See HIGH COMMISSIONER

High Commissioner Vague title of office bestowed from 1847 on Cape governors, giving them the authority to act beyond British territory. High Commissioners used this authority to extend British rule, and consequently various High Commission territories came into being. Some were short-lived, but BASUTOLAND, BECHUANALAND and SWAZILAND remained under direct rule by Britain until led to independence in the 1960s. Sir Harry SMITH was the first governor to hold the additional title of High Commissioner.

Hintsa (*c*1790-1835) ▷XHOSA chief and martyr. During the FRONTIER WARS of 1834-5, British troops invaded Hintsa's territory east of the Kei River. Persuaded to enter the British camp to negotiate, he was captured instead and, when he tried to escape, killed. His death shocked the Xhosa as well as those whites opposed to colonial expansion.

Hobhouse, Emily (1860-1926) Philanthropist from England who in 1901 made a tour of the CONCENTRATION CAMPS into which the British had herded Boer women and children during the SOUTH AFRICAN WAR. Shocked by the conditions in the camps, she publicized the British Government's 'methods of barbarism,' and the Boers held her in high esteem.

❖ Ironically, the South African Defence Force named a naval submarine after Hobhouse – who as a pacifist campaigned against all warfare, including World War I. She wrote an anti-war book of narrations, published as *War Without Glamour* in 1927.

BOERS' PLIGHT *Emily Hobhouse acquired fame among Afrikaners for her exposé of conditions in British concentration camps.*

Huguenots (HEW-ge-nohz) French Protestant refugees brought to the Cape by the DUTCH EAST INDIA COMPANY between 1688 and 1700. About 200 settled not far from Cape Town and though they soon merged into the Dutch population, and took to speaking Dutch, they made a distinctive contribution to the development of the colony. (See also ▷HUGUENOTS in 'World history'.)

❖ The Huguenots are credited as founders of the Western Cape's wine industry. A memorial was erected to them in the region's winelands at Franschhoek, their main place of settlement.

hunter-gatherers The original inhabitants of southern Africa lived by hunting and gathering. Made up of small separate bands, they had no common name for themselves, but were known to KHOIKHOI pastoralists as San. The Khoikhoi themselves had originally lived by hunting and gathering, and when they lost their cattle they had to revert to being hunter-gatherers. Whites used the term 'Bushmen' to refer to all those who lived off 'the bush' by hunting and gathering. Those who hunted did not distinguish game from stock kept by pastoralists, and often raided such stock. As hunter-gathering people came under pressure, they retreated to the deserts and the mountains. From the Drakensberg, in particular, they launched raids on cattle-keeping people and their stock in the 19th century, before being overpowered and all but eliminated. (See also ▷HUNTER-GATHERERS in 'Human society'.)

hut tax Imposed in the late 19th century by both British and BOER colonialists on each African hut, this levy was aimed primarily at forcing male Africans to work for whites in order to pay the tax. A secondary purpose was to reduce polygamy, for in polygamous households each wife had her own hut.

Immorality Act A first Act of 1927 prohibited sexual relations between whites and Africans. An amendment in 1950 forbade such relations between white and coloured people. Under the APARTHEID regime, the police undertook widespread snooping to detect offences under the Act. The resulting appalling publicity helped lead eventually to the scrapping of the Act – along with the MIXED MARRIAGES ACT – in 1985.

indentured labour Meaning literally contracted labour, the term was applied to indentured labourers brought from India to work on Natal's sugar-cane fields from 1860 to 1911. After the SOUTH AFRICAN WAR, indentured Chinese labourers were brought to work on the gold mines, but, unlike the Indians, all were repatriated soon after.

Indian Congress Mahatma GANDHI founded the Natal Indian Congress in 1894 to champion the cause of Indians, particularly to protest against laws that restricted immigration, trade and the franchise. A broader South African Indian Congress led the PASSIVE RESISTANCE CAMPAIGN of 1946. Both Indian congresses later supported the ANC in its opposition to APARTHEID, and joined with it in the CONGRESS ALLIANCE of the 1950s, but they continued to exist as separate ethnic opposition movements into the 1990s.

Industrial and Commercial Workers' Union of South Africa Trade union formed by Clements KADALIE in 1919. It grew into the first modern African mass movement in South Africa, with numerous branches especially in the rural areas of Natal, the Transvaal and the Orange Free State. In 1927 it claimed a membership of 100 000, but thereafter fell apart, partly because Kadalie fell out with his advisers, partly because of mismanagement, and also because it was considered to have failed to deliver on its promises. By 1933 it had virtually disappeared.

❖ The movement was one of several that took inspiration from the 'Back to Africa' campaign of Marcus ▷GARVEY.

influx control Control of the entry of Africans into the urban areas by PASS LAWS and other legislation. The philosophy behind it was that Africans were to be allowed into the towns and cities only to serve the labour needs of whites and in proportion to the work available for them. Such laws were gradually tightened from the 1920s, after passage of the NATIVES (URBAN AREAS) ACT of 1923. By a 1937 amendment to that Act, African males were allowed only 14 days to find work in towns. In 1952 the notorious 'Section 10' legislation denied the right to live in an urban area to any African not born there, unless he or she had lived there continuously for 15 years or had served the same employer for ten years. In the Western Cape, the COLOURED LABOUR PREFERENCE POLICY was an additional influx control device. Despite all these controls, the numbers of Africans in towns steadily increased, and in 1986, when it was clear that the whole system had effectively broken down, it was abolished by the government of P W ▷BOTHA.

Information scandal (Muldergate) Scandal concerning the misuse of state funds by the Department of Information to white-wash APARTHEID. Details of what had been going on surfaced in 1978, thanks to 'leaks' to investigative journalists. The Minister, Dr Connie Mulder, then lied to parliament, denying that state money had funded the progovernment newspaper 'The Citizen', and he was subsequently forced to resign.

❖ If Mulder had not left the government he might have become prime minister in succession to John VORSTER; instead Vorster was followed by P W ▷BOTHA.

Iron Age The Early Iron Age in southern Africa, which lasted from 3 000 years ago until about 800-900 years ago, was marked by settlement of BANTU-SPEAKING PEOPLE in the low-lying areas of Mozambique and the regions formerly known as the Transvaal, Natal and Transkei. In the Later Iron Age, people settled in virtually the whole region, establishing large communities that reared livestock, worked the land for food and practised trade. STONE AGE lifestyles survived in Africa beside Iron Age cultures until colonial times. (See also ▷IRON AGE in 'World history'.)

❖ Pottery relics of the Early Iron Age include the Lydenburg Heads, seven terracotta depictions of human heads unearthed in Mpumalanga (Eastern Transvaal) in the 1950s. They are thought to date from *c*500 AD.

❖ Archaeological sites surviving from the Later Iron Age include those at MAPUNGUBWE and GREAT ZIMBABWE.

Isandlwana, Battle of (1879) First battle of the ANGLO-ZULU WAR, fought at Isandlwana hill near the present-day town of Nqutu in KwaZulu-Natal. It was a resounding Zulu victory that shocked the British, but a Pyrrhic victory, because not many months later the ZULU KINGDOM was conquered.

❖ Embarrassed British authorities created a myth that their men had been hampered by a lack of screwdrivers to open ammunition boxes. In truth, the box lids were each held by a single screw, and it was a failure to build proper defences that contributed to the defeat of the British forces.

Jabavu, John Tengo (1859-1921) Founder and editor from 1884 of 'Imvo Zabantsundu' ('Native Opinion'), an influential African Eastern Cape newspaper, and the most prominent spokesman for Cape Africans in the late 19th century. When he opposed the SOUTH AFRICAN WAR, his newspaper was banned for a short period. He did not participate in the events leading to the establishment of the ANC, and his actions were often divisive. He was, however, instrumental in the establishment of the University of Fort Hare in 1916.

TRIUMPH FOR ZULU FIGHTERS *A monument marks the site of the overwhelming Zulu victory at Isandlwana, when the British lost more than 1 200 men in the first battle of the Anglo-Zulu War.*

Jameson, Dr Leander Starr (1853-1917) Doctor and politician who aided the expansion of the interests of Cecil Rhodes's BRITISH SOUTH AFRICA COMPANY. As BSAC administrator in Mashonaland in the 1890s, he incorporated Matabeleland into what became the colony of RHODESIA. He was arrested in the Transvaal for leading the JAMESON RAID, but was soon released and served as prime minister of the Cape from 1904-8.

Jameson Raid (1895) Abortive attempt by Cape prime minister Cecil RHODES to overthrow the Transvaal Government of Paul KRUGER. Rhodes conspired to send Dr Leander Starr JAMESON with an armed force into the Transvaal, where he was to be joined by rebelling UITLANDERS. The raid was a fiasco, and Rhodes had to resign as prime minister.

❖ A telegram from the German Kaiser to Kruger, congratulating him on repulsing the raiders, was the cause of much British anger.

job reservation Use of the law to reserve jobs for whites, first in the mining industry but much more widely under the APARTHEID regime. In the 1980s job reservation disappeared in most industries – partly under international pressure, partly because of the need for skilled and semiskilled labour.

Johannesburg Station bomb Planted in 1964 by John Harris, a member of the African Resistance Movement, a mainly white organization then engaged in an anti-APARTHEID sabotage campaign. Two people were killed

ABORTIVE RAID *Leander Starr Jameson led the force that failed to overthrow Paul Kruger.*

ON THE BRINK *The city of Kimberley spreads across the veld in this early view over the Big Hole, once the world's richest source of diamonds. The Premier Rose diamond (inset) was cut into a pear shape from a rough stone of 353,94 carats.*

and 23 injured in the blast. Harris was sentenced to death and executed in 1965.

Kadalie, Clements (*c*1896-1951) Malawi-born teacher and trade unionist who launched the INDUSTRIAL AND COMMERCIAL WORKERS' UNION OF SOUTH AFRICA in Cape Town. He was its first secretary and the driving force behind its successful expansion in the 1920s. The union later fell apart, and he spent his last years trying in vain to build it up again.

Kat River Settlement An area of relatively fertile land in Eastern Cape, previously occupied by MAQOMA, which was given to KHOIKHOI people for settlement in 1829. The settlers became prosperous, but were required to fight on the colonial side in FRONTIER WARS, and whites coveted their land. A considerable number of the settlers went into rebellion in 1851, then lost their land. Some who remained were forced out in the 1970s and 1980s, when the area became part of the CISKEI Bantustan.

Khama, Sir Seretse (1921-80) Leader of Botswana. Born heir to the Ngwato chiefdom in BECHUANALAND, he wanted to free all the people of the colony from British rule. After his marriage to a white Englishwoman, however, he was banned by the British Government from taking up his chieftainship, and had to live in exile until 1956 and then return as an ordinary citizen. Ten years later, as leader of the largest political party, he saw his country become independent. He remained president of Botswana until his death, and under his rule the country witnessed a new prosperity and remained stable. In the late 1970s he urged upon his fellow southern African presidents the establishment of what eventually became the ▷SOUTHERN AFRICAN DEVELOPMENT COMMUNITY.

Khama, Tshekedi (1905-59) Charismatic regent of the Ngwato in BECHUANALAND from 1926 until 1950. Second son of Khama III (Khama the Great, chief 1872-3 and 1875-1923), Tshekedi became regent at the age of 20 and worked with great energy to preserve the economic independence of the chiefdom. In 1949 a tribal meeting (*kgotla*) voted him out as regent in favour of his nephew, Seretse KHAMA, but the British Government banished both men from the country. In 1956 Tshekedi and Seretse Khama were allowed to return to Bechuanaland as ordinary citizens.

Khoikhoi (Quena) Name, meaning 'men of men', which those whom Europeans called Hottentots used for themselves. Pastoralists, they lived over large areas of southern Africa when the Dutch arrived at the Cape. Some fought the Dutch, some reverted to being HUNTER-GATHERERS, others took to working for whites. In the course of time they became part of the coloured population of the Cape.

Kimberley diamond rush In 1866 alluvial diamonds were found along the Orange River, drawing a rush of prospectors to the area, as well as to later diggings along the Vaal River. The rush became a stampede and a boom town sprung up at Kimberley after the discovery in 1871 of the rich pipe of diamondiferous 'blue ground' at Colesberg Kopje, which was to become the deepest excavated hole and richest diamond mine in the world – the Kimberley Mine.

❖ The first large gem in South Africa was found near Hopetown and identified as a 21,25-carat diamond in 1867.

❖ South Africa has fallen to fifth place among the largest producers of diamonds in the world (see ▷GEMSTONES in 'Earth and the environment'). However, the ▷DE BEERS group, which grew out of the company formed by Cecil Rhodes and bought the Kimberley Mine in 1889, is the world's largest producer and distributor of rough diamonds.

Kimberley, Siege of (1899-1900) The town, important for being the headquarters of Cecil RHODES's De Beers Consolidated Mines and the main trading centre in the northern Cape, was besieged by BOER forces for four months in the early stages of the SOUTH AFRICAN WAR. Relief for the besieged colonists in Kimberley, as well as MAFEKING and of Ladysmith in Natal, became a matter of national pride among ordinary people in Britain.

King, Dick (1813-71) British settler who gained fame in 1842 when he and a Zulu retainer, Ndongeni, undertook a 10-day, 960 km ride from Port Natal (later Durban) to Grahamstown to summon reinforcements to relieve a siege by VOORTREKKER forces. King was rewarded with a sugar farm at Isipingo in Natal for his efforts, while Ndongeni received a plot of land outside Durban.

Kitchener, Herbert, Lord (1850-1916) Commander-in-Chief of the British forces during the SOUTH AFRICAN WAR. He tried to bring the war to an end using methods such as CONCENTRATION CAMPS and scorched earth tactics – burning Boer crops and farmsteads. He went on to serve as War Secretary in Britain at the start of World War I.

Kok, Adam III (1811-75) Leader of the GRIQUA community at Philippolis from 1837. With his people under pressure from BOER expansion, he sold the Philippolis lands to the ORANGE FREE STATE and in 1861 led his people on a two-year journey across the Drakensberg mountains into that portion of the TRANSKEI then known as 'Nomansland'. There he established what became known as Griqualand East, which in 1874 was brought under magisterial rule by the CAPE Colony.

Krotoa (also known as Eva) (*c*1642-72) Intermediary between the Dutch of the early Cape and her people, the KHOIKHOI. She was married briefly to a Dutch surgeon, but soon fell

DEFEATED REPUBLICAN *'Oom Paul' Kruger fought in vain to preserve the independence of the Boer republics, especially after the discovery of the Transvaal's rich gold deposits.*

out with the Dutch and ended her days as a prisoner on ▷ROBBEN ISLAND.

Kruger, Paul (Stephanus Johannes Paulus) (1825-1904) BOER leader and president of the SOUTH AFRICAN REPUBLIC from 1883 until 1900. One of those who led opposition to the annexation of the Transvaal by Sir Theophilus SHEPSTONE in 1877, he went to England to protest, and then joined the ANGLO-TRANSVAAL WAR against British rule. After the discovery of gold on the Witwatersrand, he had to deal with the problems of a rapidly changing country and protect his government against Cecil RHODES, who conspired to overthrow him. After the unsuccessful JAMESON RAID, Kruger made some concessions to the mine-owners, but not enough to prevent the outbreak of the SOUTH AFRICAN WAR with Britain in 1899. He fled his capital, Pretoria, in 1900, in advance of the arrival of the British forces, and sailed from Lourenço Marques to Europe to try to win support for the Boer cause. After the war he remained in exile and died in Switzerland. (See ▷KRUGER MILLIONS in 'Myths and legends'.)

BOERS' ADVERSARY *Lord Kitchener commanded Britain's forces in the South African War.*

KwaZulu BANTUSTAN in what was Natal and which became self-governing in 1977, though it was broken into many separate pieces. Its Chief Minister, Mangosuthu ▷BUTHELEZI, refused to consider accepting 'independence', but later threatened secession before South Africa's first democratic election in 1994. For much of the 1980s and early 1990s the Bantustan was plagued by political rivalry that resulted in bloody warfare between supporters of the ANC and of the ▷INKATHA FREEDOM PARTY. Fighting abated after KwaZulu was reincorporated into South Africa as part of the KwaZulu-Natal province in 1994 but a high incidence of violence continued.

Labour Party Formed by coloured politicians in 1965 in anticipation of the establishment of the COLOURED PERSONS REPRESENTATIVE COUNCIL, the party sought to use that body to help overthrow APARTHEID. Its tactics led to the disbandment of the CRC in 1980. It then participated in the TRICAMERAL PARLIAMENT in 1983, and became the governing party in the House of Representatives until shortly before that body disappeared in 1994. In the election of that year it allied itself with the ANC, then decided to disband.

Lancaster House Agreement Accord that ended the RHODESIAN WAR and provided for the replacement of the short-lived government of Zimbabwe-Rhodesia led by Bishop Abel Muzorewa. The agreement was reached at British-sponsored talks in London in December 1979 between the various parties involved in the conflict. It arranged for a transition period of direct British rule, during which an election would be held for the government of an independent Zimbabwe. It also ended sanctions and provided for a constitution for the new country.

Langalibalele (1818-89) Powerful Hlubi chief who lived close to the Drakensberg in Natal.

REBEL CHIEF *Langalibalele, chief of the Hlubi, was banished and his lands seized after he defied the colonial government of Natal.*

In 1873 he refused to register his people's guns, then resisted arrest. Under the orders of Sir Benjamin Pine, Lieutenant-Governor of Natal, a large force was sent to capture him and he was banished to ▷ROBBEN ISLAND, although he was in fact to remain on the mainland near Cape Town until he was allowed to return to Natal in 1887. The vengeance taken by colonial forces on Langalibalele's people caused an uproar in London, brought the Natal colonists into disrepute and cost Pine his post. The affair also encouraged the British Colonial Secretary, Lord Carnarvon, to seek the incorporation of Natal in a wider South African CONFEDERATION.

Langa march (1960) March by some 30 000 Africans from Langa and Nyanga townships into the centre of Cape Town in March 1960 to protest against police action during the anti-pass campaign of the PAC. A bloodbath was averted when the leader, 23-year-old University of Cape Town student Philip Kgosana, persuaded the marchers to return to Langa, on the basis of a promise by the police to organize a meeting with the Minister of Justice. When Kgosana arrived for the meet-

ing, however, he was arrested. He left the country soon afterwards and went into exile.
❖ Kgosana was taken unawares by the march, and was wearing shorts and a frayed jacket when he took control of the crowd.

Lembede, Anton Muziwakhe (1914-47) First president of the ANC YOUTH LEAGUE and first to articulate a philosophy of African nationalism. Son of a Zulu farm labourer, he was educated at Adams College in Natal and the University of South Africa. A strong anticommunist, he urged Africans to work together to throw off their oppression.

Liberal Party (1953-68) Nonracial political party whose founders were unhappy with the feeble opposition offered to APARTHEID by the UNITED PARTY and believed in the abolition of racial discrimination. In 1960 it adopted universal suffrage as its policy. It never obtained many white votes in elections, and it dissolved itself when multiracial parties were outlawed by the National Party Government.
❖ Among its founding members were Margaret BALLINGER and the author Alan ▷PATON.

Livingstone, David (1813-73) Scottish missionary, antislavery campaigner and explorer. Introduced to Africa by Robert MOFFAT, a colleague in the London Missionary Society, he later led a series of expeditions in which he became the first European to see the Victoria Falls and Lake Malawi.
❖ Livingstone's disappearance in 1865 while searching for the source of the Nile caused widespread concern. He was tracked down near Lake Tanganyika six years later by the journalist Henry Morton Stanley, who greeted him with the oft-quoted phrase: 'Doctor Livingstone, I presume?'

Lobengula (c1836-94) Son of MZILIKAZI and his successor as ruler of the Ndebele kingdom from 1870. He accepted the terms of the so-called Moffat Treaty in 1888, in which he undertook not to cede any part of his territory to a power other than Britain, then affixed his seal to the Rudd Concession, granting mineral rights to a group that later formed the BRITISH SOUTH AFRICA COMPANY. Company troops were later instrumental in bringing Lobengula's land under British control.
❖ A myth that Lobengula had a vast treasure – reputed to be relics of the fabled gold of ▷MONOMOTAPA – inspired fortune-hunters well into the 20th century.

London Missionary Society Interdenominational Protestant mission society active at the Cape from 1799 and known especially for its opposition to colonial policies in the early 19th century. Its superintendent in South Africa, John Philip (1775-1851), was one of the leading men of the colony. Among its other famous missionaries were David LIVINGSTONE and Robert MOFFAT. In the later 19th century its stations were gradually incorporated within the ▷CONGREGATIONAL Church.

Luthuli, Albert John (c1898-1967) Teacher, Zulu chief and politician. Luthuli, who was president-general of the ANC from 1952 until his death, was BANNED in the 1950s under a succession of restriction orders. He was awarded the Nobel peace prize in 1960 in recognition of the ANC's non-violent struggle against APARTHEID, and was troubled by the organization's decision in 1961 to adopt its policy of armed struggle.
❖ Luthuli's autobiography, *Let My People Go*, was published in 1926.

NONVIOLENT CAMPAIGNER *Albert Luthuli, winner of the Nobel peace prize in 1960, shares a joke with US Senator Robert Kennedy.*

Machel, Samora (1930-86) First president of Mozambique after its independence in 1975. He led the war against Portugal by the nationalist movement ▷FRELIMO as commander-in-chief from 1966 and as its president from 1970. As Mozambican president, he courted unpopularity with his powerful neighbours by allowing African nationalists of Rhodesia and South Africa to use his country as a guerrilla base. His later political life was characterized by increasing pragmatism, particularly in his signing of the NKOMATI ACCORD.
❖ Machel died when the aircraft in which he was travelling crashed near the border with

CURTAIN OF CATARACTS *David Livingstone was the first European to see the Victoria Falls, known to the African inhabitants of the region as* Mosi-oa-Toenja, *meaning 'the smoke that thunders'.*

South Africa. Many accused South Africa of having downed the aircraft, but an aviation inquiry cleared the country of complicity.

Mafeking, Siege of (1899-1900) The town of Mafeking (now Mafikeng in North West Province) was besieged by Boer forces in the early months of the SOUTH AFRICAN WAR. News of its relief was received with jubilation in London, where the Press had made much of the 'heroism' of the besieged Britons, especially the town's commander, Robert ▷BADEN-POWELL. In fact, the endurance of the whites was greatly aided by fairly plentiful rations throughout the seven-month siege. The suffering of the town's Africans, who were denied access to these rations, is described in the diary of Solomon T PLAATJE.

Magersfontein, Battle of (1899) Key battle in the SOUTH AFRICAN WAR in which the advancing British forces, who were attempting to relieve the Siege of KIMBERLEY, were dealt a severe defeat.
❖ The defeat, along with those at Colenso and Stormberg, was part of a series of disasters for the imperial and colonial forces known collectively as 'Black Week', which made it clear that the war would not end in the quick victory the British had hoped for.

Maherero, Samuel (*c*1854-1923) A Herero leader who, after working amicably with the Germans for many years, led his people into the HERERO REBELLION in 1904. The rebellion came against a background of German steps to reduce the authority of the chiefs, of settler occupation of vast tracts of his people's land and of an outbreak of rinderpest (a fatal viral disease) among the Hereros' cattle. With the vast majority of his people exterminated, he fled first to BECHUANALAND, then later settled in the Transvaal.

Majuba, Battle of (1881) Battle in which 400 British troops were defeated by 150 Boers during the ANGLO-TRANSVAAL WAR. By the time the battle took place, the British Government had already decided to withdraw from the Transvaal. But Majuba remained a symbol of Afrikaner victory and of the vulnerability of British forces.

Malan, Daniel François (1874-1959) Afrikaner nationalist and prime minister from 1948 until 1954. A minister in the ▷DUTCH REFORMED CHURCH, he supported J B M Hertzog's NATIONAL PARTY as editor of the Cape newspaper 'Die Burger' from 1915. He entered parliament in 1918 and joined Hertzog's PACT GOVERNMENT in 1924. He broke with Hertzog over FUSION in 1934 and created a new 'Purified' National Party, which became the official opposition and went on to win the general election of 1948. It then began to put its APARTHEID policies into practice.

Mapungubwe Hilltop capital of one of the largest precolonial states known to have existed in what is now South Africa, a state thought to have been at its peak in the 14th century. Among the items found at the site were Later IRON AGE tools, pottery, and beaten gold and copper artefacts. Today all that remains are some ruins close to the Limpopo River in the far Northern Province.

Maqoma (1798-1873) ▷XHOSA chief and a leading resistance fighter against white encroachment on the Cape's EASTERN FRONTIER. Expelled from the KAT RIVER SETTLEMENT in 1829, Maqoma fought courageously against the British in 1834 and again in 1851. He was imprisoned on ▷ROBBEN ISLAND after being found guilty of complicity in the CATTLE-KILLING. When he was released, he refused to remain at the location given him in the eastern Cape, and was returned to the island, where he died.
❖ His praise-name was Jongumsobomvu, 'he who watches the sunrise'.

Marks, Sammy (Samuel) (1843-1920) Entrepreneur who came to South Africa to make a fortune on the diamond fields, and prospered in numerous ventures, including mining and agriculture. He helped establish secondary industry in the Transvaal and became a confidant of Paul KRUGER.
❖ His Victorian home *Zwartkoppies*, east of Pretoria, has been restored in every detail as a museum.

NATIONALIST STALWART *D F Malan headed the government which came to power in 1948 and initiated the apartheid policy.*

Matanzima, Kaiser (1915-) BANTUSTAN leader. Believing that Hendrik VERWOERD's policy of 'separate development' was in the best interests of his people, he became first head of the TRANSKEI Government in 1963 and led his country to 'independence' in 1976. He later became Transkei president. Authoritarian in manner, he was despised by many as a collaborator.

Mendi Troopship sunk in the English Channel during ▷WORLD WAR I in 1917, with the loss of 615 African members of the South African Native Labour Contingent. They had been on their way to serve the British war effort in France.

Mfecane (Difaqane in Sotho) Term used by historians for the 'time of troubles' in southern Africa in the 1820s and 1830s, during which there was massive destruction of African communities and large-scale loss of life. It is sometimes applied more broadly to the whole process of state building in early 19th-century South Africa, including the establishment of the ZULU KINGDOM. Recent scholarship suggests that there was no single process involved, and it has therefore been suggested that the term should be discarded.

Mfengu (Fingo) Eastern Cape people thought to be descended from refugees who fled SHAKA's tyranny in the 1820s and settled first in the TRANSKEI and then in 1835 on the Cape's EASTERN FRONTIER. The Mfengu became allies of the Cape in all the FRONTIER WARS that followed, and were rewarded with grants of land, in particular a large portion east of the Kei River. This exacerbated tensions between them and the ▷XHOSA.
❖ The most prominent Mfengu politician in the late 19th-century Cape was the newspaper founder and editor John Tengo JABAVU.

migrant labour The term refers in general to workers who regularly do temporary or contract work away from home. In southern Africa, the first African migrants took jobs in the Cape Colony in the late 18th century. Then in the late 19th century it became state policy to encourage the movement of Africans to work for temporary periods on the diamond mines and later the gold mines. At that time Africans usually did not wish to leave their homes in the rural areas permanently, and white governments did not want them settling permanently in so-called white areas. As time passed, however, and the economy required more settled labour, especially for manufacturing industry, more and more controls were erected to try to prevent permanent African urbanization. These included PASS LAWS and other INFLUX CONTROL measures. Migrant labour continued to be very important even after those controls were removed in 1986. (See also ▷MIGRANCY in 'Human society'.)

Milner, Alfred, Lord (1854-1925) British Governor of the Cape and HIGH COMMISSIONER between 1897 and 1905. An ardent imperialist, he was determined to get his way with Paul KRUGER to bring the Transvaal under British control, and pushed matters in his dealings with Kruger's government towards war. After the SOUTH AFRICAN WAR, as administrator of the conquered BOER republics, Milner sought to reconstruct them in British interests through his policies of ANGLICIZATION and RECONSTRUCTION. His decision to introduce Chinese labour for the gold mines was highly unpopular both in the Transvaal and with the government in Britain.

❖ He was assisted after the war by a group of talented young Oxford-educated administrators who gained the nickname the 'Kindergarten' because of their youth. Several went on to play important roles in South Africa – among them Sir Patrick Duncan (1870-1943), who helped in the creation of UNION.

Mixed Marriages Act (1949) APARTHEID measure which followed earlier attempts to forbid sex across the colour line. It forbade marriages between whites and all other groups, although there had never been large numbers of such marriages. One of the apartheid measures to provoke the most media scorn, it was repealed (along with Section 16 of the IMMORALITY ACT) in 1985.

Moffat, Robert (1795-1883) Leading missionary of the LONDON MISSIONARY SOCIETY who first worked in Namaqualand and then among the Tlhaping at Kuruman, which became an important stepping-off point for exploration of the further interior and for the promotion of missionary work. He translated the New Testament into Sechuana and his religious scripts made Tswana the first African language to be written in South Africa.

❖ His daughter, Mary, married the Scottish explorer David LIVINGSTONE.

Moshoeshoe (Moshweshwe) (*c*1786-1870) Founder of the Sotho kingdom, he united various Sotho groups during the MFECANE upheavals of the late 1820s and 1830s on the highveld and ruled them from his capital at Thaba Bosiu ('Mountain of Night'). A man of great wisdom and foresight, he worked closely with the French missionaries he invited to his kingdom. Faced with the threat of BOER encroachment on his lands, which stretched far into what is now the Free State, he sought British protection. This was granted when his territory was annexed by Britain in 1868, but not before he had lost all the land west of the Caledon River to the Boers. Moshoeshoe's state of BASUTOLAND became the kingdom of Lesotho in 1965.

TALENTED 'KINDERGARTEN' *Lord Milner's team of young administrators of his policies after the South African War were: (from left, standing) the Hon Robert Brand, Patrick Duncan, Herbert Baker, Lionel Hichens; (middle row) the Hon Hugh Wyndham, Richard Feetham, Lionel Curtis, Peter Perry, Dougal Malcolm; (front row) John Dove, Philip Kerr and Geoffrey Robinson.*

PIONEER LINGUIST *Missionary Robert Moffat led the way in the translation and transcription of the Sechuana and Tswana languages.*

multiparty negotiations Informal name for the negotiations that led to the election of South Africa's first democratic government under a new constitution. They began in earnest in December 1991 with talks between the National Party Government and 18 other delegations at CODESA, but this forum collapsed at its second meeting. Another forum, constituted in 1993, represented more than 20 parties (the number varied as parties walked out, or factions split away from delegations). It finally reached an agreement on 18 November 1993 on a new interim constitution and the elections for and shape of a ▷GOVERNMENT OF NATIONAL UNITY, which was elected in April 1994.

❖ Argument over what the negotiating forum would be called was as fierce as the political debate, and at least 13 names were put forward and rejected. The body at which negotiations took place was finally called simply the Negotiating Council. Its decisions were ratified by a larger Negotiating Forum and then formally accepted and signed at plenary sessions of party leaders.

Murray, Andrew (1828-1917) Most influential minister of the ▷DUTCH REFORMED CHURCH in the late 19th century, he worked for nearly six decades both north of the Vaal River and in the Cape. A prolific writer of religious works, he also founded many schools, colleges and religious societies, including the Young Men's Christian Association.

❖ His father, also Andrew (1794-1866), served as a Dutch Reformed minister in Graaff-Reinet for 45 years.

Mzilikazi (c1795-1868) Thought to have been one of SHAKA's lieutenants, he fled in 1822 from Zululand into the Transvaal, and there founded a Ndebele kingdom, first in the eastern Transvaal (Mpumalanga), then with his capital not far from present-day Pretoria, and finally in the western Transvaal. After the arrival of the VOORTREKKERS and their defeat of his army at the Battle of Vegkop, he and his people moved north in 1838, via Botswana into what is now southwestern Zimbabwe. Here, in what became known as Matabeleland, he re-established his Ndebele kingdom. He was succeeded by his son, LOBENGULA.

Natal (Natal Colony) Name given by whites to the area between the Drakensberg Mountains and the Indian Ocean, land long settled by BANTU-SPEAKING PEOPLE and controlled in the early 19th century by SHAKA. The first European settlers set up a trading post in 1824 at what is now Durban. VOORTREKKERS, led by Piet RETIEF, entered the region over the Drakensberg in the 1830s and set up the short-lived Republic of NATALIA. Britain ruled Natal from 1843, a period that heralded both the expansion of the white population through the arrival of groups of settlers and the subjugation of the indigenous population, particularly after their defeat in the ANGLO-ZULU WAR. Natal was one of the four provinces of South Africa after UNION in 1910, and later several pieces were excised from it to become the KWAZULU Bantustan. After the 1994 election, the two areas were officially rejoined as KwaZulu-Natal.

❖ A number of times in the 20th century white Natalians, who had governed themselves since the 1890s, talked of cutting themselves off politically from the rest of South Africa. They were, in particular, reluctant to enter Union, and there were separatist noises when a countrywide referendum in 1961 approved the idea of South Africa becoming a REPUBLIC. A different kind of separatism emerged in the early 1990s, when Chief Mangosuthu ▷BUTHELEZI suggested a separate status for KwaZulu in a federal South Africa.

Natalia, Republic of Short-lived VOORTREKKER republic established in 1837 in part of what is now KwaZulu-Natal. When it was brought under British rule in 1843, many of the Voortrekkers there returned across the Drakensberg to settle in what became the ORANGE FREE STATE and the TRANSVAAL.

National Convention (1908-9) Meetings in Durban, Cape Town and Bloemfontein of white delegates from the four South African states to discuss unification and a new constitution. A series of compromises was made, a constitution was drawn up, and UNION followed in 1910. The National Convention agreed that the FRANCHISE policies of the various states should remain, and that the legislative capital should be Cape Town, the administrative capital Pretoria and the judicial capital Bloemfontein. Black opponents organized a SOUTH AFRICAN NATIVE CONVENTION, but were not able to prevent the colour bar being introduced in the new constitution.

National Liberation League Political body established in the mid-1930s by coloured people disillusioned with the AFRICAN PEOPLE'S ORGANIZATION. It campaigned for equal rights for all and opposed racial SEGREGATION. Most of its members went into the NON-EUROPEAN UNITY MOVEMENT in 1944.

National Party (NP) Founded in 1914 by J B M HERTZOG to further Afrikaner interests, after he had broken with fellow Boer generals Louis BOTHA and Jan SMUTS because he believed that they had become too pro-British. For a long time the NP's main support came from Afrikaner voters living in rural voters. It came to power in 1924 with the aid of the white Labour Party. When it merged with Smuts's South African Party in 1934, D F MALAN broke with Hertzog and kept alive a separate Purified National Party as the party of ▷AFRIKANER NATIONALISM. After fighting off a challenge by the OSSEWABRANDWAG during ▷WORLD WAR II, Malan led his party to victory in the 1948 election. The NP's policy was APARTHEID, and NP governments from 1948 implemented it with zeal. After F W ▷DE KLERK's change of direction in 1990, the NP quickly decided to accept members who were not white and to distance itself from apartheid. It won 20 per cent of the votes in the general election of 1994, and entered into the ▷GOVERNMENT OF NATIONAL UNITY. (See also ▷NATIONAL PARTY in 'Politics, government and the law' section.)

national stayaways Mass withdrawals of labour as a form of protest against the APARTHEID regime which began in the 1950s and continued through the 1980s. The same tactic was then used as a means of putting pressure on the National Party Government during the transition to democracy. The largest such stayaways took place in mid-1992, after the massacre of more than 40 people (mostly ANC supporters) at Boipatong in what is now the province of Gauteng. Although each stayaway lasted only a few days, they were an indication of worker power the government could not ignore.

Natives Land Acts Legislation passed by the governments of Louis BOTHA (in 1913) and of J B M HERTZOG (1936) to restrict African ownership of land to a small portion of the total area of South Africa: seven per cent by the 1913 Act; 13 per cent by that of 1936. The Acts also sought to remove African ▷SQUATTERS from white-owned farms. The Cape was excluded from the 1913 Act because of its FRANCHISE policy; the 1936 legislation provided for nationwide uniformity, but not all the land promised to Africans then was ever bought. The laws were repealed in 1991.

PARTY LEADER *J B M Hertzog, founder of the National Party, wanted Afrikaners to have total equality with the English. He played a key role in Afrikaner politics for many years.*

Natives Representative Council (NRC) Advisory body set up in 1936 as part of the UNITED PARTY Government's quid pro quo for the removal of the Cape African FRANCHISE. Successive governments took virtually no notice of what the NRC recommended, and by 1946 relations with the government had broken down. In 1951, after the advent of the APARTHEID regime, it was abolished.

Natives (Urban Areas) Act (1923) Law that complemented the NATIVES LAND ACTS. It provided for separate African townships in urban areas, and for restrictions on the entry of Africans into the cities, restrictions which were progressively tightened in many later amendments. (See also INFLUX CONTROL.)

Negotiating Forum See CODESA and MULTI-PARTY NEGOTIATIONS.

Ngqika (c1775-1829) Paramount chief of the western ▷XHOSA in the Ciskei at the time of the first major encounters between the Xhosa and the Cape colonists. He was recognized by the Cape Government in 1819, but his collaboration with the colonists helped alienate him from his own people.

Nkomati Accord Nonaggression pact signed in 1984 between South Africa and Mozambique at Nkomati on the border between the two countries. It signalled Mozambique's weakness in the face of South African DESTABILIZATION. While Mozambique ousted ANC operatives, it later became clear that elements within the South African State continued to support ▷RENAMO, the Mozambican National Resistance movement.

Nkosi Sikelel' iAfrika 'Lord Bless Africa'. Anthem composed by Xhosa teacher Enoch Sontonga in 1897. It became the national anthem of a number of African countries before becoming one of South Africa's two national anthems in 1994, the other being 'Die Stem', with verses written by C J Langenhoven and music composed by M L de Villiers.

Non-European Unity Movement Founded in Cape Town in 1943 with the aim of building unity among the oppressed, this political organization drew support especially from the coloured elite. Strongly antiracist, it advocated a strategy of noncollaboration with State structures and of boycotts. Harsh State repression in the 1960s virtually destroyed it, but it was reconstituted as the New Unity Movement in the 1980s.

Nongqawuse See The CATTLE-KILLING.

Oppenheimer, Sir Ernest (1880-1957) Entrepreneur and founder of the giant multinational ▷ANGLO AMERICAN CORPORATION. He created his fortune in diamonds (both in South Africa and Namibia), exploited the diamond monopoly of ▷DE BEERS to keep the diamond industry profitable through the ▷DEPRESSION, and worked to open up new gold mines in the Orange Free State after World War II.

❖ He was succeeded as chairman of De Beers and Anglo by his son, Harry, whose son Nicholas was next in line for the position.

Orange Free State Independent BOER republic established in the former ORANGE RIVER SOVEREIGNTY in terms of the Bloemfontein Convention of 1854. The Boers fought wars over land with the Sotho of MOSHOESHOE in 1858 and 1865 and further consolidated white ownership of land through the purchase of GRIQUA territory in the south. It joined the SOUTH AFRICAN REPUBLIC in opposition to Britain in the SOUTH AFRICAN WAR. After the war it became a British colony, until it was incorporated into UNION in 1910 as a separate province. In 1994 it became one of the nine new provinces of South Africa, now under the name Free State.

Orange River Sovereignty Name given to the territory between the Orange and Vaal rivers – inhabited by TREKBOERS, VOORTREKKERS and many different indigenous peoples – when it came under British rule in terms of a proclamation in 1848 by High Commissioner Sir Harry SMITH. The British Government was never keen to rule it, and in 1854 it reverted to the Boers, as the ORANGE FREE STATE.

Ordinance 50 (1828) Cape legislation that gave 'Hottentots (Khoikhoi) and other free persons of colour' equality under the law, and in particular did away with Passes for them. John Philip of the LONDON MISSIONARY SOCIETY had canvassed for such a law in England. It also served the colony's need for a more mobile labour force.

Ossewabrandwag (OB) 'Oxwagon sentinal'. A cultural organization established in 1939, and which during ▷WORLD WAR II became a paramilitary body propagating ▷NAZI ideas. It embarked on sabotage against the war effort during Jan SMUTS's term as prime minister, but his successor, D F MALAN, was able to prevent it from playing a dominant role in ▷AFRIKANER NATIONALISM.

❖ John VORSTER, later prime minister of South Africa, was among about 2 000 OB members interned at Koffiefontein in the Orange Free State during the war.

MINING MAGNATE *Sir Ernest Oppenheimer laid the foundations of the Anglo American business empire that is today a leading multinational.*

PAC (Pan-Africanist Congress) Established in 1959 by disenchanted ANC members. Under the leadership of Robert SOBUKWE, the PAC advocated an ▷AFRICANIST philosophy. The PAC decided to pre-empt the ANC by launching its own ANTI-PASS CAMPAIGN in March 1960. The resulting SHARPEVILLE SHOOTINGS led to the declaration of a state of emergency by the National Party Government and both the PAC and the ANC were banned. In exile, it failed to organize effectively, and was riven with internecine feuds. After it was unbanned in 1990, it again failed to organize effectively within the country, and had difficulty raising funds. Its armed wing, known as APLA (Azanian People's Liberation Army), gained notoriety for attacks on civilian targets. In January 1994, under pressure from the Tanzanian Government, the PAC agreed to suspend its armed struggle. It fared poorly in the April 1994 election. (See also ▷PAC in 'Politics, government and the law'.)

Pact Government Led by prime minister J B M HERTZOG from 1924 to 1933, it was the result of a deal between his National Party and the white Labour Party not to oppose each other in the 1924 election. The pact gradually fell apart in the late 1920s and was finally destroyed by the political crisis brought on by the advent of the Depression and Hertzog's decision to remain on the ▷GOLD STANDARD. Hertzog then went into a new deal that led to FUSION between his party and Jan Smuts's South African Party.

Pass laws Legislation used to control the movement of Africans, especially to towns. In South Africa, pass laws were developed in the late 19th century, first on the diamond mines, and then on the gold mines. They were much extended in the 20th century until, under APARTHEID, legislation provided for a 96-page 'Reference Book' that detailed residence and working rights and had to be carried at all times. Numerous ANTI-PASS CAMPAIGNS were held, to no avail. Millions of Africans were arrested in terms of Pass laws – extended in the 1950s to women – before president P W ▷BOTHA repealed them in 1986. (See also INFLUX CONTROL)

Passive Resistance Campaign (1946) Protest led by the South African INDIAN CONGRESS against the Asiatic Land Tenure and Indian Representation Bill, which curtailed property

PAC FOUNDERS *On the Pan-Africanist Congress's first national executive committee were: (from left, seated) A B Ngcobo, Robert Sobukwe, A P Mda (not a member), P K Leballo, H S Ngcobo and (standing) J D Nyaose, E Mfaxa, Z B Molete, P Molotsi, S T Ngendane and H Hlatswayo.*

rights of Indians in Natal and the Transvaal. The campaign was modelled on those of Mahatma GANDHI in Natal and the Transvaal. The measure of success achieved impressed Nelson Mandela, who was a leading member of the ANC YOUTH LEAGUE at the time.

Plaatje, Solomon T (1876-1932) Prolific writer and politician, who in 1912 was chosen as the first secretary-general of the ANC. He was an active campaigner against the NATIVES LAND ACT of 1913.
❖ Plaatje spoke eight languages, a skill he employed both as editor of the English-Tswana newspaper 'Koranta ea Becoana' ('Bechuana Gazette') and as an interpreter during the siege of MAFEKING. His diary of the siege was published more than four decades after his death. (See also Solomon ▷PLAATJE in 'Southern African literature'.)

poor whites Term used to describe unskilled, uneducated whites (mostly Afrikaners). Many of whom were *bywoners* (tenant farmers or sharecroppers) who had been pushed off the land in the late 19th century and early 20th century largely because of the discovery of gold, the 'scorched earth' tactics during the SOUTH AFRICAN WAR, and drought. These 'have-nots' were forced to move in large numbers into the cities, where they were unable to compete for employment with Africans prepared to work for lower wages. In the 1920s and 1930s the State stepped in with a so-called civilized labour policy, which favoured white over black labour.

Population Registration Act (1950) Legislation that provided for the race classification of all South Africans into categories such as 'African', 'white', 'Asian', 'coloured' and the like. It created bizarre and often hurtful rules for classification, and was much reviled as a cornerstone of APARTHEID laws. The Act was repealed in 1991.

Progressive Party Political party formed in 1959 by 11 disillusioned UNITED PARTY members of parliament. It advocated a qualified franchise and no racial discrimination. In 1975 it amalgamated with the Reform Party, and was later called the Progressive Federal Party. In 1989 it linked up with the Independent Party and the National Democratic Party to form the Democratic Party, which won 20 per cent of white support in the election of that year.
❖ For 13 years, until 1974, the only Progressive Party member of parliament was Helen ▷SUZMAN (1917-), a doughty fighter for human rights whom many saw as the only real opposition to the APARTHEID regime in those years.

Rand Revolt (1922) Rebellion that began as a strike by white workers on the coal and gold mines against a relaxation of the job colour bar, which would have given certain jobs to blacks instead of whites (at a time of depression). The strike escalated into a full-scale uprising against the government of Jan SMUTS, who used the full might of the State to suppress it, including even the air force. More than 200 people were killed. The brutal suppression of the revolt was a factor in Smuts's defeat in the 1924 election.

Randlords Name given to the mine magnates of the Witwatersrand, such as Edward Lippert, Sammy MARKS and Joseph Robinson, especially before the SOUTH AFRICAN WAR. Many of them were irked by Paul KRUGER's Government and some were involved in the JAMESON RAID conspiracy to topple Kruger. Once thought to have played an influential role in the origins of the South African War, historians today play down the importance of their role in political developments.

Reconstruction Term used for the policies applied after the SOUTH AFRICAN WAR by colonial administrator Lord Milner in the former Boer republics. It involved, among other things, bringing the gold mines back into full production, and promoting the ANGLICIZATION of the Transvaal. The term was used again by the 1994 ▷GOVERNMENT OF NATIONAL UNITY for its plans to deal with the ravages of APARTHEID. These were linked more directly to the social and economic development of the mass of the population. (See ▷RDP in 'Business and economics'.)

Republic The goal of a republic for South Africa as a whole was long advocated by

HOT NEWSREEL *'Pictures that will move the world' is the claim made by the poster advertising a film of the fighting after a miners' strike grew into the Rand Revolt of 1922.*

leading figures of ▷AFRIKANER NATIONALISM such as J B M HERTZOG and D F MALAN, and was achieved in 1961 under prime minister Hendrik VERWOERD. A new constitution provided for a State president to replace the British monarch, but otherwise the system of government remained unaltered until 1983, when a new constitution gave the State president greatly enhanced executive powers.

Reserves As whites conquered more and more territory in South Africa, they set aside small portions of land for various black groups. In Natal, Sir Theophilus SHEPSTONE was the first to elaborate a philosophy of SEGREGATION based on Reserves. They became reservoirs of MIGRANT LABOUR for the cities and white-owned farms. From the 1950s the Reserves gradually became BANTUSTANS in terms of the policies of Hendrik VERWOERD.
❖ The TRANSKEI, which was annexed by the Cape in the late 19th century, was the single largest Reserve.

Resolution 435 Passed in 1978 by the ▷UNITED NATIONS Security Council, it demanded the withdrawal of South African forces from SOUTH WEST AFRICA and provided for the establishment of a UN Transitional Assistance Group to supervize and control an election in the territory prior to its independence as Namibia. Loosely used for the entire plan for the transition to the independence of Namibia, Resolution 435 was eventually put into effect from 1 April 1989 until the day of independence – 21 March 1990.

Retief, Piet (Pieter) (1780-1838) Leader of the VOORTREKKERS and martyr. An unsuccessful businessman in Grahamstown, he left the Cape in 1837 and became leader of the trekkers, advising them to move into Natal. Promised land here by DINGANE, the Zulu king, he and his party were being entertained at the Zulu capital when the king ordered that the whites be killed. The trekkers later avenged Retief's death at the battle of BLOOD RIVER.

Rhodes, Cecil John (1853-1902) Mining magnate and politician whose vision of African colonies stretching from the Cape to Cairo had a significant impact in southern Africa. Rhodes made his first fortune on the Kimberley diamond fields, where he established De Beers Mining Company and then De Beers Consolidated Mines. His true wealth, however, derived from the Witwatersrand goldfields and his company Consolidated Gold Fields of South Africa. He was prime minister of the Cape from 1890-6, losing office after his disastrous attempt to overthrow Paul Kruger's government by launching the JAMESON RAID. His BRITISH SOUTH AFRICA COMPANY created what was virtually a personal fiefdom for him north of the Limpopo River called, appropriately, RHODESIA.
❖ He was buried in the Matobo Hills in Rhodesia, at a place he called World's View, and all his tombstone bore were the words he had requested: 'Here lie the remains of Cecil John Rhodes'.
❖ He endowed a number of Rhodes Scholarships at Oxford University. Granted to bright, sporty young men with leadership qualities from the British colonies, America and Germany, they were extended in 1977 to women.

Rhodesia (now Zimbabwe) Name given to the territory – long inhabited by BANTU-SPEAKING PEOPLE – that was settled by whites under the auspices of Cecil Rhodes's BRITISH SOUTH AFRICA COMPANY in the 1890s. In the 1920s the company handed control of the territory to Britain. Northern Rhodesia eventually became independent as Zambia. Southern Rhodesia retained the name Rhodesia after Ian Smith's UDI in 1965. This act led to a long struggle by African nationalists against the settler population, culminating in the RHODESIAN WAR. After the war ended, Robert ▷MUGABE won the 1980 election and led the first government of the independent Zimbabwe.
❖ The name Rhodesia was first coined by the newspaperman Francis Dormer (1854-1928). He was one of the founders of the giant Argus newspaper group in South Africa and founder, in 1892, of the 'Rhodesia Herald' (now 'The Herald') and of the 'Bulawayo Chronicle' (now 'The Chronicle') in 1894.

Rhodesian War (1972-9) A mainly guerrilla war in which African nationalists, organized in the Zimbabwe National Liberation Army of Robert ▷MUGABE and the Zimbabwe People's Revolutionary Army of Joshua ▷NKOMO, fought for the independence of their country. Large areas of RHODESIA were liberated by the guerrillas before the conflict was brought to an end by the LANCASTER HOUSE AGREEMENT. By then some 30 000 people, most of them Africans, had died.

rinderpest epidemic (1896-8) Outbreak of rinderpest – an acute, contagious viral disease of cattle – that passed through southern Africa, causing the death of vast numbers of livestock. The effects were devastating on people, too, especially in the Transkei and eastern Cape, where many who believed that the epidemic had been brought by whites to deprive them of their cattle refused to cooperate in innoculation programmes. The cattle deaths and attempts to halt the disease by killing infected animals also led to rebellion against white authorities in both RHODESIA and BECHUANALAND.

Rivonia Trial (1963-1964) Trial in Pretoria of the high command of UMKHONTO WE SIZWE. Those arrested at a house in Rivonia, a suburb of Johannesburg, were originally charged

CHAMPION OF EMPIRE *Cecil John Rhodes, who envisioned the British flag flying from Cape to Cairo, lies buried beneath a plain slab on the summit of a granite dome called World's View in the Matobo Hills, Zimbabwe – formerly known as Rhodesia.*

YOUTHFUL FUTURE PRESIDENT *A smiling Nelson Mandela (centre) in 1961. Two years later, he was one of the defendants at the Rivonia Trial and was eventually sentenced to life imprisonment.*

with high treason, together with Nelson ▷MANDELA, who was already in jail when the others were arrested. Eight of the accused were found guilty of sabotage and sentenced to life imprisonment after international calls for the death sentence not to be imposed.

❖ In his much-quoted statement from the dock, Mandela spoke of 'the ideal of a democratic and free society' as one for which he was prepared to die. Thirty years after the trial he became the country's first democratically elected president.

❖ The other seven imprisoned with Mandela on ▷ROBBEN ISLAND were: Walter Sisulu, Govan Mbeki, Raymond Mhlaba, Elias Motsoaledi, Andrew Mlangeni, Ahmed Kathrada and Dennis Goldberg.

Road to the North Name coined in the 19th century for the strategically important corridor of land running up the eastern side of what became BECHUANALAND (Botswana). Also known as the missionaries' road, it was the only route to the African interior which did not pass through the Boer territory of the TRANSVAAL. When it seemed that the Transvaal might expand westward and cut off the road, Britain intervened and annexed Bechualanand in 1885.

Rorke's Drift, Battle of (1879) After the British defeat at ISANDLWANA in the ANGLO-ZULU WAR, a small British force successfully resisted a large Zulu army at Rorke's Drift near Dundee in what is now KwaZulu-Natal. It was regarded as repesenting a heroic defence against overwhelming numbers.

❖ Britain conferred the Victoria Cross, its highest award for gallantry displayed in the face of the enemy, to 11 of the troops involved in the battle.

Rubicon speech Name given to a 1985 speech by P W ▷BOTHA, who was widely expected to announce reforms of APARTHEID. When the expectations were not met, Botha was said to have failed to ▷CROSS THE RUBICON, a failure that led to a slump in the local currency and large-scale disinvestment by foreign companies. Botha did abolish the PASS LAWS in 1986 and agree to the independence of Namibia in 1988, but it was his successor, F W ▷DE KLERK, who set South Africa on a new path with his reform speech of 2 February 1990.

sanctions Coercive measures used against a government deemed guilty of breaking international law, often a campaign coordinated through the ▷UNITED NATIONS. Sanctions were imposed from 1965 against the Rhodesian Government of Ian Smith after UDI, including arms and oil embargoes, and prohibitions on trade with the country. Between 1960 and 1990, many different kinds of sanctions were imposed on the APARTHEID regime. Among the most important was the mandatory United Nations ARMS EMBARGO of 1977, the financial sanctions that followed president P W Botha's 1985 RUBICON SPEECH, and those in the USA's Comprehensive Anti-Apartheid Act of 1986. Most sanctions had fallen away by the end of 1991 after the National Party Government had instituted its reforms, but the arms embargo was not lifted until after the 1994 election.

❖ Desmond Tutu, Anglican Archbishop of Cape Town, was a leading proponent of sanctions against South Africa. Among those opposed to sanctions, on the grounds that they would inflict damage to the economy and increase unemployment, were Helen Suzman of the Democratic Party and Chief Mangosuthu Buthelezi of KWAZULU.

BULLETS AGAINST SPEARS *The Rorke's Drift mission station blazes after British forces had repelled a Zulu army in a 12-hour battle. About 500 Zulus were killed, against the defenders' 17 dead.*

segregation (racial segregation) Meaning literally separation from the main group, the word is used for the policy (whether official or not) of setting aside facilities or resources for certain groups (usually black). In South Africa, some have argued that Jan VAN RIEBEECK was the first segregationist, while others find the roots of segregation in Sir Theophilus SHEPSTONE's policies in Natal in the 19th century. It is generally accepted by historians that an ideology of racial separation did not develop in South Africa until the early 20th century, and that a full-scale set of segregationist policies was not put into place until after that. Examples of racial segregation include the FRANCHISE policies of the Union of 1910 and the NATIVES LAND ACT of 1913 and 1936, while the most extreme and all-encompassing form was APARTHEID.

Sekhukhune (*c*1810-82) Leader of the Pedi people of the eastern Tranvaal from 1861 who tried, not without success, to resist BOER encroachment on his land. In 1879 he was defeated by a British force after the annexation of the TRANSVAAL.

separate development Term substituted for APARTHEID by the National Party Government from the late 1950s. It was associated especially with Hendrik VERWOERD and his BANTUSTAN plans.

settlers Literally, any person who settles in a new country or colony. The best-known group of European settlers were 5 000 from Britain who arrived in 1820 and were given land on the Cape's EASTERN FRONTIER. In time in South Africa the term 'settler' came to be given to whites in general, and those whites whose ancestors had lived in the country for centuries especially resented the term. In the early 1990s, PAC supporters frequently chanted 'One Settler, One Bullet'. The official position of the PAC was that anyone who oppressed Africans was a settler.

Shaka (*c*1787-1828) Founder of the ZULU KINGDOM. A military genius, Shaka increased the power of his state until by the 1820s it was dominant in all of the territory that roughly corresponds with KwaZulu-Natal today. His warriors used a short stabbing spear and large shield to good effect, and went into battle in tight, horseshoe formations. His kingdom was more highly centralized than any previous state, and among whites he gained the image of a bloodthirsty and tyrannical ruler. His armies were sent far afield, and many fled before them, so his influence extended far beyond the borders of his kingdom. He did not produce an heir, however, and his half-brother DINGANE assassinated him and then succeeded him.

❖ The present Zulu monarch, King Goodwill Zwelethini, is a descendant of Mpande, another of Shaka's half-brothers.

❖ Zulu traditionalists celebrate Shaka Day on 24 September, the anniversary of his death.

WORLD-SHATTERING SHOOTING *Benumbed confusion follows the death of 69 unarmed protesters at Sharpeville in 1960 – an event that focused the world's attention on apartheid policies.*

Sharpeville shootings Incident in Sharpeville, in present-day Gauteng, on 21 March 1960 when nervous police suddenly opened fire on unarmed protesters taking part in an ANTI-PASS CAMPAIGN. Sixty-nine people died, many shot in the back. In the political crisis that followed, the PAC (which organized the protest) and the ANC were banned. The Sharpeville shootings, more than any other single incident, alerted the international community to the horrors and injustices of APARTHEID policies.

Shepstone, Sir Theophilus (1817-93) Administrator of Africans in Natal. He was renowned for his segregationist policies, especially the establishment of RESERVES for Africans and their separate administration. He was much criticized for his role in the LANGALIBALELE episode. He was sent by British Colonial Secretary Lord CARNARVON to bring about the annexation of the TRANSVAAL, which he did in 1877. He subsequently

WARRIOR KING *Two impressions reflect Shaka – A painting from Nathaniel Isaacs's* Travels and Adventures in Eastern Africa *and the character played by actor Henry Cele in the TV series.*

administered the territory until shortly before the outbreak of the ANGLO-TRANSVAAL WAR.

Slagter's Nek Rebellion (1815) Uprising that followed the refusal of a Cape frontier farmer, Frederik Bezuidenhout, to appear in court on charges of maltreating a KHOIKHOI servant. It was suppressed and the leaders were publicly executed.
❖ Afrikaner nationalists often cited the event as a prime example of British oppression – particularly since the rope broke the first time the executioner attempted the hanging.

slavery The first slaves introduced to the Cape in 1658 were from Angola. The majority of the large slave population later brought to the Cape came from India and the East Indies. South African blacks were not enslaved, although some lived in conditions akin to slavery and a few were bought and sold. The British Government ended the trade in slaves in 1808 and slavery itself in 1834. The ex-slaves then became 'apprentices' for four years before final emancipation. In time they became an almost indistinguishable part of the Cape's coloured population.

Smith, Sir Harry (Henry) George Wakelyn (1787-1860) Egocentric and bombastic British Governor of the Cape and HIGH COMMISSIONER from 1847 to 1852. He extended British rule northwards to the Vaal River (with the proclamation of the ORANGE RIVER SOVEREIGNTY) and east to the Kei River (with the annexation of BRITISH KAFFRARIA). He led the colony into war with the ▷XHOSA in 1850, and was recalled by the British Government in 1852.
❖ The town of Harrismith in the Free State is named after him; both Ladismith in Western Cape and Ladysmith in KwaZulu-Natal are named after his wife.

Smuts, Jan Christian (1870-1950) Soldier, intellectual, statesman and prime minister 1919-24 and 1939-48. As a distinguished veteran of the SOUTH AFRICAN WAR and a Minister in the TRANSVAAL Government, he played an key role in the creation of the UNION. He was Louis BOTHA's right-hand man in the first Union Government, succeeding him as prime minister in 1919. During ▷WORLD WAR I he served in East Africa, and as a member of the British Imperial War Cabinet. He joined J B M HERTZOG in the FUSION Government of 1934, then in 1939 took over from Hertzog and led South Africa into ▷WORLD WAR II, during which he served in North Africa and as adviser to the British prime minister, Winston Churchill. However, his activities on the international stage – he helped create both the ▷LEAGUE OF NATIONS and its successor, the United Nations – led him to neglect his domestic constituency, and in 1948 he lost power to D F MALAN's National Party. He remained in parliament as Leader of the Opposition until his death.
❖ Among Smuts's many interests was philosophy. His most famous and influential book, *Holism and Evolution* (1926), was instrumental in bringing the words 'holism' and 'holistic' into general usage.
❖ Smuts's wife, affectionately dubbed 'Ouma' ('Granny'), is particularly remembered for her efforts on behalf of those fighting in World War II. She tirelessly campaigned for funds, knitted for her 'boys' and organized working groups in her home to pack 'glory bags' for those on the front.

SOLDIER AND STATESMAN *Jan Smuts mingles with the loyal commandos whom he assembled to end the Rand Revolt in 1922.*

Sobhuza I (Somhlolo) (*c*1790-1839) Founder of the Swazi kingdom. He relocated his small chiefdom from present day northern KwaZulu-Natal to what is now central SWAZILAND, where he consolidated neighbouring Sotho- and Nguni-speaking people into a much enlarged state. This he bequeathed to his son and successor Mswati (*c*1826-68).

Sobukwe, Robert Mangaliso (1924-78) Ardent Africanist, proponent of a United States of Africa and leader of the PAC from its establishment in 1959. He led the ANTI-PASS CAMPAIGN which the PAC launched in 1960, after which he was imprisoned on ▷ROBBEN ISLAND for nine years. After his release, he lived in Kimberley under severe restrictions.

South African Defence Force Established in 1912 as the Union Defence Force, which distinguished itself in both World War I and II, as well as other international campaigns. It was renamed in 1957, when it had three commands – army, navy and air force (medical services and special forces were added in the 1970s and 1980s). A high proportion of the army was made up of part-time soldiers in the Citizen Force and commandos. Blacks were employed only in ancilliary roles in the World wars, although they were used in full combat roles during the BORDER WAR from the 1970s. This war was the SADF's greatest test. In 1994 the SADF was superceded by a new South African National Defence Force, which included within it former members of the ANC's military wing, UMKHONTO WE SIZWE.
❖ The South African Air Force, established in 1920, is the second oldest air force in the world after Britain's.
❖ During the APARTHEID years, the SADF's image was somewhat tarnished by the deployment of troops to suppress township unrest and by the involvement of some of its members in the policy of DESTABILIZATION and in DIRTY TRICKS.

South African flag Among South African whites the issue of a new flag for the UNION became explosive in the 1920s; the outcome was a compromise in which the Union Jack was included in the flag along with the flags of the former BOER republics. With the advent of a democratic constitution in 1994, that flag was replaced with a new multicoloured flag, approved by constitutional negotiators. Although intended to be a temporary, it soon acquired general acceptance.

South African Native Convention (1908-9) Meeting of Africans convened in response to the NATIONAL CONVENTION called by whites to unify South Africa. It was unsuccessful in its opposition to UNION, but was important as a forerunner of the ANC.

South African Republic Also called the ZAR, from the initials of its Dutch name, it was the name for the BOER Government of the TRANSVAAL, established in 1860 when various groups amalgamated under a constitution. The republic was superseded when the British conquered the Transvaal during the SOUTH AFRICAN WAR.

South African War (1899-1902) Also called the Second Anglo-Boer War, fought between the Boer republics (the Transvaal and Orange Free State) and Britain. It was provoked by British determination to overthrow Paul KRUGER's Government and gain control of the Witwatersrand goldfields. The British hoped

PEACE PARLEY *Boer leader General Louis Botha (seated, second from left) meets British Commander-in-Chief Lord Kitchener in April 1902 to discuss a truce to end the South African War.*

for a quick victory, but the Boers inflicted major defeats – notably at MAGERSFONTEIN – before their republics were conquered. Even then, the British under Lord KITCHENER had to employ 'methods of barbarism' such as CONCENTRATION CAMPS and a scorched earth policy before the Boers sued for peace. The war had by then become something of a civil war, and large numbers of blacks were directly involved. It was the most costly war fought by the British between 1815 and 1914; by the time it was ended by the Treaty of Vereeniging, 22 000 imperial troops, 7 000 Boer soldiers and many blacks had been killed.

❖ The war introduced a new word into world English – commando, from the Afrikaans name for the Boer units, which were highly mobile, mounted units of irregular soldiers who lived off the land. Winston Churchill, as war correspondent for the 'Morning Post', wrote: 'We must face the facts. The individual Boer, mounted in suitable country, is worth three to five regular soldiers.'

South West Africa (now Namibia) West-coast territory north of the Orange River, which was colonized late in the 19th century by Germany. It was invaded by South Africa at the request of Britain during ▷WORLD WAR I, an event that led to the AFRIKANER REBELLION. Jan SMUTS wished to annex it to South Africa, but did not get his way: at the end of the war Woodrow Wilson, the president of the USA, insisted that it become a ▷LEAGUE OF NATIONS mandate. After ▷WORLD WAR II, the United Nations refused to agree to its incorporation into South Africa. It therefore retained its international status, although South Africa contested that status from 1946. The matter went to the ▷INTERNATIONAL COURT OF JUSTICE, which ruled that the mandate continue. In 1966 the General Assembly of the United Nations unilaterally terminated the mandate and demanded that South Africa withdraw. After the Security Council and the International Court had confirmed that decision (1971), South Africa was gradually brought to concede the idea of independence for the territory. Initially South Africa wished to take charge of Namibia's transition to independence, but in April 1978, under pressure from the major Western powers, it agreed to a plan for the transition which involved a United Nations-monitored election, a plan embodied in RESOLUTION 435 of September 1978. South Africa refused to allow the implementation of that plan until 1988. The election was held in November 1989; and Namibia become independent under a ▷SWAPO Government on 21 March 1990 with Sam Nujoma as president. (See also BORDER WAR, CUITO CUANAVALE, DESTABILIZATION, HERERO REBELLION, WALVIS BAY.)

Soweto Revolt (1976) Uprising that began in Soweto, south of Johannesburg, as a protest by school children against BANTU EDUCATION and specifically the National Party Government's insistence that Afrikaans be used as a medium of instruction in schools. The revolt spread from here across the country, and more than 600 people, most of them teenagers, were killed. Thousands of others fled abroad, where they joined the ANC and its armed wing, UMKHONTO WE SIZWE. The harsh measures used to suppress the uprising aroused much international condemnation, and some have seen the Soweto Revolt as the beginning of the end for APARTHEID.

❖ Hector Petersen, a 13-year-old schoolboy, was the first person killed in the uprising. A photograph of a fellow student carrying his limp body was used worldwide as a symbol of the tragedy.

❖ South Africa commemorates Youth Day on 16 June, the anniversary of the revolt.

Stone Age Period from the beginning of human history until the appearance of bronze or iron implements, so called because people used stone tools and weapons. In Africa this era began 2,5 million to 3 million years ago and, although the IRON AGE started on the continent about 3 000 years ago, the Stone Age survived in some cultures until the time of colonial settlement. Archaeologists divide it into the Earlier, Middle and Later Stone Ages, reflecting the developing sophistication of tools. The San HUNTER-GATHERERS, called Bushmen by early colonists, were Later Stone Age people. In many parts of the world the Stone Age was followed by the ▷BRONZE AGE, which preceded the Iron Age.

Strijdom, Johannes Gerhardus (1893-1958) NATIONAL PARTY leader and South African prime minister from 1956-8. A dour man, nicknamed 'The Lion of the North', he interpreted APARTHEID as mere 'baasskap', or domination by whites.

Swaziland Kingdom created by SOBHUZA I, it came under increasing pressure in the late 19th century from the SOUTH AFRICAN REPUBLIC, which was seeking an outlet to the sea. In

GRAPHIC SYMBOL *This dramatic picture of fatally wounded Hector Petersen was published worldwide after the Soweto tragedy.*

1907 it became a separate territory (see HIGH COMMISSIONER) and was led to independence by Britain in 1968. After signing a secret non-aggression pact with the South African Government in 1982, it clamped down on ANC activity from its territory.

Tambo, Oliver Reginald (1917-93) President of the ANC from 1967 until 1991. A prominent member of the ANC YOUTH LEAGUE in the 1940s, Tambo worked with Nelson ▷MANDELA as a lawyer and in politics in the 1950s. In 1960, when the ANC was BANNED, he was told to continue the fight in exile, and he settled first in London and later in Lusaka. He campaigned actively on behalf of the ANC and helped organize its struggle to liberate the country. He returned from exile in poor health after the ANC was unbanned and he did not live long enough to see his party come to power in 1994.

Total Strategy NATIONAL PARTY idea that the Government should resist a 'total onslaught' against it, instigated by Moscow, with all means at its disposal. Based on a misreading that the campaign against APARTHEID was a communist-inspired design to control South Africa, Total Strategy was a brainchild of the military. It was taken up by P W ▷BOTHA's Government in the late 1970s and 1980s, and used to defend apartheid and to justify, among other things, the DESTABILIZATION of neighbouring countries.

Township Revolt (1984-6) Uprising that began in the Vaal Triangle south of Johannesburg as the TRICAMERAL PARLIAMENT was inaugurated. In part it was a response to the imposition of increased service charges on residents by new township authorities, but it soon spread countrywide, and for brief periods some townships were beyond police control. The army was drafted in, and as a result of harsh repression, including the imposition of a general state of emergency, the revolt was brought under control, but not before it had produced a great international outcry against the APARTHEID regime, and the imposition of widespread SANCTIONS against it. The uprising led the National Party Government to open negotiations with the jailed ANC leader Nelson ▷MANDELA.

trade unions Relatively small craft and miners' unions for whites were founded in South Africa in the late 19th century. The first large unions in the country were the giant INDUSTRIAL AND COMMERCIAL WORKERS' UNION of the 1920s and the AFRICAN MINEWORKERS' UNION, predecessor to the NUM (National Union of Mineworkers). It was not until 1979 that African unions were officially recognized. In the 1980s union membership grew at an unprecedented rate, and unions combined in large organizations, the most important of which was ▷COSATU, launched in 1985 and closely allied with the ANC. (See also ▷TRADE UNIONS in 'Politics, government and the law'.)

WELCOME HOME *ANC veteran Oliver Tambo, seated beside Nelson Mandela, gets a hero's welcome at a rally in Johannesburg in 1990 on his return to South Africa from 30 years of exile.*

Transkei Literally, land across the Kei, it refers to the area between the Great Kei River and the southern border of what is now KwaZulu-Natal. The area was inhabited from about the 8th century by Nguni-speaking people. White encroachment in the EASTERN FRONTIER region of the Cape was resisted by the ▷XHOSA, but the territory was brought under Cape rule in the late 19th century. The largest African RESERVE in South Africa, it became the pacesetter in Hendrik Verwoerd's BANTUSTAN scheme. In 1963 it was given 'self-government' and in 1976 received 'independence' (recognized only by South Africa) in 1976. A military govenment seized power in 1987. It was reincorporated into South Africa as part of Eastern Province in 1994.

Transvaal Meaning literally beyond the Vaal, it refers to the territory between the Vaal and Limpopo rivers. The area, occupied by BANTU-SPEAKING PEOPLE for about 1 500 years, underwent major upheavals in the 1820s and 1830s during the period that became known as the MFECANE. The VOORTREKKERS began settling here in the 1830s. They clashed with MZILIKAZI, who moved across the Limpopo. The British recognized the independence of the Transvaal Boers in the Sand River Convention of 1852, but it was not until 1860 that the trekker groups organized themselves into the SOUTH AFRICAN REPUBLIC (also known as the Transvaal Republic). In 1877, to promote South African CONFEDERATION, Sir Theophilus SHEPSTONE annexed the Transvaal for Britain at a time when its weak government was under threat from SEKHUKHUNE's Pedi. British rule, though it brought the defeat of the Pedi, was resented by the majority of the whites, who rose in revolt against it in the ANGLO-TRANSVAAL WAR of 1880-1. Governed as a British suzerainty until the SOUTH AFRICAN WAR, the territory became a colony after the war, by which time the remaining African chiefdoms had also been defeated. The Transvaal was incorporated into the UNION in 1910; in 1994 it was divided into Gauteng, Eastern Transvaal (which later became Mpumalanga), North-West and Northern provinces.

Treason Trial (1956-61) Court case against 156 people charged with treason on the grounds that they had promoted revolution by organizing the Congress of the People (at which the FREEDOM CHARTER was adopted) and taking part in the DEFIANCE CAMPAIGN. The accused, including Nelson ▷MANDELA of the ANC, were all acquitted.

trekboers Dutch term for frontier farmers. Unlike the VOORTREKKERS, the trekboers went into the interior as individuals, and continued to regard themselves as colonial subjects. The great age of the trekboer was the 18th century, when they were responsible for the major expansion of the borders of the Cape; they continued to move further inland well into the 19th century.

tricameral parliament (1984-94) Parliament that brought coloured and Indian people into South Africa's central government through representation in separate houses of parliament – a House of Representatives (coloured) and a House of Delegates (Indian). The final say over the passage of legislation lay with a white-dominated President's Council, which gained notoriety for pushing through legislation opposed by all but the National Party-dominated House of Assembly (white). One of state president P W ▷BOTHA's most important reforms, it lay at the heart of the National Party's constitution of 1984 and followed a referendum seeking approval from the white electorate. The exclusion of Africans from this new arrangement helped fuel the TOWNSHIP REVOLT, and the failure of the tricameral parliament to resolve the government's crisis of legitimacy was an important reason for State president F W ▷DE KLERK's reform move in 1990, which led to the dissolution of the tricameral parliament before the general election of 1994.

UDI (unilateral declaration of independence) (1965) Declaration issued by the Rhodesian Front party of Ian ▷SMITH after the break-up of the CENTRAL AFRICAN FEDERATION, in the vain hope of being able to maintain white supremacy in Southern RHODESIA indefinitely. No other country recognized the declaration of independence, and it led directly to the RHODESIAN WAR. Legitimate, internationally recognized independence came to Zimbabwe in 1980.

uitlanders The word, Afrikaans for foreigners, was used for non-Afrikaner whites who settled in the TRANSVAAL after the discovery of gold there and who were opposed to the government of Paul KRUGER. In their attempts to humble Kruger, the British Government fought for the extension of the franchise to them – an issue that was used to justify the abortive JAMESON RAID. The status of the *uitlanders'* was a major issue in the British-Transvaal negotiations before the outbreak of the SOUTH AFRICAN WAR in 1899.

BIRTH OF A NATION *The ship of Union sails into harbour welcomed by Britannia who has lain aside her shield to launch the dove of peace – how the* Cape Times *marked Union Day in 1910.*

Umkhonto we Sizwe (MK) 'Spear of the Nation'. Military wing of the ANC, formed soon after the ANC was banned. It undertook sabotage from 1961 and then, after the RIVONIA TRIAL, moved into guerrilla training in exile. After the SOWETO REVOLT, MK – its ranks swelled by youths who had fled the country – resumed sabotage and attempted armed mobilization within the country. After the ANC agreed to suspend the armed struggle in 1990, MK was not disbanded, but in 1994 its members were integrated into a new South African National Defence Force.

Union (1910) Joining of the CAPE, NATAL, ORANGE FREE STATE and TRANSVAAL into the Union of South Africa. Attempts to unite various South African states went back to 19th-century moves for CONFEDERATION, but only after the SOUTH AFRICAN WAR did a strong movement develop within the country for unification. After the NATIONAL CONVENTION of 1908-9 had drawn up a new constitution, the Union of South Africa was inaugurated on 31 May 1910. It was succeeded by the REPUBLIC of South Africa in 1961.
❖ Many black South Africans were opposed to the Union because the colour bar was written into its constitution, including FRANCHISE policies that excluded them.

United Democratic Front Political organization established in 1983 to challenge the TRICAMERAL PARLIAMENT. An umbrella body, it was virtually a front for the ANC and for some years was the main organized opposition to the NATIONAL PARTY Government. BANNED in 1989, it went out of existence after the unbanning of the ANC in 1990.

United Party (1934-77) Political party formed when J B M HERTZOG's National Party and Jan SMUTS's South African Party merged in 1934 to form the FUSION Government. The UP governed until Smuts lost the general election of 1948, then became the leading opposition to the NATIONAL PARTY Government. Disgusted by what they saw as the party's lack of principle, 11 Members of Parliament broke with the UP in 1959 and formed the PROGRESSIVE PARTY. The UP lost more and more support, and split further in the mid-1970s, then disintegrated. The central contradiction which undermined it was its refusal to abandon white supremacy while opposing a government committed to upholding white supremacy in the form of APARTHEID.

Van der Stel, Simon (1639-1712) DUTCH EAST INDIA COMPANY Governor and commander at the Cape 1679-99, he energetically expanded the settlement and improved its administration. His son Willem Adriaan (1664-1733) succeeded him, but aroused strong opposition from the white burghers of the colony and was dismissed.
❖ Simon van der Stel was keen on promoting the Cape's wine industry. Part of his own vineyards survive around his original homestead, Groot Constantia, in Cape Town.

Van Riebeeck, Jan Anthonisz (1619-77) First Dutch commander at the Cape for the DUTCH EAST INDIA COMPANY, who brought ashore his party in Table Bay on 6 April 1652 and thus became identified for later generations with the establishment of white settlement in South Africa.

❖ Van Riebeeck and his men arrived at the Cape in three ships, the *Drommedaris*, the *Reijger* and *De Goede Hoop*.

Van Ryneveld, Sir Pierre (1891-1972) Soldier and aviation pioneer. In 1920 he was appointed the first director of air services in South Africa with the task of forming an air force – the second in the world after Britain's. A few days later he and Sir Quintin Brand (1893-1968) set off to make history as the first pilots to fly from London to Cape Town. Van Ryneveld, a veteran of World War I, led South Africa's military forces during ▷WORLD WAR II as Chief of General Staff (head of the defence force). He received many decorations for his service in both wars.

Verwoerd, Hendrik Frensch (1901-66) NATIONAL PARTY prime minister (1958-66) and APARTHEID fanatic. Founding editor of the Nationalist newspaper 'Die Transvaler', Verwoerd entered parliament in 1948 and became Minister of Bantu Affairs in 1950. He introduced the inferior BANTU EDUCATION system for blacks in 1953. A hardliner in the administration of segregation, he realized that to sell apartheid abroad it had to be repackaged as 'separate development', and therefore created the BANTUSTAN policy. He had pledged to establish a REPUBLIC when appointed prime minister, and withdrew South Africa from the ▷COMMONWEALTH shortly before the country became a republic in 1961. He survived an assassination attempt in 1960, but a second one in 1966 was successful. He was succeeded by John VORSTER.

❖ Dimitri Tsafendas, a Mozambican-born parliamentary messenger who assassinated him on the floor of the House of Assembly, said a snake in his intestines had led him to do the deed. He was not tried, but confined for three decades to mental institutions.

ARCHITECT OF APARTHEID *Hendrik Verwoerd speaks at the Rand Easter Show in 1960 shortly before an attempt to assassinate him.*

Voortrekkers Literally 'front trekkers'. Name given to those frontier farmers who left the Cape on what became known as the GREAT TREK of the late 1830s. More vaguely meaning 'pioneers', the term has also been applied to the GRIQUA and other groups who went as pioneers into the interior.

Vorster, John (Balthazar Johannes) (1915-83) NATIONAL PARTY prime minister 1966-78. Interned during ▷WORLD WAR II because of his membership of the pro-Nazi OSSEWABRANDWAG, the grim-faced Vorster became prime minister Hendrik VERWOERD's Minister of Justice in 1962 and introduced DETENTION WITHOUT TRIAL to deal with political opposition after the SHARPEVILLE SHOOTINGS. As prime minister he was more pragmatic than Verwoerd and pursued a policy of DÉTENTE abroad. As a result of the INFORMATION SCANDAL he was forced to resign, first as prime minister and subsequently as State President. He was succeeded by P W ▷BOTHA.

Walvis Bay ('Bay of whales') Natural harbour on the Namibian coast, annexed by Britain in 1878 and later administered as a part of South Africa. In the negotiations leading to independence for SOUTH WEST AFRICA, the South African Government refused to allow the future of the bay to be discussed. After Namibia's independence in 1990, the two countries entered negotiations on its future, and Walvis Bay was finally incorporated into Namibia at the end of February 1994.

Waterboer, Nicolaas (*c*1812-84) GRIQUA leader, the son of Andries (1789-1852), the first great Griqua leader at Griquatown north of the Orange River. Nicolaas was ruler when the first diamonds were discovered on Griqua land in 1866. His territory was annexed by Britain in 1871, and incorporated into the Cape Colony in 1880.

Welensky, Roy (1907-93) Prime minister of the CENTRAL AFRICAN FEDERATION from 1956 until its dissolution in 1963. A Rhodesian-born trade unionist, he founded the Federal Party in 1953 around the concept of 'partnership' between whites and Africans, and was a founder of the Central African Federation and its second prime minister after Godfrey Huggins (later Lord Malvern). When the federation dissolved, he tried unsuccessfully to challenge Ian ▷SMITH in Southern Rhodesia, and he eventually retired to England.

❖ Welensky was an outspoken and colourfully rugged character. In his youth he worked as an engine-driver for the railways and he held the Rhodesian heavyweight boxing championship for two years in the 1920s.

UNHEEDED WARNING *British prime minister Harold Macmillan delivers his famous 'wind of change' speech to a joint sitting of the South African parliament in 1960.*

'wind of change' Much-quoted phrase from a speech delivered by the visiting British prime minister Harold Macmillan to a joint sitting of both Houses of Parliament in Cape Town in 1960. He described the growth of African nationalism as a 'wind of change . . . blowing through this continent' and warned South Africa of the need to adjust to it. Prime minister Hendrik VERWOERD rejected the message.

Witbooi, Hendrik (*c*1830-1905) Nama ruler who in 1888 took charge of the people settled around Gideon in southern SOUTH WEST AFRICA (now Namibia). He led a guerrilla war against the Germans, then, after lengthy negotiations, he became an ally of theirs for 10 years, before joining the HERERO REBELLION. A man of great intellect and force of character, he became a hero for later generations of Namibians. His diary was published in 1929.

Witwatersrand gold rush Africans had exploited gold in the TRANSVAAL long before whites arrived, but it was not until 1886 that two prospectors, George Harrison and George Walker, found the Witwatersrand's main reef

EARLY BEGINNINGS *South Africa's vast gold mining industry began with simple alluvial diggings when all that was needed were rudimentary geology, pick and shovel and a lot of luck.*

while working as builders on the farm Langlaagte. Only in the 1890s did it become clear that this was the richest gold field in the world. Apart from the boom it created in the Boer republic, the discovery led directly to the SOUTH AFRICAN WAR with Britain and later motivated UNION in 1910. (See also ▷BULLION in 'Business and economics'.)

❖ Both Georges claimed credit for the discovery, but it was Harrison who staked his claim on the farm – a claim he later sold for £10.

❖ South Africa holds a number of world records in gold mining: it is the biggest producer of gold; and it has the largest mine (East Rand Proprietory Mines, Boksburg, covering 4 900 ha), the deepest mine (Western Deep Levels, Carletonville, at 3 581 m), and the richest (Crown Mines, Johannesburg, with a yield of 49,4 million fine ounces).

Woltemade, Wolraad (*c*1708-1773) Employee of the DUTCH EAST INDIA COMPANY who died rescuing survivors from the ship *De Jonge Thomas*, which ran aground in a storm near the mouth of the Salt River in Cape Town. On his eighth trip on horseback into the pounding waves, he and the horse were swept away.

❖ The Woltemade Decoration for Bravery was established in 1970 as the highest civilian honour for gallantry.

Xhosa polity A decentralised state of relatively autonomous chiefdoms, which from the late 18th century divided into two main sections. In the course of nine frontier wars between 1779 and 1878, the Xhosa were defeated by the Cape colonial and British forces, and lost most of their land. The single most serious blow the Xhosa suffered came from the CATTLE-KILLING of 1857, which led to hundreds of thousands of deaths among the western Xhosa and opened the way to colonial expansion. (See also CISKEI; EASTERN FRONTIER; HINTSA; TRANSKEI; ZUURVELD.)

Xuma, Alfred Bitini (*c*1893-1962) Physician and politician. In the 1930s, Xuma worked in the ALL-AFRICAN CONVENTION against the removal of the franchise from Africans. In 1940 he was elected president-general of the ANC, then in a sad state of disorganization. He revived the ANC and led it into an alliance with Indian antisegregationists in 1946. Essentially conservative, he did not welcome new pressures from the ANC YOUTH LEAGUE and was ousted as president in 1949.

❖ In 1946 Xuma lobbied successfully at the United Nations against South Africa's plans to incorporate SOUTH WEST AFRICA.

Youth League (ANC) Organization within the ANC founded in 1944 to represent the interests of younger, more militant members. Its first president was Anton LEMBEDE. Other ANC Youth League leaders, extremely influential in the ANC in the late 1940s and 1950s, included Oliver TAMBO, Nelson ▷MANDELA and Walter Sisulu.

Yussuf, Sheikh (Abdin Tadia Tjoessop) (1626-99) The founding father of ▷ISLAM in South Africa. A Muslim scholar from Java, he opposed Dutch occupation of the East Indies and was deported to the Cape in 1694. His spiritual leadership made a great impression on both colonists and slaves.

Zulu kingdom Powerful state consolidated among the chiefdoms of the northern Nguni under the rule of SHAKA in the early 19th century. Weakened in the five decades after his death by internal divisions as well as encroachment by VOORTREKKERS and British settlers, the kingdom was eventually split up after the ANGLO-ZULU WAR of 1879. (See also CETSHWAYO; DINGANE; MFECANE.)

Zuurveld Relatively fertile region west of the Fish River which became contested territory between the expanding Cape colonists and the settled ▷XHOSA population in the late 18th century. The Xhosa were expelled from it in 1811-12 and their subsequent efforts to recover it were unsuccessful. The region is part of the province of Eastern Cape.

SHIPWRECK HERO *Wolraad Woltemade's historic rescue of survivors of the ship* De Jonge Thomas *is vividly depicted in a painting made by an artist who had evidently never been to the Cape.*

WORLD HISTORY

The world we live in is shaped by events from the past. Empires and civilizations have risen, flourished and then withered away. Wars have many times redrawn the global map, and revolutions have brought about democracies – or dictatorships. People as diverse as Julius Caesar and Joan of Arc, Mahatma Gandhi and Mao Zedong have single-handedly changed the course of history; their influence is still felt today.

abdication crisis Events leading up to the abdication of the British King Edward VIII in 1936. He gave up the throne in favour of his brother, George VI, in order to marry Wallis Simpson, an American divorcee who, according to the conventions of the time, was an unsuitable partner for the king.
❖ Edward announced his abdication in an emotional radio broadcast to his subjects with the famous words: 'I have found it impossible . . . to discharge my duties as king as I would wish to do without the help and support of the woman I love.' He lived the rest of his life in exile with the honorary title of Duke of Windsor.

Adenauer, Konrad (1867-1976) Chancellor of the Federal Republic of Germany from 1949 to 1963 who oversaw the recovery and reconstruction of West Germany after the ravages of Nazism and defeat in World War II. Under Adenauer, West Germany regained full sovereignty and became a member of NATO and the European Economic Community (predecessor of the ▷EUROPEAN UNION).

Alamein (El Alamein), Battles of (1942) Turning points in Egypt in the campaign in North Africa during WORLD WAR II. In the first battle (June-July) the Axis forces' advance towards the Nile was halted by Allied troops commanded by General Claude Auchinleck; at Alam Halfa (Aug-Sept) and in the second Alamein battle (Oct-Nov), Allied forces commanded by General Bernard MONTGOMERY inflicted a heavy defeat on Field Marshal Erwin ROMMEL's troops, forcing him to retreat and clearing the way for a rapid Allied advance out of Egypt towards Libya.

Alcock (John)(1892-1919) and Brown (Arthur Whitten)(1886-1948) The first men to fly nonstop across the Atlantic, on 14-15 June 1919. It took Alcock, an English naval captain, and Brown, his navigator, flying a Vickers Vimy biplane, 16 hours 27 minutes to complete the 3 060 km crossing from Newfoundland to Clifden, Ireland.

Alexander the Great (356-323 BC) Macedonian king and brilliant general who conquered Egypt and defeated Persia, extending the civilization of Greece east to India. Alexander, a pupil of the philosopher ▷ARISTOTLE, is said to have wept because there were no worlds left to conquer. His empire was short-lived, however. Within 13 years of his death, the countries he had united were separate kingdoms again.
❖ According to legend, before Alexander began his conquests, he ▷CUT THE GORDIAN KNOT with his sword. He went on to fulfil the prophecy that whoever succeeded in untying the knot would rule a vast territory in Asia.
❖ Alexander founded the city of ▷ALEXANDRIA, at the mouth of the Nile in Egypt, naming it after himself.

Allende, Salvador (a-YEN-day) (1908-73) President of Chile from 1970 to 1973. Elected as Chile's first socialist president, he faced determined opposition from the military, big business and the American Central Intelligence Agency (▷CIA). He was killed, or may have committed suicide, when the right-wing general Augusto Pinochet dislodged him in a military coup.

Allies Victorious allied nations in both WORLD WAR I and II. In World War I, the Allies included Britain and its empire, France, Italy, Russia and the USA. In World War II, the Allies – who opposed the AXIS powers – included Britain and its imperial forces, France, the Soviet Union and the USA.
❖ South Africa, as part of the British empire (and later the Commonwealth), was involved on the Allied side in both world wars, creating a great deal of domestic tension. This led, among other things, to the ▷AFRIKANER REBELLION after the invasion of German ▷SOUTH WEST AFRICA by South African forces in 1914, the collapse of the ▷FUSION Government in 1939, as well as a sabotage campaign during World War II by the ▷OSSEWABRANDWAG. Hundreds of thousands of South Africans, however, fought in both wars, many distinguishing themselves in service.

American Civil War (1861-5) War fought in the USA between 23 northern (Union) and 11 southern (Confederate) states, in which the Confederacy sought to establish itself as a separate country. The war grew out of deep differences between the north and the south, notably over slavery – opposed by President Abraham LINCOLN, but an important part of the economy of the south. The Confederates opened the war by attacking Fort Sumter in South Carolina. Most of the battles took place in the south, but the Battle of Gettysburg (1863), a Union victory regarded as the turning point in the war, was fought in the north (in Pennsylvania). The Confederate leader, Robert E Lee, finally surrendered to the Unionist commander in chief, Ulysses S Grant, at Appomattox, Virginia. The war cost more than 600 000 lives.
❖ Grant, a great whisky-lover, was much criticized for drinking too heavily. However, Lincoln defended Grant, saying: 'If I knew what brand he drinks, I would send a barrel or two to some of my other generals.'

American War of Independence (1775-83) War in which the 13 British colonies in North America threw off colonial rule and formed the United States of America. The fighting came at the end of a long period of tension, mainly over the British Government's insistence on taxing colonists without consulting them. 'No Taxation Without Representation' was the slogan of the colonists. In the first major battle, at Bunker Hill (1775), the British were victorious, but the Americans inflicted severe losses, encouraging them in their determination for independence. The next year, the colonies signed the DECLARATION OF INDEPENDENCE. They were greatly aided in their

LINCOLN'S WARRIORS *General Ulysses S Grant, without hat and facing to the right, is surrounded by his generals in this 1865 painting celebrating the Union victory in the American Civil War.*

struggle by their alliance with France, which provided ships and troops. The loss of the colonies was inevitable after the British defeat at the Battle of Yorktown (1781). Britain recognized American independence in the Treaty of Paris (1783).

❖ The War of Independence is known in the USA as the Revolutionary War or the American Revolution.

❖ The original 13 colonies that formed the USA were Connecticut, Delaware, Georgia, Maryland, Massachusetts, New Hampshire, New Jersey, New York, North Carolina, Pennsylvania, Rhode Island, South Carolina and Virginia.

Amundsen, Roald (1872-1928) Norwegian explorer who in December 1911 became the first man to reach the South Pole, a month ahead of the Englishman Robert SCOTT. Later he crossed the Arctic in an airship, and became the first man to visit both the North and South poles.

Anglo-Saxons Germanic peoples, from what is now southern Denmark and northern Germany, who settled in Britain in the 4th to the 6th century AD. The Angles, Saxons and Jutes, members of three different tribes, divided England into seven kingdoms, known as the 'Heptarchy': Essex, Wessex, Sussex, Kent, East Anglia, Mercia and Northumbria. The Saxon kings included Alfred the Great (849-99), Ethelred the Unready (978-1016) and Edward the Confessor (1042-66), whose successor Harold II was overthrown in the NORMAN CONQUEST.

❖ The term 'Anglo-Saxon' is used to describe people of pure English descent or objects with simple English qualities.

appeasement Making concessions to a warlike nation in the hope of keeping the peace. The term specifically refers to Europe's (and particularly Britain's) response to Adolf Hitler's aggression during the 1930s. Appeasement reached its height in the 1938 MUNICH AGREEMENT, which allowed Germany to annex part of Czechoslovakia.

Armada, Spanish Fleet of 130 ships sent in 1588 by PHILIP II of Spain to attempt the conquest of England and the overthrow of ELIZABETH I. The 'Invincible Armada' was destroyed by a combination of bad weather and the English fleet under the command of Lord Howard of Effingham; Sir Francis DRAKE was his vice-admiral.

Armstrong, Neil (1930-) Commander of the Apollo 11 space mission in 1969, and the first man to walk on the Moon on 21 July 1969.

❖ When he took his first step onto the Moon's surface, Armstrong radioed back to Earth: 'That's one small step for a man, one giant leap for mankind.'

AWESOME POWER *The enormous mushroom cloud caused by an atomic blast, as seen during an American test explosion. The devastation of Hiroshima in 1945 (left) killed at least a quarter of a million people, either in the blast itself or by the radiation sickness that swept the city in the aftermath.*

Atatürk, Kemal (Mustafa Kemal) (1881-1938) The founder of modern Turkey and its first president. Atatürk drove out both the occupying Greeks and the OTTOMAN sultan before proclaiming the republic of Turkey in 1923. He used dictatorial methods to carry out an ambitious Westernization programme, converting his country from an Islamic to a secular state. He adopted the name 'Atatürk', which means 'father of Turkey', in 1934.

❖ Among Atatürk's reforms were the emancipation of women and the adoption of the Western instead of the Arabic alphabet. He also encouraged Turkish men to abandon their traditional fez hats.

Athens Leading city-state, or *polis*, of ancient Greece, famous for its learning, culture and democratic institutions. Its intellectual and artistic achievements are symbolized by the ▷PARTHENON, which was built in the 5th century BC – the city's golden age. The statesmen Solon and Pericles and the dramatist ▷SOPHOCLES were some of its great figures. The political power of Athens, the first European ▷DEMOCRACY, was limited after its defeat by SPARTA in the Peloponnesian wars (431-404 BC). The wars weakened Greek civilization as a whole, paving the way for the conquests of ALEXANDER THE GREAT.

❖ Athens had declined to the size of a village when it was chosen as the capital of newly independent Greece in 1834.

atom bomb Atom bombs have been used twice in warfare, when the US planes *Enola Gay* dropped 'Little Boy' on Hiroshima and *Bock's Car* dropped 'Fat Man' on Nagasaki in August 1945, at the end of World War II. Possession of the atom bomb by the USA and the Soviet Union contributed to the COLD WAR. (See also ▷NUCLEAR WEAPON in 'Technology and invention'.)

❖ The highly secret Manhattan Project, led from 1942 by Robert Oppenheimer, developed the atom bomb in the USA. The first bomb was successfully tested near Alamogordo, New Mexico, in July 1945.

Attlee, Clement (1883-1967) British Labour prime minister from 1945 to 1951. His government introduced the National Health Service and nationalized the Bank of England, the railways, coal and other industries. He began Britain's process of decolonization by granting independence to several British territories, including India and Pakistan.

Augustus Caesar (63 BC-AD 14) The first emperor of Rome, who was an adopted son of JULIUS CAESAR. His given name was Octavian, but he took the name Augustus in 27 BC, when he became emperor after defeating the allied forces of his rival Mark Antony and the Egyptian queen CLEOPATRA in the Battle of Actium off the Greek coast. During the reign of Augustus, Rome conquered Egypt.

❖ The month of August is named after Augustus; the era when the arts of a nation are at their height, as they were in his reign, is still called an 'Augustan age'.

Axis Coalition of countries formed by Germany and Italy in 1936; Japan joined them in 1940. The Axis powers opposed the ALLIES during WORLD WAR II.

Aztecs Native American people who ruled Mexico and neighbouring areas from the 12th to the 16th century, when the Spaniards led by Hernán CORTÉS conquered the region, searching for gold. The last Aztec ruler was MONTEZUMA II. The Aztecs were skilled farmers, and built up an advanced civilization with written documents and sophisticated calendars, but their religion was based on human sacrifice.

Babylon City in ancient MESOPOTAMIA, famed for its hanging gardens (one of the SEVEN WONDERS OF THE WORLD). Situated about 90 km south of modern Baghdad, on the Euphrates River, it was the capital city of HAMMURABI and is thought to have been the site of the Tower of Babel. Babylon fell to the Persians in 539 BC.

❖ The Bible tells how the Israelites were deported to Babylon and held in captivity here by Nebuchadnezzar II (*c*630-562 BC). The phrase 'Babylonian captivity' refers to a period of involuntary exile in a hostile land.

❖ Babylonians had a counting system based on 60 – the origin of the number of minutes in an hour and seconds in a minute.

HUMAN SACRIFICE *The Aztecs believed that divine wrath could be quenched with human blood. This 16th-century Aztec illustration shows a priest ripping out a victim's heart.*

Bacon, Francis (1561-1626) A philosopher and statesman and one of the leading figures of the English ▷RENAISSANCE. Bacon served as lord chancellor to King James I and wrote many books; some scholars believe that he was the true author of some of Shakespeare's plays. He also made important contributions to science and, by emphasizing the importance of experimental evidence, laid the basis for scientific thinking.

❖ Bacon died of a chill caught stuffing a dead chicken with snow to see if the meat would be preserved for longer than normal.

Baden-Powell, Robert (1857-1941) British soldier who became famous for his leadership during the seven-month Siege of ▷MAFEKING by Boers during the South African War. While at Mafeking, he had the idea of founding the Scout movement. After he resigned from the army he devoted his energies to the Boy Scouts (which he founded in 1907) and, later, the Girl Guides (1910).

❖ Baden-Powell laid down the Scouts' principles of doing duty to God, country and others, and gave them their motto 'Be Prepared'.

Balkan Wars (1912-13) Two conflicts which are widely seen as precursors to WORLD WAR I. In 1912, Serbia, Greece, Bulgaria and Montenegro attacked the OTTOMAN EMPIRE and won most of its European territories. A year later, Bulgaria and Serbia fought each other over the spoils, and others joined in. As a result of the wars, Albania was created and Serbia and Montenegro were enlarged at the expense of Macedonia. The resulting instability in the region provided the background to the assassination of the Austrian Archduke FRANZ FERDINAND by a Serbian nationalist, following which Austria declared war on Serbia. Through a combination of alliances, mobilization plans and mutual distrust, the hostilities escalated as other nations became more and more deeply involved.

❖ The term 'Balkanization' was coined at the time to describe splitting territories into small, mutually hostile states.

❖ After World War II, communist regimes kept peace in the area by imposing ▷TOTALITARIANISM. When communist power in the former ▷YUGOSLAVIA crumbled at the end of the 1980s, sectarian and nationalist tensions erupted again.

barbarians Term used to describe the GOTHS, VANDALS, HUNS and other less cultured peoples who attacked ancient GREECE and the ROMAN EMPIRE. 'Barbarian' has since come to mean brutal or uncivilized.

❖ The original Greek word *barbaroi,* meaning 'non-Greek', referred to the supposedly uncouth 'bar-bar' sound made by the invaders.

Bay of Pigs Site of a failed attempt in April 1961 by about 1 500 Cuban exiles to invade Cuba and overthrow its president, Fidel ▷CASTRO. The invaders were trained and equipped by the US Central Intelligence Agency (▷CIA), and the failure of the operation is regarded as the most humiliating episode in the presidency of John F KENNEDY.

Becket, Thomas à (1118-70) English diplomat, politician and close friend of King Henry II, who appointed him Archbishop of Canterbury, expecting him to turn a blind eye to royal interference in Church affairs. However, Becket became a staunch defender of the Church against the king's plans to bring it under royal control. When Becket excommunicated several royal servants, Henry is reported to have bellowed angrily 'Who will rid me of this turbulent priest?' Four knights mistakenly took this as an order to execute the archbishop, and murdered him in Canterbury Cathedral. Henry deeply regretted his erstwhile companion's death and even had himself flogged; Becket was made a Catholic martyr and saint.

❖ Becket's murder is dramatized in plays by T S ▷ELIOT *(Murder in the Cathedral)* and Jean Anouilh *(Becket).*

❖ Becket's tomb made Canterbury England's principal pilgrimage site. It is also the goal of the story-telling pilgrims in Chaucer's ▷CANTERBURY TALES.

Begin, Menachem (BAY-gin) (1913-92) Israeli prime minister (1977-83), who became his country's first statesman to make peace with an Arab nation when he signed the 1978 CAMP DAVID ACCORDS with Egypt's president SADAT. Both men received the Nobel Peace Prize in the same year for their efforts.

Ben Bella, Ahmed (1916-) Algerian revolutionary who led a guerrilla campaign from 1949 to 1956 to secure independence from France. The campaign ended when he was imprisoned by the French authorities. He later became Algeria's first president (1963-5) after it became independent in 1962.

Ben-Gurion, David (1886-1973) Israeli statesman who was the driving force in the campaign for an independent Jewish state. When Israel was created in 1948 he became the country's first prime minister.

Berlin airlift (1948-9) Operation to carry food and other goods into West Berlin, a Western enclave deep within communist-ruled East-Germany. From 1945, this part of the city had been jointly governed by France, Britain and the USA, while East Berlin and the surrounding territory were controlled by the Soviet Union. In 1948, the Russians tried to force the Western powers out of West Berlin by closing transport links and cutting electricity and other fuel supplies. After ten months, when the land blockade was eventually lifted, a total of 275 000 flights had carried 2,3 million tons of cargo into West Berlin.
❖ During the airlift, 10 South African crews participated, flying more than 4 000 tons of supplies into Berlin.

Bhopal City in central India which was the scene of an environmental disaster in 1984. Poisonous methyl isocyanate gas leaked from a chemical plant run by the American-owned Union Carbide company, killing more than 2 000 people and seriously damaging the health of a further 500 000.

Bhutto, Zulfikar Ali (1928-79) Pakistani statesman who became his country's president following the secession of ▷BANGLADESH in 1971. He supervised the introduction of a parliamentary constitution, and became prime minister in 1973. His ambitious reform programme upset many powerful people, and he was overthrown by General Zia ul-Haq in a military coup in 1977. He was executed after being sentenced to death on charges of conspiracy to murder. His daughter Benazir Bhutto (1953-) has twice been elected prime minister of Pakistan (1988-90; 1993-).

Biafra Oil-rich southeastern province of Nigeria, inhabited by the Ibo people, that sought independence in 1967, starting a civil war. Many died of famine before the federal government defeated the rebels.

Bismarck, Prince Otto von (1815-98) Statesman who in 1871 created a unified German empire from around 40 smaller states. As prime minister of PRUSSIA, he declared war against Denmark (1864), Austria (1866) and France (1870-1), increasing his popularity and enlarging Prussia's sphere of influence each time. After the FRANCO-PRUSSIAN WAR, he persuaded the German states to unite under Kaiser (emperor) WILHELM II and became the first chancellor of the German empire. He introduced universal male suffrage and made many social and economic reforms before the Kaiser forced him to resign over policy differences in 1890.
❖ Bismarck's stern, aggressive policies won him the nickname of 'Iron Chancellor'. He summed up his methods as 'blood and iron'.

Black Death Type of ▷BUBONIC PLAGUE which killed many millions of people in Asia, before spreading in the 14th century to western Europe, where it killed about 25 million people – about one in three of the population. The first outbreak in Europe was between 1347 and 1351. So many people died that the consequent shortage of labour created social and economic unrest, including the Peasants' revolts in Flanders (1323-28), France (1358) and England (1381). There were several further outbreaks of the disease throughout the Middle Ages. In 1665, an outbreak in London that became known as the Great Plague killed more than 70 000 people.
❖ The nursery rhyme 'Ring a ring o'roses' may have its origins in the red rash and quick death of the plague's victims.

Black Hole of Calcutta A small dungeon into which Indian troops drove British prisoners after capturing a British fort in 1756. A survivor claimed that 146 prisoners were locked in the dungeon, all but 23 of whom had died of suffocation by the next morning, but these figures have since been disputed.
❖ Cramped, stuffy, dark places are still compared to the Black Hole of Calcutta.

Black Shirts Nickname given to supporters of Benito MUSSOLINI's Fascist party in Italy, who wore distinctive black shirts in the 1920s. The name was also associated with the extreme right-wing British Union of Fascists led by Oswald Mosley in the 1930s and Adolf Hitler's much-feared SS, which both adopted a similar uniform.

Blitz (1940-1) Period in WORLD WAR II during which British cities and towns were subjected to night-time bombings by the German *Luftwaffe* (air force). The raids claimed many lives, caused great destruction and forced people to take refuge underground, often in tube stations or in shelters constructed out of corrugated iron and sandbags (the so-called Anderson shelters). London took the brunt of the bombing, but parts of Belfast, Birmingham, Liverpool, Manchester and Coventry were also badly damaged. The centre of Coventry was razed to the ground in a ferocious attack in November 1940.

blitzkrieg Form of warfare used by German forces in WORLD WAR II in which troops in tanks and armoured vehicles made fast-moving surprise attacks with close support from the air force. Strong enemy positions were encircled rather than attacked head-on. These tactics, which resulted in the swift German conquest of Poland and France, were later copied by Allied commanders.
❖ *Blitzkrieg* is German for 'lightning war'.

Bolívar, Simón (1783-1830) Venezuelan revolutionary leader who won independence from Spain for Bolivia, Colombia, Ecuador, Peru and Venezuela. Bolivia was named in his honour and he is known in South America as 'the Liberator'.

Bolsheviks Radical Marxist group who seized power in the RUSSIAN REVOLUTION of October 1917. Led by LENIN, they acted as professional revolutionaries at the helm of a dictatorship of the proletariat. The Bolsheviks defeated their opponents, the more moderate Mensheviks, who wanted to set up a government to pave the way for a gradual transfer of power to the workers. The Bolshevik Party evolved into the Communist Party, which ruled Russia and the ▷USSR from 1918 to 1991 and spread its tentacles worldwide.
❖ The word *bolshevik*, which means 'majority', is sometimes used loosely to describe any radical left-winger.
❖ The word *menshevik* means 'minority'.

Borgias (BOR-jyers) Family which achieved great power in 15th and 16th-century Rome. Rodrigo Borgia (1431-1503) was elected Pope Alexander VI in 1492. His illegitimate son Cesare Borgia (1476-1507) was a ruthless general who conquered large areas of central Italy before being captured by his enemies, although he later escaped and was killed in battle. Cesare's sister Lucrezia (1480-1519) was a patron of the arts and a sponsor of the Italian ▷RENAISSANCE, but is mainly remembered, perhaps unfairly, as a cruel, treacherous and wanton ruler. The Borgias became notorious for killing their enemies by inviting them to a banquet and then poisoning them.
❖ Cesare Borgia is thought to be the model of the unscrupulous ruler described in ▷MACHIAVELLI's *The Prince*.

Bourbons Royal family that succeeded the House of Valois (VAL-wa) as the ruling dynasty of France. The Bourbons ruled from 1589 to 1793, when LOUIS XVI was executed during the FRENCH REVOLUTION. They were briefly restored from 1813 to 1848. The Bourbons were rivals of the HABSBURG dynasty of Spain until Philip V, a Bourbon, ascended to the Spanish throne in 1700.

Boxer Rebellion (1900) Uprising of Chinese peasants aiming to expel all foreigners from China. The Boxers acquired their nickname because they practised ritual unarmed combat, which they believed would protect them from foreign weapons. They occupied the capital, Beijing, besieging foreign legations and missions for 55 days and murdering 231 foreigners before a joint European, American and Japanese force overcame them.

Boyne, Battle of the (1690) Fought on the River Boyne in Ireland between William III (William of Orange) and the army of the deposed British monarch JAMES II, who fled to France after his crushing defeat. The battle sealed the Protestant King William's conquest of Catholic Ireland.
❖ Loyalist 'Orangemen' in Northern Ireland still celebrate the anniversary of the Battle of the Boyne with parades and parties each July – the month of William's victory.

Brandt, Willy (1913-92) West German statesman who held the office of mayor of West Berlin from 1957 to 1966; he became chancellor of West Germany in 1969. He was awarded the Nobel prize for peace in 1971 for his efforts in promoting reconciliation between eastern and western Europe. In 1974 he resigned the chancellorship after one of his staff was exposed as a communist spy. He went on to chair an international commission on the world economy which in 1980 published the 'Brandt Report', recommending that the developed nations increase their level of aid to the developing world.

Brezhnev, Leonid (1906-82) Statesman who seized the leadership of the Soviet Communist Party from Nikita KHRUSCHEV in 1964, and remained the ▷USSR's head of state until his death. While Brezhnev was in office, the Soviet Union gave heavy military support to North Vietnam in the VIETNAM WAR and to Arab nations in the ▷ARAB-ISRAELI CONFLICT. He sent the Soviet army into Czechoslovakia in 1968 to depose the government of Alexander DUBČEK, and into Afghanistan in 1979 to keep its pro-Soviet puppet government in power. Brezhnev persecuted religious and political dissidents in the Soviet Union, but reached various agreements with the USA on reducing the two nations' stocks of nuclear weapons. His belief in the USSR's right to intervene in the internal affairs of WARSAW PACT countries – where there was a perceived threat to a communist regime and the communist bloc as a whole – became known as the 'Brezhnev doctrine'.

Britain, Battle of (1940) Series of air battles in WORLD WAR II between the German *Luftwaffe* under Hermann GÖRING and Britain's Royal Air Force (RAF). The Germans, poised to invade Britain after the fall of France, sought to gain control of the air by a campaign of bombing RAF airfields. Stubborn British resistance was aided by 'Chain Home' – the first radar early warning system in the world – and excellent fighter aircraft such as the Spitfire and the Hurricane. The *Luftwaffe* called off the campaign after suffering severe losses, and launched the BLITZ instead.
❖ The pilots of RAF Fighter Command won great admiration for their bravery. Winston Churchill said of them: 'Never in the field of human conflict was so much owed by so many to so few.'

READY FOR ACTION *Young Royal Air Force fighter pilots enjoy the sunshine between sorties during the Battle of Britain. In the background is one of their aircraft, a Hawker Hurricane.*

British East India Company Company set up in 1600 to trade in Asian spices. After losing much of the spice trade to the ▷DUTCH EAST INDIA COMPANY, the British company concentrated on India, where it won political power as the MOGUL empire declined. By 1765, thanks to the soldier and statesman Robert Clive ('Clive of India') (1725-74), who drove out Dutch and French interests and defeated the Indian rulers of Bengal, it had become the strongest single power in India. From 1784 the British Government supervised the running of the company. In 1858, following the INDIAN MUTINY, the British Government took direct control of India, and in 1873 it dissolved the East India Company.

British empire Group of foreign territories ruled between the 17th and 20th century by Britain, the strongest colonial power in modern times. The earliest outposts of the empire were trading settlements in the Caribbean, North America and the Indian subcontinent. In the 18th and 19th century India was conquered, whites were settled on a large scale in Australasia, Canada and southern Africa, and a vast network of protectorates, dominions and colonies was developed in every corner of the globe. The Royal Navy was the key to controlling the empire, while Britain's vast merchant fleet plied a vigorous trade that brought huge industrial wealth for Britain. The empire reached its peak in 1919, when it embraced nearly a quarter of the world's population and covered more than a quarter of the Earth's territory. As ▷NATIONALISM increased across the world, it became increasingly difficult for Britain to maintain its rule over such a large area. In 1931, the empire was officially replaced by the British ▷COMMONWEALTH of Nations, providing a looser framework for colonial ties with London. India was the first of Britain's colonies to become independent (under Jawaharlal NEHRU) in 1947, and now almost all of Britain's former possessions are independent, although some retain the British monarch as their nominal head of state.
❖ Britain's former African colonies include South Africa, Basutoland (now Lesotho), Swaziland, Bechuanaland (now Botswana), Southern Rhodesia (now Zimbabwe), Northern Rhodesia (now Zambia), Nyasaland (now Malawi), Tanzania, Kenya, Uganda, Sudan, Egypt, Nigeria, the Gold Coast (now Ghana) and Sierra Leone. Ghana was the first of the colonies to become independent – in 1957 under Kwame NKRUMAH.

Britons Pagan Celtic people who inhabited Britain before the arrival of the Romans in the 1st century AD. They lived in tribes and spoke Gaelic and Celtic languages. The name 'Briton' is thought to derive from the Latin *pritani* ('painted people'), used by the Romans to describe the tribesmen's tradition of painting their bodies with woad, a blue vegetable dye.

Bronze Age Period in many civilizations when copper and bronze were first used to make tools and weapons. In the Middle East, this stage of human development lasted from about 4000 to 1200 BC – after the STONE AGE and before the IRON AGE.

Brown Shirts Nickname of Adolf HITLER's early militant followers, the *Sturmabteilungen* (SA, or stormtroopers), derived from their uniform of brown shirts. The Brown Shirts were crushed in the 'Night of the Long Knives' in 1934, and their place as the Nazi elite was taken by the SS, or BLACK SHIRTS.

Bruce, Robert (1274-1329) Scottish hero who reneged on his oath of loyalty to Edward I and crowned himself King Robert I of Scotland in 1306. He freed Scotland from English rule after defeating Edward II at the Battle of Bannockburn (1314).

Buffalo Bill Nickname of William F Cody (1846-1917), an American frontier settler, soldier and showman. He won his name after killing buffaloes to provide meat for workers on the Kansas Pacific Railway. Cody founded a celebrated 'Wild West Show' in 1883 which featured displays of marksmanship, mock battles and demonstrations of cowboy skills and horsemanship. The show conveyed a popular image of romantic and exciting cowboy life which still endures.

Bulge, Battle of the (1944-5) Last major German counteroffensive of WORLD WAR II, mounted against the Allies in the Ardennes area of Belgium. In a surprise attack, German Panzer tanks drove a 'bulge' 80 km deep into Allied lines. They were eventually repelled after heavy fighting and 200 000 casualties.

Byzantine empire Empire that began as the eastern portion of the ROMAN EMPIRE, centred on Constantinople (previously called Byzantium, and now Istanbul). It was founded by the emperor CONSTANTINE in AD 330, and included parts of Europe and western Asia. As the western Roman Empire declined, so Byzantium grew in importance, reaching its peak in the 6th century under JUSTINIAN. The Byzantine emperor's rule was backed by the Christian Church in the region, which broke away from Rome to become the independent Greek ▷ORTHODOX CHURCH. Byzantium survived many attacks by barbarians before it was conquered by the OTTOMAN EMPIRE in 1453. (See also ▷BYZANTINE in 'Art and design' and 'Architecture and engineering'.)

caliphs Rulers of the Muslim world who, after the death of ▷MUHAMMAD, combined their secular role with spiritual leadership. At first they were elected, but from AD 680, under the Damascus-based Omayyad dynasty, the position of caliph became hereditary. The Abbassid dynasty seized power in 750, moving the seat of the caliphate from Damascus to Baghdad. In 1258 the MONGOLS conquered Baghdad and the Abbassid caliphate came to an end.

❖ The Omayyad reign saw the division of Islam into ▷SUNNI and ▷SHIAH sects.

Calvin, John (1509-64) French theologian whose writings and actions played a major role in the REFORMATION. Calvin became a convert to ▷PROTESTANTISM in 1533, subsequently fleeing to Switzerland to escape religious persecution in France. His summary of Protestant beliefs, *Institutes of the Christian Religion* (1535), became the foundation of ▷CALVINISM. Calvin spent the rest of his career trying to run the city of Geneva along strict moralistic lines, imposing a dress code and banning all public entertainments.

Camp David accords Peace agreement signed by Israel and Egypt in September 1978 at Camp David, the USA president's official retreat in Maryland. The accords were followed in 1979 by a formal peace treaty – the first made between Israel and an Arab country. The deal was signed by Menachem BEGIN and Anwar SADAT, under the auspices of President Jimmy ▷CARTER.

Canute (Cnut) (*c*995-1035) King of England, Norway and Denmark. A Dane by birth, he won the English throne in 1016 after four years of military campaigning. He married Emma, the widow of the Saxon King Ethelred the Unready, and ruled the English according to their own customs and laws.

❖ Canute is said to have silenced fawning courtiers who exalted his power by commanding, in vain, the incoming tide to turn back, thus demonstrating to them humanity's impotence before the might of God.

Carthage Ancient city, in what is now Tunisia in north Africa, that was a rival of the ROMAN EMPIRE for much of the 3rd and 2nd centuries BC. Carthage fought three wars, known as the Punic Wars, against Rome between 264 and 146 BC, when it was defeated. Its citizens were sold into slavery. The Romans destroyed Carthage and ploughed over its site, but later rebuilt it. It was finally razed by the Arabs in 697 AD.

Casement, Roger (1864-1916) Irish-born British diplomat who in 1903 issued a celebrated report detailing atrocities in the Belgian Congo. He later became a prominent member of ▷SINN FEIN and spent much of World War I in Germany, enlisting aid in the struggle for Irish independence. Casement was arrested when a German submarine put him ashore on the Irish coast shortly before the EASTER RISING. He was later tried for treason and condemned to death.

IN THE DOCK *Roger Casement was sentenced to death for treason after he had encouraged a revolt in Ireland when Britain was at war.*

Catherine the Great (1729-96) Empress of Russia from 1762, when she oversaw the deposition and murder of her husband, Peter III. Catherine encouraged the development of western European cultural influences in Russia, strengthened the power of her nobles over the serfs and extended Russian territory towards the Black Sea and into Poland.

❖ Catherine is remembered for taking many lovers during her reign.

Catholic Emancipation Movement initiated in the late 18th century to abolish discrimination in Britain against Roman Catholics. Since the REFORMATION Catholics had been unable to hold public office or sit as MPs. After the election of the Catholic Daniel O'Connell as MP in Ireland in 1828, new legislation restored these rights, but stopped short of granting Catholics full equality.

Cavour, Count Camillo Benso di (1810-61) Chief architect of the RISORGIMENTO, the unification of Italy, which had previously comprised many small states. He became prime minister of Piedmont-Sardinia in 1852, and by 1860 he had unified much of northern Italy. Cavour then made an agreement with GARIBALDI, which resulted in southern and central Italy joining the north. For four months before he died, Cavour was the first prime minister of Italy.

Ceausescu, Nicolae (chow-SHESS-koo) (1918-89) President of Romania from 1967 until his execution at the hands of rebels who overthrew his government in 1989. Ceausescu ran a ruthless communist regime which violently repressed all dissent, but his refusal to allow the Soviet Union to interfere in Romania's domestic policy won him valuable support from the West and China. His megalomaniac policies included destroying ancient rural communities and moving their inhabitants to city high-rise blocks, and demolishing much of the historic centre of ▷BUCHAREST in order to build a huge palace for himself. Eventually, this provoked an army-backed popular rebellion which even the *Securitate*, his loyal secret police force, was unable to suppress.

Celts People, originally from France, Austria and southern Germany, who expanded across Europe and into Asia Minor and Egypt between the 7th and 1st century BC. They were powerful fighters and good farmers, with a sophisticated religion and culture. Although they were conquered by the Romans in the 1st and 2nd century AD, Celtic traditions lived on in Ireland and Britain into the Middle Ages.

❖ The Celts are well known for their art, which survives in many fine metal and stone items and in the Book of Kells (*c*800), a manuscript of the Gospels, superbly illuminated, which is now in Dublin. In parts of Britain, clusters of ancient Celtic crosses can be found, often carved with intricate patterns or biblical scenes.

Chamberlain, Joseph (1836-1914) British colonial secretary (1895-1903) who was blamed for the outbreak of the ▷SOUTH AFRICAN WAR. He knew of Cecil Rhodes's plans for the ▷JAMESON RAID, but denied complicity and retained his post. In 1897 he sent Lord Milner to South Africa as High Commissioner and backed him as he pushed matters towards war. Like others in Britain, he seemed to have believed that the British would easily be victorious.

❖ He was the father of Austen Chamberlain (1863-1937), the British foreign secretary who won the Nobel peace prize for his role in settling Germany's disputed western borders in 1925; and of Neville Chamberlain (1869-1940), who, as British prime minister, declared war on Germany in 1939 after his policies of APPEASEMENT had failed.

Chappaquiddick incident (1969) Accident in which Mary Jo Kopechne, a member of US Senator Edward Kennedy's staff, was drowned in a car allegedly driven by Kennedy when it went off a bridge at Chappaquiddick Island, off the Massachusetts coast. Kennedy never provided a full explanation of the incident. Rumours that he was drunk, and that he delayed telling police in order to try to cover up the incident, put an end to his plans to run for the US presidency.

Charlemagne (SHAR-ler-main) (*c*742-814) First emperor of the HOLY ROMAN EMPIRE. Charlemagne, whose name means 'Charles the Great', was made king of the FRANKS in AD 768 and expanded his territory to build an empire that stretched from Italy to Germany and from France to Hungary. The pope crowned him Holy Roman Emperor in 800, anointing him successor to the ancient Roman emperors. Charlemagne is especially remembered for his love of culture and his encouragement of learning, literature and the arts, as well as agriculture and commerce.

❖ Throughout the Middle Ages, Charlemagne was widely considered to be a model for all Christian rulers.

Charles Martel (*c*688-741) Military leader of the FRANKS who halted Muslim expansion from Spain into western Europe at the Battle of Poitiers (AD 732). He went on to found the Carolingian dynasty, which ruled France until 987, fostering a cultural revival known as the 'Carolingian renaissance'. Charles Martel's son, Pepin the Short, was the first Carolingian king and father to CHARLEMAGNE.

Chernobyl City in Ukraine, north of Kiev, where a reactor caught fire in 1986 at a nuclear power station, causing a huge release of radiation. It was the world's worst recorded civil nuclear disaster.

Chiang Kai-shek (1887-1975) Chinese general and statesman who succeeded Sun Yat-Sen as leader of the Kuomintang (Chinese Nationalist Party) in 1925. He set up a government at Nanking and waged a series of campaigns against the rival communist group based at Beijing. In World War II, however, he joined the communists and the Allies to fight the invading Japanese. The nationalists were overthrown in 1949 by communist forces under MAO ZEDONG, who established the People's Republic of China. Chiang fled to Taiwan, where he set up a nationalist regime which he ruled as a dictator.

Churchill, Winston (1874-1965) Statesman and prime minister who led Britain through WORLD WAR II. Churchill started his long parliamentary career in 1900, having worked as a war correspondent in the ▷SOUTH AFRICAN

TAIWAN'S FUTURE LEADER *Chiang Kai-shek inspects his troops for the last time on mainland China before fleeing to Taiwan in 1949.*

WAR. He was in charge of the Royal Navy at the beginning of World War I, was ▷CHANCELLOR OF THE EXCHEQUER from 1924-9, and played a key role in breaking Britain's General Strike (1926). His opposition to various government policies, notably APPEASEMENT, kept him out of office until the beginning of World War II. When Neville Chamberlain resigned as Prime Minister in 1940, Churchill took over and his stirring rhetoric and resolute leadership of the British war effort soon came to symbolize Britain's fierce resistance to Hitler. His grasp of strategy was equalled by his skill in negotiating with other Allied war leaders such as STALIN, DE GAULLE and ROOSEVELT. He lost the 1945 general election to Clement ATTLEE, but returned as prime minister between 1951 and 1955.

❖ Churchill's oratory is still much quoted. On taking office, he told the House of Commons: 'I have nothing to offer but blood, toil, tears and sweat'; and as the Germans overran Europe he defiantly declared: 'We shall fight on the beaches, we shall fight on the landing grounds, we shall fight in the fields and in the streets, we shall fight in the hills; we shall never surrender.' As an author, he is especially remembered for two histories, *A History of the English-Speaking Peoples* and *The Second World War.* He won the Nobel prize for literature in 1953.

❖ Churchill's trademarks included a large cigar, his 'V for victory' sign and witty but brutal repartee. Rebuked by Bessie Braddock, an outspoken Labour MP, with the words, 'Winston, you're drunk!', his gruff reply was, 'Bessie, you are ugly – and tomorrow I shall be sober.' He also playfully described Attlee as a 'sheep in sheep's clothing'.

Cid, El (*c*1043-99) Nickname (meaning 'the lord') of Rodrigo Diaz de Vivar, a Spanish warrior who fought on behalf of the kingdom of Castile in a series of local wars. When the king of Castile banished him for an unauthorized raid in 1081, he fought for various Muslim leaders. He later established himself as the independent ruler of Valencia.
❖ The facts of El Cid's life have been overshadowed by many legends told about him, including the anonymous 12th-century epic *Poema del Cid*. One story says that after his death his corpse was strapped onto his horse so that he could lead his men in a final victory against the fleeing Moors.

civil rights movement Drive by American black people and their supporters, especially during the 1950s and 1960s, to eliminate racial segregation and gain the same rights as white people. Segregation in housing, public services and employment opportunities was then common in the USA, particularly in the southern states. The first major event in the movement occurred in 1955, when the refusal of a black woman, Rosa Parks, to give up her bus seat to a white person sparked off a boycott of buses in Montgomery, Alabama. Martin Luther KING emerged as the leader of the American ▷BLACK CONSCIOUSNESS movement, giving his stirring 'I have a dream' speech at a mass rally in Washington in 1963. A few years later, the US Government introduced laws intended to stop racial discrimination and remove obstacles to blacks registering to vote. The movement then focused on education and changing the attitudes of white people. After the assassination of Martin Luther King in 1968, it became more militant, giving rise to the Black Power movement.

Classical antiquity Era of European history dominated by ancient GREECE and the ROMAN EMPIRE, from about 500 BC to AD 500.

Clemenceau, Georges (KLEM-on-soh) (1841-1929) French journalist and statesman who was prime minister from 1906 to 1909 and from 1917 to 1920. After World War I he presided at the peace conference which produced the Treaty of VERSAILLES (1919). Clemenceau, nicknamed 'the Tiger', pressed for a tough peace treaty that would punish Germany for having started the war and compensate France for its economic losses.

Cleopatra (*c*69-30 BC) Egyptian queen celebrated for her beauty, charm and luxurious living. JULIUS CAESAR fell in love with her when she was deposed after a coup, and restored her to power. For several years after Caesar had been assassinated, she lived in Egypt with the Roman politician Mark Antony. When Mark Antony committed suicide after being defeated in battle by the future emperor AUGUSTUS, Cleopatra also killed herself by allowing an asp, a poisonous snake, to bite her.
❖ The story of Cleopatra's relations with Caesar and Antony inspired plays by ▷SHAKESPEARE and George Bernard ▷SHAW.

cold war Feud between the USA and the Soviet Union that dominated international politics from 1945 to the reformist era of Soviet president Mikhail ▷GORBACHEV in the late 1980s. The phrase 'cold war' refers to a state of constant hostility, espionage and counter-espionage which never erupted into a 'hot' or shooting war. The BERLIN AIRLIFT, Berlin Wall, Iron Curtain and CUBAN MISSILE CRISIS reflected the sharp polarization of the globe into Western and communist-influenced blocs which coloured other international disputes, including the ▷ARAB-ISRAELI CONFLICT and the VIETNAM WAR, and led to a nuclear-arms race between the two superpowers. Following years of negotiation, Gorbachev and US president Ronald ▷REAGAN signed a disarmament treaty in 1989 designed to end the arms race. The international cooperation demonstrated in the 1991 GULF WAR was evidence that the cold war had truly ended.
❖ The atmosphere of the cold war is captured in many thrillers, especially in the spy novels by John ▷LE CARRÉ featuring the character George Smiley.

Columbus, Christopher (1451-1506) Genoese explorer credited with being the first European to reach America in modern times. The VIKING Leif Ericsson was reported to have been there before him (in *c*1000), and there were Norse settlements in eastern Canada in the 11th century, but in the eyes of most Europeans America was just an implausible myth before the voyage of Columbus. He reached the West Indies in 1492, having sailed across the Atlantic for FERDINAND AND ISABELLA of Spain in search of a westerly passage to China. The exact place where he first landed is unknown, but likely possibilities include San Salvador and Samana Cay, in the Bahamas. In the course of four separate subsequent journeys to the Americas, Columbus explored Cuba, Hispaniola, Puerto Rico, Jamaica, Trinidad, Venezuela and the Panama isthmus. He died at Valladolid in Spain.
❖ Columbus sighted land on 12 October. Columbus Day is a national holiday, celebrated on the second Monday in October, in many South American countries as well as in the USA.

concentration camp The first concentration camps in modern times were established by the British during the ▷SOUTH AFRICAN WAR

HISTORIC LANDING *After weeks of sailing into the blue, Columbus and his men encounter the inhabitants of a West Indies island – as depicted in romanticized fashion by an unknown artist.*

in order to 'concentrate' Boer civilians where they could be guarded. Concentration camps are also particularly associated with the rule of the Nazis in Europe from 1933 until 1945, when they were used to confine and murder millions of Jews, homosexuals, gypsies, political dissidents and others. Some camps, such as Belsen and Treblinka, were purely extermination centres for the HOLOCAUST. The camp at Auschwitz – where up to 4 million prisoners were executed in gas chambers or died of starvation, exhaustion and disease – is the most notorious Nazi camp. Concentration camps were also a notorious feature of the Soviet Union under Joseph STALIN, who also sent millions to their deaths, and of Pol Pot's Cambodia. In the 1990s, the warring armies in the former Yugoslavia were also accused of setting up concentration camps. (See also ▷CONCENTRATION CAMPS in 'Southern African history'.)

conquistadors Spanish soldiers who established Spanish rule in the NEW WORLD by conquering the INCAS, the AZTECS and other native American peoples. They wanted to find the mythical land of ▷ELDORADO and make converts to Christianity. Hernán CORTÉS and Francisco Pizarro (*c*1478-1541) were among the most powerful conquistadors.

Constantine the Great (*c*AD 285-337) The first Christian Roman emperor, said to have adopted Christianity after seeing a vision of the cross at the Battle of Milvian Bridge, near Rome, which won him the western half of the empire in 312. He put an end to the official persecution of Christians. Constantine became ruler of the whole empire in 324, and moved its capital from Rome to Constantinople (modern Istanbul), which became the capital of the BYZANTINE EMPIRE.

EMPIRE BUILDER *While exploring the Pacific Ocean, Captain James Cook claimed Australia and New Zealand for Britain.*

Mulgrave

473

...after two hours Calm, in the Latitude of 39°.35' S°
...the Wind at West, the next day it fix'd at N.N.W.
...to a fresh gale, with which we steered directly
...Lizard and on
...made the Land about Plymouth, Maker Church,
...5 o'clock in the after-noon, bore N.10.W. distant
...leagues; this bearing and distance, shew'd that the
...of Mr. Kendals Watch, in Longitude was only 7'.45"
...was too far to the West—

Jam^s Cook

Cook, Captain James (1728-79) Explorer who made three voyages in the Pacific, searching for a new continent rumoured to lie between Australia and the Antarctic. Cook charted the coasts of Australia and New Zealand, skirted the Antarctic ice field and was the first European to discover many of the Pacific islands. He was killed by Hawaiian islanders whom he initially believed to be friendly.

Coral Sea, Battle of (1942) Crucial battle in the southwest Pacific during WORLD WAR II. American naval forces repelled a Japanese attempt to invade New Guinea. Although there were heavy American losses, it was the first time that Japanese advances in the Pacific were checked.

Cortés, Hernán (1485-1547) Spanish explorer and CONQUISTADOR. He overthrew the AZTEC rulers of Mexico and established Spanish rule over the country. When Cortés first landed in Mexico, the Aztecs welcomed him as a god whose arrival had been prophesied.

Cossacks People of southern Russia who first settled here in the 15th century as runaway serfs from Moscow, Lithuania and Poland. They became skilled warriors, and were particularly renowned during the 16th and 17th centuries for their horsemanship. Instead of paying taxes, they supplied the Russian TSARS with scouts and mounted soldiers. After World War II, during which the Cossacks sided with the Germans, Stalin deported thousands of them to Siberia. *Cossack* means 'adventurer' in Russian.

❖ Cossacks are known for their distinctive dress of tunics, high boots and sheepskin hats, and for their dances, which feature fast music and athletic leaps.

Counter Reformation Reform movement in the Roman Catholic Church, started when the Church summoned the Council of Trent in 1545 partly in response to the Protestant REFORMATION. The council reformed many aspects of the Church and redefined its dogma.

Crimean War (1854-6) War fought in the Crimean Peninsula by Britain, France and Turkey against Russia, whose expansion into the OTTOMAN EMPIRE sparked off the conflict. Among the Anglo-French victories was the battle of Balaclava, where a 'thin red line' of red-coated Scottish infantrymen repelled the Russians, eventually forcing them to retreat. In the same battle, the British army sustained heavy losses in the Charge of the Light Brigade. At Inkerman, British and French troops withstood a Russian assault and inflicted heavy casualties. The Russians were defeated after a long siege forced them out of the port of Sebastopol. The campaign was marked by incompetent leadership on all sides and by disease, which claimed more lives than the fighting.

❖ Florence Nightingale (1820-1910) established a battlefield hospital for sick and wounded British soldiers in the Crimea, earning the nickname 'the Lady with the Lamp' for her efforts. She used innovative techniques that remain at the heart of modern nursing, and in 1907 became the first woman to be awarded the British Order of Merit.

Crockett, Davy (1786-1836) American frontier settler and politician. He became an American hero for his bravery in fighting against the Creek Indians in 1812, and went on to serve in the US Congress. He was killed by Mexican troops at the Alamo.

❖ His distinctive headgear, a cap made out of raccoon (or coon) fur, earned him the title of the 'coonskin congressman'.

Cromwell, Oliver (1599-1658) English general who led parliamentary forces to victory over Charles I in the ENGLISH CIVIL WAR. Early in the war, he formed a regiment of soldiers called 'Ironsides', and he later created the New Model Army, which finally defeated the royalists. After signing the king's death warrant in 1649, Cromwell took the reins of power himself, as leader of the Commonwealth and Protectorate (1649-60), in which the monarchy and the House of Lords were replaced by a council of state. At first he ruled with parliament, but from 1653, with the title Lord Protector, his supreme rule was backed only by the army. He was offered the crown, but refused it. Cromwell ruled as a dictator, suppressing uprisings in Wales, Scotland and Ireland with great military skill. Despite his strong puritanism, Cromwell supported religious toleration. After his death he was succeeded as Lord Protector by his son Richard, whose inept rule led directly to the RESTORATION of the monarchy.

Crusades Series of campaigns mounted by European powers between 1096 and 1272 to wrest the Holy Land (▷PALESTINE) from Muslim control. The official aim of the Crusades was to recapture for the Christian world the land where Jesus had lived, but the expeditions were also motivated by greed for booty and new territories. The Crusaders conquered Jerusalem in 1099 and sacked Constantinople in 1204, but failed to secure the Holy Land and were driven out by the Muslims in 1291. However, the Crusades exposed Europeans to the culture of the Middle East.
❖ The best-known warriors of the Crusades included the English King Richard I ('The Lionheart') (1157-99), the Holy Roman Emperor Frederick I Barbarossa (*c*1123-90) and the Muslim sultan Saladin (1137-93), who was the main enemy of the European knights.
❖ The Children's Crusade (1212), in which some 50 000 children left Germany and France for Palestine only to be sold into slavery or prostitution, may have inspired the tale of the ▷PIED PIPER OF HAMELIN.

Cuban missile crisis (1962) Confrontation between the USA and the Soviet Union which brought the world to the brink of a third world war. Following the Cuban Revolution in 1959, Cuba came under the influence of the Soviet Union. The Soviet leader, Nikita KHRUSCHEV, installed nuclear missiles on the island, only 225 km from the American mainland. US President John F KENNEDY responded by blockading Cuba, insisting that the missiles be removed. After seven tense days of negotiations, mediated by the United Nations, Khruschev was forced to order the removal of the missiles.

Cuban Revolution (1959) Overthrow of Cuba's American-backed president Fulgencio Batista by Fidel ▷CASTRO's guerrilla forces. Castro set up a socialist government, which quickly became communist.

Cultural Revolution (1966-76) Movement led by MAO ZEDONG to reinforce communist ideals of equality in China and eliminate foreign cultural influences. Mao dismantled the complex governmental structure that had developed after the Chinese revolution of 1949 and humiliated intellectuals and government officials by sending them out to work in the fields. He also destroyed many ancient cultural institutions.

da Gama, Vasco (*c*1460-1524) Portuguese explorer who in 1497-9 led the first expedition to sail from Europe to India using the ▷CAPE SEA ROUTE. Bartolomeu DIAS had been the first European to discover the Cape in 1488.

Dark Ages Name formerly used to describe the early Middle Ages in Europe, from about AD 500 to 900. The term refers partly to the dearth of information about the period, and partly to the political, social and economic disorder that followed the fall of the ROMAN EMPIRE. For a long time it was regarded as a period of cultural decline compared with the glories of CLASSICAL ANTIQUITY, but it is now recognized that the Dark Ages produced important artistic and literary achievements.

D-Day (6 June 1944) Allied invasion of German-occupied France during WORLD WAR II. Some 5 000 ships and 9 000 aircraft took part in the operation, codenamed 'Overlord', which landed 150 000 troops between Caen and Cherbourg on the Normandy coast. This marked the start of the major Allied counter-offensive in Europe.

Declaration of Independence (1776) Document issued by Britain's 13 American colonies, rejecting British rule and establishing the USA as a nation. It was largely written by Thomas Jefferson and declares, among other things, that 'all men are created equal' and have the right to 'life, liberty, and the pursuit of happiness'. It also justified the AMERICAN WAR OF INDEPENDENCE.

de Gaulle, Charles (1890-1970) French general and statesman who, from Britain, led the 'Free French' opposition to the Nazis and to France's collaborationist VICHY GOVERNMENT during World War II. De Gaulle served briefly as president of France after the war in 1945. He became president again in 1958, when he was called back from retirement to solve the crisis in the French colony of Algeria, where French military leaders had seized power in protest against the French Government's decision to negotiate with Algerian nationalist leaders; De Gaulle eventually granted Algeria its independence in 1962. In France he introduced a new constitution (the 'Fifth Republic'), which gave him sweeping powers. He increased France's international standing, acquired nuclear weapons and reconciled France with Germany, but blocked Britain's entry into the Common Market in 1967. In 1969, after the French people voted against his plans for further constitutional reform, he resigned.
❖ De Gaulle is remembered for his high-handed manner. He once declared: 'De Gaulle is not left, De Gaulle is not right, De Gaulle is not in the centre, De Gaulle is above.'

Delville Wood, Battle of (1916) Defence of French territory by a South African brigade

BRUTAL SLAUGHTER *Richard I of England watches a mass beheading of Saracens during the Third Crusade. As bodies pile up beneath the scaffold, more prisoners are led to their execution.*

QUEUEING UP *Lines of British and French soldiers wait patiently on the beach at Dunkirk for boats to take them across the Channel.*

during the Battle of the SOMME. More than 3 000 officers and troops won glory by holding the exposed ground for nearly a week in the face of fierce German fighting. More than 750 were killed and 1 500 wounded; unwounded survivors numbered around 800.

❖ Two South African war memorials have been built at Delville Wood to commemorate the battle, the first consecrated in 1926 by prime minister J B M Hertzog, the second in 1986 by state president P W Botha. There are replicas of the main section in the Gardens, Cape Town, and in the Union Gardens, Pretoria. The weeping cross in the Garden of Remembrance, Pietermaritzburg, is made of timber obtained from Delville Wood. The cross 'weeps' droplets of resin on almost every anniversary of the battle.

Depression, The A worldwide economic slump, also known as 'The Great Depression', that followed the 1929 ▷WALL STREET Crash. Millions of people were thrown out of work and many companies went into liquidation. In America, president Franklin D ROOSEVELT introduced the NEW DEAL in an attempt to counter the worst effects of the slump. In Europe, the harsh economic conditions experienced by many people helped to fuel the rise of ▷FASCISM. South Africa's economic mainstays, agriculture and mining, took a severe knock, and the crisis led, among other things, to a split in the ▷PACT GOVERNMENT over prime minister J B M Hertzog's refusal to abandon the ▷GOLD STANDARD. Once he reversed his decision, the price of gold soared and South Africa's economy went into a long period of growth. (See also ▷DEPRESSION in 'Business and economics'.)

Desert Rats Nickname of the British 7th Armoured Division, which adopted the badge of the jerboa (a small leaping rodent) while campaigning in Libya in World War II. Part of Bernard MONTGOMERY's Eighth Army, they fought with distinction at ALAMEIN in North Africa and in Italy.

de Valera, Eamon (1882-1975) Irish statesman who was prime minister of Eire three times (1932-48, 1951-4 and 1957-9) and president from 1959 to 1973. He played a key role in the EASTER RISING in 1916, for which he was sentenced to life imprisonment, but was released under a general amnesty in 1917. He was also at the heart of Ireland's subsequent struggle for independence from British rule. He kept Ireland neutral during World War II.

Dias, Bartolomeu (*c*1450-1500) Portuguese navigator who in 1488 became the first European to discover what he called *Cabo da Boa Esperança* (the ▷CAPE OF GOOD HOPE). He rounded it unawares, driven by storms, in 1487, but sighted it on his return journey to West Africa. His discovery enabled Vasco DA GAMA to open up the ▷CAPE SEA ROUTE from Europe to India.

❖ Dias died at the 'Cape of Good Hope' when his ship was wrecked off its rocky shore.

Disraeli, Benjamin (1804-81) British Conservative prime minister in 1868, and again from 1874 to 1880. He pursued a vigorous foreign policy of imperialism, buying Britain a major share in the Suez Canal and proclaiming Queen Victoria Empress of India. He became a close friend of Victoria. His reputation in Europe received a major boost when, thanks to his diplomatic skills at the Congress of Berlin (1878), war between Russia and Turkey was averted .

❖ Disraeli was also the author of political novels, including *Coningsby* (1844) and *The Two Nations* (1845). He was known by the nickname of 'Dizzy'.

❖ One of the reasons for his defeat in the 1880 general election was dissatisfaction with the policies he adopted towards the Boer republic of the Transvaal. He was sharply criticized by William Gladstone, leader of the Liberal opposition, for refusing to reinstate the independence of the Transvaal.

divine right of kings Doctrine that monarchs have a God-given right to rule, and that rebellion against them is a sin. The excesses created by this belief are particularly associated with the *ancién regime* of France, which was overthrown in the FRENCH REVOLUTION, and with King Charles I of England, who was deposed in the ENGLISH CIVIL WAR.

Drake, Sir Francis (*c*1545-96) English seaman and navigator who started his career as a pirate, raiding Spanish treasure ships in the Caribbean. Supported by Queen ELIZABETH I, Drake crossed the Pacific in the *Golden Hind*, resulting in the first round-the-world voyage by an Englishman (1577-80). He also played a leading part in the defeat of the Spanish ARMADA in 1588. Drake's exploits marked the beginning of Britain's years as the world's greatest sea power.

❖ It is said that Drake was told of the Armada's approach while playing bowls. He calmly ordered his ships to prepare for sailing, then went on to finish his game.

Dubček, Alexander (1921-92) Czechoslovak premier who in 1968 introduced liberal reforms to the communist state, resulting in a period of relative freedom known as the Prague Spring. This was crushed by a Soviet-led invasion which removed Dubček, from the premiership. In 1989, after the collapse of the communist government, he became chairman of the Czech Parliament.

Dunkirk Scene of a remarkable retreat by the British army in WORLD WAR II. Dunkirk is the anglicized spelling of Dunkerque, on the northern coast of France, which was the last precarious refuge of the British Expeditionary Force when France fell to the Germans in 1940. In less than a week, 860 naval and civilian vessels – the 'little ships' – took 338 226 men, 130 000 of whom were French, to England, saving them to fight another day.

Easter Rising (April 1916) Rebellion in which a secret organization, the Irish Republican Brotherhood, attempted to win Irish independence from Britain. After a week of fighting on the streets of Dublin, the rebels surrendered. The harsh reprisals of the British authorities, including the execution of 14 rebel leaders, helped to strengthen demands for IRISH HOME RULE, which came about in 1921.

Eden, Sir Anthony (1897-1977) Conservative prime minister of Britain from 1955 to 1957; he resigned through ill health after he had ordered an unsuccessful military intervention in the SUEZ CRISIS of 1956.

Edwardian period The first decade of the 20th century, so called after the British King Edward VII, the reigning monarch of the time. It was a time of reaction against the puritanical values of the VICTORIAN PERIOD, marked by elegance, luxury and relaxed morals among the wealthy and privileged. The Edwardian spirit lingered until the outbreak of World War I in 1914. (See ▷EDWARDIAN in 'Architecture and engineering'.)

Egypt, ancient Civilization that flourished in the ▷NILE valley from *c*5000 BC. In *c*3100 BC the two Egyptian kingdoms – the Upper, covering the Nile delta, and the Lower, stretched out along the valley – were united. Egyptians developed a sophisticated system of writing in ▷HIEROGLYPHS and began the tradition of burying mummified bodies in tombs. The subsequent history of ancient Egypt is usually divided into three main periods. In the 'Old Kingdom' (*c*2700-*c*2200 BC), a series of strong rulers or pharaohs developed an elaborate sun-worshipping religion and built the renowned ▷PYRAMIDS and ▷SPHINX at Giza. The 'Middle Kingdom' (*c*2100-1786 BC) was marked by the conquest of Nubia and Libya, and ended when Egypt was invaded by a people called the Hyksos. The 'New Kingdom' (*c*1570-*c*1100 BC) is generally considered the peak of ancient Egyptian civilization, when Palestine and Syria were added to its territory. Magnificent temples were built and the pharaohs were buried in the 'Valley of the Kings', where TUTANKHAMUN's almost intact grave was found in 1922. After 1100 BC Egypt's power went into decline, and in 332 BC it was conquered by ALEXANDER THE GREAT. (See also ▷EGYPTIAN ART.)

❖ The Old Testament stories of Joseph and Moses, the Jews' captivity in Egypt and their subsequent return to Palestine are set in the period of Egypt's New Kingdom.

Eichmann, Adolf (1906-62) Austrian Nazi official and member of the SS who organized the transportation of Jews to the CONCENTRATION CAMPS during the HOLOCAUST. He escaped after World War II, but was captured in Argentina by Israeli agents in 1960 and smuggled back to Israel, where he was tried and hanged for crimes against humanity.

Eisenhower, Dwight D (1890-1969) Supreme commander of the ALLIES' forces in Europe during World War II and US president from 1953 to 1961. He commanded the Allied forces in Italy in 1943 and later directed the D-DAY landings in Normandy and the defeat of Nazi Germany. As president, Eisenhower conducted the COLD WAR and negotiated the end of the KOREAN WAR. He was a fierce opponent of communism, but had a flair for conciliation which helped to maintain political stability during a period of turmoil.

Elizabeth I (1533-1603) Daughter of HENRY VIII and Anne Boleyn who became queen of England and Ireland in 1558. Her reign provided a period of stability and prosperity in which the nation flourished politically, militarily and culturally. A shrewd ruler, Elizabeth restored ▷PROTESTANTISM after the reign of the Catholic Queen MARY I and ordered the execution of MARY QUEEN OF SCOTS (1587). Elizabeth also encouraged English exploration and colonization of the NEW WORLD. In 1588, PHILIP II of Spain, who had been Mary I's husband, sent out the ARMADA, partly to defend Catholicism and take revenge for English raids on Spanish shipping, but mainly to eject Elizabeth from her throne.

English Civil War (1642-8) Conflict resulting from the power struggle between the monarchy and an increasingly forceful parliament in England, in which parliamentary forces or 'Roundheads', led by Oliver CROMWELL, defeated the 'Cavaliers' of King Charles I. Charles dissolved three parliaments because they opposed him over taxation, and then reigned for 11 years without parliament, asserting the DIVINE RIGHT OF KINGS. Lack of funds eventually forced him to recall parliament in 1640, but his attempt to arrest five MPs for treason in 1642 led to the outbreak of civil war. Catholics, high churchmen and most of the aristocracy supported the king, whose heartland lay in northern and western England; parliament had the support of the PURITANS, mainly in southern and eastern England, Scotland and London. The war went well for the king until the Scots joined with Cromwell's crack regiment, the 'Ironsides', to defeat royal troops at Marston Moor in 1644. Parliament's New Model Army finally broke royalist resistance at the Battle of Naseby (1645); a year later, Charles surrendered and was placed under house arrest. In captivity, the king exploited divisions between parliament and army, English and Scots, Presbyterians and religious 'Independents'. A second bout of war ended in victory for Cromwell at Preston in 1648. Charles was tried and executed the following year.

❖ At his execution, which took place outside on a cold January day, Charles wore two shirts so he would not shiver and give the crowd the impression he was afraid.

Etruscans Most powerful culture of ancient Italy immediately preceding the Romans. At the height of their power in the 6th century BC, they were a strong cultural and religious influence on early Rome. It was trade with Greece as well as their own industry, in metalware for example, that made the Etruscans so wealthy and powerful. Their navy was one of the strongest in the Mediterranean.

Falange Spanish fascist party founded in 1933. From 1937, led by Francisco FRANCO, it was one of the principal factions in the SPANISH CIVIL WAR. After the nationalist victory in the war it provided the framework for the ruling party of Spain.

Falklands War (1982) Armed conflict following the invasion of the British-ruled Falkland Islands by Argentina, which had long claimed the islands they call *Islas Malvinas*. On 2 April, Argentinian forces easily overwhelmed the islands' small garrison. Britain declared an exclusion zone around the islands and despatched a large naval task force to retake them. They sunk the Argentinian cruiser the *General Belgrano* outside the exclusion zone, claiming that it posed a danger

PLOTTERS *Guy Fawkes (third from right) and other conspirators scheme to blow up King James I. Fawkes's lantern (left), found in the cellars of parliament when he was arrested on 5 November 1605, would have detonated the gunpowder.*

to British ships in the area. The ship's 368 sailors were among the 643 Argentinians and 255 Britons killed before the war ended with Argentina's surrender on 14 June.

Fawkes, Guy (1570-1606) Leading conspirator in the Gunpowder Plot (1605), a Catholic plan to blow up the English King JAMES I, together with the Houses of Parliament. Fawkes was arrested with a pile of explosives in the cellars under the House of Lords after a Catholic peer had been warned not to attend parliament. The plotters were either killed or executed.
❖ Although Guy Fawkes was hanged, not burned at the stake, Britons burn his effigy or 'guy' on 5 November, the anniversary of the Gunpowder Plot. The custom – along with that of lighting firecrackers – has passed on to many former British colonies.

Ferdinand and Isabella Joint rulers of the Spanish kingdoms of Castile and Aragon from 1474 until Isabella's death in 1504. Ferdinand continued to rule alone until his death in 1516. Together they united Spain and laid the foundations of its extensive empire. They introduced the Spanish INQUISITION, expelled Jews from their country and sponsored Christopher COLUMBUS to explore the New World.

Fertile Crescent Region of the Middle East in ancient times, generally regarded as one of the main 'cradles of civilization'. It stretched from Mesopotamia to Assyria, then westwards to the Mediterranean and southwards through Palestine to the Nile Valley. As early as *c*10 000 BC, people settled in the Fertile Crescent and became farmers, growing cereals, keeping sheep and goats and using water channels to divert river water for their crops.

feudalism Name given in the 19th century to the system of obligations between lord and subject, or vassal, that provided the political, social and economic framework of medieval Europe. The king owned most or all of the land, parcels of which he gave to his leading nobles as 'fiefs'. In return, they gave him 'homage' – their loyalty and military service whenever it was needed. The nobles had a similar relationship with knights and lesser nobles, and so on. Feudalism made it possible to raise an army and decentralize administration, but it also dictated that everyone's position in society was determined by birth.
❖ The lowest form of vassal was a serf – a peasant bound to his lord, receiving his protection in exchange for labour. Serfdom continued in Russia until 1861, centuries after it was superseded in other European countries.

Franco, Francisco (1892-1975) Spanish general who led the nationalist army to victory in the SPANISH CIVIL WAR (1936-9). Franco set up a fascist dictatorship, but he resisted approaches to join the AXIS powers and kept Spain out of World War II. His regime continued until his death, when democracy and the monarchy were reinstated.

Franco-Prussian War (1870-1) Conflict in which France was crushingly defeated by an alliance of German states led by PRUSSIA. The war was provoked by the Prussian chancellor Otto von BISMARCK's unsuccessful attempt to put a German prince on the Spanish throne. The Germans besieged Paris for five months before it surrendered in January 1871. Prussia's victory unified the German states under the Prussian king as Kaiser (emperor) and forced France to give up Alsace and part of Lorraine, making Prussia the leading power in continental Europe.

Frank, Anne (1929-45) German Jewish girl who spent her early teenage years, from 1942 to 1944, hiding with her family from the Nazis in a secret flat in Amsterdam after fleeing from persecution in Germany. They were eventually betrayed, and Anne was deported to Belsen concentration camp, where she died of typhus. Her diary, published after the war, provides a moving account of suffering under NAZISM.

Franklin, Benjamin (1706-90) American statesman, author and scientist, who played a leading role in the USA's struggle for independence – securing French assistance on a mission to Paris – and helped Thomas Jefferson to draft the DECLARATION OF INDEPENDENCE. Among Franklin's many inventions were bifocal spectacles and the lightning conductor – devised after he flew a kite in a thunderstorm to demonstrate that ▷LIGHTNING would flow down the wet string.

Franks Germanic people who ruled much of Europe between the 5th and 9th century. Frankish power was at its height under two dynasties, the Merovingians and their successors in 751, the Carolingians, the descendants of CHARLES MARTEL.

Franz Ferdinand, Archduke (1863-1914) Nephew and heir of FRANZ JOSEF I and heir to the throne of Austria-Hungary. His assassination by Gavrilo Princip, a Serbian nationalist, in Sarajevo in 1914, sparked off the events that led to WORLD WAR I.

Franz Josef I (1830-1916) Austro-Hungarian emperor, much of whose reign was spent struggling with the forces of nationalism. In 1866 his army was defeated by Prussia, and in 1867 he formed the 'Dual Monarchy' of Austria and Hungary, conceding autonomy to the Hungarians. His attack on Serb nationalism in the Balkans triggered WORLD WAR I, which broke out after his nephew, Archduke FRANZ FERDINAND, was assassinated in 1914.

Frederick the Great (1712-86) King of PRUSSIA from 1740 who transformed his country from a small state in northern Germany to a major power. Frederick was a brilliant soldier and doubled the area of Prussian territory in a series of campaigns, including the invasion of Bohemia in 1744-5 and the capture of Silesia during the SEVEN YEARS' WAR. At home, he made many economic and social reforms and was a generous patron of the arts.

French Revolution (1789-99) Rebellion that deposed the BOURBON kings of France and overturned the old order of French society known as the *ancien régime*, which was built

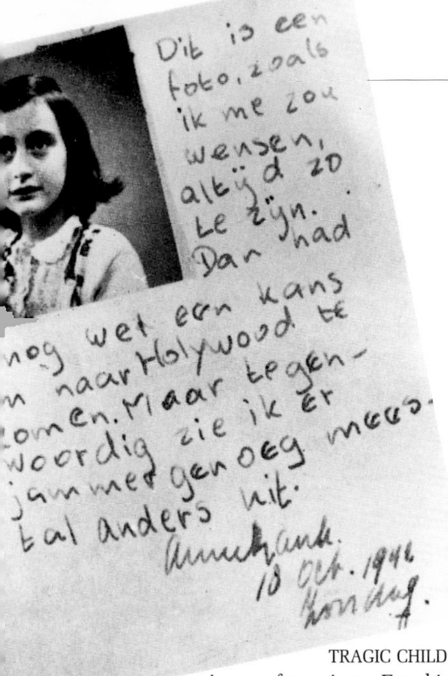

TRAGIC CHILD
A page from Anne Frank's diary, reading: 'This is a photo of me as I wish I looked all the time . . . But nowadays, I'm afraid, I usually look quite different.'

on absolute ▷MONARCHY, the DIVINE RIGHT OF KINGS and class. The revolution began in 1789, when the Estates General, or French parliament, refused to grant taxes to LOUIS XVI and his extravagant queen MARIE ANTOINETTE, and the commoners declared themselves the National Assembly – the true legislature of France. A mob destroyed the Bastille, the state prison which had become a symbol of the king's despotism, and the National Assembly abolished the privileges of the nobility, confiscating church estates and issuing a Declaration of the Rights of Man. Louis and Marie Antoinette were arrested and France was declared a republic. The king and queen were tried for treason and executed on the guillotine in 1793. Control of the government passed to the extremist Jacobins, led by Maximilien de ROBESPIERRE, who executed thousands of aristocrats and other 'enemies of the Revolution' during the Reign of Terror (1793-4). In a reaction against these excesses, Robespierre himself was executed and a new regime, run by a committee called the *Directoire*, came to power. Its incompetence and corruption allowed NAPOLEON Bonaparte, a general in the revolutionary army, to seize power in 1799 and end revolutionary rule.

❖ France's revolutionaries were so keen to sever links with the royalist past that they invented a new calendar and a new system of measurement – the ▷METRIC SYSTEM.

❖ 'Bastille Day' on 14 July, the anniversary of the attack on the prison, is the most important national holiday in France.

Gagarin, Yuri (1934-68) Soviet cosmonaut who in 1961 became the first man in space when he completed one orbit of the Earth in the spaceship *Vostok*. It was reported that he was killed in an air accident while training for the *Soyuz 3* mission.

Gallipoli (1915-16) Disastrous WORLD WAR I campaign by Allied troops to clear the Dardanelles and force a sea route through to Russia. It was Winston CHURCHILL's initiative and the costly defeats between February 1915 and January 1916 around the Gallipoli Peninsula in European Turkey led to him losing his post as First Lord of the Admiralty. But Gallipoli established the bravery of the Allied soldiers, and particularly the newly formed Australian and New Zealand Army Corps (ANZAC) which formed a large part of the Allied force and suffered heavy losses. A public holiday in both countries on 25 April marks their first landing in 1915.

Gandhi, Indira (1917-84) Prime minister of India from 1966 to 1977 and from 1980 to 1984, when she was assassinated by Sikh extremists. Her father, Jawaharlal NEHRU, was India's first prime minister; she was not related to Mahatma Gandhi. Although she achieved a reputation as a leader of developing nations, Gandhi's record as premier was marred by repeated accusations of corruption and her failure to control the sectarian violence that eventually led to her murder. Her son Rajiv succeeded her until he, too, was assassinated in 1991.

Gandhi, Mahatma (Mohandas Karamchand) (1869-1948) Indian statesman who led his country's drive for independence from Britain. After spending 20 years in South Africa fighting discrimination against Indians, Gandhi returned to India in 1914 and won international recognition for leading a campaign of nonviolent resistance and disobedience to secure Indian independence. His methods included boycotts, hunger strikes and marches to collect salt in defiance of the government monopoly. Gandhi also campaigned against India's restrictive ▷CASTE system. He was imprisoned several times for his protests. In 1947 India became independent amid strife between Hindus and Muslims, and in the next year Gandhi was assassinated by a Hindu fanatic, Nathuram Godse, who believed that Gandhi was encouraging Islam in India. (See also Mahatma ▷GANDHI in 'Southern African history'.)

❖ Gandhi was often photographed wearing a home-spun loincloth and blanket, and spinning his own thread, symbolizing his dream of Indian self-sufficiency and a return to a simpler way of life; for many years India had imported cloth from Britain.

❖ In Sir Richard Attenborough's epic film *Gandhi* (1982) the actor Ben Kingsley portrayed the man in all his saintliness and unbending determination.

Garibaldi, Giuseppe (1807-82) Italian soldier and patriot who led Italy's 19th-century RISORGIMENTO. A member of Giuseppe Mazzini's 'Young Italy' movement, Garibaldi headed a revolutionary government in Rome in 1849. In 1860 he led 1 000 red-shirted volunteers to expel the king of Naples, paving the way for the unification of Italy under King Victor Emmanuel II of Piedmont.

Garvey, Marcus (1877-1940) Jamaican-born black nationalist whose 'Back to Africa' campaign in America, creed of black pride and economic power, and slogan of 'Africa for the Africans' had a profound effect in the USA as well as on ▷AFRICANISM. In 1914 he founded the Universal Negro Improvement and Conservation Association (UNICA), which at the height of its influence boasted more than 2 million members. Its racial separatism was heavily criticized by other black leaders in the USA. Garvey slipped into virtual obscurity after he was convicted of attempted fraud in 1923.

❖ In 1921 UNICA founded four branches in South Africa. 'Garveyism' attracted a particularly strong following in the Transkei.

❖ *Black Moses*, a biography of Garvey by Edmund David Cronon, was published in 1955.

Genghis Khan (GENG-giss-KAAN) (*c*1162-1227) Mongolian general and emperor who united his people and turned them into a formidable fighting force. His armies invaded vast areas of China, Persia and Russia, and he was notorious for his cruelty to the people he conquered. He died at the helm of one of the largest empires the world has ever known, stretching from Korea to the Black Sea.

Gestapo Secret police force in Nazi Germany. The name is an abbreviation of *Geheime Staatspolizei* ('secret state police'). The Gestapo, founded by Hermann GÖRING and headed after 1934 by Heinrich HIMMLER, often resorted to blackmail and torture to deal with suspected opponents of Nazism. It also helped the SS to identify and round up Jews during the HOLOCAUST.

❖ Intimidation by officialdom is sometimes called 'Gestapo tactics'.

Gladstone, William Ewart (1809-98) British Liberal politician who served as prime minister four times between 1868 and 1894. He introduced the secret ballot and reformed the army, the Church and education, but failed to achieve IRISH HOME RULE.

❖ Gladstone, nicknamed the 'Grand Old Man'

of British politics, used to carry a small case with a hinged lid and two compartments, known as a 'Gladstone bag'.

Goebbels, Joseph (GUR-b'lz) (1897-1945) Propaganda minister of the German Nazi regime. He said that if a lie was repeated often enough, it would eventually be believed, and that a big lie was more believable than a small one. Goebbels mastered the new media of radio and film, and devised impressive events such as the Nuremberg Rallies. He had great charm and was a notorious womanizer. He poisoned his family and himself when Germany was defeated at the end of World War II.

❖ Goebbels, a superb orator, stirred Germany to wage what he called 'total war' – one which harnesses the entire resources of a country. It was he, and not (as is often thought) CHURCHILL, who first saw postwar Europe as being divided by an 'iron curtain' between the Soviet Union and the West.

gold rush The first major gold rush in modern times was in the 16th century, when Spaniards flocked to South America in search of ▷ELDORADO. The term is more usually applied to the California gold rush (1848-9), the Victoria gold rush in Australia (1851), the ▷WITWATERSTRAND GOLD RUSH in South Africa (1886) and the Klondike gold rush in Canada (1896).

Göring, Hermann (GURR-ing) (1893-1946) German military pilot and air hero of World War I who became one of Adolf Hitler's closest associates and a key member of the Nazi Government. He was the head of the *Luftwaffe* (the German air force) and founded the GESTAPO; Hitler gave him the special rank of *Reichsmarshall*. However, Göring's pilots lost the Battle of BRITAIN and failed to get supplies to German forces besieged at Stalingrad, causing his fall from favour. He was condemned to death at the NUREMBERG TRIALS, but poisoned himself the night before he was due to be hanged.

❖ Göring, a morphine addict, wore special uniforms, make-up and a vast array of medals and jewellery, and built up a huge collection of looted art treasures.

Goths General term for Germanic tribes who invaded the ROMAN EMPIRE from the Ukraine and the Balkans in the 4th and 5th century AD. They sacked Rome in 410.

❖ The term 'Gothic' was widely used by Renaissance artists to describe medieval art and ornamentation in general. Like Gothic art, the 18th-century Gothic novel and 19th-century neo-Gothic architecture have no real connection with the Goths.

Great Exhibition (1851) Display organized by Britain's Prince Albert, consort of Queen Victoria, as an exhibition of human progress in science and technology. It was held in an enormous glass-and-iron structure, nicknamed the ▷CRYSTAL PALACE, in London's Hyde Park. Six million people visited the exhibition, which was open for six months.

Greece, ancient Greek history began when powerful 'city-states' such as SPARTA, Corinth and ATHENS emerged from the prehistoric Mycenaean and Minoan cultures in the 9th century BC. Traders soon extended Greek influence over most of the Mediterranean. At the beginning of the 6th century BC, Athens became the world's first ▷DEMOCRACY and it defeated the Persians at the Battle of Marathon (490 BC). There then began a 'golden age' of Athenian culture which has been a major influence on Western civilization. It produced the dramas of ▷ARISTOPHANES, ▷AESCHYLUS, ▷EURIPIDES and ▷SOPHOCLES; the philosophy of ▷SOCRATES, ▷ARISTOTLE and ▷PLATO; and the scientific discoveries of ▷EUCLID, ▷ARCHIMEDES, Pythagoras and ▷HIPPOCRATES. Rivalry between Sparta and Athens culminated in the Peloponnesian Wars (431-404 BC), in which Athens was eventually defeated. The years of battle, however, had weakened the Greek states so much that Philip of Macedon (382-336 BC) was able to conquer and unite them into a single country. His son ALEXANDER THE GREAT extended Greek rule deep into Asia and Africa, founding the Macedonian Empire, much of which was eventually conquered by Rome in 148 BC. But Greek culture and ideas continued to flourish, and its customs permeated the ROMAN EMPIRE – a process summed up by the poet ▷HORACE as 'captive Greece made captive her rude conqueror'.

❖ The ▷VENUS DE MILO and the ▷PARTHENON are among the masterpieces of ancient Greek art and architecture.

❖ The Western alphabet evolved from the Greek alphabet and Greek words have been incorporated into many other languages – most notably English. For example, *microphone*, *nostalgia* and *hymn* are all derived from Greek words.

❖ The ▷OLYMPIC GAMES of modern times were inspired by the original Greek athletics tournament, which took place on the plains of Olympia every four years.

Grey, Earl (Charles Grey) (1764-1845) WHIG prime minister of Britain from 1830 to 1834. Grey secured the passage of the first of Britain's Reform Acts, which changed voting qualifications and abolished slavery throughout the British empire.

Guernica Basque town in northeast Spain, bombed by the German *Luftwaffe* (air force) on behalf of General Franco during the SPANISH CIVIL WAR.

❖ ▷PICASSO vividly portrayed the incident in his painting *Guernica* (1937).

Guevara, Che (g'VAAR-er, CHAY) (1928-67) Leader, together with Fidel ▷CASTRO, of the CUBAN REVOLUTION in 1959. Born in Argentina, he went on to foment communist uprisings throughout Latin America. He was killed while fighting a guerrilla war in Bolivia.

STRIKING IT RICH *Prospectors pan for gold by a stream in the 1870s Dakota gold rush. Gold diggers spent backbreaking hours sifting gravel, trying to extract tiny flakes of the precious metal.*

REBEL FIGHTER *Che Guevara's idolized face, captured in this classic 1960s poster, stared out from students' walls all over the world.*

guilds Organizations of self-employed artisans or merchants in the Middle Ages that sought to regulate the price and quality of products such as cloth and ironwork. The guilds were at their peak from the 12th to the 14th century. With the rise of ▷MERCANTILISM and ▷CAPITALISM in the 17th and 18th century the power of the guilds declined. However, some of their functions passed to the ▷TRADE UNIONS, organized to support the growing number of company employees.

Gulf War, The (1991) Battle between Iraqi forces and a USA-led coalition, following Iraq's occupation of Kuwait during a dispute over oil rights in 1990. After diplomatic negotiations failed to restore Kuwait's sovereignty, 29 countries, including the USA, Britain, France and Saudi Arabia, set out to enforce a United Nations resolution demanding an end to the occupation. The first stage was a sustained aerial bombing attack; Iraq's leader ▷SADDAM HUSSEIN responded by launching missiles at targets in Israel in a vain attempt to exploit the ▷ARAB-ISRAELI CONFLICT and disrupt the coalition by drawing Israel into the war. In February 1991, allied ground forces drove deep into Kuwait and Iraq. Iraqi troops offered little resistance before abandoning Kuwait in disarray, having set oil wells alight before they retreated. The war ended with the re-establishment of the former regime in Kuwait, but with Saddam Hussein still in power in Iraq.

Gutenberg, Johann (*c*1400-68) German printer credited with introducing the modern technique of ▷PRINTING with 'movable type' – that is, with each letter on a separate block, so that it could be reused after a page was printed. Similar printing methods already existed in the Far East, but were little known in Europe. The Gutenberg Bible of *c*1455 was the first book printed in the Western world with movable type.

Habsburg, House of Major European royal dynasty from the Middle Ages to modern times. The Habsburgs came to power in Austria in 1278 and ruled the HOLY ROMAN EMPIRE from 1493. They reached the peak of their power in the 16th century under Charles V of Spain, who ruled an empire that stretched from Prussia to South America. The dynasty's power ended after World War I with the dissolution of Austria-Hungary.

❖ The Habsburg family had a hereditary deformity of the mouth and jaw which produced a protruding lower lip, known as the 'Habsburg lip' or 'Habsburg jaw'.

Haile Selassie (HYE-lee si-LASS-ee) (1891-1975) Emperor of Ethiopia (previously Abyssinia) from 1930. He fled to England in 1936 after the Italian conquest of his country, but was restored to the throne in 1941 with the help of South African forces who invaded Addis Ababa on 6 April. Haile Selassie played a major role as an African statesman, especially in the founding of the ▷ORGANIZATION OF AFRICAN UNITY in 1963. Although he was respected abroad, he did little to alleviate the poverty and hunger at home. He was deposed by the military in 1974, after a succession of poor harvests, and the monarchy was abolished the next year.

❖ Members of the West Indian ▷RASTAFARIAN sect believe that Haile Selassie was the Messiah and that Ethiopia is the Biblical promised land. The name of their religion is derived from Ras Tafari, Selassie's name before he came to the throne.

BLAZING OIL WELLS *Iraqi troops, driven out of Kuwait by Allied troops in the Gulf War, left a trail of devastation behind them.*

Hammurabi King of ancient MESOPOTAMIA who reigned from *c*1792 to 1750 BC. He is remembered for being the first ruler to put a code of laws – the 'Code of Hammurabi' – into writing.

Hannibal (247-*c*182 BC) General of the ancient North African city of CARTHAGE. During the Punic wars, Hannibal took a massive army from Spain through southern France to Italy in an attempt to conquer Rome. This involved taking a train of elephants across the Alps in 15 days, a feat still regarded as one of the greatest operations in military history. Although he was never defeated in Italy, Hannibal was recalled to Carthage in 203 to repel a Roman invasion and did not achieve his ultimate aim of capturing Rome.

Hanover, House of German family, and electors (rulers), of Hanover, descended from the British King JAMES I's daughter Elizabeth. They received the British crown when the last STUART monarch, Queen Anne, died heirless. The first Hanoverian kings, George I and George II, took little interest in their new country; George I never even learned English. George III, George IV and William IV were the later Hanoverian kings. Queen VICTORIA used her husband Albert's family name of Saxe-Coburg and Gotha instead. This was, in turn, dropped for WINDSOR by George V.

Hanseatic League Federation of prosperous cities in northern Germany which dominated trade in the Baltic and North Sea from the 13th to the 17th century. Its main ports included Hamburg, Lübeck and Bremen.

Hastings, Battle of (1066) Battle fought at the start of the NORMAN CONQUEST of England.

Henry VIII (1491-1547) King of England from 1509 until his death. During his youth, Henry was an accomplished musician, sportsman and scholar – the perfect ▷RENAISSANCE prince. Under the influence of his ambitious chancellor, the Catholic Cardinal Thomas Wolsey, the first part of Henry's reign saw war against France. When the pope refused to dissolve Henry's marriage to Catherine of Aragon after her failure to produce a male heir, Henry broke all links with Rome and made himself head of the new ▷CHURCH OF ENGLAND in 1534, ushering in the English REFORMATION. Henry executed his second wife, Anne Boleyn; his third wife, Jane Seymour, died after giving birth to the future Edward VI. His fourth marriage, to Anne of Cleves, was a diplomatic union; Henry disliked her – calling her the 'Flanders mare' – and quickly divorced her in order to marry Catherine Howard (1540), executed two years later on a charge of adultery. In his final years Henry, now contentedly married to Catherine Parr, renewed war with France and Scotland, and ruled as a tyrant at home.

Herodotus (*c*484-*c*423 BC) Widely travelled ancient Greek historian, often called the 'Father of History'. His account of the wars between Greece and Persia was the first narrative history and the beginning of Western historical writing.

Hess, Rudolf (1894-1987) Nazi politician who was Adolf Hitler's deputy until 1941, when he flew to Scotland, apparently on his own initiative, to try to negotiate a peace treaty between Britain and Germany. He was disowned by Hitler and imprisoned until the end of World War II. At the NUREMBERG TRIALS in 1946, he was sentenced to life imprisonment and spent the rest of his life in Spandau prison, Berlin, where he was nicknamed 'Mad Rudi' because of his eccentricities; for many years he was Spandau's only prisoner.
❖ Suggestions that Hess committed suicide or was murdered, or even that the prisoner in Spandau was in fact his double, have never been substantiated.

TWO HENRYS *King Henry VIII of England swaggers in the foreground of this cartoon by the German painter Hans Holbein; his father, Henry VII, stands behind him.*

Himmler, Heinrich (1900-45) NAZI leader with special responsibility for internal security and racial policy. As head of the SS from 1929, and of the GESTAPO from 1934, he directed the repression of dissidents and the elimination of Jews and other 'undesirables' during the HOLOCAUST. He committed suicide after being captured by British troops in the last few days of World War II.

Hindenburg, Paul von (1847-1934) General who commanded German forces in WORLD WAR I and became president of the WEIMAR REPUBLIC in 1925. In 1933, the aged Hindenburg appointed Adolf HITLER chancellor; his prestige did much to make Hitler acceptable to the Germans.
❖ The *Hindenburg*, an enormous German hydrogen-filled airship named after the general, operated as a luxury transatlantic carrier before it exploded dramatically over New Jersey, USA, in 1937.

Hirohito (1901-89) Emperor of Japan from 1926 until his death. Essentially a pacifist, he presided over a period of militarism that culminated with Japan waging war on the Allies during WORLD WAR II. After the war, he gave up the emperor's traditional claim to semi-divine status.

Hitler, Adolf (1889-1945) German dictator whose expansionist policies led to WORLD WAR II. Hitler outlined his plans for Germany in his book *Mein Kampf*, which he wrote in prison after staging the failed 'Beer Hall Putsch' in Munich in 1923 against the WEIMAR REPUBLIC. His dream was to see a blond, blue-eyed 'master race' dominate 'inferior' races, such as the Slavs and the Jews. Hitler, who was born in Austria, fought in the German army as a corporal in World War I. He took over the German Workers' Party in 1921 and renamed it the National Socialist or NAZI Party. Its blend of ▷NATIONALISM and ▷ANTISEMITISM won support during the economic depression of the 1920s, and in 1933 Hitler became Germany's chancellor. He banned all other parties, took the title of *Führer* ('leader') and directed a secret arms build-up, flouting the ban on German rearmament imposed by the Treaty of VERSAILLES IN 1919. Germany occupied the Rhineland (1936), Austria (1938) and Czechoslovakia (1938-9) before marching into Poland on 1 September 1939 – the act that provoked Britain and France to declare war. Hitler's blind confidence in German military superiority and in his own skills as commander eventually led to his defeat. He escaped assassination in a bomb plot in July 1944, but committed suicide with his wife Eva Braun (1910-45) in his bunker amid the ruins of Berlin in 1945.
❖ Hitler's appearance was distinctive, with piercing blue eyes, toothbrush moustache, severe haircut and military uniform incorporating the Nazi swastika. He was a theatrical speaker, delivering ranting speeches accompanied by vigorous arm movements and emphatic blows with his fist.

Ho Chi Minh (HOH CHEE min) (1892-1969) Vietnamese revolutionary leader, and president of North Vietnam from 1954. He led the communists of Vietnam in their efforts to drive out the forces of Japan in the 1940s, France in the 1950s and the USA during the VIETNAM WAR in the 1960s. Saigon, the former capital of South Vietnam, was renamed Ho Chi Minh City after the communists finally won the war in 1975.

Holocaust Murder of some 6 million Jews by the Nazis during World War II. Heinrich HIMMLER and Adolf EICHMANN were among those who fulfilled Adolf HITLER's 'Final Solution' – the Nazi euphemism for the attempt to exterminate the Jews. Gypsies, homosexuals, political opponents and many prominent Christian leaders were also killed in CONCENTRATION CAMPS.

Holy Roman Empire Major political institution in Europe from the 9th to the 16th centuries. Intended by its founder CHARLEMAGNE to be the Christian successor to ancient Rome, it was based in Germany and included large areas of central and western Europe. At its height, it extended from Denmark to northern Italy. After the REFORMATION, the power of the Holy Roman Empire declined, and the position of Holy Roman Emperor eventually became a meaningless title of the HABSBURG family. This provoked the 18th-century French author Voltaire to write that the Holy Roman Empire was neither holy, nor Roman, nor an empire.

Hoover, Herbert (1874-1964) President of the USA from 1929 to 1933. Soon after he took office, the Wall Street Crash threw the US into the The DEPRESSION. Hoover, a Republican, was reluctant to intervene and believed that private enterprise would turn the economy around. However, mainly due to mismanagement of the country's ▷RESERVES, the economy failed to recover and he was replaced as president by the interventionist Democrat Franklin D ROOSEVELT.

Houphouët-Boigny, Félix (1905-93) First president of Côte d'Ivoire (Ivory Coast) after its independence from France in 1960. A radical in his early career, he fought for total autonomy for French colonies in the 1940s and 1950s. His five terms as president were marked by moderate policies and he won praise for his country's stability and prosperity, but drew criticism for his ties with South Africa's ▷APARTHEID regime.

Huguenots French Protestants who were persecuted by their government as well as the Roman Catholic Church during the 16th and 17th centuries. In 1572, thousands of Huguenots died in the ST BARTHOLOMEW'S DAY MASSACRE. Although they were given freedom to practise their religion in the Edict of NANTES (1598), they were still not accepted. When the edict was revoked by LOUIS XIV in 1685, many Huguenots went to live in exile in Britain and the Netherlands, from where several joined the fledgling settlement at the Cape. (See also ▷HUGUENOTS in 'Southern African history'.)

Hundred Years' War (1337-1453) Conflict between France and England which started when the English King Edward III claimed the French throne for himself. English armies mounted a series of campaigns in France, capturing much of northern France. Among the best-known English victories were those under Edward III at Crécy (1346), under Edward, the 'Black Prince', at Poitiers (1356) and under Henry V at Agincourt (1415). The tide turned after 1429, when JOAN OF ARC inspired a strong French counterattack. When the war ended, England had lost all its European possessions except Calais.

Hungarian Uprising (1956) National revolt in Hungary against Soviet domination, led by students. The protesters – who destroyed statues of STALIN and called for free elections and political independence – toppled the Hungarian Government. When the new liberal government, led by Imre Nagy, announced plans to leave the WARSAW PACT, Soviet forces invaded the country, seized Nagy and hastily restored communist rule.

Huns Asiatic people who invaded Russia in the 4th century AD and, under the leadership of Attila (*c*405-53), conquered much of central and eastern Europe and ravaged Italy in the declining years of the ROMAN EMPIRE. The Huns were known for their terrible cruelty and destructiveness.

❖ Attila, called the 'Scourge of God', died in bed in a pool of blood soon after his marriage to a Burgundian princess, giving rise to stories that she had murdered him.

Incas South American people who built a vast empire, covering modern Peru, Ecuador, Bolivia and parts of Chile. Their civilization reached its peak during the 15th and 16th centuries. The Inca emperor, who was believed to be a descendant of the sun god, ruled over a structured and disciplined society. In 1530, the Spanish CONQUISTADOR Francisco Pizarro conquered the Incas and plundered their gold.

❖ The Incas were skilled engineers and builders. Their roads, cities and temples can still be seen, notably at ▷MACHU PICCHU high in the Peruvian Andes.

Indian Mutiny (1857-8) Uprising in India against British rule. It started when the rumour spread that Indian soldiers serving in the British army had been issued with a new type of cartridge greased with pork and beef fat, offending both Muslim and Hindu religious taboos. Other grievances came to the surface, and rebels claimed several towns and army garrisons. In one incident, 200 British troops were killed at Cawnpore. The rebels were not united and British forces quashed the rebellion. The British Government took over the task of governing India from the BRITISH EAST INDIA COMPANY after the mutiny, which focused Indian nationalism.

Industrial Revolution Rapid industrialization of Britain that began in the late 18th century. Inventions that made mass production possible – Richard Arkwright's 'water frame', James Hargreaves's 'spinning jenny' and James Watt's ▷STEAM ENGINE – drove the revolution, which spread from the textile industry to all areas of manufacturing. Canals and railways were developed to move goods efficiently and imports of raw materials from the colonies were boosted. The boom was also accompanied by social problems of child labour, unhealthy hours and conditions of work, poor sanitation and squalid housing. But by the 1860s Britain had become the richest industrialized nation, the so-called 'workshop of the world'. Other advanced nations soon followed the example, and the effects were eventually felt around the globe.

❖ Demand for wool at the newly mechanized British textile mills created a 'wool boom' in the eastern Cape in the 1840s and 1850s. The boom – along with dissatisfaction with social conditions in Britain – brought new waves of settlers to southern Africa.

INCA KNIFE *The jewelled hilt of this gold ceremonial blade, made in Peru in the 12th century, shows the Incas's intricate craftsmanship.*

Inquisition Court set up by the Roman Catholic Church in the 13th century to try cases of heresy and other offences against the Church. The Inquisition was conducted by Dominican monks who could force heretics to recant or do penance, or hand them over to the civil authorities for punishment. It sometimes used torture to extract confessions; the most severe penalty was burning at the stake. The Spanish Inquisition, set up in the 15th century by FERDINAND AND ISABELLA, was particularly infamous for its harshness.

❖ The Inquisition upheld the Church's mistaken view that the Earth was fixed at the centre of the Universe and forced the astronomer ▷GALILEO to withdraw his contention that the Earth and other planets moved round the Sun.

Iran-Contra affair American scandal of the 1980s in which US Government officials supplied arms to Iran during the IRAN-IRAQ WAR and used the profits to fund 'Contra' rebels fighting Nicaragua's left-wing government. Both operations were illegal, but the arms sales helped to secure the release of American hostages held by pro-Iranian factions in Beirut. President Ronald ▷REAGAN and his vice-president George ▷BUSH denied all knowledge of the affair.

Iran-Iraq War (1980-8) War that developed from a dispute between Iran and Iraq over control of the Shatt al Arab waterway, which runs between the two countries. ▷SADDAM HUSSEIN, Iraq's leader, also accused Iran of fomenting revolt in Iraq. After early Iraqi successes, the conflict became a stalemate, with enormous loss of life on both sides. Western navies kept Gulf shipping lanes open but tension mounted, especially after an American cruiser shot down an Iranian airliner in 1988, killing all 290 passengers and crew. A ceasefire was agreed upon in 1988, and in 1990 Iraq dropped all claims to the Shatt al Arab. Iraq's use of poison gas during the conflict, especially on the Kurdish inhabitants of Halabja, caused an international outcry.

Irish Home Rule Movement demanding self-government for Ireland. Championed by Irish nationalists Daniel O'Connell (1775-1847) and Charles Parnell (1846-91), Home Rule was a major political issue from early in the 19th century until the start of World War I. British rule in southern Ireland effectively collapsed after the EASTER RISING in 1916; the Irish Republican Army (▷IRA) was created soon after, and in 1922 southern Ireland gained independence as the Irish Free State, a dominion within the British ▷COMMONWEALTH. In 1932 it was renamed Eire, and in 1949 it was proclaimed a republic and at the same time withdrew from the Commonwealth. ▷NORTHERN IRELAND gained its own parliament at Stormont, but this was dissolved in 1972.

Iron Age Period of history when iron came into general use for making weapons and tools. Organized production of iron objects developed in southwestern Asia in about 1600 BC, spreading gradually westwards and reaching Africa about 3 000 years ago. In many civilizations, the Iron Age followed the BRONZE AGE, but in Africa it followed straight after the Stone Age, with both cultures flourishing simultaneously in some regions. (See also ▷IRON AGE in 'Southern African history'.)

Ivan III 'the Great' (1440-1505) Grand prince of Moscow from 1462. Ivan won independence from the Tatars and expanded Russia's territory northwards and eastwards by his conquests which included Novgorod and part of Lithuania.
❖ Ivan the Great rebuilt the ▷KREMLIN in Moscow, using Italian architects who gave it the form it still has today.

Ivan IV 'the Terrible' (1530-84) Russia's first TSAR, who assumed the title in 1547 when he took personal power. He had been Moscow's grand duke since the age of three, but Russia had been governed by regents drawn from the boyars, or nobles. Ivan expanded his territory into the former Tatar lands of Kazan and Astrakhan, and made administrative reforms. In 1565 he started to rule by terror, introducing a secret police force and brutal methods to attack the boyars, for whom he conceived a paranoid mistrust. After killing his son in a fit of rage in 1580, he is said to have repented of more than 3 000 murders.
❖ Ivan IV's Russian nickname *Groznyi*, loosely translated as 'the Terrible', more correctly means 'awe-inspiring'.

Jack the Ripper Nickname given to the murderer of five London prostitutes in frenzied knife attacks in 1888. He mutilated four of his victims, removing organs from their corpses. His identity remains a mystery.

James I (1566-1625) The first STUART king of England, who succeeded ELIZABETH I in 1603. The only child of MARY, QUEEN OF SCOTS, he had been king of Scotland (as James VI) since 1567. Described as the scholar-king, he was an intelligent and widely read man, and his shrewd reign in Scotland brought stability and peace. As king of England, however, he was less diligent and successful, earning the unflattering epithet of 'the wisest fool in Christendom'. James's strident assertion of the DIVINE RIGHT OF KINGS and his reliance on favourites, especially the Duke of Buckingham, whom he showered with honours, brought him into conflict with parliament.
❖ The arts flourished during his reign; he commissioned the Authorized Version, or King James Bible (1611), which is one of the greatest achievements of English literature.
❖ James is remembered for writing *A Counterblast to Tobacco*, a condemnation of the new habit of smoking – introduced to Europe by Sir Walter Raleigh – as 'loathsome to the eye, hateful to the nose, harmful to the brain (and) dangerous to the lungs'.

James II (1633-1701) King of England and Scotland, who succeeded his brother Charles II in 1685. Several attempts were made to exclude him from the succession because he was a Catholic, especially following the alleged POPISH PLOT to murder King Charles. James's pro-Catholic policies aroused intense opposition, and when he produced a Catholic heir (James Edward STUART) open revolt broke out. He was deposed in 1688 in a revolution – later known as 'the Glorious Revolution' – that established the supremacy of parliament over the monarchy and put his Protestant son-in-law and daughter, William and Mary, on the throne.

Jefferson, Thomas (1743-1826) Third president of the USA, from 1801 to 1809. Jefferson was the principal author of the DECLARATION OF INDEPENDENCE. As president, he negotiated the purchase from France of 2 million km^2 of territory west of the Mississippi. This 'Louisiana Purchase' effectively doubled the size of the USA.

Jinnah, Mohammed Ali (1876-1948) Pakistan's first governor-general. A Muslim, he strove to ensure that India's Muslims and Hindus worked together in their demands for independence from Britain. However, the 1930s saw a split between Mahatma GANDHI's Indian National Congress and the Muslim League, and Jinnah negotiated for part of India to become a separate Muslim state (Pakistan) when independence was won in 1947.

Joan of Arc (c1412-31) French national heroine, nicknamed the 'Maid of Orléans', who inspired her fellow countrymen's victory over England in the HUNDRED YEARS' WAR. Claiming that she had been summoned by divine voices to drive out the English, she inspired French troops to raise the English siege of Orléans in 1429, enabling the French dauphin (crown prince) to be crowned as Charles VII and paving the way for further French victories. She was captured in 1430 and sold to the English, who burnt her at the stake as a heretic and sorcerer.
❖ Joan of Arc was made a saint of the Roman Catholic Church in 1920.

Johnson, Lyndon B (1908-73) President of the USA from 1963 to 1969. He was elected vice-president in 1960 and became president after John F KENNEDY was assassinated. Johnson continued Kennedy's programme and introduced his own initiative for social reforms and civil rights to create the 'Great Society'. He also increased the USA's involvement in the VIETNAM WAR. However, because of mounting opposition to the war and his growing unpopularity, he did not stand for a second full term and retired in 1969.

Julius Caesar (c100-44 BC) Roman general and statesman who came to power in 60 BC as part of a 'triumvirate', or three-man ruling council. From 58 to 49 BC he mounted a series of military campaigns in Gaul (modern France) and Britain which brought him much prestige. The Roman senate, fearing Caesar's power, ordered him to disband his army. He refused and went on to ▷CROSS THE RUBICON, the river that formed the boundary of his province, and march on Rome. He won a civil war against Pompey, his former colleague in the triumvirate, and declared himself dictator in 46 BC. Two years later, on 15 March – 'the Ides of March' – he was assassinated by a group of conspirators including his old friend Brutus. As he lay dying of stab wounds, he purportedly said *'Et tu, Brute?'* ('Even you, Brutus?').
❖ Caesar summed up one of his campaigns

with the celebrated message *'Veni, vidi, vici'* ('I came, I saw, I conquered').

Justinian (cAD 482-565) Emperor of the BYZANTINE EMPIRE from AD 527. He reconquered North Africa and parts of Spain and Italy from the BARBARIANS and carried out a codification of Roman law which became the basis of many European legal systems. He also built the magnificent church of ▷HAGIA SOFIA in Istanbul.

kamikaze **(KAM-ee-KAH-zee)** Japanese fighter pilots of WORLD WAR II who were trained to carry out suicide missions, deliberately crashing their aircraft packed with explosives onto enemy ships.
❖ *Kamikaze* means 'divine wind' – a reference to typhoons that wrecked MONGOL attempts to invade Japan in 1274 and 1281.

Katyn massacre (1940) Mass murder of 4 443 Polish prisoners captured by Soviet forces early in WORLD WAR II. The bodies were discovered in the Katyn forest near Smolensk, Russia, by German invaders in 1943, but the Soviets denied responsibility and blamed the Germans. In 1990, however, the more liberal Soviet government admitted that Stalin's secret police had carried out the massacre.

Kennedy, John F (1917-63) President of the USA from 1961 to 1963. A Democrat, he was the youngest president to win office. Kennedy was criticized for a bungled attempt to invade Cuba (the BAY OF PIGS episode) in 1961, but praised for his handling of the CUBAN MISSILE CRISIS. He was a campaigner for social reform, backing the CIVIL RIGHTS MOVEMENT, and a strong supporter of the American space programme; his goal of landing a man on the Moon within the decade was achieved in 1969. Kennedy's presidency ended with his assassination, apparently by Lee Harvey Oswald, as he toured Dallas, Texas, in an open-top car.
❖ Unanswered questions and inconsistent evidence about Kennedy's murder have led to speculation that Oswald may have been 'framed', or was not the sole killer. Oswald was himself assassinated two days later by Jack Ruby, a local nightclub owner.
❖ Kennedy's appeal, based on his eloquence, youthful good looks and style, was helped by his elegant wife Jacqueline, who later married the wealthy Greek shipping magnate Aristotle Onassis.
❖ Kennedy was a compulsive womanizer and had many affairs – including, it is believed, a liaison with the film star Marilyn Monroe.

Kennedy, Robert (1925-68) Brother of President John F KENNEDY and, as attorney-general, a key member of his administration. He ran for the Democratic nomination for president in 1968, but was assassinated by Sirhan Sirhan, a Palestinian-born American who opposed Kennedy's pro-Israeli stance.

Kenyatta, Jomo (c1893-1978) First president of Kenya, from 1964 until his death. An ardent anticolonial campaigner, he was also leader – along with Kwame NKRUMAH – of the Pan-African Federation, a group formed in 1945 to promote cooperation among African states. From 1952 to 1961 Kenyatta was jailed for leading the MAU MAU guerrilla campaign, which sought to remove British rule. He became prime minister in June 1963, leading his country to independence later that year and becoming its president the next year.

Khomeini, Ayatollah Ruhollah (1900-89) Political and religious leader of Iran from 1979 to 1989. Khomeini, a staunch opponent of Iran's pro-Western policies under Shah MOHAMMED REZA PAHLAVI, went into exile in 1964. He returned to Iran in 1979, following the overthrow of the shah, and set up a theocracy, or religious government, which enforced strict observance of Islam.
❖ Ayatollah is a title which literally means 'miraculous sign of God'.

Khruschev, Nikita (KROOS-chof) (1894-1971) Leader of the ▷USSR from 1953 until 1964. He caused a great sensation by denouncing his predecessor, Joseph STALIN, in 1956. Although Khruschev urged peaceful coexistence between his country and the West and relaxed the COLD WAR, the U-2 spy-plane incident in 1960 and the 1962 CUBAN MISSILE CRISIS were moments of acute international tension. Khruschev sent Soviet troops into Poland and Hungary to uphold communist rule. In 1964 he was unseated by fellow politburo members, who were led by his successor Leonid BREZHNEV.

MUSLIM REVOLUTIONARY *The Ayatollah Khomeini, who came to power in Iran on a wave of popular acclaim, enforced Islamic law through teams of zealous followers.*

King, Martin Luther, Jr (1929-68) Black minister who led the CIVIL RIGHTS MOVEMENT in the USA. He became famous in the 1950s for

FATAL INSTANT *John F Kennedy's death so shocked the world that many people can remember exactly what they were doing on 22 November 1963, when they heard the news.*

AMERICAN HERO *Dr Martin Luther King was a tireless campaigner against racial discrimination. Popular fury at his assassination triggered urban riots across America.*

leading a series of nonviolent protests, such as sit-ins and boycotts, against racial segregation. In 1963 he led a civil-rights march of more than 200 000 people to Washington, DC, ending in a rally at which he delivered his famous 'I have a dream' speech. King was awarded the Nobel peace prize in 1964. He was assassinated by James Earl Ray in Memphis, Tennessee, in 1968.

❖ King's 1963 speech outlined his vision of an America free from racial prejudice, and included the sentence: 'I have a dream that my four little children will one day live in a nation where they will not be judged by the colour of their skin but by the content of their character.'

❖ Americans commemorate Martin Luther King Day on or around his birthday – 15 January – every year.

knight Warrior who fought on horseback in medieval Europe. The knight was a key part of the social hierarchy of FEUDALISM, in between the nobles and the peasants. As well as being soldiers, knights were supposed to follow the ideals of chivalry, a code of conduct that emphasized bravery, military skill, generosity in victory, religious piety and ▷COURTLY LOVE.

❖ The word 'chivalry' is derived from the old French *chevalier*, 'knight'.

Knossos (K'NOSS-oss) Site in Crete of the capital of the Bronze Age Minoan civilization, a precursor of ancient GREECE. The heyday of Knossos was from *c*2000-1400 BC. The site was excavated, initially by the British archaeologist Sir Arthur Evans in 1899, and the buildings extensively restored.

❖ The frescoes and sculptures of Knossos, depicting ceremonies in which bulls were made to leap, wrestling, fishermen and many other themes, are notable for their lively and stylish execution. They reflect a prosperous and highly sophisticated civilization.

❖ The legend of Theseus overcoming the ▷MINOTAUR was set in Knossos.

Korean War (1950-3) War between South Korea and communist North Korea, which started when North Korean troops invaded the south. Other nations soon became involved in the conflict. The United Nations sent a mainly American force under Douglas MACARTHUR to support South Korea, while Chinese troops backed North Korea. The war became a stalemate, and a truce was eventually signed at Panmunjon in 1953.

❖ A total of 209 pilots of the South African Air Force's Number 2 Squadron and 555 South African ground personnel served in the war. The squadron, which lost more than 30 members in action, was awarded the Korean Presidential Citation in 1951, the Union of South Africa Korea Medal in 1953 and the United States Presidential Citation in 1956.

Kublai Khan (KOOB-lye KAAN) (1215-94) MONGOL emperor from 1260, and grandson of GENGHIS KHAN. Kublai Khan completed the conquest of China and made Beijing the capital of an empire that stretched as far west as the Black Sea, but he twice failed to conquer Japan. As China's first Mongol emperor, Kublai took the title of Shib-Tsu in 1279. He made Buddhism the official state religion and was a patron of learning and the arts.

❖ The splendours of Kublai Khan's court were described by the Italian explorer Marco POLO, who spent 17 years here. They also inspired the poem 'Kubla Khan', written by Samuel Taylor ▷COLERIDGE.

League of Nations International organization established in 1919 by the Treaty of VERSAILLES. The league brought about international cooperation on health, labour problems, refugees and other matters, but it was too weak to prevent the outbreak of World War II in 1939. After the war, it was replaced by a stronger and broader-based organization, the ▷UNITED NATIONS.

❖ In 1920 the league gave South Africa a mandate to govern ▷SOUTH WEST AFRICA as an integral part of the ▷UNION. It also stipulated that the government should concern itself with the well-being of the indigenous inhabitants, which it did not. The UN General Assembly, as successor to the league, terminated the mandate in 1966; in 1971 the ▷INTERNATIONAL COURT OF JUSTICE in the Hague backed the General Assembly's decision to revoke the mandate. South Africa also later resisted UN moves to bring the territory to independence as Namibia.

Lenin, Vladimir Ilyich (1870-1924) Adopted name of Vladimir Ilyich Ulyanov, the first leader of the ▷USSR, which he founded in 1922. As the leader of the BOLSHEVIKS, he played a central role in the RUSSIAN REVOLUTION of 1917, eventually emerging as Russia's leader. He took Russia out of World War I, oversaw the victory of the Red Army during the RUSSIAN CIVIL WAR, concentrated state power in the hands of the Communist Party and introduced radical economic reforms to abolish capitalism. Lenin suffered a series of strokes before dying. Against his wishes, he was succeeded by Joseph STALIN.

❖ Lenin's body was embalmed and put on display in a specially built mausoleum in Moscow's Red Square. He was the great national hero of the Soviet Union, and his image featured on coins, stamps and official art. From 1924 to 1991, St Petersburg was called Leningrad in his honour.

Lincoln, Abraham (1809-65) President of the USA from 1861 to 1865. Lincoln, a Republican, prevented his country from splitting into two nations by leading the Union (northern) states to victory over the Confederate (southern) states in the AMERICAN CIVIL WAR. He is also remembered for his Gettysburg Address in 1863, and for decreeing, the same year, that all slaves in the USA were free. While watching a play – *Our American Cousin* – in Washington, Lincoln was assassinated by John Wilkes Booth, a fanatical supporter of the Confederate cause.

❖ The Gettysburg Address, in which Lincoln dedicated a war cemetery at the site of the Battle of Gettysburg in Pennsylvania, contains the celebrated definition of democracy as 'government of the people, by the people, and for the people'.

Lindbergh, Charles (1902-74) American aviator who in 1927 made the first solo nonstop flight across the Atlantic. He took off from New York and landed in Paris 33½ hours later, flying in a Ryan monoplane called *Spirit of St Louis.* He later came under heavy criticizm for urging the USA government to stay out of World War II.

❖ The kidnapping and murder of Lindbergh's 20-month-old son in 1932 gained public attention around the world.

Lloyd George, David (1863-1945) Liberal prime minister of Britain from 1916 to 1922,

SHINING KING *Louis XIV of France carefully nurtured his image of 'Sun King', and even appeared in a ballet wearing this spectacular costume.*

at the head of a coalition government. As chancellor of the exchequer (1908-15), he triggered a constitutional crisis when the House of Lords rejected his 'People's Budget' of 1909, which introduced new taxes for the wealthy to pay for welfare measures. Consequently, the Lords were later stripped of their power to veto money bills. Lloyd George took over as prime minister halfway through World War I. When the war ended, he conducted negotiations for Britain at the conference leading to the Treaty of VERSAILLES. He provided for IRISH HOME RULE in 1921. When he died, he had been an MP for 55 years, and his energy and eloquence made a lasting impact on British political life.

Long March March across China begun in October 1934 by MAO ZEDONG with about 100 000 communist troops to escape CHIANG KAI-SHEK's forces, which had been closing in on them in southern and eastern China. It took Mao's troops a year to cover about 9 600 km and only about 10 000 completed the journey.

Louis XIV (1638-1715) King of France from 1643, known as the 'Sun King' for his power and splendour. He believed in strong personal government and absolute ▷MONARCHY, boasting *'L'etat, c'est moi'* ('I am the state'). He asserted French power in a series of wars, including the War of the SPANISH SUCCESSION.
❖ Louis ordered the lavish rebuilding of the royal palace of ▷VERSAILLES and filled it with treasures reflecting his greatness.

Louis XVI (1754-93) Last king of France before the FRENCH REVOLUTION. His failure to support reformist ministers, his expensive intervention on the rebels' side in the AMERICAN WAR OF INDEPENDENCE and the extravagance of his queen, MARIE ANTOINETTE, all helped to precipitate the revolution. Louis and Antoinette tried to flee the country, but were brought back as prisoners and beheaded for treason.

Louis Philippe (1773-1850) King of France from 1830 to 1848, known as the 'Citizen King' because of his informal manner and his support for the FRENCH REVOLUTION. He fled France in 1793, when revolutionary leaders tried to arrest him, but returned when the monarchy was restored in 1817. Elected after his predecessor, Charles X, tried to bring back absolute ▷MONARCHY, Louis Philippe was popular at first, but he became corrupt and was overthrown.

Lumumba, Patrice (1925-61) First prime minister of Zaire, previously known as the Belgian Congo. His party, which advocated national unity, was asked to form the first government after independence in 1960, although it had not won an outright majority in the election. This sparked the so-called Congo Crisis, in which troops mutinied and Katanga (Shaba) province seceded. Lumumba gained support from a United Nations peacekeeping force, but was soon ousted. He was assassinated in 1961 while being held by Katangese troops. A university in Moscow is named after Lumumba.

MacArthur, Douglas (1880-1964) American general who commanded Allied forces in the Far East and southwest Pacific during WORLD WAR II. After some initial setbacks, he oversaw the defeat and occupation of Japan and supervised the drafting of a new democratic constitution. In 1950 MacArthur was appointed to lead United Nations forces in the KOREAN WAR, but his threat to bomb China brought his dismissal by president Harry S TRUMAN in 1951.
❖ When Japan conquered the Philippines MacArthur was forced to leave, but he vowed 'I shall return'. He did so two years later, and drove out the Japanese.

Macmillan, Harold (1894-1986) British Conservative prime minister from 1957 to 1963. Taking over from Sir Anthony EDEN after the SUEZ CRISIS, he restored national confidence and for a time enjoyed considerable popularity. In 1960 his ▷'WIND OF CHANGE' speech proposed acceptance of the need for decolonization and called for an end to ▷APARTHEID.

Magellan, Ferdinand (*c*1480-1521) Portuguese explorer who rounded the tip of South America in 1520 to reach the Pacific Ocean, which he named after its peaceful waters. He was killed in the Philippines, but his crew continued the journey, returning to Spain in 1522 and completing the first round-the-world voyage in history.
❖ The Strait of Magellan, between mainland South America and Tierra del Fuego, and the ▷MAGELLANIC CLOUDS, two small galaxies in the southern night sky first recorded by Magellan, are named after the explorer.

Maginot Line (MAJ-i-noh) Supposedly impregnable chain of fortifications built by France on its eastern border in the 1920s and 1930s to stop any future invasion from the east. During WORLD WAR II the Germans simply went round it to the north.

Magna Carta (1215) List of rights and privileges – also known as the Great Charter of Liberties – sealed by King John of England after his barons met him at Runnymede Meadow on the River Thames to put pressure on him to stop his arbitrary rule and heavy taxes. A revised version, issued in 1225, became part of English law, establishing the principle that the monarch had to abide by the laws of the country and insisting that the monarch should seek the barons' permission before levying taxes.
❖ *Magna carta* means 'great charter' in Latin.

Malcolm X (Malcolm Little) (1925-65) American radical leader who opposed racial integration and preached in favour of black separatism. He encouraged black Americans to reject Christianity and embrace Islam. However, he was eventually assassinated by members of the Black Muslim group after he had left their organization and become an orthodox Muslim.

Mao Zedong (1893-1976) Chinese communist revolutionary leader who came to prominence when he led an army of workers and peasants on the LONG MARCH in 1934-5. He went on to use guerrilla tactics against both Japanese invaders and the forces of the Chinese nationalist government under CHIANG KAI-SHEK. In 1949, Mao took power and established the communist People's Republic of China. He believed that revolution must continually take place if it is not to degenerate into elitism. In the mid-1960s, he

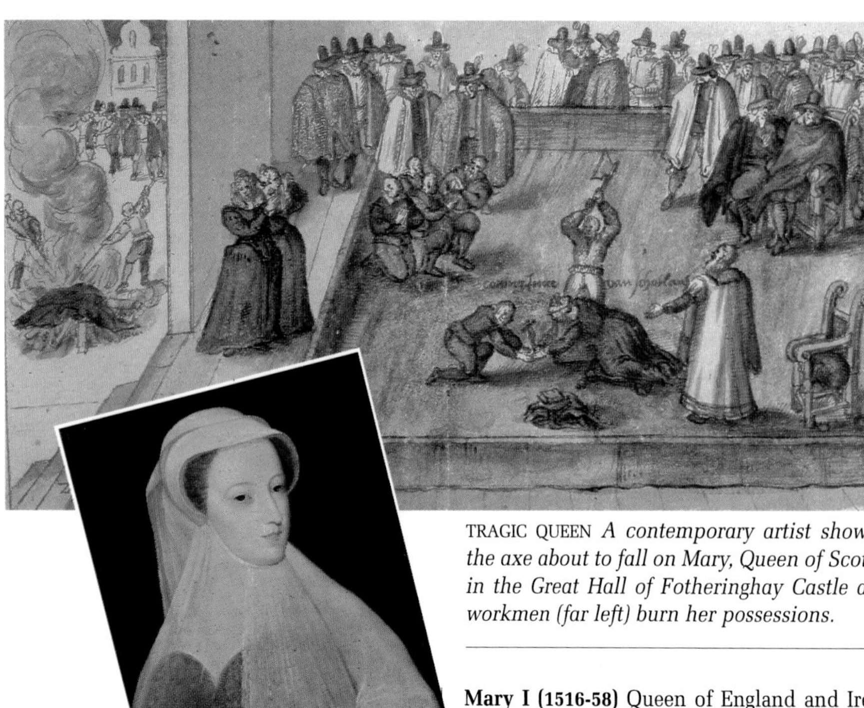

TRAGIC QUEEN *A contemporary artist shows the axe about to fall on Mary, Queen of Scots in the Great Hall of Fotheringhay Castle as workmen (far left) burn her possessions.*

launched the CULTURAL REVOLUTION, an attempt to purge China of all traces of capitalism and elitism and to encourage agriculture. During the COLD WAR he was a firm advocate of a non-aligned 'Third World'.

❖ In the 1960s, all Chinese people had to carry a copy of the *Quotations of Chairman Mao* – known as the 'Little Red Book'. Up to 800 million copies were published.

❖ After Mao's death, his wife Jiang Qing and senior advisers, known as the Gang of Four, were jailed on charges of allegedly sabotaging communism in China.

Marie Antoinette (1755-93) Wife of LOUIS XVI of France, whose expensive, frivolous tastes and resistance to reform made her deeply unpopular. Eventually, both she and Louis were overthrown and executed on the guillotine during the FRENCH REVOLUTION.

❖ Marie Antoinette was said to be so unconcerned by the problems of her subjects that when she was told that they had no bread, she purportedly replied: 'Let them eat cake.'

Marshall Aid Popular name for the European Recovery Programme, under which the USA government gave large sums of money to Britain and other European countries to help them to rebuild their devastated economies after WORLD WAR II. General George C Marshall, the American secretary of state, proposed the plan in 1947; it was wound up in 1951. A total of $14 000 million was distributed under the scheme.

Mary I (1516-58) Queen of England and Ireland, who came to the throne by ousting the Protestant Lady Jane Grey in 1553. She was the daughter of HENRY VIII by his first wife, Catherine of Aragon. A Roman Catholic, she ruthlessly persecuted Protestants, sending about 300 dissenters to be burned at the stake. Her marriage to PHILIP II of Spain provoked a rebellion and dragged England into Spain's war with France; the result was the loss of Calais, England's last foothold on the European Continent. Mary said that when she died the word 'Calais' would be found engraved on her heart.

Mary, Queen of Scots (1542-87) Queen who succeeded to the Scottish throne and staked her claim to the English throne in 1561. Her husband, Henry, Lord Darnley, murdered Mary's secretary David Riccio and was then killed himself in mysterious circumstances. In 1567, when Mary married the chief suspect, the Earl of Bothwell, the Scottish nobles forced her to abdicate in favour of her son James VI of Scotland – later JAMES I of England. Mary was imprisoned by ELIZABETH I for 20 years, but she still became the focus of Catholic plots against the English Crown. Eventually she was executed for treason.

❖ Mary was a keen ▷BILLIARDS player.

Mata Hari (1876-1917) Stage name – Malay for 'eye of the day' – of Margarete Gertrude Zelle, a Dutch-born dancer based in Paris during World War I. She is thought to have spied for both France and Germany, gathering information from the many senior military and government officials she took as lovers. The French executed her for espionage.

Mau Mau Term used for the armed revolt by Kenyan nationalists against British rule from 1952. From the 1920s, Kenyan nationalists had protested against colonial encroachment on their land and for African rights. The group that became known as the Mau Mau formed underground because of the lack of success – and prohibition – of more formal organizations. After the arrest of some 200 nationalists in terms of a state of emergency in 1952, hundreds of others waged war from the forests, creating terror and revulsion for their methods among the colonists. Protest against British treatment of detainees during the rebellion – most notably the death of 11 at a detention centre at Hola – led eventually to the calling of a constitutional conference to discuss Kenyan independence.

❖ The official death toll in the rebellion was 95 whites and 1 920 blacks killed by Mau Mau, and 11 503 killed by security forces.

Maya (MYE-a) Native American people who lived in the region of present-day Mexico, Guatemala and Honduras. They flourished from the 3rd to 10th centuries AD. The Mayas were sophisticated astronomers who made accurate calendars, built pyramids and wrote in ▷HIEROGLYPHS.

Mayflower Square-rigged sailing ship – 27 m long – that carried the Pilgrim Fathers from Plymouth, England, to Plymouth, Massachusetts, in September 1620. Problems with a second vessel delayed their departure; the consequent overcrowding and bad weather prompted one death and severe discomfort for the 102 passengers – many of them fleeing religious persecution. After 66 days, rough seas forced a landing in New England, where they formed the first permanent colony.

Medici (med-EECH-ee) Ruling family of Florence from the 14th to the 16th century. Their immense wealth came from banking, and they patronized many ▷RENAISSANCE artists, including ▷DONATELLO, ▷MICHELANGELO and ▷LEONARDO DA VINCI. Several members of the Medici family were popes, and Catherine and Marie were queens of France.

❖ The Medici remained rulers of Tuscany until its cession to Austria in 1736.

Mesopotamia Region in modern-day ▷IRAQ, known as the 'cradle of civilization'. It was in Mesopotamia in about 3500 BC that the first form of writing developed; this was the ▷CUNEIFORM script, inscribed on clay tablets. Agricultural organization also began in Mesopotamia, along with detailed work in bronze and iron. Rulers such as HAMMURABI introduced a system of codified laws.

❖ The name Mesopotamia is derived from the

Greek for 'between rivers', the area being bordered by the Tigris and Euphrates rivers.

Metternich, Prince Clemens (1773-1859) Chancellor of Austria from 1821 until he was overthrown by a revolution in 1848. Through his leadership, particularly at the Congress of VIENNA, Metternich succeeded in restoring order in Europe after the fall of NAPOLEON I. He did so, however, to the advantage of many European monarchs and at the expense of liberalism and nationalism.

❖ In the 19th century, Metternich's name became a byword for conservatism.

Middle Ages Period of European history between the fall of the ROMAN EMPIRE and the ▷RENAISSANCE, spanning the 5th to the 15th century AD. The Middle Ages was an era of chivalry (see KNIGHT), FEUDALISM and, above all, Christian spirituality. Key events in the period include the NORMAN CONQUEST, the CRUSADES, the BLACK DEATH and the building of many cathedrals.

Moguls (MOH-g'lz) Islamic dynasty, descended from the Mongols, which ruled India from 1526. The greatest of the Mogul emperors was Akbar, who reigned from 1556 to 1605. He expanded Mogul control over northern India and encouraged the arts and literature. The empire started to decline in the 18th century, and the last emperor was deposed by the British in 1857, following the INDIAN MUTINY.

❖ The ▷TAJ MAHAL is the best-known masterpiece of Mogul architecture.

DOOMED SPY *Mata Hari's revealing dance costumes cloaked her role as a double-dealing secret agent for both sides in World War I.*

Mohammed Reza Pahlavi (1919-80) Iran's last shah, who succeeded to the throne in 1941. With aid from the USA, he did much to modernize Iran. However, he also steered Iran towards authoritarian rule and allowed corruption to flourish and the economy to decline. Moreover, his programme of 'Westernization' upset religious fundamentalists, who forced him to flee in 1979 and recalled Ayatollah KHOMEINI from exile to restore strict Islamic rule.

Molotov, Vyacheslav (1890-1986) Soviet statesman who, as foreign minister, negotiated the NAZI-SOVIET PACT of 1939. He was a close ally of STALIN, and his uncompromising hostility towards the West contributed to the COLD WAR. Molotov said *niet* ('no') to so many proposals for détente that he was nicknamed 'Mister Niet' in the West. He was demoted by KHRUSCHEV following the death of Stalin in 1953. Four years later, Andrei Gromyko succeeded Molotov, serving as foreign secretary for nearly 40 years.

❖ The ironic nickname of 'Molotov cocktail' was given by Finnish troops to the improvised grenades, petrol-filled bottles stuffed with rags, with which they fought the Russian invaders in 1939.

Mongol empire Massive empire created in the 13th century by GENGHIS KHAN, who united the tribes of central Asia in 1206 and conquered an area stretching from modern Korea to Turkey and from Siberia to parts of China. The next Mongol emperor, his grandson KUBLAI KHAN, expanded the empire deep into China, where he moved the Mongol capital in 1264. After 1360, under Tamerlane, the Mongols advanced into India, where their descendants established the MOGUL dynasty.

Monroe Doctrine Statement of American foreign policy issued by president James Monroe in 1823. The USA asserted its right to oppose European attempts to colonize the American continent and confirmed its non-intervention in European disputes.

Montezuma II (1466-1520) Last emperor of the AZTECS, killed by a mob during the conquest of his kingdom by the Spanish conquistador Hernán CORTÉS.

❖ The upset stomach and diarrhoea which affects tourists in Mexico is sometimes humorously called 'Montezuma's revenge'.

Montgomery, Bernard Law (1st Viscount Montgomery of Alamein) (1887-1976) Commander of British and colonial forces in North Africa and Europe during WORLD WAR II. His first major victory, at the head of the Eighth Army, was to defeat ROMMEL at ALAMEIN; he later commanded Allied ground forces during D-DAY and the subsequent invasion of Normandy.

Moors North African Muslim people who captured Spain from the GOTHS in the 8th century AD. They went on to invade France, but were halted at Poitiers in 732. Christian rulers gradually reconquered Spain from the Moors, completing the process in 1492. Moorish Spain had a vibrant culture and a freedom of ideas and religion not permitted in Christian Europe.

❖ The ▷ALHAMBRA at Granada and the Great Mosque of Córdoba, where the Moorish CALIPHS had their capital, are splendid architectural reminders of Muslim Spain.

More, Sir Thomas (1478-1535) English statesman and scholar who served HENRY VIII until Henry's break with Rome. A loyal Catholic, More was beheaded for refusing to recognize Henry as head of the English Church. He wrote *Utopia* (Greek for 'no place'), in which he outlined his vision of an ideal society. More was made a Catholic saint in 1935.

❖ Robert Bolt wrote a powerful play about Thomas More, *A Man For All Seasons* (1960).

Mountbatten, Lord Louis (Earl Mountbatten of Burma) (1900-79) British naval commander and statesman who commanded the defence of India and the campaign to expel the Japanese from Burma during WORLD WAR II. In 1947, as viceroy of India, Mountbatten supervised India's transition to independence. He was assassinated by the ▷IRA while fishing with members of his family off the Irish coast.

Munich Agreement (1938) Pact between Britain, France, Italy and Germany, allowing Adolf HITLER to extend German territory into the Sudetenland, a frontier region of Czechoslovakia inhabited by a German-speaking minority. Neville Chamberlain, the British prime minister, claimed he had won 'peace for our time', but Germany occupied the rest of Czechoslovakia and invaded Poland less than a year later. The pact is now seen as the high point of APPEASEMENT.

Mussolini, Benito (1883-1945) Fascist ruler of Italy from 1922 to 1943. Mussolini had formed a dictatorship by 1928 and embarked on an ambitious public works programme, which included building motorways and upgrading the railways, to revive the Italian economy. He invaded Abyssinia (now Ethiopia), intervened to help General FRANCO

INTO EXILE *Napoleon stares out to sea as HMS* Bellerophon *takes him towards the island of St Helena. The defeated emperor's charm is said to have impressed the British ship's entire crew.*

in the SPANISH CIVIL WAR and annexed Albania in the 1930s. In 1940 he made an alliance with Germany as one of the AXIS powers of World War II. In 1943, after a string of military defeats, he resigned and was put under house arrest, but was freed in an audacious raid by German commandos led by Otto Skorzeny. Hitler helped to set up a puppet republic for Mussolini based at Salo, on Lake Garda, in German-occupied northern Italy. At the end of the war, Italian partisans captured and executed Mussolini and his mistress Clara Retacci.

❖ Mussolini was nicknamed *il Duce* ('the leader') by his followers and the 'bullfrog of the Pontine marshes' by Winston CHURCHILL. He was known for his proud, strutting manner and his dreams of restoring Rome's imperial greatness. It is said of him that he made the trains run on time in Italy.

Mycenae (mye-SEEN-ee) Civilization that flourished in Greece during the BRONZE AGE, especially after 1600 BC. Led by strong warrior-kings who built magnificent cities and palaces, the Mycenaeans soon became the dominant influence in the Mediterranean. Their long military expedition to conquer ▷TROY was recounted by Homer in the ▷ILIAD. By 1100 BC Mycenae was no longer powerful, probably because of natural disasters, BARBARIAN invasions and internal strife.

Nantes, Edict of (1598) Law passed by Henry IV of France giving religious freedom to the Protestant HUGUENOTS. The edict stopped the religious wars between Roman Catholics and Protestants, but it was revoked by LOUIS XIV in 1685, prompting the mass emigration of ▷HUGUENOTS, many of whom came to South Africa from 1688 onwards.

Napoleon I (Napoleon Bonaparte) (1769-1821) Emperor of France from 1804 to 1814. A brilliant general, he led French campaigns in Italy, Malta and Egypt in the mid-1790s before staging a coup and seizing power in 1799 from the *Directoire* – the regime installed during the FRENCH REVOLUTION. He set up a dictatorship and embarked on a series of legal and administrative reforms – the *Code Napoléon* remains the basis of French civil law. After crowning himself emperor of the French in 1804, Napoleon conquered much of Europe in the NAPOLEONIC WARS. However, a disastrous invasion of Russia in 1812 ended in the loss of two-thirds of his army. He was then defeated by the Allied armies at Leipzig, and France was invaded. In 1814 Napoleon was forced to abdicate and was exiled to the island of Elba. Within a year he escaped and briefly regained power, only to be defeated at WATERLOO in 1815. The British banished him to ▷ST HELENA, where he died – possibly, it is thought, from arsenic poisoning.

❖ Napoleon had a habit of tucking his right hand into his coat. At 165 cm tall, he was often nicknamed 'the Little Corporal'. Ambitious or assertive short men are sometimes said to have a 'Napoleon complex'.

❖ He angered the British by describing them as a 'nation of shopkeepers'.

❖ Napoleon divorced his wife Josephine in 1809 because she had borne him no children. She supposedly had her amorous advances rejected by Napoleon with the phrase 'Not tonight, Josephine'. The story is apocryphal: the phrase comes from a popular 1915 music-hall song.

Napoleonic Wars (1800-15) Campaigns fought by NAPOLEON Bonaparte to extend French power in Europe. Early in the wars, his army defeated Austria (in 1805 at the Battle of Austerlitz in what is now the Czech Republic), Russia and Prussia. He went on to invade Portugal and Spain, precipitating the Peninsular War (1808-14). In 1812-13, Napoleon invaded Russia and reached Moscow before being forced to retreat. He then lost two-thirds of his army due largely to the bitter winter and the Russian forces' 'scorched earth' strategy of destroying everything as they retreated.

Nasser, Gamal Abdel (1918-70) Egyptian statesman who overthrew King Farouk in 1952 and became prime minister two years later. He urged Arab nations to unite against Israel and to drive Western influence out of the Middle East. Elected president in 1956, he took control of the Suez Canal, provoking the SUEZ CRISIS. He introduced many reforms in Egypt and built the ▷ASWAN HIGH DAM. In 1967, he lost the SIX-DAY WAR against Israel. He died of a heart attack in 1970.

Nazism Political creed of Adolf HITLER and his fascist National Socialist (abbreviated to Nazi) Party. The Nazis won support in the WEIMAR REPUBLIC during the 1920s and early 1930s by promising the German people jobs and financial security after years of economic depression and inflation. They also promised that Germany, humiliated by defeat in WORLD WAR I, would become powerful again. The Nazis came to government in 1933, banned all other political parties (declaring that their party and the German state were one) and embarked on a military build-up which led eventually to WORLD WAR II. The aim was to establish the 'Third Reich', in which the 'master race' of blond, blue-eyed 'Aryan' peoples would rule the world. They relied on the SS and the GESTAPO to retain power, and are today seen as representing an extreme form of fascism, inhumanity and violence. Nazi racial policy led to the attempted genocide of the HOLOCAUST. After Germany's defeat in the war, 22 Nazi leaders were convicted of war crimes at the NUREMBERG TRIALS.

❖ The Nazis are associated with powerful symbolism and imagery, including the swastika, the stiff-armed salute, the chant *'Sieg heil'* ('hail victory'), the greeting *'heil Hitler'*, and the Nuremberg rallies, which were enormous open air meetings held in the Bavarian city of Nuremberg in the 1930s.

Nazi-Soviet Pact (1939) Nonaggression treaty between Nazi Germany and the Soviet Union, clearing the way for both countries to invade Poland a week later – an act which precipitated WORLD WAR II. The pact was broken when Germany invaded Russia in 1941.

Nehru, Jawaharlal (1889-1964) First prime minister of the Republic of India, in power from 1947 until his death. Nehru worked with Mahatma GANDHI during India's struggle to gain independence from Britain. He pursued a policy of industrialization at home and nonalignment abroad. His daughter Indira GANDHI continued the political dynasty.

Nelson, Horatio (1758-1805) British admiral who defeated the Franco-Spanish fleet off the coast of Spain at the Battle of Trafalgar (1805), so ending NAPOLEON's hopes of invading Britain. Nelson was mortally wounded at Trafalgar and died on board his flagship, HMS *Victory*.

❖ Lord Nelson had a long, scandalous relationship with Emma, Lady Hamilton, the wife of Sir William Hamilton (1730-1803), a Scottish diplomat and antiquary.

❖ Nelson had lost an arm and had a black eyepatch covering his blind right eye. When ordered to retreat during the Battle of Copenhagen (1801) against the Danish fleet, he raised his telescope to his blind eye and said that he did not see any signal.

Nero (AD 37-68) Roman emperor from AD 54, notorious for his vanity and cruelty. He had his wife and mother murdered, and kicked his pregnant mistress to death. Nero also persecuted Christians, blaming them for a fire that destroyed much of Rome in AD 64. According to tradition, he sentenced the apostles ▷PETER and ▷PAUL to death. Nero committed suicide after the army had forced him from power.

Neto, Antonio Agostinho (1922-79) Angolan statesman. A founder of the nationalist ▷MPLA, he led the organization during its war against Portuguese colonialism. He was the first president after Angolan independence in 1975, but his presidency was marred by rivalry among the MPLA and two other nationalist groups, Holden Roberto's National Front for the Liberation of Angola (FNLA) and Jonas Savimbi's ▷UNITA. The resultant civil war – and South Africa's invasion during the ▷BORDER WAR – forced him to rely heavily on Soviet aid and Cuban soldiers. He was succeeded after his death from cancer in 1979 by Eduardo ▷DOS SANTOS.

New Deal Phrase used by US president Franklin D ROOSEVELT for his policies of state intervention in the economy designed to improve conditions in America during The DEPRESSION of the early 1930s. They ranged from massive public works to sponsorship of work for artists and writers. The New Deal also brought about reforms in agriculture, finance, banking and welfare.

EVIL GLORY *The powerful imagery and ritual of Nazism is epitomized by this prewar Nuremberg rally, where Hitler ascends a triumphal staircase through ranks of loyal Brown Shirts.*

New World The Americas, especially during the time of their first exploration and colonization by Europeans.

Nicholas II (1868-1918) Last TSAR of Russia, who ascended the throne in 1894. His refusal to support liberal movements in his country, and the excessive influence wielded at his court by RASPUTIN, made him unpopular. Nicholas was forced to abdicate during the RUSSIAN REVOLUTION. The following year he and his family were shot by revolutionaries.

Nixon, Richard (1913-94) Republican president of the USA from 1969 to 1974. In 1973 the WATERGATE scandal implicated Nixon in the cover-up of a burglary and bugging operation. In August 1974 he resigned to avoid impeachment after leading members of his government had been found guilty of offences related to the scandal. As president, he visited China and the ▷USSR and withdrew US forces from the VIETNAM WAR. He published his autobiography, *Six Crises,* in 1962.

Nkrumah, Kwame (1909-72) Ghanaian statesman who led his country to independence from Britain and became its first prime minister in 1957. He did much to further Pan-African awareness, particularly while he was leader of the Pan-African Federation with Jomo KENYATTA. In 1950 his Convention People's Party launched a 'Positive Action' campaign of civil disobedience and mass action that brought the country (then called the Gold Coast) to a standstill and greatly boosted Nkrumah's reputation. The party won successive elections and led the country as it became the first African colony to gain independence. Authoritarian rule and economic crisis led to his being overthrown in a military coup while he was in Beijing in 1966.

❖ After being deposed, he lived in exile, writing several books on Pan-Africanism and Marxism and an autobiography (1957).

Norman Conquest Replacement of old English laws and practices by Norman institutions. The process began in 1066, when William the Conqueror, Duke of Normandy in France, defeated the English forces of King Harold at the Battle of Hastings and was crowned king William I of England. The Norman Conquest saw Anglo-Saxon noblemen replaced by barons from the European continent, who brought their form of FEUDALISM with them. It also heralded the reorganization of the land-holding system and the introduction of a civil service in England.

Nuremberg trials (1945-6) Trials of Nazi leaders held by the Allies after World War II. A special court tried 22 former officials, among them Hermann GÖRING, Rudolf HESS and Martin Bormann – the latter in his absence – for crimes against humanity, crimes against peace and war crimes. Bormann, appointed Hitler's deputy in 1942, had disappeared in the final days of the war and for many years was believed to be living in South America. Several of the accused offered the defence, rejected by the judges, that they were only obeying orders. Twelve of the Nazi leaders were sentenced to death; Göring killed himself to avoid execution.

Nyerere, Julius (1922-) First head of state of Tanzania. He led the movement against colonialism in what was then Tanganyika and became prime minister in 1961, then president when the country became a republic in 1962. After a revolution in the island state of Zanzibar in 1964, he successfully united the two former British colonies into the Republic of Tanzania. His socialist blueprint for the economic upliftment of his country, called the Arusha Declaration, did not bring the prosperity he had hoped it would. However, he was greatly admired for building a strong, unified country, as well as for the major role he played in the ▷OAU and the ▷COMMONWEALTH, where he took up diverse African political issues such as atrocities in Burundi and Uganda, and white minority rule in ▷RHODESIA and South Africa. In 1979 the Ugandan dictator Idi Amin tried to invade Tanzania; Nyerere sent in 20 000 troops, who ousted Amin. Nyerere retired from the presidency in 1985.

❖ Nyerere was strongly associated with the call for *uhuru* (the Swahili word for 'freedom') in Africa. A prolific writer, he expounded his political ideals in several books on *uhuru*.

Opium Wars (1839-42, 1856-60) Trading wars provoked by a Chinese ban on British merchants importing opium from India into China. The British won both wars, gaining Hong Kong, setting up trading and missionary posts in China and forcing the Chinese to legalize the opium trade.

Orangemen Members of the Orange Order, a club formed in 1795 to maintain Protestant rule in Ireland. The society is named after William of Orange, the Protestant king of Great Britain who replaced the Catholic JAMES II in 1689. Orangemen are staunch defenders of ▷NORTHERN IRELAND's separation from the Republic of Ireland.

Ottoman empire Muslim empire founded by the Turks in about 1300. The Ottomans conquered Constantinople in 1453. At its peak, in the 16th century under the sultan Suleiman the Magnificent (1494-1566), the empire included large parts of the Middle East and southeastern Europe and its navy dominated the Mediterranean. However, by the 19th century it was disintegrating, and became known as 'the sick man of Europe'. The Ottoman empire sided with Germany in WORLD WAR I, and was dismembered following its defeat. It was finally abolished by Kemal ATATÜRK in 1922.

Patton, George (1885-1945) American general known for his expertise in tank warfare during WORLD WAR II. He led operations in North Africa, Sicily and in the Allied invasion of Europe – notably during the bloody Battle of the BULGE. Only a few months after the end of the war he was fatally injured in a car crash.

Pearl Harbor United States naval base in Hawaii that was attacked without warning by the Japanese air force on Sunday, 7 December 1941. President Franklin D ROOSEVELT said it was 'a date that will live in infamy'. Nearly 2 500 people were killed and many battleships lost in the attack. Britain and the USA declared war on Japan the next day.

Perón, Juan (1895-1974) President of Argentina from 1946 to 1955. An ardent nationalist, his reforms upset the Church as well as the army, who deposed and exiled him. He returned to power in 1973 after living in Spain, but died in office. His third wife, Isabelita, continued as president in his place until a military coup in 1976. His second wife, Eva (1919-52), a former actress, held considerable power and became a popular heroine.

❖ The musical *Evita* (1978), by Andrew ▷LLOYD-WEBBER and Tim Rice, is loosely based on the life of Eva Perón.

Persian empire Ancient empire in western Asia which, under Cyrus the Great in the 6th century BC, covered the area from the Mediterranean to Afghanistan and from the Arabian Sea to the Caspian and Aral seas. The empire was extended in the 5th century BC by Darius. He and his successor Xerxes attempted to conquer GREECE, but were repeatedly defeated, notably at the battles of Marathon (490 BC) and Salamis (480 BC).

Peter the Great (1672-1725) Russian TSAR from 1682 to 1721, when he took the title of Emperor. Peter tried to transform Russia from a backward nation to a progressive one by introducing customs and ideas from western European countries. He even made his nobles cut off their long beards and adopt Western fashions. His methods were often extremely brutal and unpopular. He waged war against the Ottoman empire and Sweden, and built ▷ST PETERSBURG as his capital.

Philip II (1527-98) King of Spain from 1556, king of Portugal from 1580, and consort to MARY I of England between 1554 and 1558.

DAY OF INFAMY *American battleships blaze after the surprise Japanese attack on Pearl Harbor – the most devastating of a wave of assaults on Allied targets throughout the Pacific.*

BURIED CITY *A thick layer of volcanic ash swamped Pompeii, but protected it from decay. The hardened ash was scraped away nearly 1 700 years later to uncover houses – ornamented with superb frescoes and mosaics – preserved intact except for their roofs, which had caved in.*

He also inherited territories in the Netherlands and Italy, and his reign saw Spain reach the height of its power and influence. A HABSBURG and devout Catholic, Philip spearheaded the ▷COUNTER REFORMATION, trying to crush Protestantism throughout his territories by force of arms. He fought a series of costly wars, including a notoriously unsuccessful one in 1588, when he launched the great ARMADA against Elizabeth I of England.

❖ Philip II built the Escorial, a magnificent palace and monastery near Madrid.

Phoenicia (fa-NEESH-ah) Ancient seafaring nation situated in Canaan, in what is now Syria, Israel and Lebanon. The Phoenicians flourished from the 12th to the 9th century BC, becoming great traders and establishing Mediterranean colonies such as CARTHAGE. The Phoenicians also developed the first alphabet that used marks to represent individual sounds rather than whole words or syllables. It was adapted by the Greeks and Romans, and eventually became the modern English alphabet.

Pitt, William, the Younger (1759-1806) British politician who became his country's youngest prime minister in 1783 at the age of 24. He reorganized the country's finances but could not push through his proposals for parliamentary reform or CATHOLIC EMANCIPATION. When war broke out with France in 1793, Pitt introduced repressive measures to curb radicalism at home, and brought in the first income tax, with a top rate of 10 per cent, to pay for the NAPOLEONIC WARS. His government ordered the first British occupation of the Cape in 1795 to prevent the ▷CAPE SEA ROUTE from falling into French hands. He also passed the Act of Union (1800), which joined Ireland to England, Wales and Scotland. In his second term (1804-6) he organized an alliance with Russia and Austria to fight the Napoleonic Wars.

❖ Pitt's father, William Pitt the Elder, as foreign secretary during the SEVEN YEARS' WAR, stripped France of most of its colonial possessions and won Canada and India for Britain. He also served as prime minister for two years from 1766.

Polo, Marco (1254-1324) Venetian explorer reputed to be one of the first Europeans to cross Asia. With his father and uncle he visited the court of the Mongol emperor KUBLAI KHAN in 1275 and became a government official in China. After his return to Italy in 1295 he was captured by the Genoese in battle and spent a year in prison at Genoa, where he wrote an account of his travels.

Pompeii Ancient Roman city, near modern Naples, which was preserved when it was completely covered in ash by an eruption of the nearby volcano, Mount ▷VESUVIUS, in AD 79. Its rediscovery in 1748 yielded important information about the everyday life of Roman citizens and contributed to the emergence of ▷NEO-CLASSICISM – the revival of Classical art and architecture.

Popish Plot (1678) Alleged conspiracy by Catholics to murder the English King Charles II and replace him with his Catholic brother James (later JAMES II). The 'plot' was later exposed as the invention of a defrocked Anglican parson, Titus Oates, but by that time 35 Catholics had been executed in a wave of anti-Catholic hysteria and violence.

potato famine Widespread starvation caused by a severe outbreak of potato blight, a fungal disease, in Ireland in 1845, 1846 and 1848. The crops failed and, as the potato was the staple diet, thousands starved to death and about a million succumbed to diseases such as cholera and dysentery. The effects of the crop failures on the country's economy were felt for many years afterwards.

❖ Two million Irish people emigrated to escape the famine, many of them settling in North America or Australia.

Potsdam Conference (1945) Final conference of the Allied war leaders, held near Berlin towards the end of WORLD WAR II. It was attended by Joseph STALIN, Winston CHURCHILL (who was later replaced by Clement ATTLEE) and the recently elected Harry S TRUMAN. They fixed Poland's western frontier along the rivers Oder and Neisse and formally recognized Soviet influence in eastern Europe. They also divided Germany into zones of occupation and gave orders for the NUREMBERG TRIALS to take place.

pounds, shillings and pence British currency before decimalization in 1971 which was also the basis of currency throughout the BRITISH EMPIRE. 'Pound' referred originally to the Roman pound (0,327 kg) of sterling silver, from which Offa, an Anglo-Saxon king, was the first to mint 240 'pennies'. The shilling coin, worth 12 pennies, was introduced in the 16th century.

❖ The £ symbol is a stylized 'L' for the Latin *libra*, meaning 'pound'. The shilling was denoted by the letter 's' for *solidus*, an ancient Roman coin, and the penny by 'd', short for the Latin *denarius* or 'penny'.

❖ South Africa went 'metric' in 1961 when it became a ▷REPUBLIC, promoting the new coinage with an advertising campaign that starred the cartoon character 'Decimal Dan, the Rands-Cents Man'.

Profumo affair (1963) Sex scandal in which John Profumo, British prime minister Harold MACMILLAN's secretary of state for war, was accused of putting national security at risk by his affair with Christine Keeler, who was also having a relationship with Soviet naval attaché Eugene Ivanov. Profumo was forced to resign because he admitted misleading the House of Commons when questioned about his friendship with Keeler. In 1975 he was awarded the CBE for charitable services. Keeler served a prison sentence for offences relating to the affair.

Prohibition Outlawing of all alcoholic drinks in the USA, between 1920 and 1933. Prohibition did not stop people drinking, but merely drove them underground into 'speakeasies' where they drank illegal 'bootleg' beers, wines and spirits. The trade in alcohol was often controlled by the Mafia or gangsters such as Al Capone.

Prussia Northeastern German state which flourished in the 18th and 19th century, especially under FREDERICK THE GREAT. Under Otto von BISMARCK, Prussia led the unification of Germany in 1871. Its capital, Berlin, became Germany's capital.

❖ Prussia's strong tradition of militarism almost certainly contributed to German aggression in the first half of the 20th century, and has been blamed in some quarters for the outbreak of both world wars.

DRYING UP *An officer enforcing Prohibition inspects a hollow wooden leg used to hide liquor, while others dispose of barrels of drink. The ban on alcohol eventually proved unenforceable.*

Puritans Radical adherents of ▷PROTESTANTISM who emerged in Britain in the late 16th century and became a major force in the 17th century. 'Puritans' is a term covering many religious sects, such as ▷PRESBYTERIANISM, which wanted to 'purify' the ▷CHURCH OF ENGLAND by eliminating traces of its Catholic origins, including all images of Christ, and imposing strict adherence to the Bible. The Puritans banned the traditional English maypole and forbade Christmas celebrations as part of their strict moral code.

Quisling, Vidkun (1887-1945) Norwegian politician who collaborated with the Germans in their conquest of Norway during WORLD WAR II. The Germans rewarded him by making him leader of a puppet government which ruled the country on their behalf. After the war, he was tried, convicted of treason and executed.

❖ The term 'quisling' is sometimes used to describe people who betray their country by cooperating with an enemy.

radicals General term applied to agitators for political and social reform. It was first used in the late 18th and early 19th century to describe those who urged Britain to follow the FRENCH REVOLUTION. Radicalism brought about reforms of the franchise and of parliament in Britain, eventually evolving there into liberalism.

Raleigh, Sir Walter (1552-1618) English explorer known for his expeditions to the Americas, and for supposedly bringing tobacco and the potato from the NEW WORLD to Britain. A favourite of ELIZABETH I, he fell from favour under JAMES I and spent 13 years in the Tower of London, writing a history of the world, before being executed for treason.

❖ Raleigh was considered the near-ideal English gentleman. Legend holds that on one occasion he spread his cloak over a muddy puddle so that Queen Elizabeth would not have to soil her feet by walking through it.

Rasputin, Grigoriy (c1871-1916) Russian mystic and monk who exerted great influence over Tsar NICHOLAS II. A member of a heretical sect of flagellants, Rasputin, whose name means 'debauched' in Russian, argued that one has to sin in order to be forgiven. He was an alcoholic, and seduced many women, persuading them that they had to exhaust their sexual desires in order to achieve holiness. His apparent ability to use hypnosis to control the ▷HAEMOPHILIA suffered by Alexei, the heir to the throne, enabled him to gain a hold over the tsar's family until he was virtually able to dictate the country's affairs. Russian noblemen murdered him in 1916, but resentment of Rasputin's influence still helped to precipitate the RUSSIAN REVOLUTION.

❖ Rasputin survived being fed cakes laced with potassium cyanide and being shot through the heart: his assassins had to shoot him four more times to kill him.

Reformation Church reform movement of the 16th century that also produced widespread political changes. Martin ▷LUTHER, John CALVIN and others were instrumental in breaking with Catholicism and founding ▷PROTESTANTISM in Europe. In England, it involved the replacement of Catholicism as the official national religion by Protestantism. In 1534, HENRY VIII made himself head of an autonomous ▷CHURCH OF ENGLAND when the Pope refused to grant his request for a divorce from Catherine of Aragon. The Dissolution of the Monasteries (1535-41) – the closure of Britain's abbeys, monasteries and nunneries – and the *Book of Common Prayer* were part of the English Reformation. In Scotland, John Knox established ▷PRESBYTERIANISM – which remains the national religion – for purely theological reasons. (See also ▷REFORMATION in 'Ideas, beliefs and religion'.)

❖ The start of the Reformation is often dated from 1517, when Martin Luther set out his beliefs by nailing his '95 theses' to the church door at Wittenberg, Germany.

Resistance Any underground group fighting a foreign occupier or despotic government. During WORLD WAR II it referred to the European patriotic movements which attempted to undermine the Germans. By spying and carrying out acts of sabotage, they contributed towards the successful Allied liberation of the European continent in 1944-5.

Restoration Return of the monarchy in England in 1660 after the death of Oliver CROMWELL. King Charles II returned from exile as king of Great Britain and Ireland, presiding over a divided nation as it suffered the turmoils of the Great Plague, the Great Fire of London and the Anglo-Dutch Wars. (See also ▷RESTORATION in 'Art and design'.)

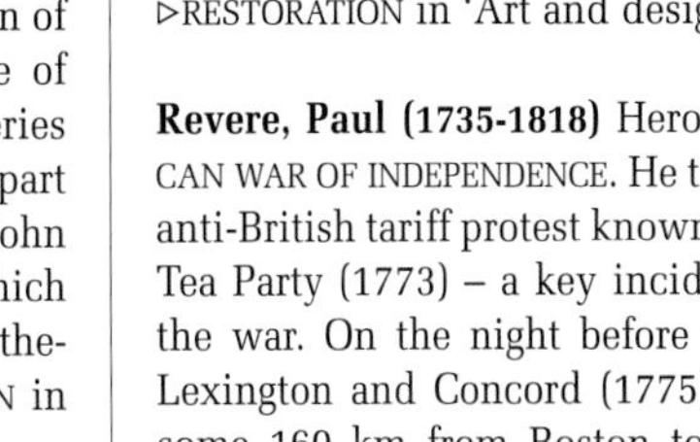

Revere, Paul (1735-1818) Hero of the AMERICAN WAR OF INDEPENDENCE. He took part in the anti-British tariff protest known as the Boston Tea Party (1773) – a key incident leading to the war. On the night before the Battles of Lexington and Concord (1775), Revere rode some 160 km from Boston to Lexington to warn colonists that British troops were preparing to seize military supplies and arrest revolutionaries.

❖ Revere's heroic mission inspired Henry ▷LONGFELLOW to write the poem 'The Midnight Ride of Paul Revere'.

Revolutions of 1848 Series of rebellions that broke out in several European nations, including France, Germany, Austria and Italy. The uprisings were unconnected events, but were inspired either by the desire for national independence from foreign domination, as in Italy, or by demands for political and social rights for the middle and lower classes, as in Germany. In France, King LOUIS PHILIPPE abdicated and the Second Republic adopted socialist policies, while in Germany the Frankfurt Assembly debated national unification of the German states.

ELIZABETHAN SEADOG *A miniature portrait gives an impression of Sir Walter Raleigh's determined character. Below, he takes prisoners during the capture of Trinidad from Spain.*

Richelieu, Cardinal (REESH-l'yer) (1585-1642) French prelate and statesman who served as chief minister of Louis XIII and became France's virtual ruler. He established a powerful absolute ▷MONARCHY in France, broke the power of the French nobility and the Protestant HUGUENOTS, and waged war against the HABSBURGS. Richelieu's efficient, sometimes ruthless, administration helped to build France into a major European power.

Richthofen, Baron Manfred von (1882-1918) German air ace of World War I, nicknamed 'the Red Baron'. He led a crack team of airmen called 'Richthofen's Flying Circus', and shot down a record 80 Allied aircraft in battle. He died when he was eventually shot down himself towards the end of the war.

Risorgimento (ri-SOR-ji-MEN-toh) Italian movement for national unification, which gained momentum in the 19th century under the leadership of GARIBALDI, CAVOUR and others. In the early 19th century, Italy was divided into small states dominated by foreign powers, but by 1870 most of Italy was united under King Victor Emmanuel II of Piedmont.

❖ *Risorgimento* is Italian for 'resurrection'.

Robespierre, Maximilien de (1758-94) Leader of the extreme radical political group, the

Jacobins, which arose during the FRENCH REVOLUTION. He was responsible for initiating the 'Reign of Terror', when thousands of aristocrats and other people deemed to be enemies of the Revolution were ruthlessly executed without trial. Public opposition to his policies grew, and he was himself eventually guillotined after a hasty trial.

Rob Roy (1671-1734) Scottish outlaw who led his clan in a series of exploits similar to those of the legendary Englishman ▷ROBIN HOOD. He was captured and imprisoned by the English Government, but was later pardoned and set free. His real name was Robert Macgregor.

Roman Empire Greatest empire in ancient Europe, centred on Rome. According to legend, Rome was founded by Romulus in 753 BC. At first, the Romans were ruled by ETRUSCAN kings, but in 509 BC they set up a republic with two annually elected consuls at its head, guided by a senate. The Roman Republic grew rapidly from its origins as a small city-state, and by the 2nd century BC it was the dominant force in the Mediterranean. In 27 BC, soon after JULIUS CAESAR was murdered, Octavian brought the republic to an end and appointed himself Rome's first emperor, adopting the name AUGUSTUS. Over the next few centuries, most of Europe and parts of Africa and Asia became subject to Rome, which set up a strong colonial government and funded massive public works such as the building of ▷AQUEDUCTS and a vast network of ▷ROMAN ROADS. But as the empire grew it became increasingly unwieldy. The Rhine-Danube frontier was exposed to remorseless BARBARIAN pressure, requiring constant and expensive campaigning. The emperor CONSTANTINE moved the capital to Byzantium and adopted Christianity early in the 4th century AD. In 395 the empire was split into two, with one emperor based in Constantinople and another in Rome. Internal weaknesses, combined with barbarian invasions from the east, led to the eventual collapse of the Roman Empire in the west in 476. In the east, however, the empire survived for another thousand years – Constantinople finally fell to the Turks in 1453.

❖ Roman citizens spoke Latin, wore togas and bathed regularly in communal bathhouses. For all their civilized trappings, their society relied heavily on slaves.

❖ The culture and achievements of ancient Rome exercised a strong influence on subsequent civilizations. The HOLY ROMAN EMPIRE and the ▷RENAISSANCE were respectively political and artistic attempts to bring back the 'grandeur that was Rome'.

❖ Edward Gibbon's 18th-century study, *The History of the Decline and Fall of the Roman Empire*, is regarded as one of the great classics of historical writing.

Rommel, Erwin (1891-1944) German field-marshal of WORLD WAR II. He led campaigns in Poland, France, Italy and North Africa, where his skilled use of BLITZKRIEG tactics won him the nickname of the 'Desert Fox'. He was eventually defeated by MONTGOMERY at El ALAMEIN. Rommel was put in command of all German forces along the English Channel, but after being implicated in the 'July plot' to kill Adolf Hitler in 1944, he was given the opportunity to take poison rather than face almost certain execution. As a great German hero, he was given a state funeral and the circumstances of his death were kept secret.

Roosevelt, Franklin D (1882-1945) President of the USA four times, from 1933 to 1945 – longer than any other president. A Democrat, Roosevelt took office during The DEPRESSION and quickly introduced the NEW DEAL in an attempt to ease its effects. Before the bombing of PEARL HARBOR, which brought the USA into World War II, he favoured the Allies by introducing the 'Lend-Lease' system to supply them with arms. Together with Winston CHURCHILL and Joseph STALIN, he led the Allies' war effort, but he died a few weeks before Germany surrendered.

❖ Roosevelt carried out his strenuous duties from a wheelchair after being crippled by polio in 1921. He was the first US president to use radio, especially in his much-loved 'fireside chats' to the American people.

Roosevelt, Theodore (1858-1919) Republican president of the USA from 1901 to 1909. As a colonel in the US Army, he led the 'Rough Riders' – a volunteer cavalry unit in the 1898 Spanish-American War. Roosevelt broke up some of America's large monopolies and brought in strict regulations on food hygiene and child labour. During his term as president, work started on the Panama Canal. Roosevelt won a Nobel peace prize in 1906 for mediating in the RUSSO-JAPANESE WAR of 1904-5.

❖ Roosevelt, popularly known as 'Teddy', was a great lover of the outdoors, and he particularly enjoyed hunting bears. The toy 'teddy bear', which became popular during his presidency, takes its name from him.

❖ Roosevelt once summed up his approach to conducting foreign policy, saying 'speak softly and carry a big stick'.

❖ Theodore Roosevelt and Franklin D Roosevelt were distant cousins.

Roses, Wars of the (1455-85) Series of wars fought by two rival branches of the Plantagenet dynasty – which ruled England after the Normans from 1154 to 1485 – for control of the throne. Each family had a rose as its emblem – white for the House of York, red for the House of Lancaster. The struggle started when Richard of York claimed the throne from the Lancastrian king, Henry VI, who had gone mad in the wake of his defeat in the HUNDRED YEARS' WAR. In 1460 Richard captured Henry, and was made heir to the throne; but Richard was killed in the same year and the Yorkist claim passed on to Edward, Duke of York – crowned Edward IV in 1461. On Edward's death, his brother Richard III usurped the throne, but alienated Yorkists helped the only remaining Lancastrian claimant, Henry Tudor (later Henry VII), to defeat Richard at the Battle of Bosworth Field (1485). He was crowned Henry VII, the first TUDOR king, and married Edward IV's daughter, Elizabeth of York, to put an end to the family rivalry. His sound administration helped to mend the damage done by 30 years of civil war and his reign is often seen as the start of modern history in England.

❖ Shakespeare's play ▷RICHARD III, which completes his historical series on the Wars of the Roses, was his first real success.

Russian Civil War (1918-20) War fought between the BOLSHEVIK Red Army, led by Leon TROTSKY, and the 'White' army, which with foreign support opposed the RUSSIAN REVOLUTION. Many parts of the Russian empire joined the battle, hoping to win independence from Moscow. At the end of the war, Poland, Finland and the Baltic states broke free from Soviet domination, but the Bolsheviks defeated the counter-revolutionary armies of Georgia, Ukraine and other states. LENIN, their political leader, declared the Union of Soviet Socialist Republics (USSR) in 1922.

Russian Revolution (1917) Two uprisings in Russia – the February Revolution and the October Revolution – which replaced the TSARS with a communist government. In February 1917, following a series of defeats in World War I, workers and soldiers rose up, forcing Tsar NICHOLAS II to abdicate. A provisional government led by Alexander Kerensky was installed. But in October the same year, LENIN and the BOLSHEVIK party led another uprising which toppled Kerensky and established rule by *soviets*, or people's councils. The revolution was followed by the RUSSIAN CIVIL WAR.

❖ The Bolsheviks shot dead the tsar and his family at Ekaterinburg in July 1918. Anastasia, the tsar's youngest daughter, may have escaped execution. Her remains do not seem to have been among the exhumed bones proved in 1993 to be those of the murdered family. For many years a woman known as Anna

Anderson tried unsuccessfully to establish her claim to be Anastasia.

Russo-Japanese War (1904-5) War fought between Russia and Japan over their rival claims to Korea and Manchuria. Japan won, becoming the first Asian country in modern times to inflict defeat on a Western power.

Sadat, Mohamed Anwar El- (1918-81) Egyptian president who succeeded Gamal Abdel NASSER in 1970. He won a Nobel prize for peace (with Menachem BEGIN of Israel) for defusing the ▷ARAB-ISRAELI CONFLICT, concluding a peace treaty with Israel in 1978. He was assassinated by Muslim fundamentalists.

St Bartholomew's Day Massacre (1572) Slaughter of French Protestant HUGUENOTS by a Catholic mob in Paris. Catherine de Medici feared that her son, King Charles IX of France, was being persuaded by Admiral Gaspard de Coligny, a leading Huguenot, to support the Dutch Protestants' rebellion against their Spanish overlords. After Catherine secretly backed a failed attempt on Coligny's life, she and Charles decided to kill Coligny and his companions. The murders by royal henchmen on 24 August sparked off mob violence in which about 3 000 Protestants were killed.

St Valentine's Day Massacre (1929) Incident in Chicago on 14 February when Al Capone's gang of bootleggers murdered seven members of 'Bugs' Moran's rival gang in an attempt to gain control of the illegal liquor traffic during the PROHIBITION period.

Salisbury, Marquess of (1830-1903) British Conservative prime minister in 1885-6, 1886-92 and 1895-1902. As DISRAELI's foreign secretary, he played a key role at the Congress of BERLIN. As premier, he introduced free public education and steered Britain through the ▷SOUTH AFRICAN WAR.

Savonarola, Girolamo (1452-98) Italian priest who crusaded against corruption in Church and state. Under his influence, the rulers of Florence instituted a stern and puritanical regime. Personal ornaments, gambling equipment and pictures were burned on a 'bonfire of the vanities'. Savonarola's enemies, including the MEDICI family, conspired with the Pope to secure his excommunication. He was convicted of heresy and duly executed.

Scott, Robert Falcon (1868-1912) British naval officer who led two expeditions in Antarctica. On his first expedition (1900-4), he explored the Ross Sea, on the west side of the continent, and made the first long journeys into the interior; the second expedition (from 1910) was a bid to be the first to reach the South Pole. Scott unwisely chose to use ponies for haulage instead of dogs, and his team arrived at the pole after more than two months of immense hardship only to find that their Norwegian rival Roald AMUNDSEN had reached it a month earlier. On the way back, the British group perished in blizzards and temperatures as low as -44°C. They were just 18 km from a supply base and safety.

Scramble for Africa (Partition of Africa) Term used for the expansion of European ▷IMPERIALISM in Africa in the late 19th century. Portugal had occupied the port of Ceuta, now an enclave in Morocco, as early as 1415, but by the 1870s Europe controlled less than 10 per cent of the continent, including the British and Portuguese colonies in southern Africa. In the last three decades of the century, however, almost all of Africa was brought under European control. Interest in exploring and 'civilizing' the continent turned into stiff competition for territory after the discovery of rich diamond and gold deposits in South Africa in the 1870s and 1880s – with Britain and France the main rivals. The 'scramble' was formalized at the Conference of Berlin (1884-5), at which the major European powers 'carved up' the continent. The new boundaries were drawn without the consent of Africa's inhabitants and with scant regard for existing states and kingdoms – the new countries often split apart previously united people or joined together bitter foes. This had repercussions during Africa's drive for independence in the 20th century, hampering unity in many former colonies and, in some cases, leading to the eruption of bitter civil strife that continues to this day.

❖ ▷LIBERIA is the only country in Africa that was never colonized. Ethiopia was occupied comparatively late, when Italy deposed HAILE SELASSIE in 1936.

❖ Portugal was the last European colonial power to withdraw from Africa in 1975, when Mozambique and Angola achieved independence. The title of 'the last African colony', however, belongs to the former ▷SOUTH WEST AFRICA, which was ruled by South Africa, in the face of international oppostion, until it became independent as Namibia in 1990.

STILL STANDING *The sun rises behind the pyramids at Giza. Built more than 4 000 years ago, they are the oldest of the ancient Seven Wonders, and the only ones that remain largely intact.*

Seven Wonders of the World Notable monuments built in ancient times, of which only the Egyptian ▷PYRAMIDS at Giza remain standing. The other six were the Hanging Gardens of BABYLON, huge stepped pyramids planted with trees and lush vegetation; the Pharos of ▷ALEXANDRIA, a magnificent lighthouse; the temple of ▷ARTEMIS at Ephesus; the tomb of King Mausolus – the origin of the word 'mausoleum' – at Halicarnassus in Asia Minor; Phidias's gold and ivory statue of ▷ZEUS at Olympia, Greece; and the Colossus of ▷RHODES, a huge bronze statue that straddled the narrow entrance to the harbour of the Greek island.

❖ There are also sometimes said to be seven wonders of the modern world. The most-favoured candidates for this honour are the ▷TAJ MAHAL, the ▷GREAT WALL OF CHINA, the statues on ▷EASTER ISLAND, the ▷EIFFEL TOWER, Chartres Cathedral, the ▷EMPIRE STATE BUILDING and the ▷PANAMA CANAL.

TRAGIC BRAVERY *British troops wait in the trenches of the Somme. Sent straight towards the German guns by their misguided leaders, more than 19 000 died on the first day of the offensive.*

Seven Years' War (1756-63) War between PRUSSIA, supported by Britain and Portugal, and an alliance that included Austria, France and Russia. Britain and France were fighting for control of North America and India, while FREDERICK THE GREAT of Prussia wanted to enlarge his kingdom at Austria's expense. After Prussia and Britain won, the French ceded Canada to Britain, which also consolidated its rule over much of India, while Prussia established itself as the dominant power in continental Europe.

shoguns Japanese caste of military leaders or *samurai*, who governed the country from the 12th century until 1867. The emperors during this period were powerless figureheads.

Six-Day War (1967) War between Israel and the forces of Egypt, Syria and Jordan. Believing that Arab armies were poised to invade, the Israelis launched a pre-emptive strike and took over the ▷GOLAN HEIGHTS in southwest Syria, the Jordanian-held portion of Jerusalem, the West Bank of the River Jordan and the Sinai peninsula. Israel returned the Sinai to Egypt in 1982 and parts of the West Bank in 1994, in terms of a settlement leading to Palestinian self-rule. In early 1995 the fate of the Golan Heights was under discussion.

slave trade Buying and selling people for forced labour, first practised in ancient Africa. The slave trade, and slavery itself, became a vital element in the economies of Egypt, Babylon, Greece and Rome. During the Middle Ages, slavery became less common in western Europe but remained important in the Arab world. In the 15th century the slave trade was revived on a large scale by European powers, who shipped black slaves from West Africa to work in their colonies in the New World. At least 12 million slaves are believed to have been brutally exported from Africa. The campaign of William WILBERFORCE helped to promote the outlawing of the slave trade in the British empire in 1807; in 1833, slavery itself was banned. In the USA, slaves were finally emancipated by president Abraham LINCOLN in 1865. Nevertheless, 200 million people worldwide are still thought to be living and working in conditions of near-slavery. (See also ▷SLAVERY in 'Southern African history'.)

Somme, Battle of the (1916) Allied offensive against the Germans during WORLD WAR I. The Allied infantry braved a nightmare of shells, machine-gun fire, barbed wire and mud, but in 20 weeks of fighting they advanced no more than 8 km. More than one million soldiers were killed – 420 000 British and colonial troops, 195 000 Frenchmen and at least 420 000 Germans, but German resistance remained strong. The Battle of the Somme, one of the bloodiest in history, was the first in which tanks were used (but not very effectively). South African troops suffered heavy losses while defending DELVILLE WOOD.

Spanish Civil War (1936-9) War between Spaniards loyal to the socialist 'Republican' government and the rebel supporters of fascism, led by General Francisco FRANCO. Volunteers from abroad joined the fighting on both sides, seeing the war as a symbolic struggle between reform and reaction. The Soviet Union helped the Republicans, while Adolf HITLER and Benito MUSSOLINI sent aid to Franco. Among the many horrific events of the war was the notorious bombing by the *Luftwaffe* of the town of GUERNICA in 1937. Eventually, the fascists won the war and set up Franco's long dictatorial rule of Spain, which lasted until his death in 1975.

❖ George ▷ORWELL's book *Homage to Catalonia* is a vivid account of his experiences as a British volunteer for the Republicans.

Spanish Succession, War of the (1701-14) Struggle for control of Spain after the last HABSBURG king died without an heir. England, Holland, most German states and Portugal, anxious to curb the power of France, formed a loose coalition to expel Philip, grandson of King LOUIS XIV of France, from the throne. The commander of the British army, the Duke of Marlborough, led the coalition armies to a series of victories, including in the Battle of Blenheim (1704). The war ended when Britain agreed to recognize Philip's rule in Spain in exchange for France handing over extensive lands in Canada.

Sparta Ancient Greek city-state, founded in *c*1000 BC, which was the great rival of ATHENS. Sparta was renowned for its rigid military discipline and lack of culture. It defeated Athens in the Peloponnesian wars (431-404 BC), but was itself beaten by a coalition of other states soon afterwards.

❖ The term 'spartan' is still used to describe rigorous or uncomfortable conditions.

❖ Spartans, or 'Laconians' as they were known in ancient times, had a reputation for terseness. When one invader warned 'If I enter Laconia, I shall destroy the city of Sparta', the Spartans returned the laconic one-word message: 'If.'

FATAL MOMENT *Photographer Robert Capa took this famous picture of a Republican soldier falling during the Spanish Civil War.*

WOMEN'S STRUGGLE *Emmeline Pankhurst is arrested outside Buckingham Palace in 1914 during a suffragette protest against the government's continued refusal to enfranchise women.*

SS Elite corps of Nazi troops originally formed as Adolf HITLER's bodyguard, and led from 1929 by Heinrich HIMMLER. After the 'Night of the Long Knives' in 1934, when the leaders of the rival SA or BROWN SHIRTS were arrested and executed, the powers of the SS included the suppression of political opponents in Germany and the persecution of Jews and any other 'undesirables'. The SS supervised the concentration camps during the HOLOCAUST. During World War II, several SS units also fought as crack troops called the *Waffen* ('armed') SS.

❖ SS stands for the German *Schutzstaffel*, meaning 'protection squad'. Its members wore a distinctive black uniform.

Stalin, Joseph (Iosif Vissarionovich Dzhugashvili) (1879-1953) Georgian dictator of the ▷USSR from 1927 until his death. Stalin was notorious for his ruthless repression of all dissent. When LENIN died in 1924, Stalin outmanoeuvred his rival Leon TROTSKY to grasp power. He later sent Trotsky into exile, and eventually ordered his assassination. Stalin's five-year plans and policies of collectivization, which abolished private ownership, were followed by political purges in which officials and army officers were put through 'show trials' on trumped-up charges of treason before being executed. In total, his actions are believed to have resulted in the deaths of more than 50 million people. Stalin signed the NAZI-SOVIET PACT in 1939 and became Hitler's early ally in WORLD WAR II, but after the German invasion of Russia in 1941 he fought with the Allies. Despite the enormous economic cost of the war and the deaths of 20 million Russians, Stalin's military and diplomatic skills expanded the Soviet Union and its sphere of influence deep into eastern Europe. He then presided over the beginnings of the COLD WAR. In 1956, Stalin's successor, Nikita KHRUSHCHEV, denounced him and his 'cult of personality'.

❖ *Stalin* is Russian for 'man of steel'. He gave his name to the city of Stalingrad (now Volgograd) and to ▷STALINISM. In the West, he was nicknamed 'Uncle Joe'.

Stone Age Period from the beginning of human history until the first smelting of metals, so called because people used stone tools and weapons. In many parts of the world the Stone Age was followed by the BRONZE AGE, while in Africa it was followed by the IRON AGE. (See also ▷STONE AGE in 'Southern African history'.)

Stopes, Marie (1880-1958) British pioneer of birth control and women's rights, whose controversial books *Married Love* (1916) and *Wise Parenthood* (1918) were the first to popularize modern methods of ▷CONTRACEPTION. She also opened the first birth control clinic in Britain in 1921. Her frankness and plain speaking about sex shocked many people.

Stuart, House of Dynasty that ruled Scotland from 1371 to 1603 and Britain from 1603 (JAMES I of England) to 1714 (Anne), except for the 11 years of Oliver CROMWELL's Commonwealth and Protectorate (1649-60). When Anne died without heirs, the crown passed to the House of HANOVER.

❖ Two Stuarts – James Edward (the 'Old Pretender', 1688-1766) and his son Charles Edward ('Bonnie Prince Charlie', 1720-88) – continued to claim the throne. With their Catholic supporters, who were called Jacobites from the Late Latin *Jacobus* for James, they mounted two rebellions – known as the 'Fifteen' (1715-16) and 'Forty-Five' (1745-6) to wrest power from the Protestant Hanoverians. Bonnie Prince Charlie was defeated at the Battle of Culloden (1746), the last battle to be fought on British soil.

Suez crisis (1956) Unsuccessful attempt by Britain, France and Israel to secure control of the Suez Canal – the vital shipping channel that links the Mediterranean and the Red Sea. It began when Egypt's president Gamal NASSER nationalized the canal, prompting fears that he might close it, cutting off oil supplies to Europe from the Persian Gulf. Three months later, Israel (later revealed to be acting as part of a previously agreed plan) invaded Egypt while British and French forces moved into the area in November 1956, ostensibly to enforce a United Nations ceasefire. Their true aim was to regain control of the canal, but international pressure – particularly from the USA – forced them to withdraw. The incident enhanced Nasser's prestige in the Arab world and led to the resignation of Sir Anthony EDEN, the British prime minister in January 1957.

suffragettes Women who campaigned in Britain for their right to vote in the late 19th and early 20th century. Led by Emmeline Pankhurst and, later, her daughters Christabel and Sylvia, the suffragettes chained themselves to railings and smashed windows to win publicity and achieve their ends. When imprisoned, they went on a hunger strike. Women over 30 won the vote in 1918, but equal franchise had to wait until 1928.

❖ Emily Davison, who was fatally injured when she dashed into the path of the King George V's horse at the Epsom Derby in 1913, was one of the movement's martyrs.

Sumeria One of the world's earliest civilizations, based in southern MESOPOTAMIA. The Sumerians built the first cities, such as Ur, before 3000 BC and probably invented writing with the ▷CUNEIFORM script.

❖ *The Epic of Gilgamesh*, an ancient Sumerian poem, tells the story of a great flood similar to the one described in the Bible in the story of Noah's Ark.

swinging sixties Nickname for the 1960s, seen in the West as a time when moral, social and economic restraints all relaxed. It was a period of intellectual and artistic rebellion, of experimentation with psychedelic drugs and of a sexual freedom fostered by the books of the psychologist Wilhelm Reich (1897-1957) and encouraged by availability of the ▷PILL.

Tereshkova, Valentina (1937-) Russian cosmonaut who in 1963 became the first woman

LONE PROTESTER *A Chinese student defies tanks sent in against fellow rebels and their 'Goddess of Democracy and Freedom' in Tiananmen Square. He was tried and shot a few days later.*

in space. She orbited the Earth for three days as solo pilot of the space capsule *Vostok 6.*

Thirty Years' War (1618-48) Struggle between France, Spain, Sweden, Denmark, Austria and numerous German states. The causes of the war were rooted in French expansionism, national rivalries, conflict between Roman Catholics and Protestants and the desire of King Gustavus Adolphus to win Swedish control of the Baltic. The war started after two Catholic members of Bohemia's ruling council were thrown out of a window in Prague by their Protestant colleagues. It ended with the Treaty of Westphalia, which limited the power of the HABSBURGS and enhanced that of France.

Tiananmen Square Massacre (1989) Incident in which Chinese troops opened fire on students staging a prodemocracy rally in the main square of China's capital, Beijing. Some 2 000 demonstrators died.

Titanic Supposedly unsinkable luxury liner which sank on its maiden voyage in 1912, after running into an iceberg in the North Atlantic. More than 1 500 of the 2 340 passengers and crew drowned, mainly because the giant ship did not have enough lifeboats.

Tito (1892-1980) Adopted name of Josip Broz, leader of Yugoslavia from 1945 until his death. Tito led communist partisan resistance to the German invasion of Yugoslavia during WORLD WAR II. His men pinned down 30 German divisions and liberated their country without the need for an Allied invasion. After the war, he imposed communist rule in his country, but in 1948 Tito broke with the Soviet Union and steered an independent course. Tito's skill in ruling Yugoslavia was underlined by its collapse into bitter civil war in 1991.
❖ The name Tito means 'this that'. He was always ordering people to 'do this . . . do that', and the nickname stuck.

Tobruk Libyan sea port where, during WORLD WAR II, 25 000 British and colonial troops (including more than 10 000 South Africans) were taken prisoner by the Germans. In June 1942 the garrison, under the command of Major General H B Klopper, surrendered to ROMMEL's forces after becoming cut off from MONTGOMERY's Eighth Army.

Tories English political party which started in 1679-80 as a group defending the right of the Catholic James, Duke of York (later King JAMES II), to succeed Charles II as king. They were opposed by WHIGS, who endorsed the revolution which deposed James and secured the Protestant succession of William and Mary. In the 1830s the Tories became known as the ▷CONSERVATIVE PARTY.
❖ 'Tory' was originally a term of abuse for dispossessed Catholic outlaws who attacked English settlers in Ireland.

Trafalgar, Battle of (1805) Naval battle in which the English under Horatio NELSON defeated NAPOLEON I's Franco-Spanish fleet, so ending his hopes of invading Britain.

Trotsky, Leon (1879-1940) Russian leader who rose to power alongside LENIN after the RUSSIAN REVOLUTION. In 1918 he founded the Red Army, which was victorious in the RUSSIAN CIVIL WAR. In favouring world communist revolution, Trotsky found himself opposed by Lenin and STALIN, both of whom insisted that communism must first develop fully within the Soviet Union. Stalin deported Trotsky in 1929, but Trotsky continued to criticize him. Eventually Stalin gave orders for a Soviet agent to assassinate Trotsky in Mexico City; the murder weapon was an ice pick.

Truman, Harry S (1884-1972) President of the USA from 1945 to 1952. As leader in the last months of WORLD WAR II, Truman ordered the ATOM BOMB to be dropped on Japan. After the war, he put forward the MARSHALL AID to promote European recovery, and formulated the 'Truman doctrine' under which the USA pledged to 'contain' communism. Truman sent troops to fight against communist forces in the KOREAN WAR, but vetoed proposals to use atom bombs in Korea.
❖ Truman is remembered for his spirited leadership. He often said: 'If you can't stand the heat, get out of the kitchen', and a sign on his desk read: 'The buck stops here.'
❖ The initial 'S' did not stand for anything. Truman had no middle name, but thought a middle initial added authority.

tsars Rulers or emperors of Russia. The first ruler to call himself 'tsar' was IVAN IV 'THE TERRIBLE' in 1547, and the last tsar was NICHOLAS II, who was deposed in the RUSSIAN REVOLUTION in 1917. In the early 20th century the absolute ▷MONARCHY of the tsars was tempered by the formation of a parliament, the Duma.
❖ The name 'tsar' is derived from caesar.

Tudor, House of Dynasty that ruled England after the Wars of the ROSES from 1485 to 1603.

GOLDEN KING *Tutankhamun's gold funeral mask is inlaid with semiprecious stones and glass beads. The vulture, cobra and his braided beard are symbols of kingship.*

The Tudor monarchs included HENRY VIII and MARY I; the last was ELIZABETH I.

Tutankhamun (*c*1361-*c*1352 BC) Pharaoh of ancient EGYPT who reigned for just six years before he died aged about 18. His reign was undistinguished, but the discovery by Englishmen Howard Carter and Lord Carnarvon in 1922 of his virtually untouched tomb at Thebes, with its magnificent array of artefacts, is among the greatest archaeological finds of all time.

U-2 American high-altitude spy plane which was shot down by a Russian missile over the Soviet Union in 1960. The pilot, Gary Powers, parachuted to safety but was arrested and found guilty by a Soviet court of spying. The U-2 incident helped to fuel the COLD WAR. Powers was released in 1962.

Vandals Baltic people who invaded the ROMAN EMPIRE in the 5th century AD, conquering North Africa and eventually plundering Rome itself in AD 455.
❖ The Vandals' pillaging of Rome made 'vandalism' a byword for wilful destruction.

V-E Day (8 May 1945) Day on which the German armies formally surrendered at the end of WORLD WAR II. It was marked by jubilant celebrations in Allied countries. V-E stands for 'Victory in Europe'. V-J DAY (15 August 1945) marked the Allied victory in Japan

Versailles, Treaty of (1919) Treaty that officially ended WORLD WAR I, signed in the Hall of Mirrors at ▷VERSAILLES, France. The leading Allied figures at the negotiations were Georges CLEMENCEAU of France, David LLOYD GEORGE of Britain and Woodrow WILSON of the USA. The treaty assigned total responsibility for the outbreak and consequences of the war to Germany, which was made to give up land, reduce its military strength, and pay extensive reparations to the Allies. It also set up the LEAGUE OF NATIONS, the forerunner to the United Nations.
❖ Generals Louis Botha and Jan Smuts of South Africa were members of the Allied delegation to the peace conference. Botha argued unsuccessfully for the annexation of German South West Africa to South Africa.

Vespucci, Amerigo (ves-POOCH-ee) (1454-1512) Italian-born Spanish explorer who, having provisioned expeditions for Christopher COLUMBUS, himself made several voyages to the NEW WORLD soon after. His name was first given to the Americas by a German cartographer, Martin Waldseemüller, who in 1507 published a map and globe based on Vespucci's account of his travels.

Vichy Government Administration of unoccupied southern France after the German invasion in 1940, during WORLD WAR II. Led by World War I national hero Marshal Philippe Pétain, who was then 84, it got its name because its seat was near the spa town of Vichy. Although ostensibly independent, Vichy France was essentially under German control. The Vichy regime continued to function after Germany occupied all of France in 1942, but in name only.
❖ After the war Pétain, who was then in his nineties, was sentenced to death for collaborating with the Nazis; the sentence was later commuted to life imprisonment on the Île de Yeu, where he died in 1951.

Victoria (1819-1901) Queen of the United Kingdom and its dominions, who succeeded her uncle William IV in 1837. Three years later she married Prince Albert of Saxe-Coburg and Gotha. After his death in 1861, she spent the rest of her life in mourning. Victoria took a keen interest in politics, especially in foreign policy – partly because of the growing BRITISH EMPIRE, and partly because her nine children married into many of the royal families of Europe. Unfortunately, several of them passed on the genetic blood disorder ▷HAEMOPHILIA, which killed one of her sons. Relations with her eldest son Edward, later Edward VII, were strained: he did not meet her strict standards of morality. In 1876, she took the title Empress of India. By the 1880s Queen Victoria had become a symbol of the empire, and her golden and diamond jubilees (in 1887 and 1897) were celebrated around the globe.

Victorian period The period from 1837 to 1901, when Queen VICTORIA reigned and Britain became the most powerful industrial and military nation in the world. Social inequalities became more apparent, with a wealthy, privileged upper class in sharp contrast to the poverty and hardship of the urban working classes. And a substantial middle class emerged, partly because of the availability of cheap manufactured goods.
❖ The term 'Victorian values' implies a strong sense of public morality and an emphasis on the importance of family life – but often with an element of hypocrisy.
❖ The period coincided with the economic boom in southern Africa after the discovery of diamonds and gold, and ▷VICTORIAN architecture is a feature of much of the new building done in this era.

Vienna, Congress of (1815) Conference of European nations held after the defeat of NAPOLEON Bonaparte. It redrew the boundaries of Europe in an attempt to restore the ▷BALANCE OF POWER and lay the foundations for peace. Under the influence of Austria's Prince METTERNICH, many European territories were given to the monarchs who had held them before the French Revolution. However, the congress largely ignored the mounting pressures of nationalism and the trend towards greater democracy in Europe.
❖ The congress formalized British rule at the ▷CAPE. The terms of this agreement, the chief among which was a British undertaking not to discriminate against former Dutch subjects, had been set out in the London Convention of 1814. However, the administration of the Cape proved to be far more autocratic than in any other British territory. For example, the Cape Governor had the power to introduce constitutional changes.

Vietnam War (1960-75) War fought between North and South Vietnam, the two parts of what was formerly the French colony of Indochina. Following the withdrawal of French troops in 1954, the communist north, under HO CHI MINH, attempted to take over the non-communist south. This war of 'liberation' was waged by the North Vietnamese army, assisted by the powerful Vietcong guerrillas. The USA became involved partly because of the domino theory – that if one vulnerable nation were to come under communist domination, neighbouring countries would naturally follow. At first it sent advisers to the South Vietnamese government and then,

INNOCENT SUFFERING *Vietnamese children flee their blazing village, bombarded with napalm by US aircraft. Phan Tim Kim (centre), her clothes burnt off, runs screaming with pain and shock.*

from 1961, troops in ever larger numbers. At the peak of America's involvement in the war in 1969, more than half a million US soldiers were fighting in Vietnam. These were withdrawn by the US government in 1973, and South Vietnam was completely taken over by communist forces in 1975, to form the present-day nation of Vietnam.

Vikings Warriors from Scandinavia who plundered much of coastal Europe from the 8th to the 10th century AD. Brutal and destructive raiders, they were the greatest seafarers of their day, travelling in longboats with high bows and sterns, ideally suited to ocean journeys. They also traded widely, and colonized Iceland, Greenland, France, Russia, Britain and Ireland. The Viking explorer Leif Ericsson (*c*970-*c*1030) even travelled to North America, and settlers followed in his wake, but they did not stay long.
❖ Leif Ericsson and his father Eric the Red were both the subjects of Icelandic ▷SAGAS.

V-J Day (15 August 1945) Day on which Japan surrendered, ending WORLD WAR II. V-J stands for 'Victory over Japan'.

Waitangi, Treaty of (1840) Agreement by which Britain annexed New Zealand. Under the treaty, native Maori chiefs accepted British rule and protection in return for a guarantee that they would keep their land and that their people would be given the same rights as British people.
❖ The treaty, signed in two versions, one in English, another in Maori, has been subjected to much legal argument. In 1877 a judge denied that the treaty had any significance, but in 1987 the New Zealand Court of Appeal confirmed its validity.

Warsaw Pact Military alliance of communist nations in eastern Europe, organized in 1955 in response to the Western ▷NATO grouping. The Warsaw Pact countries, also known as the 'eastern bloc', included Bulgaria, Czechoslovakia, East Germany, Hungary, Poland, Romania and the Soviet Union. The alliance disintegrated in 1991, following the collapse of European communism.

Washington, George (1732-99) First president of the USA, from 1789 to 1797. He commanded the colonial army during the AMERICAN WAR OF INDEPENDENCE before being elected president. Washington was known as 'Father of the Nation', and was praised after his death as 'first in war, first in peace, and first in the hearts of his countrymen'.
❖ The capital city and the northwesternmost state of the USA are both named after Washington. His portrait appears on the American one-dollar bill and 25-cent coin.

Watergate Scandal that forced US president Richard NIXON out of office in 1974. During the 1972 presidential election campaign, burglars in the pay of Nixon's Republican re-election committee were caught bugging the Democratic Party headquarters in the Watergate building in Washington, DC. Nixon's officials tried to obstruct several investigations into the break-in, but the president was eventually incriminated by tape recordings he himself had made in the White House. To avoid impeachment, Nixon resigned in August 1974.
❖ The Watergate scandal was uncovered by Bob Woodward and Carl Bernstein, two investigative journalists who worked for the 'Washington Post'. Their story is told in the film *All the President's Men* (1976), starring Robert Redford and Dustin Hoffman.

Waterloo, Battle of (1815) Battle fought on Belgian soil in which British, Prussian, Dutch and Belgian troops inflicted the final defeat on NAPOLEON Bonaparte, who had escaped from his exile on Elba after the NAPOLEONIC WARS. The allies, led by the Duke of WELLINGTON, received crucial reinforcements from Prussia late in the battle, turning Napoleon's defeat into a rout.
❖ Waterloo has become a general term to describe a decisive defeat. To meet your Waterloo is to be thoroughly beaten.

Weimar Republic (VYE-maar) Name given to Germany between the end of World War I in 1918 and the rise of Adolf HITLER in 1933. Weimar was the city in which a new democratic constitution was drawn up, replacing the old German empire with a republic. The Weimar Government was unpopular in Germany, because it accepted the harsh provisions of the Treaty of VERSAILLES and presided over a period of economic chaos and political instability. Hitler abolished the republic soon after coming to power.
❖ Weimar Germany was a place of political freedom and considerable artistic creativity, producing the ▷BAUHAUS school of design, the artists George Grosz and Otto Dix, the playwright Bertolt ▷BRECHT and many others.
❖ In the Weimar Republic ▷INFLATION made the German mark almost worthless. In November 1923 a loaf of bread cost 201 000 million marks – a load of banknotes big enough to fill a wheelbarrow.

Wellington, Duke of (1769-1852) Arthur Wellesley, soldier and statesman who won fame for driving French troops out of Spain and Portugal during the Peninsular War (1808-14) and his victory over Napoleon at WATERLOO (1815). As British prime minister (1828-30), he introduced CATHOLIC EMANCIPATION to avoid revolution in Ireland, but lost power because he opposed parliamentary reform. He was tough and outspoken – once describing his troops as the 'scum of the earth' – and was known as the 'Iron Duke'.

❖ *Wellingtonia*, the Californian redwood tree or giant sequoia; the capital of New Zealand; the waterproof Wellington boot; and beef Wellington are all named after him.

Whigs British political party formed in the late 1670s as a group seeking to exclude the Catholic King JAMES II from the succession. The deposition of James in 1688 was celebrated by the Whigs, aristocratic landowners who in contrast to the TORIES believed in a limited monarchy subject to the will of parliament. Under Charles James Fox, in the 1780s, the Whigs became the party of reform, religious toleration and commerce. In the 19th century the Whigs formed the core of the Liberal Party.
❖ 'Whig' is believed to stem from 'whiggamore', one of a group of 17th-century Scottish Presbyterian rebels who joined in an attack on Edinburgh.

Wilberforce, William (1759-1833) British evangelist, reformer and MP who campaigned against slavery for 19 years before the slave trade was abolished in British territories in 1807. Slavery itself was abolished in 1833 – only days after he died.

Wilhelm II (1859-1941) Last Kaiser (emperor) of Germany, reigning from 1888 to 1918. He was a grandson of Britain's Queen VICTORIA. After dismissing Chancellor BISMARCK in 1890, Wilhelm's aggressive foreign policy culminated in WORLD WAR I. He led Germany through the war and abdicated after his country's defeat. He lived the rest of his life as a country gentleman in the Netherlands.
❖ In Britain, especially during the war, Wilhelm was known as 'Kaiser Bill'.

Wilson, Harold (Lord Wilson) (1916-95) Labour prime minister in Britain from 1964 to 1970 and from 1974 to 1976. During his first period in office Wilson was hampered by serious economic problems, which resulted in a devaluation of the pound and harsh exchange controls. In 1965 he was faced with a unilateral declaration of independence (▷UDI) by Rhodesia (now Zimbabwe), and in 1967 he opened tough negotiations for British entry to what became the ▷EUROPEAN UNION.

Wilson, Woodrow (1856-1924) President of the USA from 1913 to 1921. He is mainly remembered for introducing PROHIBITION, and for his role in World War I and the Treaty of VERSAILLES. Wilson preserved America's neutrality until 1917, when, faced with the threat of unrestricted German submarine warfare, he declared war, saying 'The world must be made safe for democracy'. He set out 'Fourteen Points', or goals for peace, including the

IRON DUKE *Wellington, here caricatured as one of his boots, believed that victory in battle was a tragedy second only to defeat.*

establishment of the LEAGUE OF NATIONS; after the war, Wilson was disappointed when the Senate refused to allow the USA to join the league. Wilson suffered a nervous breakdown and a stroke in 1919, and his last years in office were marred by ill health.

Windsor, House of The current British royal family. George V, Queen ▷ELIZABETH II's grandfather, adopted the name as a patriotic gesture during World War I. He felt that his name of Saxe-Coburg and Gotha, which he had inherited from Queen Victoria's husband, Prince Albert, sounded too Germanic.

World War I (1914-18) War fought between the Allies (Britain and its dominions and colonies, France, Russia, Italy and the USA) and the Central Powers (Germany, Austria-Hungary and the OTTOMAN EMPIRE). The underlying causes of the war were rivalry between Austria and Russia for influence in the unstable Balkan region, and the mutual hostility of France and Germany. The assassination in Sarajevo of the Austrian heir, Archduke FRANZ FERDINAND, triggered the war. Britain entered the war when Germany invaded Belgium. Germany's westward advance was halted by the Allies at the River Marne, and the two sides formed a more or less static line, locked in trench warfare. The Central Powers were more successful to the east, where they defeated Russia at Tannenberg and invaded Poland and Lithuania. In 1915, Turkey inflicted a terrible defeat on British and Commonwealth forces at GALLIPOLI. In 1916 the bloody Battle of the SOMME and an inconclusive naval battle at Jutland brought Allied morale to a new low. German submarine attacks in the Atlantic pushed America into the war in 1917, and in the same year tanks were used effectively for the first time, at Cambrai. By this time, the use of aircraft in battle by 'aces' such as Manfred von RICHTHOFEN was also well established. Russia's heavy losses on the eastern front helped to precipitate the RUSSIAN REVOLUTION in 1917, after which Russia withdrew from the fighting. In 1918 Germany lost 750 000 men in a failed offensive in the west, and American reinforcements began playing a vital role in delivering final victory to the Allies, when Germany agreed to an armistice. The Treaty of VERSAILLES was intended to set the seal on what was believed to be 'the war to end all wars', but the punitive measures it took against Germany were partly responsible for the rise of Adolf HITLER and the outbreak of World War II, 20 years later. Some 8 million soldiers died in World War I, most of them young conscripts who became known as the 'lost generation', and 16 million men were injured.
❖ The tragedy of the war inspired many writers, including Robert ▷GRAVES and Ernest ▷HEMINGWAY, and the British war poets such as Wilfred ▷OWEN and Siegfried Sassoon.
❖ Remembrance Sunday – the Sunday nearest to Armistice Day (11 November) – is the occasion for remembering the dead of both the world wars, and other conflicts. A two-minute silence is observed at 11 o'clock on the 11th day of the 11th month, the time when the armistice came into force. Wreaths of poppies, recalling the flowers that grew in the Flanders battlefields during World War I, are laid at war memorials in many parts of the world.
❖ South Africa, as part of the BRITISH EMPIRE, was automatically involved when Britain declared war on Germany. The decision by Louis ▷BOTHA's government to invade German ▷SOUTH WEST AFRICA sparked the ▷AFRIKANER REBELLION of 1914. Many South Africans – including the later prime minister, Jan ▷SMUTS – distinguished themselves in campaigns in East Africa and in the Somme. About 12 000 South Africans died in the war.
❖ Although black South Africans were not permitted arms, 21 000 black soldiers served in noncombatant roles.

World War II (1939-45) War fought between the AXIS powers (mainly Germany, Italy and Japan) and the ALLIES (France, Britain and the ▷COMMONWEALTH, later joined by the Soviet Union and the USA). The roots of the conflict lay in the humiliating terms that were imposed on Germany by the Treaty of VERSAILLES and the economic collapse of the WEIMAR REPUBLIC, which fuelled the fascist extremism of NAZISM. HITLER demanded *lebensraum* – more living space for the German people. His *Anschluss* (union) with Austria and German demands for the Sudetenland region of Czechoslovakia were appeased by Britain and France, a policy which culminated in the MUNICH AGREEMENT. The war began when Germany invaded Poland; Britain had pledged to guarantee Poland's borders and declared war soon afterwards. For several months there was a so-called 'phoney war' with very little fighting. Germany launched a major offensive in spring 1940, conquering Norway, Denmark, the Netherlands, Luxembourg, Belgium and France by BLITZKRIEG tactics, forcing a desperate British withdrawal from DUNKIRK. Hitler called off his planned invasion of Britain after the Battle of BRITAIN, but he then ordered the BLITZ, in which the Luftwaffe (air force) bombed British cities and industrial targets. Hitler's decision to invade the Soviet Union in 1941 was a strategic mistake, breaking the NAZI-SOVIET PACT and forcing the Russians to join the Allies. Germany was now fighting a war on two fronts, while Italy's involvement brought hostilities to the Mediterranean and North Africa. The USA entered the war when the Japanese attacked the American naval base at PEARL HARBOR. Early in 1942, Japan made extensive conquests in the Pacific and invaded Burma and China, but was checked by American victories at the naval battle of Midway and elsewhere. German expansion eastwards was halted at Stalingrad and Kursk, and General MONTGOMERY and his DESERT RATS ended ROMMEL's advance in North Africa. Allied troops forced Italy to surrender and switch sides in 1943, while Royal Air Force and US Air Force bombers stepped up the strategic bombing of Germany. Hitler responded to the Allied invasion of Europe (D-DAY) in June 1944 by launching pilotless V-bombs at Britain. The Allies pushed towards Germany from both east and west, uncovering the horror of the Nazi HOLOCAUST and the CONCENTRATION CAMPS. The end of the war in Europe came on V-E DAY in May 1945. Meanwhile, US forces fought a tough island-hopping campaign across the central Pacific, while American and Australian troops pushed across New Guinea towards the Philippines. The war in the Pacific ended in August 1945, after the USA dropped ATOM BOMBS on the Japanese cities of Hiroshima and Nagasaki. About 24 million soldiers – more than half of them Soviet troops – were killed in battle, and about 12,5 million were wounded. In contrast with World War I, there were substantial civilian casualties: an estimated 40 million civilians died as a result of the hostilities, about 20 million of whom were Chinese.

❖ Of the nearly 400 000 South Africans who served in the war (including 123 000 blacks in noncombatant roles), almost 9 000 were killed. The country's troops helped oust Italy from Ethiopia (Abyssinia) and restore HAILE SELASSIE to the throne (1940-1), occupied Madagascar (1942) and fought in the North African and Italian campaigns.

❖ Codebreaking was a vital part of the Allied victory. The German 'Enigma' and Japanese 'Purple' codes were deciphered with the help of the first electronic computers.

❖ The war strengthened ties between the USA and Britain. But American airmen and soldiers stationed in Britain before D-Day, armed with nylons, cigarettes, chocolate and chewing gum, earned GIs the reputation of being 'overpaid, oversexed and over here'.

Yalta Conference (1945) Meeting between CHURCHILL, STALIN and ROOSEVELT, the British, Soviet and American Allied leaders, towards the end of WORLD WAR II. At Yalta, a resort in the Crimea, they laid plans to disarm Germany and set up the ▷UNITED NATIONS.

Yom Kippur War (1973) War triggered by a surprise attack on Israel by Syria and Egypt on ▷YOM KIPPUR, the holiest day in the Jewish calendar. The Arabs made some initial gains, but were repelled by the Israelis after three weeks. It was the last of five wars in the ▷ARAB-ISRAELI CONFLICT.

Zhou dynasty (JOH) Chinese dynasty that ousted the last king of the Shang dynasty (18th to 12th century BC) and ruled from *c*1111 BC to *c*256 BC. Under the Zhou emperors, the Chinese became a great civilization and made important advances in agriculture, technology and trade. FEUDALISM was established, and art and literature flourished. The philosopher Confucius, founder of ▷CONFUCIANISM, wrote in the Zhou period.

Zhou Enlai (JOH-en-LYE) (1898-1976) Chinese statesman who was a close ally of MAO ZEDONG and China's premier from 1949 until his death. He helped to establish closer relations between his country and Western nations in the 1970s. He was the architect of modernization programmes in 1975 and the main advocate of the policy of detente with the USA in the early 1970s.

THE BIG THREE *At Yalta, Churchill and Stalin flank a gaunt President Roosevelt, who died two months later. For eight days, the Allied leaders thrashed out how to defeat and divide Germany.*

POLITICS, GOVERNMENT AND THE LAW

A host of political systems determine how the nations of the world are governed, imposing their own pattern on society. Different frameworks of law are used to discipline the complex web of human relationships. Institutions, charismatic individuals and popular opinion play as big a role as political principles in shaping our rights, freedoms and responsibilities.

Act of Parliament Legislative proposal, or BILL, which has been approved by both houses of parliament and which has been signed into law by the president, in the case of republics. In a monarchy, a bill is signed into law by the monarch.

advocate Member of the legal profession in South Africa who gives opinions on complex legal matters and who may appear in all courts of law, especially the supreme court but barring the small claims courts, where representation by lawyers is not permitted. Instruction is given by an ATTORNEY on behalf of a client. Judges are chosen mostly from the ranks of advocates.

Advocate General In South Africa a senior official with wide powers to investigate allegations of financial misappropriation and other wrongdoing in the government and to submit reports to Parliament. The office was introduced in the wake of a series of government scandals in the 1970s.

affidavit Written statement of evidence used in a civil legal action. The author of an affidavit – the word is Latin for 'he has pledged' – swears that what is written is true and signs it before an independent witness, such as a magistrate or a court official.

African Christian Democratic Party South African political party that pursues policies based on its interpretation of biblical teachings. Among other things, it opposes abortion and homosexual rights. It polled 0,5 per cent of the vote in the 1994 election.

Africanism A political and social outlook favouring the rights and wellbeing of Africans and African culture and tradition, especially in relation to Africa's former colonial powers. Influential exponents of Africanism include Marcus ▷GARVEY, with his 'Africa for Africans' campaign of the 1920s, Kwame ▷NKRUMAH of Ghana, as well as several prominent leaders in the liberation movements of southern Africa.

Afrikaner nationalism A South African political ideology based on the promotion of Afrikaner identity and exclusivity and of Afrikaner interests, and formerly pursued by the NATIONAL PARTY and more recently by the South African CONSERVATIVE PARTY, the FREEDOM FRONT and the AFRIKANER WEERSTANDSBEWEGING, among others. It dates from the late 1870s, when a common consciousness among Afrikaners – those living in the interior and at the Cape – arose in the face of British intervention north of the Orange River, and centred on the idea that they had a distinct culture and history and faced a common foe in British oppression. In the 20th century an Afrikaner nationalist movement emerged with the goal of winning political power for Afrikaners in a new republic, which was achieved in two stages: in 1948 the National Party won political power, and in 1961 the ▷REPUBLIC was inaugurated. Nationalism lost its rationale in the next two decades, and it became clear that ▷APARTHEID could not be sustained. An extreme response to the prospect of losing political power was to talk about a separate territory (a VOLKSTAAT) for Afrikaners, but most Afrikaners rejected the idea as impractical.

Afrikaner Weerstandsbeweging (AWB) (Resistance Movement of Afrikaners) One of several ultra-right groups in South Africa that claim the country for whites, particularly Afrikaners. It projects a neo-Nazi image, operates with a paramilitary force and many of its members have engaged in protests, assault and sabotage with fatal consequences. AWB members attempted to derail the 1994 election with a series of bomb explosions which claimed lives.

❖ AWB members tarred and feathered an Afrikaans history professor at a public gathering in 1979 because he questioned the notion of divine intervention in the Battle of ▷BLOOD RIVER.

❖ In one of the most notorious attacks by one of its members, on 15 November 1988 in the centre of Pretoria, Barend Strydom went on a wild shooting spree during which seven black people died and 16 were injured. Strydom was jailed but later freed under an amnesty, seemingly unrepentant.

Amin, Idi (*c*1925-) President of Uganda from 1971 to 1979. He came to power after leading a military coup against Milton Obote, and was a brutal ruler who ordered mass arrests, massacres and other atrocities. He also expelled most of Uganda's Asian population. Amin was deposed in 1979 by a Tanzanian-backed coup, and went to live in exile in Saudi Arabia. In 1995 he was accused of plotting to overthrow the Ugandan government.

❖ Obote was restored to power soon after Amin was ousted. However, Obote was again overthrown by a military coup in 1985.

Amnesty International Organization formed in 1961 to protect HUMAN RIGHTS, gain the release of prisoners of conscience and campaign against torture and the death penalty. It works independently of all governments, and is known both for its successful lobbying campaigns and for its worldwide research into the treatment of prisoners. Its headquarters are in London. The organization was awarded the Nobel peace prize in 1977.

anarchism Doctrine that all forms of authority are evil because they are based on coercion, and that societies should be organized on the basis of voluntary association. Anarchists come in many ideological colours,

AFRIKANER MILITANCY *Eugene Terre'Blanche, flamboyant leader of the ultra-right AWB in South Africa, flanked by sycophantic followers, acknowledges crowd support.*

from left-wing communalists, who believe in self-governing local communities, to right-wing libertarians, who believe that individual freedom takes precedence over the State's right to impose taxes.

ANC (African National Congress) South African liberation movement, formed in 1912 (as the South African Native National Congress) to protect the interests of Africans and, ultimately, to pursue democratic rule. Banned in 1960, it turned to armed resistance and to pressing for sanctions. Many of its leaders, including Nelson MANDELA, were imprisoned, while others went into exile. Movements sympathetic to the ANC were formed inside the country, only to be banned in turn. The ANC, and all other political organizations, were unbanned and their leaders released in 1990, following more than a decade of internal unrest and mass protest. Talks with the NATIONAL PARTY Government and other major political parties led to agreement on an interim constitution and moderation of the ANC's support for nationalization and other socialist policies. In the 1994 election, the ANC won close to a two-thirds majority (62,65 per cent) to form South Africa's first democratic government. At its national congress in December 1994, the ANC embraced free enterprise and privatization of certain State assets. (See also ▷ANC in 'Southern African history'.)

Anglo-Irish Agreement (1985) Historic document signed by the prime ministers of Britain and Ireland, Margaret Thatcher and Garrett Fitzgerald, providing for regular conferences between their two governments. As it gave the Irish Republic a say in the affairs of Northern Ireland, the agreement was opposed by ULSTER UNIONISTS. It was followed in 1993 by another Anglo-Irish accord, the Downing Street Declaration, which implied that a cessation of violence could lead to the inclusion of SINN FEIN in official talks on Northern Ireland, but which stressed that any constitutional change affecting the province depended upon the consent of a majority of its people. The IRA's pledge to cease military operations from 31 August 1994 was seen as a significant breakthrough.

appeal courts Superior courts whose role is to hear challenges to the judgments of lower courts. The Appellate Division of the Supreme Court in South Africa is the final court of appeal in criminal and civil cases. Appeals about interpretation of the constitution are heard by the CONSTITUTIONAL COURT.

Arab-Israeli conflict Political and military struggle between Israel and the Arab world

VOICE OF THE ARABS *Yasser Arafat moved the struggle for a Palestinian Arab state from guerrilla war to the world conference table.*

that has resulted in four wars. The first was immediately after Israel's foundation in 1948, and war broke out again in 1956, 1967 (the ▷SIX-DAY WAR) and 1973. Each time Israel won and more Palestinian Arabs became refugees. Israel made peace with Egypt in 1978 (the Camp David Accord), but its invasion of southern Lebanon in 1982 increased tension in the region again. In 1987 Palestinians in the Israeli-occupied West Bank and Gaza Strip began an *intifada*, or uprising, against Israeli rule. In 1993 Israel and the PLO signed a peace accord giving the Palestinians limited self-rule in Gaza and the West Bank town of Jericho, and Israeli troops withdrew from these areas in 1994. In July 1994 Israel and Jordan signed an agreement ending the state of war that had existed between them since 1948.

Arab League Regional political grouping founded in Cairo in 1945 by seven Arab countries. There are now 22 members of the league, stretching from Morocco to Iraq, and including the PLO. Its purpose is to ensure co-operation among its member states and to protect their independence and interests. The league has had little success in resolving disputes between its members and it was divided by the 1990-1 ▷GULF WAR. Its headquarters is in Cairo.

Arafat, Yasser (1929-) Palestinian leader and chairman of the PLO since 1969 who has played a major role in the ARAB-ISRAELI CONFLICT. Arafat came to prominence after the 1967 ▷SIX-DAY WAR, when Israel made huge gains of territory. In the 1960s and 1970s he led a guerrilla campaign which aimed to destroy Israel, but in 1982 he started to cultivate diplomatic links with world leaders in order to influence opinion in favour of the Palestinians. In 1988 Arafat recognized Israel's right to coexist with an independent State of Palestine, in the hope of gaining a PLO platform in Middle East peace talks. In 1993 he signed a peace agreement with Israel's premier, Yitzhak Rabin, which secured limited self-rule for Palestinians in Gaza and Jericho. This controversial agreement has made him very unpopular amongst younger, more militant PLO members.

arms control Process of limiting the build-up of armaments and military forces by international agreement. In contrast with DISARMAMENT, the goal of which is the elimination of certain weapons, arms control aims to achieve a balance of military power between potential aggressors in order to create stability and make war less likely. A key factor in arms control talks is the extent to which each side can verify the promises of the other.
❖ During the 1970s, the USA and the USSR negotiated agreements to limit strategic nuclear weapons (SALT I and II), but this did not stop the ARMS RACE.

arms race Struggle for superiority in military systems and hardware. During the ▷COLD WAR between the USA and the USSR (1945-90), increasingly large sums of money were spent to ensure that any weapons initiative by one superpower was matched or surpassed by the other.

Asmal, Kader (Abdul Kadera) (1934-) Minister of water affairs and forestry in South Africa (1994-). He lived in exile from 1959 and was instrumental in founding the British Anti-Apartheid Movement as well as the Irish Anti-Apartheid Movement. He also served as vice-president of the International Defence and Aid Fund. He lectured law at Trinity College in Dublin and qualified as a barrister at both the London and the Dublin Bars. When he returned to South Africa in 1990, he was appointed professor of human rights at the University of the Western Cape.

Assad, Hafez al- (1930-) President of Syria who seized power in 1970 in a bloodless coup. Under Assad, Syria became a major power in the Middle East and until the early 1990s it was opposed to any peace settlement in the area. His relations with the West were damaged by alleged Syrian involvement in international terrorism, but from the late

1980s he was active in securing the release of Western hostages in Lebanon.

attorney Member of the legal profession in South Africa who usually appears on behalf of clients before any MAGISTRATE'S COURT or before certain other tribunals in virtually any type of legal work, including civil actions, criminal proceedings, debt collecting and the drafting of contracts. Attorneys have also begun acting in the supreme court.

Attorney General Senior State legal officer in several countries. In South Africa, an official in a designated area in charge of criminal proceedings who reviews evidence assembled by the police, or by other State officials, to determine whether or not the State will prosecute in a particular case, or appeal against the judgment of a court. He may also initiate police investigations.

Auditor General In South Africa, a State official charged with examining the accounts and financial transactions of all State departments and submitting regular reports to Parliament, including reports on irregularities.

authoritarianism Administrative system characterized by strong rule which calls for absolute obedience to authority. Authoritarian rulers impose their policies irrespective of the wishes of the people they govern, suppressing dissent and legitimizing their behaviour by claiming special qualities. Both ▷HITLER and ▷MUSSOLINI, for example, posed as national saviours. However, the degree of social control exerted by an authoritarian regime is less extreme than that associated with TOTALITARIANISM.

AZAPO (Azanian People's Organisation) South African political movement espousing black consciousness and founded in 1979 after the collapse of other organizations in the ▷BLACK CONSCIOUSNESS MOVEMENT and the death in police detention of student activist Steve ▷BIKO. AZAPO boycotted multiparty negotiations and South Africa's first democratic elections, and advocates nationalization of land and industry.

backbencher A member of parliament, usually of junior rank, who traditionally is seated behind ministers and deputy ministers in parliament.

bail Release of an arrested person on condition that he, or she, turns up in court on an appointed date to stand trial. Failure to appear on the specific date results in the person granted bail (or his guarantor) forfeiting a sum of money fixed by the court. South Africa's interim constitution entitles any person to demand a bail hearing upon his arrest and stipulates that bail must be granted unless the State can provide convincing evidence to refuse it. The availability of bail without the payment of excessive sums is seen as an important civil liberty throughout the world.

balance of power Situation in which rival nations or alliances perceive one another as roughly equal in power, and are therefore unlikely to gain much by waging war. Countries that wish to maintain the peace try to ensure that no single country or coalition becomes more powerful than any other in a given area.
❖ The balance of power between the USA and the USSR after World War II, maintained by a nuclear ARMS RACE, was sometimes called the 'balance of terror'.

Banda, Hastings Kamuzu (1906-) Former Malawian president who was in power for nearly 30 years. Banda qualified as a medical doctor at Edinburgh University, Scotland, in 1942. After a concerted drive for independence for the former British colony of Nyasaland and the dissolution of the ▷CENTRAL AFRICAN FEDERATION, his Malawi Congress Party won 99 percent of the vote in Malawi's first election in 1961. Five years later, he made Malawi a republic with himself the executive president and advocated contact with South Africa's apartheid regime. His one-party rule led to repression, economic stagnation and political unrest, forcing him to call a multiparty election in 1994, in which he was defeated by Bakili MULUZI. In 1995 he faced charges of ordering the murder of political opponents some years before and was placed under house arrest.

barrister Member of the senior branch of the legal profession in England, Wales and Northern Ireland, the junior branch being composed of solicitors. Barristers are called upon to give specialist opinion on complex issues and can plead cases in any court. (See ADVOCATE; ATTORNEY.)

bench Office or position of a judge. The term derives from the seat, or bench, reserved for judges in a court of law.

bill Draft of a proposed law presented for approval to parliament. In South Africa bills are introduced by cabinet ministers in either the NATIONAL ASSEMBLY or the SENATE. A bill goes through a 'first reading' in which its title and intention are tabled; a committee stage in which the appropriate standing committee of Parliament investigates, debates and, if necessary, amends it; a 'second reading' when the bill, with amendments, is fully debated and voted on; and an enactment stage in which it is signed into law, as an ACT OF PARLIAMENT, by the president. Both houses of Parliament are required to approve the same version of a bill and where differences arise these must be resolved by a joint committee of the two houses.

Bill of Rights A charter of basic rights and freedoms, entrenched in the CONSTITUTIONS of many countries, including South Africa, and proclaiming, among other things, freedom of speech, freedom of association and freedom of the press.
❖ The Bill of Rights of the USA (1791) consists of the first ten amendments to its constitution. The ones most frequently invoked are the 'First Amendment', which guarantees freedom of speech, religion, assembly and the press, and the 'Fifth Amendment', which sets out the rights of people accused of crimes.

Botha, Pik (Roelof, Frederik) (1932-) Minister of mineral and energy affairs in South Africa (1994-) and former minister of foreign affairs (1977-94). An advocate by training, Botha was a member of South Africa's legal team in the 'South West Africa case' at the INTERNATIONAL COURT OF JUSTICE. He also served as a high-profile ambassador to the United Nations in 1974, and then as ambassador to the United States. He was the world's longest serving foreign minister.
❖ Botha, who had a *verligte* ('enlightened') image and was a crowd-drawer for his party during election campaigns, was publicly humiliated on more than one occasion by former President P W Botha, once for suggesting that South Africa might one day have a black president.

Botha, P W (Pieter Willem) (1916-) Former president of South Africa (1984-1989). As defence minister (1965-78), he dramatically boosted military power; nuclear weapons were built and the armaments industry was developed into the largest manufacturing conglomerate in the country. During his presidency, military power was used for internal repression and external aggression, including an invasion of Angola in 1975, the destabilization of neighbouring countries and the 'border war' against SWAPO in Namibia. He created a nominated President's Council and a tricameral parliament with segregated white, coloured and Asian chambers, but excluding Africans. The failure of his constitutional initiatives led to domestic insurrection and to the pursuit of a repressive ▷'TOTAL STRATEGY' by the State against a perceived 'total onslaught'. Notorious for his finger-wagging style, his famous ▷RUBICON speech

PRESERVING HERITAGE *Chief Mangosuthu Buthelezi, a hereditary Zulu chief, campaigned strongly for traditional values and leadership in the KwaZulu-Natal province.*

of 1985 led to major disinvestment. He suffered a stroke in 1989 and resigned at the request of his cabinet.

❖ Some argue that Botha started the reform process that eventually led to democratic rule. He did abolish the ▷PASS LAWS in 1986, agreed to the independence of Namibia in 1988 and met jailed ANC leader Nelson MANDELA in his office in 1989. However, it was left to his successor, F W DE KLERK to carry through reform.

❖ Botha's nickname was the 'Groot Krokodil' ('Big Crocodile').

Bundestag Lower house of the German Parliament, consisting of 662 deputies elected by PROPORTIONAL REPRESENTATION for four-year terms. Together with the upper house of Parliament, the Bundesrat, the Bundestag passes legislation, elects the federal chancellor and president and oversees the activities of the federal ministries.

Bush, George (1924-) Republican president of the USA between 1989 and 1993. Bush was a former director of the CIA and served as vice-president to Ronald Reagan from 1981 to 1989. During Bush's term of office, US troops invaded Panama and deposed its president, Manuel Noriega. Bush was the leading figure behind the international force that waged the ▷GULF WAR in 1991 against Iraq. His presidency was dogged by accusations that he was involved in the ▷IRAN-CONTRA affair and that his concentration on foreign policy led to the neglect of economic and social problems at home. He was succeeded as president by the Democrat Bill CLINTON.

❖ Bush is remembered for saying during his 1988 election campaign: 'Read my lips: no new taxes' – a promise he failed to keep.

Buthelezi, Mangosuthu Gatsha (1928-) Leader of the INKATHA FREEDOM PARTY and minister of home affairs (1994-) in the GOVERNMENT OF NATIONAL UNITY in South Africa. He is hereditary chief of the Buthelezi tribe and former chief minister (1976-93) of the KwaZulu Legislative Assembly. Under apartheid, he used his position as leader of the Zulu bantustan to demand reforms, setting up the Buthelezi Commission which, in its report of 1982, called for universal franchise in KwaZulu and Natal. He joined ▷MULTIPARTY NEGOTIATIONS on a new South African constitution, but withdrew after disagreement with other parties over provincial powers. In the 1994 election he led the IFP to victory in KwaZulu/Natal and to securing the third largest number of votes nationally.

bylaw Rule made by an authority that is subordinate to parliament. The most common bylaws are those made by local councils on issues relating to the government of their areas. They may be used, for example, to curb litter or enforce parking restrictions.

cabinet government A concept of joint responsibility on the part of all ministers in the cabinet for the legislative and administrative actions of the government. Under the interim constitution the South African Cabinet is composed of members of the largest parties, proportionate to the percentage of votes which they attained in the 1994 general election. Decisions are reached by consensus, or failing that, by majority vote, and are binding on all ministers.

Callaghan, James (Lord Callaghan) (1912-) Former British prime minister (1976-9) who served in tough economic times. He brokered the ▷LANCASTER HOUSE AGREEMENT that ended the 15-year 'bush war' in former Rhodesia and brought legal independence and democracy to Zimbabwe (1980). Callaghan served in the cabinet of prime minister Harold Wilson as chancellor of the exchequer and home secretary.

capital punishment The death penalty has been phased out in most European countries but has been retained in parts of the USA, where more than 210 people have been executed since 1973. In Britain capital punishment for murder was abolished in 1965, but it still exists as the penalty for treason and for piracy at sea or in the air involving murder or attempted murder. In South Africa, mandatory death sentences were abolished in 1990 and a moratorium placed on executions. In 1995 the CONSTITUTIONAL COURT ruled for the abolition of the death penalty in face of huge public opposition to such a move.

Carter, Jimmy (1924-) US Democratic politician and 39th president of the USA from 1977 to 1981. Carter, a peanut farmer from Georgia, where he was governor (1970-4), narrowly defeated the Republican Gerald Ford in the 1976 presidential election. He brought Egypt and Israel together to sign the ▷CAMP DAVID ACCORD in 1978. He also kept US athletes out of the Moscow Olympics in 1980 as a protest against the Soviet invasion of Afghanistan the previous year. Carter lost popularity when Iranian revolutionaries took dozens of Americans hostage in Tehran and a bid to rescue them failed.

Castro, Fidel (1927-) Prime minister of Cuba from 1959, and president from 1976. Castro came to power after a three-year guerrilla war in which, with the support of Che ▷GUEVARA, he overthrew the US-backed dictator Fulgencio Batista. Castro presided over his country's transformation into a communist state, building close links with the USSR. Worsening relations with the USA led to the ▷BAY OF PIGS invasion in 1961 and the ▷CUBAN MISSILE CRISIS in 1962. The collapse of communism in the USSR and eastern Europe left Castro isolated, and Cuba's mounting economic problems forced him to seek new income from

GUNS AND ROSES *'A revolution is not a bed of roses', said Fidel Castro after seizing power in Cuba. It was one of his terser statements; his harangues sometimes lasted as long as nine hours.*

tourism. Castro has been supportive of African liberation movements, particularly in Angola, where Cuban troops were deployed for more than a decade in support of the MPLA fighting against the South African-backed forces of Jonas Savimbi's UNITA movement.

chancellor of the exchequer In Britain, the cabinet minister responsible for finance and the TREASURY and the drawing up of the government's annual budget. In South Africa, this is the task of the minister of finance.

Chaskalson, Arthur (1931-) President of the CONSTITUTIONAL COURT in South Africa (1995-) and a distinguished human rights lawyer. Chaskalson became a SENIOR COUNSEL in 1971 and practised as an advocate for some 20 years before he helped to establish the Legal Resources Centre, the base from which he fought and won many of the most important legal challenges to apartheid laws. He assisted in the drafting of the Namibian Constitution and also South Africa's interim constitution in 1993-4. He is an honorary member of the Bar Association of New York.

Chief Justice The senior judge in South Africa who swears in the president, his deputies, other judges, and members of parliament, and who advises the president and the cabinet on the selection of new judges, including some judges of the constitutional court. He presides over the general administration of the country's courts and hears petitions from persons seeking the right to appeal against the judgments of the supreme court.

Chiluba, Frederick Jacob Titus (1943-) President of Zambia and former trade union leader. He was elected chairman-general of the Zambian Congress of Trade Unions in 1974. In 1990 he took over the full-time leadership of the Movement for Multiparty Democracy, which swept to victory over Kenneth KAUNDA in 1991 in the first multiparty election in Zambia for 23 years. Chiluba supports free-market principles.

Chirac, Jacques (1932-) President and former prime minister of France who is regarded as the spiritual descendant of General Charles ▷DE GAULLE. The conservative Chirac narrowly defeated the socialists to win the presidency in 1995 after having pursued the post for nearly two decades and being dismissed as a has-been. He served two terms as prime minister – from 1974-6 and from 1986-8 – and refounded the conservative GAULLISM movement, Rassemblement pour la République (RPR), in 1976 as a personal campaign vehicle. He has a long-standing image as an impulsive leader with an inclination to elastic political views. In the 1970s, he was a left-leaning nationalist who opposed European integration; in the 1980s, he was a convinced free-marketeer who privatized state enterprises and worked for the single European market. Before his election as president, he presented himself as a crusader for social reform and undertook to change the monarchical quality the presidency acquired under the 14-year reign of his predecessor, François MITTERRAND. Within weeks of becoming president, Chirac unleashed a storm of worldwide protest when he announced that France would resume testing of nuclear weapons in the Pacific Ocean after a break of 3 years.

Chissano, Joaquim Alberto (1939-) President of Mozambique and former minister of foreign affairs. He became president after the death of Samora ▷MACHEL in 1986. Chissano had served as a FRELIMO representative in Dar-es-Salaam from 1963 before becoming Mozambique's transitional prime minister (1974-5). In the face of continuing civil war he entered into negotiations with RENAMO opponents, agreeing to a ceasefire and winning democratic elections in October 1994.

Christian democracy Set of political doctrines, shaped by 20th-century Roman Catholic ideas about social justice, which has become influential in many European countries and in Latin America. Although there are distinctions between Christian democratic parties in different countries, common themes include a strong commitment to Roman Catholic family values, hostility to communism and broad support for enlightened welfare policies.
❖ Among those countries with strong Christian democratic parties are Germany, Italy, Chile, Venezuela and El Salvador.

CIA (Central Intelligence Agency) US national security organization founded in 1947 to gather foreign intelligence information and to undertake secret political operations abroad. It was placed under the direction of the president and the National Security Council and now also reports to a number of congressional committees. The CIA is by far the biggest organization of its type in the world, employing some 3 000 field officials and about 9 000 administrators. The agency's involvement in a series of unsuccessful assassination attempts – for example, on Fidel CASTRO – as well as other subversive activities, both inside and outside the USA, damaged its reputation. The CIA's less well-publicized successes have included 'Operation Gold' in 1955 – when a tunnel was dug into East Berlin to intercept underground Soviet telephone lines, which remained undiscovered for more than a year.

circuit court South African court that is convened from time to time in outlying areas designated by the JUDGE PRESIDENT of a particular region and presided over by a judge of the supreme court of that region.

STARS AND STRIPES *The smiling image that wooed America with promises of economic recovery and domestic reform: Bill Clinton, the 42nd president of the USA, and his wife Hillary.*

CIS (Commonwealth of Independent States) Loose confederation that was created in 1991 among 12 of the 15 former republics of the USSR, excluding the Baltic States. The CIS has no common citizenship, parliament or president. With headquarters in Mensk, its sole declared purpose is to deal centrally with certain international laws and policies that apply to its members, through regular meetings of delegates from each republic.

civil case A court action involving the rights or legal obligations of a private citizen. Civil cases include litigation for damages, breach of contract, divorce and matters relating to family law. In South Africa civil cases can be initiated by an individual, or group, including the government, and the seriousness of the case – usually determined by the monetary amount of the claim for compensation – determines which court it will be heard in. Civil cases are distinct from CRIMINAL CASES.

civil disobedience Refusal to obey laws that are regarded as unjust, often by use of peaceful demonstrations, sit-ins and marches. The technique was made famous by Mahatma ▷GANDHI, in the USA by the ▷CIVIL RIGHTS MOVEMENT and opponents of the Vietnam War, and by the anticolonialists and liberation movements throughout Africa.

civil rights Freedoms given to a citizen by the State which are guaranteed either by CONVENTION or by a written CONSTITUTION. There are many such rights, among them classic freedoms, such as those of speech and religion, as well as the right to vote. Modern civil rights include protection against discrimination on grounds of race, gender or sexual orientation.

civil service The body of people employed by the State to implement laws and policies and to carry out all duties of public administration that are not of a legislative nature. Unlike politicians, who must submit their record to the verdict of voters in an election, civil servants (also known as 'public servants') are a permanent organ of administration which remains in place even when governments change. Although civil servants are supposed to be nonpartisan, they have substantial political power because cabinet ministers often depend on their advice. In South Africa, and other newly democratic countries of Africa, a policy of ▷AFFIRMATIVE ACTION has been introduced in order to make the civil service more reflective of the ethnic and social character of the country as a whole.

Clinton, Bill (William) (1946-) US Democratic politician and 42nd president of the USA (1993-). Clinton, a former governor of Arkansas, defeated Republican George Bush in the 1992 presidential election on the promise that he would lead the American economy out of recession, reduce the huge budget deficit and improve health, education and welfare programmes. After the election, he put his wife Hillary in charge of implementing health reforms, and appointed several other women to leading positions in the government. Clinton came under increasing criticism for a lack of decisiveness in foreign policy, and faced accusations of financial and sexual misconduct. The 1994 mid-term election left Clinton with both houses of Congress dominated by Republicans.

CND (Campaign for Nuclear Disarmament) Organization founded in 1958 to work for the abolition of nuclear weapons in Britain. Its tactics, which included mass marches to the Atomic Weapons Research Establishment at Aldermaston in Berkshire, achieved much

'BAN THE BOMB' *The first CND marchers endured four days of rain and icy winds before their 1,5 km-long column of 9 000 reached Aldermaston from Trafalgar Square at Easter in 1958.*

publicity and attracted considerable support from intellectuals, politicians and church leaders. Its influence declined after 1983, following the massive electoral defeat of the Labour Party, which had campaigned for unilateral nuclear disarmament.

commission of inquiry An official investigative body that inquires into any matter and submits a report containing specific findings or recommendations according to its terms of reference. Such commissions – appointed in South Africa by the president, a cabinet minister or a provincial premier – may subpoena witnesses to give evidence and may conduct their investigations in public or behind closed doors. Their recommendations, or findings, are not binding on the government.

common law A system of laws developed in England based on common custom and previous court judgments, or precedents, rather than on statute law, which is based on legal definition. Legal precedent shapes the law in Britain, most Commonwealth countries and in the USA. In South Africa, common law and statute law both contribute to the legal system.

Commonwealth Organization made up of 51 former territories of the British Empire, most of which are now independent sovereign states. The Commonwealth, which acknowledges the British monarch as its head, is a forum for international debate and technical cooperation. It is administered by a secretariat, whose secretary-general wields considerable influence on the world stage.

❖ The Commonwealth Games, an athletics contest open to all citizens of the Commonwealth, is held every four years.

❖ South Africa returned to the Commonwealth in 1994. Prime Minister Hendrik Verwoerd had withdrawn its membership in 1961 before it became a republic.

communism Political doctrine aimed at establishing – if necessary, by revolution – a classless society in which goods and the means of production, such as factories and machinery, are commonly owned. The doctrine was originally associated with the writings of Karl ▷MARX and the interpretation put on Marx's ideas by ▷LENIN and his followers. During the rule of ▷STALIN (1922-53) in the USSR, communism developed into a worldwide network of parties subordinate to the political line laid down by the Communist Party of the Soviet Union. Since Stalin's death, however, many self-styled communist countries have demonstrated wide divergences from Marxist-Leninist theory. In particular, the Chinese Communist Party developed along distinct ideological lines under the influence of ▷MAO ZEDONG and advocated outright confrontation between communism and ▷CAPITALISM, condemning Soviet negotiations with the West as 'revisionism'. Marx believed that communism was ultimately inevitable – he saw it as a natural progression from SOCIALISM that would be achieved when the coercive organs of the State had 'withered away'. Modern communist countries have been characterized by a strong State apparatus and a powerful role for the party, but only a few survived beyond the 1980s. (See also ▷COMMUNISM in 'Business and economics'.)

❖ The principles of communism were set out in 1848 by Marx and ▷ENGELS in *The Communist Manifesto*, a pamphlet that ends with the words: 'The workers have nothing to lose but their chains. They have a world to win. Workers of the world, unite!'

❖ Communism was outlawed in South Africa in 1950 under the Suppression of Communism Act. The SOUTH AFRICAN COMMUNIST PARTY, was unbanned along with the liberation movements in 1990, when the Act was also repealed.

Congress National legislative body of certain countries, including the USA, whose Congress is divided into the HOUSE OF REPRESENTATIVES and the SENATE. Congress can block a president's legislative programme, or override a presidential veto by a two-thirds majority in each house. It can also remove officials from office by IMPEACHMENT.

Conservative Party Political parties of this name exist in several countries and are generally characterized by their opposition to radical social and economic change. In South Africa, the Conservative Party has been associated with the maintenance of white power and privilege, and opposition to majority rule. It was founded in 1982 by Andries Treurnicht (1921-93) after he and others had broken away from the NATIONAL PARTY over what they saw as the NP's abandonment of some of the principles of AFRIKANER NATIONALISM. The CP became the official opposition, but after the 1989 election it found itself on the sidelines. It boycotted the 1994 election. In Britain, the Conservative Party dates from the early 19th century. The word 'conservative' was first applied to a political party in 1834 when Sir Robert Peel, leader of the formerly Catholic party known as the Tories, renamed his followers 'conservatives' in his Tamworth Manifesto. The British party's policies have generally been associated with the defence of property and support for private enterprise, the free market and opposition to nationalization.

constitution The basic law, or body of laws, which establish and govern the political system of a country. In South Africa the constitution is a written document and disputes over its interpretation are resolved by the CONSTITUTIONAL COURT. In the USA the appeal court is the final arbitrator in all matters pertaining to the written constitution. But some countries, such as Britain and Israel, have unwritten constitutions, which means that their political systems are governed by legal precedents, customs and conventions. In South Africa, an interim constitution was agreed to at ▷MULTIPARTY NEGOTIATIONS in 1993. This provided the framework for democratic elections in 1994 and the GOVERNMENT OF NATIONAL UNITY, and laid down the principles that would form the basis of the final constitution drawn up by the CONSTITUTIONAL ASSEMBLY.

constitutional assembly Body constituted after South Africa's first democratic election and charged with drafting a new constitution in terms of constitutional principles laid down in June 1993 during ▷MULTIPARTY NEGOTIATIONS. Technically comprising all members of the NATIONAL ASSEMBLY and the SENATE, the constitutional assembly reorganized itself into a management committee and a 46-member constitutional committee, working with six theme committees. The latter received submissions on different aspects of the constitution from political parties, organizations and the public. The constitutional commitee formulated positions of agreement and disagreement and processed these for debate and adoption in the assembly. The CONSTITUTIONAL COURT was constituted to have the final say over the new constitution as well as any future changes.

constitutional court A special court in South Africa whose task is to arbitrate in disputes over the interpretation of the constitution, and to hear petitions over the constitutional validity of ACTS OF PARLIAMENT or the judgments of other courts. The South African court consists of 11 members who hold office for a single nonrenewable period of seven years. The court must certify the constitutional validity of the South African Constitution and any amendments to it, and its decisions are final and binding upon the government, the president and all other courts.

❖ In 1995, in one of its first rulings, the constitutional court abolished CAPITAL PUNISHMENT – a decision that led to much debate, before and after the ruling.

contempt of court Offence that undermines the administration of justice. Criminal contempt is behaviour likely to obstruct the administration of justice – for example, unruly behaviour in court or comment on court proceedings that might prejudice the outcome of a case. Civil contempt is the refusal to obey the orders of a court.

convention Rules governing political conduct without having legal force. They are usually unwritten and are applied in a particular case because they have applied to similar cases in the past. The British constitution relies heavily on convention.

COSATU (Congress of South African Trade Unions) A federation of trade unions formed in 1985 in South Africa, broadly subscribing to the principles of the ▷FREEDOM CHARTER and maintaining close links with the ANC and the SOUTH AFRICAN COMMUNIST PARTY. The National Union of Metalworkers of South Africa, the single largest trade union in the country, forms the backbone of COSATU. In the 1994 elections COSATU formally joined the ANC and SACP in an election alliance, and several former union officials now serve in the cabinet.

❖ By the mid-1990s, COSATU represented some 1,3 million workers led by general secretary Sam Shilowa, a former security guard.

Council of Europe Organization of European countries established in 1949 to deal with issues of European society. It includes all members of the EUROPEAN UNION and the European Free Trade Association, plus Turkey, Cyprus and Malta, and has its headquarters in Strasbourg, France. In 1950 it established the EUROPEAN CONVENTION ON HUMAN RIGHTS and the EUROPEAN COURT OF JUSTICE.

Council of Ministers Body of the EUROPEAN UNION responsible for political decision-making, comprising one cabinet minister from each country chosen according to the matter under discussion.

court martial A criminal prosecution within the armed forces of a country against a member of the armed forces who is accused of breaches of military law or discipline. Senior officers serve as judges and prosecutors and the accused is entitled to legal representation. Judgments and sentences are subject to judicial review. Britain has a special appeal court for the military.

criminal case A court prosecution, distinct from a CIVIL CASE, which is initiated by the State against an individual, either alone or in concert with others, for alleged transgression of criminal laws. Criminal laws usually are aimed at protecting the safety or interests of the community as a whole, or a significant or clearly identifiable element of the community. In South Africa, the ATTORNEY GENERAL in an area determines in which court criminal cases will be prosecuted, but generally initial charges are heard in a MAGISTRATE'S COURT before a decision is taken on whether or not the matter should be referred for hearing in the SUPREME COURT.

DECOLONIALIZING AFRICA

Country	Independence	Colonial ruler	First post-colonial leader
Angola	11 Nov 1975	Portugal	Antonio Agostinho Neto
Botswana	30 Sept 1966	United Kingdom	Seretse Khama
Congo	15 Aug 1960	France	Abbé Fulbert Youlou
Ghana	6 Mar 1957	United Kingdom	Kwame Nkrumah
Kenya	12 Dec 1963	United Kingdom	Jomo Kenyatta
Lesotho	4 Oct 1966	United Kingdom	Leabua Jonathan
Madagascar	26 June 1960	France	Philibert Tsiranana
Malawi	6 July 1964	United Kingdom	Hastings Kamuzu Banda
Mozambique	25 June 1975	Portugal	Samora Moises Machel
Swaziland	6 Sept 1968	United Kingdom	King Sobhuza II
Tanzania	9 Dec 1961	United Kingdom	Julius Nyerere
Uganda	9 Oct 1962	United Kingdom	Apollo Milton Obote
Zaïre	30 June 1960	Belgium	Patrice Lumumba
Zambia	24 Oct 1964	United Kingdom	Kenneth Kaunda
Zimbabwe	19 Apr 1980	United Kingdom	Robert Mugabe

Crown The monarch, or monarchy. In Britain, the term is also used to refer collectively to government ministers and their departments. The British monarch retains some powers under the ROYAL PREROGATIVE, but these must be exercised in accordance with ministerial advice.

customary law Traditional rules of social behaviour, often governing marriage and inheritance. These are usually subservient to the constitution of a country, although in some countries of southern Africa customary law has been embodied in the national law and the constitution. However, in most countries there is a move to diminish the influence of customary law.

damages Financial compensation that is awarded by a court to a successful plaintiff in a CIVIL CASE. Sometimes a court may award exemplary damages – designed to punish the defendant as well as to compensate the plaintiff – but, assuming it is possible, damages are usually calculated on the basis of the amount needed to restore the plaintiff to the position in which he or she would have been if the wrong had not been done.

De Klerk, F W (Frederik Willem) (1936-) Deputy president (1994-) and former president of South Africa (1989-94), and leader of the NATIONAL PARTY. A lawyer by profession, he served in the cabinet in several portfolios and was elected president after the resignation of P W BOTHA. Generally regarded as a conservative, he caused surprise when on 2 February 1990 he lifted the 30-year ban on the ANC as well as restrictions on several political parties and organizations, and announced the release of Nelson MANDELA and other political prisoners. He entered into negotiations with the ANC and other parties which led to South Africa's first democratic election in April 1994, in which the National Party won the second largest number of votes. These results qualified De Klerk under the interim constitution to become one of the two deputy presidents.

❖ In 1993, De Klerk and Mandela jointly received the Nobel peace prize.

democracy Rule by the people. Except in very small communities, direct democracy is impossible, so that most countries have a system in which people make their will known through elected representatives. An elected government, however, does not by itself guarantee democracy. Other essential features include PLURALISM, CIVIL RIGHTS and the RULE OF LAW.

❖ The concept of democracy originated in Athens in the 5th century BC. At that time its central doctrine was that every free-born male citizen should participate directly in making laws and decisions, and that this function should not be delegated to others.

Democratic Party Several parties by this name exist. During the ▷APARTHEID era in South Africa, the Democratic Party (a union of the Progressive Federal Party, the Independent Party and the National Democratic Movement) emerged as the strongest parliamentary opposition to the National Party. The DP, which supports free enterprise and human rights, attracted only 1,73 per cent of votes in the 1994 election. In the USA, the Democratic Party is one of the two major political parties. The party evolved between 1812 and 1836 and became the representative of the agricultural southern states. By the 1920s it was also championing the interests of urban dwellers in the north. During Franklin Roosevelt's presidency, (1933-45) a radical programme of economic and social reform consolidated the Democrats' hold on the US electorate. Two Democrats, John Kennedy and Lyndon Johnson, occupied the White House for much of the 1960s, but their backing for civil rights and desegregation legislation alienated supporters in the south. After 1968 the Democrats found it hard to win the presidency, although they maintained their domination of congress. Today the Democratic Party is linked with reform of health care and social services, economic intervention and support for a tax system that places a proportionately greater burden on rich individuals and large corporations. Bill CLINTON, a Democrat, was elected president in 1992.

❖ A cartoonist in the 1870s gave the Democratic Party in the USA its symbol of a donkey.

Deng Xiaoping (1904-) Chinese communist politician who became the effective leader of China in 1978. Originally Deng welcomed foreign investment in China, encouraged his country to open up to the outside world and oversaw a vigorous economic revival. However, China's economic experiment began to go wrong in the mid-1980s. Growing financial hardship, coupled with demands for political reform, culminated in mass protests which led in 1989 to the ▷TIANANMEN SQUARE MASSACRE and a subsequent widespread purge of dissidents. The massacre was sanctioned by Deng – a fact which greatly damaged his international reputation. He retired from his last official position in 1990.

détente Reduction of tension between countries. The term was used especially of the period in the 1970s when the US presidents Richard Nixon and Gerald Ford tried to draw the USSR into a closer relationship with the USA. The last and most fruitful period of détente between the superpowers occurred during Mikhail Gorbachev's presidency of the USSR, which saw disarmament agreements and the end of the ▷COLD WAR. The term was also used for South African prime minister John Vorster's attempts at closer ties with the rest of Africa. (See ▷DÉTENTE in 'Southern African history'.)

devolution Transfer of certain legislative or executive powers from a central to a regional authority. In the late 1970s, Britain's Labour government put forward a plan to create separate assemblies for Scotland and Wales within the United Kingdom, but referendums in the two countries in 1979 failed to endorse the proposals. Devolution re-emerged as an important issue at the British general election of 1992, when both the Labour Party and the Liberal Democratic Party promised to introduce a Scottish parliament.

❖ Northern Ireland was governed by a devolved parliament at Stormont from 1921 to 1972, when direct rule was imposed from Westminster to curb conflict.

Dhlakama, Afonso Mechacho Marisetta (1953-) Mozambican politician, leader of RENAMO. He deserted from the Portuguese Army in 1972 to join FRELIMO in Tanzania, serving with the movement there and in Mozambique until 1977 when, disillusioned, he crossed into what was then Rhodesia (now Zimbabwe) to join Renamo. In 1979 he became president of Renamo, and launched a war against the Frelimo government. After negotiations, he agreed to a ceasefire and elections, but was defeated by Frelimo in Mozambique's 1994 multiparty ballot.

diplomacy Management of international affairs by reconciling differences between countries or by promoting the interests of a particular country. All countries maintain a specialist group of diplomats to represent their interests abroad, but international crises are increasingly influenced and mediated by the intervention of such institutions as the UNITED NATIONS.

Director General In South Africa a senior civil servant who heads a government department and is responsible for the day-to-day planning and administration of that department under the direct supervision of the cabinet minister, to whom he or she is answerable. They are generally required to be experts in their fields and provide advice and information to the cabinet.

disarmament Reduction or elimination of some part of a country's military forces and weapons in an effort to promote peace, save money or reduce tensions. The advent of nuclear weapons caused a growth in support for unilateral disarmament in some countries. However, the main disarmament successes were brought about by multilateral talks and the strategic arms limitation and reduction talks (SALT and START) in the 1970s and early 1990s.

dissolution Process whereby a parliament is ended and a general election called. In democracies, a general election must be held at regular intervals. In many countries the head of government chooses the time of the election – or may be forced into calling one by defeat in parliament.

Dos Santos, José Eduardo (1942-) President of Angola (1979-). He joined the MPLA in 1961 and went into exile, commencing studies as a petroleum engineer in the former Soviet Union in 1963. He served with MPLA forces inside Angola from 1970 to 1974 and, on the assumption of power by the MPLA, became its chairman. He served as Angola's minister of foreign affairs (1975) and was elected president after the death of Agostinho ▷NETO. After a long civil war against UNITA rivals, Dos Santos agreed to a ceasefire in 1991, and UN-supervised elections, which the MPLA won in 1992, confirming Dos Santos as president. He played an important role in negotiating the withdrawal of South African troops from Namibia in the late 1980s.

election The process whereby a government is chosen by the people. Generally, elections take place at regular intervals under the rules of a constitution and allow all adults (usually those over the age of 18) to vote in secret for candidates or political parties. The votes are counted in the presence of the contending parties and the candidates, or parties, with the largest number of votes forming the new government, while those with fewer votes form the opposition. The first fully democratic election in South Africa took place in April 1994, when voters chose between 26 contending parties competing on the basis of a form of PROPORTIONAL REPRESENTATION. National and provincial representatives were elected at the polls.

Elizabeth II Queen of the United Kingdom and symbolic head of the COMMONWEALTH since 1952, when she succeeded her father, George VI. The Queen has certain ROYAL

WORKING DAY *Television has given Britons a new insight into the role played by the Queen in the nation's affairs. The first major royal occasion to be televised was her coronation in 1953.*

PREROGATIVES, which she exercises only on the advice of her ministers. She is briefed weekly by the British prime minister and presides at the opening of Parliament and at meetings of Commonwealth heads of government. She must give the royal assent to ACTS OF PARLIAMENT before they can become law. Elizabeth II heads the Royal House of Windsor, whose members include her husband Prince Philip, Elizabeth, the Queen Mother, her son and heir apparent, Charles, Prince of Wales, and her daughter Anne, the Princess Royal. She has two younger sons, Prince Andrew, and Prince Edward. Charles and Andrew are separated from their wives, Diana, the Princess of Wales, and Sarah, the Duchess of York. Anne is divorced and has remarried. ❖ Prince Philip is the Queen's third cousin.

emergency powers Special powers which are taken by a government to deal with a grave and unforeseen crisis, or state of emergency. In South Africa, numerous national and regional states of emergency were declared in response to popular political resistance against apartheid. The special powers assumed by the government included media censorship, the right to arrest and interrogate any person, the banning of public gatherings and demonstrations, the right to enter and search any premises, and wide indemnity from prosecution for the police and military in applying the emergency regulations, which were condemned by the world.

European Convention on Human Rights Statement of rights drawn up by the COUNCIL OF EUROPE in 1950 and signed by almost all European countries. It came into force in 1953 and includes a code of individual rights, among them freedom of thought and religion. The convention is administered and enforced by the European Commission on Human Rights and a European Court of Human Rights.

European Court of Justice Court based in Luxembourg whose role is to ensure that the law of the EUROPEAN UNION (EU) is implemented and harmonized throughout the EU countries. Actions may be brought to the court by or against member states and it may also be asked to hear cases arising from member states' domestic courts, which must defer to its decisions. The court is made up of 13 judges appointed by the member states for renewable six-year terms. The court issues a single judgment and there is no leave to appeal against sentences.

European Union (EU) Association of western European countries which replaced the European Community (EC) in 1993. A European Parliament, whose members are directly elected every five years in EU countries, is largely a forum of discussion, but it can veto the EU budget. The EU has a secretariat and an administrative corps (the European Commission) in Brussels. The goal of the EU is to promote closer economic and political cooperation between its members and to achieve monetary union by 1999. It had its origins in the 1950s when France, West Germany, Belgium, the Netherlands, Italy and Luxembourg – 'The Six' – formed the European Coal and Steel Community (ECSC), the European Atomic Energy Community (Euratom) and the European Economic Community (EEC). The most important of these, the EEC, was formed in 1957 by the Treaty of Rome with a view to eliminating tariffs and promoting trade between the six members of the 'Common Market'. In the late 1960s it became the European Community. Britain, Ireland and Denmark joined in 1973, Greece in 1981 and Portugal and Spain in 1986. Austria, Finland and Sweden were to become members in 1995, and Norway, Cyprus and Malta have also applied for membership. Several Eastern European countries have associative agreements with the EU, whose other institutions include the COUNCIL OF MINISTERS and the EUROPEAN COURT OF JUSTICE.

executive Branch of government that puts into effect a country's laws. In the USA the executive (the president) is distinct from the legislature (congress) and the judiciary in accordance with the SEPARATION OF POWERS. In South Africa the executive consists of the president and the cabinet. In Britain there is no such separation between the executive and the legislature.

extradition Formal legal proceedings for removing a person from one country to stand trial in another, provided that both countries have signed extradition treaties. It does not usually apply to political offences.

family court Special court in South Africa where intimate and private family disputes, barring divorce, but including abuse of children under the age of 18, are heard and arbitrated in private.

fascism Doctrine that emphasizes the authority of the head of State, treats DEMOCRACY with contempt and advocates NATIONALISM, often expressed in aggressively racist terms, as a way of building national unity. It is linked with extreme right-wing militaristic views and virulent hatred of COMMUNISM, but it has traditionally attracted strong working-class support. Fascism flourished between the two world wars in ▷MUSSOLINI's Italy, ▷HITLER's Germany and ▷FRANCO's Spain. The characteristic fascist institution was the 'corporative state' – so called because the people elected to its governing assembly represented particular institutions and power groups rather than geographical constituencies. After World War II fascism declined, but neofascism sprang up in Germany and elsewhere in the 1990s.

FBI (Federal Bureau of Investigation) Organization created in 1908 as the investigative branch of the US Department of Justice. The FBI, which employs more than 6 000 agents, developed responsibilities for criminal investigations, especially in the politically sensitive fields of organized racketeering, espionage and domestic security.

❖ J Edgar Hoover was director of the FBI from 1924 until he died in 1972. Since Hoover's death it has been revealed that he used his power to make himself invulnerable to political control, and blackmailed presidents and other top politicians with his knowledge of their sexual indiscretions.

federalism System of government in which power is divided between a national (federal) government and various regional governments. Federalism combines the benefits of size for purposes such as defence with those of self-government at local level for functions such as education. The federal system is well developed in countries such as the USA, Germany and Australia.

first past the post Voting system in which the candidate for whom the most votes have been cast is elected, even though he or she may not have won an absolute majority over the other candidates. This system, which was used by South Africa before the 1994 election, has been criticized for its failure to reflect support for minority parties in election results. Another system, used in South Africa in 1994, is PROPORTIONAL REPRESENTATION.

Freedom Front A rightist South African political movement launched in 1993 to campaign for the rights of whites, and led by a former head of the South African Defence Force, General Constand VILJOEN. It broke with other rightist groups to participate in the 1994 elections, winning representation in parliament on the basis of polling 2,2 per cent of the vote as well as dominance of the statutory Volkstaat Raad, a forum for negotiations with the government on the establishment of a white 'homeland' (VOLKSTAAT).

Frelimo (Frente de Libertaçao de Moçambique) Ruling party of Mozambique, which won a majority in the first multiparty election of October 1994. Frelimo was the major liberation movement in the country and fought a long guerrilla war against Portuguese colonial power. It assumed power on the collapse of the Portuguese empire in 1974, but soon faced armed internal resistance from RENAMO and ▷DESTABILIZATION by the South African regime in the 1980s. Originally a Marxist party, which nationalized property and other assets, it has embraced many free-market principles and multiparty democracy.

Gaddafi, Muammar (1942-) Libyan political and military leader who in 1969 helped to overthrow the monarch, King Idris, in a coup d'état. Colonel Gaddafi emerged as the most important figure in the ruling military council. In 1978 he initiated the Revolutionary Committee Movement, which became a vehicle for international political intrigue and terrorism. Gaddafi's association with terrorist incidents and airline hijacking isolated him from the international community in the 1980s. In 1986 the USA retaliated against Libyan terrorism with a series of air raids and an economic blockade of the country. Although Libya has since made efforts to improve relations with the West, Gaddafi is still treated as an international pariah.

FACE OF DEFIANCE *The rugged features of Colonel Gaddafi, Libya's leader since 1969. His persistent support for terrorist groups during the 1980s enraged Western powers.*

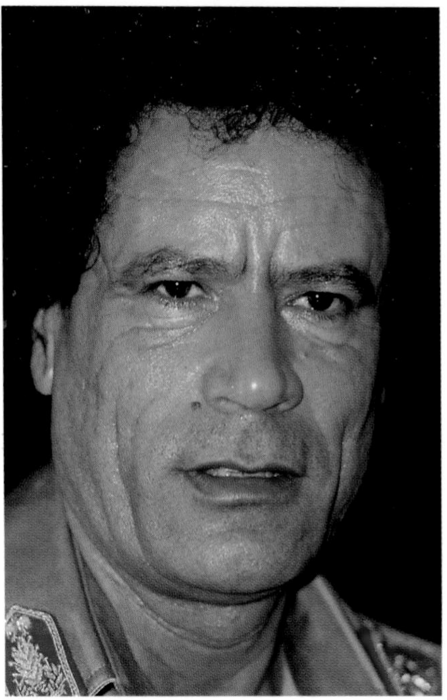

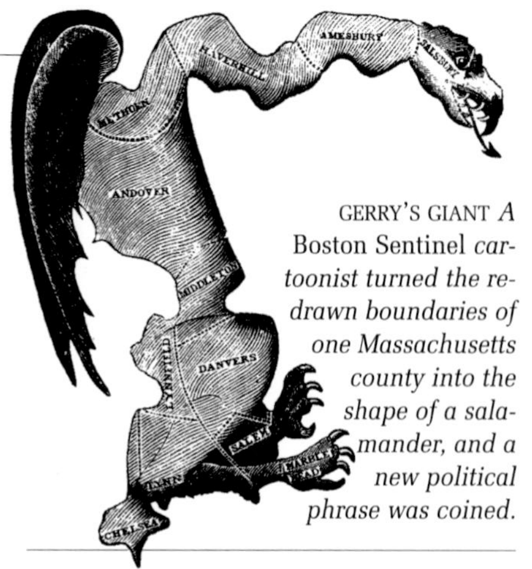

GERRY'S GIANT *A* Boston Sentinel *cartoonist turned the redrawn boundaries of one Massachusetts county into the shape of a salamander, and a new political phrase was coined.*

Gaullism French political movement originated by Charles ▷DE GAULLE during the 1950s. It stands for strong leadership within a highly centralized state. It also attaches great importance to French national independence, and is wary of international movements that might weaken that independence. In 1966 de Gaulle removed France from the unified military structure of NATO, and his followers maintain an ambivalent attitude to closer ties between France and the other members of the EUROPEAN UNION. Gaullism is the inspiration behind the main conservative force in France today, Rassemblement pour la République (RPR), which was founded in 1976 by Jacques CHIRAC (1932-). He succeeded François MITTERRAND as France's president in 1995.

Geneva Convention Series of international agreements on the rules of warfare, signed between 1864 and 1949. All the agreements have tried to lay down minimum standards for the treatment of the wounded and sick, prisoners of war and, more recently, civilians in wartime conditions. From the start, the convention has been linked with the activities of the International Red Cross movement, which works to ensure that the Convention's principles are applied – as does the UNITED NATIONS. The crisis in the former Yugoslavia has led to calls for a new Geneva Convention.

❖ There are now more than 160 signatories to the Geneva Convention. As well as sovereign states, these include such bodies as the Palestine Liberation Organisation.

gerrymandering Drawing up of electoral boundaries deliberately to give an advantage

GOOD OLD DAYS *Mikhail Gorbachev (centre, front) celebrates the 40th anniversary of the German Democratic Republic with East German leader Erich Honecker (right) in 1991.*

to one party. The term originated in the USA in 1812, when Eldridge Gerry, the governor of Massachusetts, divided the state into new electoral districts in a bid to ensure that his supporters were elected. One of the district's was so oddly shaped that it looked like a salamander and so the term 'gerrymander' was coined. Most of the world's democracies have regulations to prevent at least the most blatant forms of gerrymandering.

❖ The NATIONAL PARTY in South Africa was accused of gerrymandering when it used the Delimitation Commission (1947) to weight constituencies, so that urban constituencies, where the party had less support, carried a large number of voters, while rural constituencies, where the party was strong, were much smaller. The move allowed the party for many years after 1948 to govern with a parliamentary majority far greater than its majority of election votes.

Ginwala, Frene Noshir (1932-) Speaker of parliament in South Africa (1994-) and the first woman in the country to hold the position. She is a trained lawyer who previously headed the ANC's research department. She spent 30 years in exile, working as a journalist in East Africa and serving as an ANC official in Tanzania, Zambia, Mozambique and the United Kingdom, where she was a spokesperson on key issues. Ginwala has been influential in the formation of the Women's National Coalition and has put women's issues on the agenda of the ANC, also heading its emancipation commission.

glasnost Policy adopted by Mikhail GORBACHEV of allowing greater intellectual freedom in Soviet society. Gorbachev, who came to power in 1985, introduced both *glasnost* and *perestroika* ('restructuring') – a wide-ranging reform strategy – with the intention of modernizing Soviet society, reviving a collapsing economy and bringing the USSR closer to the West.

❖ Examples of *glasnost* have included the admission of official responsibility for millions of deaths of Soviet citizens during the rule of Joseph Stalin, and the opening of State archives to journalists.

Gorbachev, Mikhail (1931-) Soviet leader who initiated the transformation of the USSR's society and economy as well as its role on the international stage. Gorbachev succeeded Konstantin Chernenko as general secretary of the Communist Party in 1985. Gorbachev became executive president, with increased powers, in 1990. He forged good diplomatic relations with the USA and helped bring about the end of the ARMS RACE. He encouraged greater intellectual freedom and industrial efficiency through the policies of GLASNOST and *perestroika*. His long-term goals were the introduction of freedom of speech and a market economy. During his leadership, many former Soviet satellite countries in eastern Europe, such as Czechoslovakia and Poland, were allowed to dismantle their communist regimes and become democracies. Meanwhile the USSR experienced nationalist conflict within its own borders, resulting in its break-up in 1991 into 15 republics. Gorbachev's radical agenda generated opposition among conservatives and there was an attempted coup d'état in 1991. Although the coup failed, Gorbachev's power was broken and he was forced to hand over control to Boris YELTSIN, who had successfully defeated the coup.

Government of National Unity Coalition of all parties that won significant support in South Africa's 1994 election. It is dominated by the ANC and includes the NATIONAL PARTY and the INKATHA FREEDOM PARTY. Under a pre-election agreement and in terms of the interim CONSTITUTION, parties were granted cabinet portfolios in proportion to their support in the election. The second largest party in the election, the NP, was entitled to nominate one of two executive deputy presidents. The cabinet or government reaches agreement by consensus or, failing that, by simple majority vote in the cabinet. It is due to remain in power until 1999.

governor Chief executive in each of the 50 states of the USA. A governor, who serves for a two or four-year term, has extensive powers, including the right to declare a state of emergency or to call out troops to quell riots. The office of governor, especially in large states such as California, is seen as a useful preparation for the presidency. Of recent presidents, Jimmy Carter, Ronald Reagan and Bill Clinton had all been governors. The title of governor is also given to the CROWN representative in a British dependency such as Hong Kong. By contrast, a governor-general is the Crown representative in certain independent territories within the COMMONWEALTH, such as Australia.

green paper A government document tentatively outlining options for proposed legislation, opening the way for wide consultation and producing a WHITE PAPER.

Greens Name given to political parties which are part of the environmental movement. Most of these parties were formed in the late 1970s and 1980s, when the world became increasingly conscious of the ▷GREENHOUSE EFFECT, ▷ACID RAIN and the destruction of the ▷OZONE LAYER. Green parties have found it easier to make a political impact in countries which operate a system of PROPORTIONAL REPRESENTATION, such as Germany.

❖ Pressure groups such as Greenpeace and

Friends of the Earth have campaigned on a wide range of issues and helped to promote the use of products such as lead-free petrol and ozone-friendly aerosols.

habeas corpus A court order for the release from prison, or other form of detention, of an individual. In practice it requires the person to be presented to the court which has issued the order so that the court can determine whether or not the individual is being wrongly held. In many countries the right to habeas corpus has been curtailed, or suspended, by special security legislation. During the apartheid years, thousands of detainees in South Africa were denied this right, which has since been restored.

Hanekom, Derek André (1953-) Minister of land affairs in South Africa (1994-). A former smallholder in the Magaliesberg near Johannesburg, he served three years in prison for leaking information about South African Defence Force support for the Mozambican rebel movement RENAMO to the ANC. After his release he worked for development projects and was the ANC's spokesperson on agricultural matters.

Hansard The official, usually verbatim, record of proceedings in parliament. The name derives from Luke Hansard, the printer of the HOUSE OF COMMONS in Britain, who began publishing reports of debates in the British parliament in 1812. It has been adopted in the parliaments of many COMMONWEALTH countries, including South Africa. In the USA, the official record of proceedings in both houses of congress is the Congressional Record.

Havel, Václav (1936-) Czech dramatist and politician who was elected president of Czechoslovakia after the overthrow of the Communist Party in 1989. During Czechoslovakia's period of communist rule, he became known as a HUMAN RIGHTS activist. He had been arrested several times and was twice jailed for alleged subversive activities. Following the partition of Czechoslovakia in 1993, he remained president of the Czech Republic, adopting a conciliatory attitude towards Slovak separatists and the communists of the old regime.

head of state Person, usually a monarch or president, who acts as a country's formal or ceremonial head, in contrast with the head of government. Depending on the country's constitution, a head of state may be simply a figurehead or may, like the US and South African presidents, wield executive power.

Herstigte Nasionale Party (Re-established National Party) Far-right South African party founded in 1969 by Albert Hertzog (the son of J B M ▷HERTZOG) and others opposed to certain of the race policies of John ▷VORSTER, including the decision to allow Maori rugby players from New Zealand to tour South Africa. The HNP seeks a return to total ▷APARTHEID and undiluted Afrikaner hegemony, but has never fared well in elections.

House of Commons Lower house of the British parliament which debates government policy, effectively makes all laws and scrutinizes the activities of government. The Commons has 651 members, each representing a single constituency and elected by a FIRST PAST THE POST system for a maximum of five years – although the prime minister may call an election within that period.

House of Lords Unelected upper house of the British parliament, composed of some 775 hereditary peers and 400 life peers, including 19 Law Lords and 26 bishops, which is presided over by the LORD CHANCELLOR. The Lords review and, if necessary, amend legislation sent to them by the House of Commons, but may hold up a law, other than one concerning public funding, only for up to a year. The House of Lords is also the supreme APPEAL COURT in Britain.

House of Representatives Lower house of the US Congress consisting of 435 members directly elected for two-year terms. Its seats are apportioned relative to each state's population. Both the SENATE and the House of Representatives take part in virtually every aspect of policymaking and lawmaking in the USA, but the 'House' – which has more than four times as many members as the senate – tends to be more closely linked with local political concerns.

❖ The coloured house in South Africa's ▷TRICAMERAL PARLIAMENT of the 1980s and early 1990s also went by this name.

human rights Individual rights or freedoms thought to be fundamental to a civilized society. They include freedom of expression, movement and association, implementation of the due process of law, equality before the law, and the right not to be subjected to cruel or degrading punishment. In 1948 the United Nations adopted a Universal Declaration of Human Rights, and in 1950 the EUROPEAN CONVENTION ON HUMAN RIGHTS was signed. Human rights in wartime are covered by the GENEVA CONVENTION. In South Africa, human rights activists were instrumental in opposing ▷APARTHEID and revealing the abuses to which citizens were subject.

hung parliament Parliament in which no single party has an overall majority.

WARRIOR'S GRAVE *The flagship of Greenpeace,* Rainbow Warrior, *sinks with the loss of one crew member after an explosion in Auckland, New Zealand, in 1985. The environmental group had protested against French nuclear tests in the South Pacific. Two detained French agents were returned to France.*

DAYS OF THE RAJ *At the state entry into Delhi of Britain's Viceroy, Lord Curzon, in 1903, Indian splendour combined with imperial might. During these glory days the empire – usually marked in red on maps – embraced a quarter of the world's population and land mass.*

impeachment Process of removing an official such as a president, judge or viceroy from office for serious wrongdoing. In the USA, the procedure requires the HOUSE OF REPRESENTATIVES to submit articles of impeachment (effectively a list of complaints) which are examined by the SENATE. In 1974 the House voted to impeach president Richard Nixon following the ▷WATERGATE affair, but he resigned before the case could be tried by the Senate. Several members of the US federal judiciary have been impeached.

imperialism System of rule by which one country extends its authority over other territories through military force or political and economic control. One of the earliest known empires, extending from Greece to India, was created in the 4th century BC by ▷ALEXANDER THE GREAT. One of the most recent was the Soviet empire, consisting of the 15 republics of the former USSR and its satellite states in eastern Europe, which broke up in 1991. (See also ▷BRITISH EMPIRE and ▷SCRAMBLE FOR AFRICA in 'World history'.)

industrial court In South Africa, a special court which hears cases involving breaches of labour laws and disputes over agreements negotiated between workers and management. The court may hear petitions from individual workers and usually conducts its hearings behind closed doors, although judgments are announced.

Inkatha Freedom Party (IFP) South African political party with strong Zulu links established as the Inkatha National Cultural Liberation Movement in 1975, building on a Zulu cultural organization of the same name founded in the 1920s. Under the leadership of Mangosuthu BUTHELEZI, Inkatha resisted the ▷BANTUSTAN system, but it was also strongly opposed to SANCTIONS and critical of armed struggle. The IFP, which draws almost all of its support from the inhabitants of KwaZulu-Natal, initially opposed the holding of the 1994 election because the interim constitution did not provide for sufficient regional powers. It was, however, persuaded to take part in the poll and drew the third largest number of votes (10,5 per cent) and won the KwaZulu-Natal provincial election. It supports strong regional powers in a federal constitution and champions the cause of a Zulu kingdom and a free-market economy.

interdict (injunction) Court order either obliging or preventing a particular action. An interdict may be sought to ensure that a named individual does not visit another, for example, or that a newspaper does not publish material which might impede a fair trial or which could be defamatory. In urgent cases a temporary interdict may be granted and the final outcome of the case decided at a later hearing. Anyone who fails to abide by an injunction is guilty of CONTEMPT OF COURT.

International Court of Justice Chief judicial body of the UNITED NATIONS, based at The Hague, whose main task is to arbitrate between member countries in international disputes. The court consists of 15 judges elected for nine-year terms by the UN General Assembly and Security Council. All UN members can use the court, but only those which have formally accepted its jurisdiction – wholly or in part – can be sued in it. Britain excludes all disputes involving members of the COMMONWEALTH from the court's jurisdiction. Although the UN cannot enforce a court decision, it often succeeds in influencing public opinion.

❖ The legality of South Africa's jurisdiction in the former South West Africa (Namibia) was the subject of a five-year wrangle in the International Court of Justice in the 1960s. The court's verdict, that it had no power to decide the case, heralded the start of armed resistance by SWAPO.

international law Branch of law that governs relations between countries and their rights and duties with regard to one another. It deals with issues such as HUMAN RIGHTS, the recognition of states and the acquisition of territory. The bodies responsible for administering international law include the UN, the European Commission on Human Rights, the International Labour Organization and the Inter-governmental Maritime Consultative Organization. The usual sources of international law are conventions, treaties and international custom.

interpolation debate A snap debate in the South African Parliament on a matter of immediate and compelling importance. Of short duration, such debates are allowed at the discretion of the SPEAKER, usually at the request of a member of parliament whose party is not in the government.

IRA (Irish Republican Army) Irish republican guerrilla force bent on securing a united Ireland. The IRA was founded in 1919, and in the run-up to the partition of Ireland in 1921 its members killed more than 700 policemen and soldiers. The organization, which consistently refused to accept the existence of a separate Northern Ireland, was outlawed throughout Ireland when it backed Germany in World War II. It then went into decline. Following civil unrest in Northern Ireland in 1969, the IRA divided into 'Official' and 'Provisional' wings. The former declared a unilateral cease-fire in 1972, but the Provisionals, or Provos, emerged as an active terrorist force. The IRA is represented in the political arena by SINN FEIN. Since 1969, more than 3 400 people have died and more than 35 000 have been injured in terrorist activities and sectarian violence involving the IRA and Northern Ireland's LOYALIST groups. On 31 August 1994, the IRA issued a cease-fire statement, a first step towards a settlement.

isolationism Policy of self-sufficiency by which one country deliberately avoids political, diplomatic or military commitments to other countries. When the USA declared its independence in 1776, it hoped to remain a peaceful trading nation independent of European quarrels. Since then, isolationist sentiments have intermittently dominated US foreign policy, but after its reluctant entry into World War II in 1941 the USA was obliged to assume a world role from which it did not retreat once the war was over.

❖ From the 1870s Britain took pride in its foreign policy of 'splendid isolation'. It was based on the unassailable strength of the ▷BRITISH EMPIRE and navy, but was brought to an end when Germany began to build up its navy in the early 20th century.

Judge President In South Africa, the senior judge in a provincial division of the SUPREME COURT who orders the affairs of the bench under his jurisdiction. The Judge President swears in senior public representatives and other judges in the region.

judicial review Process whereby judges scrutinize legislation to see if it accords with the intentions of the lawmaking body or parliament. In the USA, judicial review is a crucial instrument of the SUPREME COURT, which since 1803 has had the power to strike down Acts of Congress which are incompatible with the US constitution. In South Africa, the CONSTITUTIONAL COURT is empowered to perform this function.

Judicial Services Commission A commission of legal specialists in South Africa which performs various services for the government in the administration of justice, including drawing up nominations for judges of the APPEAL COURT and the SUPREME COURT, and some judges of the CONSTITUTIONAL COURT.

Kaunda, Kenneth David (1924-) Former president of Zambia (1964-91). Kaunda was a schoolteacher and welfare officer before entering politics. In 1951, he joined the Northern Rhodesian African National Congress, a 'sister' organization of the ANC in South Africa which was later banned. In 1960 he was elected president of UNIP (United National Independent Party). He became prime minister of Northern Rhodesia in 1964 and the first president of Zambia in the same year. Nationalization and the collapse of the copper price led to grave economic hardship, and domestic and international opposition to his one-party rule led, in 1991, to multiparty elections in which he and his party were ousted from power. After initially withdrawing from politics, Kaunda became active again, accusing his successor, Frederick CHILUBA, of attempting to frustrate his reentry into politics.

Keating, Paul (1944-) Prime minister of Australia from 1991. He has campaigned to transform Australia from a parliamentary monarchy into a republic by the year 2000 and to replace the British monarch – who is also Queen of Australia – with an elected Australian head of state.

❖ Keating caused a stir in 1992 by putting his arm around Queen Elizabeth II at a reception in Canberra. The gesture was seen as an embarrassing breach of protocol.

Knesset Israeli parliament, whose 120 members are elected every four years by a system of PROPORTIONAL REPRESENTATION in a single constituency. This system results in many different parties and coalition governments. Since the 1970s, the religious parties, although winning only a small number of seats, have been able to exert considerable influence over the different governments of Israel.

Kohl, Helmut (1930-) German Christian Democratic politician who was chancellor of the Federal Republic of West Germany (1982-90) and of a united Germany from 1990. Although Kohl has been seen to lack charisma and diplomatic skill, he has proved to be a shrewd political operator. He encouraged the reunification of Germany in 1990 as a long-term policy for his country, although he knew that the aftermath of integration would bring serious economic and political difficulties.

Labour Party Several parties by this name have existed. In South Africa a white Labour Party was part of the ▷PACT GOVERNMENT in the 1920s; while a coloured party by the name was active during the apartheid era. (See ▷LABOUR PARTY in 'Southern African history'.) Britain's Labour Party was founded in 1900 as an alliance of trade unionists and socialist clubs. The Labour Representation Committee, as it was originally called, changed its name to the Labour Party in 1906, when it won 29 seats in the general election, under the leadership of Keir Hardie. By 1922 Labour had replaced the Liberals as the main opposition to the Conservative Party. Ramsay MacDonald formed the first Labour Government in 1924, but the party did not secure an overall majority in the House of Commons until Clement Attlee won the general election of 1945. Attlee's government (1945-51) created the WELFARE STATE and nationalized Britain's major industries. The party formed governments in the 1960s and 1970s under Harold Wilson and James Callaghan. In 1979, increasingly left-wing policies led to a long period of opposition, and in 1981 a group of Labour right-wingers (the 'gang of four') broke away to form the SDP (Social Democratic Party). In 1983 Neil Kinnock took over the leadership from Michael Foot and sought to broaden the party's electoral appeal and abandon some of its more radical policies. After two more election defeats for Labour, Kinnock resigned and John Smith took over. Smith built on the work of Kinnock, moving the party further to the right, but died of a heart attack in 1994. He was succeeded by Tony Blair, a modernizer, also on the right wing of the party.

land rights In many former colonies indigenous populations have campaigned to have their land rights restored. Under segregation policies, blacks in South Africa lost virtually all access to land and millions were forcibly removed from their homes in the NATIONAL PARTY government's pursuit of apartheid. In 1994 a law was passed setting up a land commission and a land claims court for the purposes of restitution and compensation.

Leader of the House Member of the governing party in a chamber of parliament who is responsible for supervising the business of the chamber.

left wing Term usually associated with individuals or parties which represent radical opposition to tradition and the established order, and which seek change in the direction of equality, SOCIALISM or MARXISM. It also distinguishes a shade of opinion within a political party, as in the left wing of the British Conservative Party. (See RIGHT WING.)

Leninism Doctrine associated with ▷LENIN and the Bolshevik faction of the (Marxist) Social Democratic Party in Russia at the end of the 19th century. Lenin's most influential theories concerned the methods by which a Marxist revolution could be achieved and the way in which a Marxist society should be governed. He stressed the importance of a strong central party and the need to reconstruct industry and bring about a cultural revolution. After Lenin's death in 1924, his doctrines were transformed by the dictatorial rule of ▷STALIN. In recent times, Leninism has been used to justify an authoritarian party structure on the grounds that it was necessary for the achievement of a socialist revolution.

Leon, Tony (1956-) Leader of the DEMOCRATIC PARTY (DP) and a member of parliament in South Africa. He practised as a lawyer and started his political career as a city councillor in Johannesburg. A supporter of free enterprise and fundamental human rights, he and other DP leaders played an active role in promoting the ▷MULTIPARTY NEGOTIATIONS that culminated in the first fully democratic election of 1994.

Liberal Democratic Party British political party (1988) formed from a merger between the Liberal Party and the Social Democratic Party with the aim of combining the best elements of LIBERALISM and SOCIAL DEMOCRACY. It is officially named Social and Liberal Democrats. The party won several by-elections under the leadership of Paddy Ashdown but did not achieve similar success in the general election of 1992.

liberalism Doctrine that champions individual freedom and progressive social reforms. Although liberals oppose dogma and too much State intervention, they believe that government should have a major role in regulating capitalism and enhancing social welfare. Elements of liberal tradition have been crucial to the development of democracy.

lobby Group of people representing a particular interest who seek to influence legislation. In the USA, full-time lobbyists are employed to represent to the government the interests of corporate clients or pressure groups, such as a pharmaceutical company or an environmental organization. Other countries have a less structured lobby system. In Britain and South Africa, the term 'lobby' is also used to refer to the political journalists who have access to cabinet ministers and senior civil servants, from whom they acquire confidential information on condition that they are discreet in their disclosures.

local government Government in its local or regional form; in South Africa, it is the third tier of government after the national and provincial levels and having responsibility for the administration of city, town and rural community affairs.

Lord Chancellor Britain's most senior judge, charged with the administration of British courts, and who also acts as SPEAKER of the HOUSE OF LORDS.

loyalist In Northern Ireland, a person loyal to the British Crown in wishing the province to

REDS ON THE MAP *Senator McCarthy indicts the communist influences he claimed to have unearthed. Witnesses at an 'Un-American Activities' probe included stars Danny Kaye, Humphrey Bogart and Lauren Bacall.*

remain part of the United Kingdom. Loyalists are represented in the political arena by the ULSTER UNIONISTS. The term has been devalued by its link with those who are prepared to use terrorism to achieve their ends, including illegal groups such as the Ulster Volunteer Force (UVF) and the Ulster Freedom Fighters (UFF).

Maastricht, Treaty of (1992) Agreement creating the EUROPEAN UNION (EU) signed by the 12 member states of what was formerly called the European Community. One of the principal aims of the treaty was to establish a single European currency and a European central bank by 1999. It also provided for common EU citizenship and the implementation of a common foreign and defence policy. Britain opted out of the treaty's Social Chapter on employment conditions, and secured the right to opt out of a future single currency. Ratification of Maastricht by all 12 members was completed in 1993, after referendums were held in several countries.

❖ The movement towards monetary union suffered a setback in 1993 through the effective collapse of the European exchange rate mechanism (ERM), which was intended to manage exchange rates within the EU.

McCarthyism Arbitrary persecution of alleged communist sympathizers for political or economic gain. The term derives from the activities of the US senator Joseph McCarthy (1909-57), who said in 1950 that he had a list of 205 communists in the STATE DEPARTMENT. Feeding on fears about the Soviet threat, McCarthy quickly gained national publicity for his campaign against subversive influences on the US government. Most of his accusations of communist links were later shown to be false and were generated by a desire for self-aggrandizement. Nevertheless, his inquiries destroyed the careers of individuals in many different walks of American life, including the diplomatic corps, the universities and Hollywood. McCarthy was censured by the senate in 1954.

magistrate The presiding judicial officer in a MAGISTRATE'S COURT. In South Africa, magistrates have limited judicial powers as well as administrative functions in a district, such as performing marriage ceremonies.

magistrate's court A lower court, presided over by a MAGISTRATE, which hears criminal and civil cases. In South Africa, a magistrate may – with the approval of the ATTORNEY GENERAL – refer a case to the SUPREME COURT for trial. The matters which may be heard by a magistrate's court generally involve less serious criminal charges and civil claims not exceeding a set amount. Its judgments may be appealed against and the range of sentences passed are generally less severe than those of higher courts.

Major, John (1943-) British Conservative politician who succeeded Margaret THATCHER as prime minister in 1990. Major's rise to power was swift. In 1987 he was appointed

HIGH FLYER *From a modest home in Brixton, Tory leader John Major rose through the ranks to end up at London's No 10 Downing Street, with his wife Norma.*

chief secretary to the TREASURY in Thatcher's government. He became foreign secretary in 1989 and CHANCELLOR OF THE EXCHEQUER a few months later. In 1992 Major led the Conservatives to a fourth successive election victory, but doubts surfaced about his effectiveness as a leader when divisions opened up in his party over the MAASTRICHT treaty. His Citizen's Charter, an attempt to improve the quality of public services, was criticized for its lack of effectiveness. ▷PRIVATIZATION schemes, so popular under Thatcher, ran into difficulties, and in 1994 his government was shaken by scandals and resignations over sexual and financial affairs.
❖ In 1993, opinion polls showed that Major was the most unpopular British prime minister since such surveys began.

Makwetu, Clarence Mlamli (1928-) Leader of the Pan-Africanist Congress (PAC) in South Africa. He was president of the Pan Africanist Movement, and was elected PAC leader in 1991 and re-elected at the PAC's national congress in 1994. A former political prisoner, he persuaded the PAC to join ▷MULTIPARTY NEGOTIATIONS and to participate in South Africa's first democratic election in 1994. He has attempted to soften the organization's perceived anti-white stance.

Mandela, Nelson Rolihlahla (1918-) President of South Africa (1994-) and leader of the ANC who spent 27 years in prison. Mandela began studies at the University of Fort Hare and completed his BA degree by correspondence in 1941, followed by legal studies at the University of the Witwatersrand. With the former president of the ANC, Oliver ▷TAMBO, he opened the first African legal firm in South Africa in Johannesburg in 1952, by which time he was deeply involved in the ANC, having become a founder, and later (in 1950) national president, of its Youth League and a leader of the ▷DEFIANCE CAMPAIGN of 1952. Mandela was banned under the Suppression of Communism Act in 1952, when he became national deputy president of the ANC. In 1956 he was among 156 people charged with high treason and during the four years of the ▷TREASON TRIAL he undertook much of the defence. When the trial ended in 1961 all the accused were found not guilty. In the ▷RIVONIA TRIAL of 1963 he and eight others were sentenced to life imprisonment. Released from prison in 1990, Mandela led the ANC in ▷MULTIPARTY NEGOTIATIONS with the National Party government which led to agreement on an interim majority rule constitution. In the ensuing 1994 election, the ANC won close to a two-thirds majority and Mandela was inaugurated as president. In 1993 he and F W DE KLERK were awarded the Nobel peace prize.
❖ His autobiography, *Long Walk to Freedom*, was published in 1994.

Mandela, Nomzamo Zaniewe Winifred (1934-) Former deputy minister of arts, culture, science and technology in South Africa and estranged wife of President Nelson Mandela. A social worker, Mandela married the ANC leader in 1958 and during his imprisonment was severely harassed by the government, being banned repeatedly and banished to Brandfort in the Free State in the late 1970s. Her defiance of the government won her international admiration, but she later became a divisive figure in the ANC when representatives of COSATU and the ▷UNITED DEMOCRATIC FRONT accused her of involvement in the kidnapping and murder of a young activist, Stompie Seipei, in 1989. Mandela was acquitted of involvement in the murder, but convicted of being an accessory to the boy's kidnapping. She has built a significant support base in the poverty-stricken, strife-torn townships of the East Rand but her fortunes within the ANC have been mixed since the kidnapping trial and she has faced accusations of undemocratic tendencies. She holds office in the ANC Women's League, SANCO and the Congress of Traditional Leaders. In April 1995 she was dismissed from her cabinet post by President Mandela.
❖ Mandela's international popularity waned after she defiantly declared in April 1986 that the liberation movement, with the aid of 'sticks', 'matches' and 'necklaces', would free South Africa. Many alleged police informers were executed with the notorious 'necklace' (burning car tyre) during the 1980s.

Maoism Doctrines associated with the revolutionary communist leadership of ▷MAO ZEDONG in China. Maoism is characterized by a belief in the need for continuous revolution and a rejection of the Marxist assumption

CLENCHED FIST *The stern resolve which enabled Nelson Mandela to conduct his own defence in the* Treason Trial *and, later, survive 27 years in jail was still much in evidence on his release.*

that socialism can occur only after a capitalist society has been established. It has particular appeal for revolutionary movements in developing countries because it argues that revolution can be achieved without an industrial working class or 'proletariat'.

martial law Rule by military authorities imposed on a population in wartime or when the civilian authority is considered to be working inadequately. Martial law is distinct from military law, which covers the rules pertaining to the discipline and administration of the armed forces.

Marxism Political and economic theories, based on the writings of Karl ▷MARX and Friedrich ▷ENGELS, which are principally concerned with the establishment of a communist state. At the root of Marxism is the concept of class struggle between those who control the means of production (the 'bourgeoisie') and those who are exploited in the economic system (the 'proletariat'). Marx and Engels believed that the abolition of private property was a necessary prelude to the achievement of equality. They wrote about how the inequities of capitalism would be overcome and replaced by a 'dictatorship of the proletariat', leading to SOCIALISM and then to COMMUNISM – an idea later developed by ▷LENIN. Marxism has been interpreted and expounded by many theorists, so while the writings of Marx and Engels still constitute a core of Marxist thought, they no longer entirely define Marxism. Its practical application by governments committed to Marxism, notably the former USSR, has added further dimensions to its interpretation.

❖ Marx believed that, in a fully developed communist state, goods would be distributed 'from each according to his ability, to each according to his needs'.

Masire, Quett Ketumile Joni (1925-) President of Botswana (1980-). A former journalist and founder member of the Botswana Democratic Party, he was elected prime minister in the pre-independence legislative assembly in 1965 and joined the Botswana delegation at independence talks in London in 1966. After independence he served almost continuously in the cabinet, in various portfolios, including finance, and was elected president after the death of Sir Seretse ▷KHAMA. Masire supports free enterprise and multiparty democracy.

mass mobilization A term used in South Africa and some other countries for the organization of large demonstrations and protests, and 'mass action', including strikes and marches.

Mbeki, Thabo Mvuyelwa (1942-) Deputy president of South Africa (1994-) and chairman of the ANC. He went into exile in 1961 and obtained a master's degree in economics from Sussex University in England, before undergoing military training in the USSR. While in exile he was a close advisor to former ANC president Oliver ▷TAMBO, represented the ANC in London and at its African headquarters in Lusaka, and served as head of the organization's international and information departments before returning to South Africa in 1990. He was closely involved in all negotiations leading to the country's first democratic election in 1994.

MEC (member of the executive committee) In South Africa, a member of a provincial cabinet or executive committee, charged with specific powers, responsibilities and functions of government as devolved to the nine provinces under the interim constitution.

Meyer, Roelf (Roelof Petrus) (1947-) South African politician, lawyer and businessman. He won election to parliament in 1979, becoming deputy minister of law and order in 1986. After the unbanning of the ANC and the release from prison of Nelson Mandela and other political prisoners, Meyer emerged as the National Party's chief negotiator at multiparty talks, championing the interim constitution. He was appointed minister of provincial affairs and constitutional development in the GOVERNMENT OF NATIONAL UNITY.

minister of state Assistant to a senior minister in the British government, who is not head of a department nor, usually, a member of the cabinet.

Minister of the Crown Senior minister in the British government who is usually in the cabinet. Ministers of the Crown, of whom there are about 20, are chosen by the prime minister but appointed by the monarch. More than a dozen of them hold the position of SECRETARY OF STATE in the most important government departments.

Mitterrand, François (1916-) French socialist politician who was elected president of France in 1981, defeating Valéry Giscard d'Estaing. Mitterrand introduced a number of radical economic and political reforms, including nationalization and decentralization measures, but he had to modify his programme in 1983 because of worsening economic conditions. In 1986 the socialists lost their majority in the national assembly, forcing Mitterrand to accept a period of 'cohabitation', when the left-wing president had to work with a right-wing majority in the assembly led by Jacques CHIRAC. Mitterrand was re-elected president in 1988. Throughout his term of office he sought to combine support for European integration with mildly reformist social policies. From 1993 the right wing again had a majority in the assembly, and Mitterrand had to work with the Gaullist prime minister, Edouard Balladur. Plagued by ill health, Mitterrand did not stand for re-election in 1995, when he was succeeded by Chirac.

WILY LEADER *François Mitterrand doggedly pursued European unity and socialist reform during his 14 years as French president.*

Mobutu Sésé Seko (1930-) President of Zaire (1970-) and reportedly one of Africa's richest autocrats. Mobutu was appointed deputy minister of defence by prime minister Patrice ▷LUMUMBA at independence in June 1960. Within months he staged his first coup, with American backing, declaring Lumumba and President Joseph Kasavubu 'neutralized' and installing an interim government with himself and other officials as the powers behind the scenes. He put down resistance in the Katanga province and a national Lumumbist insurrection with the help of international mercernaries and finally ousted Kasavubu. Mobutu was elected president unopposed in 1970, 1977 and 1984, and his regime has been bolstered by external patrons. In 1990 he lifted a 20-year ban on opposition parties. A transitional parliament elected a new prime minister, Kengo Wa Dondo, in 1994.

❖ In personalizing the state Zaire, Mobutu adopted grand titles and extravagant praise-names such as 'guide of the revolution', 'helmsman', *'mulopwe'* ('emperor' or 'god-king') and even 'messiah'.

Modise, Joe (Johannes) (1929-) Minister of defence in South Africa (1994-) and former commander of the ANC's armed wing, UMKHONTO WE SIZWE (MK), since 1965. His early political activities included resisting the Sophiatown removals and he was also one of the 156 accused in the ▷TREASON TRIAL of the 1950s. Modise received military training in Czechoslovakia and the USSR. He was involved in the planning and execution of MK operations, such as the joint manoeuvres with Joshua Nkomo's Zipra guerrillas during the Wanki Campaign of 1966 in what was then Rhodesia (now Zimbabwe) and implementing the strategy of 'armed propaganda' in South Africa after 1976.

Moi, Daniel arap (1924-) President of Kenya (1978-). Moi, the successor to Jomo ▷KENYATTA, adopted an increasingly hard line towards political opposition. Domestic unrest and pressure from donors of foreign aid eventually forced him to hold multiparty elections in 1992, which he won against a fragmented opposition.

monarchy Two forms of monarchy exist, absolute monarchy and constitutional monarchy. In the absolute form, the monarch wields power without constitutional controls. In constitutional monarchies, the monarch is the titular and ceremonial head of state with powers that are limited and defined by the country's constitution.
❖ The few remaining absolute monarchies include the Gulf states of Oman and Qatar.

MPLA (Movimento Popular de Libertaçao de Angola) The Angolan political party and liberation movement which waged a lengthy war against Portuguese colonialism and, in 1974, after the collapse of the Portuguese empire, unilaterally assumed power. With support from the former Soviet Union and the backing of Cuban troops, it became embroiled in a civil war against UNITA, which received assistance from the USA and South Africa. Following a ceasefire, United Nations-supervised elections took place in 1992 and the MPLA won a convincing victory. It has renounced many of its Marxist policies and has actively sought the support of the USA and other Western countries.

Mugabe, Robert Gabriel (1925-) First democratically elected prime minister of Zimbabwe (1980) who became president in 1987. Before independence, Mugabe spent 10 years in detention for resistance activities (1964-74) and then fought the liberation war from Mozambique. In 1988, after the merger of the two leading political parties, ZANU and ZAPU, Zimbabwe effectively became a one-party state under Mugabe's leadership. He was a driving force, with Sir Seretse ▷KHAMA, in the Southern African Development Coordinating Conference (later re-established as the SADC) to reduce the dependence of southern African states on South Africa.

Muluzi, Bakili (1943-) President of Malawi (1994-) and leader of the United Democratic Front, a coalition of five political parties. Muluzi, a tobacco farmer and businessman, began his political career in the Malawi Congress Party of former president Hastings BANDA. He became its secretary general, but resigned in 1982 and began campaigning for a multiparty democracy. An outspoken critic of Banda's administration, he won 84 of 177 seats in the national assembly in Malawi's first multiparty elections in 1994 and formed a coalition government with a strong emphasis on rural economic upliftment and the promotion of human rights.

Naidoo, Jay (1954-) Minister without portfolio responsible for implementing the RDP in South Africa. Naidoo stood for parliament in 1994 after more than a decade in the trade union movement and heading the powerful trade union federation COSATU. When he laid down the post of general secretary, COSATU, with 1,3 million members, was the fastest-growing federation in the world. Under his leadership, COSATU's political role deepened and it also became a major player in the National Economic Forum (now ▷NEDLAC).

national assembly The larger of the two chambers of the South African parliament, the other being the SENATE. The 1994 interim constitution provided for 400 members of the national assembly (MPs) to be elected according to a form of PROPORTIONAL REPRESENTATION based on party lists. The assembly debates and votes on all legislation and decisions are reached by majority vote. The presiding officer is the SPEAKER, with a Deputy Speaker, and members fall under the disciplinary control of party WHIPS.

nationalism Sense of belonging to a specific nation, or a particular community, distinguished from other countries or groups by such factors as a common language, religion, historical tradition and the occupation of a clearly defined geographical region. Nationalism has its origins in the collapse of feudalism in western Europe. However, it adopted a coherent form only during the French Revolution, spreading through Europe in the 19th century, and through Africa and Asia in the 20th, to become one of the most potent political forces of modern times. Nationalism has often been used by rulers to direct opposition towards 'foreign' threats. Although it was tarnished in the early 20th century by its links with ▷NAZISM and FASCISM, nationalism has undergone a revival in recent years, exemplified most dramatically in the break-up of the former USSR. Unresolved nationalist tensions were exposed by the GLASNOST policy. (See also AFRIKANER NATIONALISM.)

National Party Former ruling party of South Africa, and after the 1994 election the second largest party in the GOVERNMENT OF NATIONAL UNITY. After its victory in the 1948 whites-only general election, the NP launched its policy of ▷APARTHEID, an extreme form of racial segregation, introducing complex legislation to separate the country's citizens along racial lines and to promote the interests of whites, especially Afrikaner nationalists. Under pressure from the international community, including sanctions and embargoes, and internal pressure and unrest, the party began a slow process of reform, culminating in the formal abandonment of apartheid and the acceptance of majority rule. In the country's first democratic election held in 1994, it polled 20,4 per cent of the vote, and won the majority in the PROVINCIAL PARLIAMENT of the Western Cape. It supports free-market principles and the federal devolution of powers. (See also ▷NATIONAL PARTY in 'Southern African history'.)
❖ The party opened its membership to all races in October 1990, and has built up significant support among coloured voters in the Western Cape – a factor in its victory in the region in 1994.

NATO (North Atlantic Treaty Organization) International defence organization founded in 1949 in response to the expansion of Soviet influence in Eastern Europe and to the Soviet blockade of Berlin (1948-9). During the ▷COLD WAR, NATO provided the countries of western Europe and North America with a defence umbrella against aggression from the Soviet bloc. The understanding that an attack on any member of NATO was an attack on the whole organization meant that the USA would come to the aid of its allies, if necessary with nuclear weapons. However, differences of opinion over nuclear strategy between the USA and the European members, and the end of the Cold War in 1990, encouraged NATO to re-examine its role in the world and consider transforming itself from a military to a political organization devoted to the promotion of European stability.
❖ The formation of NATO led to the Soviet bloc countries signing the ▷WARSAW PACT in 1955. In the early 1990s, after the collapse of communism in eastern Europe, some former republics of the USSR, which had previously been allied to the Warsaw Pact, applied to join NATO.

NAZI TWIST *Fans and members of the British neo-Nazi rock band 'Screwdriver' at a secret concert in London, one of the European centres affected by a resurgence of fascism.*

natural rights Rights which are rooted in the concept of fair play and safeguarded by natural law, a moral code thought to derive from an instinctive sense of right and wrong which underlies all law. The concept originated with the ancient Greek philosophers and permeates the concept of natural justice. Natural justice assumes, among other things, that an accused person is entitled to a court hearing, that a judgment cannot stand unless the accused was given a fair chance to state his or her case and to answer the other side's case, and that a judgment is invalid if it was made by a person with a financial or other interest in the outcome.

neo-Nazism Political ideology originating from, and sympathetic to, the policies and practices of the National Socialist (Nazi) party in Germany from 1932 to the end of World War II in 1945, and especially its veneration of Aryan racial purity.

New Right Name given to a broad movement in the 1970s and 1980s which stressed the benefits of ▷MONETARISM and free-market solutions to economic problems. The New Right sought to promote individual freedoms and in some cases placed a strong emphasis on traditional religious and moral values. Although New Right influences permeated many parts of the developed world, the movement was particularly linked with the governments of Ronald REAGAN and Margaret THATCHER. In Britain, Thatcher's government represented a sharp break with earlier traditions of conservatism. For example, it adopted a radical approach to the public sector with its vigorous policy of ▷PRIVATIZATION.

Nkomo, Joshua Mquabuko Nyongdo (1917-) Vice-president of Zimbabwe (1990-). Nkomo was elected president-general of the Rhodesian African National Congress in 1957 and president of the Zimbabwe African People's Union in 1961. As a black nationalist leader, he was under almost continuous banishment or imprisonment from 1963 to 1974, and became joint leader with Robert MUGABE of the Patriotic Front in 1976. At the conclusion of the ▷RHODESIAN WAR he returned to Zimbabwe, but was defeated by Mugabe in the country's first democratic election in 1980. He was appointed to several cabinet portfolios before becoming vice-president.

Nujoma, Sam (Shaffishuna Samuel) (1929-) President of Namibia (1990-) and founder and president of SWAPO (1957). In the face of South Africa's refusal to give up jurisdiction of ▷SOUTH WEST AFRICA, he went into exile in 1960 and set up a SWAPO exile headquarters in Dar-es-Salaam. On his return to South West Africa in 1966 he was arrested and deported. He resorted to armed resistance and a lengthy 'bush war' ensued from Angolan bases, ending with a South African agreement to accept Namibia's independence. Nujoma returned to his country in 1989, winning the first democratic election in 1990. He was returned with an increased majority in the December 1994 election.

OAS (Organization of American States) Association created in 1948 to provide mutual defence and assistance for the countries of North, Central and South America. The USA saw the OAS as a bulwark against communist threats in the Americas, while the Latin American countries were more concerned with economic and social issues. Although its international influence declined in the 1980s, the OAS, which has more than 30 members, remains a useful forum for the discussion of problems such as drug trafficking.

OAU (Organization of African Unity) Association of African countries established in 1963 to promote African unity and solidarity, to coordinate political, economic, defence and social policies, and to eliminate colonialism in Africa. The OAU, which now has 53 members, has its administrative headquarters in Addis Ababa, Ethiopia. The chairman is elected annually, normally the head of state from the country hosting the annual conference, which takes place in a different country every year. Its secretary general is Salim Ahmed Salim of Tanzania. After introducing democracy in 1994, South Africa could at last join the OAU.

Official Secrets Act A law aimed at safeguarding matters which the State has classified as secret, and frequently including matters of a military or strategically important nature. In many countries such legislation has been used to protect the State from the scrutiny of its critics, and of the media, or to avoid embarrassing disclosures. Many countries, including South Africa, are reviewing such laws to improve parliamentary supervision; in the West this was prompted by the end of the Cold War.

oligarchy Greek word, meaning rule by the few, used to denote a small, unrepresentative faction, or a country governed by such a group. The Greek philosophers ▷PLATO and ▷ARISTOTLE used the term as a contrast to monarchy, the rule of one, and democracy, the rule of the people. Both saw oligarchy as a degenerate form of aristocracy, the rule of the best. Recent oligarchies have included the Philippines under Marcos and Romania under ▷CEAUSESCU. White minority governments in the former Rhodesia (Zimbabwe) and South Africa were also oligarchies.

opinion polls George Gallup first developed sampling techniques in the USA during the 1930s. They are now a staple part of any election and are often commissioned by newspapers and television as part of their coverage of current events – although they have often given rise to a number of objections. The way in which poll questions are worded, for example, can have an important effect on the responses they produce. Poll results may influence voters and they have often been inaccurate. In some countries, such as France, surveys are banned in the final stages of an election. South Africa also took this step in the run-up to the 1994 election.

opposition Political party or organized group opposed to the government in power. In Westminster-style parliaments the term – which originated in the late 18th century – is traditionally used to refer to the second largest party in the lower house, whose duty is to challenge the party in power and to make preparations to form its own government should the opportunity arise.

PAC (Pan-Africanist Congress of Azania) South African liberation movement formed in 1959 when a group within the ANC broke away in protest against the growing influence of whites and of the Communist Party in the organization. It mounted a national campaign against the pass laws, culminating in the ▷SHARPEVILLE SHOOTINGS of 1960, after which it was banned along with other liberation movements. Beset by schisms while in exile, and by a lack of funds, the PAC reached agreement on participation in ▷MULTIPARTY NEGOTIATIONS and the 1994 election but drew little support (1,25 per cent of the vote). Its electoral failure was widely ascribed to its antiwhite slogans and the pursuit of socialist economic policies. (See also ▷PAC in 'Southern African history'.)

pacifism Opposition to all war, as a matter of principle. Pacifists believe that individuals should refuse to fight in national wars, even if conscripted. There is a strong religious aspect to pacifism and some sects, notably the Quakers, have made it a part of their faith.

Paisley, Ian (1926-) Northern Irish Protestant minister and fiery ULSTER UNIONIST politician. Paisley, a charismatic demagogue, has been leader of the Democratic Unionists since he helped to found the party in 1972. He has resolutely opposed all initiatives to involve the government of the Irish Republic in the affairs of Northern Ireland.

parliament An assembly where the laws of a country are made. Parliaments generally draw up their own rules of procedure and are sovereign bodies subject only to the limitations placed on their power by the constitution. Under the interim constitution in South Africa parliament is composed of two chambers: the NATIONAL ASSEMBLY, presided over by the SPEAKER, and the SENATE, presided over by the president of the senate. Legislation may be introduced in either chamber, but both must approve a measure before it can become law and differences must be resolved by a committee of both houses. (See also PROVINCIAL PARLIAMENTS.)

parliamentary privilege Special privileges and freedoms enjoyed by members of parliament, including immunity from legal proceedings over their actions, statements or decisions in parliament.

parliamentary standing committee A group of MPs, broadly representative of all parties in proportion to their representation in parliament, which considers legislation on a clause by clause basis, making any necessary amendments before referring it to parliament for further debate and voting. Different standing committees exist for many of the ongoing functions of government and committee members usually have applicable expertise or interest. The committees may call for expert evidence and advice. A parliamentary select committee may be appointed to investigate and report on a specific matter.

PLO (Palestine Liberation Organization) Body founded in 1964 to act as a focus for the rights of Palestinians displaced by the creation of Israel in 1948. It consists of several distinct groupings and has been dominated since the late 1960s by Yasser ARAFAT. The PLO resorted to guerrilla activity and terrorism for a time, but from the 1980s there was an increasing emphasis on diplomatic activity. Following the PLO's renunciation of violence, talks culminated in 1993 in the signing of an agreement in terms of which Israel granted limited self-rule to Palestinians in the Gaza Strip and Jericho.

pluralism Dispersal of political power among a wide variety of groups, such as trade unions, employers' associations and religious, ethnic, cultural and regional minorities, as well as political parties. Pluralists argue that public policy should emerge as a result of discussion between all interested groups. (See also ▷PLURALISM in 'Ideas, beliefs and religion'.)

police force Individuals authorized, and required, to uphold the law, investigate crimes and apprehend offenders. In the negotiations leading to democratic rule in South Africa it was agreed that each of the nine provinces would have some control over police within its area, sharing power with a national commissioner of police who also plays a coordinating role.

Pol Pot (1925-) Cambodian leader of the pro-Chinese communist Khmer Rouge movement from 1963. After becoming prime minister in 1976, Pol Pot set up a dictatorial regime which perpetrated one of the worst campaigns of mass murder in history: at least 2,5 million people – about one in three of the entire population – were killed. Many thousands of others were forced to move out of the towns to worksites in the countryside. Pol Pot was overthrown in a Vietnamese-backed coup in 1979 and resumed guerrilla warfare. The Khmer Rouge enjoyed a resurgence in the 1990s and agitated for a share in the Cambodian government.

precedent Previous ruling by a court that influences the decision in a case where the issues are similar. The rules of precedent in the English COMMON LAW system have become increasingly strict since the 19th century and require that, with a few exceptions, courts must follow their previous decisions and those of the courts above them in the hierarchy. The system has influenced South Africa's ROMAN-DUTCH LAW.

premier Another title for prime minister. In South Africa the premier is the senior politician in each of the nine provinces, who is elected by the members of the PROVINCIAL PARLIAMENT and appoints members of the executive committee, or provincial cabinet. He, or she, presides over meetings of the executive committee and also has ceremonial powers and functions.

president The head of state and of government in a republic, who is either directly elected by voters or elected by parliament. Some are assisted by one or more executive deputy presidents. South Africa has two deputy presidents, who are also members of the cabinet. Under the interim constitution's provisions the deputy presidents are elected by parliament and have powers and responsibilities delegated to them by the president, for whom they also deputize.

prime minister The senior minister normally of the largest party in a British-style parliamentary system, but sometimes also in republics where the president has only ceremonial functions. Prime ministers appoint members of the cabinet and preside over cabinet meetings. The prime minister is a constitutional link between the government and the head of state.

prison Secure institutions where offenders are incarcerated, or where persons awaiting trial sometimes are accommodated. Generally, long-term prisoners are housed in prisons with high security. The most secure South African prisons are on Robben Island, where Nelson MANDELA and many other political prisoners served life sentences, and Pretoria Central, where some political prisoners were held and where executions of condemned prisoners took place.

MEDIUM AS MESSAGE *A child's last crust of bread was one of the propaganda images used in Germany during the Nazis' rise to power. In America the shadow of the swastika was invoked to aid the war effort. During the Cultural Revolution of China in 1966, everyone had to carry a* 'Little Red Book'.

private member's motion In the South African Parliament, a motion proposed by an ordinary MP, as opposed to a member of the cabinet. Although debated and voted on, it does not have legal or constitutional standing but is a vehicle for expressing the sentiments of MPs on a particular issue. Former opposition MP Alf Widman for years tried to get parliament to pass his anti-smoking bill.

Privy Council Group of some 400 senior British politicians, lawyers and bishops who rarely meet as a body. The Privy Council, which has its roots in the 14th century, was originally the executive through which the monarch ruled, but this role was superseded in the 18th century by the cabinet, and the council's status is now largely formal. The Privy Council's remaining duties are carried out by a small inner group which, among other functions, meets to issue proclamations and orders in council. These may be made under the ROYAL PREROGATIVE, such as an order declaring war, or to implement legislation passed by parliament. The Privy Council operates with several standing committees, including the judicial committee, which is the supreme appeal court for some Commonwealth countries.

propaganda Information systematically produced and disseminated to influence public opinion by changing values and attitudes, with little regard to whether it distorts the truth. Interest in political propaganda grew in the period 1919-39, when the fascist movements of Italy and Germany manipulated symbols and arguments to promote their cause. Mass media such as newspapers and television can greatly enhance the influence and impact of propaganda.

❖ During the apartheid era, the South African government waged a pro-apartheid and anti-communist propaganda campaign. The use of taxpayers' money for this purpose led to the ▷INFORMATION SCANDAL in the 1970s.

proportional representation (PR) Electoral system which aims to reflect accurately all shades of political opinion in an elected assembly. One form of PR is the party list system, in which seats are given to each party in proportion to the number of votes they have won nationally. It is used by many European nations, including Germany and Italy. Under the single transferable vote system – used by, for example, the Irish Republic – voters rank candidates in order of preference. Once a candidate has enough votes to be elected, extra votes for that candidate are redistributed among other candidates according to the voters' second preferences, and so on. PR has been adopted by most democracies, but not by Britain, which favours the FIRST PAST THE POST system. The party list form of PR was introduced in South Africa with the first democratic election in 1994. All parties produced lists of candidates from which MPs were chosen, starting at the top.

prosecutor State law official who is authorized to represent the State in criminal, and some civil, cases. In South Africa prosecutors are briefed by the ATTORNEY GENERAL in the region in which they serve to put the State's case against accused persons in magistrate's courts and the supreme court.

provincial parliaments In South Africa, the nine regional legislatures which form part of the federal structure under the constitution. They govern their own region and executive power is vested in an executive committee appointed by a PREMIER. The premier is elected by the provincial parliament.

Public Protector A State official in South Africa who has wide powers to investigate complaints which have been submitted by the public against a State department or official. The Public Protector has the power to order the department or official to correct what are deemed to have been mistakes and to provide relief in instances where the petitioner has been unfairly or unjustly treated.

question time A regular time set aside in parliament during which members of the cabinet are called on to answer questions put to them by MPs. Notice of the questions is usually required and, while the answers are often drawn up by civil servants, the minister may be called on to answer a supplementary question. In South Africa some ANC MPs have tried to relieve President Mandela of his obligations to question time.

Ramaphosa, Cyril Malamela (1952-) Chairman of South Africa's CONSTITUTIONAL ASSEMBLY and secretary-general of the ANC. Ramaphosa became active in the ▷BLACK CONSCIOUSNESS MOVEMENT while a law student, and was held in detention as an office-bearer of the Black People's Convention. He became a skilled trade union organizer and negotiator, rising to the position of secretary-general of the National Union of Mineworkers. He organized a national miners' strike and persuaded the NUM to join forces with COSATU, thus abandoning his black consciousness roots. He was a key figure in forging the alliance between the ANC, COSATU and the SOUTH AFRICAN COMMUNIST PARTY and was also the ANC's key negotiator in the ▷MULTIPARTY NEGOTIATIONS which produced an interim constitution that led to the first democratic election in 1994.

ratification Formal approval of a treaty by a parliament or another legislative body. Sometimes ratification may depend on the outcome of a REFERENDUM.

RDP (Reconstruction and Development Programme) Government programme of economic development in South Africa which aims to meet basic needs, develop human resources, build the economy and democratize the State and society. The RDP originated in the ranks of the ANC, COSATU, the SOUTH AFRICAN COMMUNIST PARTY and the South African National Civic Organization. It was the ANC's main platform during the 1994 election and is supported by civil society.

Reagan, Ronald (1911-) Republican president of the USA from 1981 to 1989. He cut taxes and spent heavily on defence, which caused a rapid growth in the national debt. He sent troops into Grenada to suppress a revolution, provided aid for the Contra rebels in Nicaragua and ordered the bombing of Libya in retaliation for acts of terrorism against Americans. A leading figure of the NEW RIGHT, Reagan maintained a close relationship with the British prime minister, Margaret THATCHER. In spite of his support for the defence programme known as STAR WARS, he agreed to a series of arms reductions with the Soviet president, Mikhail GORBACHEV. The Reagan administration pursued a policy of 'constructive engagement' with South Africa, not aligning itself with apartheid but maintaining relations in a manner that would not allow the country to be 'destabilized' by communist forces. The term was coined by the Assistant Secretary of State for Africa, Chester Crocker, who claimed that it was not America's task to 'choose between black and white' but to actively defend Western interests. Reagan survived an assassination attempt in 1981.

❖ The fact that no disaster or scandal, such as the ▷IRAN-CONTRA AFFAIR, seemed to 'stick' to Reagan, or to dent his immense personal popularity, led some critics to label him 'the Teflon president'.

referendum Direct popular vote on an issue of public concern. Referendums have been much used in Switzerland and in the USA. Three landmark referendums were held in South Africa in 1961, 1983 and 1992 to test public support respectively for a republic, for the extension of the franchise to coloureds and Indians, and for a reform process leading to majority rule.

regional courts Intermediary courts in South Africa, which can hear more serious cases and impose heavier sentences than MAGISTRATE'S COURTS but not more than the SUPREME COURT may hear or impose. They tend to deal more with criminal offences.

remand Detention of an accused person awaiting trial. A person who is to be remanded for more than a specified number of days – varying according to the circumstances – must normally be freed on BAIL. Under certain special circumstances an accused could be denied access to bail.

STAR PERFORMER *Ronald Reagan, a former actor, was the oldest ever US president, leaving office at 77. Wounded in an assassination bid in 1981 he told his wife Nancy: 'Honey, I forgot to duck.'*

Renamo Nickname of the Mozambique National Resistance Movement. Former rebel movement which was formed in the mid-1970s and given financial and military assistance by the white regime in the former Rhodesia (now Zimbabwe) with the object of harassing its guerrilla opponents based in Mozambique. After the collapse of white rule in Zimbabwe in 1980, the National Party Government in South Africa took over the arming and training of Renamo with the object of destabilizing Mozambique, and Renamo's war against the FRELIMO Government intensified. After peace talks with Frelimo and the cutting off of South African support in 1990, Renamo agreed to a ceasefire and multiparty elections, in which it was defeated but demonstrated significant support.

Republican Party One of the two major political parties in the USA. It was established in the 1850s to oppose slavery. The party's first great leader was Abraham ▷LINCOLN, who was president from 1861 to 1865. The party dominated the US Government between 1860 and 1933, with prominent leaders such as Lincoln, Theodore Roosevelt (president 1901-09) and Herbert Hoover (1929-33). Recent Republican presidents have included Richard Nixon (1969-74) and Ronald Reagan (1981-9). Guided by a commitment to individualism and free enterprise, the Republican philosophy is RIGHT WING by comparison with that of the rival DEMOCRATIC PARTY. Republicans generally believe that economic and political stability can best be achieved by minimal federal government intervention.

❖ The symbol of the Republican Party is an elephant. It was devised in the 1870s by the cartoonist Thomas Nast, who was also responsible for the Democratic Party's donkey symbol. Nast based his creations on characters from Aesop's *Fables*.

right wing Term that has no absolute definition but has come to be linked with the forces of traditional authority and with the defence of privilege and the status quo. In Western democracies, right-wingers give a higher priority to economic than to social policies, seeking to cut taxes and reduce public spending, except on defence. More generally, right-wingers tend to oppose social and political change unless it represents a return to what is perceived as a rosier past. In Russia, for example, the term right wing has been used to denote communists who oppose the liberalization of society and desire a return to the certainties of the former Soviet system.

❖ The terms 'right wing' and 'left wing' first came into use during the ▷FRENCH REVOLUTION, when those who supported the king took their places on the right in the Estates-

General (French parliament) and their opponents sat on the left.

❖ In South Africa the right wing ranges from the former governing National Party to the Conservative Party and the Freedom Front, which seek self-determination for whites, and several small ultra-right groups, such as the *Blanke Bevrydingsbeweging* (White Liberation Movement), which proclaims the superiority of the 'white master race'.

Roman-Dutch Law A system of law in South Africa which has its roots in Roman law and in the legal tradition of the Netherlands. It differs from COMMON LAW in that it is written in the form of statutes and is based upon principles rather than on precedents, but since the 1806 British occupation of the Cape it has been influenced by English law.

royal prerogative Range of powers formally enjoyed by a monarch. In Britain, these powers are now normally exercised by the CROWN, meaning that they are exercised in the monarch's name and under the monarch's signature by government ministers. The powers include the royal assent, the signature of the monarch which gives legal and constitutional status to an ACT OF PARLIAMENT, the prerogative to pardon a criminal offence and the right to declare war. In accordance with the royal prerogative, the British monarch is immune from all legal proceedings.

rule of law Belief in the supremacy of law over everyone, including officials and the government. The rule of law is thought to prevent the government from having too much power and to protect personal freedoms. The concept is particularly important in countries such as Britain that have no written constitution. Disregard for the 'rule of law' facilitated the repression of black people in South Africa during the apartheid years.

SADC (Southern African Development Community) Economic union established in 1992 to replace the Southern African Development Coordinating Conference (1979), which unsuccessfully attempted to reduce economic reliance on South Africa. Its members were the so-called Frontline states of Angola, Botswana, Lesotho, Malawi, Mozambique, Swaziland, Tanzania, Zambia and Zimbabwe, later joined by Namibia. They aimed to reduce their dependence on South Africa for rail and air links and port facilities, imports of raw materials and manufactured goods, and the supply of electric power. Although projects were started to this end, by 1985 the region had become even more dependent on South Africa for its trade outlets. Progress was hampered by the severe drought of the early 1980s, a lack of drive from the top and the political instability in the region. The 1992 treaty establishing the SADC lists among its objectives deeper economic cooperation and integration and the strengthening of regional solidarity, peace and security. By July 1992 SADC had acquired some US$3,7 billion of the US$8,5 billion required for funding projects in sectors ranging from culture, information and energy to food security, mining and transport. South Africa became a member of SADC in 1994 and has been elected to head the important financial and investment sector of the union.

Saddam Hussein (1937-) President of Iraq since 1979, by which time he had already established dictatorial control over the country through the Ba'ath Party. Saddam built up a network of ruthless internal security forces and used terror to wipe out dissent. In 1980 he invaded neighbouring Iran, starting an eight-year war, which ended in stalemate but which devastated the economies of both countries and claimed some 367 000 lives, with more than 700 000 wounded. During the war Saddam developed chemical weapons, which he used against Iraq's Kurdish population, attempted to build a 'supergun', probably to use against Israel, and started a nuclear weapons programme. In 1990 he invaded Kuwait, triggering the ▷GULF WAR. Despite defeat in the war, Saddam stayed in power. Since 1991 he has forced many thousands of Marsh Arabs to flee the country by the systematic destruction of their homelands in southern Iraq.

SANCO (South African National Civic Organization) National umbrella body of predominantly township-based civic associations in South Africa. The 'civics', as they are commonly known, emerged as community forums for the anti-apartheid struggle during the 1980s, while at the same time providing an alternative to the local government structures of the apartheid regime. They were instrumental in instigating a national rent and service payment boycott that remained in force for many years. SANCO was established in 1992 to co-ordinate and represent the civics on a national level and to assist their transformation into vehicles for development and local government reform. Although the civics, and SANCO, claim non-partisan status, they are strongly aligned with the ANC and there has been an overlap in the leadership in the past. SANCO formally supported the ANC in the 1994 election.

sanctions Actions, often including a trade embargo, taken against one country by others in reprisal for a breach of international law or act of aggression. Sanctions, applied against South Africa by opponents of ▷APARTHEID, were lifted in 1993. They were also imposed against the white-dominated former Rhodesia (now Zimbabwe) in 1965 by countries seeking to thwart Ian SMITH's unilateral declaration of independence from Britain. Sanctions are not easy to enforce; they may also take a long time to produce results, or they can bring hardship to people whom they were not meant to hurt. (See also ▷SANCTIONS in 'Southern African history'.)

TAKE FIVE *Unita's charismatic Jonas Savimbi elaborates at a press conference with a display of characteristic showmanship.*

Savimbi, Jonas Malheiro (1934-) Leader of UNITA, one of the three liberation movements of Angola. Savimbi studied medicine in Portugal in the late 1950s, but police harassment caused him to flee to Switzerland, where he switched to political science and graduated from the University of Lausanne in 1965. After involvements with the Union of the People of Angola and the FNLA (Frente Nacional de Libertaçao de Angola), Savimbi founded UNITA in 1966. From his bases in the remote wilderness of southeastern Angola, he has fought first against Portuguese colonial rule and then against the Cuban and Soviet-backed MPLA in a war which has devastated the country. Savimbi is reviled by his opponents as a power-hungry opportunist and right-wing revolutionary but is idolized by his supporters as a charismatic crusader for African social democracy.

SDP (Social Democratic Party) British political party founded in 1981 by the so-called 'gang of four' – Roy Jenkins, David Owen, William Rodgers and Shirley Williams – all of whom had been prominent members of the Labour Party. The new party opposed the growing power of Labour's left wing, advocating instead policies of SOCIAL DEMOCRACY. It formed an alliance with the Liberal Party and enjoyed an initial surge of support among the electorate, but this was never translated into a substantial number of seats in the HOUSE OF COMMONS. After the 1987 election the party merged with the Liberals, forming what became the LIBERAL DEMOCRATIC PARTY, although an SDP rump continued under David Owen until 1990.

secretary of state Title given to senior ministers in the British cabinet who are in charge of the most important government departments, and in the USA to the minister responsible for conducting foreign policy.

security services Government agencies responsible for the protection of State security and the gathering of intelligence, and loosely used in South Africa to include the police and the military. In South Africa the intelligence-gathering operations of the government have been drastically reformed since the advent of majority rule to make the security services – the National Intelligence Service and Military Intelligence – more accountable and to subject them to parliamentary scrutiny and supervision. (See also ▷BOSS in 'Southern African history'.)

senate The upper house of most two-chamber legislatures, such as those in South Africa, the USA and Canada. A senate's method of election, terms of office and powers vary from one political system to another. Under the interim constitution in South Africa the senate (90 members) has the same lifespan as the NATIONAL ASSEMBLY (400 members), and is composed of members appointed on the basis of PROPORTIONAL REPRESENTATION and according to votes cast for the provincial legislature. A major task envisaged for the senate, in addition to being an instrument of legislative review, is that it should act as guardian of provincial interests.

Senior Counsel In South Africa senior advocates of some 10 years' experience who have been appointed by the state president. Advocates apply for this status to the Bar Council and the application is submitted to the relevant JUDGE PRESIDENT, the minister of justice and, finally, the state president. Some South African advocates still hold the British equivalent of this title, Queen's Counsel, which is given to advocates in COMMONWEALTH countries. It was discontinued in South Africa when the country became a republic in 1960. QCs are appointed by the LORD CHANCELLOR to become 'one of Her Majesty's counsel learned in the law'.

❖ An advocate who has been granted the status of Senior Counsel is said to have 'taken silk'. The expression is derived from the silk on the advocate's gown.

TOAST TO TOKYO *Gauteng Premier Tokyo Sexwale, voted the most desirable male by local women, steps out with wife Judy (left) and Limpho Hani, widow of ANC activist Chris Hani.*

separation of powers Principle embodied in the constitutions of some countries by which the judicial, legislative and executive functions are separated from one another. Maintaining the independence of each function is intended to safeguard liberty by introducing checks and balances into the system. The idea of such a division originated in the 18th century and is particularly associated with the writings of ▷MONTESQUIEU. It is embodied in the US Constitution, which requires that the executive (the president) be elected for a fixed term separately from the legislature (congress) and vests judicial power in the SUPREME COURT. In South Africa, the functions of the executive (president and cabinet), legislature (national assembly and senate) and the judiciary (supreme court and CONSTITUTIONAL COURT) also reflect the principle of separation of powers.

Sexwale, Tokyo (Mosima Gabriel) (1953-) Premier of the Gauteng Province (formerly the PWV region) in South Africa (1994-) and a member of the national executive committee of the ANC. After a short spell in the ▷BLACK CONSCIOUSNESS MOVEMENT, Sexwale went into exile in 1975 and underwent military training in the USSR. Afterwards, he was convicted of conspiracy and terrorism and spent 13 years in jail on Robben Island. The assassination of Chris ▷HANI, his close friend, catapulted Sexwale to national prominence and he played an important role in controlling expressions of public anger at the time.

shadow cabinet Leading members of the main opposition party in the House of Commons who sit on the front bench opposite the government. In effect, the shadow cabinet forms a 'government in waiting' – each member 'shadows' a government minister, taking charge of issues relating to that minister's department and portfolio.

sheriff In South Africa, the sheriff is an officer of the supreme or magistrate's court, who serves, processes and executes the judgements and other orders of the court. In England and Wales, the sheriff is the chief officer of the CROWN in every county, formally known as the high sheriff. The sheriff, whose office dates from pre-Norman times, retains certain legal powers, but his role is now mainly ceremonial. In Scotland the term denotes a judge presiding over a sheriff court. In the USA, the chief law-enforcement officer of a county and the chief executive of certain courts is also known as sheriff.

Sinn Fein (SHIN FAIN) Irish political party dedicated to the establishment of a united and independent Ireland. Sinn Fein, meaning 'We ourselves', was founded in 1902 to lobby for Home Rule. Its first leader was Arthur Griffith, who was succeeded in 1917 by Eamon de Valera. The party played a key role in winning independence for the Irish Republic, but it did not accept the Anglo-Irish treaty of 1921, because it excluded independence for the 'six counties' of Ulster. Sinn Fein is still active as the political branch of the IRA. From 1983 to 1992 its leader, Gerry

IRA IN SA *Gerry Adams, leader of Sinn Fein, visits a scene of much violent conflict, the Phola Park squatter settlement near Johannesburg, while in South Africa in 1995.*

Adams, was MP for West Belfast, but he never took his seat at Westminster. In 1993 the British Government offered Sinn Fein a role in discussions on Northern Ireland's future in return for an unequivocal condemnation of violence. In August the following year the IRA issued a ceasefire statement.
❖ A ban on broadcasting voices of Sinn Fein members, imposed by the British Government in 1988, was lifted in September 1994.

small claims court Courts of law in South Africa where civil claims for damages of less than R2 000 are arbitrated. Litigants and respondents must represent themselves, without the services of lawyers, through all stages of the case.

Smith, Ian Douglas (1919-) Prime minister of Rhodesia (now Zimbabwe) before independence. He was a steadfast opponent of black majority rule and a founder member of the Rhodesian Front, which swept to power in the 1962 legislative assembly election with Smith becoming prime minister in 1964. Lengthy independence negotiations with the British Government failed over the issue of black constitutional advancement, and Smith declared independence unilaterally (▷UDI) on 11 November 1965. This was followed by international sanctions and the commencement of the war of liberation. Sanctions, the 'bush war', pressure from South Africa and the diplomatic intervention of the USA, brought the Smith Government to the Lancaster House negotiations with Britain and Zimbabwean liberation movements. Smith lost power in an internationally monitored election in 1980, which ushered in majority rule. He remained politically active as leader of the Conservative Alliance (the renamed Rhodesian Front), from which he resigned in 1987 though retaining his position as MP. In 1987 he was suspended from parliament for a year after making negative statements about Zimbabwe in South Africa.

social democracy Form of SOCIALISM that rejects the goal of common ownership of property and nationalization, and argues that liberal capitalism is the most efficient means of generating wealth. Social democrats believe that policies to enhance social welfare and equality should be pursued on the basis of expediency rather than ideology. Since 1980, most Western socialist parties have moved towards social democracy.

socialism Doctrine that advocates the collective ownership of the means of producing and distributing goods and the abolition of all forms of social inequality. The most influential writer on the socialist ideal was Karl ▷MARX, who saw socialism as a transitional stage between ▷CAPITALISM and COMMUNISM. However, many socialist movements later adopted programmes that were radically different from MARXISM and LENINISM, particularly in their rejection of the need for, or inevitability of revolution.

South African Communist Party (SACP) Party formed underground in 1953 as the successor to the banned ▷COMMUNIST PARTY OF SOUTH AFRICA. Members remained active, some in the ▷CONGRESS ALLIANCE, others in ▷UMKHONTO WE SIZWE. The SACP was unbanned in 1990 and a number of its members played an important role in the ▷MULTIPARTY NEGOTIATIONS that followed. In particular, Joe Slovo (1926-95), its general secretary, proposed the compromise that led to the establishment of the GOVERNMENT OF NATIONAL UNITY. In the 1994 election, the SACP gave its support to the ANC as a member of the tripartite alliance with COSATU, gaining 50 seats for its members in the government.

sovereignty of parliament Power of a parliament to take the final decision and to be the ultimate legal authority in a country. Membership of the EUROPEAN UNION (EU) means that EU law takes precedence over an individual country's law if there is a conflict – leading some people to argue that this implies that sovereignty effectively has been transferred to the European Union.

MADAM SPEAKER *Frene Ginwala, South Africa's first female Speaker of Parliament, introduced several changes in the House, including a more relaxed dress code.*

Speaker A member of parliament elected by other MPs to preside over debates and to keep order. In South Africa the Speaker presides over the NATIONAL ASSEMBLY; in the USA over the HOUSE OF REPRESENTATIVES, and in Britain over the HOUSE OF COMMONS.
❖ Dr Frene GINWALA became South Africa's first female speaker in 1994.

Stalinism Doctrine derived from Joseph ▷STALIN's highly personal and autocratic adaptation of MARXISM and LENINISM in the Soviet Union. Stalin's policies in the 1920s and 1930s involved the collectivization of agriculture, rapid industrialization and the enforcement of ambitious 'five-year plans' for the economy. He used ruthless methods, including the suppression of all opposition and the use of terror, involving periodic purges of the party, the armed forces and society.

Star Wars Defence programme, officially known as the Strategic Defense Initiative (SDI), adopted by the USA during the presidency of Ronald Reagan. It centred on the development of a 'shield' in space to save the USA from attack by strategic nuclear weapons. After consuming a total budget of some US$29 000 million, it was discarded in 1993.

State Department Branch of the US Government responsible for foreign policy, headed by the SECRETARY OF STATE. Located in an area of Washington DC known as Foggy Bottom, the State Department has frequently been viewed with suspicion by some US politicians as a source of elitist views and policies. It was a target of MCCARTHYISM.

statute law Body of law derived from ACTS OF PARLIAMENT rather than from traditional use and the decisions of courts and judges, which make up COMMON LAW.

sub judice (sub JUDE-issee) Rule limiting comment on a case that is being heard in court, or that is about to come before the courts, in order not to prejudice the decision. Failure to obey the rule may be interpreted as CONTEMPT OF COURT or conspiracy to pervert the course of justice – either of which could attract a prison sentence.

supreme court In South Africa, the court that hears cases of a serious criminal or civil nature and is empowered to pass the severest sentences and the heaviest fines of all the courts in the country. It is precluded from interpreting the constitution, which is the preserve of the CONSTITUTIONAL COURT, and its judgments and sentences may be appealed to the APPEAL COURT. The supreme court is organized into provincial divisions, each presided over by a JUDGE PRESIDENT, under whom the provincial judges serve. Judges are appointed by the government mostly from the ranks of senior advocates, usually on the advice of a JUDGE PRESIDENT, the CHIEF JUSTICE and the JUDICIAL SERVICES COMMISSION.

Suzman, Helen (1917-) South African politician and an internationally acclaimed champion of HUMAN RIGHTS. She was a founding member of the ▷PROGRESSIVE PARTY in 1959 and the only member of the party to be returned to parliament in the 1961 general election. For the next 13 years she was a lonely but distinguished liberal voice in parliament, opposing increasing repression and the abuse of human rights. She initiated visits to Nelson MANDELA and other political prisoners of the time. Suzman retired from active politics in 1989, but served as a member of the Independent Electoral Commission in 1994.
❖ Helen Suzman and P W BOTHA did not speak for years after he insinuated opposition complicity in the assassination of former prime minister Hendrik ▷VERWOERD.

SWAPO (South West Africa People's Organization) Namibian liberation movement and political party founded in 1958 to bring independence to ▷SOUTH WEST AFRICA, then ruled by South Africa. It was first known as the Ovambo People's Organization. In the face of the South African Government's refusal to heed United Nations' calls for movement towards independence, SWAPO began a guerrilla war in 1966 backed by the OAU. In 1973 the UN recognized it as the 'sole and authentic representative of the Namibian people'. Five years later, SWAPO agreed to a Western plan for the independence of the territory, but it was not until 1988 that the South African Government agreed to implement the plan, known as ▷RESOLUTION 435. A ceasefire was followed by a UN-supervised election in 1989 in which SWAPO won a clear majority to form the first independent government of Namibia. In the election of December 1994 it was returned to office with a larger majority.

SIMPLY SUZMAN *In the heyday of apartheid, Helen Suzman was one of a handful of opposition politicians to whom oppressed South Africans could turn for assistance.*

Taoiseach (TEE-shach) Official title of the prime minister of the Republic of Ireland, adopted in the 1930s. Taoiseach is an old Gaelic word for a clan leader.

Thatcher, Margaret Hilda (Baroness Thatcher of Kesteven) (1925-) British Conservative Prime Minister from 1979 to 1990. She became Conservative leader in 1975 and led the party to three election victories, in 1979, 1983 and 1987, carrying through many radical reforms. Thatcher curbed trade union power, reduced income taxes, restricted the powers of local government, encouraged private enterprise and returned several nationalized industries to private ownership, thereby increasing the number of shareholders. Her popularity was increased by Britain's victory in the ▷FALKLANDS WAR of 1982, and by legislation allowing council house tenants to buy their homes. However, Thatcher's authoritarian style and her opposition to any loss of British sovereignty to the EUROPEAN UNION brought her into conflict with some of her closest colleagues. These factors, combined with the unpopularity of a new poll tax, contributed to her downfall in 1990, when Geoffrey Howe's resignation speech precipitated a party leadership challenge led by Michael Heseltine, but from which John MAJOR emerged as victor. Thatcher was Britain's first woman prime minister, and she became the longest-serving British prime minister of the 20th century. She forged close links with several world leaders, in particular Ronald Reagan and Mikhail Gorbachev. Her firm opposition to imposing punitive sanctions against South Africa in the 1980s isolated Britain in the COMMONWEALTH. She argued that sanctions would not benefit blacks in any way and would also cause the loss of some 120 000 British jobs.
❖ Thatcher's forthright policies and sometimes confrontational manner earned her the nickname 'the Iron Lady'.

totalitarianism Form of government in which the State has total control over almost all aspects of society – with the result that citizens have hardly any individual freedom. History's starkest example of totalitarianism include the USSR in the 1930s under Joseph ▷STALIN's regime.

trade unions Associations first formed by workers in the late 18th century to protect their members from exploitation and improve their pay and working conditions. Trade unions developed from the medieval artisans' ▷GUILDS whose power declined with

IN AND OUT *On becoming prime minister in 1979, Margaret 'Iron Lady' Thatcher showed herself to be a leader of firm principles, telling the Conservative Party conference in 1980, 'The lady's not for turning.'*

the rise of ▷CAPITALISM. In South Africa, trade unionism took hold only in the 20th century. By 1910 union membership numbered little more than 10 000 countrywide. The unions were dominated by British immigrants and, together with newly urbanized Afrikaners, they blocked labour rights for black workers. The first black union was the Industrial and Commercial Workers' Union of South Africa, formed in 1919 under Clements ▷KADALIE. Until 1979, when the government adopted the recommendations of the Wiehahn Commission, blacks were excluded from labour legislation permitting collective bargaining and strikes. The 1980s saw a resurgence in black union activity which also served as an important vehicle of political mobilization at a time when most political organizations were banned or restricted. The resurgence of union activity culminated in the formation of COSATU in 1985, and of the National Council of Trade Unions, which supported the black-consciousness position, in 1986.

traditional leaders Usually hereditary elders and chiefs in most countries in southern Africa, who have social powers and functions within their communities and who sometimes have limited statutory recognition. The Congress of Traditional Leaders of South Africa (CONTRALESA), formed in 1990, brought together traditional leaders throughout the country who identified broadly with the liberation movement, although officially maintaining a nonaligned stance. The interim constitution allows for the appointment of a House of Traditional Leaders in each province as a consultative body with no legislative powers, although it may make recommendations to government.

Treasury British government department responsible, in cooperation with its ▷CENTRAL BANK, the Bank of England, for economic policy. The prime minister is nominally First Lord of the Treasury, but its effective head is the CHANCELLOR OF THE EXCHEQUER. The Treasury controls the purse strings of government, and therefore wields great power. In South Africa the Department of Finance of the central government has financial authority and is also often referred to colloquially as the Treasury.

tribunal Public body with the power to decide the outcome of civil conflicts, especially in specialist areas of welfare policy. Tribunals were introduced in the early 20th century to provide a relatively easy way of resolving disputes about such matters as compensation for industrial injuries. They now cover a range of subject areas, including industrial disputes and social security payments. Apart from the chairman, who usually has legal qualifications, a tribunal's other members are often lay rather than professional judges.

Truth Commission Abbreviated form of a statutory body (the Truth and Reconciliation Commission) in South Africa aimed at achieving national healing. It intends establishing the facts about certain repressive or illegal actions and HUMAN RIGHTS abuses perpetrated during the apartheid era and by the liberation movements. (See also ▷DIRTY TRICKS in 'Southern African history'.)

Ulster unionist Supporter of the union of Northern Ireland and Great Britain. The Ulster Unionist Party, which for much of the 20th century has been in formal alliance with Britain's Conservative Party, is almost exclusively Protestant. It dominated Northern Irish politics during the province's period of devolved government (1921-72). Its ties with the Conservatives were broken in 1972, when the British prime minister, Edward Heath, suspended the devolved government, imposed direct rule from Westminster and put forward plans for self-government on the basis of power-sharing between Protestants and Catholics. These changes prompted Ian PAISLEY to form a splinter group, the Democratic Unionist Party. In the 1992 general election, the Ulster Unionist Party, led by James Molyneaux, won nine of the 17 Northern Irish seats in the House of Commons; other unionist parties won four.

unilateralism Belief that countries possessing nuclear weapons should abandon them of their own accord – whether or not other countries do the same.

UNITA (União Nacional para a Independência Total de Angola) Former Angolan liberation movement and political party which operated largely in the south of the country during the latter stages of the liberation struggle against Portuguese colonialism. After the collapse of Portuguese rule in 1974, UNITA became embroiled in a civil war against its main rival, the MPLA, and formed an alliance with the FNLA (Frente Nacional de Libertaçao de Angola). UNITA was given military, financial and logistical support by the United States and South Africa. A ceasefire led to a UN-supervised election in 1992 in which UNITA was defeated. It rejected the outcome of the election, but signed a second ceasefire agreement in 1994.

United Nations (UN) International organization founded in 1945 as successor to the

SYMBOL OF UNITY *Flags of the world's nations flutter in the breeze at the United Nations Building in New York City from where peacekeeping efforts are launched.*

League of Nations to promote world peace and international justice and security. The UN is governed by a Security Council of 15 members, of which five – the USA, Britain, France, China and Russia – have permanent seats on the council. Permanent members have the power to veto any UN initiative they dislike – a course that is often resorted to by the USA. The UN General Assembly includes representatives from all member states, which number more than 180. The UN has committed troops to peace-keeping operations in such places as Lebanon, Korea, Cyprus, the Congo, Somalia and Bosnia. It also aims to encourage peace by improving, for example, education, health and literacy through the work of subsidiary bodies such as UNESCO (United Nations Educational, Scientific and Cultural Organization) and WHO (World Health Organization). Since 1992 the secretary-general of the UN has been Boutros Boutros-Ghali of Egypt. The UN played an important role in forging the independence of Namibia, whose first democratic elections were held under the auspices of the United Nations in 1989.

❖ A former South African prime minister, Jan Christian ▷SMUTS, was instrumental in the formation of the UN.

❖ A mandatory UN ▷ARMS EMBARGO against South Africa was effective between 1977 and 1994, when the country resumed full membership of the General Assembly after a long period of absence and isolation.

veto Power to block legislation. In Britain the monarch theoretically has the power of veto by withholding royal assent, but this has not been done since 1707. In the USA the president can veto legislation sent to him from CONGRESS. This power is frequently used, especially when the president does not have a majority in Congress. However, a presidential veto may be overturned by a two-thirds majority in each chamber of congress. The South African Constitution does not allow the president an independent veto of legislation.

Viljoen, Constand Laubscher (General) (1933-) Leader of the FREEDOM FRONT, a right-wing South African political party, and former head of the South African Army and the South African Defence Force. As director of general operations from 1975, he was responsible for conducting military operations along South Africa's borders, including during the ▷BORDER WAR in Namibia and Angola. After retiring from the military, he became active in far-right white politics. Viljoen's constructive approach in talks has been hailed by the ANC. He eventually broke with extreme groups to form the Freedom Front and participate in the 1994 election, in which his party polled 2,2 per cent and he won a seat in parliament. Viljoen advocates a negotiated settlement with the black majority on Afrikaner demands for social and communal autonomy in a VOLKSTAAT.

***volkstaat* (People's state)** The concept of a geographical area in which white Afrikaners would exercise sovereignty over their own political, social and economic structures. Advocated by far-right groups in South Africa, the idea has been rejected as unrealistic by all other groups, including the ANC-led government, but the ANC has agreed to negotiate possible alternatives with a statutory Volkstaat Raad.

welfare state Social and economic system in which the State takes primary responsibility for the welfare of its citizens, especially the needy. Every welfare state includes some system of social security to provide state pensions, child benefits, health care, unemployment benefits and assistance for the disabled.

Westminster system The British style of government which, unlike the US system, allows for a greater fusion between the executive and legislative branches of government. The president or prime minister as well as cabinet members are elected MPs and elections are decided FIRST PAST THE POST and conducted on a constituency basis. Parliamentary standing committees play a less prominent role in the Westminster system.

❖ South Africa's 1983 constitution produced a shift away from the Westminster system in that it introduced a ▷TRICAMERAL PARLIAMENT and assigned considerable powers to an executive president.

whip Post based on the British practice of appointing a member of a political party to be responsible for party discipline, especially for ensuring attendance and supervising the voting behaviour of members in important debates. The parties' chief whips organize the day-to-day running of parliamentary business in each house. In the case of South Africa, each party represented in the NATIONAL ASSEMBLY is allocated whips according to the size of its representation.

white paper Document issued by the government containing proposals for legislation. Although more firmly formulated than a GREEN PAPER, its contents may still be substantially modified after public discussion.

Yeltsin, Boris (1931-) President of Russia from 1990. In the late 1980s, disillusioned by the slowness of Mikhail GORBACHEV's reforms, Yeltsin campaigned for the USSR's speedy transformation into a more liberal country with a capitalist-style economy. He was elected to the newly created national legislature in 1989, and to the Russian parliament in 1990. In 1991 he was elected president of Russia after putting down a coup attempt against Gorbachev. Mounting domestic problems prompted another coup attempt in 1993, which was suppressed only after violent clashes. In December 1993 a referendum on the constitution strengthened Yeltsin's powers.

FRIEND AND FOE *Defying the anti-Gorbachev plotters, Boris Yeltsin shows his support for a president whom he would later supplant.*

Zionism Doctrine of Jewish nationalism developed in the late 19th century. The inspiration behind the spread of Zionist ideas and the creation of a mass movement was Theodor Herzl (1860-1904). Zionists encouraged immigration to Palestine – the 'Promised Land' of the Bible – as a first step towards a Jewish state. A key turning point was the Balfour Declaration of 1917, which expressed British support for a national homeland for the Jews. The massacres of the Nazi ▷HOLOCAUST increased international backing for such a homeland. In 1948 another key figure in the development of Zionism, David Ben-Gurion, became the first prime minister of an independent Israel.

Zwelethini, Goodwill (1948-) Eighth monarch of the Zulu people installed in 1971. His relations with INKATHA FREEDOM PARTY leader Mangosuthu BUTHELEZI became shaky in the 1980s and he has also been a victim of the power struggle between the ANC and IFP.

BUSINESS AND ECONOMICS

For centuries, theories on market forces, inflation and exchange rates have influenced governments' handling of the economy. Ordinary people, as well as businesses, make economic decisions every day when they buy something, or plan their budgets and investments. In doing so they become increasingly familiar with terms and practices once understood only by financiers. Bulls, bears and white knights have lost their mystique.

accounts Set of figures, usually produced annually, which reflects a company's financial affairs. Accounts are divided into two parts – a profit and loss account and a balance sheet. They give a picture of the company's trading position, its ASSETS and LIABILITIES and its profit or loss.

actuary Person employed by an insurance company to assess risks and set the level of premiums, or payments, by those insured. The higher the risk of a claim, the greater the premium charged.

Afrikaanse Handelsinstituut (AHI) Body representing Afrikaner interests in commerce, industry, mining and finance in South Africa and Namibia. Established in 1942, the AHI is recognized as the primary representative of Afrikaner business.

Anglo American Corporation The largest company in South Africa, predominantly a mining and finance conglomerate. Anglo was established in 1917 by Sir Ernest Oppenheimer with considerable backing from the American financier, J P Morgan, for the prime purpose of developing the East Rand gold mines. Oppenheimer soon expanded the Anglo empire into the diamond industry with the formation of Consolidated Diamond Mines in South West Africa (now Namibia) and with the purchase of controlling shares in DE BEERS in South Africa. The corporation also extended its interests to the South African coal and chemical industries and the development of the Zambian copper fields. In the 1950s and 1960s Anglo further diversified into property and finance. Today the conglomerate has extensive international investments through Minorco, its offshore investment company, as well as being one of the largest mining groups in the world.

annual general meeting (AGM) Meeting which must be held each year by every company for the shareholders to receive and approve the ANNUAL REPORT and ACCOUNTS submitted by the directors.

annual report Document issued by companies which sets out their financial position and reviews their performance over the previous 12 months. Annual reports must contain the company's audited profit and loss accounts and BALANCE SHEET, usually accompanied by a statement from the chairman of the board of directors.

arbitrage Attempt to make a profit by buying and selling the same shares or commodities in different markets. For example, if shares of a company are slightly higher on the Johannesburg Stock Exchange than in London, speculators can make a risk-free profit by buying shares in London and immediately selling them in Johannesburg. Another form of arbitrage involves buying shares in a company likely to be the object of a TAKEOVER bid, which tends to push up its share price.

AIRBORNE FIRE POWER *South Africa's Rooivalk helicopters, world leaders in military technology, are among the defence industry's products for which Armscor is an international broker.*

Armscor South African state-owned armaments corporation. In response to the international arms embargo against South Africa the government set up Armscor as part of its strategic defence movement during the apartheid era. Armscor's initial objective was to meet all the country's diverse military needs. It is now in the forefront of technology and its primary function is still to serve as the official armaments organization for the government of the day.

assembly line Line of factory workers and equipment along which a product being assembled passes from operation to operation until completed. The assembly line, together with automation, is the basis of mass production. The principle behind the production line, that manufacturing can be speeded up by being divided into simple operations, was established in the 19th century. Henry FORD developed the moving assembly line in 1913. In the classic assembly line, the product being manufactured moves on a conveyor belt past teams of workers, each of whom performs a single operation.

❖ An alternative strategy to mass production developed in recent years is flexible specialization. This is the use of multipurpose equipment and skilled labour to produce a continually changing range of products that are semi-customized. It has been proposed as a way to alleviate the stagnation of formal economic sectors in developing countries.

asset Something of value which can be used to cover a LIABILITY or debt. 'Current' assets include cash or anything that can easily be sold. Buildings or land, which take longer to sell and turn into cash, are known as 'fixed' assets. Assets may also be 'intangible', such as a trade name or GOODWILL.

asset stripping Taking over a company in order to sell off its assets at a profit rather than run it as a going concern. This usually leads to the break-up or closure of the company that has been taken over. If it is quoted on the stock exchange, it could also become a 'cash shell', no longer operating but retaining its listing for a limited period.

audit Examination by an independent accountant, or auditor, of the ANNUAL REPORT and ACCOUNTS of a company. It is a legal requirement. The auditor's certificate should state that the accounts are a true reflection of a company's financial position, or 'qualify' them by setting out any serious reservations. Legally, auditors are employed by the shareholders, in whose interests they should act.

bad debt Debt which a lender is unable to recover, usually because the debtor is unable to pay. Most companies make provision for bad debts in their accounts.

❖ The biggest ever bad debts were recorded by leading banks in the late 1980s after they lent large sums of money to developing countries such as Mexico, Brazil and Argentina.

These countries proved unable to meet even the interest payments on the loans, let alone repay the debt itself.

balance of payments Difference between the value of what a country buys from abroad and what it sells to overseas countries. If a country exports more than it imports, it is said to have a strong balance of payments or a balance of payments surplus. If it imports more than it exports, it has a balance of payments deficit. There are two main elements to a country's balance of payments: 'visible' trade, in goods and raw materials, and 'invisible' trade, in services.

balance sheet Account showing all the ASSETS and LIABILITIES of a company which, as the term implies, must balance.

banker's acceptance (BA) Term applied to a form of short-term financing used particularly in import and export trade. An importer is usually allowed a certain period of time to pay for a consignment of goods, typically about three months from the date of their loading. However, an exporter who is owed R100 000 for goods may not wish to wait out that period and may sell the BILL OF EXCHANGE confirming the deal to a discount house for a little less than R100 000, the amount depending on the 'BA rate', the prevailing rate of interest for such transactions. The exporter retains his liquidity, while the discount house obtains the interest. Often the discount house will, in turn, pass on the bills it has accumulated to a merchant bank, which 'accepts', for a fee, responsibility for payment should the debtor default.

bank rate Rate of INTEREST at which the CENTRAL BANK lends money to a country's other financial institutions, also called the minimum lending rate. Commercial banks base their interest rates for loans on the bank rate, but generally charge more because there is a risk that a loan will not be repaid, and also because they want to make a profit. Directly linked to the bank rate is the 'prime rate', which is the rate a bank charges on overdrafts to its best customers and which determines the interest rate offered on deposits.
❖ Changes in the bank rate can have a profound effect on the economy. If the rate goes up, borrowing becomes more expensive and investment in industry suffers. If the rate goes down, foreign investors may take their money to other countries where they can get a better return on it, which affects the BALANCE OF PAYMENTS and the value of the currency. Central banks often increase the bank rate in order to reduce the MONEY SUPPLY and so curb inflation.

bankruptcy Being unable to pay one's debts – a synonym for INSOLVENCY, which is the term used in legal procedures in South Africa.
❖ The word 'bankrupt' is derived from *banca rupta*, Latin for 'broken bench' – the symbol of a bankrupt moneylender.

bear Investor who believes that share prices are going to fall and therefore sells in anticipation of being able to buy them back at a lower price. Bears sometimes sell shares they do not own in the hope that they will be able to buy them at a lower price before they have to deliver them to the buyer. A period when share prices are falling is known as a 'bear market'. Its opposite is a BULL market.
❖ The term 'bear' is short for 'bearskin jobber', alluding to their tendency to 'sell the bear's skin before catching the bear'.

big bang Computer-based changes in the London stock market introduced on 27 October 1986. Many traditional practices of the stock market (including dealing on the floor) were abolished overnight, making London a more competitive and responsive market for investors. The impact of the reforms was likened to the ▷BIG BANG theory explaining the origin of the universe.

bill of exchange Written order, similar to a cheque, which requires the holder to pay on demand, or in the future, a specified amount to another person. Bills are just a more complicated sort of IOU used to provide credit in trade. The holder of a bill can either redeem it or sell it to someone else at a discount in order to obtain the money ahead of the due payment date. (See also OPEN ACCOUNT.)

blue chip Stock of a financially sound company with a long history of profit, growth and good management. It is therefore thought to be a low-risk investment. Prominent South African blue-chip companies are DE BEERS, ANGLO AMERICAN and the REMBRANDT GROUP.
❖ The term originated from the gambling chip having the highest value in poker, which is usually blue.

Board of Tariffs and Trade (BTT) An advisory board to the South African Minister of Trade and Industry, formed by representatives of the public and private sectors, appointed by the president. Its main function is to set tariffs for imports into the SOUTH AFRICAN CUSTOMS UNION.

bond Financial document issued by a corporation or public body at a fixed rate of interest and usually redeemable on a fixed date. Bonds issued by companies are sometimes converted into EQUITY over a certain period.

budget Forecast of future income and expenditure. Companies must set out their plans for future operations so that they can assess their cash flow and trading position. Governments, too, provide annual budgets setting out their proposals for balancing their estimated revenue and expenditure.
❖ The Minister of Finance presents South Africa's annual budget to parliament in March, when he outlines the government's economic stance for the coming fiscal year.

built-in obsolescence Incorporation into products of features that will make them out of date or useless prematurely, so as to guarantee demand for replacements in the future.

bull Investor who expects share prices to rise and therefore buys shares anticipating that he can sell them at a higher price in the future. Bulls may also contract to buy shares at current prices for future delivery, hoping that they will be able to sell them at a profit. A period when share prices generally are rising is known as a 'bull market' – the opposite of a BEAR market.

bullion Gold and silver of great purity, usually sold in bars. London and Zürich are the world's main bullion markets. Bullion becomes more attractive to investors in times of war and instability, because it is a tangible and a relatively inflation-proof form of wealth. In South Africa, dealing in bullion is legally the sole preserve of the Reserve Bank, but a popular medium for investment in gold by individuals is the Krugerrand. This coin contains one troy ounce (31,1 grams) of fine gold; its price varies in line with the international gold price.
❖ The worldwide demand for Krugerrands, at its height in the 1970s, diminished after the introduction of sanctions, and when countries such as the USA, Australia and Canada began producing similar coins. In 1978 the proportion of South Africa's gold output used

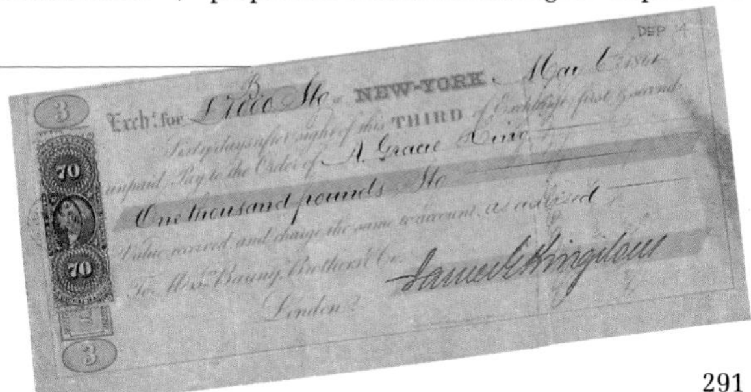

OLD BILL *Originally introduced as a means of providing credit, particularly for foreign trade, a bill of exchange is really little more than a sophisticated type of IOU ('I owe you').*

for Krugerrands rose to a record 26,5 per cent. By 1994 the proportion was only 1,6 per cent.

buyers' market Market in which buyers are in a position to bargain prices downwards because supply exceeds demand at current prices. For a buyers' market to emerge, the supply of a product generally has to be inflexible, or 'inelastic'. A buyers' market in baked beans, for example, will not occur because manufacturers can cut output to meet reduced demand. There is a limited supply of housing, however, so a buyers' market can develop if more people wish to sell houses than buy them. (Compare SELLERS' MARKET.)

capital Material wealth, including machinery and buildings, owned by companies. The term also refers to the money needed to buy machinery and premises, and thus any asset or resource.

capital gain Difference between the price paid for an asset such as shares or real estate and the selling price.
❖ Although South Africa has no capital gains tax, the idea has been mooted as a way to redistribute wealth.

capitalism Political and economic system which allows open competition between companies in a free market. Under capitalism, the means of production and distribution are held by private individuals or corporations rather than by the government.

cartel Group of producers or suppliers who work together as a MONOPOLY and set volumes and prices to enhance profits.
❖ An example is OPEC, which attempts to increase the price of oil by restricting the exports of its members.

caveat emptor Latin for 'let the buyer beware'. It is the buyer's responsibility to be alert to the possibility that he may be cheated; the seller is not required to point out defects in goods for sale (except for latent defects – those not apparent on close inspection), although it is illegal for him to make false representations about them.

central bank Financial institution which acts as banker for a government, advises on monetary policy and is 'lender of last resort' (the source of all the money lent and borrowed by other financial institutions). Central banks oversee the banking business of a country and usually supervise the printing of banknotes. They also sometimes intervene in the currency markets to manipulate exchange rates. South Africa's central bank is the SOUTH AFRICAN RESERVE BANK.

Chamber of Mines of South Africa Established in 1889, soon after the discovery of gold on the Witwatersrand, as a central coordinating body to advance and protect the interests of its members. The mining houses soon realized the advantages of such an employers' organization in the negotiation of labour recruitment and wage policies, and in the provision of essential services such as procurement of supplies, legal advice, gold refining and the marketing of by-products. The chamber has played a major role in the region's politics and economics.

close corporation (CC) Type of business operation formed as a separate legal entity comprising from one to ten members. The particular advantage of the formation of a close corporation for small business ventures is that the LIABILITY of the members is limited to their individual capital contributions.
❖ Legislation providing for the formation of close corporations was passed in South Africa in 1984.

commodity Product, usually in a raw or unprocessed state, such as tin, cocoa, rubber or bananas. Commodities can be traded in many ways, FUTURES and OPTIONS being particularly important. Because transactions in commodities are all on paper, the merchandise can be bought and sold many times without it ever moving. Tin in the ground or wheat yet to be sown can also be traded in this way.

communism Economic and social system in which all the means of production, distribution and exchange are nominally owned by the workers and controlled by the communist party and state in their name. A communist system usually has a PLANNED ECONOMY, although countries such as China are now trying to combine communist party control with a market economy. (See also ▷COMMUNISM in 'Politics, government and the law'.)

competition policy In South Africa this is prescribed by the Maintenance and Promotion of Competition Act (1979) and applied by the Competition Board. It aims to ensure the efficient working of a market-orientated economy. The role of competition policy in South Africa is contentious because of the increasing levels of ECONOMIC CONCENTRATION and CONGLOMERATION.

conglomeration The DIVERSIFICATION of a company into more than one product market, often in response to volatile conditions in its original product market, or to satiation of that market. It may also be viewed as a growth strategy away from declining industries into emergent or highly profitable industries.
❖ It is estimated that the six dominant conglomerate groups in South Africa (ANGLO AMERICAN, DE BEERS, REMBRANDT, Old Mutual, Sanlam and Liberty Life) effectively control around 80 per cent of the assets quoted on the Johannesburg Stock Exchange.

consumer credit Money borrowed to finance purchases of consumer goods. It includes credit cards, store cards, bank loans and HIRE

EMPIRE BUILDER *Cecil Rhodes (centre, seated) began the expansion of the De Beers empire in 1889 when he bought the Kimberley Central Company from Barney Barnato (at right of Rhodes) for £5 338 650. With them are the directors of De Beers in 1891.*

PURCHASE. Consumer credit tends to increase when people are optimistic about their financial position, and shrink during a RECESSION.
❖ The Usury Act (1968) regulates the maximum interest rate charged on monetary loans by South Africa's banks, building societies and other money-lenders.

cooperatives Worker or producer cooperatives are business operations manufacturing goods or providing services, but which are owned and controlled by the workers or producers themselves. Worker cooperatives are generally formed around a particular set of ideological beliefs and in response to specific socioeconomic conditions. The mix of their socioeconomic objectives often involves complex trade-offs and consequently the success of self-management systems is regarded as highly controversial.
❖ Producer cooperatives, an example being the KWV, were established in South Africa in the early 1900s to promote agriculture.

CPI (Consumer Price Index) Index of the cost of a representative basket of consumer goods and services measured at the final transaction stage. South Africa's CPI is estimated and published monthly by the Central Statistical Service, and is used as an indicator of domestic INFLATION rates.

credit rating Assessment of an individual's ability to repay a loan. It is based on salary, existing financial commitments and debt record, as well as factors such as age.

credit squeeze Deliberate attempt by a government or CENTRAL BANK to curb purchases of consumer goods on credit in order to reduce the level of economic activity and curb INFLATION. The most common way of doing this is to raise INTEREST rates.

dawn raid Where a bidder for a company suddenly buys as many shares as possible, often using a third party to conceal the bidder's identity and motive, usually before mounting a full TAKEOVER bid. A method of acquiring control of a company that was popular in Britain in the 1980s, it derives its name from the fact that, to pre-empt rival bids, the shares are bought rapidly at the beginning of a working day.

De Beers The De Beers group is the world's largest seller of rough diamonds. With its partners, it owns 18 diamond mines in four countries and produces 50 per cent by value of the world's gemstones. De Beers was formed in 1888 by Cecil John ▷RHODES and fellow financier and diamond magnate Barney Barnato. By 1891 it had bought out rival mining companies, effectively obtaining complete control over the South African diamond industry. In the 1920s De Beers became part of the ANGLO AMERICAN group, whose chairman, Ernest Oppenheimer, succeeded in uniting the interests of diamond producers and merchants worldwide. Today, De Beers is still the leader in the international rough diamond market. Most of the world's major rough diamond producers sell their output through De Beers' Central Selling Organization (CSO), which is based in London.

THE HUMAN COST *The Depression of the 1930s brought despair to millions of unemployed workers – from the soup kitchens of America to the streets of Wigan, England.*

deflation Fall in prices, almost always related to a decrease in economic activity and consumer spending. This occurs particularly during a DEPRESSION.

depression Period of drastic decline in the national economy. Business activity plummets, prices fall and the level of unemployment soars to unacceptable levels.
❖ The most severe such period was the ▷DEPRESSION of the 1930s. However, many economists think that the RECESSION of the early 1990s was sufficiently deep and prolonged to be considered a depression.

devaluation Fall in the value of a country's currency against others. This may be as a result of market pressures or of government policy to make a country's exports cheaper.

developing country Country with a small GROSS NATIONAL PRODUCT (GNP) per capita which has not yet developed a mature industrialized economic base. In terms of the WORLD BANK's classification, any country which had a GNP per capita of less than US$7 910 in 1992 qualified for the term and was entitled to a specific category of financial aid and privileges under trade agreements. South Africa's position is in doubt as it has a highly developed industrial base, but a large proportion of its population have a relatively low level of productivity, which puts its GNP per capita on the borderline between the 'developing' and 'developed' categories.
❖ Most of the world's developing countries, also called 'Third World' countries, are in Africa and Asia.

diminishing returns Law of economics first propounded by David RICARDO. It argues that adding one unit of input (such as labour) to fixed amounts (such as of land or CAPITAL) will produce successively smaller increases in production.

❖ In common usage, the 'point of diminishing returns' is a supposed point at which additional effort or investment in a given endeavour will not yield a correspondingly improved end result, especially when a higher yield is taxed at an excessively high rate.

disposable income The amount of money available for an individual or population to spend. This is calculated by subtracting all taxes and social insurance contributions such as to unemployment and medical funds from gross income.

diversification Expansion of a company's products and activities into areas unconnected with its core business. The term also applies to spreading the risk in a share portfolio by investing in a wide variety of shares. (See also CONGLOMERATION.)

dividend Payment made to shareholders as their share of company profits. Dividends are usually expressed as a certain number of cents per share.

Dow Jones index Refers to the Dow Jones Industrial Average, an index of the selling price of the shares of 30 major industrial companies on the New York Stock Exchange. It is used worldwide as an indicator of trends in share markets.

dual exchange rate A system of two distinct nominal FOREIGN EXCHANGE rates: a free market rate for capital transactions and a fixed official rate (set by the CENTRAL BANK) for trade transactions on the current account of the BALANCE OF PAYMENTS. The aim is to protect the economy from volatile capital movements. For many years a dual exchange rate system was imposed in South Africa to deter the flight of capital in response to political developments. It ended in 1995. Until then, the 'commercial rand' rate was the official rate for current account transactions managed by the SOUTH AFRICAN RESERVE BANK, and the 'financial rand' rate, applying to foreign investments, was set by the market. This tended to discourage foreign investors who required the assurance that they would be able to withdraw their capital and income without restriction.

dumping Selling goods at a loss to eliminate competition, acquire HARD CURRENCY or open up new markets. The term usually refers to the sale of goods by one country in another country at a large discount. The price is often even lower than that charged in the country in which the goods originated.

economic concentration Refers to the degree to which the three or four largest companies in a particular industry dominate the market for their products.

❖ There is relatively high concentration in the South African manufacturing industry.

economics Study of the production, distribution and consumption of goods and services. The word economics derives from a Greek word meaning 'household management'. Economics touches on many disciplines – including mathematics, sociology, psychology, accounting, geography and political theory. The attempt to build economic models is notoriously difficult, because predictions of human behaviour en masse have proved unreliable, and many economists regard their subject as being more of an art than a science.

elasticity Extent to which SUPPLY AND DEMAND are affected by the response to changes in price. Demand is said to be elastic when it responds considerably to fluctuations in prices, and inelastic when it responds only slightly or not at all.

❖ Demand for luxury goods is usually more elastic than that for everyday necessities. For products which are marketed on their exclusiveness, however, demand can sometimes fall if prices fall.

embargo A government's restriction on trade, aiming to put pressure on other governments by prohibiting exports to, or imports from, those countries. Embargoes are often ineffective because countries not party to the ▷SANCTIONS may supply the goods, often at inflated prices. Consumers can also boycott companies to bring pressure on them to change their pricing policies or other practices.

embezzlement Theft of money that has been entrusted to one's care.

❖ One of the worst cases of embezzlement in history was the theft of at least £400 million from the pension fund of the Mirror Group of British newspapers by the group's chairman Robert Maxwell (1923-91).

endowment policy Form of LIFE ASSURANCE which pays out a guaranteed sum either on death or at a fixed date, usually 10 to 30 years after the policy starts.

equity In stock market terminology, the SHARES of a company. Equity also refers to the financial value of someone's property over and above the amount owed in a MORTGAGE. For example, if a house is bought for R80 000, of which R10 000 is put down and R70 000 is borrowed, the equity in the house is R10 000. The equity will rise if property prices rise.

SMILING CROOK *After British press baron Robert Maxwell was found drowned in the Atlantic, investigators discovered he had embezzled money on a massive scale.*

European Monetary System (EMS) Financial system set up by members of the ▷EUROPEAN UNION (EU) in 1979 to limit fluctuations in the exchange rates of European currencies. Its main elements are the European Currency Unit, or ECU, and the Exchange Rate Mechanism (ERM). The ECU is the currency used by countries of the EU for commercial transactions and BOND issues. It is derived from all the currencies in the EMS weighted according to the size of each member state's economy. Because of this, it is a more stable currency than those of most member states. Currencies in the ERM must maintain parity with the ECU, which is planned to become the basis of a single currency for all member countries of the European Union.

excise Duty levied on goods produced locally. Alcohol, petrol and cigarettes are sources of excise duty in South Africa.

extraordinary general meeting Special meeting of shareholders of a company. It may be called by the directors to approve a course of action, or by the shareholders to protest against decisions made by the board.

Federal Reserve System The central banking authority of the USA, commonly called 'the Fed'. The Federal Reserve has a board of governors consisting of seven members appointed by the US president, and it exercises broad supervisory authority over the 12 regional reserve banks, one of which (New York) is responsible for all foreign exchange dealings. Its policy decisions are constitutionally independent of the government.

financial year Any period of 12 months on which company ACCOUNTS are based. The financial year should not be confused with the fiscal year, which is the accounting period used by governments for rates of tax and other matters, as set out in the annual BUDGET – although many companies' financial year coincides with the fiscal year.

❖ In the USA, companies call their financial year a fiscal year.

fiscal drag Term applied to the effect of INFLATION on the economy through the increase in income tax payments. As inflation reduces the value of money and salaries and wages rise, more people are brought into the tax net, while those already paying tax are lifted into a higher tax bracket. The resultant reduction in the population's spending power places a drag on economic growth.

fiscal policy A government's plans to control its own expenditure and taxation, which together make up the BUDGET. Another function of fiscal policy, combined with monetary policy (the control of the MONEY SUPPLY), is to regulate the level of economic activity and the BALANCE OF PAYMENTS.

Ford, Henry (1863-1947) American industrialist who revolutionized industrial mass production by introducing the first really successful moving ASSEMBLY LINE. In 1908 he produced the Model T – the first affordable car for the mass market. By the time production ceased in 1927, more than 15 million Model Ts had been sold.

❖ 'They can have any colour as long as it's black,' Ford said of customers for his low-priced Model T.

foreign direct investment (FDI) The purchase or establishment by a foreign resident of a commercial venture in the domestic economy. This has become critically important to the economic welfare of DEVELOPING COUNTRIES, which usually cannot raise enough capital locally for major projects. FDI facilitates the transfer of finance, technology, skills and managerial expertise, and gives the access to international markets that is essential to the success of an industrializing country.

foreign exchange Global trading of currencies. Exchange rates vary according to the economic standing of the countries concerned; they are most directly affected by a change in interest rates.

❖ When South Africa's interest rates rise in relation to the rates prevailing in other countries – which makes investment in South Africa more attractive – the value of the rand will tend to rise in terms of the other countries' currencies.

MOTOR MAN *Henry Ford (below) shows off one of his earliest models, made in a small workshop. His assembly line, devised for the Model T in 1913, was adapted and improved for the Ford Hudson (bottom) in the 1920s.*

franchise Licence to manufacture or market a product with an established trade name, according to an agreed format. The franchisor provides the product or raw material, sales techniques and other kinds of managerial assistance, in exchange for a fee and the loyalty of the franchisee.

❖ The Spur chain of restaurants and Master Maths supplementary education services are examples of established South African franchises. Franchising can be a viable form of joint venture to stimulate entrepreneurship.

free enterprise Freedom of private businesses to operate competitively with the minimum of legal restrictions and government involvement. LAISSEZ FAIRE is the principle underlying free enterprise.

Friedman, Milton (1912-) American economist who has championed FREE ENTERPRISE. His major popular work is *Capitalism and Freedom* (1962), in which he argues that welfare services discourage individual effort, and emphasizes the importance of keeping the MONEY SUPPLY and INFLATION under tight control. He won the Nobel prize for economics in 1976.

❖ Friedman's brand of MONETARISM was adopted with enthusiasm by the British prime minister Margaret Thatcher and American president Ronald Reagan in the 1980s.

futures Contract to deliver COMMODITIES or SECURITIES at a certain price on a fixed date in the future. The futures market enables companies to control their costs by HEDGING against possible price changes in the future. By buying copper futures, for example, a company knows some of the costs involved in future production because they have already been incurred – even though it may not need the copper for 18 months. Most contracts for future delivery, however, are traded by speculators who have no intention of taking possession of the goods. If they expect prices to rise, they buy a futures contract in the hope of selling it on for a higher price and making a profit. If they expect prices to fall, they sell a contract to make a profit by buying back when prices fall. In this way, supermarket chains now buy (and possibly sell) many foods before they have been harvested – or even before they have been grown.

G7 Popular name of the group of seven leading industrialized countries – the USA, Japan, Germany, France, Britain, Italy and Canada – which meets regularly to discuss world economic strategy.

Galbraith, John Kenneth (1908-) Canadian-born American economist who advocates strong intervention by governments to promote economic growth and to counterbalance over-powerful corporations and trade unions.

GATT (General Agreement on Tariffs and Trade) International body which aimed to boost world trade by reducing trade barriers. GATT was set up by international treaty in 1948, and its member states, who account for more than 80 per cent of world trade, conduct tariff negotiations through a series of 'rounds'. The 'Uruguay Round' of 1986-94 became bogged down in arguments over the European Union's protectionist policies, especially the Common Agricultural Policy, which guaranteed prices for farm products such as milk, butter, meat and cereals. The participants finally agreed to implement progressive cuts in import tariffs and farm subsidies. The Uruguay Round was finally concluded by the signing of the Marrakesh Agreement in April 1994. As a signatory to this agreement, South Africa undertook major trade policy reforms.
❖ Frustration at the slow pace of negotiations gave GATT the nickname of 'General Agreement to Talk and Talk'.
❖ The World Trade Organization (WTO) came into operation on 1 January 1995 as a successor to GATT, with 81 members and headquarters in Geneva. Membership remained open to all those of the 125 GATT member countries who ratified the terms of the Marrakesh Agreement. The WTO covers a wider field, regulating activities which were beyond GATT's jurisdiction, such as trade in services, intellectual property rights and investments.

gearing The ratio of a company's fixed interest debt to the value of its share capital. A company with a high gearing is more vulnerable to INSOLVENCY and therefore a riskier investment than one with low gearing.

General Mining Union Corporation (Gencor) Second largest mining CONGLOMERATION in South Africa, after the ANGLO AMERICAN CORPORATION. Formed in 1980 by the merger of Union Corporation with General Mining and Finance Corporation, Gencor is predominantly involved in mining (gold, coal, minerals, platinum, and ferro-alloy products), but has diversified its interests into energy (oil and gas), manufacturing (paper and packaging), engineering and construction, among others.

Getty, Jean Paul (1892-1976) American oil magnate who was dubbed the 'richest man in the world'. Getty, the son of an oil millionaire, accumulated a fortune of US$4 billion in the Oklahoma oil fields. He moved to Britain in the 1940s.
❖ Getty's great legacy is the Getty Museum in California, a vast collection of art treasures housed in the reconstruction of a Roman villa. The museum is the wealthiest buyer of art in the world.

gilts Special type of SECURITIES issued by governments in the form of interest-bearing certificates, which provide an important way of borrowing money. Gilts pay a guaranteed level of interest, and most must be redeemed, or cashed in, at a specified date.
❖ Gilts were so named because the original certificates issued in Britain were printed with gold borders.

gold The discovery of extensive gold reefs in the Witwatersrand in 1886 catalysed modern industrialization of the South African economy, and led to the country's becoming the largest gold producer in the world. Gold production and export has provided substantial State revenue and foreign exchange. This has meant that the prospects of the economy have depended on the volatile movements of the international gold price. It is only in recent decades that consistent efforts have been made to promote manufacturing exports in an attempt to reduce dependence on gold alone. (See also BULLION; MINING.)
❖ A market price for gold is 'fixed' twice every weekday by a group of London bullion dealers. Usually quoted in US dollars per troy ounce (31,1 grams), it determines the price South African gold mines receive for their production. In January 1980 gold reached an all-time high of US$850.

gold standard Monetary system which obliged governments to be able to exchange paper currency for gold on demand. The gold standard was first adopted early in the 19th century by Britain and the USA to correct imbalances in international trade. International debts were always settled in gold. When a country had a deficit in its BALANCE OF PAYMENTS, more gold had to be paid out for imports than it earned in exports. Gold reserves fell, forcing the authorities to lessen the MONEY SUPPLY to cover the debt. This caused prices to fall (making exports more attractive) and wages to drop (reducing demand for imports), so bringing the economy back into balance – but often at a depressed level of activity. Most currencies, led by sterling, came off the gold standard in the 1930s in response to the worldwide DEPRESSION, when the financial discipline it imposed was seen as too stringent, preventing governments from borrowing large amounts to reflate their economies and reduce the miseries of unemployment.
❖ South Africa, whose economy was so dependent on gold, came off the gold standard on 27 December 1932, more than a year after Britain. The delay by the government in coming to a decision caused a huge outflow of capital and provoked a political crisis which led eventually to a realignment of parties and change of government.
❖ Today, many countries are happy to run long-term balance of payments deficits, which they could not have done in the days of the gold standard.

goodwill Value of a business over and above that of its physical assets. It includes the company's reputation for quality and service, links with clients, suppliers and others and the value of its brand names. It is hard to calculate, but can be substantial.

Gresham's law Principle that bad money will drive good money out of circulation, proposed by Sir Thomas Gresham, one of Queen Elizabeth I's advisers. If a government minted gold pound coins and later began to mint the coins out of cheaper metals, the public would hoard the gold pounds (possibly for later sale at a higher price) rather than use them as a medium of exchange. Gold pounds would stop circulating, and indeed this is what happened to the gold sovereign, issued until 1931, with a face value of one pound but a market value in recent years of about £60.
❖ In times of high INFLATION central banks have often had to withdraw coins made of metal that has become worth more than the face value of the coins.

gross domestic product (GDP) Total value of all goods and services produced in a country in a 12-month period.

gross national product (GNP) The sum of GROSS DOMESTIC PRODUCT plus the net income and interest brought in by foreign investments. GNP is an important indicator of a country's economic health.
❖ A country's relative wealth is measured by the 'GNP per capita' – its gross national product divided by its population figure.

hard currency Any freely exchangeable currency of relatively stable value which is widely used in international trade. Where local currencies are weak or prone to fluctuation, traders may prefer to deal in US dollars, German marks or Japanese yen. There is always more demand for a hard currency than there is supply, which means its value on the black, or unofficial, market tends to be higher than the official exchange rate. This has happened in many African countries.
❖ In weak economies, especially those with high INFLATION, hard currencies can virtually drive out the national currency.

LOADS OF MONEY *In 1923 Germany experienced disastrous inflation and the mark plummeted in value. Banknotes became virtually worthless, forcing some customers to collect their cash from the bank in laundry baskets.*

Harmful Business Practices Act Law passed in South Africa in 1988 to prevent the exploitation of the consumer by misleading advertising or practices of dubious legality. The Act provides for the formation of a committee of experts in commerce, consumer affairs, law and economics to investigate consumers' complaints, which may brought to its notice by organizations such as the South African Coordinating Consumer Council.

Hearst, William Randolph (1863-1951) American newspaper publisher who built a vast and influential news empire. He was a leading exponent of 'yellow press' sensationalism, and introduced the large 'banner headline' to newspapers.

hedging The attempt to counterbalance the risk of loss in one form of investment by investing in some other form. FUTURES and OPTIONS are important methods of hedging on commodity prices, which can fluctuate sharply. A company selling to Germany in Deutschemarks may hedge its anticipated receipts by selling the Deutschemarks in a forward contract for a known value of rands.
❖ Gold, which tends to retain its value relative to other investments, is usually regarded as a hedge against inflation.

hire purchase (instalment sale) Method of buying something with a loan, which is paid off in regular instalments. The repayment usually includes INTEREST on the value of the loan. Although the buyer takes possession of the product on payment of the first instalment or deposit, he does not legally own it until he has made the the final payment.
❖ Hire purchase is sometimes known as 'the never-never' because the payments can sometimes seem to go on for ever.

income distribution Division of income among persons or households. Governments often make the distribution less inequitable by taxing high incomes more than low ones; COMMUNISM aims at equal distribution.

income tax Direct tax imposed on income. A 'progressive' income tax is one in which those with higher incomes pay more tax than those with lower incomes. In South Africa there has been a shift in recent years towards higher taxation of individuals, which has placed an increasing burden on upper and middle-income earners. This reflects the narrow tax base, with a relatively small proportion of income earners contributing the largest share of tax.
❖ A loan levy, a percentage of the total tax bill charged in addition to income tax and paid as a loan to the fiscus, was imposed in South Africa on individuals or companies during the 1970s and 1980s. The taxpayer was reimbursed, with interest, after a specified period.
❖ A 'transition levy' was imposed in the 1994-5 tax year to help finance specific projects during the transition to a postapartheid democracy. This was a once-off charge of 5 per cent of total taxes payable.
❖ A tax of 98 per cent on unearned income was imposed by Britain's Labour Party government in 1974.

inflation General increase in price levels, or fall in the value of money, over a period of time. If goods which cost R100 a year ago now cost R110, the annual rate of inflation is 10 per cent. High inflation not only reduces the value of people's savings, but it also damages the economy by pushing up the price of imports, which can lead to a BALANCE OF PAYMENTS crisis. Governments try to control inflation by restricting pay increases, while CENTRAL BANKS may regulate the MONEY SUPPLY through the imposition of higher INTEREST rates. Inflation can enter a self-sustaining spiral, when price rises fuel wage demands, which in turn bring a further increase in prices. South Africa had double-digit inflation rates (although below 20 per cent) from the early 1970s to the mid-1990s. Only in recent years have anti-inflationary policies shown a measure of success, bringing the rate to single-digit levels.
❖ Both the CPI and the PPI are used in the measurement of inflation in South Africa.
❖ Countries such as Argentina and Russia have in the past experienced hyperinflation of 1 000 per cent. In 1994 Zaire's inflation rate reached 2 000 per cent.

informal economy Economic activities that are not recorded in the official national accounts. In developed countries, so-called 'black market' dealings are done in cash to evade tax or to obtain HARD CURRENCY. In DEVELOPING COUNTRIES, such as those in southern Africa, the informal economy has for the most part evolved as a response to the stagnation of formal sector employment. Informal sector entrepreneurs include vegetable hawkers, shantytown artisans, drug dealers, shebeen queens and those engaged in many other money-earning activities.

infrastructure Entire system of roads, railways, ports, airports, energy supplies and communications which underpins the efficient functioning of a country or region.

insider trading Use of information not available to most shareholders or the general public to make profits in share and commodity markets. Insider trading is illegal in most countries, exceptions being Japan and Germany. Defenders of the practice claim that it makes the market more active and efficient, and hurts no-one. However, it can give some traders an unfair advantage. An unexplained increase of activity in a share ahead of a profits announcement, a takeover bid or a restructuring of a company is often a sign of insider trading.

insolvency The state of being unable to pay one's debts when they are due. A court may order that a company be liquidated when it does not have enough ASSETS to cover its total

LIABILITIES. Similarly, the estate of an individual may be sequestrated on the grounds that it is insolvent. In both instances, the court appoints somebody to sell the assets and use the proceeds to pay the creditors as much as possible, often only a portion of their claims. For example, if the assets amount to only half of what is owed, the debts will be paid off at 50c in the rand. By law, certain creditors have preference, among them the Department of Inland Revenue for any tax owing. In the case of a company or CLOSE CORPORATION, where it appears that there could be a return to profitable trading, the court will place it under judicial management and appoint judicial managers to take charge of it until it returns to profitability.

institutional investors Groups such as insurance companies, pension funds, banks and investment trusts or UNIT TRUSTS, which use their funds to buy shares and other securities. These investors now dominate many of the world's stock markets.
❖ Old Mutual, Sanlam and Liberty Life, South Africa's largest insurance companies, dominate local institutional investment.

insurance Method of protecting oneself against risks by paying a premium to an insurer, who undertakes to indemnify the insured against a specified loss or course of events. The most common forms of insurance are against accidental death or ill health, or against loss, damage or destruction of property by theft, fire or accident. LLOYD'S OF LONDON is the world's biggest and most important insurance market.
❖ Almost any risk can be insured against. Dancers and athletes can insure their legs and musicians can insure their hands against damage or loss. An American radio station even took the precaution of taking out insurance against having to pay out a $1 million prize it offered to anyone who succeeded in finding Elvis Presley alive.

interest Payment made for the use of borrowed funds. There are two types of interest: simple or compound, the latter meaning that interest is calculated not only on the principal amount of the loan or deposit, but also on any accumulated interest. In referring to the amount earned on a bank deposit, the 'flat' rate is the rate quoted assuming the interest is withdrawn, while the 'effective rate' assumes the interest is added to the capital.

internal market Arrangements within a large organization intended to mimic competitive markets. Departments compete against each other and bill each other for services as if they were independent bodies. Some people believe that internal markets bring greater efficiency to organizations.

International Development Association (IDA) Body set up in 1960 under the auspices of the ▷UNITED NATIONS to help DEVELOPING COUNTRIES by providing them with interest-free or low-interest loans.

International Monetary Fund (IMF) United Nations agency associated with the WORLD BANK. It was set up in 1947 to promote international monetary cooperation and to expand world trade. It also lends money to countries with short-term BALANCE OF PAYMENTS difficulties. The IMF can attach conditions to its loans, as it does when it insists that a government carry out spending cuts or reform its economy in return for a loan. Its occasional insistence that countries also carry out social and political reforms in return for help with debt has been controversial, particularly in Africa. Members of the IMF in good standing are considered for membership of the World Bank.
❖ South Africa's re-entry into international capital markets after the removal of apartheid was heralded by the availability of an IMF loan of US$850 million in December 1993.

interventionism Government action to moderate the effects of the free market. Enterprise zones – districts where special grants are available to encourage business growth – and COMPETITION POLICY, which provides for action against the abuse of market power by large companies or MONOPOLIES, are examples of government intervention. Economists, like governments, disagree on how much intervention is desirable.

investment trust Company listed on the STOCK EXCHANGE whose business is to invest in the shares of other companies. The value of an investment trust's shares is related to the value and earnings of the shares it owns.

invisibles Imports and exports which are not physical goods, such as earnings from foreign investments and from the supply of services, and which can be vital in redressing a deficit in the country's physical balance of trade.

Johannesburg Stock Exchange (JSE) The South African stock market, formed in 1887 soon after the discovery of the Witwatersrand gold fields. It is governed by the Stock Exchanges Control Act (1985) as well as its own internal regulations. With the listing of an increasing number of industrial companies as the economy has expanded, it has grown immensely, facilitating the development of an integrated capital market.

VINTNERS' SANCTUM *Wine matures in huge wooden casks in the KWV's 'Cathedral Cellar' at Paarl, in Western Cape.*

junk bond Specialized type of BOND issued by companies in order to raise capital against inadequate security. They are issued in huge numbers, and give holders a very high rate of INTEREST to compensate for the low credit rating of the issuer, which entails a high risk of total loss. Junk bonds were used to finance a number of TAKEOVER bids in the late 1980s, especially in the United States, and frequently brought about the immense enrichment of issuers at the expense of investors.

Keynes, John Maynard (1883-1946) British economist whose ideas dominated economic policy in Britain and the United States from the 1930s to the 1960s. His *General Theory of Employment, Interest and Money* (1936) revolutionized economic thought by suggesting that national economies need not aim to balance their budgets.
❖ In 1944 Keynes played a major part in the Bretton Woods conference, which sought to organize post-World War II finance and trade.

Keynesian economics Branch of economics associated with the theories of John Maynard Keynes which seeks to establish a mix of CAPITALISM and INTERVENTIONISM. Keynesian economists reject the theory that the free market will provide employment for everyone, and instead advocate tax cuts and government spending on public works in times of RECESSION to fuel demand and create jobs. In order to do this, it may be necessary to run a budget deficit. When the economy booms, on the other hand, Keynesians believe governments should raise taxes or cut spending in order to dampen down demand, and use any budget surplus to pay off their borrowings. This 'stop-start' policy has been criticized for exaggerating the cycles of alternating economic booms and slumps.

KWV The Koöperatiewe Wynbouwers-vereniging van Suid-Afrika Bpk (Co-operative Winegrowers' Association of South Africa Ltd) was established in 1918. It is now largely a commercial organization marketing South African wines and spirits worldwide. Its 4 400 members are shareholders, participating in profits. Nonmembers are able to share in the organization's communal distilling wine pool. The KWV owns extensive cellars, wineries and distilleries in the Western Cape. It conducts research and development and handles production superfluous to the needs of the domestic wine, brandy or grape juice concentrate markets. It also negotiates wine exports, stabilizes primary producer prices and sets standards of quality.

labour Human resources used in the production process. According to the 'labour theory of value', the value of an item is determined by the amount of labour used to produce it.
❖ The labour recruitment policies of the gold mines tended to entrench racially discriminatory policies that, although politically and economically expedient, were to have tragic and lasting social effects. (See ▷MIGRANT LABOUR in 'Southern African history'.)

labour relations (industrial relations) A broad field of study and practice that considers all aspects of the employment relationship and seeks to achieve conflict resolution and cooperation within the workplace.
❖ Labour relations in South Africa has been highly politicized and consequently characterized by extreme volatility and hostility, as disenfranchised workers have struggled to voice political as well as economic rights through industrial disruption and conflict. (See also ▷TRADE UNIONS in 'Politics, government and the law'.)

laissez faire French phrase meaning 'allow (people) to do (as they choose)'. Laissez faire economics advocates the minimum regulation or interference in the economy so the FREE ENTERPRISE system can operate according to its own laws.

Land Bank The Land and Agricultural Bank of South Africa was formed in 1912 to satisfy the special financial needs of the agricultural sector. It provides financing for the buying of seeds and raw material, capital equipment, and land. The dual nature of agriculture in South Africa has meant that the Land Bank has predominantly supported the white-owned commercial farms without consideration of the needs of black subsistence farming. It has consequently been targeted for reorganization under a land reform and rural restructuring programme in postapartheid South Africa.

liability An obligation or debt. On a company's BALANCE SHEET, its liabilities should be offset by its ASSETS.

life assurance Insurance policy covering individuals, families and business partners against death. It is called assurance, not insurance, because the event will definitely happen sooner or later; the element of risk lies only in the timing of death. The policy provides a lump sum when it matures or when the assured person dies.
❖ Financial institutions usually require mortgagees to have life assurance to guarantee payment of a loan should the mortgagee die before it has been fully repaid.

limited company Business in which each shareholder's personal liability for the company's debts is limited to the amount he has paid for his shares. Should the company go into liquidation, the shareholders may lose their money but cannot be called on to meet its debts. Without the principle of limited liability, the development of the large joint stock company – the bedrock of the modern economic system – would not have been possible, because shareholders would have been exposed to excessive risks.
❖ In South Africa privately owned (proprietary) limited companies add the abbreviation '(Pty) Ltd' after their names.

liquid asset An ASSET which can quickly be converted into money. Cash itself is a completely liquid asset, and finished goods are nearly as liquid – provided that a market can be found for them. Buildings, machinery and land are fixed, not liquid, assets because they could take years to sell.

liquidity The amount of cash available for the day-to-day running of a business. Liquid companies have enough money on hand to meet their financial obligations without having to sell fixed ASSETS.

Lloyd's of London The world's most important INSURANCE market. Lloyd's does not transact business itself, but provides the facilities for independent underwriters, or 'names', to do so. Underwriters work in syndicates to spread the risk, but face unlimited liability in case of loss. Lloyd's evolved from informal meetings of merchants at Edward Lloyd's coffee-house in the City of London, first held in the late 17th century. There, traders who dealt in cargo would find other businessmen who would agree to pay for losses in return for a small premium.
❖ In the 1990s, Lloyd's faced a crisis after risks had been badly underestimated. In 1994 it reported that losses declared over the previous four to five years had amounted to more than £8 billion (then equal to more than R40 billion).
❖ Lloyd's produces a *Register of Shipping* which inspects ocean-going ships and classifies them according to the degree of risk they represent to insurers. A ship which is 'A1 at Lloyd's' is well maintained and run, presenting the minimum risk to insurers.
❖ The Lutine Bell, taken from HMS *Lutine*, which sank in 1799 with a still unrecovered cargo of gold, hangs in the underwriting room at Lloyd's. In former times it was rung for important announcements: once for bad news, twice for good.

Lomé Convention An agreement, first signed in Lomé, capital of Togo, in 1975, giving 46

OLD AND NEW *The Lloyd's building is a high-tech masterpiece, but the 18th-century Lutine Bell remains at its centre, and entries in the 'loss book' are still written with a quill.*

DEVELOPING COUNTRIES in Africa, the Pacific and the Caribbean free access to the markets of the ▷EUROPEAN UNION. It has since been revised several times and the number of countries participating raised to 70.

loss leader Product sold at or below cost price in order to entice customers into buying other items. It is common practice in supermarkets, where very competitive prices for basic foodstuffs such as milk and bread are used to attract customers.

macroeconomics Study of the broad economic picture, involving the analysis of national income and expenditure, MONEY SUPPLY, BALANCE OF PAYMENTS and how they interrelate. (Compare MICROECONOMICS.)

Malthus, Thomas (1766-1834) British economist who was one of the first people to warn of the dangers of overpopulation. Malthus's often pessimistic theories hold that populations tend to grow faster than food production, that therefore much of the world's population will always go hungry and that eventually overpopulation will be checked by famine, disease or war.

manufacturing industry In contrast to countries in the rest of Africa, South Africa has a manufacturing sector that is by far the largest sector of the economy and has earned it its description of 'the powerhouse of Africa'. Manufacturing production, particularly of consumer goods, grew steadily in the late 1920s and in the 1930s after the government adopted a policy of protecting local industry and began promoting heavy industry with the founding of Iscor (the Iron and Steel Corporation). But it was not until early in the 1940s that manufacturing overtook mining as the leading sector. In the boom years of the 1960s industrial expansion was particularly rapid when the gold price was relatively high and huge amounts of foreign capital, particularly from West Germany, flowed into the country. By 1965 the contribution of manufacturing to the GROSS DOMESTIC PRODUCT (GDP) exceeded that of mining and farming together; by 1993 the manufacturing sector contributed nearly 25 per cent of GDP.

market economy System in which most economic activity is controlled by individuals and private companies rather than by the government.

market research Investigation of the needs and preferences of a particular group or market, usually by means of consumer surveys. It enables companies to estimate the strength of demand for a product before they go to any expense and expose themselves to the risk of producing and distributing it.

REVOLUTIONARY ECONOMIST *Karl Marx's ideas led to communist revolutions around the world, but they failed to create the ideal and classless societies of which he dreamed.*

Marx, Karl (1818-83) German political and economic theorist whose ideas were the basis of ▷MARXISM, the theory that underlies COMMUNISM. He believed history was shaped by economic contradictions that caused economic and social systems to collapse, and that CAPITALISM was inherently flawed. Marx's theories of revolution were applied in Russia by ▷LENIN and his successors after the 1917 Russian Revolution. After initial success in industrial development and during World War II, the Marxist governments of Russia and eastern Europe collapsed in the 1980s. Communist systems still remained in China, North Korea, Vietnam and Cuba. (See also ▷MARX in 'Ideas, beliefs and religion'.)

mercantilism Economic doctrine that flourished in Europe from the 16th to the 18th century. Mercantilists believed that a nation's wealth and ability to conduct war depended largely on the amount of gold and silver in its treasury. Accordingly, mercantilist governments imposed extensive economic restrictions in order to ensure an adequate surplus of exports over imports.

❖ The European quest for gold-yielding colonies in Asia, Africa and America was in part a product of mercantile economics.

microeconomics Study of economics at the level of individuals and households, companies and specific industries. It examines mainly consumer and producer behaviour, including the psychology of economic decisions. Microeconomics seeks, for example, to explain why people buy expensive cars but not why exports rise and fall – an area of MACROECONOMICS.

mining Mining has been the engine of growth behind the modern capitalist economy in South Africa, and in many other African countries. The discovery of diamonds at Kimberley in the late 1860s and of GOLD on the Witwatersrand in 1886 attracted the attention of international financiers to the rich natural resources of southern Africa and transformed the region's economy. Mining was by far the largest contributor to South Africa's gross domestic product until the 1940s, when MANUFACTURING INDUSTRY superseded it. Besides gold, of which it is the world's largest producer, and diamonds, for which it now ranks third in value terms and fifth in volume, South Africa has an abundant wealth of other minerals. It has huge reserves of coal and iron ore and is among the world's three or four top producers of chromium, manganese, vanadium, platinum, vermiculite, antimony, asbestos, fluorspar and uranium.

❖ South Africa's neighbours, too, are rich in minerals. Namibia is the world's second largest producer of gem-quality diamonds, has the world's largest uranium mine and is a leading producer of lead, cadmium, zinc and copper. Gold, nickel, asbestos, coal, copper and tin are among the 40 minerals Zimbabwe produces. Botswana is the world's top producer of diamonds in value terms and third in volume, and has copper, nickel and coal. Mozambique has large reserves of coal. Further north, Zambia mines predominantly copper, while Angola produces diamonds and oil and has large reserves of many other, largely unexploited, minerals.

mixed economy Most developed countries have mixed economies: economies that contain both private and state-owned businesses, and combine FREE ENTERPRISE with some degree of state control.

❖ Since the 1970s, there has been a steady worldwide swing, led by Britain, towards PRIVATIZATION and away from government intervention and ownership of industry, which has often proved inefficient and uneconomic.

monetarism Doctrine which asserts that the control of the MONEY SUPPLY should be the foremost instrument by which governments regulate the economy. Monetarists such as Milton FRIEDMAN claim that INFLATION can be best controlled by limiting growth in the money supply rather than by taxation or the

artificial control of prices, incomes or the availability of credit.
❖ During the 1980s many governments embraced monetarism; however, by the 1990s many of their successors had opted for a more flexible policy, varying taxation and government expenditure, in addition to controlling the money supply.

money laundering The process by which money obtained through criminal activity or as a result of tax evasion is converted into untraceable bank balances.

money supply Amount of money in circulation in a country at any given time, usually controlled by the country's CENTRAL BANK. Because the supply of money affects price levels, controlling it is an important tool in restricting INFLATION.
❖ The widespread use of credit cards – which tend to increase the holder's purchasing power and in effect put more money into circulation – has made it more difficult for central banks to measure the money supply.

monopoly Exclusive control of a product or service. By restricting output, the monopolist can raise prices and profits. A firm that has a substantial market share can also influence prices. Some control over monopoly is exerted in South Africa through COMPETITION POLICY, which can block mergers or acquisitions that might create overpowerful companies. A 'natural monopoly' arises in an industry which lends itself automatically to being controlled by a single producer who can operate at a lower cost than competitors. This happens particularly when the capital investment required to start the industry is so huge that it can be provided only by the state or corporations backed by state funds.
❖ Several of South Africa's parastatals, such as Eskom (electricity), Iscor (iron and steel) and Sasol (oil from coal) are natural monopolies, with no prospect of any genuine competition in the immediate future.

mortgage Long-term loan usually used to finance the purchase of property. The lender owns the property, which acts as security for the loan, but the borrower has secure possession of it. Interest rates on mortgages are lower than on many other types of loan, because the property is usually good security against the sum borrowed.
❖ There are two main types of mortgage. With an endowment mortgage, the borrower pays off only the interest on the loan and relies on the proceeds of an assurance policy to pay off the debt eventually. With a repayment mortgage, the borrower pays off both the interest and the debt directly.

multinational Industrial or commercial enterprise which operates in several countries. Multinationals can take advantage of cheap labour or raw material costs in different countries, and can avoid import duties by producing goods in the country in which they are to be sold. It is sometimes claimed, however, that they use their international presence to bypass legal restrictions. Some multinationals are wealthier and more powerful than many nations.
❖ Unilever, Royal Dutch/Shell and Nestlé are among Europe's leading multinational companies. Other well-known multinationals are Ford, Sony, Toyota and Exxon (Esso).

Murdoch, Rupert (1931-) Australian-born media tycoon whose company, News Corporation, produces magazines, newspapers, books, feature films and cable television programmes. Its holdings include Sky satellite television, Twentieth Century Fox film studios and six television stations in the United States which form Fox Broadcasting – one of America's major television networks.

NAFCOC (National African Chamber of Commerce and Industry) Representing African business people in South Africa, the chamber aims to develop the business and management skills of black entrepreneurs. It holds management and leadership courses and liaises with other national institutions.

national debt Sum owed by the government to its own citizens and to foreign creditors. Governments borrow money by selling SECURITIES, on which interest is paid, in order to cover their budget deficits – the difference between expenditure and the amount raised by taxation.

nationalization Takeover by a government of a privately owned business. In Britain, many industries (such as the railways, collieries and electricity supply) were nationalized by the Labour government in the late 1940s. This was for ideological reasons – ▷SOCIALISM prescribes state ownership of certain industries – as well as to achieve economies of scale while preventing the formation of a privately owned MONOPOLY. It also allowed the rescue of essential industries that were close to financial collapse. (See also PARASTATAL.)
❖ Nationalized industries are often criticized for being inefficient, uncompetitive and badly managed.

national savings Government scheme to raise funds by borrowing personal savings. Most countries have some form of national savings, which pay investors interest in the same way as bank or building society accounts.

NEDLAC (National Economic Development and Labour Committee) A body launched in South Africa on 18 February 1995 to replace the National Economic Forum (NEF), comprising representatives of labour, business and government. The NEF was set up in October 1992 to address – on a consultative basis – critical economic and socio-economic development issues arising in the post-apartheid era.

Nikkei index Share index of the Tokyo Stock Exchange. The main Nikkei index charts the share movements of Japan's 300 top-rated listed companies.

no-claim bonus Reduction in insurance premiums because no claim has been made. The system is well established in motor insurance, where premiums can be reduced by as much as 60 per cent if the driver has not made any claims for several years. It is also becoming common in insurance policies for personal possessions.

OECD (Organization for Economic Cooperation and Development) International body comprising most of the world's advanced industrialized countries. The OECD, which replaced the Organization for European Economic Cooperation in 1961, aims to promote economic growth and stability for its members and to help DEVELOPING COUNTRIES build up their trading capacity.

oligopoly Any market dominated by a small number of individuals or companies. An example is the international market for rough diamonds, which is dominated by major producers who sell their output through DE BEERS' Central Selling Organization.

Onassis, Aristotle (1906-75) Greek shipping magnate who owned the largest fleet of supertankers in the world. At his death, his assets were estimated at US$500 million.
❖ Onassis's flamboyant lifestyle included a liaison with the opera singer Maria ▷CALLAS and marriage in 1968 to Jackie Kennedy, widow of US president John F Kennedy.

OPEC (Organization of Petroleum Exporting Countries) Group of oil-rich countries, mainly in the Middle East, which operates as a CARTEL to control oil production and to secure favourable prices for the oil placed on the market by its members.
❖ OPEC raised oil prices sharply in 1973. The result was a severe oil shortage and global economic disruption and INFLATION.

open account Term for the sale of goods or services paid for on the basis of a periodic statement of account. Open account financing is the predominant method of payment used in the settlement of South Africa's international trade transactions.

option Right to buy or sell a share or a COMMODITY at a specified price at a future date. Options are a sophisticated method of HEDGING against possible price movements: instead of buying the goods, or even a FUTURES contract for delivery at a later date, traders buy a much cheaper 'call' option to buy, or a 'put' option to sell, the goods in the future. They will exercise their option only if the price at the time of the transaction makes it worth while.

parastatal State-owned corporation. Government intervention in the South African economy through the establishment of parastatals has been extensive. It has occurred in industry, services, broadcasting and through licensing and control boards. Examples of corporations owned by the state have been: SASOL (oil from coal), Soekor (oil prospecting), Iscor (steel), Eskom (electricity), SATS (railways), SAA (airways) and broadcasting (SABC), among others.

Parkinson's law Proposition that work expands to fill the time available for its completion. It was put forward in 1955 by the British economist C Northcote Parkinson as a partly satirical attack on civil servants: he believed that they expanded their work unnecessarily, increasing their numbers and the amount of bureaucratic paperwork at the expense of the taxpayer.

partnership Business or professional venture owned by two or up to 20 people. The attributes of a partnership are similar to those of the SOLE PROPRIETORSHIP, except that ownership and control of the venture is vested in more than one person. Each partner is committed to contributing either skills or capital to the venture and is liable for actions taken and debts incurred by the partnership. (See also CLOSE CORPORATION.)

pension fund Non-profit-making institution that manages the financial provisions of employees and employers for the time when they retire or are no longer capable of working. Income is derived from the contributions of employees and employers, investments and cash from the sale of assets. Pension funds in South Africa are governed by the Pensions Act (1956).

❖ Pension funds have in the past been viewed as more attractive than PROVIDENT FUNDS because employees' contributions are tax deductible up to certain limits. However, only one-third of the total value of money accumulated in the fund may be paid out on retirement or in the event of death; the balance is paid monthly or as an annuity.

❖ Pension funds invest heavily in the stock market and in property, and their managers can exert considerable influence on the money markets.

perfect competition Theoretical economic scenario in which there are so many producers and consumers in a market that no individual trader is large enough to affect the price. Although in reality there is no such thing as perfect competition, the markets for some commodities, such as wheat and tin, come close to the ideal.

petrodollars US dollars that are earned from exports by oil-producing countries and are held in banks or other institutions outside those countries.

❖ In the 1970s, OPEC countries accumulated enormous reserves of petrodollars, which at times threatened the stability of exchange rates throughout the world as they were continually moved from country to country in search of higher interest rates.

planned economy System in which prices, wages and production levels are set by a central authority, usually the government, as part of its political programme. The former Soviet Union and other communist countries had planned economies, but most of those countries have now adopted at least some degree of FREE ENTERPRISE.

PPI (Producer Price Index) The index of the cost of a representative basket of wholesale goods, including capital and intermediate goods, which are inputs in the production process. As the PPI is a measure of 'wholesale' prices, it may act to forecast the trend of the CPI (Consumer Price Index).

❖ The South African Producer Price Index is estimated and published monthly by the Central Statistical Service.

price control Legislation limiting consumer and industrial price increases to control INFLATION. It is often introduced as part of a general prices and incomes policy – allowing incomes to rise only in line with prices.

❖ Price controls were unsuccessfully applied in South Africa in the 1970s in an attempt to curb inflation.

price-earnings (PE) ratio Figure relating the market value of a share to historic or prospective company profits. It is calculated by dividing the company's profit by the number of shares to give earnings per share. The current price of the share is then divided by its earnings per share. If a company has 1 million shares and makes a profit of R100 000, the earnings are 10c a share. If the price of the shares is 100c, the PE ratio is 10; if the price is 200c, the ratio is 20. Investors use PE ratios to decide whether the shares of a company are expensive or cheap compared with those of similar companies. The higher the PE ratio, the faster, generally, investors and analysts expect profits to grow.

primary sector Section of the economy that produces and processes raw materials, fuel and foodstuffs, as opposed to manufactured goods (in the SECONDARY SECTOR) or services (in the tertiary sector).

❖ Many primary goods are produced in developing countries, and their prices fluctuate with the level of demand from the industrialized world. In recent years, prices for raw materials such as copper and iron ore and other commodities such as cocoa and cotton have been depressed, which has held back economic growth in the developing countries which produce them.

private sector Part of the economy which is not owned or controlled by the government. In most developed countries, the greater part of economic activity is in private hands. The trend towards PRIVATIZATION during the 1980s and 1990s has enlarged the private sector in Britain and many other countries.

privatization Sale of government-owned corporations and industries to private investors; the opposite of NATIONALIZATION.

❖ Privatization of parastatals was first seriously placed on the South African agenda in 1987. The objectives were to encourage economic growth, raise revenue for the State and spread asset ownership. Until recently, privatization of major parastatals was limited to Iscor (1989) and Telkom (1991). A few smaller sales have occurred, such as that of National Sorghum Breweries (1991).

profit A company's profit margin is the amount by which its sales revenue exceeds the cost of producing and distributing its goods or services. Profits can be retained and ploughed back into the company, or, alternatively, distributed among its shareholders, and sometimes its staff.

❖ The 'profit motive' – the urge to earn money by selling goods or services – is said to drive the FREE ENTERPRISE system.

protectionism Raising the price of imports by imposing duties and QUOTAS, in order to protect domestic industries from foreign competition. Other schemes, such as the stringent imposition of safety regulations, are also sometimes used to make importing difficult. Governments can also subsidize domestic industry to make its goods cheaper than goods that are imported.

provident fund Institution performing a similar function to that of the PENSION FUND. However, the provident fund provides a lump sum to its members on retirement or in the event of disability or death. Provident funds in South Africa are regulated by the Insurance Act (1943). Although contributions paid by employees to the fund are not tax deductible, the merit of the provident fund has been that the total value of money accumulated is paid out. This feature made this type of fund increasingly attractive during the period of political and economic uncertainty in the 1980s and 1990s.

public expenditure Spending by the government and the public sector. Increasing public spending may create jobs and reduce unemployment, but also usually fuels INFLATION by encouraging the demand for goods and increasing the MONEY SUPPLY.
❖ In many Western countries, the rise in public spending after World War II caused huge national budget deficits which led to a reaction against socialist policies. Britain's postwar Labour government was reputed to have brought the country to the edge of bankruptcy and its economy was saved only by the timeous discovery of North Sea oil.

public goods Products or services whose consumption by one person does not preclude consumption by another – for example, street lighting, the police force or defence services. Such goods produce social benefits which are not easy to assess in terms of simple profit and loss, and are usually paid for or subsidized by governments. If matters are left to the free market, public goods may be inadequately supplied, particularly if it is difficult for suppliers to charge consumers for them.

public sector borrowing requirement (PSBR) Amount of money a government needs to borrow in a given year. The PSBR is equivalent to the difference between the government's income and expenditure. It is mostly funded through the sale of GILTS and by NATIONAL SAVINGS. The accumulated PSBRs of the past make up the NATIONAL DEBT.

quota Limit imposed by governments on imports, or by business CARTELS on production. Import quotas, often used in the past by South Africa, aim to protect domestic industry from foreign competition, while production quotas aim to keep prices high.

real cost Term which can have two meanings in economics. Sometimes it is used to describe the 'opportunity cost' of something – the value of the resources used to produce a good, plus the cost of foregoing some alternative course of action. It can also mean the price of a product adjusted for INFLATION.

real income Income measured in terms of what it will buy. If incomes rise more quickly than prices, real incomes increase.

recession Fall in economic activity characterized by declining demand, lower production and rises in unemployment. A country is said to be in recession when its GROSS DOMESTIC PRODUCT has shrunk for nine consecutive months. Deep and prolonged recessions become DEPRESSIONS.

reflation Increase in economic activity, fuelled by a general increase in demand which may be spontaneous, or brought about by government action such as cutting taxes or investing in large-scale public works. Governments are cautious about reflating their economies, because it can lead to INFLATION.

Rembrandt Group A conglomerate formed by Dr Anton Rupert in 1941. Previously operating as the Rembrandt Tobacco Corporation (SA), the formation in 1969 of Rembrandt Group (Remgro) as the group's primary investment holding company acknowledged the diversification of its interests. Remgro now has considerable interests in a wide range of industries through its subsidiaries and associated companies. These include the tobacco, spirits, food and wine, petrochemicals, medical services, banking and life assurance industries.

rescheduling Change in the original terms for repayment of a loan when the borrower has run into repayment difficulties. Banks may agree to accept smaller repayments spread over a longer period.
❖ In the 1980s, banks agreed a series of debt reschedulings for various countries in Latin America and sub-Saharan Africa; devaluations of local currencies and falls in commodity prices had left them unable to pay even the interest on their debts, let alone repay the loans themselves. In December 1994 Mexico faced a similar situation after the value of its currency, the peso, fell 40 per cent against the US dollar in 10 days, due mainly to loss of confidence in its political and economic prospects.
❖ South Africa's debts had to be rescheduled in the late 1980s after political events set off a sharp devaluation of the rand and a huge flight of capital through disinvestment.

reserves Currencies and gold held by a country's CENTRAL BANK in order to provide backing to national currencies and to finance international trade. Reserves are kept in stable and easily exchangeable currencies such as US dollars, Deutschemarks and yen, and also often in gold. In a company's accounts, reserves comprise profits and other funds held back by a company for further development and not distributed as DIVIDENDS.

retail price maintenance Practice by which a retailer can obtain a product from a supplier only if the retailer guarantees to sell it at a certain price. This is illegal in South Africa, with certain exceptions. A related practice, also illegal, is 'horizontal price collusion', which is the agreement between two or more suppliers of a commodity to charge a particular or a minimum price for their product.

retirement annuity Fixed regular income paid in return for the investment of a lump sum. The payments usually stop when the beneficiary dies, so the income is based on life expectancy. Men normally obtain higher annuity rates than women of the same age, because on average men do not live as long.

reverse takeover Process by which a large company takes over a smaller one, but in effect the smaller gains control of the larger, perhaps supplying new management. Companies can use reverse takeovers to gain a stock market quotation without having to issue shares or go through the complicated process of meeting the stock exchange's criteria for a quotation.

Ricardo, David (1772-1823) British economist who developed the theory of comparative advantage as an explanation of international trade. This held that countries which are more efficient at producing goods will still trade with those who are less efficient. Efficient countries will export goods in which their comparative efficiency is high, and import goods where it is low. This became an important argument in support of LAISSEZ FAIRE economics.
❖ Ricardo's pessimistic views about overpopulation, diminishing returns and the 'iron law of wages' (that population growth will depress wages by producing an excess supply of labour), along with those of Thomas MALTHUS, led to economics being dubbed the 'dismal science'.

risk Element of chance which all investors must consider when making financial decisions. The higher the perceived risks of an investment, the higher the return is expected to be. Speculators and investors can opt for a safe, but modest return by putting their money into BLUE CHIP companies or building societies. Alternatively, they can invest in a new business venture which has the possibility of much higher returns, but a corresponding high risk of total loss. Investors spread risk by having a balanced portfolio of investments; for example by buying GILTS as well as SHARES in many different companies.

Rockefeller, John D (1839-1937) American industrialist who founded the Standard Oil Company in 1870. By 1880 he controlled virtually the entire oil industry in the USA. Although he had to break up the company in 1892, following antimonopoly legislation, he continued to dominate the oil industry until his retirement in 1911.
❖ At one time the richest man in the world, Rockefeller gave more than US$500 million to charity. He funded the Rockefeller Center in New York; his heirs still own the building.

Rothschild Banking dynasty founded in the 18th century by Meyer Amschel Rothschild in Frankfurt, Germany. He and his sons made much of their wealth by lending money to the warring parties in the Napoleonic wars, during which their intelligence service was a step ahead of Britain's. The Rothschilds helped to finance the growth of industry during the Industrial Revolution and continued to dominate European banking until World War II, when the Nazis confiscated many of their ASSETS. Members of the family still own private banks in London and Paris.

SACOB (South African Chamber of Business) Formed in the late 1980s by the unification of the Associated Chambers of Commerce and the Federated Chamber of Industry, it is a national coordinating body representing the interests of business and commerce in South Africa. It has a network of regional and local chambers.

Sasol Acronym derived from the Afrikaans name of the South African Coal, Oil and Gas Corporation. Sasol was established by the government in 1950 to produce oil and petrol from ▷COAL – with technology considered revolutionary at the time – so as to build up strategic reserves during the apartheid era. Although formed primarily to produce petrol, Sasol today is a world leader in the synthetic organic chemicals industry.

scarcity Fundamental idea behind all conventional economic theory. It is assumed that human wants will always exceed the resources available to fulfil them, forcing individuals to choose which of their desires will be satisfied from resources which are rationed – usually by way of their higher prices.
❖ John Kenneth GALBRAITH challenged this traditional assumption with his theories on the affluent society.

seasonal adjustment Modification made to economic statistics to compensate for seasonal changes in demand, supply, price or any other factors, which might otherwise obscure the long-term trend. Fruit and vegetables, for example, may become more plentiful every spring or autumn, causing prices to fall. The CPI is calculated on a seasonally adjusted basis to allow for this effect.

seasonal unemployment Periodic unemployment created by changes in the demand for different products or services at different times of the year. Holiday resorts, for example, experience seasonal unemployment outside the tourist season.

secondary sector Manufacturing and construction industries, which turn raw materials from the PRIMARY SECTOR into finished goods ready to be transferred to a SERVICE INDUSTRY in the tertiary sector for distribution, promotion and sale.

securities Documents recording ownership of ASSETS or property which can be lodged as collateral for a loan. The term can also be used more broadly to cover BONDS, STOCKS, SHARES and EQUITIES. These are negotiable securities which can be bought and sold, and yield either INTEREST or DIVIDENDS.

sellers' market Market in which demand exceeds supply, allowing sellers to ask higher prices for their goods. It is the opposite of a BUYERS' MARKET.

service industry Any industry which does not make anything, but provides services to other industries or members of the public. Banking, hairdressing, transport and theatre are all examples of service industries and part of the tertiary sector.
❖ Since 1945 the service industries in the highly industrialized countries such as Britain and the United States have grown enormously relative to manufacturing.

shares Units of investment that represent part ownership of a company. They are also called EQUITY or equities. People who hold shares in a company are entitled to a portion of its net profits, paid in the form of a regular DIVIDEND. As the providers of a substantial amount of the company's CAPITAL, shareholders may also have some say in the way it is run. A company may issue any number of shares: small, privately owned companies may have as few as two shares, while Iscor has issued more than 2 billion.

single European market Agreement between the members of the ▷EUROPEAN UNION to allow the free movement of goods, labour and capital between member states. The system aims to ensure that industries operate on equal terms in any member state, and can sell their goods freely throughout the EU. It also dictates common health and safety standards.

Small Business Development Corporation (SBDC) A public company controlled by the private sector whose aim is to stimulate entrepreneurship in southern Africa. The SBDC provides financing, advisory services and help in the location of business premises, and promotes the interests of small business at a national level.
❖ In several South African centres the SBDC has set up premises for light industries and crafts that are available to entrepreneurs at reasonable rentals.

Smith, Adam (1723-90) Scottish economist whose book *An Inquiry into the Nature and Causes of the Wealth of Nations* (1776) argued for minimal interference in the workings of the free market. It asserted that individuals working in their own interest will be guided by an 'invisible hand' which will automatically further the interests of their community. He also proposed that wealth was mainly created by labour, and the more labour that was put into a product, the higher its value would be.
❖ Adam Smith is considered the father of modern LAISSEZ-FAIRE economics.

social cost Cost seen from the perspective of society as a whole, not from an individual or corporate standpoint. For example, the cost of pollution may not be felt by the company producing it, but will affect society generally because of the decline in air and water quality. Unemployment also carries a social cost: low morale and potentially increased delinquency among the unemployed could be added to the economic cost of social security payments, lost income tax revenue and lost production. However, social costs, like the value of PUBLIC GOODS, are often difficult to measure in financial terms.

sole proprietorship Business owned by a single individual. The attraction of forming a sole proprietorship is the absence of legal formalities involved. Disadvantages are that the sole proprietorship is not a separate legal entity, so the owner is personally liable for business operations, the owner is taxed as an individual on the profits that accrue to the

PAPER ART *In the past, share certificates were of elaborate design with splendid engravings romanticizing industry and commerce. Today, they are usually a simple record of ownership.*

business, and scope for growth is limited to the owner's capital contribution.

South African Customs Union (SACU) Customs agreement of 1903 joining the South African colonies (Cape, Orange Free State, Transvaal and Natal), Bechuanaland (now Botswana), Basutoland (now Lesotho) and Swaziland. Renegotiated after the formation of the Union in 1910 and amended to include South West Africa (now Namibia) in 1920, the agreement stipulates a currency linked to the rand and a common monetary policy (implemented by the South African Reserve Bank). The SACU has aided economic integration in southern Africa, with South Africa playing the dominant role.

South African Reserve Bank (SARB) The CENTRAL BANK of South Africa, initially formed in 1921 to facilitate the country's financial development. The SARB fulfils the traditional central bank functions. It is the bank of the government and of the commercial banks, and the currency issuer. It is responsible for the conduct of monetary policy to ensure optimum performance of the economy while safeguarding the value of the rand. It also controls the sale of gold BULLION from South African mines and supervises the banks and building societies.

speculation Short-term capital movements arising from expectations of future exchange rate movements. If the local currency is expected to devalue, speculators will buy foreign currency now, expecting to sell it for local currency at a profit at some future date. Speculators may also deal in COMMODITIES.

stag STOCK EXCHANGE speculator who buys new share issues in the hope of selling at a quick profit when dealings begin.

stagflation Combination of low economic growth and high INFLATION, when prices and unemployment rise and investment in industry is low. The word is a blend of 'stagnation' and 'inflation'.

stamp duty Special tax payable on certain transactions, including property leases, the term deriving from the revenue stamps that must legally be affixed to documentation during the sale as proof of payment.

stock Type of repayable, interest-bearing debt issued by governments and companies to raise money. In South Africa and Britain, stockholders are creditors of a company; unlike the shareholders, they do not own any EQUITY in the company. In the USA they are equivalent to shareholders.

stock exchange Place where stocks, shares, bonds and other securities are bought and sold. The world's major stock exchanges are in London, New York (WALL STREET) and Tokyo. Smaller, but nevertheless important, stock exchanges include Johannesburg, Hong Kong, Frankfurt and Zürich.

❖ Southern Africa is served by the JOHANNESBURG STOCK EXCHANGE, and smaller exchanges in Zimbabwe and Namibia. The Zimbabwe Stock Exchange, re-established in 1946 after World War II in Bulawayo and Harare, provides a secure basis for capital market dealings in that country. A stock exchange was established Windhoek in 1992 to meet capital market requirements in the newly-independent Namibia.

stock exchange index An average that measures changes over a certain period of time in the prices of shares on a particular exchange. Key stock exchange indices are: the DOW JONES Industrial Average (New York), the NIKKEI Industrial Average (Tokyo), and the FTSE-100, or Financial Times-Stock Exchange 100-share index (London).

subsistence Bare minimum needed to stay alive. In a subsistence economy, people produce almost all their necessities themselves and rarely have any left over with which to trade for other goods.

supply and demand In economic theory, the two main factors which determine price. Supply refers to the willingness of producers and others to offer goods and services for sale, while demand refers to the willingness and ability of consumers to buy these goods. The price of the goods, and the amount sold, is the result of the interaction of these two forces. Demand is affected by such factors as income and fashion.

supply-side economics Idea that supply rather than demand is the key element in a country's economy. Supply-side economists say governments should concentrate on improving the quality of labour and boosting capital supply and productivity. They believe that stimulating investment in industry by lowering taxes on businesses will raise production, which in turn will bring down prices and control INFLATION.

takeover Acquisition of a company by another company or, sometimes, an individual. The aim is usually to boost profits, to eliminate competition, or to achieve economies of scale (the reduction in unit costs resulting from a larger volume of production in relation to basic overheads). Takeover bids of publicly quoted companies, which are sometimes signalled by the bidder building up a large shareholding in the company concerned, are watched very carefully by dealers on the STOCK EXCHANGE. In Britain, they are monitored by a Takeover Panel; South Africa has a Securities Regulation Panel.

taxation Compulsory levy imposed by central and local government. Most taxes are levied on income, expenditure or wealth.

Taxes on income and capital gains are called direct taxes, while those on expenditure, such as VAT (valued added tax), are called indirect taxes. Taxes may be charged to individuals or to companies.

tax avoidance Minimizing one's tax bill by legitimate means. Wealthy individuals and businesses sometimes avoid tax by exploiting loopholes in the tax rules. Another way is to invest or base a business in a tax haven – a country with no taxation, or very low levels of taxation, such as the Cayman Islands, the Channel Islands or Liechtenstein.

❖ Some wealthy people avoid tax by becoming 'tax exiles' – leaving their home countries to live where tax rates are lower. Others constantly travel between countries so that they never reside anywhere long enough to qualify as a taxpayer.

❖ Tax evasion is the illegal counterpart of tax avoidance. Taxes are commonly evaded by people not declaring their true income, or by making false claims for tax relief.

Thebe Investment Corporation Black-owned investment corporation, formed in mid-1992 by a non-profit community trust. The trustees of Thebe include President Nelson Mandela and Walter Sisulu of the African National Congress. Thebe was established with the primary aim of increasing the stake held by black business in all sectors of the South African economy.

trade barrier Any government measure that discourages international trade. Trade barriers range from outright bans on products to import duties which make a product difficult to sell by raising its price.

❖ Since its formation in 1947, GATT (the General Agreement on Tariffs and Trade, now the World Trade Organization) has sought to dismantle trade barriers throughout the world.

trade cycle Natural tendency of an economy to waver between boom periods of high production, investment and employment, and times of RECESSION or DEPRESSION.

treasury bills Specialized BILLS OF EXCHANGE used by the government as a short-term method of raising money. They are sold every week to discount houses, which are institutions that specialize in buying and selling bills of exchange.

UIF (Unemployment Insurance Fund) Provides for unemployment insurance in South Africa, in accordance with the Unemployment Insurance Acts of 1946 and 1966. The fund comprises contributions by certain employees, their employers, and the ministry of labour. The fund distributes benefits to contributors during periods of unemployment, provided they are available and able to work.

underwriting Process of sharing INSURANCE risks, by which syndicates of underwriters accept liability for part of any eventual loss. Each underwriter is paid a premium for bearing his share of the risk: the more money the underwriters guarantee, or the higher risk their syndicate insures, the higher the premiums will be. By extension, INSTITUTIONAL INVESTORS underwrite new issues of shares, promising to buy surplus shares if they are not taken up by private investors.

unemployment The level of unemployment in an economy depends on the demand for labour, and is therefore an important economic indicator. Most economists now agree that the ideal of full employment is almost impossible to achieve.

❖ In South Africa, structural deficiencies and the stagnation of the formal economy, increased rural-urban migration, the unequal distribution of income, and the encouragement of capital-intensive production techniques have allowed unemployment to reach extremely high levels since the 1960s.

unit trust (mutual fund) Institution that invites small investors to buy 'units', which are pooled to buy STOCKS and SHARES. The value of each unit is that of the total fund divided by the number of units issued. Investors can sell their units back to the fund at any time. The term 'mutual fund' is preferred in the USA and Canada. Both terms are used in South Africa.

usury Charging excessive INTEREST on loans. In medieval Europe, usury was common, but in most countries it is now illegal to charge more than a specified maximum interest rate.

❖ In many Muslim countries, moneylending at interest is considered to be usury and is forbidden. Instead of lending money, Islamic banks levy fees or enter leasing and profit-sharing deals with their customers.

VAT (value added tax) Sales tax levied on goods and services. VAT replaced General Sales Tax (GST) in South Africa in 1991 as a more efficient system of indirect taxation. However, only certain basic foods are exempt from VAT and the imposition of VAT on all other basic needs, goods and services is still the subject of political controversy. In 1995, the rate was 14 per cent. VAT-registered companies can generally claim back VAT they have paid on purchases, so the tax is paid only on the value they add to the goods they produce or the services they provide.

voetstoots The legal stipulation, often specified in a contract or deed of sale, that an article is sold 'as it stands', with any defects. The seller is then not liable for any defects in the article sold that are unknown to him. However, he is liable for defects known to him at the time of sale. This practice, common among dealers in South Africa, is open to much abuse and is therefore criticized by the South African Coordinating Consumer Council.

Wall Street Financial district of New York, home of many banks and investment companies, and often referring specifically to the New York Stock Exchange. Its name comes from the stockade, or wall, the original Dutch settlers built in 1653 to protect themselves from native American attackers.

❖ The historic collapse of New York stock prices on 24 October 1929, when many investors lost their fortunes, is known as the Wall Street Crash. Stocks continued to fall until, by late 1932, most were worth only 20 per cent of their 1929 value. The Crash marked the beginning of the worldwide ▷DEPRESSION of the 1930s.

white knight As the name implies, someone who rescues a business. It specifically refers to a third party who prevents a hostile TAKEOVER bid by either making a friendly bid or else acquiring a large enough shareholding to pre-empt the predator.

World Bank International financial organization set up in 1945 after the Bretton Woods conference of 1944, which sought to organize postwar world finance and trade. Officially called the International Bank for Reconstruction and Development, it was originally concerned with providing capital for the postwar reconstruction of Europe. Since the 1950s its main priority has been to promote the economic development of its member countries. It lends money to governments and arranges finance for a wide variety of projects, especially in DEVELOPING COUNTRIES.

❖ To join the World Bank countries must be reputable members of the INTERNATIONAL MONETARY FUND (IMF).

yield Income derived from an investment, expressed as a percentage of its current value. Yield is important for investors in STOCKS and SHARES, who use it to calculate the likely return on their portfolio of holdings, relating the original or 'par' value of a share to its market price and its DIVIDEND by a simple formula. A 200c share paying a dividend of 20c would have a yield of 10 per cent if its market value were still 200c; if the share value had risen to 400c, however, the yield would then have fallen to 5 per cent.

FILMS, ENTERTAINMENT AND THE MEDIA

Mass entertainment is the creation of modern technology. The talent and glamour of Hollywood brought stars of the theatre to a wider cinema audience, and created new stars of its own. Today, television has a mission to inform as well as to amuse. Radio remains a powerful medium, while newspapers and magazines thrive on the continuing appeal of words and pictures.

PATRIOTIC PARTNERS *Humphrey Bogart and Katharine Hepburn plan to use their dilapidated 9 m steam launch,* The African Queen, *as a makeshift torpedo to sink a German gunboat.*

42nd Street Backstage musical comedy film in which the leading lady of a Broadway show falls ill and a girl from the chorus takes over. 'You're going out there a youngster,' the director tells her. 'But you've got to come back a star!' It was made in Hollywood in 1933 and has some spectacular song-and-dance numbers devised by choreographer Busby BERKELEY.

A-Team, The American television serial which was the most popular series screened on TV1 in South Africa. Starring George Peppard (Colonel Hannibal Smith) and Dirk Benedict (The Face), it involved an odd assortment of soldiers on the run – including a psychopath and a black giant with 'bad attitudes' – who assist victims of injustice.

Abbott and Costello American comedy duo of the 1940s, who moved to the cinema from vaudeville, taking many of their crosstalk routines with them. Lou Costello (1906-59) was the chubby, buffoonish half, while Bud Abbott (1895-1974) was the thin, bullying 'straight man'. *In Society* (1944), in which they play a pair of incompetent plumbers who wreck a mansion, is generally considered to be their funniest film.

African Mirror South African-produced newsreel thought to be the world's oldest regular film newsreel. The first weekly release by I W SCHLESINGER's African Film Productions took place on 5 May 1913. It brought the drama of World War I to the relatively isolated towns of South Africa. African Mirror was produced for many years, becoming bilingual and later going international under the name Mirror International/Spieël Internasionaal.

African Queen, The Romantic adventure film directed by John Huston in 1951, starring Katharine Hepburn and Humphrey Bogart. Based on a novel by C S Forester, it concerns the disreputable, gin-swigging captain of a Congo river launch, *The African Queen*, who helps a prim-and-proper missionary to escape from the hostile German forces in East Africa at the beginning of World War I.

All Quiet on the Western Front Classic antiwar film about a group of young German volunteers experiencing front line action in World War I. Their youthful patriotism turns to cynicism as one after another they are killed. Taken from Erich Maria Remarque's best-selling novel, it was made in Hollywood in 1930 by the Oscar-winning director Lewis Milestone.

❖ An unforgettable image in the film shows the hero, played by Lew Ayres, being shot by a sniper as he reaches out for a butterfly.

Allen, Woody (Allen Stewart Konigsberg) (1935-) Brooklyn-born comedian who has been writing, directing and acting in his own films since the late 1960s. Early movies such as *Bananas* (1971) are pure slapstick, but the romantic comedies he made with Diane Keaton, such as *Annie Hall* (1977) and *Manhattan* (1979), reveal greater depth. *Interiors* (1978) and *September* (1987) show the sobering influence of his idol, Ingmar Bergman. *Manhattan Murder Mystery* (1993) marked a return to light-hearted humour.

❖ Mia Farrow was Allen's partner and leading actress during the 1980s, when they co-starred in the marital drama *Hannah and her Sisters* (1986). However, their relationship broke up over a much-publicized child custody case in 1993.

alternative media Concept of media that emerged in opposition to the mainstream commercial media with social consciouness as its *raison d'être*. During the 1980s in South Africa the term was used for new progressive media which campaigned against apartheid. Newspapers and magazines, such as the MAIL & GUARDIAN, *New Nation*, *Die Suid-Afrikaan* and *Vrye Weekblad*, predominated alongside mainly DOCUMENTARY films – prohibited for public viewing – and independent radio stations such as CAPITAL RADIO and Radio 702.

Amadeus Dazzling 1984 film version of Peter Shaffer's stage play about the life and death of ▷MOZART. Starring Tom Hulce as Mozart, with a high-pitched giggle, it highlights the feud between him and his embittered and self-professed rival, the ▷HABSBURG court composer Antonio Salieri.

American in Paris, An Highly acclaimed Hollywood musical about an ex-GI trying to succeed as a painter in Paris shortly after World War II. Directed by Vincente Minnelli in 1951, it starred Gene Kelly and Leslie Caron and featured music by George Gershwin. It contained a long ballet sequence which was considered an artistic breakthrough in the cinema. The sequence was choreographed by Kelly and danced by Caron.

Andrews, Julie (1935-) Wholesome British singing star who won hearts throughout the world in *Mary Poppins* (1964) and *The Sound of Music* (1965). Her less sugary roles, as in Alfred Hitchcock's spy thriller *Torn Curtain* (1966) and *That's Life* (1986), directed by her husband Blake Edwards, have generally been disappointing. On stage she was the original Eliza Doolittle in *My Fair Lady*.

Apocalypse Now Spectacular Vietnam War epic co-written, produced and directed in

DEADLY ENEMIES *Good and evil are epitomized by the 1989 screen Batman, Michael Keaton, and the most sinister of Jokers, Jack Nicholson, who earned a record US$6 million for the role.*

1979 by Francis Ford Coppola. Martin Sheen portrays an American captain sent to assassinate a renegade US Army officer, played by Marlon Brando, who is waging his own war in the hills. The most memorable scene is of a beach being strafed to the accompaniment of Wagner's *The Ride of the Valkyries.*

❖ Plagued by Sheen's heart problems, and Brando's weight problem, the film took so long to make that show business journalists retitled it 'Apocalypse Later'.

Arende Afrikaans TV drama series based on the traumatic experiences of Boer prisoners on ▷ST HELENA during the ▷SOUTH AFRICAN WAR. A Cape rebel (Ian Roberts) is exiled for life on the island. Written by Paul Venter and produced by Dirk de Villiers, it was among the first of a number of quality historical dramas produced for TV. Its two parts (1989 and 1991) were seen by over 2 million viewers.

Ashcroft, Dame Peggy (1907-91) British stage actress renowned for her Shakespearean roles in the 1930s. She played Desdemona to Paul Robeson's *Othello* (1930) and was an outstanding Juliet in John Gielgud's production of *Romeo and Juliet* (1932). She appeared in the British TV series *The Jewel in the Crown* (1984) and a handful of films, most notably Alfred Hitchcock's *The 39 Steps* (1935) and David Lean's *A Passage to India* (1984) – for which she won the Oscar for Best Supporting Actress. She was made a Dame of the British Empire in 1956.

Attenborough, Lord Richard (1923-) Baby-faced British character actor who made a memorable 'Pinkie', the heartless young gangster in the 1947 film version of Graham Greene's *Brighton Rock.* He later became a leading director of epics, including *Oh! What a Lovely War* (1969), *Young Winston* (1972), *Gandhi* (1982) and *Chaplin* (1992). He was knighted in 1976 and made a peer in 1993. He is the brother of the zoologist and television personality Sir David Attenborough.

❖ Attenborough's *Cry Freedom* (1987) about black consciousness leader Steve ▷BIKO, caused a controversy when ▷AZAPO and other activist groups complained that the film was more concerned with Biko's associate, exiled newspaper editor Donald Woods. They accused Attenborough of bias, distortion and over-simplification.

Bardot, Brigitte (Camille Javal) (1934-) Sultry French actress who was billed as a 'sex kitten' when she starred in her husband Roger Vadim's 1956 film *And God Created Woman.* In it she played a sexually obsessed young woman – a type she concentrated on throughout her career. She retired in 1973 and devoted herself to campaigning for animal rights.

Batman Cartoon superhero created in an American comic strip in 1939. It was turned into a children's television show in the 1960s, with Adam West as the Caped Crusader and Burt Ward as his partner Robin. They appeared in the first *Batman* film (1966). The title role was taken by Michael Keaton in two big-budget sequels: *Batman* (1989) and *Batman Returns* (1992). Val Kilmer took the part in the 1995 sequel called *Batman Forever.*

Battleship Potemkin, The Highly influential Russian silent film directed by Sergei Eisenstein in 1925. It tells of a naval mutiny in Odesa in 1905 and has one of the most admired sequences in cinema history: the massacre of innocent civilians on the Odesa Steps, during which a runaway pram with a baby trundles downwards. A similar sequence appears in *The Untouchables* (1987) with Kevin Costner as Elliot Ness.

BBC The British Broadcasting Corporation, Britain's public service radio and television station. BBC radio began in London in 1922 and the television service started in 1936: this was suspended when war broke out in 1939 and resumed in 1946. A second television channel, BBC2, followed in 1964. The corporation operates under Royal Charter and is run by a Board of Governors appointed by the monarch. It is funded by the annual TV and radio licence fee paid by those who own or rent sets.

Beatty, Warren (1937-) American 'heart-throb' actor and brother of Shirley MacLaine. He starred in major productions such as *Bonnie and Clyde* (1967), *Shampoo* (1975) and *Heaven Can Wait* (1978). He directed and played the lead in *Reds* (1981), an account of John Reed, an American journalist who covered the Russian Revolution in 1917 and later cofounded the American Communist Party. It won Beatty a Best Director Oscar. He has

MELODY MAKERS *An illuminated pattern of women with violins croon 'The Shadow Waltz' – one of the highlights of choreographer Busby Berkeley's musical hit* Gold Diggers *of 1933.*

since played the leads in *Dick Tracy* (1990), the comic-strip detective, and *Bugsy* (1991), the true-life story of a Hollywood gangster.

Becky Sharp First feature film made in three-colour Technicolor. Produced in Hollywood in 1935, and based on William ▷THACKERAY's novel *Vanity Fair*, it starred Miriam Hopkins in the title role.

Bergman, Ingmar (1918-) Swedish film and theatre director renowned for his haunting imagery, mystical themes and stark view of life. Bergman deals with complex moral, psychological and metaphysical problems. In 1956 he made his best-known film, *The Seventh Seal*, a parable about a knight who plays chess with Death. His other films include the comedy *Smiles of a Summer Night* (1955), *Wild Strawberries* (1957), *Through a Glass Darkly* (1961), *Persona* (1966) and *Fanny and Alexander* (1982).

Bergman, Ingrid (1915-82) Swedish actress who went to Hollywood in 1938, hailed as the new Greta Garbo. Among the films that made her a star were *Intermezzo* (1939), *Casablanca* (1942), *Notorious* (1946) and *Joan of Arc* (1948). She made her last film appearance in Ingmar Bergman's *Autumn Sonata* (1978), a moving story of a bereaved woman's reunion with her daughter. She won Best Actress Oscars for her roles in *Gaslight* (1944) and *Anastasia* (1956), and a Best Supporting Actress Oscar for *Murder on the Orient Express* (1974).

Berkeley, Busby (1895-1976) American choreographer and director whose films are marked by their lavish dance routines. These were often photographed from above so that the lines of chorus girls formed fanciful, kaleidoscopic designs. His films were a tonic during the Depression years of the 1930s, and included *The Gold Diggers* series (1933-7), 42ND STREET (1933), *Footlight Parade* (1933) and *Babes in Arms* (1939).

Berks, John (1941-) One of the most popular and highest paid disc jockeys in South Africa during the 1980s. Berks, who also hosted his own TV show and who now broadcasts on Radio 702, has offended hordes of faithful listeners by refusing to pander to their vanity and prejudices. He has become something of a specialist in adult talks shows.

Birth of a Nation, The Hollywood's first and most renowned historical epic. Made in 1915 and set in the American Civil War, it was hailed for its masterly use of long-shots, close-ups, fade-outs and fade-ins – techniques pioneered by the director, D W Griffith. But it was criticized for glorifying the Ku Klux Klan and for its harsh view of blacks.

Blade Runner Bleak but visually stunning 'thriller of the future', in which a former policeman and licensed killer, played by Harrison Ford, is commissioned to hunt down and destroy a group of homicidal, outer space robots. Made in 1982, the film had a happy ending and an obtrusive commentary. In 1992 British director Ridley Scott produced a new release with a more realistic finale and without the commentary.

Bogarde, Sir Dirk (Derek van den Bogaerde) (1921-) British film actor of Dutch ancestry who rose to prominence in crime melodramas such as *The Blue Lamp* (1951) and light comedies and adventure tales such as *Doctor in the House* (1953) and *Campbell's Kingdom* (1957). His later, more celebrated roles include a bisexual barrister in *Victim* (1961), a sinister valet in Joseph LOSEY's *The Servant* (1963), a cynical Oxford don in *Accident* (1967) and a dying composer in Luchino Visconti's DEATH IN VENICE (1970). He was

SUPER SPY *Dapper and dangerous, Sean Connery is ready for action as trigger-happy secret agent James Bond, also known as 007.*

knighted in 1992. Bogarde is also a writer of note, with several novels and volumes of an autobiography to his credit.

Bogart, Humphrey (1899-1957) Taciturn American actor who played to perfection two hard-boiled private eyes: Dashiel Hammett's Sam Spade in *The Maltese Falcon* (1941) and Raymond Chandler's Philip Marlowe in *The Big Sleep* (1946). He appeared in four films with Lauren Bacall (1924-), including *To Have and Have Not* (1944). He married Bacall in 1945. His films – in many of which he played a gangster wearing a snap-brimmed hat and a trench coat – include *The Petrified Forest* (1936), *Angels with Dirty Faces* (1938), *The Roaring Twenties* (1939), *High Sierra* (1941), *Casablanca* (1942), *The African Queen* (1951) for which he won a Best Actor Oscar, and *The Caine Mutiny* (1954).

Bond, James Hero of Ian ▷FLEMING's spy novels – the film versions of which were noted for their spectacular stunts and gadgets. Bond was first portrayed by Sean CONNERY, who made seven films, from *Dr No* (1962) to *Never Say Never Again* (1983). The second Bond, former model George Lazenby, appeared in only one film: *On Her Majesty's Secret Service* (1969). Roger Moore became the third Bond, starting with *Live and Let Die* (1973). Timothy Dalton took over in *The Living Daylights* (1987) and *Licence to Kill* (1989) and Pierce Brosnan filmed *Goldeneye* in 1995. The films featured exotically named villains, such as Dr No and Goldfinger, and a succession of beautiful women.

Bonnie and Clyde Violent gangster film based on the real-life exploits of two of America's most ruthless and daring bank robbers, who terrorised the Midwest in the early 1930s. Starring Warren Beatty and Faye Dunaway, and directed in 1967 by Arthur Penn, it used a variety of stylistic tricks to tell its brutal story.

Brando, Marlon (1924-) Moody American actor trained in 'The Method' school of acting which aims at a complete identification – physical and mental – with the character being portrayed. His early and most notable films include *The Men* (1950), *A Streetcar Named Desire* (1951), *The Wild One* (1953) and *On the Waterfront* (1954), for which he won a Best Actor Oscar. He made an impressive Mark Antony in *Julius Caesar* (1953) and his singing gambler in *Guys and Dolls* (1955) contrasted with his menacing Mafia boss in *The Godfather* (1972). His other films include the sexually explicit *Last Tango in Paris* (1972) and *Apocalypse Now* (1979). His life has been dogged by personal problems, including the conviction of his son for the murder of his daughter's lover, and her subsequent suicide.

❖ Brando once commented on the vast fees he commands for cameo film roles: 'Another day, another million dollars!'

❖ Brando took a cameo part as a world-weary human rights lawyer in *A Dry White Season* (1987) based on the novel of André P ▷BRINK about a naive white South African schoolteacher who discovers the brutality of apartheid when his gardener's son disappears after the 1976 school riots.

Bryceland, Yvonne (1926-92) South African actress associated with the plays of Athol ▷FUGARD. She acted with Fugard himself in the 1960s and 1970s, and her performance in his *Boesman and Lena* was widely acclaimed. Her career took off when she settled in London in the 1970s. She made her debut on Broadway in Fugard's *Road to Mecca* (1988). Bryceland died of liver cancer in London a month after it was diagnosed.

❖ The Space Theatre in Cape Town was founded by Bryceland and her husband, Brian Astbury, in 1972.

Bugs Bunny Brash cartoon rabbit created by Warner Brothers in 1937. He was said to have been inspired by a scene in the comedy film *It Happened One Night* (1934), in which Clark Gable eats a carrot with gusto.

Burton, Richard (1925-84) Welsh stage and screen actor admired for his brooding presence and rich voice. Among the highlights of his theatrical career were *Hamlet* at London's Old Vic in 1954, and King Arthur in the Broadway musical *Camelot* (1960 and 1980). He made his film debut in 1948 and his many films include *My Cousin Rachel* (1952), *Becket* (1964), *The Night of the Iguana* (1964), *The Spy Who Came in from the Cold* (1965) and *Who's Afraid of Virginia Woolf?* (1966). He gave a fine performance as the narrator in the BBC radio production of Dylan Thomas's *Under Milk Wood*, first broadcast in 1954.

❖ While making *Cleopatra* in 1962 Burton had a well-publicized relationship with his leading lady and future wife, Elizabeth TAYLOR. In the midst of it Laurence Olivier sent him a cable asking if he wanted to be 'a great actor or a household name'. Burton's reply was: 'Both!'

❖ Burton and other stars such as Roger Moore and Richard Harris took the leading parts in *The Wild Geese* (1978), a mercenary adventure which was shot on location in Tshipise, Northern Province and which also starred South Africa's Winston Ntshona as a deposed African leader.

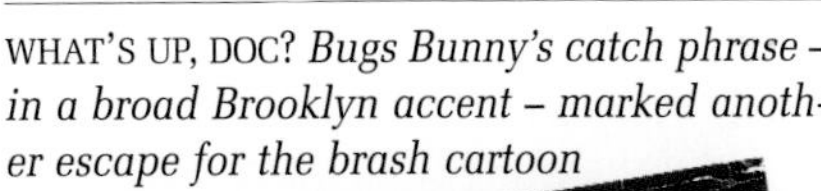

WHAT'S UP, DOC? *Bugs Bunny's catch phrase – in a broad Brooklyn accent – marked another escape for the brash cartoon superstar.*

Butch Cassidy and the Sundance Kid Witty, tongue-in-cheek account of two of America's most celebrated train robbers, played with great charm and style by Paul Newman as Cassidy and Robert Redford as the Kid. The film, directed by George Roy Hill in 1969, tells how the outlaws flee to Bolivia – where they come to a violent end.

Cagney, James (1899-1986) Pint-sized American actor who epitomized the screen gangster in a series of fast-paced crime dramas such as *The Public Enemy* (1931), *Angels with Dirty Faces* (1938), *The Roaring Twenties* (1939), *White Heat* (1949) and *Kiss Tomorrow Goodbye* (1950). He showed his versatility as the song-and-dance man George M Cohan in *Yankee Doodle Dandy* (1942), for which he won an Oscar. After making the Cold War comedy *One, Two, Three* (1961), he retired to his Texas ranch. He made a dynamic comeback, at the age of 82, in *Ragtime* (1981), a story of political life in New York before World War I.

❖ Although Cagney was best-known for his tough guy roles, he began his career as a chorus boy and female impersonator.

Capital Radio First independent radio station in South Africa, previously owned by the Transkei ▷BANTUSTAN. Established in December 1979 with a special dispensation from the South African Government, it offered an alternative music station, broadcasting to the Eastern Cape and KwaZulu-Natal. Listeners in the Western Cape and Gauteng receive the service after 6 pm. Broadcasts are made from studios in Durban via a transmitter in Port St Johns. In addition to music and extensive sports coverage, it offers news bulletins. These were particularly valuable during the apartheid years, and provided coverage of issues and events suppressed by the progovernment SABC.

Carry On . . . Series of bawdy British film farces which began in 1958 with *Carry On Sergeant*. Unsubtle and full of innuendo, there have been more than 30 titles, the most recent being *Carry on Columbus* (1992). The cast members included Kenneth Williams, Sydney James, Barbara Windsor, Bernard Bresslaw, Charles Hawtrey, Joan Sims and Hattie Jacques.

❖ Sydney James was a South African actor who moved to London in 1946 and perfected the character of the stubborn, earthy Cockney on stage, films and television.

Casablanca Evocative wartime romance and adventure film directed in 1942 by Michael Curtiz, starring Humphrey Bogart, Ingrid Bergman, Paul Henreid and Claude Rains. Set largely in Rick's nightclub in the Vichy-controlled Casablanca in World War II, it tells of the obsession of the owner (Bogart) with a married woman (Bergman) with whom he had an affair with in prewar Paris and who works for the Resistance. It builds to a tense climax at the city's fog-shrouded airport. The haunting theme tune, 'As Time Goes By', sums up the film's bittersweet quality.

❖ One of the cinema's most misquoted catchphrases, 'Play it again, Sam', is often wrongly attributed to Humphrey Bogart. It is in fact Bergman who says: 'Play it, Sam.'

Chaney, Lon (1883-1930) American silent-film star and master of disguise whose roles included *The Hunchback of Notre Dame* (1923) and *The Phantom of the Opera* (1925). In 1957 James Cagney starred in a biographical film about him aptly called *Man of a Thousand Faces*. His son, Lon Chaney Junior (1906-73), gave a moving performance as the dim-witted Lennie in the film *Of Mice and Men* (1939).

Chaplin, Sir Charles (1889-1977) British comic genius whose 'little tramp' figure – complete with baggy trousers, bowler hat, skimpy frockcoat, turned-up shoes, bamboo cane and toothbrush moustache – captivated the world. Chaplin travelled to America in 1910 as a variety performer and became a film actor, director, producer, choreographer and composer. His films include *Shoulder Arms* (1918), *The Kid* (1921), *The Gold Rush* (1925), *City Lights* (1931), *Modern Times* (1936), and *The Great Dictator* (1940), in which he spoke on screen for the first time. His last four films were *Monsieur Verdoux* (1947), *Limelight* (1951), *A King in New York*, (1957), which was a bitter attack on the American way of life, and *A Countess from Hong Kong* (1966), with Marlon Brando, Sophia Loren and Chaplin as a seasick ship's steward. His left-wing sympathies made him a victim of the McCarthy anti-Communist witch-hunt of the early 1950s, and he moved from America to Switzerland – where he lived quietly with his fourth wife, Oona O'Neil, daughter of the American playwright Eugene O'Neil. He received an honorary Oscar in 1971 and was knighted in 1975.

Citizen Kane Influential film about the rise and fall of an unscrupulous American newspaper tycoon – based on William Randolph Hearst – who sacrifices personal happiness for commercial success. It is told in flashback, using a bag of brilliant technical tricks – such as mock newsreel accounts of Kane's career. Proclaimed by many critics as the best film ever made, it is the masterpiece of Orson WELLES, who, in 1941, at the age of 26, co-wrote the script, directed and produced the film – as well as making his screen acting debut as Kane.

***Clockwork Orange*, A** Bleak and brutal film version of Anthony ▷BURGESS's horror novel about a Britain of the future in which law and order have broken down and violence rules. Directed in 1971 by Stanley Kubrick, it starred Malcolm McDowell as a young murderer and rapist loose in a society in which gangs prowl the streets torturing and killing for pleasure, using a slangy, futuristic language to a background accompaniment of Beethoven. After being scientifically brainwashed in prison, McDowell becomes a helpless victim himself.

comics Two of Britain's oldest and best-loved children's comics, *The Dandy* and *The Beano*, were launched in 1937 and 1938 respectively. They featured perennial favourites such as Korky the Cat, Desperate Dan and Dennis the Menace. They were the first British comics to use American-style speech bubbles instead of captions.

commercial radio Radio service that operates for profit. Revenue comes from advertising, sponsorships and subscriptions (in the case of encoded services) but not licence fees, which accrue to public service broadcasting. With an independent income, the programme content of commercial radio stations is less

MAN OF MIRTH *Chaplin satirizes the soulless nature of assembly-line work in* Modern Times *(1936). Starving in Alaska, he dines on shoe leather (inset) in* The Gold Rush *(1925).*

circumscribed than that of public broadcasting and COMMUNITY RADIO.

community radio Radio owned, controlled and run by the community it serves. It aims to counter the commercialization of information and to improve popular participation. Operating on subsidies and limited advertising income, the station's transmission range is usually limited. The world-wide community radio movement was pioneered by pacifists in the USA after World War II. A number of community radio stations went on air in South Africa in 1995 after receiving licences from the INDEPENDENT BROADCASTING AUTHORITY. The campaign for community radio was spearheaded by Cape Town's Bush Radio, which made two broadcasts in 1993 before its transmitter was sealed by the authorities.

Connery, Sean (1930-) Rugged Scots superstar who created the role of James Bond in the early 1960s. He successfully threw off this image in a string of international hits, including Alfred Hitchcock's *Marnie* (1964), *The Anderson Tapes* (1971), *Robin and Marian* (1976), *The Name of the Rose* (1986), *The Untouchables* (1987), for which he won an Oscar as Best Supporting Actor, and Steven Spielberg's *Indiana Jones and the Last Crusade* (1989).

Cooper, Gary (1901-61) Quietly spoken and affable star, best known for Westerns, including the classic *High Noon* (1952), which won him a Best Actor Oscar. A former cowboy, Gary Cooper began his career as a stunt rider and, after a series of small parts in silent films, played the lead in *The Virginian* (1929). He displayed a deft talent for comedy in movies such as *Mr Deeds Goes to Town* (1936). He was equally at ease in serious dramatic roles, including a pacifist war hero in *Sergeant York* (1941), for which he won his first Oscar, and a guerrilla in Ernest Hemingway's Spanish Civil War saga, *For Whom the Bell Tolls* (1943).

Costner, Kevin (1955-) Intense leading man descended partly from Cherokee stock who directed and starred in *Dances With Wolves* (1990), about a US Army officer during the Civil War who becomes a Sioux brave. The movie won seven Oscars, including Best Film and Best Director. Costner shot to stardom in 1987 in the thrillers *No Way Out* and *The Untouchables*. Among his other films are two baseball stories, the realistic *Bull Durham* (1988) and the modern fairy tale *Field of Dreams* (1989), *Robin Hood, Prince of Thieves* (1991), *JFK* (1991), *The Bodyguard* (1992) and *A Perfect World* (1993), with Clint Eastwood.

❖ Costner starred in *Waterworld* (1995) which, at about US$180 million, is the most expensive film ever made – a futuristic, post-greenhouse clash between good (Costner) and evil (Dennis Hopper).

COMIC CAPERS *British boys and girls grew up with their own favourite comics, following the picture stories avidly from week to week.*

Crawford, Joan (Lucille Le Sueur) (1904-77) Emotional American film actress, whose staring eyes were once compared to car headlamps. She won a Best Actress Oscar for *Mildred Pierce* (1945), in which she played an ambitious waitress who succeeds in running her own restaurant. Her films include *A Woman's Face* (1941), *The Story of Esther Costello* (1957) and the grotesque horror film *Whatever Happened to Baby Jane?* (1962), in which she appears with Bette DAVIS.

Cruise, Tom (1962-) Clean-cut American film actor hailed as the world's Number One male pin-up in the early 1990s. After playing juvenile leads in the early 1980s, he graduated to adult stardom and won critical acclaim in *The Color of Money* (1986), *Rain Man* (1988), *Born on the 4th of July* (1989) and *The Firm* (1993). He is married to Nicole Kidman, co-star in *Far and Away* (1992).

Dallas Glossy drama serial (1978-91) which started a Hollywood trend for television sagas about the seriously rich and powerful. It concerned the loves and rivalries affecting the wealthy Ewing family and their oil empire based in Dallas, Texas. Larry Hagman played the man whom audiences loved to hate, the ruthless J R Ewing.

❖ 'Who shot J R?' was a much-posed question in 1980. The answer was a pregnant ex-lover, Kristen, played by Mary Crosby.

Davis, Bette (1908-89) Formidable American actress whose unconventional looks and powerful personality enlivened a long series of so-called 'women's pictures'. She won Oscars for her roles in *Dangerous* (1935) and *Jezebel* (1938). Among her other notable films were *The Private Lives of Elizabeth and Essex* (1939), *The Letter* (1940), *Now Voyager* (1942), *Mr Skeffington* (1944) and *All About Eve* (1950). She later won acclaim for her roles as an ageing former child star in *Whatever Happened to Baby Jane?* (1962), opposite Joan Crawford, and a deranged suspected murderess in *Hush, Hush, Sweet Charlotte* (1964). She made her last film *The Wicked Stepmother* in 1989, the year of her death.

Dean, James (1931-55) Idolized American actor whose screen image of petulance and moody rebellion made him a hero with youngsters in the rock'n'roll era. His only major films, made in little more than a year, were *East of Eden* (1955), based on John ▷STEINBECK's sombre novel about an adolescent who discovers that his mother, thought to be dead, is the madam of a local brothel; *Rebel Without a Cause* (1955), a study of juvenile delinquency among the middle classes; and the Texas-set epic, *Giant* (1956). Dean died at the age of 24 when his sports car crashed in southern California in 1955.

Death in Venice Sumptuous and moving Italian film about the last, lonely days of a composer holidaying in a plague-threatened Venice shortly before the outbreak of World War I. Based on a short novel by the German author Thomas ▷MANN, it was directed in 1971 by Luchino Visconti. The film stars Dirk BOGARDE and tells of the composer's doomed, idealistic love of a beautiful boy whom he sees at a distance.

De Mille, Cecil B (1881-1959) Autocratic American film producer-director and one of the founders of Hollywood. He went to Hollywood in 1913 to make the Western, *The Squaw Man* – generally regarded as Hollywood's first feature-length film – and stayed to direct lavish biblical epics such as *The Ten Commandments* (1923), *King of Kings* (1927) and *The Sign of the Cross* (1932). His many later films include *Samson and Delilah* (1949), the Oscar-winning circus spectacular, *The Greatest Show on Earth* (1952), and a grandiose remake of *The Ten Commandments* in 1956, lasting more than three hours.

❖ He played the tireless, all-powerful film tycoon to the hilt, telling his staff: 'You are here to please me. Nothing else matters!' During World War II there was a saying in Hollywood: 'Anyone who leaves De Mille for the armed forces is a slacker!'

Dench, Dame Judi (1934-) Distinguished British stage and screen actress who made her debut as Ophelia in *Hamlet* (1957) at London's Old Vic theatre. Highlights from her theatrical career include playing Sally Bowles in the musical *Cabaret* (1968), and Cleopatra in Shakespeare's *Antony and Cleopatra* (1987) with Anthony HOPKINS. She has appeared in television comedy series such as *A Fine Romance* (1981-5) with her husband Michael Williams. Her films include *A Room with a View* (1985) and *84 Charing Cross Road* (1986).

De Niro, Robert (1943-) Versatile American actor whose roles have ranged from a Jesuit priest in *The Mission* (1986) to a psychopathic hoodlum in *GoodFellas* (1990). He has worked with director Martin Scorsese on several harrowing films, playing a disturbed ex-Vietnam War veteran in *Taxi Driver* (1976), a grotesque boxing champion in *Raging Bull* (1980) and a vengeful ex-convict in *Cape Fear* (1991). Among his other outstanding films are *The Godfather Part II* (1974) for which he won a Best Supporting Actor Oscar, *The Deer Hunter* (1978) and *A Bronx Tale* (1993), which he also directed.

Depardieu, Gérard (1948-) Imposing French actor who has been acclaimed for his sensitive portrayals of eccentrics and social misfits. A school drop-out at the age of 12, he later became an amateur boxer, lifeguard and dishwasher. His early roles were undistinguished and it was not until the 1980s that he found parts worthy of his talent – such as the husband who comes back from the dead in *The Return of Martin Guerre* (1981) and the tragic hunchback in *Jean de Florette* (1986). The doomed romantic poet *Cyrano de Bergerac* followed in 1990, as did his first Hollywood role, a wily musician in the romatic comedy *Green Card*.

❖ South African actress Alice Krige took a lead role in a London stage production of *Cyrano de Bergerac*.

De Sica, Vittorio (1902-74) Italian director and character actor whose quartet of films after World War II – *Shoeshine* (1946), *Bicycle Thieves* (1948), *Miracle in Milan* (1950) and *Umberto D* (1952) – helped to set a trend of social realism in film-making. He later directed Sophia Loren in three of her finest and most popular films: *Two Women* (1960), *Yesterday, Today and Tomorrow* (1963) and *Marriage Italian Style* (1964).

Dietrich, Marlene (Maria Magdalene von Losch) (1901-92) German-born American singer and actress whose ageless beauty, high cheekbones and husky voice made her a screen goddess. Dietrich's international reputation was made in 1930 with Germany's early first talking picture, *The Blue Angel*, in which she played a temptress called Lola-Lola. The film was directed by Josef von Sternberg, who made a further six films with Dietrich when she went to Hollywood. A sultry singing voice added to Dietrich's appeal.

Dirty Harry Tense and violent police thriller in which an unprincipled San Francisco policeman tracks down an insane sniper. Clint EASTWOOD played the detective, Harry Callahan, who is as brutal and ruthless as the killer he is out to destroy. Made in 1971 by director Don Siegel, the film inspired four sequels: *Magnum Force* (1973), *The Enforcer* (1976), *Sudden Impact* (1983) and *The Dead Pool* (1988).

Disney, Walt (1901-66) American film producer and animator who created the cartoon characters Mickey and Minnie Mouse, Donald Duck, Goofy and Pluto. He began his career as a commercial artist and moved to Hollywood in the 1920s, where he made *Steamboat Willie* (1928), the first cartoon with sound and music – with Disney himself providing Mickey's voice. After *Three Little Pigs* (1933) came the world's first feature-length cartoon with sound and colour – SNOW WHITE AND THE SEVEN DWARFS (1937). He masterminded four more full-length children's classics: *Fantasia* (1940), *Pinocchio* (1940), *Dumbo* (1941) and *Bambi* (1942). In the 1940s he combined cartoon animation and live action – a technique he later used to great effect in *Mary Poppins* (1964). Among other Disney cartoons were *Pinocchio* (1940), *One Hundred and One Dalmatians* (1960), *The Jungle Book* (1967) and *The Prince and the Pauper* (1990). In 1955 Disney opened the first theme park, Disneyland, in California.

documentaries South Africa's burst of ALTERNATIVE MEDIA of the 1980s included many fine documentaries with apartheid themes that received overseas honours but were prohibited for local viewing. Works of note included Kevin Harris's *Cry of Reason* on the life of Afrikaner cleric Beyers Naude (1987), Jürgen Schadeberg's *Have You Seen Drum Recently?* (1989) about the destruction of Sophiatown culture and Mark Newman's *The Two Rivers* (1985). Independent films received a boost with the formation of the Film and Allied Workers' Organisation in 1987.

MOVIE MOUSE *Mickey Mouse, seen here in* The Prince and the Pauper *(1990), was introduced to movie audiences by Walt Disney (right) in 1928.*

Donat, Robert (1905-58) British stage and film actor renowned for his Oscar-winning performance as the elderly schoolmaster in *Goodbye, Mr Chips* (1939). Donat's looks – and his dashing roles as *The Count of Monte Cristo* (1934) and Richard Hannay in HITCHCOCK's spy thriller *The 39 Steps* (1935) – made him a heart-throb. Dogged by ill health, he made his last film appearance as a Chinese mandarin in *The Inn of the Sixth Happiness* (1958), with Ingrid BERGMAN.

Douglas, Kirk (Issur Danielovitch) (1916-) Dimple-chinned Hollywood star whose many notable films include *Champion* (1949), *Ace in the Hole* (1951), *Lust for Life* (1956), in which he played the painter Vincent van Gogh, *Gunfight at the OK Corral* (1956) and *Spartacus* (1960). He is the father of leading actor Michael Douglas (1944-), who starred in two of the most erotic thrillers of recent times: *Fatal Attraction* (1987) and *Basic Instinct* (1992). Michael Douglas rose to prominence in the popular TV police series *The Streets of San Francisco* (1972-5). Among his best-known films are *Romancing the Stone* (1984) and *Wall Street* (1987), for which he won a Best Actor Oscar.

Dracula films Hungarian actor Bela Lugosi was the first Hollywood star to don the Transylvanian count's cloak in *Dracula* (1931). Since then dozens of vampire films have appeared with leading actors such as Lon Chaney, Jnr, Christopher Lee, Klaus Kinski and Gary Oldman, who starred in Francis Ford Coppola's spectacular *Dracula* (1993).
❖ At his express wish, Lugosi, who died in Los Angeles in 1956, was buried in his long, silklined black Dracula cloak.

HIT MAN *Clint Eastwood played the cheroot-chewing gunman, who shot first and asked questions later in the first batch of 'spaghetti Westerns'.*

E.T. – The Extra-terrestrial Heart-warming fantasy film about an American boy who befriends a scared and lovable being from outer space who is stranded on Earth. With the loving help of his brother and sister, the youngster helps E.T. – a charming special effects creation, part pet and part 'human' – to return to his own planet. The film was directed by Steven Spielberg in 1982, and has one of the screen's most touching and tearful endings.

Eastwood, Clint (1930-) Craggy-faced American actor-director who became an international star as The Man With No Name in the 'SPAGHETTI WESTERN' *A Fistful of Dollars* (1964) and its two sequels: *For a Few Dollars More* (1965) and *The Good, the Bad and the Ugly* (1966). He originally made his name on TV as the cowboy Rowdy Yates in *Rawhide* (1959-66). Later he starred in *Coogan's Bluff* (1968), *Where Eagles Dare* (1969) and *The Beguiled* (1971). Then came the DIRTY HARRY sequence of thrillers and two crazy comedies, *Every Which Way But Loose* (1978) and *Any Which Way You Can* (1980). As a director he created and played the leads in the thriller *Play Misty For Me* (1971), *High Plains Drifter* (1972), *Pale Rider* (1985), *White Hunter, Black Heart* (1990), a study of an egocentric film director based upon John HUSTON, and *Unforgiven* (1992), a powerful and innovative Western which won four Oscars, including Best Picture and Best Director.

Easy Rider Trend-setting film about two drop-out, drug-taking motorcyclists who travel from Los Angeles to New Orleans Mardi Gras in pursuit of 'freedom'. Their attitude and appearance, however, bring them little but abuse, hatred and scorn. Made in 1969 on a shoestring budget, the film starred Peter Fonda and Dennis Hopper, who co-wrote the script and was also the director. It made an overnight star of Jack Nicholson in a small but telling role as a philosophical drunk.

Egoli – Place of Gold South Africa's first daily television serial (1992), starring many well-known local actors. It is broadcast during open time on M-NET and centres on life around a Johannesburg car manufacturing firm, Walco. Glamour, everyday drama and lifelike characters who speak in English and Afrikaans make for part of its appeal. It is produced by Franz Marx and directed by Danie Odendaal and more than 100 people and a full-time cast of 24 actors work on the production.

Emmy Prestigious award which is TV's version of the Oscar. It is presented annually by the American Academy of Television Arts and Sciences.

STATION STALWART *Springbok Radio veteran Esmé Euvrard does duty at Radio Jukebox, a programme that was on the air – like the presenter herself – for three decades.*

Euvrard, Esmé (1919-93) Imposing radio personality who hosted an Afrikaans magazine programme, *So Maak Mens*, with Jan Cronjé on SPRINGBOK RADIO for 28 years. She joined the SABC in 1937, at the age of 17, and was an accomplished singer, performing also in Italian, French, Portuguese and Spanish.

Evans, Dame Edith (1888-1976) Imposing British actress best remembered for her majestic performance as Lady Bracknell in Oscar Wilde's comedy *The Importance of Being Earnest*, which she played on the stage in 1939 and in the 1952 film version. She was made a Dame of the British Empire in 1946.

Fairbanks, Douglas (1883-1939) Athletic American actor known for his flamboyant performances in silent films such as *The Mark of Zorro* (1920), *The Three Musketeers* (1921), *Robin Hood* (1922), *The Thief of Bagdad* (1924) and *The Black Pirate* (1926). His career declined with the coming of sound. His son, the debonair Douglas Fairbanks, Jnr (1909-), played similar swashbuckling roles in films such as *The Prisoner of Zenda* (1937), *Gunga Din* (1939), *The Corsican Brothers* (1941) and *Sinbad the Sailor* (1947).

Fantasia Revolutionary Walt Disney film, made in 1940, featuring cartoon sequences set to the music of Bach, Beethoven, Schubert and Stravinsky, among others, and performed by the Philadelphia Orchestra conducted by Leopold Stokowski – who has a brief conversation with Mickey Mouse. The movie's most memorable sequences feature Mickey Mouse and many bucket-carrying broomsticks in

FAULTLESS FAURE *Pioneering South African director Bill Faure at work on the set of* Salomé *(1979), one of the many delights he created for the entertainment starved public.*

Paul Dukas' *The Sorcerer's Apprentice*, and the ballet-dancing animals – including elephants, ostriches and hippopotamuses – in Ponchielli's *Dance of the Hours.*

Faure, Bill (1949-94) Well-known South African television director. In the early days of SABC-TV the versatile Faure gave viewers a variety of fare, including the soapie, *The Dingleys*, excellent productions of *Carmen* and *Salomé*, and a range of documentaries. As a freelancer he created the weekly live magazine programme *Prime Time* and the documentary news update *Carte Blanche*, and also produced two Miss World pageants. His lengthy TV series *Shaka Zulu* was received favourably worldwide. Faure was a recipient of numerous awards, including one of the Ten Outstanding Persons of the World.

Fawlty Towers Uproarious BBC television series (1975-9) about a bullying, devious and frequently panic-stricken seaside hotel proprietor. It was written by comedian John Cleese, who played Basil Fawlty, and his then wife Connie Booth, who played Polly the maid. The other main characters were Sybil Fawlty (Prunella Scales) and Manuel the Spanish waiter (Andrew Sachs). The character of Basil Fawlty was based on a hotel owner whom Cleese had once encountered in Torquay.

Fellini, Federico (1920-93) Stylish Italian director whose films are admired for their dazzling camera work and arresting imagery. A former cartoonist, Fellini won worldwide acclaim for *La Strada* (1954), starring his wife Guiletta Masina, *La Dolce Vita* (1960) and *8½* (1963), starring Marcello Mastroianni.

film noir Term borrowed from the French, literally meaning 'dark film' and used to describe the murky, doom-ridden Hollywood crime thrillers of the 1940s. Classic examples include Billy Wilder's *Double Indemnity* (1944), *The Killers* (1946), starring Burt Lancaster and Ava Gardner, *Crossfire* (1947), with Robert Mitchum, Robert Ryan and Gloria Grahame, and *White Heat* (1949), the story of a psychopathic gangster played by James Cagney, who has a fixation about his mother.

Fleet Street Road in central London which became the heart of Britain's newspaper industry in the 18th century. The last remaining national newspaper offices moved to other sites in the 1980s. The street was named after the Fleet River, which now runs underground.

❖ Fleet Street is also known as 'The Street of Ink' or 'Street of Shame'.

Flynn, Errol (1909-59) Dashing, Tasmanian-born film star who became a Hollywood legend – as much for his hard drinking, fist fights and womanizing as his acting. Even so, his good looks, charm and infectious sense of humour gained Flynn fans throughout the world in films such as *The Charge of the Light Brigade* (1936), *The Adventures of Robin Hood* (1938), *The Sea Hawk* (1940), *They Died With Their Boots On* (1941) and *Gentleman Jim* (1942).

Fonda, Henry (1905-82) Dignified American stage and screen actor. He worked with director John Ford on films such as *The Young Mr Lincoln* (1939), *The Grapes of Wrath* (1940), the Western *My Darling Clementine* (1946), in which he played the sheriff Wyatt Earp; and the comedy *Mister Roberts* (1955), in the title role of an officer aboard a US cargo ship in World War II who longs for action. Other notable films include: *Twelve Angry Men* (1956), *Fail Safe* (1964) and *Once Upon a Time in the West* (1968), in which he appeared as a sinister villain. He eventually won an Oscar for his part in *On Golden Pond* (1981), opposite Katharine Hepburn and his daughter, Jane Fonda. His son, Peter Fonda, is also an actor.

Fonda, Jane (1937-) American actress who shot to international fame in the title role of *Barbarella* (1967). Based on an adult science-fiction comic strip, she played a voluptuous 'sex symbol' in an array of revealing costumes. She moved on to more serious and rewarding roles in *They Shoot Horses, Don't They?* (1969), and two films for which she won Oscars: *Klute* (1971) and *Coming Home* (1978). Her later films include *The China Syndrome* (1979), *On Golden Pond* (1981), *The Morning After* (1986) and *Old Gringo* (1989). She has also created extremely successful health and fitness books and videos. She is the daughter of Henry Fonda.

Ford, Harrison (1942-) American actor who found success with his sympathetic portrayal

FLIGHTS OF FANCY *In Fellini's autobiographical* 8½, *a renowned film director attempts to break through a persistent creative block by recalling dreams and fantastic scenes from his past.*

of two mercenary heroes: the pilot Han Solo in the *Star Wars* trilogy (1977-83), and the archaeologist Indiana Jones in *Raiders of the Lost Ark* (1981.) His other films include: *Blade Runner* (1982), *Indiana Jones and the Temple of Doom* (1984), *Witness* (1985), *Indiana Jones and the Last Crusade* (1989) and *The Fugitive* (1993).

Ford, John (Sean Aloysius O'Feeney) (1895-1973) Irish-American director of more than 100 feature films, including many Westerns. These include classics such as *Stagecoach* (1939), starring John Wayne, *My Darling Clementine* (1946), *Fort Apache* (1948), *She Wore a Yellow Ribbon* (1949), *The Searchers* (1956) and *The Man Who Shot Liberty Valance* (1962), with James Stewart. Ford's Oscar-winning films were *The Informer* (1935), *The Grapes of Wrath* (1940), *How Green Was My Valley* (1941) and *The Quiet Man* (1952). He also made patriotic documentary films in World War II.

Formby, George (1904-61) Ukelele-playing Lancashire comedian who was one of Britain's biggest stars during World War II. He portrayed an innocent abroad in a flock of cheaply made and cheerful films. These include: *Let George Do It* (1940), *Spare a Copper* (1941), *Bell-Bottom George* (1943), *Get Cracking* (1943), *I Didn't Do It* (1945) and *George in Civvy Street* (1946).

Fortune, Charles (1905-94) Doyen of South African sports broadcasters known to generations of fans for his eloquent, verbose word pictures, particularly in the days before television. Fortune qualified as a mathematics and science teacher, but shortly before World War II swiftly made a name for himself as a broadcaster after standing in for a commentator who had taken ill. He joined the SABC in 1955 and was noted particularly for his cricket commentary, covering four South African tours of England and two of Australia; he later became secretary of the South African Cricket Association. He continued commentating until 1989.

Foster, Jodie (1962-) Former American child actress who won Best Actress Oscars for her performances as a rape victim in *The Accused* (1988) and as an FBI agent in *The Silence of the Lambs* (1991) opposite Anthony Hopkins. Her earlier films include *Alice Doesn't Live Here Any More* (1974), *The Little Girl Who Lives Down the Lane* (1976) and Martin Scorsese's *Taxi Driver* (1976), in which she portrayed a teenage prostitute. She made her debut as a director with *Little Man Tate* (1991), the emotional film about a seven-year-old boy genius in which she also starred.

LONELY GODDESS *With her chiselled beauty and air of mystery, Greta Garbo played remote and ethereal heroines. She later became the world's best-known – and most photographed – recluse.*

Frankenstein films Series of monster movies based upon Mary Shelley's 19th-century Gothic novel. The most influential of these, *Frankenstein* (1931), was made in Hollywood with British-born Boris Karloff as the monster created by Baron Frankenstein. It was followed by *The Bride of Frankenstein* (1935) and *Son of Frankenstein* (1939). In 1957 the original Hollywood film was remade in England by Hammer Films as *The Curse of Frankenstein*, with Peter Cushing as the scientist and Christopher Lee as the monster.

Gable, Clark (1901-60) Robust American actor known as the 'King of Hollywood'. He made his greatest hit as the dashing Rhett Butler in *Gone with the Wind* (1939). Gable was a star for some 30 years and appeared in more than 90 films. His other films include the romantic comedy *It Happened One Night* (1934), for which he won an Oscar, *Mutiny on the Bounty* (1935), *San Francisco* (1936), *Adventure* (1945), *Run Silent, Run Deep* (1958) and the posthumously released *The Misfits*, in which he played an ageing, modern-day cowboy opposite Marilyn Monroe.

❖ Gable's ears were so large and protruding that they had to be taped back for his film roles. He also confessed that, 'I haven't a single tooth of my own in my head!'

Garbo, Greta (1905-90) Aloof, Swedish actress who went to America in 1925 and became a star of silent films and one of Hollywood's first 'legends'. Starting with *The Torrent* (1926), she made a quick succession of silent films which displayed her as an alluring vamp. These include *Flesh and the Devil, Love*, and *A Woman of Affairs*. In 1930 came her first talking picture, *Anna Christie*, in which her opening words were, 'Gimme visky, ginger ale on the side. And don't be stingy, baby!' She followed this with romantic roles in *Grand Hotel* (1932) – in which she cried, 'I vant to be alone!' – and in *Queen Christina* (1933), *Anna Karenina* (1935) and *Camille* (1937). Her first comedy, *Ninotchka* (1939), was billed as the film in which 'Garbo laughs!' She played another comic role in *Two-Faced Woman* (1941), which was savaged by the critics, prompting her abrupt retirement from the screen.

Garland, Judy (Frances Gumm) (1922-69) Vivacious American actress and entertainer who made her greatest film impact as Dorothy, the little girl who sings 'Over the Rainbow' in *The Wizard of Oz* (1939). She teamed up with Mickey Rooney for several brash and energetic 'youth' musicals including *Babes in Arms* (1939), *Strike Up the Band* (1940) and *Babes on Broadway* (1941). She then starred in *For Me and My Gal* (1942), with Gene Kelly, *Meet Me in St Louis* (1944), in which she sang the celebrated 'Trolley Song', and *Easter Parade* (1948), with Fred Astaire. However, the pressures of stardom, weight problems, alcohol and drugs played havoc with her life. Her studio contract was cancelled, but she made a powerful comeback in *A Star is Born* (1954), opposite James Mason. Her daughter is the singer and actress, Liza Minnelli (1946-).

Gere, Richard (1949-) American actor and sex-symbol who rocketed to stardom as a male escort in the film *American Gigolo* (1980). He consolidated his reputation as an actor and pin-up as a naval recruit in *An Officer and a Gentleman* (1982). After several commercial flops, Gere re-established himself as a corrupt cop in *Internal Affairs* (1989), a love-struck millionaire in the romantic comedy *Pretty Woman* (1990), and a supposedly long-lost husband in *Sommersby* (1993), an American remake of the Gérard Depardieu film *The Return of Martin Guerre*.

Gibson, Mel (1956-) American-born film actor who became an international star in the title role of the *Mad Max* trilogy (1979-85). Made in Australia, the films dealt with a vengeful policeman in a lawless, gang-ridden society of the future. In America Gibson starred as a violent and ruthless detective in *Lethal Weapon* (1987), *Lethal Weapon 2* (1989) and *Lethal Weapon 3* (1992). In contrast, he was a convincing Prince of Denmark in Franco Zeffirelli's film version of *Hamlet* (1990). He directed and starred in two films, *The Man Without A Face* (1993) and *Braveheart* (1995).

Gielgud, Sir John (1904-) Veteran British actor and director hailed as one of the greatest Hamlets of the century – a role he has played more than 500 times. His wide variety of films date from the 1920s; the more recent ones include *Julius Caesar* (1953), as the 'lean and hungry' Cassius, *The Charge of the Light Brigade* (1968), *Murder on the Orient Express* (1974), *Arthur* (1981) for which he won an Oscar as Best Supporting Actor, and *Prospero's Books* (1991), a fanciful version of Shakespeare's *The Tempest*. Gielgud was knighted in 1953.

FILM EPIC Gone with the Wind *became the longest ($3^1/_2$ hours), most expensive film when released in 1939. It cost $4,25 million.*

Godfather, The First of a trilogy of violent Mafia films about the corrupt Corleone family, directed in 1971 by Francis Ford Coppola and based on a best-selling novel by Mario Puzo. It starred Marlon Brando in the title role and Al Pacino as his son and heir. It won three Oscars, including Best Picture and Best Actor (Brando). *The Godfather, Part Two* (1974) won six Oscars, including best director (Coppola) and best supporting actor (Robert De Niro). *The Godfather, Part Three* (1990) again starred Pacino, but the film collected no honours.

Goldwyn, Samuel (Samuel Goldfisch) (1882-1974) Polish-born American producer of mainly family films who set up his own company – Goldwyn Pictures – in 1917. After he left the company it merged with Louis B Mayer Productions and Metro Pictures in 1924 to form Metro-Goldwyn-Mayer. From then on Goldwyn worked as an independent producer. His most notable films include *Wuthering Heights* (1939), *The Westerner* (1940), *The Best Years of Our Lives* (1946), *Hans Christian Andersen* (1952), *Guys and Dolls* (1955) and *Porgy and Bess* (1959).
❖ Among the so-called 'Goldwynisms' attributed to the producer are: 'Anyone who goes to a psychiatrist should have his head examined!', 'Include me out!', 'In two words: impossible!' and 'A verbal contract isn't worth the paper it's written on!'

Gone with the Wind Hollywood's most ambitious prewar talking film, based on the best-selling novel by Margaret Mitchell (1900-49). Made in 1939, it recounts the romantic adventures of a southern belle named Scarlett O'Hara at the time of the American Civil War. For three years before filming began, producer David O Selznick (1902-65) bombarded the American people with publicity about the forthcoming epic. He held a nationwide competition to find the 'ideal' Scarlett O'Hara, finally settling for the relatively unknown English actress Vivien Leigh. He fought the censors to allow Clark Gable, who played Rhett Butler, to use a mild swear word in the line, 'Frankly, my dear, I don't give a damn!'

Goon Show, The **(1952-60)** Eccentric British radio comedy show that was the brainchild of Spike Milligan. It involved a cast of freakish characters such as Eccles, Bluebottle and Neddy Seagoon. The show began in 1951 as *Crazy People* with Milligan, Peter Sellers, Harry Secombe and Michael Bentine. It was renamed *The Goon Show* in 1952; Bentine left shortly afterwards.

Grable, Betty (1916-73) Blonde American song-and-dance star whose legs – which she insured for $1 million – made her the leading Allied pin-up of World War II. Among her many colourful musicals were *Tin Pan Alley* (1940), *Coney Island* (1943), *Mother Wore Tights* (1947) and *Three for the Show* (1955).
❖ She said of her career that: 'There are two reasons why I'm in the movies – and I'm standing on both of them!'

Grahamstown Arts Festival Annual arts jamboree which offers substantial exposure to established artists and emerging talent alike and is widely acknowledged as the clearest indicator of the state of the arts in South Africa. Virtually every art form is represented at the midwinter event which takes place in the university town of Grahamstown and is officially known as the Standard Bank National Arts Festival. It has been held since 1974 with the brief of enriching the cultural and educational life of all South Africans. The Festival has experienced phenomenal growth over the years – in 1994 there were 241 events on the main programme and 370 on the Fringe, a total of 1 500 live performances scheduled, and 62 000 tickets sold for the main programme alone. The 1820 Settlers' National Monument is the main venue of the Festival but the rapid growth has seen it expanding to occupy virtually every available hall, theatre, club, coffee bar and nook in the town which gets flooded by visitors.

Grant, Cary (Archibald Leach) (1904-86) Witty and elegant British-born actor with an accent all of his own, noted for his polished romantic performances. He went to America in 1920 with a troupe of acrobats working in circuses and in vaudeville. He entered films in 1932 and had his first leading roles opposite Marlene Dietrich in *Blonde Venus* (1932) and Mae West in *She Done Him Wrong* (1933). Later comedies include *Bringing Up Baby* (1938), *Arsenic and Old Lace* (1943) and *Mr Blandings Builds His Dream House* (1948). Alfred Hitchcock chose him to costar with some of Hollywood's most glamorous leading ladies in films such as: *Suspicion* (1941), with Joan Fontaine, *Notorious* (1946), with Ingrid Bergman, *To Catch a Thief* (1954), with Grace Kelly, and *North by Northwest* (1959), with Eva Marie Saint. His later films include *That Touch of Mink* (1962), with Doris Day, *Charade* (1963), with Audrey Hepburn, and *Father Goose* (1964), with Leslie Caron. He received a 1970 Academy Award for general excellence.

❖ A journalist once wired Grant's agent, asking: 'How old Cary Grant?' Grant replied to this himself, saying: 'Old Cary Grant fine. How old you?'

Great Train Robbery, The Cinema's first Western, made in New Jersey, USA, in 1903 – it lasted for 11 minutes. Writer and director Edwin S Porter used new techniques such as panning – moving the camera to follow the action. Audiences jumped in their seats as a bandit raised his gun and – in realistic close-up – fired it straight into their faces.

Guinness, Sir Alec (1914-) Versatile British stage, screen and television actor. He was a notable Shylock in *The Merchant of Venice* (1937) at London's Old Vic theatre and, after war service, was an unforgettable Fagin in David Lean's film version of *Oliver Twist* (1948). He scored a triumph in the macabre comedy *Kind Hearts and Coronets* (1949) and starred in four more Ealing comedies: *The Lavender Hill Mob* (1951), *The Man in the White Suit* (1951), *The Ladykillers* (1955) and *Barnacle Bill* (1957). He won an Oscar as a fanatical army officer in *The Bridge on the River Kwai* (1957). He also starred in two major BBC television series: *Tinker, Tailor, Soldier, Spy* (1979) and *Smiley's People* (1981). He was knighted in 1959.

Hanks, Tom (1956-) Fifth actor in history to win Hollywood's OSCAR award two years in a row. Hanks won Best Actor awards for his sensitive and moving portrayal of a homosexual lawyer with Aids in *Philadelphia* (1994) and playing a lovable simpleton in the box-office smash hit *Forrest Gump* (1995). The other actors who won consecutive Oscars were Spencer Tracy, Jason Robards, Katharine Hepburn and Luise Rainer.

Hepburn, Audrey (Edda van Heemstra Hepburn-Ruston) (1929-93) Beguiling Belgian-born actress who played the cockney flower-girl Eliza Doolittle in the film version of *My Fair Lady* (1964). After playing small parts in British films, including *Laughter in Paradise* (1951) and *The Lavender Hill Mob* (1951), she moved to America and made her Oscar-winning Hollywood debut as an 'off-duty' princess in *Roman Holiday* (1953), with Gregory Peck. She had leading roles in films such as *Sabrina* (1954), *War and Peace* (1956), *The Nun's Story* (1958), *Breakfast at Tiffany's* (1961) and *Charade* (1963). She retired from the screen in 1968, and made a come-back in *Robin and Marian* (1976), with Sean Connery. Her last screen appearance was as an angel in Steven Spielberg's film fantasy *Always* (1989).

FESTIVE SUNDOWNER *A marimba band whets the cultural appetites of festival goers during a sundowner concert in the Settlers' Monument at the Grahamstown Arts Festival.*

Hepburn, Katharine (1907-) American star whose portrayals of spirited, free-thinking women have won her an unsurpassed four Best Actress Oscars from a record 12 nominations. Her winning roles were in the films *Morning Glory* (1933), *Guess Who's Coming to Dinner* (1967), *The Lion in Winter* (1968) and *On Golden Pond* (1981). Hepburn had a long relationship, both on and off screen, with Spencer Tracy – with whom she made several 'war-of-the-sexes' comedies, including *Woman of the Year* (1942), *Adam's Rib* (1949), *Pat and Mike* (1952) and *The Desk Set* (1957). Among her other notable films are *Bringing Up Baby* (1938), *The Philadelphia Story* (1940), *The* AFRICAN QUEEN (1951) and *Suddenly Last Summer* (1959).

Heston, Charlton (1924-) Rugged American star mostly cast in historical, adventure and science fiction epics. Among his films are: *The Greatest Show on Earth* (1952), *The Ten Commandments* (1956), as Moses, *The Agony and the Ecstasy* (1965), as Michelangelo, *Khartoum* (1966), as General Gordon, and *Planet of the Apes* (1967).

Heyns, Katinka (1949-) Versatile South African actress who became a film and TV director of note in the 1980s. Heyns made an impressive debut in the 1969 film about interracial love, *Katrina*, which shocked conservative South African audiences. Her first project as director was *'n Rand 'n Droom* made for Afrikaans TV. *Fiela se Kind* (1987), a period film that examined racism critically, was hailed as a work of pioneering success. It was sold in several overseas countries.

Hitchcock, Sir Alfred (1899-1980) British film director renowned for the dazzling 'shock' effects in his films – and for the brief and witty appearances he made in many of his classic thrillers. He directed the first British 'talkie', *Blackmail* (1929), and among his other early thrillers were *The 39 Steps* (1935), *Secret Agent* (1936), *Sabotage* (1936) and *The Lady Vanishes* (1939). He then went to Hollywood

JUNGLE TROUBLE *Bob Hope (right), Dorothy Lamour and Bing Crosby face danger in their 1941 safari comedy* The Road to Zanzibar.

and made a host of critical and box office successes. These include *Rebecca* (1940), *Shadow of a Doubt* (1943), *Spellbound* (1945), with its remarkable dream sequence designed by Salvador Dali, *Notorious* (1946), *Strangers on a Train* (1951), *Rear Window* (1954), *North by Northwest* (1959), PSYCHO (1960), *The Birds* (1963) and *Marnie* (1964). The films of his final period – *Torn Curtain* (1966), *Topaz* (1969), *Frenzy* (1972) and *Family Plot* (1976) – had their quota of excitement, humour and suspense. His portly figure, double-chin and funereal voice became well known to television viewers through *Alfred Hitchcock Presents* (1955-61), a series of short dramas which he introduced and occasionally directed. He was knighted in 1980.

Hoffman, Dustin (1937-) Adroit, short-statured American screen and stage actor who sprang to prominence portraying a sexually naive former student in the film *The Graduate* (1967). He then appeared as a tubercular cripple in *Midnight Cowboy* (1969), a 121-year-old soldier of fortune in *Little Big Man* (1970) and a doting single parent in *Kramer vs Kramer* (1979), for which he won a Best Actor Oscar. He showed his gift for comedy in *Tootsie* (1982), as an unemployed actor who disguises himself as a woman in order to get work. He won his second Oscar for his performance as an autistic innocent in *Rain Man* (1988). He also played the title role in Steven Spielberg's *Hook* (1991), a contemporary Peter Pan tale, and in *Outbreak* (1995), dealing with a worldscale medical crisis.

Hollywood Capital of the film world since 1913, when Cecil B DE MILLE made *The Squaw Man* in what was then a lawless desert area which had recently become part of Los Angeles. Early film-makers were lured by the promise of 350 days of sunshine a year and terrain that could be used to film anything from Foreign Legion epics to Wild West dramas. By the early 1930s, when sound had revolutionised the cinema, Hollywood was a thriving, self-contained community. Known as 'Tinsel Town', it was renowned for its opulent lifestyle, parties and scandals. The 'Golden Age' lasted until the early 1960s, when most of the studios – or 'dream factories' – were making films for television.

❖ Marilyn MONROE once said of Hollywood: 'It's a place where they pay you $50 000 for a kiss – and 50 cents for your soul!'

Hope, Bob (1903-) British-born film comedian famed for his 'ski-slope' nose, immaculate sense of timing and skill in playing the complete screen coward. He went to America with his family in 1907. After a spell as a vaudeville dancer and a fast-talking radio comic, he appeared in several Broadway musicals. He made his feature film debut in *The Big Broadcast* of 1938 and consolidated his reputation as a funny man in *Thanks for the Memory* (1938), *The Cat and The Canary* (1939) and *The Ghost Breakers* (1940). He then teamed up with Bing ▷CROSBY and Dorothy Lamour (1914-) in the hugely popular 'Road' films, starting with *The Road to Singapore* (1940). He also made a series of 'solo' comedies, including *My Favourite Blonde* (1942), *My Favourite Brunette* (1947), *The Paleface* (1948) and *Fancy Pants* (1950).

Hopkins, Sir Anthony (1937-) Welsh stage, screen and TV actor who became an international star in Hollywood, winning a Best Actor Oscar for his chilling portrayal of a serial killer, Dr Hannibal Lecter, in *The Silence of the Lambs* (1991). His early films included *The Lion in Winter* (1968), *Young Winston* (1972) and two supernatural thrillers made in America: *Audrey Rose* (1977) and *Magic* (1978), directed by Richard Attenborough. Intense and stockily built, he played leading roles in *Howard's End* (1992), Attenborough's production of *Chaplin* (1992), *Dracula* (1993) and *The Remains of the Day* (1993), with Emma Thompson. Highlights of his British stage career include *King Lear* (1986) and *Antony and Cleopatra* (1987).

Huston, John (1906-87) Colourful American director, screenwriter and actor who was the son of veteran character actor Walter Huston (1884-1950) and the father of actress Anjelica Huston (1952-). He directed the first of his own scripts with *The Maltese Falcon* (1941), a hard-boiled detective story starring Humphrey Bogart. He followed this with two classic gangster films: *Key Largo* (1948), with Bogart and Edward G Robinson, and *The Asphalt Jungle* (1950), in which Marilyn Monroe had a small but eye-catching part. *The Treasure of the Sierra Madre* (1948) won Huston Oscars for Best Director and Best Screenplay, while Walter Huston got the Best Supporting Actor award. John Huston gained more acclaim for *The* AFRICAN QUEEN (1951), in which Bogart won an Oscar. Huston's other films include the quirky *Beat the Devil* (1954), again with Bogart, *The Night of the Iguana* (1964) and *Prizzi's Honor* (1985), in which Anjelica Huston won an Oscar as Best Supporting Actress.

Independent Broadcasting Authority (IBA) Independent body established during the transition to democracy in South Africa to usher in a new dispensation in broadcasting free of the domination of the SABC and independent of the State. The IBA must redefine public, commercial and community broadcasting and issue licences accordingly. The first new licences for radio and TV stations were issued during 1995. The IBA must promote a diverse range of radio and television services on a national, local and regional level, catering for all language and cultural groups and providing entertainment, education and information. It must place limitations on cross-media control of private broadcasting services, and can make regulations for local television and music content. IBA decisions may be reviewed by the courts.

Independent Newspapers of South Africa (formerly Argus Printing and Publishing Co) Biggest and oldest newspaper group in South Africa which owns and publishes most major English language newspapers. It was renamed Independent Newspapers of South Africa in 1995, a year after the Dublin-based Independent Newspapers Group headed by Tony O'Reilly, Irish food and media magnate, took over control from the ▷ANGLO AMERICAN CORPORATION, which had held the majority shareholding since the 1950s. Argus Printing and Publishing was formed in 1888 after a merger of *Cape Argus* and *The Star* and its first shareholders were dominated by mining interests. Independent Newspapers main titles include *The Star, Saturday Star, The Sunday Independent, Pretoria News, Cape Times, The Argus* (including two weekend editions), *The Daily News, Natal Mercury* and *Diamond Fields Advertiser.*

Jaws Nail-biting suspense film about the devastating effect a killer shark has on a crowded

CHARACTERISTIC KANI *The hardships suffered on Robben Island are articulated by stage veterans John Kani (right) and Winston Ntshona in the original 1973 stage production of* The Island.

New England beach resort. Directed in 1975 by Steven Spielberg, the film cleverly builds up tension and is two-thirds under way before the shark is fully seen – after it has claimed its first victims. The movie's runaway success led to three sequels – *Jaws II* (1978), *Jaws III* (1983) and *Jaws – The Revenge* (1987), none of which was directed by Spielberg, and none of which captured the terror of the original.

Jazz Singer, The World's first 'talking' feature film, made in America in 1927, starring the singer ▷AL JOLSON (1886-1950), whose opening lines were: 'Wait a minute, wait a minute. You ain't heard nothin' yet! You wanna hear *Toot, Toot, Tootsie?* All right, hold on . . . ' The film was a box-office sensation with its sentimental story about the son of a cantor who becomes a popular entertainer – which reflected Jolson's own life. Audiences wept when Jolson, in blackface, knelt on one knee and serenaded his 'Mammy'. With its synchronized music and snatches of dialogue, the film changed the cinema.

Jurassic Park Highly exciting monster film released in 1993, which is the most commercially successful film so far made. Directed by Steven Spielberg, it tells how a fanatical millionaire, played by Richard Attenborough, creates a theme park inhabited by genetically reproduced dinosaurs which go on the rampage. The film cost US$60 million to make.

Jones, Trevor (1949-) District Six-born composer who has written the scores of many international film hits, including *The Black Angel*, a short film for the supporting bill to the *Star Wars* sequel, *The Empire Strikes Back*, *Excalibur* (1981), *Labyrinth* (1986), *Mississippi Burning* (1988) and *The Last of the Mohicans* (1992). Jones left South Africa at 18 on a Royal Academy of Music scholarship. He became a BBC reviewer of classical music at 21 but diversified his studies at York, adding rock, avant-garde, electronics, jazz and ethnic music to his repertoire. He later became resident composer at London's National Film School.

Kani, John (1943-) Distinguished South African actor best known for appearances in the acclaimed work of Athol ▷FUGARD. In the 1970s, he collaborated with Fugard and fellow actor Winston Ntshona on plays that showed the suffering caused by apartheid, most notably *Sizwe Bansi is Dead*, for which he won a Tony Award (1975). Kani was named best actor at the Sicilian Film Festival (1987) for his portrayal of a terrorized roadhouse waiter in *Saturday Night at the Palace.* In the same year he played the title role in Janet SUZMAN's production of Othello. Kani is an artistic director at the Market Theatre.

❖ The 1986 production of August Strindberg's *Miss Julie* caused a stir – one of the scenes required that Kani kiss actress Sandra Prinsloo and few South African audiences had seen this type of interracial intimacy on stage.

Kaye, Danny (David Daniel Kaminsky) (1913-87) Exuberant American film comedian and stage and television entertainer, noted for his mimicry and tongue-twisting musical numbers. He sprang to stardom with his first film, *Up in Arms* (1944). This was followed by a host of hits, including *Wonder Man* (1945), *The Kid from Brooklyn* (1946), *The Secret Life of Walter Mitty* (1947), *Hans Christian Andersen* (1952) and *The Court Jester* (1956). He is also remembered for his high-spirited one-man performances at the London Palladium in the 1950s.

Keaton, Buster (1895-1966) Poker-faced Hollywood clown who wrote and directed many of his own comedy films. These included *The Boat* (1922), *Our Hospitality* (1923), *The Navigator* (1924) and *The General* (1926), hailed as his best – about a young engineer's attempts to enlist for the Civil War. His career declined with the arrival of talking pictures.

Kelly, Grace (1929-82) American cinema actress and former society beauty whose cool charm brought her stardom. Her films include the classic Western *High Noon* (1952), three Hitchcock thrillers, *Dial M for Murder* (1954), *Rear Window* (1954) and *To Catch a Thief* (1955), and the melodramatic *The Country Girl* (1954), for which she won an Oscar for Best Actress. In 1956 she gave up her film career to marry Prince Rainier III of Monaco. She was killed when her car plunged off a mountain road on the Riviera.

Keystone Cops, The Frenzied troupe of comics formed in 1912 by Hollywood's 'comedy king', producer Mack Sennett (1880-1960). Their silent shorts were famed for their car chases, stunts and custard-pie battles. They disbanded in 1920.

King Kong Classic monster film, made in 1933, about a giant ape known by his captors as King Kong. Shipped from a remote Pacific island to New York, Kong is put on show in a circus – from which he escapes. He goes berserk, wrecking cars, terrorizing the city and abducting a scantily-clad blonde played by Fay Wray (1907-). With screaming girl in hand, he makes his last desperate stand on top of the Empire State Building, fighting off the planes sent to shoot him down.

❖ Although he appeared to stand some 15 m

high on screen, King Kong was actually a 40,6 cm animated model.

❖ *King Kong* was also the title of a 1959 township musical based on the life of a heavyweight boxing champion which boosted the development of black theatre in South Africa. It was taken to London with Ken Gampu playing the leading part.

knock 'n drop Community interest newspapers that are driven by local advertising and distributed free to residents in the area. In South Africa, many regional and suburban free sheets are tied to the big newspaper groups. Examples include the *Southern Suburbs Tatler*, which has been distributed in the southern suburbs of Cape Town since 1979, the *South Coast Sun, Northcliff and Blackheath Times* and *Kempton Express.*

Kubrick, Stanley (1928-) American director, writer and producer who caused a public outcry with his disturbing film *A* CLOCKWORK ORANGE (1971). His other films – all of which have caused controversy – include the black comedy *Dr Strangelove: Or How I Learned to Stop Worrying and Love the Bomb* (1963), the spectacular science fiction epic *2001: A Space Odyssey* (1968), the horror film *The Shining* (1980), in which Jack Nicholson played a deranged writer intent on murdering his wife and son, and the harrowing Vietnam drama *Full Metal Jacket* (1987).

Kurosawa, Akira (1910-) Best-known Japanese film director who deals with the major themes of the post-World War II culture. Kurosawa first attracted attention in the West with his 1951 Venice Festival Grand Prize winner, *Rashomon*, which depicted the destruction of the Heian court society. His international reputation grew with numerous awards, including an OSCAR for best foreign language film for the Siberian epic *Dersu Uzala* (1975). His 1980 Cannes Grand Prize winner, *Kagemusha,* was distributed worldwide by 20th Century-Fox. Kurosawa invented realistic swordfighting on screen and serious portrayals of violence.

Lancaster, Burt (1913-94) Brawny American film star who began his show business career as a circus acrobat. He sang and danced in US Army shows during World War II and made a compelling film debut in *The Killers* (1946). Other leading roles followed in *Brute Force* (1947), *Criss Cross* (1949), *Trapeze* (1956), in which he played an acrobat, *Gunfight at the OK Corral* (1957), *Sweet Smell of Success* (1957), *Elmer Gantry* (1960), for which he won an Oscar for his portrayal of a hypocritical evangelist; and *The Birdman of Alcatraz* (1962). He later played an ageing gangster in *Atlantic City* (1980), a Texas oil magnate in the British-made *Local Hero* (1983), and a train robber in *Tough Guys* (1986), which also starred Kirk Douglas.

Laurel and Hardy Bowler-hatted comedy duo whose screen antics kept audiences laughing for more than a quarter of a century. The thin, nervous one – Stan Laurel (1890-1965) – was born Arthur Stanley Jefferson in England. The fat, bullying one – Oliver Hardy (1892-1957) – was born Norvell Hardy Junior in America. They teamed up in 1927 and made scores of films, including *The Music Box* (1932), which won a Best Short Film Oscar, *Bonnie Scotland* (1935), *Way Out West* (1937) and *A Chump at Oxford* (1940). They toured Britain after World War II as a music-hall act, delighting their old admirers and winning many new ones.

Lawrence of Arabia Sweeping adventure film about the enigmatic British soldier-scholar T E Lawrence, dashingly played by Peter O'Toole, who fought as an Arab guerrilla leader in the Middle East in World War I. Directed in 1962 by David Lean, the $3^1/_2$ hour picture combined breathtaking desert scenes with high action – such as the blowing up of a railway train. Its superb cast included Jack Hawkins as General Allenby, Alec Guinness as Prince Faisal, and Anthony Quinn as an arrogant Arab chief. It won a string of Oscars, including the Best Film award.

Lean, Sir David (1908-91) Illustrious British director whose masterpiece, LAWRENCE OF ARABIA, set a new standard in screen epics, gaining him a Best Director Oscar. His early, small-scale films included *This Happy Breed* (1944), *Blithe Spirit* (1945), two magnificent Dickens adaptations – *Great Expectations* (1946) and *Oliver Twist* (1948) – *Hobson's Choice* (1953) and *Summer Madness* (1955), a touching romance set in Venice with Katharine Hepburn and Rossano Brazzi. He won his first Oscar for *The Bridge on the River Kwai* (1957), with Alec Guinness. His next two epics, *Dr Zhivago* (1965) and *Ryan's Daughter* (1970), were slated by many of the critics – although the public flocked to see them. Disheartened, Lean did not make another film until *A Passage to India* (1984), from E M Forster's novel about the clash of eastern and western cultures in British-ruled India. He was knighted in 1984.

Leigh, Vivien (1913-67) Radiant English stage and screen actress who played the vivacious Southern belle, Scarlett O'Hara, in GONE WITH THE WIND (1939) – for which she won an Oscar. She made her film debut in the British comedy *Things Are Looking Up* (1934) and

BUDDIES *Stan Laurel smiles innocently, while Oliver Hardy looks ready to scold: 'Here's another fine mess you've gotten me into!'*

played opposite Laurence Olivier in *Fire Over England* (1937). The couple married in 1940 after starring together in *Romeo and Juliet* in New York. They continued their partnership in the wartime morale-raiser *That Hamilton Woman* (1941), in which she played Emma Hamilton to Olivier's Lord Nelson. Her later films included *Caesar and Cleopatra* (1945), *Anna Karenina* (1948), *A Streetcar Named Desire* (1951), in which her performance as another Southern belle, the neurotic Blanche Dubois, gained her a second Oscar, *The Deep Blue Sea* (1955), *The Roman Spring of Mrs Stone* (1961), and *Ship of Fools* (1965). Her career and marriage were blighted by physical and mental illness.

Lemmon, Jack (1925-) American comic actor who made his name playing highly strung

GOOD FRIENDS *Insurance clerk Jack Lemmon woos elevator girl Shirley MacLaine in* The Apartment, *a cynical comedy of office life.*

LOVE MATCH *Sophia Loren showed her comic flair in* The Millionairess *(1960), a romance between the world's richest woman and a poor Indian doctor, played by Peter Sellers.*

misfits before turning to more serious dramatic parts. He worked with director Billy Wilder in a string of comic hits, including *Some Like it Hot* (1959), *The Apartment* (1960) and *The Fortune Cookie* (1966), with Walter Matthau (1920-). He also appeared with Matthau in the film version of Neil Simon's *The Odd Couple* (1967) and in *The Front Page* (1974), again directed by Wilder. Lemmon showed his dramatic talents as an alcoholic in *Days of Wine and Roses* (1962) and a garment manufacturer fighting middle age in *Save the Tiger* (1973), for which he won a Best Actor Oscar.

Lion King, The A Zulu version was made of this popular Walt Disney animated feature. The project was initiated by the managing director of Ster-Kinekor, Dave Krynauw, and produced by Katinka HEYNS with Victor Ntoni as the musical director.

LM Radio Lourenço Marques Radio became the first commercial station to broadcast in southern Africa in 1935. The station was started by C J McHarry, a South African who ran broadcasting in Portuguese East Africa. The station broadcasted mainly in English and its pop music slots had a keen audience among young people in South Africa. The SABC acquired the station in 1972 and replaced it with Radio 5 three years later.

Loren, Sophia (Sofia Villani Scicolone) (1934-) Voluptuous Italian actress and former beauty queen who became an international star and sex symbol in Hollywood productions in the 1950s. They included *The Pride and the Passion* (1957) and *Desire Under the Elms* (1958). She blossomed as a serious actress in Vittorio De Sica's war drama *Two Women* (1960), for which she won a Best Actress Oscar, and starred in major epics such as *El Cid* (1961), *The Fall of the Roman Empire* (1964) and *Operation Crossbow* (1965). She also made two hit comedies with actor Marcello Mastroianni (1924-), *Yesterday, Today and Tomorrow* (1963) and *Marriage Italian Style* (1964). In the 1980s she turned to television work, including a remake of *Two Women* (1989).
❖ Modest about her figure, Loren was quoted as saying, 'Everything you see, I owe to spaghetti!'

Losey, Joseph (1909-84) American film director who was driven out of the USA during the Communist witch-hunt of the 1950s. He moved to Britain, where he made some of the finest films of the 1960s. They include *The Servant* (1963), *King and Country* (1964) and *Accident* (1967) – all of which starred Dirk Bogarde. He also directed *The Go-Between* (1971) and a sumptuous version of Mozart's *Don Giovanni* (1979).

Loy, Myrna (1905-93) Elegant American film actress who was hailed as the 'Queen of Hollywood' in the late 1930s. She first worked in silent films, including *Ben-Hur* (1925), and moved smoothly into talking pictures, in which her charm and sophistication were much in demand. In 1934 she costarred with William Powell (1892-1984) as the husband-and-wife detective team, Nick and Nora Charles, in the first of *The Thin Man* series. She later appeared in the popular comedies *Mr Blandings Builds His Dream House* (1948) and *Cheaper by the Dozen* (1950).

Lumière brothers French pioneer film-makers – Auguste (1862-1954) and Louis (1864-1948) – who in December 1895 presented the first-ever moving pictures to a paying audience. The venue for the presentation was a café in Paris and the short films – one of which showed workers leaving the brothers' photographic plate factory in Lyons – were shown by means of a combined motion-picture camera and projector which the brothers had invented.

M*A*S*H Highly popular American television series, inspired by the hilarious 1969 Hollywood film of the same name. The initials stand for 'Mobile Army Surgical Hospital'. The series, which ran from 1972-82, starred Alan Alda as Captain 'Hawkeye' Pierce, chief surgeon of an eccentric medical unit serving in the Korean War. Although awash with blood, guts, sex and often cynical black humour, *M*A*S*H* reflected some uncomfortable truths about the horrors of modern warfare.

M-Net (Electronic Media Network Limited) South Africa's first pay television station which has nearly a million subscribers in Africa. M-Net was launched by the major press groups in 1986 to curb the flow of advertising revenue to the SABC's television services. Its shareholders include NASIONALE PERS, TIMES MEDIA LTD, INDEPENDENT NEWSPAPERS OF SOUTH AFRICA, PERSKOR, Natal Witness and Dispatch Media. In 1995 a separate company, MultiChoice, was formed for technical and support services. M-Net concentrates on films, sport and children's programmes and local productions such as its popular magazine programme *Carte Blanche* and daily serial, EGOLI – PLACE OF GOLD. It sponsors two major annual awards for books and films.

MacLaine, Shirley (1934-) Ebullient American actress, singer and dancer who began her career as a Broadway chorus girl. She made her film debut in Alfred Hitchcock's black comedy *The Trouble With Harry* (1955) and starred in a string of comedies and musicals, including *The Apartment* (1960) and *Sweet Charity* (1968). She won an Oscar for her performance opposite Jack Nicholson in the marital drama *Terms of Endearment* (1983). MacLaine is the sister of the equally famous American star Warren Beatty.

Mail & Guardian Leading independent newspaper in South Africa and part of a range of ALTERNATIVE MEDIA started in the mid-1980s at the height of political repression. It has a branch, Weekly Mail Television, producing television documentaries that have been screened around the world. A periodically made documentary series, *Ordinary People*, is made for national television. In 1987 the newspaper organized a South African film festival and a conference of independent local film producers to drum up public support for that sector of the film industry. It also initiated an annual short film festival in 1992 which recognizes independently made local short films. Since 1992, it has carried the southern African edition of *The Guardian Weekly* of London, which is now fully incorporated into the paper.

Mapantsula Term used to describe a particular kind of music and dance. Young, black male adherents, known by the same term, are recognized by their expensive and elaborate clothing. Female adherents are known as Mshaza. Thomas Mogotlane stars as Panic, a petty thief, in the 1988 film *Mapantsula*,

MAGAZINES TO INFORM AND ENTERTAIN

Sales figures are one measure of a magazine's success and popularity. But some of the smaller circulation journals have an influence that has made them household names – and some that are no longer published live on in the memory of the reading public.

Bona Black consumer magazine with the largest circulation in South Africa. It was founded in 1956 and appears monthly. Circulation 258 265.

Cosmopolitan South African edition of the glitzy American women's magazine. It appears monthly and also has a large male following. Glamour is combined with quality topical articles. Founded in 1984. Circulation 97 574.

Drum Black magazine founded in 1951 by Jim Bailey which spawned a generation of talented black writers in South Africa, producing a potent mix of politics, entertainment and social news. Now owned by Nasionale Media, its content is less upmarket. Circulation 181 516.

The Economist Weekly international news and business journal, with comment on politics, economics and finance. Founded in 1843. Circulation (UK) 103 268.

Fair Lady Best known South African women's magazine. Published fortnightly, its first editor and publisher, Jane Raphaely, now produces two other women's magazines, *Cosmopolitan* and *Femina* (1982-), with 109 574 circulation. Founded in 1965. Circulation 142 526.

Financial Mail Leading South African business weekly published since 1965, preceded by *Southern African Financial Mail* (1959-64). Circulation 32 330.

Hello! Glossy weekly packed with gossipy articles on royalty and other celebrities. Founded in 1988. Circulation (UK) 441 656.

Huisgenoot Oldest Afrikaans weekly and magazine with the largest circulation in South Africa. Founded in 1916, it played an important educational role, but from the 1980s it became more sensational. Circulation 516 941. An English version of the magazine, *You*, started appearing in 1987. Circulation 301 411.

National Geographic Magazine International glossy monthly on travel, wildlife, environment and anthropology, noted for its photography. Founded in 1988. Circulation (UK) 354 429.

Reader's Digest General interest monthly with accessible, accurate writing on almost any subject. The world's most widely read magazine. Founded in the USA in 1922 and in Britain in 1938. Circulation (worldwide) 27 million; (UK) 1 784 733; (SA) 370 000.

Scope General interest fortnightly magazine with a reputation for pin-ups, sensationalism and risqué articles. It frequently fell foul of South Africa's old censorship laws. Founded in 1966. Circulation 102 697.

Style Up-market, progressive monthly of general interest with editions for Gauteng, Western and Eastern Cape and KwaZulu-Natal. Founded in 1981. Circulation 47 600*.

Time International news and general interest weekly, noted for its brisk writing style and strong pictures. Founded in the United States in 1923, and in Europe in 1946. Circulation (UK) 107 000; (SA) 69 000 claimed.

Tribute Authoritative black monthly which mixes serious investigative journalism with articles of general appeal. Its editor is the controversial columnist of *The Star*, Jon Qwelane. Founded 1987. Circulation 16 286*.

Vogue Influential fashion, trends and lifestyle monthly. The British edition was founded in 1916, when war prevented the importation of glossy American magazines. Circulation (UK) 183 439.

Circulation figures (international): June-Jan 1994, Source: ABC; South Africa: Jan-June 1995. Source: ABC.
** July-Dec 1994: SARAD 1995*

directed by himself and Oliver Schmitz. The film explores life in the conflict-ridden townships of South Africa, with Panic's political education as focal point.

March of Time, The Extremely influential film-documentary series founded in America by *Time* magazine in 1935 and shown as part of cinema programmes. Each month the 20-minute films explored subjects such as the growth of Nazism in Germany and the climb to power of the dictators ▷MUSSOLINI and ▷STALIN. The series ran until the late 1940s, when it gradually gave way to current affairs programmes on television, including *CBS Report* in the USA and *Panorama* and *World in Action* in Britain.

Marx Brothers Family of American film comedians who were at their anarchistic peak in the early 1930s. Best-known were the piano-playing Chico (Leonard, 1886-1961), who chased women and assumed a ludicrous Italian accent; the silent Harpo (Adolph, 1888-1964), who played the harp and communicated by means of a bicycle horn; and the wise-cracking, woman-chasing Groucho (Julius, 1890-1977), who loped around with a painted-on moustache and an outsize cigar. The straight man Zeppo (Herbert, 1901-79), appeared in their first five films and then became a show-business agent. The lesser-known Gummo (Milton, 1893-1977), left the act before the first Marx Brothers film was made and became their business manager. Their films include *Animal Crackers* (1930), *Monkey Business* (1931), *Horse Feathers* (1932), *Duck Soup* (1933), *A Night at the Opera* (1935), *A Day at the Races* (1937) and *A Night in Casablanca* (1946). Groucho later appeared in a handful of films such as *A Girl in Every Port* (1952) and hosted the popular American quiz show *You Bet Your Life* on radio (1947-58) and on television (1956-61).
❖ On declining a membership offer from a club, Groucho Marx wrote to the secretary, stating: 'I don't care to belong to any club which would accept me as a member!'

Mason, James (1909-84) Suave and sinister villain of a host of British-made costume dramas including *The Man in Grey* (1943), *Fanny by Gaslight* (1944) and *The Wicked Lady* (1945), which entertained audiences during World War II. He made his film debut in *Late Extra* (1935) and his services were constantly in work on both sides of the Atlantic for the rest of his long career. Among his most memorable films were: *The Seventh Veil* (1945), *Odd Man Out* (1947), *The Desert Fox* (1951), in which he played Field Marshal Rommel, *Julius Caesar* (1953), as Brutus, *A Star is Born* (1954), *Lolita* (1961), *Georgy Girl* (1966), *The Verdict* (1982) and *The Shooting Party* (1984).

McQueen, Steve (1930-80) Poker-faced American film actor – and former reform-school inmate – who specialized in rugged, he-man roles. He starred in action films such as KUROSAWA's *The Magnificent Seven* (1960), *The Great Escape* (1963), *Bullitt* (1968), which featured a roller-coaster car chase over the hills of San Francisco, *The Getaway* (1972), *Papillon* (1973), and *The Towering Inferno* (1974). He extended his acting range in a film version of Ibsen's *An Enemy of the People* (1977). Despite suffering from terminal cancer, he gave typical, tight-lipped performances in the Western *Tom Horn* (1980), and as a modern-day bounty hunter in *The Hunter* (1980).

Merchant-Ivory Independent British film company headed by American director James Ivory (1928-) and Indian producer Ismail Merchant (1936-), who are renowned for their stylish period films and adaptations of novels by E M Forster. These include *A Room With a View* (1985), *Howard's End* (1992), which won an Oscar for Emma Thompson, and *The Remains of the Day* (1993), with Emma Thompson and Anthony HOPKINS.

Milligan, Spike (1918-) Eccentric Irish comedian who was the creative genius behind the bizarre humour of the GOON SHOW. His offbeat comedy series for BBC Television, *Q*, began in 1965 with *Q5* and ended in 1980 with *Q9*. Among his films are *The Bed Sitting Room* (1969), a surreal post-Nuclear War comedy adapted from a play by Milligan, *Monty Python's Life of Brian* (1979), a religious satire, and *Yellowbeard* (1983), a farcical pirate tale.

Mills, Sir John (1908-) Upright British film actor who went from playing a plucky able seaman in *In Which We Serve* (1942) to a stiff-upper-lip army officer in *Tunes of Glory* (1960). He began his career in the 1930s as a chorus boy in musical comedies. Among his best-known movies are *Scott of the Antarctic* (1948), *The History of Mr Polly* (1949), *Hobson's Choice* (1953), *Ice Cold in Alex* (1958), and David Lean's Irish melodrama, *Ryan's Daughter* (1970), for which he won an Oscar for his portrayal of a village simpleton. He is the father of actresses Juliet Mills (1941-) and Hayley Mills (1946-) who made her screen debut opposite him in the thriller *Tiger Bay* (1959). He was knighted in 1977.

Mitchum, Robert (1917-) Strapping, droopy-eyed American star of gangster classics such as *Crossfire* (1947), *Out of the Past* (1947) and *Where Danger Lives* (1950). In 1943, his first year in Hollywood, he appeared in some 18 films, starting as an extra in *Hoppy Serves a Writ* and ending with a supporting role in *Gung Ho*. He made his mark in *The Story of GI Joe* (1945) and played the lead in a host of major productions, including *Night of the Hunter* (1955), *The Sundowners* (1960), *Cape Fear* (1961), *Ryan's Daughter* (1970), *The Friends of Eddie Coyle* (1973) and two private-eye films: *Farewell My Lovely* (1975) and *The Big Sleep* (1978). On TV, he starred in the mini-series *The Winds of War* (1983) and its sequel *War and Remembrance* (1989).

Monroe, Marilyn (Norma Jean Baker) (1926-62) Sultry American actress who became an international sex symbol during the 1950s. After working as a photographic model – and posing in the nude for a pin-up calendar – she went to Hollywood and got small but telling parts as the mistress of a crooked lawyer in *The Asphalt Jungle* (1950) and a would-be actress in *All About Eve* (1950). She sparkled in films such as *Gentlemen Prefer Blondes* (1953), *How to Marry a Millionaire* (1953), *The Seven Year Itch* (1955) and Billy Wilder's classic gangster spoof, *Some Like It Hot* (1959). Her last finished film was *The Misfits* (1961), written by her third husband, the playwright Arthur Miller. Unpunctual and unreliable, she was fired from *Something's Got to Give* in 1962. Shortly afterwards she died of a drug overdose in mysterious circumstances.

❖ She was renowned for her pert exchanges with the press. These included: 'What do you wear in bed?' Answer: 'Chanel No 5!' 'You had nothing else on?' Answer: 'Sure – I had the radio on!'

LEG SHOW *Comedian Tom Ewell admires Marilyn Monroe's legs as she straddles a New York air grating in* The Seven Year Itch *(1955). Barriers held back the crowds at the filming of the scene.*

Monty Python's Flying Circus BBC television comedy series (1969-74) noted for the lunatic humour of its sketches such as 'The Dead Parrot' and 'The Ministry of Silly Walks'. It was written and performed by a team of former university humorists, including John Cleese, Graham Chapman, Eric Idle and Michael Palin. The imaginative and witty graphics were the work of American animator Terry Gilliam. The team's feature films include *Monty Python and the Holy Grail* (1974) and the irreverent *Monty Python's Life of Brian* (1979).

Namibian Broadcasting Association National broadcaster of Namibia. Its TV service, in English, reaches Windhoek, Swakopmund and Oshakati, centres where half of the Namibian population lives. Eight radio channels broadcast in 11 indigenous languages. Broadcasting was originally introduced as an extension of the SABC's Bantu Radio Service. The NBA was formed in 1979 and is controlled by the State.

Nasionale Pers Major Afrikaans-orientated press group which, along with PERSKOR, boosted the apartheid government. Its newspaper and magazine division is known as Nasionale Media. The company was founded in 1915, also the year in which its flagship, the Cape Town-based *Die Burger*, was established. In the 1980s the group started competing in the black market, acquiring an important national black weekly *City Press* and magazines such as *Drum* and *True Love*. Newspaper titles include *Beeld*, *Die Volksblad* and *Rapport*, owned with Perskor. It also owns women's magazines such as *Sarie* and *Fair Lady*.

❖ The first editor of *Die Burger*, D F Malan, later became the first National Party leader and prime minister.

New Wave Name given to a group of young French film directors in the late 1950s and early 1960s who used outdoor locations and hand-held cameras and who oversaw each aspect of film-making, from script to editing, claiming to be the sole 'authors' of the finished works. Their films included Francois Truffaut's *The Four Hundred Blows* (1959),

NEWSPAPERS OF SOUTHERN AFRICA

Newspaper	Circulation	Description
Sunday Times 1906	505 505	Largest-circulation newspaper and first Sunday paper. Its first editor was George Kingswell, a rolling stone and near-genius.
Rapport 1970	390 669	Sunday newspaper with sensationalist and right-wing political leanings. Edited by a controversial former minister of religion and woman's magazine editor, Izak de Villiers.
Business Day 1985	36 960	Only national business daily in the country, established in part to fill the vacuum left by the closure of the *Rand Daily Mail* in 1985.
The Star 1887	182 119	Leading daily with 24-hour editions, regarded as an authoritative voice in the SA newspaper world.
Sowetan 1981	208 358	Largest-circulation daily newspaper in South Africa. It is directed at a black readership.
The Citizen 1976	117 983	Popular Johannesburg daily which has survived its odious beginnings as a government-created organ for apartheid propaganda.
Beeld 1974	98 997	Most progressive of Afrikaans dailies now committed to value journalism rather than pushing a particular political viewpoint.
New Nation 1986	17 824	Alternative black weekly which campaigned against apartheid. It appeared as a Sunday paper for a while.
City Press 1983	267 550	Weekly, directed at a black readership and the fastest growing newspaper in South Africa.
Mail & Guardian 1985	28 603	Leading independent weekly which consistently exposed the abuses of the apartheid regime.
The Argus 1886	89 014	Western Cape afternoon paper which claims the biggest readership in the Cape metropolitan area. Also published on weekends.
Die Burger 1915	105 841	Afrikaans daily, which was the foundation stone of the Nasionale Pers publishing empire. Based in Cape Town.
Cape Times 1876	54 947	Oldest surviving daily newspaper in South Africa. It was relaunched with a more up-market appearance in 1995.
The Natal Witness 1846	27 645	Oldest existing newspaper in South Africa, initially established as a weekly. Now a daily, it is also one of three independent papers in the country.
Imvo Zabantsundu 1884	19 350	Oldest black newspaper in the country, founded by John Tengo Jabavu in King William's Town. Now producing weekly English and Xhosa editions.
Eastern Province Herald 1845	31 387	Daily newspaper distributed throughout the Eastern Cape. It started off as a weekly and is based in Port Elizabeth.
The Chronicle 1894	74 032*	One of Zimbabwe's two main daily newspapers. Bulawayo-based, it was founded by the Argus Printing and Publishing Company. The majority shareholder is the Zimbabwe Mass Media Trust.
The Herald 1891	134 000*	Zimbabwe's largest circulation daily newspaper, printed in Harare. It was founded by the Argus Printing and Publishing Company. Majority shareholding now with the Zimbabwe Mass Media Trust.

*Circulation: Jan-Jun 1995. Source: ABC; * Africa South of the Sahara 1995.*

Alain Resnais's *Hiroshima Mon Amour* (1959) and Jean-Luc Godard's *Breathless* (1960).

Newman, Paul (1925-) Blue-eyed American actor and sex symbol who became one of Hollywood's leading film stars from the mid-1950s onwards. His numerous films include *Somebody Up There Likes Me* (1956), *Cat on a Hot Tin Roof* (1958), *The Hustler* (1961), *Hud* (1962), *Cool Hand Luke* (1967); and two enormously popular films with Robert Redford: *Butch Cassidy and the Sundance Kid* (1969) and *The Sting* (1973). These were followed by *The Towering Inferno* (1974), *Absence of Malice* (1981), *The Verdict* (1982), *The Color of Money* (1986) which won him an Oscar, *Blaze* (1989) and *Mr and Mrs Bridge* (1990). He directed his wife Joanne Woodward (1930-) in *Rachel, Rachel* (1968).

Ngema, Mbongeni (1955-) South African playwright, director and actor who has achieved international success since the early 1980s. A factory 'tool-boy' turned actor and musician, Ngema is best known for his Broadway hit musical *Sarafina!* His play *Woza Albert*, cowritten with Percy Mtwa, received the London *City Limits* Best Play of the Year Award in 1983 and he also wrote and directed the award-winning *Asinamali.* He has been nominated for five Tony Awards and has won Best Director awards in Los Angeles and Edinburgh. He runs a recording company for local music and has won the OKTV Award for the best contribution to South African music. Ngema was apppointed head of the music theatre department of the Natal Performing Arts Council in 1994.

Nicholson, Jack (1937-) Magnetic American film star who specializes in portraying bizarre characters, such as an axe-wielding maniac in *The Shining* (1980), a sex-obsessed Satan in *The Witches of Eastwick* (1987) and the malign Joker in *Batman* (1989). He scored his first major success in EASY RIDER (1969). His other outstanding films include *Five Easy Pieces* (1970), *The Last Detail* (1973), *Chinatown* (1974), *One Flew Over the Cuckoo's Nest* (1975) for which he won an Oscar, *Terms of Endearment* (1983), which won him another Oscar, *Prizzi's Honor* (1985), *Ironweed* (1987), *The Two Jakes* (1990), which he also directed, and *Wolf* (1994).

Niven, David (1910-83) Sophisticated British actor who worked as a Hollywood extra before being signed as a typical English gentleman. He appeared in *The Charge of the Light Brigade* (1936) and *Bachelor Mother* (1939). Commissioned in the British army in World War II, he was released to make two stirring propaganda films: *The First of the Few* (1942), about the birth of the Spitfire, and *The Way Ahead* (1944). Among his many other films were *A Matter of Life and Death* (1946), *Around the World in Eighty Days* (1956), *Separate Tables* (1958), for which he won an Oscar, *The Guns of Navarone* (1961) and *The Pink Panther* (1963). He wrote two witty, best-selling autobiographies: *The Moon's a Balloon* (1971) and *Bring on the Empty Horses* (1975).

Nommer Asseblief (Number Please) Comic Afrikaans television serial which charmed viewers with its accounts of *dorp* life, as filtered through a small community's manual telephone exchange. It was directed by Henk Hugo and screened in 1979 and 1980.

Olivier, Lord Laurence (1907-89) Outstanding British actor and director who brought Shakespeare to the cinema-going public with his film versions of *Henry V* (1944), *Hamlet* (1948), for which he won a Best Actor Oscar, and *Richard III* (1955). He came to prominence in *Fire over England* (1936) and went to Hollywood to film *Wuthering Heights* (1939), *Rebecca* (1940), *Pride and Prejudice* (1940) and the morale-boosting *That Hamilton Woman* (1941), in which he played the British naval hero Lord Nelson, opposite the Emma Hamilton of his second wife, Vivien Leigh. Another memorable performance was his portrayal of the seedy music-hall comedian Archie Rice in the stage and film versions of John Osborne's *The Entertainer* (1957 and 1960). He later costarred with Michael Caine in the thriller *Sleuth* (1972). Among his many theatrical highlights were his 1964 portrayal of *Othello* at London's National Theatre, of which he was the first director (1963-73). On television he gave virtuoso performances in *Brideshead Revisited* (1981), *A Voyage Round My Father* (1982) and in the title role of Shakespeare's *King Lear* (1983). Olivier and Vivien Leigh were divorced in 1960 and the following year he married the British actress Joan Plowright (1929-). He was knighted in 1947, and in 1970 became the first actor ever to be made a peer.

***Orkney Snork Nie! (Orkney isn't snoring!)* (literal)** Most popular South African television serial (it was screened in 1987 and 1990), which also became a hit film. A family comedy set in the mining town of Orkney, it portrays the comings and goings of the quirky Van Tonder family. Written by Willie Esterhuizen, it starred Zack du Plessis, Annette Engelbrecht and Jacques Loots.

Oscar Popular name for the American Academy Award, a gold-plated statuette given since 1929 by the Academy of Motion Picture Arts and Sciences to each of the winners of its annual trophies.

❖ The statuette is said to have been 'christened' by a Hollywood secretary, who said it reminded her of her Uncle Oscar.

FAMILY QUIRKS *Annette Engelbrecht is puzzled by her 'children' in* Orkney Snork Nie!

O'Toole, Peter (1932-) Volatile Irish stage and screen actor who became an international star in David Lean's LAWRENCE OF ARABIA (1962). He appeared in a quick succession of major productions, including *Becket* (1964), *Lord Jim* (1965), *Night of the Generals* (1966) and *The Lion in Winter* (1968). His later films include *The Stunt Man* (1980), *My Favourite Year* (1982) and *The Last Emperor* (1987). On stage, he is best remembered for his title roles in *Hamlet* (1963) and *Jeffrey Bernard is Unwell* (1989).

Pacino, Al (1940-) Dynamic American actor of Sicilian descent who was ideally cast as the urbane Mafia don Michael Corleone in *The Godfather* films of 1972, 1974 and 1990. He also starred in crime films such as *Serpico* (1973), *Dog Day Afternoon* (1975), *Sea of Love* (1989) and the comic-strip *Dick Tracy* (1990). He won an Oscar for his role as a blind ex-military officer who introduces a greenhorn to life in *Scent of a Woman* (1992).

Peck, Gregory (1916-) Dignified American star in films for 20 years before winning an Oscar as a lawyer who defends a Negro on a rape charge in *To Kill a Mocking Bird* (1962). He found stardom in his first film, *Days of Glory* (1943), and brought distinction to dozens of top-line productions, including *Gentlemen's Agreement* (1947) and *Twelve O'Clock High* (1949), as well as Westerns such as *The Big Country* (1958). Later roles include that of the father of the antiChrist in the occult thriller *The Omen* (1976).

Perskor The second biggest Afrikaans newspaper group after NASIONALE PERS. The more conservative Perskor, founded in 1931, dominated the newspaper industry in the north with newspapers such as *Die Transvaler* and *Die Vaderland*. Perskor agreed in the 1980s to leave the morning newspaper market to Nasionale Pers. Between 1977 and 1980 the group distorted figures to show higher circulation in conservative Afrikanerdom's heartland of Pretoria. Newspaper titles include *Die Transvaler, The Citizen, Tempo* and *Rapport* (50 per cent share). It owns black titles, including the weekly *Imvo Zabantsundu* and magazines *Bona* and *Tandi*, as well as others such as *Rooi Rose, Farmer's Weekly, South African Garden and Home, Keur* and *Scope*.

Pink Panther, The Riotous comedy film starring Peter Sellers as the accident-prone Inspector Clouseau on the trail of a master criminal called The Phantom who has stolen a priceless jewel known as The Pink Panther. Made in 1963 by the American director Blake Edwards (1922-), the film's success inspired seven sequels and a highly popular cartoon series.

Planet of the Apes Chilling science fiction film starring Charlton Heston in which astronauts trapped in a time warp land on an alien planet ruled by a race of intelligent but often brutal apes. The film, made in 1967 by American director Franklin Schaffner (1920-), has a surprise ending which punches home its moral message. It spawned five sequels and a television series made in 1974.

Poitier, Sidney (1924-) Black American film star whose screen success played a significant part in promoting racial equality in the 1950s and 1960s. Several of his films dealt with racial issues and prejudice. They included *No Way Out* (1950), *The Defiant Ones* (1958), *Lilies of the Field* (1963), for which he won an Oscar, *To Sir with Love* (1967), *In the Heat of the Night* (1967) and *Guess Who's Coming to Dinner* (1967), the first film to deal with a mixed marriage.

Polanski, Roman (1933-) Controversial Polish director whose films often portray people in the throes of sexual and mental torment. They include *Knife in the Water* (1962, Poland) and a crop of movies made in Britain, America and France, such as *Repulsion* (1965), *Rosemary's Baby* (1968), *Macbeth* (1971), *Chinatown* (1974), *Frantic* (1988) and *Bitter Moon* (1992).

Price, Vincent (1911-93) Sepulchral-voiced American actor who was the undisputed 'King of the Horror Film'. After a distinguished Hollywood career, he made the chilling *House of Wax* (1953), in which he played a homicidal sculptor who exhibits his embalmed victims in an eerie wax museum. This was followed by *The House of Usher* (1960), *The Masque of the Red Death* (1964), *The Abominable Dr Phibes* (1971) and *Theatre of Blood* (1973).

❖ A notable art collector, Price was reputed to be the highest-paid lecturer on painting in the USA.

Prior, Chris (1948-) Radio 702 presenter noted for his phenomenal knowledge of popular music, especially rock, and often referred to as the 'Professor of rock'. Prior is a former 5FM late-night veteran who has been on the air for a quarter of a century. He started out as a reporter and has freelanced in India, Indonesia and Singapore.

Psycho Director Alfred Hitchcock's masterpiece of horror, dark humour and suspense.

Made in 1960, the film featured Janet Leigh as a thief-on-the-run and Anthony Perkins (1932-92) as a young man obsessed with his mother who runs a remote motel in which the fugitive spends the night. The heroine is then slashed to death in the shower by a maniac wielding a knife. It started a trend for so-called 'slasher' films.

Puttnam, David (1941-) London-born producer hailed as the 'saviour' of the ailing British film industry in the 1980s. His movies include the Oscar-winning *Chariots of Fire* (1981), *Local Hero* (1983), *The Killing Fields* (1984) and *The Mission* (1986).

Radio Metro Popular national commercial radio station with mainly urban black listeners. It projects an up-market contemporary image with music programmes, phone-in slots, chat shows and actuality programmes. Among its presenters are radio's most popular personalities such as Bob Mabena, Lawrence Dube and Tim Modise. It was launched by the SABC in 1986 and has the third highest listenership (after Radio Zulu and Radio Xhosa).

Redford, Robert (1937-) American actor and director who rose to superstar status opposite Paul Newman in the Western *Butch Cassidy and the Sundance Kid* (1969) and the crime caper *The Sting* (1973). His later films include *The Great Gatsby* (1974), *All the President's Men* (1976), *Out of Africa* (1985), *Havana* (1990) and *Indecent Proposal* (1993). He directed the domestic drama *Ordinary People* (1980), which won a number of Oscars, including one for Best Director, and *A River Runs Through It* (1992).

Redgrave, Vanessa (1937-) Statuesque English stage, film and TV actress. She starred in the film *Morgan – A Suitable Case for Treatment* (1966), a satirical portrait of London in the 'Swinging Sixties'. Among her other films are *Blow Up* (1966), *Isadora* (1968), *Julia* (1977) and *Steaming* (1985). Highlights of her theatrical career include Henrik Ibsen's *The Lady from the Sea* (1976) and Tennessee Williams' *Orpheus Descending* (1988). She won an EMMY for her performance in Arthur Miller's harrowing TV drama about survival in Auschwitz, *Playing for Time* (1980). She is the daughter of the distinguished actor Sir Michael Redgrave (1908-85), and the sister of actress Lynn Redgrave (1943-). She was once married to the Oscar-winning film-maker Tony Richardson (1928-91), director of *Tom Jones* (1963).

Reed, Sir Carol (1906-76) Renowned British film director who made three highly acclaimed postwar movies: *Odd Man Out* (1947), *The Fallen Idol* (1948) and *The Third Man* (1949). Among his later films were *Outcast of the Islands* (1951), *Trapeze* (1956), *Our Man in Havana* (1959) and the bright musical *Oliver!* (1968), which won Oscars for Best Picture and Best Director. Reed was knighted in 1952, the first British film director to be so honoured.

Richardson, Sir Ralph (1902-83) Highly regarded British stage and screen actor with a rich voice and theatrical manner, and also an accomplished deadpan comic. Among his many films were *The Fallen Idol* (1948), *Outcast of the Islands* (1951) and *Dr Zhivago* (1965). Highlights on stage included *Flowering Cherry* (1958), *What the Butler Saw* (1969), *Home* (1970) and Harold Pinter's *No Man's Land* (1975). He was knighted in 1947.

Robinson, Edward G (Emanuel Goldenberg) (1893-1973) Romanian-born American film actor specialising in 'tough guy' and gangster roles. He shot to stardom in *Little Caesar* (1930), a thinly disguised portrait of the Prohibition racketeer Al Capone. His other crime films included *Bullets or Ballots* (1936), *Double Indemnity* (1944), and *Key Largo* (1948), in which he gave a memorable performance as a tenacious insurance investigator.

Room at the Top Pioneering English film which, in 1959, dealt with sex in an adult and open way. Based on John Braine's best-selling novel, it starred Laurence Harvey as a brash young Yorkshireman on the make – socially and financially – and Simone Signoret in an Oscar-winning performance as the worldly wise married woman with whom he has a passionate affair. Director Jack Clayton faithfully captured the look and feel of life in the industrial North. The film received a string of nominations, including Best Picture.

Rossellini, Roberto (1906-77) Highly influential Italian film director. His trilogy of newsreel-like films – *Open City* (1945), *Paisa* (1946) and *Germany, Year Zero* (1947) – used amateur actors and real-life settings to bring everyday realism to the European postwar cinema. His later films included *Stromboli* (1949), which starred Ingrid Bergman, whom he married the following year. He is the father of actress Isabella Rossellini (1952-).

Russell, Ken (1927-) Provocative British film and TV director who caused an outcry with his bold film adaptation of D H Lawrence's *Women in Love* (1969). He followed this with a bizarre version of Tchaikovsky's life and loves in *The Music Lovers* (1970), the sacrilegious *The Devils* (1971) and the raucous rock opera *Tommy* (1975). Later films include *Crimes of Passion* (1984) and *Whore* (1991). In 1993 he directed an explicit TV version of D H Lawrence's erotic novel *Lady Chatterley's Lover*.

Rutherford, Dame Margaret (1892-1972) Eccentric British character actress who made her name playing 'dotty old ladies'. These included Agatha Christie's spinster detective Miss Marple in the film *Murder She Said* (1961) and its sequels, the irrepressible medium Madame Arcati in Noël Coward's *Blithe Spirit* both on stage and screen (1941 and 1945), and the upright Miss Prism in Oscar Wilde's *The Importance of Being Earnest* – on stage in 1939 and on screen in 1952. She won an Oscar for her supporting role as the scatter-brained Duchess of Brighton in Terence Rattigan's *The VIPs* (1963). She was made a Dame of the British Empire in 1967.

SABC South African Broadcasting Corporation, the State-owned broadcasting network which monopolized broadcasting in South Africa until the birth of the INDEPENDENT BROADCASTING AUTHORITY in 1993. The SABC was founded in 1936 on the advice of BBC director-general Sir John Reith, who recommended that it remained independent. It took over the assets and staff of I W SCHLESINGER's African Broadcasting Company which consolidated independents that had been on the air since the 1920s. Afrikaans was added to the solely English programmes in 1937 and Zulu, Xhosa and northern Sotho followed in 1940. The first commercial service of the SABC, SPRINGBOK RADIO, was launched in 1950, and Radio Bantu, broadcasting in four indigenous languages, was inaugurated in 1960. FM (frequency modulation) services began two years later. Radio RSA, an external service to Africa, was broadcasting worldwide by 1964. After years of resistance by conservative forces, television broadcasts started and SABC-TV was formed in 1976. By the 1990s the corporation operated 23 national and regional radio services, including Radio Orion, Radio Allegro, Radio 2000 and RADIO METRO. Independent services such as M-NET, CAPITAL RADIO and 702 had also emerged. In 1993 a representative SABC board, headed by Dr Ivy Matsepe-Casaburri, replaced its progovernment predecessor. First to introduce major changes was the English-language Radio South Africa, which was relaunched as SAfm in March 1995. Its new inclusive identity caused an outcry among many longtime listeners.

SABC-TV Television network of the SABC, offering three services in nine languages to a daily audience of 11 million viewers. About

50 per cent of programmes are locally produced and services are relayed by ground and satellite transmitter systems. Television finally began on 5 January 1976 – after decades of resistance by successive governments who thought it either too expensive or a morally destructive influence. Five years' preparation included the erection of an extensive new broadcasting complex in Auckland Park. The initial 37½ hours of viewing weekly, with evenings divided equally between English and Afrikaans, changed lifestyles. International blockbusters such as *The World at War* and *Rich Man Poor Man* emptied restaurants, theatres and cinemas. Among the first popular local serials were *The* VILLAGERS and NOMMER ASSEBLIEF. TV2 and TV3, a single channel shared between Nguni and Sotho languages, started broadcasting in the early 1980s. The channel was relaunched as CCV in 1990 with a vernacular time-slot and an English time-slot. A third channel, NNTV (formerly TSS-TV), started in October 1993, focusing on sport, documentaries and educational programmes. Bophuthatswana started a television service in 1983, offering a service augmented by the international news service CNN. Independent pay television began with M-NET in 1986. Community television licences were issued in 1995.

❖ The name of a Johannesburg landmark, the 253 m Hertzog Broadcasting Tower, was changed to SABC Tower after TV was introduced because it carried the name of a fiery opponent of television, Dr Albert Hertzog, a cabinet minister from 1958-69.

Sarafina! Mbongeni Ngema's stage musical about the 1976 school boycotts which was turned into a film by Darrell Roodt, featuring stars such as Whoopi Goldberg, John KANI and Miriam ▷MAKEBA. It translated political injustices into popular idiom and presented white audiences with images of predawn raids, detention and torture of schoolchildren, all of which had been suppressed. It received a 10-minute standing ovation at the 1992 Cannes Film Festival, was nominated for a Grammy award, and won Best Film in the M-Net Awards. The play, portraying the boycotts through the eyes of a teenage girl, Sarafina (Leleti Khumalo in the film), had a successful two-year run on BROADWAY. (See also ▷SARAFINA! in 'Music, song and dance'.)

Schlesinger, Isidore William (1871-1947) Pioneer of the South African entertainment industry and film mogul credited with producing the world's oldest film newsreel, AFRICAN MIRROR. The son of a Hungarian-Jewish immigrant, Schlesinger grew up in New York and in 1894 moved to South Africa, becoming a highly successful insurance salesman and financier. He developed Johannesburg's Empire Theatre into a flourishing company of theatres and founded African Film Productions, which produced a dozen short fiction films in 1915-16, including the acclaimed epic *De Voortrekkers* (1916). Schlesinger set up an organization for the national distribution of films and variety acts and also owned an impressive network of cinemas. The country's first chain of radio stations from which the SABC evolved was sponsored by him.

❖ Rushes of *De Voortrekkers* proved to be dramatically realistic: the Zulu mineworkers hired as 'warriors' for the battle scenes, instead of falling 'dead', carried on their attack, forcing the police to intervene.

DEFECTIVE DETECTIVE *The hapless Inspector Clouseau (Peter Sellers) is on the track of a jewel thief in* The Pink Panther *(1963).*

Schuster, Leon (1951-) South African actor and creator of SLAPSTICK for local television and film. Schuster was the scriptwriter and star of *There's A Zulu on my Stoep* (1994), a slapstick comedy about inter-racial relationships which became the biggest local film success ever. A month after its release, the film had grossed R8,5 million. It generated better revenues per print than *Jurassic Park* and *Basic Instinct*.

Schwarzenegger, Arnold (1947-) Austrian bodybuilder and former Mr Universe whose appearance in an American film documentary called *Pumping Iron* (1977) led to a Hollywood career. Among his best-known films are *Conan, the Barbarian* (1981), *The Terminator* (1984), *Predator* (1987), *Total Recall* (1990), *Twins* (1988) and the comedy *Kindergarten Cop* (1990).

Scorsese, Martin (1942-) Virtuoso American director who has worked with actor Robert De Niro on several violent and harrowing films such as *Mean Streets* (1973), *Taxi Driver* (1976), *Raging Bull* (1980), *GoodFellas* (1990) and *Cape Fear* (1991). He also made *The Color of Money* (1986), the controversial *The Last Temptation of Christ* (1988) which infuriated Christians worldwide and the romantic *The Age of Innocence* (1993), with Daniel Day-Lewis and Michelle Pfeiffer. In 1987 he directed the Michael ▷JACKSON video *Bad*.

Sellers, Peter (1925-80) Versatile British comic actor who became an international star in two films directed by Stanley Kubrick: *Lolita* (1962) and *Dr Strangelove: Or How I Learned to Stop Worrying and Love the Bomb* (1964). Sellers started out as a comedian and impressionist and was a member of the GOON SHOW radio team (1952-60). He then enjoyed great success as the bumbling French detective, Inspector Clouseau, in the PINK PANTHER movies of the 1960s and 1970s. His other film comedies included *The Ladykillers* (1955), *I'm All Right, Jack* (1959), *Only Two Can Play* (1962), *The Party* (1968), *There's a Girl in My Soup* (1970) and *Being There* (1979).

❖ 'If you asked me to play myself,' Sellers once stated, 'I wouldn't know what to do. I don't know who I am or what I am!'

Shaka Zulu South African mega-production on the life of the great warrior king Shaka which was lauded by the international media. The epic tale was produced by Bill FAURE and first serialized locally in 1986. Henry Cele, a local professional soccer player who became a superb actor, appeared in the title role, with Dudu Mkhize and the British actor, Edward Fox, taking other key parts.

Sher, Anthony (1949-) Outstanding South African actor who is also an accomplished writer, painter and musician. Sher, who has lived in England since 1968, achieved success in London's West End and in Royal Shakespeare Company productions. He was acclaimed in the role of Harry Kirk in the BBC's *The History of Man*. In 1985 he received the Laurence Olivier Award for his performance as Richard III and later the best actor award for his part in Harvey Fierstein's *Torch Song Trilogy*. Among his novels are *Middlepost* and *Cheap Lives*. His first professional visit to South Africa was made with the Royal National Theatre Studio in 1994 to do workshops at the Market Theatre, Johannesburg. In 1995 he returned for a production of Shakespeare's *Titus Andronicus*.

slapstick Boisterous comedy characterised by physical activity. Jamie UYS and Leon SCHUSTER brought slapstick to the South African screen with their candid camera and sight

gags. *The Gods Must be Crazy* (1981) brought South Africa, and Uys, international acclaim.
❖ A slapstick is the flexible divided lath used by a clown.

Smith, Dame Maggie (1934-) Flamboyant British actress and comedienne who in 1969 won an Oscar for her performance as the unorthodox Scottish schoolteacher in the film version of Muriel Spark's *The Prime of Miss Jean Brodie*. Her other films include *Travels With My Aunt* (1972), *A Room With a View* (1985), *The Lonely Passion of Judith Hearne* (1987) and *The Secret Garden* (1993). Highlights from her distinguished stage career include Desdemona in *Othello* (1964), *Lettice and Lovage* (1987) and Lady Bracknell in Oscar Wilde's *The Importance of Being Earnest* (1993). She was made a Dame of the British Empire in 1990.

Snow White and the Seven Dwarfs Walt Disney's full-length cartoon masterpiece, it was completed in 1937 after two years' production work and at a cost of some US$1,5 million. Taken from a story in *Grimms' Fairy Tales*, it featured a beautiful maiden, a handsome prince, an evil and terrifying stepmother and the seven lovable dwarfs, each with his own distinctive personality: Doc, Bashful, Dopey, Grumpy, Happy, Sleepy and Sneezy.

Spaghetti Westerns Name given to a batch of bloodthirsty cowboy films made in Italy and Spain. Italian director Sergio Leone began the trend with *A Fistful of Dollars* (1964) and its sequels *For a Few Dollars More* (1965) and *The Good, the Bad and the Ugly* (1966).

CLOSE ENCOUNTER *Steven Spielberg gets together with E.T., a stranded alien who loves people but longs to return to his own planet.*

STAR-TREKKERS *The starship* Enterprise *was crewed by (standing) the communications officer, Lieutenant Uhura, Dr 'Bones' McCoy, and (sitting) pointed eared Mr Spock and the ship's commander, Captain Kirk.*

Spielberg, Steven (1947-) Phenomenally successful American film director and producer responsible for a string of financially record-breaking movies. They include JAWS (1975), *Close Encounters of the Third Kind* (1977), *Raiders of the Lost Ark* (1981), ET (1982), *Indiana Jones and the Temple of Doom* (1984), *Indiana Jones and the Last Crusade* (1989), *Hook* (1991), JURASSIC PARK (1993) and *Schindler's List* (1994) – a moving account of how one man saved a group of Jews from the Holocaust – which won Oscars for best film and best director.
❖ Spielberg began as one of television's youngest ever directors, and was only 23 when he made *Duel* (1971), a gripping story about a motorist who is pursued by the unseen driver of a mammoth and menacing petrol tanker.

Springbok Radio South African commercial radio service whose romantic serials and audience participation shows enjoyed a huge following. Programmes such as *Radio Juke Box*, *Lux Radio Theatre* and *Hospital Time* which began with the service in 1950, were still on the air 30 years later. The *Pick-a-Box* quiz, with 600 000 listeners, remained on the air for 17 years. Broadcasting in English and Afrikaans, Springbok Radio promoted the growth of local drama by scrapping imports in favour of local serials. The first English language serial of note was *Brave Voyage*; *Liefdeslied*, the first Afrikaans serial, ran from 1953 to 1959. The station closed down in 1985 due to rationalization at the SABC.

Stallone, Sylvester (1946-) Robust American film actor who shot to fame in *Rocky* (1976), a boxing drama which he wrote himself and which won a Best Picture Oscar. It inspired four sequels all written by Stallone, three of which – *Rocky II* (1979), *Rocky III* (1982) and *Rocky IV* (1985) – he directed. Stallone's 'Rambo' film series, about a violent Vietnam veteran, have also proved popular. He has described Rocky and Rambo as 'money-making machines that can't be switched off'.

Star of the South South Africa's first locally made film. The melodramatic tale about a big diamond was produced by the Springbok Film Company, shown at Christmas time in 1911 and regarded as rather amateurish.

Star Trek American science fiction television series set aboard the starship USS *Enterprise* in the 23rd century. Commanded by Captain James T Kirk (played by William Shatner), and with the pointed-eared half-alien Mr Spock (Leonard Nimoy) as the first officer, the *Enterprise* and its crew met danger and hostility wherever they ventured. The series ran from 1966-9 and was followed by *Star Trek: the Motion Picture* (1979) and five film sequels.

ILL-FATED *Elizabeth Taylor as the queen of Egypt, and Richard Burton as the Roman general Mark Antony, mix politics and passion in* Cleopatra *(1963), the story of their doomed romance.*

Star Wars Spectacular space-age adventure film with stunning special effects. Directed by George Lucas in 1977, it told of a fight between the forces of good and evil. It made a star of Harrison Ford as space pilot Han Solo and gave Alec Guinness his most unusual – and best-paid – role as the space knight Obi-Wan Kenobi. Its international success led to two equally exciting sequels: *The Empire Strikes Back* (1980) and *The Return of the Jedi* (1983).

Stewart, James (1908-) Lanky, slow-speaking American actor who came to prominence in two classic comedies directed by Frank Capra: *You Can't Take It With You* (1938) and *Mr Smith Goes to Washington* (1939). He later appeared as a cynical reporter in *The Philadelphia Story* (1940) for which he won an Oscar, and a would-be suicide in Capra's small-town fantasy *It's a Wonderful Life* (1947). He starred in several Westerns, including the classic *Destry Rides Again* (1939), with Marlene Dietrich. He also played the lead in three Hitchcock thrillers: *Rear Window* (1954), *The Man Who Knew Too Much* (1955) and *Vertigo* (1958). His other notable films include *Harvey* (1950), in which he played the intoxicated friend of an invisible rabbit, *Anatomy of a Murder* (1959), *The Flight of the Phoenix* (1965) and the Civil War drama *Shenandoah* (1965).

Streep, Meryl (1951-) American film star able to assume a variety of accents. She gave outstanding supporting performances in *The Deer Hunter* (1978) and *Manhattan* (1979) before graduating to leading roles. These include a vindictive ex-wife in *Kramer vs Kramer* (1979), for which she won a Best Actress Oscar, a fallen Englishwoman in *The French Lieutenant's Woman* (1981), a Polish, ex-concentration camp inmate in *Sophie's Choice* (1982), which won her a second Oscar, a Danish aristocrat in *Out of Africa* (1986) and an Australian murder suspect in *Cry in the Dark* (1989).

Sunset Boulevard Bitter but brilliant Billy Wilder film, made in 1950, about a former silent-film star desperate to stage a comeback and a frustrated screenwriter hired to write a script that will make her 'big' again. The leads were played by Gloria Swanson (1897-1983), herself a former silent-screen goddess, and William Holden (1918-81). Among the supporting cast were silent comedian Buster Keaton, silent director Eric von Stroheim and pioneering director Cecil B DE MILLE, who played himself.

Suzman, Janet (1939-) South African born actress who became a polished Shakespearian player. She received an Oscar nomination for her performance in a filmed version of *Nicholas and Alexandra* (1971). Suzman has acted in South Africa only twice (1971 and 1978), in productions directed by Barney Simon. Her *Othello*, produced at the Market Theatre in 1987, was screened by BBC Channel Four during the prime Christmas viewing period the next year.

Tarzan More than 80 feature films, as well as a TV series, have been made about the athletic English nobleman, Lord Greystoke, who is abandoned in the African jungle as an infant and is brought up by apes. Based on a character created by the American novelist Edgar Rice Burroughs (1875-1950), the first Tarzan film, *Tarzan of the Apes*, was made in 1918 and the most recent, *Greystoke*, in 1984. Among the best-known Tarzans have been the former Olympic swimmer and gold medallist Johnny Weissmuller (1904-84), Lex Barker (1919-73) and Gordon Scott (1927-).

Taylor, Elizabeth (1932-) British-born actress who became a child star in Hollywood at the age of 10 after being evacuated to California during World War II. She went from playing wholesome young girls in films such as *Lassie Come Home* (1943) and *National Velvet* (1944) to sensual women in *Cat on a Hot Tin Roof* (1958) and *Butterfield 8* (1960), for which she won an Oscar. Among her other films are *Father of the Bride* (1950), *Suddenly, Last Summer* (1959), *A Little Night Music* (1977) and *The Mirror Crack'd* (1980).

❖ Taylor has been married eight times – twice to Richard BURTON (1964-74 and 1975-6),

FILMING FRENZY *Jamie Uys directs operations on the set of* The Gods Must be Crazy *which was shot in a KwaZulu-Natal banana plantation bought especially for the production of the film.*

whom she met when they were filming *Cleopatra* (1963). They later costarred in several films, including *Who's Afraid of Virginia Woolf?* (1966), for which Taylor gained her second Oscar.

Temple, Shirley (1928-) Hollywood's most popular child star of the 1930s. Her cheerful personality, sunny smile and bubble curls provided welcome relief from the gloom of the Great Depression, in films such as *Little Miss Marker* (1934), *Curly Top* (1935), *Dimples* (1936), *Rebecca of Sunnybrook Farm* (1938) and *The Little Princess* (1939). As a teenager her appeal waned, although she continued making films until the late 1940s.
❖ In the 1960s she began a successful political career in the Republican Party as Mrs Temple Black, serving as the US representative to the United Nations (1969-70), ambassador to Ghana (1974-6), chief of protocol at the White House (1976-7) and ambassador to Czechoslovakia (1989-92).

Times Media Ltd South Africa's second major English language newspaper group, previously known as South African Associated Newspapers. For years its flagship, the *Rand Daily Mail*, was a vociferous opponent of apartheid. However, the newspaper ceased publication in 1985, offically because of poor financial performance. Times Media is controlled by the ▷ANGLO AMERICAN CORPORATION. In 1994, the rival INDEPENDENT NEWSPAPERS OF SOUTH AFRICA acquired TML's holdings in the *Cape Times*, Argus Newspapers, Natal Newspapers and the *Pretoria News*. TML is part of the newspaper consortium which controls M-NET and MultiChoice and also owns major magazines such as *Financial Mail* and *Playboy*. Newspaper titles include *Sunday Times*, *Business Day*, *Eastern Province Herald*, *Evening Post*, *Weekend Post* and *Algoa Sun*.

Tom and Jerry Cartoon series about the running battle between a belligerent cat named Tom and his harassed opponent, Jerry the mouse, who always comes out on top. Created in Hollywood in 1937 by animators William Hanna and Joe Barbera, the series has been criticized for its emphasis on violence. Even so, its highly imaginative animation helped it to win Best Cartoon Oscars for seven of the shorts, including *Mouse Trouble* (1944) and *The Two Mouseketeers* (1951).

Tracy, Spencer (1900-67) Sturdy American film actor noted for his natural and realistic performances. He became a major star in 1937 when he won an Oscar for *Captains Courageous*, in which he played a Portuguese fisherman. He gained a second Oscar portraying the real-life Father Flanagan, head of a community for juvenile delinquents, in *Boys' Town* (1938). He later teamed up with Katharine Hepburn – with whom he had a long personal relationship – in a series of witty, war-of-the-sexes comedies. Hepburn also costarred in his last fim, *Guess Who's Coming To Dinner* (1967). His other notable movies included *Bad Day at Black Rock* (1955) and *Inherit the Wind* (1960).

Truffaut, François (1932-84) French film director whose key movie is the autobiographical *The Four Hundred Blows* (1959), telling how a boy, played by Jean-Pierre Leaud, escapes from a brutal reform school and roams the streets of Paris. It ends abruptly with a static close-up of the boy's face – a device much imitated by other directors. He also made a series of films about the amatory adventures of a sensitive young man – again portrayed by Leaud. These include *Stolen Kisses* (1968), *Bed and Board* (1970) and *Love on the Run* (1979).

Ustinov, Sir Peter (1921-) All-round British show business personality known for his portrayal of Agatha Christie's detective Hercule Poirot in *Death on the Nile* (1978) and *Evil Under the Sun* (1982). Ustinov directed a film version of his Cold War stage comedy *Romanoff and Juliet* (1961), in which he also starred. He won Best Supporting Actor Oscars for his roles in *Spartacus* (1960) and in *Topkapi* (1964), as the dupe of a gang of jewel thieves. He was knighted in 1990.

Uys, Jamie (1921-) South African film-maker noted for humourous, SLAPSTICK and candid camera films that won him international fame. Many of his early films were made with Uys himself in the role of scriptwriter, cameraman, director and lead actor, and often also responsible for editing and sound arrangements. His first film, *Daar Doer in die Bosveld (Far Away in the Bushveld)* (1950), was also the first Afrikaans colour film. Favourite themes were Boer vs Brit, the fumbling farmboy and civilization vs wilderness. His most successful films were the 1970s' productions of *Funny People*, *Beautiful People* and *The Gods Must Be Crazy*, which became the highest-grossing foreign film of all time when released in the USA in 1984. Its depiction of blacks as incompetent politicians and idiotic terrorists earned Uys accusations of racism.

Uys, Pieter-Dirk (1945-) Outstanding South African contemporary satirist and actor. Uys is best known for his portrayal of Evita Bezuidenhout, SA ambassadress to the fictitious bantustan of 'Bapetikosweti', with whom he has entertained audiences locally and abroad since the 1980s. Other revues and plays include *Adapt or Dye*, *Farce About Uys*, *Paradise is Closing Down*, *God's Forgot-*

LAST RESPECTS *US cavalrymen, led by veteran captain John Wayne, give a military funeral to a trooper and former Confederate general killed by Indians in* She Wore a Yellow Ribbon *(1949).*

ten, Karnaval and, before the 1994 democratic election, *One man one volt.*

Valentino, Rudolph (1895-1926) Silent-film star of Italian-American origins whose so-called 'animal magnetism' gained him the title of The Great Lover. His sensuous mouth, flaring nostrils and staring eyes – displayed in films such as *The Four Horsemen of the Apocalypse* (1921), *The Sheik* (1921) and *Blood and Sand* (1922) – captivated women around the world and caused a vogue for dark-haired, dark-eyed Latins.

❖ Valentino's death from peritonitis caused several of his female fans to commit suicide, and 80 000 hysterical mourners attended his lying-in-state in New York. He was commemorated in a popular song of the time, titled 'A New Star in Heaven Tonight'.

Van Rensburg, Manie (1945-93) Talented South African film director who produced films of note for cinema and TV since the 1970s. They present a complex picture of Afrikaners during significant periods of their history, including the urbanization of the 1930s, the revival of Afrikaner nationalism during World War II and the emergence of modern, urban Afrikaners after the 1970s. His work has been highly praised and included the TV comedy series *Willem* and dramas such as *Verspeelde Lente, Heroes* and *The Mantiss Project.* From the mid-1980s he shifted towards the international film scene with productions such as *The Native Who Caused All the Trouble* (1989), *The Fourth Reich* (1990) and *Taxi to Soweto* (1991). He committed suicide in 1993.

Villagers, The The first weekly television series with which South African viewers identified. Broadcast in 1976, the story, created by John Cundill and Noel Harford, dealt with life on a Reef goldmine and its characters were ordinary, human and warm. When Buller Wilmot (played by Brian O'Shaughnessy) was killed in a mine explosion, thousands of homes mourned and wept at his televised 'funeral'. The series had a regular following of some 1,2 million viewers.

RADIO REALISM *Orson Welles' radio version of* The War of the Worlds *(1938) was so realistic that many Americans panicked, fearing that Martians had landed in New Jersey. The story was also filmed, in 1952.*

Viviers, Gerhard (1926-) South African radio sports commentator whose vivid and spirited commentary in Afrikaans was synonymous with Springbok rugby for decades and brought him a legion of followers. Viviers, who was frequently accused of bias in his career, joined the SABC in 1962 and covered some 600 rugby matches, including 51 tests, as well as national and international boxing and cricket. He also appeared in local TV productions such as *Sonkring* and *Rustelose Jare.* He lost his voice when he contracted cancer of the throat in 1990, but learnt to speak again after surgery.

Wayne, John (Marion Michael Morrison) (1907-79) Robust American film actor known for his rolling walk and drawling speech. He graduated from singing-cowboy parts to an Oscar-winning performance as the hard-drinking, overweight, one-eyed lawman Rooster Cogburn in the Western *True Grit* (1969). Nicknamed 'Duke' after a dog he had as a boy, he was chosen by director John Ford to play the Ringo Kid in *Stagecoach* (1939). He then starred in scores of Western, war and action films, including *Red River* (1948), *Sands of Iwo Jima* (1949), *The Quiet Man* (1952), *The High and the Mighty* (1954), *The Searchers* (1956) and *Rio Bravo* (1958). He gave a moving performance in his last film, *The Shootist* (1976), a portrait of an ageing gunfighter dying of cancer at the start of the century.

❖ As an actor-director Wayne made the patriotic *The Alamo* (1960) and the *The Green Berets* (1968), in which he expressed his support for American military involvement in Vietnam.

Welles, Orson (1915-85) 'Boy genius' of Hollywood who, at the age of 26, directed, produced, cowrote and starred in the trailblazing CITIZEN KANE (1941). His second film, *The Magnificent Ambersons* (1942), a sombre family saga, was also hailed as a masterpiece. Although he lost some of his early brilliance,

SEX SYMBOL *Fur-clad Mae West symbolizes feminine allure in* Goin' to Town *(1935), as an oil heiress who breaks into high society.*

he directed and starred in some stylish thrillers such as *The Stranger* (1946), *The Lady from Shanghai* (1948) and *Touch of Evil* (1958). He also made three highly personal Shakespeare films: *Macbeth* (1948), *Othello* (1952) and *Chimes at Midnight* (1966), in which he was a swaggering Falstaff. Among his other notable roles were the crooked Harry Lime in *The Third Man* (1949), a fanatical preacher in *Moby Dick* (1956) and a melodramatic courtroom lawyer in *Compulsion* (1959).

West, Mae (1892-1980) American stage and screen actress renowned for her buxom figure – after which an inflatable life-jacket was named in World War II – and for the sexual innuendo of her dialogue. The most famous instance of this is the often misquoted 'Why don't you come up sometime and see me?' from the film *She Done Him Wrong* (1933).
❖ Among Mae West's sayings were: 'It's not the men in my life, it's the life in my men that counts.' And, 'When I'm good I'm very good, but when I'm bad I'm better.'

Weyers, Marius (1945-) South African actor who snapped up leading male parts in local stage, film and television productions of the 1970s and 1980s. A talent in classical and contemporary drama, Weyers was seen in *Hedda Gabler, The Crucible, Hello and Goodbye, The Guest* and *Othello*, among others. In the late 1980s he left for Hollywood, where some of his first appearances were in the television sitcoms, notably *The Golden Girls, Good and Evil* and *Designing Women.*

Widmark, Richard (1914-) American actor with a chilling, high-pitched giggle who specialized in portraying cold-blooded killers. He made a memorable film debut in *Kiss of Death* (1947) as a psychopathic murderer seeking vengeance on a stool pigeon. He followed this with *Road House* (1948) and *Night and the City* (1950), an atmospheric thriller set in the postwar London underworld. He scored another major hit with *Madigan* (1968), in which he played a dedicated New York cop. He also starred in a 1970s television series based on the character.

Wilder, Billy (1906-) Austrian-born director and writer who has made some of Hollywood's most sparkling and cynical sex comedies. These include *The Seven Year Itch* (1955) with Marilyn Monroe, *Some Like It Hot* (1959), with Monroe, Jack Lemmon and Tony Curtis and the Oscar-winning *The Apartment* (1960), with Lemmon and Shirley MacLaine. Among his other notable films are *Double Indemnity* (1944), *The Lost Weekend* (1945), a grim study of an alcoholic with Ray Milland in the starring role which won Best Director, Best Screenplay and Best Actor Oscars, SUNSET BOULEVARD (1950) and two lurid newspaper stories: *Ace in the Hole* (1951), starring Kirk Douglas, and *The Front Page* (1974), with Jack Lemmon and Walter Matthau.

Williams, Kenneth (1926-88) Outrageous British comedian who, with his saucy voice, haughty demeanour and shocked expression, was one of the mainstays of the CARRY ON film series. He made his name in long-running radio shows such as *Round the Horne* and *Hancock's Half Hour*, on which he coined the catchphrase, 'Ere, stop messin' about!'

Wizard of Oz, The Enchanting musical fantasy film which, in 1939, made a star of the young Judy Garland. In it she plays Dorothy, a little girl from Kansas whose farm is hit by a tornado, which transports her and her dog Toto from their dull, sepia world to the Technicolor land of Oz, ruled by the Wizard in the Emerald City. Despite sharing some wonderful adventures with the Scarecrow (played by Ray Bolger), the Tin Man (Jack Haley) and the Lion (Bert Lahr), Dorothy finally realises that there is no place like home. Her song, 'Over the Rainbow', won an Oscar. It was also nominated for Best Picture. Directed by Victor Fleming, the film was based on the classic children's book *The Wonderful Wizard of Oz* (1900) by Frank L Baum.

Zeffirelli, Franco (1923-) Italian stage and film director whose lively, fast-moving Shakespeare films are aimed squarely at the youth market. He began with a rumbustious version of *The Taming of the Shrew* (1966) with Richard Burton and Elizabeth Taylor, and followed this with *Romeo and Juliet* (1968) starring the young Leonard Whiting and Olivia Hussey. He chose the American-born actor Mel Gibson to play the title role in *Hamlet* (1990). Zeffirelli also directed the internationally successful television series *Jesus of Nazareth* (1977), with Robert Powell as Christ.

Zimbabwe Broadcasting Corporation State-controlled broadcasting service of Zimbabwe. It consists of two television channels, one of them educational, which broadcasts some 200 hours of television per week in colour from Harare and Bulawayo. Radio broadcasts are in English and six local languages on three semicommercial stations and one station broadcasting informal and formal educational programmes. The ZBC's predecessor, the Rhodesia Broadcasting Association, was formed in 1964, although radio services had operated in the country since 1933.

Zimbabwe Mass Media Trust Nongovernmental organization which has the majority shareholding in Zimbabwe Newspapers, publishers of the main newspapers in Zimbabwe. It was established in 1981 to increase local influence in the press and took over the South African-based Argus Printing and Publishing Company's shareholding of 45 per cent in Zimbabwe Newspapers. Its two main dailies are the Harare-based *The Herald* (circulation 134 00) and *The Chronicle* (circulation 74 032), published in Bulawayo. Other important regional titles include the *Manica Post* (Mutare), *The Times* (Gweru), *Masvingo Star* (Masvingo), *Chaminuka News* (Marondera) and *The Telegraph* (Chinoyi).

Zinnemann, Fred (1907-) Veteran Austrian-born director whose films include the classic Western *High Noon* (1952), *From Here to Eternity* (1953), for which he won a Best Director Oscar, *The Nun's Story* (1958) and the historical drama *A Man For All Seasons* (1966), which gained him another Oscar. In the 1970s he turned to political subjects, making the thriller *The Day of the Jackal* (1973) and *Julia* (1977), set in Nazi Germany in the 1930s.

MUSIC, SONG AND DANCE

The appeal of music is ageless and universal: it makes us want to sing and dance, and stirs the human soul. From Beethoven to the Beatles, from Bach to the blues, melody, rhythm and harmony have been interpreted by great singers, instrumentalists and conductors to excite, to sadden and to haunt our memories long after the last note has been played.

Abba Swedish pop group of the 1970s who became the most successful group since the Beatles. It consisted of two married couples – Anni-Frid Lyngstad and Benny Andersson, and Bjorn Ulvaeus and Agnetha Fältskog. In 1974 they won the Eurovision Song Contest with the song 'Waterloo'. The group's name was derived from the initials of their first names. Abba split up in 1983 when the couples divorced.

a capella Term meaning 'in church style' applied to choral music or a vocal ensemble sung without instrumental accompaniment; traditional African choirs are an example.

African pop Exemplifying African pop is an artist such as Chicco (Sello Twala) (1963-) – the biggest pop musician in South Africa – who went solo in 1985 with the song 'Chicowena'. Brenda Fassie (1963-) set the crossover ball rolling in 1983 with the disco song 'Weekend Special', released by her band, Brenda and the Big Dudes. Fassie started out as preteen lead singer of The Cosmos, an Elsie's River disco group. Yvonne Chaka Chaka (1965-), who began as a township punk with zebra-striped hair, grew to achieve wide success in Africa.

Afrikaans pop Popular music created by Afrikaans musicians covers a wide range of styles from the sweet sentimentality of the romantic balladeers Bles Bridges and Sonja Heroldt, through the middle-of-the-road Steve Hofmeyr to the so-called 'Alternative wave' of the 1980s, represented by the highly individualistic David Kramer with his satirical 'Boland blues', the iconoclastic Johannes Kerkorrel (Rolf Rabie) with his Gereformeerde Blues Band and the outrageous cabaret of pianist-singer Nataniël.

Albinoni, Tomaso (1671-1750) Italian violinist and prolific composer of vocal and instrumental works. He wrote more than 40 operas, and was one of the first composers to write concertos for the solo violin. The tragic Adagio in G Minor ascribed to Albinoni, made popular by the film *Gallipoli* (1981), was expanded by his biographer Remo Giazotto (1910-) from a small fragment.

alto In choral singing, the lowest range of the female singing voice (a shortened form of contralto) – or the highest adult male voice apart from COUNTERTENOR. The word is Italian for 'high'.

aria Song for a solo voice in an opera, oratorio or cantata. An example is 'Nessun Dorma' from Puccini's opera *Turandot*. The word is Italian for 'air' or 'melody'.

PERFECT PARTNERSHIP *Fred Astaire's imaginative routines looked easy, but they took weeks to perfect. In the background, he and Ginger Rogers go through their paces in a scene from the film* Top Hat *(1935), one of their many classics of the screen.*

Armstrong, Louis (*c*1900-71) New Orleans jazz trumpeter and singer, considered to be one of the greatest jazz musicians of all time. His nickname was 'Satchmo' or 'Satchelmouth'. He became renowned in the 1920s for his inspiring improvisations and gravelly voice. Armstrong brought jazz to a global audience and is credited with the invention of SCAT singing. He appeared in more than 50 films, including *High Society* (1956) and *Hello, Dolly!* (1969).

Ashton, Sir Frederick (1904-88) Distinguished British dancer, choreographer and ballet director, who helped to make ballet popular and to build the career of Margot FONTEYN. Ashton was director of the Royal Ballet from 1963 to 1970, a prolific choreographer of ballets in widely varied styles. They include such established works as *Façade* (1931), *Les Patineurs* (1937), *Symphonic Variations* (1946), *La Fille mal Gardée* (1960), *Enigma Variations* (1965) and the ballet film *Tales of Beatrix Potter* (1971).

Astaire, Fred (Frederick Austerlitz) (1899-1987) American entertainer who revolutionized the film musical with his innovative tap-dance routines. He was admired for his charm, grace and seemingly effortless dancing. From 1916 to 1932 Astaire was partnered by his sister Adele, who appeared in Broadway shows with him until she married and retired from the stage. Astaire then turned to

Hollywood and met newcomer Ginger Rogers. They made ten musical films together, including *Flying Down to Rio* (1933), *Top Hat* (1935) and *Follow the Fleet* (1936).
❖ In 1932, Fred Astaire received a disappointing appraisal for his Hollywood screentest. The verdict was: 'Can't act. Can't sing. Can dance a little.'

Bach, Johann Sebastian (1685-1750) German organist and choirmaster, generally considered to be the greatest composer of the BAROQUE era. A staunch Protestant, his religious faith colours his work, notably in the Mass in B Minor (1733) and the *St John* (1724) and *St Matthew* (1729) passions. He also wrote more than 200 church and secular cantatas and many works for organ, including the dramatic *Toccata and Fugue in D minor.* Bach's enormous output also includes the six *Brandenburg Concertos* (1711-20) and four orchestral suites: Suite No 3 in D includes the popular *Air on the G String* melody. Bach fused intense feeling with supreme musical logic: he was a master of counterpoint – the subtle interweaving of two or more melodies into a unified and satisfying whole. After his death, his music was largely forgotten until Mendelssohn launched the Bach revival with a performance of the *St Matthew Passion* in Leipzig in 1829.
❖ Bach was a member of the most remarkable family in musical history, consisting of 40 professional musicians spanning seven generations. Twice married, Bach had 20 children. Two of his sons, Karl Philipp Emanuel (1714-88) and Johann Christian (1735-82), were composers who played an important part in the development of the symphony, which initially was a relatively short work.

Bacharach, Burt (1928-) American popular composer who teamed up with lyricist Hal David to write classic hits, including 'Raindrops Keep Fallin' on My Head' from the film *Butch Cassidy and the Sundance Kid* (1969) for which he won an Oscar.

Balanchine, George (Georgi Balanchivadze) (1904-83) Russian-born American ballet dancer, and one of the greatest choreographers in the history of ballet. He became chief choreographer of Sergei DIAGHILEV's *Ballets Russes* in 1925 and formed a lifelong friendship with the composer Stravinsky; their collaboration began in 1928 with the ballet *Apollon Musagète.* In 1933, Balanchine went to America, where, as artistic director, he raised the New York City Ballet to a company of international standing.

ballet Artistic dance form which originated in the formal dances of French court entertainments, notably under Louis XIV (1638-1715). Dancing on the tips of the toes was introduced early in the 19th century, and modern ballet developed in the early 20th century, influenced by Russian dancer and choreographer Mikhail Fokine (1880-1942) and Russian impresario Sergei DIAGHILEV.

TIMELESS GENIUS *In his lifetime, Bach was better known as an organist. His fame as a composer came nearly two centuries later.*

Barker, Joyce (1931-92) South African dramatic soprano who, in 1956 while training in London, became the first winner of the Kathleen Ferrier Scholarship. She later sang leading roles at Covent Garden. After returning to South Africa in 1963 she appeared frequently in the opera productions of the performing arts councils, notably in Puccini's *Turandot.*

baritone Middle range of the male singing voice, higher than BASS and lower than TENOR. The word is from the Greek *bari* meaning 'deep' and *tone* meaning 'sound'.

baroque In music, the term applied to the elaborate and much ornamented music of composers between 1600 and 1750. Baroque composers include Monteverdi, Purcell, Vivaldi, Bach and Handel.

Bartók, Béla (1881-1945) Hungarian composer and pianist, who collected Eastern European folk songs and adapted them to produce an individual style of music. His most important works include six string quartets, three piano concertos and the opera *Bluebeard's Castle* (1911). In 1940 he moved to America, where he lived on the verge of starvation until he was commissioned by the conductor of the Boston Symphony Orchestra Serge Koussevitzky to write the *Concerto for Orchestra* (1943), his most popular and tuneful work. He died in poverty just as his work was beginning to receive wider recognition in America and Western Europe.

Basie, Count (William Basie) (1904-84) American jazz pianist and bandleader noted for his

BALLET TERMS

à terre Various floor steps which do not entail any jumps.

batterie, battu Jump during which a dancer beats the calves sharply together.

corps de ballet Group of dancers who support the principal dancers.

divertissement Separate dance within a ballet, designed as entertainment or to show off a dancer's technique.

élevation Any high jump in ballet.

entrechat Vertical jump during which the dancer beats the calves together, landing on one or both feet.

fouetté Spectacular pirouette in which the dancer whips the raised leg out to the front and side to achieve impetus for more turns.

jeté Jump from one leg to the other.

pas Basic ballet step in which the weight is transferred from one leg to another. The term is also used in combination to indicate the number of performers in a dance; a *pas seul* is a solo and a *pas de deux* for two.

pirouette Complete turn on one leg, which is performed on the ball of the foot by men, or on the toes by women.

plié Bending the legs from a standing position; *demi-plié* involves bending the knees as far as possible while keeping the heels on the ground.

relevé To rise, with a slight spring, off the heel and onto the ball of one or both feet.

soutenu A prolonged movement, executed at a slower tempo than usual.

FAB GEAR *By the end of 1963, the Beatles were the most influential group in Europe, setting fashions in hairstyles and clothing with their clean-cut image of 'mop tops' and collarless jackets.*

part in developing the big-band sound. He formed his first orchestra in 1936 and led a band until his death in 1984. The Count Basie Orchestra was one of the most important and successful SWING bands, playing a style of jazz popular in the 1930s and 1940s.

bass Lowest range of the male singing voice. Also an abbreviation for the lowest-stringed instrument, the double bass. The word is Italian for 'low'.

Beach Boys, The (Brian Wilson, Dennis Wilson, Carl Wilson, Mike Love, Al Jardine, Bruce Johnston) The most commercially successful American pop group of the 1960s, whose melodic pop songs idealized the sun-and-surf Californian lifestyle. Brian Wilson was one of the first producers to use electronic music effectively; he gave the band their sophisticated, technical sound, notably on the album *Pet Sounds* (1966).

Beatles, The British pop group, the leading exponents of the Liverpool sound or 'Mersey beat' which emerged in the 1960s. The Beatles grew out of a group formed by John Lennon in 1956, with Paul McCartney and George Harrison joining in 1957 and Ringo Starr in 1962. Lennon and McCartney proved to be one of the most successful song-writing teams in history. Their first single, 'Love Me Do', was released in 1962; in 1965 the band were awarded MBEs – in recognition of their contribution to Britain's export earnings – and by 1966 they had become the most successful and respectable pop group in the world. Influenced by drugs and 'flower power', their music took a new direction with the album *Sergeant Pepper's Lonely Hearts Club Band* (1967), an experimental adventure in music and technology that captured the psychedelic spirit of the time and included 'Lucy in the Sky with Diamonds' (which spelt LSD). The demise of the 'Fab Four' began in 1968 when McCartney became disillusioned with Lennon's relationship with girlfriend Yoko Ono, and the group split up in 1970. Fans hoped for a reunion until Lennon was shot dead outside his New York apartment in December 1980.

❖ John Lennon (1940-80) was a figurehead of the peace movement of the 1960s. He married Yoko Ono in 1969 and settled in New York. When his son Sean was born in 1975, Lennon became a reclusive 'house-husband' until the release of his comeback album *Double Fantasy* (1980). A track called 'Starting Over' topped the charts after Lennon was killed by a mentally unbalanced fan.

❖ McCartney (1942-) formed the band Wings in 1971 with his wife Linda on keyboards. Wings had a series of successful albums and the song 'Mull of Kintyre' (1977) became the first single to sell more than two million copies in Britain.

bebop Style of jazz developed by black jazz musicians in the 1940s. With its fast driving rhythms, complex harmonies and sophisticated improvisations, bebop, or bop, evolved into the modern jazz of the 1950s and 1960s. Dizzy GILLESPIE and Charlie PARKER were its most prominent exponents.

Beecham, Sir Thomas (1879-1961) English conductor and renowned interpreter of the composer Frederick DELIUS. Beecham, known for his acid wit, founded the London Philharmonic Orchestra in 1932, later became artistic director of Covent Garden's Royal Opera House and founded the Royal Philharmonic Orchestra in 1946.

❖ Beecham inherited a baronetcy from his father, a manufacturing chemist and prominent patron of the arts.

Beethoven, Ludwig van (1770-1827) German composer and pianist who led music into the ROMANTIC era. Building on the foundations laid by Haydn and Mozart, he enlarged the scope of all the major musical forms. At the age of 30 Beethoven began to lose his hearing – a fact which he tried to conceal. By 1824 he was totally deaf. He was often said to shout and curse as he composed, but the wild emotion in his music was tempered by his great respect for musical discipline and logic. His works include nine symphonies, 16 string quartets, five piano concertos and 32 piano sonatas. Among Beethoven's most popular compositions are the Third or *Eroica* Symphony (1803-4), the Sixth or *Pastoral* Symphony (1807-8), the Ninth or *Choral*

CULT COMPOSER *Beethoven, shown in this drawing made in 1818, was hailed as a musical demigod during the Romantic era.*

Symphony (1817-23), the *Moonlight Sonata* (1800-1), the opera *Fidelio* (1805-14) and the Mass in D or *Missa Solemnis* (1819-22).
❖ The opening bars of Beethoven's Fifth Symphony (1804-8) contain the best known sequence of four notes in classical music. They have been described as 'The sound of Fate knocking at the door'.

Berlin, Irving (Israel Baline) (1888-1989) Russian-born American composer and lyricist. He wrote the unofficial American anthem 'God Bless America' (1918, revised 1938) and 'White Christmas' (1942), one of the best-selling songs in history. Berlin also wrote BROADWAY musicals such as *Annie Get Your Gun* (1946) and the songs for Hollywood films such as *Top Hat* (1935).

Berlioz, Hector (1803-69) French composer, music critic, leading exponent of the Romantic movement and father of the modern orchestra and the art of conducting. His originality and imaginative orchestration were first displayed in his bizarre *Symphonie fantastique* (1830), which is notable for its freedom from classical form and expansive scoring for a very large orchestra. Berlioz was attracted by the sublime and wrote a monumental Requiem Mass known as *Grande messe des morts* (1837), requiring a huge orchestra and choir; but he could also produce delicate work, as in the oratorio *The Childhood of Christ* (1854). His masterpiece is generally considered to be the two-part opera *The Trojans* (1856-8).

Bernstein, Leonard (1918-90) American conductor and composer, who worked in both the classical and the popular fields of music. He wrote a number of serious choral and symphonic works, but is best remembered for his musicals *On the Town* (1944, filmed in 1949) and *West Side Story* (1957, filmed in 1961). He wrote the music for several Hollywood films, including *On the Waterfront* (1954), and was conductor of the New York Philharmonic (1958-70).

Berry, Chuck (1926-) American singer, songwriter and guitarist, renowned for his sharp, witty lyrics. A key figure in the evolution of popular music, Berry pioneered ROCK'N'ROLL with songs such as 'Roll Over Beethoven' and 'Johnny Be Goode' (1958). Both the Beatles and Rolling Stones helped to turn Berry into a cult hero by recording many of his songs.

Bizet, Georges (BEE-zay) (1838-75) French composer whose reputation rests chiefly on the opera *Carmen* (1875). He wrote several other operas and an early symphony (1855) which lay undiscovered for 80 years. His orchestral suites from *Carmen* and from Alphonse Daudet's play *L'Arlésienne* are his most famous concert works.

blues Style of American folk music that evolved from the folk songs of black southern Americans, especially 'work songs' lamenting their oppression. The blues song form has often been used in jazz and rock. Bessie Smith (1894-1937) was the outstanding blues singer of her generation.

boeremusiek The traditional light music of the Afrikaans community, popular particularly in the country areas of South Africa. Its distinctive style, based on 19th-century European dance music, has been developed by successive generations since about 1830, when the accordion and concertina became popular instruments. It is characteristically associated with the concertina or accordion, guitar and violin, but is also played by larger *vastrap* (dance) orchestras.

Bolshoi Ballet Moscow-based ballet company formed in 1776, renowned for an athletic and vigorous style of dancing. The Bolshoi's most celebrated productions include modern versions of *Spartacus* (1968) and *Ivan the Terrible* (1975).

Bosman, Gerry (1936-95) South African musician, an accomplished organist, whose bigband arrangements and performances of light music were popular on radio, records and TV. He wrote and directed the theme music for several TV shows and films in South Africa and Hollywood and conducted concerts by South Africa's symphony orchestras.

Boulanger, Nadia (1887-1979) French composer, famous as the teacher of several of the 20th century's leading composers and many other outstanding musicians.

Brahms, Johannes (1833-97) German composer who was born in Hamburg and made his career in Vienna. As a young man he wrote expansive and passionate music, but as he grew older his works became more formal. From the 1860s he was hailed as the saviour of classicism by opponents of WAGNER's so-called modernism. His works include four symphonies, two monumental piano concertos and a lyrical violin concerto, quantities of chamber music and songs, and choral works, among them his colossal *A German Requiem*.

Bream, Julian (1933-) British guitarist and lute player who won international popularity

BROADWAY MAESTRO *A vibrant scene from the musical* West Side Story *conveys the energy of Leonard Bernstein's forceful score.*

and acclaim in the 1950s. He has made a major contribution to the revival of interest in Renaissance music.

Brel, Jacques (1929-78) Belgian songwriter and singer whose combination of anger, romanticism and world-weariness, strongly influenced many of those who came after him. His recordings reached a global market and his musical *Jacques Brel is Alive and Well and Living in Paris* (1968) had a three-year run on BROADWAY.
❖ South African actress, producer and theatre personality Taubie Kushlick (1910-91), a friend and great admirer of Jacques Brel, keenly promoted his music in South Africa; she staged his Broadway musical in Johannesburg and Cape Town.

Britten, Lord Benjamin (1913-76) British composer who made his name in 1945 with his tragic opera *Peter Grimes*. He was a child prodigy – by the age of ten he had already written string quartets and piano sonatas. Among his many works are the operas *The Turn of the Screw* (1954) and *Death in Venice* (1973); the orchestral work *A Young Person's Guide to the Orchestra* (1946); and the choral *War Requiem* (1962). Leading tenor roles in Britten's operas and song cycles were written for – and definitively recorded by – his lifelong companion, Sir Peter Pears (1910-86).
❖ In 1948, Britten founded the annual summer music festival held at Aldeburgh in his native Suffolk.

DYNAMIC DIVA *Maria Callas was a compelling singer and actress, but had a reputation for being temperamental and unreliable.*

Broadway Principal theatre district of New York City, centred on part of the street called Broadway in Manhattan.

Brown, James (1928-) American singer known as the 'Godfather of Soul'. Brown has played a key role in the development of soul music since the 1960s. Political songs such as 'Say it Loud, I'm Black and I'm Proud' (1968) also made him an important figurehead of the black rights movement. His electrifying dance routines inspired many people, including Michael JACKSON, as well as the exponents of RAP MUSIC.

Bruckner, Anton (1824-96) Austrian composer and organist. Bruckner did not write his first important work until he was in his forties, and it was not until his sixties that he gained recognition. His most important works are his nine symphonies and large choral works, especially the three masses and the *Te Deum*.

Cahn, Sammy (1913-92) Witty American lyricist and performer of his own material with his one-man stage and TV show, *Words and Music*. He was renowned for providing material for Frank Sinatra. He won Oscars for his lyrics for several films, including *Three Coins in the Fountain* (1954) and *A Hole in the Head* (1959).

Callas, Maria (Maria Kalageropoulou) (1923-77) American-born Greek soprano who became one of the most celebrated and controversial performers of the 20th century. She was renowned for her dramatic interpretations of Italian Romantic composers. Although the quality of her voice and her vocal technique were considered faulty, she gave some of the most passionate and memorable performances of all time – especially in the title role of Puccini's *Tosca*.
❖ Callas's personal life was as colourful as her career. At the height of her fame she became the mistress of the Greek shipping millionaire Aristotle ▷ONASSIS, but after ten years together Onassis abandoned her to marry Jackie Kennedy, widow of the assassinated American president. Three years later, after making an unsuccessful comeback tour, Callas died alone in her Paris flat from a heart attack – or 'a broken heart', her friends said.

Calloway, Cab (1907-94) American band leader, composer and singer, renowned for his eccentric showmanship and big-band jazz sound. In the 1930s he worked at the celebrated *Cotton Club* in Harlem, New York.
❖ Newspaper critics called Calloway 'The King of Hi-De Ho' because of his bizarre style of SCAT singing.

cantata Musical composition for voice and instruments: normally a small-scale oratorio for solo singers accompanied by a small chorus and orchestra.
❖ The master of this form was J S BACH, who composed more than 200 cantatas – among them the humorous *Coffee Cantata*, to words of a play about a young woman's attempts to overcome her addiction to coffee.

Carreras, José (1946-) Spanish tenor who, together with PAVAROTTI and DOMINGO, became one of the leading tenors of the 1980s and 1990s. The onset of leukaemia interrupted his career in 1987 but he made an emotional and triumphant return to the stage in 1990.

Caruso, Enrico (1873-1921) Italian opera singer, generally considered to be the finest tenor in the history of the art. He made his debut in 1894 and sang most of the great tenor roles in French and Italian opera.
❖ Caruso was one of the first artists to appreciate the commercial possibilities of the gramophone. In 1902, sales of '*Vesti la Giubba*' from the opera *Pagliacci* made him the earliest recording artist to sell more than a million copies of a record.
❖ The Italian tenor Beniamino Gigli (1890-1957) was regarded as Caruso's successor.

Casals, Pablo (1876-1973) Spanish cellist, composer and conductor. He raised the status of the cello as a major instrument with his performances of concertos, chamber music and the unaccompanied cello suites of J S BACH, which he rescued from near-oblivion.

Cash, Johnny (1932-) American singer, songwriter and guitarist, of part Cherokee descent, renowned for his gravelly baritone voice. Cash was one of the first stars of COUNTRY AND WESTERN music. In the USA by the mid-1990s he had a total of 129 country and 50 pop hits. A champion of Native American rights, he recorded an album of protest songs in 1964 called *Bitter Tears*. In the 1970s he returned to the fundamentalist Christianity of his youth and moved into GOSPEL MUSIC.

Charles, Ray (1930-) American singer, songwriter and pianist, blind from the age of seven. An outstanding RHYTHM AND BLUES singer, he has also performed jazz, soul, country and pop music. His biggest hits include 'Georgia on my Mind' (1960) and 'I Can't Stop Loving You' (1962).

BLEND OF TRADITIONS *The groups Juluka and Savuka formed by Johnny Clegg integrated the styles of Europe and Africa. Here Clegg and Dudu Zulu do a powerful dance in Zulu style.*

Charleston Popular dance, characterized by frantic arm movements and side kicks. It was originally popular with black people from the Southern states of America and is named after the city of Charleston in South Carolina. The dance featured in the black revues of the 1920s in New York, and turned into a worldwide craze following a musical called *Runnin' Wild* (1923).

Chopin, Frédéric (1810-49) Polish pianist and composer, almost exclusively of piano music. In Paris, Chopin became a celebrated figure of the Romantic era. His friends and admirers included BERLIOZ, LISZT and MENDELSSOHN, and he had a long romance with the novelist George Sand (Amandine Dupin), who called herself by a man's name and wore men's clothes. Chopin died of tuberculosis.
❖ Chopin was fiercely patriotic. He carried a silver urn filled with Polish earth wherever he went.

Clapton, Eric (1945-) British guitarist and a leading figure in RHYTHM AND BLUES. His first success was with the rock band Cream, whose music paved the way for bands such as LED ZEPPELIN and later generations of heavy-metal groups. As Derek and the Dominoes, he had a big hit with 'Layla' in 1972. Having overcome heroin addiction, he resumed his career with a recording of Bob MARLEY's 'I Shot the Sheriff' (1974).

classical Term often used to describe any European or American music written in a scholarly tradition but, strictly speaking, it refers to the period of European music written between 1750 and 1820. Classical composers include HAYDN and MOZART. The music of BEETHOVEN marks the transition from the classical to the ROMANTIC era.

Clegg, Johnny (1931-) Singer, songwriter, guitarist and founder of the ground-breaking singing, dancing and instrumental groups Juluka and Savuka, which pioneered the integration of white and black musical traditions. Savuka performed internationally and in the late 1980s Clegg was more popular in France than Michael JACKSON; the French dubbed him *le Zoulou Blanc* (the White Zulu).
❖ The Juluka hit 'Scatterlings' was included on the soundtrack of the Academy Award-winning film *Rain Man* (1988).

Coertse, Mimi (Maria Sophia) (1932-) South African opera singer, the first to become an international success. She achieved fame in her early twenties in the exacting role of Queen of the Night in Mozart's *The Magic Flute*, a role she later sang more than 500 times. She was appointed a permanent member of the Vienna State Opera in 1956 and became known as one of the world's top four coloratura sopranos (able to sing rapid, highly ornamented music requiring great agility in the voice). She also appeared at most of the major opera houses of Europe. In 1973 she returned to South Africa, where she continued to perform in opera and recitals.

Cole, Nat King (1917-65) American singer and pianist. Although he began his career as a jazz pianist, Cole made his name as a popular balladeer with his smooth and romantic singing style, epitomized in songs such as 'Mona Lisa' (1950), 'Unforgettable' (1951) and 'When I Fall in Love' (1957).

concert pianists The popularity of the piano as a solo and concerto instrument and the huge demand for recordings has resulted in a proliferation of concert pianists having a uniformly high standard of technical and interpretative ability. As a result few pianists can now acquire the fame of the great virtuosi with individual styles who flourished in the first half of the 20th century. Among the biggest names, acclaimed worldwide, were Claudio Arrau (1903-91) Vladimir Horowitz (1904-89), Artur Rubinstein (1887-1982) and Artur Schnabel (1882-1951). Prominent after World War II have been Vladimir Ashkenazy (1937-), Alfred Brendel (1931-), Emil Gilels (1916-85), Glenn Gould (1932-82) and Sviatoslav Richter (1914-).
❖ The long-lived Artur Rubinstein was still appearing on the concert platform when he was in his nineties.
❖ Claudio Arrau, noted for his powerful tone and effortless technique, was the protégé and pupil of Martin Krause (1853-1918), who was a pupil of Franz LISZT.
❖ Glenn Gould, famous for his recordings of works by J S BACH and his eccentricity, ended his concert career in 1964 and from then on refused to perform in public.

Connell, Elizabeth (1946-) South African-born opera singer who has won international acclaim. She has sung mezzo-soprano and soprano roles at Covent Garden in London, the Metropolitan in New York, La Scala in Milan and other major European opera houses, including Bayreuth.

contralto Lowest range of the female singing voice, usually called alto in choral music.

Copland, Aaron (1900-90) American pianist, conductor and composer, whose use of folk song established the 'Americanist' style of modern concert music. He produced his most popular work in the late 1930s and 1940s: two cowboy ballets called *Billy the Kid* (1938) and *Rodeo* (1942) his masterpiece *Appalachian Spring* (1944) and his highly acclaimed *Third Symphony* (1946). He also wrote music for films.

countertenor Highest naturally produced adult male voice, with a range above that of TENOR. Countertenors today take parts previously given to the surgically created castrato voice, which was common in 17th and 18th-century opera.

JAZZ GIANT *Miles Davis, who took up the trumpet at the age of 13, developed a pensive style that launched the 'cool jazz' movement.*

country and western Commercial form of American folk music. Jimmie Rodgers (1897-1933) is credited as the first artist to merge rural hillbilly music with American popular song. Well-known country and western songwriters and singers include Hank Williams Jnr (1949-), Tammy Wynette (1942-) and Dolly Parton (1946-).
❖ 'King' of South African country music was Bobby Angel (1937-), who began singing when he was six and retired in 1988.

Coward, Sir Noël (1899-1973) British actor, director, playwright and composer who was renowned for his foppish sophistication and quintessential Englishness. He wrote the music and words for the operetta *Bittersweet* (1929) and the revue *Words and Music* (1932). Among his wittiest songs are the satirical 'Don't Put Your Daughter on the Stage Mrs Worthington' and 'Mad Dogs and Englishmen'. He was noted for his one-man cabaret performances in London and Las Vegas in the 1950s.

Crosby, Bing (Harry Lillis Crosby) (1904-77) One of the most successful American recording artists of the 20th century, with sales of more than 400 million records. Crosby called himself 'The Groaner' and he popularized a new, relaxed style of singing. In the late 1920s the microphone was a recent invention, and Crosby was the first solo singer to use it to good effect – influencing crooners such as Frank SINATRA. Crosby's greatest hits include 'White Christmas' (1942), 'Silent Night' (1942) and 'Swinging on a Star' (1944).
❖ Crosby was nicknamed 'Bing' because of his childhood obsession with an American comic-strip character called 'Bingo' that appeared in a local newspaper.

crossover music A fusion of two or more different styles, such as between classics, jazz, rock, pop or blues. In Africa it is also applied to music combining elements of traditional African music with popular American and European styles.
❖ Pioneers of crossover in South Africa have been the groups led by Johnny CLEGG (Juluka and Savuka) and P J ('Thandeka') Powers. More recently the group Tananas, led by guitarist Steve Newman, has carried crossover far beyond its predecessors; its sound blends folk, jazz, African, oriental and various other ethnic influences with contemporary classical elements.

Davis, Miles (1926-91) American jazz trumpeter and composer, one of the most influential musicians in jazz. He launched the 'cool jazz' movement (a lighter style with less impassioned improvisation) with his recordings of 1948-9, which were reissued under the title *The Birth of the Cool.* Davis later experimented with electronic instruments and fused jazz with rock.

Debussy, Claude (1862-1918) Influential French composer, a musical revolutionary who set out to free music from the 'barren traditions' which he felt were stifling it. His intoxicating use of harmonies created a sensual musical dream world, and had a profound influence on modern Western music. Debussy lived a bohemian life in Paris, where he was idolized by young students and artists. The critics described him as a musical impressionist – a label which Debussy disliked but which has stuck; it is applied also to composers whom he influenced such as Maurice RAVEL and Frederick DELIUS. Debussy had his first success with the sensuous orchestral piece *Prélude à l'après-midi d'un faune* (1892-94) (later made famous by Vaslav NIJINSKI's ballet to the music). His only completed opera *Pelléas and Mélisande* (1892-1902) won him international acclaim. Among his best-known orchestral works are *Nocturnes* (1897-9) and *La Mer* (1903-5). He also produced an extensive repertoire of piano music.

de Groote, Steven (1952-89) South African concert pianist whose promising international career was cut short by his early death, four years after he sustained serious injuries in a plane crash in the USA. He won the famous Van Cliburn piano competition – a pinnacle of achievement for a pianist – in 1977, performed widely, held university appointments in the USA and was appointed an honorary professor of music at the University of Stellenbosch in 1986.
❖ Steven de Groote came from a musical family. His father, Pierre, was an outstanding violinist; his brothers André, Oliver and Phillip are, respectively, professor of piano at Brussels Conservatoire, a clarinettist (formerly in the Cape Town Symphony Orchestra) and a cellist in the British Chilingirian String Quartet; his sister Tessa is also a pianist.

Delius, Frederick (1862-1934) British composer of German parentage who made his home in France in 1889. Influenced by Debussy and Grieg, his works were impressionistic in style. Delius was championed by Sir Thomas BEECHAM, who called him 'the last great apostle of romance, emotion and beauty in music'. His output included the orchestral works *Brigg Fair* (1907) and *On Hearing The First Cuckoo in Spring* (1913).

Diaghilev, Sergei (Dee-AH-gi-lev) (1872-1929) Russian impresario who, as the founder of the Ballets Russes, was the greatest single influence on ballet in the 20th century. Diaghilev introduced Russian ballet to the West in 1909 with a historic season in Paris. For the next 20 years his Ballets Russes dominated the world of ballet. Diaghilev's unique position resulted from his insistence on using only outstanding talents among dancers (Pavlova, Nijinsky) and composers (Debussy, Satie, Ravel, Stravinsky and Prokofiev) and artists (Matisse, Picasso and Cocteau). Among Diaghilev's most notable productions were *The Firebird* (1910), *Petrushka* (1911) and the sensational *The Rite of Spring* (1913).

District Six: The Musical Record-breaking show, set against the political background of the apartheid era (see ▷DISTRICT SIX in 'Places and landscapes of southern Africa'), with music and script by David Kramer and Taliep Petersen and direction and design by Fred Abrahamse. First staged at the Baxter Theatre, Cape Town, in 1987, it became the longest-running show in the city's theatrical history. It later moved to Johannesburg and the Edinburgh Festival and was revived in Cape Town. Kramer and Petersen collaborated on three more musicals, *Fairyland* (1991) *Poison* (1994) and *Kat and the Kings* (1995).

diva Italian word for 'goddess', usually reserved for great operatic sopranos such as Maria CALLAS, Kiri TE KANAWA and Jessye

NORMAN. The term can also be applied to mezzo-sopranos and contraltos.

Domingo, Placido (1941-) Spanish operatic tenor renowned for his fine acting and musical versatility. He has sung more than 75 different roles, from the works of Puccini to Wagner, and recorded many solo albums of popular songs. Domingo was only 21 years old when he was made lead tenor with the Israeli National Opera in Tel Aviv, and by the 1970s he had become one of the biggest international opera stars.

Domino, Fats (Antoine Domino) (1928-) American singer, pianist and songwriter, who pioneered the New Orleans style of RHYTHM AND BLUES in the 1950s. His boogie-woogie piano playing style, characterized by a repeated rhythmic and melodic pattern in the bass, influenced ROCK'N'ROLL music.

Doors, The (Jim Morrison, John Densmore, Robbie Krieger, Ray Manzarek) American rock band formed in 1965, whose controversial songs were inspired by the drug culture of the time. The band's focus, Jim Morrison (1943-71), was noted for his bizarre personality and lurid poetry. He achieved commercial and critical success with songs such as *Light My Fire* (1967), but the use of drugs and alcohol made Morrison's behaviour increasingly erratic. He died of a suspected overdose.
❖ The film *The Doors* (1991), directed by Oliver Stone, vividly depicted Morrison's extraordinary lifestyle.

Duncan, Isadora (1877-1927) American dancer whose 'natural' style proved to be the starting point of the modern dance tradition. Inspired by Classical Greek dancing, she championed an expressive style of movement, dancing in bare feet and flowing draperies. Duncan made her Chicago debut in 1896, toured all over Europe and opened schools in Russia.
❖ She was strangled by her scarf when it caught in the rear wheel of a moving car.

du Plessis, Hubert (1922-) Prolific South African composer and former senior lecturer in music at the University of Stellenbosch, who in 1963 was awarded the South African Academy for Science and Arts' Gold Medal for Music. His output includes songs and song cycles, choral works (notably the unaccompanied *Requiem aeternam*, Opus 39), piano sonatas and orchestral works.

du Pré, Jacqueline (1945-87) British cellist who mesmerized audiences with her passionate interpretations, particularly of the Elgar Cello Concerto. She married the Israeli pianist and conductor Daniel Barenboim (1942-) in 1967. Stricken by multiple sclerosis in 1973, she taught until her death.

Dvořák, Antonín (DVORR-zhack) (1841-1904) Czech composer who used the folk songs of his Bohemian peasant background to inject colour and gaiety into his music. He loved the countryside, and his orchestration often reflects pastoral elements. His Czech nationalism is particularly evident in the *Slavonic Dances* (1878; 1887) and *Slavonic Rhapsodies* (1878). When he went to New York as head of the National Conservatory (1892-5) he was inspired by Native American chants and African American spiritual melodies to write his Ninth Symphony, *From the New World* (1893).

NOSTALGIA FOR A LOST HOME District Six: The Musical, *filled with colourful characters and vibrant music, recaptured the spirit of an area of Cape Town destroyed by apartheid laws.*

Dylan, Bob (Robert Zimmerman) (1941-) American folk singer and songwriter who became a spokesman for millions of disaffected young people of his generation – while his artistry was a major influence on his musical peers. A strong supporter of the civil rights and antiwar movements, Dylan wrote protest songs such as 'Blowin' in the Wind' (1963) and 'The Times They Are a-Changin' (1964).

Elgar, Sir Edward (1857-1934) British composer who enjoyed only modest success with his early choral works but made a great impact with the orchestral *Enigma Variations* (1899). The oratorio *The Dream of Gerontius* (1900) was initially unpopular, but later confirmed his stature. Among his best-known works are a violin concerto, a cello concerto, and the five *Pomp and Circumstance* military marches (1901-3), the first of which provided the tune for 'Land of Hope and Glory'. From 1924 he was Master of the King's Music.

Ellington, Duke (1899-1974) American jazz composer, songwriter and bandleader. He began his career as a jazz pianist and formed his own band in 1924. In the 1930s his orchestra became renowned for its residency at the Cotton Club in Harlem, New York. The band travelled the world, recording, broadcasting and playing concerts until his death. Ellington was a prolific composer, writing jazz pieces, standard ballads and fullscale suites. Some of his most popular songs include: 'Mood Indigo', 'Sophisticated Lady' and 'Don't Get Around Much Anymore'. He wrote several film scores including the dramatic music for *Anatomy of a Murder* (1959).

Fauré, Gabriel (1845-1924) French composer and organist, noted particularly for his Requiem Mass (1887-1900). He wrote many lyrical songs and piano pieces. His best-known compositions include the song cycle *La Bonne Chanson* (1892-4), the opera *Pénélope* (1913) and incidental music to the play *Pelléas and Mélisande* (1898).

Fields, Gracie (1898-1979) British singer, comedienne and actress. Her Lancashire humour and flair for singing comic songs such as 'I Took My Harp to a Party' and 'The Biggest Aspidistra in the World' won her great popularity in the 1930s. Fields toured the world during World War II to entertain the troops.

Fitzgerald, Ella (1918-) American jazz singer, known for the clarity of her voice and SCAT singing style. With songs such as 'A Tisket a Tasket' and 'Ev'ry Time We Say Goodbye' she built up a reputation as the finest female jazz vocalist after Billie HOLIDAY.

folk music Simple form of popular music that originated with ordinary people of a particular region singing about their experiences. Because the songs were seldom written down until many years later and the authors were forgotten, true folk music is considered timeless. Modern folk revivalists include Woody GUTHRIE, Bob DYLAN and Joan Baez (1941-).

❖ Composers such as DVOŘÁK, GRIEG, VAUGHAN WILLIAMS and BARTÓK made use of folk tunes and rhythms in their compositions.

Fonteyn, Dame Margot (Margaret Hookham) (1919-91) British ballerina renowned for her perfect technique and seemingly effortless dancing. She established an unequalled reputation in such classic roles as Aurora in *The Sleeping Beauty* (1939), as well as in the many ballets created for her by Frederick ASHTON. Her legendary partnership with Rudolf NUREYEV was formed in 1962 when they first danced together in *Giselle*; Fonteyn was almost twice his age. In 1964 Fonteyn's husband, the Panamanian diplomat Roberto Arias, was the victim of an assassination attempt which left him paralysed. Because Fonteyn had to help nurse and support him, she was in financial difficulty when he died in 1989, and a benefit gala was held for her at Covent Garden the following year.

GRACE AND POISE *Dame Margot Fonteyn dances Juliet to Rudolf Nureyev's Romeo in Vienna in 1967. Their artistry transcended their age gap; Fonteyn was almost 20 years older than Nureyev.*

fugue An instrumental or vocal composition in which individual tunes, or voices, are harmoniously interwoven. A fugue begins with a short tune which is sung or played alone: this tune is called the subject and recurs throughout as the main theme. As the first voice finishes the subject, a second voice picks it up in a different pitch – usually at an interval of a fifth – and this second entry of the subject is called the answer. While the second voice goes through the answer, the first voice continues with a new thematic figure that combines with the answer. If third and fourth voices enter, they repeat the process, eventually creating a four-part texture. The fugue continues in a similar manner, with everything evolving from the basic theme.

Gershwin, George (1898-1937) Versatile American pianist and composer who bridged the gap between popular and classical music. Gershwin often worked with his brother Ira (1896-1983), who was a gifted lyricist. Together they wrote the musical comedies *Lady, Be Good* (1924) and *Funny Face* (1927). Ira also worked with George on the groundbreaking folk opera *Porgy and Bess* (1935). George Gershwin sprang to prominence in his own right with the symphonic work *Rhapsody in Blue* (1924) for piano and orchestra, followed by the concert piece *An American in Paris* (1928), which inspired the film of the same name in 1951.

Gilbert and Sullivan Sir William Schwenck Gilbert (1836-1911) and Sir Arthur Seymour Sullivan (1842-1900), librettist and composer respectively, were the English authors of a series of popular comic OPERETTAS, still often performed. They first worked together on a play in 1871 and, encouraged by the theatrical agent Richard D'Oyly Carte, continued their partnership with the operetta *Trial by Jury* in 1875. Carte built the Savoy Theatre in 1881 to stage their works, and the three of them began a series of operettas, known as the Savoy operas. Notable works include *The Pirates of Penzance* (1879), *The Mikado* (1885) and *The Gondoliers* (1889).

Gillespie, Dizzy (John Birks Gillespie) (1917-92) American jazz trumpeter, band leader and composer. Gillespie played a major part in

AGE OF AQUARIUS *The two heads on the original poster for* Hair *form the figure ∞, which is the mathematical symbol for infinity.*

establishing the trends of modern jazz and was a leading exponent of BEBOP. He played with many bands in the 1930s and early 1940s before forming his own band in 1944. His compositions include 'Night in Tunisia' (1942) and 'Groovin' High' (1944). He continued to play and record into the 1980s.

❖ Gillespie was nicknamed Dizzy because of his penchant for clowning. He originated the jazz 'uniform' of dark glasses and beret.

Glass, Philip (1937-) American composer and leading exponent of 'minimalist' music which is based on extensive repetition of a theme and rhythmic pattern, using synthesized sounds, amplified wind instruments and voices. Among his works are the four-and-a-half-hour opera *Einstein on the Beach* (1976), which was well received in Europe but shocked audiences at the Metropolitan Opera, New York, and *Satyagraha* (1980), an opera based on the life of Mahatma ▷GANDHI in South Africa.

Glyndebourne Small opera house in Sussex, home of the annual Glyndebourne Festival. The festival was founded in 1934 and is noted for its high standard of production, particularly of the works of Mozart.

Goodman, Benny (1909-86) American band leader, composer and clarinet virtuoso who was known as the 'King of Swing' – a style of jazz played by big bands in the 1930s and 1940s. In New York in 1935 he formed the Benny Goodman trio with Gene Krupa and Teddy Wilson; a year later Lionel Hampton made it a quartet. For 30 years Goodman maintained his reputation as one of the finest jazz musicians.

❖ Benny Goodman was also an outstanding performer of classical music; he recorded music of Mozart and Weber and commissioned works from, among others, Béla BARTÓK and Aaron COPLAND.

gospel music Joyful, jazz-inspired religious music, associated with the Protestant revivalism of the late 19th century, when black slaves of America evolved a repertoire of gospel and SPIRITUAL songs. In 1928 a pianist called Thomas A Dorsey (1899-1993) – not to be confused with Jimmy or Tommy – began writing popular gospel songs: he founded the National Convention of Gospel Singers and came to be known as the 'Father of Gospel Music'. He discovered and toured with Mahalia JACKSON, who was nicknamed the 'Gospel Queen'. In recent years 'white' gospel music, which has stylistic affinities with country and western music, has gained popularity among evangelists and at religious revival meetings.

Grieg, Edvard (1843-1907) Norwegian composer whose music reflects the influence of folk song. His most famous works are the two orchestral suites based on his incidental music for Ibsen's epic play *Peer Gynt* (1875), and the Piano Concerto in A minor (1868), which is one of the most often-performed works in the piano concerto repertoire.

Guthrie, Woody (1912-67) American songwriter and folk singer who flourished in the 1930s. A champion of the poor, he wrote numerous songs about social injustice and the hardships of the Depression years, and travelled throughout America as a street singer. One of Guthrie's best-remembered songs is 'This Land Is Your Land', regarded by many Americans as a second national anthem.

Hair Ground-breaking American musical, concerned with the Vietnam war and hippie lifestyle of the 1960s, with score by Galt MacDermot and book and lyrics by Gerome Ragni and James Rado. *Hair* opened in London in 1968 on the night that Britain's stage censorship was abolished: it was the first time that nudity had been allowed on a West End stage, and the first attempt to bring rock music to the theatre. A film version was made in 1979. The show had a brief revival at London's Old Vic in 1993; it was also staged at the Nico Malan Theatre in Cape Town later that year. Memorable songs include 'Aquarius' and 'Good Morning Sunshine'.

Haley, Bill (1925-81) American singer and guitarist. Haley was known as the 'Father of ROCK'N'ROLL'. Although he did not invent the style, he was the first artist to bring it to the masses. In 1953 he formed the band Bill Haley and the Comets, and their recording of 'Rock Around The Clock' was used in the film *The Blackboard Jungle* (1955). Haley's sound was so revolutionary that it led to cinema riots, with young people dancing in the aisles and ripping up seats. The record sold 22 million copies worldwide and re-entered the charts in 1968 and 1974, but Haley soon lost his crown to the new king of rock'n'roll, Elvis PRESLEY.

Hammerstein II, Oscar (1895-1960) American songwriter, renowned for his poetic and sentimental lyrics. He collaborated with Richard RODGERS on a series of big-scale musicals, from *Oklahoma!* (1943) to *The Sound of Music* (1959). He also worked with several other composers, including Jerome KERN, with whom he wrote *Show Boat* (1927), the first American musical to be based on a serious work of fiction.

Handel, George Frideric (1685-1759) German-born composer of the BAROQUE era, who became a naturalized British subject in 1726. He wrote 46 operas, but he is best known for his *Water Music* suite (1717) and his magnificent *Messiah* oratorio (1742). Beethoven admired Handel above all other composers, saying: 'To him only I bow the knee.'

❖ It is traditional for the audience to stand during the 'Hallelujah Chorus' of Handel's *Messiah*. This tradition began at the oratorio's

GRAND SCALE *Handel represented music at its most majestic and sublime. Many regard his* Messiah *as the finest oratorio ever written.*

LADY SINGS THE BLUES *Billie Holiday was renowned for her searching and intense interpretations of torch songs, but personal insecurity and the pressures of club life led to her career's tragic decline.*

first London performance in 1743 before George II, when the king was so moved by the exultant chorus that he rose to his feet and was followed by the rest of the audience.

Haydn, Joseph (1732-1809) Austrian composer who was prominent in the development of the string quartet and the symphony: his 107 symphonies and 68 string quartets revealed the rich possibilities of both musical forms. Haydn also wrote operas, concertos, masses and oratorios. His popular oratorios, *The Creation* (1799) and *The Seasons* (1801) were prompted by listening to performances of oratorios by Handel during visits to England. Haydn's music reflects his own genial and endearing character; because of his generous, fatherly nature, he was known as 'Papa'.

heavy metal Style of guitar-based rock music characterized by loud, fast and intense playing. It developed in the 1960s with blues-based groups such as Cream (whose guitarist was Eric CLAPTON) and rock guitarist Jimi HENDRIX, who used heavily amplified music. The term 'heavy metal' was inspired by the song 'Born To Be Wild', recorded by a hard-rock band called Steppenwolf in 1968 and adopted as a rebellious anthem by motorcycle gangs. The song contains the phrase 'heavy metal thunder' from the William Burroughs novel *The Naked Lunch* (1959).

Helpmann, Sir Robert (1909-86) Australian born ballet dancer, choreographer and actor, renowned for his dramatic style. He moved to England in 1933 and became one of the first stars of the Sadler's Wells Ballet, partnering Margot FONTEYN. In 1965 he became artistic director of the Australian Ballet. He appeared in the ballet films *The Red Shoes* (1948) and Rudolph NUREYEV's *Don Quixote* (1973).

Hendrix, Jimi (1942-70) American electric guitarist of the 1960s. His experimental guitar style, using special effects such as feedback and distortion, revolutionized the use of the instrument in rock music and helped to inspire HEAVY METAL music. Hendrix was one of the first black rock stars, but his audience was mainly white. In 1966 he went to London and formed a group called the Jimi Hendrix Experience. Hendrix was a flamboyant showman; as part of his stage act he would play the guitar with his teeth. He died at the height of his fame after taking drugs.

Holiday, Billie (Eleanora Fagan) (1915-59) American singer and leading jazz vocalist of her day. Although Holiday was not a true BLUES singer, everything she sang had a blues 'feel'. She was a gifted interpreter of lyrics and her voice had a unique, coarse timbre. She had her first recording session with the Benny Goodman band in 1933 and her first solo concert in 1946, but Holiday cut a tragic figure in the music world; her genius was never appreciated by the general public in her lifetime, and her career was blighted by drugs and alcohol. By the 1950s her voice and her health began to fail, and she died of a drug-related illness.

Holly, Buddy (1936-59) American singer, guitarist and composer, one of the great pioneers of ROCK'N'ROLL. Holly produced some of the most innovative pop songs of the 1950s, experimenting with production techniques and developing his 'hiccuping' vocal style. His first solo hit record was 'Peggy Sue' (1957); he died in a plane crash the following year.

Holst, Gustav (1874-1934) English composer of partly Swedish descent, with a somewhat mystical musical style. He is best known for his orchestral suite *The Planets* (1917), inspired by the characteristics traditionally applied to the heavenly bodies by astrologists, the choral *Hymn of Jesus* (1920) and the opera *The Perfect Fool* (1923).

Howes, Dulcie (1908-93) Prominent teacher and promoter of ballet in South Africa. In 1934 she was instrumental in forming the University of Cape Town Ballet School, of which she became principal and from which grew the UCT Ballet Company, later to become the CAPAB Ballet Company, of which she was artistic director from 1963 to 1970. She was awarded an honorary doctorate of music by UCT in 1976.

Ibrahim, Abdullah (Dollar Brand) (1934-) Virtuoso South African jazz pianist and composer of worldwide fame. Born in Cape Town, he had piano lessons from the age of seven and began his musical career in the mid-1950s when he sang with the vocal group The Steamline Brothers and later played the piano for the Tuxedo Slickers. In 1960 he formed the Jazz Epistles, which included Hugh MASEKELA on trumpet. Two years later he, Jonny Gertze, bass, and Makaya Ntshoko, drums, left for Europe, where they performed widely as the Dollar Brand Trio. Here they were discovered by Duke ELLINGTON who sponsored the recording of an album and persuaded them to move to America. Brand (he later changed his name to accord with his conversion to the Muslim faith) was the first jazz pianist to be given a Rockefeller grant to study music and he became a stylistic innovator who at one time was considered 'too modern' until popular taste caught up with him. He was soon touring the world, solo or with groups, and made innumerable recordings. Since 1991 Ibrahim has lived and performed mainly in South Africa. In 1994 he was awarded an honorary doctorate by the University of the Western Cape.

❖ Ibrahim's Cape Town-born wife, who performs under the name Sathima, is a jazz singer acclaimed by critics in the USA particularly for her renditions of the music of Duke Ellington.

Iglesias, Julio (1943-) Spanish crooner whose multilingual records and romantic image made him an international superstar. By the end of the 1980s his albums had sold more than 100 million copies in seven languages – including Japanese. 'Begin the Beguine', his first big hit in English, topped the British charts in 1981.

Ipi-Tombi Musical featuring African traditional performing arts that played for longer both in Johannesburg (where it had its premiere in 1974) and London than any other South African theatrical show. It also toured in Australia.

❖ South African singer Margaret Singana (1938-) made her name in this show, later producing many recordings and featuring in stage, film and television shows in Britain and the USA.

Jackson, Mahalia (1911-72) American GOSPEL singer, considered one of the greatest of all time, with a powerful contralto voice of great emotional intensity. During the 1930s her services were in demand as a church singer and

LIVING LEGEND *Much speculation has grown up around Michael Jackson's personal life. The media often portray him as a lonely victim of his fame and success.*

Decca invited her to make a recording in 1937. From 1946 she began recording regularly. In the 1950s she began appearing on television and gave the first all-gospel concert at Carnegie Hall in New York. She made a European tour in 1952 and in the last 20 years of her career sang in concert halls, at jazz festivals, at the White House, and before European royalty. She refused to appear in nightclubs or sing blues or pop music. She appeared in several feature films.

Jackson, Michael (1958-) American pop singer who began singing with his brothers in the Jackson Five when he was only five years old, and proved to be a natural showman. Jackson released his first hit solo album *Off The Wall* (1979) and had instant success with the single 'Don't Stop Till You Get Enough'. In 1982 his *Thriller* album became the most successful album of all time, with sales of more than 40 million. Seven of the tracks became Top 10 hits, including 'Billie Jean' and 'Beat It'. In 1993 Jackson, whose face has been remodelled by plastic surgery, gave a rare television interview in which he denied some bizarre rumours – including the suggestion that he had taken drugs to whiten his skin. Later that year he faced allegations of child abuse; he denied them, but made a substantial out-of-court settlement.

❖ In 1994 Jackson married Lisa Marie Presley, daughter of Elvis PRESLEY.

Janáček, Leoš (YAN-a-check) (1854-1928) Czech composer who derived inspiration from folk song and the rhythms and inflections of the Czech language. His work includes the operas *The Cunning Little Vixen* (1924) and *The Makropoulos Affair* (1925), the orchestral piece *Sinfonietta* (1926) and the *Glagolitic Mass* (1926).

jazz Musical style created by black Americans in New Orleans at the start of the 20th century. Jazz has its roots in black folk songs, SPIRITUALS, BLUES and RAGTIME. It evolved via the big-band jazz of the SWING era in the 1930s with band leaders such as Duke ELLINGTON, Count BASIE, Cab CALLOWAY and Benny GOODMAN, through the experimental BEBOP jazz of the 1940s developed by musicians such as Dizzy GILLESPIE and Charlie PARKER, to the lighter 'cool jazz' movement of the late 1940s launched by Miles DAVIS.

Jolson, Al (Asa Yoelson) (1886-1950) American singer and actor, renowned for his dynamic stage presence and black make-up. Jolson joined a minstrel show in 1909 and became the star attraction. He began recording and touring; some of his best-known songs included 'Mammy', 'Swanee' and 'Sonny Boy'. In 1927 Jolson became a big box-office attraction when he made the first full-length talking picture *The* ▷JAZZ SINGER. A fresh wave of popularity began when Jolson entertained American troops during World War II. Two films were made about Jolson's life, both featuring his recorded voice: *The Jolson Story* (1946) and *Jolson Sings Again* (1949).

Jones, Tom (1940-) Welsh pop singer known for his powerful voice and masculine image. Jones started singing in working-men's clubs (billed as 'Tiger Tom') and had hit singles with songs such as 'It's Not Unusual' (1965) and 'Delilah' (1968). In the 1970s he became a cabaret star in Las Vegas.

Joplin, Scott (1868-1917) American pianist and composer who in the 1890s helped to evolve RAGTIME, a musical style that swept the world until it was displaced by JAZZ towards the end of World War I. Joplin wrote two operas, which were not commercially successful, and even planned a ragtime symphony. One of his best-known works is 'Maple Leaf Rag' (1899).

❖ Joplin's work enjoyed a revival after his piano composition 'The Entertainer' was used in the film *The Sting* in 1973.

Kaapse Klopse Participants in the festival of street processions and rallies held in and around Cape Town at New Year, a spectacle of colourful costumes and lively music, widely known as the Coon Carnival. The origins of the carnival date back to the late 1880s when black North American minstrels visited the Cape and local groups emulated their costumes, songs and dance. In 1906 the

FESTIVE TIME *Features of Cape Town's annual minstrel carnival are troupes in costumes of vivid colours, singing and dancing to the music of trumpet, saxophone, banjo and percussion.*

UPBEAT DOWNPOUR *Gene Kelly happily weathers a Hollywood storm, in the unforgettable scene from* Singin' in the Rain.

first formal Minstrel Carnival was held at the Green Point Track. Since then carnival boards have coordinated the activities of competing troupes – some of whom have had up to 1 500 members – and organized events with prizes in various categories.

❖ The carnival is a valuable source of income for tailors, who every year turn out thousands of costumes for performers.

Karajan, Herbert von (1908-89) Austrian conductor and opera impresario, known for his precision and faithfulness to the composer's intentions. In 1955 he became conductor of the Berlin Philharmonic Orchestra – resigning only three months before his death. In 1956 he was appointed artistic director of the Salzburg Festival. He was also closely associated with the Vienna State Opera.

Kelly, Gene (1912-) Versatile American musical star and director, renowned for his athletic dancing, inventive choreography and winning smile. Some of his most memorable films were *Anchors Aweigh* (1945) in which he danced with Jerry the cartoon mouse, *On the Town* (1949), *An American in Paris* (1951) and *Singin' in the Rain* (1952). He directed the film musical *Hello, Dolly!* in 1969.

Kern, Jerome (1885-1945) Celebrated American songwriter who was a founding figure of the 20th-century American musical. His early musical comedy successes such as *Oh Boy!* (1917) and *Sally* (1920) were surpassed by his musical masterpiece *Show Boat* (1927), which he wrote with Oscar HAMMERSTEIN II. After 1939 Kern devoted himself to film music and later the concert platform. Kern's best-known songs include 'The Way You Look Tonight', 'Ol' Man River' and 'Smoke Gets in Your Eyes'.

King Kong Jazz opera composed by Stanley Glasser (1926-) featuring the music of Todd Matshikiza, the first South African theatrical production to gain international fame. An example of CROSSOVER music with its fusion of black American, African and European styles, it received critical and popular acclaim when it was produced in Johannesburg in 1959, starring black performers. It moved in 1961 to the West End of London, where it ran for a year.

❖ *King Kong* helped to launch Miriam MAKEBA, who played the female lead, on her international career.

Kirov Ballet Russian ballet company based at the Kirov State Theatre of Opera and Ballet in St Petersburg. The company succeeded the Imperial Russian Ballet and inherited its elegant style of dancing. Three of its most notable dancers – Rudolf NUREYEV, Natalia Makarova (1940-) and Mikhail Baryshnikov (1948-) – defected to the West and gained international reputations.

Klatzow, Peter (1945-) South African composer and associate professor at the University of Cape Town, whose works have won several awards in international competitions and are widely performed. In 1993 he received an Artes Award for his score of the Capab ballet *Hamlet*, performed in Cape Town and later in London and broadcast on SABC-TV. Born in Springs, he began taking piano lessons at the age of four and within a few years had begun composing piano pieces. He studied at the Royal College of Music in London (1964-5), where he won numerous prizes, and with the famous teacher of composition Nadia BOULANGER in Paris in 1966. In 1985 UCT honoured him with the title of Fellow of the University.

❖ The choreography of *Hamlet* by Veronica Paeper (1944-), artistic director of CAPAB Ballet, was also recognized by an Artes Award in 1993. Two other ballets with music by Klatzow were choreographed by her: *Drie Diere* and *Still life with Moonbeams*.

Klemperer, Otto (1885-1973) German conductor and composer, famous for highly individual interpretations of Beethoven. Klemperer's outstanding career began in 1907 in Prague, where he became conductor of the German Opera on the recommendation of Gustav MAHLER. In 1933 he moved to America and conducted many major orchestras in all parts of the world. He was principal conductor of the Philharmonia Orchestra in London from 1955 until his death.

kwela A form of urban African penny-whistle music popular in the 1950s, composed of elements of traditional, MARABI and American swing-jazz music.

Ladysmith Black Mambazo South African unaccompanied choral group, originally made up of 12 brothers and cousins from the Shabalala and Mazibuko families. They came to prominence in the USA when they toured with Paul Simon (of SIMON AND GARFUNKEL fame) in 1987 to promote his *Graceland* album and in the same year their album *Shaka Zulu* soared into the top 30 of the British charts.

❖ *Graceland* won Grammy awards in both 1986 and 1987.

Last, James (Hans Last) (1929-) Popular German conductor and composer who has sold more than 50 million albums worldwide with his big-band arrangements of classic pop hits. He formed his own orchestra in 1964 and achieved international popularity with his 'Non-Stop Dancing' albums.

Led Zeppelin (Robert Plant, Jimmy Page, John Paul Jones, John Bonham) British heavy-rock band formed in 1968, renowned for the sheer volume of their sound. They grew out of the British BLUES scene and became one of the biggest acts of the 1970s, especially in America. Robert Plant's passionate vocals and Jimmy Page's screeching virtuoso guitar inspired later generations of

INTERNATIONAL HITS *Choral group Ladysmith Black Mambazo's style of unaccompanied singing has brought them enthusiastic acclaim from audiences in many countries.*

HEAVY METAL groups. The group disbanded in 1980 after the death of drummer John Bonham from alcohol poisoning.

Lee, Peggy (Norma Egstrom) (1920-) American popular singer, songwriter and actress. Her clear yet husky voice suited many forms of music, including jazz, Latin American and folk. She was discovered by band leader Benny GOODMAN in Chicago in 1941 and worked with him for a few years until she went solo. In the 1950s, Lee appeared in films and was nominated for an Oscar for her performance in the role of a fading singer in *Pete Kelly's Blues* (1955).

Lehár, Franz (1870-1948) Austro-Hungarian composer of operetta and light music. After Johann Strauss, Lehár was the greatest figure in Viennese operetta. His most popular work, *The Merry Widow* (1905), brought him international fame. Before the theatre came to dominate his life, he wrote many songs and orchestral pieces, including the well-known 'Gold and Silver' concert-waltz (1902).

Les Misérables Operatic musical based on the novel by Victor ▷HUGO, with score by Claude-Michel Schonberg, libretto by Alain Boublil and lyrics by Herbert Kretzmer. The musical was first produced in Paris in 1980 and opened in London in 1985.

❖ Schonberg and Boublil also wrote the highly successful musical *Miss Saigon* (1989), which is based on the story of Giacomo PUCCINI's opera *Madam Butterfly*.

Liberace (Wladziu Valentino Liberace) (1919-87) American pianist and entertainer, renowned for his flamboyant presentation with glass pianos, ornate candelabras and sequinned costumes. A child prodigy of Polish-Italian stock, Liberace was a talented classical musician. His natural showmanship, and spirited and extravagant interpretations of the popular classics, made him one of the most commercially successful pianists of the 1950s, and he was still filling concert halls in the 1980s.

libretto Text of an opera, oratorio or musical comedy: the book of words that are sung and spoken. The word is the diminutive of the Italian for 'book'.

lied German word for 'song' (plural: lieder) applied in English to a ROMANTIC art song for solo voice, usually with piano accompaniment. Beethoven, Schubert, Schumann, Brahms and Richard Strauss wrote many exceptionally beautiful examples.

Liszt, Franz (1811-86) Hungarian virtuoso pianist, composer and teacher, generally regarded to have been the greatest performer of his time and possibly the greatest pianist of all time. In his youth Liszt was a flamboyant showman, renowned for his often fiery style of composition and performance. He ended his career as a concert pianist at the age of 37 at the height of his fame as a performer. In later life he assumed minor orders in the Roman Catholic Church, becoming known as the Abbé Liszt. A great innovator in composition, he created the 'symphonic poem' – an orchestral piece interpreting a theme from literature, art or nature – and he influenced many other composers, including Richard WAGNER and Claude DEBUSSY. His prodigious output included numerous transcriptions or arrangements for the piano of orchestral and operatic works by other composers, which he helped to popularize.

❖ Liszt was the 19th-century equivalent of a pop star. Crowds besieged him and women swooned over him, cherishing mementos of him, such as locks of his hair, and even his cigar butts.

❖ Liszt championed the compositions of Wagner, who became a close friend and married Liszt's daughter Cosima.

THREE OF THE BEST *Among Andrew Lloyd Webber's many successful shows are* Jesus Christ Superstar, Cats *and* Phantom of the Opera, *in which actor Michael Crawford (below) played the sinister yet sensitive 'Phantom'.*

Lloyd Webber, Sir Andrew (1948-) British composer of some of the longest-running musicals in the history of British theatre. In 1968 Lloyd Webber and lyric writer Tim Rice wrote the rock musical *Joseph and the Amazing Technicolor Dreamcoat*; it was staged in the West End in 1973 and revived in 1992. In 1969 Lloyd Webber and Rice wrote another biblical rock opera, the controversial *Jesus Christ Superstar*. Next came *Evita* (1978), based on the life of Eva Peron, wife of the Argentinian president; the show, staged in London, contained the memorable song 'Don't Cry For Me, Argentina'. Lloyd Webber parted company with Rice to work on *Cats* (1981), a feline fantasy based on T S ▷ELIOT's poems from *Old Possum's Book of Practical Cats*, containing the hit song 'Memory'. More successful shows followed: *Starlight Express* (1984), *Phantom of the Opera* (1986) and *Aspects of Love* (1989). A stage production of Billy Wilder's classic Hollywood film *Sunset Boulevard* had its premiere in London in 1993. In the same year Lloyd Webber was knighted for his services to the arts and was given a star on the Hollywood Walk of Fame.

❖ In September 1991 Lloyd Webber made theatre history by becoming the first person to have six shows running simultaneously in London's West End.

Lynn, Dame Vera (1917-) British singer who became known as 'The Forces' Sweetheart' of World War II with sentimental songs such as 'We'll Meet Again' and 'White Cliffs of Dover'. In the 1940s she entertained the troops in war zones and made her first film,

MORALE BOOSTER *In World War II, Vera Lynn was every soldier's favourite singer and a nostalgic link with home for troops abroad.*

also called *We'll Meet Again*. In the 1950s she topped the British charts with 'My Son, My Son'. She continued in later life to make regular appearances at soldiers' reunions and commemorations.

Madonna (Madonna Louise Ciccone) (1958-) American pop star who was one of the most successful female singers and songwriters of the 1980s. Madonna rose to fame with the catchy pop song 'Holiday' in 1984. She was adopted as a symbol of sexual liberation by millions of young women fans, known as 'wannabes'. Madonna's overtly sexual image and expert manipulation of the media was highlighted in 1992 by her book *Sex*, in which she appeared nude. Her film career – in which she sought to become a modern-day Marilyn Monroe – has been less successful.

Mahler, Gustav (1860-1911) Austrian composer and conductor, who wrote long, intensely emotional works for large orchestras. Mahler earned his living as an operatic conductor and for many years was conductor and artistic director of the Vienna State Opera, where he set high standards. From 1908 he was conductor of the New York Philharmonic and spent his summers in Austria composing. His works include nine symphonies (and an unfinished tenth), the cantata *Das Klagende Lied* (1880-9), the song-symphony *Das Lied von der Erde* (1909), and the haunting song-cycle *Kindertotenlieder* (1904). Several of his works, especially his eighth symphony *(Symphony of a Thousand)* (1910), employ huge orchestral and vocal resources.

❖ The slow movement of Mahler's Fifth Symphony accompanies the opening of Luchino Visconti's film ▷DEATH IN VENICE.

Makeba, Miriam (1932-) Singer of international fame – called the 'Empress of African Song' – who grew up in Johannesburg and became a symbol of the anti-apartheid movement when her records were banned in South Africa. After appearing in the film *Come Back Africa* and in the musical KING KONG, she established her career in the USA, where she toured and recorded with the calypso star, singer and actor Harry Belafonte (1927-). She remarried after her divorce from Hugh MASEKELA and in 1969 moved to Conakry in Guinea, from where she continued to tour. She returned to South Africa in 1990. In 1994 she received an honorary doctorate in music from the University of Cape Town and became a member of parliament.

❖ In 1964 Miriam Makeba addressed the General Assembly of the UN, and in 1962 sang at President John Kennedy's Madison Square Gardens birthday party.

Mancini, Henry (1924-94) American composer and conductor who wrote the scores for more than 100 films. In 1961 he won an Oscar for his music to *Breakfast at Tiffany's* which included the ever-popular song 'Moon River'. Mancini also wrote the theme tune for *The Pink Panther* in 1964.

Mantovani, Annunzio Paolo (1905-80) Italian-born British composer, conductor and arranger. He created an ethereal sound with his orchestra, known as the 'cascading strings', which made him one of the most successful album sellers in the history of popular music. His arrangement in 1951 of an old song called 'Charmaine' became the first of several million-selling singles.

BLONDE BOMBSHELL *Madonna sports her trend-setting 'bullet-bra' on her 1990 world tour. It was designed by Jean Paul Gaultier.*

EMPRESS OF SONG *During her spectacular international singing career Miriam Makeba became a symbol of opposition to apartheid.*

Mapfumo, Thomas (1945-) Zimbabwean singer-composer and band leader whose recordings of Shona compositions won eight gold discs in the 1970s. His *chimurenga* ('music of the struggle') was regarded as the distinctive and authentic sound of Zimbabwe. By the mid-1980s he was established as an international star and, with his band, toured widely in Europe and Africa.

marabi Form of music that developed among urban black communities in South Africa in the 1920s, combining elements of distinctive African rhythms and polyphonic principles with harmonization based on the Western three-chord system.

Marley, Bob (1945-81) Jamaican singer and songwriter who became the first international REGGAE superstar with his group Bob Marley and the Wailers, formed in 1964. The group had their first hit in Britain with 'No Woman No Cry' (1975), followed by songs such as 'Jamming' (1977) and 'One Love' (1984). Marley, who was a devout Rastafarian, died of cancer while touring America; he received a state funeral in Jamaica.

Masekela, Hugh (1939-) South African trumpeter, band leader, composer and singer, whose musical career began with the encouragement of the anti-apartheid campaigner

VERSATILE MUSICIAN *South African Hugh Masekela, who began playing the trumpet as a boy, achieved success also as a band leader, singer and composer. He wrote the score for* Sarafina!

Father Trevor Huddleston. Huddleston gave him a trumpet when he was 14, helped him form the Huddleston Jazz Band and secured a gift of a trumpet for him from Louis ARMSTRONG. Later he was associated with Dollar Brand (Abdullah IBRAHIM) and Miriam MAKEBA, whom he married, but later divorced. A scholarship from calypso star Harry Belafonte (1927-) enabled him to study at the Manhattan School of Music in New York. In the 1980s he settled in Botswana, where he founded a school of music. He was guest star on American singer-songwriter Paul Simon's *Graceland* tour of America in 1987 and wrote the score for the hit South African musical and film SARAFINA! He returned to South Africa in 1990.

ZIMBABWE SOUND *Thomas Mapfumo's Shona recordings won eight gold discs in the 1970s.*

mass Roman Catholic service of Communion. 'High Mass' (*Missa Solemnis*) has been the principal form of religious music since the Middle Ages, and inspired composers such as Bach, Mozart and Beethoven to write some of their finest work.

mbaqanga Zulu word for maize bread, originally a term for popular commercial African jazz in South Africa in the 1950s that developed from KWELA and blended African melody, MARABI and American jazz. In the 1960s it described a new style combining urban neo-traditional music and marabi played on electric, guitars, saxophones, violins, accordions and drums.

❖ Miriam MAKEBA built her local reputation with mbaqanga as lead singer with the Manhattan Brothers and later with her own quartet, the Skylarks.

Mendelssohn, Jacob Felix (1809-47) German Romantic composer. He was a keen traveller and his overture *The Hebrides* (1830) and *Italian* and *Scottish* symphonies (1833, 1842) were inspired by his extended tours. He was a great favourite of Queen ▷VICTORIA; during her lifetime his oratorio *Elijah* (1846) rivalled Handel's *Messiah* in popularity.

❖ Mendelssohn helped to revive the music of J S BACH, which had been virtually forgotten since Bach's death in 1750.

Menuhin, Lord Yehudi (1916-) American-born violin virtuoso of Russian parentage, who took British nationality in 1985. He made his professional debut at the age of seven as soloist with the San Francicsco Symphony Orchestra, toured internationally as a child and made a famous recording of Elgar's Violin Concerto (with the composer conducting) when he was 16. Bartók's Sonata for Solo Violin (1945) was one of many works written for him.

❖ Menuhin, a champion of oppressed minorities, refused to appear in South Africa during the apartheid era, but in 1995 conducted performances and gave master classes in Johannesburg and Cape Town.

Messiaen, Olivier (1908-92) French composer whose highly distinctive music, often incorporating birdsong, influenced many younger composers, several of whom, among them STOCKHAUSEN, were his pupils. His works, particularly the six-hour-long opera *St Francis of Assisi*, reflect his love of nature and his interest in mysticism and medieval and oriental rhythms.

Michael, George (1963-) British singer and songwriter who formed Wham! with Andrew Ridgely in 1981. After many hits, including 'Careless Whisper' (1984), Michael went solo. His next album *Faith* reached No 1 in Britain and America. In 1994 Michael lost a legal battle with Sony over the level of his royalties but the two parties later reached a settlement.

Miller, Glenn (1904-44) American band leader, trombone player and composer. His orchestra, formed in 1938, was noted for its smooth, sophisticated performances of dance numbers such as 'Moonlight Serenade' and 'In the Mood'. Miller joined the army during World War II and entertained the Allied forces in England in 1944. On the way with his band to a posting in France, the plane disappeared over the English Channel.

Moeketsi, Kippie (1925-83) South African alto saxophone virtuoso who played with the orchestra of KING KONG in London in 1961. On his return to South Africa later in the 1960s, he strove to promote jazz in African areas, but the difficulties imposed by apartheid blighted his career and he died in poverty.

Monteverdi, Claudio (1567-1643) Italian composer, usually considered to have written the first major operas. In 1613 he became musical director at St Mark's Basilica, Venice, where he remained until his death. His greatest works include the operas *Orfeo* (1607) and *The Coronation of Poppea* (1642), as well as the religious choral work *Vespers* (1610).

Motown Black independent record company formed by songwriter Berry Gordy in 1959, which influenced the sound of the 1960s by blending pop music with RHYTHM AND BLUES and GOSPEL. The Detroit-based label became a mini-music industry, discovering new talent and employing its own songwriters and producers. Gordy sold the label to MCA in 1988. ❖ Motown was named after 'Motortown', the nickname for the city of Detroit, the centre of the American car industry.

Mozart, Wolfgang Amadeus (1756-91) Austrian composer and one of the great geniuses of Western music. As a boy, accompanied by his violinist father, Leopold, he toured the courts of Europe, dazzling kings and courtiers with his brilliant keyboard playing. In 1781, after an unhappy period of musical employment in the service of the Archbishop of Salzburg, Mozart settled in Vienna as a freelance composer, and became the toast of the city. The head of the Vienna Opera, Antonio Salieri, tried to obstruct his young rival's career, but Mozart was befriended by the composer HAYDN. Mozart wrote more than 600 compositions, including 41 symphonies, 27 piano concertos, 23 string quartets, and several operas. Well-known compositions include the short work for strings *Eine kleine Nachtmusik* (1787), and the operas *The Marriage of Figaro* (1786), *Don Giovanni* (1787) and *The Magic Flute* (1791). The obvious charm and technical brilliance of Mozart's music are deceptive; although he was often full of boyish spirits, his letters and operas reveal him to be someone who understood human nature in all its complexity.

CHILD PRODIGY *Mozart (insert) was four when he began giving concerts. Among his many works was* Eine kleine Nachtmusik *(above).*

Musorgsky, Modest Petrovich (1839-81) Russian composer of great originality, who wanted his music 'to portray the soul of man in all its profundity'. His works include the opera *Boris Godunov* (1868-72), the orchestral work *Night on the Bare Mountain* (1867) and the piano suite *Pictures at an Exhibition* (1874), made famous by Maurice RAVEL's orchestration of it (1922).

My Fair Lady Musical based on George Bernard ▷SHAW's comedy *Pygmalion* – about a cockney flower girl who is transformed into a 'lady'. With music by Frederic Loewe (1901-88), and book and lyrics by Alan Jay Lerner (1918-86), it opened on Broadway in 1956 with Julie ▷ANDREWS as the flower girl, Eliza Doolittle, Stanley Holloway as her dustman father, and Rex Harrison as the phonetics expert who teaches Eliza how to talk and behave in polite society. It was successfully filmed in Hollywood in 1964.

Napier, Marita (1939-) South African opera singer, a dramatic soprano, whose first big success was as Sieglinde in Richard WAGNER's *Die Walküre* at Bayreuth in 1974. She has sung major roles also at Covent Garden, London, La Scala, Milan, the Vienna State Opera, the Liceo, Barcelona, and the Metropolitan Opera, New York, and has returned frequently to sing at South African opera houses. In 1989 she was the winner of a Grammy Award for classical music.

Nijinsky, Vaslav (*c*1889-1950) Russian ballet dancer and choreographer whose superb technique and exceptional dramatic gifts made him the greatest male dancer of his time. As leading dancer with DIAGHILEV's Ballets Russes in Paris, he excelled in such contrasting ballets as *Schehérazade* (1910) and *Petrushka* (1911). As a choreographer, his radically original style caused a sensation when the *Rite of Spring* to music by STRAVINSKY was first produced in Paris in 1913. Nijinsky retired in 1917 after he had been diagnosed as mentally ill and he spent most of the rest of his life in institutions.

Norman, Jessye (1945-) American soprano who has been one of the greatest opera stars and lieder singers since the 1980s. She combines tremendous power with exquisite control and is renowned for her interpretations of WAGNER, MAHLER and Richard STRAUSS.

Novello, Ivor (1893-1951) Welsh composer, playwright and actor, who wrote one of the most popular tunes of World War I, the patriotic 'Keep the Home Fires Burning'. With his matinée idol good looks, he starred in films in the 1920s and 1930s. His romantic musicals included *The Dancing Years* (1939) and *Perchance to Dream* (1945).

Nureyev, Rudolf (1938-93) Russian dancer and choreographer who trained with the KIROV BALLET and defected to the West in 1961. Through his vibrant presence and versatility he quickly established himself as one of the outstanding male dancers of the post-war era. He joined the Royal Ballet in 1962 and formed a memorable partnership with Margot FONTEYN. Despite ill health and advancing years, Nureyev never wanted to retire from dancing; he gave his last performance in Berlin in 1992.

Offenbach, Jacques (1819-80) Composer, born in Germany, whose highly successful French operettas include *Orpheus in the Underworld* (1858) and *La Belle Héléne* (1864). In 1876 he began a more serious work, *Tales of Hoffmann* (1881), but died during rehearsals of the production.

Oliver! Musical by the British composer Lionel Bart (1930-), based on Dickens' ▷OLIVER TWIST. It opened in London's West End in 1960. It was made into an Oscar-winning film in 1968 and has often been revived on stage.

Memorable songs include 'Food, Glorious Food' and 'Consider Yourself'.

operetta Comic or light-hearted opera, with a good deal of spoken dialogue, such as GILBERT AND SULLIVAN's *The Mikado* (1885) and Franz LEHÁR's *The Merry Widow* (1905).

Orbison, Roy (1936-88) American singer and composer of country-influenced ROCK'N'ROLL, a kind of music also known as 'rockabilly'. His mournful falsetto voice made him one of the most distinctive singers of the 1960s.

Osibisa African pop group formed in London in 1969 that became one of the most commercially successful African groups. The group's core of three Ghanaians, led by Teddy Osei, was initially joined by two other Ghanaians, a Nigerian and three West Indians. Their music is described as having 'criss-cross rhythms which explode with happiness'.

Paderewski, Ignace Jan (1860-1941) Polish concert pianist, composer, patriot and politician, renowned for his interpretations of Chopin. In 1919 he became liberated Poland's first prime minister.

Paganini, Niccolò (1782-1840) Italian violinist and composer, considered the greatest violin virtuoso of all time whose brilliance and technical mastery raised violin playing to new heights. A gaunt figure, dressed always in black, Paganini so astonished audiences that there were rumours that he was in league with the devil. His works include six violin concertos and 24 caprices (compositions that do not follow any strict form).

❖ One of Paganini's striking effects was to play a melody with the bow while plucking the accompanying harmony with the unused fingers of his left hand.

Parker, Charlie (1920-55) American jazz saxophonist and composer, also known as 'Bird', renowned for his technical agility, adventurous improvisation and melodic invention. In the early 1940s, along with Dizzy GILLESPIE, Parker developed a modern jazz form known as BEBOP with fast driving rhythms, complex harmonies and sophisticated improvisations. An addiction to heroin and alcohol contributed to his early death.

Pavarotti, Luciano (1935-) Ebullient Italian tenor whose powerful voice and outgoing personality made him an international star soon after his operatic debut in 1961. In 1990 Pavarotti had a hit record with the aria 'Nessun Dorma' from Giacomo PUCCINI's oriental opera *Turandot*, which was used as the theme song for the soccer World Cup tournament in 1990. That same year, his concert in Hyde Park in London attracted an enthusiastic audience of 150 000.

Pavlova, Anna (1885-1931) Russian ballerina who was the most celebrated dancer of her day. She danced all the major roles with the Imperial Russian Ballet, appeared with DIAGHILEV's Ballets Russes and formed her own company in 1913. She toured the world, mesmerizing audiences particularly with her poignant solo 'The Dying Swan' to music by Camille SAINT-SAËNS.

OPEN-AIR ARIAS *The concert by Italian tenor Luciano Pavarotti in London's Hyde Park in 1990 was one of his most successful – bringing the music of opera to a huge audience.*

THE LANGUAGE OF MUSIC

adagio Slow and leisurely.

allegretto Briskly, but more slowly than allegro.

allegro Quick, lively.

amoroso Lovingly.

andante Moving gently, flowing.

animato Animatedly.

cadenza Unaccompanied, virtuoso passage by a soloist in a concerto.

chord Group of two or more notes played together.

coda Short additional passage at the end of a movement or composition.

counterpoint Set of two or more melody lines played together and in harmony.

crescendo Rising in volume and intensity.

forte Loudly.

fortissimo Very loudly.

grave Solemnly.

largo Slowly, stately.

legato Smoothly and evenly.

leitmotif Musical phrase associated with a particular character or situation, used extensively by Wagner.

pianissimo Very softly.

piano Softly.

pizzicato Played by plucking rather than bowing the strings of an instrument, such as a violin or cello.

presto Fast.

rallentando Gradual slowing down.

recitative Sung narrative in opera or oratorio, in the rhythm of ordinary speech.

reprise Repetition of a phrase, or return to an earlier theme.

staccato Crisply, sharply.

syncopation Accentuation of a beat in each bar that is normally unaccentuated.

tempo Pace at which a work is performed.

tutti All together.

vibrato Slight wavering of pitch, used in singing and on some instruments, usually to add emotion.

vivace Lively.

Piaf, Edith (1915-63) French cabaret singer of the 1950s renowned for her waiflike appearance, strong voice and emotional delivery. Born into poverty, Piaf was singing on the streets of Paris when she was 15. She was discovered by a cabaret owner who nicknamed her *La môme piaf*, or 'little sparrow'. Her best-known songs were 'La Vie en Rose', 'M'lord' and her personal anthem 'Non, je ne regrette rien' ('No regrets'). She published two volumes of memoirs (1958 and 1964).

Pink Floyd (Roger Waters, David Gilmour, Nick Mason, Rick Wright and Syd Barrett) British rock band formed in 1966 specializing in concerts with fantastic light shows. Their album *Dark Side Of The Moon* (1973) – one of the most successful records of all time – sold more than 25 million copies. In 1979 they had their first No 1 hit single with 'Another Brick in the Wall', from their album *The Wall*.

Poole, David (1925-91) South African ballet dancer, teacher, choreographer and producer. After training under Dulcie HOWES at the University of Cape Town Ballet School, he made his mark as a character dancer in the Sadler's Wells Theatre Ballet and Ballet Rambert in

COURT DRAMA *A scene from Verdi's* Don Carlos *(1867) sumptuously produced at Milan's opera house, La Scala.*

STORIES OF BEST-LOVED OPERAS

The Marriage of Figaro (1786) Mozart's greatest comic opera centres on the intrigues surrounding the approaching marriage of Figaro (Count Almaviva's servant) and Susanna (Count Almaviva's maid). The Count tries to seduce Susanna before she marries, but Figaro manages to outwit his master. Upon hearing *Figaro* for the first time, the Austrian Emperor Joseph II told Mozart it had 'too many notes'.

La Traviata (1853) Romantic opera by Verdi. Violetta Valéry, a Parisian courtesan suffering from consumption, is so moved by the devotion of the young man Alfredo Germont, that she leaves town to set up home with him. Germont's father persuades her to renounce his son, who in turn denounces her as faithless. In the final deathbed scene, the two lovers are reconciled, only for Violeta to collapse and die in Alfredo's arms.

Der Ring des Nibelungen (1869-76) Four separate operas: *Das Rheingold, Die Walküre, Siegfried* and *Götterdämmerung*, make up this massive 15-hour cycle, which took Richard Wagner 25 years to complete. The story revolves around a ring that gives it's wearer supreme power. In *Das Rheingold*, Wotan, the ruler of the gods, forces a dwarf called Alberich, the forger of the ring, to surrender it to him. The curse that the vengeful dwarf lays on all the wearers of the ring is the subject of the next three operas. Eventually the curse is lifted by the self-sacrifice of Wotan's favourite daughter Brünnhilde.

Aïda (1871) Verdi's grand opera of the Egyptian warrior Radames and the slave Aïda – who is in fact the daughter of the ruler of Ethiopia. As they plan to run away together Radames accidentally betrays his country by revealing some military secrets. He is overheard and is condemned to be buried alive. Aïda smuggles herself into his tomb to die with him.

Carmen (1875) Now one of the world's most popular operas; *Carmen* was a flop when it was first performed in Paris in 1875 (the audience was shocked by its daring realism), and its disappointed composer, Georges Bizet, died soon afterwards. It tells the story of the beautiful gypsy Carmen who bewitches a corporal called Don José. He deserts his regiment for her, but Carmen soon tires of him and takes up with the bullfighter Escamillo. The rejected José stabs Carmen to death.

La Bohème (1896) Puccini's first international triumph, which has some of the best known arias ever written. Set in Paris, a Bohemian called Rodolfo falls in love with a consumptive seamstress called Mimi. They later quarrel and part – as do Rodolfo's friend, the artist Marcello, and his mistress Musetta, with whom he has just been reunited. Both men are pining for their former loves when Musetta returns, closely followed by Mimi, who has collapsed and is dying. The opera ends tragically with Rodolfo embracing her lifeless corpse.

Tosca (1900) Set in Rome in Napoleonic times, Puccini's tragic epic tells the story of Tosca, a great opera singer who is in love with Cavaradossi, a painter. He helps a revolutionary escape and is arrested by Scarpia, the sadistic police chief who himself desires Tosca. The singer agrees to let Scarpia have his way with her, if he will spare Cavaradossi's life. Tosca stabs him but the dead Scarpia manages to have the last laugh. Although he had assured Tosca he would fake Cavaradossi's execution, he had in fact ordered the firing squad to use real bullets. The betrayed Tosca kills herself as Scarpio's minions arrive to arrest her.

Madam Butterfly (1904) Puccini's tear-jerking masterpiece tells the story of the doomed relationship between Cio-Cio-San, a young Japanese geisha girl, and Pinkerton, a lieutenant in the US navy. Pinkerton sees his Japanese-style marriage as a temporary arrangement, while she considers the ceremony to be binding and bears him a child. When Pinkerton returns to Japan with his new American wife to reclaim his son, Butterfly commits suicide.

Turandot (1926) Puccini's last opera features the aria 'Nessun Dorma' and is set in ancient Peking. Calaf, the disguised son of an exiled ruler, wins the hand of the cruel and haughty Princess Turandot by answering three riddles correctly; the penalty for failure is death. Calaf goes on to win her love with a passionate kiss.

London. He returned to South Africa in 1957. At the UCT Ballet School and later as artistic director of CAPAB Ballet he played a dominant role in the production of a wide range of classical and modern ballets. He became director of the UCT Ballet School in 1973 and was appointed the first full professor of ballet in South Africa. He was also a vice-president of the Royal Acadamy of Dancing.

❖ Under apartheid legislation David Poole and a brother were classified 'white', while other members of his family were classified 'coloured'. After retiring in 1990, he devoted himself to the teaching and promotion of ballet in black areas.

Porter, Cole (1891-1964) American songwriter noted for his witty, sophisticated lyrics. He established his reputation with musicals such as *The Gay Divorcée* (1932) and *Anything Goes* (1934). As the result of a riding accident, he was a semi-invalid for the last 27 years of his life. During this time, however, he produced his masterpiece *Kiss Me Kate* (1948) and the film score for *High Society* (1956). Among Porter's best-known songs are 'Night and Day' and 'I Get a Kick Out of You'.

Presley, Elvis (1935-77) American singer and guitarist, widely regarded as the embodiment of ROCK'N'ROLL. Presley was renowned for his remarkable vocal range and ability to sing the BLUES. His music was a unique mixture of RHYTHM AND BLUES, GOSPEL and COUNTRY AND WESTERN. In 1956, when Presley had hits with 'Heartbreak Hotel' and 'Hound Dog', his rebellious image made him the archetypal pop idol. After being drafted into the US Army from 1958 to 1960, Presley re-emerged as a clean-cut crooner with ballads such as 'Are You Lonesome Tonight?' His popularity suffered when, seduced by Hollywood, he made a stream of lightweight musical films. He managed to revive his career in the late 1960s with songs such as 'In the Ghetto' and 'Suspicious Minds'. Presley spent his last years as a cabaret artist in Las Vegas. Dependent on drugs, his bloated body attired in vulgar costumes, Presley seemed to have become a symbol of decadence. It is a testament to his enduring fame, however, that more than 20 million of his records were sold in the 24 hours after his death. He remains the biggest selling solo artist of the 20th century.

❖ Presley's provocative hip-swivelling routine was deemed too suggestive for television in the 1950s, and he was shown only from the waist up. He was nicknamed 'Elvis the Pelvis' and later 'The King'.

REBEL ROCK *With his sultry blues voice, sullen curled lip and gyrating hips, Elvis Presley became the greatest exponent of rock'n'roll. His image was seen everywhere – even on American stamps.*

Prince (Prince Rogers Nelson) (1958-) American singer, songwriter and actor who is renowned for his sexual lyrics, his outrageous image and his mixing of elements of soul, funk, disco and rock. His many hits since his first major album and film *Purple Rain* (1984) include 'The Most Beautiful Girl in the World' (1994).

❖ On a visit to Britain in 1987 Prince offended the popular press, who dubbed him 'a toothpick in a purple doily'.

Prokofiev, Sergei (1891-1953) Russian composer and pianist whose work was both classical and experimental. He won international renown with his first symphonic work, the *Classical Symphony* of 1917. Prokofiev lived abroad from 1918 and was associated with DIAGHILEV's Ballets Russes. He returned to Russia in 1934, when his work became less adventurous. His works include the fantasy opera *The Love for Three Oranges* (1919), and the ballet *Romeo and Juliet* (1935-6).

Puccini, Giacomo (1858-1924) Italian opera composer, whose music is notable for its romantic melody and strong sense of drama. Puccini achieved overnight success with the opera *Manon Lescaut* in 1893. He wrote three of the world's most popular operas: *La Bohème* (1896), *Tosca* (1900) and *Madam Butterfly* (1904). His final masterpiece *Turandot* was completed by Franco Alfano after the composer's death, and staged in 1926.

punk rock Subversive musical movement, launched as a reaction to rock bands who 'took themselves too seriously'. The name 'punk' comes from the American slang for something rotten and worthless. The music, prevalent in the late 1970s, was characterized

by its aggressive, anti-establishment lyrics.
❖ Punk fashions feature outlandish spiked hair, ghoulish make-up and ripped clothes.

Purcell, Henry (1659-95) Organist and one of the greatest of English composers. He was the only significant English composer of the BAROQUE period, his works including chamber and church music and music for state occasions. He wrote Britain's earliest full-scale opera *Dido and Aeneas* (1689).

Queen (Freddie Mercury, John Deacon, Brian May, Roger Taylor) British rock band, renowned for the flamboyant showmanship of their lead singer Freddie Mercury (1946-1991). Formed in 1970, Queen had a major success with the single *Bohemian Rhapsody* (1975), which was accompanied by one of the first pop videos. The band split up after Freddie Mercury died.

Rachmaninoff, Sergei (1873-1943) Russian composer and virtuoso pianist who excelled at the interpretation of the late Romantic composers, and dazzled audiences with his own technically brilliant concertos and solo pieces. He moved to Switzerland and later America after the Russian Revolution of 1917. His works include four piano concertos, three symphonies, three operas, a choral work and the *Rhapsody on a Theme of Paganini* (1934) for piano and orchestra.
❖ One of Rachmaninoff's most popular and often-played works, the Piano Concerto No 2, was written after a hypnotist enabled him to overcome a block to composition.

ragtime Style of Afro-American music composed particularly by Scott JOPLIN which became internationally popular from the 1890s until about 1920, when it was displaced by JAZZ. Often performed on the piano, ragtime, or 'ragged' music, usually featured a syncopated right hand – in which strong beats become weak, and vice versa – with a steady rhythm in the left hand.

Rambert, Dame Marie (1888-1982) Polish-born dancer and teacher, one of the great pioneers of modern British ballet. In 1913 she began to work for DIAGHILEV's Ballets Russes. She became a British citizen in 1918 and founded a ballet school in 1926. From 1935 her company was called the Ballet Rambert.

rap music Style of music and dance which originated in black New York street culture as 'performance' poetry, with themes of social comment and satire. Rap became a musical form when an instrumental backing was added. One of the first examples was 'Rapper's Delight' (1979) by the Sugar Hill Gang.
❖ Popular exponents of rap in South Africa are the vocal group Prophets of the City, who, contrary to many American rappists, take a strong antidrug, antiviolence stance.

Raubenheimer, Marc (1952-83) South African concert pianist who was establishing an international career when he was killed in an air crash in Spain. In 1980 he won the important Paloma O'Shea piano competition in Santander, Spain.

Ravel, Maurice (1875-1937) French impressionist composer who is usually paired with DEBUSSY, although Ravel's compositions are more classical in style. He wrote scintillating piano music of great technical difficulty, two small-scale operas and the ballet *Daphnis and Chloé* (1912).
❖ Ravel reputedly wrote his often-played ballet score *Boléro* (1928), in which he repeats the same short theme over and over again with unvarying rhythm for 20 minutes, in answer to a friend's challenge that he could not do exactly that without boring his audience.

Redding, Otis (1941-67) American singer and songwriter of the 1960s, regarded as one of the greatest male SOUL MUSIC singers because of his emotional vocal style. His best-known hit single is the pensive '(Sittin' on the) Dock of the Bay' (1968).

Reeves, Jim (1923-64) American singer renowned for his smooth, velvety voice. Often referred to as 'Gentleman Jim', Reeves created a style of CROSSOVER MUSIC that appealed to both country and pop fans. His hits included 'He'll have to go' (1960) and 'Distant Drums' (1966).

reggae Popular music of Jamaican origin, characterized by a strong offbeat rhythm. Reggae is used by black movements and the followers of ▷RASTAFARIANISM to express social issues. It became popular with white audiences in the late 1960s and was widely promoted by Bob MARLEY in the 1970s.
❖ South African singer Lucky Dube (1964-), reputedly the country's highest paid performer, is known as Africa's 'King of Reggae'.

requiem A MASS with biblical passages and prayers for the admission of the dead to heaven. Celebrated requiems have been written by BERLIOZ, FAURÉ, MOZART and VERDI. An outstanding modern example is Benjamin BRITTEN's *War Requiem* (1962).

rhythm and blues Style of black popular music, also known as R&B, which originated in America in the 1940s. A fusion of BLUES and JAZZ using drums, electric guitars and saxophones, R&B was the first black music to become widely popular with white audiences. Attracted by its powerful rhythms, white musicians used R&B as an important element of ROCK'N'ROLL. In the early 1960s an R&B movement developed in London, influencing rock groups such as the Rolling Stones. Early pioneers of R&B include Ray CHARLES, Muddy Waters (1915-83), B B King (1925-) and Bo Diddley (1928-).

Richard, Sir Cliff (Harry Webb) (1940-) Singer who began his career as Britain's answer to Elvis PRESLEY. In 1958 he formed a group called the Drifters, who evolved into The Shadows, and had a No 2 hit with a rock-'n'roll number called 'Move It', soon followed by 'Living Doll' (1959), the first of many No 1s. He went on to cultivate a middle-of-the-road image in the 1960s, with a string of family film musicals such as *The Young Ones* (1962) and *Summer Holiday* (1963). He professed his Christianity in 1966 and became known for his gospel tours. In 1968 he was runner-up in the Eurovision Song Contest with 'Congratulations'. Having survived the ever-changing musical trends of four decades, Richard has established himself as Britain's most durable pop artist.
❖ The Shadows was the most influential instrumental rock'n'roll group in Britain during the late 1950s and early 1960s.

DURABLE STAR *Through the changing trends of four decades Cliff Richard has retained his popularity – and his youthful appearance.*

❖ In 1995 Cliff Richard was knighted for his services to charity.

Rimsky-Korsakov, Nicolai (1844-1908) Russian composer noted for his vivid orchestration and his frequent use of oriental subject matter, as exemplified in the symphonic suite *Scheherazade* (1888) and the opera *The Legend of Tsar Sultan* (1900). The latter contains the famous orchestral interlude, 'The Flight of the Bumble Bee'.

Robeson, Paul (1898-1976) American singer and actor of the stage and screen, one of the most important black performers of his time, with a bass voice of operatic quality. He made his mark as Joe in the musical *Show Boat* in 1928, and became associated particularly with the song 'Ol' Man River'. Robeson promoted GOSPEL MUSIC, recorded a great many SPIRITUALS and was an active campaigner for black civil rights.

rock'n'roll Music craze of the late 1950s which combined elements of white American COUNTRY AND WESTERN with black RHYTHM AND BLUES and boogie woogie – a style of jazz piano-playing characterized by a bass line played eight beats to the bar. Bill HALEY (1925-81) and The Comets launched the era with the song 'Rock Around the Clock' in 1955, and a year later Elvis PRESLEY emerged as 'The King' of the genre. Other important artists include Chuck BERRY, Fats DOMINO and Buddy HOLLY.

Rodgers, Richard (1902-79) American popular composer. He collaborated with the librettist Lorenz Hart (1895-1943) on *Pal Joey* (1940) and other musicals, but is especially remembered for those he produced with Oscar HAMMERSTEIN II, including *Oklahoma!* (1943), *Carousel* (1945), *South Pacific* (1949), *The King and I* (1951) and *The Sound of Music* (1959), which were all turned into successful films after they had been staged.

Rolling Stones British group often hailed as the greatest rock'n'roll group in the world. The band was formed in 1962 by Mick Jagger (1943-) and Keith Richards (1943-), who became one of the most successful songwriting teams of all time. They were later joined by Brian Jones (1942-69) on guitar, Bill Wyman (1936-) on bass and Charlie Watts (1941-) on drums. Their music was inspired by RHYTHM AND BLUES artists such as Bo Diddley (1928-) and Muddy Waters (1915-83), and by their rock'n'roll hero, Chuck BERRY. The Stones had early No 1 hits with 'Little Red Rooster' (1964), '(I Can't Get No) Satisfaction' (1965), and 'Get off of my Cloud' (1965). While their rivals, The Beatles, were considered to be cleancut and fairly conventional at the time, the Stones wore their hair long and had an anti-establishment image. Brian Jones left the band in 1969 with a drug problem, and was found dead in his swimming pool shortly afterwards. He was replaced by Mick Taylor (1948-) until 1974, and then by Ron Wood (1947-). The band made two of their finest albums in the 1970s: *Sticky Fingers* (1971) and *Exile on Main Street* (1972). During the 1980s the group remained among the biggest live attractions in rock, and they began the 1990s with a successful international tour.

Romantic In music, the period between 1820 and 1910, an era of emotional expressiveness when European composers used their music to depict moods, images, spiritual aspirations or themes drawn from literature. The era was introduced predominantly by the late music of Beethoven. Prominent Romantic composers include Berlioz, Brahms, Chopin, Dvořák, Liszt, Mahler, Rossini, Schubert, Schumann, Tchaikovsky, Verdi and Wagner. An important aspect of romanticism was 'nationalism', particularly in Russia and Eastern Europe, in which composers drew on the musical heritage of their countries.

Ross, Diana (1944-) American soul singer who started out as a member of the most successful 'girl group' of all time, The Supremes, and who became the greatest black woman artist of the rock era. The Supremes' hits included 'Stop! In the Name of Love' (1965). In 1970 Ross went solo and hit top spot in America with 'Ain't No Mountain High Enough' and in Britain with 'Chain Reaction'.

Rossini, Gioacchino (1792-1868) Italian opera composer, known throughout Europe for his vivacious melodies and sparkling comic writing. He wrote 38 operas, both comic and serious, within 19 years, and was only 24 when he wrote his masterpiece *The Barber of Seville* (1816). After writing *William Tell* (mainly known for its overture) in 1829, Rossini composed no more operas and very little other music.

Royal Ballet National ballet company of Britain, based at the Royal Opera House, Covent Garden, London. Founded in 1931 by Dame Ninette de Valois (1898-) as the Vic-Wells Ballet. The company later became known as the Sadler's Wells Ballet before being granted its present name by Royal

OLD-TIMERS *The Rolling Stones made their debut in 1962 and are seen here 30 years later, having enjoyed possibly the longest and most consistent success of any rock group.*

AWARD-WINNING MUSICAL *Soweto children gather at a protest rally in the film* Sarafina!, *starring Whoopi Goldberg and Leleti Khumalo. The stage production in America won a Tony Award.*

Charter in 1956. Its most memorable dancers have included Sir Robert HELPMANN, Margot FONTEYN and Rudolph NUREYEV.

Saint-Saëns, Camille (1835-1921) French composer noted for his constant experimentation, which prevented him from developing a recognizable personal style. Some critics claimed that his beautiful harmonies and elegant musical forms and scintillating piano writing were superficial, but they are the reasons why his music has remained popular. His works include the opera *Samson and Delilah* (1877), the descriptive suite *The Carnival of the Animals* (1886) and his Symphony No 3 (with organ) (1886).

Sarafina! South African musical by playwright Mbongeni ▷NGEMA and composer Hugh MASEKELA, first staged in Johannesburg in 1987 and later that year in Lincoln Centre, New York. It moved to Broadway early in 1988 and played for two years before beginning a US tour. It received a Tony Award and in 1992 was made into a film directed by Darrell Roodt. (See also ▷SARAFINA! in 'Films, entertainment and the media'.)

Satie, Erik (1866-1925) French pianist and composer, chiefly of piano works and ballets. An eccentric but truly original composer, he led a bohemian life in Paris, participating in many avant-garde projects. Satie's music used simplicity of technique to achieve novel and surreal effects: his ballet *Parade* (1917) for DIAGHILEV's Ballets Russes included parts for typewriters and steamboat whistles and caused an outcry at its premiere. In the 1920s he became something of a cult figure among young French composers who were influenced by his uncluttered music.

scat A jazz vocal style, reputedly invented by Louis ARMSTRONG, in which the performer improvises meaningless sounds and syllables instead of using words.

Schoenberg, Arnold (1874-1951) Austrian composer who abandoned his earlier lush romanticism in 1908 for a harsh, dissonant style, using all 12 notes of the chromatic scale and written in no particular key. He became one of the most influential of 20th century musicians but his music provoked much public hostility. His works include *Transfigured Night* (1899) and the vast choral work *Gurrelieder* (1911), for about 400 performers.
❖ A disapproving critic coined the term 'atonal' for Schoenberg's later music. It has remained in use for music that is not written in any fixed key.

Schubert, Franz (1797-1828) Austrian composer renowned for his melodic genius. A short, shy and podgy man, Schubert lived an unconventional life in Vienna, supported by a circle of devoted friends who called themselves 'Schubertians'. He was amazingly prolific; in his brief lifetime he wrote more than 600 songs, nine symphonies and 25 major chamber works, as well as piano music, operas and choral music. His Symphony No 8, called *The Unfinished* (1822), is one of the most popular orchestral works ever written.

Schumann, Robert (1810-56) German Romantic composer with a genius for harmony. His gentle, poetic music is most clearly represented by his songs and piano pieces which reflect his love for his wife, the pianist Clara Wieck (1819-96), who was also a close friend of Johannes BRAHMS. A period of great creativity preceding and following Schumann's marriage in 1840 was followed by mental illness, and in 1854 he attempted suicide and was confined to an asylum. Among his best-known compositions are his four symphonies, the song cycle *Dichterliebe*, his piano works, especially *Carnaval* and Davidsbundlertänze and his piano concerto, one of the most often performed in the repertoire.
❖ Schumann was also an influential music critic, who hailed the publication of one of Chopin's earliest works with the words: 'Hats off, gentlemen – a genius!'

Schwarzkopf, Dame Elisabeth (1915-) German operatic soprano and lieder singer, known for her interpretations of MOZART and Richard STRAUSS. She made her first appearance at Covent Garden in London in 1947.
❖ When Schwarzkopf was a guest on BBC radio's *Desert Island Discs*, all the records she chose were her own.

Segovia, Andrés (1893-1987) Spanish guitarist who initiated the 20th century revival of the guitar as a classical instrument. He transcribed many keyboard works by Bach and other BAROQUE composers for the guitar.

Shostakovich, Dmitri (1906-75) Russian composer – one of the most prolific and widely acclaimed of the 20th century. Shostakovich wrote his first symphony in 1926 when he was only a student, making him world famous at the age of 20. Because he was influenced by Western avant-garde music, his compositions often clashed with Soviet musical policy, and Shostakovich was forced to appease the communist regime by confessing to 'unworthy stylistic tendencies'. In later life he was said to be in constant terror of offending the authorities and felt his freedom to compose as he wished greatly restricted. His works include 15 symphonies, 15 string quartets, three violin concertos, a concerto for piano, trumpet and orchestra and an opera *Lady Macbeth of Mtsensk* (1934).

Sibelius, Jean (1865-1957) Finland's leading composer. Born at a time when his country was under Russian domination, he was inspired by ancient Finnish legends to write stirring patriotic works such as *Finlandia* (1899). His greatest achievements are his seven symphonies (1899-1924) which evoke the lakes and pine forests of Finland, and a violin concerto (1903). He once said: 'It pleases me to be called an artist of nature, for nature has truly been the book of books for me.'

Simon and Garfunkel American vocal duo of the 1960s and early 1970s. With Paul Simon's thoughtful folk-rock songs and Art Garfunkel's angelic voice, they became one of the most popular duos in the history of rock. In 1970 their album *Bridge Over Troubled Water* became one of the best-selling albums of all time, but the duo split up at the peak of their career. They reunited in 1982 to give a concert in Central Park, New York.

Sinatra, Frank (1915-) American singer and actor, widely regarded as the greatest lyric interpreter of his time. He rose to fame during World War II and became the first popular singer to induce hysteria among his teenage fans. Sinatra's first stage appearance in New York in 1942 caused a sensation and led to film roles in musicals such as *On the Town* (1949). His popularity waned in the early 1950s, but he revived his film career with a dramatic role in *From Here to Eternity* (1953), for which he won an Oscar. Sinatra also made a comeback as a singer; his voice and style had mellowed on albums such as *Songs For Swingin' Lovers* (1956). More film musicals followed, including *High Society* (1956) and *Pal Joey* (1957). Among his most memorable hits are 'My Way' (1969) and 'New York, New York' (1980). Although he announced his retirement in 1971, 'Ol' Blue Eyes' gave many subsequent 'farewell' performances.

Sondheim, Stephen (1930-) American composer and lyricist, widely regarded as one of the most influential popular music composers of modern times. He wrote the lyrics for Bernstein's *West Side Story* (1957) and had his first success as both lyricist and composer with *A Funny Thing Happened on the Way to the Forum* (1962). His many successful shows include *A Little Night Music* (1973) featuring the song 'Send in the Clowns'.

soprano Highest range of the woman's singing voice, from the Italian *sopra*, meaning 'above'. Famous sopranos include Maria CALLAS, Jessye NORMAN, Joan SUTHERLAND and Kiri TE KANAWA. The term 'dramatic' soprano is applied to the powerful type of voice required for forceful roles such as those in the operas of Wagner. Mezzo-soprano is the middle range of the female voice, lower than soprano and higher than alto.

soul music Style of black American popular music combining elements of GOSPEL MUSIC and RHYTHM AND BLUES, which had its golden age in the 1960s. Sam Cooke was the first gospel singer to turn pop star; his No 1 record 'You Send Me' (1957) marked the beginning of the soul era, and he became a model for the soul stars who followed.

ELEGANT PARTNERSHIP *Phyllis Spira and Eduard Greyling formed a popular duo in CAPAB productions. They danced leading roles, particularly in classical ballets, with great distinction.*

Spira, Phyllis (1943-) South African ballerina, known for her technical brilliance, musicality and sense of humour and versatility in roles ranging from the lyrical to the dramatic. She became a soloist with the British Royal Ballet in 1961, was principal ballerina for PACT (1963-4) and CAPAB (1965-6) and toured Canada, the USA and Mexico with the Canadian National Ballet (1967-8). She returned to South Africa permanently in 1968, becoming principal ballerina for CAPAB and, after her retirement as a dancer in 1988, ballet mistress of CAPAB.

❖ Spira's most popular partnerships were with Gary Burne (1934-76) and Eduard Greyling (1948-).

spiritual Type of religious song originated by African Americans in the early 19th century.

Many of the songs allude to the days of slavery and are concerned with biblical themes of deliverance. Several spirituals have become standard pieces of music for concert singers, such as 'Nobody Knows the Trouble I've Seen' and 'Swing Low, Sweet Chariot'. Negro spirituals gained widespread popularity when they were promoted by a group called the Fisk Jubilee Singers in the 1870s, and by the American singer and actor Paul ROBESON in the late 1920s.

Springsteen, Bruce (1949-) American rock singer and songwriter, known as 'The Boss'. In 1974 the American critic Jon Landau (who later became Springsteen's manager) wrote the now-famous words, 'I have seen the future of rock'n'roll – it's called Bruce Springsteen'. Springsteen lived up to this prediction with energetic performances and thoughtful songs about the state of America. His most successful albums were *Born To Run* (1975) and *Born In The USA* (1984) which sold more than 12 million copies.

Staff, Frank (1918-71) South African ballet dancer and choreographer whose first success was with the Ballet Rambert in London. He later danced with the Sadler's Wells Ballet and various British, French, and American companies, choreographed many West End of London and Broadway theatrical productions and directed an award-winning film *All Halloween*. After returning to South Africa in the 1960s he was choreographer for the University of Cape Town Ballet Company, the PACT ballet company and the Brian Brooke Company, for which he produced many musicals. His ground-breaking ballet *Raka* (1967) was based on the poem by NP van Wyk ▷LOUW to music by Graham Newcater. Several of his ballets have remained in the repertoire of South African companies.

❖ Veronica Paeper (1944-), artistic director and choreographer of the Capab Ballet Company, was trained by and married to Frank Staff. She revived some of his ballets after his death and choreographed and produced many successful works of her own, notably *Hamlet*, for which she received an Artes Award in 1993 and which was staged in London that year.

Stockhausen, Karlheinz (1928-) German avant-garde composer and theorist. His *Gesang der Junglinge* (1955-6) was the first and one of the greatest masterpieces of electronic music; it combines electronic sounds with the voice of a boy soprano and has a mystical streak which often runs through his music. In later years he concentrated on dramatic music and opera and experimented with weird combinations of instrumental and vocal sound, including banging, singing, speaking babbling and whispering.

❖ A seven-evening musical theatre work called *Light* which Stockhausen began in 1977 is scheduled for completion in 2002.

RARE FIDDLE *This Stradivarius violin came from the workshop of instrument maker Antonio Stradivari. His surviving violins are now regarded as virtually beyond price because of their incomparable tone and projection.*

Stradivarius Any stringed instrument made by Antonio Stradivari (1644-1737), who was born in Cremona, Italy. Stradivari is generally considered to be the greatest violin maker of all time and his instruments are still highly prized by performers today. He also made superb violas and cellos.

❖ A violin-maker whose instruments today rank with those of Stradivari was Giuseppe Guarneri del Gesù (1698-1744).

Strauss II, Johann (1825-99) Austrian composer, also known as Johann Strauss the Younger. He was the son of Johann Strauss I (1804-49), a famous composer of light music known as 'Father of the Waltz'. Strauss II was hailed as 'The Waltz King' when his dance music became fashionable all over Europe. He wrote 400 waltzes, including 'The Blue Danube' (1867), and many polkas, mazurkas and marches. He also composed the popular operetta *Die Fledermaus* (1874).

Strauss, Richard (1864-1949) German composer and conductor. He wrote eight symphonic poems, nine operas, including *Der Rosenkavalier* (1911), one of the most popular operas written in the 20th century, and *Also Sprach Zarathustra* (1896), a piece for orchestra, part of which was later used to great effect in the science-fiction film *2001: A Space Odyssey* (1968). His beautiful *Four Last Songs* were composed at the age of 84.

Stravinsky, Igor (1882-1971) Russian-born American composer who was one of the

BALLROOM FAVOURITE *The waltz is a flowing dance in rapid triple time, dating from the 18th century. With the help of composer Johann Strauss II (inset), the dance became universally popular in the 19th century.*

greatest musical innovators of the 20th century. He founded his international reputation with his music for DIAGHILEV's Ballets Russes, beginning with the ballet *The Firebird* (1910), but his work was not readily accepted. The harsh and discordant score for *The Rite of Spring* (1913) caused a riot when it was first performed in Paris. Later pioneering works include the oratorio *Oedipus Rex* (1927), the *Symphony of Psalms* (1930) and the opera *The Rake's Progress* (1951).

Streisand, Barbra (1942-) American singer and actress, one of the world's most successful performers. She sprang to fame in the Broadway musical *Funny Girl* (1964), in which she played the role of entertainer Fanny Brice. She repeated the role in the film of 1968, which won her an Oscar. Among her later hits were songs such as 'The Way We Were' (1974) and 'Evergreen' (1977).

❖ Streisand wrote, produced, directed and starred in the film *Yentl* (1983).

Sutherland, Dame Joan (1926-) Australian operatic SOPRANO, renowned for her vocal range. Her coloratura voice enabled her to excel in *bel canto*, a florid style of singing that demands great agility and is exemplified in the operas of Vincenzo Bellini (1801-35) and Gaetano Donizetti (1797-1848). She was coached by her husband, the conductor Richard Bonynge (1930-), and with him helped to popularize Bellini and Donizetti masterpieces. She retired in 1990.

swing Style of jazz popular in the 1930s and 1940s, characterized by a lively rhythm suitable for dancing. Swing was played in an organized fashion by big bands, as opposed to the improvised jazz played by smaller groups. The 'Swing Era', which had its heyday between 1935 and 1944, featured the bands of Count BASIE, Duke ELLINGTON, Benny GOODMAN and Glenn MILLER.

Tchaikovsky, Peter Ilyich (1840-93) Russian composer whose Romantic music expressed the emotional extremes he felt, from brooding melancholy to a magical sense of elation. He wrote six symphonies, three piano concertos, a violin concerto and ten operas, including *Eugene Onegin* (1878). His ballets *Swan Lake* (1875), *Sleeping Beauty* (1888) and *The Nutcracker* (1892) are among the foundation works of classical dance. Tchaikovsky also wrote the rousing *1812 Overture* (1880) which incorporates the 'Marseillaise' and the Tsarist Russian national anthem – and, sometimes, a cannon in the orchestra.

❖ Biographers have speculated whether Tchaikovsky, whose death was attributed to cholera, in fact committed suicide.

Te Kanawa, Dame Kiri (1944-) New Zealand singer, one of the leading sopranos of modern times. She arrived in England in 1965 and joined the Royal Opera three years later. Her first major success was as the Countess in Mozart's *Marriage of Figaro* in 1971. Te Kanawa sang in BERNSTEIN's 1985 recording of *West Side Story*, and topped the pop charts with the Rugby World Cup theme song 'World in Union' in 1991.

❖ In 1995 Dame Kiri, herself a rugby fan, performed in South Africa – that year's venue for the Rugby World Cup.

Temmingh, Roelof (1946-) South African composer who has specialized in music incorporating sounds generated by a computer and electronic devices, but whose more conventional opera *Enoch, the Prophet*, incorporating traditional African choruses, has won him a wider audience outside of academic circles. Temmingh was born in Amsterdam but came to South Africa with his family in 1958. In 1972 he attended the International Course for New Music in Darmstad, Germany, where the teachers included STOCKHAUSEN. Since 1973 he has lectured in composition and musicology at the University of Stellenbosch.

tenor Highest normal range of the male voice, apart from ALTO. The *Heldentenor*, or heroic tenor, is one with a powerful enough voice to carry over a large orchestra, as in the operas of Richard WAGNER.

Tippett, Sir Michael (1905-) British composer who, with Benjamin BRITTEN, led the revival in British music after World War II. Tippett was greatly influenced by jazz music and the composers PURCELL and STRAVINSKY. He won international success with the poignant oratorio *A Child of Our Time* (1941). His other works include five operas, some with librettos written by himself, four symphonies and several concertos.

Toscanini, Arturo (1867-1957) Italian conductor, renowned for his imperious manner and fiery interpretations of Beethoven, Verdi and Wagner. Because he was extremely short sighted, he committed all scores to his phenomenal musical memory. He was artistic director of La Scala, Milan's opera house, at various times between 1898 and 1929, and of the Metropolitan Opera, New York (1908-15); and conductor of the New York Philharmonic Orchestra (1928-36).

Turner, Tina (1938-) American rock and soul singer. She was discovered by guitarist Ike Turner in 1956, when she joined his rhythm-and-blues band and later became his wife and co-star, recording hits such as 'River Deep, Mountain High' (1966). Their marriage broke up in 1976 and Tina Turner went solo. She became one of the biggest stars of the 1980s with her album *Private Dancer* (1984).

RUGBY FAN *Famous operatic soprano Kiri Te Kanawa topped the pop charts with the Rugby World Cup theme song in 1991 – and she avidly enjoys watching the game.*

van Wyk, Arnold (1916-83) South African composer, the first to win wide recognition internationally. Born in Calvinia, Northern Cape, he began improvising at the piano when he was six. In 1938 he won a scholarship to the Royal Academy of Music in London and later worked for the BBC. During his years in Britain he composed a symphony which was conducted by Sir Adrian Boult in a broadcast performance and his *Saudade* for violin and orchestra was performed at a promenade concert at the Albert Hall. After his return to South Africa in 1946 he lectured in music, first at the University of Cape Town and later at Stellenbosch. Outstanding among his works is the *Missa in illo tempore* for unaccompanied choirs composed to commemorate the tercentenary of Stellenbosch in 1979.

Vaughan Williams, Ralph (1872-1958) English composer who became one of the leaders of the 20th-century revival of English music. Vaughan Williams was greatly influenced by folk tunes and Tudor music, as can be heard in his *Fantasia on a Theme of Thomas Tallis*, for strings (1910). His works include nine symphonies, among them *Sinfonia Antarctica* (Number 7), based on his score for the film *Scott of the Antarctic* (1948).

Verdi, Giuseppe (1813-1901) Italian composer and one of the masters of Italian opera. After being rejected as a student by the Milan Conservatory in 1832 for being insufficiently talented, he studied privately. His first opera *Oberto* (1839) was only a moderate success, but fame came three years later with *Nabucco*. With his gifts for melody, drama and orchestral colour, Verdi wrote a series of popular operas, including *Rigoletto* (1851), *La Traviata* (1853) and *Aïda* (1871). By 1882 Verdi had retired to work on his beloved farm, but he was tempted back to composition by two Shakespeare adaptations – *Otello* (1887) and *Falstaff* (1893) – which were in a more contemporary style, reflecting the influence of WAGNER and which are widely regarded as his masterpieces. The patriotic fervour of his early operas linked him closely with the movement for Italian unification; he became a symbol for Italian liberty and died a national hero.

Vivaldi, Antonio (1678-1741) Italian virtuoso violinist and leading BAROQUE composer. After entering the priesthood he was nicknamed the 'Red Priest' because of the colour of his hair. Energetic and prolific, Vivaldi wrote 447 concertos, 46 operas and many works for the church. By the time he had written his best-known work, a set of four violin concertos entitled *The Four Seasons* (1725), he was recognized and admired throughout Europe. In 1741 he left Venice, where he had been musical director at a conservatory, for Vienna, where he died in obscure circumstances.

Wagner, Richard (1813-83) (VAHG-ner) German composer who revolutionized opera with his richly expressive music. Wagner dreamed of merging words, drama and music into a total work of art, with a series of vast, highly dramatic works which he called 'music dramas'. He wrote his own texts, and used the orchestra to help tell the story by writing a score of continuous music (rather than the traditional division into arias and recitatives) and by developing a device called the *leitmotif* – a recurring musical theme identified with a particular person, emotion, event or idea. His ideal of 'music drama' inspired generations of composers including Claude DEBUSSY and Richard STRAUSS. Wagner's best-known composition is his monumental cycle of four operas (or three music dramas and a prelude, as he termed it), *Der Ring des Nibelungen*. This is an epic based on German mythology which lasts about 15 hours and is intended to be performed over four successive nights. It was written over a period of 25 years. *Der Ring* was first performed at Wagner's own opera house at Bayreuth in 1876. Other works include *The Flying Dutchman* (1843), *Tristan and Isolde* (1865) and *Die Meistersinger von Nürnberg* (1868).

❖ Only Wagner's works are performed in the Bayreuth Festival Theatre which has become an exclusive shrine to the composer and draws audiences from all parts of the world.

Waller, Fats (Thomas) (1904-43) American jazz composer, pianist and entertainer, remembered for his exuberant performances. He was a prolific composer of shows and hit songs such as 'Ain't Misbehavin'' (1929).

Waters, Muddy (McKinley Morganfield) (1915-83) American BLUES singer, guitarist and composer. In the 1940s he established himself as 'King of the Chicago Blues' with his unique moaning and shouting style. He was the greatest single influence on the British blues boom of the 1960s, inspiring enthusiasts such as the ROLLING STONES. His songs include 'Hoochie Coochie Man' (1954) and 'I've Got my Mojo Working' (1957).

Williams, John (1941-) Australian guitarist, based in Britain from 1952. He and fellow guitarist Julian BREAM helped to re-establish the classical guitar as a solo instrument.

Wonder, Stevie (1950-) American singer, songwriter and multi-instrumentalist who has been the most successful black recording artist of the rock era. Blind from birth, Wonder was a child prodigy and joined MOTOWN Records in 1962 as 'Little Stevie Wonder', when he had an American No 1 hit single with 'Fingertips'. In the late 1960s Wonder began to cowrite his own material and to experiment with electronic technology, pioneering the use of the synthesizer in black music on songs such as 'Superstition' (1972). In 1983 he wrote one of his most popular songs, 'I Just Called To Say I Love You' for the film *The Lady in Red*.

Wynette, Tammy (1942-) Country singer who has been hailed as 'The First Lady of Country Music'. She is renowned for her impassioned songs about loneliness, which are infused with her bitter experience of a string of stormy marriages and health problems. She is best known for her songs 'Stand By Your Man' and 'D.I.V.O.R.C.E.' (both 1968).

MULTI-TALENTED *Born blind, Stevie Wonder began making waves at the age of 12 when his first LP and single were No 1 hits. He has been making music – and numerous hits – ever since.*

SPORT AND LEISURE

Ever since the ancient Greeks held the first Olympic Games, individuals and teams have enjoyed pitting their strengths and skills against each other in competitive sports. Every age has produced its sporting personalities and national champions. Ardent fans urge them on to set new standards of excellence, sharing the drama and the emotion of great sporting moments.

DOUBLE VICTORY *Muhammad Ali (left) beat Joe Frazier in 1974 on his way to regaining the world title. As Cassius Clay he defeated Britain's Henry Cooper (inset) in 1963, despite being floored in the fifth round.*

Agassi, Andre (1970-) US tennis player who won the Wimbledon singles title in 1992, the US Open singles championship in 1994 and the Australian Open in 1995. Agassi built up a cult following among young people attracted by his appearance and style – flashy tennis clothing and aggressive play. He is known for his charm and good manners on the court.

Albertyn, Greg (1972-) South African motorcyclist and triple motocross world champion, who left school in Std 8 to pursue a career in Belgium. He won the 125 cc world championship in 1992, and the 250 cc world championship in 1993 and 1994, before moving to the USA to campaign in the supercross series in 1995. He is known for his strongly-held Christian beliefs.

❖ Motocross is a motorcycle race across very rough ground; in supercross, motorcyclists compete over an indoor obstacle course.

Ali, Muhammad (1942-) American heavyweight boxer who proclaimed himself 'the Greatest' and proved it by dominating the world championship scene between 1964 and 1979. Sensationally, he first won the title at the age of 22 by defeating Sonny Liston. Born Cassius Marcellus Clay in Louisville, Kentucky, he was known as the 'Louisville Lip' for his repartee and boasts of being able to 'float like a butterfly and sting like a bee'. During a colourful and controversial career he joined the militant 'Black Muslim' sect and changed his name accordingly. In 1967 Ali became a rallying point for opposition to the Vietnam War when he refused to serve in the US Army – for which he was deprived of his world title. He returned to the ring in 1970 and regained the title four years later. Ali made his last winning comeback in 1978, when he beat Leon Spinks. He retired in 1981 and has suffered for some years from Parkinson's disease.

American football National sport of the USA, played by two teams of 11 whose aim is to pass or run the oval ball over their opponents' goal line, for a touchdown, worth six points. A kick through the goal, or touchdown conversion, earns one point, and a field goal – kicked like a penalty in rugby union, but taken as an option by the attacking side – earns three points. Professional teams have a squad of 45 players to choose from, with different teams for offence and defence, and specialist kickers. The season reaches a climax each January with the SUPER BOWL. The game was first played in Canada in 1874.

America's Cup International yachting contest held every three or four years culminating in the best of seven races between two ocean-going yachts, the defender and the challenger. The yachts have a crew of 11 and are about 20 m long. Countries wishing to challenge the cup-holders take part in a series of elimination races. The contest is named after the schooner *America*, which beat Britain's best in a race round the Isle of Wight in 1851. The cup stayed in US hands for the next 132 years. Then, in 1983, the Australian yacht *Australia II* beat the US defender *Liberty*. However, the USA won the trophy back in 1987 with *Stars and Stripes* and retained it in 1992 with *America III*. In 1995 the cup was won by the New Zealand yacht *Black Magic*, whose skipper, Peter Blake, started a craze for red socks.

❖ In 1990, after a controversial legal battle, the New York appeals court ruled that, although *Stars and Stripes* was a catamaran, it had not violated the original race rules – which stated that the competing yachts should be monohulls.

angling Fishing with rod and line which takes three main forms. In game fishing, or fly fishing – mainly for trout or salmon – fish are attracted to the hook with lures or flies. Flies are known as 'wet', 'dry' or 'nymphs'. Nymphs and wet flies are fished under water and resemble tiny water creatures. Dry flies are fished on the surface of the water and are meant to look like insects alighting momentarily. In coarse fishing – for freshwater fish other than those of the salmon family – the hook is baited with food (for example, maggots, worms or bread) and is held on the bottom with a weight or suspended just below the surface by a float. Teams compete in coarse-fishing contests for the total weight of fish caught. Sea fishing from a beach, pier or boat generally uses the same techniques as coarse fishing. It may yield anything from a black steenbras weighing less than 3 kg to a shark weighing half a ton.

archery Olympic sport in which a competitor fires arrows at a fixed target. There are two recognized divisions – the Olympic bow (previously the recurve bow) and the compound bow. A standard target round consists of 144 arrows fired from various distances. Men shoot from 90 m, 70 m, 50 m and 30 m, whereas women shoot from 70 m, 60 m, 50 m and 30 m. The South African Archery Association was formed in 1949.

Ashe, Arthur (1943-93) US tennis player, famous as the first black man to win the Wimbledon championship. He was also a widely respected social activist. Early in his career he faced racial discrimination but eventually broke all barriers to win both the US national singles championship and the US Open championship in 1968. He turned professional in 1969 and defeated Jimmy Connors in the men's singles final at Wimbledon in 1975. After having suffered the first of several heart attacks at the age of 36, he was forced to retire in 1980. Eight years later he discovered he had contracted AIDS from a blood transfusion during heart surgery – a fact which he announced publicly in 1992. He spent much of his remaining years campaigning to lessen the stigma attached to the disease.

❖ Arthur Ashe was a founder member of Artists and Athletes Against Apartheid; he played in South Africa in 1973 with the proviso that there would be no racial segregation at his matches.

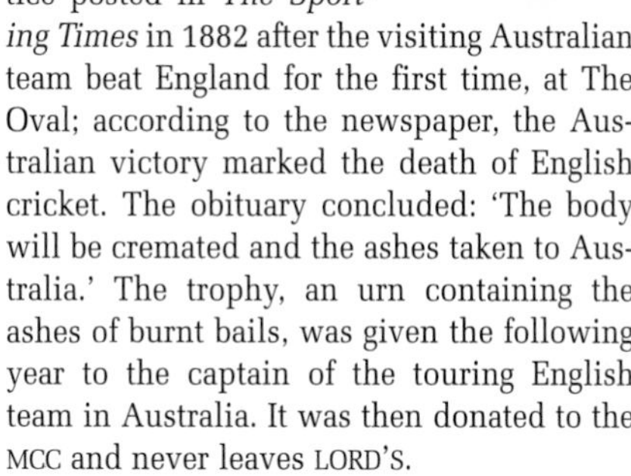
REST IN PEACE *The ashes of England's cricketing pride repose in this urn.*

Ashes, The Trophy in a cricket contest played between England and Australia, usually consisting of a series of five Test matches. Its name derives from a mock obituary notice posted in *The Sporting Times* in 1882 after the visiting Australian team beat England for the first time, at The Oval; according to the newspaper, the Australian victory marked the death of English cricket. The obituary concluded: 'The body will be cremated and the ashes taken to Australia.' The trophy, an urn containing the ashes of burnt bails, was given the following year to the captain of the touring English team in Australia. It was then donated to the MCC and never leaves LORD'S.

athletics Sports encompassing track and field events, cross-country and road running, and walking, which are widely regarded as the leading events of the OLYMPIC GAMES. Track and field events also have their own world championships. Road events include the MARATHON, run over 42,195 km.

❖ Egypt provides the first known evidence of organized running, in *c*3800 BC, and athletic prowess was highly valued at the ancient Olympic Games, in Greece. Modern athletics contests date from 1812, when the Royal Military College at Sandhurst in Berkshire, UK, founded its annual sports day. Five years later the world's first athletics club, the Necton Guild, was established in Norfolk.

Bacher, Ali (1942-) Former South African cricket captain who became one of the game's leading administrators. The son of Lithuanian immigrants, he made his first-class debut aged 17, scored 679 runs in 12 Tests, and led South Africa to a 4-0 series whitewash over Australia in 1970. He orchestrated a series of 'rebel' tours during South Africa's isolation due to ▷APARTHEID. But, faced by violent protests against Mike Gatting's England 'rebels' of 1990, he renounced this route and campaigned vigorously to take cricket to South Africa's black townships.

backgammon Board game for two players in which counters are moved according to the throw of two dice. The board is divided into two identical sides, one for each player, consisting of 12 elongated triangles, called points, divided by a central strip, the bar. Players aim to manoeuvre their own set of 15 counters from one triangle to another around the board, without being sent back to the start or being blocked by their opponent, and so be the first to take them off. When gambling, a doubling dice can be used by each player alternately to double the stakes.

badminton Court game, played as singles or doubles, in which players volley a shuttlecock (a cork stub with feathers) over a high net with light, strung rackets. Points may be scored only by the server, who forfeits the serve when he or she loses a rally. A game runs to 15 points or, in women's singles, 11. A match is decided over three games.

❖ The game originated in the 1870s at Badminton – seat of the dukes of Beaufort.

Bailey, Gary (1958-) South African goalkeeper who played football for the University of the Witwatersrand in Johannesburg before joining England's Manchester United in 1978. He played 294 league games for United, winning FA CUP medals in 1983 and 1985. He won two full caps for England, against Ireland and Mexico, and was a member of their 1986 World Cup squad in Mexico. Bailey's career in England ended in 1987 after a serious knee injury. He returned to South Africa and spent two seasons (1988-9) with KAIZER CHIEFS, before retiring for good. Again he followed in the footsteps of his father Roy, who played in goal for Ipswich Town in the 1960s, by opting for a career in sports broadcasting.

Ballesteros, Seve (Severiano) (1957-) Spanish golfer who first won the British Open Championship in 1979 and became the leading European player in the early 1980s. He played a major part in Europe's Ryder Cup successes against the USA. He won the US Masters event in 1980 and 1983, as well as two more British Open Championships, in 1984 and 1988.

Ballington, Kork (1951-) South African motorcyclist who won world titles four times in the late 1970s. He clinched the 250 cc championship in 1978 and the 350 cc title the following year. Ballington, who competed in more than 230 races worldwide riding Grand Prix and Superbikes, notched up 31 victories in Grand Prix races between 1976 and 1980. His world championship victories were all achieved on a Kawasaki.

Bannister, Sir Roger (1929-) British athlete who was the first man to run a mile in under four minutes. He did so on 6 May 1954, at Oxford, clocking 3 min 59,4 sec for the distance. A medical student at the time, Bannister believed that there was no physical reason to prevent a man or woman from breaking the psychological barrier of the four-minute mile.

Barlow, Eddie (1940-) South African cricket all-rounder noted for his competitiveness. He was an opening batsman who took risks and a medium-pace bowler who specialized in breaking stubborn partnerships. He played his first Test against New Zealand in Durban in 1961 and in his total of 30 Tests scored 2 516 runs at an average of 45,74 and took 40 wickets. He played county cricket for Derbyshire in England for many years. At home, Barlow scored 6 413 Currie Cup runs and took 264 wickets. He also played rugby for Transvaal. He stood as a political candidate for the Progressive Federal Party in Simon's Town, and was sports ambassador to London in the early 1980s. He returned to South Africa in 1987 and coached Free State and Transvaal before retiring to tend his Cape wine farm in 1994.

RECORD MILER *Roger Bannister hits the tape at the end of his record-setting sub-four-minute mile at the Oxford University track in 1954.*

HARD-HITTING HEROES *Baseball fans in America have been thrilled by the exploits of legendary batters such as (left to right): Ted Williams, Joe DiMaggio, Babe Ruth and Jackie Robinson.*

baseball US sport, developed in the mid-19th century from the old English game of rounders. It is played nine-a-side on a 27,4 m (90 ft) square 'diamond' infield with a large outfield. The batter stands in front of the 'home plate', one point of the diamond, with 'bases' at the three other points. At the middle of the diamond is a small mound from which the pitcher throws the ball. The batter's aim is to hit the ball and run round the bases – right back to the home plate, if possible, to score a home run. Alternatively, he may stop at any base, and complete his run when another batter hits the ball. There are a number of ways in which the fielding side can get a batter out, and when three batters are out, that innings ends. Each side has nine innings. American professional baseball is played in two leagues, and the season culminates in a feverishly followed world series between the respective champions.

basketball Five-a-side court game in which opposing teams hand-pass or dribble, by bouncing, a ball and try to throw it through the opposing team's basket. A 'basket' earns from one to three points depending on how it is made. A game can be divided into two periods of 20 minutes or four 12-minute quarters, and a team may have up to seven substitutes. The baskets are fixed at a height of 3 m to a backboard at each end of the court. The world's most renowned basketball team, the Harlem Globetrotters of New York, was founded in 1927 to play exhibition games.

Becker, Boris (1967-) German tennis star who became the youngest Wimbledon men's singles champion when he won the title in 1985 at the age of 17 (and was the first unseeded player to achieve this). He retained the title in 1986 and regained it in 1989. A powerful serve-and-volley player, he led Germany to their first ever Davis Cup triumph in 1988.

Betrix, Gonda (1943-) South African show-jumper whose career spanned almost four decades. As Gonda Butters, she started her equestrian career at the age of 14 in the late 1950s and quickly achieved an impressive string of victories at home and abroad. Betrix won the FEI (Fédération Equestre Internationale) world title four times, the South African Derby six times and the national championship on ten occasions. She won the State President's Sport Award in 1974. In 1992, she became one of only two South African riders ever to have competed in showjumping events at the Olympic Games.

billiards Game played with one red and two white balls on a baize-covered table measuring 3,7 m by 1,8 m with six pockets. Players strike a cue ball (white or spot white) and score points by potting another ball, going 'in-off' (sending the cue ball into a pocket off another ball) or making a 'cannon' (hitting both the other balls with the cue ball). A player continues to build up 'breaks' until he or she fails to score, when it becomes the other player's turn. Games are usually played up to a certain number of points.

❖ Famous players of the game have included Mozart, who composed mentally while relaxing at billiards, and Mary, Queen of Scots, who was greatly distressed to be parted from her billiards table while she was imprisoned.

blackjack Casino card game based on pontoon, or vingt-et-un (twenty-one), in which the 'bank' (dealer) deals out cards – each of which has a value in points – to players round the table. The object is to get nearer to a total of 21 points, without exceeding it, than the dealer.

Blankers-Koen, Fanny (Francina) (1918-) Sprinter, hurdler, jumper and pentathalon competitor, one of the greatest all-rounders among women athletes. Representing the Netherlands in the 1946 European championships, the 1948 Olympics and the 1950 European championships, she won a total of nine gold medals. Between 1942 and 1951 she set many world records.

bobsleighing Winter sport in which a two or four-man crew sit in a sleigh and shoot down a twisting track of solid ice with steeply banked bends at speeds of more than 145 km/h. The driver steers the bob by moving the front runners by means of ropes or a type of steering wheel. The brakeman at the back uses the brakes only to stop the bob at the end of a run or to correct skids. In a four-man bob, the two middle men help to steer by shifting their weight at bends. The first run was built at St Moritz, Switzerland – home of the Cresta Run – in 1904.

❖ Bobsleighing acquired its name from the way in which members of early teams 'bobbed' their bodies back and forth in order to increase the speed of their sleighs at the start of a run.

Border, Allan (1955-) Australian all-round cricketer who captained his country in 93 of his 156 Tests, scoring a world record 11 174 runs at an average of 50,56. Known for his courage and tenacity at the crease, he was also a reliable slow left-arm bowler, taking 39 Test wickets – including 7/46 against the West Indies in 1989. Border retired from Test cricket in May 1994.

Borg, Björn (1956-) Swedish tennis player who set a modern record by winning five successive Wimbledon men's singles titles between 1976 and 1980. In a period dominated by serve-and-volley champions, Borg reigned supreme on grass with a counter-attacking baseline game based on topspin, demonstrating an ice-cool temperament. He excelled on European clay, and won the first of his six French Opens in 1974 at the age of 18. In 1975 he led Sweden to their first success in the DAVIS CUP tournament.

Botha, Naas (1958-) Springbok flyhalf who spent most of his record-breaking career either much-loved or much-maligned. A prodigious kicker, Botha made his debut for Northern Transvaal at 19 in 1977 and first played for South Africa against the South American Jaguars in 1980. He played in 28 Tests for South Africa, including eight as captain, and scored a South African record of 312 points in internationals, including a world record of 18 drop goals. Botha turned out in 11 Currie Cup finals and led Northern Transvaal to victory on four occasions. He scored a record 2 511 points in 123 Currie Cup matches. After leading the Springboks on their tour of England and France in 1992, he retired from the game.

❖ Botha had a trial as kicker for the Dallas Cowboys AMERICAN FOOTBALL team in 1983 and during South African summers played professional rugby in Italy.

Botham, Ian (1955-) English cricketer who made his Test debut in 1977 and broke many all-round records with his big hitting and penetrating swing bowling. He became the first player to score a century and take more than 10 wickets in a Test, hitting 114 and taking 6/58 and 7/48 against India in Bombay in 1980. A controversial and colourful character, known as 'Beefy' for his strapping physique, Botham was often in the news for his flamboyant off-field behaviour. He is well remembered for his role in the 1981 Ashes Test matches, when his batting and bowling feats almost single-handedly snatched victory from the Australian team.

bowls Game played with biased bowls (large balls) sometimes called woods, which take a curved path when rolled. A bowls game ranges from singles to four-a-side. In singles, each player has four bowls; in fours, each has two. A small white ball known as a jack is the target. A point is scored for each bowl nearer the jack than the nearest of an opponent's.

boxing Fighting with gloved fists inside a raised ring. Boxers fight in weight divisions, ranging from strawweight (47,627 kg) to heavyweight (over 81 kg). In amateur boxing, a major Olympic sport, competitors fight three three-minute rounds. Lengths of professional fights vary, with a maximum of 12 three-minute rounds for title bouts. A fight may be won by a knockout, when a floored boxer is unable to get to his feet during a count of 10 seconds, on points after it has 'gone the distance', meaning the maximum time has elapsed, or by a technical knockout, through the intervention of the referee.

❖ Boxing gave birth to the phrase 'the real McCoy', or genuine article. It was coined in the USA by Charles 'Kid' McCoy, the world welterweight champion in 1896, who used it to distinguish himself from another fighter named Al McCoy.

Bradman, Sir Donald (1908-) Australian cricketer, known as 'the Don', regarded by some as the greatest batsman of all time. In a career which lasted from 1927 to 1948, he scored 28 067 runs at an average of 95,14; in Tests he made 6 996 runs at an average of 99,96. His highest score was 452 not out for New South Wales against Queensland in the 1929-30 season; his highest score in a Test was 334 against England in 1930 – both world records at the time. He captained Australia in five series of Test matches.

Brand, Esther (1926-) South African athlete who as Esther van Heerden broke the world record for the high jump in 1951 and went on to win a gold medal in the event at the 1952 Olympic Games in Helsinki with a leap of 1,69 m. This turned out to be the last Olympic gold medal won by a South African before the country's suspension from international contests. Brand first showed her potential when breaking the Western Province record by 12,7 cm at the age of 14. She won national titles in the high jump from 1938 to 1948 and in 1946 also won the national title in discus-throwing.

Budd, Zola (1966-) South African known for competing barefoot as a long-distance runner. In 1984 she took British citizenship and was a finalist in the 3 000 m at the Los Angeles Olympics, in which she accidently tripped the American favourite Mary Dekker (later Dekker Slaney) who fell and retired from the race; Budd ended in 7th place. She won the world cross-country titles in 1985 and 1986. She returned to South Africa in 1988, married, and as Zola Pieterse came 4th in the 1993 world cross-country race.

SCORING POINTS *Naas Botha, renowned for his kicking prowess, takes a shot at the goalposts in fine style. He captained South Africa against the touring Australians in 1992.*

FINAL RUN *Donald Campbell was killed on Coniston Water in the Lake District in 1967, when his speedboat* Bluebird *somersaulted and broke up at almost 530 km/h.*

Campbell, Sir Malcolm (1885-1949) and Donald (1921-67) British father and son racing-car and speedboat drivers. Malcolm was the first person to hold both the world land and water speed records at the same time and Donald was the second. Malcolm called his boats *Bluebird* and his son used the same name for his boats and cars. Malcolm broke the land speed record nine times between 1924 and 1935 and was the first to smash the 482 km/h (300 mph) barrier. He broke the water speed record three times between 1937 and 1939. Donald broke the water speed record seven times between 1955 and 1957 and the land speed record once when he broke through the 643 km/h (400 mph) barrier, on the Lake Eyre salt flats, South Australia, in 1964.
❖ In 1929 Sir Malcolm attempted to break the world land speed record at Verneukpan in the northern Cape, South Africa. The pebbles and rocks of the pan tore *Bluebird's* tyres to shreds, and at the last moment he learnt that Henry Segrave had pushed the speed to 373,2 km/h – an impossible target at Veneukpan's altitude. Campbell settled instead for breaking the 8 km (5 mile) and 5 km world records.

Campese, David (1962-) Flamboyant Australian rugby union player who scored a record number of tries in international games as wing-threequarter. Regularly in the headlines from the time he made his Test debut against New Zealand in 1982 aged 19, he inspired Australia to their 1991 World Cup victory, when he was joint leading scorer in the tournament with six tries. He had scored 63 tries in 92 Tests up to the middle of 1995.

chess Game that originated in India or China in about the 6th century. It is played on a checkered board by (usually) two players, each starting with 16 especially designed pieces that have fixed restrictions on their movement. The object of the game is to enforce the opposition's principal piece, the King, into a position, known as checkmate, in which it is unable to escape capture.

Christodoulou, Stan (1944-) Boxing referee who is the only South African to have been referee of a world title fight outside the country. He also was the youngest referee ever to decide a world title bout, a feat he accomplished at age 29 in the match between Arnold Taylor and Romeo Anaya in Johannesburg in 1973. He became executive director of the South African National Boxing Control Board in 1979. By early 1995 Christodoulou had officiated in 66 world title fights in 16 countries.

Coe, Sebastian (1956-) British runner in the middle distance category who was the first athlete to win the Olympic 1 500 m twice, in 1980 and 1984. Coe set an unrivalled nine world records between 1979 and 1981, including records for the 800 m, 1 500 m and the mile. He retired in 1990 and in 1992 became a Conservative MP.

Coetzee, Gerrie (1955-) South Africa's first world heavyweight boxing champion. He won the title in September 1983, knocking out Michael Dokes in the 10th round of their contest in Virginia, USA. He had previously failed in two title bids against John Tate and Mike Weaver. However, the 'Boksburg Bomber', as he was known to fans, lost his first title defence against Greg Page at Sun City. In the late 1980s, he switched to promoting and at one stage was agent for South African world champion Dingaan Thobela.

Comaneci, Nadia (1961-) Romanian gymnast who, at the age of 14, became the first person to attain a perfect score of ten at the Olympic Games, which she did in Montreal in 1976. She escaped from the ▷CEAUSESCU regime in 1987 and eventually acquired the status of a refugee in the USA.

Comrades Marathon South Africa's premier annual road race, an 89 km stretch between Durban and Pietermaritzburg which is run in one direction one year and the other direction the next year. It was started in 1921 by engine driver Vic Clapham as a way of honouring his fallen friends from World War I. The first race attracted only 34 participants, but by the 1990s there were about 12 000. The first winner, Bill Rowan, racing in flimsy tennis shoes, covered the distance in 8 hr 59 min. Legendary nine-times winner Bruce FORDYCE's record of 5 hr 27 min 18 sec was set in 1984. Frith van der Merwe set the women's record of 5 hr 54 min 43 sec on her way to finishing 11th overall in 1989.

Connolly, Maureen (1934-69) Diminutive US tennis player known as 'Little Mo'. She won the US Open singles title in 1951 at the age of 16, and two years later became the first female player to achieve the GRAND SLAM. She won the Wimbledon singles championship three times (1952-4), retiring a short while later after crushing a leg in a riding accident.

Craven, Danie (1911-93) Springbok rugby scrumhalf, flyhalf and captain who became a legendary figure in South African rugby administration and was known throughout the world as 'Doc'. Craven played 16 Tests for South Africa, four as captain against New Zealand in 1937 and the British Lions the following year. He became president of the

South African Rugby Board in 1949 and, in a reign that spoke volumes for his tenacity and leadership style, stayed at the helm of the game in the country until his death. He had a lengthy association with the University of Stellenbosch, arriving as an 18-year-old and staying there for 63 years. He moulded the university rugby team into one of the best club sides in the country. In his time at Stellenbosch, nine Springbok captains, including Craven himself, were 'Matie' (the university's nickname) products.

❖ The Craven Week, launched in 1964 to honour Danie Craven, is an annual tournament for talented schoolboy rugby players and regarded as 'a junior CURRIE CUP'. Some 25 teams are fielded and the week's activities include coaching sessions and talent-spotting by clubs and provincial unions.

cricket Eleven-a-side game in which a hard leather ball is bowled from a crease, or line, at one end of a 20 m long pitch to a batsman defending the wicket at the other, who then attempts to score runs. The object is to score more runs than the opposing team. Six balls bowled in succession constitute an 'over'. If the ball dislodges at least one of the two bails set on the three stumps of the wicket, the batsman is bowled out. Other ways of dismissal include being caught (when the ball is caught by a player after it is hit but before it touches the ground) and lbw, or leg before wicket (when a ball that, in the umpire's opinion, would have hit the stumps hits a batsman). A batsman can also be 'stumped' if he plays at the ball, misses, and is out of his crease when the wicketkeeper strikes the stumps with the ball in his hand, or by throwing the ball. Batsmen score four runs by hitting the ball past the boundary, and six runs if it clears the boundary without bouncing first. Provincial matches last up to four days and Test matches up to five. Since the 1980s, one-day cricket has become a money-spinning favourite with crowds around the world. The game is played as normal, except that each side receives a limited number of overs, usually 50.

croquet Game played on a lawn, or court, in which players use long-handled mallets to drive coloured balls through a series of hoops, then on to a wooden peg. The first player or doubles team to hit the peg wins.

curling Team game in which players slide disclike granite stones, known as curling stones, across a long, narrow ice rink towards a target called a tee. Competitors carry special brooms with which they vigorously 'soop', or sweep, the ice in front of the moving stones to try to correct their speed and direction. As the game progresses, players and spectators give loud cries of 'Soop! Soop!'. Since 1969 curling has had its own world championships, contested by teams from countries such as Scotland, the USA, Canada, Sweden and Norway.

LONG WAY TO GO *Comrades Marathon veteran Bruce Fordyce, flanked by two other competitors, sets the pace during the 89-km Durban-Pietermaritzburg run. He won the race nine times.*

Currie Cup Trophies donated in 1888 by Sir Donald Currie, then chairman of the Union Castle Mail Steam Ship Company, for provincial sporting competitions in South Africa. The five trophies – for cricket, rugby, soccer, swimming and water polo – were initially awarded to the South African province which showed best form against early English sports teams, but later became the prizes for interprovincial competition.

cycle racing Bicycle sport that takes place on road or track. Road events include stage races, long-distance races on circuits on the open road, shorter races on closed circuits, and time trials, in which competitors set off at intervals. Races held on specially banked tracks include sprints, pursuit and time trials. In sprints, the two competing riders jockey for position, sometimes almost coming to a standstill as they try to manoeuvre into the best position just above and behind the other rider, for the sudden, final dash. In pursuit, riders, or teams of riders, start at opposite sides of the track and chase each other over several laps. Cycle racing is also held off-road. In cyclo-cross, road racing machines are used on short but difficult circuits where riders often have to carry their cycles. Contests for mountain bikes are held on larger circuits. South Africa's premier cycling event is the Rapport Tour, which has been staged annually since 1973 and continues to attract top class local and international cyclists. Another popular local event is the annual 105 km Argus cycle race held in the Cape Peninsula on the second Sunday in March.

darts Pub game that has become a worldwide international sport through the influence of television. Players take turns to throw three darts at a circular board divided into scoring sectors numbered 1 to 20. Darts that land in the 'bull's-eye' in the centre of the board score 50, and 25 for an outer bull. Normally, scores are deducted from a starting number, usually 501 or 301, and the game is won by the first player to throw a 'double' that brings his or her score exactly to zero.

Davis, Steve (1957-) English snooker player who won his first world title in 1981 at the age of 23, and went on to dominate the game in the 1980s. He was overtaken as the world's number one in the early 1990s by Stephen Hendry, but continued to be rated among the top five internationally.

Davis Cup International tennis team event for men, held annually since it was established in 1900 by the US player Dwight Davis. Teams must qualify for inclusion in a world group comprising the top 16 tennis-playing nations, which take part in a yearly knock-out tournament. Each round of the tournament consists of five matches, two pairs of singles and one doubles, played over a three-day period and not necessarily involving the same players in each match. South Africa won the tournament in 1974 when India refused to play in the final for political reasons. South Africa returned to the elite world group in 1994.

decathlon Athletics competition in which men take part in 10 track and field events over two days. The events, in the order in which they are contested, are: 100 m, long jump, shot-put, high jump, 400 m, 110 m hurdles, discus, pole vault, javelin and 1 500 m. Points are awarded, according to scoring tables, for each performance.
❖ Tests of all-round sporting ability have their origins in the ancient Greek Olympics. The decathlon was revived at contests in the USA in the 1880s.

de Villiers, Dawie (1940-) Springbok scrum-half who first led his country to New Zealand and Australia in 1965, and captained the Springboks for the 22nd and final time against the All Blacks in 1970. He played a total of 25 Tests and turned to politics after hanging up his boots. He was elected to parliament in 1972 and appointed ambassador to Britain in 1979. In 1994 he became minister of environmental affairs and tourism in the ▷GOVERNMENT OF NATIONAL UNITY.

DiMaggio, Joe (1914-) US baseball star who led the New York Yankees to ten World Series titles between 1936 and 1951. He is best known for two things: his unrivalled streak of safe hitting (securing at least one base hit) in 56 consecutive games in 1941 and his brief and highly publicized marriage in 1954 to the film star Marilyn Monroe.
❖ DiMaggio's grace and style as a player, as well as his outstanding ability, made him the idol of a generation. Paul Simon's popular song 'Mrs Robinson', written in 1967 for the Dustin Hoffman film *The Graduate*, included the words: 'Where have you gone, Joe DiMaggio? A nation turns its lonely eyes to you.'

diving Sport in which competitors dive into the water from high springboards and platforms, performing graceful acrobatics as they descend. Judges award points for take-off, technique, grace and entry into the water. The points are then multiplied by a factor reflecting the degree of difficulty of each dive to arrive at the diver's score.
❖ Between 1982 and 1988 Greg Louganis of the USA won four Olympic gold medals and five world titles, making him the most successful diver of all time.

Dladla, Teenage (Nelson Tutu) (1956-) Award-winning South African soccer player, a member of KAIZER CHIEFS for 12 years and their assistant coach after his retirement in 1992. He was regarded as a world-class player, but never had the opportunity to display his skills overseas.

D'Oliveira, Basil (1931-) South African-born cricketer who made his name playing for England, but whose place in sporting history is guaranteed for a different reason. Classified coloured in South Africa, D'Oliveira was chosen to tour the country with England in 1968, but was refused entry by the apartheid government of the day because of his skin colour – a decision which marked the start of South Africa's isolation in world sport when the British cancelled their tour. D'Oliveira went on to play 44 Tests for England, in which he scored 2 484 runs at an average of 40,06 and took 47 wickets.

dressage Equestrian sport in which horses perform a series of disciplined movements at the walk, trot and canter. Judges mark horses and riders, both of which must be well groomed as well as proficient. Dressage is an event in its own right as well as being the first phase in a THREE-DAY EVENT.

Du Plessis brothers Brothers Willie (1955-), Michael (1958-) and Carel du Plessis (1960-) all played Test rugby for the Springboks in the 1980s. Willie made his debut at centre against the 1980 Jaguars and went on to score three tries in 14 Tests. Carel, a left wing, made his debut the following year against the All Blacks, and scored four tries in 12 Tests. Michael played flyhalf and centre and scored one try in his eight Test appearances. A fourth brother, Jacques, played provincial rugby for Western and Eastern Province.

du Plessis, Morné (1949-) Springbok rugby player who followed in the footsteps of his father Felix by captaining his country. He was born in the year his father led South Africa against the All Blacks. His mother, Pat, was a hockey international. The Springboks were victorious in 13 of the 15 Tests in which Du Plessis was captain. A rangy eighthman, he played in 22 Tests, from 1971 to 1980; he captained Western Province in 103 of his 112 matches. He also played cricket for the South African schools and Western Province teams.

LOST TO SA *Basil D'Oliveira seen in action playing for England. His refusal of re-entry to South Africa in 1968 set off the country's many years of isolation from world sport.*

He was manager of the victorious Springboks in the 1995 World Cup rugby tournament.

du Preez, Frik (1935-) Springbok rugby player who shares the record for the most-capped player with loose-forward Jan Ellis. Both made 38 Test appearances. Between 1961 and 1971 Du Preez played for South Africa in a total of 87 matches, another record. He made his Test debut as a flank against England in 1960-1, but earned a reputation as a bullocking lock forward who made rampaging runs. He played 31 times at lock but had no fewer than eight different partners. He scored one try in his 38 Tests.

Durban July South Africa's premier horse race which takes place annually over 2 200 m at Greyville, Durban, on the first Saturday in July. The race was first run in 1897 and was won in the first two years by Campanajo, one of only four horses that have twice been winners. The others were Corriecrian, in 1907 and 1908, Pamphlet in 1918 and 1920, and Milesia Pride in 1949 and 1950. The race is as much a fashion rendezvous and social event as a sporting occasion.

Els, Ernie (1969-) South African golfer who won his first Major, the US Open, in 1994 at the age of 24. Germiston-born Els was a teenage prodigy who won his first golf title at 13 and the Under-14 World Junior title the following year. He turned professional in 1989 and made his mark in 1992 by walking off with both the PGA and South African Open – one of only three players to have accomplished this in one season. In 1993 he won his first tournament abroad, the Phoenix Masters in Japan, and the following year he began fulfilling his potential, winning the US Open, the World Matchplay title and the unofficial World Championship of Golf.

FA Cup (Football Association Challenge Cup) Annual knock-out competition in England in which more than 500 senior clubs linked to the Football Association take part. Five qualifying rounds are held before the first round proper, when clubs from the lower divisions of the Football League enter the competition. Clubs from the FA Premier League and the First Division of the Football League enter in the third round proper in early January. The final, played at London's Wembley stadium in May, is watched by millions on television in many countries.
❖ The first FA Cup final took place in 1872 at the Kennington Oval, in London. It drew 2 000 spectators.

Fangio, Juan Manuel (1911-95) Argentinian racing driver of Italian descent, regarded by many as the greatest of all time. His record of five world drivers' championships (in 1951 and 1954-7) still stood in 1995. Fangio won his first title in an Alfa Romeo and also triumphed in a Maserati, a Mercedes and a Ferrari. He won a total of 24 major Grand Prix events – a record bettered only ten years later by Scottish racing driver Jim Clark (1936-68).

TEENAGE PRODIGY *Ernie Els won the US Open in 1994, when he was only 24. He won his first title at the age of 13.*

fencing Sport developed from duelling in which there are three classes, each named after the type of sword used: foil, épée and sabre. Fencers wear white padded uniforms and faceguards. The object in a bout – which usually lasts for a specified period – is to make a 'hit' on your opponent by touching a particular target area of the body with the sword. In foil and épée, only the point may be used; in sabre, the blade edge may also score hits. Target areas are the trunk for foil, the whole person for épée, and the body, arms and head for sabre. In competitions hits are registered electronically.

Fischer, Bobby (1943-) US chess player who in 1972 became the first – and, so far, only – American to win the world championship, beating Boris Spassky of the former USSR. In 1975 he was stripped of the title after refusing to defend it against Anatoly Karpov of the USSR, and became a recluse. An eccentric genius, Fischer won his first US championship at 14, and at 15 became the youngest ever International Grandmaster. Hungarian Peter Leko, aged 14, has since become the youngest grandmaster. In 1992 Fischer beat Spassky in a rematch by ten games to five.

fishing See ANGLING.

football Team game in which a ball is kicked, carried or sometimes thrown. The term may refer to rugby and other variants, but is most commonly used for association football, or soccer, the world's most popular sport, which is played in more than 190 countries. Soccer is an 11-a-side game that originated in its present form in late 19th-century England. The soccer WORLD CUP is held every four years.
❖ The word 'soccer' derives from Oxford student slang for 'association'.

Fordyce, Bruce (1955-) South African ultradistance runner who won the COMRADES MARATHON nine times, from 1981-8 and again in 1990. In 1989 he opted not to run. Fordyce set records for both the Up (Durban to Pietermaritzburg) and Down (Pietermaritzburg to Durban) runs of the marathon. His 1986 Down run record stands at 5 hr 24 min and 7 sec. His Up run record set in 1988 stands at 5 hr 27 min and 42 sec. Fordyce also won the London-to-Brighton race in 1981, 1982 and 1983. On his way to winning in 1983, he broke the world 80 km (50 mile) record in a time of 4 hr 50 min and 21 sec, which still stood in 1995. In 1987 he won the 84 km High Arctic Midnight Sun Marathon in Canada in a record time of 6 hrs 33 min.

Formula One The major class of Grand Prix motor racing. The Fédération Internationale de l'Automobile (FIA) lays down conditions and standards – 'formulae' – of engine, fuel, design and the like for various classes of single-seater racing cars. Formula One standards are changed regularly, a prime concern being to keep speeds within safety limits.

CHAMPION SPRINTER *Namibian Frankie Fredericks took the world 200-m title in Stuttgart in 1993 and the next year won the event at the Commonwealth Games in Canada.*

Fosbury flop Revolutionary style of high-jumping invented by US athlete Dick Fosbury, who used it to win the high-jump event in the 1968 Olympics in Mexico City. Competitors approach the bar from an angle in a wide arc, turning as they reach the bar, clearing it head first and face up and landing on their backs (on a sponge pad). All leading high-jumpers now use the 'flop'.

Fredericks, Frankie (1967-) Namibian sprinter who won his country's first major gold medal by taking the world 200 m title at Stuttgart in August 1993. At the 1992 Barcelona Olympics, Fredericks picked up silver medals in both the 100 m and 200 m. He first attracted attention when he won the South African 200 m championships in 1987. He won a scholarship to study in America, where he completed a master's degree in business administration at Brigham Young University. In 1991 he set an African record of 9,95 sec for the 100 m and also set his best 200 m time of 19,85 sec at Stuttgart.
❖ In 1993 Fredericks had a street named after him in the Namibian capital of Windhoek.

Gerber, Danie (1958-) South Africa's record try-scorer in Test rugby. A powerful strong-running centre, he scored 19 tries in 24 Tests

between 1980 and 1992. He played for Eastern Province and Western Province and, towards the end of his career, in Italy. Gerber made his Test debut against the South American Jaguars in 1980.
❖ Gerber twice scored 'hat tricks' of tries in Test matches – against the Jaguars in 1982 and against England in 1984.

Gleneagles Agreement Pledge made in 1977 by leaders of Commonwealth countries to discourage sporting contacts with South Africa because of apartheid. Commonwealth members pledged to 'vigorously combat the evil of apartheid by withholding any form of support for, and by taking every practical step to discourage, contact or competition by our nationals with sporting organizations, teams or individuals from South Africa or any other country where sports are organized on the basis of race, colour or ethnic origins'. The agreement was made during a meeting at the Gleneagles Hotel, Tayside, Scotland, and was intended to end official rugby and cricket tours to South Africa by Australian, British and New Zealand teams; however, several official and unofficial or 'rebel' tours were arranged in the following years in defiance of the agreement.

gliding Sport in which light aircraft are kept aloft and guided by skilful use of rising air currents called thermals. Most gliders are launched by tow from an aeroplane and operate without engines, but motor-gliders – in which an engine is used to launch or land the craft or to sustain it in flight – are becoming more popular. Gliding world championships are held, with competitions for distance and speed of flight.
❖ In hang-gliding, a pilot hangs in a harness attached to an unpowered aircraft consisting of a large cloth wing stretched over a light (usually aluminium) framework. The flight is controlled by means of a horizontal bar.

golf Game played on grass courses which, full-size, consist of 18 holes, each set in a smoothly mown green and, normally, approached by a roughly mown fairway 90 m to 550 m long. The object is to hit a golf ball from the tee (a plastic peg set in the ground by the golfer) along the fairway to the green and finally into the hole, in as few strokes as possible. A target number of strokes is set for each hole, according to its distance from the tee. This is called the par for the hole. A score of 1 over par for a hole is known as a bogey; 1 under par is a birdie; 2 under par is an eagle; 3 under par is an albatross or double eagle. Clubs with varying degrees of loft (slant) are used for the various types of shot, such as driving off the tee, chipping out of a bunker or putting on the green. The accepted international authority on the rules of the game is the Royal and Ancient Golf Club at St Andrews in Scotland, which organizes the British Open Championship. Other leading international competitions include the US Open and the Ryder Cup.
❖ Club golfers earn a 'handicap' based on their performances in competition. This is the number of strokes a player may subtract from his or her score, and enables players to compete in amateur golf on equal terms.

Grace, W G (William Gilbert) (1848-1915) Most influential English cricketer of the 19th century. A physician by profession and larger-than-life character, 'WG' dominated the cricket field and the game itself, becoming a national figure. He played in 22 Tests, all against Australia, and led England in 13. He was a forceful batsman and medium-pace bowler, scoring 54 211 runs, including 124 centuries, and taking 2 809 wickets in a career lasting nearly 44 seasons. He did not retire from first-class cricket until he was 60.

Graf, Steffi (1969-) German tennis player who in 1987, at the age of 17, became the youngest woman ever to win the French Open. In 1988 Graf was only the third woman ever to achieve the GRAND SLAM, breaking Martina NAVRATILOVA's six-year dominance of Wimbledon. However, at Wimbledon in 1994 Graf became the first top-seeded woman to be defeated by an unseeded player – American Lori McNeil – in an opening round match. She won the Wimbledon singles title in 1989, 1991, 1992, 1993 and 1995. In 1988 she became the only player to have won a 'golden grand slam' – the four events of the grand slam plus the Olympic Games gold medal in the same year.

CRICKETING DOCTOR *With his bushy beard, W G Grace was one of the best-known people in Victorian England. He was a doctor of medicine, but cricket was his passion in life.*

Grand National World's most famous steeplechase, held annually at Aintree, near Liverpool, since 1839. It is the most severe test of jumping and stamina in British horse racing. Each of the 16 fences is jumped twice over a distance of 7,25 km (4 miles 4 furlongs), except the Chair (the highest jump) and the water jump which are jumped once.

grand slam Term used in several sports to indicate victory in all the major events in one year or season. The grand slam in tennis means winning a Wimbledon singles title and the US, French and Australian Open championships; in golf, it means winning the British Open and the three major US championships – the Masters, PGA (Professional Golfers Association) and Open.

Grobbelaar, Bruce (1957-) Zimbabwean goalkeeper who played for Durban City in South Africa before making his name with Liverpool in England. He played for Liverpool for 13 years before transferring to Southampton in 1994. During that time he played 628 league games and helped Liverpool win six league championships, three FA Cups, three League Cups and the European Cup. A great favourite with fans, as much for his eccentric clowning as his shot-stopping ability. Grobbelaar helped Zimbabwe come close to a World Cup finals place in 1994.

gymnastics Competitive gymnastics is at least 2 500 years old, but its modern revival dates from 1811 when the first open-air gymnasium was inaugurated in Germany. Several gymnastics events were included in the first modern Olympics in 1896. Since World War II, the sport has been dominated by competitors from Japan, China, eastern Europe, the former USSR and, more recently, the USA.

Hadlee, Sir Richard (1951-) New Zealand all-round cricketer who played in 86 Tests between 1973 and 1990. As a right-arm fast bowler, Hadlee took 431 Test wickets – a world record that stood until 1994, when it was overtaken by India's KAPIL DEV. An aggressive left-handed batsman, he scored 3 124 Test runs, averaging 27,16. He played ten seasons in England for Nottinghamshire.

heptathlon Athletics competition in which women take part in seven track and field events spread over two days. Day one consists of the 100 m hurdles, shot-put, high jump and 200 m. Day two includes the long

FAVOURITE WITH FANS *Virtuoso goalkeeper Bruce Grobbelaar, then playing for Liverpool, strikes a crowd-pleasing pose in an FA Cup match in 1994. He was famous for his eccentric clowning.*

jump, javelin and 800 m. American Jackie Joyner-Kersee holds the world record and won Olympic heptathlon titles both in 1988 (when she also won gold in the long jump) and in 1992. She won 14 consecutive heptathlons from 1985 until pulling up injured in the 1991 world championships in Tokyo.

Hewitt, Bob (1940-) and Frew McMillan (1942-) South African doubles tennis team who won three Wimbledon titles, the French Open and the US Open. The pair were dissimilar. Hewitt, a former Australian, was broad, bald and temperamental. McMillan was slim, quiet and always sported a baggy white cap. Between them the pair also won 11 GRAND SLAM mixed doubles titles. Hewitt won four other Grand Slam doubles titles with Fred Stolle. Hewitt and McMillan were elected to tennis's Hall of Fame in 1992. After retirement, both maintained contact with the game, Hewitt as a commentator and McMillan as captain of South Africa's Davis Cup team until late 1994.

hockey Fast 11-a-side team game played with curved wooden sticks in which the object is to hit a hard leather ball through the opposing team's 3,6 m wide goal. A hockey stick has one flat side, which must be used to hit the ball. Fouls include raising the stick above the shoulder when striking the ball and using the stick in any way that might obstruct or endanger an opponent.

horse racing Equestrian sport embracing both flat racing and (in Britain) National Hunt racing, in which only thoroughbreds take part. A race may be a handicap, in which the weight a horse must carry is calculated according to its past form, or a nonhandicap, in which the weight carried is based simply on the horse's age and sex.

Howa, Hassan (1922-92) Veteran cricket administrator and anti-apartheid stalwart who coined the phrase 'no normal sport in an abnormal society'. Howa, as president of the South African Council of Sport (SACOS) and the South African Cricket Board, campaigned vigorously for the isolation of South African sport as long as the playing fields remained racially segregated.

ice hockey Fast six-a-side team game played on a 61 m by 30 m ice rink with a goal at each end. The puck – a small, hard rubber disc – travels at speeds of up to 160 km/h, and players may reach up to 45 km/h on their skates. During a game there are three 20-minute periods of playing time. With regular substitution, players are seldom on the ice for more than two or three minutes at a time, except for the goalkeeper, who is heavily padded and protected

❖ A feature of ice hockey is the 'sin bin', a glass pen in which over-aggressive players who have been awarded time penalties are obliged to sit before rejoining the game.

Indianapolis 500 Best-known motor race in the USA, first run in 1911. The 805 km race – one of 16 races in the Indy car series – is held in May at the Indianapolis Motor Speedway, Indiana, a track known as 'the Brickyard' as it was paved in 1909 with 3,2 million bricks. Indy cars are about 50 per cent heavier than FORMULA ONE cars, because they have to sustain average speeds of more than 320 km/h.

Johanneson, Albert (1943-95) South African who became Britain's first black soccer star. Born in Germiston, he was an exceptionally talented player from his mid-teens and won the nickname 'Black Panther'. After playing for Germiston Callies and Hume Zebras, he moved to Britain in 1960 and for the next ten years played for Leeds United.

judo Sport developed from the Japanese martial art of ju-jitsu – the idea of which is to turn an opponent's strength to one's own advantage. Judo means 'gentle way', and the aim is to win by throwing an opponent on his or her back or by forcing a submission – or, failing that, to win on points. Players are graded according to skill by a system of coloured belts, progressing to a series of advanced 'dan' grades that are marked by the wearing of black belts.

jukskei Sport of South African origin played by teams of four who throw a wooden object called a skei (the pin of an ox-yoke) at a pin standing in a sandpit a set distance away – 16 m for men, 14 m for women and veterans. The object is to score 23 points. Three points are awarded for knocking the pin down, one point is scored if a player lands nearer than 4,6 cm from the pin and closer than their opponent's pin. Each game consists of three innings or 'skofte' (shifts). In 1940 the South African Jukskei Union was formed in the coffee house of the Dutch Reformed Church Synod in Bloemfontein. A provincial competition is held annually at Jukskei Park in Kroonstad. Similar games, in which a horseshoe may replace the skei, are played in Zimbabwe, Zambia, Australia and the USA.

Kaizer Chiefs South Africa's most successful soccer club, also affectionately known as the AmaKhosi. It was founded in 1969 by Kaizer Motaung and a group of disenchanted players as a rebel offshoot of another famous team, Orlando Pirates. Motaung had been playing in America for Atlanta Chiefs at the time, and he borrowed part of that club's name in launching his own team. The club won the old National Professional Soccer League title five times and, by 1994, the National Soccer League championship three times since the launch of that league in 1985. The club's distinctive gold and black colours are as well known as the team's stylish manner of play. Their fan-club is the biggest in the country, with more than 80 000 registered members and the total number of its supporters is estimated to be more than 750 000.

Kapil Dev (1959-) Indian allrounder who has taken the highest number of wickets in the history of Test cricket. When he announced his retirement in 1994 after a 17-year Test career, his fast-medium outswingers had earned him 434 wickets in 131 Tests at an average of 29,64 runs. He is the only player in Test history to have scored more than 5 000 runs and taken more than 400 wickets. An aggressive middle order batsman, he scored 5 248 Test runs at an average of 31,05. In 1983 he captained India to victory in the World Cup tournament, during which he scored the second highest individual one-day international score of 175 not out against Zimbabwe.

karate Japanese form of unarmed combat – karate means 'empty handed' – in which sharp blows are struck with the hands, feet, elbows or legs. It is now practised worldwide as a sport. There are two kinds of competitive karate. 'Kumite' are carefully controlled sparring matches, divided into different weight categories, in which points are awarded for attacking moves. In 'kata' events, contestants do not fight each other but are marked for their individual routines of kicks, punches and strikes. The first world karate championships were held in Tokyo in 1962.

Khan, Imran (1952-) Pakistani all-round cricketer who captained his country 48 times between 1982 and 1992. In 88 Tests he scored 3 807 runs and took 362 wickets. His career reached a climax in 1992, when he led Pakistan to victory over England in the World Cup limited-overs tournament. Khan also played county cricket for Worcestershire (1971-6) and for Sussex (1977-88).

Khan, Jansher (1969-) Pakistani squash player who until 1995 had won six world championships and claimed 62 victories on the world circuit. He is a great rival of compatriot Jahangir Khan (1963-), who also won six world championships. When he first appeared on the world tour, to be beaten by Jahangir in March 1987, the 17-year-old Jansher claimed he would beat the great master within a year. At the Hong Kong Open the following September he did just that, and went on to win nine of their next ten meetings. In all, the pair clashed 37 times in tournament play, with Jansher edging Jahangir 19-18. Jansher's success was built on a tireless fitness regime and incredible ability as a retriever. Officials even redesigned the professional game, lowering the tin and changing the scoring system, in an attempt to limit his capacity to wear opponents down.

RECORD SCORER *Trinidadian star Brian Lara holds the records for the highest individual score in first-class and Test cricket, and for scoring seven centuries in eight innings.*

King, Billie Jean (1943-) US tennis player who won a record 20 Wimbledon titles between 1961 and 1979 and was a pioneer of the movement to gain more recognition for women's tennis. King developed an aggressive serve-and-volley game which, allied to an unquenchable spirit, brought her 39 GRAND SLAM victories, including 12 singles titles, and a world number one ranking five times between 1966 and 1974. In 1970 King became one of the founders of the women's professional tennis tour.

Korbut, Olga (1955-) Belorussian gymnast who caught the imagination of millions of television viewers around the world with her performances at the 1972 Munich Olympics, when she was 17. She won individual gold medals on the beam and in the floor exercises. She was the first gymnast to perform a back somersault on the beam.

lacrosse Team sport in which players catch, carry and pass a ball in a net on the end of a stick called a 'crosse'. Rules for the men's game (ten-a-side) and the women's (12-a-side) differ, although the object is the same – to score goals.

❖ The sport developed in North America in the 18th century from an indigenous game called 'baggataway'. It received its French name from the stick's resemblance to a bishop's staff – 'la crosse'.

Laker, Jim (1922-86) English off-spin bowler best known for an achievement unique in first-class cricket: in 1956, he took 19 wickets for England against Australia at Old Trafford. His 9/37 in the first innings was the best Test bowling analysis for 60 years; his 10/53 in their second was the best ever. The same season, while playing for Surrey, Laker had taken all ten wickets in an innings against the Australian tourists. He helped Surrey to win the county championship every year from 1952 to 1958, and also played for Essex (1962-4). He later became a broadcaster.

land speed record Fastest speed achieved on land by a manned vehicle. The contest for the land speed record began in 1898, with two drivers outdoing each other until one of them, Camille Jenatzy, a Belgian, reached 106 km/h in an electric car. Steam and petrol provided the power for later records, but rocket or jet engines are now used. Over the past 70 years, the record has been fought out between British and American contenders. In October 1983 the British driver Richard Noble roared across the Black Rock Desert in Nevada, USA, to set a record of 1 019 km/h in *Thrust 2*, powered by a Rolls-Royce jet engine.

Lara, Brian (1969-) Trinidadian batsman, a left-hander, who set a world individual scoring record in first-class cricket with his 501 not out for Warwickshire against Durham in June 1994 – on his way to another world record of seven centuries in eight innings. In April 1994 he had made the highest score in Test history with 375 for the West Indies against England in Antigua.

Lauda, Niki (1949-) Austrian racing driver who won his first world drivers' championship in 1975. A horrifying crash in the 1976 German Grand Prix at the Nurburgring circuit left him trapped in his blazing Ferrari. Lauda suffered severe facial burns, but six weeks after receiving the last rites he was back on the track – and won two more world titles, in 1977 and 1984.

Laver, Rod (1938-) Australian left-handed tennis player who is the only person to have won the GRAND SLAM twice. He won his first Wimbledon singles title in 1961, and completed the grand slam in 1962 before turning professional, which excluded him from major tournaments. When the rules of tennis were changed in 1968 to allow amateurs and professionals to compete, he won Wimbledon that year and completed his second grand slam in 1969.

Le Mans A 24-hour race for sports cars held annually at Le Mans in north-west France. Created in 1923 as a test of endurance for standard four-seaters, Le Mans is now dominated by two-seater sports cars, the most powerful of which are faster on the straight than FORMULA ONE cars. Each car has two or three drivers who take turns at the wheel as the race progresses through the day and night. The most successful drivers have been Jacky Ickx of Belgium, who won the race six times, and Derek Bell of Britain, who won it five times.

Lenglen, Suzanne (1899-1938) French tennis star regarded by some as the finest woman player ever. Lenglen had a magnetic personality and thrilled the crowds as she leapt about the court like a ballerina. In the seven years from 1919 to 1926 she lost only one singles match, when she was forced to withdraw because of illness. She won 15 Wimbledon titles, including six singles, and the Olympic singles and mixed doubles in 1920.

Lewis, Carl (1961-) US sprinter and long-jumper who won eight Olympic gold medals – making him one of the most successful athletes of all time. Lewis won four golds at the Los Angeles Olympics in 1984, for the 100 m, 200 m, 4 x 100 m relay and long jump. At the Seoul Olympics in 1988 he won the 100 m (after Canadian Ben Johnson had been disqualified for using drugs) and the long jump. In the 1991 world championships in Tokyo, he set a world record in the 100 m with 9,86 sec, but suffered his first long-jump defeat for more than a decade at the hands of team-mate Mike Powell. Lewis got his revenge at Barcelona in 1992, winning his third long-jump gold, and then his eighth Olympic gold, helping the US 4 x 100 m relay team to a world record.

Lillee, Dennis (1949-) Australian cricketer widely acknowledged as the finest fast bowler of his generation. Between 1971 and 1984 he took 355 wickets in Test cricket, including 167 against England – the most by any bowler against one country.

Lindenberg, Peter (1955-) South African powerboating champion who in 1989 won the British Grand Prix to become the first South African to win a leg of the World Series. He recovered from a near-fatal accident after barrel-rolling in the Malaysian leg of the World Series in Penang in 1991. By 1995 he had won 11 South African powerboat championship titles and had scored 83 victories in 218 Grand Prix events. He finished third in the 1989 world championships.

❖ In 1980 Lindenberg set a new world record (which stood until 1990) for the barefoot waterskiing ramp-jump with a leap of 17,4 m.

Little, Sally (1951-) South African-born golfer who left the country in 1971 to join the US LPGA tour and won 15 tournaments and more than a million dollars. She became an American citizen in 1982, the year in which she also celebrated her best performance of four wins, and third place on the money list. In 1983, abdominal surgery and other injuries almost curtailed her career. After an unsuccessful spell of five years, she again won a tournament in 1988.

Locke, Bobby (1917-87) South African golfer who won four British Opens – in 1949, 1950, 1952 and 1957. He also landed nine South African Opens. In all, he won 38 South African titles, 18 British tournaments, 15 US tournaments and ten other overseas titles. In 1948 he won the Chicago Open by 16 strokes, which has remained the widest margin of victory in a US tour event. He had an unusual style which made him hook almost all his shots, even putts. During World War II, Locke flew more than 100 missions over the Mediterranean as a South Africa Air Force pilot. He was elected to golf's Hall of Fame in 1977.

long jump Track-and-field event performed with a running start about 30 m from the take-off board. If the athlete starts the jump beyond the board, the effort will be disallowed. The men's record for the long jump is held by Mike Powell of America, who jumped 8,95 m in Tokyo in August 1991. He broke one of the longest-standing athletics records of 8,90 m set by fellow-American Bob Beamon in Mexico City in 1968. The long jump was first held in the Greek Olympics in 708 BC and introduced into the modern Olympics in 1896.

Lord's Cricket ground in northwest London and headquarters of cricket's ruling bodies – the MCC (Marylebone Cricket Club), the TCCB (Test and County Cricket Board) and the ICC

SOARING *US athlete Bob Beamon set a world long-jump record of 8,90 m in 1968, which stood for 23 years.*

SETTING THE STYLE *Suzanne Lenglen shocked people in the 1920s with her daringly short calf-length skirts and fiery temperament. She was also known for the bandanna around her head.*

DIVINE HELP *Diego Maradona handles the ball past Peter Shilton to put England out of the 1986 World Cup. Maradona later said the goal had been scored by the 'Hand of God'.*

(International Cricket Council). It is also the main home ground of the Middlesex county side. The ground was opened in 1814 by the entrepreneur Thomas Lord.

Louis, Joe (1914-81) Idolized American boxer who was world heavyweight champion from 1937 to 1949. He held the title for longer than anyone else and was a wonderful ambassador of the sport. The 'Brown Bomber', as he was known, became champion at the age of 23, and retired undefeated after defending his title against 25 challengers. He returned to the ring in 1950 at the age of 36, but failed to regain the title.

Luyt, Louis (1932-) Controversial South African rugby administrator who was the guiding force behind the 1995 Rugby World Cup in South Africa. A provincial player with Free State, Luyt rose from being a railways clerk to making his fortune in fertilizer. In 1976 he was elected president of Diggers Rugby Club and in 1984 he became president of the Transvaal Rugby Union, turning the struggling province into CURRIE CUP champions in the 1990s. He became president of the South African Rugby Football Union in 1994. Luyt, who has a reputation for being uncompromising, had a public fallout with Springbok team manager Jannie Engelbrecht after South Africa lost a Test series against New Zealand in 1994. Engelbrecht was dismissed a few months later.
❖ Luyt acted as a front-man for the South African Government in setting up 'The Citizen' newspaper, one of the ▷INFO SCANDAL projects which was launched in 1976 to disseminate apartheid propaganda, and which is estimated to have cost South African taxpayers R35 million.

McArthur, Ken (1882-1960) South African who won the 1912 Olympic Marathon in Stockholm. With teammate Chris Gitsham, he provided a South African one-two in the race, the only time in Olympic history that one country has provided both winner and runner-up in the marathon. McArthur, a policeman from Potchefstroom, won in 2 hr 36 min 54 sec. Gitsham, a miner from Germiston, finished second with a time of 2 hr 37 min 52 sec. McArthur was rewarded for his heroics with a plot of land in his home town.

McEnroe, John (1959-) US tennis star who was one of the most talented and exciting players of modern times. A fast left-hander, McEnroe was particularly admired for his deft and delicate touch play and his extraordinary range and imagination on court. He reached the Wimbledon semi-finals in 1977, at the age of 18. He won the US title in 1979 and ended Björn BORG's supremacy at Wimbledon in 1981 to become world number one, a position he held until 1984. McEnroe won four US Open titles and three Wimbledon singles titles, and helped the USA to four triumphs in the Davis Cup.
❖ McEnroe was notorious for his on-court tantrums. His outbursts included the remarks – directed at linesmen and referee respectively – 'You guys are the pits of the world!' and 'You *cannot* be serious!'

McKenzie, Precious (1936-) South African-born bantamweight weightlifter who broke innumerable British, Commonwealth and world records. Unable to represent South Africa during the apartheid era, he settled in Britain, which he represented at the Olympic Games in 1968, 1972 and 1976. He also became the first man in the history of the Commonwealth Games to win four consecutive gold medals. He was elected to the International Powerlifting Federation's Hall of Fame in Arlington, Texas and in 1974 was awarded the MBE (Member of the Order of the British Empire). He later moved to New Zealand, from where he toured the world as a back injury prevention consultant. He has featured – and broken records – in many TV shows.
❖ Precious McKenzie appeared in the *Guiness Book of Records* as the first man in the world to have totalled 11 times his own body weight in the three power lifting disciplines.

Maradona, Diego (1960-) Argentinian footballer who led his country to victory in the 1986 World Cup and was widely acknowledged as the world's most gifted player of the 1980s. A midfielder, Maradona could wriggle through the tightest of defences. He joined Italian club Napoli in 1984 for a then world record fee of £6,9 million (at that time the equivalent of about R14 million). In 1991 he was twice arrested for possession of cocaine and suspended from football for 15 months. He made a comeback in 1993 with the Spanish club Sevilla. However, in 1994, while playing for Argentina in the World Cup, he was barred from the game after testing positive for the banned drug ephedrine.

marathon Longest Olympic running event, contested over 42,195 km. Marathons are also held annually in several major cities, including Boston, London and New York. These events have sometimes attracted more than 25 000 runners of all standards, including many who run for charity. In 1995 the world record for the men's marathon – 2 hr 6 min 50 sec – was held by Belayneh Dinsamo of Ethiopia; the women's record of 2 hr 21 min 6 sec was held by Ingrid Kristiansen of Norway.
❖ A marathon was introduced in the first modern Olympics in 1896 to commemorate the legendary run of Pheidippides, who brought the news to Athens of the Greek victory over the Persians at Marathon in 490 BC – and then died.

Marciano, Rocky (1923-69) US boxer who was world heavyweight champion from 1952 to 1956. He made his name when he defeated former world champion Joe LOUIS in 1951. Known for his outstanding stamina and relentless two-fisted slugging, he beat Jersey Joe Walcott for the title in his 43rd fight, and successfully defended it six times. Marciano, who retired undefeated, with a record of 49 bouts and 49 victories, died in a plane crash on the day before his 46th birthday.

Maree, Sydney (1956-) South African-born track star who rose from an underprivileged life in Atteridgeville township near Pretoria to break the world 1 500 m record. Maree won a scholarship to Villanova University in Pennsylvania, where he graduated with an economics degree. In 1981, he ran the mile in 3 min 48,72 sec, then the third fastest time in history. Maree broke the world 1 500 m

GOING FOR SILVER *Elana Meyer heads for a long-distance win at the Barcelona Olympics in 1992. She won a silver medal here and at the 1994 Commonwealth Games in Canada.*

record in a time of 3 min 31,34 sec on 28 August 1983. He became a US citizen and ran in the 1988 Olympic Games in Seoul, finishing 5th in the 5 000 m. He lives in Philadelphia and works as a stockbroker in New York.

martial arts Physical skills derived from Asian techniques of armed or unarmed combat. Some martial arts are linked to religious beliefs derived from ▷TAOISM and ▷ZEN BUDDHISM; others are practised for self-defence or sport. They include JUDO and KARATE, from Japan, and kung fu, from China. Kick boxing and SUMO WRESTLING, often grouped as martial arts, are primarily competitive sports.

MCC (Marylebone Cricket Club) Governing body of cricket from 1787 to 1969, which, as a private club, remains responsible for the laws of the game. The MCC's headquarters is LORD'S cricket ground in London.

Meyer, Elana (1966-) South African track athlete who broke the world record for the 15 km distance in November 1991. Her time of 46 min 57 sec took 20 seconds off Ingrid Kristiansen's earlier record. In May that year, she had broken the half-marathon record set by Kristiansen, clocking 1 hr 7 min 59 sec. She won silver medals at the 1992 Olympics and at the 1994 Commonwealth Games in Canada. She made her marathon debut in Boston in 1994 and won the World Half-Marathon Championships in Oslo that year.

mile Classic middle-distance running race, the Blue Riband of the track, which has survived metrification. A four-lap test of stamina, speed and tactics, the mile (1,6 km) race has retained the prestige it acquired after World War II, when breaking the four-minute barrier became the ultimate goal of athletics. Long after Roger BANNISTER's historic run in 1954, the four-minute mile was a measure of excellence. New Zealander John Walker was the first to break 3 min 50 sec in 1975. By the mid-1990s the men's world record had been reduced to 3 min 44,39 sec (by Nourredine Morceli of Algeria) and the women's to 4 min 15,61 sec (by Paula Ivan of Romania).

❖ The mile is neither an Olympic nor a world championship event.

Mitchell, Brian (1961-) South Africa's most successful boxing world champion. Mitchell won the World Boxing Association junior lightweight world title by defeating Alfredo Layne on a 10th-round technical knockout on 27 September 1986 and went on to defend his title 13 times, a record in the junior lightweight division. He was never knocked out and retired undefeated in 1991. Never a devastating puncher, Mitchell relied on fitness and workrate. Most of his title fights took place during South Africa's sports isolation and he had to compete in foreign, and often hostile, arenas. He made a comeback in late 1994 but retired again in 1995.

Mitchell, Bruce (1909-95) South African whose Test cricketing career spanned almost 20 years, and who was the country's highest Test scorer, with 3 471 runs at an average of 48,88. In 42 Tests he scored eight centuries and 21 half-centuries from 80 innings. His highest Test score was 189 not out against England in 1947. Although renowned for his batting skills, he took five wickets for 42 runs in a Test against England in 1929.

modern pentathlon Four-day competition involving five sports – showjumping, épée fencing, pistol shooting, swimming (300 m freestyle) and cross-country running (4 km). Points are awarded for each discipline. The contest – which in ancient Greece was based on the skills needed by a battlefield messenger – was devised for the 1912 Olympics.

Mokone, Steve (1938-) South African soccer player who excelled abroad in the 1950s and 1960s. Nicknamed 'Kalamazoo', his attacking skills earned him comparisons with greats of the day such as Stanley Matthews and Alfredo di Stefano. He travelled to Britain in 1955 and spent two years with Coventry City. This was followed by spells in Holland, France and Italy, where he spent five years. He later attained a master's degree in psychology from the University of Pennsylvania, where he taught until 1974, and eventually opened a private practice on the East Coast of America.

Monopoly World's most popular board game, in which from two to six players throw dice and buy or sell the property on which their tokens land. Some players become 'rich' in

WORLD TITLE HOLDER *Brian Mitchell (right), world junior light-weight champion, drew with Tony Lopez at Sacramento, California, in 1991 but beat Lopez in a re-match at Sun City.*

WHEELER-DEALERS *According to psychologists, dealing in property when playing Monopoly appeals to the tycoon in everyone.*

the process and others go 'bankrupt'. It was invented in America in 1932 by Charles Farrow, then an unemployed heating equipment salesman. Some two million sets are sold each year throughout the world.

motorcycle racing Chiefly, Grand Prix racing on motorbikes, but also encompassing motocross, speedway, drag racing and trials. Classes of motorcycle have varied from 50 cc to 1 000 cc or above. There are world championships for 125 cc to 500 cc and also for motorcycles with sidecars.

Muir, Karen (1952-) South African swimming prodigy who, between the age of 12 and 16, broke 17 world records. Her first world mark came in Blackpool, England in 1965 at the age of 12. Entered in the girls' event and not the senior race, she broke the world 100 m backstroke record with a time of 68,7 sec. At the time she was the youngest person ever to hold a world record in any sport. Muir won 22 South African championships and set 15 national records. In 1980, when she had qualified as a doctor, she was inducted into swimming's Hall of Fame in Fort Lauderdale, Florida.

Nash, Paul (1947-) South African sprinter who equalled the world record of 10 seconds for the 100 m distance at Krugersdorp in April 1968. Nash was then a 20-year-old commerce student at the University of the Witwatersrand. He later repeated this time in Zürich, where he also ran 20,1 sec for the 200 m, an unprecedented combination in Europe at that time. South Africa's sports isolation as a result of apartheid prevented Nash from competing in the Olympic Games in Mexico in 1968. After being afflicted by arthritis he retired from the track in 1970.

Navratilova, Martina (1956-) Czech-born, left-handed tennis player who dominated the women's game for most of the 1980s and won the Wimbledon singles title a record nine times. Navratilova defected to the USA in 1975, won the Wimbledon title in 1978 and 1979, and became a US citizen in 1981. She was ranked number two behind Chris Evert for a couple of years, but remoulded her playing style and came back even more strongly. Her all-round game kept her at the top of the rankings for five years, between 1982 and 1987 and again in 1990. By 1993 she had won a record 164 singles titles as well as 162 doubles titles. She retired in 1994, the year in which she lost in the Wimbledon final to Conchita Martinez of Spain.

netball Seven-a-side game played mainly by women, indoors or outdoors, on a hard court. The object is to score goals by throwing a large ball through a hoop set 3 m from the ground at each end of the court. The ball is passed by throwing with one or both hands. Players may not take a step while holding the ball, but are permitted to pivot on one foot before passing it.

Newby-Fraser, Paula (1962-) Durban-born triathlon runner who won the prestigious Iron Man title in Hawaii seven times before retiring in late 1994. Holder of the women's record, she once came 11th overall in the event, which consists of a swim of 3,8 km, 180 km of cycling and a 42,2 km marathon. She was the first woman to complete the Iron Man in less than nine hours. A born achiever, she broke the senior Natal 100 m butterfly record at 13, matriculated at the age of 15 and graduated with an honours degree in social science from Natal University. Her link with the Iron Man began after she won the South African triathlon championships in 1985, for which the prize was a trip to Hawaii.

Nicklaus, Jack (1940-) US golfer hailed as the greatest ever player of the game. He won the US Amateur title in 1959 and 1961 before turning professional. In his first pro tournament he beat Arnold Palmer in a play-off for the 1962 US Open. He won a record 18 GRAND SLAM tournaments – three Open Championships, six US Masters, five US PGAs and four US Opens.

Ntsoelengoe, Ace (Patrick) (1952-) One of the best soccer players South Africa has produced, a striker or midfielder with speed and expert dribbling skills. He played mainly for KAIZER CHIEFS and attracted attention in the USA when he played for Minnesota Kicks in the North American Soccer League. In 1987 he captained a South African eleven which played a team of overseas players and in 1990 became assistant coach for Chiefs.

Nurmi, Paavo (1897-1973) Finnish athlete who dominated middle-distance running in the 1920s, setting 35 world records. The 'Flying Finn', who ran with a stopwatch in his hand, won nine gold medals in three Olympics, over distances that ranged from 1 500 m to 10 000 m.

YOUTHFUL RECORD BREAKER *At the age of 12 South African Karen Muir broke the world 100 m backstroke record and became the youngest person ever to hold a world record in any sport.*

Olympic Games Held every four years, the modern games were inaugurated in Athens in 1896 at the instigation of Baron Pierre de Coubertin, a French scholar who was inspired by the excavation of the ancient Olympic site – where the games were first held in about 776 BC. In the 1896 games, 311 male contestants from 13 countries took part in nine sports. Almost 100 years later, in 1992 at Barcelona, close to 10 000 competitors from 169 nations took part in 257 events. In 1996 the Olympic Games will be held in Atlanta, USA, and in 2000 in Sydney, Australia. The WINTER OLYMPICS are also staged every four years.

❖ The Paralympic Games, international games for the disabled, are now held immediately after the Olympics, usually at the same venue. Men and women – who may be, for example, partially sighted or wheelchair-bound – compete in 18 different sports, including basketball, judo and sailing, against people with disabilities similar to their own. Winners are awarded medals equivalent to those presented at the Olympic Games.

orienteering Running sport in which competitors must find the quickest route through woods and rough country. Starting a minute apart, runners armed with a special compass and map have to check in at all the control points marked. There are always several possible routes to the next checkpoint, none of which runs in a straight line. Competitors need good judgment and map-reading skills, as well as the stamina to cover up to 20 km. The sport, which originated in Sweden in 1918, now has its own world championships.

Owens, Jesse (1913-80) US athlete whose record-breaking feats at Ann Arbor, Michigan, on 25 May 1935, are unparalleled in sport. In 45 minutes he set five world records and equalled another. First he equalled the 91 m (100 yd) record of 9,4 sec. He then, with a leap of 8,13 m, set a long-jump record that stood for 25 years. His last four records were set in two races, the 200 m (220 yd) sprint and the 220 yd hurdles; his times of 20,3 sec and 22,6 sec also counted as records for the 200 m sprint and 200 m hurdles.

❖ In 1936, at the Berlin Olympics, Owens won four gold medals – for the 100 m and 200 m sprints, the sprint relay and the long jump. Because his success meant that, as a black, he invalidated the Nazi belief in Aryan supremacy, Adolf ▷HITLER, who attended the Games, refused to acknowledge him and left the stadium in a rage.

GREEK RACE *Athletics were part of the ancient Greek Olympics.*

GREEK GRACE *Throwing the discus, an event in the pentathlon, was mentioned by the ancient Greek epic poet Homer.*

RECORD BREAKER *Jesse Owens starts the 200 m race at the Berlin Olympics of 1936. He won in an Olympic record time of 20,7 sec.*

Palmer, Arnold (1929-) US golfer whose flair and style attracted a huge following, dubbed 'Arnie's army'. His popularity with the crowds helped to make golf one of the fastest growing sports of the 1960s. He won 80 tournaments, including four US Masters, two British Open Championships and one US Open. By 1968 Palmer had become the first player to amass earnings of US$1 million from golf. He continued to play at the highest level until the late 1980s.

Pelé (Edson Arantes do Nascimento) (1940-) Brazilian footballer who is universally acknowledged as the greatest and most popular player of all time. From his explosion onto the international scene as a 17-year-old in the 1958 World Cup finals in Sweden to his thrilling performances 12 years later in Mexico, he played what he called his 'beautiful game' with infectious joy. In his 18-year career he scored 1 281 goals in 1 363 games and scored 77 goals in 92 internationals – in the process helping Brazil to victory in three World Cup tournaments

❖ A plaque in Rio de Janeiro's Maracana stadium commemorates 'the most beautiful goal ever seen'. It was scored by Pelé for his club Santos in March 1961, when he beat every man in the Fluminense team before putting the ball in the net. In 1994 he was appointed Brazil's Minister of Sport.

pelota Fastest ball game in the world, originating in Spain, in which players hit a ball with a scoop-shaped wicker racket, known as a chistera, against any of three walls of a court – at speeds of more than 300 km/h. A version of the game known as jai-alai (pronounced hie-a-lie) is popular in Latin America and the USA.

pentathlon Athletics competition made up of five events – the 60 m hurdles, high jump, shot put, long jump and 800 m race – completed over two days.

Player, Gary (1935-) South African golfer, possibly his country's most famous athlete. Nicknamed the 'Black Knight' because of his fondness for all-black clothing in his prime, Player cut a swathe through world golf after turning professional in 1953. With Jack Nicklaus and Arnold Palmer he became known as one of the legendary 'Big Three' of the game. Player won nine Majors, his first coming in the 1959 British Open. He won that tournament again in 1968 and 1974, the US Open in 1965, the US Masters in 1961, 1974 and 1978, and the US PGA in 1962 and 1972. In 1965, at the age of 30, he had completed golf's GRAND SLAM. A highly disciplined keep-fit fanatic, Player was named South African Sportsman of the Year eight times and was crowned South Africa's sportsman of the century in 1990. At the end of 1994 he had won 170 tournaments and his combined US earnings in regular and senior tours totalled more than US$5 million. He is much in demand as a course designer.

Pollock, Graeme (1944-) South African cricketer rated by some as the finest left-handed batsman of all time. He set the record for the highest individual score by a South African

FINEST LEFT-HANDER *Record-breaking Graeme Pollock gets going on his way to notching up more runs for South Africa. He scored a total of 2 256 runs in 23 Test matches.*

in Test cricket when he struck 274 against Australia at Kingsmead, Durban, in February 1970. He scored 2 256 runs in 23 Tests at an average of 60,97. This tally included seven centuries. In 1964 Pollock, aged 19, became the youngest South African to score a Test hundred when he hit 122 against Australia in Sydney. In the following Test in Adelaide, he notched a South African record partnership for any wicket of 341 runs in 283 minutes with Eddie BARLOW. Pollock represented Eastern Province and Transvaal and played first-class cricket until the age of 45.

❖ Graeme Pollock's brother, Peter Pollock (1941-), who was a devastating fast bowler and useful lower order batsman, took 63 Test wickets before he retired and turned to cricket administration.

polo Game played on horseback between teams of four. Riders use long wooden mallets to strike a small white ball into goals at either end of a grass field measuring 274 m by 183 m. Of Indian origin, the game gets its name from the Tibetan word for ball, 'pulu'. A full game consists of as many as eight seven-minute periods called 'chukkers'. Special horses called 'polo ponies' are trained for the game. Riders usually change onto fresh ponies between chukkers. Polo is popular in South and North America. In Britain it has traditionally been regarded as a fashionable upper-class sport. The Prince of Wales remains a keen player, despite having sustained a number of injuries in games.

pool Any of several games played on a six-pocket billiard table measuring 2,1 m by 1,2 m. There are 15 'object' balls – two sets of seven balls, differentiated by colour or numbers, and one black – and a white cue ball that must be struck by the cue. Two players compete, and the first to pocket one set of coloured balls, followed by the black, wins.

Price, Nick (1957-) Number one ranked golfer in the world in 1994. Price, who was born in Durban but grew up in Zimbabwe, showed early promise when he won the Junior World tournament in California at the age of 17. He clinched his first tournament overseas in 1984 but had to wait until 1991 for his second win in America. He won two tournaments during that year and became one of the top ten money winners on the US tour. In 1992, he won his first Major, the US Professional Golfers' Association title. He topped the US money list in 1993 and in 1994 won back-to-back Majors – the British Open and the US PGA – to move to the top of the world rankings. Price is known for his friendliness and fondness for returning to Zimbabwe to indulge in his other passion – tiger-fishing.

Procter, Mike (1946-) South African cricketer, an all-rounder who also coached the South African team. As a player for Natal, Western Province and Rhodesia, he was a swashbuckling batsman and fast bowler who bowled off the 'wrong' foot. He played seven Tests for South Africa before its isolation, scoring 226 runs and taking 41 wickets. He then played for Gloucestershire in England for many years with such success that the county became known as 'Proctershire'. In 1970-1 he became only the third batsman ever to hit six successive first-class centuries. He coached the South African team when the sports embargo was lifted and international events resumed, leading them to the World Cup semifinals in 1992. He was ousted after the 1994 England tour.

professional foul Euphemism commonly used in association football to denote an offence committed deliberately in order to gain an advantage. When a player uses a professional foul to prevent an attempt at goal, he can be sent off.

Prost, Alain (1955-) French racing driver who has triumphed in a record number of FORMULA ONE Grand Prix events. A shrewd tactician, Prost – known as 'the Professor' – was world drivers' champion in 1985, 1986, 1989 and 1993. By the summer of 1993, he had won 51 out of 200 races, mostly in a McLaren. He also scored a record number of points. After switching to Ferrari he joined the Williams team in 1993 before retiring. In 1995 he again started becoming involved in the sport as a test driver.

Queensberry rules Set of regulations formulated in England in the mid-1860s that transformed prize fighting into the modern sport of boxing. The rules were drawn up by the Amateur Athletic Club and published under the name of the 8th Marquess of Queensberry, a patron of the sport. They banned throwing and wrestling, limited rounds to three minutes, and allowed a fighter 10 seconds to get to his feet after being knocked down.

rally Motor race contested in stages on public and closed roads, much of it over rough terrain. Standard road vehicles are strengthened and modified for rally conditions and fitted with a range of special equipment, such as extra lights and lightweight driving seats. Drivers must complete each stage in a set time or lose points. A navigator uses a route map to warn the driver of corners, bumps or inclines. Some rallies last several days, the most famous being the Monte Carlo Rally, first held in 1911. Other major rallies include the Paris-Dakar Rally and the longest annual event, the Safari Rally, in Kenya, which has extended over as much as 6 234 km. There are world rally championships based on performances in a number of specified events.

Ramsamy, Sam (1938-) Staunch anti-apartheid campaigner who returned from an 18-year exile to head the National Olympic Committee of South Africa (NOCSA). Ramsamy studied in England before he started a teaching job in Durban in 1969. In 1972 he returned to England, where he became deputy principal of a school in London. He returned to South Africa in 1990 and the following

HOME FROM EXILE *Sam Ramsamy (left) is welcomed to Cape Town by the Mayor, Patricia Kreiner, and Minister of Sport Steve Tshwete.*

ELECTRIFYING FIELDER *South African Jonty Rhodes, whose feats as a fielder brought him international fame, scored a match-saving century for South Africa against Sri Lanka in 1993.*

year he was elected chairman of the South African Co-ordinating Committee on Sport, which later became NOCSA. Ramsamy was general manager of the 1992 South African Olympic team in Barcelona.
❖ Ramsamy, a founder member of SANROC (the South African Non-Racial Olympic Committee), was its chairman from 1986 to 1989.

Rhodes, Jonty (1969-) South African cricketer known particularly for his electrifying fielding. Rhodes shot to fame during the 1992 World Cup when his diving run-out of Pakistani batsman Inzamam-ul-Haq was captured by television and beamed around the world. A middle-order batsman, Rhodes, who suffers from epilepsy, silenced critics of his technique with several gutsy Test innings, including a match-saving century in Sri Lanka in 1993. He set a world record of five catches in a one-day international against the West Indies in India in 1993.

Rice, Clive (1949-) Tigerish and outspoken South African who never played official Test cricket but was widely regarded as one of the game's best all-rounders in the 1980s. He won the world single wicket title three times. He played in the Kerry Packer series in the late 1970s and captained Nottinghamshire to the 1981 and 1987 county championships. Rice led the Transvaal 'Mean Machine' of the 1980s to five Currie Cup, five Nissan Shield and three Benson and Hedges night series titles. In 1991 he captained South Africa on their historic post-isolation tour of India, but the following year he was controversially dropped from the World Cup squad. Rice was also released by Transvaal that season after more than two decades of service and ended his playing career with Natal. He later headed the South African Cricket Academy.

Richards, Barry (1945-) Classically gifted South African batsman who played just four Tests for his country before its isolation during the apartheid era, scoring 508 runs at an average of 72,57, including two centuries. In a first-class career which spanned 18 years, Richards scored more runs than any other South African – 28 358 at an average of 54,74. He played for a decade with the English county Hampshire, had one profitable season with South Australia and was a star of the Kerry Packer series. In 1982 he captained South Africa in the second and third tests of the first 'rebel' series against Graham Gooch's English team. He later emigrated to Australia, where he coached South Australia before becoming the chief executive officer of Queensland Cricket Association.

Richards, Vivian (1952-) West Indian cricketer who was an exciting batsman and an inspiring captain of his country. He played in 121 Tests, accumulating 8 540 runs, with an average of 50,23, to beat Gary Sobers' West Indian record. His best season was against England in 1976, when he scored 829 in only four Tests. During that year he made a world record 1 710 Test runs. In England, Richards played for Somerset (1974-86) and later Glamorgan (1990-3). He made his highest score – 322 for Somerset against Warwickshire in 1985 – in just under five hours, becoming the first West Indian to score 300 runs in a day. He holds the record for the highest innings in a one-day game – 189 not out against England at Old Trafford in 1989. From 1985 to 1991 he captained the West Indies to 27 victories in 50 Tests.

Roberts, Muis (Michael) (1954-) South African jockey, an 11-times South African champion who also achieved extraordinary success in Britain. After capturing his 11th South African title in 1984, Roberts pursued his sport in Britain. In 1988 he rode 121 winners in the flat-racing season and was voted Britain's Jockey of the Year. In 1992 he became British champion and the following year he clinched a deal as No 1 rider to Sheik Mohammed Al Maktoum, who ran the most powerful stable in Europe. Roberts is known as 'Mighty Mouse' in Britain.
❖ Roberts survived a plane crash in July 1992. He left hospital the following day and rode three winners that afternoon.

Robinson, Sugar Ray (1920-89) US boxer who was possibly the greatest of all time. An all-round fighter, with a devastating punch and brilliant ringcraft, he was world welterweight champion from 1946 until 1950, before moving up to middleweight. He established a record by winning the world middleweight crown on five separate occasions, once after retiring for more than two years. In 1961, at the age of 41, he almost won it for a sixth time, but was held to a draw by Gene Fullmer. A professional boxer for 20 years, he was said to have shown few signs of his many bouts in the ring.

rodeo Traditional North American sport that developed out of ranching skills in the late 19th century. Rodeo shows include the riding of broncos – wild or half-tamed horses – steer wrestling and bull riding.

Roos, Paul (1888-1948) South African rugby player who led the Springboks (a name originated by him) on their first overseas tour. Of the four Test matches in Britain the team won two, lost one and drew one. They lost only two of the 29 matches they played and scored a total of 608 points against 84 conceded. Roos had a distinguished career in education, giving his name to the Stellenbosch Gymnasium, of which he was principal; he became an MP shortly before he died.

roulette Gambling game in which a small metal ball is spun in a horizontal wheel before settling into a section numbered 1-36 (alternately red and black) plus a green zero (there are two zeros in the US game). Players make their bets by placing chips, or counters, on the betting layout, which is a table top marked into numbered sections corresponding to those on the wheel. Odds vary according to the type of bet, of which there are many. For example, long odds (35-1) are given on any one single number, known as 'en plein'; short odds (even money) are given on black or red, on high numbers (19-36), known as 'passe', or low numbers (1-18), known as 'manque'.

Roux, Mannetjies (Francois du Toit) (1939-) Small but powerful Springbok centre known best for his fearsome crash-tackling. He played 27 Tests for South Africa between 1960 and 1970 and scored six tries, including two against the British Lions in the Bloemfontein Test of 1962. Roux played 56 times for his country, scoring 13 tries.

rowing Sport which originated in Britain, in which each oarsman or oarswoman in a boat, or 'racing shell', rows with one oar or, in the case of sculling, two oars. Competitive events involve coxed boats, in which a lightweight cox steers and controls the pace, or coxless boats, which are steered by a member of the crew operating a rudder with his feet. The number of oarsmen in a boat can be one, in sculling only (singles), two (pairs, or double sculls), four (fours, or quadruple sculls) or eight (eights). Championship races are usually contested over a distance of 2 000 m for both men and women. Rowing has been an Olympic sport since 1900; there are also world championships.

❖ The world's best-known rowing events are the Oxford and Cambridge Boat Race and Henley Royal Regatta which are held on the ▷THAMES every year.

rugby league Game created in 1895 when a group of rugby football clubs in the north of England broke away from the amateur world of RUGBY UNION. Among several changes to the rules, the number of players in a team was reduced in 1906 from 15 to 13. A unique feature of rugby league is the play-the-ball rule, which comes into force when a player is tackled while in possession. The tackled player keeps the ball, puts it on the ground and heels it to a team-mate who is positioned behind him. Each side retains the ball for a period of six tackles. If the side in possession has not scored or kicked away the ball when the sixth tackle is made, the opposition restart the game with a play-the-ball at the site of the sixth tackle. A scrum is called when the ball is kicked out of play, or when there has been a 'knock-on', which is when the ball has been hit, dropped, or otherwise played with hand or arm, in the direction of the opposition's goal-line. A try is worth four points, a conversion and a penalty goal two each and a drop goal one point. The game is played on a limited scale in South Africa.

NIFTY WORK *South Africa's world-rated scrumhalf Joost van der Westhuizen prepares to feed his backline in the World Cup final against New Zealand in June 1995. South Africa won 15-12.*

rugby union Fifteen-a-side rugby football game. The oval ball may be handled and passed as well as kicked – but it may not be thrown or knocked forward. A try, when the ball is touched down over the opposing team's goal line, scores five points. A try may be 'converted' for an extra two points if the kick at goal that follows is successful. Three points are given for a penalty goal or drop goal. One of the features of the game is the set scrum, in which the two sets of forwards interlock together against each other, the ball is thrown in and the opposing 'hookers' try to kick the ball backwards out to their own team. If the ball goes over the touchline, the game is restarted with a 'line-out', when the opposing forwards group themselves into two parallel lines and try to gain possession of the ball when it is thrown back into play

❖ A highlight of the rugby union calendar in South Africa is the CURRIE CUP competition, staged annually between provincial teams.

❖ The growing popularity of the sport around the world was reflected by the launch of the World Cup series in 1987. South Africa was included for the first time in 1995, when it was also the venue for the tournament – and its team won.

❖ Rugby union is said to have originated in the early 19th century at Rugby public school in Warwickshire, where, during a football match in 1823, a boy named William Webb Ellis picked up the ball and ran with it. It was not until 1871 that the Rugby Football Union was founded, after the FOOTBALL Association had banned the handling of the ball.

Ruth, Babe (George Herman) (1895-1948) Baseball star whose big hitting made him the greatest American sporting hero of the 1920s. Babe Ruth began his baseball career as a highly successful pitcher in 1914 for the Boston Red Sox, but his hitting steadily improved, and in 1919 he set a major-league home-run record of 29. He signed for the New York Yankees the following year and slugged a stupendous 54 home runs. A left-hander and a fine outfielder, Ruth set record after record with the Yankees. He led the American league in home runs 12 times, achieving his milestone record 60 in 1927, and hit a record 714 'homers' in a 22-year league career.

Sampras, Pete (1971-) US tennis star who, since 1990, has never been ranked lower than number six in the world. One of the game's best serve-and-volley players (and almost unbeatable on grass), Sampras has swept the boards in some of the world's most prestigious tournaments, including the US Open in 1990 (when he was the youngest ever US men's singles champion), 1993 and 1995, Wimbledon in 1993, 1994 and 1995 and the Australian Open in 1994.
❖ In 1993 Sampras won eight titles in major tournaments around the world, bringing him prize money of nearly US$5 million.

Scheckter, Jody (1950-) South African racing driver who achieved ten victories in his first season in Europe in 1971. In 1979 he won the Formula One world championship at Monza, Italy, in a Ferrari. East London-born Scheckter, who early in his career had a reputation for recklessness, drove for Tyrrell, Wolf, Ferrari and McLaren in an eight-year spell. He finished third in the world championship twice, and was runner-up in 1977, before landing the title. He drove in 113 Grand Prix events, won ten and scored 246 championship points. He retired in 1980.

Scrabble Board game in which two to four players score points by forming interlocking words with lettered tiles on a 225-square board. Invented in 1931 as Criss Cross, it was redesigned and named Scrabble in 1948.

Sea Cottage (1963-87) South African race horse that was shot three weeks before the 1966 July Handicap. The favourite to win, he was shot by nightclub bouncer Johnny Nel, who had been hired by a bookmaker who stood to lose a fortune. However, Sea Cottage recovered from the bullet wound to the right upper quarters and ran the race. Two weeks later he won the Clairwood Winter Handicap. The following year, Sea Cottage dead-heated with Jollify in the July Handicap. Trained by Syd Laird, and usually ridden by Laird's brother-in-law Bobby Sivewright, Sea Cottage won 20 of 24 races before being retired.

Seles, Monica (1973-) Serbian-born tennis player who in 1992 briefly overtook Steffi GRAF as the world's number one. A left-hander with double-handed forehand and backhand, she won the French Open in 1990 at 16, becoming the youngest winner of a GRAND SLAM tournament. Between 1991 and 1993 she achieved six more grand slam victories, taking her career earnings to nearly US$7 million. Seles attributed her defeat by Steffi Graf in the 1992 Wimbledon final to her efforts to curb her habitual on-court 'grunt'.
❖ Seles withdrew from the game after she was stabbed in the back by a spectator – a fanatical supporter of Steffi Graf – while on court in a tournament in Hamburg in April 1993. In 1995 she began her comeback in an exhibition game against Martina Navratilova.

Senna, Ayrton (1960-94) Brazilian racing driver who triumphed in the world drivers' championship in 1988, 1990 and 1991. He was killed in May 1994 when his Williams-Renault crashed at more than 305 km/h at the Imola track in Italy during the San Marino Grand Prix.

shooting Gun sport involving a variety of weapons and targets; it falls into four broad categories – pistol, airgun, clay-pigeon and rifle shooting.

show jumping Equestrian sport in which competitors jump a number of fences over a set course. Mistakes are penalized by faults, which in some competitions may also be incurred by taking longer than a specified time limit to complete the course. If a horse knocks down any part of a fence or puts a foot in a water jump, it incurs four faults. Refusal to jump a fence incurs three faults, while fall of horse or rider is worth eight. If two or more riders are tied at the end of a round with no faults or the same number of faults, there may be a jump-off to decide the winner, usually over a shortened course, against the clock.

ski racing Sport classified as either Alpine or Nordic. Alpine ski racing, first included at the Olympic Games in 1936, embraces slalom and downhill events. Competitors start at intervals and races are decided purely on time. In slalom, skiers speed down a steep mountainside, twisting and turning in and out of as many as 75 gates – pairs of poles bearing coloured pennants. In the downhill competitions, skiers take the fastest route to the finish. Nordic skiing – which includes ski jumping and langläufing – formed part of the first Winter Olympics, at Chamonix, France, in 1924. In langläufing, skiers race across country on long, lightweight skis over distances ranging from 5 to 50 km.
❖ Freestyle is a form of competitive skiing popularized in the early 1970s which includes 'aerials' (spectacular jumps from special ramps), ballet performed to music (like figure skating on skis) and acrobatics, or 'hot-dogging', on bumpy slopes (moguls).

snooker Game played on a standard billiard table with one white cue ball, 15 red balls and six balls of different colours. Players try to strike the white cue ball in such a way that it hits a coloured ball into any of the six pockets. The balls of differing colours must be potted alternately with the reds (worth one point). Once potted, red balls remain in the pockets, but other colours are returned to their starting spots on the table until all 15 reds have been potted. Then the colours are potted in sequence: yellow (two points), green (three), brown (four), blue (five), pink (six) and black (seven). A sequence of successful shots is called a break. The highest

WIMBLEDON HAT TRICK *Reputed to be unbeatable on grass, a balletically poised Pete Sampras shows the form that took him to a third successive Wimbledon singles title in 1995.*

FORMER PIRATE *South African soccer star Jomo Sono, who started off with Orlando Pirates before moving to Cosmos, scored 200 goals during a seven-year career in America.*

possible score for potting all the balls in one break (assuming there has been no previous foul by an opponent) is 147. The 'frame', or game, ends when all balls have been potted or one of the players concedes. A 'snooker' is a position in the game in which the cue ball comes to rest at a point where a player cannot hit the coloured object ball or balls directly.
❖ Snooker was devised in 1875 by British Army officers in India, who were tired of playing billiards. The name is thought to have come from 'Snookers', the nickname given to first-year cadets at the Royal Military Academy in London at that time.

Sobers, Sir Gary (Garfield) (1936-) West Indian cricketer who was possibly the best all-rounder in the history of the game. An elegant left-handed batsman, he scored 8 032 runs (including 26 centuries) in his 93 Test matches – a record at the time – at an average of 57,78. His 365 not out against Pakistan in 1958 beat Len Hutton's Test record by one run. In turn, this was beaten by the West Indian batsman Brian LARA, with 375 against England in 1994. Sobers was the first player to hit six sixes in an over – for Nottinghamshire against Glamorgan in 1968. He was also a fine left-arm fast, medium and slow bowler, taking 235 Test wickets and 110 catches. He captained the West Indies between 1965 and 1972. He was knighted when her retired from cricket in 1975.

Sono, Jomo (1955-) South African soccer player who played alongside legends of the game such as PELÉ and Franz Beckenbauer at New York Cosmos in the 1970s. Sono's father Eric played for Orlando Pirates in the 1960s and Jomo made his debut for the same club in 1970. He moved to Cosmos in 1977 and scored 200 goals during a seven-year career in America. On his return to South Africa, he bought the old Highlands Park football club, which he later renamed Jomo Cosmos. With Sono still an influential figure in midfield, the club won the league championship in 1987 and the BOB Save trophy in 1990, and progressed to the semifinals of the African Cup Winners' Cup trophy in 1993, despite being relegated from the first division that season. He is a successful businessman, owning a promotions company and several fast food franchises.

Spitz, Mark (1950-) US swimmer who won an unprecedented seven gold medals at the 1972 Olympics in Munich. His victories, in individual and relay events, were all in world-record times. He had previously won two golds, a silver and a bronze at the 1968 Olympics in Mexico City.

sports boycott A concerted sanction on athletes to and from South Africa that lasted more than two decades and prevented most of the country's white athletes of the 1970s and 1980s from competing at an international level. It affected mainly team sports, although individual golfers and tennis players who could still partake on world circuits were made to feel unwelcome in some countries, and refused entry in others. The boycott had its genesis in the treatment meted out to Basil D'OLIVEIRA in 1968 and was later strengthened by anti-apartheid activists such as Peter Hain, who led disruptive demonstrations against the Springbok rugby tour of Britain in 1969-70. In 1981 the United Nations Committee Against Apartheid released a blacklist of prominent athletes around the world who had maintained links with South Africa, which further entrenched the country's sporting isolation. On his return to the country in 1991, ANC leader Steve Tshwete, who became Minister of Sport after the democratic election of 1994, played a significant role in ending the boycott by helping broker solutions between fractious South African sporting bodies. First to compete after the boycott ended was the national cricket team that undertook a short tour of India in late 1991.
❖ In 1995 the seal was set on South Africa's reacceptance into the international community when it was host to the World Cup rugby tournament.

squash Racket game played with a small, soft rubber ball on an indoor court with four walls. The rackets have smaller heads than those used in tennis. The ball is served from boxes marked on the floor, and only the server can score points. If he or she loses a rally, service goes to the opponent. Players take alternate shots and the ball must hit the front wall before it touches the floor. However, it can hit any of the other walls before or after the front wall. The ball may be played on the volley, but must not be allowed to bounce on the floor more than once. The first player to score nine points wins the game. However, if the score reaches eight-all, the receiver of the serve can extend the game to ten points. Matches are played over five games.

sumo wrestling Traditional Japanese form of wrestling in which two huge contestants grapple together with the aim of being the first to throw, push, pull, twist or slap the other onto the floor or out of the small ring. Bouts rarely last for more than a few seconds. Professional Japanese wrestlers belong to 'stables', where they train for big tournaments which last 15 days and are held six times a year in Japan.

Super Bowl Contest in AMERICAN FOOTBALL between the champions of the two national leagues: the American Football Conference (AFC) and the National Football Conference (NFC). It was first held in January 1967 in the Los Angeles Coliseum. In January 1995 the San Francisco 49ers beat the San Diego Chargers to become the first team to win the Super Bowl five times.

surfing Water sport in which participants stand or lie on special boards, using them to 'catch' and 'ride' big waves while performing graceful moves, stunts and other routines. The best surfing beaches are in the Pacific. The sport is widely practised on the coasts of Australia, California, Hawaii and South Africa. World championships are held annually. Body surfing, without boards, is particularly popular in Australia.

swimming Major Olympic sport, involving a variety of strokes and distances. In freestyle events, swimmers may officially swim any stroke, but most choose the front crawl – the fastest. Backstroke, breaststroke and butterfly are the other strokes, all four being used in medley events. Freestyle distances range from 50 m to 1 500 m and for other strokes from 50 m to 200 m. Swimmers must touch the end of the pool at each turn, and rules govern how a turn should be made. Races are timed to one-thousandth of a second.
❖ In synchronized swimming, the swimmers

MAN MOUNTAIN *The world's heaviest sumo wrestler, 263 kg Konishiki – known as the 'Dump Truck' – prepares to take on an opponent. He owes his weight to eating vast quantities of a special high-protein stew.*

perform graceful, ballet-like routines in the pool. There are solo, duet and team competitions, in which synchronization plays a vital part. Points are awarded according to the degree of difficulty and quality of manoeuvres.

table tennis Game played with small wooden bats and a light celluloid ball on a wooden table measuring 2,7 m by 1,5 m with a 15 cm high net across the middle. The aim is to score points by hitting the ball across the net so that an opponent cannot hit it back. Each player has five serves in succession, and the first player to reach 21 points (with a lead of two points) wins a game. In doubles, players must hit the ball alternately. Top-ranking players can retrieve smashes from as far as 6 m behind the table.

Tayfield, Hugh (1929-94) Highly competitive South African off-spin bowler who held the record for the most number of Test wickets for his country. In a career that spanned 37 Tests, Tayfield took 170 wickets at an average of 27,91. His best performance was a match-winning 9/113 in the fourth Test at the Wanderers against England in 1957. Nicknamed 'Toey', Tayfield was known for his tight control of length and his ability to bowl marathon spells.

tennis World's leading racket sport, played on courts with the standard dimensions of 23,77 m (78 ft) long by 8,23 m (27 ft) wide but on a variety of surfaces – including grass, cement, clay, tarmac and rubberized carpet on most indoor courts. The original surface used for tennis was grass, and the sport is still sometimes called lawn tennis. At the start of each point the ball is served from behind the baseline into a service court on the other side of the net. A valid service that is not returned is often called an 'ace'. The rally then continues until one player fails to return the ball into the opponent's side of the court. On fast surfaces such as grass, the powerful serve-and-volley game is dominant: as soon as a player has served a ball, he or she moves up towards the net to try to volley the return. On slower surfaces, the 'baseline' game, marked by long rallies of groundstrokes, prevails. Matches are divided into sets and games. A set is won by the first player to be two games ahead and win six games. If a set reaches six-all, then a tie-break is played, unless it is the deciding set, in which case play sometimes continues until one player wins by being two games ahead. A match is usually the best of three sets – although in major events, such as Wimbledon and other GRAND SLAM tournaments, men play the best of five.

❖ The tie-break operates when the score reaches six games all in any set except, on occasions, the final set of a three or five-set match. The first player to win seven points takes the game and set, providing he or she leads by two points. If the score reaches six points all, the game is extended until this margin is achieved.

tenpin bowling Indoor game in which players roll a heavy ball down a wooden alley and try to knock over ten upright wooden clubs known as 'pins'. Players have ten frames, or turns, in a game and are allowed two attempts at each frame. If all ten pins fall on the first ball, it is called a 'strike'. If it takes two deliveries to knock down all ten pins, it is called a 'spare'.

❖ Tenpin bowling started in the USA in the 1800s to beat a law banning ninepins, which had become dominated by gamblers.

Thompson, Daley (1958-) British athlete who won the DECATHLON gold medals at the 1980 and 1984 Olympics and broke the world points record for the event four times. He won the decathlon in the first world athletics championships in 1983, as well as three Commonwealth and two European titles. Plagued by injury later in his career, he retired in 1992 and turned to commentating on athletics.

Thomson, Shaun (1955-) South African champion surfer known for his fast, sweeping turns and brilliant tube riding. Thomson became world champion in 1977, spent 13 years in the world's top 12 and won 11 world tour events, including three victories in the Gunston 500, South Africa's premier surfing event. He took part in more than 220 professional events worldwide, set a record of 19 wins in major events, and had earned more than US$200 000 when he retired in 1989.

Thorpe, Jim (1888-1953) US athlete, baseball and football star who was one of the greatest ever all-round sportsmen. Part American Indian, part French and Irish, Thorpe won both the DECATHLON and the PENTATHLON in the 1912 Olympics in Sweden by huge margins. But his record was later expunged and his medals withdrawn for having received a few dollars for playing baseball during a college vacation, thus infringing his amateur status. He played major-league baseball (1913-19) and American football in the 1920s, when he was one of the game's star players.

❖ Thorpe, who died in poverty in 1953, was portrayed by Burt Lancaster in the film *Man of Bronze* (1951). In 1982 his medals were returned to his family and his name was restored to the Olympic champions' roll.

three-day event Demanding equestrian challenge for both horse and rider. Points are awarded in three separate disciplines, DRESSAGE, speed and endurance, and SHOWJUMPING, each of which is contested on separate days. The second stage, called speed and endurance, is divided into four phases: roads and tracks, steeplechase, another round of roads and tracks, and cross-country. It is an Olympic and world championships sport.

Tour de France World's best-known cycling race, staged annually over three weeks in summer and covering some 4 000 km of France and parts of neighbouring countries. Every stage is a race in itself, but riders' times for each stage are added together to determine the overall winner. Sponsored riders compete in teams of 12. Team members help each other, especially their top rider or riders. Some, called '*domestiques*', carry drinks and help with punctures, as well as acting as pace-setters – they even give up their own

PEDAL POWER *Competitors in the Tour de France turn on the power at the Perpignan stage of the race. Miguel Induráin of Spain (inset) won the race five years in succession, from 1991 to 1995.*

bikes to team mates if necessary. The race leader traditionally wears a yellow jersey.

Toweel, Vic (1928-) South Africa's first boxing world champion and a member of the famous Toweel boxing family. In his fourth fight as a professional, Toweel won the national bantamweight title and in his seventh fight won the national featherweight title. He won the British Empire title when he beat Stan Rowan in November 1949, and a month later became South Africa's first world champion when he beat Mexico's Manuel Ortiz for the world bantamweight title. He defended it three times – against Ireland's Danny O'Sullivan (whom he knocked down 14 times before winning on a technical knockout), the Spaniard Louis Romero and Scotland's Peter Keenan. Toweel lost his title in 1952 to Australia's Jimmy Carruthers. He fought 32 times, winning 28 matches, losing three and drawing one. Later he moved to Australia, where he made news in 1993 by donating one of his kidneys to a grandson.

Tyson, Mike (1965-) US boxer who, at 20, was the youngest man ever to win a world heavyweight title. He took the heavyweight division by storm and became undisputed world champion in 1987. Tyson – whose neck measurement is a massive 49,5 cm – looked set to be champion for years to come. But his career was affected by the collapse of his marriage to an actress, followed by late-night brawls and arrests. After winning ten world heavyweight title fights, he lost his title in 1990 to the little-known American James 'Buster' Douglas in Tokyo.
❖ In 1992, after a sensational trial, Tyson was sentenced to six years' imprisonment for the rape of an 18-year-old student. He was released in 1995.

Visagie, Piet (1943-) South African flyhalf who played 25 Tests for his country between 1967 and 1971, scoring 130 points, a tally exceeded only by Naas BOTHA. Visagie scored six Test tries. In a total of 44 representative matches for South Africa, he scored 240 points. He played provincial rugby for the unfashionable Griqualand West team that won the Currie Cup in 1970. South Africa lost only four Tests in which Visagie was flyhalf.

volleyball Outdoor or indoor team game that was invented in 1895 to improve the health of out-of-condition American businessmen. It became an Olympic sport in 1964 and is now played by men and women at all levels. Two six-member teams compete to score points by hitting a large inflated ball over a net into the opposing team's court, so that they cannot return it or are forced to play the ball out of court. After a ball has been served, each team is allowed to hit it three times in the air with their hands or arms before sending it over the net. The first team to reach 15 points wins the set, but they must have a two-point lead or play on until one is established.

CATCHING THE BREEZE *The popularity of wind-surfing has grown rapidly world-wide since the first sailboard was invented in 1952. It was introduced as an Olympics event in 1994.*

water polo Seven-a-side team game played in a pool measuring from 20 to 30 m long and from 8 to 20m wide, with water at least 1 m deep. Team members can swim with the ball and pass it to each other with the aim of throwing it into their opponents' goal. Except for the goalkeeper, they may not touch the ball with both hands or punch it, and only the goalkeeper may stand to play the ball.

Watson, Doug (1943-) South African bowls player who won the world singles title in front of his home crowd in 1976. He also won five South African Masters titles and was named South African Sportsman of the Year in 1976. He competed for Eastern Transvaal (now ▷MPUMALANGA) from 1967 onwards.

weightlifting Sport in which participants compete in many categories according to their bodyweight. There are two main recognized lifts: the snatch, a lift from floor to overhead in one continuous movement; and the clean and jerk, a lift in two stages – first to the shoulders (the clean) and then overhead (the jerk). A contestant may have three attempts. Once the weight on the bar has been increased, subsequent contestants may not attempt a lighter lift.
❖ In 1988 Leonid Taranenko of the former USSR set a clean and jerk record of 266 kg.
❖ A world record-breaking weightlifter is South African born Precious MCKENZIE.

Wessels, Kepler (1957-) South African cricketer who emigrated to Australia to fulfil his sports ambitions. Wessels made 162 on his debut for Australia against England in 1982 and went on to score 2 550 runs in 37 Tests for his adopted country. He returned to South Africa to lead Eastern Province from the doldrums to Currie Cup success in 1989. Wessels was chosen to captain South Africa at the 1992 World Cup. His captaincy and batting style were sometimes criticized as being too negative, but under Wessels South Africa never lost a Test series. He scored 1 027 runs in 16 Tests for the country before retiring from international cricket at the end of 1994.

Wimbledon Tennis club in southwest London that has become synonymous with the All-England Lawn Tennis Championships – the world's most prestigious tennis event. The first championships were held at Wimbledon in 1877. All the singles finals have been played on the centre court, which now holds 20 000 spectators. There are 18 grass courts at Wimbledon, and some 20 other courts. The championships are held annually in the last week of June and the first week of July. As well as men's and women's singles, doubles, and mixed doubles, the fortnight includes tournaments for juniors and veterans.

windsurfing Water sport, also known as boardsailing, in which participants stand on a board in the water and steer by tilting a sail which is attached to a small mast connected to the board by a universal joint. There are freestyle windsurfing competitions, in which contestants perform tricks, balances and other manoeuvres. Windsurf racing was introduced into the Olympics in 1984.

❖ The windsurfing sailboard was invented in 1958 by a 12-year-old English schoolboy, Peter Chilvers.

Winter Olympics International games held separately from the OLYMPIC GAMES since their inauguration in 1924. Before that, ice skating and ICE HOCKEY had sometimes been included in the summer games. Since 1994 the winter games have been held in the middle of the four-year cycle of the summer games – instead of, as previously, the winter and summer games being staged in the same year. Major events include ski jumping, figure-skating, speed skating, cross-country skiing and BOBSLEIGHING.

World Cup International association football tournament, first held in 1930, when it was contested by 13 countries and won by the hosts, Uruguay. More than 140 countries now take part in qualifying stages, of which 24 reach the finals. The first round of the finals is played in six groups of four teams, and all the teams within a group play each other. The top two from each group, together with the best four of the others, make up the last 16, and thereafter it becomes a knock-out competition. The first World Cup was the Jules Rimet Trophy, named after the Frenchman who pioneered the tournament. Brazil won the trophy outright in 1970, when they became the first country to win three World Cups. Italy and Germany later achieved the same feat, and in 1994 Brazil achieved a record fourth World Cup victory. The present trophy is the FIFA (Fédération Internationale de Football Association) World Cup.

❖ A cricket World Cup, started in 1975, takes place every four years; Pakistan took the honours in 1992.

❖ A rugby World Cup series was begun in 1987; it was won by South Africa in 1995.

world drivers' championship International competition for FORMULA ONE Grand Prix racing drivers. Its inaugural race was the British Grand Prix at Silverstone in 1950. Points are awarded for placings in each of the season's major Grand Prix events: ten for a win, six for second place, four for third, and three, two and one for the minor positions. Juan Manuel FANGIO of Argentina won the championship a record five times between 1951 and 1957. More recent winners include Nelson Piquet (Brazil), Alain PROST (France), Ayrton SENNA (Brazil), Nigel Mansell (Britain) and Michael Schumacher (Germany).

wrestling Group of sports in which two contestants attempt to throw or immobilize each other. Wrestling formed part of the ancient Greek Olympics, and it was one of the original sports in the modern Games. The two Olympic styles are freestyle and Greco-Roman. The main differences between them is that use of the legs and holds below the waist are not allowed in Greco-Roman. There are ten weight categories for each style. Many cultures practise their own form of wrestling, including SUMO in Japan; 'glima' (Iceland), in which wrestlers grasp each other by means of a hip harness; 'yagli' (Turkey), in which the wrestlers are covered in oil; and 'Cumberland and Westmorland' (northern England), in which each wrestler joins his own hands behind the other's back, and the two contestants try to wrestle each other to the ground from a chest-to-chest clinch. In professional all-in wrestling there are almost no restrictions on the type of holds.

yacht racing Water sport comprising both 'one-design' events – in which strict rules govern the yachts' shape and sail area – and handicap races for various classes of vessel. Race distances cover anything from a couple of nautical miles in a one-man dinghy to the four-yearly Whitbread Round the World race over a course of some 32 000 nautical miles that takes some six months. Crews, which range from one to a dozen depending on the size of vessel, work to make the best use of the wind. Yachting has been an Olympic sport since 1900. The first women-only class was introduced in 1988. One of the world's best-known yachting competitions is the AMERICA'S CUP. One of the best known yacht races in South Africa is the Cape-to-Rio race, 3 640 nautical miles long, which takes competitors an average of 25 days to finish. The first race was held in 1971. Political problems diverted the race to Uruguay in the late 1970s and early 1980s, but the race returned to the Rio endpoint in 1993. Bertie Reed and John Martin were two outstanding South African trans-ocean yachtsmen of the 1980s. Reed was notable for his skilful and often successful handling of the ageing yacht *Voortrekker*, which he sailed to a remarkable second place in the BOC round-the-world race in 1983. Martin's finest accomplishment was his two victories out of four legs of the BOC in 1986.

Zatopek, Emil (1922-) Czech athlete who was one of the greatest long-distance runners of all time. Between May 1948 and July 1954 he ran 38 races at 10 000 m and won them all, including two Olympic finals. In 1952 he won three Olympic golds: the 5000 m, the 10 000 m and the marathon – a unique treble. Despite an ungainly style on the track, he set 18 world records at distances ranging from 5 000 m to 30 000 m. He ran with his arms flailing and head rolling, and a look of agony on his face, as if he might collapse at any moment. However, he was a master tactician who built up his stamina by arduous training.

TRANS-OCEAN NAVIGATORS *In the BOC solo round-the-world race in 1991, Bertie Reed (right) came to the rescue when the yacht sailed by fellow South African John Martin foundered.*

FOOD AND DRINK

Mealtimes are milestones in the day: they divide it into smaller, manageable periods, and offer a break in routine and a chance to relax. The human race has turned nourishment into an elaborate social ritual and a sensual indulgence. Never before has such a range of foods and drinks from across the world been so widely available. Baklavas, blinis and sushi, tequila, cassis and schnapps are no longer foreign to us.

al dente (al DEN-tay) Italian term meaning 'to the tooth'. It is used to describe pasta that is cooked through but remains firm enough to bite. Slightly crisp vegetables may also be described as al dente.

Angostura bitters Reddish-brown spicy tonic mostly used to flavour drinks – for example, pink gins.

anise Aromatic plant whose seeds, called aniseeds and which have a liquorice flavour, are used to flavour food as well as drinks such as pastis and OUZO. Its leaves can be used in salads and fish soups.

antipasto Italian term, meaning 'before the meal', used to describe appetizers.

artichoke The heart and fleshy part of the leaves of globe artichokes, shaped like large thistle heads, are usually eaten steamed or boiled, with a vinaigrette sauce. Jerusalem artichokes, knobbly tubers with a nutty-flavoured flesh – commonly grown in South Africa – are often used in soups. Chinese artichokes are similar to Jerusalem artichokes.

atjar A hot pickle or relish containing chunks of whole fruit or vegetables and served with Cape Malay curries.

au gratin Dishes served 'au gratin' are usually sprinkled with a mixture of grated cheese and breadcrumbs and are browned under a grill or in the oven until crusty.

bagel Ring-shaped traditional Jewish roll which is boiled for a few seconds before being baked, giving it a slightly chewy texture. Bagels are often filled with smoked salmon and cream cheese.

baklava Greek or Turkish triangular sweet made of alternate layers of thin filo pastry, chopped pistachio nuts and almonds mixed with sugar and spices. A boiling syrup of honey, sugar, rose water and lemon juice is poured over the dish after cooking.

béarnaise Creamy sauce made from egg yolks, white wine vinegar and butter, and flavoured with chopped spring onions, chervil, tarragon and peppercorns. It is typically served with steak, poached salmon or fresh asparagus.

béchamel White sauce made with butter, flour and milk infused with bay leaves, onion, peppercorns and nutmeg.

Beeton, Mrs (Isabella) (1836-65) British cookery writer who, during her short life (she died after the birth of her fourth child) wrote the definitive Victorian book on cookery and the art of housekeeping, the *Book of Household Management* (1860). Although much of it is now out of date and inapplicable to modern households, it remains a classic that many people still find useful and entertaining.

VICTORIAN STANDARDS *Mrs Beeton's* Book of Household Management *was the housewife's bible. Beeton wrote it because 'there is no more fruitful source of family discontentment than a housewife's badly cooked dinners and untidy ways'.*

bhajia (chilliebite) Indian savoury dish made from chillies, other vegetables, herbs – usually including fresh coriander – and spices. Onion bhajias are rolled into balls, covered in flour and deep-fried.

biltong Popular South African snack of spiced beef, buck or ostrich meat, traditionally dried and cured in the sun. It was once regular fare for the nomadic ▷TREKBOERS.

biriani (breyani) Among the best of exotic Indian rice dishes, which has become a Cape Malay favourite. Meat (usually mutton), chicken or fish is combined with rice, lentils, eggs and spices, usually including saffron. Vegetarian versions have also been created.

bisque Thick soup that is usually made from shellfish and enriched with cream, wine, egg yolks and brandy. The basic ingredient of the classic bisque is usually rock lobster.

blini Small leavened pancake made with buckwheat flour and often served with soured cream and CAVIAR.

bobotie Spiced dish of minced beef or mutton with an egg custard topping. It was introduced by Malay slaves and has become a traditional meal in South Africa.

boerewors Original farm-style sausage of South Africa, made usually from a mixture of beef and pork. There are stringent criteria for what may be labelled boerewors.

Bombay duck Small fish found off the west coast of India which are dried on racks in the sun and flavoured with the pungent and garlicky herb asafetida.

bouillabaisse (BOO-ya-bess) French soup or stew made with fish stock, fish fillets, vegetables and herbs. Traditionally, this is separated into two courses: as a broth poured over slices of dry, stale bread, and then as a dish of fish and vegetables.

bourguignon (bor-gin-NYON) Method of cooking food in red wine with mushrooms, onion, bacon pieces and herbs.

bredie Cape Malay meat and vegetable stew, subtly spiced and prepared in a minimum of liquid. It is named after the vegetable used, for example WATERBLOMMETJIES bredie.

bresaola (brezz-OW-la) Cured reddish-brown beef tenderloin from Italy. It is dried for two months before being sliced very thinly and served with olive oil, lemon juice, black pepper and parsley.

calzone Italian savoury, made with pizza dough which is folded over a filling and sealed before being baked.

Cape Malay Distinctive, spicy cuisine of the Muslim community of Cape Town. Although named after the original Malay slaves who introduced their recipes to South Africa, the style evolved locally and was also influenced by several other Eastern styles of cooking, including Indian.

carob Bean with a sweet pulp which is often used as a chocolate substitute because it has a lower fat content and contains no caffeine.

cassis Sweet blackcurrant liqueur. A small amount of cassis – one part in 20 – mixed with white wine makes Kir; with Champagne it is called Kir Royale.

cassoulet French casserole made with haricot beans and goose, pork or duck.

caviar Ripe eggs of sturgeon, a bony variety of fish. It is typically served from a dish that sits on a bed of crushed ice, and eaten with soured cream on a BLINI or on fresh white toast. There are many substitutes, the most common being lumpfish roe which are dyed red or black.
❖ The most expensive food in the world is beluga caviar from sturgeons, which live mainly in the Caspian and Black seas.

challah Bread traditionally eaten on the Jewish Sabbath. A plaited loaf, often decorated with poppy or sesame seeds, is also called *kitke* in South Africa.

chicory (endive) White and crisp salad vegetable which has a slightly bitter taste, especially if it is old. Curly endive looks more like a lacy, pale green lettuce. Radicchio is a purple-and-white chicory.

chocolate Mixture made from roasted and ground cocoa (cacao) seeds and sugar, often with added milk, fruit or nuts.
❖ The percentage of cocoa in chocolate varies from 2 per cent in white chocolate to 70 per cent in dark chocolate.

chorizo Dry Spanish sausage made from cured pork or beef and seasoned with garlic and red pepper. It can be eaten raw, fried, or added to a white bean stew called *fabada*.

chowder Thick soup or stew, usually made with clams, shellfish or fish.

cognac Brandy made from the double distillation of white wine. The alcohol from the first distillation is distilled again. It is matured in seasoned oak casks, where it may remain for up to 60 years. Strictly speaking, only brandy produced in the area round the town of Cognac, in the Charente region of western France, may be called cognac.
❖ Three-star cognac is aged for between three and five years, VSOP (very special – or superior – old pale) cognac for five to 15 years and Napoleon for a minimum of 30 years.

consommé Clear, thin soup made from clarified stock, and served hot or cold.

cordon bleu Term used for an outstanding cook or a very high standard of cooking.
❖ The term means 'blue ribbon' and was originally the highest order of knighthood in France, the members of which wore a blue sash. The term probably became used in cooking because French cooks often wore an apron with blue ribbons.

coulis Purée of fruit or vegetables which is thin enough to pour.

POPULAR CHEESES

Blaauwkrantz	South Africa; cow's milk	Blue-veined, Roquefort-style cheese. It is granular and has a sharp, tangy, salty taste.
Brie	France; cow's milk	Flat round, with a white, downy rind and mild-flavoured centre which should be soft, almost runny, when ripe.
Camembert	France; cow's milk	Small, flat round with a soft, white rind. The centre has an earthy flavour, and should be soft but firm when eaten.
Cheddar	England; cow's milk	Hard and golden. It has a smooth taste and should be matured for at least 12 to 18 months.
Drakensberg	South Africa; cow's milk	Semi-soft, dark yellow, with a soft, creamy texture and rich flavour.
Feta	Greece; goat's, cow's or sheep's milk	Snow-white, crumbly and slightly salty. Very moist, ripened in a mixture of its own whey and brine.
Gouda	Netherlands; cow's milk	Mild, yellow and firm. A similar cheese, made in a large ball shape with a red wax rind, is Edam.
Gruyère	Switzerland; cow's milk	Waxy, mild cheese with small holes. Emmenthal – a similar cheese – has much larger holes.
Jarlsberg	Norway; cow's milk	Semi-hard with large holes and a dry rind. It has a nutty, sweet flavour.
Mozzarella	Italy; water-buffalo's or cow's milk	Handmade fresh cheese, shaped into balls and kept in salted whey or brine. It is soft and white, with a bland milky flavour, and provides the 'stringy' topping for pizzas.
Parmesan	Italy; cow's milk	Rock-hard salty cheese. To enjoy the full, almost spicy flavour of *Parmigiano Reggiano* – Parmesan matured for at least three years – it must be freshly grated.
Ricotta	Italy; cow's or sheep's milk	White and crumbly whey which is low in fat – similar to cottage cheese.
Roquefort	France; sheep's milk	Semi-hard blue cheese which is matured in the damp, cool Combalou caves. It is widely regarded as one of the world's finest cheeses.
Stilton	England; cow's milk	A firm cheese, which can be either white or blue. When ripe, it has a sharp, tangy flavour.

couscous (coose-coose) Type of semolina made from coarsely ground wheat rolled into pellets. When soaked or steamed, it swells like rice. It is a staple food in North Africa.

crème fraîche Slightly sharp or sour-tasting thick cream made from cow's milk.

creole The cuisine of the West Indies. Savoury creole dishes of shellfish, salt cod, chicken and pork are typically cooked in a spicy tomato, pepper and onion sauce and served with rice. Sweet Creole dishes often use banana or pineapple with rum.

croissant French pastry, made by layering butter with enriched yeast dough.
❖ Croissants were first made in Budapest in 1686. Bakers working at night heard Turkish assailants digging underground and gave the alarm. The city was saved and the bakers created the pastry to mark the victory, choosing the crescent shape after the emblem on the flag of the Ottoman empire.

crudités Hors d'oeuvre of raw vegetables – for example carrots, cucumber, celery and peppers – sliced or cut into sticks and eaten with dips such as TZATZIKI or HUMMUS.

Daiquiri Cocktail made with four parts white rum to one part lime juice, a dash of sugar syrup and crushed ice.

dauphinoise (doe-fin-WAHZ) French method of oven-baking thinly sliced potatoes covered with milk or cream.
❖ *Gratin dauphinoise* is made by adding beaten egg and grated cheese to the dish.

dhal Indian word for various kinds of split lentils, beans or other pulses, and the term used to describe their cooked state. Dhal is served seasoned with garlic and spices such as cumin and coriander, and may be puréed.

dolmades (dol-MAH-dez) Minced lamb and rice rolled in vine leaves and cooked in stock, olive oil and lemon juice. The dish originates from Turkey and Greece.

Dry Martini Cocktail with two parts gin to one of dry vermouth, and a green olive or twist of lemon. The drier the martini, the smaller the proportion of vermouth.

enchilada (EN-chill-AH-da) Spicy Mexican corn pancake, or TORTILLA, filled with meat, beans or chicken and topped with chilli sauce and cheese.

en croûte A dish cooked in a pastry case. It is a French term, meaning 'in a crust'.

Escoffier, Auguste (1846-1935) French chef who began his career at the age of 13 in his uncle's restaurant in Nice. He went on to work in Paris and ran the kitchens in the Savoy Hotel in London in 1890, before moving to the Carlton Hotel in 1898. Escoffier invented many recipes, including peach melba, and wrote several influential books, including *Ma Cuisine* (1934). France awarded him both the Legion and the Officer of Honour in recognition of his work.
❖ Escoffier is known as 'the king of chefs and the chef of kings'.

felafel (fell-AFF-ul) Middle Eastern dish of deep-fried patties made from spiced, crushed beans or chickpeas. Felafel is often served in pitta bread with salad and TAHINI dressed with chilli sauce.

florentine Any dish made, served or garnished with spinach and coated in a mornay (cheese) sauce; the name comes from the Florence region, formerly a spinach-growing area. A florentine is also a round, flat biscuit made with dried fruit and nuts, coated on one side with chocolate.

focaccia (fo-CATCH-ee-a) Soft and savoury Italian flat bread made with olive oil and usually topped with garlic and rosemary.

foie gras (FWA GRAH) Goose or duck liver, usually gently poached or braised, or made into pâté. Goose foie gras is a creamy white or light pink, while duck foie gras tends to be darker and has a slightly stronger flavour. Both have a very high fat content as birds are force-fed to enlarge the liver artificially. Foie gras is normally served as an hors d'oeuvre.

fondue Swiss speciality prepared at the table. Cheese (usually Gruyère), white wine, kirsch and seasonings are melted in a dish over a spirit lamp. Diners dunk cubes of bread into the fondue sauce.
❖ In a fondue bourguignonne, cubes of raw meat are cooked in hot oil in the fondue dish and then dipped into sauces such as mustard, horseradish or mayonnaise.

fricassee (fri-cass-AY) Stew of chicken, veal, lamb or fish in a white sauce containing small onions and mushrooms.

fromage frais Fresh soft cheese made with fermented skimmed milk, which sets like yoghurt. It can be used as a slightly lighter and sharper substitute for cream.

gazpacho Chilled or iced Spanish soup of tomato, cucumber, red peppers, onions, garlic, olive oil and bread.

ghee Clarified butter used in Indian cooking. It has a sweet, slightly nutty flavour.

gnocchi (NYOCK-ee) Italian dumplings made from potatoes, semolina pasta or a flour and egg mixture, and served in soup or with a cheese or tomato sauce.

goulash Rich meat, tomato and onion stew seasoned with paprika. The term derives from the Hungarian *gulyás hus*, meaning 'herdsman's meat'.

grappa Clear spirit – similar to South Africa's home-distilled *witblitz* ('white lightning') – made in Italy by distilling what remains of grapes (such as skins, pulp and stalks) after being pressed to extract the juice for wine.

gravlax Scandinavian dish of thinly sliced raw, marinated salmon, traditionally served with a sweet mustard and dill sauce.

guacamole (gwacka-MO-lay) Mexican dish of mashed avocado, tomato and seasoning served with helpings of crisp TORTILLA or as an accompaniment to meat.

gumbo Thick soup from Louisiana made with okra and a variety of other ingredients such as ham or fish.

haggis Scottish speciality of sheep's stomach stuffed with oatmeal, onions, fat and spiced sheep's offal. Haggis is boiled and served with mashed turnip, or 'neeps', on Burns' Night, 25 January.

halva Middle Eastern sweetmeat made from roasted, ground sesame seeds mixed with boiled sugar. It is often flavoured with pistachio nuts, honey or vanilla.

Harvey Wallbanger Cocktail made with one measure of vodka to two measures of fresh orange juice, a dash of Galliano liqueur and crushed ice.

hollandaise Rich sauce of butter, egg yolk and lemon juice served hot or cold with fish, vegetable or egg dishes.

hummus (GHOO-muss) Middle Eastern purée of chickpeas, TAHINI, garlic, lemon juice and olive oil. It is usually served with PITTA bread or as a dip with crudités.

julienne Fine vegetable strips, used as a garnish, sautéed in butter, or served as a salad.

kassler rib German-style pickled and smoked pork chops that are grilled, fried or barbecued, often served with SAUERKRAUT.

kebab (brochette) Chunks of meat and sometimes vegetables or fruit threaded on a skewer and roasted, grilled or barbecued. The South African equivalent, the *sosatie*, is made with spiced meat and fruit. The word may have entered Afrikaans from *sisateh*, Malay for minced or chopped meat.

kedgeree English breakfast dish of flaked fish – usually smoked haddock – rice, hard-boiled eggs and onions.
❖ The term derives from an Indian rice and lentil dish called *khichari*. Anglo-Indian chefs adapted this in the 19th century, using fish and eggs instead of lentils.

HERBS AND SPICES *Many herbs, used for garnishing dishes and adding flavour, are also valued for their medicinal properties. Most recipes call for spices – some as exotic as saffron, others as common as salt and pepper.*

konfyt Preserves or conserves of whole or large pieces of fruit in syrup, typically made with green figs or watermelon.
❖ In Afrikaans, *konfyt* refers to any jam. *Korrelkonfyt* is grape jam made from the hanepoot variety; *moskonfyt* is made from grape must.

Leipoldt, C Louis (1880-1947) Versatile South African intellectual, author and medical doctor. His culinary gifts gave rise to the Afrikaans classic, *Kos vir die Kenner* (1933), as well as collections of his recipes and articles on food and wine published posthumously.
❖ Leipoldt, an expert on Cape wines, once recommended the use of good wine as a healthy component of infants' diets.

mabela (amabele) Nguni word for millet and grain sorghum, Africa's indigenous grains which were the staple food in southern Africa until modern, disease-resistant maize was widely cultivated. It is still grown for making porridge and brewing beer, and is commercially available.

macrobiotic Term given to diets for healthy living which consist mainly of grains and vegetables, and sometimes fish. Meat, fruit, milk products and alcohol are forbidden.
❖ This system derives from the ancient Chinese principle of balancing the feminine (Yin) and the masculine (Yang).

Margarita Cocktail made with four parts TEQUILA to two parts lemon or lime juice. Traditionally, it should be served chilled with salt around the rim of the glass.

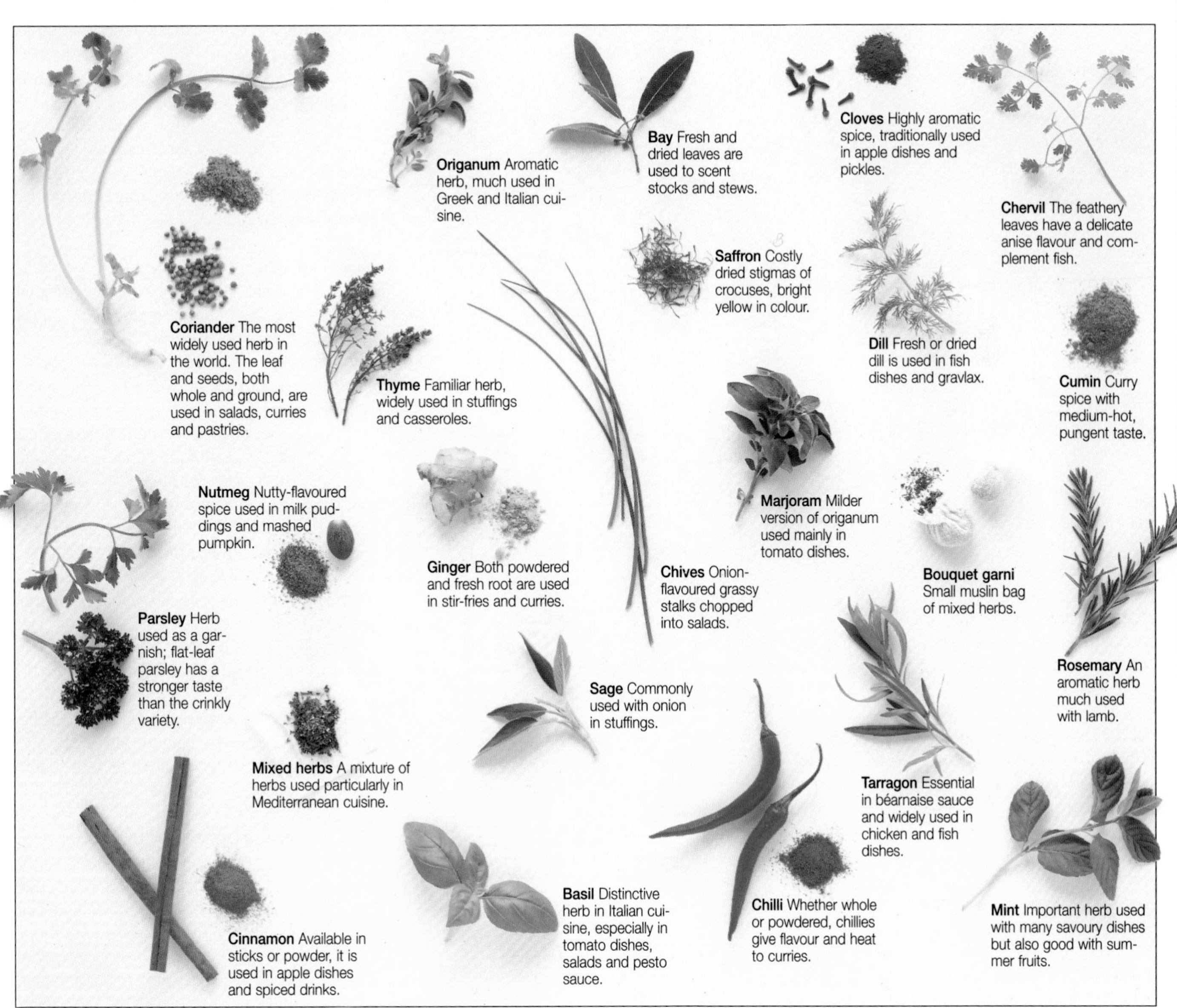

Coriander The most widely used herb in the world. The leaf and seeds, both whole and ground, are used in salads, curries and pastries.

Origanum Aromatic herb, much used in Greek and Italian cuisine.

Bay Fresh and dried leaves are used to scent stocks and stews.

Cloves Highly aromatic spice, traditionally used in apple dishes and pickles.

Chervil The feathery leaves have a delicate anise flavour and complement fish.

Saffron Costly dried stigmas of crocuses, bright yellow in colour.

Thyme Familiar herb, widely used in stuffings and casseroles.

Dill Fresh or dried dill is used in fish dishes and gravlax.

Cumin Curry spice with medium-hot, pungent taste.

Nutmeg Nutty-flavoured spice used in milk puddings and mashed pumpkin.

Marjoram Milder version of origanum used mainly in tomato dishes.

Ginger Both powdered and fresh root are used in stir-fries and curries.

Chives Onion-flavoured grassy stalks chopped into salads.

Bouquet garni Small muslin bag of mixed herbs.

Parsley Herb used as a garnish; flat-leaf parsley has a stronger taste than the crinkly variety.

Rosemary An aromatic herb much used with lamb.

Sage Commonly used with onion in stuffings.

Mixed herbs A mixture of herbs used particularly in Mediterranean cuisine.

Tarragon Essential in béarnaise sauce and widely used in chicken and fish dishes.

Basil Distinctive herb in Italian cuisine, especially in tomato dishes, salads and pesto sauce.

Chilli Whether whole or powdered, chillies give flavour and heat to curries.

Mint Important herb used with many savoury dishes but also good with summer fruits.

Cinnamon Available in sticks or powder, it is used in apple dishes and spiced drinks.

masala General term for the spices used in curries or for a prepared curry mixture. Garam masala is a mixture of hot spices usually added to Indian curries before serving.

mealie meal Finely ground maize (corn) which, cooked as a porridge, is a staple food to most people in South Africa. The porridge may be stiff (*phuthu* in Zulu, *stywepap* in Afrikaans) or crumbly (*mphokoqo* in Xhosa, *krummelpap* in Afrikaans). It is sometimes eaten with MFINO and sour milk (*amasi*). (See also MABELA.)

❖ Maize was introduced to Africa by the Portuguese from North America and was cultivated in southern Africa before the arrival of the Dutch colonists at the Cape.

mebos Old Cape confection made from salted and sugared dried apricots, enjoyed on its own or used in fruitcakes or chutney.

❖ Hildagonda Duckitt (1840-1905), the Cape cookery writer and author of *Hilda's Diary of a Cape Housekeeper*, recommended mebos as an antidote to seasickness.

VERSATILE PASTA *The best pasta is made from durum wheat and water, sometimes with added egg, spinach or other colourings and flavourings. It is available fresh or dried, in various shapes.*

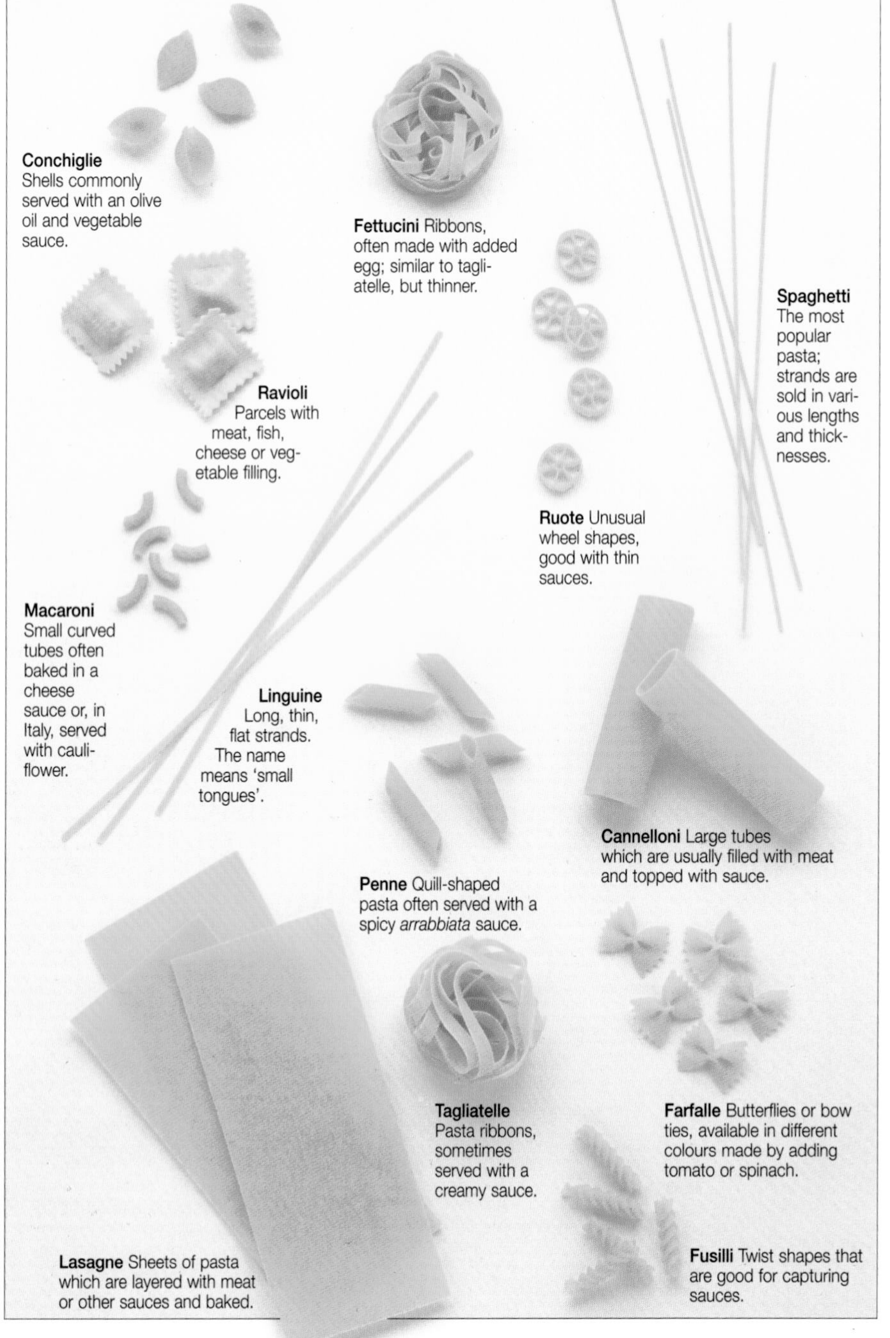

Conchiglie Shells commonly served with an olive oil and vegetable sauce.

Fettucini Ribbons, often made with added egg; similar to tagliatelle, but thinner.

Spaghetti The most popular pasta; strands are sold in various lengths and thicknesses.

Ravioli Parcels with meat, fish, cheese or vegetable filling.

Ruote Unusual wheel shapes, good with thin sauces.

Macaroni Small curved tubes often baked in a cheese sauce or, in Italy, served with cauliflower.

Linguine Long, thin, flat strands. The name means 'small tongues'.

Cannelloni Large tubes which are usually filled with meat and topped with sauce.

Penne Quill-shaped pasta often served with a spicy *arrabbiata* sauce.

Tagliatelle Pasta ribbons, sometimes served with a creamy sauce.

Farfalle Butterflies or bow ties, available in different colours made by adding tomato or spinach.

Lasagne Sheets of pasta which are layered with meat or other sauces and baked.

Fusilli Twist shapes that are good for capturing sauces.

meze (mezz-AY) Selection of spiced hors d'oeuvres traditionally served with OUZO or raki in Greece or Turkey. Meze often include DOLMADES, olives and dried meats.

❖ Meze is Turkish for a 'small bite'.

***mfino* (*imifino*)** Nguni word for wild green vegetables, which are cooked into a stew and served with MEALIE MEAL porridge. Different plants are used, depending on the region. They are also sometimes called 'African spinach'. The Sotho word is *morogo*.

nan (naan) Leavened Indian flat bread that is cooked in a charcoal or *tandoori* oven and is served with curry.

niçoise Dishes from Nice or the surrounding region in southeast France and typically made with tomatoes, olives, anchovies, garlic and green beans.

noisette French word for hazelnut, used to describe small, boneless lamb steaks, usually tied with string; also something flavoured or made with hazelnuts.

osso bucco Italian stew made from deboned knuckle of veal, tomatoes and onions, served with pasta or rice and *gremolata* – a spiced mixture of citrus peel, garlic and parsley.

ouzo Greek aniseed-flavoured clear spirit which becomes milky when water is added to it. It is traditionally served with MEZE.

paella Spanish dish of rice, shellfish, chicken and vegetables flavoured with saffron and cooked in a flat pan or *paellara*. Ingredients vary according to the region.

pastrami Highly seasoned smoked beef, traditionally thinly sliced and eaten on rye bread. The word comes from the Yiddish word *pastra*, meaning 'preserve'.

pesto Italian sauce made from basil, garlic, pine nuts, Parmesan cheese and olive oil, which is served with pasta. A French version called *pistou* can be added to soups.

pilaf (pilau) Eastern method of cooking rice. The rice is browned with spices before stock and vegetables are added. The rice is covered and cooked slowly without stirring until it has absorbed all the liquid.

Pina Colada A sweet, creamy cocktail usually made with three parts white rum, four parts pineapple juice and two parts coconut milk, with a dash of sugar syrup.

pitta Flat, slightly leavened bread which originated in the Middle East. It is chewy and faintly sweet, and can be slit open after heating to take a variety of fillings.

polenta Italian cornmeal which can be boiled and served soft, like semolina, or baked into a firm cake which can be served plain or topped with a sauce.

pot-au-feu Traditional French stew flavoured with aromatic herbs which can be served in two parts: as a soup (the broth) and then as a main dish (the meat).

potjiekos Literally 'pot food'. A Boer style of cooking in a three-legged iron pot (*potjie*) over a fire. It was revived in the 1980s as an alternative to braaivleis because of soaring meat prices. Today's potjiekos is a one-dish meal of meat or fish and vegetables.

pretzel Dry, crusty traditional German bread, typically hard-baked in the shape of knots, salted and served as a snack.

prosciutto (pro-SHOOT-oh) Italian cured ham which is matured for eight months to two years. The most famous is Parma ham, often sliced very thinly and served with fresh melon or green figs.

rijstafel Dutch for 'rice table'. The term is used for a meal made up of rice dishes which are served with a variety of Indonesian dishes made of spicy meat, fish and chicken, accompanied by fruit and vegetable side dishes, and garnished with pickles.

risotto Italian dish made by gently frying onions and *arborio* or 'risotto' rice (a short-grain variety) in butter and gradually stirring in stock and any other ingredients until the rice is cooked and can absorb no more liquid.

rocket (arugula) Green salad leaves shaped rather like those of the dandelion and having a clean, peppery flavour.

roti (chapatti) Unleavened bread of Indian origin which is cooked on a flat surface. In the Cape, a roti rolled around a filling of curry is known as a *salomi.*

sambal Any of a variety of side dishes served with Indian or Cape Malay curries. These may include ATJAR, pickles, chutneys and salads flavoured with vinegar, chilli and onion. The word comes from the Malay *sambal* or *sembal* for condiment.

samoosa (samosa) Indian savoury of deep-fried triangular pastry pockets filled with a mixture of spiced meat or vegetables.

sangria Citrus fruit punch of Spanish origin, made with red wine and served hot or cold. Brandy or liqueur may be added to the mix.

satay Malaysian or Indonesian dish of grilled spiced meat skewered on wooden sticks, usually served with a peanut sauce.

sauerkraut German dish of shredded cabbage preserved by being layered with salt and allowed to ferment. It is often served hot with potatoes and meats.

schnapps (schnaps) In Europe a term applied to a variety of strong spirits, including a Dutch gin made from potatoes.
❖ In German *schnaps* means 'snatch' or 'gasp', which evokes the manner in which it should be drunk – and the subsequent effect.

Screwdriver Cocktail of two parts gin or vodka and one part orange juice. If gin is used, a dash of sugar should be added.

shwarma (doner kebab) Middle Eastern dish in which slices of lamb are spit-roasted, then carved into slivers which are served in PITTA bread with raw onions, chilli or garlic sauce and salad dressed with TZATZIKI.

Singapore Sling Cocktail made with three parts gin to one part cherry brandy, the juice of a lemon or lime, water, sugar, fresh mint and a slice of orange.

smorgasbord Scandinavian savoury selection of hot or cold dishes served either as hors d'oeuvres or a full buffet meal.

sushi Japanese savoury delicacy which usually consists of seaweed rounds filled with seasoned rice and raw fish or shellfish, served with pickled ginger and a type of horseradish paste. Sashimi is thinly sliced raw fish without the rice or seaweed.

sweetbreads Culinary term for the thymus gland and the pancreas of pigs, lambs or calves. These are typically blanched and then fried in butter.

tabbouleh Middle Eastern cold dish of steamed cracked wheat (known as bulgur) mixed with mint, parsley, tomatoes, onions and lemon.

taco Mexican dish of fried TORTILLAS filled with meat or beans with GUACAMOLE and black-bean or chilli sauce.

tahini (tahina) Thick sesame seed paste used in Greek and Lebanese cooking, and an important ingredient in HUMMUS.

tapas Spanish selection of savoury hors d'oeuvres, which might typically include potato omelette, smoked sausage, spinach with pine nuts, garlic, chickpeas, olives, grilled prawns and fried calamari (squid).

tapenade Salty purée of black olives, anchovies, capers, lemon juice and garlic often used in pasta sauces.

taramasalata Greek speciality; a pale pink purée made from smoked cod's roe, blended with olive oil and lemon juice.

tequila Mexican spirit made from the pulp of the agave plant. It is often used in cocktails, but is also served as a 'short' which is traditionally knocked back in one gulp after sucking a slice of lime or lemon and putting a pinch of salt on the tongue.

teriyaki Japanese style of cooking. Fish or meat is marinated in soya sauce and rice wine and then grilled over charcoal.

terrine Any food cooked in a terrine – a deep earthenware dish with a tight-fitting lid. Terrines are most commonly used to make pâté. They are usually placed in a *bain-marie*, or large pan of hot water, in the oven, which gently cooks the contents.

tiramisu Layered Italian dessert consisting of sponge cake flavoured with coffee and Marsala wine or rum and brandy and creamy, soft mascarpone cheese.

tofu (bean curd) White purée of soya beans which is set solid. It has little taste but absorbs other flavours and can be used in creamy puddings or stir-fries. Tofu is high in protein and is eaten by many vegetarians, as well as being a staple food in Japan and other East Asian countries.

tortilla (tor-TEE-yah) Thin cornmeal pancake used in South America to make TACOS, tostadas (deep-fried flavoured crisps), and ENCHILADAS (meat and sauce wrapped in tortilla and baked).

truffles Walnut-sized and highly valued fungi with an unmistakable scent and distinctive flavour which grow underground on the roots of some trees. There are three types of edible truffle in Europe: the White Winter, the Black Winter (or Perigord) and the Black Summer. White truffles, the best of which come from Alba in Italy, are the most expensive. Truffles are located by pigs or trained dogs which sniff them out.

tzatziki Greek dip made with thick yoghurt, cucumber, garlic and herbs and served with pitta bread or crudités.

Van der Hum South African liqueur made with the loose-skinned local *naartjie* (tangerine). Farmers made it from the early days of settlement at the Cape.

vichyssoise (vee-shee-SWAAZ) French soup made with leeks, potatoes, chicken stock and cream, usually served chilled.

vinegar Oxidized beer (malt vinegar), wine or cider used as a condiment, in salad dressings (vinaigrettes) and in sauces. It is often flavoured with herbs, garlic, fruit or chilli.

vitello tonnato Classic Italian dish consisting of cold, poached veal with a caper, tuna and anchovy sauce.

waterblommetjies Cape pond weed, now commercially grown for the flower sections which are used as a vegetable, particularly in a BREDIE, regarded by many as a gourmet dish.

whisky Spirit made by distilling fermented grain, such as barley and wheat. It is the main spirit produced in Scotland and also in Ireland, where it is spelt 'whiskey'. A single malt is the product of a single distillate; but most brands are blended. Popular American whiskies include Rye (distilled from rye) and Bourbon, which has to have at least 51 per cent maize, and which gets its dark colour from the oak barrels in which it is aged.
❖ The word 'whisky' comes from the Gaelic *uisge beatha*, meaning 'water of life'.

wok Large Chinese steel frying pan with a rounded bottom and a domed lid, used for stir-frying, deep-frying and steaming.

zabaglione (za-bah-lyee-OWN-eh) Light Italian dessert made by whisking together egg yolks, sugar and Marsala wine in a bowl resting over a pan of simmering water.

zucchini Italian word, commonly used in North America, for courgette or baby marrow.

THE LANGUAGE OF WINE

Appelation Contrôlée System of regulations used to authenticate claims made on wine labels in France. In South Africa, the Wine of Origin certification system is used.

Blanc de Blanc White wine made from white grapes only. Traditionally it was the French term for champagne made from white grapes.

Blanc de Noir Literally 'white from black'. Wine made from black grapes, where the skin is removed soon after extraction of the juice and leaves only a slight pink blush. Vin gris is similar, while rosé is a darker pink from longer contact with the skins.

Bordeaux Major wine-making region in south-west France, producing classic reds and whites.

bouquet Fragrance in wine produced by the process of fermentation, ageing and mellowing. This is different from the aroma, which is the smell of the original grape carried over into a wine. The bouqet is a test of a wine's quality.

Bukettraube German white grape with a prominent bouquet, used to produce off-dry and dessert-style wines in South Africa.

Cabernet Sauvignon Grape producing the finest of red wine varieties. In South Africa, some 120 wines are made of this grape as well as about 50 Bordeaux-style blends.

Cape Riesling (Paarl Riesling) Fruity white variety widely used for blending, especially in dry and sparkling wine. Internationally it is known as Cruchen Blanc.

Chardonnay White grape variety used in the Champagne and Burgundy regions of France and around the world to produce elegant wines. These have become the premium whites in South Africa since good propagating material became available.

Chenin Blanc (Steen) The most widely planted white grape variety in South Africa.

Cinsaut (previously Hermitage) Red grape variety that is light-bodied when grown for bulk but medium-bodied and fruity if grown correctly.

Colombard White grape which was used mainly for brandy until its potential as a natural wine was discovered by chance in the 1970s. It produces dry and off-dry to semi-sweet wines with a fragrant aroma.

Cuvée French term meaning literally the contents of a cask, but usually referring to an individual batch or blend of wine.

fortified wine Wines boosted in alcoholic strength by adding spirits, such as Port, Sherry, Hanepoot, Muscadel and Jerepigo. Before improved cellar techniques, fortification was also a way of preserving wine.

Hanepoot (Muscat d'Alexandrie) Grape grown widely in South Africa for the table, for raisin-making and juice, as well as for dessert and fortified wine. It produces mellow, sweet wines with a strong 'muscat' (musky) flavour.

Gewürztraminer White grape that produces spicy white wines, usually made in sweeter styles in South Africa.

Late Harvest South African term for a medium- to full-bodied white wine with high sugar levels obtained without adding sweetening.

Merlot Noir Black grape used to produce the rich, fragrant red Merlot wine as well as in classic Bordeaux-style blends.

méthode champenoise The method of making sparkling wine according to the traditions of the Champagne region of France, which involves a second fermentation in the bottle. The sweetest wine is labelled Doux, followed by Demi Sec, Sec and Extra Brut – the driest. Many Cape wine makers have adopted the method, describing their sparkling wines as Cap Classique. The name Champagne may be used only for the wines of that region.

noble rot (*botrytis cinerea*) Fungus that causes ripe grapes to shrivel and increase in relative sugar content. Wine makers use it to make rich, sweet wines such as Nederburg Edelkeur.

noble wine Wine of exceptional quality. A noble grape variety is one that produces good wine almost wherever it is planted.

Pinotage Cross of Pinot Noir and Cinsaut (Hermitage) developed in South Africa in 1925. The grape produces a light, medium and sometimes full-bodied wine which can be enjoyed relatively young.

Premier Grand Crû Term used in South African wine classification for blended wines which are as dry as wine-making techniques allow.

Sauvignon Blanc The premium South African white wine before the rise of Chardonnay, bottled unwooded as well as wooded.

Sémillon Previously Green Grape (*Groendruif*). Grape used in sweet white wines. It is used mainly in blends, particularly in the great Bordeaux whites such as Sauterne, which is made chiefly from Sémillon with some Sauvignon Blanc.

Shiraz Of Persian origin, this grape produces a medium to full-bodied wine. It has good ageing potential and is popular in red blends.

Stein Semi-sweet, fruity German-style wine. It should not be confused with Steen (Chenin Blanc), although South African Stein is usually predominantly Chenin Blanc.

Weisser Riesling (Rhine Riesling) Noble German grape variety, producing an aromatic, full-flavoured white wine.

Wine of Origin A wine bearing a seal which, in terms of South African legislation, certifies its origin, vintage, cultivar, whether it is an estate wine and whether the Wine and Spirit Board consider it to be of superior quality.

PLACES AND LANDSCAPES OF SOUTHERN AFRICA

With its serene lakes, thundering waterfalls, towering mountains, game parks containing an incomparable selection of wild animals and birds, and kilometres of pristine beaches, few other regions in the world can match the scenic beauty of southern Africa. To add to these attractions, the subcontinent also boasts a rich heritage of historic towns, villages and buildings, each with a fascinating selection of stories to tell.

TIP OF A CONTINENT *Cape Agulhas lighthouse, a beacon for navigators, built in 1849, stands at the southernmost point of Africa.*

Agulhas, Cape An isolated spot 200 km southeast of Cape Town to which visitors travel to experience the thrill of standing at the southernmost point of Africa. Its lighthouse was erected in 1849.
❖ The nearby Agulhas Bank, where the Indian and Atlantic oceans meet, is the richest fishing ground in the southern hemisphere.

Ai-Ais Oasis and tourist resort amid the barren mountains of southern Namibia, where mineral-rich water wells to the surface at a temperature of 57°C. It is the end point of an 80 km hiking trail along the floor of the FISH RIVER CANYON.

Albany Magisterial district of Eastern Cape that became home to most of the 1820 British settlers. Its first magistrate, Jacob Cuyler, named it after his birthplace, Albany, New York. Grasslands and scrub are the natural cover of the undulating, sometimes mountainous terrain, which produces cattle, sheep, citrus fruit, pineapples and chicory. The chief town is GRAHAMSTOWN.

Alberton Industrial town near JOHANNESBURG, established in 1904 and named after Hendrik Alberts, a republican general of the ▷SOUTH AFRICAN WAR. The black residential areas of Kathlehong and Thokoza, lying to the east of the extensive industrial areas, form part of Alberton.

Alexander Bay Town in Northern Cape on the ORANGE RIVER estuary, opposite Oranjemund (Namibia), where rich deposits of alluvial diamonds are found. The diamonds are recovered from state-owned diggings on raised beaches along the Atlantic shore.

Alexandra African township that was once several kilometres northeast of JOHANNESBURG but is now almost surrounded by the city's northern suburbs. As a 'black spot' in terms of apartheid legislation, Alexandra was destined for demolition and for many years was allowed to degenerate.

Algoa Bay Wide, shallow bay on the EASTERN CAPE coast, dominated by the city of PORT ELIZABETH. It was here that 5 000 British immigrants – the '1820 Settlers' – were landed in 1820-1. Some fine beaches stretch from Cape Recife to Cape Padrone.

Alice Eastern Cape town on the Tyume River, site of the University of Fort Hare, founded in 1916 as the South African Native College. Lovedale Institute, founded here by the Glasgow Missionary Society, now a technical college, runs a printing and publishing house.
❖ Presidents Nelson Mandela (South Africa) and Robert Mugabe (Zimbabwe) are among the distinguished graduates of Fort Hare.

Allanridge Town on the Free State goldfields where promising ore was found in 1896 but was lost in a shipwreck while on its way to Britain for assessment. The borehole was reevaluated 50 years later and found to be directly above the main gold-bearing reef. A monument marks the site.

Amanzimtoti Seaside town lying south of Durban on the NATAL SOUTH COAST with a large rock pool of filtered sea water, a tidal lagoon and a long, sandy beach. After Durban, it is KwaZulu-Natal's largest holiday resort and a favourite venue for surfing.

Amatole mountains Range extending east and west to the north of KING WILLIAM'S TOWN, with large indigenous forests and plantations. The area was the scene of bitter fighting between white settlers and Xhosa graziers in the 19th century. The Xhosa name means 'weaned calves', possibly suggested by the rounded outliers close to the main range. The range's outlines are notably softer than those of Western Cape mountains.

Arniston (Waenhuiskrans) An archetypal Western Cape fishing village of thatched, whitewashed cottages, depicted by generations of watercolourists. Lying about 20 km northeast of Cape AGULHAS, it was the scene of the catastrophic wreck of the troopship *Arniston,* en route from India, in 1815.
❖ Although the village is commonly called Arniston, its official name is Waenhuiskrans

('wagon-house cliff'), which refers to a coastal cave about 1,5 km from the village.

Atteridgeville Large town and municipal area of mainly black residents adjoining PRETORIA. It was founded in 1939.

Auas mountains Highest range in the rugged, high-lying country in the district of WINDHOEK, Namibia, with a mean elevation of more than 2 000 m. The highest peak is Moltkeblick (2 509 m).

Auckland Park Old JOHANNESBURG suburb, now the site of the headquarters of the South African Broadcasting Corporation (▷SABC).

Augrabies Falls Here, near UPINGTON in Northern Cape, the ORANGE RIVER plunges 91 m into a barren, rocky gorge. In legend, it is the home of spirits and of more than one lost treasure. The falls are the central feature of the Augrabies Falls National Park, in which the barren landscape is relieved by botanical specimens such as the kokerboom *(Aloe dichotoma)*. Animals in the park include black rhino, baboon, springbok and smaller buck species.

Badplaas Spa resort in Mpumalanga (formerly Eastern Transvaal) with mineral springs, reputed to have healing properties, at temperatures of up to 50°C.

Bain's Kloof Pass Scenic road across the DRAKENSTEIN mountains in Western Cape, named after its builder, Andrew Geddes ▷BAIN. It is little changed – apart from its resurfacing – since it was opened in 1853.

Bambandyanalo Late Stone Age hillsite on the south bank of the LIMPOPO RIVER in Northern Province, settled for four centuries from about 1055. It lies across a valley from the better-known site of MAPUNGUBWE.

Barberton LOWVELD town in Mpumalanga where South African gold mining began in 1884, two years before the discovery of the Main Reef on the WITWATERSRAND. The Barberton bubble burst within a few years when the shallow reefs and alluvial gold were worked out; but living was riotous while it lasted. The Sheba Mine, the world's oldest working gold mine, is a few kilometres outside Barberton.

❖ The town has a statue of Jock (of the Bushveld), the dog made famous by Sir Percy ▷FITZPATRICK, who for a time was editor of Barberton's *Gold Field News*.

Barkly West Pioneering diamond town, formerly known as Klipdrif, where a territorial dispute between the Cape Colony, Orange Free State and the Griquas led to the diggers proclaiming a short-lived republic in 1870. It lies on the VAAL RIVER, northwest of KIMBERLEY. A museum displays mining relics and prehistoric artefacts, abundant in the area. Historic buildings include St Mary's Church (1885), the first Anglican church to be built on the diamond fields.

Bathurst Eastern Cape village on the Kowie River noted for its historic buildings associated with the 1820 British settlers. These include churches, an inn, a mill and a powder magazine. A hilltop toposcope commemorates land allocations made to the settlers. The village also has an agricultural museum. A forest reserve encloses a horseshoe bend in the river. The district is an important pineapple growing region.

battlefields In its turbulent recorded history, South Africa has often been a battleground. But there have been relatively few pitched battles and not many of the scenes of conflict have been preserved. Most of the famous battles were in KwaZulu-Natal, where local municipalities have devised a 'Battlefields Route'. They include BLOOD RIVER (1838), ISANDLWANA (1879), MAJUBA (1881), Talana Hill at DUNDEE (1899) and SPIOENKOP (1900). Northern Cape battle sites include Belmont, Graspan and Magersfontein (all 1899). In Free State are Vegkop (1836) and Boomplaats (1848). Several sites may be visited around the towns of MAFIKENG, LADYSMITH and KIMBERLEY, all besieged in 1899-1900; but most sites have been obliterated by urbanization.

Beaufort West Western Cape town and railway junction in the central Great KAROO, adjoining the Karoo National Park. The dry climate – its annual rainfall is about 200 mm – has made it a favourable area for sufferers from chest complaints. The main streets are lined with pear trees.

❖ Memorabilia of Chris Barnard, the pioneer heart-transplant surgeon, who was born here, are exhibited in the town's museum.

Beitbridge Zimbabwean town and customs and immigration post on the northern bank of the LIMPOPO RIVER, near the halfway point between PRETORIA and HARARE.

Bellville City often mistakenly referred to as one of Cape Town's 'northern suburbs'. Forming part of the metropolitan area of greater Cape Town, it is a residential, educational, commercial and industrial centre.

❖ Other so-called 'northern suburbs' are Parow and Goodwood.

ROARING TORRENT *The Orange River plunges 91 m into a narrow gorge at the Augrabies Falls. In full flood the river forms 19 separate cascades, and a huge column of spray rises into the air.*

ARCHITECTURAL GEM *Gravestones around the tiny church of Belvidere provide a record of its founding family and of early residents of this 19th-century village and Knysna.*

Belvidere Picturesque GARDEN ROUTE village on the Knysna River, noted for a tiny church (the nave is only 5,4 m wide) consecrated in 1855. It was built in a 12th-century Norman style by Thomas Duthie, son-in-law of George Rex, founder of KNYSNA.

Benoni East Rand town where gold mining came to an end in 1967, by which time the local economy had switched its base to industry. It is noted for its fish-stocked lakes and bird sanctuary.
❖ The name Benoni, meaning 'son of my sorrows' (Genesis 35:18), alludes to the difficulty of making the original land surveys because of the irregular shape of the farm on which the town was founded.

Berea Residential suburb of Durban on a ridge overlooking the city and the sea, the first of among several places bearing this biblical name to be established. It was named in 1835 by the missionary Captain Allen Gardiner, the site of whose mission is now marked by St Thomas's Church and its historic cemetery.

Berg River Major river of the Western Cape, flowing 300 km from the Jonkershoek Mountains at STELLENBOSCH to the Atlantic Ocean at Laaiplek in St Helena Bay. As part of a major irrigation project the 12 km Franschhoek Mountain Tunnel links the Berg River valley to the Riviersonderend valley.
❖ A challenging four-day canoe race, the Berg River Marathon, is held annually in July.

Bethlehem Agricultural and industrial centre and resort town of eastern Free State. Lying at 1 650 m above sea level, it is close to Lesotho, the Golden Gate Highlands National Park and the DRAKENSBERG. Attractions include boating and angling at Loch Athlone and Saulspoort Dam, and a nature reserve.
❖ The district, a major grain-producer, is appropriately named – the biblical Bethlehem means 'house of bread'.

Bethulie Town and resort in the southern Free State that, since the establishment of a mission school in 1829, has had seven changes of name. However, Bethulie, taken from the Apocrypha and meaning 'chosen by God', refers to the site rather than the name. The town is on the Bethulie Dam and adjoins the Gariep Dam, which is crossed here by the country's longest road and rail bridge, with a span of 1 163 m. There was a large concentration camp here during the ▷SOUTH AFRICAN WAR and the town has a memorial cemetery.

Betty's Bay Coastal village and resort, 90 km from Cape Town, in the heart of a rich area of mountain and coastal vegetation (fynbos). The Harold Porter Botanic Garden, one of the National Botanic Gardens of South Africa (see panel below), is situated here.
❖ Betty Youlden was the daughter of one of the area's property developers.

Bisho Capital of Eastern Cape province since 1994. Adjoining KING WILLIAM'S TOWN, it was established and developed as the capital of the former 'independent' Ciskei.

Bishopscourt Cape Town suburb of high-priced properties situated on the lower eastern slopes of Table Mountain. Formerly Jan ▷VAN RIEBEECK's farm Boschheuwel, it was later known as Protea until acquired in 1851 by Robert Gray, the first Anglican Bishop of Cape Town. The suburb takes its name from the official residence, Bishopscourt, of the Archbishop of Cape Town, who is head of the ▷CHURCH OF THE PROVINCE OF SOUTH AFRICA.

Bloemfontein Capital of Free State province and judicial capital of South Africa, founded in 1846. Africans know it also by its Sotho name of Mangaung – 'place of the cheetah'. Renowned for its roses, it is an important centre for education, transport, communications, agriculture, sport and commerce.
❖ The National Women's Monument, in the grounds of the War Museum of the Boer Republics, commemorates the 26 000 Boers (mainly women and children) who died in concentration camps run by the British military authorities from 1900-2. The museum is a valuable source of objects and information relating to the ▷SOUTH AFRICAN WAR.

Blood River Battlefield near Dundee in KwaZulu-Natal where, on 16 December 1838, a Zulu army shattered itself against a wagon

NATIONAL BOTANIC GARDENS OF SOUTHERN AFRICA

Ewanrigg National Park
Harare district
Large collection of cycads and 50 species of aloes from Africa; trees, cacti, bougainvillea, shrubs, fuchsias and herbs from all parts of the world; a stream full of aquatic plants.

Free State National Botanic Garden
Bloemfontein
Set among the shady trees and colourful flowers of the region, it has a permanent exhibition of grasses from the surrounding plains and of the bulbous plants and ferns found high up in the mountain ravines.

Harold Porter National Botanic Garden
Betty's Bay
In a mountainous setting near the sea and an area with one of the densest concentrations of fynbos in the Western Cape; natural flora of the coastal region and host to ferns and ericas; there are scenic trails to kloofs and waterfalls.

Karoo National Botanic Garden
Worcester
Devoted to semidesert and succulent flora, especially aloes, that do not survive at Kirstenbosch; a splendid spectacle of colour in September and October.

Kirstenbosch National Botanic Garden
Cape Town
World famous gardens covering 560 ha on the slopes of Table Mountain; it grows about a third of South Africa's 24 000 indigenous plant species; headquarters of the South African National Botanic Gardens; it has a library, herbarium, restaurant and tourist shop.

Lowveld National Botanic Garden
Nelspruit district
On the junction of the Nel and Crocodile rivers, it has a series of waterfalls, cliffs and gorges providing magnificent views; also a large collection of indigenous trees and a fern garden.

Natal National Botanic Garden
Pietermaritzburg
Started for the acclimatization of timber trees and allied plants, it contains fine specimens of imported trees, including planes and wild figs; also flowering shrubs.

National Botanic Gardens
Harare
Indigenous plants, including most of the 750 species found in Zimbabwe, plants typical to the African continent, among them rare and endangered species, and exotics from South America, India, Australia and the Far East.

Pretoria National Botanic Garden
Pretoria
Plantings that reflect all major types of southern African vegetation.

Witwatersrand National Botanic Garden
Roodepoort district
Mountainous area with an imposing waterfall and plantings of trees and aloes.

laager defended by 464 Voortrekker riflemen, of whom only four sustained injuries. Full-scale bronze replicas of the wagons and cannons used mark the site.

❖ Although the battle demonstrated the futility of an attack with spears against a sound position resolutely defended with firearms (see RORKE'S DRIFT), it acquired almost religious significance for many Afrikaners. It is celebrated annually as a public holiday, now known as the Day of Reconciliation.

Bloubergstrand Seaside residential area and resort within the greater Cape Town area, north of the city. It takes its name from the sandy hill (formerly Blaauwberg) below which the brief engagement was fought in 1806 that led to the second British occupation of the Cape.

❖ The panoramic view of Cape Town and Table Mountain is often photographed from Bloubergstrand.

Bluff, The Promontory and residential area forming the southern bank (opposite The Point) of the channel entering Durban harbour. Rising to a height of 77 m, it shields the harbour facilities along its inner shore from the southeasterly winds.

❖ The Zulu name for the Bluff is *isiBubulungu*, meaning 'the long bulky thing'.

Blyde River Perennial river rising near PILGRIM'S REST in Mpumalanga (formerly Eastern Transvaal) and flowing northwards to join the Olifants River. Along its course are potholes and rock formations with extraordinary colours and shapes. At Blyde River Canyon it plunges into a gigantic gorge that offers spectacular views. Its run-off of more than 40 per cent of the precipitation is the highest of any South African river.

Bochabela Large residential area forming the southeastern part of Bloemfontein and including the smaller areas of Phahameng and Batho. Many people apply the name Bochabela ('refuge') to Bloemfontein as a whole.

Bo-Kaap Residential area above the city centre of Cape Town, on the slopes of Signal Hill, noted for steep, narrow streets lined with small, late-Georgian terraced houses that are the subject of continuing conservation efforts. Traditionally the home of Cape Town's Muslim community, it has many mosques and is also called the Malay Quarter – although very few of its inhabitants are of Malay descent.

Bokkeveld Geographical regions of the southwestern Great KAROO, with the Kouebokkeveld lying east of the Bokkeveld Mountains and the Warmbokkeveld to the south. CERES, in the Warmbokkeveld, has become the hub of a deciduous-fruit industry.

Boksburg Town on the EAST RAND, named in 1887 after Eduard Bok, state secretary of the South African Republic. It is the site of one of the world's largest gold mines and of South Africa's first coal mine (*c*1888). The Transvaal's first railway service, opened in 1890, ran between Johannesburg and Boksburg. The nearby Boksburg Lake and Cinderella Dam are resort areas.

Boland Literally 'upland', the rural area inland from Cape Town, including STELLENBOSCH, PAARL and FRANSCHHOEK. It is a scenic area noted for wine production.

Border Former name of a region in the eastern Cape. After the creation of the Transkei and Ciskei 'states', it was applied to the narrow corridor of towns occupied mostly by whites extending north from East London, bounded by the Kat and Great Fish rivers in the west, the KwaZulu-Natal border and Indian Ocean to the east, and the Stormberg and Drakensberg ranges in the north.

Botshabelo Nature reserve in Mpumalanga (formerly Eastern Transvaal) and museum noted for its brightly painted Ndebele village and for Fort Merensky, a fine example of indigenous building techniques in stone. It was formerly a mission station founded in 1865 by the Berlin Missionary Society as a refuge for christianized Pedi.

Botswana Landlocked independent Commonwealth republic enclosed by South Africa, Namibia and Zimbabwe. It extends over 500 000 km^2, two-thirds of which is covered by the scrubland of the Kalahari Desert. To the north are the green plains of the Okavango waterway and to the east a fertile region along the banks of the Limpopo River. Abounding in wild life, the country has several major game parks, notably the Chobe, MAKGADIKGADI PAN and Central Kalahari reserves. Botswana's capital is Gaborone.

Brakpan Town on the East Rand which flourished in the first half of the century as a coal and gold-mining centre. It claims to have the world's highest mine dump, rising to 110 m above ground level. This claim may not stand for long, however, because mine dumps are being reprocessed with new technology to extract whatever gold remains in them.

Brandberg Mountain massif at the edge of the NAMIB DESERT, northwest of Windhoek. Königstein peak, at 2 585 m, is the highest point in Namibia. The mountains are known for the plants that survive in the barren dryness and for their ▷ROCK ART, including the famous 'White lady of the Brandberg'.

❖ The 'white lady' is now believed to be neither white nor a lady.

Bredasdorp Town of the Strandveld area of Western Cape, on the slopes of a hill known as Preekstoel ('pulpit'). The district, which includes the coastal fishing centres of AGULHAS, Hotagterklip and Struisbaai, produces

HOME TO MUSLIMS *This mosque is one of many that distinguish the Bo-Kaap residential area of Cape Town, where several streets of late-Georgian terraced houses have been restored.*

ZIMBABWE'S SECOND CITY *Flamboyant trees provide vivid patches of colour in the streets of Bulawayo. In the background the Supreme Court's architecture offers a reminder of colonial days.*

wool and cereals. One of the town's earliest buildings houses a Shipwreck Museum.

Breërivier (Breede River) Major river of the southern part of Western Cape, flowing about 320 km from its source near CERES to Witsand, on St Sebastian Bay, southeast of SWELLENDAM. Storage dams in the river basin irrigate land around Ceres, Worcester, Robertson, Bonnievale and Swellendam. Regularly in the 19th century and occasionally until 1908, the river was navigated by ocean-going steam ships as far as Malgas, 48 km from the sea.
❖ South Africa's last pont still operating on demand is at Malgas.

Bronkhorstspruit Town, east of Pretoria, where the opening battle of the first Anglo-Transvaal War was fought on 20 December 1880. It is the centre of a well-watered mixed farming region and is known for its attractive holiday resort and nature reserve – and a large Buddhist community.

Buffalo River (Buffelsrivier) Name of several important rivers in South Africa: (1) The largest tributary of the Tugela in KwaZulu-Natal. (2) A river in the central Great KAROO which, having become the Groot River, joins the Gourits River south of Calitzdorp. In flood, it destroyed much of the town of Laingsburg in 1981. (3) A river of Eastern Cape, rising in the AMATOLE MOUNTAINS and entering the Indian Ocean at East London, South Africa's only river port.

Bulawayo Zimbabwe's second city after HARARE and the commercial, industrial and administrative centre of Matabeleland. Originally the Ndebele capital of King ▷LOBENGULA, it was abandoned and razed in 1893 on the approach of white invaders, who re-established it. It is an important railway junction and the centre of a large mining and ranching district.

Burgersdorp Town in the northern part of Eastern Cape named after the burghers who founded it in 1847. Its Taalmonument, unveiled in 1893, commemorates the right to use Dutch in the Cape Parliament.
❖ The country's first theological college (of the Gereformeerde Kerk) was founded here in 1869, but moved to Potchefstroom in 1905.

Bushmanland Old term for a loosely defined, very arid area in Northern Cape, lying east of NAMAQUALAND, south of the Orange River and north of Calvinia. The name has no political or demographic significance.

Bushveld Warm, inland area of southern Africa with vegetation mainly of tall, rank grass and trees of the acacia and ficus species. It receives summer rainfall. Lying between 700 m and 1 300 m above sea level, it includes parts of Northern Province, North-West, Botswana and Namibia.

Butha Buthe Town in Lesotho, site of the ancestral home of ▷MOSHOESHOE. It lies 1 965 m above sea level and south of the Free State town of Fouriesburg.
❖ The district has many caves that contain San ▷ROCK ART.

Cabinda Seaport and detached district of Angola lying north of the Zaire (Congo) River. The enclave has vast offshore and mainland oilfields, Angola's main source of income.

Cahora Bassa Huge hydroelectric and irrigation scheme in Mozambique, intended also to provide a waterway for landlocked Malawi, Zambia and Zimbabwe. It lies in a narrow gorge of the Zambezi River, northwest of Tete. Civil war in Mozambique has delayed the project's completion.

Caledon River River that for some 300 km of its 500 km length forms the boundary between Free State and Lesotho. Its source is 3 333 m above sea level in the DRAKENSBERG in Lesotho and it joins the Orange River near BETHULIE at the Gariep Dam. After the Vaal, it is the Orange River's most important tributary. Its use for irrigation is limited by a lack of suitable land close to its course.

Calvinia Principal town of the semiarid area known as the Hantam, in the southwest corner of Northern Cape. The district, which produces wool and wheat, is renowned for its spring flowers.

Camdeboo Southeastern part of the Great KAROO, consisting mainly of the flat plains between the Camdeboo and the Winterberg ranges. The principal towns are GRAAFF-REINET, Pearston and Somerset East.

Camps Bay Cape Town suburb and seaside resort on the western, or Atlantic, side of the Cape Peninsula, overlooked by Lion's Head and the TABLE MOUNTAIN buttresses known as the Twelve Apostles. It is noted for the scenic Victoria Road and Camps Bay Drive.

Cango Caves Extensive series of limestone caverns in the SWARTBERG north of OUDTSHOORN. Known to prehistoric people, who ventured little further than the entrance, the caves were rediscovered in 1780 and are a major tourist attraction. About 2,5 km of the cave sequence has been explored; its full extent is unknown. One of the chambers is 98 m long, 49 m wide and 15 m high.
❖ The caves' dripstone formations, imaginatively illuminated in colour, are among the world's most beautiful and extensive.

Cape Agulhas See AGULHAS, CAPE.

Cape Flats Low-lying, sandy plain between the Cape Peninsula and the mainland of Africa that was once a channel of the sea between Table Bay and False Bay. It is now for the greater part not more than 30 m above sea-level. Cape Town International Airport is sited here, close to the N2 highway.

Cape folded mountains Ranges of the southern parts of Western and Eastern Cape noted for the intensely convoluted folding of sedimentary strata that took place from the Carboniferous to the Jurassic periods, ending about 135 million years ago.

Cape of Good Hope Southern tip of the Cape Peninsula lying within the Cape of Good Hope Nature Reserve. A rocky, windswept area of 7 750 ha, it is home to troops of baboons, the rare Cape platanna frog and a rich variety of flowering plants.

WORLD-FAMOUS SIGHT *Devil's Peak, Table Mountain, Signal Hill and Lion's Head form Cape Town's splendid backdrop. In the city, Greenmarket Square is the site of a crowded flea market.*

Cape Peninsula Popular resort and holiday area, extending southwards from Cape Town, with beaches, harbours, mountains and historic sites among its many attractions. A fingerlike projection from the African mainland, it encloses the sweep of FALSE BAY.
❖ Sea bathers in the Peninsula can choose between the relatively warmer water of the False Bay coast on the Peninsula's eastern side and the often icy water of the Benguela Current on the western side.

Cape Point Spectacular high, rocky promontory on the southernmost tip of the Cape Peninsula, to the east of the Cape of Good Hope. It is popularly (but incorrectly) regarded as the meeting place of the Atlantic and Indian oceans. Lying within the Cape of Good Hope Nature Reserve, it is exposed to strong winds from the sea for most of the year.
❖ The Cape Point lighthouse overlooks storm-tossed seas ploughed by the legendary 17th-century phantom ship the ▷FLYING DUTCHMAN, reputedly seen by many travellers – including King George V of England when he served as a midshipman.
❖ The Atlantic and Indian oceans meet off Cape AGULHAS.

Cape Town South Africa's 'Mother City', its oldest and southernmost early settlement, now capital of Western Cape and legislative capital of the country. It was initially founded as a refreshment station for ships en route to the East. From the magnificent setting of its city centre below TABLE MOUNTAIN, Devil's Peak, Lion's Head and Signal Hill, its suburbs sprawl along almost the whole of the CAPE PENINSULA and northwards to BELLVILLE. Near the Company Gardens, developed by the ▷DUTCH EAST INDIA COMPANY, are the Houses of Parliament, the Tuynhuis (the presidential residence) the South African Library, the South African National Gallery, the South African Museum, the South African Cultural History Museum and St George's Cathedral. Another focal point for tourists and residents is the popular flea market on Greenmarket Square, which is surrounded by coffee bars and restaurants. The main business centre is on and adjoining the Foreshore, a large tract of land reclaimed from the sea.
❖ Part of Cape Town's harbour area has been developed as the VICTORIA AND ALFRED WATERFRONT, a tourist centre housing shops, restaurants and one of the world's few Imax cinemas, with a screen several storeys high.

Caprivi Strip Narrow strip of land (up to 80 km wide) that has a profusion of game in reserves set in rich savannah country. It lies in the northeast corner of Namibia, bordered by Angola, Zambia and Botswana.

Carletonville Gold-mining town in Gauteng, adjoining the black residential area of Khutsong, near Johannesburg. It has grown rapidly in spite of the sinkholes in the area.

Castle of Good Hope (Cape Town) The second oldest building in South Africa (after the ▷POSTHUYS), built by the Dutch on the shores of Table Bay to boost fortifications when war with England seemed imminent. Work began in 1665 and was officially completed in 1679. It is in the shape of a five-pointed star. It now houses military headquarters and cultural and military museums.

Cathedral Peak A 3 004 m peak, the easiest to climb of the major peaks of the DRAKENSBERG range and centre of a popular resort area.

Cederberg Mountain range about 250 km north of Cape Town named after the cedar trees (*Widdringtonia* species) that once grew here in profusion. Extreme weathering has produced weird rock formations, such as the Maltese Cross and Wolfberg Arch, near Sandrif. Near the southern end of the range is the extraordinary Stadsaal – a mass of rock with chambers and caves, some containing San ▷ROCK ART. Its attractions include the spring flowers of the Biedouw Valley.

Ceres Farming centre and resort town set among mountains in the Warmbokkeveld northeast of Cape Town, founded in 1854 and named after the Roman goddess of agriculture. One of South Africa's rare earthquakes – in 1969 – had its epicentre close to Ceres.

'SLEEPING POOL' *Zimbabwe's Chinhoyi Caves are famous for the mirrorlike surface of the blue waters in a deep subterranean pool.*

Champagne Castle Table-topped peak, rising to 3 348 m, in the Drakensberg range, near the border between Lesotho and KwaZulu-Natal.

Chapman's Peak A 592 m peak south of Hout Bay in the Cape Peninsula, falling precipitously to the sea. A spectacular scenic drive skirts the peak high above the sea.

Chimanimani Village (formerly Melsetter) in the province of Manicaland, Zimbabwe, south of Mutare in an area of forestry and mixed farming. Chimanimani National Park encompasses majestic mountain scenery at the southern end of the Eastern Highlands.

Chinhoyi Town in Zimbabwe famous for the Chinhoyi Caves, where the action of water over a long period has created an enormous circular sinkhole. Looking 50 m down from the top, the viewer sees the mirrorlike surface of the so-called Sleeping Pool, which is 90 m deep, with crystal-clear water of a vivid blue colour. There are also bizarre limestone formations. Chinhoyi is in a prosperous mining and farming area northwest of Harare.

Clanwilliam Town in Western Cape, the centre of the rooibos tea industry. The herb buchu (*Agathosma* species) is also harvested in the surrounding CEDERBERG mountains and processed for medicinal use. An annual skiboat angling regatta is held on the vast Clanwilliam Dam on the Olifants River.

Clarens Town in the eastern Free State named after the Swiss town in which president Paul ▷KRUGER died in exile in 1904. Founded in 1912, the town has attractive, sandstone buildings.

Clifton Fashionable seaside residential suburb 8 km from central Cape Town with four small, sandy beaches known for offering sunbathers shelter from the southeasterly wind.

Coffee Bay Picturesque resort on the WILD COAST in Eastern Cape, noted for bathing and angling. According to local legend, it was so named after a ship that was wrecked here in 1863 and deposited its cargo of coffee beans on the beach.

Colenso Town in KwaZulu-Natal, the site of a British defeat in 1899 during an attempt to lift the Boer siege of LADYSMITH in the ▷SOUTH AFRICAN WAR. Urban and industrial expansion has covered the battlefield, but a museum in the town and the military cemeteries at Clouston Koppie and Chieveley nearby are much visited.

Colesberg Town in the Great KAROO in Northern Cape, almost midway between Johannesburg and Cape Town. The survival of many Cape Dutch and Georgian houses, early churches and water furrows lining the streets has helped to preserve a restful, old-time atmosphere. Sheep and horses are raised on large farms in the district.

Company's Garden (Cape Town) Originally a vegetable garden established by the settler-servants of the Dutch East India Company in 1652, now a mid-city haven of lawns, shady shrubs, flowerbeds and exotic trees, occupying less than 6 ha of the original 18 ha. In or adjoining the gardens are the Houses of Parliament and many other buildings of historic and cultural interest.
❖ The Houses of Parliament, built in the Classical style and opened in 1885 as the meeting place for the parliament of the Cape Colony, have been extended several times over the years; but the basic style of red brick and white plaster has been retained.

Constantia Semirural residential area in a fertile valley in the Cape Peninsula, site of Groot Constantia, the 17th-century farm and wine estate established by the Cape governor Simon van der Stel.
❖ The Groot Constantia homestead is a classic example of Cape Dutch architecture, parts of it dating from 1692. Its magnificent setting on vine-clad mountain slopes offers a panoramic view of FALSE BAY and beyond.

Cradock Town on the Great Fish River in the area formerly known as the Eastern Cape Midlands, a district producing sheep, cattle and lucerne. The Mountain Zebra National Park lies west of the town.

Cubango River Angolan name for the Kavango (OKAVANGO) River forming the boundary between Namibia and Angola. The vast inland delta, in northern Botswana, forms swamps and other habitats for an immense variety of wildlife.

Darling Town in the wheat-growing area of the SWARTLAND, noted for the local variety of beautiful indigenous flora, especially bulbous types. The 20 ha Tienie Versveld Flora Reserve west of the town is a vivid exhibition of the area's natural flora in springtime.

De Aar Karoo town in Northern Cape, South Africa's second biggest railway junction after GERMISTON. With lines from Western and Eastern Cape, Gauteng and Namibia meeting here, it has about 110 km of track within its precincts, and trains pass through at the rate of around 90 a day. A holiday resort at Vanderkloof Dam is nearby.
❖ The house in De Aar in which the writer Olive ▷SCHREINER lived from 1907 to 1913 is open to visitors.

De Kaap Valley and former gold-mining village in Mpumalanga (formerly Eastern Transvaal), south of Nelspruit. A short-lived stock exchange was established at De Kaap in 1884. The chief town of the valley is BARBERTON. The area is associated with Sir Percy ▷FITZPATRICK's famous *Jock of the Bushveld*.
❖ The De Kaap Valley is the natural home of the blood-red flowering Pride of De Kaap *(Bauhinia galpinii)* and the Barberton Daisy *(Gerbera jamebonii)*.

Dingaan's Kraal The site in KwaZulu-Natal of the former Zulu royal town of Hlomo Amabutho. It has monuments to the king ▷DINGANE and to the Voortrekker leader Piet ▷RETIEF, who was killed here with many of his followers in 1838 during an attempt to persuade the king to grant land to the migrant Boers. Meticulous excavation and reconstruction have been undertaken for several years.

District Six Part of Cape Town that grew in late Victorian times into a densely populated area of close-packed, terraced houses at the edge of the city centre on the western slopes of Table Mountain. By the 1960s the poor but vibrant community consisted almost entirely of coloured people who, in terms of the ▷GROUP AREAS ACT, were forcibly resettled in new suburbs on the CAPE FLATS. Their old homes were broken down and for a long time the site remained a bare scar close to the heart of South Africa's 'Mother City'.

RESORT CITY *Sun-seekers on Durban's North Beach contrast with the serenity of the Temple of Understanding in nearby Chatsworth (above right) and the bustle of a traders' arcade (right).*

Drakensberg mountains Range stretching in an arc for more than 1 000 km from Eastern Cape to Northern Province, the focus of many resort areas with spectacular scenery. Though much of the country's interior lies in its rain shadow, the range has a relatively high rainfall and most of the subcontinent's important perennial rivers rise in or near it. The highest point is Thabantshonyana (3 482 m) in the Lesotho-KwaZulu-Natal section, where many peaks are snow-covered in winter.

Drakenstein Fruit-growing, wine-making and scenic region of Western Cape bordered by the Drakenstein Mountains, with the town of FRANSCHHOEK at its centre. A European settlement was established here in 1687 and reinforced the next year by the arrival of the French Huguenots.

Dullstroom Town in Mpumalanga (formerly Eastern Transvaal) established by Dutch immigrants in 1883 and known for the district's well-stocked trout streams and for having the highest railway station in South Africa, at 2 077 m above sea level.

❖ Elms and beeches planted in Dullstroom by the original settlers have survived well – reputedly because the winters are as cold here as in Europe.

Dundee Coal-mining town in KwaZulu-Natal. Museums on the nearby site of the battle of Talana Hill (1899) display the techniques of coal-mining, glass-making and brick-making, as well as local and military history.

Durban Africa's busiest port and the biggest city in KwaZulu-Natal, with beaches and entertainment facilities that have made it a great holiday resort, particularly for residents of Gauteng, and tourist centre. It is especially popular in the winter, when its mild weather makes sea bathing still pleasurable. Apart from its sand and surf, a few of its other attractions include the Umgeni River Bird Park, the Botanic and Amphitheatre gardens, Seaworld, Juma Mosque and the Temple of Understanding, the Fitzsimons Snake Park, museums, galleries and libraries. Durban handles more than half the country's imports and exports of general cargo. Its population is about 3 million.

❖ Durban's Indian Market, in Warwick Avenue, is frequented as much by local people as by tourists. Its range of wares includes curries and spices, cloth, jewellery, curios, fruit and vegetables and imported delicacies.

Dzata Site of the ruins of stone structures, erected in the late 17th century by emigrants from Zimbabwe, in the Soutpansberg range of Northern Province, near the present town of Louis Trichardt. The ruins, covering about 7,5 ha, are venerated by the Venda people.

East London Industrial and resort city and South Africa's only river port, at the mouth of the BUFFALO RIVER in Eastern Cape. It lies at the heart of some of the country's most beautiful coastline, with lagoons and sheltered, sandy beaches. It is the chief town of the former BORDER region, with five industrial areas.

East Rand Industrial and gold-mining area immediately east of Johannesburg in Gauteng. The principal towns are Benoni, Boksburg, Brakpan, Germiston and Springs.

Eastern Cape South African province, home of the Xhosa people and of the descendants of British and German settlers who arrived here in the 19th century. It is bounded in the west by the Western Cape, in the east by KwaZulu-Natal, and extends inland from its southern coast to the Free State and Lesotho. It includes an area of semiarid Karoo, with rolling grasslands to the east. The province's economy is based on agriculture, but Port Elizabeth-Uitenhage and East London form an important industrial complex, particularly for the motor industry. The capital is Bisho.

❖ Eastern Cape's WILD COAST has numerous holiday resorts.

Eastern Transvaal See MPUMALANGA.

Elgin (Grabouw) Elgin is the name only of the railway station for the town and district of Grabouw, but the region's prime products are known worldwide as Elgin apples. Forests and orchards of deciduous fruit trees cover the rolling hills of this scenic area. A museum in Grabouw features the apple industry.

Elim Scenic, old-world village, established in 1824 as a mission station near BREDASDORP in Western Cape by the Moravian Brethren who gave it its biblical name. Elim is also the name of a mission station, which has a tuberculosis hospital, in Northern Province near Louis Trichardt.

❖ Elim in Western Cape is known for the skill of its artisans, especially the thatchers.

Elizabeth Bay Small bay and ghost town on the coast of Namibia, south of Lüderitz. The town was established because of nearby diamond terraces but, with KOLMANSKOP, was abandoned soon after World War I.

Empangeni Town and centre of the KwaZulu-Natal sugar industry. Cotton, cattle and timber are also produced in the district. Places of interest nearby include RICHARDS BAY and Enseleni Nature Reserve.

ANCIENT SURVIVOR *In the wilderness of Erongo, weird plant forms, such as the* Welwitschia mirabilis *which survives up to 2 000 years, have adapted to their arid habitat.*

Ermelo Town in the highveld of Mpumalanga (formerly Eastern Transvaal) destroyed in the ▷SOUTH AFRICAN WAR 20 years after its foundation. Rebuilding began in 1902. It is the centre of a farming district noted for cattle, sheep and forestry. Its coal is railed to RICHARDS BAY for export and also supplies several large power stations locally.

Erongo (Damaraland) Central part of Namibia, with the South Atlantic to the west and the Kalahari Desert to the east. Walvis Bay and SWAKOPMUND are the principal towns on the coast. Parts of the Skeleton Coast and Namib-Naukluft parks fall into this area.

Eshowe Town in KwaZulu-Natal with a forest reserve covering 162 ha within its municipal area. In the late 19th century it was the capital of Zululand. Fort Nonqayi, built by the British administrators after the ▷ANGLO-ZULU WAR, houses an historical museum.

Estcourt Industrial and commercial centre in KwaZulu-Natal and gateway to the central Drakensberg resorts. It lies on the Boesmansrivier and is on the main rail route between Durban and Johannesburg. There are several historical sites in the area. The town's meat-processing factory is one of Africa's largest.

False Bay Large coastal indentation east of the CAPE PENINSULA, stretching eastwards from CAPE POINT to Cape Hangklip (formerly known as False Cape) and northwards to the white sands of Muizenberg. On the shores of False Bay are the fishing harbours of KALK BAY and Gordon's Bay and many extended and popular beaches.

❖ False Bay was named by early mariners who, on their way home from the East, wrongly identified Cape Hangklip as Cape Point, and turned north after passing it, only to find their passage blocked by the mainland at the centre of the bay.

Ficksburg Picturesque town in the Free State on the Caledon River where it forms the border with Lesotho. Founded in 1867, it is the main point of entry from Lesotho. A colourful Cherry Festival is held annually in November during the cherry harvest.

Fish Hoek Suburb of Cape Town on the FALSE BAY coast, with an attractive beach and walkway built on the rocks edging the bay. For many years a municipality separate from Cape Town, it was noted for its adherence to a clause in the early 19th-century land grant that forbade the public sale of liquor. This clause has now been repealed.

Fish River Canyon Majestic, rocky cleft some 160 km long and rarely more than 2 km wide, carved by Namibia's longest river in the south of the country. A rugged hiking trail of 80 km, ending at the hot-springs resort of AI-AIS, is open from May to August to groups of at least three people (who must have a certificate of medical fitness). A view site is reached by gravel road from the main road between Springbok and Grünau.
❖ The Fish River Canyon is the world's second largest after the 350-km Grand Canyon in the USA.

Fort Beaufort Town in Eastern Cape, originally an outpost built in 1822 to garrison the eastern frontier of the Colony of the Cape of Good Hope. Among its relics are a multiple-arch bridge over the Kat River and a martello tower, believed to be the world's only example of this type of coastal fortification not built at the sea. It is the centre of an area noted for cattle raising and citrus growing.

Franschhoek Town (the 'French corner') in Western Cape, picturesquely set among the mountains of the BERG RIVER valley. The centre of a farming district devoted mainly to wine-making, it was established in 1688 with the settlement of Huguenot refugees as a farming community. A Huguenot Memorial was erected here in 1938 to commemorate the 250th anniversary of the settlers' arrival. The accompanying Huguenot Memorial Museum, opened in 1965, is an important historical and genealogical source.
❖ Franschhoek was initially named Olifantshoek because of the elephants found here.

Free State Land-locked province (formerly Orange Free State) of South Africa, with rolling grasslands and fields of maize, wheat and sunflowers in the west and flat-topped mountains in the east. It lies in the centre of the country between the Orange and the Vaal rivers and forms part of the inland plateau. It is rich in minerals, with a gold-mining industry, centred on WELKOM vying in importance with that of the Witwatersrand.
❖ Before the ▷SOUTH AFRICAN WAR, the Orange Free State was a Boer republic. Its capital, BLOEMFONTEIN, became South Africa's judicial capital after ▷UNION.

Fundudzi, Lake Lake in Northern Province regarded with veneration by the Venda people as the home of their python god of fertility, who is placated annually in a famous *domba* ceremony. Remotely situated in the SOUTPANSBERG range, it was created in ancient times when a landslide blocked the course of the Mutale River. Access is not generally allowed to the public.

'VALE OF GRACE' *A Cape Dutch homestead in Genadendal, dating from the early 19th century, typifies the tranquillity of this Western Cape village founded by Moravian missionaries.*

Gaborone National capital of Botswana, developed from a village since 1965, the year before the country's independence. (Colonial government had been conducted from within South Africa.) It is the site of both Anglican and Catholic cathedrals and the campus of the University of Botswana. The National Museum is a major attraction in this modern, tree-shaded city.
❖ Being close to the South African border, Gaborone was home to a large community of political exiles during the ▷APARTHEID years.

Garden Route Mountains, lakes, rivers, forests and beaches combine to make this plateau between the Indian Ocean and the coastal ranges of Western and Eastern Cape provinces one of the country's major resort areas and tourist attractions. The area is traversed by the N2 national road from Swellendam in the west to Humansdorp in the east. Vast natural forests, centred on KNYSNA, are home to the few survivors of Africa's southernmost herd of elephants. An air of romance and mystery pervades the forests, site of a 19th-century gold rush, of occasional and unexplained human disappearances and former home of a hardy, reclusive breed of woodcutters. The relatively high rainfall favours the cultivation of forest plantations and vegetable farming. Principal towns include MOSSEL BAY, GEORGE and the fashionable PLETTENBERG BAY.

Gauteng South African province, created in 1994, centred on its capital, JOHANNESBURG, and formed by the area previously known as the PWV – the intensely industrialized region encompassing PRETORIA, the WITWATERSRAND and VEREENIGING. It is the smallest in area of the nine provinces, but is the financial, commercial and industrial hub of the country, with the densest population.

Genadendal Tranquil, oak-shaded village in Western Cape, a treasure of ▷VERNACULAR architecture, its apt name meaning 'Vale of Grace'. It was founded by Moravian missionaries in 1737 as a centre for evangelism and training. Many of the buildings are proclaimed national monuments.
❖ President Nelson Mandela gave the name Genadendal to the presidential residence, formerly called Westbrooke, in the Cape Town suburb of Rondebosch.

George Cathedral town in an incomparable setting among lakes, forests and mountains, on the GARDEN ROUTE, 10 km from the Indian Ocean. A reputed 'sleepy hollow' until the 1960s, it has grown immensely over the past few decades. It has been the seat of an Anglican (Church of the Province of South Africa) bishopric since 1911.

Germiston Industrial city in Gauteng, centre of the world's most intensive gold-mining area, a few kilometres southeast of JOHANNESBURG. It has the world's largest gold refinery, handling more than 70 per cent of the world's gold production. It also has Africa's largest railway junction. It was laid out on the farm Elandsfontein in 1887 and officially named Germiston in 1904 after a farm of the same

RECREATING THE PAST *The bygone pleasure of riding in a horse-drawn omnibus is one of the many attractions offered visitors to Gold Reef City, the reconstruction of a gold-rush town.*

name outside Glasgow, the birthplace of John Jack, a gold-mining pioneer.

Giant's Castle Peak rising to 3 314 m above sea level, and a game reserve and resort area of the Drakensberg, in the district of ESTCOURT in KwaZulu-Natal. Scenic beauty, game viewing, climbing and trails for hiking and horse riding are among the attractions.
❖ Caves in the area around Giant's Castle are rich in San ▷ROCK ART; one of them contains more than 500 paintings.

Gobabis Principal town of Namibia's main dairy and cattle-farming area, on the banks of the Nossob River. It is known to the ▷HERERO people as ePako ('the pool').

Gold Reef City Reconstruction of a gold-rush town at Crown Mines, south of Johannesburg's city centre. Among its attractions are rides on steam trains and a horse-drawn omnibus, an underground tour of a gold mine, fun fairs and live entertainment – including tribal dancing and can-can girls.

goldfields South Africa's landscape and history are scattered with goldfields exploited by small-scale operators who moved on when most of the (mainly alluvial) gold had been won. Sites extend from Western Cape to the far Northern Province. Gold became a permanent feature of the national economy with the discovery in 1886 of the Witwatersrand Main Reef. Until 1930, the accepted limits of the Main Reef were confined to central Gauteng, but new prospecting methods showed new and deeper reefs towards POTCHEFSTROOM and KLERKSDORP. Later, the reef was traced into northwestern Free State, where the first big strike was made, near WELKOM, in 1939. The Free State goldfields now produce a substantial proportion of the country's output.

Graaff-Reinet Karoo town lying in a loop of the Sundays River in Eastern Cape. A substantial part of its late 18th-century nucleus survives. Its eventful history includes proclamation of the first South African 'republic' in 1795, ten years after the town was founded. Near the town are the isolated village of NIEU-BETHESDA and the VALLEY OF DESOLATION, which has dolerite-capped shale heights that have eroded into bizarre shapes.

Grabouw See ELGIN.

Grahamstown Cathedral town and campus of Rhodes University in Eastern Cape. Grahamstown was the administrative centre for the old eastern frontier and the British settlers of 1820 were encouraged to settle here to augment the population and provide defence reinforcements. The ALBANY Museum in the town is an important centre for historical and genealogical information.
❖ Known as the 'City of Saints' because of its 40 churches, Grahamstown usually has a restful and rustic atmosphere – except in July, when its National Festival of the Arts attracts hundreds of thousands of visitors.

Groote Schuur Estate and official State residence at the eastern foot of Devil's Peak in Cape Town, on the site of an early settlers' barn *(schuur)*. Sir Herbert ▷BAKER, inspired by the Cape Dutch style, designed the main dwelling. The entire estate and all the other land belonging to him on Table Mountain was bequeathed by Cecil ▷RHODES (1853-1902) to a future 'federal' South Africa.
❖ Groote Schuur Hospital, in which the world's first human heart transplant was performed by Dr Chris Barnard in 1967, was built on part of the original estate and opened as a training hospital in 1938.
❖ Rhodes Memorial, designed by Baker and Francis Masey and completed in 1908, overlooks Groote Schuur from the slopes of the mountain. It is an imposing granite structure in the style of a Grecian temple and has a famous equestrian statue, sculpted by G F Watts, of which there is a replica in Kensington Gardens, London.

Guano Islands Small islands off the south and west coast of South Africa and the coast of Namibia. Occupied only by birds and seals, they are collectively named after the many tons of guano (bird dung) deposited here during the nesting season. Individual island names include Plum Pudding, Ichaboe, Roast Beef, Marcus and Malgas. 'Harvesting' of the guano, a valuable concentrated fertilizer, began in the 1840s. Recently it has been collected only from platforms erected on a few of the islands.

Gweru Zimbabwe's third largest city, a cattle-ranching centre in a region rich in minerals (including gold, chrome, asbestos and coal). Formerly called Gwelo, the town is an important railway centre and has Zimbabwe's biggest container-handling facility.

Harare Capital and largest city of Zimbabwe, lying 1 470 m above sea level in the province of Mashonaland East. It has an international airport, is the centre of road, rail and air services and a major industrial, educational and tourist centre. Features of this modern and attractive city include the 15 ha Harare Gardens, Anglican, Catholic and Greek Orthodox cathedrals and the national archives containing David ▷LIVINGSTONE's diary and paintings by Thomas ▷BAINES. The city was formerly called Salisbury.

Harrismith Eastern Free State town on the main road from Bloemfontein to Durban, named in honour of the mid-19th century governor Sir Harry Smith. The district, noted for fine mountain scenery, produces maize and wool.

Hartbeespoort Dam Major storage dam in Gauteng sited below the confluence of the

Magalies and Crocodile rivers, a popular resort for anglers and water sports enthusiasts from Pretoria and the Witwatersrand. The shores are dotted with hotels, clubs, cottages and caravan parks. The township of Kosmos extends along part of its northern shore.

Hel, Die Deserted village, properly known as Gamkaskloof, in a remote valley of the Swartberg Mountains in the southern part of Western Cape. It was named Die Hel ('The Hell') by outsiders because of the difficult access. The narrow, fertile valley was settled in the early 19th century when the only way in or out involved a long and laborious journey over rocks and rivers, part of it undertaken by donkey-cart. Long content and self-sufficient, the inhabitants abandoned their homes in the 1960s after a road was built to the village from the summit of the SWARTBERG PASS. Its remoteness – the 'new road' is a daunting drive of 57 km – is perhaps the chief fascination of Gamkaskloof, apart from the grandeur of the mountain scenery.

Hermann Eckstein Park Area of more than 100 ha in Saxonwold, Johannesburg, given to the city in 1903 by a mining house and including Zoo Lake, the Johannesburg Zoological Garden, the South African National Museum of Military History and extensive picnic grounds.

Hereroland Former name for the traditional home of the pastoral Herero and Mbanderu peoples in northern Namibia. Lying south of the Ugab River and north of the Swakop and White Nossob rivers, it now falls into two areas – Otjozandjupa and Omaheke. The Great Place of the Herero is Okahandja, a road and rail centre on the main route from WINDHOEK to Walvis Bay.

❖ The Herero led a determined rebellion against German colonizers in 1903-7 and suffered banishment and near-extermination.

Hermanus Seaside resort town and fishing harbour on Walker Bay in Western Cape. Hermanus is famous as an angling centre, and the

BIZARRE SHAPES *Dolerite-capped shale heights formed by ages of erosion dominate the typical Karoo landscape of the aptly named Valley of Desolation near Graaff-Reinet.*

LINK WITH THE PAST *Now a fashionable resort, Hermanus's harbour museum maintains a record of its history as a fishing village.*

old harbour has been restored as an open-air museum recording the history of the town and its fishing boats. The lagoon is popular for water-sports. Scenic walks and drives include Fernkloof Nature Reserve, where there is an abundance of indigenous vegetation.

❖ A centre of the WHALE ROUTE, Hermanus boasts a 'whale crier', who announces the arrival of these great mammals within the sweep of the bay.

❖ Its former name, until postal officials objected to its length, was Hermanuspietersfontein, after an itinerant herdsman who watered his animals here.

Hex River A tributary of the BREËRIVIER giving its name to the Hex River Mountains which enclose the beautiful Hex River Valley, near WORCESTER in Western Cape. This fertile valley has been farmed since the early 18th century and the vines and fruit trees stretching as far as the eye can see against their mountainous backdrop present a splendid view, especially in autumn.

highveld Plateau, between 1 200 and 1 800 m above sea level, including most of Free State and the southern parts of Gauteng and Mpumalanga (formerly Eastern Transvaal). Rain, often accompanied by thunder storms, falls here in summer. The natural treeless grassland of the highveld makes it ideal for maize and wheat farming. With its deposits of diamonds, gold and coal, the highveld may well be one of the richest areas in the world.

Hillbrow One of the oldest suburbs of Johannesburg, situated close to the city centre. It has always been densely populated and was formerly known for its cosmopolitan and bohemian atmosphere. The number of residents has now risen to 420 people per hectare – more than 10 times the figure for Johannesburg as a whole. Occupation density is more

JOHANNESBURG LANDMARK *The brightly lit Hillbrow Tower, soaring above its densely populated suburb, provides an infallible direction-finder for newcomers to the city.*

than two people per dwelling unit, which is often only a small room in one of the many high-rise blocks.

Hilton High-lying residential village and educational centre overlooking Pietermaritzburg. Described in the 19th century as 'a paradise of grass and bush with cool aisles of tall gum tree', it retains much of the atmosphere of an early English village.

Hogsback Village and holiday resort lying at 1 200 m above sea level in the AMATOLE MOUNTAINS of Eastern Cape, near ALICE. It is noted for its forests and many waterfalls. The thatched church of St Patrick-on-the-Hill is reputed to be the world's smallest nondenominational church. Easter services are held regularly in the vast 'outdoor cathedral' among the forests, with fallen trunks for pews. Contributing to its English atmosphere are gardens with fruit, nuts and berries introduced by early settlers.

Hole in the Wall Spectacular natural rock feature and tourist attraction on the WILD COAST of Eastern Cape, southwest of Coffee Bay. Erosion of a detached cliff has produced a large, tunnel-like hole through which the sea surges violently and noisily.

Holy Circle Area formed by a ring of at least six *kramats*, the burial-places of esteemed Islamic leaders, around Cape Town. Some are on the slopes of Table Mountain, others on Signal Hill, on Robben Island and in Constantia. Local Muslim tradition says that followers of the Prophet who live within the circle are safe from fire, famine, plague, earthquake and tidal waves. The *kramats* are often covered by a domed structure suggesting a mosque in miniature.

❖ The most famous of the Holy Circle *kramats*, drawing many pilgrims to Macassar, is that of the exiled Sheikh ▷YUSSUF of Indonesia (1626-99).

Hondeklipbaai A small bay on the coast of NAMAQUALAND in Northern Cape, north of Port Nolloth. The bay was used to export copper mined at Springbok and later at Okiep and Spektakel. It is now a fishing centre.

Hottentots Holland mountains Range of CAPE FOLDED MOUNTAINS partly enclosing the outlying areas of greater Cape Town and the Cape Flats. A barrier to early exploration, once known as 'the mountains of Africa', they are now crossed by Sir Lowry's Pass.

Irene Former village, now a suburb of Pretoria, the site of the farm *Doornkloof*, one-time home of General Jan Christian ▷SMUTS. The homestead is now a museum.

Isandlwana Hill in northern KwaZulu-Natal, formerly in the old kingdom of Zululand, which was invaded by the British army in January 1879. Failure to consolidate a defensive position led to a shattering British defeat on 22 January, when about 24 000 Zulus attacked. Losses included some 800 British soldiers, mostly of the 24th Regiment (South Wales Borderers) and 470 African levies. The Zulus, pitting spears against fire power, probably suffered at least 2 000 dead. (See also RORKE'S DRIFT.)

Ixopo Small town in southern KwaZulu-Natal, near Pietermaritzburg and centre of a major dairy-farming and forestry region. It is a place name familiar to millions through the opening sentences of Alan Paton's *Cry, the Beloved Country* (1948): 'There is a little road that runs from Ixopo into the hills. These hills are grass-covered and rolling, and they are lovely beyond any singing of it.'

❖ A Buddhist retreat centre in the hills near Ixopo draws many visitors.

Johannesburg City lying at 1 740 m above sea level, literally founded on gold, now the mining, financial, commercial, engineering and manufacturing heart of South Africa and capital of Gauteng province. Developed from a tent town in 1886 with the discovery of a surface outcrop of the Main Reef, Johannesburg became the focus of foreign or 'uitlander' expression. The population, including SOWETO and other adjacent municipalities, now exceeds 5 million. The city centre undergoes continuous vertical expansion to meet demand for office space. Contrasting suburbs

SURGING SEA *Waves rush turbulently through the Hole in the Wall, an unusual rock formation in a detached cliff on the Wild Coast, to create a spectacular – and noisy – attraction for tourists.*

include crowded HILLBROW and parklike Houghton and Sandton. Johannesburg was founded about 60 km south of Pretoria, but the two cities have been rapidly growing closer together.

❖ Johannesburg is known to many Africans as eGoli ('City of Gold').

Kadoma Principal town (formerly Gatooma) of a rich mining region of Zimbabwe, producing gold, magnesite, copper and nickel. It is also the centre of the country's cotton and textile-manufacturing industry. There is an important mineral refinery at Eiffel Flats, near Kadoma.

Kalahari Arid region of central southern Africa, its flat sandy expanse of 65 000 km² encompassing parts of South Africa, Angola, Namibia and Botswana. There are almost no permanent springs and, in the south especially, drought is the normal condition. The northern parts are better endowed with water, vegetation and game.

Kalk Bay Cape Town suburb on the FALSE BAY coast, with a picturesque fishing harbour and tranquil old thatched church (Holy Trinity). Antique shops line the crowded Main Road. Caves in the mountain behind it are a potholer's delight. Its name is derived from the Dutch *kalk* ('lime') because of kilns set up in the 17th century to make lime for whitewash and plaster from shells gathered here.

Kame Village, formerly Khami, and site of Iron Age ruins, in Zimbabwe, near BULAWAYO. The main ruins occupy a site of 1,5 km² and are believed to be all that remains of the capital of a state that emerged in the 15th century, when ▷GREAT ZIMBABWE was in decline.

Kanoneiland Settlement and largest of the islands in the lower Orange River, downstream of UPINGTON in Northern Cape. The island is 14 km long and up to 3 km wide, with an area of 2 533 ha.

❖ Kanoneiland's name comes from an event in 1878, when the Cape Police bombarded refugee Korana people with artillery.

Kariba Resort town in Zimbabwe and lake on the Zambezi River, which forms the border between Zimbabwe and Zambia. The dam wall, which spans a narrow gorge about 280 km northwest of Harare, holds back a lake 280 km long with a width of up to 40 km. National parks and safari areas with a lake or river boundary include Matusadona, Mana Pools, Charara and Chete.

Karoo, Great Arid geographical region of central South Africa, including parts of Western, Eastern and Northern Cape and Free State, most of it lying between 600 m and 1 350 m above sea level. Throughout much of the Karoo, water may be pumped to the surface – usually by the ubiquitous windmills – but the natural flora includes many unique succulent species adapted to conditions of extreme dryness. Its mountain ranges include the Sneeuberg, Roggeveld and Nuweveld, but the characteristic scenery is of baking plains dotted with flat-topped hills or koppies. The Great Karoo is one of South Africa's main regions for sheep rearing.

FINANCIAL HUB *The Johannesburg Stock Exchange, flanked by First National House on the left, is the focal point of the city's – and South Africa's – financial centre; nearby are the headquarters of many of the country's leading mining, banking and industrial groups.*

Karoo, Little Area of the southern parts of Western and Eastern Cape lying between the coastal ranges and the mountains that form the southern limits of the Great Karoo. Its mountain passes and scenery attract visitors. The area is the centre of ostrich farming and also produces port wines and a range of crops, including tobacco and deciduous fruits. The principal town is OUDTSHOORN.

Katberg Well-watered mountain region in the FORT BEAUFORT district of Eastern Cape, with extensive forest plantations and holiday resorts. Katberg Pass, built in the 1860s (it has a gravel surface for much of its length), reaches 1 700 m, providing outstanding views.

Keetmanshoop Namibia's unofficial 'capital of the south', situated on the main road and railway south of WINDHOEK. Its buildings, a mixture of German colonial and modern architectural styles, include a church converted to a museum and the *Alte Kaserne* or old barracks. Near the town is a forest of kokerbome *(Aloe dichotoma)*, a tree-like succulent growing up to 7 m tall.

❖ The district of Keetmanshoop supports huge flocks of karakul sheep.

Keiskammahoek Forestry centre and village in the AMATOLE MOUNTAINS, near BISHO, with a large hospital and a stone fort dating from the mid-19th-century frontier wars.

Kimberley Diamond-mining centre and capital of Northern Cape, 2 000 m above sea level at the geographical centre of the Republic of South Africa. Founded as diamond-diggings on the farm Vooruitzicht in 1871, it was named after the British colonial secretary, the Earl of Kimberley. It was unsuccessfully besieged by the Boers from November 1899 to February 1900 while their arch-enemy, Cecil ▷RHODES (who called Kimberley his 'foster mother'), was in residence. It has several cultural and industrial museums.

❖ Kimberley is famous for its Big Hole, the

world's largest excavation dug by hand, with a mean diameter of 457 m and a depth of 366 m. It is now partly filled with water.

King William's Town Eastern Cape town, for decades a 'frontier garrison town'. It is the home of the Kaffrarian Museum, which has one of the world's finest collections of mammal specimens (the Shortridge Mammal Collection). Its many attractive historic buildings contrast with the modernity of the adjacent town of BISHO, the provincial capital.

Klerksdorp City laying claim to be the oldest town north of the Vaal settled by Europeans (in 1837). It is the centre for gold mining in North-West province and of the largest agricultural cooperative (producing maize, peanuts, cattle and sunflower seeds) in the southern hemisphere.

Knysna Resort and forestry town on the GARDEN ROUTE, in an idyllic lagoon-side setting where the Knysna River flows to the sea through a narrow channel below towering cliffs called the Knysna Heads. It is the terminus of a regular scenic steam-train journey from GEORGE (68 km away). The town is at the edge of one of the world's largest protected forest areas, containing many trails and the venue for an annual Forest Marathon that coincides with an Oyster Festival. Old goldworkings in the forest also draw tourists, as do the beaches, rivers and mountains.

❖ Knysna was founded in about 1800 by a wealthy Englishman known as George Rex, about whom there has grown an enduring legend that he was the son of George III of England and the Quaker Hannah Lightfoot. Extremely hospitable to travellers, Rex was reticent about his background and took his secret – if he had one – to his grave, which lies in a small, wooded clearing near the N2 national road.

❖ George Bernard Shaw spent a year in Knysna in 1932 while writing *The Adventures of a Black Girl in Search of God.*

Kokstad Historic Eastern Cape town and capital of the former province of Griqualand East, set among forested mountain slopes in a district noted for dairy farming and horse rearing. The town is associated with the epic but little-known trek of the ▷GRIQUA people, who arrived here in 1862. It is an attractive holiday resort, with broad oak-lined streets and a healthy, bracing climate.

Kolmanskop Namibian ghost town of buildings in the German colonial style amid sand dunes southeast of Lüderitz. It is in the *Sperrgebiet,* or diamond area, to which access is granted only in special circumstances. Established in 1908 and once inhabited by about 700 families, it was abandoned some 20 years later. It is now battered by wind and flung sand that piles up to roof height and, sometimes, moves on.

COUNTLESS SHOVELFULS *Pick and shovel were used to dig Kimberley's 366-m-deep Big Hole, which had workings below that going to a depth of 1 km. Today it is partly filled with water.*

Komatipoort Town, railway and customs centre on the MPUMALANGA-Mozambique border, 105 km east of NELSPRUIT on the main road and rail route to MAPUTO. The Crocodile Bridge Gate to the Kruger National Park is some 13 km from the town.

Kosi Bay Resort area and nature reserve with a series of lakes on the coast of KwaZulu-Natal close to the Mozambique border. It is an angler's paradise, has abundant bird life and is the breeding ground for the world's largest marine turtles, some of which exceed 2 m in length and 600 kg in mass.

Kroonstad Principal town and railway junction of northern Free State, with a holiday resort on the banks of the Vals River. The area produces cattle, sheep, grains and fruit.

Krugersdorp Gold-mining and industrial centre in Gauteng. It is the site of the STERKFONTEIN CAVES, where remains of the apelike primate *Australopithecus africanus* were found. The 1 400 ha Krugersdorp Game Reserve is 7 km from the town centre.

Kunene (formerly Kaokoveld) Fairly barren and sparsely populated mountainous region of northwestern Namibia. The Skeleton Coast Park and the Etosha National Park fall in this area. The Etosha Pan, a dried-up lake, is a 120 km by 50 km shallow depression which fills after rainy periods, attracting huge numbers of game and flocks of flamingoes.

Kunene River River rising in Angola near Nova Lisboa and flowing south before turning west to form the border with Namibia. A hydroelectric station on the border taps the power of the 123-m-high Ruacana Falls.

Kuruman Better known as the mission station of Robert ▷MOFFAT than as a progressive town in the far Northern Cape, 230 km northwest of Kimberley. The mission is a popular tourist attraction, as is the dolomitic spring, known as the Eye of Kuruman, in the town's main street. The district is noted for cattle and sheep rearing, and for dairy farming.

KwaZulu-Natal One of the nine provinces of South Africa, it is an area famous for its temperate weather and warm sea currents. The coastline is dotted with resorts and seaside villages perched between subtropical forests and golden beaches. KwaZulu-Natal's midlands stretch between the coast and the majestic Drakensberg mountains, where wild flowers grow in profusion and snowfalls transform the landscape overnight. The province is the traditional home of most of South Africa's Zulu people.

GHOST TOWN *Derelict and forlorn, the remnants of once-opulent colonial-style homes are all that remain of the town of Kolmanskop, abandoned when its diamond diggings closed.*

Ladysmith Principal town of the Klip River district, now in KwaZulu-Natal, brought to world fame when besieged by the Boers during the ▷SOUTH AFRICAN WAR. Bungled attempts to lift the siege added to the battlefields and military cemeteries in the district, which are regularly visited by local and foreign tourists. The Siege Museum is housed in the old town hall. Lying in the Drakensberg foothills, the town is a gateway to resort areas.

Langa African residential area and sprawling suburb of Cape Town with a population of more than 76 000. It was laid out in 1927 as one of the first model 'townships' for migrant workers and their families.
❖ In 1960 Langa made world headlines when Philip Kgosana, a young Pan-Africanist Congress activist, led a march by about 30 000 people protesting against the Pass laws from the township to the centre of Cape Town.

Langebaan Village and shallow lagoon northwest of Cape Town. The lagoon is a long and narrow (15 km by 2,5 km) inlet of SALDANHA Bay separated from the Atlantic Ocean by a long, narrow peninsula and is acknowledged as one of the great wetlands of the world. It forms part of the West Coast National Park, which in springtime attracts thousands of visitors who come to see the blaze of flowers.
❖ Environmentalists fiercely opposed plans by the Iron and Steel Corporation (Iscor), disclosed in 1995, to site a steelworks near Langebaan. However, Iscor withdrew its proposition shortly before a commission of inquiry was due to report on the project's effect on the environment. The commission subsequently recommended that the steelworks be sited further away from the lagoon.

Langkloof Narrow valley of Western and Eastern Cape, 160 km long, that has been farmed since 1760 and is a big apple-growing region. The valley is well watered, most of the rivers rising in the Tsitsikamma mountains and flowing from south to north.

Lebombo mountains Range of low (600 m) mountains forming part of South Africa's boundary with Swaziland and Mozambique. Eight east-flowing rivers have cut deep gorges, in one of which – the Pongola – a large storage dam has been built.

Lesotho Tiny mountain kingdom entirely surrounded by South Africa on which it is economically dependent. Its inhabitants – the Basotho – were forged as a nation in the early 19th century by King Moshoeshoe I who, from his mountain headquarters of Thaba Bosiu, unified thousands of people fleeing Zulu expansionism. The country became a British protectorate in 1868 and achieved full independence in 1966. The first prime minister was Leabua Jonathan, who was deposed in a military coup in 1986. In elections in March 1993 – the first since 1970 – the Basotho Congress Party under the leadership of Ntsu Mokhele scored a landslide victory. The capital is MASERU.

Limpopo River For about 700 km of its 1 600 km course the Limpopo forms South Africa's northern border with Botswana and Zimbabwe and reaches the Indian Ocean about 80 km north of MAPUTO. Over much of the catchment area the annual rainfall is below 500 mm and irrigation is not extensively practised. In years of drought the river may cease flowing.

Long Tom Pass Scenic road winding through the DRAKENSBERG between Sabie and Lydenburg in Northern Province. It reaches an altitude of 2 148 m, one of the highest points on a major road in South Africa. Its name comes from the heavy Creusot artillery pieces used by the Boers during the South African War; a full-scale replica of one of the guns has been placed near the summit.

Lowveld Region east of the great escarpment in Northern Province and MPUMALANGA, extending north into Zimbabwe, never rising to more than 600 m above sea level. The climate and vegetation are subtropical, with rain falling in summer, when malaria is prevalent in the area. The principal town is NELSPRUIT.

Lüderitz Seaport in Namibia, north of the mouth of the Orange River, on a shallow bay recorded as Angra Pequena (little bay) by Portuguese sailors in 1487. The town, a centre of the fishing industry, derives charm from its setting of German-style buildings with an uncompromisingly rocky Namibian backdrop.

Mafikeng Town, formerly Mafeking, with an eventful history, including a siege (1899-1900) that, while of no military significance, held readers of British newspapers spellbound. It is now part of Mmabatho, the capital city complex of North-West Province.
❖ The besieged town was held by a garrison of 800 men commanded by Robert ▷BADEN-POWELL, who organized the boys of the town into a noncombatant corps, giving birth to the idea of the Boy Scout movement.

Magaliesberg Low range of mountains in Gauteng. The highest peak is 1 780 m above sea level, although the range rarely rises more than 300 m above the surrounding ground level. Including Hartbeespoort Dam, it is a popular recreation area extending from RUSTENBURG to east of PRETORIA.

Magoebaskloof Scenic drive which snakes down the Drakensberg escarpment through forests and tea plantations between Haenertsburg and Tzaneen, Northern Province, dropping about 600 m in 6 km. It is named after Chief Makgoba (Magoeba) of the Tlou people.

Majuba Mountain between Volksrust and Newcastle in KwaZulu-Natal that is symbolic of Boer prowess at arms. As at the nearby

BATTLEFIELDS of Ingogo and Laing's Nek, Majuba saw the defeat of British professional soldiers by Boer sharpshooters. The battle took place in February 1881 and led to the end of the Anglo-Transvaal War and to the Transvaal's regaining some degree of independence from Britain. There are memorials on the sites, which are on the KwaZulu-Natal battlefields route.

Makgadikgadi Pan Ancient lake in northeast Botswana, now almost permanently dry and believed to be the largest salt pan in the world, covering 6 500 km². When the pan is flooded after good summer rains, it draws vast herds of game and huge flocks of birds. Makgadikgadi Pan Game Reserve, to the west, is a vast grassland. To the northwest, Nxai Pan National Park consists mainly of forest and savanna woodland.

Maluti Mountains Range, mostly in Lesotho, that runs parallel to that country's border with the Free State and forms part of the watershed incorporated in the Lesotho Highlands Water Project. For the greater part above 2 700 m, the mountains are covered in snow in winter.

Mamelodi A thriving residential area, east of Pretoria, which began in 1951 as a dormitory suburb for Africans. The proposed administration of Pretoria and Mamelodi by a single authority may result in the name (a nickname for president Paul Kruger) being applied to the entire complex.

Mapungubwe Flat-topped hill in the MESSINA district of Northern Province, close to the Limpopo River, where relics of a Zimbabwean culture skilled in gold-working have been found. With Makapansgat, it is an important site for palaeontological research. Permits to visit the site may be obtained from the University of Pretoria.

Maputaland Coastal area in the far north of KwaZulu-Natal, including the Maputaland Marine Reserve and Sanctuary and Kosi Bay Nature Reserve and, inland, Tembe Elephant Park and Ndumo Game Reserve. To the south are the Greater St Lucia Wetland Park and Mkuze Game Reserve. For fishermen and lovers of nature and the outdoors, it offers an abundance of delights.

Maputo National capital and major seaport of Mozambique and capital of Maputo Province. It was formerly known as Lourenço Marques. Only 100 km from the South African border, it was once a major tourist destination for people of the present-day Gauteng, Mpumalanga (formerly Eastern Transvaal) and Northern Province. Its infrastructure deteriorated during the almost 20 years of civil war that ended in 1994. It is Mozambique's leading manufacturing centre, with food-processing and textile industries.

VICTORIAN VINTAGE *In keeping with the rest of the tiny village of Matjiesfontein in the Great Karoo, the Lord Milner Hotel, restored to its former splendour, recaptures the atmosphere of a more gracious and tranquil era. The entire village has been proclaimed a National Monument.*

Margate Holiday resort on a lagoon on the south coast of KwaZulu-Natal so popular with residents of Gauteng that it has been called a seaside suburb of Johannesburg.

Maseru Capital and seat of government of Lesotho, near the Free State town of Ladybrand. The main point of entry to this mountain kingdom, it is an interesting blend of old and new, British colonial and African. It has a Catholic cathedral.

Matjiesfontein Small Victorian-vintage village in the Great KAROO, close to the N1 highway. It was established in the 1880s on the main rail route to the north as a dining stop and later developed into a place of recuperation for sufferers from lung complaints. The village and its hotel have been restored to their early splendour and are a popular weekend retreat for Capetonians.

Matobo Hills Range of hills (familiarly known as the Matopos) within the Matobo National Park near Bulawayo in southern Zimbabwe. There are many prehistoric caves and shelters, some with ancient paintings.
❖ Cecil ▷RHODES, principal colonizer of Zimbabwe (formerly Rhodesia), is buried here, in a simple grave on the commanding summit of a huge granite dome known as World's View.

Mbabane Capital of Swaziland, 17 km from that country's western border with Mpumalanga (formerly Eastern Transvaal). Well sited amid greenery and mountains, Mbabane has all modern amenities. It is close to Mlilwane Wildlife Sanctuary and many scenic sites.

Messina South Africa's northernmost town, 16 km south of the Zimbabwe border, in Northern Province. The district has many Stone Age and Iron Age village sites, some of them within the extensive Baobab Reserve, which contains at least 100 of these curious and ancient trees. Copper is mined here and the district produces cattle and fruit.

Middelpos Rare and somewhat whimsical example of an unevolved Karoo dorp, remotely situated midway between the towns of SUTHERLAND and CALVINIA in Northern Cape. Rare and beautiful bulbous plants abound in the dry and dusty surroundings.

Midrand Commercial, industrial and business centre situated in Gauteng, 20 km from Pretoria and 30 km from Johannesburg. It was formerly known as Halfway House.
❖ In 1995 Midrand was mooted as an alternative site for the South African parliament.

Mmabatho Capital city of North-West Province, former capital of the 'independent' state of Bophuthatswana. It was built as a modern extension – primarily for the tourist trade – of Mafikeng, which was formerly capital (as Mafeking) of the Bechuanaland Protectorate (now Botswana).

Mossel Bay GARDEN ROUTE town, east of Cape Town, now better known for its offshore gasfields. From the 15th to the 17th century it was a regular stopover for Portuguese navigators. History is well-displayed in the museums and the town and bay are popular holiday resorts. The sheltered harbour is too shallow for ocean-going vessels but is the haven to an important fishing fleet.

Mozambique Poor agricultural country in southeast Africa that was plagued by civil strife from the late 1970s to the early 1990s. Mozambique's problems were aggravated by drought in the 1980s. The country was a Portuguese colony until 1975, and then a Marxist state until 1990. The capital, Maputo, is a major port; formerly called Lourenço Marques, it was once a popular holiday resort for South Africans – a role it is hoping to regain.

Mpumalanga Province, formerly Eastern Transvaal, bounded by Gauteng, Northern Province, Free State, KwaZulu-Natal and Lesotho. Mozambique forms the eastern boundary. The capital is Nelspruit, 320 km east of Pretoria. The province includes coalfields and major thermal power stations in the west, with large forest plantations above the escarpment and on the lowveld. The southern part of the Kruger National Park falls within the province, which has many resort areas.

Muizenberg Residential suburb of Cape Town, once a premier seaside resort, with a sandy beach extending many kilometres along the FALSE BAY coast. It is the site of the ▹POSTHUYS, South Africa's oldest European building, dating from 1673.

Msunduzi River Scene of an annual canoe race called the Duzi Canoe Marathon, from Alexander Park in PIETERMARITZBURG to the confluence with the Mgeni River and then to the mouth of the Mgeni in DURBAN.

Murchison Range Low range of hills in the lowveld of Northern Province near the town of Gravelotte. Gold was mined in the area in the 1880s and the former ghost town of Leydsdorp is being revived as a tourist attraction. A great baobab tree nearby once had a bar for thirsty miners in its trunk.

Mutare Zimbabwe's fourth largest city (formerly Umtali), situated in the Eastern Highlands in Manicaland Province, 8 km from the border with Mozambique. The town has lush gardens and avenues lined with flowering trees. There are many viewing sites in the mountains nearby.

Namaqualand Near-desert region of Northern Cape which, despite its aridity, is famous for profuse and colourful displays of spring flowers. The principal town is SPRINGBOK, near which copper is mined.

❖ The northern part of Namaqualand, especially the Richtersveld, is renowned for the beauty and variety of its semiprecious stones.

Namib Desert Arid 'sea of dunes' stretching north along the Atlantic coast from Northern Cape into Angola. In Namibia the desert stretches up to 100 km inland to the edge of the central plateau. The sand dunes, up to 300 m high, are reputed to be among the world's highest.

Namibia Arid, sparsely populated country in southwest Africa, ruled by South Africa from the end of World War I until 1990. From the mid 1960s SWAPO, the South West Africa People's Organisation, conducted a guerrilla war against South African rule. Inland is the Namib Desert – a strip of harsh wilderness where frequent fogs often supply the only moisture. In the north, off the Skeleton Coast, treacherous currents, strong winds and fog have caused many shipwrecks. Namibia is a major diamond producer. In the capital, Windhoek, many German buildings survive.

SOUTHERN AFRICAN NATURE RESERVES AND GAME PARKS

Addo Elephant National Park
Eastern Cape
Has about 100 elephants of the same species as the African elephant, but more reddish in colour, the females rarely having tusks; also 50 mammal species, including black rhino.

Etosha National Park
Northern Namibia
Vast saline desert plain surrounded by open grassland with belts of deciduous trees and bushes where a wide variety of mammals and birds gather around water holes in large numbers: elephant, lion, leopard, cheetah, hyena, black rhinoceros, giraffe, gemsbok, springbok, eland, blue wildebeest, kudu, Burchell's zebra and the rare black-faced impala; and 325 bird species, ranging from ostrich to sunbird.

Chobe National Park
Northern Botswana
Predominantly the domain of large herds of elephant and buffalo; also lion, leopard, cheetah, spotted hyena, warthog, white rhinoceros, giraffe, hippo, crocodile and 350 bird species.

Golden Gate Highlands National Park
Free State
Mainly scenic park, with hiking trails through foothills and spectacular orange-yellow sandstone cliffs of the Maluti mountains; black wildebeest, eland, red hartebeest, blesbok and Burchells' zebra; prolific bird life, including black eagle and bearded vulture.

Hwange National Park
Zimbabwe
Said to contain the widest variety and greatest density of wildlife in the world, with up to 26 000 elephant in winter; black and white rhinoceros and 25 predator species, including lion, leopard and spotted hyena; 16 antelope species; more than 400 bird species.

Kalahari Gemsbok National Park
Northern Cape
Large nomadic antelope herds, including eland, gemsbok, blue wildebeest, red hartebeest and springbok; lion, leopard, cheetah, hyena, jackal; 215 bird species.

Kruger National Park
Mpumalanga and Northern Province
One of the world's largest national parks, covering 19 455 km^2 and stretching 350 km with an average width of 60 km; several major rivers flow across it; it has five main botanical divisions, with the environment and natural foods of each division determining the variety of wildlife within it; home to 138 mammal species, including elephant, lion, rhinoceros, giraffe, zebra, wildebeest, buffalo, hyena and a wide variety of antelope, and 115 reptile species; also 480 bird species, including waterbirds, raptors, owls, louries, cuckoos, parrots and hornbills; and 200 tree species.

Matobo National Park
Zimbabwe
Area of scenic beauty and unique flora in the Matobo Hills (Matopos), having the world's greatest concentration of rock art and, among 300 bird species, the world's largest number and variety of raptors, including more than 30 per cent of the world's eagle species; also rhino and southern Africa's largest number of leopard.

Mountain Zebra National Park
Eastern Cape
Protecting some of the last remaining concentrations of Cape mountain zebra, numbering about 200; also eland, hartebeest, wildebeest, blesbok, springbok and mountain reedbuck; 200 bird species, including martial, black and booted eagle, blue crane and pale-winged starling.

Royal Natal National Park
KwaZulu-Natal
Scenic park in the Drakensberg mountains, with extensive network of footpaths, climbs, and horse trails and trout fishing; variety of buck and 200 bird species.

Tsitsikamma Forest National Park
Eastern Cape
Coastal park of indigenous forest and fynbos, with cliffs falling to the sea and deep, narrow valleys cut by rivers flowing from the Tsitsikamma mountains; bushbuck, duiker, baboon, vervet monkey, mongoose and otter; 280 bird species, including 25 of seabirds.

Natal North Coast Popular name for the coastline and resorts of KwaZulu-Natal to the north of Durban. Among the main centres are Ballito, Umhlali, Umhlanga and Umdloti.

Natal South Coast Popular name for the coastline and resorts of KwaZulu-Natal to the south of Durban, extending for 170 km to Port Edward. Among the main centres are MARGATE, PORT SHEPSTONE, Bendigo, Hibberdene, Southbroom and Uvongo.

Nelspruit Capital of Mpumalanga, on the main road and rail routes to MAPUTO. It is an important commercial and tourist centre in a district producing citrus and other fruits, vegetables, tobacco and timber.

Nieu-Bethesda Village near GRAAFF-REINET in Eastern Cape, set in the foothills of the Sneeuberg range under the 2 503 m Kompasberg peak, often snow-capped in winter. An outstanding feature is Owl House, once the home of the reclusive eccentric Helen Martins (1898-1977). She covered the walls and ceilings with ground glass of various colours and filled its garden with sculptures of mythical figures she created with chicken wire and cement. The house is now a museum.
❖ A play by Athol ▷FUGARD, *Road to Mecca,* features the life of Helen Martins.

Northern Cape Largest of the nine provinces of South Africa created in 1994. It extends from the Atlantic coast eastwards to the borders of Free State, Eastern Cape and North-West Province, and borders Namibia and Botswana in the north. Its semi-arid Karoo-type terrain is sparsely settled and used mainly for stock rearing. Besides extensive deposits of diamonds and semiprecious stones, it has vast reserves of iron ore. The capital is KIMBERLEY.

Northern Province South African province, formerly the northern part of the Transvaal, with its capital at PIETERSBURG and embracing about half of the Kruger National Park. It extends southwards from the international boundaries of Botswana and Zimbabwe to the borders of Gauteng, Mpumalanga (formerly Eastern Transvaal) and North-West. Much of it consists of grassy highveld separated by the Drakensberg escarpment from the lowveld, which extends to the boundary of Mozambique. WARM BATHS, near the southern border of the province, is a popular spa resort with a modern, well-equipped hydro.

North-West Province of South Africa that includes the former Bophuthatswana, homeland of the Tswana people. Its terrain ranges from rich arable land in the northeast, producing wheat, maize, sunflowers, peanuts and cotton, to the arid northwestern part, close to the KALAHARI DESERT. The rest of the province is fine ranching country. Major tourist attractions are the SUN CITY hotel resort and the Pilanesburg Game Reserve. The province also has two of the world's largest platinum mines at RUSTENBURG. The modern capital is Mmabatho.

Okavango Delta Flood plain of 10 000 km^2 in northwest Botswana, abounding with wildlife. The delta is not – contrary to popular belief – a swamp, and there is excellent fishing in its clear waters. Game viewing from boats is a special attraction; the best months to visit are from May to October.

Orange River South Africa's longest river, flowing about 2 000 km from its source in Lesotho to the Atlantic Ocean. Previously called the Gariep, it was renamed after the former Dutch royal house.

Orange River Scheme Huge water-storage and hydroelectric project, one of the most ambitious projects of its type in the world. It includes the Gariep and Vanderkloof dams, as well as the dams and tunnels of the Lesotho Highlands Water Project, which will provide a link with the VAAL RIVER system.

WILD LIFE HAVEN *A circle of dry ground emerges from the Okavango Delta, home to deer, hippo, lion and huge flocks of birds.*

THE WAY IT WAS *Residents of Pilgrim's Rest, an early gold-mining town which has been preserved intact, built their houses of corrugated iron, not knowing how long they would retain possession.*

Oribi Gorge Spectacular ravine on the Mzimkulwana River, a tributary of the Mzimkulu in southern KwaZulu-Natal. The gorge, about 25 km long and 180 m to 300 m deep, lies 20 km west of PORT SHEPSTONE within a proclaimed nature reserve.

Oudtshoorn Principal town of the Little KAROO and 'ostrich capital' of the world. Ostrich show-farms are a popular attraction, as are the CANGO CAVES, near the town. The district produces fruit, wine, lucerne and tobacco – and its ostrich products include feathers, fertilizer, leather and meat.

Paarl Town in the valley of the BERG RIVER, north of Cape Town, surrounded by mountains, some of which are topped by huge granite domes. On one of these is the TAALMONUMENT. The town and district have many gracious old Cape Dutch buildings. The main products are fruit and wine.

Panorama Route Scenic circular route of some 70 km in Mpumalanga (formerly Eastern Transvaal), taking in the edge of the Drakensberg escarpment, several waterfalls and the quaint old mining town of PILGRIM'S REST. Diversions can be made to include resorts, tea rooms and other attractions.

Peddie Town in Eastern Cape midway between the Great Fish and Keiskamma rivers and southwest of King William's Town. Fort Peddie stands on a ridge overlooking the town, where there are old cemeteries with memorial inscriptions worthy of preservation or record.

Pelindaba Site of the South African Atomic Energy Board's first nuclear reactor and nuclear research station, a short distance from the N4 highway southwest of Pretoria. Radio isotopes produced here are supplied to industry, medical institutions and agriculture.

Pella Mission station (1814) and village in the northeastern corner of NAMAQUALAND in Northern Cape, near the Orange River. Fruits, including dates, are produced under irrigation and the district is rich in minerals and semiprecious stones.

Pietermaritzburg Historic city situated northwest of Durban. With ULUNDI, it is proposed as the capital of KwaZulu-Natal. Many gracious and stately Victorian buildings survive in the city centre and shady parks are an attractive feature. The district yields timber and dairy produce.

Pietersburg Capital of Northern Province, northeast of Pretoria, and gateway to the Kruger National Park via MAGOEBASKLOOF. The town is an educational centre and has the University of the North at Turfloop a few kilometres to the east. The district is noted for cattle rearing.

Pilgrim's Rest The earliest mining town in South Africa (1874), preserved in its setting of wooded mountain scenery near the Drakensberg escarpment in Mpumalanga (formerly Eastern Transvaal). A popular tourist destination, it is close to other scenic attractions, including the PANORAMA ROUTE.

Plettenberg Bay Town on the GARDEN ROUTE in Western Cape, with beaches, lagoons, rivers and forests providing the attractions that make 'Plet' one of the prime holiday resorts in South Africa.

Port Elizabeth City and harbour in Eastern Cape and, with the nearby town of Uitenhage, forming the hub of the motor manufacturing and ancillary industries. It is also a popular holiday centre; attractions include beaches, parks and gardens, an oceanarium (with performing dolphins), snake park, museums, art galleries and a 'Heritage Trail'.
❖ Port Elizabeth's oldest house, which has been preserved as a domestic museum of the city's earliest days, is located on Castle Hill.

Port St Johns Holiday resort at the Mzimvubu River mouth on the WILD COAST in Eastern Province. It is set in a landscape of beautiful beaches and mountains covered with subtropical forest.

Port Shepstone Town (no longer a port) at the mouth of the Mzimkulu River in KwaZulu-Natal. Founded in 1880, long before the vogue for seaside holidays, it is a combination of old-style commercial centre and modern resort. The town is on the route of the narrow-gauge Alfred County Railway.

Potchefstroom Historic town, founded in 1838 by Voortrekker leader Andries Hendrik Potgieter, in North-West Province on the banks of the Mooi River. Museums and buildings of the old republican era, the University of Potchefstroom and a holiday resort and yacht club are among its attractions.

Pretoria Executive capital of South Africa. Set among hills and overlooked by the ▷UNION BUILDINGS (1910) and Voortrekker Monument (1949), the city is spaciously laid out with many public parks. In springtime it is ablaze with the lilac flowers of the jacaranda trees lining many of its streets. It has many government buildings (and employees), three universities – of Pretoria, South Africa and Medunsa (Medical University of South Africa) – and a wide variety of museums. Among the recreational facilities it offers are bird-watching at Austin Roberts Bird Sanctuary, picnics at Wonderboom Nature Reserve and Fountains, and boating, angling and camping at HARTBEESPOORT DAM.
❖ Kruger House Museum, an unpretentious dwelling in Pretoria occupied by president Paul ▷KRUGER from 1884 until his exile in 1900, contains many of Kruger's personal possessions and the original furniture.
❖ Church Square, the city's centre, is dominated by a statue of Kruger by Anton ▷VAN WOUW. Its southern side is styled after Trafalgar Square in London and its northern side after the Place de la Concorde in Paris.

Prince Albert Great Karoo town noted for its individual style of gabled architecture at the foot of the SWARTBERG PASS, northwest of OUDTSHOORN. The district produces sheep and fruit, especially peaches and apricots.

Prince Alfred's Pass Gravel road of some 80 km passing through the Outeniqua Mountains between Avontuur and KNYSNA, encompassing incomparable scenery of mountain, forest and sea.
❖ Prince Alfred, later Duke of Edinburgh, was the second son of Queen Victoria and twice visited South Africa in the 1860s. On the second occasion, he shot an elephant near Knysna. (See VICTORIA AND ALFRED WATERFRONT.)

Qacha's Nek Picturesque village in mountainous country in the southeast of LESOTHO, 1 066 m above sea level. Bridle paths linking outlying posts provide superb trails for horse riding in the surrounding area, which produces cattle, goats, maize and wheat.

Queenstown The chief town of the area formerly known as the Eastern Cape Midlands. It was laid out in 1853 in the form of a hexagon, for easy defence. It is an important agricultural and educational centre in a district that produces sheep and cattle.

Qunu Village of huts scattered across rolling hills south of UMTATA in Eastern Cape, notable for being the place where president Nelson ▷MANDELA grew up.

Rehoboth Principal town of the Bastergebiet and the District of Rehoboth and now also the principal town of Hardap in Namibia. The term 'baster' (half breed) is proudly acknowledged by people who are descended from the original settlers of 1868.
❖ Hot mineral springs are a feature of the surrounding country.

Rhodes Village in the foothills of the southern DRAKENSBERG in Eastern Cape. At an altitude of 1 700 m, it is a centre for skiing and other winter sports.

Richards Bay Town and harbour at the mouth of the Mhlatuze River in northern KwaZulu-Natal. In terms of tonnage, the port handles more than twice as much as Durban; it exports up to 50 million tons of coal and 10,5 million tons of other mineral commodities a year. The lagoon is the home of hippos and aquatic birds.

Richtersveld Remote and extremely arid area and national park of far northwestern NAMAQUALAND in Northern Cape, inhabited by a few Nama people. Rainfall ranges between 5 and 200 mm annually, and temperatures between freezing point and 52°C.

Robben Island Low-lying island (the Dutch name means 'seals') with an unhappy history, 7 km from the mainland in TABLE BAY. It served for more than three centuries as a leper colony, mental asylum and maximum security prison. Still a prison in 1995, its future had yet to be decided. The creation of a nature reserve incorporating the old village and part of the prison was proposed.
❖ The island acquired worldwide notoriety as the site of the prison in which Nelson ▷MANDELA spent 18 years.

Roodepoort Mining and industrial city northwest of Johannesburg. Attractions include the Transvaal Botanic Gardens and Florida Lake (formed by water pumped from the mines). Its annual Eisteddfod draws participants from many countries and opera performances are given regularly in its theatre.

Rorke's Drift Art centre, village and mission on the Buffalo River in the DUNDEE district of northern KwaZulu-Natal. The day after their victory at ISANDLWANA in 1879, the Zulu army was repelled here by a small British garrison.

Rustenburg Town, a popular holiday and health resort, west of Pretoria. Two of the world's largest platinum mines adjoin the town in a district that produces fruit, cattle, tobacco, maize and wheat.
❖ The Gereformeerde Kerk was founded in the town – a memorial marks the spot.

St Lucia, Lake Shallow lake and estuarine area on the coast of northern KwaZulu-Natal. Four separate nature reserves make up a vast complex of lakes, dunes and beaches with a great diversity of habitats. Fishing, both in the lake and out at sea, is among the attractions that include game-spotting and bird-watching, hiking and camping.
❖ The eastern shore of Lake St Lucia, subject of a long debate over proposed opencast mining on its dunes, has been declared a conservation area.

Saldanha Town, fishing harbour and bay, northwest of Cape Town on the Atlantic coast. The bay leads into the LANGEBAAN Lagoon. Tourism, fishing and fish-processing (especially rock lobster) are economically important. The Naval Gymnasium and the Military Academy of the South African National Defence Force are both at Saldanha.

Salem Tiny old-world village in the ALBANY district of Eastern Cape, established by Hezekiah Sephton's party of 1820 Settlers. Methodism in South Africa had its roots here. The name means 'peace'.

Sandveld Coastal plateau between the CAPE PENINSULA and SALDANHA, once known as 'the great desolate plain' and renowned for the springtime colour and profusion of its wild flowers. The development of coastal resort areas at Yzerfontein and places north of Saldanha accelerated in the 1990s.

Sani Pass Challenging 93-km route over the DRAKENSBERG from KwaZulu-Natal to Lesotho for which four-wheel-drive vehicles are the best option. It reaches an altitude of 2 865 m.

Sasolburg Town in Free State, south of Johannesburg, built to serve Sasol (the South African Coal, Oil and Gas Corporation) and its employees. It is near vast deposits of low-grade coal, from which Sasol produces oil, petrol and petrochemicals.

Serowe Principal town in the district of Ngwato, Botswana, near Palapye, which is on the Mafikeng-Bulawayo road. Established in 1902 in the style of an African village-town, it still has many traditional *kgotlas*, or outdoor meeting places.

Sharpeville Town in Guateng near VEREENIGING where on 21 March 1960 police fired on a crowd of African demonstrators against the pass laws, killing 69 and injuring 180. The incident provoked international outrage.

Simon's Town Long-established naval base and town on the FALSE BAY coast, 36 km south of Cape Town. The base was occupied by the British Royal Navy from 1806 until 1957, when it was transferred to South Africa.

Sophiatown Former African suburb of Johannesburg with a vibrant community life and a night life of music and dancing centred on the shebeens. Sophiatown set the pace of urban African life for three decades until, in terms of the ▷GROUP AREAS ACT in 1955, it was razed to make way for the development of a white suburb called Triomf (triumph).

South Africa Country occupying the southern tip of the African continent. Parliament sits in CAPE TOWN between January and July, but the administration is based in PRETORIA and the highest court is in BLOEMFONTEIN. The largest city is JOHANNESBURG. South Africa is the continent's most developed country, much of its wealth coming from gold, diamonds and other minerals. Nearly three-quarters of South Africans are black. The biggest group are the Zulus, most of whom live in the province of Kwazulu-Natal. Whites make up 16 per cent of the population. Slightly more than half of them are Afrikaners, the Afrikaans-speaking descendants of early Dutch settlers who arrived in Cape Town from 1652. Britain first took control of the Cape in 1795. Many ▷BOERS, as the settlers of Dutch descent were then called, resented British rule and antislavery legislation, and in the 1830s Boer Voortrekkers moved northwards in a migration known as the ▷GREAT TREK. Boers and British clashed again in the ▷SOUTH AFRICAN WAR of 1899-1902. In 1948 the Afrikaner-dominated Nationalist government was elected, which implemented a policy of ▷APARTHEID for more than 40 years. The ANC and other black political parties were banned in 1960, and the ANC leader Nelson Mandela was imprisoned in 1962, a year after South Africa left the ▷COMMONWEALTH. The ban on ANC activity was lifted on February 2, 1990, and Mandela was released after 27 years of imprisonment. The apartheid system was officially abandoned in 1992. Other countries then eased trade, cultural and sports sanctions imposed since 1977. Conflict arose between supporters of the ANC and those of the dominantly Zulu Inkatha Freedom Party, led by Chief Mangosuthu Buthelezi. The first nonracial elections were held in 1994, 342 years after the arrival of the first whites in the Cape. On 2 May 1994, Nelson Mandela was elected president, and the following month South Africa rejoined the Commonwealth. Spectacular South African scenery includes the Garden Route – a stretch of the southern coast luxuriant with trees and flowering plants – and the Drakensberg range in the northeast. The country has an abundance of wildlife.

❖ South Africa's first wine was made in 1659, from vines planted by Dutch settlers soon after their arrival seven years earlier.

Soutpansberg Range of mountains extending east-west in Northern Province bordering on Zimbabwe. The well-forested slopes are the site of several hotels and a popular hiking trail. The chief town is Louis Trichardt. The district produces timber, cattle and fruit.

Soweto South Africa's largest African municipality, adjoining Johannesburg, with suburbs ranging from the near-opulent to shack settlements. Events in Soweto made world headlines during the struggle against ▷APARTHEID. The name is an acronym of South Western Townships.

Spioenkop Hill within a nature reserve of the same name overlooking the TUGELA RIVER, near Colenso in KwaZulu-Natal. Scene of an abysmal defeat of the British army in January 1900 on the road to the relief of LADYSMITH.

Springbok Commercial and administrative centre of the copper-mining area of NAMAQUALAND in Northern Cape, where once herds of springbok drank at a spring and where wild flowers still transform the veld into a blaze of colour in springtime. Its Hester Malan Nature Reserve preserves the fauna and flora of the area.

ARCHITECTURAL FANTASY *Not an ancient despot's residence, but the Palace of the Lost City, a luxury hotel, set in a forest of exotic trees, at the Sun City resort in North-West Province.*

Springs Mining and heavily industrialized EAST RAND town in Gauteng. It is the core town of the East Rand Metropolitan Transport Area (ORMET).

Stellenbosch Historic and scenic university town in the valley of the Eerste River in Western Cape. It is known for its oak-lined streets and fine examples of ▷CAPE DUTCH architecture and as the centre of a region famous for its wine production.

Sterkfontein Caves Fossil site at KRUGERSDORP in Gauteng where remains of the ape-like primate *Australopithecus africanus* were found in the 1930s. The attractions include a museum, restaurant and picnic grounds and regular tours are conducted through the chambers. A large underground lake lies 40 m below the surface.

Sterkfontein Dam Dam near Harrismith in Free State in the valley of the Nuwejaarspruit. It has the largest wall in South Africa. Its lake, which is open to anglers and water sports enthusiasts, covers 6 940 ha. It is adjoined by the Sterkfontein Dam Nature Reserve. The dam is part of a vast water transfer scheme in which water from the TUGELA RIVER is pumped into it for diversion into the VAAL RIVER, which supplies Gauteng.

Sudwala Caves A popular tourist attraction, with stalactites, stalagmites and fossilized remains, about 10 km north of the highway between NELSPRUIT and Waterval Onder in Mpumalanga (formerly Eastern Transvaal). The facilities include a museum, dinosaur park, swimming pool and restaurant.

Suikerbosrand Range of hills running more or less parallel to the WITWATERSRAND south of Johannesburg, near the town of Heidelberg in Gauteng. A nature reserve provides amenities for recreation for the inhabitants of the highly industrialized Witwatersrand.

Sun City Glossy tourist resort with hotel, sporting, gambling and theatrical entertainment facilities in the Pilanesberg Game Reserve in North-West province.

❖ A more recent addition, with an 'African fantasy' theme, is the Lost City. This includes a luxury hotel, a beach with a stretch of water that resembles a seaside bay, complete with waves, and a bridge that is lined with stone elephants and which shudders at intervals to simulate an earthquake.

Sutherland Small Karoo town in Northern Cape, founded in 1857. It is the site of the South African Astronomical Observatory.

PRISTINE CAPE DUTCH *Historic houses in Church Street, Tulbagh, were reconstructed after an earthquake destroyed a large part of the town in 1969. It is the centre of a wine-growing region.*

Swakopmund Coastal town and former harbour in Namibia at the mouth of the Swakop River. Fine old German-style houses are incorporated into a lively resort close to the Skeleton Coast National Park.

Swartberg Pass Majestic crossing of the Swartberg range between OUDTSHOORN and PRINCE ALBERT, with magnificent vistas. The summit is at 1 577 m and the mountain peaks are often snow covered in winter. Built in the 1880s, the pass has hardly changed since then. Its narrow, sometimes wet and slippery, gravel road, with its steep gradients, is daunting to nervous motorists.

Swartland District north of Cape Town in Western Cape, so called ('black land') because of the dark-coloured renosterbos *(Rhinocerotis elytropappus)* that formerly covered the reddish soil. Malmesbury is the main town of the area, which is noted for wheat production.

Swaziland Southern African monarchy, one of only three remaining in Africa. Surrounded on three sides by South Africa and to the north-east by Mozambique, Swaziland boasts a beautiful climate, splendid scenery and a plentiful water supply. However, since independence it has battled to balance traditional politics with modern developments – and this has had a depressing effect on its economy. The present monarch is Mswati III, who ascended the throne in 1986. The previous king, Sobhuza II, who died in 1982, reigned for 61 years. Mbabane is the capital. (See also ▷SWAZILAND in 'South African history'.)

Swellendam Historic town and former magistracy, established in 1747, south of the Langeberg range in Western Cape. It is noted for the beauty of its mountain scenery, the adjacent Bontebok National Park and many old buildings that have been well preserved.

Taalmonument Afrikaans language monument, unveiled in 1975 on one of the great granite rocks of PAARL, where 100 years earlier the Genootskap van Regte Afrikaners (the Association of True Afrikanners) had begun its campaign for the recognition of Afrikaans. It is composed of linked columns that symbolize the contribution of Western languages and culture and acknowledge the large parts played by the languages and influences of African and Eastern cultures.

❖ An earlier Taalmonument was erected in BURGERSDORP in 1893 to commemorate the right to use the Dutch language in the formerly English-only Cape Parliament.

Table Bay Large inlet north of Table Mountain with the city of Cape Town situated on its shores. Some 221 ha of level ground, now forming the city's Foreshore, was recovered from the sea in 1880 and in 1934. The harbour and breakwater provide shelter for shipping from the violent northwest gales of winter. ROBBEN ISLAND is located in the middle of the bay.

Table Mountain Famous landmark and tourist attraction overlooking Cape Town and Table Bay. It is 1 086 m high. Its sheer cliffs offer a challenge to mountaineers, but there are also several easier climbs and an aerial cableway carries visitors to the top in six minutes. The mountain and adjoining Devil's Peak and Lion's Head exert a profound influence on the city's weather, especially by their effect on the southeasterly gales in summer.

❖ The first recorded ascent of Table Mountain was by Antonio de Saldanha, a Portuguese fleet commander, in 1503.

Taung Village (formerly Taungs) and lime quarry north of KIMBERLEY in Northern Cape. Site of the discovery (in 1924) of the first fossil remains to be identified as those of the apelike primate *Australopithecus africanus.*

Thaba Bosiu Historic site in Lesotho, 1 804 m above sea level, the mountain fortress and home of ▷MOSHOESHOE who successfully defended it against attacks by Boers and British. It is venerated as the site where the Sotho kingdom was founded and as the burial place of Moshoeshoe and other Sotho kings.

Thohoyandou Modern town in the Soutpansberg of the far Northern Province. The former capital (until 1994) of the 'independent' state of Venda, it is centred on a shopping centre, hotel and casino.

Troutbeck Resort and reputedly the finest trout-fishing area in southern Africa, north of Nyanga National Park in the Eastern Highlands of Zimbabwe. The angling season is from November to the end of May, but some lakes may be fished all year round.

Tsumeb Namibian mining town north of Windhoek yielding a range of more than 200 minerals, including copper, lead (the world's largest output), zinc, cadmium and silver. It is the northern terminus of Namibia's rail system and some 90 km from Etosha National Park. An adequate water supply and the subtropical climate help to make this one of the prettiest towns in Namibia.

Tugela River Third most important river in South Africa after the VAAL and the ORANGE rivers. Rising on the eastern slopes of the KwaZulu-Natal Drakensberg, it flows 560 km to the sea. Close to its source the river drops 2 000 m in a series of falls and cascades. Storage dams in the basin include Chelmsford, Spioenkop and Wagon Drift and water is pumped via STERKFONTEIN DAM into the Vaal River system to the Witwatersrand.

Tulbagh Historic Western Cape town, founded in 1743 and rebuilt after near-destruction by an earthquake in 1969.

Tzaneen Town at the foot of MAGOEBASKLOOF in the Letaba district of Mpumalanga (formerly Eastern Transvaal), east of Pietersburg. It is central to resort areas of the Kruger National Park and Drakensberg. Research on malaria and bilharzia is conducted at the Siegfried Annecke Institute.

DOCKSIDE DEVELOPMENT *Cloud-bedecked Table Mountain forms the backdrop to Cape Town's Victoria and Alfred Waterfront. Launches moored at the quay offer trips around the docks, the bay and along the coast. The spacious Victoria Wharf Shopping Mall (left), containing cinemas, a theatre, a craft market and numerous restaurants overlooking the harbour, was once a warehouse.*

Uitenhage Highly industrialized town north of PORT ELIZABETH with motor-vehicle assembly plants and factories producing tyres, car components and textiles. Founded in 1804 under the brief ▷BATAVIAN REPUBLIC regime, it has interesting museums and an old railway station with exhibits of locomotives and rolling stock.

Ulundi Administrative centre until 1994 of the former self-governing state of KwaZulu and recently a contender (with PIETERMARITZBURG) for the position of capital of the province of KwaZulu-Natal. A memorial marks the site of the Battle of Ulundi, fought between British and Zulu in 1879.

Umtata Eastern Cape university town northeast of East London and former capital (until 1994) of the 'independent' state of Transkei. It is the seat of an Anglican bishopric.

Upington Town on the north bank of the Orange River, west of KIMBERLEY in Northern Cape, at the centre of a prosperous area in which extensive irrigation schemes have been implemented. It is conveniently situated in relation to the Kalahari Gemsbok and AUGRABIES FALLS national parks and on the road and main rail route to Namibia.

Vaal Dam An extensive series of artificial lakes formed where several tributaries meet the Vaal River and where the borders between Gauteng, Mpumalanga (formerly Eastern Transvaal) and Free State come together. It is a popular fishing and watersports area.

Vaal River The most important tributary of the Orange River, which it joins near Douglas, southwest of Kimberley in Northern Cape. Up to that point it flows 1 355 km from its source on the western slopes of the Drakensberg near ERMELO in Mpumalanga (formerly Eastern Transvaal). Its water, which supplies the heavily industrialized, mining and densely populated areas of Gauteng and the northern Free State, is supplemented by water transferred to it from the TUGELA RIVER.

Valley of a Thousand Hills Majestic valley traversed by the Mgeni River between Pietermaritzburg and Durban in KwaZulu-Natal, with panoramic views eastwards for about 50 km to the coast and westwards across the midlands of KwaZulu-Natal. The valley is rich in flowering plants, especially aloes.

Valley of Desolation A landscape of crumbling cliffs and huge, dolerite-capped pillars which forms an extraordinary sight from the viewpoint on Spandau Kop near GRAAFF-REINET in Eastern Cape. The valley is a national monument.

Vanderbijlpark Modern industrial town established in 1941 on the Vaal River in Gauteng, southwest of Johannesburg. It is the headquarters of the South African Iron and Steel Corporation (Iscor). It has many parks and gardens and the river, which has select residential areas along its banks, is a popular recreational amenity.

Vereeniging Industrial town on the Vaal River in Gauteng. The Treaty of Vereeniging that ended the ▷SOUTH AFRICAN WAR was negotiated here but signed in Pretoria. A museum displays relics of the war and a collection of fossil plants. There are resorts along the river.

Victoria and Alfred Waterfront Retail, entertainment and commercial development of Cape Town's old docklands, including the Victoria and Alfred basins, begun in 1988. Its shops, hotels, restaurants, cinemas, theatres, markets, museums and aquarium, set against the authentic background of a working harbour, have become a major tourist attraction. ❖ Prince Alfred, Queen Victoria's second son, inaugurated Cape Town's first breakwater for the new harbour in the 1860s. His name has been given also to PRINCE ALFRED'S PASS.

Victoria Falls Series of cataracts, the world's largest known curtain of falling water, on the Zambezi River where it forms the boundary between Zambia and Zimbabwe. In April and May, when the river is at its fullest, about 340 000 m^3 of water pass over the falls every minute and its roar can be heard 20 km away.

Warm Baths (Warmbad) Spa resort in Northern Province. Its extensive and luxurious modern hydro development has an hotel,

NAMIBIAN CAPITAL *A clock tower amid contemporary buildings in Windhoek's Independence Avenue stands as a reminder of the time the former South West Africa was a German colony.*

self-catering bungalows, indoor and outdoor swimming baths and treatment centre for rheumatic complaints. The temperature of the water, which is mildly radioactive, ranges between 32° and 46°C.

Waterval Boven Town and railway station on the main road and rail route between Johannesburg and the Mozambique border. Here the Transvaal highveld comes to an end and the railway line drops 228 m in 7,5 km on the way to Waterval Onder. The original route of the line, passing the Elands River falls and going through a century-old, 213 m tunnel, is a national monument.
❖ Krugerhof, seat of president Paul ▷KRUGER's government in 1900, brings tourists to Waterval Onder.

Welkom Gold-mining town, established in 1948, and centre of the Free State goldfields, which contribute about 20 per cent of the world's gold production and almost 50 per cent of South Africa's output.

Wellington Town in the Berg River valley in Western Cape adjoining PAARL. It was one of the areas of settlement of the 17th-century French ▷HUGUENOTS and is the centre of a fruit-growing district with several wineries and factories producing canned foods, textiles and leather.

Western Cape Province of South Africa extending to the east and north of its capital, CAPE TOWN, and embracing the country's earliest European settlements. It abounds in splendid beaches, forests, vineyards and wheatlands and spectacular mountain and coastal scenery contrasting with the wide open spaces and koppies of the northern strip in the semiarid Karoo. It is also famous for the great variety of its flora. Its climate in the southern part is Mediterranean, with winter rainfall, while across the mountain ranges that run parallel to the coast, the winters are dry, with rain falling in the summer.

West Coast Informal name applied to the coast north of Cape Town from Bloubergstrand to Velddrif. It is washed by the cold Benguela Current and offers excellent fishing, both from boats and from the shore. The area is noted for its magnificent carpet of spring flowers.

Whale Route Whimsical name given to the coast from False Bay eastwards to HERMANUS, where Southern Right whales come close inshore at various points to calve or mate.

Wild Coast Stretch in Eastern Cape between the Great Kei River in the south and Port Edward in the north, characterized by deep river gorges and forested mountain slopes hung with flowers and creepers. There are several resorts in this anglers' paradise.
❖ The 'wild' element in the Wild Coast is the sea that has accounted for many shipwrecks and mysterious disappearances off the coast.

Windhoek Capital of Namibia and industrial city, founded in 1890 when the former South West Africa was a German protectorate. Many German names and buildings survive and a German carnival held annually adds to the colourful atmosphere. Its industries include food processing, brewing, engineering, diamond sorting and processing of the much-prized karakul lamb pelts.

wine routes The soils and climate of Western Cape are well suited to growing grapes and wine routes have developed as a marketing and publicity tactic to allow people to taste a variety of wines at their source in a short time. Among the districts boasting a wine route are Stellenbosch, Paarl, Franschhoek, Worcester, Robertson, Olifantsrivier, Swartland, Calitzdorp, Karoo and Upington.

Witwatersrand Highly industrialized area in Gauteng and the world's greatest goldfield. Lying for the most part at least 1 700 m above sea level, it comprises an almost continuous succession of towns, with Johannesburg in the centre. Roodepoort, Krugersdorp and Randfontein lie to the west and Germiston, Boksburg, Benoni, Brakpan and Springs to the east. It is also called the Rand ('ridge').

Witbank Mining and industrial town in Mpumalanga (formerly Eastern Transvaal), in a district that produces about two-thirds of South Africa's coal output. Some of the country's largest thermal power stations are situated nearby. A pleasant recreational area at a dam on the Orange River is on the outskirts.
❖ Winston ▷CHURCHILL, then a war correspondent, found refuge here after escaping from a Boer prison camp in 1899.

Worcester Attractive and spacious town in the BREËRIVIER valley in Western Cape. The town is surrounded by mountains, many of which are snow-clad in winter. It is noted for specialized schools for the deaf and the blind and for its Karoo garden of succulent plants. The district produces wine and brandy.

Zimbabwe Landlocked country of south-central Africa, much of which is savannah dotted with massive granite hills. Zimbabwe was the British colony of Southern Rhodesia from the end of the 19th century until 1953, when it joined in a federation with Northern Rhodesia (now ▷ZAMBIA) and Nyasaland (now ▷MALAWI). The federation broke up in 1963 and in 1965 Southern Rhodesia's white minority government made a unilateral declaration of independence. After a protracted guerrilla war, legitimate independence was secured in 1980, with black majority rule and Robert Mugabe as prime minister. The capital is HARARE, formerly known as Salisbury.
❖ The country takes its name from Great Zimbabwe, the ruins of massive stone buildings occupied by the Shona-Karanga civilization (*c*AD 1200-1450).

NATIONS AND PLACES OF THE WORLD

Our world has grown smaller. Remote corners of the Earth can be reached in only a few hours. Scenes of distant wars, droughts and disasters appear daily on television, compelling immediate interest. Holiday resorts and places rich in culture, architecture or history lure us abroad, while deserts, mountains, exotic isles or icy wastes astound us with their natural beauty.

Acapulco Resort on Mexico's south coast, renowned for its cliff-divers who plunge from more than 37 m into a rocky shallow cove. To avoid hitting the rocks, divers take off as a large wave comes in.

Aegean Sea Arm of the Mediterranean Sea situated between Greece, Turkey and Crete. The Aegean is studded with islands in three groups: the Cyclades, the Sporades and the Dodecanese, of which the largest one is RHODES.

Afghanistan Country in southwest Asia, divided by the Hindu Kush mountain range. Its capital is the ancient city of KABUL. Afghanistan is one of the world's least developed countries and many of its people are seminomadic livestock herders. Nearly all Afghans are Muslims.

❖ Troops of the former USSR occupied Afghanistan from 1979 to 1989.

Alaska Largest of the states of the USA in area but the second smallest in population, after Wyoming, with just over 550 000 inhabitants. Alaska was bought from Russia in 1867 for US$7,2 million, but became a state only in 1959. Extensive oil reserves along the Arctic coast are its chief source of wealth. The biggest city is Anchorage but the state capital is Juneau, which is accessible only by sea and air.

Albania Poorest European nation, with more than half its population working on the land. The capital is Tirana. Hard-line communists controlled Albania from 1944 to 1990, since when economic, political and social reforms have been introduced. However, Albania remains the country in Europe least accessible to foreigners.

Aleutian Islands Chain of 14 large and 55 small islands forming part of and extending westwards from ALASKA. These rainy, mountainous, treeless islands are the home of some 1 000 Aleuts, whose main source of income comes from fishing.

Alexandria Port on the Nile delta and second largest city of Egypt, founded by Alexander the Great in 332 BC. The Pharos, or Lighthouse, of Alexandria was one of the Seven Wonders of the Ancient World.

❖ In ancient times Alexandria was a centre of learning with a famous library holding more than 500 000 manuscripts.

Algeria North African country – the continent's second largest after Sudan – which gained independence from France in 1962 after a long war. More than 85 per cent of the country is in the SAHARA desert, where there are huge deposits of natural gas and petroleum. Berbers established a kingdom here in about 2400 BC and Arabs arrived from the 7th century bringing Islam, now the faith of most Algerians. Military governments have ruled the country since 1965. When the first round of parliamentary elections held in 1991 was decisively won by the fundamentalist Islamic Salvation Front, the second round was cancelled and the movement banned. This led to violent conflict between the military and the fundamentalists, who also targeted foreigners for attack.

Alps The 1 200 km-long range of mountains extending from the Mediterranean coast of France and northwestern Italy through Switzerland, northern Italy and Austria, famous for its snow-covered peaks and skiing resorts, among them St Moritz. The Alps' and Western Europe's highest peak is Mont Blanc (4 807 m) on the French-Italian border near Geneva. The Matterhorn, a magnificent, pyramidlike mountain on the Swiss-Italian border near Zermatt, is 4 478 m high.

Amazon World's second longest river (after the Nile), flowing for some 6 440 km across Peru and northern Brazil. Seven of the Amazon's tributaries are more than 1 600 km long, and it ends in a delta so vast that two channels are separated by an island which is about the size of Switzerland.

❖ The Amazon rain forest covers an area of 6,5 million km² – nearly five times the size of South Africa.

Amritsar Indian city whose Golden Temple is the most sacred shrine of ▷SIKHISM. In the Amritsar Massacre of 1919, troops under a British officer, General Reginald Dyer, fired into a crowd of unarmed Indian protesters, killing about 400. In 1984 Indian troops

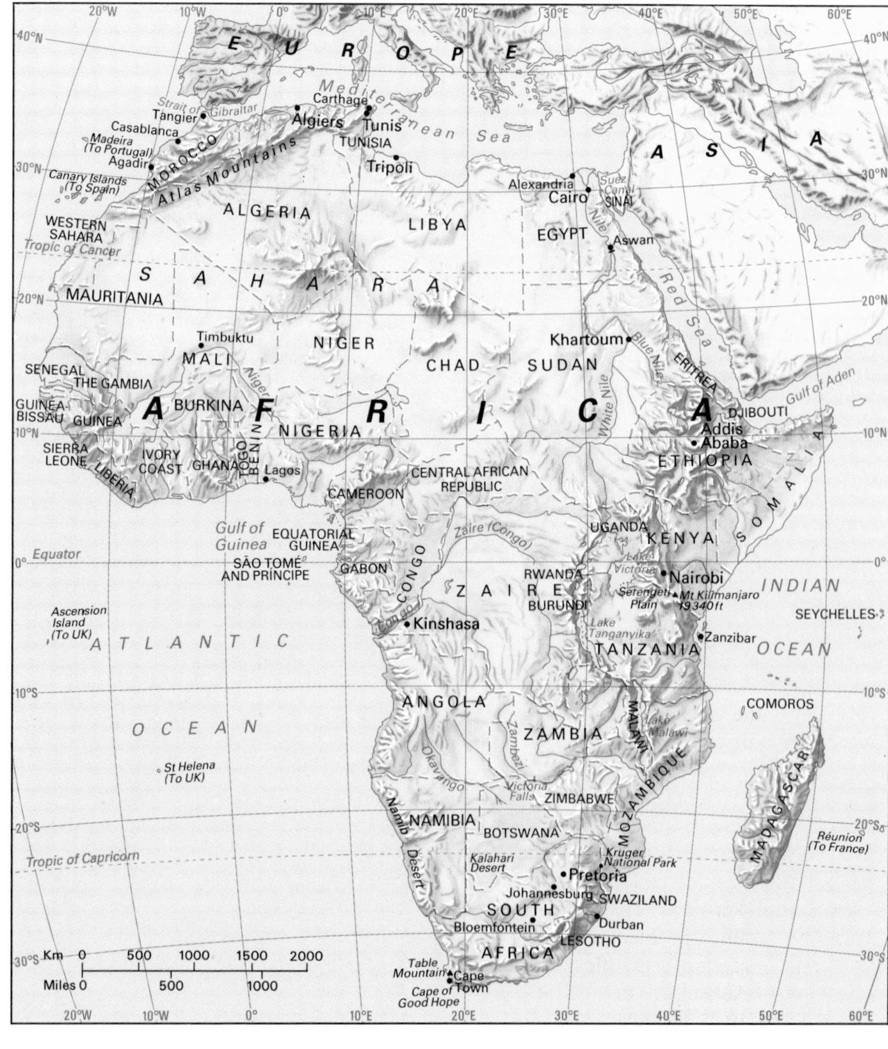

HOT CONTINENT *Harsh deserts cover one-third of Africa and hot and humid rain forests lie along the Equator. Only 6 per cent of the land is arable, yet two out of three people work on the land.*

NIGHT SCENE *Lights outline gables in Amsterdam and one of the city's 1 000 bridges that cross more than 100 canals.*

stormed the Golden Temple, which had been occupied by a group of Sikh extremists.

Amsterdam Capital and largest city of the Netherlands. The old city of canals and gabled houses dates mainly from 1650-1720. Amsterdam was the home of the painter, ▷REMBRANDT, and, during World War II, of the Jewish refugee Anne ▷FRANK. It has been a diamond-cutting centre since the 1570s.

Andes World's longest mountain range, running along South America's Pacific coast for 8 000 km. The highest point is at Aconcagua (6 960 m). The ▷INCA empire embraced much of the northern Andes, and the ruins of the Inca city MACHU PICCHU are located 2 280 m up in the mountains.

Andorra Tiny principality in the PYRENEES between Spain and France, known for its ski resorts and duty-free goods.

Angel Falls World's highest waterfall, with a drop of 979 m, on a tributary of the River Caroní in Venezuela.
❖ The falls are named after Jimmy Angel, an American pilot who, in 1935, was the first white man to see them.

Angola Country in southwestern Africa with vast but untapped mineral resources (apart from its oil and diamonds). Luanda is the capital and largest city. The country's independence from Portugal in 1975 was followed by civil war between the marxist government and the pro-Western opposition group UNITA, which was given military assistance by the USA and South Africa. The war ended only in 1994.

Antarctica Barren continent almost twice the size of Australia surrounding the South Pole. Even in the summer, ice and snow cover 98 per cent of Antarctica, and in places the ice is more than 4 km deep. The 1959 Antarctic Treaty has resulted in international cooperation in the interests of scientific research, and scientists are Antarctica's only inhabitants.
❖ As one of 19 signatories to the Antarctic Treaty, South Africa maintains a base here, at Sanae in New Schwabenland. Its biologists and meteorologists have also done extensive research on the sub-Antarctic Marion Island, which is a South African possession.
❖ A Norwegian team led by Roald ▷AMUNDSEN was the first to reach the South Pole in 1911, a month before a British team led by Captain Robert ▷SCOTT.

Ararat Highest mountain in Turkey, rising to nearly 5 165 m, not far from Turkey's eastern border. It is traditionally regarded as the resting place of Noah's Ark.

Arctic Area extending from the North Pole to the Arctic Circle at latitude 66°32´, the southernmost latitude at which the Sun does not set at the northern midsummer and remains below the horizon all day at midwinter. Much of the Arctic Ocean, which surrounds the North Pole, is permanently covered by pack ice, 2-3 m thick in places. The Arctic is the natural habitat of polar bears.
❖ Robert Peary, an American naval officer and explorer, led the first party to reach the North Pole, on 6 April 1909.

Argentina Second largest country in South America, after Brazil. The Andes stretch along its western border. BUENOS AIRES is the capital and largest city. Most of the Spanish-speaking people live in towns and cities, but much of the country's wealth comes from its fertile plains, including the almost treeless pampas, where massive numbers of cattle are reared. The barren highland of Patagonia is in southern Argentina.

Ascension Island Tiny British-owned volcanic island in the South Atlantic Ocean, only 88 km² in area. It is 1 130 km from the nearest land – the island of ST HELENA, which is only slightly larger – and some 1 530 km from Africa.
❖ Ascension Island was an important air-sea

ICE AND FIRE *A plume of smoke rising above Antarctica's McMurdo Sound marks Mount Erebus, a 3 794 m volcano named after a ship of Sir James Ross's Antarctic expedition of 1841.*

staging post during World War II and the 1982 conflict over the Falkland Islands.

Aswan High Dam Massive dam on the Nile in Egypt, completed in 1971 and built to keep the river level constant throughout the year to control flooding. The dam has brought drawbacks as well as advantages; previously the annual floods deposited fertilizing silt on the land, but now farmers must use expensive chemical fertilizers. Lake Nasser formed behind the 109 m high dam.

❖ The Soviet Union provided the funds for the temple of Abu Simbel, among many other Ancient Egyptian structures, to be moved to make way for the dam.

❖ The USA and Britain, concerned about Egypt's purchase of arms from communist sources, withdrew their pledges of financial aid for the dam in 1956. President Gamal Nasser then nationalized the Suez Canal, which precipitated the ▷SUEZ CRISIS.

Athens Historic capital of Greece. The sprawling, bustling, congested, modern city is built around the rocky hill of the Acropolis, dominated by the majestic ▷PARTHENON, temple of the goddess Athena, built in the 5th century BC, the golden age of ancient Greece. Air pollution by traffic and industrial fumes are seriously eroding the city's ancient ruins.

Atlanta Capital of Georgia in the USA and host of the 1996 Olympic Games. During the American Civil War the city was burned by Union troops led by General William Sherman. In the 1960s it was the centre of the Civil Rights Movement.

Atlantic Ocean World's second largest ocean, after the PACIFIC OCEAN, almost three times the size of Africa. The Atlantic stretches from the North Pole to the South Pole, and from Europe and Africa on one side to the Americas on the other. It meets the INDIAN OCEAN at Cape ▷AGULHAS, the southernmost point of Africa. It grows about 25 mm wider each year as two of the Earth's tectonic plates gradually move apart. Molten rock which wells up to fill the space has slowly formed an immense ridge that runs down the length of the ocean.

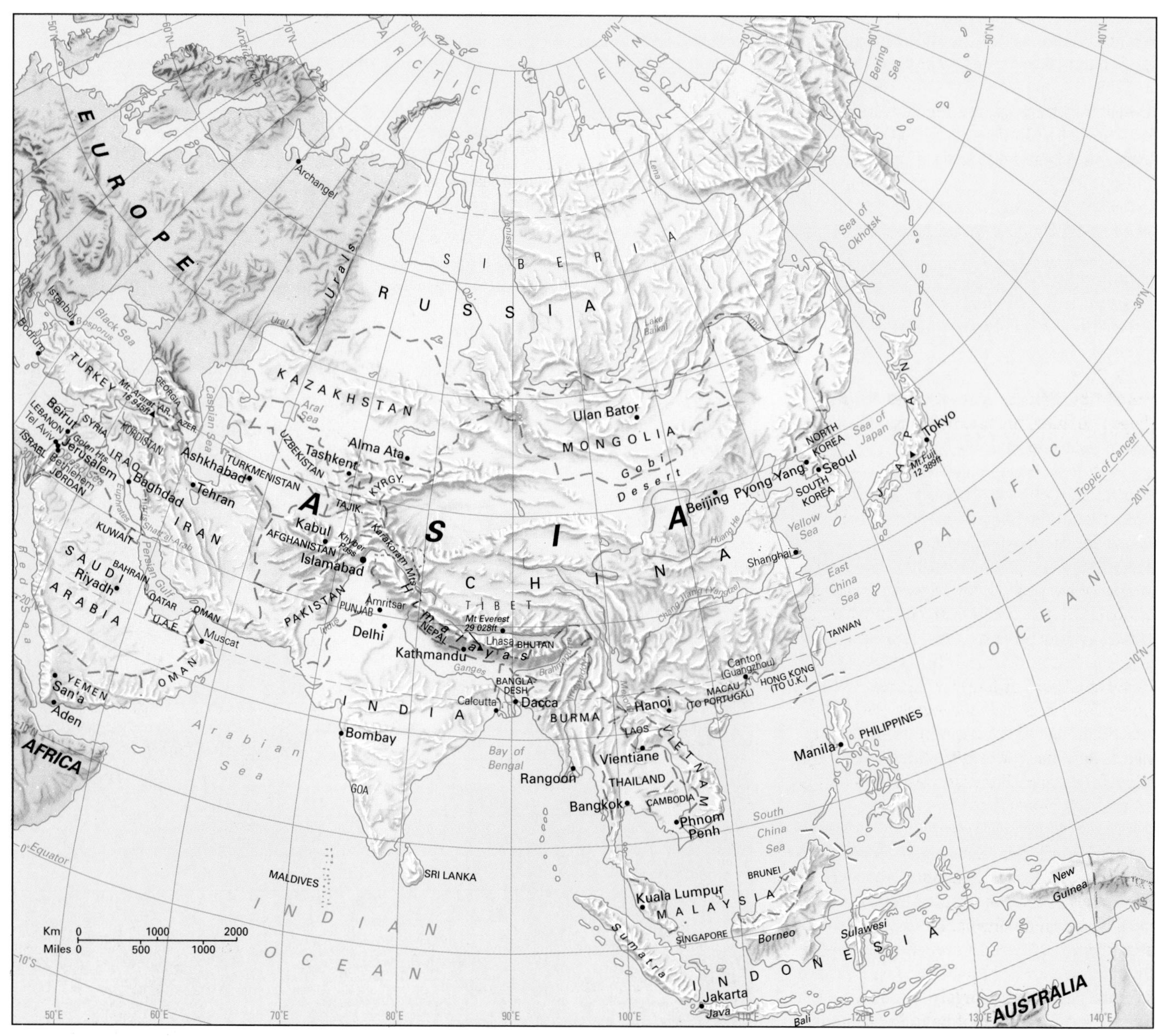

LARGEST CONTINENT *Asia makes up a third of the Earth's land area, and is home to three-fifths of world population. It has both the highest and lowest points on land – Mount Everest and the shores of the Dead Sea.*

ICELAND and ASCENSION ISLAND are peaks on the growing ridge.

Auckland New Zealand's largest city, chief port and former capital, lying on a narrow isthmus in the north of North Island. It was founded by British settlers on a Maori site in 1840. It has a population of nearly 950 000, of which more than 205 000 are Maoris and Pacific islanders.

Australia World's sixth largest country in area but with a population of only 17,8 million, most of whom are concentrated in towns and cities around the coast. Few people live in the vast arid interior of deserts, scrub and enormous sheep and cattle stations. CANBERRA is the country's capital, but its largest cities are SYDNEY and Melbourne. ▷ABORIGINES have lived in Australia for about 50 000 years, but they now make up only one in 65 of the population. The first British settlers – many of whom were convicts – landed in 1788. Since the mid-1960s immigrants have arrived from Europe and countries such as Hong Kong, China and Vietnam – and in recent years from South Africa.

Austria Small, mountainous and politically neutral country in central Europe. Austria was once the centre of a vast empire, ruled by the ▷HABSBURG dynasty from the 13th century until the end of World War I. The capital city is VIENNA.

Ayers Rock Giant rock near Alice Springs in central Australia, rising 348 m from the plains and with a circumference of 9 km. It is a sacred place to the Aborigines.

Azerbaijan Country, formerly part of the USSR, west of the Caspian Sea. Baku, the capital, is the centre of oil production, Azerbaijan's main industry. Conflict over the Armenian-dominated territory of Nagorno-Karabakh, in the west of the country has resulted in many deaths.

Baghdad Capital of Iraq, on the banks of the Tigris. The city centre has modern hotels, international banks and department stores; farther out are narrow, dusty alleys lined with colourful bazaars. Baghdad was bombed during the 1991 ▷GULF WAR.

Bahamas Caribbean state made up of some 700 islands. Most Bahamians live on New Providence, where the capital Nassau is located, and Grand Bahama. The main industry is tourism.

Bahrain Small and largely barren Persian Gulf emirate, made up of Bahrain Island and 32 smaller islands. In 1931 Bahrain became the first Arab country to strike oil.

FLOATING MARKET *Shopping, like many other daily activities, takes place on the water in the canal-webbed centre of old Bangkok.*

Baikal, Lake World's deepest lake, in southern Siberia. It holds as much water as all five American GREAT LAKES combined.

Bali Indonesian island off Java's east coast. The hot climate, long beaches, ancient Hindu monuments and traditional art, music and dancing attract many tourists.

Balkans Mountainous area of southeast Europe, encompassing Albania, Bulgaria, Greece, Romania, the former Yugoslavia and European Turkey. Turks occupied parts of the Balkans from the 15th century until the ▷BALKAN WARS of 1912-13; Austro-Hungary also ruled territory here during the 19th century. Sectarian tensions erupted after the fall of communism at the end of the 1980s.

Baltic Sea Almost landlocked sea in northern Europe linked to the NORTH SEA by narrow straits between Denmark and the Scandinavian Peninsula. Once a freshwater lake formed when glaciers melted at the end of the last Ice Age about 10 000 years ago, it still has a low salt content because so many rivers flow into it.

Bangkok Capital of Thailand whose old city is known for its *klongs* or canals and its temples. The streets are clogged with traffic, including *tuk-tuks* – three-wheeled mopeds with a rear passenger seat. There is also a seedier side to Bangkok, which has been called the 'Sex capital of the world'.

FAR APART *Distances are vast in Australia, which measures 4 350 km from east to west. At least 1 450 km of ocean separate Australia from its 'neighbour' New Zealand.*

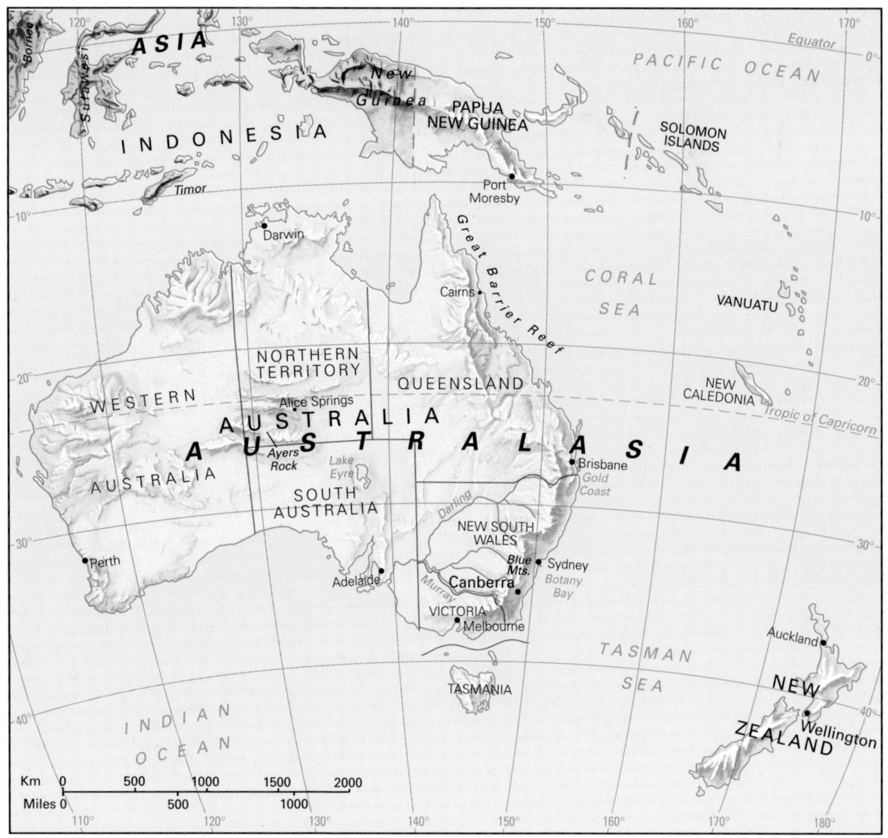

BAVARIAN FANTASY *The fairy-tale Neuschwanstein Castle was the work of Ludwig II, king of Bavaria from 1864 to 1886. Inside, paintings of scenes from Wagner's operas decorate the rooms.*

Bangladesh One of the world's poorest and most densely populated countries, straddling the Ganges-Brahmaputra delta and subject to floods and to cyclones that sweep in from the Bay of Bengal. The country's 123 million people are mostly rural Muslims. Bangladesh was formerly East Pakistan and became independent in 1971 after a war that cost more than a million lives.

Barcelona Spain's second largest city after Madrid, capital of Catalonia and a major port, known for its nightlife and for the flamboyant art nouveau buildings of the Spanish architect Antonio ▷GAUDÍ. Barcelona staged the 1992 Olympic Games.

Bath Beautiful British city renowned for its Roman baths and ▷GEORGIAN architecture. The baths still receive hot spring water through the original plumbing provided in the period between the 1st and 5th century AD when Rome ruled Britain.

Bavaria Large south German state, whose lakes, mountains, forests and picturesque towns and villages draw many tourists. Germany's highest peak, the Zugspitze (2 963 m), is in the Bavarian Alps. Industry is centred on the state capital MUNICH, and Nuremberg, where Nazi war criminals were tried after World War II.

❖ BMW stands for Bayerische Motoren Werke (Bavarian Motor Works), founded in 1929.

Bay of Bengal Arm of the Indian Ocean between India and Burma that experiences dramatic tropical cyclones. In 1970 a cyclone and tidal wave in the bay killed 300 000 people in the coastal region of Bangladesh.

Beijing (formerly Peking) Capital of China and its second largest city after Shanghai, with a population of nearly 11 million. The Mongol leader Kublai Khan made the city the capital of his empire in 1267, and it was renamed Beijing, 'Northern Capital', in 1403. Today, the wide streets throng with pedestrians, cyclists and buses; private cars are rare. In the city centre are Tiananmen Square, one of the world's biggest public squares, the site of the ▷TIANANMEN SQUARE MASSACRE and of Mao Zedong's mausoleum. It is also the site of the Forbidden City, the private domain of China's emperors from 1421 to 1911 which commoners entered on pain of death. The palace buildings, which together have 9 999 rooms, are surrounded by an 11 m wall; they are now open to visitors.

Beirut Capital of Lebanon. The city was founded by the Phoenicians in the 14th century BC and later became an important Greek and Roman trading centre. Before 1975 Beirut was the trade and financial centre of the Middle East. In the late 1970s and 1980s parts of the city were badly damaged during civil wars and the Israeli invasion.

Belfast Capital of Northern Ireland on the River Lagan, with Black Mountain rising in the background and fine public buildings that recall its prosperous past. The linen industry flourished in Belfast in the 17th century, and the Industrial Revolution once again brought prosperity, with engineering and shipbuilding among the main industries. From 1969 to the early 1990s it was the site of a violent conflict between its Catholic (Nationalist) and Protestant (Unionist) inhabitants, which has severely damaged the city.

Belgium Small European kingdom which comprises two distinct regions – the Flemish-speaking north and the French-speaking south. The dividing line runs roughly east-west through the capital, BRUSSELS. The Battle of ▷WATERLOO was fought just south of Brussels. During World War I Allied troops fought the Germans from muddy trenches across this low-lying country. Belgium was again a battlefield during World War II, when Allied troops fought the Germans in the Battle of the Bulge in the Ardennes region. Nevertheless, historic towns, including Antwerp, Bruges and Ghent, have largely survived the many wars.

❖ Belgium is known for its fine cuisine, chocolate and lace.

Belgrade Capital of Serbia and of the former Yugoslavia, with its oldest part built on hills overlooking the confluence of the Danube and Sava rivers. Its strategic position has led to various occupations throughout its history. In 1941 the city was devastated by the Germans during World War II, and it suffered more damage when it was liberated by Soviet and Yugoslav forces in 1944.

Belize Warm, humid Central American country whose Caribbean coast has long stretches of sandy beaches protected by coral reefs. The beaches and the spectacular ruins of Mayan temples attract tourists. Formerly British Honduras, Belize achieved independence in 1981.

❖ The coast is subject to hurricanes; in 1961 Belize City was so badly damaged that the capital was moved from here to Belmopan in the mountainous and jungle-covered interior.

Bering Strait Channel connecting the Bering Sea and the Arctic Ocean. In 1728 the Danish explorer Vitus Bering discovered that North America and Asia were two separate continents. He later died on Bering Island.

❖ During the Ice Ages, people crossed from Asia to colonize North America; sea levels were lower and a land bridge existed between the two continents.

Berlin Germany's capital city before 1945 and since 1990. In the interim years the infamous Berlin Wall separated East Berlin, capital of the communist East Germany, from the western half of the city, which was a West German enclave within East Germany. The wall was built by the East German government to stop the movement of its citizens to the free, more prosperous West. Anyone who tried to cross it without permission from the East German authorities risked being shot by border guards; more than 500 people were killed while trying to escape between 1961 and 1989. With the collapse of communism in Eastern Europe, the wall was reopened in November 1989 and soon demolished. At the centre of the reunited city stands the Brandenburg Gate, the ceremonial entrance to the Unter den Linden – a wide boulevard named after its lime trees and lined with stately public buildings. A 335 m television tower dominates the city's skyline of modern buildings, the result of rebuilding after massive wartime damage. A string of lakes surrounded by pine woods brings tranquillity to the outskirts.

Bermuda British colony made up of 150 western Atlantic islands, 20 of which are inhabited, lying 1 400 km east of Charleston in the US state of South Carolina. The capital, Hamilton, is on Great Bermuda, the largest island. Bermuda's economy depends almost entirely on year-round tourism, but lenient tax laws have also attracted wealthy people and financial institutions to the islands.
❖ Ships and aircraft are reputed to have disappeared mysteriously in the ▷BERMUDA TRIANGLE, an area of the Atlantic between Bermuda, Puerto Rico and Florida.

Bern Capital of Switzerland, with many well-preserved 18th-century buildings. Bears – Bern's heraldic symbol – are kept in a large pit by the River Aare.

Bethlehem Birthplace of Jesus, 8 km south of Jerusalem, and an important place of Christian pilgrimage. A grotto beneath Bethlehem's Church of the Nativity is reputed to be the site of the manger in which Jesus lay.

Bhutan Small Himalayan kingdom which admits few tourists. Bhutan was ruled by monks until 1907 and villages grew up around fortified Buddhist monasteries or *dzongs*. Most of the Bhutanese are farmers, although less than one-tenth of the land is cultivated; three-quarters of Bhutan is covered with forest.

Birmingham Britain's second largest city, situated in the West Midlands in the heart of England. In the 19th century its factories and many thriving small businesses made it 'the workshop of the world', producing everything from pen nibs to the first rotary steam engines. It is still an important commercial and industrial centre. Extending north of Birmingham is the industrial area of the West Midlands, known as the 'Black Country' because of the soot and grime produced by numerous mines and factories that sprung up here in the 19th century.

Black Forest Pine-clad mountain range in southwest Germany. Its distinctive houses, with eaves stretching almost to the ground, and spa towns such as Baden-Baden, make it popular with tourists. The River Danube rises in the Black Forest.
❖ The cherries that grow in some Black Forest valleys led to the creation of the Black Forest gâteau – a chocolate cake filled with cream and cherries and flavoured with *Kirsch*, a cherry liqueur.

Black Sea Tideless sea connected to the Mediterranean by the Bosporus, the Sea of Marmara and the Dardanelles. The Crimean peninsula extends into the Black Sea.

Blue Mountains Range of mountains, with sheer-sided valleys, that lies inland from Sydney, Australia, and rises to 1 100 m. The mountains are named from the blue haze surrounding them, which is formed by oil droplets given off by eucalyptus trees.

Bogotá Capital of Colombia, built on the plateau E Cordillera 2 800 m up in the Andes. It was founded in the 16th century (1538) by Gonzalo Jiménez de Quesada, a Spanish conquistador seeking the mythical ▷ELDORADO. Bogotá's Gold Museum houses many artefacts of the Chibcha people who lived on the plateau before the arrival of the Spaniards.

Bolivia Landlocked South American country that was part of the powerful Inca empire conquered by the Spanish in the 16th century. Half of Bolivia's population lives on a windswept, treeless plateau 3 700 m up in the Andes. Many people are farmers, growing maize and potatoes. The main cash crop, however, is coca, whose leaves are the source of cocaine – Bolivia is one of the major suppliers of the drug. La Paz, the world's highest capital city – 3 610 m above sea level – lies southeast of Lake TITICACA.
❖ Bolivia is named after Simón Bolívar, who helped to win independence from Spain for several South American countries, including Bolivia.

Bologna North Italian city and medieval university town, with two 12th-century leaning towers and streets lined with *portici* – covered sidewalks that protect pedestrians from summer heat and winter rains. It is an important publishing centre and has an international children's book fair every spring.
❖ Bologna is famous for pasta – its nickname is 'La Grassa' or 'the Fat City' – and gives its name to 'bolognese' sauce.

Bombay (Mumbai) Hot, humid and cosmopolitan city on India's west coast, the country's financial and commercial centre and also the centre of its film industry. Its main growth took place after the Suez Canal opened in 1869, when the city became known as the 'Gateway to India'. Many Victorian public buildings bear witness to the days of British rule.

Bonn Historic German city on the Rhine, founded as a Roman fort. It was heavily bombed during World War II and in 1949 was transformed from a dignified university town into the West German capital. In 1991 it was decided that berlin should once again be the capital and seat of government, although the Bundestag, or parliament, and federal ministries would remain in Bonn until the end of the decade.
❖ The composer ▷BEETHOVEN was born in Bonn in 1770.

Bordeaux French port on the Gironde estuary and the heart of the Bordeaux, or claret, wine-growing region.

Borneo Densely forested and mountainous Southeast Asian island – one of the world's largest – influenced by Dutch and British colonialism. The northern part of the island comprises the sultanate of BRUNEI and the Malaysian states of Sarawak and Sabah; the south, Kalimantan, is part of INDONESIA.

Bosnia-Herzegovina Country that was part of the former YUGOSLAVIA and declared its independence in 1991. From 1482 to 1878 the mainly mountainous land was controlled by Turks, who had an enormous influence. It was noted for its superb Islamic art and architecture, including mosques, covered bazaars, baths, fountains and bridges. At the outbreak of civil war in 1992 some 40 per cent of the people were Muslims, 32 per cent were Serbs and 18 per cent Croats. The capital, SARAJEVO, was badly damaged during the civil war.

Boston Port and capital of Massachusetts in the northeast USA. It was founded in 1630 by English Puritans who named it after Boston

in Lincolnshire, where many of them had come from. It has some elegant 18th-century buildings. In Cambridge, across the Charles River from Boston, are Harvard – America's oldest university, founded in 1636 – and the Massachusetts Institute of Technology.
❖ In 1773 angry citizens boarded a ship and threw a cargo of tea overboard, a gesture of resistance to British taxes that became known as the BostonTea Party.

Brasília Purpose-built capital of Brazil, founded in 1960. It is laid out on an open plateau in the heart of Brazil in the form of an aeroplane. Residential areas form the 'wings', and an avenue of public and government buildings the 'fuselage'.

Brazil Very large country occupying almost half of South America. The capital is BRASÍLIA, but the biggest cities are SÃO PAULO and RIO DE JANEIRO. Brazil's population, a melting pot of different races, is largely Portuguese-speaking. In 1494 the Treaty of Tordesillas, signed by the Spanish and Portuguese kings, granted to Spain all newly found land west of a fixed line of longitude. Land to the east of the line, which included Brazil, went to Portugal. One-third of the country is covered by the Amazon basin's humid ▷RAINFOREST, which is known as the *inferno verde*, or green hell. The clearance of areas of rain forest is a major cause of concern for conservationists. Elsewhere, there are arid scrublands, fertile savannahs, remote highlands and prairie grasslands where gauchos, or cowboys, herd cattle on vast ranches. The IGUAZÚ FALLS are on the border of Brazil and Argentina. Brazil produces more than a quarter of the world's coffee and pioneered the production of fuel from sugar.
❖ Brazil has produced the great Formula One motor racing drivers Emerson Fittipaldi, Nelson Piquet, and Ayrton Senna, and footballers such as Pelé, Jaïrzinho, Sócrates and Romario. Brazil's soccer stadiums together have a total capacity of 4 million people.

Bristol British city, 11 km from the mouth of the Avon River on the Bristol Channel, once a principal port of western England. In the 18th and 19th centuries it prospered through trade with America, including the traffic in slaves. Its docks house the steamship *Great Britain*, built in 1843 – the first iron ocean-going ship with a screw propeller.

Brunei Oil-producing state on the north coast of Borneo, ruled by a sultan who is said to be one of the world's richest people. In many villages on the swampy coastal plains the houses are raised on stilts. Brunei was a British protectorate between 1888 and 1984.

TWIN CITIES *Budapest straddles the Danube: the fairy-tale turrets of the Fisherman's Bastion on the Buda shore, or west bank, frame parliament's floodlit dome on the Pest side, east of the river.*

Brussels Capital of Belgium, and headquarters of the European Union and NATO. Many of the buildings in the old part of the city date back to the 15th century, including the city hall with its 96 m spire in the central square. Brussels is an industrial city, producing textiles, machinery and chemicals. Signs in the city are in both Flemish and French, reflecting Belgium's two language groups, though Brussels is predominantly French speaking.
❖ Brussels sprouts, first grown in the 13th century, are named after the city.

Bucharest Capital of Romania, with tree-lined boulevards, shady parks and handsome houses and public buildings. In the 1980s, President Nicolae ▷CEAUSESCU cleared 6 km² of the older part of the city centre to make way for a new civic centre whose main boulevard leads to a massive parliament building.

Budapest Capital of Hungary with two distinct parts – Buda on the west side of the River Danube and Pest on the east side. They are linked by several bridges, the oldest of which is the Chain Bridge (1839-49). Much of old Buda was devastated during World War II, but its medieval churches, town houses and royal palace have been beautifully restored. Pest has wide avenues, large open squares and bustling street cafés. Its river frontage is dominated by the vast domed parliament building.

Buenos Aires Lively river-port capital of Argentina on the River Plate, founded by Spanish settlers in 1536. It has been nicknamed the 'Paris of Latin America' because its traditional architecture resembles that of late 19th-century France.
❖ The name Buenos Aires is a shortened form of the city's full name: Ciudad de la Santísima Trinidad y Puerto de Nuestra Señora la Virgen María de los buenos aires (City of the Most Holy Trinity, and Port of Our Lady the Virgin Mary of good winds).

Bulgaria Country in southeast Europe, under Turkish rule from 1396 until the last links were severed in 1912, and under communist rule from 1946 to 1989. The capital is Sofia. Tobacco and wine are major products, and Bulgaria's Black Sea coastline attracts many international tourists.
❖ Bulgaria produces nearly three-quarters of the world's rose oil, used for making perfume. The petals are picked before dawn so that they keep their fragrance.

Burgundy Region of hills and valleys in east-central France whose vineyards produce some of the world's finest and most popular wines, including Côte de Beaune, Chablis and Beaujolais.

Burkina Faso Small overpopulated, impoverished, landlocked country in West Africa, formerly the French colony of Upper Volta. Much of it lies in the Sahel, the arid fringe of the Sahara, and it has been repeatedly crippled by severe drought and famine. Since its independence in 1960 military and civilian governments have followed one another in quick succession. Its capital is Ouagadougou.

Cairo Cosmopolitan capital of Egypt and largest city in Africa, on the River Nile. The bazaars and mosques of the crowded older areas contrast with the wide streets and modern office blocks of the newer parts.
❖ The Great ▷PYRAMID and the ▷SPHINX are in the Cairo suburb of El Gaza.
❖ Cairo's Al-Azhar University, founded in about AD 970, is one of the world's oldest.
❖ The first performance of Guiseppe ▷VERDI's opera *Aïda* was staged here to mark the opening of the Suez Canal in 1869.

Calcutta India's largest city, with a population of more than 11 million people, and the capital of the state of West Bengal. Lying on the Hugli River, Calcutta was founded in 1690 by the East India Company, and the prosperous trading centre was India's capital city until 1911 when the capital was transferred to New Delhi.
❖ In 1979, Mother Teresa received a Nobel prize for her work with Calcutta's poor.

California Prosperous western state, the most populous and third largest in the USA. It is subject to earthquakes, especially along the San Andreas fault on which SAN FRANCISCO lies. The SIERRA NEVADA range rises in the east of the state. California's sunny climate attracts tourists and is ideal for growing fruit and vegetables. LOS ANGELES is the biggest city; the state capital is Sacramento.
❖ Gold drew early settlers to California, giving it the nickname of 'The Golden State'.
❖ Hollywood, Disneyland and SILICON VALLEY are all in California.

Cambodia Rural, rice-growing Southeast Asian country. The 1970s were a particularly bloody decade for the country. It was drawn into the ▷VIETNAM WAR and then ruled by the brutal regime of ▷POL POT and the Khmer Rouge, who evacuated entire towns, including the capital, Phnom Penh.
❖ At ▷ANGKOR, deep in the jungle of northwest Cambodia, are the magnificent ruins of the Khmer civilization that dominated the area from the 9th to the 15th century. There are more than 600 elaborately carved Hindu temples, some as big as cathedrals, and extensive irrigation canals.

Canada World's second largest country after Russia. Canada extends over six time zones and it takes four and a half days to cross from coast to coast by train. Much of the country is uninhabited; more than half is covered by forests broken by thousands of lakes; the Rocky Mountains tower to more than 3 000 m in the west; and the far north, including the huge Baffin Island, is a frozen, treeless wilderness. Wheat and other grains are grown on the prairies in the south of the interior. Most Canadians live in the far south, especially around VANCOUVER in the west and in the eastern urban area near the Great Lakes and the St Lawrence Seaway which includes OTTAWA, Canada's capital city, TORONTO and MONTREAL. The official languages are English and French, reflecting the origins of early European settlers. The ▷SEVEN YEARS' WAR (1756-63) resulted in France surrendering its colonies to Britain, with which Canada, as a Commonwealth country, retains its ties. However, many French speakers in QUEBEC favour independence for their province. Inuit (Eskimos) and Native Americans now make up only two per cent of the population.
❖ The Mounties – Royal Canadian Mounted Police – nowadays travel in motor vehicles. Horses, and the traditional wide-brimmed hats and scarlet tunics, are used only on ceremonial occasions.
❖ In 1896 gold was discovered at Bonanza Creek, a tributary of the Klondike River in Yukon Territory, in the far northwest of Canada. Thousands of prospectors joined the ▷GOLD RUSH.

Canary Islands Group of seven volcanic islands and several islets off Africa's northwest coast which all belong to Spain. They include Tenerife, Gran Canaria, Fuerteventura and Lanzarote. The warm climate all year round attracts many tourists.
❖ Tenerife is dominated by the 3 718 m volcano Pico de Teide, the highest point in Spanish territory.
❖ The Canary Islands are named after the fierce dogs that lived there – the name comes from *canis*, the Latin word for dog.

TEEMING STREETS *Traders pack the narrow streets of Calcutta, a densely populated and cosmopolitan centre of commerce.*

Canberra Australia's capital city, which is laid out on a formal plan with many parks. Canberra was founded primarily as the seat of federal government, rather than a business or commercial centre. With a population of about 300 000, it is much smaller than SYDNEY or Melbourne.

Canton (Guangzhou) Vibrant, cosmopolitan city in south China. Between 1759 and 1842 Canton was the only Chinese port open to Europeans, except for the Portuguese, who traded from Macau. Europeans exported silk, porcelain, tea and other goods, but the Chinese showed little interest in imports. Attempts by the British to expand trade in opium and China's attempts to stop them led to the ▷OPIUM WARS of the mid-19th century.

Cardiff Seaport at the mouth of the River Taff, the capital of WALES since 1955. It was a modest market town until the coal and iron industry developed in the 19th century; by 1900 it produced more coal than any other city in the world. The coal industry has declined since, but the city's docks still handle general cargo.

Caspian Sea World's largest inland body of water, which is fed by Europe's longest river, the Volga. The Caspian Sea is bordered by Russia in the northwest and Iran in the south and is bigger than Germany. Its famed sturgeon is the source of ▷CAVIAR.

Central African Republic Small, landlocked, impoverished country in the heart of Africa. Formerly known as Ubangi-Shari, a territory of French Equatorial Africa, it became independent in 1960. In 1977 the country's ruler Jean-Bedel Bokassa – who had gained a reputation for brutality and amassed a huge fortune from trade in ivory and diamonds while reducing the country to bankruptcy – crowned himself emperor in a wildly extravagant ceremony. He was overthrown in 1979.

Central Park Large park in the centre of New York in the USA. It contains a zoo and also Cleopatra's Needle, one of a pair of Egyptian obelisks that are 3 500 years old (the other is on London's Victoria Embankment). The park

FANTASY LAND *The improbably sculpted domes and towers of southwest China's Guilin Hills rise above patterned paddy fields. Caves beneath the hills are rich in stalagmites and stalactites.*

has a reputation for being unsafe after dark because of frequent muggings.

Challenger Deep Deepest known spot in the oceans, in the Marianas Trench east of the Philippines. The greatest recorded depth is 11 033 m below sea level.
❖ In 1960 a Swiss-American team made a record descent of 10 915 m into the Marianas Trench in a bathyscaph.

Chang Jiang (Yangtze) World's fourth longest river, after the Nile, Amazon, and Mississippi, and the longest in China. It flows for 5 980 km down narrow valleys, across farmland and through impressive gorges before it enters the East China Sea near Shanghai.

Chicago Third largest city in the USA after New York and Los Angeles. Sited at the southern end of Lake Michigan, it is known for its innovative architecture, including that of Frank Lloyd ▷WRIGHT in the city's suburbs, and has the world's tallest office building, the ▷SEARS TOWER.

Chile Long, narrow South American country sandwiched between the Andes and the Pacific Ocean. The capital is Santiago. In between the barren Atacama Desert in the north and the cold and windswept forests and glaciers of the south is the fertile area that produces Chile's wine. In 1973 right-wing military leaders under General Augusto Pinochet overthrew the marxist government of President Salvador ▷ALLENDE.
❖ EASTER ISLAND, 3 780 km away in the Pacific Ocean, is part of Chile.

China World's third largest country in area, but by far the most populous with more than 1 160 million inhabitants – one in five of the world's population. The majority are Han, or Chinese, but there are 55 other ethnic groups. Most of the fertile land and the largest cities, including SHANGHAI and the capital BEIJING, are in densely populated eastern China. Western China has bleak plateaus, high mountains, including the Himalayas, and barren deserts. China has one of the world's oldest civilizations – one dynasty of rulers succeeded another from about 1766 BC until AD 1911. After a power struggle between communists and nationalists led by ▷CHIANG KAI-SHEK, China became a communist state in 1949 under the leadership of ▷MAO ZEDONG, who introduced the ▷CULTURAL REVOLUTION in 1966. Since the early 1980s China has encouraged free enterprise but has avoided any far-reaching political reform. Agriculture employs about 60 per cent of China's workers.
❖ Early Chinese inventions include the compass, paper, porcelain, gunpowder, silk, and printing from movable type.

Cologne City on the Rhine in Germany, founded by the Romans; the city takes its French and English name from *colonia*, the Latin word for colony. Cologne cathedral, one of Europe's most splendid Gothic buildings, survived World War II bombing. The city's name in German is Köln.

Colombia South American country with the fertile valleys and snow-covered peaks of the Andes mountain range in the west, and hot grassy plains and tropical jungles in the east.

CITY SLICKERS *Ice skating is just one of many facilities in New York's Central Park, which also has an open-air theatre, sports facilities, woods and boating lakes within its varied landscape.*

The capital is BOGOTÁ. Coffee, grown mostly on small farms, is the leading export.
❖ Colombia's production of cocaine and other illegal drugs, based around Medellin, grew immensely in the 1980s.

Comoros Volcanic islands in the Indian Ocean between ▷MOZAMBIQUE and the northern tip of MADAGASCAR. The group comprises four islands, three of which – Njazidja, Mwali and Nzwani – became independent from France in 1975 and formed the Islamic Republic of the Comoros, with Moroni on Njazidja as its capital. The fourth, Mayotte, remains a French dependency. Tourism is a growing industry.

Congo Country in west-central Africa straddling the equator and bordering the Congo River (called the Zaïre River in neighbouring Zaïre). Its capital is Brazzaville. After gaining independence from France in 1960, it was the first country in Africa to declare itself a communist state. After a series of military coups, counter-coups and political assassinations, the communist era ended with multiparty parliamentary elections in June 1992. Periodic clashes between opposition groups and government security forces have continued. It has vast offshore oil reserves and oil is the mainstay of its economy. Many of its small urban middle class are French-speaking and have been educated abroad.

Copenhagen Capital of Denmark, with many buildings dating from the 16th and 17th centuries. The Tivoli Gardens amusement park is in the city centre; a statue of the Little Mermaid of Hans Christian Andersen's story is on the waterfront. Royal Copenhagen porcelain has been made in the city since 1775.

Corfu Fertile Greek island, popular with tourists. Corfu is the most northerly of the Ionian Islands off Greece's Adriatic coast; the northern part of the island is less than 8 km from the coast of Albania. Corfu Town (Kerkira) has 16th-century Venetian fortifications and a cricket ground – the island was ruled by Britain between 1815 and 1864.

Corsica Mountainous Mediterranean island, north of Sardinia, part of France. Much of the interior is covered with aromatic shrubs and cork oaks, with forests higher up. The capital is Ajaccio.
❖ Corsica was the birthplace, in 1769, of the French emperor Napoleon I.

Costa Rica Mountainous and heavily forested country located between Nicaragua and Panama in Central America. Coffee and bananas are the main exports. Costa Rica abolished its army in 1948 in a bid to stop military coups and its governments have been unusually stable for the region.

ISLAND FORTRESS *Huddled behind its massive walls at the southern tip of Corsica, the town of Bonifacio perches on a white limestone cliff, offering spectacular views over the sea to Sardinia.*

Côte d'Azur Fashionable Mediterranean coastal strip which includes Monte Carlo (in Monaco) and the French resorts of Nice and Cannes, the site of an international film festival each northern spring.

Côte d'Ivoire Formerly known also as Ivory Coast, this West African country is a rare phenomenon in Africa – one that since gaining its independence has experienced a long period of prosperity under a stable government. Ruled by France until 1960, it still has about 50 000 French people living here – French is the official language and the French influence remains strong. For 33 years its government was dominated by president Félix Houphouët-Boigny (1905-93), who pursued a policy of liberal capitalism and encouraged Western investment. Its capital was moved in 1984 from Abidjan to Yamoussoukro, which has become a prestigious city with palatial buildings and Africa's largest cathedral, rivalling St Peter's Basilica in Rome in size.

Crete Largest of the Greek islands, lying south of the mainland. The main town is Heraklion. The Minoan civilization with its palace at ▷KNOSSOS flourished here between 3000 and 1100 BC.

Crimea Peninsula of UKRAINE extending into the Black Sea. It was the scene of the Crimean War between Russia and the forces of England, France and Turkey in 1854-6, remembered particularly for the Charge of the Light Brigade and the dedication of the English nurse Florence Nightingale.

Croatia South European country that was one of the more prosperous parts of the former YUGOSLAVIA. Many tourists used to visit the sunny beaches along its Dalmatian coast. But both tourism and industry suffered severely as a result of civil war in the early 1990s. The country was under Hungarian, and later Habsburg, control from 1102 until 1918. Croatia declared its independence from Yugoslavia in 1991. The capital is Zagreb.

Cuba West Indian country and the largest island in the Caribbean. The capital is Havana. A communist government led by Fidel ▷CASTRO came to power in 1959. In 1961, Cuban exiles, supported by the USA, landed at the island's ▷BAY OF PIGS in an unsuccessful attempt to overthrow Castro's regime, and the following year the world was brought to the brink of war by the ▷CUBAN MISSILE CRISIS. The economy was weakened in the early 1990s by the collapse of communism in the former USSR and the subsequent loss of aid.
❖ Havana cigars, rolled by hand, are made from tobacco grown in northwest Cuba.

Cyprus Dry, sunny Mediterranean island in the east, whose beaches and mountains attract large numbers of tourists. The capital is Nicosia. Greeks make up 80 per cent of the population and Turks 19 per cent. Archbishop Makarios was the island's first president after its independence from Britain in 1960. Turkish forces invaded northern Cyprus in

1974 and in 1983 the Turks declared the occupied area to be the 'Turkish Republic of Northern Cyprus', which is recognized only by Turkey.

❖ The Greek name of the island, *Kypros*, means copper, which has been extensively mined here since prehistoric times.

Czech Republic Central European country founded on 1 January 1993 when the former republic of Czechoslovakia split into the Czech Republic and SLOVAKIA. The capital is PRAGUE. The republic is known for crystal made in Bohemia, the western part of the country, and for its beer, especially Pilsener lager which originated in the western city of Plzen in 1842. Among its famous spa towns are Karlovy Vary (Carlsbad) and Mariánské Lázne (Marienbad).

❖ Wenceslas I – the 'Good King' of the popular Christmas carol – ruled Bohemia in the early 10th century.

Dallas One of the largest cities in the USA, on the Texas plains. It is a centre of the American oil and electronics industries, and also a major cotton market. It inspired the television soap opera *Dallas*.

❖ President John F Kennedy was assassinated in Dallas in 1963.

Damascus Capital of Syria and reputed to be the world's oldest continuously inhabited city, important since the third millennium BC. The old walled city has a mosque built in AD 708; in the modern part of Damascus there are high-rise hotels and office blocks.

❖ Damask cloth, a fabric with a complex patterned weave, has been made in Damascus since the Middle Ages.

Danube Europe's second longest river after the Volga and a major transport route, flowing from the slopes of the BLACK FOREST in southern Germany to its delta in the Black Sea. Cities on its banks include Vienna, Budapest and Belgrade.

Dead Sea One of the world's saltiest lakes, lying between Israel and Jordan. Its shores, 396 m below sea level, are the lowest point on the world's land surface. The Dead Sea is rich in minerals, which are said to provide those who bathe in it with therapeutic effects, especially for arthritis and respiratory problems. The sea's black mud is also claimed to be beneficial for the skin.

Death Valley Major depression in California that includes North America's hottest, driest and lowest place, 86 m below sea level. It is bordered by mountains 3 000 m high.Temperatures can reach more than 52°C.

Delhi Capital of India, with two distinct parts. Old Delhi is a crowded maze of narrow streets centred on the 17th-century Red Fort built by the Mogul emperor Shah Jahan, who also built the ▷TAJ MAHAL. New Delhi, planned by the British architect Sir Edwin ▷LUTYENS, was laid out from 1912-31 as a new capital city, with broad tree-lined avenues, gardens and government buildings – some of which were designed by Sir Herbert ▷BAKER, architect of South Africa's Union Buildings.

PILLARS OF SALT *Dotting the mineral-rich waters of the Dead Sea are tiny islands – the tips of columns of salt that form as water evaporates in summer temperatures as high as 50°C (122°F).*

Denmark Small, densely populated kingdom in northern Europe, consisting of the Jutland Peninsula and more than 400 islands. The capital, COPENHAGEN, stands on Zealand, the largest island. Denmark is prosperous, with a well-organized farming industry known for its butter and bacon.

Djibouti Small desert country on the Gulf of Aden with a strategically placed free port and capital of the same name. It became an independent republic in 1977 after 96 years as a French colony. Economically it depends on its role in providing transit for trade with landlocked Ethiopia.

❖ Djibouti has one of the world's hottest climates, with temperatures averaging 30°C and often exceeding 40°C.

Dresden Historic city in eastern Germany. It was once one of the most beautiful cities in Europe, with many baroque buildings, but Allied bombing raids in February 1945 destroyed more than half the city. Most of the best-known buildings have been restored.

❖ Dresden china, a delicate porcelain, is made in nearby Meissen, where the industry moved in 1710.

Dublin Capital of the Republic of Ireland, at the mouth of the River Liffey. Its many fine Georgian buildings include Leinster House, where the Dail (Parliament) sits. Trinity College library houses the Book of Kells, an illuminated Celtic manuscript of around AD 800. Dublin's Phoenix Park is one of the biggest urban parks in Europe, and includes a zoo, a racecourse and the president's residence. Guinness stout has been brewed in Dublin since 1759.

East Timor Eastern part of an Indonesian island that gained independence from Portugal in 1975 but was taken over by the Indonesian government. Since then more than 200 000 Timorese have been killed in guerrilla warfare between Indonesian forces and an independence movement.

Easter Island Tiny, remote volcanic island of 120 km^2 situated in the Pacific 3 780 km west of the coast of Chile, to which it belongs. The island is known for the 1 000 or so giant stone statues carved between AD 1000 and 1500, the largest of which are 21 m high.

Ecuador South American country straddling the Equator, from which it takes its name. The capital is Quito. The Andes mountains, which run down the centre of the country, contain several snow-capped volcanoes. To the west is a large plain and to the east are dense tropical forests and savannah, where oil is exploited.
❖ The Galapagos Islands lie 1 100 km west of Ecuador, to which they belong. Their distinctive wildlife helped to inspire ▷DARWIN's theory of evolution.

Edinburgh Capital of SCOTLAND on the Firth of Forth, famous for its majestic castle, parts of which date from 1100, and its annual international festival of music and drama which has earned it the nickname of 'Athens of the North'. The festival, first held in 1947, takes place in late August and early September. Some medieval buildings survive in the Old Town, while the Georgian New Town is noted for its fine neoclassical architecture.

Egypt Arab country in North Africa whose capital is CAIRO. Desert makes up 96 per cent of the land. Most Egyptians live in the densely populated valley and delta of the NILE or along the ▷SUEZ CANAL, where the green irrigated land contrasts with the desert beyond. Rural dwellers of the valley and delta are known as *fellahin*. The ▷PYRAMIDS, the Sphinx and the temples at Luxor are among the many remains of the civilization of ancient Egypt. The port of ALEXANDRIA was a major city in ancient times. ▷CLEOPATRA ruled Egypt in the 1st century BC.

El Salvador Small but densely populated Central American country, with rugged highlands and volcanoes. The capital is San Salvador. From 1979 to 1992 the country was torn by civil war between left-wing guerrillas (FMLN) and the US-backed, right-wing government. The conflict ended after United Nations intervention. Two out of every five people work on the land and coffee is the most valuable crop.

England Southern part of Britain, the largest constituent and most densely populated area of the UNITED KINGDOM, whose people gave their name to the language that has become the international medium of communication. LONDON is its capital. The climate is mild relative to its northerly latitude, due to the warming effect of the Gulf Stream over which the prevailing southwesterly winds blow. England was cut off from the European continent by the Strait of Dover about 7 500 years ago, when the retreat of the last Ice Age allowed the NORTH SEA to submerge the lowlands, forests and marshes that linked them. Throughout its history it has been subject to waves of immigration. Neolithic settlers arrived about 6 000 years ago and built the great megalithic circles, such as that at ▷STONEHENGE, that still stand. The Celts (pronounced Kelts) came between 2200 BC and the first century AD and their languages survive in Welsh, Gaelic and the Cornish dialect of southwestern England. The Romans, who occupied Britain from AD 43 to 408, established their order, built a road network and defensive walls and laid out the first Roman towns. Then came the ▷ANGLO-SAXONS, who for the next five centuries kept the native Celtic ▷BRITONS confined to the north and west. Meanwhile, the Anglo-Saxons established the English language, the Christian church and central kingship. In the 9th and 10th centuries ▷VIKINGS conquered the eastern part of the country. In 1066 came the last great invasion of England, the ▷NORMAN CONQUEST. In later centuries, culminating in the formation of the United Kingdom, England led the development of parliamentary institutions and the ▷RULE OF LAW.

MOORLAND GIANT *Each of the 170 grey granite outcrops on Dartmoor, such as Combestone Tor near Dartmeet, has a distinctive shape, sculpted by the weather over thousands of years.*

English Channel Waterway, part of the Atlantic Ocean, between England and France, known in France as La Manche, ranging in width from 34 km to 180 km. It is the world's busiest sea passage with about 350 ships passing through it every day. The 50 km ▷CHANNEL TUNNEL linking the two countries by road and rail was opened in 1994.
❖ The Channel Islands, consisting of Jersey, Guernsey, Alderney, Sark and several smaller islands, lie towards the western end of the English Channel close to the French coast. They are British dependencies but have their own legislative and legal systems.

Eritrea Small African country on the Red Sea, once an Italian colony that was one of the most industrialized countries of Africa, now impoverished by nearly 30 years of civil war and drought. After World War II it was joined in a federation with Ethiopia, whose attempt to revoke its autonomy in 1962 began a vicious war which ended only with the fall of Ethiopia's military dictator, Mengistu Haile Mariam, in 1991. In 1993 a transitional government was elected to rule for four years.

Ethiopia Mountainous northeast African country, formerly known as Abyssinia. It is one of the largest countries in Africa, with an area of more than 1 million km² and a population of some 60 million. Ethiopia has existed for 2 000 years. It became a Christian country in 330 but was cut off from the main centres of Christianity for 800 years, and was presumably the source of a legend in the Middle Ages of a king called Prester John who

ACROSS EUROPE *Rich in culture and cities, Europe stretches from the Atlantic to the Ural Mountains. Russia spans Europe and Asia.*

ruled over a Christian empire in the heart of Africa. During the 19th century it was one of the few parts of Africa not colonised by Europe, although the Italians controlled it from 1936 to 1941. Emperor ▷HAILE SELASSIE, a member of a line of monarchs said to have descended from King Solomon (972-932 BC), was overthrown in 1974. The monarchy was replaced by a marxist military republic which was itself overthrown in 1991. In the 1970s and 1980s Ethiopia suffered from civil war, drought and severe famine. Its capital Addis Ababa is also the headquarters of the ▷OAU (Organisation of African Unity).

Euphrates River rising in Turkey and flowing through Syria and Iraq into the Persian Gulf. The Mesopotamian cities of Babylon and Ur were on the Euphrates.

Finland North European country where forests and 55 000 lakes form the greatest part of the surface area. Forestry and the production of paper and other wood products are central to the economy. About 1 700 Lapps live in Lappland in the far north. In 1939-40 Finnish troops led by Marshal Carl Mannerheim put up a heroic resistance to Russian forces. The capital is Helsinki.

❖ The sauna originated in Finland.

Florence Beautiful city in north central Italy whose churches, Renaissance palaces and works of art have attracted visitors for centuries. ▷LEONARDO DA VINCI, ▷MICHELANGELO and ▷RAPHAEL were all Florentine artists. The wealthy Medici family were rulers of the city and patrons of the arts from the 15th to the 18th century.

Florida 'Sunshine State' in the southeast USA. The swamps and mangrove forests of the Everglades in southern Florida are rich in wildlife. The Florida Keys, a string of coral islands, stretch southwest from MIAMI to Key West. The city of Orlando, in central Florida, is a base for visiting the John F Kennedy Space Centre and Walt Disney World.

❖ The sunshine has attracted many emigrants from South Africa who have made their home in Florida.

France Western Europe's largest country, noted for its culture, food and wine. PARIS, the romantic capital, the châteaux of the Loire valley, the scenery of the ALPS and Pyrenees, and the sunshine of the CÔTE D'AZUR all attract many tourists. Gaul, roughly equivalent to modern France and Belgium, was conquered by the Romans by 50 BC. In the late 5th and early 6th centuries the land was invaded by the Franks, who gave France its name and whose king, ▷CHARLEMAGNE, built up the first great French empire. In 1066 the Duke of Normandy, in northern France, conquered England and became King William I. During the next four centuries England and France fought many battles, most notably during the ▷HUNDRED YEARS' WAR (1337-1453). Over the next 200 years France became increasingly powerful, reaching its height during the reign of ▷LOUIS XIV. The absolute rule of the French kings came to an end with the ▷FRENCH REVOLUTION (1789-99), after which ▷NAPOLEON I ruled France, and much of western Europe, until his defeat at ▷WATERLOO in 1815. Later in the 19th century France acquired large tracts of northwest Africa and colonies in Southeast Asia. After World War II, during which the greater part of France was occupied by the Germans, a *rapprochement* with Germany led to the creation of the European Economic Community, now the ▷EUROPEAN UNION (EU), in which France plays a leading role. The crisis over the independence of Algeria (1958-62) led to Charles ▷DE GAULLE's re-emergence as his country's leader. In the 1960s France became a leading industrial nation. The country is divided into 22 regions and 96 *départements*, two of which make up CORSICA.

❖ As well as the world's finest wines, such as those from BURGUNDY and Champagne, France produces nearly 400 cheeses.

Ganges River that rises in the Himalayas and flows through northern India to end in the world's biggest delta. To Hindus the Ganges is the holiest river; the dead are cremated on its banks and their ashes scattered in the water.

Gaza Strip Land on the eastern Mediterranean coast, formerly part of Palestine and administered by Egypt until it was occupied by Israel in 1967. In May 1994 Israel handed over the Gaza Strip to a ▷PLO (Palestine Liberation Organization) authority with limited powers while negotiations on its future status continued.

Geneva Swiss city on the shores of Lake Geneva (Lac Léman), where a 145 m fountain rises into the air. The Red Cross has its headquarters in Geneva, as do several United Nations agencies, including the World Health Organization, the International Labour Organization and the World Trade Organization (the successor to ▷GATT).

Germany West European country that is one of the world's leading industrial economies and the dominant economic force in the ▷EUROPEAN UNION (EU). The capital is BERLIN, although the Bundestag (parliament) and the federal ministries are in BONN. Frankfurt is the financial centre, MUNICH is the largest city of south Germany, and Hamburg is the biggest port. Before 1871 Germany consisted of many small states, the strongest of which were ▷PRUSSIA and BAVARIA. When the German states united and Prussia's prime minister, Otto von ▷BISMARCK, became chancellor, the Prussian king became Germany's Kaiser Wilhelm I. His grandson, Kaiser Wilhelm II, took Germany into World War I. Germany experienced hyperinflation in the 1920s, which led to the rise of ▷NAZISM under Adolf ▷HITLER, who became chancellor and assumed dictatorial powers in 1933. Germany's invasion of Poland in 1939 led to World War II. In 1949 the country was divided into the communist German Democratic Republic (East Germany), and the Federal Republic of Germany (West Germany) whose chancellor, Konrad ▷ADENAUER, oversaw his country's spectacular economic recovery. The two Germanys were reunited on 3 October 1990. The west's chancellor, Helmut ▷KOHL, became leader of the united country, and the east's leader, Erich Honecker, went to Chile. He died in exile on 29 May 1994.

OLD BRIDGE *Florence's shop-lined Ponte Vecchio has spanned the River Arno since 1345. The cathedral dome (inset) dates from 1461.*

Ghana West African country with tropical forests in the south and arid plains in the north. The capital is Accra. Ghana's name is all that remains of the rich ancient empire of Ghana, which was founded in the 4th century and reached the peak of its power in the 10th century. It lay further to the north than the present-day state. Ghana was the first black African country to achieve independence from European colonial rule; before 1957 it was the British colony of the Gold Coast. Its first prime minister, Kwame ▷NKRUMAH, encouraged all Africans to throw off colonial rule. In 1966 the despotic Nkrumah was deposed by a military coup. A series of coups followed which led to long periods of military dictatorship interspersed by short periods of civilian rule. Ghana was a relatively prosperous country at the time of independence, but its fortunes steadily declined, as political instability, corruption, mismanagement and ethnic strife ruined its economy. However, its prospects have improved since 1992 when a new democratic constitution was approved and multiparty elections held for the first time in 13 years.

Gibraltar Peninsula of southern Spain that is only 5 km long, but rises to 425 m at the Rock of Gibraltar. It has been a British colony since 1713, but Spain still lays claim to it.

❖ Barbary apes live on the rock. Folklore has it that Britain will retain control as long as the apes survive.

Glasgow Scotland's largest city, on the River Clyde. The city prospered after Scotland's union with England in 1707, especially through trade in New World tobacco and sugar. It continued to expand during the Industrial Revolution and became famous for its Clydebank shipyards. But by the end of the 19th century its fortunes had declined and areas such as the Gorbals became notorious slums.
❖ The stately ocean liners known as the Cunard 'Queens' were built at Clydebank.

Golan Heights Strategically important bare hills in southwest Syria, rising to 2 225 m, occupied by Israelis in 1967 and annexed by Israel in 1981. Israel acknowledged Syrian sovereignty of the Golan Heights in 1994, but they continued to be the subject of dispute and international negotiation.

Gough Island Small island (90 km^2) belonging to Britain in the South Atlantic, 354 km south of TRISTAN DA CUNHA. It is a base for scientific research and South Africa has a meteorological station on it.

Grand Canyon Spectacular gorge in Arizona, in the southwest USA, which is 450 km long.

Great Barrier Reef World's longest coral reef system, 2 000 km long, off the northeast coast of Australia. Colourful fish live in large numbers among the 350 species of coral. Tourism is carefully controlled, for the delicately balanced ecosystem is easily harmed by human activity. It is a World Heritage Area.

Great Lakes Freshwater North American lakes that cover an area equal to about one-fifth of South Africa. Lakes Superior, Huron, Erie and Ontario straddle the border between Canada and the USA. Lake Michigan is situated within the USA. Niagara Falls lies between lakes Erie and Ontario.

Greece South European country that was the cultural centre of the Mediterranean world some 2 500 years ago. The capital and by far the largest city is ATHENS. Greece consists of a mountainous mainland and about 1 400 islands, including the Ionian Islands to the west of the mainland, the Sporades, Cyclades and Dodecanese to the east, and Crete to the south. After World War II communist guerrillas and nationalist troops fought a civil war here. A military coup in 1967 was followed by another soon afterwards and the country was ruled by an oppressive military junta until 1974, when democratic government was restored. A quarter of the population of Greece work on the land, growing olives, grain and vines on small farms.

NATURE'S HANDIWORK *The Colorado River cut through many layers of rock to produce the Grand Canyon, which is 1,6 km deep in places.*

❖ Greece has a long seafaring tradition and today it has the world's third largest merchant marine fleet, after Liberia and Panama. Some of its shipowners – among them Aristotle ▷ONASSIS – have become famous for their great wealth.

Greenland The world's largest island – called Kalallit Nunaat (Land of the People) by its inhabitants – the greater part of which lies within the Arctic Circle. Its area is more than 2 million km^2 (almost twice the size of South Africa), all but one-tenth of which is permanently covered with an ice cap with an average depth of 1 500 m, leaving a coastal belt 20 km in width. Although nominally a part of Denmark, the country has had home rule since 1979. The people are a mixture of Inuit (Eskimo) and Danish extraction. The capital is Godthåb (or Nuuk).

Greenwich London borough on the south bank of the River Thames, which has given its name to Greenwich Mean Time (GMT) and the Greenwich meridian, used as the basis for determining time throughout most of the world. This results from it being the site of Britain's first Royal Observatory, founded in 1675, the beginning of an era in which new techniques of navigation and cartography were developed. Scientists decided that the prime meridian (0°), from which longitude east and west is measured, would pass through the observatory. GMT is local solar time at the Greenwich meridian.

Hague, The The seat of government of the Netherlands since 1590. The name derives from the former hunting lodge of the Counts of Holland in a wooded area known as The Haghe ('hedge'). At the heart of the city is a castle built in 1248, around which grew a palace, known as the Binnenhof. Beside it an artificial lake, the Hofvijer, was built in 1350. This area is surrounded by government buildings and embassies. Beyond is a spacious city of canals, parks and woods, also linked by canal with Amsterdam.
❖ The Hague is the site of the International Court of Justice, established in 1922.

Haiti Poor agricultural country making up the western third of the West Indian island of Hispaniola; the rest of the island is the Dominican Republic. Port-au-Prince is the capital. From 1957 to 1986 Haiti was oppressively ruled by members of the Duvalier family – first by Dr François ('Papa Doc') Duvalier and his special police, the *Tontons Macoutes*, and then by his son Jean-Claude ('Baby Doc'), who was deposed in 1986. A military coup in 1991 ousted the democratically elected president Jean-Bertrand Aristide. In 1994 US forces intervened to restore democracy.

❖ ▷VOODOO is still practised in Haiti.

Hawaii Group of volcanic north Pacific islands that became the 50th US state in 1959. Hawaii is also the name of the largest island. The capital, Honolulu, and ▷PEARL HARBOR are both on the island of Oahu.

Hebrides Group of 500 islands, also known as the Western Isles, off the west and northwest coast of Scotland, 20 of which are inhabited. Iona was an ancient druidical shrine and became a cradle of Christianity when St Columba founded a monastery here in AD 563. It is the burial place of 60 kings of Scotland, Ireland and Norway.

❖ Fingal's Cave on the tiny island of Staffa is regarded as one of the scenic wonders of Britain. It is 20 m high and 69 m deep and its six-sided, black basalt formations create a spectacular forest of columns, some 11 m tall. It inspired ▷MENDELSSOHN to compose the overture *The Hebrides*.

Himalayas World's highest mountain range, curving across southern Asia for 2 400 km and containing the world's highest peak, MOUNT EVEREST (8 846 m). Of the Earth's 109 peaks rising to more than 7 300 m, 96 are in the Himalayas.

Hong Kong Densely populated, prosperous British territory on China's south coast due to be returned to China in 1997. Hong Kong Island and part of the Kowloon Peninsula were acquired by Britain between 1841 and 1860. In 1898 the New Territories comprising north Kowloon and many islands were leased from China for 99 years. Hong Kong Island, its waterfront lined with high-rise banks and offices, is connected by road and rail tunnels to Kowloon and the New Territories.

Huang He China's second longest river, after the CHANG JIANG (Yangtze). The name means yellow river and refers to the enormous amount of silt that colours the water.

Hungary Landlocked country in central Europe, with vast, intensively farmed plains. The capital is BUDAPEST and the people are Magyars, whose language is related to Finnish. Austro-Habsburgs controlled Hungary from 1699 until 1867, when the Austro-Hungarian dual monarchy was established. From the late 1940s until 1989 Hungary was a communist country. In 1956 the former USSR crushed the ▷HUNGARIAN UPRISING.

CROWDED COLONY *Hong Kong, with its innumerable skyscrapers, is one of the most densely populated places in the world. More than half the population lives on or above the tenth floor.*

Iceland European island country in the North Atlantic Ocean. The country's economy is based on fishing. One-ninth of the island is permanently covered by snow and ice, but there are also volcanoes and hot springs. The capital is Reykjavík.

Iguazú (Iguaçu) Falls Spectacular waterfall on the border of Brazil and Argentina, made up of some 275 cascades which plunge over a crescent of cliffs.

Ilha do Sal Small island in the Cape Verde group, 620 km off West Africa, a fuelling stop for South African Airways aircraft in the years of sanctions when South Africa was denied landing rights in most of Africa. It is still sometimes used by planes flying to and from New York. It has beautiful beaches, undiscovered by tourists.

India Second most populous country in the world after China, with 903 million inhabitants – one in six of the world's people. Nearly 83 per cent of the population are Hindus. ▷HINDUISM probably developed from beliefs brought by invaders from the northwest after about 2000 BC. Islam, followed by 11 per cent of Indians, was introduced in the 12th century and in the 16th century most of India came under the control of the Muslim Mogul empire. The Moguls brought new art and architecture, which reached its peak with the ▷TAJ MAHAL. There are also 18 million Christians and 17 million Sikhs, as well as Buddhists, Jains and others. Hindi is the official and most widely spoken language and English is also in general use in government and commerce, but some 17 other major languages, including Urdu and more than 1 000 minor languages and dialects, are spoken. British influence, which began with the British East India Company, a trading company established in 1600, increased as the power of the Mogul empire declined. In 1857, after the ▷INDIAN MUTINY, Britain assumed direct responsibility for India, which became the 'jewel' of its empire. The drive for independence from Britain, achieved in 1947, was led by Mahatma ▷GANDHI. The capital is DELHI, but the largest cities are BOMBAY (Mumbai) and CALCUTTA. Three-quarters of the people live in rural villages. The Himalayas are in the far north of India, and the GANGES flows down from the mountains and across a vast plain. India has a summer monsoon season when most of the rain falls.

Indian Ocean World's third largest ocean, after the Pacific and Atlantic; it lies between Asia, Antarctica, Africa and Australia. Indian Ocean islands include the Seychelles, the Maldives and Mauritius.

Indonesia Southeast Asian country, consisting of more than 13 600 islands, most of them forested and mountainous. The capital, Jakarta, is on Java, where three-fifths of Indonesians live. The country also includes Sumatra, Sulawesi and parts of BORNEO and New Guinea. Indonesia's 300 ethnic groups speak 250 different languages, but most people follow Islam, brought by Muslim traders in the 14th century. With a population of more than 185 million, Indonesia is the world's largest Muslim nation. European spice traders arrived in the 16th century, and the Dutch East India Company made Jakarta (then Batavia) the centre of its trading empire. Dutch rule lasted until 1949. Oil, natural gas and rubber are major exports; tourism is also important – especially for BALI which draws about a million visitors every year.

❖ Krakatoa, a volcanic island blown apart in an eruption in 1883, lay between the islands of Java and Sumatra. It is uninhabited now.

Iran Islamic republic in western Asia where the ancient ▷PERSIAN EMPIRE was founded. The country's interior is a vast desert. Iran's wealth comes mainly from oil and natural gas, and in the 1960s and 1970s the Shah of Iran used oil revenue to finance the country's modernization. A revolution against the Shah's rule led in 1979 to the establishment of an Islamic republic led by Ayatollah Ruholla ▷KHOMEINI. From 1980 to 1988 Iran fought its neighbour in the ▷IRAN-IRAQ WAR. The capital is Tehran.

Iraq West Asian country crossed by the EUPHRATES and TIGRIS rivers. Much of Iraq was formerly the ancient region of ▷MESOPOTAMIA. Its inhabitants are Arabs, Kurds and Turks. In 1979 ▷SADDAM HUSSEIN became president; he took his country into the ▷IRAN-IRAQ WAR of 1980-8, and his invasion of Kuwait led to The ▷GULF WAR in 1991. The capital of Iraq is BAGHDAD.

❖ The early Mesopotamian civilizations of ▷SUMERIA and Assyria, and the city of ▷BABYLON, were all in present-day Iraq.

Ireland, Republic of (Eire) Country making up about five-sixths of the island of Ireland (the rest, NORTHERN IRELAND, is part of the United Kingdom). A mild, humid climate is responsible for the landscape's countless shades of green which earn Ireland the popular name of 'Emerald Isle'. DUBLIN is the capital. The official languages are Irish, spoken in the Kerry and Connemara regions of the west, and English. English rule of the whole island began in the 16th century when Henry VIII wanted to establish Protestantism in place of Roman Catholicism. In 1800 the Irish Parliament was abolished and Ireland was united with Britain. A growing campaign for Home Rule entered a violent phase with the 1916 ▷EASTER RISING, organized by the secret Irish Republican Brotherhood, which ended with the surrender of the rebels after a week a fighting on the streets of Dublin. In later years a terrorist war against Britain was waged by the ▷IRA, founded in 1919. The Irish Free State came into being in 1922, but without the six counties in the north where Protestant descendants of 16th and 17th-century English and Scottish settlers wanted to retain ties with Britain. The last constitutional ties with Britain were severed in 1949 when Ireland became a republic. Formal direct links were re-established in 1985 with the signing of the ▷ANGLO-IRISH AGREEMENT. Ireland has experienced massive emigration, starting in the 1840s during the ▷POTATO FAMINE caused by crop failure and continuing this century. Before the famine the population was 8 million; now it is 3,5 million.

Israel Country at the eastern end of the Mediterranean Sea. It was formerly proclaimed on 14 May 1948 as a homeland for the Jews who have vigorously defended its existence against the hostility of its powerful Arab neighbours – a situation that has led to five wars and innumerable terrorist attacks from both sides. The country's 4 million Jews now make up more than 80 per cent of the population, the remainder being mostly Palestinian Arabs. The DEAD SEA and the Sea of Galilee are both on Israel's border, and water from the Sea of Galilee is channelled southwards to irrigate the arid Negev region. Kibbutzim (communal settlements) produce 35 per cent of Israel's crops; many also have factories. The capital is JERUSALEM; the second largest city is TEL AVIV-JAFFA. (See also ▷ARAB-ISRAELI CONFLICT in 'Politics, government and the law'.)

Istanbul Turkey's largest city, on the Bosporus. The oldest part of this ancient city is built beside an inlet known as the Golden Horn. The Blue Mosque, named after the blue tiles decorating its interior, is one of nearly 500 mosques whose domes and minarets rise above the city; the ▷HAGIA SOFIA has been in turn a cathedral, a mosque and a museum. The city was called Byzantium until AD 330, when the Roman emperor Constantine moved his capital here and renamed it Constantinople. The ▷BYZANTINE EMPIRE retained

TASTE OF IRISH *A perfectly preserved public facility of yesteryear such as this traditional pub at Oranmore in Galway county, western Ireland, is not an unfamiliar sight.*

it as capital until 1453, followed by the ▷OTTOMAN EMPIRE until 1922, when the capital was moved to Ankara by Kemal Ataturk. Constantinople was renamed Istanbul in 1930.
❖ The barracks in the suburb of Usküdar (Scutari) is where Florence Nightingale tended the wounded in the ▷CRIMEAN WAR.

Italy Country consisting of a boot-shaped peninsula extending into the Mediterranean and including the islands of SICILY, just off the boot's toe, and Sardinia, to the west of its ankle. Italy is rich in art and architectural treasures – frescoes and bronze sculptures left by the ▷ETRUSCANS, impressive ruins that recall the glories of the ▷ROMAN EMPIRE, and churches and museums packed with Renaissance art. After the fall of Rome, the peninsula was politically fragmented for 15 centuries until the mid-19th-century ▷RISORGIMENTO – the movement for unification, whose leading figures were Giuseppi Garibaldi and Camillo Cavour. Unification took place in 1870. From 1922 to 1943 the Fascist dictator Benito ▷MUSSOLINI ruled Italy. Among Italy's many splendid cities are FLORENCE, VENICE and the capital, ROME. Now the country is a major industrial power, with industry and commerce concentrated in the north; the southern part is less prosperous.

Jamaica West Indian island country with palm-fringed beaches and a tropical climate that attract many tourists. Sugar is an important crop, and so is the coffee grown in the Blue Mountains. Jamaica became independent from Britain within the Commonwealth in 1962. The capital is Kingston.

Japan Country in the north Pacific Ocean made up of four main islands: Honshu, Hokkaido, Kyushu and Shikoku. Much of the land is mountainous and most people are crowded into towns and cities around the coast, especially in and around TOKYO, the capital. Earthquakes, volcanic eruptions and tsunamis (tidal waves) are a constant threat. The stately Mount Fuji (3 776 m), Japan's highest mountain, is a volcano that last erupted in 1707. From the 12th century until 1867 shoguns ruled the country and samurai made up a warrior caste. Japan was virtually closed to foreigners from the 1630s until the 1850s, when an American fleet under Commodore Matthew Perry forced it to open its ports. The Japanese occupied Korea in 1910 and Manchuria in the 1930s, and embarked on a war against China in 1937. In 1941 they bombed the American military base of ▷PEARL HARBOR and by mid-1942 had conquered much of Southeast Asia. After the Americans dropped atomic bombs on Hiroshima and Nagasaki in 1945, forcing Japan's surrender, Emperor ▷HIROHITO renounced his divine status and assumed the role of a constitutional monarch. Japan's economy made a dramatic recovery and the country is now one of the world's top industrial and financial powers.

Jerusalem Capital of Israel and a holy city for Jews, Christians and Muslims. Jerusalem's walled Old City is divided into Armenian, Christian, Jewish and Muslim quarters. It has many historic religious sites, including the western wall, or Wailing Wall, the only remnant of the Jewish temple destroyed by the Romans in AD 70; the Church of the Holy Sepulchre, built where Jesus is thought to have been buried; and the Dome of the Rock, an octagonal mosque built on the site of the Jewish temple and over the spot where the prophet Muhammad was reputed to have ascended into heaven. The Knesset, the Israeli parliament, is in the newer part of the city.

Jordan Arab kingdom in southwest Asia, four-fifths of which is desert. The capital, Amman, is a major financial centre for the region. As a result of the ▷ARAB-ISRAELI CONFLICT Jordan has received many refugees since World War II. In 1967 Jordan lost the WEST BANK – territory west of the River Jordan and Dead Sea – to Israel. In 1988 King Hussein, Jordan's monarch since 1952, renounced administrative responsibility for the West Bank. In 1994 Jordan and Israel signed an agreement ending 46 years of war.

Kabul Capital of Afghanistan, standing in a valley flanked by steep hills. The city is more than 3 000 years old. During the 16th century it was the capital of the Mogul empire.

Karakoram Mountain range in the disputed border area of India, Pakistan and China. Eighteen of the craggy peaks are over 7 600 m high. The highest peak in the Karakoram, and second highest in the world, is the 8 611 m K2, given that name because it was the second Karakoram peak to be measured.

Kathmandu Capital of Nepal, lying 1 324 m above sea level in a fertile valley in the Himalayas. The old part of Kathmandu is a maze of narrow streets lined with buildings with carved wooden balconies; elsewhere there are European-style buildings. During the 1960s many ▷HIPPIES were attracted to Kathmandu by the easy availability of drugs in the area.

Kazakhstan Huge central Asian country, formerly part of the USSR, almost the same size as India but with only 17 million people. Much of it is rather dry; the flat or rolling land is used as pasture for sheep and goats. The Muslim Kazakhs are the country's biggest ethnic group, closely followed by Russians. The capital, Alma-Ata, has twice been rebuilt after earthquakes.

Kenya East African country whose capital is Nairobi. Tea and coffee are grown in the fertile southwest of the country, but much of the rest of Kenya is scrub and desert. In the 1950s the ▷MAU MAU conducted a violent campaign against British rule; Jomo ▷KENYATTA, once jailed as the leader of the Mau Mau, became Kenya's first president after independence in 1963. Many tourists visit Kenya on safari to see wildlife that includes elephants, cheetahs and giraffes. Some of the oldest fossil remains of modern human ancestors – 2 million years old – have been found in northern Kenya, particularly near Lake Turkana. Mombasa, Kenya's second largest city, was occupied by Arab traders in the Middle Ages.

Kiev Capital of Ukraine, dating from the 6th century AD. In the 9th century Kiev was the capital of the original Russian state; its grand prince converted to Christianity and made it the state religion in 988. The modern city, a major centre of industry, was severely damaged in World War II; it was rebuilt, with tree-lined boulevards.

Kilimanjaro Africa's highest mountain, an extinct volcano rising to 5 895 m in Tanzania. It is snow-capped all year, even though it is little more than 320 km from the Equator.

Kurdistan Hilly region around north Iraq and the neighbouring parts of Turkey, Iran and Syria, inhabited by some 18 million Muslim Kurds. The Kurds have often been victims of suppression and have fought for their independence. In 1991, after The ▷GULF WAR, many Kurds fled from Iraqi forces after rising against the regime of ▷SADDAM HUSSEIN. More recently, Turkey and Iraq have cooperated in their war against Kurdish rebels.

Kuwait Small emirate at the head of the Persian Gulf, with immense reserves of oil which have been used to develop its economy. The capital is Kuwait City. Iraq's invasion of Kuwait in August 1990 led to The ▷GULF WAR six months later. Nearly all the land is desert; sea-water distillation plants supply most of the country's water.

Lake District Area of scenic grandeur in northwestern England comprising 16 major lakes, set among the Cumbrian mountains. The area has been a National Park since 1951.
❖ The Lake District's attractions were popularized by the so-called 'Lake Poets' who

included the writers William ▷WORDSWORTH, Samuel Taylor ▷COLERIDGE and Robert Southey. Wordsworth's home at Grasmere in the Lake District is now a museum.

Laos Mountainous, forested and poor communist country in Southeast Asia. It lies to the west of Vietnam and during the Vietnam War (1960-75) suffered from bombing raids and troops moving through the country. The capital is Vientiane.

Las Vegas City in Nevada, in the USA, known for its neon lights and gambling casinos which attract more than 20 million people from all parts of the world every year.

Lebanon Small country at the eastern end of the Mediterranean Sea, with spectacular mountains separating the coastal plain from the fertile Beqa'a valley. The capital, BEIRUT, is on the coast. Complex religious and political differences caused civil war between 1975 and 1990 and seriously damaged the economy of this once-prosperous country. Lebanon was still unstable in the mid-1990s.
❖ Cedars of Lebanon, the country's national symbol, were used to build Solomon's Temple in Jerusalem, and were imported by the ancient Egyptians. There are only a few cedar forests left in the country.

Leipzig City in eastern Germany, a centre of trade and culture for many centuries. Leipzig's international trade fair was first held in 1165. Martin Luther, who launched the Protestant Reformation, was active here; composers such as J S ▷BACH and Felix ▷MENDELSSOHN worked in the city and Richard ▷WAGNER was born here; the writer Johann Wolfgang von ▷GOETHE studied at Leipzig University.

Liberia Small West African country founded in 1847 as a place of settlement for freed slaves from the USA. It is the only African country that has never been ruled by a foreign power. For many years descendants of Americo-Liberians were a privileged elite and formed strong governments in a one-party system. In 1980 a bloody military coup ended their dominance. In 1989 civil war began between rival factions in the army, leading to the loss of at least 150 000 lives, the displacement of more than a third of the population, protracted anarchy and the destruction of the economy. After international intervention, a transitional government was formed in 1994 to pave the way for elections, but these were repeatedly postponed after renewed fighting.
❖ Ships of many nationalities have been registered in Liberia because of the tax advantages and lax safety requirements offered by its 'flag of convenience'.

HOME FOR A SAINT *In AD 685 an early Christian saint, Herbert, established his hermitage at Derwent Water; visitors have sought out the seclusion of the Lake District's widest lake ever since.*

Libya Large north African country, nearly all of which lies in the Sahara Desert. Most of its inhabitants live near the Mediterranean coast around the capital, Tripoli, and the city of Benghazi. Oil dominates the economy. Since 1969 Libya has been ruled by Colonel Muammar ▷GADDAFI. On the coast east of Tripoli are the ruins of Leptis Magna, an ancient city inhabited successively by the Phoenicians, Carthaginians and Romans.

Liechtenstein Tiny principality between Austria and Switzerland, covering 160 km^2, and with fewer than 30 000 inhabitants, 38 per cent of whom are foreigners living and working here. It has been a sovereign state since 1342. The capital is Vaduz.

Lilongwe National capital of MALAWI since 1975, replacing Zomba because of its central position. With a population of 350 000, the country's second largest city after Blantyre, it is a trading centre for a fertile area that produces maize, peanuts and tobacco.

Lisbon Capital of Portugal spreading over seven hills beside the estuary of the Tagus River. In the 15th century Lisbon's trade links with newly discovered lands in Africa brought wealth and great splendour. An earthquake in 1755 destroyed much of the city, but some fine old buildings remain.

Liverpool City and port on the River Mersey in northwest England. By the middle of the 18th century it was one of the biggest and most prosperous ports in the world and in the 19th century was the main port for British, German and Scandinavian emigrants to the USA. Its importance declined after World War II and today the Victorian Albert Dock, which closed in 1972, has been renovated as a complex of museums and galleries and a centre for water sports.
❖ The story of the ▷BEATLES, the musicians who were born in Liverpool and brought it worldwide fame in the 1960s, is told in an elaborate walk-through exhibition in the dock complex.

London National capital of the UNITED KINGDOM on the banks of the River THAMES, one of the world's largest and most cosmopolitan cities with a population of nearly 7 million, spread over 1 580 km^2. Once the hub of the vast ▷BRITISH EMPIRE, it is still a world cultural, financial and trade centre and with its wealth of historic landmarks draws many millions of overseas and British visitors every year. The Romans founded Londinium in AD 43 in an area now occupied by the city's business heart, known as 'the City'. In the 11th century a royal palace and minster were built to the west at what became known as Westminster, now the centre of government. The cities were merged only in the 17th century. The Great Plague struck London in 1664-5 and in 1666 the Great Fire largely destroyed its medieval buildings. The City developed over the centuries as an international centre of banking and commerce, the basis of its wealth being the docks from which ships sailed to trade almost everywhere in the world. Today, after redevelopment following the ▷BLITZ of World War II, its contemporary buildings have all but obscured the splendour of landmarks such as Sir Christopher ▷WREN's St Paul's Cathedral. The Bank of England, founded in 1694, and Mansion House, the official residence of the lord mayor of London, are sited here, as are the stock exchange and the headquarters of many banks, insurance companies, stockbrokers and other financial institutions. In the western part of central London are Buckingham Palace, official London residence of the sovereign, the Houses of Parliament, the government ministry buildings of Whitehall, the medieval Westminster Abbey, the National and Tate galleries and – in a dominant position along one side of Trafalgar Square, the imposing South Africa House, seat of the South African ambassador. Among other outstanding features and landmarks of London are: Covent Garden, now a large piazza which for more than 300 years housed the capital's main fruit, vegetable and flower market, with the Royal Opera House, also referred to as 'Covent Garden', nearby; the East End, once a poorer area of London centred on the docks and home of the cockneys; Heathrow, the world's busiest international airport, with 48 million passengers passing through every year; Hyde Park, with its Serpentine lake and Speaker's Corner where aspiring orators have expounded since Victorian times; Petticoat Lane and Portobello Road, large Sunday markets selling clothes, leather goods and bric-a-brac; Piccadilly Circus, the heart of the city's theatreland; Soho, traditionally thought of as the 'red light' district but now known for its cafés, bars and restaurants; the Tower of London, a Norman fortress dating from the 11th and 12th centuries housing the Crown Jewels and guarded by yeoman warders, also known as 'beefeaters', since 1326; and ▷WIMBLEDON, where international tennis championships have been held yearly since 1877. The city also offers a rich cultural fare, with five full-time symphony orchestras, major concert halls such as the Festival and Royal Albert, more than 40 major theatres and many smaller ones, famous museums such the British Museum, with its associated British Library, and the Victoria and Albert Museum, and numerous art galleries. The city's underground rail system was the world's first and is the world's largest; a new extension also links it to the Docklands, where opulent office and residential areas, such as Canary Wharf, have been developed.

CITY TREASURES *The Tower of London stands by the mighty Tower Bridge completed in 1894. Upstream, a World War II cruiser, HMS* Belfast, *is moored for the public to visit.*

Los Angeles Sprawling American city in southern California. Most people drive to work on the multilane freeways and the city

suffers from traffic jams and severe air pollution caused by exhaust fumes. One of its districts is Hollywood, renowned as the centre of the American film and television industries. Beverley Hills, home of many celebrities and wealthy people, is also a district of Los Angeles. Disneyland is in Anaheim, south of the city.

❖ Early in 1994 the North Ridge earthquake devastated part of the city, which, like SAN FRANCISCO, lies on the San Andreas Fault.

Louisiana Mostly low-lying state of the southern USA, which includes the Mississippi delta. The capital is Baton Rouge and the largest city is NEW ORLEANS.

❖ Louisiana was named after Louis XIV of France – French settlers began arriving here in 1699. The French sold their territory, extending from the Mississippi to the Rockies and from the Gulf of Mexico to Canada, to the USA in 1803 for US$11,25 million. This so-called Louisiana Purchase doubled the area of the USA.

Lourdes French town in the foothills of the Pyrenees where in 1858 a peasant girl, Marie-Bernarde Soubirous, known as Bernadette, said that she had seen a vision of the Virgin Mary. A healing shrine every year attracts some 5 million pilgrims.

Lusaka Capital of ZAMBIA since 1935, with a population of about 1 million, it is the centre of a fertile cotton and tobacco farming area.

Luxembourg Small, prosperous grand duchy, lying between Belgium, Germany and France – at one time the point of entry to Europe for many South Africans travelling by air. Of its 390 000 inhabitants about a third are foreigners. It is the seat of the European Court of Justice. The capital is also called Luxembourg. Luxembourgish, French and German are the official languages.

Macau Tiny Portuguese enclave on the southern China coast, only 16 km² in area (about three times the size of ▷ROBBEN ISLAND). Portuguese merchants used it as a trading post from the 1520s, but its importance declined as nearby Hong Kong flourished. However, it is still a major trade centre and its casinos attract many tourists. It is due to be returned to China in 1999, with the protection of the Portuguese culture guaranteed by China for the next 50 years

Machu Picchu Magnificently sited ruins of an ▷INCA city, 2 280 m up in the Peruvian Andes. They were brought to the world's attention in 1911 by Hiram Bingham, an American archaeologist.

INCA RUINS *Machu Picchu, which remained out of the reach of plundering Spanish invaders, covers 13 km² in the Peruvian Andes.*

Madagascar (Malagasy Republic) Indian Ocean island country off Africa's east coast, the world's fourth largest island (after Greenland, New Guinea and Borneo), about half the size of South Africa. The Malagasy people, whose 18 ethnic groups all speak the same language, are mostly of mixed Indonesian, African and Arab descent. A poor country, it relies heavily on tourists – particularly from southern Africa – attracted by its beautiful beaches and tropical forests. The capital is Antananarivo.

❖ Madagascar has many unique plants and animals that evolved in isolation after the island broke away from the African continent some 150 million years ago – including the lemur, a long-tailed arboreal ▷PRIMATE.

Madeira Mountainous island in the Atlantic Ocean, with subtropical vegetation, 710 km west of the African kingdom of Morocco. Madeira and its neighbouring islands are possessions of Portugal; it gained partial autonomy in 1980. Although now less prosperous than in the days when passenger liners travelling between South Africa and Britain called here regularly, it is still a popular winter resort. The capital is Funchal

Madrid Capital and largest city of Spain, situated on dry plains in the centre of the country. Madrid is the home of one of the world's major art galleries, the Prado, which contains works by leading Spanish artists, including ▷GOYA, ▷EL GRECO and ▷VELÁSQUEZ.

Malawi Long, narrow country in southeast Africa, bordering Lake Malawi. The capital is LILONGWE. It has great natural beauty, but poverty is widespread. Dr Hastings Banda became president in 1964, when Malawi gained independence from Britain. His 30-year dictatorship ended with the country's first multiparty elections in May 1994, when Bakali Muluzi was elected president.

Malaysia Kingdom in Southeast Asia, consisting of a peninsula of the mainland and the more rural states of Sabah and Sarawak, which are in the northern part of the island of BORNEO. Much of the land is mountainous and covered with luxuriant forest. Malays, who are mostly Muslims, make up 60 per cent of the population and dominate politics; the Chinese, who make up 30 per cent, dominate business. The capital is Kuala Lumpur. Malaysia is one of the world's leading rubber producers. It has adopted an economic programme which seeks an eightfold increase in national income by 2020.

❖ The term 'Cape Malay' has been incorrectly applied to the Muslim population of the Cape. The first Muslims at the Cape were political exiles, convicts and slaves brought mainly from Indonesia. Relatively few came from the Malay Peninsula.

Maldives Country of about 1 300 low-lying coral islands in the Indian Ocean, 640 km southwest of Sri Lanka. Sandy beaches, palm trees and lagoons attract many tourists; fishing is the other main source of income. The capital is Malé.

Malta Mediterranean island country, about 90 km south of Sicily and 330 km east of Tunisia, made up of Malta, the smaller island of Gozo and tiny Comino. The capital, Valletta, is on Malta. Many foreign powers have dominated the islands, including the Knights of St John from 1530 to 1798, and the British, who had a naval dockyard here that closed in 1979. Malta achieved full independence from Britain in 1964.

❖ Malta was awarded the George Cross, Britain's highest civilian award for bravery, in recognition of the islanders' courage in withstanding German and Italian bombardment during World War II.

Man, Isle of Island midway between England and Ireland which, although it belongs to the British Crown, is self-governing. Its parliament, the Tynwald, is one of the world's oldest legislative assemblies, having met regularly for more than 1 000 years. The capital and main port is Douglas.

❖ The Manx cat, a tailless breed, is unique to the island.

Manchester City on the River Irwell in northwest England. In the 14th century Flemish weavers settled here and in the late 18th and 19th centuries Manchester's cotton manufacturing made it a major centre of the ▷INDUSTRIAL REVOLUTION – with its accompanying evils of pollution, slums and exploitation of labour. The city benefited from a network of railways and canals, one of which linked it to the estuary of the River Mersey, bringing ocean-going ships to the thriving textile factories. Coinciding with its decline as an industrial city in the 1920s it became an important banking centre.
❖ In Roman times Manchester was called Mancunium and residents are still known today as Mancunians.

Maputo Capital of ▷MOZAMBIQUE and major seaport, formerly known as Lourenço Marques. Its large natural harbour contributed to its development based on transport trade which began in 1895 when it was linked by rail to Johannesburg. In the days of Portuguese rule it was an elegant city popular with tourists from southern African countries, but tourism collapsed as a result of the guerrilla war that followed independence. It has a population of more than 1 million.

Marshall Islands Pacific island country of some 1 250 coral islands, more than 4 000 km east of the Philippines. In the late 1940s and 1950s the USA exploded 64 nuclear weapons on Bikini and Enewetak atolls.
❖ The bikini bathing garment was named after Bikini atoll, reputedly because of the 'atomic' impact it had on onlookers.

Massachusetts Northeast coastal state of the USA. After sailing from England on the ▷MAYFLOWER in 1620, the Pilgrim Fathers established a settlement here at Plymouth on Cape Cod Bay. In 1626 they founded the city of Salem, notorious for the witchcraft trials it held in 1692 that led to the execution of 20 townsfolk, most of them women. The state capital is BOSTON.

Mauritius Large volcanic island east of Mozambique, separated from the mainland by a channel between 400 and 970 km wide. Occupied by Britain in 1810, it became an independent Commonwealth state in 1968 and a republic in 1992. It was once relatively prosperous as a producer of sugar, molasses and rum, but its economy declined as a result of changing world markets. Sugar is still a major export, the second biggest after cotton. Since the 1980s tourism has developed rapidly, now contributing one-third of the country's foreign earnings. The island is surrounded by coral reefs, making scuba diving a big attraction, and it has superb tropical beaches along 117 km of its coastline.

WARM SKIES *A fine cluster of art deco buildings on Ocean Drive in South Beach, Miami, complements the warm evening light which draws visitors to the Florida resort throughout the year.*

Mediterranean Sea Almost tideless sea between Europe and Africa connected to the Atlantic Ocean by the Strait of GIBRALTAR. Several ancient civilizations – Egyptian, Minoan, Mycenaean, Phoenician, Greek and Roman – arose around the Mediterranean.

Memphis US city and major cotton market on the Mississippi River in the state of Tennessee. The singer Elvis ▷PRESLEY spent much of his life here and was buried at his mansion, Graceland, now a museum.
❖ The civil rights leader Martin Luther King was assassinated in Memphis in 1968.

Mexico Predominantly mountainous Central American country that has both harsh deserts and tropical forests. The south has active volcanoes and is sometimes hit by earthquakes. Magnificent ruins of early civilizations include those of the ▷MAYA, who lived in the low-lying Yucatan Peninsula, and the ▷AZTECS, who were conquered by the Spaniards between 1519 and 1521. The country has rich oil fields and silver mines.

Mexico City Capital of Mexico and the world's largest city, with about 16 million people. It lies 2 240 m above sea level. It has Aztec ruins, palaces built in Spanish colonial times and many modern buildings. New buildings are constructed to withstand earthquakes; a strong quake in 1985 killed more than 7 000 people.

Miami Large city on Florida's Atlantic coast, where numerous Cuban exiles have settled and where many drugs from South America enter the USA. Its Art Deco District has impressive architecture. The warm temperatures all year round draw holidaymakers to the Miami Beach resort.

Milan Italy's second largest city and the country's centre of finance, industry, fashion and publishing. Older buildings include the Gothic cathedral, and the convent of the late 15th-century church of Santa Maria delle Grazie, where Leonardo da Vinci painted his fresco *The Last Supper*. The Galleria, a huge 19th-century glass-roofed building, now a shopping arcade, is near the famous La Scala opera house.

Mississippi Major river in the USA which flows 3 779 km from northwest Minnesota to its delta in the Gulf of Mexico. At St Louis it is joined by the Missouri, and the 6 019 km Mississippi-Missouri is the world's fourth longest river system. The muddy waters of 'Old Man River' carry vast amounts of freight. A system of levees and side channels usually helps to prevent flooding, but in 1993 two months of heavy rain brought floods to an area a quarter of the size of South Africa.

Monaco Tiny, rich principality on the French Riviera, stretching along the coast for just over 3,2 km. The palace of the ruling Grimaldi family is on the rocky headland of Monaco town, and further along the coast is the resort area of Monte Carlo, with its ornate casino.
❖ Prince Rainier III succeeded to the throne of Monaco in 1949. He married the film star Grace ▷KELLY in 1956.
❖ The Monaco Grand Prix takes place in the town's winding streets every May.

Mongolia High, arid country between Russia and China, much of it covered with grassland or the wastes of the Gobi Desert. The capital is Ulan Bator. Mongolia was a communist country from 1924 to 1990.
❖ Some of Mongolia's nomadic herdsmen live in circular, dome-topped tents called *gers* in Mongolian or *yurts* in Russian.

Montreal Canadian industrial city, in Quebec province, built around a wooded hill called Mount Royal, from which it takes its name. It is an inland port on Montreal Island, at the junction of the Ottawa and St Lawrence rivers. Montreal has tall, modern buildings, picturesque cobbled streets and underground shops and restaurants that give protection from the bitterly cold, snowy winters and the hot summers.
❖ Montreal claims to be the world's second largest French-speaking city after Paris.

Morocco Kingdom in northwest Africa. The Atlas Mountains rise to more than 4 000 m behind the fertile coastal lands; further inland is the harshness of the ▷SAHARA. The capital is Rabat, but the largest city is Casablanca, scene of a World War II meeting between Allied leaders and the inspiration for the film starring Humphrey Bogart and Ingrid Bergman. Marrakech, the former capital at the foot of the Atlas Mountains, is a bustling and colourful city whose *souks* – markets and bazaars – attract many tourists.

Moscow Capital of Russia and previously of the USSR. The 12th-century ▷KREMLIN, in the heart of Moscow, is a fortress with government buildings, palaces and cathedrals within its walls. Just outside the walls are Red Square, the site of military parades during the Soviet era, the 16th-century St Basil's Cathedral, with its magnificent colourful domes and the department store GUM. The city was besieged by Napoleon I in 1812.
❖ Moscow is known for its vast underground railway stations.

Mount Everest World's highest mountain (8 846 m) in the Himalayas on the border of China and Nepal. It was named after Sir George Everest, a British surveyor general of India. Edmund Hillary, a New Zealander, and Tenzing Norgay, a Sherpa, were the first people to reach the summit, in 1953.

Mount Rushmore Mountain in the Black Hills of the state of South Dakota, USA, where the faces of four former US presidents – George Washington, Thomas Jefferson, Abraham Lincoln and Theodore Roosevelt – were carved in a granite cliff between 1927 and 1941. The heads are 18 m high, with mouths about 5,5 m wide.

Mount St Helens Large ▷VOLCANO in Washington state, USA, that erupted violently in 1980. Ash rose 24 km into the air, and trees were flattened over an area of about 600 km^2.

Munich Germany's third largest city, and capital of the state of Bavaria. Its name in German is München. It has impressive public buildings and churches, and many museums, art galleries, theatres and concert halls.
❖ Munich is known for its beer gardens, and also for the *Oktoberfest*, a beer festival held in late September and early October which attracts over 6 million people. Some 5 million litres of beer are consumed at the festival.

Myanmar (Burma) Buddhist country in Southeast Asia, known as Burma until 1989. The capital, Yangon (previously called Rangoon), is at the swampy mouth of the Ayerarwady (Irrawaddy) River. Trees cover two-thirds of the country, providing teak and rubber. In the east, where the borders of Myanmar, Thailand and Laos meet, opium poppies are grown in the 'Golden Triangle', which supplies 70 per cent of world production. Feudal warlords fight for control of the drug trade. The country has been wracked by political turmoil since the late 1980s.
❖ Mandalay, immortalized in a ballad by Rudyard ▷KIPLING, is Burma's second city and the country's cultural heart.

Naples Beautifully sited Italian city built around the Bay of Naples, with VESUVIUS in the background. It has fine churches and museums that contain many works of art, as well as narrow streets and densely populated alleys lined with decaying buildings.

Nepal Kingdom which runs along the southern slopes of the HIMALAYAS. Its southern border with India is only just above sea level, but 160 km to the north are MOUNT EVEREST and other mighty peaks that lie on the northern border with China. Sherpas, a group of people from northeast Nepal, often act as guides

ROOM WITH A VIEW *A wintry Moscow sun, seen through the wrought iron of a hotel balcony, outlines the impressive snow-touched turrets of the Kremlin on the far side of Red Square.*

and porters to mountain expeditions. The capital is KATHMANDU.

Netherlands Prosperous and densely populated kingdom where more than one-fifth of the land has been reclaimed from the sea over the past three centuries. The Netherlands was a major sea power and wealthy nation in the 17th century, when the ▷DUTCH EAST INDIA COMPANY's trade in spices led to the Dutch settlement at the Cape and the colonization of what is now Indonesia. Trade brought prosperity to AMSTERDAM, which is the capital, although The HAGUE is the seat of government. ROTTERDAM is the world's biggest port. Agriculture employs a tiny proportion of the workforce but is intensive and scientific, with dairy farms, huge areas of glasshouses, and fields of tulips and other flowers.
❖ The Netherlands has produced many great painters, including ▷VAN EYCK, ▷HALS, ▷REMBRANDT, ▷VERMEER and ▷VAN GOGH.

New Orleans Inland port city on the Mississippi River in the southern state of Louisiana, USA, known for its annual Mardi Gras festival. The city's French Quarter has buildings in the French and Spanish colonial styles, with iron trellis balconies.
❖ ▷JAZZ originated in New Orleans.

New York Cosmopolitan, vibrant city, the biggest in the USA, with more than 7 million inhabitants. The heart of New York, the borough of Manhattan, contains the city's major business and cultural institutions. These include the financial sector of Wall Street; the twin-towered World Trade Centre; Times Square, named after the building formerly occupied by *The New York Times*; Greenwich Village, the haunt of students and artists; the theatres of Broadway; and a multitude of museums. Central Manhattan is laid out as a grid of numbered streets. The smartest shops and the 381 m high ▷EMPIRE STATE BUILDING are on Fifth Avenue, and CENTRAL PARK lies between 59th Street and 110th Street. The residential area of Harlem lies to the north of Central Park. New York's other four boroughs are Brooklyn and Queens, both on Long Island, and the Bronx and Staten Island. The Brooklyn Bridge, the world's longest suspension bridge when it opened in 1883, spans the East River and connects Brooklyn to Manhattan. The Statue of Liberty, another famous landmark, stands in New York Harbour.
❖ Europeans arrived at the site of New York in 1609 and the Dutch bought Manhattan Island in 1624, calling it New Amsterdam. It was taken over by the English in 1664 and renamed New York. The name was also given to one of the original 13 states of the USA in 1777.
❖ New York's nickname, 'The Big Apple' – which was the name of both a dance and a Harlem night club – was probably coined by jazz musicians in the 1930s. It was adopted in the 1970s as a slogan to promote the city.

New Zealand Country slightly larger than the UK, but with only 3,5 million inhabitants (compared with Britain's 58 million). Three-quarters of New Zealanders live on North Island, the slightly smaller of the two main islands where the largest city, Auckland, and the capital, Wellington, are located. North Island has hot springs and geysers at Rotorua, and active volcanoes. South Island is dominated by the Southern Alps where 14 peaks exceed 3 000 m. The first people to arrive in New Zealand, 1 000 years ago, were Polynesians; they adopted the name ▷MAORI, meaning normal, to distinguish themselves from Europeans, who arrived in large numbers from the 1830s. The country achieved independence from Britain in 1931. Sheep outnumber people by almost 16 to 1.

Newcastle upon Tyne City and port on the River Tyne in northeast England. It has been at the centre of the English coal trade since the 13th century – and has given the name Newcastle to coal-mining towns in South Africa, Australia, Canada and the USA. It lies in Tyneside, an industrial region which was once one of the largest shipbuilding centres in the world.

Nicaragua Central American country whose agricultural economy has been undermined by civil war. Sandinista guerrillas opposed to President Anastasio Somoza overthrew the government in 1979. Civil war, which broke out in the 1980s between the Sandinista government and the US-backed Contras, ended in June 1990 with the election of a new president and approval of a new constitution. But fighting between left-wingers and right-wingers resumed in 1993 and a peace agreement the following year remained fragile. The capital, Managua, was badly damaged by earthquakes in 1931 and 1972.

Nigeria Most populous African country with more than 100 million people made up of about 250 ethnic groups. Since obtaining independence from Britain in 1960, this federation of 30 states has been plagued by political instability, a civil war that claimed a million lives, and continuing ethnic conflicts. Despotic military juntas have ruled it for 25 of the first 35 years of its existence. Nigeria has oil fields around the Niger River delta and oil and gas dominate the economy, although more than half of the people work on the land, with major crops including cocoa, peanuts, palm oil and cotton. In 1991 the capital moved from Lagos, a city of nearly 6 million people notorious for its traffic congestion, to Abuja, a new city on a politically neutral site in central Nigeria.

SHEEP COUNTRY *New Zealand, the world's largest exporter of lamb, also has some of the finest pastures, as seen here at South Otago.*

Nile World's longest river, flowing 6 695 km from its most distant headstream, in the African state of Burundi, to its delta in the Mediterranean. The White Nile flows out of Lake Victoria and on through lakes and swamps to Khartoum, where it is joined by the Blue Nile, which rises in the Ethiopian highlands. The river's annual floods brought fertility to its valley and allowed the civilization of ancient Egypt to flourish. The ASWAN HIGH DAM, completed in 1971, now regulates the river's flow.

North Korea Communist country in the northern half of the Korean peninsula in east Asia. The state was formed in 1948, and fought the ▷KOREAN WAR against South Korea between 1950 and 1953. Kim Il-sung was the country's leader from 1948 until his death in 1994, when his son Kim Jong Il took over. North Korea lost a major ally with the collapse of communism in the USSR and tension between North and South Korea, which had persisted, began to ease. Until an accord was signed with the USA in 1994, the North's nuclear potential attracted worldwide concern. The capital is Pyongyang.

North Sea Shallow sea, lying between Britain and mainland Europe, a major shipping lane and a rich fishing ground. It is also a source of oil and natural gas, whose main beneficiaries are Britain and Norway.

Northern Ireland Province of the United Kingdom, made up of six counties: Antrim, Armagh, Down, Fermanagh, Londonderry and Tyrone. All except Fermanagh lie around Lough Neagh, the largest lake in the United Kingdom. The magnificent coastal scenery includes the Giant's Causeway, composed of thousands of hexagonal basalt columns packed together. In 1921 the mainly Protestant counties of Ulster withdrew from the newly established Irish Free State. In 1969 deep-rooted hostility between Northern Ireland's Catholics and Protestants erupted in violence which continued intermittently for 25 years. The capital is BELFAST; the second-largest city is Londonderry.

Norway Prosperous Scandinavian kingdom with impressive mountain scenery. About a third of Norway lies north of the Arctic Circle, but the coast, deeply indented with fjords, is kept almost entirely ice-free by the northward extension of the Gulf Stream. Its seafaring tradition dates back to ▷VIKING times, and fishing is an important industry. North Sea oil is a major source of revenue. The capital is OSLO.

Oberammergau Small town in the far south of Germany. A Passion play was performed here in 1634 to celebrate deliverance from the plague, and has been staged by the townspeople every ten years since then – apart from a few exceptions during wars. The next performance of the play will be in 2000.

Oklahoma Southwestern state of the USA, forming part of the Great Plains. Drought struck in the 1930s, when dust storms blew away the dry, over-cultivated top soil, and the barren land of northwestern Oklahoma and neighbouring states became known as the Dust Bowl.

❖ The migration of 'Okies' to seek their living elsewhere was the subject of John ▷STEINBECK's novel *The Grapes of Wrath.*

Oman Sultanate on the southeast coast of the Arabian Peninsula, most of whose income comes from oil. Rugged mountains in the north and south flank a vast desert plain. A small region of Oman, overlooking the Strait of Hormuz, is isolated from the rest of the country by part of the United Arab Emirates. The capital, Muscat, was a major trade centre in the 5th century BC.

Ontario Province in central Canada. Most people live in the southeast corner which includes OTTAWA, Canada's capital, and TORONTO, the state capital, and also the Niagara Falls. Few people live in the heavily forested north of the province.

Oslo Capital and main port of Norway, spreading over a large area at the head of the vast Oslofjord. The city has also been known as Christiania, after Christian IV, king of both Norway and Denmark, who had the city rebuilt after a disastrous fire in 1624. Maritime exhibits on the waterfront include reconstructed Viking ships; the ship *Fram* in which Roald ▷AMUNDSEN travelled to the Antarctic for his 1911 polar expedition; and the raft used by Thor Heyerdahl in his Kon-Tiki expedition.

❖ A collection of work by the Norwegian artist ▷MUNCH can be seen in Oslo.

Ottawa Spacious, leafy capital of Canada in the province of Ontario. In 1857, when Ottawa was a lumber town, Queen Victoria proclaimed it Canada's capital and dashed the hopes of Montreal, Toronto and other contenders for the position. Ottawa's industries include timber, pulp, paper and publishing.

Oxford Historic university city in England, lying at the junction of the River Thames and the River Cherwell. Oxford is Britain's oldest university; its first college, University College, was founded in 1249. It now has 36 colleges and more than 25 000 students. The university's Bodleian Library, founded in 1602, is one of the most important libraries in the world.

❖ President Bill Clinton of the USA won a ▷RHODES scholarship to Oxford, as have many South Africans.

Pacific Ocean World's largest ocean, covering one-third of the surface of the Earth; its area of 166 million km² is greater than that of all the planet's land surface combined. It stretches from the Arctic to the Antarctic and is bounded by Asia, Australia and the Americas. The ocean floor has vast underwater mountain ranges and trenches, including CHALLENGER DEEP – the deepest known spot in

VAST LANDS *The two huge countries that make up North America – Canada and the USA – cover an area nearly as large as that encompassed by all 43 countries in Europe.*

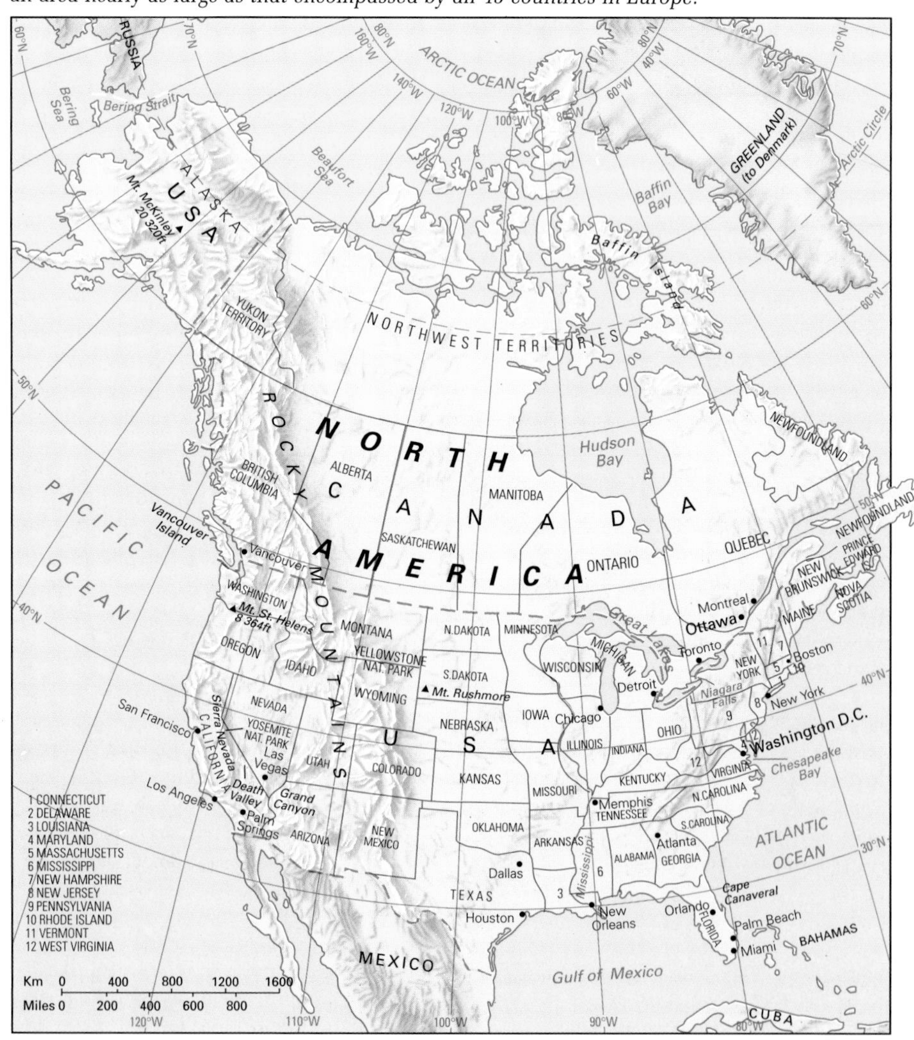

any ocean. There are three main groups of volcanic and coral islands: Melanesia, Micronesia and POLYNESIA.
❖ The Portuguese explorer Ferdinand ▷MAGELLAN, leader of the expedition which circumnavigated the world in 1519-22, gave the ocean its name because it was relatively free of violent storms.

Pakistan Largely rural country in southern Asia. Part of Pakistan is a dry plain crossed by the River Indus, but the north has some of the world's highest mountains. When India gained independence from Britain in 1947, Pakistan was created for the Muslim minority and then consisted of West Pakistan and East Pakistan, 1 600 km apart. In 1971 East Pakistan became the separate state of BANGLADESH. Soon afterwards, Zulfikar Ali ▷BHUTTO became the first president of the new Pakistan. His daughter Benazir Bhutto has twice been elected prime minister. The capital is Islamabad.
❖ A major early civilization flourished at Mohenjo Daro in the Indus valley.

Palestine Land at the eastern end of the Mediterranean Sea. In biblical times Palestine was the homeland of the Jews. Since then it has been ruled by many powers, including the Romans, Arabs and Turks. After World War I Palestine was administered by Britain under a League of Nations mandate until the state of Israel was born in 1948. During the war that followed almost 600 000 Palestinian Arabs fled from their homes. In 1994 the ▷PLO, which had for many years campaigned for the rights of Palestinians, was granted limited powers of government over the GAZA STRIP, which had been occupied by Israel since 1967.

Panama Small, narrow Central American country cut into two by the ▷PANAMA CANAL. In 1989 US troops invaded the country to overthrow the regime of General Manuel Noriega, whom the US accused of drug-trafficking on a huge scale and who was later sentenced to 40 years' imprisonment. The capital is Panama City.

Papua New Guinea Pacific country northeast of Australia, made up of the mountainous mainland – the eastern half of New Guinea – and many islands. The country's rain forests are home to a wide range of animals, including birds of paradise and giant butterflies. It achieved independence from Australia in 1975. The capital is Port Moresby.

Paraguay Landlocked South American country. Nearly all Paraguayans live in the east of the country, especially around the capital, Asuncion; very few people live in the west, amid the dry forest and thorny scrubland of the Gran Chaco. In 1954 General Alfredo Stroessner seized power and ran a fascist dictatorship until he was ousted by a coup in 1989. The country's first free elections were held in 1993.
❖ Josef Mengele – the Nazi 'Angel of Death' who conducted grotesque medical experiments at the Auschwitz concentration camp – lived in hiding in Paraguay until his death in 1978.

CLASSIC CLASH *The Pyramide entrance to the Louvre, designed by the Chinese American I M Pei, was built in 1989 despite misgivings about a stylistic clash with the 16th-century building.*

Paris Elegant capital of France on the River Seine. One of the world's major tourist centres, its attractions include: the ▷EIFFEL TOWER; the Arc de Triomphe and Champs Elysées; the Gothic ▷NOTRE DAME Cathedral, begun in 1163; the white-domed Sacre Coeur on top of the artists' hill, Montmartre; the ▷POMPIDOU CENTRE; the Louvre museum, which houses the *Mona Lisa* and the ▷VENUS DE MILO; and its many pavement cafés. Many of the city's boulevards and parks date from the 1850s and 1860s. It has attracted artists, musicians and writers for centuries and is still the centre of the fashion industry. At the start of the ▷FRENCH REVOLUTION rebels stormed the city's Bastille fortress on 14 July 1789. In World War II German forces occupied Paris unchallenged: in a bid to prevent destruction, the French government had declared it an open city. It was liberated by the Allies in August 1944.

Pennsylvania State in the eastern USA named after its founder, William Penn. The capital is Harrisburg, but the largest city is Philadelphia, where the ▷DECLARATION OF INDEPENDENCE from Britain was signed in 1776.

Persian Gulf (Arabian Gulf, or simply The Gulf) Arm of the Indian Ocean, surrounded by oil-producing countries. The Persian Gulf is linked to the Gulf of Oman by the Strait of Hormuz, and is an important shipping lane. The ▷GULF WAR took place in 1991.

Perth Sunny capital of Western Australia. It was named after the Scottish county of Perth, birthplace of Sir George Murray, Britain's secretary of state for the colonies when the city was founded in 1829. It is the commercial and cultural centre of the state and produces textile, furniture and vehicles.
❖ Perth is the world's most isolated major city; SYDNEY is a four-hour flight away.

Peru South American country with high peaks in the Andes and hot, wet, forested lowlands. The capital is Lima. Peru was the home of the ▷INCAS before their empire fell to the Spanish conquistadores in the 1530s. It became independent in 1824. Half of all Peruvians are Amerindians, some of whom live at high altitudes, herding alpacas for their wool and using llamas as beasts of burden. The Maoist Shining Path organization conducted a violent terrorist campaign in Peru in

LEANING TOWER *The remarkable 55 m high bell tower of Pisa's cathedral started to lean even before it was finished, in 1174.*

the 1970s and 1980s; the group's leader, Abimael Guzman, was imprisoned in 1992.

Philippines Southeast Asian country made up of more than 7 000 islands which are subject to earthquakes, volcanic eruptions and typhoons. About half of all Filipinos work on the land. The country is named after King Philip II of Spain, and was ruled by Spain for more than three centuries. Ferdinand Marcos ruled the Philippines for two decades, aided by his wife Imelda, who was known for her large collection of shoes. An election in 1986 swept Corazon (Cory) Aquino to power. She was succeeded in 1992 by Fidel Ramos, an army general who had remained loyal to her government through several failed coups. The capital is Manila.

❖ The paper used to make Manila envelopes was originally made from the fibre of a plant grown in the Philippines.

Pisa Italian city on the River Arno in Tuscany, whose leaning tower is a major tourist attraction. ▷GALILEO, the astronomer and mathematician, born in Pisa in 1564, is reputed to have used the tower to show that objects fall at the same rate whatever their mass. In Roman times Pisa was a port, but silting of the river has left it 10 km inland.

Poland Central European country whose borders have moved many times. At the end of the 18th century Poland was divided between Russia, Prussia and Austria, and it regained sovereignty only in 1918. Its invasion by Germany in 1939 sparked World War II, during which 6 million Poles, half of them Jews, were killed. Many of them died in Auschwitz concentration camp; others died in the ▷KATYN MASSACRE. The capital, WARSAW, and the historic city of Cracow are both on the Vistula – Poland's longest river. In 1980, strikes in the shipbuilding city of Gdansk led to the formation of Solidarity, headed by Lech Walesa. Multiparty elections were held in 1989, ending more than 40 years of communist rule.

❖ In 1978 Cardinal Karol Wojtyla of Cracow became Pope John Paul II, the first pope since 1523 not to be an Italian.

❖ Notable Poles include the astronomer ▷COPERNICUS; Marie ▷CURIE, who discovered radium; and the composer, ▷CHOPIN.

Polynesia Largest of three groups of islands in the Pacific Ocean; the others are Melanesia and Micronesia. The Polynesian islands are scattered between New Zealand, Easter Island and the Hawaiian islands, and include TAHITI, TONGA and Western Samoa. New Zealand's Maoris are Polynesians. Melanesia means 'black islands' and refers to the inhabitants' dark skins; the people of the Solomon Islands, New Guinea and Fiji are predominantly Melanesians. The MARSHALL ISLANDS and Kiribati (formerly the Gilbert Islands) are part of Micronesia.

Portugal Country on the Iberian Peninsula's Atlantic coast. Around the coast, fishermen catch sardines, tuna and anchovies, and fish canning is an important industry. The warm climate and sandy beaches of the Algarve, in the far south, attract holidaymakers. In the 15th century Prince Henry the Navigator (1394-1460) encouraged early explorers; Vasco da ▷GAMA and Bartolomeu ▷DIAS made notable voyages, and the Portuguese were the first Europeans to reach China and Japan by sea. In 1500 the Portuguese reached BRAZIL, which they governed until 1822. Two African countries, ANGOLA and ▷MOZAMBIQUE, later became part of their empire. During the 20th century Portugal was ruled for more than 40 years by right-wing dictators – António Salazar (1933-68) and Marcello Caetano – until a military coup in 1974, which led eventually to the restoration of democratic government. The capital is LISBON.

❖ Portuguese wines include *vinho verde* and port, named after the city of Oporto.

Prague Capital of the Czech Republic. The 14th-century Charles Bridge, lined with statues, crosses the Vltava River. On one side of the river, the castle, cathedral and royal palace crown Hradčany hill. On the other side are the town hall, with its 15th-century astronomical clock, and Wenceslas Square, a broad boulevard with a statue of St Wenceslas on horseback. Since the collapse of communism in 1989 Prague has attracted many more tourists.

Puerto Rico Fertile, mountainous Caribbean island to the east of Hispaniola. Puerto Rico's predominantly Spanish-speaking inhabitants who have been US citizens since 1917, have been given the option of becoming the 51st US state, of retaining the country's status as a self-governing commonwealth or of becoming a fully independent country. The capital is San Juan.

Punjab, India Prosperous Indian state where most of the country's Sikhs live. The city of AMRITSAR contains the holiest Sikh shrine, the Golden Temple.

Punjab, Pakistan Province that is mostly flat and crossed by several great rivers that supply water for irrigation; the main crop is wheat. It was part of the pre-independence Indian province of Punjab, which in 1947 was divided between Pakistan and India. Nearly all the inhabitants are Muslims.

Pyrenees Mountain range lying between France and Spain and rising to 3 404 m at Pico de Aneto. The tiny Catalan-speaking state of ANDORRA is in the eastern Pyrenees; the Basque people live in the western Pyrenees, in both Spain and France.

Quebec Canada's largest province. The far north is a treeless frozen tundra; much of the remainder is covered with forest broken by lakes. Most people live in the south, along the St Lawrence River. More than 80 per cent of the population of Quebec are French speakers, many of whom have been pressing for self-government. The largest city is MONTREAL. The provincial capital is Quebec City, founded in 1608 by French settlers.

Red Sea Long, narrow arm of the Indian Ocean and a major trade route, linked to the Mediterranean Sea by the Suez Canal.

❖ The Red Sea's name comes from occasional blooms of algae which turn the sea a reddish-brown colour. It is also known for its colourful underwater life.

Reykjavík Capital of Iceland, said to have been founded by Viking settlers in AD 874. Buildings in Reykjavík are heated by hot water piped from nearby volcanic springs, which also give the city its name, which means 'smoking bay'.

Rhine European river flowing north from Switzerland to the North Sea. Barges carry freight – mainly iron ore, coal and oil – along the Rhine. The river was once heavily polluted, but this has been reduced since the mid-1970s. As it flows towards Bonn, the Rhine passes through a gorge with vineyards and castles on its slopes. Basle and Cologne are also on the Rhine.

❖ The Lorelei rock rises above the Rhine gorge. In German legend, the rock was the home of a nymph whose singing lured boatmen to their deaths.

Rhodes Largest of the Greek Dodecanese islands, off Turkey's southwest coast. The Colossus of Rhodes – a 33 m statue of the sun god Helios – was one of the Seven Wonders of the Ancient World. From the 13th to the 16th century, Rhodes was the headquarters of the Knights of St John, a Christian order established to care for pilgrims and the sick which took on a military role during the ▷CRUSADES. The island attracts many tourists.

Rhône European river flowing south from Switzerland to its delta in the Mediterranean Sea, via Lake Geneva (Lac Léman) and Lyons. The Camargue, a region of marshes, lagoons and farmland known for the black bulls and small white horses that live here, is in the Rhône delta. Vineyards on the Rhône's hilly banks south of Lyons are the source of Côtes-du-Rhône wines.

Rio de Janeiro Spectacularly sited Brazilian city, overlooked by the Sugar Loaf Mountain and Corcovado, crowned with a statue of Christ with outstretched arms. Large numbers of tourists visit the wide, sandy beaches of Copacabana and Ipanema, and also the colourful carnival which takes place just before Lent every year. Shanty towns climb the city's steep slopes. Rio was Brazil's capital city until 1960, when the new city of BRASÍLIA became the capital.

Riviera Region along the Mediterranean coast from Hyères in southeast France to La Spezia in Italy, known for its trendy resorts of Monte Carlo, Nice, Cannes and St Tropez.

Rocky Mountains Mountain range, with magnificent scenery and vast forests, that stretches for 4 800 km along the western side of North America, from Mexico to Alaska. The highest point is Mount Elbert (4 399 m) in the US state of Colorado. Areas of particular beauty which are protected from development include Yellowstone National Park in the USA, and Banff National Park in Canada. Bighorn sheep, mountain lions and grizzly bears still live wild in the Rockies.

Romania Former communist country in Eastern Europe. The forested Carpathian Mountains sweep in an arc around Transylvania, the setting for the story of ▷DRACULA. Moldavia, the northeast region of Romania, has monasteries with exterior wall paintings that date from the 16th century. The River Danube reaches the Black Sea in Romania, and its delta has abundant wildlife. Many tourists visit the Black Sea coast. Romania's ruthless dictator, President Nicolae ▷CEAUSESCU, was shot with his wife Elena on Christmas Day 1989 after a short revolution that started in Timisoara, in western Romania. BUCHAREST, the capital, is on a plain in the south.

Rome Italy's capital on the River Tiber. Modern Rome spreads well beyond the seven hills on which the ancient city was built after it was founded in the 8th century BC, supposedly by the mythical ▷ROMULUS AND REMUS. Surviving relics of the time when the so-called Eternal City was the capital of the Roman Empire include the Colosseum, where gladiators fought and Christians were thrown to the lions; the Forum, which was the centre of government; and the ▷PANTHEON, a temple dedicated to all the gods. Many of Rome's palaces and churches date from the 16th and 17th centuries. ▷ST PETER'S BASILICA is part of the VATICAN CITY, a walled state within the city.

Rotterdam The largest city in the Netherlands, with a population of nearly 600 000, and the world's largest and busiest port. Europoort, the western part of the city's port and industrial complex, was created in 1958 as 'the Gateway to Europe'. It can berth the world's largest bulk carriers of oil, ore and grain. The main port of entry to the ▷EU (European Union), about 32 000 ships call at Rotterdam every year.

Russia World's largest country, nearly as big as Canada and the USA combined and stretching almost halfway round the globe. Russia is home to some 75 different ethnic groups, although Russians make up more than 80 per cent of the population. The Russian language is written in the Cyrillic alphabet. The second biggest group of people are the Tatars, who are Muslims. MOSCOW, the capital, ST PETERSBURG and almost all the other major cities lie west of the Ural Mountains. Few people live east of the Urals, in SIBERIA. The far north of Russia is a frozen, treeless wilderness dotted with lakes and bogs, and much of the remainder of the country is covered with vast tracts of forest. Almost all of Russia has intensely cold winters, and in the centre of the country January temperatures regularly fall below -40°C. Moscow rose to prominence in the 14th and 15th centuries, when its grand prince effectively became Russia's leader. Grand Prince Ivan, known as ▷IVAN THE GREAT, greatly strengthened Moscow's position, and it was his grandson, ▷IVAN THE TERRIBLE (1533-84), who first took the title of tsar. In the following years nobles were given land and the services of peasants in return for obedience to the tsar. Serfdom was established in 1649. ▷PETER THE GREAT (1682-1725) introduced Western ways and built the capital of St Petersburg. His reforms were continued by ▷CATHERINE THE GREAT (1762-96). Serfdom was abolished in 1861, but a huge gulf remained between the peasants, who made up the vast majority, and the elite. A revolution in 1905 resulted in the introduction of the Duma, or parliament, but

CITY GUARDIAN *Since 1931 the 30 m statue of Christ the Redeemer has kept watch over Rio de Janeiro from the 710 m summit of Corcovado, known locally as the 'Hunchback'.*

continued unrest and the rigours of World War I led in 1917 to the abdication of Tsar ▷NICHOLAS II and the ▷RUSSIAN REVOLUTION. A communist state was subsequently set up after a devastating civil war, when Joseph ▷STALIN began a dictatorship that ended only after World War II. With the break-up of the USSR in 1991 the Russian Federation, set up in 1922, lost most of its member states. It still consists, however, of 21 independent republics and autonomous regions or districts, and is the largest member of the ▷CIS (Commonwealth of Independent States). The first president of the new state of Russia was Boris ▷YELTSIN.

Rwanda and Burundi Two Central African countries in which hundreds of thousands of people have been massacred in conflict between the Hutu majority and their former Tutsi overlords. In both countries, administered by Belgium until the early 1960s, the Tutsi, a tall people originating in Uganda and Ethiopia, had dominated the shorter Hutus in a feudal system dating from the 16th century. In 1959 a Hutu uprising overthrew the Tutsi hierarchy in Rwanda and the conflict soon spread to Burundi. In the years of fighting and political instability that followed, both sides were accused of atrocities and the attempted genocide of their ancient enemies. In April 1994 the Hutu presidents of both Rwanda and Burundi were killed in an aircraft allegedly shot down by Tutsis. A new campaign of mass slaughter by Hutu death squads erupted in both countries, while 2 million refugees fled into disease-ridden camps in neighbouring countries, where thousands died. In July 1994 a Tutsi-led movement gained control of Rwanda and early in 1995 Tutsis massacred thousands of Hutus in a refugee camp. Between 1956 and 1995 about 500 000 people were estimated to have been killed in Rwanda and 2 – 5 million people became refugees as a result of the conflict.

ROAD WAYS *Lights outline the 1 280 m long Golden Gate Bridge of San Francisco, and cable cars (inset) climb the steep streets.*

Sahara Desert in north Africa, the world's biggest, almost as large as the USA. Sand dunes cover only about 15 per cent of the Sahara, and much of the rest is bare rock or gravel. The highest mountains, the Tibesti, rise to more than 3 350 m; the lowest point is in Egypt's Qattara Depression, 133 m below sea level. In summer, ground temperatures can reach 70°C and most places receive less than 125 mm of rain a year. Saharan peoples include the Tuareg and the Berbers. The desert has substantial deposits of oil and other minerals.

❖ Deep in the Sahara, on the Tassili N'Ajjer plateau, rock paintings more than 6 000 years old show elephants and cattle, indicating that the land was once fertile.

St Helena Remote, mountainous island, only 122 km² in area, in the South Atlantic Ocean, 1 930 km west of Africa's southwest coast. It is a British colony whose dependencies include ASCENSION ISLAND and TRISTAN DA CUNHA. St Helena has no airport. The Royal Mail ship *St Helena* calls only every second month on a round trip from England to South Africa, which includes Ascension Island – and, once a year, Tristan da Cunha.

❖ Napoleon I was exiled to St Helena from 1815 until his death in 1821. Boer prisoners were held here during the South African War.

St Petersburg Grand Russian city with wide avenues, many canals and bridges, and neoclassical baroque buildings. St Petersburg was founded in 1703 by Tsar ▷PETER THE GREAT, who wanted to open a 'Window on the West' and bring European culture to Russia. It was built on marshy islands in the River Neva delta by large gangs of forced labour. Russia's capital from 1712 to 1918, it was known as Petrograd from 1914 to 1924 and then Leningrad until 1991, when its name reverted to St Petersburg. Nevsky Prospekt is the city's main shopping street. The Russian Revolution began in St Petersburg in 1917 and during World War II more than a million people died here during a siege by German and Finnish forces.

❖ The composer Peter Ilyich ▷TCHAIKOVSKY, the goldsmith Carl ▷FABERGÉ and the ballerina Anna ▷PAVLOVA all worked in St Petersburg. The ▷KIROV BALLET is based in the city.

Salzburg Austrian city whose castle, the 11th-century Hohensalzburg, crowns a craggy hill and overlooks the towers and domes of the city's many churches. A world-renowned music festival is held here every summer.

❖ The city's music academy is called the Mozarteum after ▷MOZART, who was born in Salzburg in 1756.

❖ The musical and film *The Sound of Music* were based on the story of Maria von Trapp, who was a postulant in the Nonnberg Abbey, situated near the castle.

San Francisco Hilly and sometimes foggy city in California, standing on the tip of a peninsula between the Pacific Ocean and San Francisco Bay. The ▷GOLDEN GATE BRIDGE spans the bay's entrance. San Francisco lies on the San Andreas Fault and was almost destroyed by an earthquake in 1906. A severe earthquake in 1989 caused much less damage, partly because newer buildings had been constructed to withstand earthquakes. In the late 1960s and early 1970s the city was adopted by ▷HIPPIES as the centre for 'flower power'. Tourists flock to San Francisco to ride on the cable cars that climb the steep streets, to visit the seafood restaurants and to wander around its Chinatown.

❖ Alcatraz, a rocky island in San Francisco Bay, was a prison from 1861 to 1963; the gangster Al Capone was one of its inmates.

San Marino Tiny country, dating from the 13th century, surrounded by Italy. It is only 62 km² in area and has a population of about 23 000. The capital, also called San Marino, is a walled town with towers and ramparts built on a steep hill. Much of the country's revenue comes from the sale of stamps and duty-free goods.

São Paulo Brazilian city, the largest in South America and one of the largest in the world, with more than 10 million inhabitants. It has attracted people from several countries, and many Paulistas, as the citizens are called, are of German, Japanese and Italian descent. Its prosperous centre has impressive skyscrapers, but it also has extensive slums.

Sarajevo Capital of Bosnia-Herzegovina, which was formerly part of Yugoslavia. The assassination in the city in 1914 of Archduke ▷FRANZ FERDINAND, heir to the Austro-Hungarian throne, sparked off World War I. The city was heavily shelled during fighting in the civil war of the early 1990s.

Saudi Arabia Desert kingdom with vast reserves of oil; its capital is Riyadh. The prophet ▷MUHAMMAD was born in the western city of ▷MECCA, and Saudi Arabia's legal system is based on Islamic law; alcohol is forbidden, for non-Muslims as well as Muslims, and theft and adultery are severely punished. Turks ruled the land from the early 16th century. In 1902 Ibn Saud started a campaign to free the land from Turkish rule and unite the tribes of Arabia. He became king of the new state of Saudi Arabia in 1932. During World War I Lawrence of Arabia helped in the campaign against the Turks. Nearly all the country is harsh desert; the Rub al-Khali, or Empty Quarter, in the south of the country is particularly forbidding.

Scotland Northern part of Britain and constituent country of the United Kingdom. Its original inhabitants were Picts, called *picti* by the Romans because they painted or tattooed their bodies. But the country took its name from Scots, a Celtic people who came from Northern Ireland and settled here in the 5th and 6th centuries AD. They were later joined by Scandinavians. The kingdom of Scotland was formed in the 9th century and united with England in 1707. Its capital is EDINBURGH and main industrial cities are GLASGOW, Aberdeen and Dundee.

Senegal Predominantly Muslim country that was France's first West African colony and has retained its French character, French being the official language. It gained independence in 1960 and since 1974 has had a multiparty system, dominated by the socialist party of President Abdou Diouf. Diouf was re-elected in 1993 for a third five-year term. Drought and famine in the 1970s and 1980s were a setback to its economic development and it remains heavily dependent on food imports and international aid. Although the country has been relatively stable politically, there have been violent clashes between government troops and secessionist forces in the south. Its modern capital, Dakar, is one of West Africa's largest industrial centres, and an important cultural centre.

Seoul Capital of South Korea. The city has risen from the ashes of the 1950-3 Korean War, when it was largely destroyed and its population shrank dramatically. Now Seoul is a bustling modern high-rise metropolis with thriving industry, appalling traffic congestion and a population of nearly 10 million. Seoul hosted the Olympic Games in 1988.

Serbia Formerly the largest and most populous state of Yugoslavia, with two autonomous regions: Vojvodina, which was once part of Hungary, and Kosovo, which is predominantly Albanian. The capital of this mountainous land is BELGRADE, on the River Danube. In the Middle Ages Serbia was the dominant state in the Balkans. It was then ruled by Ottoman Turks until it became independent in 1878. After the break-up of Yugoslavia in 1991-2, Serbia and Montenegro claimed to be the successor state to Yugoslavia, and Serbia pursued aggressively expansionist plans in Bosnia and CROATIA, which led to international sanctions.

Serengeti Plain Vast area of northern Tanzania. Huge herds of wildebeest, zebras and gazelles live in the Serengeti and follow the rains to new grazing grounds. Part of the plain is a national park covering 14 500 km².

Severn Britain's longest river, which rises in Wales and meanders for 354 km through the cities of Shrewsbury, Worcester and Gloucester, and into the Bristol Channel. The birthplace of the ▷INDUSTRIAL REVOLUTION was at Ironbridge Gorge on the River Severn in Shropshire. At Coalbrookdale in 1709 Abraham Darby revolutionized ironmaking by smelting iron ore with coke and in 1779 the world's first cast-iron bridge was built across the gorge. The Ironbridge Gorge Museum includes a completely reconstructed 19th-century industrial town.

Seville Main city of Andalucía on the Guadalquivir River in southern Spain. Muslim Moors lived here from the 8th to the 13th century, and Moorish architecture survives in the narrow twisting streets of the old town and in the Alcázar fortress and palace begun in 1181. Seville's 15th-century cathedral, where Christopher Columbus is said to be buried, is built on the site of a mosque. The Giralda bell tower next to it was one of the mosque's minarets.

Seychelles Scattered group of 115 tropical islands in the Indian Ocean with idyllic, palm-fringed beaches. The islands became an independent republic in 1976 after 162 years of British rule. Most of its people, descendants of French settlers and African slaves from Mauritius, live on Mahé, which is more than 1 800 km east of Mombasa on the Kenyan coast. The isolated islands have several unique species of plants, birds and animals, including giant turtles that used to be slaughtered for their tortoiseshell. Since an

MODERN HERITAGE *The ornate buildings round Seville's Plaza de España belie appearances. They do not date from the city's distant past but were built for the Spanish-American Fair of 1929.*

international airport was built at Mahé in 1971 the Seychelles have become a popular tourist resort, particularly for South Africans.

Shanghai China's largest city and main port, with a population of more than 12 million. In 1842 Shanghai was one of the first Chinese ports opened to foreign trade. People from Britain, France, America and Japan made it a major trade and finance centre and built impressive European-style banks, hotels and business premises. In the 1930s Shanghai was noted for both its wealth and its decadence. Today it is an important manufacturing centre.

❖ Shanghai's Yu Yuan Garden of Happiness is the model for the design on 'willow pattern' chinaware.

Siberia Extensive, inhospitable region of tundra, swamps and forests in eastern Russia. Siberian winters are exceptionally severe: in the Yakut region of eastern Siberia, January temperatures average -43°C, and have fallen to a Northern Hemisphere record of -70°C. Yet in summer the temperatures rise to 19°C. The region's enormous mineral wealth includes coal, oil and gas, and also diamonds, iron ore and gold. Siberia has been a place of enforced exile for political prisoners and criminals, especially during the Stalin era; The dissident writer Alexandr ▷SOLZHENITSYN was interned in Siberia during the 1940s and 1950s and graphically described his experiences in his novel *One Day in the Life of Ivan Denisovich.*

Sicily Largest of the Mediterranean islands, at the tip of the Italian 'boot'. Mount Etna, Europe's largest and most active volcano, is at the eastern end of the island; repeated eruptions – most recently in 1991-2 – vary its height of around 3 323 m. The capital is Palermo. The ▷MAFIA originated in Sicily.

Siena Beautiful medieval city in Tuscany, central Italy. Siena's central square, the Piazza del Campo, is surrounded by historic buildings that include a massive 13th-century palace, the Palazzo Pubblico. The Palio horse race takes place in the city streets each summer, with the riders and their mounts decked in medieval regalia.

Sierra Leone Former British colony that developed around its capital Freetown, which began as a place of settlement for Africans freed from slave ships by the British navy in the 18th and 19th centuries. The liberated slaves became one of the most highly educated and influential elites in West Africa. After independence in 1961 their political dominance waned. The country became involved in the civil warfare in neighbouring Liberia in the 1980s and a military government took over in 1992, installing a 27-year-old army captain, Valentine Strasser, as president.

Sierra Nevada Range of magnificent mountains in the western USA, mainly in east California. The Sierra Nevada's highest point, the 4 418 m Mount Whitney, rises above the Sequoia National Park, where the world's biggest tree – named after General William Sherman – stands 83,8 m high and measures 31,4 m round the base. Yosemite National Park is also in the Sierra Nevada. Gold was discovered in the mountains in 1848 and attracted thousands of prospectors.

Silicon Valley Area of western California, USA, between Palo Alto and San José. It is named after the silicon chips used in the electronics and computing industries, of which it is a major centre.

Sinai Desert peninsula of Egypt, between the two northern arms of the Red Sea. The Bible describes how Moses was leading the Israelites out of Egypt when he received the Ten Commandments at Mount Sinai, thought to be the 2 285 m Jebel Musa. After the formation of Israel in 1948, Sinai became a region of conflict between Arabs and Jews; it was occupied by Israel in 1967 and returned to Egypt in 1982.

Singapore Hot, prosperous island country, covering only 632 km^2 (less than a third of the size of Gauteng), comprising 60 islands off the tip of Malaysia's mainland peninsula. Formerly the UK's biggest Far East naval base, it gained self-government in 1959, briefly joined the Federation of Malaysia, then became an independent republic in 1965. Densely populated Singapore is a major international port and business centre. It is a strictly regulated country which has almost entirely eliminated unemployment, poor housing and illiteracy. It has few natural resources; its success can be attributed to its strategic position and its industrious and highly disciplined population, who are now considered to be among the richest in Southeast Asia. The capital, Singapore City, has many gleaming glass-and-concrete skyscrapers. Chinese people make up about 75 per cent of the population, Malays 14 per cent and Indians 7 per cent.

Slovakia Central European country that came into being on 1 January 1993 after Czechoslovakia split into the CZECH REPUBLIC and Slovakia. The capital, Bratislava, is on the Danube. The High Tatras in the north, rising to 2 655 m, attracts many tourists.

Slovenia Small central European country, formerly the most prosperous republic of Yugoslavia. It became an independent country in 1992 with Ljubljana as the capital. Tourists visit Slovenia's mountains and Lake Bled in the Julian Alps.

Somalia Country extending round the easternmost tip of Africa whose extreme poverty has been aggravated by repeated droughts and years of war between rival clans. The capital is Mogadishu. In colonial times the northern part was occupied by Britain and the southern by Italy. The two territories were joined to form an independent republic in 1960. Its president Mohammed Siad Barre, who had ruled tyrannically after seizing power in a military coup in 1969, was ousted in 1991 after three years of civil war. Fighting continued among various groupings of about 14 factions and there was large-scale looting of international food aid for the drought-stricken country. In December 1992 a UN peacekeeping force was deployed to disarm the warring factions and ensure that food reached 4,5 million famine victims. This intervention failed to end the fighting and the peacekeepers, 70 of whom had been killed, withdrew early in 1995 with the country still in political disarray. In 1991 the north of Somalia broke away and declared itself the Somaliland Republic.

South Korea East Asian country that since the early 1960s has changed from an agricultural society into a major industrial power. The ▷KOREAN WAR (1950-3) left the country exhausted, but now textiles, cars, electronic goods and ships are produced efficiently and cheaply. Industry is concentrated in the densely populated northwest – centred on the capital SEOUL – and in the south; few people live in the forested mountains of the east.

Southampton British city and port on the south coast of England. The port dates from Roman times but its importance grew in the 19th century with the development of its docks. It eventually became the point of departure for the great transatlantic liners, such as the ill-fated ▷TITANIC, the *Queen Mary* and the mailships to South Africa. Since the decline of ocean travel parts of the docklands have been transformed into opulent housing and business complexes.

Spain Large country with many distinctive regions, occupying most of the Iberian Peninsula and separated from France by the PYRENEES. Spain's sunny coastline has made it the most popular holiday destination in Europe, with more than 40 million tourists arriving every year. Away from the busy coastline is a mostly dry, often mountainous country, cut through by valleys and gorges. Muslim Moors conquered most of Spain in the 8th century. Christians started to reconquer it in the 11th century, and the Moors were finally driven out in 1492, the year in which the Italian-born Christopher ▷COLUMBUS sailed under a Spanish flag to North America. Spanish conquistadors and explorers followed him, and by the 1560s Spain's New World empire extended from Argentina to California. Spain's power began to decline after England defeated the Spanish ▷ARMADA in 1588. The ▷THIRTY YEARS WAR (1618-48) and wars with France proved equally disastrous for Spain. In 1701, further conflict, involving England, the Netherlands, a number of German states and Austria against France, broke out over the question of succession to the Spanish throne. It was only in 1713 that peace was concluded. Napoleon's bid to conquer Europe in the early 1800s caused further upheaval in Spain, with British, Spanish and Portuguese soldiers taking on the French army and turning the country into a battlefield. The early 1800s also saw Spain losing a number of its Latin American colonies, including Argentina (1810), Paraguay (1811), Peru and Mexico (1821). The ▷SPANISH CIVIL WAR of 1936-9 was followed by the dictatorship of General Francisco ▷FRANCO, which ended with his death in 1975, when democracy was restored with King Juan Carlos on the throne. Spain's capital, MADRID, is in Castile, the heart of the country. Its second city, BARCELONA, is in hilly Catalonia, part of whose coast is the Costa Brava. Farther south are Valencia and the resort of Benidorm. The southern part of Spain is Andalucía, the land of flamenco dancers, bullfights, Moorish architecture and the Costa del Sol; its biggest city is SEVILLE. In the western Pyrenees live the Basques, whose separatist militant wing, the ETA, has waged a campaign of murder and bombings. La Rioja, south of the Basque country, produces Spain's best table wines. Galicia and Asturias, in the northwest, are green, fertile areas.

❖ The CANARY ISLANDS and the Balearic Islands – Majorca, Minorca, Ibiza, Formentera and Cabrera – are part of Spain.

❖ Paella, one of Spain's best-loved dishes, is made from rice flavoured with saffron and shellfish, chicken and vegetables .

CIVILIZATIONS *Before Europeans arrived in the Americas the Maya flourished in Mexico, Guatemala and Honduras, the later Aztecs in Mexico and the Incas in the northern Andes.*

Sri Lanka Island country shaped like a teardrop off the southern tip of India. Tea, rubber and coconut are among Sri Lanka's main exports. Colombo, the capital, has European-style buildings that date from the time of British rule, when the country was called Ceylon. The Sinhalese, who make up 75 per cent of the population, are mostly Buddhists; Tamils – 18 per cent of Sri Lankans – are mostly Hindus and live mainly in the north. Tension between Sinhalese and Tamils has led to violence.

❖ Sri Lanka had the world's first woman prime minister, Sirimavo Bandaranaike (1960-5 and 1970-7).

❖ One of Sri Lanka's former names is Serendip, from which the word serendipity – the faculty of making happy discoveries by accident – was later coined by the English writer Horace Walpole.

Stockholm Clean, graceful and beautifully sited capital of Sweden, spanning several islands. In the Old Town are 16th and 17th-century buildings, the Royal Palace and the Parliament building, which stands on its own island. The City Hall has a massive square tower and a Golden Hall whose walls are clad in gilded mosaic tiles.

❖ Nobel prizes, founded by the Swedish chemist Alfred ▷NOBEL (1833-96), are awarded in Stockholm, except for the peace prize, which is awarded in Oslo.

Strasbourg Historic French city only 4 km from the border with Germany. It is the headquarters of the Council of Europe; sessions of the European Parliament are also held here.

IDYLLIC ISLAND *Tahiti, the original South Sea paradise, rises from a ring of coral atolls in the Pacific. Traditional lifestyles (inset) are being eroded by tourism and the motor car.*

Sudan Africa's largest country, crossed by the Nile. Muslim Arabs live in the north, and black Africans speaking many different languages live in the south. World attention has focused on the Sudan in recent years as a result of its major drought, famine and civil war. It has also had a huge influx of refugees fleeing famine and war in Ethiopia, Eritrea and Chad. The capital is Khartoum.

Sweden North European kingdom with many forests, lakes, waterfalls and rivers. The forests provide the raw material for factories which produce all kinds of wood products. Sweden is also known for the clean design of its furniture, glass and cutlery. The arctic north has heavy snow for eight months of the year and the temperatures here can fall to -40°C. Most people live in the south, especially around the capital, STOCKHOLM. The standard of living is generally very high, but so are taxes. Sweden last fought a war in 1814. It remained neutral in both world wars.
❖ Smörgåsbord is a buffet meal of fish (especially herring), meat, salads and cheese.

Swindon Town in Wiltshire, England, that became important after the 19th-century railway boom, when Isambard Kingdom ▷BRUNEL made it the headquarters of his Great Western Railway. Swindon grew again between 1960 and 1980 when many companies moved here to take advantage of its good road and rail communications. It also became the home of Galileo, the international airways reservations computer centre.

Switzerland Mountainous country in the Alps. Switzerland's many magnificent peaks include the Eiger, the Jungfrau and the Matterhorn on the Italian border, all of which are more than 3 960 m high. The capital of this prosperous and efficient country is BERN, but the biggest cities are Zürich, Basle and GENEVA. Switzerland is made up of 26 cantons. Four languages are spoken: 73 per cent of the people speak German, 20 per cent French, 4 per cent Italian, and fewer than 1 per cent Romansch, a dialect spoken in eastern Switzerland and also in northern Italy. The country is an important financial centre – its code of banking secrecy encourages enormous foreign investment – and is also known for watchmaking and chocolate, and for Gruyère and Emmenthal cheese. Switzerland is not a member of the United Nations, NATO or the European Union, but despite its long-standing political neutrality, every Swiss man is liable for military service.
❖ Swiss women were granted the vote only in 1971. The Swiss constitution allows for national referendums to be held on any legislative issue if requested by a sufficient number of citizens.

Sydney Australia's biggest city and oldest settlement and state capital of New South Wales. The striking ▷SYDNEY OPERA HOUSE, its roof shaped like white sails, stands on the harbour near the broad ▷SYDNEY HARBOUR BRIDGE. British settlers, some of them convicts, arrived in 1788 in Botany Bay, now in the city's suburbs, and made their first settlement very close to the spot where the Opera House now stands. The cosmopolitan city has many beaches, including Bondi Beach, which is renowned for its good surfing and is popular with tourists.
❖ The Olympic Games will be held in Sydney in the year 2000.

Syria Oil-exporting country in the Middle East, extending inland eastwards from the Mediterranean Sea. Away from the coast and the coastal mountains much of the land is arid grassland that turns green after the sparse rain. Nearly all Syrians are Muslims. The capital, DAMASCUS, is one of the world's oldest cities, and Phoenician traders sailed from what is now Syria's coast from about 1200 BC. Crusaders intent on recovering Christian holy places from Muslim control built castles that include the magnificent Krak des Chevaliers in the coastal mountains. Syria has been involved in the conflict between Arab countries and Israel and in 1967 Israel occupied the GOLAN HEIGHTS in Syria's mountainous southwest. Archaeological sites include the ruins of Palmyra, an oasis city destroyed by the Romans in AD 273.

Tahiti South Pacific island nearly 4 000 km northeast of New Zealand's North Island. Tahiti is the largest island of French Polynesia; the capital is Papeete.
❖ Tahiti's idyllic beauty was depicted by the French painter Paul ▷GAUGUIN, who lived here from 1895 to 1901.

Taiwan Island off China's southeast coast. In the late 1940s, 2 million Chinese supporters of ▷CHIANG KAI-SHEK's Nationalist Party fled to Taiwan from ▷MAO ZEDONG's communist forces on the mainland. Now the former mainlanders and their descendants make up 15 per cent of the population. Since the 1960s Taiwan has grown rapidly to become a major economic power, exporting electronic goods, clothes, shoes and many other products. It maintained close links with South Africa during the period of anti-apartheid sanctions and remains an important trading partner. Taiwan has luxuriant vegetation and mountains rising to more than 4 000 m. The island was formerly known as Formosa, derived from the description given by Portuguese travellers in the 16th century of *Ilha Formosa* ('Beautiful Island'). The capital is Taipei.

Tanzania East African country that came into being in 1964 when Tanganyika united with the hot, humid island of Zanzibar. Africa's highest mountain, the snow-capped KILIMANJARO, rises in northern Tanzania, and lakes Victoria, Tanganyika and Malawi lie round the country's borders. Much of the interior is dry grassland. Tanzania has abundant wildlife and there are vast national parks and game reserves such as the 18 km wide crater of the extinct Ngorongoro volcano and the Serengeti National Park. Tanzania's first president was Julius Nyerere, who ruled the country until he retired in 1985. In the early 1970s he engineered a costly socialist experiment in which huge numbers of people were moved to new villages that were intended to supply everything necessary for communal agriculture. The country's food production declined sharply and people later drifted back to their original homes. Dodoma has replaced Dar es Salaam as capital.

Tasmania Island off Australia's southeast coast, one of the country's six states. The Dutch explorer Abel Tasman landed a party here in 1642 and named it Van Diemen's Land after the governor general of the Dutch East Indies who had sent him on the voyage. In 1788 the island was annexed to Britain as part of New South Wales; the penal settlement of Port Arthur was established in 1830 and received 12 000 convicts during the 40 years it lasted. The state capital is Hobart.

Tel Aviv-Jaffa Israeli city on the Mediterranean Sea, the country's centre of business and culture. Tel Aviv was founded in the early 20th century by Jewish settlers from the ancient and crowded port of Jaffa – the biblical port of Joppa – and the two settlements have now merged.

Texas Large southern state of the USA, more than half the size of South Africa. Oil has generated wealth in Texas since 1901. The state capital is Austin, but the biggest cities are DALLAS, San Antonio and Houston, which is the headquarters of NASA (the National Aeronautics and Space Administration). Texas was part of Mexico until 1836, when it broke away after a revolution; for a brief while it was an independent republic until it became part of the USA in 1845.

❖ In 1836 the folk hero Davy ▷CROCKETT and 186 other Texans were besieged by the Mexican army in the Alamo, a Spanish mission in San Antonio. All were killed.

Thailand Buddhist kingdom in Southeast Asia, called Siam until 1939, the only country in the region that was never a European colony. King Bhumibol, who has reigned since 1946, is treated with great reverence. The centre of Thailand is a vast expanse of paddy fields. In the north are forested mountains rich in teak, where elephants are used to handle heavy logs in the more difficult country. Main exports include textiles and rubber. Tourists visit the capital BANGKOK – which the Thais call Krung Thep – and resorts such as Ko Samui and Phuket island.

❖ During World War II Thailand was occupied by the Japanese, whose prisoners of war and slave labourers built a railway bridge over the River Kwai in the west of the country. An estimated 65 000 people died while building the bridge and the railway line. The story was told in the 1957 film *The Bridge on the River Kwai*.

Thames River rising in the Cotswolds of England and flowing east for 338 km through Oxford (where it is also known as the Isis), Reading and central London, southeast of which it joins the North Sea in a wide, tidal estuary. Ocean-going ships used to sail up the Thames to dock in the Pool of London in the heart of the city, but today most ships berth at ports such as Tilbury on the river's lower reaches. The Thames flows past so many celebrated historic sites that it has been aptly described as 'liquid history'. Among them are Windsor, which is dominated by Windsor Castle, home of English monarchs for the past 900 years, and Eton, a small town in Berkshire, opposite Windsor, home of Eton College, the world-renowned private boys' school, founded in 1440. At Runnymede, a meadow on the banks of the Thames near Egham in Surrey, King John put his seal on the ▷MAGNA CARTA.

❖ Tower Bridge, the landmark bridge spanning the river next to the Tower of London, has two halves, each weighing 1 000 tons, that can be raised hydraulically to allow large ships to pass through.

Tibet High, remote part of China, making up the Xizang Autonomous Region to the north of the Himalayas. Mount Everest is on the border of Tibet and Nepal. Tibet is often referred to as the roof of the world. Much of it is a virtually uninhabited, windy and bitterly cold plateau, about 4 500 m high. Most people live round the south and east of the plateau, where the climate is milder and the land can be cultivated. Tibet has been part of China at various times in the past and also since a Chinese invasion in 1950. Before that it was ruled from its capital, Lhasa, by a Buddhist priestly aristocracy headed by their spiritual leader, the ▷DALAI LAMA. Many monasteries were destroyed during China's Cultural Revolution.

Tierra del Fuego Group of islands at the extreme south of Argentina and Chile, between which countries they are divided. The Portuguese navigator Ferdinand ▷MAGELLAN saw fires lit by the native peoples as he passed through the strait – named after him – between the main island and the mainland. He called the land Tierra de los Fuegos, meaning 'Land of Fire'; it was later changed to the Spanish equivalent.

Tigris Major river of southwest Asia, flowing for nearly 1 850 km through Turkey, Syria and Iraq. It joins the Euphrates to form the Shatt-al-Arab waterway. Some of the earliest civilizations developed in ▷MESOPOTAMIA between the Tigris and Euphrates; the Assyrian cities of Ashur and Nineveh were on the banks of the Tigris.

Timbuktu West African town on the edge of the Sahara, in central Mali. Timbuktu was founded in the 11th century and quickly became a major trading centre for salt carried by Saharan caravans and goods traded along the Niger River. Timbuktu's gold and salt were known in Europe in the Middle Ages. The city was also a centre of Islamic teaching. Tribal wars from the 16th century onwards sent it into decline.

Titicaca, Lake South America's largest lake, which is 3 812 m up in the Andes on the border of Bolivia and Peru and surrounded by ice-capped peaks. Remains of the Inca and pre-Inca civilizations survive on the lake's Islands of the Moon and the Sun, as well as at the ancient city of Tiahuanaco to the south. The Uru people live on the lake on vast floating 'islands' made from totora reeds, which they also use to build their houses and boats.

❖ The local people have larger hearts and lungs than normal to cope with the effects of oxygen deficiency at the high altitude.

Togo Small West African country, once a German colony, later administered by France, from which it gained independence in 1960. From 1967 it was ruled by a military regime, which effectively remained in control after a return to constitutional but one-party government in 1980. Political turmoil in the early 1990s led to multiparty elections in February

1994 and the installation of Edem Kodjo, former secretary-general of the Organization of African Unity, as prime minister. Togo's capital, Lomé, has given its name to the Lomé conventions – trade and aid agreements between the EEC and African, Caribbean and Pacific states – the first of which was held here in 1975.

Tokyo Prosperous, crowded, expensive capital of Japan and one of the world's largest cities, with more than 11 million people. Tokyo, formerly Edo, replaced Kyoto as Japan's capital in 1868, when it was given its present name, meaning 'Eastern Capital'. The city has been rebuilt twice this century: first after an earthquake in 1923 which destroyed much of the city, and then after damage during World War II. Now Tokyo is one of the world's major financial centres, with high-rise office buildings constructed to withstand earthquakes. The city's neon-lit Ginza district, not far from the Imperial Palace, has restaurants, night clubs and shops.

Tonga Pacific kingdom made up of 169 coral and volcanic islands, 3 200 km northeast of Sydney, Australia. The British explorer Captain James Cook visited the islands in 1773 and called them the Friendly Islands because of the welcome he received here.

Toronto Canada's biggest city and the capital of the province of Ontario, built on the shores of Lake Ontario. Toronto has the tallest free-standing structure: the 553,4 m CN (Canadian National) Tower, a communications tower with a revolving restaurant 346 m above the ground. Toronto is Canada's business and manufacturing centre, and a cosmopolitan city whose Italian, Chinese, Greek and Portuguese immigrants have created distinctive 'villages' within the city.

Trinidad and Tobago Hot Caribbean island country lying just off the coast of Venezuela. The capital, Port of Spain, is on lively Trinidad, which is by far the larger of the two islands and the home of calypso music and steel bands. Oil has been tapped on Trinidad since 1867 and the revenue makes the islands one of the more prosperous Caribbean countries. Palm-fringed beaches sheltered by coral reefs attract many tourists – especially to the more tranquil Tobago.

Tristan da Cunha Remote, windswept Atlantic Ocean island, 98 km^2 in area and some 2 400 km west of Cape Town. Tristan da Cunha is part of the British dependency of ST HELENA. When the volcano which forms the greater part of the island erupted in 1961 most of the 300-odd inhabitants were taken to Britain and some came to South Africa; but most islanders chose to return two years later.

Tunisia North African country, which in the past has been ruled by many peoples – including Phoenicians, Romans, Byzantines, Arabs and Turks. From 1881 to 1956 Tunisia was a French protectorate. Today it is one of the most Europeanized parts of the Arab world, with a pro-western Islamic society. Every year more than 3,5 million tourists flock to Tunisia for the sun and superb beaches and also to visit the fine Roman remains and the site of ▷CARTHAGE, in a suburb of Tunis, the capital.

Turin North Italian city on the River Po and the first capital of a united Italy (1861-5). The city centre has fine piazzas, a Roman city gate and 17th and 18th-century buildings. It is the home of the Fiat and Lancia cars.

Turkey Country bridging the continents of Europe and Asia, with beautiful coasts, historic sites and fine Islamic architecture. The European part, Thrace, is separated from Anatolia, the considerably larger Asian part, by the narrow Dardanelles and Bosporus straits, and the Sea of Marmara. Remains of ancient civilizations include Catal Huyuk, one of the earliest towns, and the cities of ▷TROY, Ephesus and Pergamum. During World War I Allied troops fought on the beaches of Gallipoli, a peninsula in European Turkey overlooking the Dardanelles. After World War I, Kemal ▷ATATÜRK introduced major reforms to westernize the country. Now many tourists visit Mediterranean and Aegean coastal resorts such as Bodrum and Marmaris. The capital is Ankara, but the largest city is ISTANBUL.

Uganda East African country which, although crossed by the Equator, has a surprisingly temperate climate, since much of the land lies at least 900 m above sea level. The capital is Kampala. Lake Victoria, Africa's largest lake, lies partly in Uganda and is one of the main sources of the Nile, which flows across the country. Four out of five Ugandans work on the land. Since the late 1980s Uganda's economy has begun to recover from more than 20 years of political instability and civil war, and the brutal rule of Idi ▷AMIN, Uganda's leader from 1971 to 1979.

Ukraine Southeast European country, formerly part of the USSR, whose capital is KIEV. The Ukrainian steppes, and especially the 'black earth' land in the west, are intensively cultivated, but Ukraine also has heavy industry, a result of rich deposits of iron ore, coal, gas and oil. In 1986 the ▷CHERNOBYL nuclear

HOMES IN THE ROCK *At Üçhisar, in Cappadocia, central Turkey, soft volcanic rock weathered into an other-worldly landscape has been hollowed out to make homes.*

disaster took place in northern Ukraine. Ukraine's Crimean Peninsula extends into the Black Sea and has many holiday resorts.

United Arab Emirates (UAE) Rich oil-producing federation of Persian Gulf emirates, formed in 1971. The largest emirates are Abu Dhabi and Dubai; the capital is Abu Dhabi City. The coast was once known as the Pirate Coast because Arab pirates preyed on European ships. After a truce arranged by Britain in the 19th century ended piracy, the area became known as the Trucial Coast or Trucial States.

United Kingdom (UK) The world's 17th largest country in terms of its population of about 58 million, but with an area about one-fifth of South Africa. It nevertheless became one of the most powerful nations in the world through its naval and military strength, and – through the vast ▷BRITISH EMPIRE, which at one time dominated a quarter of the world's populations – spread its political, economic and cultural influence across the globe. It is an archipelago of islands stretching from the Shetlands and Orkney in the extreme north to the Isle of Wight and the Channel Islands in the south. Its full name is the United Kingdom of Britain and Northern Ireland, but it is also referred to as Great Britain, or simply Britain, which is the name of the main island, made up of ENGLAND, SCOTLAND and WALES. Wales was merged with England in the 16th century and Scotland in the 17th. Attempts to bring Ireland under Anglo-Norman control, which had begun in the 12th century, finally came to fruition in 1801 when the Act of Union created the United Kingdom. When the southern part of Ireland won its independence from the UK in 1921, six counties in the north, popularly known by the ancient name of Ulster, chose to remain part of the UK. Britain's rich mineral resources, especially coal, tin, iron, and lead, fuelled the ▷INDUSTRIAL REVOLUTION which began in the 18th century. Aiding this development, before the days of railways, were England's abundant rivers and the close proximity of its coastline to the places of manufacture – no place in the country is more than 200 km from the sea. The UK was the world's first highly industrialized and densely urbanized nation. Its prosperity in the heyday of Queen ▷VICTORIA's empire was based on the heavy 'smokestack' industries, such as coal, textiles and shipbuilding, and on the easy availability of a more or less captive imperial market overseas. But two world wars and the world-wide movements for national liberation brought drastic changes. ▷WORLD WAR I left the empire largely intact, with one-quarter of the world's people still under allegiance to the British crown, but its economic ascendancy had begun to fade. ▷WORLD WAR II left it seriously overstretched militarily and financially. By the mid-1960s most of its overseas possessions had won independence. Already a rich mixture of stocks, the country has since 1945 experienced yet another wave of immigration, mostly from the former states of the empire, especially India, Pakistan and the West Indies. In the 1991 census 3 million citizens, or 5,5 per cent of the population, described their ethnic status as not 'white'. The late 20th century has brought a transformation in the British economy. Mining and agriculture have declined, while employment in the booming service industries has doubled in the past 50 years to 73 per cent of the workforce, partly due to the growth of tourism, which in 1994 was the second largest industry, bringing more than 20 million visitors from overseas every year. A great boost to the economy was the discovery in the 1960s of oil and gas reserves in the NORTH SEA. These contributed greatly to the boom years of the 1980s, when the economy grew without interruption for eight years. LONDON is the UK's capital; other important cities are EDINBURGH, CARDIFF, BELFAST, BIRMINGHAM, LIVERPOOL and MANCHESTER.

United States of America (USA) World's fourth largest country, after Russia, Canada and China. It is nearly eight times the size of South Africa. The most populous areas are the eastern seaboard and the California coast. The capital is WASHINGTON DC, but the biggest cities are NEW YORK, LOS ANGELES and CHICAGO. The USA has almost every type of landscape and climate: tundra in Alaska, deserts with tall cacti in Arizona, snow-capped peaks in the Rocky Mountains and rich farmland in the Midwest states south of the GREAT LAKES. The first Americans came from Asia over a land bridge across the Bering Strait about 25 000 years ago. Spaniards explored the south and west of what is now the USA in the early 16th century. The first permanent English settlement was Jamestown, founded in Virginia in 1607. Thirteen years later, the Pilgrim Fathers landed at Plymouth in Massachusetts. Settlement spread rapidly westward, driving ▷NATIVE AMERICAN Indians from their tribal territories. The immigrants who flocked to the 'land of opportunity' were mainly Europeans until the second half of the 20th century, when Asians, Africans and South Americans arrived in larger numbers. On 4 July 1776 the 13 British colonies adopted the ▷DECLARATION OF INDEPENDENCE from Britain which resulted in the formation of the United States of America. In the southern states cotton plantations were worked by African slaves and slavery was a major issue in the ▷AMERICAN CIVIL WAR. After the Civil War the economy grew rapidly, uninterrupted by World War I, until the ▷WALL STREET Crash of 1929 marked the start of the ▷DEPRESSION. After World War II the USA emerged as a superpower. A champion of capitalism, it adopted a policy of opposing communism which led to involvement in the ▷KOREAN WAR (1950-3) and the ▷VIETNAM WAR (1960-75) and also to a campaign, in which Senator Joseph McCarthy was prominent, of accusing citizens of communist sympathies. Today the USA is a republic made up of 50 states and the District of Columbia (Washington's 'DC'); the last states to join were ALASKA in 1867 and HAWAII in 1959. Each state represented in both ▷SENATE and ▷CONGRESS is responsible for making its own laws about, for example, drinking, divorce, gambling and the death penalty, which is retained by 36 states. The ▷DEMOCRATIC and ▷REPUBLICAN parties dominate US politics. Democrat presidents have included Woodrow ▷WILSON, who promoted the idea of a League of Nations, Franklin D ▷ROOSEVELT, whose 'New Deal' brought recovery from the Depression and John F ▷KENNEDY, president at the time of the 1962 ▷CUBAN MISSILE CRISIS. The first great Republican president was Abraham ▷LINCOLN, who led the northern states to victory in the American Civil War. The Republican President Dwight D ▷EISENHOWER was supreme commander of Allied forces in World War II. Richard ▷NIXON improved relations with the USSR and China before resigning over the Watergate scandal in 1974. Bill ▷CLINTON, who beat incumbent George ▷BUSH in the 1992 election, was the first Democrat president for 12 years.

❖ America is named after the Italian explorer Amerigo ▷VESPUCCI.

❖ The US flag – the stars and stripes – has 50 stars representing the present states, and 13 stripes representing the original states.

Uruguay One of the smallest countries in South America, with a predominantly Spanish-speaking population of nearly 3 million, half of whom live in the capital, Montevideo. Independent since 1828, it disintegrated from being a model of democracy and prosperity during most of the 20th century to being a prime example of South American civil warfare, poverty, hyperinflation and repressive military governments. However, that trend has been reversed since the restoration of democracy in 1984.

USSR (Union of Soviet Socialist Republics) Former country that from 1922-91 covered nearly one-sixth of the Earth's land surface, and had inhabitants of more than 100 different nationalities. It was established after the

▷RUSSIAN REVOLUTION nominally as a federation, but in fact MOSCOW, the capital, kept control of all the USSR's constituent republics. Soviet leaders included Vladimir ▷LENIN, Joseph ▷STALIN, Nikita ▷KHRUSHCHEV, Leonid ▷BREZHNEV and Mikhail ▷GORBACHEV. After World War II the ▷COLD WAR developed between the USSR and the West. Gorbachev's appointment as general secretary of the Communist Party in 1985 introduced an era of *glasnost*, or political 'openness', and *perestroika*, or economic 'restructuring' – in effect a liberalization of communist policies. In 1991 one after another of the USSR's 15 republics broke with Moscow, and became the independent countries of Armenia, AZERBAIJAN, Belarus, Estonia, Georgia, KAZAKHSTAN, Kyrgyzstan, Latvia, Lithuania, Moldova, RUSSIA, Tajikistan, Turkmenistan, UKRAINE and UZBEKISTAN. All except Estonia, Latvia and Lithuania became members of the ▷CIS (Commonwealth of Independent States).

Utah State in the western USA which has extraordinary rock formations, including those of Monument Valley where many Western films were shot. The capital, Salt Lake City, was founded in 1847 by ▷MORMONS led by Brigham Young, and is the headquarters of the Mormon Church. Nearby is the Great Salt Lake; land speed records have been set on the Bonneville Salt Flats west of the lake.

Uzbekistan Central Asian country of deserts and plains, formerly part of the USSR. Tashkent, the capital, was rebuilt after an earthquake in 1966. The ancient city of Samarkand, in southern Uzbekistan, was an important place on the Silk Road between China and Europe and in the 14th century became the capital of the Tatar warlord Tamerlane. Uzbeks, who are Muslims, make up 70 per cent of the population; Russians are the country's biggest minority. The Aral Sea is on the northern border of Uzbekistan.

Vancouver Canada's third largest city (after Ottawa and Montreal) and its chief Pacific port, close to the border with the USA. The cultural, commercial and industrial centre of British Columbia, it is the western terminus of the trans-Canadian railways, roads and airways. Its metropolitan area has a population of about 1,5 million.

Vatican City Walled city within Rome, which is the home of the Pope and headquarters of the Roman Catholic Church. It is the world's smallest state, with an area of about 0,5 km² and a population of fewer than 1 000. Many tourists visit the Vatican City to see ▷ST PETER'S BASILICA and Michelangelo's frescoes in the Sistine Chapel.

MASTERPIECE *In the Vatican City, a shaft of sunlight illuminates the sumptuous interior of St Peter's Basilica. Much of it was designed by Michelangelo, who was appointed architect in 1546.*

Venezuela South American country with oil fields in the north around Lake Maracaibo (a pear-shaped inlet of the sea). The capital is Caracas. Most Venezuelans live along the Caribbean coastline; inland lie the *llanos* – undulating plains where cowboys herd cattle. South of the Orinoco River, and making up about half the country, are the Guiana Highlands whose massive flat-topped mountains loom above lush jungle. The world's highest waterfall, ANGEL FALLS, is in the eastern highlands.

Venice North Italian city, one of the world's great architectural and cultural treasures, built on 118 low islands in a lagoon. The islands are separated by narrow canals and linked by more than 400 bridges. The wider Grand Canal, lined with palaces, winds through the heart of Venice. It is crossed by the late 16th-century Rialto Bridge. Around its Piazza San Marco are St Mark's Basilica, the 99 m high Campanile, and the Doge's Palace, built in the 14th to 15th century as the official residence of the city's elected leader. The Bridge of Sighs spans the canal between the Doge's Palace and the State prison. The city was founded in the 5th century AD and became a major trading state that reached the height of its power in the early 15th century. Venice suffered disastrous floods in 1966. At one time the city was sinking, but measures have been taken to prevent further damage.

❖ Venice was the birthplace of the artists ▷BELLINI, ▷TITIAN, and Giorgione and the city was immortalized in the detailed paintings of ▷CANALETTO. Paintings and frescoes adorn many Venetian churches.

❖ Venice's famous gondolas have been painted black since 1562, when a law was passed to curb excessive decoration.

❖ Glass has been made on Murano, an island in the lagoon, since the 13th century.

Vesuvius Volcano, 1 277 m high, rising behind the Italian city of Naples. Vesuvius last erupted in 1944, but its best-known eruption was in AD 79, when the city of ▷POMPEII was buried under ash and lava, and Herculaneum under mud flows. The volcanic soils are fertile and vines are grown on the lower slopes.

Victoria, Lake Africa's largest lake, lying between Kenya, Tanzania and Uganda and covering nearly 70 000 km² (about four times the area of Gauteng). The British explorer John Speke became the first European to see the lake, in 1858, during his search for the source of the Nile. He named the lake in honour of Queen Victoria.

Vienna Capital of Austria, on the Danube. Before 1918 Vienna was the capital of the mighty Austro-Hungarian empire. Many imposing buildings, such as the Opera House and the Hofburg palace, line the 4 km long Ringstrasse boulevard which replaced the old city walls in the late 1850s. Adolf Hitler's march into Vienna in 1938 temporarily united Austria and Germany and Vienna was severely damaged by Allied bombing during World War II. The Allies controlled the city from 1945 to 1955 and divided it into four sectors occupied by Britain, France, the USA and the USSR.

❖ Vienna is known for the waltz, its pastries and also for music – especially opera, the Vienna Philharmonic Orchestra and the Vienna Boys' Choir.

Vietnam Communist country in Southeast Asia. Vietnam was a French colony from the 1880s. In 1954, after the French finally withdrew, the country was divided into communist North Vietnam and noncommunist South Vietnam. The North's attempt to reunite the country under communist rule resulted in the ▷VIETNAM WAR (1960-75). Despite American intervention, South Vietnam fell to the communists in 1975 and the unified state was set up in 1976. Two million Vietnamese were killed during the war and afterwards many thousands of 'boat people' fled by sea. The capital is Hanoi, the former capital of North Vietnam; Saigon, the former capital of South Vietnam, is now called Ho Chi Minh City.

Virgin Islands Group of about 100 Caribbean islands, most of them uninhabited, east of Puerto Rico. About two-thirds of the islands are owned by the USA; the rest form a British colony. Tourists enjoy the sandy beaches, tropical climate and good sailing.

Virginia Historic eastern seaboard state of the USA. Its capital is Richmond. English settlers arrived here in 1607, and the state was named after Queen Elizabeth I, the 'virgin queen'. Williamsburg, the state capital from 1699 to 1780, has renovated and reconstructed colonial buildings. In Virginia also are Mount Vernon, the home of George Washington, the first president, and battlefields of the War of Independence and the American Civil War.

Volga Europe's longest river and a trade route between Europe and Asia since the Middle Ages. The Volga flows for 3 688 km through forest, steppe and semidesert to its delta in the Caspian Sea. Dams across the river have created a string of huge lakes. The city of Volgograd – known as Stalingrad from 1925 to 1961 – was virtually destroyed in the 1942-3 Battle of Stalingrad.

❖ The Volga Boat Song tells the story of Stepan Razin, the 17th-century leader of a popular uprising who sailed along the Volga with his followers.

Wales Principality and constituent of the UNITED KINGDOM lying west of England, with which it was united in 1536-42. The British sovereign's eldest son is usually the Prince of Wales. Its people, many of whom are descendants of the original Celtic inhabitants, have a strong feeling of nationalism and about a quarter of them know the Welsh language. In the 19th and early 20th century it was a major coal-mining and industrial region. Its capital is CARDIFF.

MOORING PLACES *Beyond the gondolas tied to their mooring posts is Venice's Church of Santa Maria della Salute, begun in 1631-2 and built in thanksgiving for release from the plague.*

Warsaw Capital of Poland on the River Vistula. During World War II Warsaw was occupied by the Germans who confined 500 000 Jews to a walled ghetto. Many died of disease or were transferred to death camps, and the ghetto was razed after an abortive uprising in 1943. By the end of the war more than half of the city's prewar population had been killed or deported, and only one in ten of its buildings were fit for use. After the war, part of the city's historic centre was restored, and a modern new city was created beyond it.

Washington DC Capital of the USA. The city's civic buildings are grouped around The Mall, a long park. The domed white Capitol and the Library of Congress stand at one end of The Mall on Capitol Hill. Near the Potomac River at the other end of The Mall is the Lincoln Memorial, which resembles a Greek temple and houses a statue of Abraham ▷LINCOLN. The White House, the president's official residence, is set back from The Mall. DC stands for District of Columbia – the territory ceded by the states of Maryland and Virginia in 1788-9 to provide a site for the new capital city; it was first used by Congress in 1800. The name Columbia – taken from Christopher Columbus – is the poetical name for America and was used more liberally in the 18th century. Washington DC is not part of any state and is under federal jurisdiction.

Wellington New Zealand's national capital on the south-west coast of North Island, with a population of about 330 000. A major port for the country's foreign trade, it is built around a deep sheltered harbour on a steep, often windswept, slope. It was founded in 1840 and has many impressive Victorian buildings. Its industries are centred on the nearby Hutt Valley and town of Porirua.

West Bank Area of land about 130 km long and 50 km wide lying to the west of the River Jordan and the northern half of the Dead Sea. It was governed as part of Jordan from 1950 to 1967, when it was seized by Israel during the ▷SIX-DAY WAR. An Israeli military administration was set up and Jewish settlements established, leading to conflict between the Jewish settlers and the West Bank's Palestinian population. In 1988 Jordan's King Hussein renounced administrative responsibility for the West Bank. In 1993 Israel agreed to a limited form of self-rule for Palestinians in the West Bank town of Jericho and the GAZA STRIP. A timetable was set for elections and further negotiations, which appeared to be going according to plan, despite continued acts of violence on both sides.

West Indies Group of islands to the east of Central America. The main islands are CUBA,

JAMAICA, Hispaniola (the states of HAITI and the Dominican Republic), PUERTO RICO and TRINIDAD AND TOBAGO. Smaller islands include Barbados, Grenada, St Vincent, St Lucia and the VIRGIN ISLANDS. After the voyages of Christopher Columbus, Spain, France, Britain and the Netherlands all claimed islands for themselves, and introduced West African slaves to work on sugar plantations. Several islands are still European colonies.
❖ Columbus called the islands 'the Indies' because he thought he had reached the Indies of east Asia. The name of the islands were later changed to the West Indies to distinguish them from the East Indies.

Western Australia Largest of Australia's six states, more than twice the size of South Africa yet with fewer inhabitants than Durban. In the interior there are sand dunes and salt lakes that form after rain. The north-west coast is subject to hurricanes. Sheep farming is the major enterprise in less arid areas. Gold prospectors flocked to Western Australia in 1886 and gold is still mined here. Most people live in and around PERTH, the capital. The main port is Freemantle and other important centres include Bunbury and Geraldton.

Yellowstone National Park World's first national park, established in 1872. Nearly all the park is in the US state of Wyoming. It is known for its geysers, bubbling mud pools and rock terraces deposited by mineral-laden hot springs; but it also has canyons, waterfalls and lakes. The best-known geyser, Old Faithful, erupts once about every 70 minutes, sending a jet of boiling water and steam more than 40 m into the air.

Yemen Country created in May 1990 when the Yemen Arab Republic merged with the People's Democratic Republic of Yemen (South Yemen). The mountainous west has enough rainfall to support forests and crops, but much of the country is dry. The capital is the walled city of San'a, but part of Aden is the commercial centre.
❖ The ruined city of Marib, in western Yemen, was once the capital of the ancient kingdom of Sheba. The Bible describes how the Queen of Sheba visited King Solomon to test his wisdom.

Yugoslavia South European country that was formed in 1918 and broke up amid much bloodshed and destruction in 1991. The name is now claimed by the association formed by two of its former constituent states, SERBIA and Montenegro. The other constituents, now existing as separate states, are BOSNIA-HERZEGOVINA, CROATIA, Macedonia and SLOVENIA. The former capital, Belgrade, is now the capital of Serbia and Montenegro. Marshal ▷TITO, Yugoslavia's communist leader from 1945 to 1980, broke with the USSR and developed the country's own brand of communism. Tourists flocked to sunny islands and beaches along the Dalmatian coast, to the medieval port of Dubrovnik and to resorts in the mountains that make up three-quarters of the country. Slovenes and Croats, whose countries were once part of the Habsburg empire, are predominantly Roman Catholic. Centuries of Turkish rule had an enormous influence in Bosnia-Herzegovina, and many people there are Muslims. Serbs, Montenegrins and Macedonians are predominantly Orthodox Christians and use the Cyrillic alphabet. After Tito's death, nationalism resurfaced. Slovenia, Croatia and Bosnia-Herzegovina declared their independence from Yugoslavia in 1991, with the former Yugoslav republic of Macedonia following in 1992.

SUNSET CROSSING *Pedestrians and a cyclist cross the Upper Zambezi by the suspension bridge at Chinyingi Mission Station, which is a landmark in western Zambia.*

Zaire Large country in central Africa, one-third of which is covered with thick, luxuriant rainforest in which about 100 000 pygmies, the descendants of Zaire's first inhabitants, live. The capital is Kinshasa. The Zaire River, Africa's second longest river after the Nile, is 4 670 km long and much of it is navigable. From 1885 to 1908 Zaire was the personal colony of Belgium's King Leopold II and was known formerly as the Belgian Congo. Independence in 1960 brought political chaos as rival nationalist factions fought for control. In 1965 General Joseph Mobutu (later known as Mobutu Sese Seko when first names were abolished) seized power – and retained it for three decades in the face of repeated attempts to overthrow him, while amassing huge wealth as the country became increasingly impoverished. The early 1990s were marked by attempts at political reform, fostered by the international community, and outbreaks of ethnic conflict in which some 10 000 people died and hundreds of thousands were displaced. Despite being the second largest producer of industrial diamonds, Zaire remains one of the poorest nations of the world. In 1994 the inflation rate in the capital, Kinshasa, reached a staggering 2 000 per cent.

Zambia Country in south-central Africa, whose name comes from the Zambezi river which forms part of the border with Zimbabwe. The capital is Lusaka. Much of Zambia is high woodland and savannah that becomes increasingly dry towards the southwest. The Copperbelt in the northeast, where about 40 per cent of Zambians live, is the source of the ore that is the basis of the economy. Zambia is second only to the USA in its copper reserves and is one of the world's largest producers; but falling prices – added to its difficulties as a landlocked country in transporting its exports through Zimbabwe, South Africa, Angola and Mozambique – have caused it severe economic hardship. Before independence in 1964 the country was the British colony of Northern Rhodesia. Kenneth Kaunda was the head of state from independence until 1991, when he was swept from power in the first multiparty elections held in 19 years. As one of the Front Line States, Zambia was a prominent and outspoken opponent of apartheid in South Africa. It is also a member of the Southern African Development Community.

THE EARTH AND THE ENVIRONMENT

Our planet has been moulded by massive cycles of creation and destruction over 4 600 million years. Human life remains at the mercy of awesome natural phenomena over which we have no control. But increased understanding of our environment has shown us the challenge we face in ensuring that human activities do not threaten the delicate balance that sustains life on Earth.

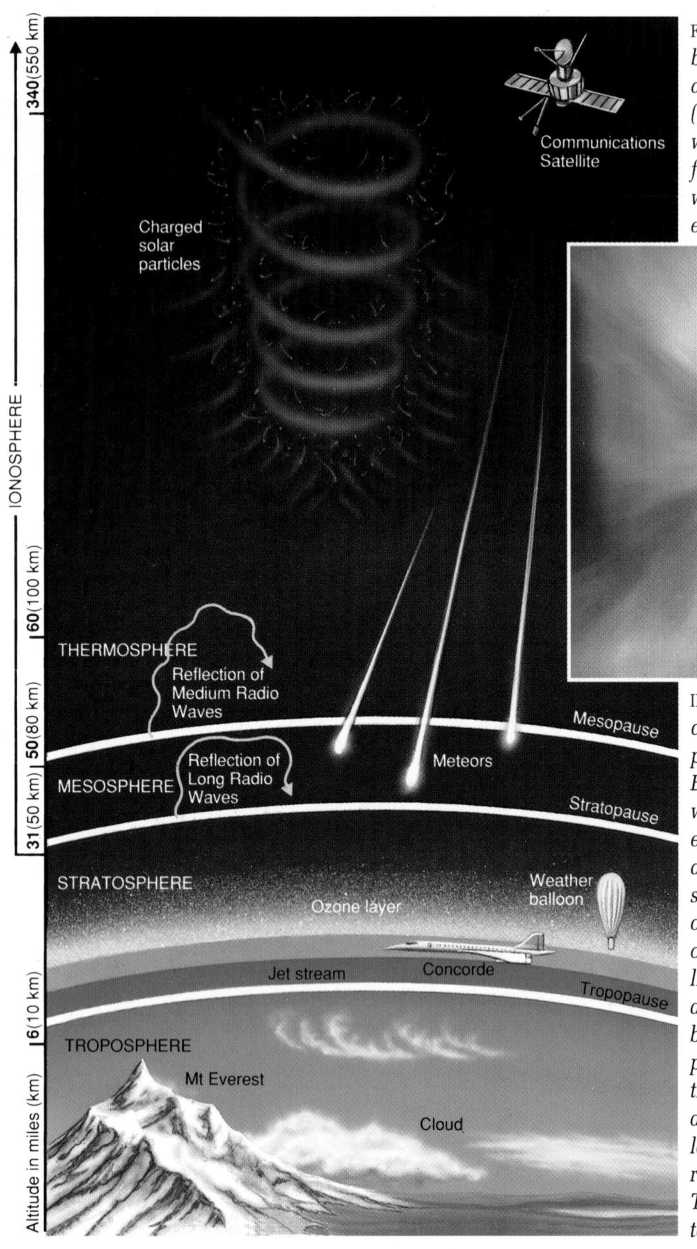

FIERY SKIES *The aurora borealis (northern lights) and the aurora australis (southern lights) occur when charged particles from the Sun interact with ionized air molecules near the poles.*

INVISIBLE LAYERS *The densest air in the atmosphere is closest to the Earth in the troposphere, where weather systems exist. To avoid weather, airliners fly in the calm stratosphere, which also contains the protective ozone layer, essential to life. Shooting stars occur as debris from space burns up in the mesosphere, the lower layer of the ionosphere, which is also where long-wavelength radio waves are reflected back to Earth. The thermosphere contains very diffuse air.*

acid rain Corrosive rain which damages the outside of buildings, destroys trees, kills freshwater fish and causes loss of vegetation through increased acidity in soil. It is caused by sulphur dioxide from coal-burning power stations and nitrogen oxides from car exhausts reacting with oxygen in the air and dissolving in rain droplets in clouds. This forms dilute but lethal solutions of sulphuric acid and nitric acid. Acid rain can be carried a long way from the source of the pollution by the prevailing winds. Active volcanoes, which release quantities of sulphur dioxide and hydrogen sulphide, also cause acid rain. Acid rain was first recognized in 1859, but its effect on vegetation was not fully realized until the 1970s.

air mass Huge body of air that is nearly uniform in temperature and humidity, and which is separated from other air masses by a cold or warm FRONT. An air mass can extend for hundreds of kilometres. There are three types: tropical (warm), polar (cold) and arctic/antarctic (very cold and dry). The first two are categorized as either 'maritime' (formed over the sea, and moist) or 'continental' (formed over land, and dry). The movement of air masses, and of the fronts between them, is responsible for weather.

anticyclone Area or system of high pressure in the atmosphere, sometimes known as a 'high'. Winds blow outwards from the centre of an anticyclone, spiralling anticlockwise in the Southern Hemisphere and clockwise in the Northern – the opposite direction to a CYCLONE. Anticyclones bring settled weather: warm and dry in summer, and cold and clear in winter.

atmosphere Narrow layer of gases that surrounds the Earth and enables life to exist. Retained by the Earth's gravitational pull, it contains about 78 per cent nitrogen, almost 21 per cent oxygen and 1 per cent argon, about 0,2 per cent water vapour and 0,03 per cent carbon dioxide, with trace amounts of other gases. The atmosphere shields the Earth from the Sun's harmful rays, the cold of outer space, and bombardment by meteoroids. Closest to Earth is the troposphere, where air density is at its greatest. Temperature decreases with height and weather systems form here. Above the troposphere's ceiling, or tropopause, temperature increases with height, preventing air from moving vertically. The IONOSPHERE, which contains electrically charged particles, extends outwards from the upper atmosphere, or stratosphere. Charged particles are captured by the magnetic field of the Earth and drawn towards the poles, causing MAGNETIC STORMS and auroras.

❖ A primordial atmosphere consisting of nebular gas (mainly hydrogen) left over from the formation of the solar system would have been stripped from the Earth by intense radiation from the Sun. The atmosphere replacing it, formed from volcanic gases, had little free oxygen and a hundred times more carbon dioxide than it does now. Much of the carbon dioxide has been removed by living things: over many millions of years it has been 'locked up' in the bodies of long-dead organisms and turned into sedimentary rock and fossil fuels. The atmosphere's oxygen content has increased mainly due to plants' ▷PHOTOSYNTHESIS.

atmospheric pressure Weight of air above the Earth's surface that creates pressure on it. The standard atmospheric pressure at sea level – defined as one atmosphere – is 1,04 kg/cm^2, or 1 013,25 millibars. As altitude increases there is less air overhead, which causes atmospheric pressure to fall off at a rate of about 3,5 millibars for every 30 m climbed. Above 2 400 m, air pressure and oxygen supply are low enough to cause altitude sickness. Above 300 km, the pressure is as low as any man-made vacuum. Air pressure also varies with different meteorological conditions, and its measurement using a barometer is a principal means of WEATHER FORECASTING. Places of equal pressure are linked on weather maps by lines called isobars. There are no fixed levels that distinguish high pressure from low; rather, a level is high or low in relation to another system nearby. Areas of high pressure are associated with settled weather, while low-pressure systems bring unsettled weather. Rapid falls in atmospheric pressure herald storms.

Beaufort scale Measure of wind speed that relies on observed indicators such as the height of waves. Devised by Admiral F B Beaufort in 1805 and modified in 1926, it ranges from force 0, calm with a wind speed of less than 1 knot (1,852 km/h), to force 12, a hurricane with wind speeds of more than 64 knots (117 km/h). Forces 13 to 17 were added by the US Weather Bureau in 1955 to describe the most severe storms. Originally based on the effects of wind on a fully rigged man-of-war, the scale is still used at sea. In meteorology it has been largely replaced by the direct measurement of wind speed.

biosphere Uppermost layer of the Earth's surface, plus its lower ATMOSPHERE, which is inhabited by organic life. The term also refers to an artificially closed environment where interdependent plants and animals form a self-sustaining ECOSYSTEM.

❖ Between 1991 and 1993, eight volunteers spent two years isolated inside Biosphere 2 (Biosphere 1 is Earth), a sealed 1,2 ha glass and steel structure outside Tucson, Arizona. The experiment, the first of a series, was designed to investigate the feasibility of building a settlement on Mars.

cave Natural cavity or series of underground chambers and passages usually eroded by water. Caves are formed by underground streams, by wave EROSION along coasts and by water dissolving rock, as in limestone cave systems with their distinctive STALACTITES AND STALAGMITES. Caves also form in glaciers and in solidified volcanic LAVA.

❖ The world's most extensive cave system is under the Mammoth Cave National Park in Kentucky, USA. Potholers can explore more than 480 km of charted passages.

CFCs (chlorofluorocarbons) Chemical compounds, also known as Freons, containing carbon, chlorine and fluorine, used in making insulators, solvents, refrigerants and aerosol propellants. CFCs, known to be partly responsible for 'holes' in the OZONE LAYER, are being replaced by isobutanes. However, CFCs are likely to be used for many years to come, particularly in the developing world.

climate Long-term weather conditions of a particular place, including temperature, rainfall, humidity, sunshine and WIND. Climate is largely determined by latitude, altitude and location in relation to major landmasses and oceans: in coastal regions temperature is modified by proximity to the sea, while in the centre of a continent it will reach great extremes. The most widely used classification of climates is: tropical (hot and wet), desert (dry), warm or cool temperate, polar or mountain. Within this scheme there are specific types. For example, Cape Town has a warm temperate Mediterranean-type climate with a dry summer; Britain's climate, which is also warm temperate, is maritime type – mild and moist.

Cirrus

Altostratus above nimbostratus

Cumulonimbus

Altocumulus

CLOUD PATTERNS *Feathery plumes of cirrus, or mare's tails, often herald bad weather. Altostratus clouds often cover the entire sky and can turn into rain clouds, such as nimbostratus. Anvil-shaped cumulonimbus bring thundery storms and altocumulus usually indicate fair weather.*

climatic change Throughout the Earth's history, major fluctuations in climate have been caused by many factors: volcanic eruptions that obscure the Sun, the impact of METEORITES, the changing positions of the landmasses caused by CONTINENTAL DRIFT, variations in the Earth's orbit, and changes in the Sun's temperature as well as in the composition of gases in the ATMOSPHERE. Some periods of change such as the ICE AGES, when the general climate was 10-12°C colder than at present, continued for thousands of years. Within these huge cyclical changes are smaller variations, such as the 'little ice age' that lasted from about 1430 to 1850. Since the 1880s, temperatures across the world have risen, prompting theories on GLOBAL WARMING. By the 1980s the Earth's temperature was rising at more than 0,2°C per decade.

cloud Mixture of minute water droplets and ice crystals in the atmosphere. Clouds form when warm, moist air rises and cools, and the water vapour it contains condenses around microscopic particles of dust or smoke. Clouds typically contain one million water droplets per cubic metre, and one million cloud particles are needed to form a single raindrop. Clumps of cloud form when air rises quickly, while slow-rising air forms cloud sheets. Cirrus, cirrostratus and cirrocumulus clouds, which form at 6 000-15 000 m, are composed almost entirely of ice crystals. White altocumulus clouds, which indicate fine weather, and grey altostratus clouds, which produce rain, form at 2 000-6 000 m. Nimbostratus, at 1 000-2 000 m, are also rain clouds associated with a cold FRONT. Dark, anvil-shaped cumulonimbus clouds rise to above 15 000 m, and herald approaching THUNDERSTORMS. Hazy, low-level stratus clouds produce overcast skies, and low-level cumulus clouds often bring drizzle.

coal Black sedimentary rock formed from vegetation which partially decomposed in swamps, predominantly during the Carboniferous period (see GEOLOGICAL TIME SCALE). It built up into thick peat beds which compacted when other rock formed on top. Pressure and underground heat slowly transformed the peat into coal. The main types of coal are anthracite, the hardest coal, with more than 90 per cent carbon; bituminous coal, used as house coal, containing more than 80 per cent carbon; and lignite or brown coal, which contains around 70 per cent carbon and many impurities.

❖ Coal fuelled the ▷INDUSTRIAL REVOLUTION, and still supplies more energy and has larger reserves than OIL and NATURAL GAS. It is the 'dirtiest' of the fossil fuels – more than 3 000 million tons are burnt annually, producing 'greenhouse gases', such as carbon dioxide and sulphur dioxide, which are blamed for contributing to GLOBAL WARMING and also to ACID RAIN.

❖ South Africa has some of the shallowest deposits of coal in the world, making its coal mines among the most economical. ▷SASOL's oil-from-coal process is the world's most economical and successful, and is a large foreign exchange earner.

cold front See FRONT.

continent One of seven landmasses of the Earth's crust – Asia, Africa, North America, South America, Australasia, Europe and Antarctica – which cover nearly 30 per cent of the Earth's surface. Continental features include margins or boundaries (typically undersea), chains of old and young fold mountains, a central sediment-covered platform and the shield – the oldest part. Shield areas, such as north Canada and central Africa, are remnants of former continents that broke up and recombined – part of a process explained by PLATE TECTONICS.

continental drift The theory of continental drift was first comprehensively outlined by the German meteorologist Alfred Wegener in 1912. He based his ideas partly on the fact, noted three centuries earlier, that the eastern bulge of South America fitted almost exactly into the bight of Africa's west coast, but mainly on the similarities between fossils found in the coalfields of Europe and North America. Wegener believed that for most of the Earth's history there had been a single continent, Pangaea, surrounded by an ocean, Panthalassa. It is now believed that Pangaea became two proto-continents, separated by the Tethys Sea: Gondwanaland, comprising South America, Africa, India, Australia and Antarctica; and Laurasia, which combined North America, Europe and the rest of Asia. Despite steadily mounting evidence, Wegener's theory was not generally accepted until it was incorporated into the theory of PLATE TECTONICS which was developed in the 1950s and 1960s.

coral reef Undersea ridge or hillock built from the skeletons of coral, a marine animal related to jellyfish and sea anemones that lives in warm seas. Coral colonies grow on skeletons of previous generations, and huge submarine structures, such as Australia's ▷GREAT BARRIER REEF, have slowly built up.
❖ Atolls are large ring-shaped coral reefs that enclose a lagoon.

Coriolis effect Apparent force acting on an object moving across the Earth's surface, due to the EARTH's rotation. The apparent velocity of an object at rest on the Earth's surface rises from zero at the poles to a maximum at the Equator. When an object moves away from the Equator, the object appears to deflect to the left in the Southern Hemisphere and to the right in the Northern. Consequently, something moving in a north-south direction also appears to be moving east or west. The Coriolis effect is responsible for the pattern of WINDS and OCEAN CURRENTS and is an important consideration in air travel, missile guidance and spacecraft launching.

cyclone Area or system of low pressure in the atmosphere, often called simply a 'low'. Winds blowing inwards to 'fill' the depression adopt a spiral pattern because of the CORIOLIS EFFECT, moving clockwise in the Southern Hemisphere and anticlockwise in the Northern – the opposite of an ANTICYCLONE. In mid to high latitudes a cyclone is referred to as a depression and is associated with unsettled weather. In tropical regions it is associated with high winds and torrential rain. (See also HURRICANE.)
❖ An elongated area of low pressure, particularly of a depression, is called a 'trough'.

MOVING CONTINENTS *An original landmass, Pangaea, split into two proto-continents, Laurasia and Gondwanaland. The Tethys Sea became the Mediterranean. The movement continues – North America is moving away from Europe, and India is pushing into the Himalayas. Calculations show that in about 250 million years' time Australia could collide with North America.*

225 million years ago

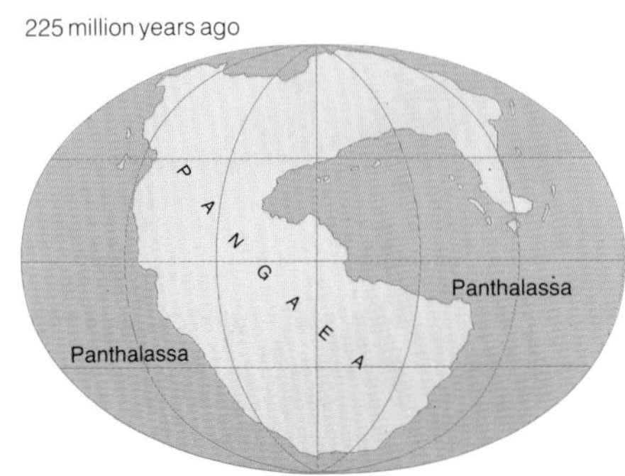

135 million years ago

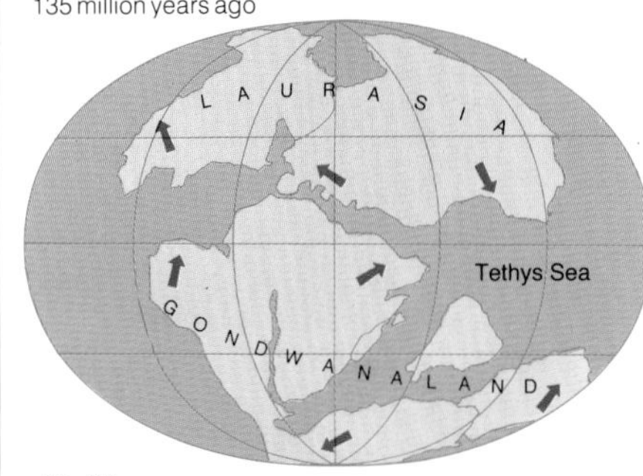

40 million years ago

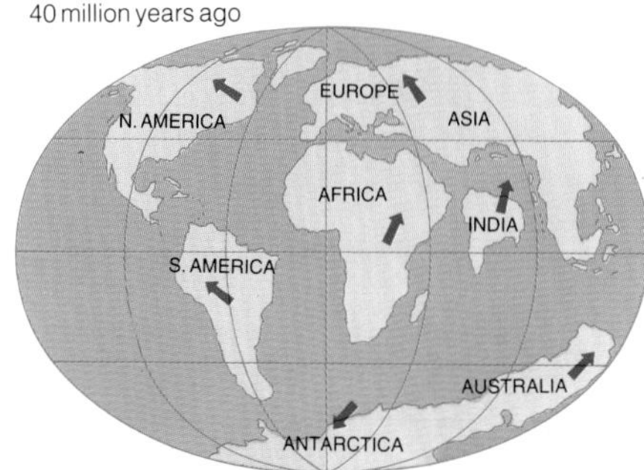

250 million years from now

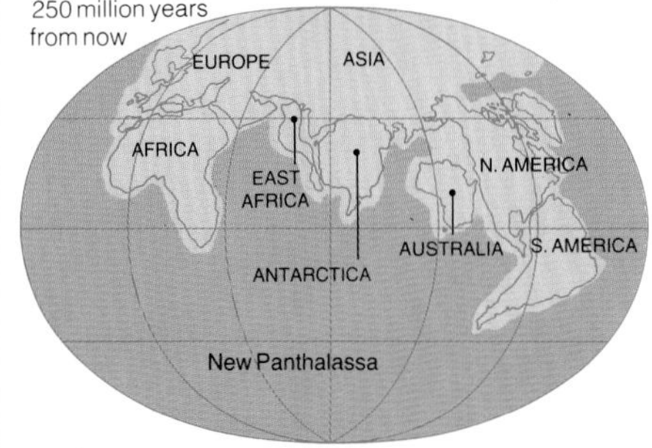

DDT (Dichlorodiphenyltrichloroethane) A powerful insecticide used widely during World War II to kill lice, fleas and mosquitoes – greatly reducing the incidence of typhus, ▷MALARIA, plague and yellow fever which these insects carry. Later, DDT was used widely as an all-purpose agricultural pesticide, but resistant strains of insect pests soon developed. It was then found that DDT was picked up by insect-eating animals and became concentrated as it passed along the food chain. The link between DDT and the deaths of large numbers of birds – including many wagtails in South Africa and peregrine falcons in Britain – caused many countries around the world to ban its use in the 1960s.
❖ South Africa banned the insecticide for agricultural use in 1976, but it is still occasionally used in southern Africa against mosquitoes when there is a severe outbreak of the potentially fatal disease malaria.

deforestation Felling and clearing of forest, usually for timber or to make way for agriculture. Over the past 5 000 years the great forests that once covered the temperate zones of Europe and North America have been steadily cleared. Today, the loss of RAINFOREST in Southeast Asia and South America is causing widespread concern.
❖ Reforestation is the replanting of trees in an area that has been stripped of forest cover, while afforestation is the planting of trees in an area that has not previously been forested, such as a WETLAND.

desert Arid region where average rainfall is less than 250 mm a year, usually where there are persistent belts of high-pressure ANTICYCLONES, such as in the Sahara Desert in northern Africa, or where mountains prevent the passage of rain, such as in the Gobi Desert of Mongolia and northeast China. In the Sahara, daytime temperatures can reach 51°C. The Gobi has a winter night-time temperature that can fall to -40°C. True deserts cover only 5 per cent of the Earth's land area, but with their associated arid and semi-arid regions, they affect around one-third of the land surface. Deserts spread largely because of over-grazing and drought, such as in the Sahel region, in the southern Sahara.
❖ The Atacama Desert in northern Chile is

POWER OF NATURE *The San Francisco earthquake of October 1989 registered 7,1 on the Richter scale and caused buildings and highways to collapse. Amazingly only 24 people were killed.*

the driest in the world: in the town of Calama there was no rain from 1570 to 1971.
❖ The Namib, covering 310 km² of Namibia, is the oldest coastal desert in the world, dating back some 50 million to 80 million years.

Earth The only inhabited planet orbiting the Sun. It has three major parts: the ATMOSPHERE; the OCEANS; and ROCK made up of an inner and an outer core, a mantle and a crust. The inner core, some 2 400 km across, is thought to be solid iron and nickel – reaching a temperature of 4 500°C. Around it is an outer core, about 2 200 km thick, composed of molten iron, probably mixed with sulphur and oxygen, at a temperature of approximately 2 200°C. The mantle, between the core and the crust, is about 2 900 km thick, and is composed of hot rock – mainly iron-magnesium silicates (peridotite). The continental crust is largely granite and supports the continents. It is an average of 32 km thick, although it can be more than 60 km thick at mountain ranges. The oceanic crust is made largely of basalt and gabbro and is 6-16 km thick. Newer than continental crust, it is constantly being formed along OCEAN RIDGES. The Earth is not a perfect sphere: because of its rotation, it bulges slightly at the Equator, having an equatorial circumference of 40 076 km and a polar circumference of 40 008 km. Its total surface area is 510 100 000 km². Land covers 29 per cent, or 148 000 000 km². As the Earth orbits the Sun, it tilts by about 23½ degrees on its axis from the perpendicular. This is the reason for seasons outside the tropics, as the sun appears to move north or south of the equator as the Earth moves along its elliptical orbit. (See also ▷EARTH in 'Science, space and mathematics'.)
❖ The human race has been in existence for less than one-thousandth of the Earth's 4 600 million-year history (see GEOLOGICAL TIME SCALE illustration, p 468).

earthquake Violent tremor in the Earth's crust caused by the sudden release of stresses at the edges of the Earth's crustal plates, a process explained by PLATE TECTONICS. Earthquakes occur most frequently around the rim of the Pacific Ocean and along the trans-Asiatic belt, which extends through the Mediterranean Sea and eastward via Asia to the Pacific. The energy from these disturbances is transmitted to the surface of the Earth by SEISMIC WAVES.
❖ The magnitude, or energy, of an earthquake is measured on the RICHTER SCALE.

ecosystem Community of interdependent plants and animals and the physical environment they occupy. A pond or the entire world can be viewed as a single ecosystem, but usually the term refers to a single type of habitat, such as DESERT or fresh water. Each organism occupies a specific 'niche' which determines its relationship with other living things in the ecosystem – for example, its position in the food chain.

El Niño Effect when an area of abnormally warm water in some years partly replaces the normally cold, rich fishing waters of the Pacific Ocean off northern Peru in December or January. It occurs when northerly winds replace the prevailing southerlies, driving warm water shoreward and downward. As a result, the marine life cycle cannot be supported and great numbers of sea birds and fish die, with devastating effects on the local economy. The cause of these changes is not known, but it is linked with anomalous weather around the world. In 1992, for example, it was associated with drought in southern Africa, Indonesia, eastern Australia and northeastern Brazil, a hurricane in Samoa, freak storms in California and months of heavy rain in Alaska and Canada.
❖ The El Niño phenomenon was also responsible for southern Africa's most severe drought spell in the early 1980s.

environment Surroundings in which an organism lives, including the CLIMATE, the physical and chemical conditions of its habitat, and its relationship with other living things. Since the 1960s, 'Green' or environmental concerns, such as POLLUTION and the need to recycle materials and reduce waste, have become major political issues. Some industrial countries now have environmental protection agencies to police the producers of pollution. (See also ECOSYSTEM.)

erosion Gradual breaking down of landforms and removal of the debris to another place, by ice (especially during periods of GLACIATION), rivers, waves, rain and wind. Over hundreds of years, the processes of erosion can reshape entire landscapes and play an important part in the ROCK cycle.

eutrophication Build-up on lakes, ponds and slow-moving rivers of microscopic ▷ALGAE which may block sunlight and deplete levels of oxygen in the water – killing other forms of aquatic life. The algae result from excess fertilizers and human waste.

fault Fracture in the Earth's crust where forces transmitted through the movement of tectonic plates displace the two sides of the crust relative to each other. Faults may range from mere centimetres to hundreds of kilometres – such as the San Andreas Fault in California, which is 965 km long. Horizontal or vertical movement along a major fault line causes EARTHQUAKES.
❖ The 1969 earthquake that devastated the

towns of Tulbagh and Ceres in the Western Cape originated along the prominent fault line running through Worcester.

flood Several factors may cause flooding, such as excessive rain, sudden spring thaws, TSUNAMIS and storms at sea. Flash floods are caused by sudden THUNDERSTORMS in dry valleys, where the volume of rainfall overwhelms the natural or constructed drainage, as happened in Laingsburg in the Western Cape in 1981, when the Buffels River burst its banks, drowning 104 people and leaving only 23 of the town's 208 houses intact.

❖ There was widespread flooding in KwaZulu-Natal in 1984 in the wake of the tropical CYCLONE Demoina. South Africa's record rainfall in 24 hours was measured at the time: 597 mm at Lake St Lucia.

❖ Engineers designing dams, bridges and drainage channels, calculate the magnitude of a flood in terms of how often it is likely to occur. The Thames Barrier, for example, should protect London from a flood likely to occur only once in 1 000 years.

❖ In 1993, the Mississippi River rose 10 m, overtopping levees and flooding over two-thirds of its flood plain – an event estimated as likely to occur once every 500 years. The cost of the resulting damage was estimated at some US$10 billion.

fold Bending or buckling of ROCK strata under intense pressure, for example where the Earth's plates collide, forcing the land to rise, as in MOUNTAIN BUILDING. When the rocks are eroded, the effects of the folding action can be seen in the diagonal or twisted forms of the exposed strata – once the flat sedimentary floors of ancient seas.

FAULT LINE *Two enormous parts of the Earth's crust slide slowly past each other at the San Andreas Fault, causing earthquakes and making a dramatic scar across California.*

front Leading edge of an advancing cold or warm AIR MASS. In a cold front, relatively dense cold air undercuts warmer, thinner air, leading to a rapid drop in ground temperature. Showers or sometimes THUNDERSTORMS follow. The rain stops abruptly for a short while after the front passes, then resumes before tailing off. Warm fronts, which are rare in southern latitudes, produce a wide band of CLOUD and gentle persistent rain and, sometimes, widespread fog. Warm fronts tend to travel slowly and can easily be caught up by cold fronts (which can move at speeds up to 60 km/h). When this happens, an occluded front occurs, in which the warm air is pushed upwards, causing cloud and rain.

Gaia hypothesis Theory, proposed by the English scientist James Lovelock in 1979, that the Earth can be regarded as a single integrated living organism composed of a delicate web of interconnected ECOSYSTEMS. This network, named 'Gaia' after the 'Earth Mother' of Greek mythology, regulates the global environment, but POLLUTION created by human beings may be upsetting this stability, damaging the OZONE LAYER and giving rise to GLOBAL WARMING. (See also ▷GAIA in 'Myths and legends'.)

gemstones Crystals that are prized for their rarity, form, iridescence and hardness. Of some 3 000 minerals, no more than 100 are used as gemstones. Only the finest specimens are considered precious, including aquamarine and emerald (from the mineral beryl), alexandrite and cat's-eye (chrysoberyl), ruby and sapphire (corundum), diamond (carbon), amazonite and moonstone (feldspar), garnet, lazurite, opal, peridot (olivine), quartz, spinel, topaz, tourmaline and zircon. Others such as jade, serpentine and turquoise are popular for carving. Some organic materials – amber, jet, coral and pearl – are also considered to be gemstones.

AEONS OF TIME *Precambrian rock represents 85 per cent of the Earth's history, but contains few fossils. Life forms developed and proliferated during the other three eras – the Palaeozoic 'ancient life', the Mesozoic 'middle life' and the Cenozoic 'modern life'. The Cenozoic is divided into the Tertiary and Quaternary periods. The Quaternary is further split into the Pleistocene epoch, when the Earth underwent a series of ice ages during which* Homo sapiens *– modern man's ancestors – appeared; and the current Holocene epoch, which began 10 000 years ago.*

PRECAMBRIAN ERA *The Earth was formed about 4 600 million years ago. The first primitive single-celled animals appeared 600 million years later.*

PALAEOZOIC ERA *Creatures emerged from the sea at about the same time that flying insects evolved – approximately 500 million years ago. The first mountains and trees thrust towards the sky from the previously flat landscape.*

MESOZOIC ERA *Flowering plants, dinosaurs, mammals and birds developed in the three Mesozoic periods – the Triassic (225-190 million years ago), Jurassic (190-130 million years ago) and Cretaceous (130-65 million years ago).*

CENOZOIC ERA *In the current geological era, the Himalayas and the Rockies were formed as the Earth's huge continental 'plates' collided with each other. Life on Earth took its present form with the evolution of a wide variety of mammals, including human beings.*

❖ Some diamonds are 3 000 million years old. Southern Africa's largest diamond – the Cullinan, found in 1905 – measured 100 mm across and had a mass of 3 025 carats. It was cut into 105 stones, with the two biggest – the Star of Africa (530,2 carats) and the Lesser Star of Africa (317,4 carats) – being set in the British Crown Jewels.
❖ Africa produces more than half of the world's diamonds, with Namibia the top producer of gem diamonds at 30 per cent of world output. Zaïre is the second largest producer (after Australia) of industrial diamonds. (See also ▷MINING in 'Business and economics'.)

geological time scale History of the Earth as revealed by the ▷FOSSIL record and the stratification, or sequence of ROCK layers. By the end of the 18th century, the processes of deposition and EROSION that produced rock strata were partly understood and it became clear that the Earth must be vastly older than the 6 000 years estimated from the Bible. During the early 1800s, fossils found in sedimentary rock were organized into their chronological sequence, which made possible the development of a geological time scale, divided into eras, periods and epochs. Potassium-argon dating is now used to determine the age of rock, even the oldest formed some 4 500 million years ago.

geothermal energy Heat obtained from hot rocks lying close to the EARTH's surface. It is used to heat buildings directly and to generate electricity in countries such as Italy, Japan and Iceland. Steam from hot springs, or water pumped into boreholes, which quickly turns to steam – reaching temperatures of up to 350°C – may be used to drive turbines.

glaciation Large accumulation of ice, such as glaciers and ice sheets formed from compacted snow during ICE AGES. The term also describes the EROSION caused by ice, sometimes hundreds of metres thick, moving over the Earth's surface. Ice sheets, now confined to Greenland and Antarctica, are the source of ICEBERGS. Like ice sheets, glaciers move slowly under the enormous weight of ice, scouring the landscape, carving out valleys and depositing mounds of debris called moraine. Retreating ice leaves U-shaped valleys such as the fjords of Scandinavia and the firths of Scotland.
❖ The Antarctic ice cap is up to 3 800 m thick in places, and contains more than 90 per cent of the Earth's ice.

global warming Theory that the world is warming up due to the GREENHOUSE EFFECT. Levels of carbon dioxide in the ATMOSPHERE have risen since the ▷INDUSTRIAL REVOLUTION took effect in the 1780s. More recently, the clearing of RAINFOREST has added to the problem, because there are fewer trees to absorb carbon dioxide during ▷PHOTOSYNTHESIS. If the emission of carbon dioxide and other 'greenhouse gases' – produced by power stations, industry and cars – continues to grow at the present rate, the average global temperature could increase by 1,8°C by 2030, causing other unpredictable effects on the CLIMATE and SEA LEVEL. The governments of many countries are committed to stabilizing carbon dioxide emissions by the year 2000.

DEADLY STORM *Trees at Palm Beach, Florida, bend before 200 km/h winds in 1945. Hurricanes on land are mercifully short-lived; they usually blow themselves out after one day.*

greenhouse effect Gases in the ATMOSPHERE act in the same way as glass in a greenhouse, trapping the Sun's heat and effectively keeping the planet more than 30°C warmer than it would otherwise be. This maintains the surface of the Earth at temperatures where water is liquid and life is possible. However, there are fears that the steadily increasing levels of 'greenhouse gases' such as carbon dioxide and methane will cause GLOBAL WARMING.

hail Ice balls created by updrafts which carry water droplets to the tops of storm clouds, where they freeze. More water condenses and freezes around these ice particles, until they become too heavy and fall to the ground. Hail stones are commonly spherical and stones up to 10 cm in diameter are not uncommon in parts of southern Africa.
❖ The heaviest hail stones recorded (in Bangladesh in 1986) were reported to have a mass of 1 kg.

humidity Amount of water vapour in the ATMOSPHERE. Air at 30°C can hold six times as much water vapour as it can at freezing point. Humidity is therefore expressed as a percentage of the maximum amount of moisture the atmosphere can carry at a given temperature, and is thus termed relative humidity.
❖ Air conditioning aims to keep humidity at 50 to 60 per cent. Humidity below 20 per cent dries the throat, leaving it vulnerable to infection. In Singapore City humidity sometimes reaches 98 per cent.

hurricane Name for a tropical CYCLONE in the north Atlantic, the Caribbean and the northeast Pacific, accompanied by high winds and torrential rain. In the northwest Pacific and the China seas they are called typhoons; in the Indian Ocean and southwest Pacific they are known as cyclones. They form over warm water with a surface temperature of at least 27°C and at latitudes high enough for the CORIOLIS EFFECT to be appreciable. At their centre is the 'eye', an area of calm air around which winds blow at up to 290 km/h. Winds of 120 km/h – BEAUFORT SCALE force 12 – are designated hurricanes.

hydrologic cycle Constant circulation of water between air, land and sea. Water evaporates from the oceans, some falls back into the sea again, but the rest falls on land as rain, snow or hail. Some evaporates again directly, some passes back to the atmosphere through plant transpiration, some finds its way back to the oceans through streams and rivers, and some goes into the ground, where its upper limit is known as the WATER TABLE. A small but vital amount is taken up by living things and incorporated into their tissues.

ice ages Long periods of CLIMATIC CHANGE when temperatures fall and GLACIATION occurs over a wide area. There have been a number of ice ages over the past 3 000 million years. During the Pleistocene epoch, the most recent period of extensive glaciation, the polar ice caps advanced and retreated at least four times to cover most of northern and central Europe – at one time covering as much as 30 per cent of the Earth. The last ice sheet retreated about 11 000 years ago, leaving debris as far south as London. With more of the Earth's water frozen in ice sheets, the SEA LEVEL was as much as 130 m lower than it is today. The English Channel was dry and a land bridge between Alaska and Siberia allowed early Mongoloid peoples to colonize the Americas.

iceberg Floating mass of freshwater ice that has calved from an ice shelf, the seaward end of a glacier, or from an ice sheet. Some 12 000 icebergs are calved each year from the glaciers of west Greenland. About 375 a year drift south into the Atlantic Ocean, where some, towering up to 170 m above sea level, are a hazard to shipping. Most melt within two years. On average the ice in icebergs is about 5 000 years old. The tip of an iceberg, visible above the water, represents only about one-ninth of its total volume. The Ross Ice Shelf, off the Antarctic coast, is more than half the size of Zimbabwe, making it the world's largest body of floating ice.

❖ The 'unsinkable' SS *Titanic* sank on her maiden voyage in 1912 after hitting an iceberg – 1 500 people lost their lives.

ionosphere Region of the upper ATMOSPHERE between 60 km and 300 km above the Earth, where air molecules or atoms are charged electrically (ionized) by absorbing short-wave radiation from the Sun. Ionized layers reflect radio signals and are thus of great importance in communications, but higher frequency VHF and UHF signals pass straight through them without reflection and can be received only in the line of sight of the transmitter or satellite. The ionosphere is affected when there are MAGNETIC STORMS.

irrigation Artificial distribution of water by canals, pipelines and ditches to land that would otherwise be too dry for crops to flourish. Worldwide, an area about the size of western Europe is irrigated. Some 65 per cent of it is in the rice-growing areas of China, India, Pakistan and Southeast Asia.

❖ The Orange-Fish River Tunnel which takes water from the Gariep (previously known as the Hendrik Verwoerd) Dam in the Free State to the upper valley of the Fish River, is the world's longest hydroelectric irrigation tunnel, at 82,9 km.

lava Molten ROCK or magma that flows from volcanic vents and fissures at a temperature of 1 100°C, which is high enough to melt steel. When lavas cool, they solidify to form igneous rock. Froth on the surface solidifies into pumice – the only rock that floats.

lightning Giant electric spark of up to 100 million volts produced by a variation in the electric charge of different thunder clouds (sheet lightning) or between clouds and the ground (forked lightning). It is caused by a build-up of static electricity generated by particles of snow, hail or rain buffeted about by warm, rising air currents within thunder clouds. Forked lightning begins with a faint leader stroke branching and darting from side to side, taking the route of least resistance to the ground, quickly followed by a massive luminous return stroke. The peak current of the return is around 100 000 times the current flowing through a normal light bulb. Air in the lightning's path superheats to 16 000°C and expands supersonically before contracting rapidly, causing a clap of thunder.

❖ Benjamin ▷FRANKLIN invented the lightning conductor, a metal rod which helps to prevent a strike by gradually discharging electricity, or conducts the strike along the rod into the ground.

STROKES OF BRILLIANCE *The central core of a lightning bolt is estimated to be up to five times hotter than the surface of the Sun.*

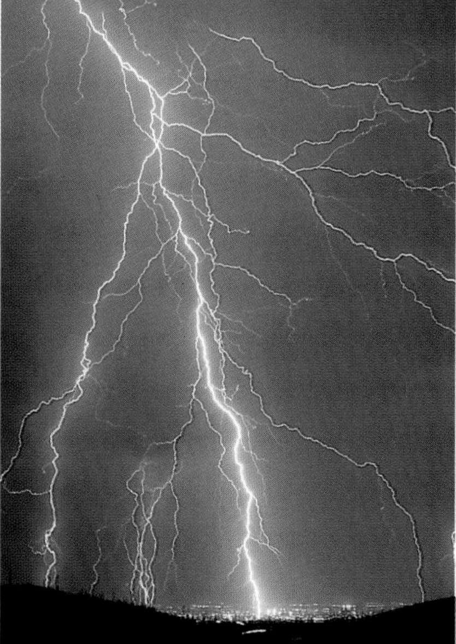

magnetic poles Two points on the surface of the EARTH where its magnetic lines of force meet; a compass needle is drawn to the north magnetic pole. The Earth acts as a large magnet because of a mass of iron at its core. Electric currents in the core generate most of its magnetic field, though about 10 per cent is produced by currents in the IONOSPHERE. The magnetic poles change position slowly, but remain around 1 600 km from the geographic poles – the Earth's axis of rotation.

❖ Simple compasses have been used in navigation at sea since the 12th century.

magnetic reversal Switch in direction of the Earth's magnetic field – the magnetic north pole becomes the magnetic south pole and vice versa. The last switch was about 30 000 years ago, but many more are known to have occurred during the Earth's history. The reversals are recorded by the magnetic basalt rock that forms where SEA-FLOOR SPREADING takes place. As molten basalt oozes from the sea floor and solidifies, it takes up the magnetic orientation of the Earth at that time, forming bands, or strata, magnetized first in one direction, then the other. From this the rock's geographical latitude and place of origin can be determined.

❖ During an occurrence of magnetic reversal, cosmic-ray particles that would normally be deflected by the Earth's magnetic field reach the surface of the planet, causing genetic mutation in living things. This may explain the sudden extinction of some species or the sudden appearance of others.

magnetic storm Disturbance of the Earth's magnetic field caused by ▷SOLAR WIND – charged particles from the Sun – which is responsible for auroras in the ATMOSPHERE. Magnetic storms can disrupt computer systems, radio and satellite communications, cause failure of electrical transmission lines, and increase doses of radiation to people on transpolar flights.

meteorite Rock or metal that has fallen to Earth from meteoroids – parts of asteroids or comets. Unlike ▷METEORS – another name for shooting stars – meteorites reach the Earth's surface without completely burning up. The commonest are stone meteorites (aerolites), which may contain particles of iron. Iron meteorites (siderites) often contain nickel as well as other metals. The largest meteorites found intact each weighed 60 tons. One landed at Hoba, near Grootfontein in Namibia, the other in Kansas, USA.

❖ In 1992 a 12 kg meteorite was found embedded in the bonnet of a car at Peekshill, in New York State. Though such an occurrence is rare, statistically a meteorite impact large enough to kill 100 people is likely to happen every 100 years.

❖ A crater at Chicxulub, Mexico, 180 km wide was caused when a meteorite measuring some 10 km across exploded. This impact would have released energy equivalent to 10 000 atom bombs, and its aftermath may have destroyed half the Earth's living creatures, including the dinosaurs.

monsoon Large-scale reversal of WINDS in the tropics. The word, from the Arabic *mausim* meaning 'season', originally applied to the winds of the Arabian Sea, which blow for six months from the northeast and six months from the southwest. It is now used for any wind system that reverses seasonally, especially the winds of south and Southeast Asia. These blow cool and dry from the north from November to April, then warm and wet from the southwest from May to September when they carry torrential rain.

mountain building Deformation of the Earth's crust by warping, faulting or folding, or by deposition of volcanic material – processes which are all explained by PLATE TECTONICS. Dome mountains occur where the crust warps upwards without fracturing. At fracture zones, FAULT-block mountains are forced upwards. FOLD mountains (such as the Langeberg and Swartberg ranges in the Western Cape) result from layers of sedimentary ROCK being forced upwards by lateral pressure. The Earth's largest volcanic ranges are the OCEAN RIDGES, which are still being built, as are two major fold mountain systems on land which were formed during the last 50 million years. One, stretching from the Himalayas to the Alps, Pyrenees and Atlas Mountains, is caused by India colliding with the rest of Asia, and by Africa colliding with Europe, due to continuing CONTINENTAL DRIFT. The other, responsible for creating the Andes, results from Pacific crustal plates sliding under the Americas.

❖ Some hills and mountains (such as the Drakensberg range) are created by the slow EROSION of softer rock resulting in a hard core being exposed.

natural gas Fossil fuel which is a mixture of methane and other gases such as propane, butane and helium that occurs in underground reservoirs of porous rock. Natural gas is often found near OIL deposits, as it is made by the same processes.

nuclear waste Items that are dangerously radioactive, most notably spent fuel rods from nuclear power stations. There is controversy over the disposal of nuclear waste, especially since the effects of widespread contamination have become known following accidents such as that at ▷CHERNOBYL in 1986. Some dumping has taken place at sea, for example in the Arctic and the deep Marianas Trench off the Philippines, but an international treaty now forbids this. High-level waste from the chemical reprocessing of spent fuel rods from power stations and decommissioned nuclear weapons causes huge problems as it remains radioactive for thousands – even millions – of years.

❖ Waste from Koeberg nuclear power station near Cape Town, is stored in specially constructed bunkers at Vaalputs, 100 km south-east of Springbok in the Northern Cape.

❖ The Waste Isolation Pilot Plant in New Mexico, USA, has been designed to store contaminated material until AD 12 000.

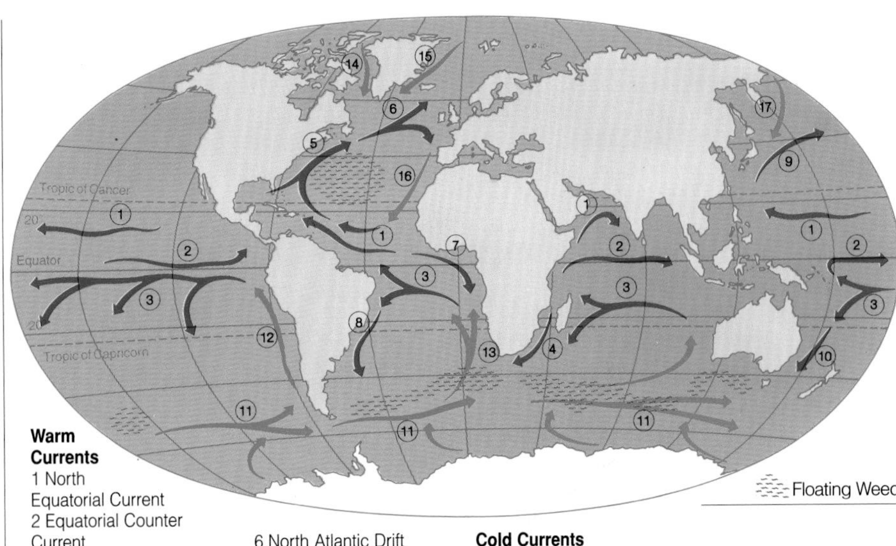

EVER-MOVING OCEANS *The oceans' surface currents carry great bodies of cold or warm water to different parts of the globe and have long been used by trading ships. Most remain fairly constant, but some can suddenly change course – usually during unseasonal or extreme weather.*

oasis Area in a DESERT surrounding a well or a natural spring where there is enough water to support plantlife. The water is supplied from deposits, or aquifers, in underlying sandstone; its source is sometimes as far as 800 km away.

ocean Salt water oceans originally formed when water vapour escaped from the Earth in huge volcanic eruptions. As it fell it cooled, covering nearly 71 per cent of the Earth's surface with water. Run-off from the land dissolved minerals from the rocks, producing a salty sea. The three principal oceans are the Pacific (which covers a third of the globe), the Atlantic and the Indian. The ice-covered Arctic and the waters surrounding Antarctica, called the Antarctic or Southern Ocean, are much smaller.

ocean currents Surface currents are driven by prevailing WINDS and form part of huge ocean gyres – circular movements of water in each of the great ocean basins which flow anticlockwise in the southern seas and clockwise in the northern seas, due to the CORIOLIS EFFECT. Major surface currents along the southern African coast are the cool, northward-flowing Benguela Current along the west coast and the warm South Equatorial Current which flows southwards along the east coast. The latter becomes compacted as it squeezes into the channel between the east coast of southern Africa and the island of Madagascar, creating the unusually warm, fast-flowing Mozambique-Agulhas Current that makes this part of the coast so treacherous for shipping. Other examples of ocean currents are the Peru (Humboldt) Current, which in some years produces EL NIÑO. Deep ocean currents result from contrasts in the density of different water masses – for example, dense cold water is carried from the polar areas, and gradually warms to emerge at the tropics.

ocean depths The average depth of the oceans is nearly 4 km; the greatest depths are recorded in the Pacific Ocean trenches – 11 km in the Marianas Trench near the Philippines. The continental shelf regions, with an average depth of 200 m, are of greatest economic importance, for their fishing and OIL deposits. The continental slope also holds an enormous abundance of marine life – down to a depth of around 1 000 m, below which light does not penetrate and photosynthesizing plants cannot exist. But even below this depth, down to about 2 000 m, there is a substantial animal population, including giant squid and angler fish. Beyond the continental slope is the ocean floor, with depths of 6 000 m, characterized by the sediment-covered abyssal plain. Here scavenger fish such as the rat-tails live.

ocean ridges Series of volcanic mountains forming a 80 000 km chain along the ocean floors – the largest single feature on the Earth's crust. Sometimes the mountains rise more than 3 000 m to form islands such as Iceland along the Mid-Atlantic Ridge. The ridges, which form where SEA-FLOOR SPREADING takes place, help to confirm the theory of PLATE TECTONICS.

❖ Hydrothermal vents on ocean ridges, produced by undersea volcanic activity, may have been the source of the earliest life forms on Earth. Water is driven by convective circulation and rises to temperatures above 100°C. Heat-loving microbes thrive here, providing food for giant tube worms.

oil Naturally occurring viscous mixture, including fossil hydrocarbons which yields combustible fuels, petrochemicals and lubricants which are extracted at different stages of ▷OIL REFINING. Crude oil consists of the partially decomposed remains of tiny sea plants and animals which have been buried under layers of rock.

❖ Offshore oil production, which began as early as 1896 off California, now accounts for 25 per cent of total output.

ore ROCK containing minerals that yields metals or any other important elements in quantities sufficient to make mining economical. One example is bauxite, the chief ore of aluminium. Gold, silver, platinum and copper can be mined as pure metals, but most metals are found as alloys or as chemical compounds. They are deposited in veins in rocks by water containing dissolved salts. Different minerals crystallize out at different water temperatures. After ores are mined, metals are extracted by crushing, heating, electrolysis and other chemical methods, and also by using bacteria. (See also GEMSTONES.)

❖ The average grade of gold ore mined in South Africa yields 5 to 6 g of gold per ton of rock. The minute particles of gold in the ore are generally in too low a concentration to be seen with the naked eye.

ozone layer Thin concentration of ozone gas, O_3, in the upper ATMOSPHERE – 15-40 km above the Earth. Ozone is formed by the action of ▷ULTRAVIOLET RADIATION from the Sun on atmospheric oxygen. It shields the Earth from the harmful effects of this radiation which would otherwise kill or injure most living things on the planet. Ozone can easily be destroyed by chemical reaction, especially by CFCs and nitrogen oxides from car exhausts. Satellite surveys show large 'holes' in the ozone layer around the poles, and over large urban conurbations, especially in summer. It is feared that these may be linked to an increase in skin cancers and eye cataracts, which are associated with overexposure to ultraviolet radiation.

plate tectonics Theory that the EARTH's crust is made up of distinct plates whose movement causes CONTINENTAL DRIFT and MOUNTAIN BUILDING. There are nine main plates, and as many as 16 smaller ones. Some plates diverge at OCEAN RIDGES, pushed apart by molten rock, or magma, forcing its way up between the plates. This process can throw up volcanic mountains above sea level. Where plates collide, or converge, one plate can sink under another, forcing the other upwards. This is called a subduction zone, and these zones circle the Pacific in a so-called 'ring of fire', where volcanoes erupt and EARTHQUAKES occur with great frequency. The plates are thought to float on denser matter beneath the crust of the Earth, carried by convection currents in the hot mantle. Over millions of years they have moved around the globe, reconstructing the landmasses.

❖ Hotspots occur where there are isolated magma vents within the Earth's plates; 16 of them have been identified. When a plate moves slowly over a hotspot, a chain of volcanic islands forms – such as the Hawaiian Islands, where Mauna Kea rises 10 000 m from the ocean floor.

pollution Contamination by poisonous or harmful matter, as in the discharge of sewage or toxic waste, such as heavy metals, into rivers or the sea. Other forms of pollution include NUCLEAR WASTE, the emission of gases that cause ACID RAIN, GLOBAL WARMING and photochemical SMOG, and CFCs which damage the OZONE LAYER. High levels of heat, light and noise generated by industrial processes, traffic noise and amplified music are also forms of pollution. Many industrialized countries are introducing tougher laws to control pollution.

radiocarbon dating The age of organic material can be determined by measuring the extent of the decay of the radioactive isotope carbon-14 in it. Radiocarbon dating is used extensively by geologists, palaeontologists and archaeologists. Carbon-14 is produced naturally in the atmosphere by the action of cosmic rays on nitrogen. During ▷PHOTOSYNTHESIS it is absorbed by green plants as carbon dioxide and spreads to animals through the food chain. As long as organisms continue to live, they absorb carbon-14. When they die, the absorption ceases. Carbon-14 has a radioactive ▷HALF-LIFE of 5 700 years – that

EARTH-SHAKING *Movement of the Earth's tectonic plates builds mountains, fuels volcanoes, unleashes earthquakes (particularly around the Pacific plate) and renews the Earth's crust.*

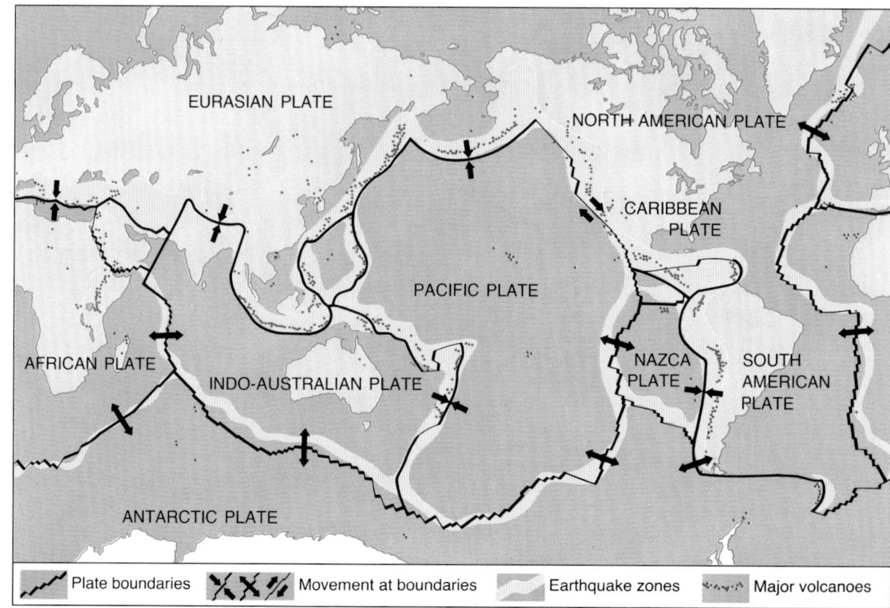

is, in 5 700 years half the carbon-14 will have turned back into nitrogen. So by measuring how much carbon-14 remains in a sample, it is possible to work out its age. Rocks can be similarly dated using potassium-argon.

rainbow When sunlight falls on rain, spray or fog, the droplets split light into its constituent colours (red, orange, yellow, green, blue, indigo and violet), or ▷SPECTRUM, because of ▷REFRACTION. In the sky, a rainbow always appears in the opposite direction to the Sun. Sometimes a double (or even triple) rainbow appears, the fainter rainbow appearing higher in the sky with the order of the colours reversed.

rainforest Thick forest that grows where rainfall typically averages above 1 500 mm a year. Equatorial, or tropical, rainforests are wet all year round. Subtropical rainforests have a MONSOON, or a wet season, and a season of drought. Rainforests are particularly rich in plant and animal life, possibly because the habitat has remained unaltered for millions of years, allowing an enormous number of species to evolve. A typical equatorial rainforest has a many-layered tree canopy. The tallest trees tower at 50 m, with a lower layer at about 20 m and a third up to 15 m. The highest level is occupied by leaf-eating monkeys, woodpeckers and flying squirrels. Inhabiting the lower canopy are immensely varied insects, fruit-feeders such as bats and hummingbirds that rely on nectar. Epiphytes, such as orchids and bromeliads, grow on tree hosts without harming them.

❖ A current annual loss (now mainly in Asia) of some 52 000 km^2 of rainforest from logging and agriculture may have damaged the Earth's ability to absorb carbon dioxide, contributing to GLOBAL WARMING. It has also caused the extinction of many plants and insects. Since most nutrients and energy are locked up in the vegetation, its destruction exposes thin, poor soils to erosion.

Richter scale Measure of magnitude of an EARTHQUAKE detected on a seismograph. Introduced by C F Richter in 1935, the scale begins at 0 – the smallest earthquake Richter could detect – and increases by one unit for each tenfold increase in magnitude. For example, an earthquake measuring 6 on the Richter scale is 1 000 times more powerful than one measuring 3. The worst recorded earthquake in South Africa, which hit the town of Tulbagh in the Western Cape in 1969, measured 6,5 on the Richter scale. One of the largest recorded quakes, measuring 8,3, hit Chile in 1960; the 1995 earthquake in the Japanese city of Kobe measured 7,2.

❖ Another scale – the Mercalli scale – grades earthquakes from 1 to 12 according to the disturbance felt by people, from tiny tremors to total destruction.

rift valley Steep-sided, flat-bottomed valley formed by subsidence of the Earth's crust between two FAULTS.

❖ The East African Rift Valley is part of a rift system that runs from the valley of the River Jordan and the Dead Sea, through the Gulf of Aqaba, and across eastern Africa to the coast near Beira in Mozambique – a distance of about 6 400 km. It can be seen clearly in photographs of the Earth taken from space.

river Originating in run-off from mountains, lakes, springs or meltwater from snow fields or glaciers, rivers shape the landscape. They play an important part in the HYDROLOGIC CYCLE and in the EROSION of land both above ground and below the surface, where cave systems are formed. The speed of water flow in rivers, which determines the amount of sediment eroded and transported, varies greatly; maximum flow usually occurs at the centre of the channel – nearer the banks it is reduced by friction. Some rivers fan out into a delta of several channels as they reach the sea, while others flow through a single estuary. Near the sea, rivers often cross a flat area where the river slows, depositing sediments as it meanders across a flood plain. An oxbow, or crescent-shaped, lake may form after a period of flood when the river cuts through its banks, bypassing the loop of a meander. An upheaval of the landmass may raise the flood plain, whereupon the process of erosion begins again.

❖ Rivers deposit up to 8 000 million tons of sediment into the oceans every year.

rock Main material of the EARTH's crust, composed chiefly of various minerals. Rock can be classified into three types: igneous, sedimentary and metamorphic, according to its origin. Igneous rock is cooled magma ejected from the mantle as LAVA. Examples of igneous rock include granite, the basis of continental rock and much used in building and road construction, and basalt, generated at OCEAN RIDGES. These are made up principally of the minerals quartz, feldspar, mica and hornblende, and vary in their crystal size according to how near the Earth's surface they were formed; glass-like obsidian is a surface-cooled rock, while gabbro, a basalt that cooled deep below the Earth's crust, is made up of crystals larger than 10 mm. Sedimentary rock results from layers of muds and sands being deposited at the bottom of

UNSEASONAL SANCTUARY *This Venezuelan rainforest is home to a vast range of wildlife, but like other rainforests, it has no seasonal rhythm – every plant has its own life cycle.*

ROCK OF AGES *Layers of sedimentary rock line canyons in Arizona, USA (top left); the hexagonal columns of Antrim's Giant Causeway are igneous basalt (left); and marble at Pilbara, Australia, is metamorphic rock (above).*

ancient seas and compressed, leaving clearly defined strata. Sandstone, shale, limestone and COAL, which is formed from organic matter, are all examples of sedimentary rock. Metamorphic rock is a result of the transfomation of sedimentary or igneous rock by heat, pressure and chemical action underground. Slate, schist and marble are examples; marble is metamorphosed limestone with the same chemical composition, but much denser and harder.

❖ Another example of igneous rock is Kimberlite, 'blue ground' that occurs in cylindrical veins and often contains diamonds.

❖ In the process known as the rock cycle, igneous rock is eroded and laid down as sedimentary rock, which in turn may be transformed by the action of heat and pressure into metamorphic rock, before volcanic activity turns it back into igneous rock. An entire cycle takes millions of years.

❖ Potassium-argon is used to date rock, in a method similar to RADIOCARBON DATING. By measuring the ratio of rates of decay of potassium-40 and argon-40, one meteorite was found to be 4 500 million years old. The oldest rock on Earth (4 000 million years) was found in Greenland, while rock in the Limpopo Valley dates back more than 3 850 million years.

sea-floor spreading Enlarging of the sea floor on either side of an OCEAN RIDGE. It occurs where tectonic plates are moving apart and hot magma wells up from the Earth's interior. At some ocean ridges, the sea floor is spreading by as much as 17 cm a year. (See also PLATE TECTONICS.)

sea level The mean surface height of the sea, measured from a fixed point on land over a period of at least 19 years, and used as a reference point for all other altitudes. Sea level is constantly fluctuating due to TIDES, ATMOSPHERIC PRESSURE, WINDS and OCEAN CURRENTS; the density of sea water can also affect it. Satellite surveys are now used to measure changes in sea level.

❖ Major climatic changes such as ICE AGES caused a lowering of sea level because sea water was locked up in ice caps. During the last ice age, the huge weight of ice caused much of northern Europe and North America to sink. When the ice retreated, these areas started to rise, sometimes leaving coastal features well inland. Stockholm is still rising at a rate of 40 cm a century. Sea level has also continued to rise since the last ice age – at a rate of about 13 mm a year this century. Some scientists believe this may also be partly due to the melting of polar ice caps as a result of GLOBAL WARMING.

seismic wave Shock wave transmitted through the Earth from an EARTHQUAKE or explosion, which can cause giant waves or TSUNAMIS. The reflection and refraction of artificial seismic waves are used to locate OIL, NATURAL GAS and minerals, as well as to study the Earth's inner structure.

smog Mixture of smoke and fog that hangs in a pall over large cities. There are two types: sulphurous smog, produced by coal burning, and photochemical smog, caused by sunlight acting on hydrocarbons and nitric oxides from car exhausts. The gases formed, including ozone, which is toxic at low altitudes, damage plants, irritate the eyes and cause distress to people with lung complaints.

soil Agriculturalists classify soils as sands, clays or loams. Sands have large particles (0,02-2 mm) and dry out quickly in the sun. Clays have tiny particles (0,002 mm) and are heavy, sticky and easily waterlogged. Loam is a fertile mixture of sand, clay, humus (dead and rotting organic material) and living organisms. Geologists classify soils according to their origin: alluvial soils are formed by particles of eroded rock deposited by rivers; drift, or till, is left by glaciers; loess is soil that has been carried by the wind; and sedimentary soil comes directly from the breakdown or weathering of the underlying bedrock. In horticulture, soil is measured in terms of its acidity or alkalinity – its pH value. This can vary in a garden, depending on how the soil has been treated, but ranges from pH5 (acid) to pH8 (alkaline) with most plants preferring pH6,5.

stalactites and stalagmites Tapering rock formations in limestone caves which hang from the roof (stalactites) or grow from the floor (stalagmites). They form mainly from calcium carbonate, although other carbonates and sulphides are also deposited. Taking thousands of years to grow, stalactites and stalagmites do not necessarily form in pairs, but where they do, they eventually join to form a column.

NATURE'S SCULPTURE *Stalactites and stalagmites in the Cango Caves near Oudtshoorn.*

❖ Cleopatra's Needle, a 10 m stalagmite in the Cango Caves near Oudtshoorn, was formed over some 150 000 years.

temperature inversion A rise in the temperature of the atmosphere with increasing altitude – the reverse of the usual situation in which air temperature drops with altitude. Temperature inversions prevent air circulating freely in convection currents and often occur at a cold or warm FRONT. They can often happen over cities where air pollution prevents much sunlight from reaching the ground: warm air in the upper atmosphere traps cooler, polluted air near the ground, causing SMOG. Nocturnal temperature inversions frequently lead to fog.

thunderstorm Storm caused by strong, rising air currents, accompanied by LIGHTNING. When a deep layer of moist air is forced to rise by a cold FRONT or by heating from warm ground, the water vapour in it condenses, releasing heat and accelerating the updraft. Higher still, the water droplets freeze, releasing yet more heat. The clouds rise until they reach the tropopause (see diagram p 464) in the ATMOSPHERE, where hot air can rise no further, giving them their flat-topped anvil shape. This generates a down-current, leading to heavy rain or hail.
❖ Although thunder and lightning occur at the same time, light from a stroke travels nearly 700 times faster than sound so that the thunder is heard up to a few seconds later.
❖ Thunderstorms are rare in polar regions where the ground produces little heat, but in Java they occur on up to 320 days a year.

tidal wave Common but incorrect name for the giant wave called a TSUNAMI.

tide Regular rise and fall of sea level caused by differences in the gravitational pull on different points on the Earth's surface. Because it is nearer to the Earth, the Moon's effect is more than twice that of the Sun, while other planets produce much slighter effects. Where the Moon's pull is dominant, tides occur 52 minutes later each day, because of the Moon's motion. Where the Sun is dominant, as at Tahiti, tides occur at the same time each day. When the Sun and Moon are both in the same direction, at a new or full Moon, their effects reinforce one another, producing a particularly high or spring tide. At the first and last quarters of the Moon, the Sun and Moon pull in opposite directions, producing a low or neap tide. The shape and size of the oceans moderate the effects of the Moon's gravitational force. Tides range from 16,6 m at the Bay of Fundy, Nova Scotia, to 60 cm around the shores of the Mediterranean.
❖ A tidal range of 3 m or more can be harnessed to generate electricity.
❖ Tidal friction has slowed the Earth's rotation. Daily growth lines on fossilised corals from the Devonian period 400 million years ago show that, within one year, which lasted about the same length of time as now, there were more than 400 days.

tornado Narrow, rapidly spinning funnel of air that descends from a thundercloud – an extreme example of spiralling air in a CYCLONE. Tornadoes, also called twisters, are stronger than HURRICANES, blowing at speeds of up to 800 km/h, with a violent updraft that lifts lorries and even entire buildings.
❖ Tornadoes occur commonly in 'Tornado Alley' which runs northeastwards across Oklahoma and Kansas, USA. Warm, moist air from the Gulf of Mexico meets cold, dry air from the Rockies on the Great Plains, giving rise to daily storms in late spring.
❖ Southern Africa's worst tornado hit the town of Roodepoort on the West Rand on 26 November 1948. Within five minutes it had laid waste to a strip of residential land 300 m wide and 3 km long, killing three people.

tsunami Japanese word for a giant wave caused by an earthquake. At sea the wave may be hundreds of kilometres long and may travel at speeds of more than 650 km/h. In deep water it is relatively harmless, but in shallow water its speed and length diminish rapidly, causing it to rear up as high as 80 m as the waters surge inland.

volcano Vent in the Earth's crust from which molten rock, or magma, in the form of LAVA, is ejected, together with gases and ash. Active volcanoes usually lie along plate boundaries and their existence is explained by PLATE TECTONICS. The shape of the volcano depends on the composition of its lava. In Hawaii eruptions occur slowly with fluid, low-silica lava, flowing over large areas. Stromboli, off northern Sicily, and also Mount Fuji, Japan, erupt more strongly, expelling ash and rivers of more viscous, high-silica lava, resulting in a steeper sided, cone-shaped volcano. Some eruptions such as Mount St Helens in California, which blew in 1980, and Mount Pinatubo in the Philippines, which erupted in 1991, make huge explosions. They throw rock, ash and clouds of gas into the atmosphere, probably causing GLOBAL WARMING (by stopping heat from the Earth escaping), and other long-term changes to the weather. The most violent explosions blow out the interior of the volcano, forming a crater, which is called a caldera if it is more than 1 km wide. Lava domes occur where the lava is so viscous that it simply piles up over the vent. Fissure vents are narrow cracks emitting lava; they can be several kilometres long.
❖ In 1883, the eruption of Krakatoa – a volcanic Indonesian island – had 26 times the power of the greatest H-bomb test.

waterspout TORNADO that occurs at sea. The vortex can suck water vapour hundreds of metres into the air. Most waterspouts occur in the tropics but they can also occur at higher

VOLATILE VOLCANO *The Hawaiian volcano Kilauea spewing volcanic ash 300 m high into the air. Kilauea erupts about every three weeks, for just a few hours or for days at a time.*

WATERWAY *The Okavango Delta, Africa's largest oasis, 15 000 sq km in area, provides a wetland habitat for birds and animals.*

latitudes in summer. Waterspouts more than 35 m in diameter can overturn boats and cause damaging winds.

❖ In a few cases, showers of fish have been known to fall on land after a waterspout had sucked them into the sky.

water table Upper level of ground water in subterranean rock. If a layer of rock that holds water, such as sandstone, is underlaid by a layer of impermeable rock, it forms an aquifer, or underground reservoir from which water can be extracted via bore holes. If the rock surfaces, the water will emerge as a spring. Where water pressure in an aquifer is high enough to force the water above the water table, an artesian well can be sunk to extract water without the need for pumping.

❖ Overuse of water or drought may cause a fall in the water table from which it may take years to recover. In some arid regions resources of 'fossil' water that existed for thousands of years in underground reservoirs cannot be renewed. In the Middle East, scarcity of ground water, as well as diversion of water from rivers upstream, is a cause of conflict as populations swell. Similar disputes have also arisen in drier rural regions of southern Africa.

weather forecasting Scientific weather forecasting began in the 17th century with the development of barometers to measure ATMOSPHERIC PRESSURE. This became practical only in the 1830s, when the telegraph permitted the rapid transmission of data. First attempts at shipping forecasts were made in the 19th century. Forecasters today use charts produced by computers from data collected from weather balloons (radiosondes), high-flying aircraft and satellites. The rate of approaching weather or wind speed is measured with an anemometer; at sea it is given according to the BEAUFORT SCALE.

westerlies Dominant wind system that normally blows from the 'horse' latitudes – 30° North or South – towards the poles. The wind is from the northwest in the Southern Hemisphere and from the southwest in the Northern Hemisphere. The westerlies are associated with changeable weather.

wetland Area where the water level is near or above the surface of the ground for most of the year, creating a habitat for a wide range of aquatic bird and animal life. In southern Africa, wetlands occur mainly along the east coast of Mozambique and KwaZulu-Natal, in the Okavango Delta and in northern Namibia.

whirlpool Strong, swirling eddy or maelstrom where two tidal currents meet. Notable whirlpools occur in the Naruto Strait between Japan's Inland Sea and the Pacific; in the Strait of Messina between Sicily and mainland Italy; and off Sicily's north coast – the Charybdis whirlpool.

whirlwind Swirling column of air created when an overheated layer of air near the ground causes a localized low pressure area. These 'dust devils' are common in the hot, dry interior of southern Africa in summer.

wind Movement of air from areas of high ATMOSPHERIC PRESSURE to areas of low pressure. Differences in atmospheric pressure are largely due to the Sun warming the atmosphere and the Earth unequally. Winds do not blow directly from a place with high pressure to places with low pressure; their path is curved due to the CORIOLIS EFFECT. There are three main belts of prevailing wind either side of the Equator: the trade winds, the WESTERLIES and the polar easterlies, which strongly influence OCEAN CURRENTS. Along the Equator there is a region of low wind, known as the Doldrums, where the northeast and southeast trade winds meet. Sailors were dependent on the trade winds for their voyages west from Europe, hence their name. In some areas seasonal reversal of the wind results in a MONSOON. As well as the seasons, the Earth's physical features affect winds, especially local winds such as the cool summer mistral, which blows along the Rhône Valley in France, and the hot, dry, turbulent winter berg winds that blow seawards from the escarpment of southern Africa a day or two ahead of an approaching cold FRONT. In coastal areas winds often reverse daily. Strong winds may combine with high tides, causing storm surges and flooding.

❖ Wind turbines are increasingly being used to produce electricity.

wind-chill Index of the degree of atmospheric cooling felt by a person. The stronger a cold wind blows, the quicker a body cools. It is easier to survive low temperatures in calm air than considerably higher temperatures in a strong wind. Wind-chill is sometimes incorporated in weather forecasts by giving the equivalent temperature in calm air. At 0°C, a 40 km/h wind gives a wind-chill equivalent of -16°C. At -40°C, the same wind gives a wind-chill equivalent of -75,5°C.

THE WAY THE WINDS BLOW *Wind systems often start near the Equator where air – heated by the land and sea – rises, leaving an area of low pressure beneath it which 'sucks in' surrounding air.*

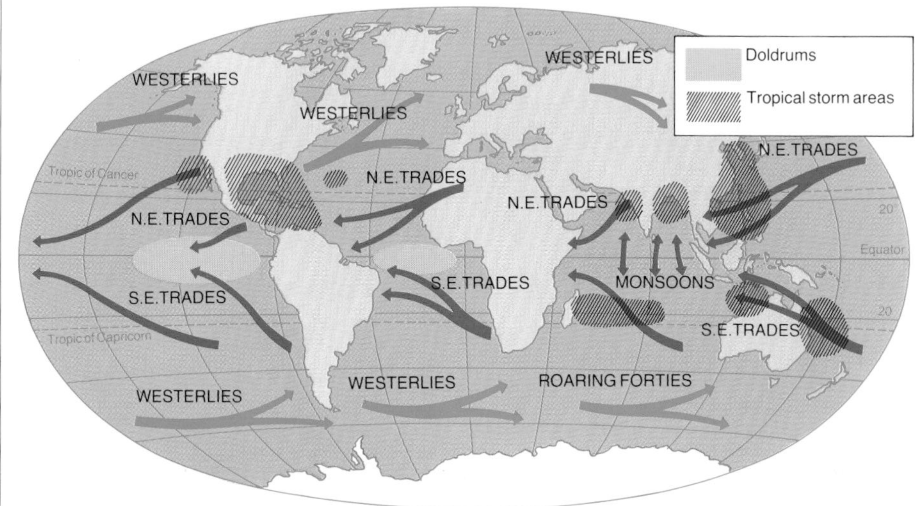

THE LIVING WORLD

Since the first living cells appeared on Earth some 4 000 million years ago, evolution has produced more than 1,5 million species of living organisms. Wild plants, from tiny algae to huge trees, and wild animals, from lowly insects to proud lions, have been supplemented by forms domesticated for human uses. Uniting the natural world is the discovery that one type of molecule, DNA, controls all forms of life.

HEADSTRONG RIVALS *Two male springboks lock horns in a show of fierce aggression during the mating season. The winner will have the pick of the female members of a herd.*

acquired characteristics Features that an organism acquires during its lifetime. The muscles developed by a body builder are one example. In the early 19th century, the French biologist Jean Baptiste Lamarck (1744-1829) suggested that parents might pass on such acquired characteristics to their offspring, and so bring about evolutionary change. Lamarck believed, for example, that giraffes 'stretched' their necks by browsing on tall trees, and that each generation 'inherited' slightly longer necks from their parents. However, his theories were superseded by those of British naturalist Charles DARWIN.
❖ During the communist era in the Soviet Union, Darwin's theories were rejected in favour of those of Jean Baptiste Lamarck.

adaptation Any feature or special ability that improves an organism's chances of survival in its environment. Adaptations can be anatomical, physiological or behavioural. The fins of fishes and whales are adaptations to water; the wings of bats and birds are adaptations to air; hibernation is an adaptation to cold winters. Such adaptations are usually the result of natural selection over many generations. Adaptations of individuals during their own lifetime – for example, the development of greater lung capacity by people who move to mountain areas where there is less oxygen – are not passed on to their offspring, and they are more properly called ACQUIRED CHARACTERISTICS.

aestivation Dormancy in response to heat or drought; the summer counterpart of HIBERNATION. Breathing almost ceases and the animal stops eating. Aestivators are usually cold-blooded. For example, some African lungfish species spend the summer buried in dried swamp mud, becoming active again when the autumn rains come.

aggression Animals use aggression to attack, to defend and to threaten opponents, usually of the same species. Aggression is used to establish and defend a territory, as well as during courtship, when rival males compete fiercely for females. It is also used to establish and maintain a position within a social hierarchy. Between members of the same species, aggression generally takes the form of ritualized fighting, where injury is unlikely to occur. However, fighting between members of different species, over food, for example, often results in injury or death.

algae Simple plantlike organisms which live mainly in water, although some species are found in damp conditions on land. There are more than 25 000 species of algae, ranging from microscopic single cells to seaweeds up to 60 m in length. Algae belong to the kingdom Protista.

alternation of generations Phenomenon among all plants and some animals of alternating between asexual and sexual REPRODUCTION from one generation to the next. Among plants, mosses and ferns show alternation of generations most clearly. The green moss plant reproduces sexually to produce a spore-producing capsule. This reproduces asexually, releasing spores that grow into a new sexually reproducing stage. Animals showing alternation of generations include the aphid, which during the summer reproduces asexually, producing large numbers of offspring; in the autumn, aphids reproduce sexually, which ensures variation in their young.

amino acids Building blocks of PROTEINS, which are found in all living things. All amino acids are made up of combinations of carbon, hydrogen, nitrogen and oxygen; some also contain sulphur. Plants and some microorganisms can make all the amino acids they require through PHOTOSYNTHESIS. Animals can make only some of the amino acids they need; the rest have to be supplied by their diet.

amoeba Single-celled protozoan that can be up to 1 mm in length. Most species of amoeba live in water, mud or soil; some are parasitic, and one species is responsible for human amoebic dysentery. Amoebae move by sending out projections called pseudopodia ('false feet'). They feed on other tiny organisms and bacteria by surrounding and engulfing them. Amoebas, which belong to the kingdom Protista, reproduce asexually, simply by splitting in two.

amphibians Cold-blooded vertebrates such as frogs, toads, newts and salamanders that typically spend part of their lives on land and part in water. Most amphibians begin life as water-dwelling LARVAE before changing, by METAMORPHOSIS, into air-breathing adults. They have moist, soft skin, often with poison glands, but without scales, which would inhibit respiration. Amphibians evolved from fish some 370 million years ago and were the first vertebrates to emerge from the sea – where life began – and to walk on land.
❖ The term 'amphibian' derives from the Greek *amphibios*, 'living a double life'.

angiosperms Flowering plants belonging to the phylum Angiospermophyta and comprising by far the largest group of plants, ranging from the daisy to the oak tree. All angiosperms (literally 'cased seeds'), which include the aloe and the protea, produce seeds within a mature ovary, or fruit, unlike the other seed-bearing plants, or GYMNOSPERMS.

animal Unlike plants, animals cannot manufacture their own food. They obtain it by eating either plants (herbivores), animals (carnivores) or both (omnivores). With some exceptions, such as coral, most animals are also able to move from one location to another. They usually have specialized senses and respond quickly to stimuli. They range in complexity from simple sponges to human beings, but they all belong to the kingdom Animalia. (See panel below.)

annelids Soft-bodied, segmented worms belonging to the phylum Annelida. Annelids have a simple circulatory and nervous system. Some 9 000 species are found in sea and fresh water as well as in most habitats on land; these include earthworms, ragworms and leeches. The giant earthworm of Eastern Cape can reach a length of up to 3 m.

annual Flowering plant which completes its life cycle within one year. (Compare BIENNIAL and PERENNIAL.)

antennae Pair of long, thin sensory organs which project from the heads of ARTHROPODS. The antennae can be moved around and are normally used to touch, smell and judge air and water currents. Some crustaceans also use them for swimming.

arachnids Class of ARTHROPODS, mostly land-living, characteristically having four pairs of legs, simple eyes and no antennae. They include spiders, scorpions, ticks and mites. Spiders have poisonous fangs, while scorpions have claws and a poisonous sting; both are carnivores, or flesh-eaters. Most mites and ticks are parasites.

arthropod Organism belonging to the phylum Arthropoda, a group of invertebrates which have a hard external segmented skeleton that supports and protects the body. Its antennae, mouthparts and jointed legs are all arranged in pairs. Arthropods make up about 85 per cent of all animal species. The main arthropod groups are INSECTS, ARACHNIDS such as spiders and mites, CRUSTACEANS, centipedes and millipedes.

autotroph Organism that can make all the complex organic molecules necessary for it to survive from simple inorganic molecules. The most familiar autotrophs are green plants, which make food and materials for growth and repair using sunlight energy, water and carbon dioxide in the process of PHOTOSYNTHESIS. Other autotrophs include ALGAE and some BACTERIA. All other organisms are HETEROTROPHS.

bacteria (singular: bacterium) Microscopic, mostly single-celled organisms that are among the simplest living creatures and lack the nucleus found in more complex cells. They make up the kingdom Monera. Simple bacteria were the first forms of life to appear on Earth 4 billion years ago. Some types of bacteria are HETEROTROPHS, living as parasites, or as SAPROTROPHS which play a vital role in breaking down dead matter and recycling it into the soil. Other types are AUTOTROPHS, using light or chemicals as their source of energy. Many parasitic bacteria cause diseases, such as tetanus in human beings, and crown gall in plants, which affects the leaves of trees. The genetic manipulation of bacteria for commercial purposes – for example, the mass production of human insulin – is an important aspect of biotechnology.

biennial Flowering plant which requires two growing seasons to complete its lifecycle. Food reserves built up in the first season are used to produce flowers and seeds in the second. Biennials include wild stock, Sweet William, Canterbury bell and the Cape forget-me-not. (Compare ANNUAL and PERENNIAL.)

THE ANIMAL KINGDOM

The animal kingdom's wide embrace includes birds, fish, insects and human beings. Invertebrates evolved from single-celled organisms more than 600 million years ago; vertebrates evolved from invertebrates some 100 million years later. Animals may be as different as leeches and lions, but the vast majority share typical characteristics, such as the power of locomotion, fixed structure and limited growth. They are grouped into around 35 phyla and then into classes such as mammals and birds, as this simplified chart shows.

ANIMALS
Kingdom Animalia

(* = number of species)

INVERTEBRATES

- **SPONGES** – *Phylum Porifera* – * 9 000
- **COELENTERATES** – *Phylum Coelenterata* – * 9 000 – e.g. jellyfish, coral
- **ROUNDWORMS** – *Phylum Nematoda* – * 12 000 – e.g. eelworm
- **FLATWORMS** – *Phylum Platyhelminthes* – * 20 000 – e.g. tapeworm
- **MOLLUSCS** – *Phylum Mollusca* – * 100 000 – e.g. snail, octopus
- **TRUE WORMS** – *Phylum Annelida* – * 15 000 – e.g. earthworm, leech
- **ECHINODERMS** – *Phylum Echinodermata* – * 7 000 – e.g. starfish, sea urchin 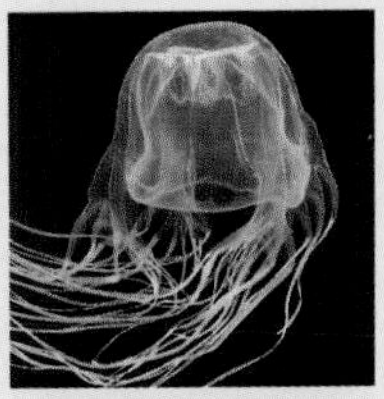
- **ARTHROPODS** – *Phylum Arthropoda* 
  - **INSECTS** – *Class Insecta* – * 800 000 + – e.g. mosquito, butterfly, aphid
  - **MILLIPEDES** – *Class Myriapoda* – * 7 500
  - **CENTIPEDES** – *Class Chilopoda* – * 2 500
  - **SPIDERS/SCORPIONS** – *Class Arachnida* – * 70 000 – e.g. spider, scorpion,
  - **CRUSTACEANS** – *Class Crustacea* – * 32 000 – e.g. crab, lobster, shrimp

VERTEBRATES

- **CHORDATES** – *Phylum Chordata*
  - **CARTILAGINOUS FISH** – *Class Chondrichthyes* – * 620 – e.g. shark, ray, dogfish
  - **BONY FISH** – *Class Osteichthyes* – * 25 000 + – e.g. salmon, elf, angelfish, cod
  - **AMPHIBIANS** – *Class Amphibia* – * 4 000 – e.g. frog, salamander, toad
  - **REPTILES** – *Class Reptilia* – * 6 000 – e.g. snake, crocodile
  - **BIRDS** – *Class Aves* – * 9 000 – e.g. ostrich, vulture, pigeon
  - **MAMMALS** – *Class Mammalia* – * 4 000 – e.g. lion, monkey, elephant

bioluminescence Production of light by certain living organisms. Some animals use the light to attract a mate, others to attract a meal. Glow-worms and fireflies as well as some algae and deep sea fish are bioluminescent.

birds There are more than 9 000 species of birds. They range in size from the bee hummingbird, which weighs just 1,6 g, to the flightless North African ostrich, which may weigh as much as 125 kg and stand 2,4 m tall. Birds can be found in almost all the Earth's habitats. Scientists now believe they evolved from flesh-eating dinosaurs around 220 million years ago. They became adapted to flight by evolving feathers, hollow bones for lightness, and feet modified as claws. Feathers not only permit flight, they also insulate the body, enabling birds to maintain their constant high body temperature of up to 40,5°C, which allows them to be so active. Most birds incubate their eggs in nests, sometimes in huge colonies, and care for their young, which generally are born naked and helpless. Many birds migrate in autumn to warmer feeding grounds, returning in spring to breed. Birds are warm-blooded vertebrates and belong to the class Aves. (See also MIGRATION.)

bivalve Mollusc with a shell made of two parts or valves connected by an elastic hinge. Bivalves, which include mussels, oysters and clams, live in sea and fresh water; some attach themselves to rock, while others bury themselves in sand or mud. Most feed on small particles extracted from water. Some bivalves are hermaphrodites with male organs developing first.

bulb Short underground stem wrapped in fleshy leaves which enclose a young shoot. In spring, the shoot grows upwards, using food from the fleshy leaves. After flowering, the plant dies back, storing food in the bulb during the winter ready to grow again next spring. Tulips, daffodils and onions all grow from bulbs. (Compare CORM.)

camouflage Most animals use camouflage to escape their predators, but avoiding detection can also be useful for animals waiting to ambush prey. Leopards, for example, are difficult to see in dappled sunlight. Countershading – a dark back and a light stomach – is used as camouflage by many fish, such as sharks and barracudas. Seen from above, the fish blends into the dark water, while from below, the light belly disappears into the sunlit surface. Chameleons change colour to blend with their surroundings by using pigment cells that can produce different patterns as well as colours.

carbohydrates Group of organic compounds which are the main source of energy for living things. Energy is derived by breaking down carbohydrates in RESPIRATION. The simplest carbohydrates are sugars, such as glucose and sucrose. But they are stored in complex forms – as glycogen in animals and as starch in plants.

CLEVER COLOURING *The horned toad adopts a convincing camouflage to avoid detection and merges into the leafy background of its natural habitat in the rainforests of Malaysia.*

cell Basic unit of life and the smallest part of a living organism that can lead an independent existence. Some simple organisms, such as BACTERIA, consist only of single cells, but all higher animals and plants are composed of large numbers of cells, organized into specialized tissues and organs; the human body contains 50 billion cells. All cells are enclosed within a thin membrane, which controls the passage of water, chemicals and waste products in and out of the cell. Within the membrane is the protoplasm which, in almost all cells, is divided into a nucleus and the watery cytoplasm. The nucleus is the control centre of the cell. It is here that the genetic material DNA, which contains the coded instructions for the growth and maintenance of the cell, is stored. The manufacturing centre of the cell is the cytoplasm, which is scattered with a number of structures called organelles. Among these are the mitochondria, where the reactions involved in RESPIRATION, the universal source of energy for the cell, take place, and the RIBOSOMES, where instructions from the DNA are used to assemble ENZYMES and other proteins. Plant cells differ from animal cells in having a tough outer wall of cellulose, which helps support the plant, and a central vacuole filled with sap, which keeps the cell rigid. Green plant cells also contain lens-shaped organelles, called chloroplasts; these are filled with the pigment chlorophyll, which captures the Sun's energy during PHOTOSYNTHESIS.

cell division The process that enables living things to grow, maintain themselves and reproduce. When a cell divides, it passes on a copy of its paired CHROMOSOMES, which contain the genetic material DNA, to each of its two offspring. In ordinary cell division, known as mitosis, each 'daughter' cell receives an exact copy of the parent cell's chromosomes. Mitosis is the form of cell division that takes place when a single fertilized cell develops into a complex multicellular organism such as a human being. The mechanism by which cells differentiate during growth to become, for example, nerve, muscle or bone, is still one of the great mysteries of biology. A different form of cell division, called meiosis, is used to produce sex cells, such as sperm or eggs: the daughter cells receive only half the full complement of chromosomes, so that when the egg is fertilized by a sperm, the full complement is restored. In meiosis, the initial duplication of chromosomes is followed by a mingling of genetic material between the two strands of each chromosome pair; the

ANIMAL AND PLANT CELLS

The cell is the microcosm of life. It builds up and breaks down molecules, stores energy and releases it, sends and receives messages, and reproduces. Its nucleus, containing DNA, floats in cytoplasm enclosed in a membrane. Although their structure is different, both animal and plant cells grow and develop by replicating themselves and dividing the cells created.

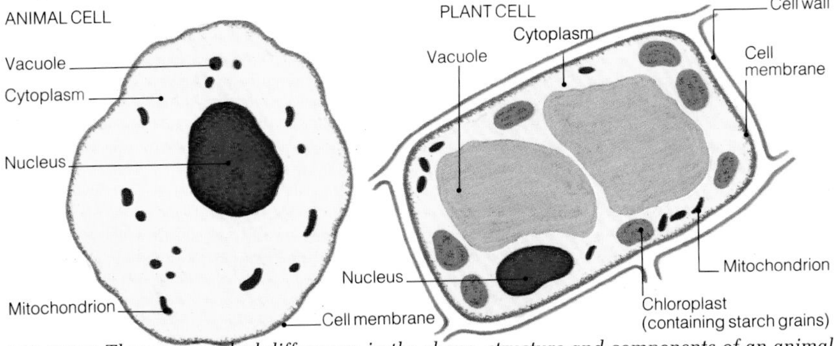

CELL TYPES *There are marked differences in the shape, structure and components of an animal cell (left) and a plant cell (right) with chloroplasts for photosynthesis and a rigid wall.*

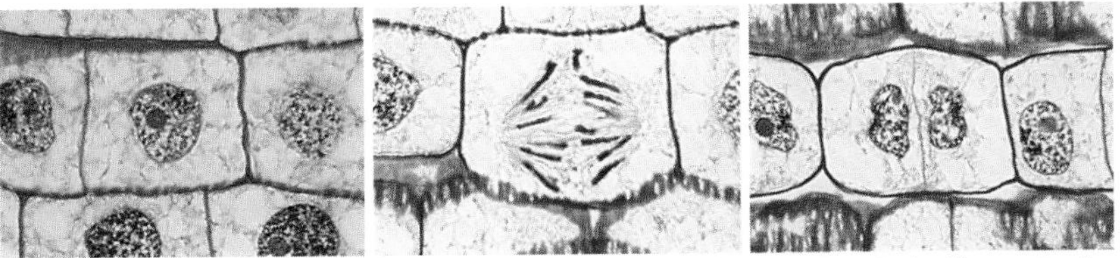

DIVISION *Images of an onion root cell during mitosis – cell division. First it duplicates its chromosomes. These are pulled apart, each set is encircled by a separate nuclear membrane, and two new nuclei are formed. The cell is then ready to divide into two identical cells.*

cell then divides to give two daughter cells, both of which divide once again with no further duplication of chromosomes to give a total of four daughter cells, each containing only a single strand of each chromosome pair.

cellulose Major component of plant cell walls which helps to support plants. Cellulose is a complex CARBOHYDRATE.

❖ Animals lack the enzymes to break down cellulose, so those with a diet high in cellulose – such as rabbits, cattle, horses, sheep and termites – use the services of specialized bacteria in their digestive systems. Without these bacteria, such animals would die.

cephalopod Class of marine mollusc, including squid, cuttlefish and octopus. They are distinguished by the mobile 'arms' around their heads used for catching and holding their prey, as well as by their excellent eyesight and their beaks. All cephalopods are predators and excellent swimmers. They swim by squirting out water in a form of jet propulsion.

cetaceans Group of aquatic mammals that includes whales, porpoises and dolphins. Unlike fish, cetaceans breathe air, do not have scales, are warm-blooded, they give birth to live young and suckle them. Cetaceans breathe through a blowhole in the top of the head, and some whales can hold their breath for several hours.

chlorophyll See PHOTOSYNTHESIS.

chromosomes Coiled structures in the nucleus of cells which carry the GENES that determine the characteristics of every organism. Chromosomes always come in pairs, except in sex cells, and all members of a species have the same number. Human beings have 23 pairs. Chromosomes become visible only under a microscope when the DNA molecules from which they are formed become shorter and thicker just before the cell splits in two, during CELL DIVISION. Mammals, which reproduce sexually, have a pair of sex chromosomes that are identified as X and Y; females have two Xs and males have an X and a Y.

❖ Sometimes during meiosis – the process of cell division that produces sex cells – chromosomes fail to separate, leaving the offspring with an extra chromosome in each cell. In human beings, an extra chromosome in pair 21 causes Down's syndrome, a particular manifestation of mental retardation.

circadian rhythm A 24-hour cycle of behaviour, as for example in sleep patterns and in the movement of flowers' petals. It is usually determined by the presence or absence of light. Normal patterns of behaviour continue for a few days if a subject is deprived of the normal cycle of light and dark, but then a new circadian rhythm emerges. (See also ▷BIORHYTHMS.)

classification System of arranging organisms into groups according to their physiological, anatomical or other characteristics. Organisms are divided into five kingdoms; animals, plants, fungi, protists (single-celled organisms and seaweeds), and monerans (bacteria and blue-green algae). Each kingdom is divided into phyla (singular: phylum), each phylum is divided into classes, each class into orders, each order into families, and each family into genera (singular: genus). Each genus is made up of one or more species; species are organisms which are very similar and which can interbreed to produce fertile offspring. Human beings *(Homo sapiens)*, for example, are members of the genus *Homo*, the family Hominoidea (together with gorillas and chimpanzees), the order Primates (with apes, monkeys and lemurs), the class Mammalia (all mammals), the phylum Chordata (with birds, reptiles, amphibians and fishes) and the kingdom Animalia (all animals).

❖ The modern system of classification and naming of species was devised by Swedish botanist Carolus Linnaeus (1707-78).

climax community A group of interdependent plants and animals growing and living in the same environment that have reached the final stage of their development in which the balance between them will remain stable almost indefinitely, barring human intervention or natural disaster. Examples are forests, such as the Brazilian rainforest, areas of the African savannah or the prairies of the American west, where there are large herds of grazing animals.

clone Organism that is genetically identical to its parent because it has been produced by asexual REPRODUCTION. Some plants, such as strawberries, blackberries, beeches and horse chestnuts, clone themselves by means of vegetative propagation, sending out horizontal shoots, or runners, that root themselves, and produce new plants. Single-celled organisms which reproduce by budding, or splitting in two, such as yeast or amoebas, are also cloning. Some invertebrates, such as aphids, reproduce rapidly by cloning.

❖ The possibility of cloning human beings or extinct organisms, such as dinosaurs, is a favourite theme of science fiction writers. While such a process is possible in theory, many biologists doubt that it will ever be achieved in practice.

cocoon Protective covering of eggs or larvae produced by some invertebrates. Many insect larvae spin a cocoon around themselves in preparation for turning into pupa during their METAMORPHOSIS.
❖ Most commercial silk is obtained from the cocoon of the Chinese silk moth.

coelenterate Animals that belong to the phylum Coelenterata are mostly sea-dwelling, and include jellyfish, anemones and corals. They have a central digestive cavity with a single opening that takes in food and expels waste. The opening is surrounded by tentacles with stinging cells which inject poison into prey.

cold-blooded (exothermic) Term that describes an animal whose body temperature is largely dependent on its environment. In fact, the blood of a cold-blooded animal may be very warm. All animals, apart from birds and mammals, are cold-blooded. Creatures who are cold-blooded become more active as their body temperatures increase. Lizards, for example, bask on warm rocks until they are warm and active enough to search for food.

conifers Cone-bearing trees such as cedars, pines and firs, most of which have needle-like leaves and are EVERGREEN, although some, such as larches, drop their needles once a year. They fall into the phylum Coniferophyta. The oldest trees are conifers, the 5 000-year-old bristlecone pines. A sequoia known as 'General Sherman' in California is the most massive single living thing; it has a girth of 24 m and stands 81 m high. The Californian redwood – 113 m high – is the tallest living tree.
❖ The yellowwood tree (Podocarpus) is a conifer indigenous to southern Africa; the 'Big Tree' of the Knysna forest is the Outeniqua yellowwood.

corm Swollen stem at the base of a plant which forms an underground food store during dormant periods. It is surrounded by protective scale leaves. In spring, the corm provides energy for the growth of leaves and flowers. Gladioli and freesias grow from corms. (Compare BULB.)

cotyledons First seed leaves of a plant after germination. They form part of the embryo plant and provide the food for it to grow into a seedling. Flowering plants are classified either as MONOCOTYLEDONS, which have one cotyledon in their seeds, or as DICOTYLEDONS which usually have two.

courtship Pattern of behaviour which an animal adopts to show it is ready to mate with one of its own species. The distinctive pattern is designed to attract a mate and also to counter the potential partner's natural fear or aggression. Ostriches use their wings in a characteristic way, peacocks give elaborate displays, while some male frogs and toads puff up their throats and croak. Courtship displays are also an important part of sexual selection in animals.

crustacean Group of mainly aquatic ARTHROPODS, which includes crabs, crayfish, lobsters, prawns and barnacles; woodlice are terrestrial crustaceans. Crustaceans typically have a thorax covered by a hard shieldlike carapace, or EXOSKELETON, made from chitin or bone, jointed limbs used for movement and capturing food, and a body divided into an abdomen and a head with compound eyes.
❖ The world's largest crustacean is the Japanese spider crab, which measures 46 cm across its body and up to 3 m from the tip of one leg to the tip of the leg opposite. Lobsters, which are marine creatures, are more commonly measured by weight; some giants weigh more than 18 kg.
❖ Rock lobsters, often incorrectly called

Tyrannosaurus One of the largest known flesh-eating land animals that lived more than 65 million years ago. It was almost 12 m long, 5,5 m high and weighed 7 tons.

Diplodocus This huge dinosaur lived in the Jurassic period, 150 million years ago. It was about 27 m long and would have weighed 12 tons.

crayfish (which are freshwater crustaceans) are measured by size in South Africa, where legally only specimens with a carapace of 80 mm or more in length may be caught.

cultivar Cultivated variety of plant developed as a result of agricultural or horticultural intervention. Strains of many plants, such as wheat, have been bred to be resistant to pests and bad weather conditions, while still producing a high yield.

Darwin, Charles Robert (1809-82) British naturalist whose concept of natural selection formed the basis for his theory of EVOLUTION. Darwin began to develop his ideas in the 1830s during an expedition to South America and the Galapagos Islands on HMS *Beagle*. In 1859 he published *On The Origin of Species by Means of Natural Selection*, in which he set out his theory that species evolve because nature selects those characteristics that help an individual to survive and breed. This, and his later work, *The Descent of Man* (1871), which suggested that human beings and apes shared a common ancestor, provoked violent opposition from the Church, since it challenged the Biblical account of the Creation and implied that human beings had not been created in God's image. Most scientists adopted Darwin's theories, which today are readily accepted by almost all but the most conservative of religious fundamentalists. The original theories have, however, been modified and extended in the light of advances in genetics.

EVOLUTIONIST *Charles Darwin who conceived the once provocative theory that human beings and apes share a common ancestry.*

deciduous Term describing plants that, unlike EVERGREENS, shed their leaves at the end of each growing season – in autumn in temperate regions, or at the start of the dry season in the tropics. Leaf fall helps prevent water loss when water is scarce, because the soil is either frozen or dry. The term may also describe deer antlers, or children's milk teeth, that are shed at a specific stage.

dicotyledons (dicots) Most abundant of the two groups of flowering plants, with some 170 000 species. Dicotyledons have two or more COTYLEDONS in their seeds, net-veined leaves, and flower parts arranged in multiples of four or five. They include most deciduous trees, cactuses and roses. (Compare MONOCOTYLEDONS.)

dinosaurs Group of REPTILES, now extinct, which were the dominant land animals on Earth from around 230 million to 65 million years ago. The name comes from the Greek for 'terrible lizard'. They lived on every continent and at least 1 000 species have been recorded, ranging from fiercesomely equipped predators such as *Tyrannosaurus rex* to giant browsing herbivores, or plant-eaters, such as the 20 m long *Brachiosaurus* and the armour-plated *Stegosaurus massospondylus*, which was found in southern Africa. The greatest number of dinosaur fossils found in southern Africa belong to *Massospondylus*. Up to 6 m in length, it had a small head and a long neck for its size. It walked on its four legs, although it probably stood on its hind legs for long periods while stretching to reach the leaves at the top of trees. Some dinosaurs were probably endothermic (warm-blooded), unlike modern-day reptiles. They laid eggs and some showed parental care. The two main divisions of the dinosaurs were the Saurischia, or lizard-hipped dinosaurs, which included the flesheaters, as well as huge planteaters such as *Apatosaurus*; and the Ornithischia, or bird-hipped dinosaurs, which included herbivores such as *iguanodons* and duck-billed *hadrosaurs*. The reason for the extinction of the dinosaurs remains a mystery. The fact that many other species became extinct at around the same time – including such groups as the giant flying *pterosaurs* and the marine *plesiosaurs* – suggests that some cataclysmic event, such as an

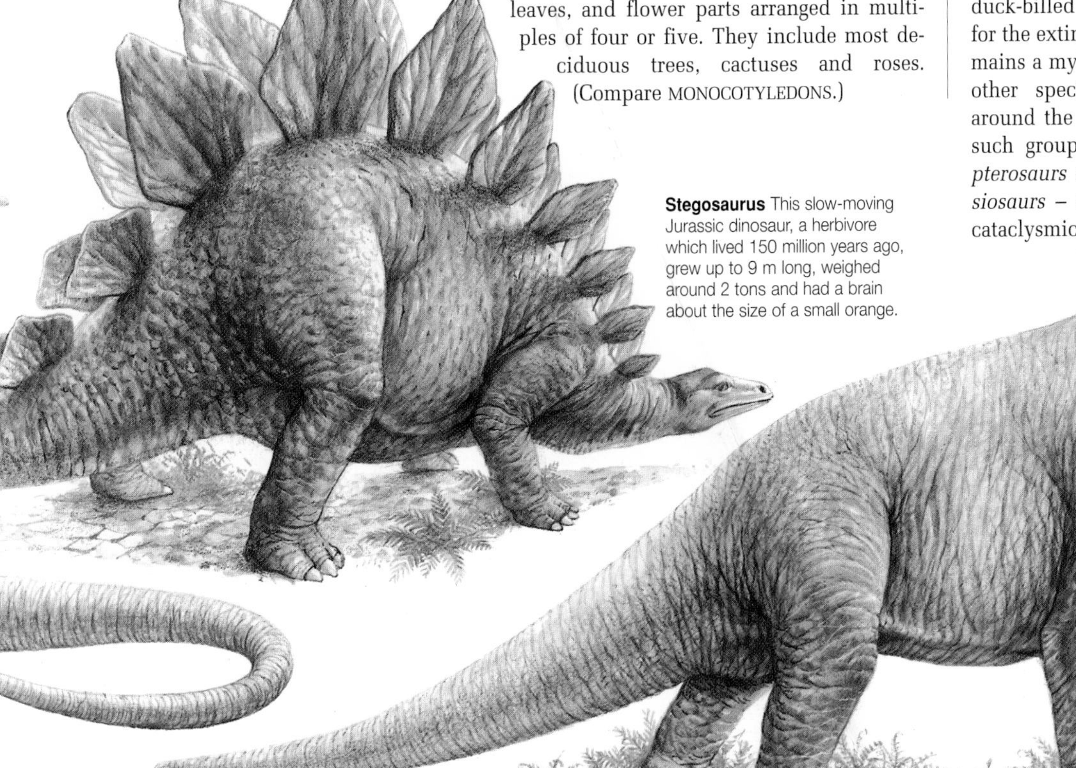

Stegosaurus This slow-moving Jurassic dinosaur, a herbivore which lived 150 million years ago, grew up to 9 m long, weighed around 2 tons and had a brain about the size of a small orange.

Brachiosaurus This Jurassic herbivore measured up to 25 m long, 16 m high and weighed about 70 tons.

asteroid colliding with earth, resulting in a sudden change in climate, might have been responsible.

❖ In his film *Jurassic Park* (1993), Steven ▷SPIELBERG invented a new 'type' of the *Velociraptor* family because none of the species then known about were large enough for the film's dramatic purpose. After the film was made, fossils were discovered of a dinosaur that matched his invention in almost every detail. It was named *Utahraptor* after the North American state in which it was found.

❖ The largest of the dinosaur bones so far found in southern Africa were similar to those of the 21 m *Apatosaurus*, previously called *Brontosaurus*.

DNA (deoxyribonucleic acid) Molecule in the cells of all living things, which contains the genetic information that makes individuals different from one another but similar to their parents and others of the same species. In all except the most primitive cells, DNA is found in the CHROMOSOMES in the cell nucleus. It consists of two long chains of organic compounds, called nucleotides, joined together in a double helix structure – like a twisted rope-ladder. Before CELL DIVISION, the DNA molecule 'unzips' down the middle and each half acts as the template for the creation of the missing half; in this way, two molecules are created where there was one before. There are only four kinds of nucleotides, and many thousand are required to make up one gene. Each gene controls the manufacture of a single protein, for example an ENZYME, using a closely related 'messenger' molecule called RNA to carry the genetic message from the nucleus to the cytoplasm, where it ensures that AMINO ACIDS are linked in the correct order to produce a specific protein. The arrangement of nucleotides copied from DNA onto RNA determines which amino acids are used: this is the genetic code. The combined effect of many different genes can determine eye or hair colour, or whether the organism will become a flower or a human being.

❖ The unravelling of DNA's structure in 1953 won Nobel prizes for James Watson, Francis Crick and Maurice Wilkins, and led to genetic engineering, DNA 'fingerprinting' and the attempt to map the entire human DNA.

dodo Extinct bird which lived on Mauritius, with several related species on other islands in the Indian Ocean. Its numbers dwindled after people settled in these areas; flightless and ponderous, it was an easy target for hunters. The last dodo was sighted in 1681.

dormancy Period in the life cycle of a plant or animal during which normal functions are slowed down or suspended.

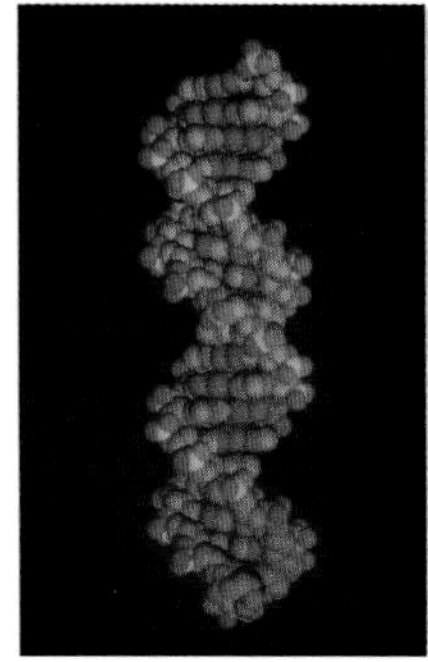
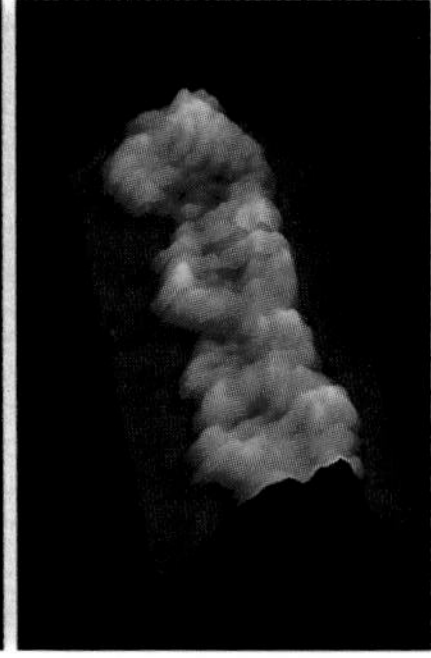

COIL OF LIFE *The double helix structure of DNA, modelled by computer (left) and seen through an electron microscope (right), contains the inherited genetic code that controls all life.*

echolocation Method used by bats, dolphins and some other animals to detect objects using hearing rather than sight. They emit sounds, usually as high-pitched clicks or pulses, and form a picture of their surroundings from the returning echoes.

egg Reproductive cell of the female animal; after fertilization, it contains the developing EMBRYO and its food supply. Birds and most reptiles deposit the egg externally in a protective shell, and normally incubate their eggs until hatching, called oviparity. Mammals and a few other animals nurture the embryo within the body and give birth to live young – a process called viviparity.

embryo Developing plant or animal, from the time the fertilized egg or ZYGOTE begins to divide until germination, birth or hatching. In mammals, the embryo is called a foetus once organs start developing; this occurs after eight weeks in human beings.

enzyme Protein molecule that acts as a biological catalyst. Enzymes speed up virtually every chemical reaction that takes place in living things; without them, the processes of life would grind to a halt. They work by a type of 'lock and key' mechanism, in which only certain molecules will attach to a particular enzyme. The reaction – the combining, changing, or breaking down of molecules – then takes place. Some enzymes operate only in the presence of other factors known as coenzymes. In mammals these are often derived from vitamins. (See also ▷CATALYST in 'Science, space and mathematics'.)

TAME FOOL *Dodos were named after the Portuguese word for idiot,* doudo. *The birds became extinct because they were so trusting and could easily be caught and killed.*

ephemeral Plant that completes its life cycle in the space of a few days or weeks. Many garden weeds, such as groundsel and willowherb are ephemeral, as are plants that bloom in the desert after rain.

epidermis Outermost layer of cells covering a plant or the body of an animal and providing a waterproof, protective cover.

epiphyte Plant that grows on another plant without harming or helping it, as many mosses and orchids do. Epiphytes are common in rainforests, where airborne moisture is plentiful and minerals can be obtained from the surface of the plants they are growing on. (Compare PARASITE.)

evergreen Term describing trees and shrubs that apparently keep their leaves all year round; in fact, their leaves are lost and replaced, but not all at the same time. In hot countries most trees are evergreen. In temperate or cold climates most evergreens are CONIFERS or GYMNOSPERMS.

evolution Process by which living things change and diversify over time to produce new forms of life. Scientific theories of evolution emerged during the 19th century, as geologists and biologists began to question the biblical account of Creation. An early and now discredited proposal, by the Frenchman Jean Baptiste Lamarck, was that species had evolved through the inheritance of ACQUIRED CHARACTERISTICS. The modern theory of evolution, however, derives from the concept of natural selection put forward by Charles DARWIN (and at about the same time by the British zoologist A E Wallace) in 1859. Darwin noted that organisms always produce more offspring than are needed to maintain the population, and that there are differences between individuals within a species. He argued that, in the competition for food and mates, those organisms best suited to the environment would be most likely to survive and pass on their individual characteristics to their offspring: successful or advantageous characteristics would survive, whereas unsuccessful ones would be bred out – the process of natural selection. As the environment changed, or as new individual variations arose, so new characteristics would become desirable and the species would change. Eventually, entirely new species would emerge. The rediscovery of the work of the Austrian monk and botanist Gregor MENDEL in 1900 provided a genetic basis for natural selection, and set the seal on the acceptance of Darwin's concept.

exoskeleton Hard external covering shown most clearly by the largest group of invertebrates, the ARTHROPODS which includes INSECTS and CRUSTACEANS. It performs many of the functions of an internal skeleton – protecting and supporting the internal organs and providing attachment for the muscles. Bony exoskeletons are found in tortoises, although they also have internal skeletons.

extinction Disappearance of a species from the Earth. In the past, extinction has generally been the result of failure to adapt to changing climate or habitat, or to the success of some species at the expense of others. In recent times, the extinction of most species has been caused by human interference; the disappearance of many large mammals around 10 000 years ago was probably due to hunting by prehistoric human beings. Modern destruction of rainforests is estimated to account for the extinction of as many as 6 000 species a year.

❖ In southern Africa the quagga and the blue antelope became extinct after the arrival of European settlers.

fats See LIPIDS.

fermentation Breakdown of glucose and other sugars that releases energy, without using oxygen. Yeast is used in the production of wine and beer to ferment sugars, producing carbon dioxide and ethanol (alcohol). (Compare RESPIRATION.)

ferns Group of nonflowering plants belonging to the phylum Filicophyta. Unlike MOSS, they have true roots, stems and complex leaves. Approximately 8 000 species of fern have been identified, the largest of which, the tree ferns, grow to 24 m. The fern plant reproduces by ALTERNATION OF GENERATIONS, releasing spores from the undersides of certain leaves. The spores germinate and eventually produce male and female sex cells which fuse to produce a ZYGOTE, which grows into a new fern plant.

fertilization Fusion of male and female sex cells during sexual REPRODUCTION to form a single cell or ZYGOTE. Fertilization can take a number of forms, either inside the female's body, as with birds and mammals, or externally, as with most amphibians and fish, where the male fertilizes the eggs after the female has laid them. In flowering plants, fertilization takes place after the POLLINATION process. A pollen tube grows towards the ovule, and carries the male sex cell to the female sex cell.

fish Diverse group of cold-blooded aquatic vertebrates. There are more than 25 000 species of fish. They breathe by extracting oxygen from the water through GILLS. Fish are divided into three types: cartilaginous, bony and jawless. Cartilaginous fish, such as sharks and rays, have a skeletal system made out of cartilage instead of bone. By far the most numerous and successful group are the bony fish, whose skeleton is made of lightweight bone; these range from minnows to ocean sunfish which can weigh more than two tons. Jawless fish, such as the lamprey, have a funnel-shaped, sucking mouth. They have neither jaws nor paired fins. Fish usually reproduce by the female laying eggs, which the male then fertilizes; most fish then abandon the eggs, but some will care for them either by guarding them, incubating them, or, as in the case of the seahorse, by tucking them in a pouch. In cartilaginous fish, fertilization takes place within the female's body, after which some species lay eggs with horny cases ('mermaid's purses'), while others give birth to live young as mammals do.

flight Only insects, birds and bats are capable of true flight, using either one or two pairs of wings. All flying animals have extremely lightweight bodies and strong muscles. Birds' wings are adapted to their lifestyles. For example, songbirds, which use flapping flight, have short, stumpy wings, whereas albatrosses, which travel long distances using gliding flight, have long, tapering wings. In order to hover, as hummingbirds and some insects do,

THE ANATOMY OF A FLOWER

Flowering plants – or angiosperms – are the most abundant and varied group of plants on Earth. Whether large or small, colourful or inconspicuous, every flower has the same basic function: to produce seeds so that its genes can survive. The typical flower consists of concentric rings of sepals, petals and stamens, with one or more pistils at the centre.

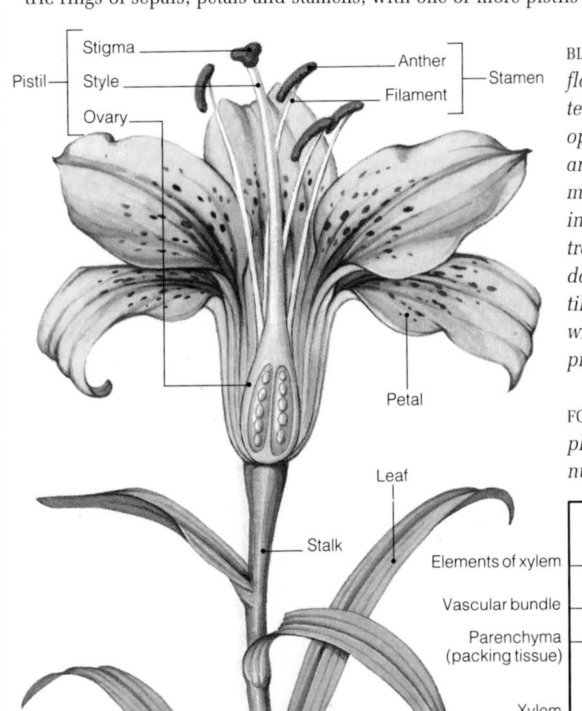

BLOOM AND GROW *All parts of a flower are crucial. Sepals protect the bud until the flower opens. Petals attract insects and other pollinators. Filaments support pollen producing anthers. The sticky stigma traps pollen. A tube then grows down through the style and fertilizes egg cells in the ovary, which matures into a fruit that protects the seeds.*

FOOD AND WATER *Xylem and phloem cells carry water and nutrients throughout the plant.*

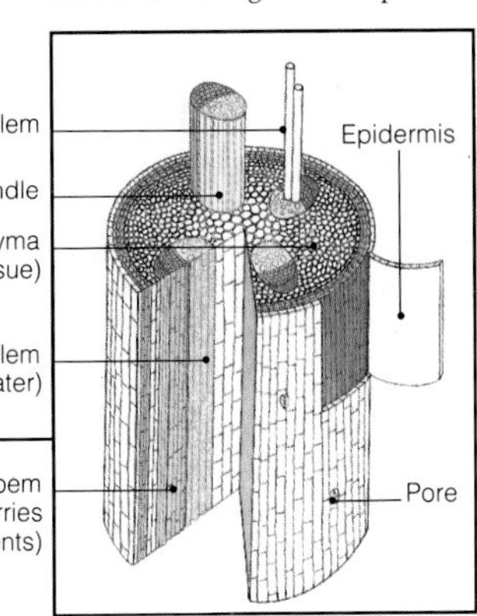

the wings are flapped very rapidly and vertically instead of diagonally.

flower Reproductive structure of ANGIOSPERMS, or flowering plants. Most flowers have brightly coloured petals to attract the insects that pollinate them, but those pollinated by the wind are normally small and inconspicuous. Most plants have male and female organs in the same flower, but some plants have separate male and female flowers. The male part, the stamen, produces pollen which contains male sex cells. The female part, the carpel, is made up of the stigma, the style and the ovary. The stigma, at the top of the style, usually has a sticky surface which receives the pollen. The style leads into the ovary within which are ovules containing the female sex cells. After FERTILIZATION the ovule becomes a SEED, surrounded by the ovary which becomes the FRUIT.

fossil Remains or traces of an organism that existed in the past, preserved in rock, peat, ice, or other material. Usually only the hard parts of the body such as the bones, shells or teeth are found as fossils in rocks; soft parts usually decay before they are fossilized. However, dinosaur footprints and prints of ferns, made in mud before it turned to rock, have been found.
❖ The oldest fossils date back some 4 000 million years and provide the earliest evidence of the ORIGIN OF LIFE.

fruit Seed-bearing part of a plant; many foods that are thought of as vegetables are technically fruits. The fruit is usually formed from the ovary of the flower after fertilization, and its biological role is to enclose and protect the seed, and help in seed dispersal. Fruit and seeds may be dispersed whole, or the fruit may open to release the seeds. Fruits are divided into two main groups: dry, such as poppy or sycamore, and succulent, such as pineapple or tomato.

fungi Like animals, fungi are unable to make their own food. Some, such as mushrooms, are SAPROTROPHS which feed on and break down dead animals and plants in the soil; others are parasites. Fungi also include moulds, rusts, toadstools, puffballs, mildews and yeasts.

gamete Sex cell, such as a sperm or an egg. One gamete joins with another – of the opposite sex – to form a ZYGOTE during FERTILIZATION. Gametes are formed by a type of CELL DIVISION called meiosis.

gastropod Class of MOLLUSCS which includes snails, limpets, whelks (marine snails) and slugs. Typically, gastropods have a head with eyes and tentacles, a rasping tongue or radula, and a large, muscular 'foot' on which they move. Many have a spiral-shaped shell.
❖ The name gastropod derives from Latin and means 'stomach-foot' – from the way they appear to walk on their stomachs.

gene Section of DNA which forms the basic unit of inheritance. Each gene controls, on its own or with other genes, a particular characteristic. During REPRODUCTION, genes are passed on from parents to offspring. Genes occur in pairs on separate chromosomes; genes within pairs may be identical, or one gene may be dominant and the other recessive, in which case the characteristic controlled by the dominant gene will be the one shown by the organism. For example, if a human being has one gene for brown eyes, and one for blue eyes, the brown eye gene dominates and that individual will have brown eyes. Each chromosome is composed of thousands of genes. Genetics, pioneered by Gregor MENDEL, is the study of how genes are inherited.

germination Beginning of a seed's growth into a seedling. Germination takes place only when conditions such as moisture and temperature are suitable.

gills Internal or external respiratory structures in aquatic animals, including crustaceans, fish and some amphibians. Gills are far more efficient than lungs, taking in about 80 per cent of the oxygen in the water which passes through them.

gizzard Part of the digestive tracts of some toothless animals, such as birds and many invertebrates, where food is broken down by a grinding action before chemical digestion. In crustaceans the gizzard's tough lining is drawn out to form 'teeth'; birds swallow stones to assist the process.

glucose Simple sugar produced by plants during PHOTOSYNTHESIS. The energy locked inside glucose is released during RESPIRATION to power all life activities.

grasses One of the commonest groups of flowering plants. They are MONOCOTYLEDONS, and their fruits are grains, many of which are cultivated as sources of food, such as wheat, maize, barley and oats.

growth Process usually achieved by CELL DIVISION and cell enlargement. All multicellular (many-celled) organisms begin life as a single cell which divides repeatedly. Groups of cells form different tissues, such as muscle or nervous tissues. In animals, growth takes place at different rates in almost all parts of the body. Plant growth is restricted to meristems – at the tips of roots and shoots, and around the stem. Plants continue to grow throughout their lives although, as in the case of some perennials, they may die back during the winter season.

gymnosperms Group of plants, including CONIFERS, that are nonflowering but produce seeds. The name gymnosperm, meaning 'naked seed', refers to the seeds not being enclosed in an ovary. (Compare ANGIOSPERM.)

heterotroph Organism that needs an external source of food to provide energy and materials for growth and repair. All animals and fungi, many bacteria and a few plants are heterotrophs. All are ultimately dependent on AUTOTROPHS, organisms that can make their own food.

hibernation Dormant state in which some creatures, including hedgehogs, insects and snails, survive winter. Their metabolism slows right down and, in warm-blooded animals, body heat drops to just above ambient temperature. (Compare AESTIVATION.)

hybrid Offspring produced by crossing parents with distinct genetic differences. F1 and F2 hybrids are the first and second generation of offspring, produced by crossing different varieties of the same species. When different species are crossed, the offspring may be sterile, as when a horse and a donkey mate to produce a mule.

insects There are more than 800 000 known species of insect, and probably several million yet to be identified. Insects, which are ARTHROPODS, have three body parts: head, thorax and abdomen. The head has two antennae and a pair of compound eyes. Attached to the thorax are six legs and, typically, two pairs of wings, although some insects have no wings at all. Insects breathe through holes in the thorax called spiracles. They do not have teeth, and their mouthparts vary according to the way they live. For example, grasshoppers have chewing mandibles for eating vegetation, mosquitoes have piercing mouthparts for sucking blood, and butterflies have coiled tubes which they unroll to feed on nectar. All insects can reproduce sexually. Female insects lay eggs. After hatching, insects develop from juvenile stages to adults by METAMORPHOSIS. Different insects communicate in different ways. Cicadas, for example, use sound, fireflies use light, and many insects, including moths, make use of PHEROMONES.

THE STRUCTURE OF A LEAF

Leaves are the most specialized and efficient food factories in a plant because they are the site of photosynthesis. When sunlight strikes a leaf, energy is absorbed by the green pigment, chlorophyll. Chlorophyll acts as a catalyst to bring about chemical reactions between water and carbon dioxide – the raw materials plants use to manufacture food.

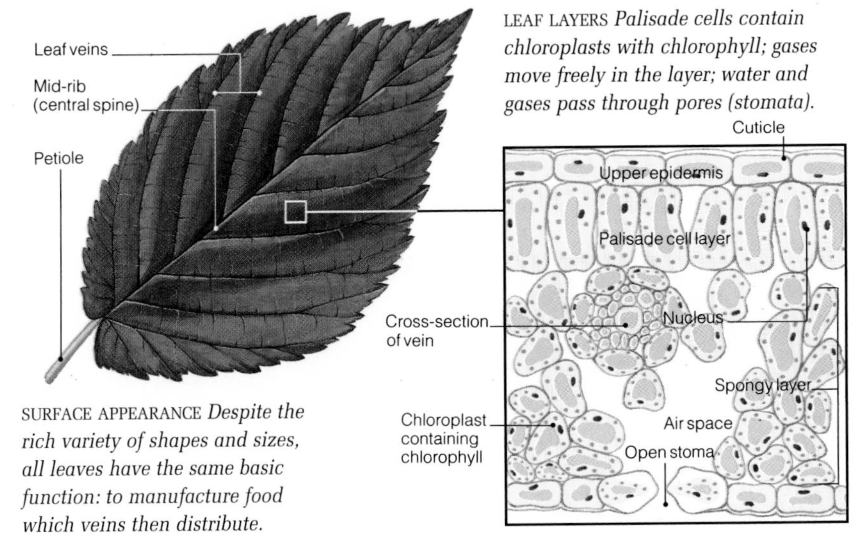

LEAF LAYERS *Palisade cells contain chloroplasts with chlorophyll; gases move freely in the layer; water and gases pass through pores (stomata).*

SURFACE APPEARANCE *Despite the rich variety of shapes and sizes, all leaves have the same basic function: to manufacture food which veins then distribute.*

instinct (innate behaviour) Behaviour that is inherited, not learned or modified by environmental influences. Many animals are born with responses to stimuli they will meet in their environment already incorporated in their nervous systems. It enables them to perform actions impossible for each generation to learn afresh. Examples of instinctive behaviour include worker bees constructing combs or newlyhatched turtles digging themselves out of the sand and making for the sea.

invertebrate Any animal without a backbone. (See The Animal Kingdom panel, p 479.)

larva Juvenile form of an animal that is very different from the adult, such as a frog tadpole or a fly maggot. A larva develops into an adult through METAMORPHOSIS.

leaf Food factory of most plants, where PHOTOSYNTHESIS takes place. The cells that make up the inner part of the leaves contain chloroplasts packed with chlorophyll, the green pigment that traps sunlight during photosynthesis. Above and below these cells are the upper and lower epidermis which, with the thin outer cuticle, protect the leaf and make it waterproof. Pores, or stomata, in the lower epidermis can be opened or closed by the guard cells that surround them. Carbon dioxide, one of the raw materials for photosynthesis, enters the leaf via the stomata, while oxygen, one of the products, passes out through them. Veins carry water and the products of photosynthesis to and from a leaf. In DECIDUOUS plants, flat leaves expose a large area of photosynthetic cells to sunlight to ensure efficient food production; and in many EVERGREENS, needlelike leaves minimize water loss.

lichens Symbiotic association between FUNGI and ALGAE. The algae produce food for the fungi by PHOTOSYNTHESIS, and the fungi give protection to the algae and absorb water and minerals from their surroundings. Lichens can survive in harsh environments, such as arctic regions and deserts, where few plants can exist. (See SYMBIOSIS.)

lipids Group of compounds found in living organisms that include fats, oils and steroids, such as ▷CHOLESTEROL. Fats in animals are used for energy storage and, in mammals, for insulation. Some plants store oil in seeds to fuel their future growth. A type of lipid, called phospholipid, forms part of the structure of all cell membranes.

mammals Class of warm-blooded vertebrates which evolved more than 225 million years ago from mammal-like reptiles and is characterized by adult females that suckle their young. Today there are three types. Monotremes, which include the duck-billed platypus, are the only surviving mammals that lay leathery eggs and suckle their young from glands in the skin. The other two types of mammal, the MARSUPIALS and the placental mammals, both have mammary glands. Placental mammals, which during prenatal development, are nourished in the womb by a placenta, are by far the most successful of the three mammal types; they have 17 orders as opposed to the single order of marsupials. Although some mammals such as human beings, elephants, seals, pigs and CETACEANS are relatively hairless, most species are covered in fur or hair, which helps them to regulate their body temperature.

❖ The largest mammals are female blue whales, which can be more than 34 m long and weigh as much as 180 tons.

marsupials Group of mammals, found in Australasia and the Americas, which includes kangaroos, koalas and opossums. They differ from other mammals in that their young are born in a relatively undeveloped state and, guided by smell, find their way from the birth canal to an external pouch. Here the tiny marsupial remains, latched onto a teat during its early development. Later, it may leave the pouch for brief periods, returning for food and shelter until its development is complete.

Mendel, Gregor (1822-84) Austrian monk and botanist who first devised a theory of heredity in 1866. He proposed that individual characteristics were determined by 'factors' which are passed from parent to offspring. He based his ideas on experiments he conducted with pea plants. His work remained unnoticed until it was rediscovered in 1900. His

FATHER OF GENETICS *The plant-breeding experiments of the Austrian monk, Gregor Mendel, conducted in his monastery garden, formed the basis of modern genetics.*

theories were proved to be largely correct when scientists identified GENES.

metamorphosis Transformation from juvenile to adult form that takes place in insects, amphibians and other animals. In complete metamorphosis, a larva changes into a pupa and on to an adult stage, or imago; insects such as the beetle and the butterfly, for instance, look quite different from any of their earlier stages. In incomplete metamorphosis, as in the grasshopper, the adult looks very similar to the juvenile stage, or nymph. Metamorphosis can also occur in amphibians, such as the frog which grows from a legless, lungless tadpole into an animal that can live on land.

migration Periodic two-way movement of an animal population, commonly birds, grazing animals, seals, turtles and some fish. Animals migrate to follow a food source, to breed and to avoid cold winters. Migration is usually prompted by seasonal changes in the weather or in the hours of daylight. Frogs may move only a few hundred metres, whereas some birds migrate thousands of kilometres. The longest annual migrators are the Arctic terns which fly from pole to pole every year, a round trip of more than 32 000 km. Migrating birds use a variety of navigational aids, including the position of the Sun and the stars and the Earth's magnetic field.
❖ The European swallow *(Hirundo rustica)*, a familiar sight in South Africa from September onwards, migrates every year from as far away as Siberia.

Caterpillar feeding on milkweed — Larva changing into a pupa — Pupa suspended from milkweed

Adult emerging from its pupa — Metamorphosis is almost complete . . . — Adult monarch butterfly

DRAMATIC CHANGES *In the monarch butterfly, the transformation from egg to adult may take only two weeks. Eggs hatch into caterpillars which eat, grow and moult several times. The caterpillar, or larva, changes into a pupa, from which emerges the spectacular winged adult butterfly.*

mollusc Soft-bodied invertebrates, often with shells, which include GASTROPODS, such as snails, BIVALVES, such as oysters, and CEPHALOPODS, such as squid.

monocotyledons (monocots) One of two groups of flowering plants. Monocotyledons have one COTYLEDON in their seeds and their flower parts are arranged in multiples of three. They include lilies and grasses. (Compare DICOTYLEDONS.)

moss Simple land plant without true leaves, stems or roots. Mosses, which belong to the phylum Bryophyta, do not have a vascular system like other plants. Instead, they absorb moisture directly through their 'leaves' and 'stems'; this explains why most live in wet habitats. Mosses show ALTERNATION OF GENERATIONS in their life cycle.

mutation Change in the genetic material (DNA) of an organism that alters the characteristics it passes on to its offspring. Mutations occur at random in all organisms during the replication of DNA; they are the raw material on which natural selection and hence EVOLUTION operate. However, mutations can also be brought about by radiation and certain chemicals; most are harmful.

nitrogen cycle Constant recycling of nitrogen between the atmosphere and living things. Nitrogen is converted to nitrates 'fixed' by bacteria in the root nodules of leguminous plants, such as peas and beans. Plants absorb nitrates from the soil and incorporate them into proteins and other essential materials, which are then eaten by animals. Nitrogen is released back into the air by SAPROTROPHS and other decomposers in the soil.

nymph Juvenile stage of an insect such as the grasshopper or dragonfly that resembles the adult, except that its wings and reproductive organs are undeveloped.

origin of life The first signs of life probably appeared some 4 billion years ago as the Earth, which had formed around 4,6 billion years ago, cooled and the oceans filled. The crucial step was the appearance of AMINO ACIDS – the building blocks of proteins – and the nucleic acids, molecules that can replicate themselves and control the assembly of proteins. There are several theories as to how these organic molecules were formed. One suggests that methane, ammonia and carbon dioxide in the early atmosphere reacted together during violent electrical storms; the resulting molecules dissolved in the oceans to produce a primeval 'soup' in which, over millions of years, the first living systems evolved. Alternate theories suggest that life began around hot water vents in the deep oceans, or that it arrived on meteorites from space. The first living organisms were single cells that resemble the most primitive forms of bacteria in existence today.

ovary Female reproductive organ in animals and some plants, where egg cells are produced. (See also FLOWER.)

parasite Organism which lives on or in the body of another larger organism, known as a host, on which it feeds. Parasitism differs from SYMBIOSIS in that only the parasite benefits from the association; the host generally suffers. (Compare EPIPHYTE.)

perennial Plant that continues to grow and flower each year. Herbaceous perennials die back each autumn and survive the winter underground as BULBS, CORMS or RHIZOMES. Woody perennials, such as trees and shrubs, have permanent woody stems, but may lose their leaves in winter. (Compare ANNUAL and BIENNIAL.)

pheromone Chemical released by an organism which has a specific effect on a member of the same species. Pheromones play an important role in the behaviour of many animals, in particular insects and mammals. For example, the queen in a termite colony produces a pheromone that stops the reproductive development in the ovaries of other females.

❖ Research shows that a male emperor moth is able to detect a pheromone released by a female from 11 km away.

photosynthesis Process by which plants and some other organisms use sunlight to make glucose. In plants, photosynthesis takes place in the chloroplasts, which are concentrated in the cells of the LEAF. Chloroplasts are packed with chlorophyll, a green pigment, which captures the Sun's energy. This energy is then used to split hydrogen molecules from water and combine them with carbon dioxide to form GLUCOSE. Glucose can be stored as starch or converted to other substances, such as LIPIDS and proteins, needed by the plant. The simple raw materials, water and carbon dioxide, are obtained from the soil and air respectively. During the day, when photosynthesis is occurring, oxygen is released into the air as a waste product.

❖ Most oxygen in the atmosphere has been produced by photosynthesis.

plankton Collective term for all the minute organisms that drift with the current in seas and lakes. Plankton is an important source of food in aquatic communities; the world's largest living animal, the blue whale, feeds solely on plankton.

plant One of the five main divisions of the living world, plants are distinguished from other organisms in two ways: they can manufacture their own food, and they have no means of locomotion. Plants range in size and complexity from simple mosses to the giant sequoia trees indigenous to the USA. The most successful and numerous group of plants are flowering plants or ANGIOSPERMS.

plant hormones Substances that regulate the growth and development of plants. Auxins, for example, which are produced at the growing tips of stems, roots and young leaves, encourage cells to elongate. Their effects also include growth responses, or TROPISMS, such as phototropism – growing towards light. Other plant hormones help to initiate the germination of seeds, trigger fruit ripening and promote leaf fall and dormancy in seeds.

plant tissues Most multicellular green plants, except mosses, have roots, stems and leaves. These are all made up of three basic types of tissue: vascular, ground and epidermal. The transport or vascular system in plants carries two lanes of traffic. Xylem carries water and minerals from the roots and phloem carries sucrose and other nutrients from the leaves. Surrounding the vascular system is the ground tissue which, depending on its site in the plant, is used for PHOTOSYNTHESIS, support or water absorption. The surface of the plant is covered by the EPIDERMIS – a single outer layer of cells for protection.

pollen Tiny structures that contain the male sex cells of a seed-bearing plant. They are usually produced in huge numbers in pollen sacs located on the anthers of flowers and on the male cones of conifers. In order for a plant to be fertilized, the POLLINATION process must take place.

pollination Transfer of pollen from a male to a female organ of a plant, usually of a different plant of the same species. Some plants, such as conifers, grasses and some deciduous trees, are wind pollinated; pollen is blown by the wind to another plant. But most flowering plants have evolved a complex interdependent relationship with animals, especially insects, that feed on the FLOWERS and pollinate them at the same time. The bright colours and scents of flowers attract insects, which come to obtain the flower's nectar. In reaching the nectar, the insect brushes against the anthers – picking up pollen which it carries to the stigma of another flower. Other animals that

THE PLANT KINGDOM

All plants, from the smallest moss to the tallest tree, share a common feature – they make their own food by trapping energy from the sun. Plants, which evolved from green algae more than 450 million years ago, make up one of the five kingdoms of living organisms. They are divided into various phyla, the largest of which contains the flowering plants.

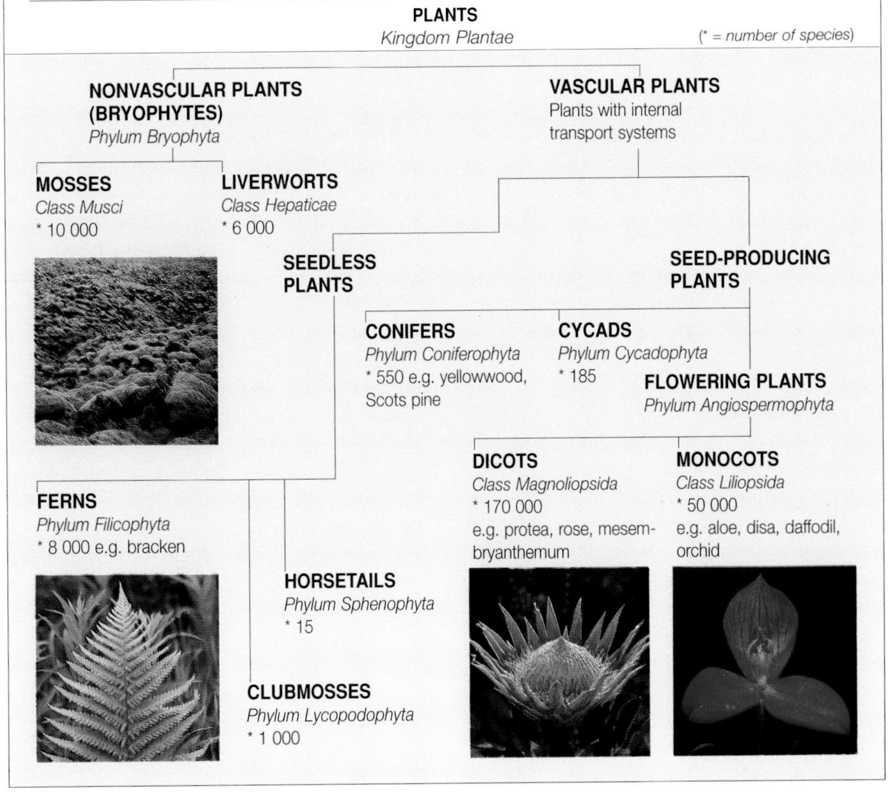

PLANTS
Kingdom Plantae

(* = number of species)

NONVASCULAR PLANTS (BRYOPHYTES)
Phylum Bryophyta

MOSSES
Class Musci
* 10 000

LIVERWORTS
Class Hepaticae
* 6 000

VASCULAR PLANTS
Plants with internal transport systems

SEEDLESS PLANTS

FERNS
Phylum Filicophyta
* 8 000 e.g. bracken

HORSETAILS
Phylum Sphenophyta
* 15

CLUBMOSSES
Phylum Lycopodophyta
* 1 000

SEED-PRODUCING PLANTS

CONIFERS
Phylum Coniferophyta
* 550 e.g. yellowwood, Scots pine

CYCADS
Phylum Cycadophyta
* 185

FLOWERING PLANTS
Phylum Angiospermophyta

DICOTS
Class Magnoliopsida
* 170 000
e.g. protea, rose, mesembryanthemum

MONOCOTS
Class Liliopsida
* 50 000
e.g. aloe, disa, daffodil, orchid

pollinate plants include bats, hummingbirds and honey possums.

predation Killing and eating of one animal (the prey) by another (the predator). Many predators' main hunting sense is vision; animals such as the dragonfly, hawk and cat have particularly keen eyesight. Most others track their prey by scent.

primates Group of mammals that includes monkeys, apes and human beings. Primates are distinguished by large brains, opposable thumbs – giving them dexterous hands – three-dimensional colour vision, a reduced snout and two mammary glands.

proteins Group of organic compounds found in all living things. Proteins are made from long chains of AMINO ACIDS, linked together in a set sequence controlled by GENES in the cell's nucleus. A particularly important group of proteins are ENZYMES, which control all the cell's chemical reactions. Proteins such as keratin and collagen give strength and elasticity to hair, feathers and scales, as well as to skin and tendons. Proteins are an important part of muscles and also involved in the clotting of blood. A living organism may contain more than 10 000 different kinds of protein, each with an individual task.

❖ Eating foods that provide a good balance of proteins is vital to people's health.

protists Microscopic organisms, most of which are single-celled, that are divided into two groups: protozoans and algae. Protozoans, such as AMOEBA, are described as animal-like because most eat other organisms. This group also includes the PARASITES that cause malaria and sleeping sickness. ALGAE are plantlike because they make their own food by photosynthesis. Protists belong to the kingdom Protista.

❖ England's white cliffs of Dover are made from the remains of billions of foraminiferans – protists with microscopic shells made from calcium carbonate.

reproduction There are two types of reproduction: asexual and sexual. Asexual reproduction involves only one parent producing offspring, or CLONES identical to itself. Some simple organisms, such as the amoeba, reproduce asexually by just splitting in two. Many plants reproduce asexually by vegetative reproduction – sending out shoots which take root to produce independent offspring. Sexual reproduction requires the production of male and female sex cells which fuse to produce a ZYGOTE during FERTILIZATION. The offspring that are produced by sexual reproduction receive half of each parent's GENES and so are not identical to either parent, but a 'cross' between the two.

HOW SEEDS TRAVEL

Plants have evolved many strategies to send their seeds far away and ensure that young plants colonize new areas instead of crowding around them and competing for light and nutrients.

Dandelion

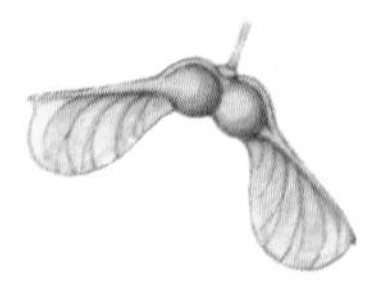

Sycamore

BLOWING IN THE WIND *Parachute and wings propel many types of seeds through the air.*

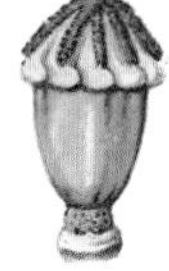

Poppy

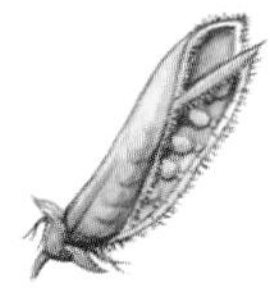

Broom

MOVERS AND SHAKERS *Breezes shake seeds from poppy 'heads'; pods burst to fling contents away.*

reptiles Class of cold-blooded VERTEBRATES, which includes turtles, lizards and snakes, crocodiles and alligators. Reptiles, which live predominantly on land, typically have scaly skins and lay leathery eggs. The largest living reptiles are the Komodo dragon, a carnivorous lizard that can grow to be nearly 5 m long, and saltwater crocodiles which can weigh more than 2 tons. Reptiles' eyesight varies: some snakes can distinguish only between light and dark, whereas most lizards have keen eyesight for hunting. Crocodiles and alligators have excellent hearing when their heads are out of the water; some lizards and snakes can hear only deep sounds. Both snakes and lizards use their tongues to detect odour molecules in the air. They can track prey by flicking their tongue out and transferring the molecules it has picked up into special sensory organs in the roof of the mouth. Some snakes, such as rattlesnakes, can hunt by detecting the body heat of their prey. Most reptiles lay eggs, but some give birth to live young.

respiration Process occurring in all cells which releases energy from organic compounds such as glucose. This energy is used to power all cell reactions and all activity, although some is lost as heat. Anaerobic respiration does not require oxygen but releases only small amounts of energy; it occurs during fermentation, and in muscles during exercise. Aerobic respiration requires oxygen and produces more energy.

rhizome Underground horizontal stem of some plants which acts as a food store during the winter. In spring the rhizome produces buds from which new leaves and flowers grow. Plants with rhizomes include irises, ferns and many grasses.

ribosome One of many tiny structures known as organelles found in the cytoplasm of all CELLS. Ribosomes provide the site for the assembly of proteins from their building blocks – amino acids – using 'construction plans' provided by the genetic material DNA located in the cell nucleus.

RNA (ribonucleic acid) Complex organic compound which carries and translates the genetic information contained in DNA. It implements DNA's instructions to build specific proteins, so determining all an organism's characteristics. There are three types of RNA – messenger, transfer and ribosomal. Messenger RNA transcribes the message from DNA in the nucleus, linking up with the RNA in the RIBOSOME. Transfer RNA lines up AMINO ACIDS in the correct order to construct a specific protein.

root Part of a plant which absorbs water and minerals from the soil. Basically, roots divide into two types – tap roots and fibrous roots. Tap roots reach vertically down into the soil. Dandelions have large tap roots, but in carrots and parsnips they are larger still – swollen with food reserves. Fibrous roots form a dense, threadlike web underground. Grasses all have fibrous roots. In some cases, roots grow directly from shoots or leaf cuttings; these are called adventitious roots and are found, for example, in strawberry plants that spread by sending out shoots, or runners, that take root.

ruminants Even-toed MAMMALS which include deer, giraffes, cattle and goats. The success of this group – Artiodactyla – is a result of its complex and efficient digestion of vegetation, which is not normally a very nourishing food source. The digestive system consists of four or more 'chambers' or stomachs. Grazed food passes to the first chamber or rumen, where its cellulose is partly digested by bacteria. The partly digested food – the cud – is then returned to the mouth for further chewing, or rumination, before being swallowed and further digested.

saprotroph Organism that obtains its nutrition by absorbing the dead remains of other organisms in the earth surrounding it. Saprotrophs are important 'decomposers' – recycling nutrients for plants and animals to re-use. Most saprotrophs digest their food externally by secreting ENZYMES onto the food, turning it into a solution which they can then absorb. Included among saprotrophs are many bacteria and fungi.

seed Part of a plant that develops from the ovule after fertilization and which contains the EMBRYO capable of germinating to produce a new plant. The seed also contains the embryo's store of food, in the form of COTYLEDONS or oil, and it is enclosed by a protective seed coat. The seeds of flowering plants are protected within a fruit. Some seeds can lie dormant for several years. When the embryo starts to grow, the seed splits open; this is called GERMINATION.

seed dispersal Plants disperse their seeds in a variety of ways to ensure they do not grow too close to the parent plant and thereby compete with it for water, light and nutrients. Seeds dispersed by the wind are either very light, such as dandelion 'parachutes' or, like sycamores, have fruits flattened as wings to help them glide. The fruit of the gorse bush dries, twists and then bursts open explosively, catapulting out its seeds. Some fruits have burs with hooks that stick to animals which distribute the seeds. Animals also eat succulent fruits such as rose hips or blackberries; the seeds pass through their intestines unharmed and are deposited in droppings. Coconuts can float for long distances in the sea until they land on a beach, where their seeds germinate.

senses The five main senses are sight, hearing, touch, taste and smell, but not all animals have all of them. The more complex eyes of insects, higher molluscs such as the octopus, and vertebrates, focus light onto light-sensitive cells which send a message to the brain, where it is interpreted as an image. The compound eyes of insects are made up of many separate 'mini-eyes' which are very good at detecting sudden movements – making it difficult to swat flies. Many animals communicate using sound; invertebrates do not have ears, although some detect sounds with their antennae. Fish use their lateral line – an earlike organ – to detect vibrations in the water. Birds sing to attract a mate or declare their territories. The sense of smell – chemical molecules in the air activate receptors in the animal – is crucial to most animals; it is especially useful for identifying mates and often provides the means for finding food.

social insects Termites and hymenopterans (bees, ants and wasps) live in large colonies, whose members are organized into castes. All social insects have a queen, which is the only fertile female, and workers, which are sterile. Hymenoptera workers are all female; the only function of the males is to fertilize the queen, after which they die. The queen is little more than an egg-laying machine, totally dependent on the workers for food and grooming. Termites and some species of ants have a soldier caste, that attack prey and defend the nest. If a nest gets too full, all or part of the population must move, which is why bees swarm. Control of the colony is often achieved through the production of PHEROMONES released by the queen.

species Group of organisms that share many similarities and which breed with each other. 'Species' and below them 'subspecies' form the lowest category in the CLASSIFICATION hierarchy. Each species has a scientific name which, unlike its common name, is recognized internationally. The scientific name is made up of a generic name, giving the genus to which the organism belongs, and a specific name, which defines the species. The trout, for example, is *Salmo trutta*, while the name for its close relative, the salmon, is *Salmo salar*.

sperm Male reproductive cell. The sperm of animals and spermatozoids of simple plants consist of a head section containing CHROMOSOMES which penetrates the ovum at fertilization, and a tail section with which they swim. Because sperm needs liquid in which to swim, plants, such as ferns, can reproduce only in damp conditions.

spore Reproductive cell that can develop into a new organism. Spores are produced by bacteria, fungi and seedless plants, such as FERNS. They can be spread far and wide by wind, water and animals. Spores are minute – a single mushroom may produce billions. Some PROTISTS produce dormant spores to survive unfavourable periods of weather.

starch Complex carbohydrate consisting of glucose subunits, used as an energy store in plants. Potatoes are an example of starch being stored in tubers; cereals and legumes are other sources. Starch is a major energy source for human beings and other animals.

QUEEN BEE *At the centre of her colony, the queen bee is surrounded by dozens of sterile workers who feed and groom her. Charged with reproduction, she lays up to two thousands eggs a day.*

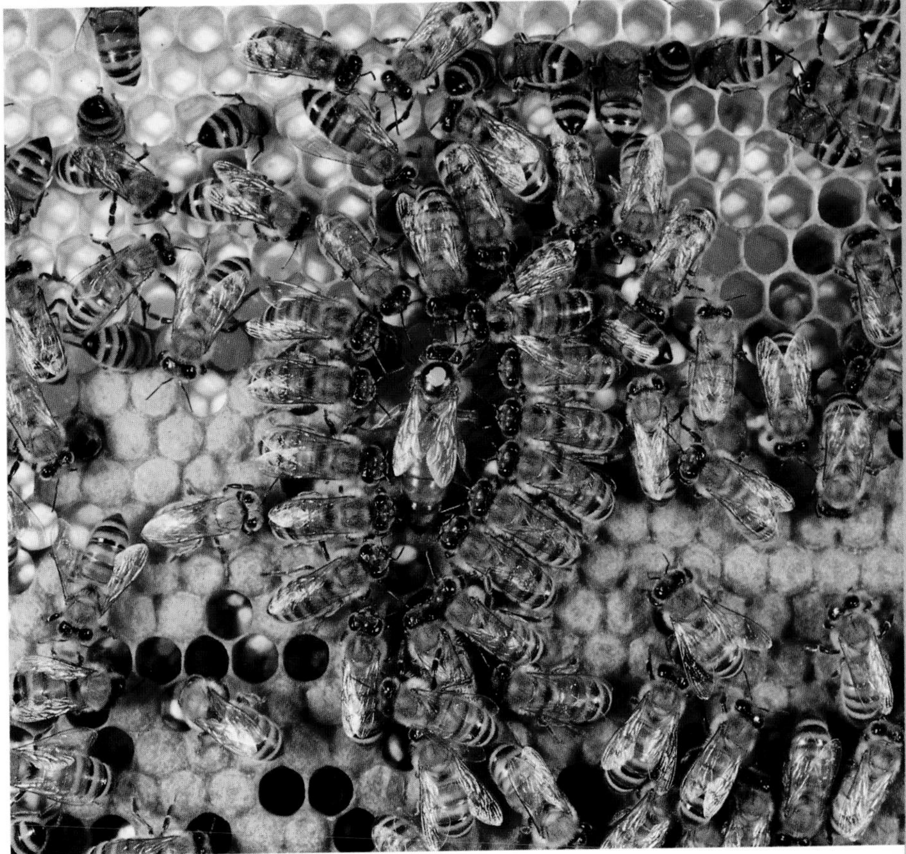

HOW A VIRUS MULTIPLIES

A virus, a submicroscopic entity consisting of a shell of proteins surrounding a mass of genetic material, has the ability to 'instruct' cellular machinery to produce more viruses in a short time. When this happens, the host becomes ill.

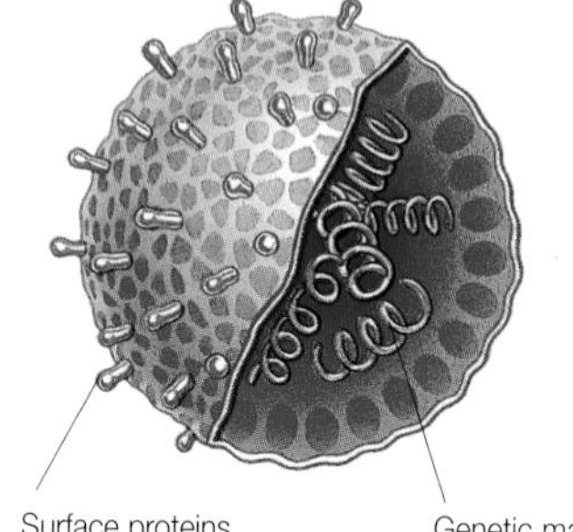

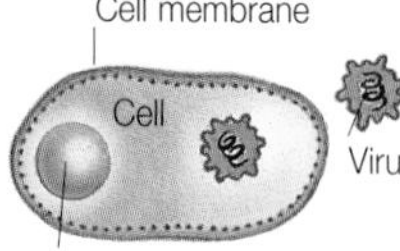

1 A virus zooms in on a host cell, where it either enters the cell itself or injects its genetic material (known as genome) into it.

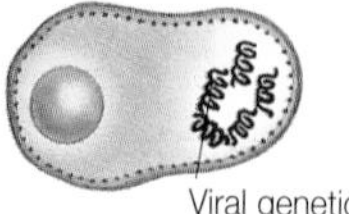

2 The genome, using the host cell's machinery, replicates again and again.

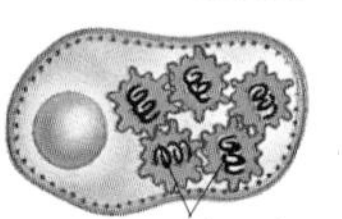

3 Each new genome is turned into a protein shell by the cell.

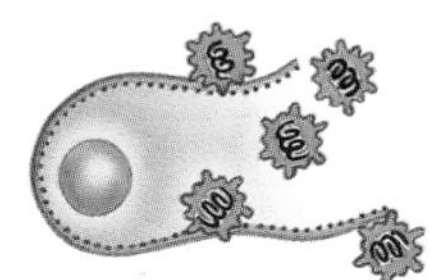

4 New viruses, capable of infecting other cells, emerge from the host cell.

succulents Plants usually found in areas of low rainfall, having thick, fleshy leaves and stems which are used to store water. Succulents – their name comes from the Latin word *succus* which means juice – have adapted in various ways to minimize water loss. For example, some have developed leaves with thickened cuticles, others have reduced breathing pores; still others are protected by spines to discourage thirsty animals. The Little Karoo and Namaqualand in South Africa have the highest concentration of succulents in the world. Well-known types include euphorbias, stapelias and aloes.

symbiosis Permanent or long-term association between individuals of different species, especially one that is to their mutual benefit. One example is LICHEN, a symbiotic relationship between a fungus and an alga. Where only one benefits, the relationship is commensal; if one gains at the other's expense, it is parasitic.

❖ The relationship between flowering plants and their pollinating insects may be regarded as symbiotic: the insect obtains food from the plant, which is in turn fertilized by the insect. This is also known as mutualism.

territory Many animals, especially birds, fish and mammals, establish their own exclusive territories for feeding or breeding. Even in densely populated bird colonies, each couple will create a small territory around its nest. Some large mammals, such as lions, may establish territories of several square kilometres for hunting. Members of the same species usually maintain their personal territory by displays of AGGRESSION.

tissue Group of similar cells which perform a specific function for an organism, such as muscle tissue or nerve tissue.

transpiration Loss of water vapour to the atmosphere from plants, mainly through the stomata, or 'pores', of the LEAF. As water is lost, the plant replaces it by drawing more up its stem through its roots – creating a transpiration stream. In a healthy plant with adequately moist soil this poses no problem, but plants in drier areas may suffer water loss and wilt. Plants can control transpiration by opening and closing their stomata; stomata generally close at night or when the daytime heat becomes too intense. A large tree may transpire 87ℓ of water each day.

tree All trees are classified as either flowering ANGIOSPERMS or nonflowering GYMNOSPERMS. Hardwood trees are angiosperms, most of which are DECIDUOUS, and all softwood trees are gymnosperms, which include most EVERGREENS. A chief characteristic of the tree is the trunk of WOOD, which grows outward as well as upward. Some CONIFERS live for up to 5 000 years, but the oldest living thing is a 10 000-year-old regenerating creosote bush, found in the Mojave Desert.

tropism Ability of the root or stem of a plant to grow towards, or away from, a stimulus. Most plant shoots grow towards the light, while some, such as sunflowers, turn towards it – a process known as phototropism. Gravity's effect on plants is known as geotropism; roots grow downwards in response to it (positively geotropic), while shoots grow upwards (negatively geotropic).

tuber Enlarged underground stem or root which acts as a food store. Potatoes are stem tubers, while dahlias have root tubers.

vertebrate Animal that has a bony or cartilaginous backbone, such as fish, birds and mammals. Over 40 000 species are vertebrate. (See The Animal Kingdom panel, p 479.)

virus Simple biological 'system' which is not really a living organism because it cannot reproduce without the assistance of living host cells. Viruses are PARASITES of animals, plants and some bacteria. Viruses frequently lead to disease and are responsible for the common cold, herpes, polio, rabies, ▷AIDS and many other diseases.

warm-blooded (endothermic) Term describing an animal which has a constant body temperature, independent of the external temperature. All birds and mammals are endotherms. Both have a high metabolic rate which releases heat to maintain body temperature. Heat loss is reduced by feathers in birds and by hair, and a layer of fat, in most other animals. Internal mechanisms monitor body temperature constantly and control it by triggering automatic processes which help to lose or retain heat, such as sweating or shivering.

wood In cross-section there are four main parts to wood – bark, cambium, sapwood and heartwood. Just inside the protective bark lies the thin layer of cambium where growth takes place, leaving a new ring every year. Between the bark and the cambium lies the phloem, PLANT TISSUE that carries sucrose and other nutrients around the tree or shrub. The sapwood is xylem – tissue that carries water up from the roots and which turns into heartwood when it dies. Wood is divided into two types: hardwood, produced by flowering trees (ANGIOSPERMS), and softwood, from nonflowering trees (GYMNOSPERMS). Although some so-called hardwoods, such as balsa, are softer than softwoods, such as pine, most – like teak and mahogany – are much harder.

yeast Type of single-cell fungus that obtains its energy through FERMENTATION and reproduces asexually by budding – 'growing' another organism. Yeasts are used in brewing to ferment sugars into alcohol, and in baking to produce the carbon dioxide which causes bread to rise.

zygote Fertilized EGG that results from the joining of the nucleus of an ovum with that of a SPERM in animals, or of a female gamete with a male gamete in plants. It develops, by CELL DIVISION, into an embryo.

MEDICINE, HEALTH AND THE HUMAN BODY

The human body is a natural machine far more complex and subtle than any we have been able to invent for ourselves. In more than 2 000 years of observation and experiment we have learnt to eradicate some of the diseases that once afflicted us and to alleviate and cure many others. Yet all the advances of medical science have only reinforced our sense of wonder at the body's capabilities.

abortion Premature ending of pregnancy either naturally, through miscarriage, or artificially, by medical termination. Although medical abortion is practised widely, it is controlled in most countries by legislation, and in some countries it is forbidden altogether. In South Africa, abortion is restricted to cases where conception results from an illegal act such as rape, incest or intercourse with a mentally handicapped woman, or where doctors certify that there is a serious risk of physical or mental harm to the mother or of severe physical defect in the child. However, illegal (or 'back street') abortions are common, and may result in serious illness or even death.

❖ Pressure groups in favour of legalized abortion are termed 'pro-choice' groups, those against call themselves 'pro-life'.

Achilles tendon Body's largest and strongest tendon, which connects the calf muscles to the heel bone. It is sometimes torn during strenuous exercise.

acne Skin disorder most common during adolescence, when increased levels of sex HORMONES cause glands in the skin to overproduce sebum, an oily secretion. Sebum accumulates in skin pores to produce whiteheads and blackheads, especially on the face, chest, upper back and shoulders. Blocked pores may become infected with bacteria, producing reddened, inflamed spots filled with pus. Picking or scratching spots spreads infection and may cause scarring. Acne cannot be prevented, but it can be controlled. Exposure to sunlight is effective, and severe cases can be treated with antibiotics. The condition also improves with age and usually clears up by the mid-twenties. Acne is not caused by dirty skin and harsh cleansing may even exacerbate the condition.

acupuncture Traditional Chinese technique in which needles are inserted into the skin to cure illness or relieve pain. Practitioners claim that the needles unblock the body's invisible energy channels, known as meridians. Acupuncture has been practised for more than 3 500 years in the Far East, but it has only recently gained acceptance in the West and is still not fully understood.

acute illness Sudden or short-lived condition that may, or may not, be severe. (Compare CHRONIC ILLNESS.)

adenoids Pads of tissue at the back of the nose which, with the TONSILS, prevent germs from entering the respiratory system. They form part of the LYMPHATIC SYSTEM. Infected adenoids swell, and if they begin to interfere with breathing and speech, they may need to be surgically removed (commonly along with the tonsils).

adrenaline HORMONE that increases heart rate, air supply to the lungs and blood supply to muscles, and promotes the release of glucose into the blood for immediate energy – preparing the body for action and helping it to cope with fear, stress or exercise. Adrenaline is released by the adrenal glands located near the top of each kidney, in response to signals from the autonomic NERVOUS SYSTEM.

ageing Natural deterioration of the body, which begins during the reproductive years and accelerates after middle age. Its underlying cause is the steadily decreasing ability of body cells to divide and repair themselves. Skin becomes wrinkled as it loses its elasticity, short-term memory may become impaired, CATARACTS and GLAUCOMA become a risk, and bones become increasingly brittle. (See OSTEOPOROSIS.)

AIDS (Acquired Immune Deficiency Syndrome) A fatal condition in which the body's IMMUNE SYSTEM breaks down as a result of infection by the Human Immunodeficiency Virus (HIV). It is possible to carry the virus – or be HIV positive – for ten years or more without developing AIDS. The virus is carried in blood, semen and other body fluids, and is typically transmitted during unprotected sexual intercourse, by transfusion of infected blood or through sharing an infected hypodermic needle. It is also transmitted from mother to foetus. HIV cannot be transmitted through casual physical contact. Once in the bloodstream, the virus attacks cells that are part of the immune system. Sufferers eventually die of opportunistic infections – those that do not normally affect people with healthy immune systems – such as rare forms of pneumonia and skin cancer. There is no cure. The disease is most prevalent in southern and central Africa, where it affects 1 in 12 people and where the increasing incidence is one of the most serious health problems.

alcoholism (alcohol dependence) Mental or physical addiction to alcohol produced by its heavy and long-term consumption. There are two main types of alcoholic: steady drinkers; and bingers or dipsomaniacs. Severe alcoholics may experience symptoms including memory lapses and hallucinations. Sudden withdrawal can produce severe trembling and convulsions, known as delirium tremens or 'DTs'. Long-term alcohol abuse leads to CIRRHOSIS, liver failure and general physical and mental ill health. There is some evidence that alcoholism has a genetic link, but social and psychological factors are regarded as far more important. Researchers recommend a maximum alcohol consumption of 21 units a week for an adult male and 14 for an adult female. One unit is the equivalent of a measure of spirits, a glass of wine or 250 ml beer. During pregnancy women should be particularly careful about drinking more than four units a week as this increases the chance of foetal alcohol syndrome, when the baby's brain fails to develop properly.

❖ Alcoholics Anonymous (AA) is a self-help organization for alcoholics who are trying to

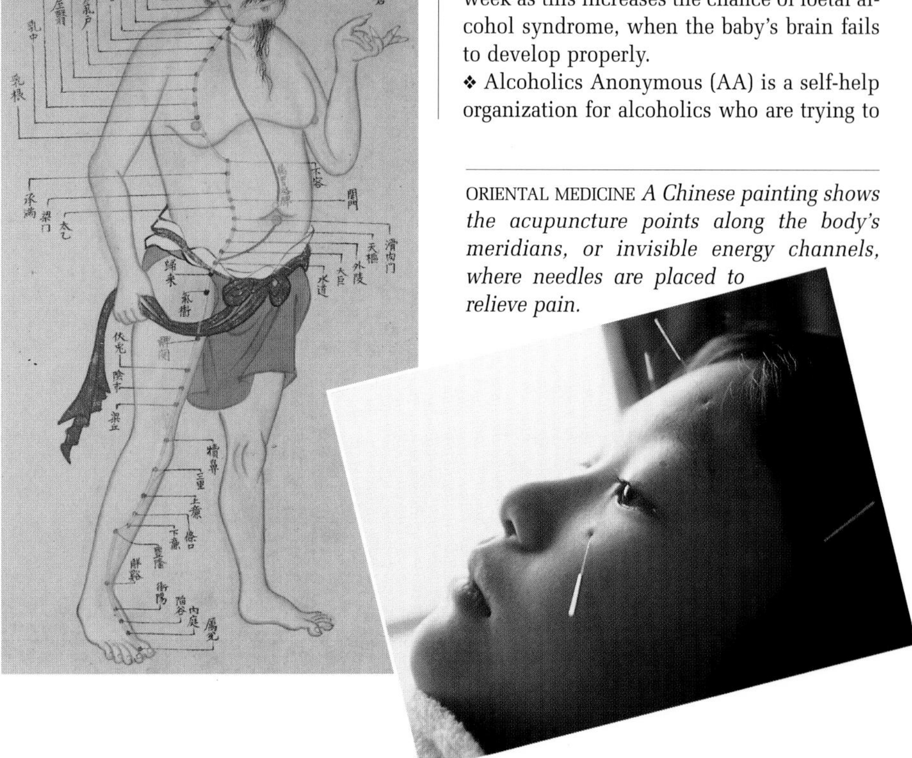

ORIENTAL MEDICINE *A Chinese painting shows the acupuncture points along the body's meridians, or invisible energy channels, where needles are placed to relieve pain.*

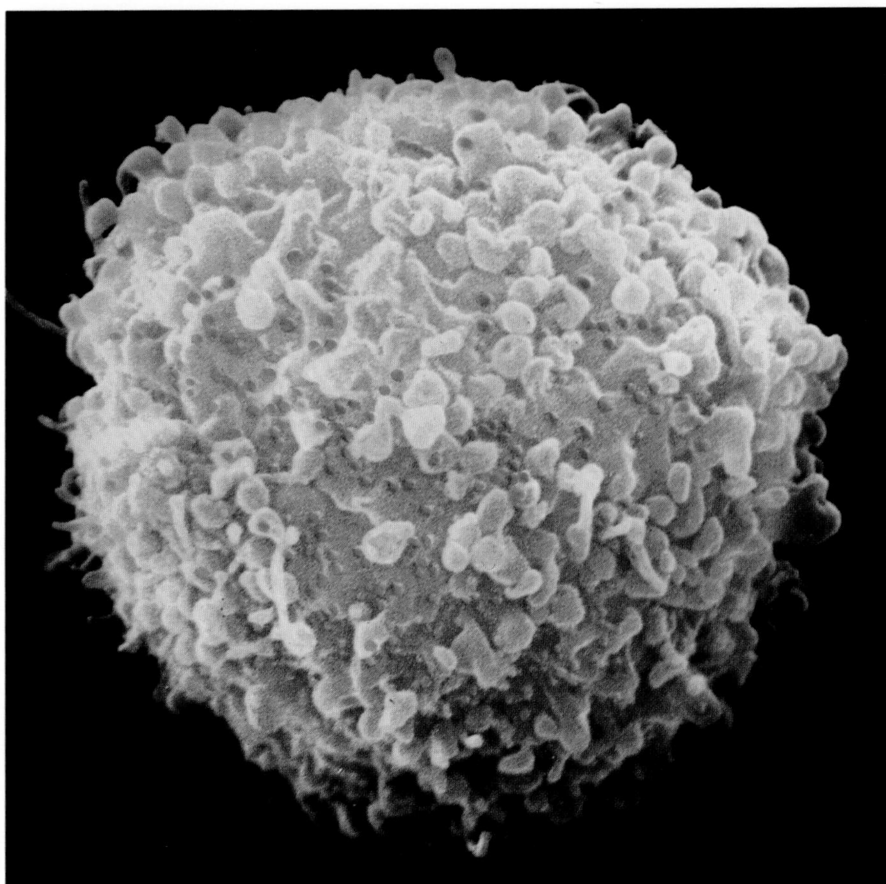

KILLER VIRUS *A false-colour image shows a T-lymphocyte cell – the body's basic unit of defence against infection – being 'attacked' by green particles of HIV, which causes AIDS.*

stop drinking. The first step for members is to admit they have a drinking problem. AA calls alcoholism a disease for which the only cure is total abstention.

allergy The IMMUNE SYSTEM of people with allergies misidentifies harmless substances as harmful and its subsequent defence produces an allergic reaction. Symptoms include itchy eyes, a runny nose, rashes or vomiting, brought on by the release of HISTAMINE in the body. Among the most common allergies are HAY FEVER – caused by inhaling pollen – and those caused by exposure to dust mites or eating gluten or dairy products. Allergies are usually relieved with antihistamines, but severe reactions may be life-threatening and require an injection of ADRENALINE.

alternative medicine Any form of treatment outside the range of orthodox medicine, such as HOMEOPATHY, OSTEOPATHY, CHIROPRACTIC and ACUPUNCTURE. It is also known as complementary medicine.

Alzheimer's disease Progressive deterioration of the brain, which is one of two causes of DEMENTIA. The other is multiple STROKES. Alzheimer's can occur at any age, but becomes increasingly common with advancing age; more than 20 per cent of people over the age of 75 may have it. It is characterized by increasing confusion, memory loss, apathy and depression. Suggestions that excessive aluminium in the blood contributes to the disease has led to warnings about cooking in aluminium saucepans, especially acid foods that react with the metal. This is not, however, generally accepted to be a major risk.

amniocentesis Test taken to detect abnormalities in an unborn child, usually between the 16th and 18th week of PREGNANCY. Some of the amniotic fluid surrounding the FOETUS is drawn off by inserting a hollow needle into the uterus. Foetal cells in this fluid are then checked for evidence of several conditions, including DOWN'S SYNDROME. The test, which carries less than a 1 in 50 risk of miscarriage, is performed where a risk of foetal abnormality is suspected.

anaemia Most common disease of the blood in which not enough red cells are produced. Anaemia is usually caused by excessive bleeding, for example, heavy periods; or a form of malnutrition, such as a lack of iron, vitamin B_{12} or folic acid. Some pregnant women become anaemic because the developing FOETUS depletes their iron or folate level. (See also SICKLE-CELL ANAEMIA.)

anaesthetic Local anaesthetics block nerve signals to the brain from a particular part of the body and are used for minor surgery. General anaesthetics – which cause the patient to lose consciousness – are used for major, or very painful, surgery.

❖ Before the introduction of anaesthetics in 1846, it was not uncommon for patients to die of shock from the pain even if an operation was otherwise successful. The first anaesthetics were ether and chloroform.

aneurysm Abnormal swelling of an artery in a region that has been weakened by injury or ATHEROSCLEROSIS, although sometimes it can be congenital (that is, there from birth). If an aneurysm bursts, it can be fatal.

angina Chest pains sometimes accompanied by a choking feeling as a result of an inadequate supply of blood to the HEART, and often brought on by exertion, since this increases the heart muscle's demand for blood.

anorexia nervosa Psychological eating disorder known as the 'slimmer's disease', typically affecting teenage girls. No matter how emaciated she becomes, the sufferer believes she is overweight and refuses to eat enough. The condition often persists for years and a normal eating pattern may never be regained; a high proportion of sufferers go on to develop BULIMIA.

antibiotic Drug used to fight bacterial infection. The first modern antibiotic to be used medically was PENICILLIN, originally obtained from a mould by the Scottish bacteriologist Alexander Fleming (1881-1955) in 1928. Antibiotics can now be produced synthetically. They may dissolve the bacterium, impair its ability to take in nutrients, or prevent it from dividing. A wide range of antibiotics is now available; not all are suitable for a particular infection, since bacteria become resistant to antibiotics through continued exposure

❖ Primitive antibiotics have been used for many centuries. In ancient Egypt, a poultice of rotting material was used to treat skin problems or infected wounds.

antibodies Proteins manufactured by certain white blood cells to fight foreign invaders in the body, such as bacteria, viruses and parasites. They play a major part in the IMMUNE

SYSTEM. Each antibody combats a particular infection: for example, a measles antibody would not fight a cold virus. Marker molecules called antigens, carried by the invader, enable the antibody to identify and destroy it; the invader either dissolves, or is engulfed by white blood cells. Once the body has an effective antibody, it becomes immune to that disease. This is the basis of IMMUNIZATION.

anticoagulant Any substance that slows down or prevents the clotting of BLOOD. Artificial anticoagulants are used to treat blood clots. (See THROMBOSIS.)

appendix (vermiform appendix) Closed tube, the length of the middle finger, joined to the beginning of the large intestine. It is believed to be associated with the immune system in human beings, and is involved in digestion in some plant-eating animals. Appendicitis, or inflammation of the appendix, is fairly common and the usual cure is surgical removal. A burst appendix, which usually goes on to cause peritonitis – the inflammation of the abdominal cavity's membrane – can be fatal without swift and appropriate action.

arthritis Inflammation of the tissues in the joints, resulting in stiffness and pain. The two most common forms of the disease are osteoarthritis and rheumatoid arthritis. Osteoarthritis results from wear and tear on joints – usually the knees, hips and spine. Rheumatoid arthritis, which affects three times as many women as men, is caused by the body's IMMUNE SYSTEM acting abnormally and may damage tendons, ligaments and tissues as well. In extreme cases, feet and hands can become deformed.

asthma Difficulty in breathing, caused by narrowing and inflammation of the bronchial tubes. An attack may be brought on by many factors, including exercise, anxiety or an allergic reaction to pollen or house dust. Sufferers can relieve attacks by breathing in a bronchodilator drug – which makes the bronchial tubes wider – from an inhaler. The incidence of childhood asthma has increased rapidly since the early 1980s; some experts believe this is due to air pollution, others blame a rise in allergies, smoking during pregnancy or a poor diet.

atherosclerosis Narrowing of the arteries caused by fat building up along the walls of the arteries and solidifying into obstructive mounds containing CHOLESTEROL and other substances, resulting in reduced blood flow. This increases the risk of HEART ATTACK, STROKE and ANEURYSMS. A heart attack, caused by blood clotting on these fatty obstructions called plaque, is the commonest cause of death in people in Western countries who are over the age of 40.

autism Behavioural disorder that affects 1 in 2 000 children. The causes of autism are still unknown; some experts believe they are probably physical, others consider that early psychological traumas play a part. It affects significantly more boys than girls. An autistic child is unable to relate socially and seems to be absorbed in his or her own private world. The child will often display obsessive behaviour and repeatedly copy other people. At the same time the child may have 'islets' of skill, usually in areas that involve abstract thought such as music and mathematics. About one-third of autistic children have average IQs; the remainder are of subnormal intelligence. Although there is no known cure for autism, a great deal can be done to help with appropriate education and support.

back pain Most people suffer back pain at some time in their lives, but it is seldom a sign of serious disease and usually goes away within a week. Often the cause is muscle or ligament strain, especially when the lower, lumbar, region is affected. Any pain in the lower back is classified as lumbago. Severe, persistent pain may be a symptom of a SLIPPED DISC or occasionally of a disease affecting internal organs, such as gallstones.

WORLD APART *Stephen Wiltshire sits beside his drawing of the financial district of New York. An extraordinary ability to retain and reproduce architectural images is one of the pleasures in this young autistic artist's world.*

benign Term describing a condition that is not life-threatening. It is most often used to describe tumours or growths that are not MALIGNANT or cancerous.

beta blockers Drugs used to treat HEART disorders and high BLOOD PRESSURE. They reduce the heart's workload by blocking signals from the autonomic nervous system that would otherwise increase both heart rate and blood pressure.

bile Greeny-brown fluid produced by the liver and stored in the gall bladder. It is released into the small intestine to excrete waste and to help digest fats. (See JAUNDICE.)
❖ A bilious attack has nothing to do with bile and is usually the result of overeating.

bilharzia (schistosomiasis) Tropical disease, affecting the blood vessels of the liver, spleen, bladder and bowel. It is caused by flukes (parasitic worms) hosted by snails and the infection is contracted when a person wades, swims or washes in infected water. Common symptoms are blood in the urine or faeces, fever and tiredness. More than 200 million people in 70 countries – mainly in Africa, South America and Asia – are affected. The disease is now easily treated. The parasite can be killed by boiling water that is to be used for washing or drinking.
❖ Bilharzia is found in many rivers and dams in southern Africa, particularly in Mpumalanga and Northern Province, parts of KwaZulu-Natal, the Eastern Cape coast, Caprivi in Namibia, the northern and eastern regions of Botswana, and most of Mozambique and Zimbabwe.

biorhythms Functions of the brain or body that follow a regular cyclical pattern. Some, such as sleepiness and wakefulness, follow a 24-hour, or circadian, cycle.
❖ When the ▷CIRCADIAN RHYTHM is disrupted – for instance, by flying across several time zones – people often find it difficult to adjust, and so suffer from jet lag.

blood Fluid that acts as a transport medium around the CIRCULATORY SYSTEM, and which also helps to defend the body against infection. The average adult male has 5,5-6,5 litres of blood; an adult female usually has 4,5-5,5 litres. It is made up of blood cells suspended in plasma. Plasma, the fluid part of the blood, carries food, ANTIBODIES, blood-clotting proteins, HORMONES and waste around the body. Red blood cells contain HAEMOGLOBIN, a protein that picks up oxygen in the lungs – giving blood its bright red colour – and releases it in the tissues. White blood cells fight infection. Platelets play an important role in blood clotting. Common diseases of the blood include ANAEMIA and LEUKAEMIA.

DYING BLOOD CELL *After 120 days and thousands of trips through the bloodstream, the red blood cells begins to expire. A white blood cell is seen here engulfing and digesting an ageing cell.*

blood group There are four basic BLOOD groups – A, B, AB and O. In a blood transfusion, donor and recipient must share the same blood group, otherwise the recipient may have a serious, possibly fatal, reaction. Individuals are also classified as Rh+ (Rhesus positive) or Rh- (negative). An Rh- mother may need an injection after her first pregnancy to avoid antibodies killing a future unborn baby's red blood cells. All blood types are determined genetically and may be used to help prove parentage.

blood pressure The pressure exerted by blood as it travels through the main arteries of the body. Blood pressure is determined by the elasticity of arteries, and the volume of blood forced into them at any time by the heart. When the heart contracts, pressure is at its highest (systolic) and when it relaxes, pressure is at its lowest (diastolic). Pressure is expressed by putting the systolic number over the diastolic. The average reading for a healthy adult is roughly 120/80, but this increases with age. Women tend to have slightly lower blood pressure than men. High blood pressure or hypertension increases the risk of HEART ATTACK and STROKE. Low blood pressure, hypotension, is often the cause of fainting and dizziness.

blood vessels Flexible tubes through which the blood flows around the CIRCULATORY SYSTEM. All arteries carry blood away from the heart under high pressure. The thick elastic muscular walls of the arteries expand when the heart forces blood into them, then contract to push blood onward round the body. The pressure wave passing along an artery with each heartbeat can be felt as the pulse. Veins carry blood towards the heart. Veins have thinner walls and carry blood at low pressure; valves prevent blood flowing backwards. The smallest and most numerous blood vessels, the capillaries, link arteries and veins.

bones See SKELETON.

brain The brain and spinal cord together form the central NERVOUS SYSTEM, linked by nerves to all parts of the body. As well as thought, memory and emotion, the brain controls the running of the body, constantly monitoring blood pressure, breathing and balance. It is divided into three main sections: the cerebellum; the brainstem; and the cerebrum. The cerebellum controls balance, coordination and posture. The brainstem controls breathing, blood pressure and digestion, and links the brain to the spinal cord. The complexity of the cerebrum is what differentiates human brains from those of other animals. Its thin outer layer is a mass of 'grey matter' called the cerebral cortex. It is here that conscious thought takes place, information from sensors, such as eyes and skin, is analysed and voluntary movements are initiated. Inside it is 'white matter' – a mass of nerve fibres that connects the cortex to the rest of the brain. The left hemisphere controls the right side of the body and communication skills such as writing and speech, mathematics and reasoning. The right hemisphere controls the left side of the body, spatial skills, artistic and musical activities, and creativity. Immediately beneath the cerebrum, the hypothalamus controls hunger, thirst, sex drive, aggression and sleep, and is directly connected to the PITUITARY GLAND. An insufficient supply of oxygen to the brain at birth, or at a later stage in life, can cause permanent brain damage. STROKE, EPILEPSY and MENINGITIS are all disorders of the brain.

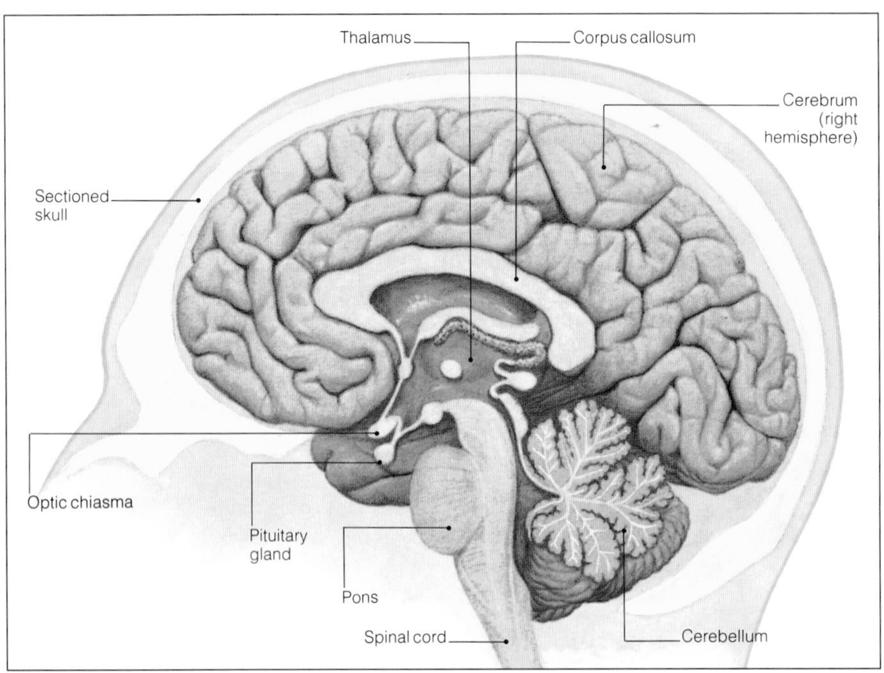

BRAIN POWER *A cross-section of the brain shows its three main sections – the cerebellum, the brainstem and the cerebrum. Below, two scans, using radioactive dye, show how much glucose the brain uses to power thinking. The brain of a highly intelligent person, on the right, uses less glucose (yellow) to find the correct answer to an abstract problem than the brain of someone with lower intelligence, on the left, suggesting that brain efficiency is a mark of intelligence.*

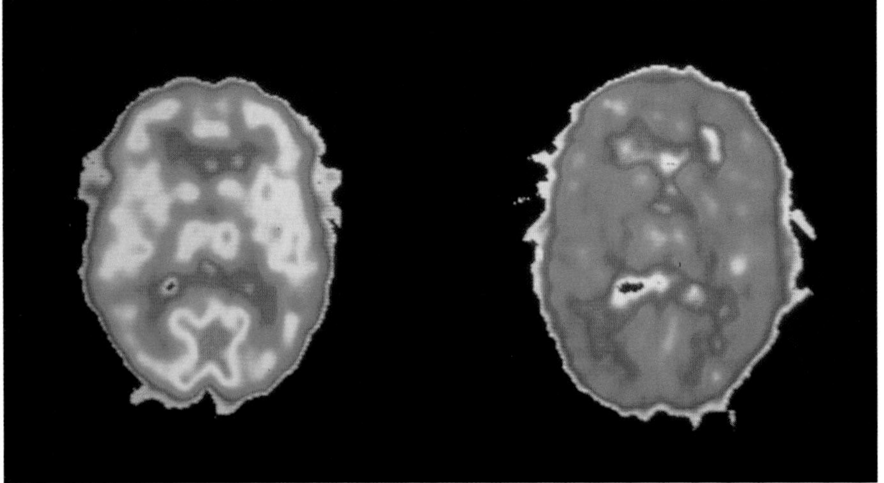

bronchitis Inflammation of the bronchi – the large air passages that connect the windpipe to the lungs – causing coughing, breathlessness and increased phlegm. Acute bronchitis is an infection caused by bacteria or viruses. Chronic bronchitis is a serious disease usually caused by smoking. It may lead to EMPHYSEMA and HEART FAILURE.

bubonic plague Highly infectious, sometimes fatal bacterial disease affecting the lymphatic system. The bacteria are carried by rat-borne fleas. The lymph nodes become swollen, creating buboes or lumps, and the victim suffers a high fever, severe thirst and blood poisoning, and becomes confused. Today, the disease is easily treated with antibiotics, but in the Middle Ages the so-called ▷BLACK DEATH killed millions of people across Europe. It is still found in southern Africa. In the early 1990s there were several outbreaks in Mozambique and a major epidemic in India.

bulimia Eating disorder characterized by binging followed by induced vomiting. The condition typically affects women in their late teens and early twenties and is often linked with ANOREXIA NERVOSA.

Caesarean section Operation to deliver a baby by cutting through the mother's abdomen. It is often necessary when the baby is in an awkward position. If the mother's pelvis is too small for the baby's head to pass through, it is safer for the baby to be delivered by surgery than to be forced through the birth canal.

cancer Disorder caused by rogue cells multiplying unchecked in a tissue, organ, or the blood, often resulting in a MALIGNANT tumour. It may spread throughout the body and kills by preventing normal functioning. Cancer may be triggered by environmental factors such as diet, pollution, smoking, a virus, or stress; in some cases, the tendency to develop cancer is inherited. Orthodox treatment includes RADIOTHERAPY, CHEMOTHERAPY and surgery. Some cancers usually affect only people over 40 years old but some forms of LEUKAEMIA are most common in children. In South Africa, cancer of the oesophagus and the SKIN CANCER known as basal cell carcinoma are the most common cancers among men; cervical and breast cancer are the most common among women.

❖ A substance, such as tobacco smoke, that can cause the body's cells to become cancerous is known as a carcinogen.

cartilage Tough connective tissue that covers the ends of bones and enables joints to move smoothly. It also forms the shock-absorbing discs between the vertebrae. Ears, the end of the nose and the rings of the windpipe are cartilage. In unborn babies, most of the skeletal structure begins as cartilage and gradually turns to bone.

cataract Painless condition of the eye that occurs when the lens becomes opaque. Many elderly people suffer some degree of cataract. It is part of the normal ageing process, but sometimes it is the result of diabetes or injury. Symptoms include deteriorating vision and better vision in half-light than daylight. Cataracts can be treated by replacing the lens of the eye.

cellulite Fatty deposits usually found on the thighs and buttocks. It can be reduced by exercise and eating a healthy diet.

cerebral palsy Any disorder affecting muscle control which is caused by damage to a child's developing brain. The most common cause is lack of sufficient oxygen to the foetal brain, but damage may result from injury before or during birth. Many children with cerebral palsy are of normal intelligence. Effects vary from slight clumsiness to spasticity. PHYSIOTHERAPY, occupational therapy and speech therapy can help.

cervical smear A test to detect pre-cancerous cells in the tissue of the cervix. A minute specimen of tissue is scraped from the cervix with a spatula for examination. The test, which takes only a few seconds, is almost always painless. Doctors suggest that women who have been sexually active should have a test once a year.

❖ The test is also commonly called a 'Pap' smear after its inventor, American anatomist George Papanicolaou (1883-1962).

❖ South Africa has one of the highest rates of cervical CANCER in the world.

chemotherapy Any treatment using anti-cancer drugs which specifically attack cancer cells by interfering with their reproduction and absorption of nutrients. Chemotherapy

BLOOD ON THE MOVE *Above, an image magnified 600 times, shows red blood cells packed into a tiny capillary. Below, the body's network of major arteries and veins. Arteries carry oxygenated blood (red) from the heart; veins carry deoxygenated blood (blue) back to the heart. The pulmonary artery and vein carry blood to and from the lungs.*

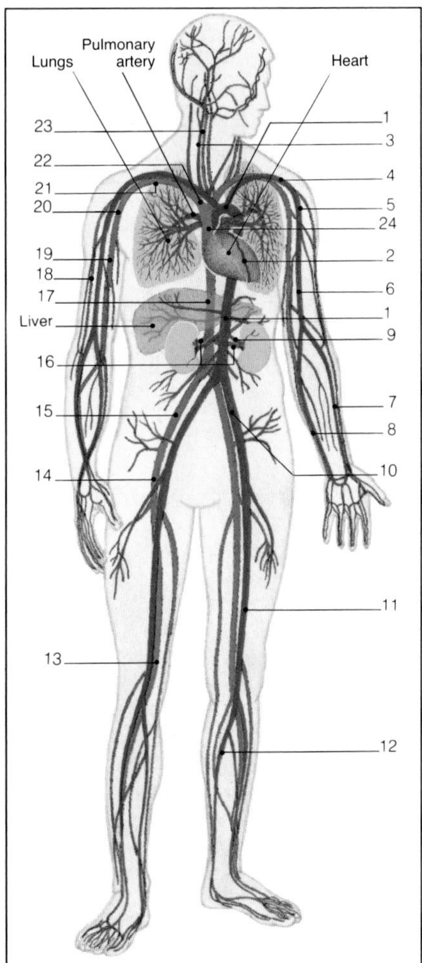

Arteries	Veins
1 Aorta	13 Saphenous
2 Coronary	14 Femoral
3 Common carotid	15 Common iliac
4 Subclavian	16 Renal
5 Axillary	17 Inferior vena cava
6 Brachial	18 Cephalic
7 Radial	19 Basilic
8 Ulnar	20 Axillary
9 Renal	21 Subclavian
10 Common iliac	22 Brachiocephalic
11 Femoral	23 Internal jugular
12 Tibial	24 Superior vena cava

may also disturb the activity of normal cells, causing distressing side effects such as hair loss or nausea.

chickenpox Highly infectious childhood viral disease. Symptoms include a temperature and a rash on the body and, often, in the mouth and ears. These form blisters and then itchy scabs. The virus may resurface in later life to cause SHINGLES.

childbirth After nine months of PREGNANCY, the womb begins to contract and the cervix opens up. As contractions become longer and stronger, the baby will be forced (normally head first) down into the vagina and out into the world. After delivery, the umbilical cord is clamped and cut. About ten minutes after the baby is born, the PLACENTA – or afterbirth – is expelled. Breech babies are born bottom or feet first. A CAESAREAN SECTION may be necessary if the baby is in this position, or if the mother's pelvis is too narrow. Lack of oxygen during birth may cause birth defects.

chiropractic Form of holistic, alternative medicine based on adjustment of the spine. It is founded on the idea that disease or pain is caused by interference with the NERVOUS SYSTEM. (Compare OSTEOPATHY.)

cholera Acute, sometimes fatal, bacterial infection prevalent in Africa and Asia. It is caused by swallowing contaminated water or food. Symptoms include diarrhoea, vomiting and muscle cramps. If untreated, the patient may die of dehydration.

cholesterol Substance found in all body cells. It is also involved in the manufacture of hormones and vitamin D, and the transportation of fats around the body. Most cholesterol is manufactured in the liver; the remainder is obtained from cholesterol-rich foods such as eggs and dairy products. An excessive level of cholesterol in the blood – a condition known as hypercholesterolaemia – is associated with ATHEROSCLEROSIS.

❖ South Africa's whites have one of the highest rates of heart disease in the world, largely due to a diet that contains too much saturated fat, as well as the presence of a hereditary form of hypercholesterolaemia that is common in people of Afrikaner descent.

chronic illness Long-term condition or a recurring illness which may or may not be severe. (Compare ACUTE ILLNESS.)

circulatory system System of BLOOD VESSELS through which the blood is circulated around the body by the pumping action of the heart. It supplies all parts of the body with food and oxygen, and also removes wastes. There are two parts to the circulatory system: the pulmonary circulation connects the heart to the lungs; the systemic circulation connects the heart with the rest of the body. Dark red blood – with low levels of oxygen – enters the pulmonary circulation when it is pumped by the right side of the heart to the lungs. Here it picks up oxygen before travelling back to the left side of the heart, which pumps the bright red oxygen-rich blood into the main arteries of the systemic circulation. The blood passes along smaller and smaller vessels, finally reaching the microscopic capillaries where it gives up its nutrients and oxygen. Blood that is poor in oxygen flows from the capillaries into the veins that carry it back to the right side of the heart.

circumcision Removal of the foreskin of the penis. In some Western countries, such as the USA, and among Jews, it is performed on most male babies as a matter of course. In many African cultures it is part of the ritual surrounding entry into manhood. The operation results in reduced sensitivity and is medically necessary only when the foreskin is too tight. Female circumcision, a brutal and unnecessary operation, ranges from removal of the tip of the clitoris to the complete removal of the outer genitalia, causing permanent damage and a possible risk to life. It has been performed, however, on more than 100 million women in some 30 countries.

cirrhosis Chronic disease of the LIVER in which liver cells are replaced by scar tissue, which prevents the organ from functioning properly. Cirrhosis is usually caused by ALCOHOLISM or HEPATITIS. If discovered early, it may be arrested, but when advanced a transplant may be the only cure.

colostomy Operation in which part of the colon is pulled through the abdomen wall and made into an artificial opening. A disposable bag is attached to the opening to hold the faeces as they are discharged. A colostomy may be necessary if the colon is cancerous, blocked or injured.

colour blindness Inability to distinguish between colours, most commonly between red and green. This condition is hereditary, and much more common in men; it can be genetically carried by women who are not themselves colour blind.

coma State of deep unconsciousness in which all response to stimuli is lost. A coma can be caused by a head injury, a disease such as MENINGITIS or DIABETES, a STROKE or a drug overdose. A coma may last for hours, days and even years, or the patient may never regain consciousness.

❖ The longest coma recorded was that of a woman who died in the United States in 1978 at the age of 43. She had been in a coma for 37 years.

concussion Dizziness or a temporary loss of consciousness caused by a blow to the head or a loud explosion. Anyone suffering from concussion should be kept under observation for 24 hours in case any new symptoms develop that may indicate brain damage. Repeated concussion can lead to permanent brain damage – one of the main hazards of professional boxing.

congenital Term meaning 'present at birth'. It is used to describe conditions that develop before or during birth, such as CEREBRAL PALSY, DOWN'S SYNDROME or a HARELIP. (See also HEREDITARY.)

Congo fever Viral infection, related to Lassa fever, which is spread by ticks in some regions. Infection results in severe and often fatal illness, with rash, SHOCK and bleeding. It is also highly contagious among people.

conjunctivitis Inflammation of the conjunctiva – the transparent covering of the white of the eye and inner lining of the eyelid. The eye becomes red and itchy. It may be caused by infection or allergy, and can be treated with ointment or eyedrops. In children it is often known as 'pink eye'.

contraception Prevention of pregnancy by mechanical, chemical or hormonal methods. The diaphragm and the condom stop the sperm and the egg from meeting. The IUCD (intrauterine contraceptive device) prevents the implantation of the fertilized egg in the womb. Spermicides are chemicals that kill sperm. The most successful method is the PILL, which contains hormones that prevent ovulation. New methods include female condoms and hormonal implants.

❖ The Roman Catholic Church forbids its members to use artificial contraception.

cornea Transparent, protective front part of the EYE which helps focus light on the retina. Tears keep the cornea moist and healthy. A damaged or diseased cornea can usually be replaced in a corneal transplant.

cot death (Sudden Infant Death Syndrome [SIDS]) Inexplicable and sudden death of a previously healthy baby, usually between one and six months old. Breathing stops for no apparent reason. Doctors believe that risk factors include: the temperature of the room; smoking; bottle feeding; a sudden viral infection; bedding that is too soft or too warm; or the position in which the baby sleeps – it should lie on its back.

cyst Abnormal lump or swelling, formed by the growth of a small sac filled with fluid or semisolid matter. Cysts are generally harmless, although they may have to be removed if they interfere with the functioning of the tissues in which they grow.

cystic fibrosis Hereditary disease that causes the mucus-secreting glands of the lungs, pancreas and intestines to produce large amounts of thick, sticky mucus. This causes chronic lung infection and prevents the absorption of fats and other nutrients from the small intestine. With modern treatment, most sufferers survive to adulthood. The gene that causes cystic fybrosis was identified in 1989 and it may become the first disease to be treated by ▷GENETIC ENGINEERING.

COLOUR CHECK *Below left, colour blind people see a number; those with normal vision see patches of colour. Below right, those with normal vision see the number 57; the colour blind see 35.*

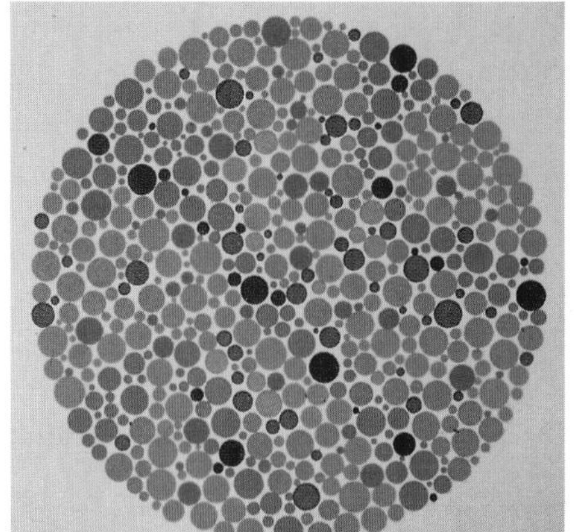

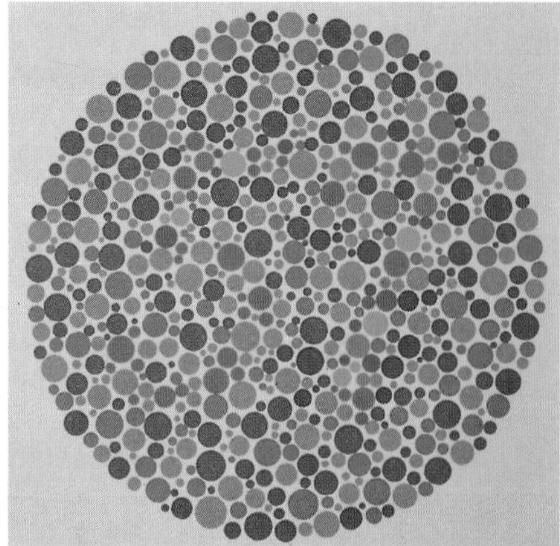

cystitis Inflammation of the bladder lining, usually caused by bacteria travelling up the urethra. Its main symptoms are a frequent urge to urinate, and a burning pain when urine is passed. It is far more common in women, because their urethras are shorter than those of men and more easily infected.

dementia Any progressive loss of mental functions. The commonest causes are strokes and ALZHEIMER'S DISEASE. One in five people over 75 is affected by dementia. Memory loss and confusion are the first symptoms. Sufferers from dementia eventually become unable to care for themselves.

dentistry Stopping tooth decay, curing gum disease, repairing damaged teeth and providing false teeth are all part of dentistry. Specialized treatments include orthodontics – the straightening of teeth – oral surgery, and denture design and construction. Advances in technology have greatly improved the general condition of tooth care, but better diet and oral hygiene are equally important. (See also TEETH.)

depression Symptoms include insomnia, lethargy, poor appetite, irritability, crying and an inability to enjoy pleasurable activities. There may be a reason for depression, such as redundancy or the death of a spouse, and it is a normal part of the grieving process. It is only when there appears to be no outside cause, when the condition appears to be chronic or when it is part of MANIC DEPRESSION, that it is regarded as a mental illness. Depression is common at any stage of adult life, and often responds well to treatment.

detached retina An injury may cause the retina to become detached from the back of the EYE, but it also happens spontaneously that fluid builds up between the retina and the outer layer of the eye. If diagnosed in time, the condition may be reversible; otherwise blindness may result.

diabetes Disorder caused by the body's inability to regulate the level of glucose in the blood by means of the hormone INSULIN. Symptoms include thirst, excessive urination, and weight loss. If untreated, the person may go into a diabetic COMA. Treatment usually involves a careful diet and may include taking tablets or injections of insulin. Long-term effects include heart and artery problems, impaired vision, kidney disease and nerve disorders.

dialysis Process of removing wastes from blood through a membrane, used in the treatment of kidney disease. In one method, haemodialysis, blood enters the dialysis machine, or artificial kidney, from the patient. Wastes, toxic substances and excess water pass through the membrane from the blood into dialysis fluid. Cleaned blood is returned to the patient, and the dialysis fluid is discarded. It takes between two and six hours to purify or clean an adult's blood. Dialysis normally has to be carried out two or three times a week. Few sufferers from kidney disease are able to afford to acquire the necessary equipment to avoid frequent visits to a hospital.

diarrhoea Usually caused by infection or food poisoning, diarrhoea can also be the result of stress or excess alcohol. Those affected should drink plenty of soft drinks to rehydrate the body and replace lost sugar and mineral salts.

❖ Dehydration caused by diarrhoea is the biggest cause of infant mortality in the developing world. About 45 million children die of it every year.

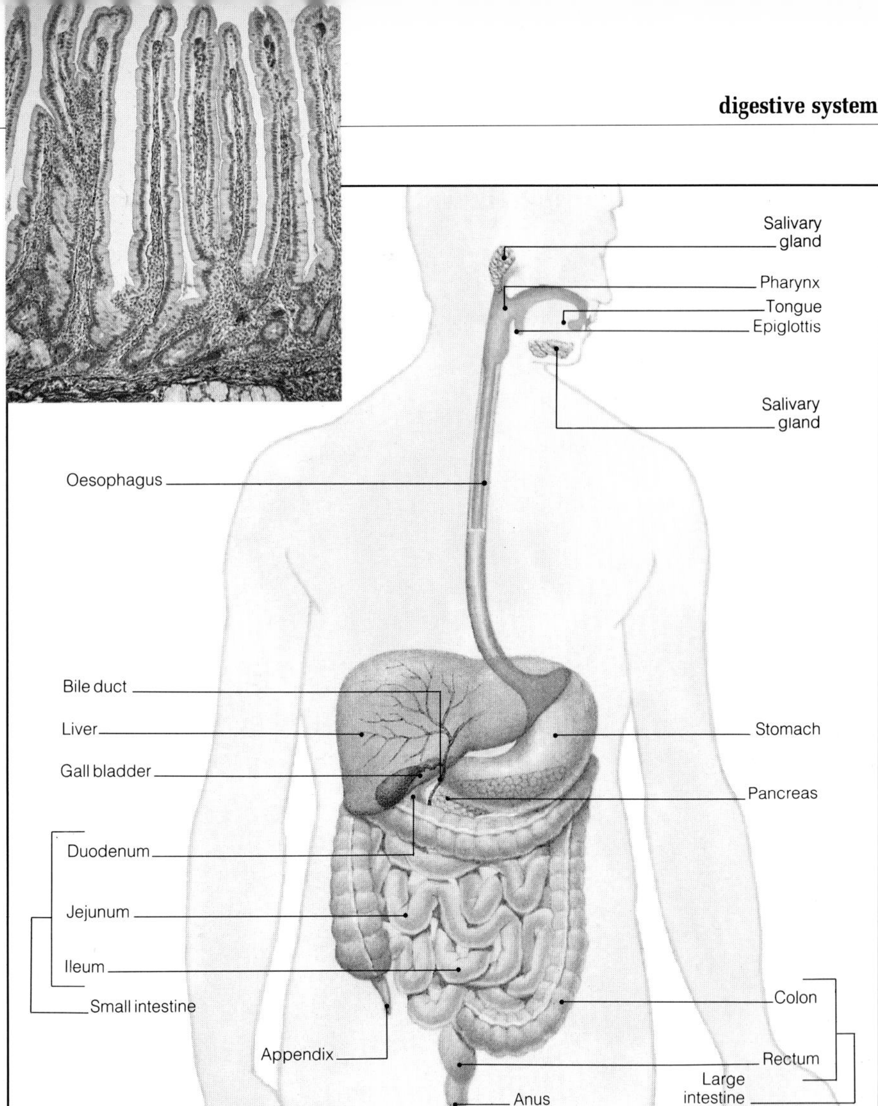

DIGESTING FOOD *The diagram shows the body's digestive system. Above is a false-colour image of a section through the small intestine. This secretes intestinal juice which contains enzymes which break down food. Nutrients from the food are then absorbed from the intestines into the blood through capillaries in tiny villi, seen here as fingerlike projections in the intestinal wall.*

digestive system Group of organs that breaks down food into a form that can be absorbed and used by the body. A few foods, such as vitamins and minerals, can be absorbed directly into the bloodstream, but most need to be broken down by enzymes into smaller and simpler molecules. Fats become fatty acids, proteins become amino acids and carbohydrates are turned into simpler sugars such as glucose. The process begins in the mouth, where chewing pulps food, which travels down the oesophagus and arrives in the stomach where it is mixed with hydrochloric acid and the enzyme pepsin, which breaks down proteins. The churning action of the stomach reduces food to a souplike liquid called chyme. The stomach stores chyme, passing small amounts at intervals to the small intestine. Here digestion is completed by enzymes secreted by the PANCREAS into the small intestine and by the wall of the small intestine itself. Fat digestion is aided by the release of BILE from the gall bladder. Simple food substances are then absorbed into the blood or LYMPHATIC SYSTEM. The remaining waste passes through the large intestine, where water is absorbed, then moves into the rectum, from which it is expelled as faeces. Food usually takes one or two days to go through the whole digestive system.

diphtheria Rare, and sometimes fatal, bacterial infection. Symptoms include a sore throat and a greyish-black film at the back of the throat, from where bacterial toxins may spread, damaging the heart and nervous system. The disease, which occurs commonly in children, can be prevented by immunization.

Down's syndrome CONGENITAL condition caused by the existence of an extra ▷CHROMOSOME. It leads to moderate or severe learning difficulties and is characterized by certain physical features. People with Down's syndrome may have a flat facial appearance, eyes that slant upwards on the outside edge of the eye, and with an extra fold of skin on the inner edge, as in Mongolian races. This led to the condition being called mongolism, but the term is no longer used. The condition can be detected during the early stages of pregnancy by carrying out an AMNIOCENTESIS test. One in every 700 babies is born with Down's syndrome. The incidence rises with the age of the mother, especially after 35.

dreams People dream during a stage in their sleeping called rapid eye movement (REM) sleep. This occurs about five times a night when the brain's electrical activity suddenly increases dramatically. Dreams may be a way for the brain to sort out the events and emotions of the previous day and many psychologists believe they also offer guidance from the unconscious mind on problems encountered in the waking state. Newborn babies appear to dream more than twice as much as adults. Several forms of psychotherapy involve an examination of the patient's dreams.

drug Any chemical substance that changes the functioning of the body or affects a disease. Drugs can be naturally occurring, such as caffeine in tea and coffee, or synthetic, such as paracetamol.

drug addiction Physical or psychological dependence on a drug. Not only illegal drugs such as heroin are addictive; people who take prescribed medicines such as tranquillizers or painkillers for prolonged periods may become addicted. Many smokers are, in fact, addicted to the nicotine in cigarette smoke. Drugs such as heroin create a physical dependence. To end the dependency, the addict will either have to be weaned slowly off the drug itself and onto a less harmful substitute, or go 'cold turkey' – stop completely. Sudden withdrawal from heroin may produce symptoms including cramps, diarrhoea, vomiting and even fits. Some people seem to be far more prone to addiction than others. There may be a genetic link, but social factors are also important.

dysentery Inflammation of the intestines which causes severe abdominal pain, fever, and bloody diarrhoea. It is usually contracted in tropical and subtropical regions following ingestion of food or water contaminated with faeces. Dysentery is usually bacterial or amoebic. Treatment of the condition involves the replacement of body fluids and sometimes a course of antibiotics.

❖ Dysentery is ENDEMIC in several countries (including in parts of southern Africa), and as many as 1 in 10 people are affected by it throughout the world.

dyslexia Difficulty in recognizing words, letters and sometimes numbers. A dyslexic sees characters interchanged, such as *folwer* for *flower*. Dyslexics are slow readers, but this is not a reflection of their intelligence.

ear Organ of hearing and balance. The visible part of the ear, the pinna, collects sound and funnels it down a short canal to the eardrum. The eardrum is a thin membrane, like the skin of a real drum, which vibrates in response to sound. Tiny bones in the middle ear transmit vibrations from the eardrum to the fluid-filled cochlea in the inner ear. Vibrations travelling through the fluid stimulate nerve cells that send impulses along the auditory nerve to the brain, where they are interpreted as sound. The inner ear also contains three fluid-filled semicircular canals concerned with balance. When the body moves, the fluid shifts, stimulating hair cells which send nerve impulses to the brain that keep it informed about the body's posture and movement. Earaches, most common in childhood, are usually caused by an infection of the middle ear. Conductive deafness – when the bones of the middle ear are malfunctioning or the canal is blocked – can sometimes be helped by surgery. Perceptive deafness, when the inner ear or the auditory nerves are damaged, sometimes after too much exposure to loud noise (as for instance in the operation of machinery or the firing of heavy artillery), is incurable. However, it can usually be alleviated with a hearing aid.

❖ Sudden changes in altitude, in an aeroplane for example, can cause the ears to 'pop'. This is caused by the equalizing of uneven pressure on each side of the eardrums.

ectopic pregnancy Development of the embryo outside the uterus, usually in a Fallopian tube. About 1 in 200 pregnancies is ectopic. As there is a considerable risk that the Fallopian tube may rupture, it is usually

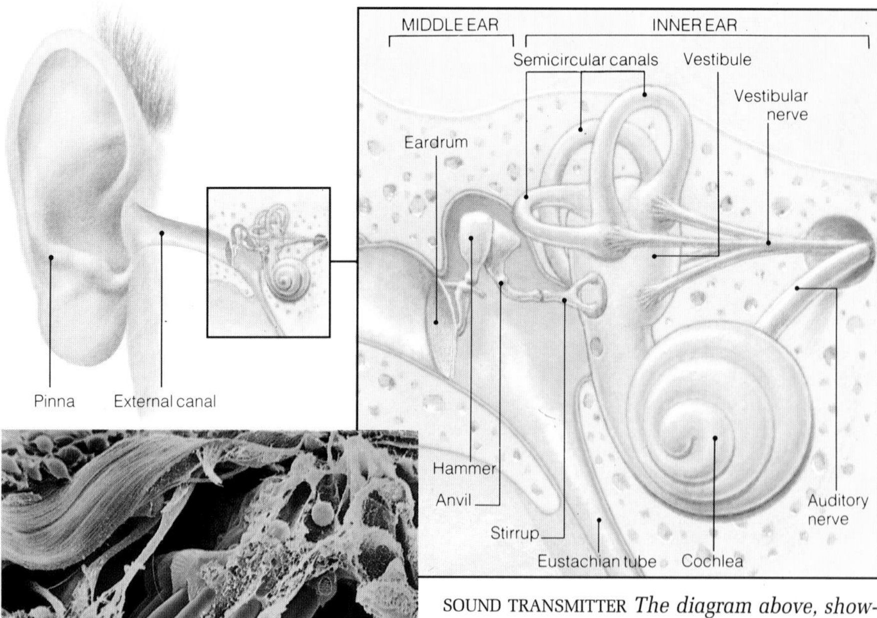

SOUND TRANSMITTER *The diagram above, showing the middle and inner ear, is expanded from the diagram on its left. The photograph (magnified 830 times) shows four rows of hair cells in the cochlea. Each cell contains about 100 hairs that turn sound waves into electrical impulses, which the brain can then interpret as sound.*

necessary to operate and terminate the pregancy so as to prevent internal bleeding.

eczema (dermatitis) Inflammation of the skin which causes redness, itching and cracking. The skin can become infected. Usual causes are ALLERGY or STRESS. It is common in babies and children, but most grow out of it. Treatment includes emollients to keep the skin moist and steroid ointments and creams. Eczema is often coupled with asthma or hay fever and is often resistant to treatment.

electrocardiogram (ECG) Recording of the electrical activity of the heart detected by electrodes attached to the chest and limbs. The read-out of the heart's electrical impulses on a monitor or graph paper helps doctors to assess accurately the condition of the heart and how well it is functioning.

embolism Blockage of an artery caused by a blood clot, gas bubble or some other substance. Embolisms can sometimes cause a STROKE or a HEART ATTACK.

emetic Substance that induces vomiting, which may be used when a person has swallowed a poison or an irritant. Typical emetics are concentrated salt water solution or the drug Ipecac. Use of an emetic without medical supervision can be dangerous.

emphysema Disorder in which the air sacs in the lungs become damaged and lose their elasticity, reducing the uptake of oxygen into the bloodstream. It is usually caused by smoking, although air pollution may make the condition worse. Symptoms include shortness of breath and frequent coughing or 'smoker's cough'. Emphysema may put a strain on the heart, increasing the likelihood of heart disease. The damage is irreversible, although the condition can sometimes be halted if treated in time.

encephalitis Inflammation of the brain, most often caused by infection with the herpes simplex virus (which usually causes cold sores or fever blisters), or occasionally results as a complication of MUMPS or MEASLES. Most people recover in response to treatment. However, in rare cases, the condition can lead to brain damage or even death.

endemic Term which describes a widespread disease or condition that is constantly present in a population or region, an example being malaria in parts of southern Africa. (Compare EPIDEMIC and PANDEMIC.)

endocrine system Glands that secrete HORMONES directly into the blood. Among other functions the endocrine system regulates growth, metabolism, sexual development and response to stress. Most endocrine glands are controlled by hormones from the PITUITARY GLAND, which is, in turn, influenced by the hypothalamus in the brain. The endocrine system includes the adrenal and THYROID glands, the ovaries, pancreas and testes.

endorphins Natural painkillers which are produced by the body. Endorphins are released at times of stress such as trauma, and also during strenuous exercise, such as marathon running.

❖ Opium-based drugs, such as morphine and heroin, have a similar chemical structure to that of endorphins.

endoscope Tube-shaped instrument, usually flexible, used for viewing the body's interior. The most commonly used include the gastroscope (for inspecting the inside of the stomach), the sigmoidoscope and colonoscope (large bowel), and the bronchoscope (windpipe and large airways of the lungs). Each consists of a bundle of ▷FIBRE-OPTIC tubes, with a light at the tip and an eyepiece or camera at the viewing end. Specialized attachments can be used to take tissue samples for biopsy – that is, a laboratory examination to check the extent of disease.

epidemic Rapid and extensive spreading of a contagious disease. Unlike ENDEMIC diseases, epidemics usually last for no more than a few weeks or months. (Compare also PANDEMIC.)

epilepsy Disorder of the brain which leads to fits or seizures and sometimes loss of consciousness. Epilepsy is the result of abnormal electrical activity in the brain. It sometimes runs in families, or can develop after brain damage. Attacks may be triggered by anxiety, fatigue or flashing lights. Epilepsy affects 1 person in every 200. The condition can usually be controlled with anti-convulsant drugs. Types of epilepsy include: petit mal, a momentary loss of concentration or consciousness; and grand mal, a more prolonged loss of consciousness which is accompanied by convulsions.

❖ The ancient Greeks called epilepsy the sacred disease and believed it was a punishment from the gods.

eye Organ of sight. The mechanism of the eye is similar to that of a camera. The CORNEA and the lens focus light through the pupil onto the retina. The pupil is like a camera's aperture; tiny muscles in the coloured iris adjust its diameter so that the right amount of light is let in. The central cavity is filled with jelly-like vitreous humour, which maintains the shape of the eye. The retina is made of sensitive nerve tissue connected to the optic nerve. It contains 130 million light receptors – rods, which register black-and-white vision, and cones, which are concerned with colour vision. Nerve impulses travel along the optic nerve to the brain, where images are analysed. When the eyeball is too long, the cornea and the lens cannot properly focus the image onto the retina, causing short-sightedness or myopia. Long-sightedness or hypermetropia, is the result of an eyeball that is too short. Astigmatism – vision that distorts the image – is caused by a misshapen cornea. Total or partial blindness is due to malfunctions of the eye, optic nerves or the part of the brain that processes the image.

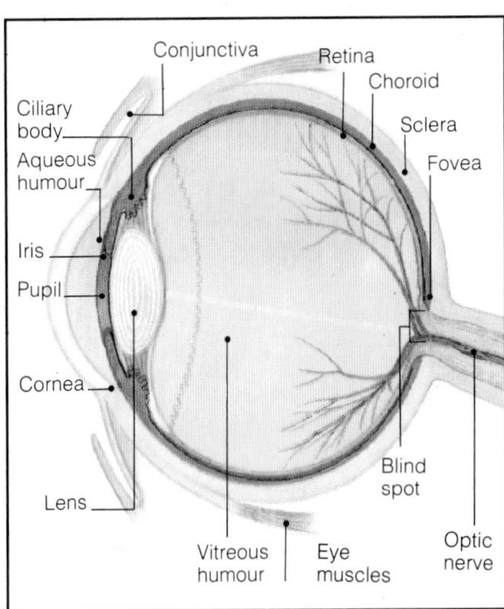

EYE MAKE-UP *A cross-section of the eyeball shows its three layers: the tough, white, outer sclera protects the eye; the middle, choroid is dark and stops light reflecting within the eyeball; and the inner layer, or retina, has light-sensitive cells called rods and cones.*

fainting Momentary loss of consciousness due to a reduction in oxygen supply to the brain. People faint for a variety of reasons: shock, fear, a stuffy atmosphere, pain, the sight of blood, or blowing too hard into a wind instrument. People with low blood pressure are especially prone to fainting.

fever Raised body temperature often caused by the immune system fighting infection. It is a symptom of many acute illnesses, one of the most common being influenza. Any temperature higher than 37°C is classified as a fever. High fevers may be accompanied by delirium (or confusion) and sometimes, especially in children, by convulsions.

foetus Term for an unborn child after the eighth week of pregnancy when it becomes

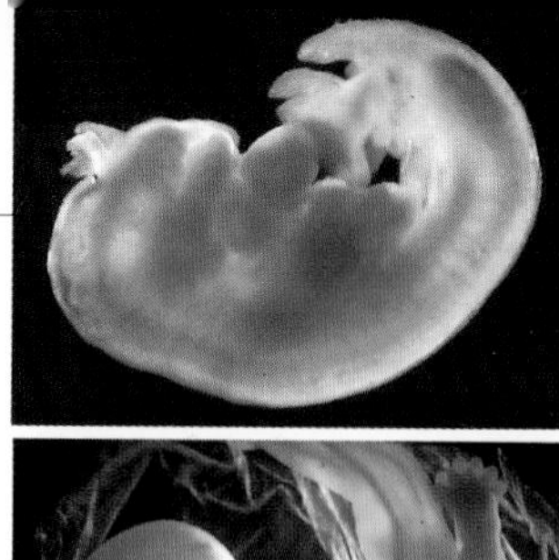
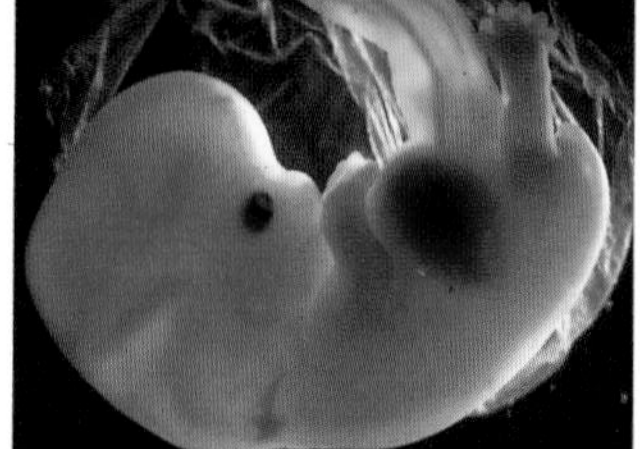
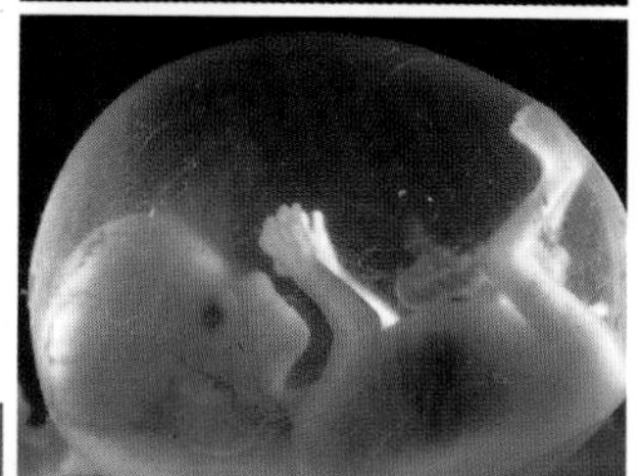
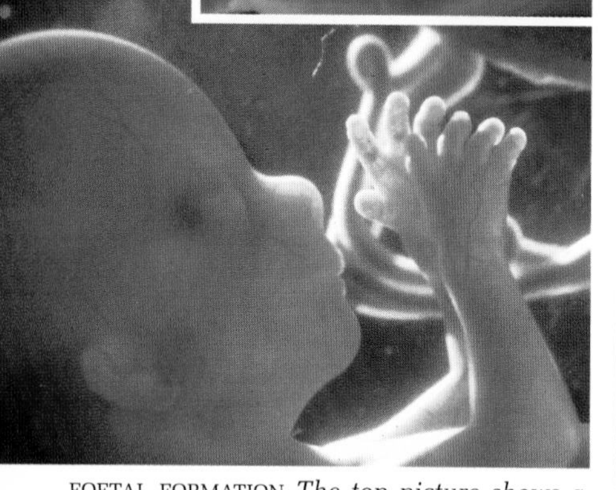

FOETAL FORMATION *The top picture shows a 28-day-old human embryo. At seven weeks, it is little more than 25 mm long and has arm and leg buds. At 14 weeks, facial features and limbs are evident. At four months, the ears, nose and mouth are formed.*

recognizably human. For the first eight weeks it is called an embryo.

fontanelles Two soft areas on the top of a newborn baby's head where the skull bones do not fully form until the age of about a year.

food poisoning Illness caused by eating food contaminated with poison, a bacteria such as SALMONELLA, or a virus. Symptoms may include abdominal pain, vomiting and diarrhoea. Botulism is a rare and usually fatal form of food poisoning caused by botulin, the most poisonous bacterial toxin known.

fracture Break or crack in a bone, usually caused by injury. Fractures are called greenstick when the bone splits but does not break. Bone regenerates naturally, and in healthy people a fracture will mend perfectly if the bones are properly aligned with, for example, pins or by a plaster cast.

gall bladder Small pear-shaped sac attached to the underside of the liver, which stores and concentrates BILE until it is discharged via the bile duct into the small intestine when food enters from the stomach. Gallstones – hard, pebblelike chemical deposits – can build up and cause severe pain or obstruct the flow of bile if they become lodged in the bile duct. Although they can sometimes be removed with special instruments without surgery, the whole gall bladder is usually removed (an operation called cholecystectomy). This is now frequently done by laparoscopic or 'keyhole' surgery in which only small cuts are made in the abdomen, resulting in less pain and a shorter hospital stay than with the conventional operation.

gangrene Death of body tissue due to lack of blood supply. The affected area becomes discoloured or black. Gangrene may lead to infection, in which case antibiotics may help. Amputation of a limb is sometimes necessary to stop the gangrene spreading to other parts of the body.

gastroenteritis Inflammation of the stomach and intestines. Symptoms are mild stomachache, diarrhoea and vomiting.

German measles See RUBELLA.

germs Common term for microscopic living organisms – including ▷BACTERIA and ▷VIRUSES – which cause disease. Germs were not recognized as a cause of illness until the 19th century, when the French scientist Louis PASTEUR identified the bacterium that causes anthrax.

gingivitis Inflammation of the gums caused by a bacterial infection. It is often the result of inadequate brushing and flossing of the teeth. The gums tend to bleed easily and in severe cases may become ulcerated.

glands Organs or groups of cells that produce a secretion, such as enzymes or hormones. Glands are either part of the ENDOCRINE SYSTEM or exocrine. Exocrine glands, which include sweat, salivary and digestive glands, release secretions directly to the body's outer and inner surfaces. Lymph nodes, an important part of the immune system, are also called glands. Lymph nodes swell noticeably in the neck, groin and armpits when the LYMPHATIC SYSTEM fights infection.

glandular fever (infectious mononucleosis) Viral infection common in young adults. Symptoms include fever, headache, sore throat and swollen glands in the neck, armpits and groin. The victim may feel lethargic for several weeks or months before fully recovering from the illness.

glaucoma Disorder of the EYE which usually occurs after the age of 40. Vision at the edge of the visual field is gradually lost and may result in 'tunnel vision' and eventual blindness. The condition is caused by blockage in the eyes' internal drainage ducts, leading to increased pressure of the fluid in the eyeball. If diagnosed early, it can usually be controlled with eye-drops.

gout Disorder causing attacks of ARTHRITIS often in only one joint at a time, especially in the hands and feet. Crystals of uric acid collect in the joint and cause severe pain, redness and swelling. The big toe is often affected. The condition is associated with kidney stones and is caused by a high level of uric acid in the blood. It is easily treated, but drugs must usually be taken for prolonged periods or even for life to prevent the condition recurring.

❖ Contrary to popular belief, gout is not caused by drinking too much port.

haemoglobin Pigment in blood that carries oxygen. Haemoglobin gives blood its red colour: the more oxygen present, the brighter the red. A person who is anaemic has too little haemoglobin in the red blood cells.

haemophilia Hereditary disorder caused by a lack of the blood-clotting agent Factor VIII, which results in excessive bleeding when any blood vessel is even slightly injured. Painful bleeding into joints is common. Haemophilia is transmitted down the maternal line, but affects only male offspring. It is treated with regular infusions of Factor VIII.

haemorrhoids (piles) Condition in which VARICOSE VEINS form inside or outside the anus, leading to bleeding and pain. A common cause is insufficient fibre in the diet, but pregnant women often suffer from haemorrhoids due to pressure on the large intestine.

hair Made up of dead cells composed largely of the protein keratin, hair is divided into three types: downy hair called lanugo that covers the foetus; fine vellus hair on the body; and longer terminal hair on the scalp. Terminal hair appears in the armpits, pubic area and, in men, on the face after puberty. Hair is always falling out and being replaced, but permanent hair loss leading to baldness is common in men. Hair goes grey because of a lack of the pigment melanin.

halitosis (bad breath) Chronic bad breath may be a symptom of some disorder, such as

GINGIVITIS, of a digestive complaint or a lung disease. But sometimes it is due simply to eating strong-smelling food.

harelip Congenital defect in which the upper lip is split down the middle, because the skin did not fully fuse as the baby developed in the womb. The condition can usually be repaired with plastic surgery when the baby is about three months old. A harelip is often associated with a cleft palate, which is when the roof of the mouth is divided into two halves from front to back.

Harvey, William (1578-1657) English physician and anatomist who first accurately described the circulation of the blood. In 1628 he published his theory that blood was pumped around the body along the blood vessels by the heart. Until then it had been almost universally believed that blood ebbed and flowed like the tide.

hay fever Allergy to pollen which usually affects sufferers in the spring and early summer. The pollen irritates the mucous membrane of the nose and throat. Symptoms include sneezing, a runny nose, watering eyes and, sometimes, CONJUNCTIVITIS. Antihistamines are commonly prescribed.

❖ Children born just before the pollen season seem to be more prone to hay fever.

heart The average human heart beats 2 500 million times in a 70-year lifespan. The heart is divided down the centre by a thick, muscular wall. Each side is subdivided into two connecting chambers: the atrium above and the ventricle below. One-way valves separate each atrium from its ventricle, and each ventricle from the artery that leaves it. BLOOD is pumped by both sides of the heart working in unison to maintain even pressure. First the atria squeeze the blood they have collected into the ventricles below. The right ventricle then contracts to pump blood through the arteries to the lungs and back to the left side of the heart; the left ventricle pumps it round the rest of the body. The heart gets its own blood supply from the coronary arteries. The most common disease of the heart is an insufficient blood supply, caused by partially blocked coronary arteries. This can cause ANGINA and lead to a HEART ATTACK. Although defects in the heart's structure are quite common at birth, these can often be repaired with surgery. TRANSPLANT SURGERY may be necessary if any of the heart's chambers are damaged beyond repair.

❖ In a total heart transplant, the back wall of the two atria and major blood vessels of the patient's own heart are left behind to attach the donor heart. In a 'piggy back' transplant the entire heart is kept in place but supplemented by the donor heart, which operates in tandem with the diseased heart.

heart attack (myocardial infarction or coronary thrombosis) Sudden loss of blood supply to an area of the heart, resulting in the death of some heart muscle. This is the most common cause of death in developed countries. In South Africa an average of 30 people die every day of heart attacks. It is usually caused by a blockage in a coronary artery narrowed by ATHEROSCLEROSIS. Symptoms include severe pain and pressure in the chest, which may spread to the left arm, neck and jaw, but sometimes the attack goes unnoticed. A heart attack may lead to cardiac arrest, when the heart stops completely. A heart bypass operation may be considered for someone who has ANGINA; blood vessels are taken from another part of the body and grafted beside the blocked coronary arteries. A triple or double bypass refers to the number of arteries bypassed in the surgery.

heartburn Burning feeling in the chest, produced when stomach acid flows up into the oesophagus, often after a heavy meal.

heart failure Condition in which the heart is unable to pump enough blood round the body, usually because of a HEART ATTACK, high BLOOD PRESSURE, ANAEMIA, an irregular heart rhythm, or a thyroid condition. Symptoms include difficulty in breathing, especially when lying down flat, fatigue and swelling in the legs. Heart failure may also have an effect on the functioning of other organs, such as the kidneys. Drugs can be taken to reduce the work the heart has to do and improve its performance.

hepatitis Inflammation of the liver, usually caused by a virus but sometimes induced by drugs and other chemical substances, including alcohol. Severe cases can lead to permanent liver damage. Symptoms include fever and JAUNDICE. The two most common viral forms are hepatitis A and B. Hepatitis A is spread through contaminated food and water and is common in tropical and subtropical countries. Hepatitis B, which is more serious, is spread through contaminated syringes, sexual intercourse and blood transfusions, although often the route of infection is unknown. Both forms of hepatitis are very common in South Africa, and the country has one of the highest rates of hepatitis B in the world. IMMUNIZATION against both hepatitis A and B is available.

❖ Hepatitis B is ENDEMIC in sub-Saharan Africa, and the continent is estimated to have 50 million carriers of the disease.

SANGOMA'S MUTI *A traditional South African healer pounds the root of a plant, one of the sources of his many herbal medicines.*

herbal medicine Use of plants and their extracts as drug treatment. Herbalism dates back to prehistoric times, and is still commonly practised by traditional African herbalists, who may be consulted in addition to a ▷PRIEST-DIVINER.

❖ Many of today's drugs are based on plant extracts. For example, digitalis, a drug used to treat HEART FAILURE, is extracted from foxglove leaves. The first contraceptive pill was based on extracts from the Mexican yam.

hereditary Any characteristic, such as eye colour, or any condition, such as HAEMOPHILIA, that can be passed on through the genes. Not all CONGENITAL conditions – those that are present at birth – are genetically transferred, but the HUMAN GENOME PROJECT is finding that many conditions have a hereditary component, such as certain forms of CANCER and ALZHEIMER'S DISEASE. These discoveries have prompted renewed interest in the ▷NATURE-NURTURE DEBATE.

hernia Abnormal protrusion of an organ through the muscle wall containing it, usually of the intestine through the abdominal wall. The condition is dangerous only if the blood supply to the protruding part is cut off, in which case surgery is required. If the stomach protrudes through the diaphragm into the chest cavity, it is called a hiatus hernia. This may lead to heartburn.

herpes Blisterlike sores on the skin or mucous membranes caused by the herpes simplex virus. There are two main types of herpes that are caused by different forms of

MEDICINE MAN *While many of his Greek contemporaries believed sickness was an affliction sent by the gods, Hippocrates recognized that disease had a natural cause.*

the virus: cold sores and genital herpes. Some people have only an initial attack, while others suffer repeated outbreaks. If a pregnant woman has an outbreak of genital herpes when she is about to give birth, she should be given a CAESAREAN SECTION to avoid harm to the baby. The diseases CHICKENPOX and SHINGLES are caused by a virus closely related to herpes simplex.

Hippocrates (*c*460-*c*370 BC) Greek physician who is regarded as the founding father of Western medicine. Although the writings once ascribed to Hippocrates are now known to have been written by more than one person, his contribution to the study of disease and the understanding of the doctor's role were nonetheless quite considerable. Unlike his predecessors, who were magicians as much as physicians, Hippocrates was convinced that diseases had natural causes. He was the first to keep case notes – the systematic chronicling of a patient's disease which doctors still use today. He also established the ground rules for the doctor/patient relationship, which are still the root of all modern codes of medical ethics. An extract from the Hippocratic oath reads as follows: 'Whatsoever house I enter, there will I go for the benefit of the sick, refraining from all wrongdoing. Whatsoever things I see or hear in my attendance on the sick which ought not to be voiced abroad, I will keep silence thereon.' The writings of Hippocrates are full of aphorisms, some of which have become household phrases, such as 'Desperate diseases require desperate remedies'.

histamine Chemical in the body that can cause inflammation, narrow the airways into the lungs, and stimulate the stomach's production of acid during allergic reactions. Histamine may be countered by the use of antihistamine drugs.

HIV See AIDS.

hives (nettle rash or urticaria) A condition marked by the sudden appearance of large, itchy, red or white bumps on the skin. These may be caused by an allergic reaction to a particular food or drug, or exposure to heat, cold or sunlight.

Hodgkin's disease Cancer of the lymph tissues. The lymph nodes, LIVER and SPLEEN become enlarged. Its cause is unknown, but it is most common in men between the ages of 20 and 30. If the disease is identified in its early stages, the prognosis (forecast of the outcome of the disease) is favourable.

holistic medicine Branch of ALTERNATIVE MEDICINE that aims to treat the whole person – mind and body together – instead of treating a problem in isolation.

homeopathy Branch of ALTERNATIVE MEDICINE based on the premise that like cures like. Practitioners prescribe a minute amount of the same substances which, given in large doses to a healthy person, would produce the symptoms of the disease.

hormones Chemical messengers produced by the ENDOCRINE SYSTEM and by other organs including the kidneys, intestines, brain and the placenta, which secretes hormones during pregnancy. Some hormones maintain a constant environment inside the body – INSULIN, for example, regulates the amount of glucose in the blood. Other hormones – for example, OESTROGEN, TESTOSTERONE and growth hormones – effect long-term changes, including a child's growth and sexual maturation. ADRENALINE triggers swift responses in the body when danger, injury or illness occur.
❖ Hormone replacement therapy (HRT) is used when the production of female sex hormones falls off: women are given oestrogen and progestogen to relieve the symptoms of their MENOPAUSE.

Human Genome Project Worldwide programme to identify all human genes. The project is coordinated from Washington, DC, but scientists from all over the world are participating. There are about 70 000 human genes: by 1995 more than 2 500 had been identified, including the genes for ALZHEIMER'S DISEASE, breast cancer and CYSTIC FIBROSIS.

hyperactivity Constant overactivity, usually in prepubescent children. They are unable to concentrate, and sleep for only a few hours a night. Hyperactivity has only recently been recognized as a real disorder, so little is known about causes or cures. Paradoxically, stimulants have been found to have a calming effect in some cases.

hyperventilation Rapid breathing pattern, usually caused by anxiety, which leads to too much carbon dioxide being taken from the blood. This results in a rapid heart beat, dizziness and tingling of the lips, fingers and toes. Sometimes the person faints. Sufferers should breathe slowly in and out of a paper bag for a few minutes to build up carbon dioxide in the blood.

hypnosis Waking state of extreme relaxation in which the person enters a trance, loses touch with the environment and becomes extremely susceptible to suggestion. Hypnotism was used as a form of therapy, mainly for 'hysteria', in the 19th century and is still used today to help people abandon such habits as smoking and to get over phobias.

hypothermia Abnormally low body temperature which can lead to unconsciousness and death. It is most common in infants, vagrants forced to sleep out in cold weather and drowning victims, but it can affect anyone exposed to cold for a long period. Hypothermia is diagnosed when body temperature falls below 35°C.

hysterectomy Surgical removal of the uterus and cervix or only the body of the uterus because of cancer or menstrual abnormalities. If the operation is to stop the spread of cancer, Fallopian tubes and ovaries may also be removed. It is one of the most frequently performed operations. After a hysterectomy, MENSTRUATION ceases and the woman can no longer bear children.

immune system Body's defence system against infection and cancer. The system is usually highly efficient. Foreign organisms and cancers are usually detected and killed without any noticeable effect on the person. Only during prolonged battles will the victim develop fever, inflammation or swollen lymph glands. The first line of defence consists of physical barriers such as skin, liquids such as mucus that trap microorganisms, and white blood cells called phagocytes that 'eat' foreign invaders that get into blood or tissues. The second line of defence is the immune system proper, which targets specific invaders. The immune system has two types of response to intruders: humoral and cellular, both controlled by cells called lymphocytes. In a humoral response, B-lymphocytes are stimulated by the presence of the invader to release specific killer chemicals called ANTIBODIES. These lock onto the invader and immobilize it, allowing phagocytes to move in and engulf it. The cellular response involves two types of T-lymphocytes. T-helper lymphocytes recognize abnormalities within body cells, such as cancer or the presence of a virus. These then stimulate T-killer lymphocytes to destroy the abnormal body cell. The B and T lymphocytes that survive a battle are the memory of the immune system. They will act immediately if the same threat appears, sometimes providing immunity to the disease for good. Transplants are usually rejected as foreign bodies by the immune system unless its activity is suppressed by drugs. The AIDS virus attacks the T-helper cell directly, so wrecking the immune system.

immunization Introduction of a mild dose of an infection into the body, which stimulates resistance to it. The germs used have usually been killed or weakened. Young children may be immunized against certain diseases, including DIPHTHERIA, POLIO and TETANUS.

❖ The British physician Edward Jenner (1749-1823) pioneered the process in 1796 with a vaccine against SMALLPOX. The World Health Organization successfully eradicated smallpox in 1979 through a global immunization programme. It was the first disease to be totally eradicated by human effort. (See also VACCINATION.)

incubation period The time between infection and the appearance of symptoms. This may be a few hours, as with some food poisoning, or many years, as with AIDS.

infertility treatment In men, infertility is usually caused by a failure to produce enough healthy sperm. In women, it may be a failure to ovulate. Sometimes fertility treatment is simply a matter of a change in diet, and relaxation exercises. In women, and occasionally in men, there may be a hormonal imbalance for which HORMONE treatment may be the solution. If the problem is not hormonal, there are several options available. With artificial insemination, sperm can be injected into the cervix with a syringe. Microsurgery may be used to repair the Fallopian tubes if they are blocked. Another possible option is *in vitro* fertilization, when the egg is fertilized by sperm in the laboratory and then placed in the womb; babies conceived this way are often called test-tube babies.

❖ In 1987 Pat Antony of Tzaneen in Northern Province became the first woman to give birth to her own grandchildren. She was implanted with her daughter's ova which had been fertilized *in vitro* by her son-in-law's sperm and was 48 when she gave birth to triplet babies.

influenza An acute, infectious disease caused by any of a large number of related viruses. Symptoms of 'flu' include fever, muscle pain, headache, loss of appetite, coughing and a sore throat. Vaccines are available against some strains, but owing to the rapid mutation of the virus, they may be effective only for short periods.

❖ In the flu pandemic of 1918-19, an estimated 15 million people died worldwide. The only countries unaffected were New Guinea, St Helena and a few Pacific islands. It was the worst global plague since the 14th-century ▷BLACK DEATH. (See also ▷FLU EPIDEMIC in 'Southern African history'.)

insulin Hormone secreted by the pancreas which enables the body to use glucose and so control glucose levels in the blood. People with DIABETES have difficulty producing insulin and may need regular injections.

intravenous Term meaning literally 'within a vein'. An intravenous drip can be used to supply drugs, fluids or nutrients directly into a patient's vein.

irritable bowel syndrome (irritable colon or spastic colon) Both constipation and diarrhoea can be caused by this condition, in which the bowel muscles function spasmodically. The lower abdomen may also become distended and painful. It is thought that the condition is often caused by STRESS and it is particularly common among women aged between 20 and 40.

jaundice Yellowing of the skin and eyes, caused by an excess of BILE pigment in the blood. It is a symptom of liver disease, blockage in the bile duct or the excessive destruction of red blood cells. Newborn babies often develop jaundice before their livers have started to work efficiently.

kidneys Pair of organs that filter waste from the blood and excrete it, together with excess water, as urine. They also maintain the body's chemical balance and produce a hormone that stimulates production of red blood cells. Human beings can survive perfectly well with only one kidney. People with kidney disorders may need to have regular DIALYSIS to artificially filter out the waste. Inflammation of the kidneys is called nephritis. Kidney stones are small lumps of calcium salts that form in the kidneys. Stones cause pain as they pass through the urinary tract and larger ones may obstruct the kidney or ureter (the tube taking urine from the kidney to the bladder), causing severe pain and back pressure on the kidney. They can usually be removed surgically or destroyed by ultrasound.

kwashiorkor Disease of severe MALNUTRITION found particularly in children in impoverished rural areas. Caused mainly by too little protein (and sometimes vitamins) in the diet, it is characterized by a swollen belly, stunted growth, loss of hair-colour, diarrhoea, weakness and irritability.

❖ The word is Ghanaian for 'displaced child'. The disease is often found when a baby is weaned early because of the arrival of a younger sibling who 'displaces' it at its mother's breast and the first child's milk protein is not replaced from another source.

laryngitis Strained or inflamed vocal cords which give the sufferer a hoarse, whispery voice. The condition is caused by overuse or infection. Singers may develop benign nodes on their vocal cords. The nodes may have to be surgically removed.

larynx (voice box) Framework of cartilage, muscles and ligaments which contains the vocal cords. The entrance is guarded by the epiglottis, which prevents food from going down the trachea. Sound is produced when air passes between the vibrating vocal cords. The pitch of the note varies as the controlling muscles contract and relax. The Adam's apple is the front of the larynx. When boys reach puberty, the larynx grows, causing the voice to deepen.

lentigo Flat, discoloured areas of skin which usually appear after the age of 50. They are harmless. Unlike freckles, they are not stimulated by exposure to the sun.

leprosy Bacterial infection that causes damage to the nerves and sometimes disfigurement. Large, hard patches appear on the skin. Because of the loss of feeling, some sufferers injure themselves and become repeatedly infected. Eventually this may lead to the loss of extremities. Leprosy has a long incubation period of about three to five years, and by the time there are any symptoms – loss of feeling in the hands and feet, muscle weakness, or paralysis of parts of the body – the disease is well established. Antibacterial drugs (or antibiotics) will kill the bacteria, but any disfigurement is irreversible. In 1995 there were about 2,5 million registered cases in the world, mainly in India and Brazil. Each year more than 600 000 new cases are reported, of which about 100 are in South Africa.

❖ Contrary to popular belief, leprosy is not very contagious. It can be caught only through intimate contact with someone in the early stages of the disease.

leukaemia Cancer of the white BLOOD cells. Abnormal white blood cells multiply at the expense of red blood cells and platelets, causing ANAEMIA, bruising and bleeding. In severe cases, white blood cells may take over the bone marrow entirely, stopping any other blood cells from being produced. Leukaemias can be ACUTE or CHRONIC; the form of leukaemia also depends on the type of white blood cell involved. People who have been exposed to radiation are more likely to suffer from it. CHEMOTHERAPY and RADIOTHERAPY may cure certain forms of leukaemia. In children, treatment can now provide a complete cure for more than half of those affected.

lice Parasitic insects which feed on blood and live on the surface of the skin. Their bites cause severe itching and a skin irritation called pediculosis. Three species of lice infest human beings: head lice, body lice and pubic lice, or crabs. Body lice are pin-head sized and lay their eggs in clothing. Head and pubic lice are smaller. All three can be got rid of with medicated shampoos or ointments. Head lice lay grey eggs, or nits, in the hair and commonly infest schoolchildren whose heads often come into close contact.

ligament Tough band of fibrous, flexible tissue that connects bones to one another and supports some internal organs. Ligaments ensure that joints move only in the right direction – preventing the knee from twisting, for example. If a ligament is torn, it can take several weeks or months to heal.

Lister, Joseph (1827-1912) British surgeon who revolutionized surgery in 1865 with the introduction of antiseptics. Lister used carbolic acid to demonstrate that antiseptics kill germs and so reduced the incidence of wounds becoming infected. He was inspired by the contemporary work of the French bacteriologist Louis PASTEUR, who discovered that germs cause disease.

liver The body's chemical factory and largest organ after the skin. The liver performs at least 22 major functions. Human beings can survive with just a quarter of their liver, and the tissue can regenerate if part of the liver is damaged. Blood flows into the liver through the hepatic artery from the aorta, and through the portal vein directly from the intestines. The liver stores glucose and vitamins A, D and B_{12}. It converts excess amino acids – the building blocks of proteins – into urea, which is excreted in the urine. It removes poisons, drugs and alcohol from the blood and renders them harmless. It also manufactures important proteins and breaks down old red blood cells. Liver disorders include HEPATITIS and CIRRHOSIS. Cancers from elsewhere in the body commonly spread to the liver.

STERILE SURGERY *Joseph Lister, seated centre, with staff in King's College Hospital, London, 1891. By persuading other surgeons to use antiseptics he almost certainly saved thousands of lives.*

lungs Pair of spongy, air-filled organs that form the main part of the RESPIRATORY SYSTEM. The lungs are made up of millions of minute air sacs called alveoli. Oxygen from the air taken into the lungs passes through the thin membranes of the alveoli into the blood; carbon dioxide passes in the opposite direction into the air which is breathed out. The lungs are extremely delicate, and long-term irritation such as smoking or pollution damages them permanently, and may cause EMPHYSEMA, BRONCHITIS or CANCER.

❖ Lung disease is a common occupational hazard in South Africa. Miners, sandblasters and quarry workers may develop silicosis (hardening of the lungs) from inhaling small particles; asbestos workers may develop lung disease (asbestosis) or cancer from inhaling asbestos fibres if appropriate precautions are not taken.

lymphatic system Network of small vessels through which lymph, derived from excess tissue fluid, is carried from the body's tissues back to the bloodstream. Lymph is a clear yellowish fluid made up of proteins, fats and white blood cells – mainly lymphocytes that play an important part in the IMMUNE SYSTEM. Lymph nodes or GLANDS, situated along lymphatic vessels, act as a barrier to infection by filtering out harmful bacteria. The nodes are small and soft but become swollen when fighting infection. The lymphatic system also transports fats from the small intestine.

malaria Tropical disease caused by parasites carried by mosquitoes and injected into the bloodstream when the mosquito bites. About 300 million people a year contract malaria, and it is the greatest medical hazard facing travellers to the tropics. Once in the bloodstream, the parasites travel to the liver, where they reproduce. Malaria is characterized by a particular type of recurring fever; this starts with chills, after which the temperature soars, then the patient is drenched with sweat as the body tries to cool down. Severe cases may develop kidney failure or coma. Malaria is ENDEMIC to Mozambique and occurs seasonally in several other parts of the southern African region, including Northern Province, Mpumalanga, KwaZulu-Natal,

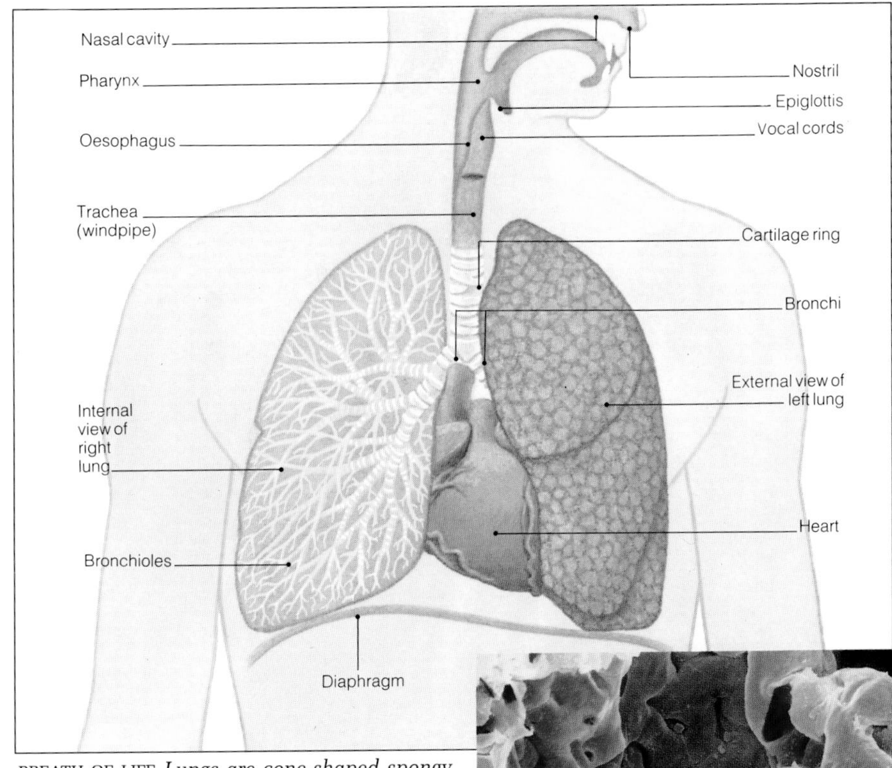

BREATH OF LIFE *Lungs are cone-shaped spongy organs protected by the ribs, spine, breastbone and respiratory muscles. Capillaries surrounding alveoli – microscopic air sacs – allow oxygen to pass into the blood from air that has been breathed in, and carbon dioxide to pass from the blood into the lungs before exhalation. Each lung has about 300 million alveoli, one of which is magnified 1 050 times on the right.*

northern parts of Namibia, Botswana and Zimbabwe. The parasite has become resistant to some commonly used antimalarials, including chloroquine. Medical advice should be obtained before travelling to these areas.

malignant Term for conditions that may be life-threatening as opposed to those that are BENIGN. It is usually used to describe cancers, or any illness that is fast-developing and likely to be fatal.

malnutrition Lack of adequate nutrients due to a poor diet or diseases which impede the body's ability to digest food. Malnutrition retards growth, leaves the body susceptible to infection, causes ANAEMIA and hampers the function and regeneration of cells, leading to muscle wastage and damage to organs and bones. Some 1,5 billion people in the world, or one in four, suffer from malnutrition.

mammogram Breast X-ray used to check for TUMOURS. It is recommended every three years for women aged between 50 and 64.

manic depression Mental disorder characterized by abnormal mood swings, from euphoria to deep DEPRESSION. In a manic period, a sufferer may be hyperactive, speak rapidly, have delusions, go on wildly extravagant spending sprees, and be irritable although elated. The drug lithium, whose benefits were first reported in 1949, has been used to counteract the mood swings, with a success rate of nearly 80 per cent.

❖ Artists, writers and creative people generally have been found to be six times more likely to suffer mood swings than the rest of the population.

mastectomy Surgical removal of all or part of a breast, usually performed to treat breast CANCER. Radical mastectomy may also include taking out the muscles and lymph nodes in the armpit.

mastitis Bacterial infection that causes a breast to become red, swollen and tender. Mastitis usually occurs when a mother is breastfeeding her baby.

ME (Myalgic encephalomyelitis or post-viral fatigue syndrome) A condition characterized by extreme fatigue. There may also be dizzy spells, headaches, muscle pains, DEPRESSION and anxiety; but these last two symptoms may be due to the difficulty of diagnosis and the long duration of the disease. ME also tends to get worse the more the victim exercises; active people seem to be more prone to the syndrome. It can last from two months to more than two years and, since there is no definitive test, diagnosis is by a process of elimination. ME usually develops after a viral infection, but the exact cause of the disease is still unknown. It was first identified in 1934 in the USA and its diagnosis increased rapidly in the 1980s.

measles Acute contagious disease, caused by a virus. Symptoms include a fever, sore eyes, a dry cough and a rash of red spots on the limbs, face, chest and back. An attack of measles can lead to pneumonia, ear infections and, rarely, inflammation of the brain. It is a major cause of infant mortality in the developing world, including South Africa. IMMUNIZATION is possible when a child is about 15 months old.

melanin Dark brown pigment in the skin and hair which determines the tone of the complexion. Melanin is produced by cells in the skin that are sensitive to sunlight. The pigment absorbs the sun's harmful ultraviolet rays and protects the body from burning and developing SKIN CANCERS. A sun tan is the result of stimulated melanin production. People with white hair and pink eyes who have no melanin and therefore no colouring are known as 'albinos'.

❖ Red hair is caused by a special red pigment, which competes with melanin. People who have very red hair produce very little melanin in their skin, which is why they burn easily in the sun.

memory Little is known about how memory works, but its main seat is believed to be the hippocampus in the centre of the forebrain, although long-term memory is believed to be stored throughout the brain. Memory works in three phases. First a piece of information or an impression such as a sound or an image is registered and goes into short-term memory a few seconds or this may last a few hours. Then, if it has made a deep impression, or if it crops up repeatedly – such as a friend's telephone number – it is stored in the long-term memory. The majority of people can hold about six to eight pieces of information in their short-term memory. When asked to remember more than that, the more recent facts tend to push out those which were stored earlier. The final phase, retrieval of the information, may be stimulated by a smell or an emotion, for example, or it may be done at will. Gradual loss of memory is associated with the onset of DEMENTIA.

meningitis Inflammation of the meninges – the membranes surrounding the brain and spinal cord. The disease is usually due to infection by a virus or bacterium. Symptoms include severe headaches, a stiff neck or back, high fever, vomiting, sensitivity to light, and a dark, blotchy rash. Viral meningitis is usually mild, but bacterial meningitis can, without early diagnosis and treatment with large doses of antibiotics, result in brain damage or even in death.

menopause Cessation of MENSTRUATION, marking the natural end of a woman's fertile years, and the physical changes associated with it caused by the reduction in levels of the hormone OESTROGEN. Periods may stop abruptly, gradually get farther apart, or become progressively lighter. Many women have hot flushes and night sweats, which may continue for two to five years. Others find menopause passes almost unnoticed. Hormone replacement therapy (HRT), using oestrogen patches or tablets, is usually an effective remedy. During and after menopause, the bones become more brittle (see OSTEOPOROSIS) and fat levels rise in the blood; this can lead to ATHEROSCLEROSIS. The average age for menopause is between 45 and 55.

THE MAIN BRANCHES OF MEDICINE

Cardiology	Area of medicine that deals with the heart.
Chiropractic	Branch of medicine that relieves pressure on the nerves by adjustment of the spine and joints and so removes the source of pain or discomfort.
Endocrinology	Study and treatment of the body's hormone-producing glands, such as the pituitary, thyroid and pancreas.
Epidemiology	Study of disease in communities, including control of epidemics.
Gastroenterology	Branch of medicine concerned with disease of the stomach and intestines.
Gynaecology	Branch of medicine that deals with the female reproductive system.
Haematology	Study of the blood and treament of blood diseases such as leukaemia.
Immunology	Study of the body's immune response to disease.
Neurology	Study and treatment of the nervous system, including the brain, spinal cord and nerves. It deals with conditions such as epilepsy and Parkinson's disease.
Obstetrics	Care of a woman during her pregnancy and childbirth. Modern technology, such as ultrasound scanning, helps to ensure a safer birth and a healthy baby.
Oncology	Treatment of cancer by means of surgery, radiotherapy or drugs.
Ophthalmology	Medical and surgical treatment of disorders of the eye, including injuries, cataracts and glaucoma and the prevention of blindness.
Orthopaedics	Branch of surgery concerned with treatment of bones, muscles, ligaments and tendons. It also includes manipulation, exercise and the fitting of braces.
Osteopathy	Practice of therapy based on manipulation of bones and muscles.
Otolaryngology	Branch of medicine concerned with disease of the ear, nose and throat.
Paediatrics	Branch of medicine dedicated to the physical and emotional health of children and young people. It deals with childhood diseases, growth and development.
Pathology	Study of disease, including postmortem examinations.
Psychiatry	Study and treatment of abnormal behaviour and disorders of the mind.
Radiology	Branch of medicine concerned with the diagnosis of disease through the use of X-rays and similar techniques.
Rheumatology	Area of medicine that deals with joints, muscles and connective tissues and seeks to treat diseases such as arthritis and gout.
Urology	Study and treatment of the urinary tract, which includes the kidneys and bladder.

menstruation (periods) Monthly discharge of the blood-enriched lining of the womb via the vagina, which normally lasts from three to seven days. This marks the beginning of a menstrual cycle – changes which prepare the uterus for pregnancy. The monthly cycle lasts for about 28 days and is controlled by the hormones oestrogen and progesterone secreted by the ovaries. About two weeks after menstruation, the womb lining has built up again and one of the ovaries releases an egg. If fertilized, the egg implants in the womb lining and pregnancy begins. Otherwise, the cycle continues.

metabolism Chemical processes occurring in the body's cells. When complex substances are broken down to provide the body with energy, the process is called catabolism. When they are built up, during protein synthesis, for example, it is called anabolism. The metabolic rate is the amount of energy the body uses. Naturally thin people often have a high metabolic rate.

microsurgery Surgery in which the surgeon can view the operation through a binocular microscope. It has dramatically improved the success rate for operations on CATARACTS, lazy eyes and some disorders of the ear. Microsurgery makes it possible to sew severed limbs back on to the body, because each minute blood vessel and nerve ending can be individually reconnected.

migraine Severe headache, often accompanied by nausea or vomiting. It may be preceded by sparks of light in the field of vision. Light and noise increase the pain. Some people may have one migraine in a lifetime, others are afflicted often. It can be quite disabling, lasting for as long as two days. Treatment is of variable success; some migraine sufferers are greatly helped by drugs; some little or not at all.

motor neuron disease (MND) Progressive form of PARALYSIS which occurs usually in those aged over 50. The cause is unknown. Nerves that control the body's muscle action degenerate, leading to muscle wastage. Eventually the muscles controlling speech, swallowing and breathing may become impaired. In the most severe cases, the victim dies within a few years, but in others the advance of the disease may be very slow or, in some instances, may stop altogether.

❖ In 1963, when he was 21, the physicist Stephen Hawking was diagnosed as having motor neuron disease. However, he has continued to conduct research and write books, despite being severely disabled and having a computer-generated voice.

mucous membrane Thin lining of the passages and cavities of the body such as the mouth, respiratory system and the digestive tract. The lining secretes mucus – a slippery, sticky fluid which lubricates and serves to protect the membrane.

multiple pregnancy There are two types of twin pregnancy. Either two eggs are released from the ovary at once, in which case the twins are no more similar than normal brothers or sisters; or the egg divides at an early stage in the pregnancy, resulting in 'identical' twins. The presence of more than two foetuses in the womb is rare and usually due to fertility treatment.

multiple sclerosis (MS) Progressive disease of the NERVOUS SYSTEM which typically affects adults aged between 20 and 40 living in a temperate climate. In Britain, 1 in every 1 000 people suffers from MS, although in South Africa the condition is uncommon. Nerves in the brain and spinal cord lose their protective covering, becoming unable to function. This may lead to problems with vision, sensation and muscle control. MS occurs with different degrees of severity and speed. In severe cases it can lead to crippling paralysis: however, the condition is usually interspersed with periods of remission and improvement for many sufferers.

mumps Acute viral disease, usually contracted during childhood. Symptoms include a fever and swollen salivary glands. If the disease occurs in teenage or adult males, it may cause inflammation of the testes, sometimes resulting in sterility. A vaccine is available for children more than a year old.

muscles Body tissues, made up of bundles of muscle fibres, that can contract – or shorten – usually when they are stimulated by a nerve impulse. The human body has three types of muscle. The most widely distributed is skeletal or striped muscle. There are about 650 skeletal muscles in the body, most attached to bones; they produce voluntary movements such as walking or nodding the head. The largest skeletal muscle is the gluteus maximus in the buttocks; the smallest is the stapedius in the ear. Smooth or involuntary muscle is found inside organs and works under automatic control. In a process called peristalsis, for example, food is gradually pushed along the intestine. Cardiac muscle, found only in the heart, beats automatically, nonstop throughout a person's life – an average of 2 500 million beats in a 70-year lifetime. Nerve impulses from the autonomic NERVOUS SYSTEM speed up or slow down contractions according to the body's needs.

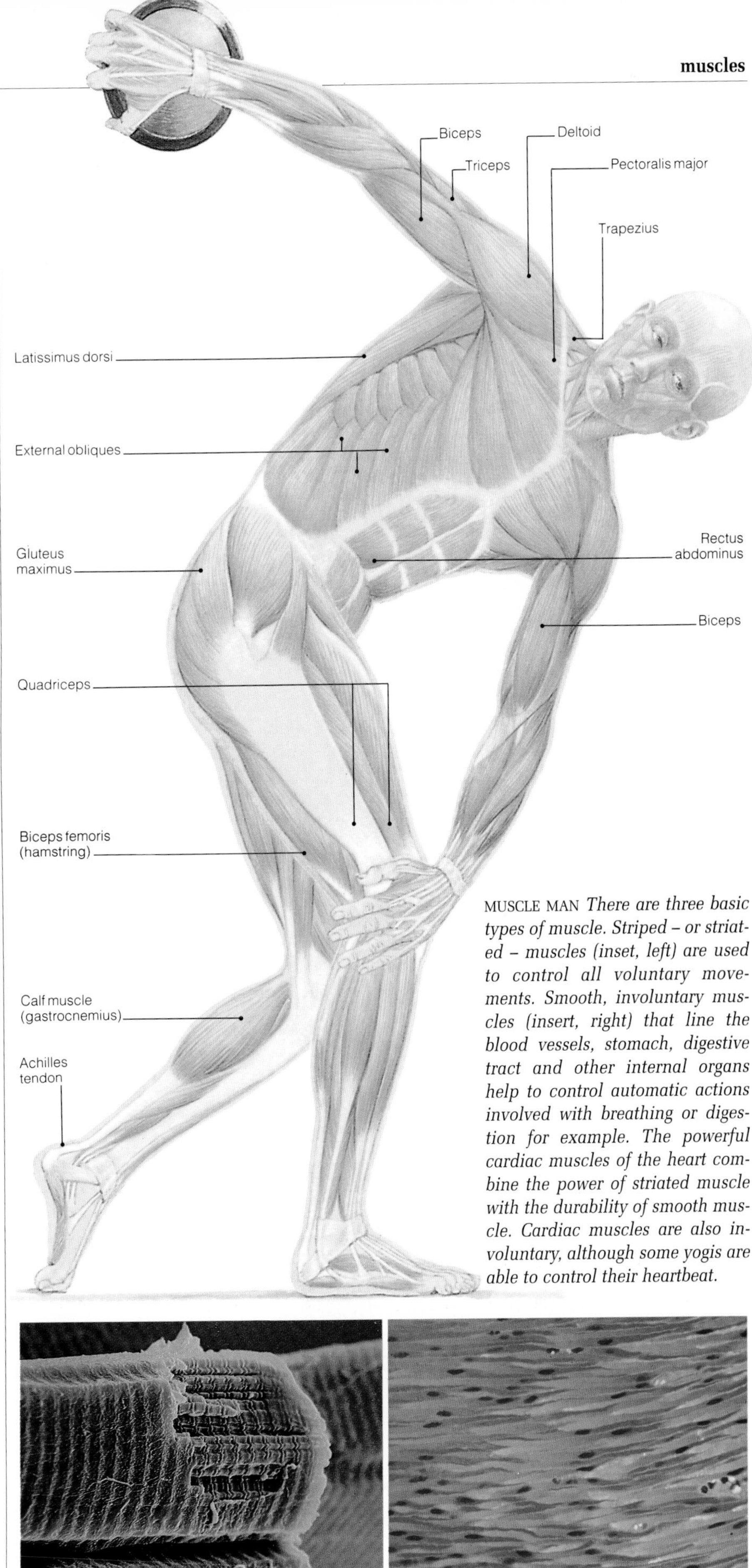

MUSCLE MAN *There are three basic types of muscle. Striped – or striated – muscles (inset, left) are used to control all voluntary movements. Smooth, involuntary muscles (insert, right) that line the blood vessels, stomach, digestive tract and other internal organs help to control automatic actions involved with breathing or digestion for example. The powerful cardiac muscles of the heart combine the power of striated muscle with the durability of smooth muscle. Cardiac muscles are also involuntary, although some yogis are able to control their heartbeat.*

muscular dystrophy (MD) Hereditary disease in which the muscles are enlarged but weak. Children with some forms of MD may survive into late middle age, although they are likely to be disabled. But children with the most common form of MD, which affects only boys, rarely survive into their 20s. Adults who contract MD have quite a good chance of never suffering severe disability.

nervous system Network that controls and coordinates all the body's activities. At its core are the BRAIN and SPINAL CORD, forming the central nervous system (CNS). The CNS consists of billions of interconnected nerve cells that receive information from sense organs – eyes, ears, nose, tongue and skin. The brain processes and stores information before sending out appropriate instructions to muscles and body organs. Simple reflexes are controlled by the spinal cord. The autonomic nervous system automatically regulates involuntary functions such as heart rate and breathing rate. Linking the CNS to the rest of the body is the peripheral nervous system (PNS). This consists of a network of nerves, composed of bundles of neurons up to 1 m long. Impulses are relayed electrically and chemically along neurons at more than 100 m per second. Impulses pass from one neuron to the next across a SYNAPSE. Disorders of the nervous system include STROKE, MOTOR NEURON DISEASE, POLIO, MULTIPLE SCLEROSIS, DEMENTIA, and some kinds of deafness or blindness. Trapped nerves – causing NEURALGIA – are extremely painful; SCIATICA, occurring in the spinal cord, is a common example.

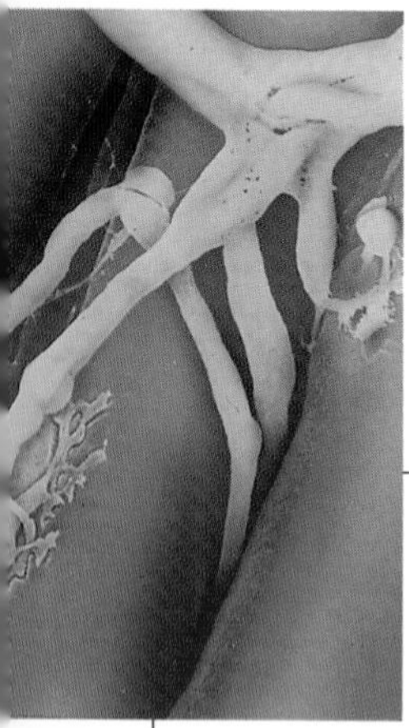

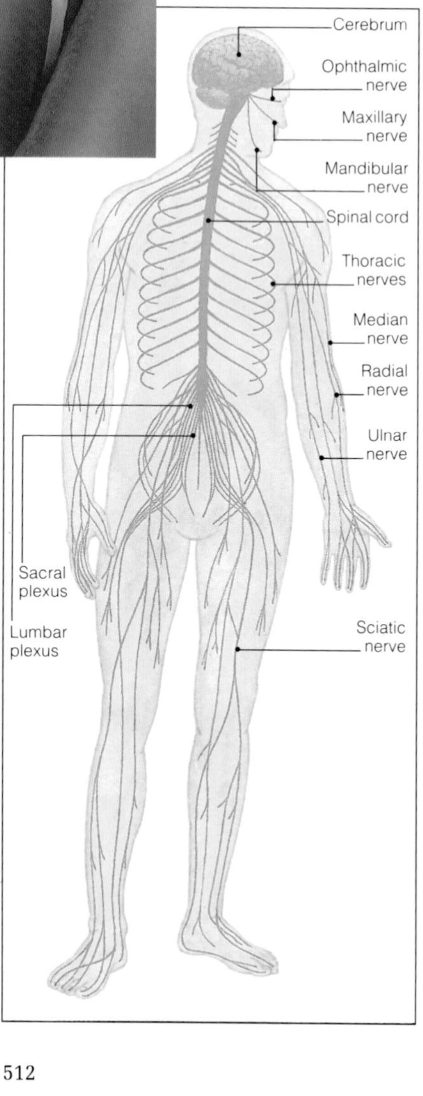

NERVOUS SYSTEM *The diagram shows the brain, spinal cord and the network of nerves. Signals, or electrical impulses, are carried from one end of a nerve cell to the other. Signals are passed on, chemically, to the next nerve at a synapse (left).*

neuralgia Spasmodic and severe pain, caused by the irritation or compression of a nerve. Neuralgia sometimes occurs after an attack of SHINGLES.

neurosis Mental disorder which has no physical basis. Victims still have a grip on reality, and are usually aware of their own abnormal feelings. Phobias, OBSESSIVE-COMPULSIVE DISORDERS and eating disorders are all neuroses.

obesity An obese person is someone who weighs more than 20 per cent above the maximum recommended weight for their sex and height. Reasons may be dietary, genetic or hormonal, or stem from a mental disorder. Obesity carries with it an increased risk of conditions such as high blood pressure and heart disease.

obsessive-compulsive disorder Neurosis, or mental illness, characterized by repetitive, ritualized behaviour. This may, for example, manifest itself as an obsession with germs. Sufferers may wash themselves, their house or their car over and over again, no matter how clean things are and even if they are aware that their behaviour is bizarre. Other sufferers may dress or undress in a ritualized sequence or repeatedly check that a door is locked or a stove has been turned off. Though many people show such behaviour to a mild degree, it is considered a disorder only if sufficiently severe to interfere with normal life.

oestrogens Group of hormones secreted mainly by the ovaries, but also by the adrenal glands and, during pregnancy, by the placenta. Oestrogens help to control MENSTRUATION and the smooth running of the female REPRODUCTIVE SYSTEM, and also stimulate development of secondary sexual characteristics at puberty. Synthetic oestrogen is used in the PILL, and in drugs that treat menstrual disorders, as well as some cancers.

osteopathy Branch of alternative medicine that involves adjustment of the body to restore normal usage. Osteopathy differs from CHIROPRACTIC which aims to treat many conditions mainly by manipulation of the spine.

osteoporosis Condition in which bones become brittle and susceptible to fracture. Osteoporosis is most common among women after they have been through the MENOPAUSE. This is because their ovaries then stop producing oestrogen which, among its other functions, helps to maintain bone density. Without this hormone, bones lose calcium and become weaker.

ovaries Pair of female sex glands located on either side of the pelvis. These are a vital part of the female REPRODUCTIVE SYSTEM because they secrete the sex hormones OESTROGEN and progesterone and produce eggs. Every woman is born with about 700 000 immature egg cells in her ovaries, about 450 of which will ripen during her lifetime. At ovulation an egg is released into the Fallopian tube about 14 days before the next period of MENSTRUATION. This is the most likely time for becoming pregnant. Ovarian cysts, which are common in women between the ages of 25 and 60, can usually be removed easily. If the cyst is large, the whole ovary may need to be removed, although the woman's fertility is usually maintained by her remaining ovary. Most ovarian cysts are benign.

pacemaker Electronic device that regulates the heart rate, first introduced in the USA in 1952. In a healthy heart, a node at the top of the right ventricle sends out electrical impulses which control the contractions of the heart. If this fails, an artificial pacemaker can be implanted. Some 'demand' pacemakers function only when the heart is not producing its own electrical impulses at the correct intervals. A pacemaker is sensitive enough to detect these delays and, by filling in the gaps, maintains a normal rhythm. Some models include a radio transmitter and receiver, which means a doctor can adjust the rate of the pacemaker from outside the patient's body.

pancreas Large gland, located behind the stomach, which plays a dual role. As part of the ENDOCRINE SYSTEM, the pancreas secretes INSULIN directly into the bloodstream to control the blood glucose level. As a part of the

DIGESTIVE SYSTEM, it produces pancreatic juice, an enzyme-laden fluid that breaks down fats, carbohydrates and proteins in the small intestine. The pancreas also produces sodium bicarbonate, which neutralizes stomach acid when it reaches the small intestine.

pandemic Infectious disease that spreads quickly among the population of a large area, such as a continent. The INFLUENZA pandemic of 1918-19 affected the whole world. (Compare EPIDEMIC and ENDEMIC.)

paralysis Loss of voluntary movement due to the NERVOUS SYSTEM being damaged – somewhere between the brain and the nerves controlling the muscles of the affected area. Paralysis can be caused by a condition such as MOTOR NEURON DISEASE, PARKINSON'S DISEASE, MUSCULAR DYSTROPHY or a STROKE. It is classified according to which parts of the body are affected. Paraplegia is the paralysis of both legs and sometimes part of the trunk; hemiplegia affects one side of the body; and quadriplegia affects all four limbs.

paranoia Feeling of persecution or belief that all events are connected to, and conspiring against, oneself. Paranoiacs often believe that they have a mission, or that they are superior to the rest of the world. SCHIZOPHRENIA, brain damage, ALCOHOLISM and MANIC DEPRESSION may all lead to the development of paranoia.

Parkinson's disease Chronic disease of the nervous system that usually occurs in late middle age. Symptoms include unsteadiness, shaking, partial paralysis of the face and stiffening of the muscles, causing a shuffling gait. It appears to be caused by a deficiency of dopamine – a chemical that transmits nerve impulses – in part of the brain that controls normal muscle contraction. Symptoms of the disease can be minimized by administering the drug L-dopa, a precursor of dopamine. Transplant of healthy brain tissue may be a future option.

Pasteur, Louis (1822-95) French scientist who discovered that GERMS cause disease. Pasteur's most important contribution to science was his discovery of microorganisms, which he first identified when studying the spoilage of wine during its fermentation. He discovered that by gently heating the wine he killed the bacteria that were turning it into vinegar; this process became known as pasteurization. Pasteur also perfected IMMUNIZATION, pioneered by the British doctor Edward Jenner (1749-1823). He found that, if he allowed bacteria or viruses to die before using them in a vaccine, it was just as effective and posed no danger. He discovered vaccines for anthrax and rabies. Today, the Pasteur Institute, founded by Pasteur himself, remains one of the world's most important research institutes. Its researchers were among the first to identify HIV, the virus that causes AIDS.

penicillin First ANTIBIOTIC – discovered by Alexander Fleming (1881-1955) in 1928. Penicillin, derived from a common mould that grows on fruit, is effective against a host of different bacteria, including some of those that cause tonsillitis, bronchitis and syphilis. ❖ Although Fleming discovered penicillin, it was the pathologist Howard Florey and biochemist Ernst Chain who realized its importance in fighting infection. They managed to isolate and produce the active ingredient in the mould early in World War II and consequently thousands of lives were saved. The three jointly received the Nobel prize for medicine in 1945.

physiotherapy Treatment of disorders by physical means, such as massage, manipulation, ultrasound, heat treatment and breathing exercises. Physiotherapy is often necessary after an injury, a major operation, or for arthritis. Children with learning disabilities have also been found to respond to activities which teach balance and coordination and to a method of postural correction known as the Alexander technique.

pill, the Oral contraceptive. The most common type works by regulating a woman's production of OESTROGEN and progesterone, so that she fails to ovulate. Adverse side-effects continue to be a subject of debate. It appears, for instance, that women using certain types of the pill may have a slightly higher risk of developing a THROMBOSIS. The first oral contraceptive was developed in 1956.

pituitary gland Master gland of the ENDOCRINE SYSTEM, which regulates the functioning of many other glands. The pituitary is directly connected to, and controlled by, part of the brain called the hypothalamus. Pituitary hormones influence growth, production of skin pigment, contraction of the womb during labour and many other activities.

placebo Substance with no medicinal powers used in place of a drug. In drug trials, some of the subjects are given placebos while the others are given the real drug. This is to combat the 'placebo effect', which occurs when a person's belief in the effectiveness of a medicine, even though it might be only a sugar pill, leads to the cure of his or her ailment. Research has shown, in fact, that the placebo effect plays a part in the success of any drug.

placenta Fleshy, disc-shaped organ that develops in the womb and is attached to the

PASTEURIZATION *Louis Pasteur, one of France's greatest scientists, proved infections were caused by living organisms, and his discoveries led to the development of antiseptics. Among the many tributes paid to him, the engraving (inset), dated 1895, hails him as a benefactor of humanity.*

womb lining during pregnancy. The baby is attached to the placenta by the umbilical cord. The placenta contains a dense network of blood vessels and passes oxygen and nutrients from the mother's blood to that of the baby, carrying waste back the other way. After the baby is born, the placenta separates from the uterus wall and is expelled, as the afterbirth, by the muscular contraction of the womb. Some diseases, such as RUBELLA, and some drugs, such as nicotine, can pass across the placenta.

plaque Thin layer of bacteria and mucus that forms on teeth even when they are brushed regularly. Bacteria in plaque break down sugary food, releasing acids that erode the teeth and cause decay. Plaque also refers to a fatty deposit on an artery wall – a symptom of ATHEROSCLEROSIS.

pneumonia Inflammation of the lungs caused by bacteria or viruses. Symptoms include fever, pains in the chest and coughing. Most forms can be treated with antibiotics, but pneumonia can become severe and the patient may require hospital treatment. It can be a complication of several other illnesses such as bronchitis, chickenpox or measles.

polio (poliomyelitis) Acute viral infection which can cause inflammation of the central NERVOUS SYSTEM. Polio may be mild, with symptoms amounting to no more than a fever and headache, or severe, leading to paralysis or death. The first vaccine against polio was prepared by a Pittsburgh physician, Jonas E Salk, in the early 1950s and used in 1954. It contained polio virus that had been killed with formalin. Three years later a Cincinatti virologist, Albert Bruce Sabin, began IMMUNIZATION with his weakened live polio virus. Polio has almost disappeared in South Africa as a result of vaccination. Two cases – said to be the last – were reported in 1991.
❖ The World Health Organization hopes to eradicate polio by the year 2000.

porphyria Group of diseases in which substances called porphyrins accumulate in the body to cause skin disease, severe abdominal pain or both. Most forms are HEREDITARY. The disease is more common in South Africa than in any other country – the gene was introduced into the Cape in 1688 when two Dutch settlers married. It is believed that more than 20 000 South Africans now living are carriers of the affected gene.

postnatal depression State of despair that can affect a woman in the first year after having a baby. She may have to be treated for DEPRESSION. This reaction is not only associated with a first child; equally, a mother who has suffered from postnatal depression with her first baby might have no adverse reaction after subsequent births.

post-traumatic stress syndrome Anxiety that comes on after a particularly violent event, such as war, rape, torture, a natural disaster or a crash. Sufferers may have flashbacks, recurring nightmares, DEPRESSION and feelings of alienation or guilt.
❖ Many antiapartheid activists subjected to ▷DETENTION WITHOUT TRAIL reported post-traumatic stress syndrome.

pregnancy At conception a woman's egg is fertilized by a sperm and implants in the womb, where it develops into an embryo, and then a foetus. Pregnancy usually lasts for approximately 280 days. With today's medical knowledge, babies that are born two and even three months prematurely often survive. If the foetus starts to grow outside the womb – usually in one of the Fallopian tubes – it is called an ECTOPIC PREGNANCY. The foetus is most vulnerable to infection, poisoning and miscarriage during the first three months of pregnancy.

premenstrual syndrome (PMS) Also known as premenstrual tension (PMT). Irritability, fatigue, clumsiness and DEPRESSION brought on by hormonal changes after ovulation and before MENSTRUATION. For most sufferers, PMS may last a few days before and during a period, but some women suffer for two weeks every month. Taking evening primrose oil or vitamin B_6 seems to help some sufferers; progesterone tablets or suppositories, prescribed by a doctor, may help others.
❖ Premenstrual syndrome has been successfully used as a defence in murder trials.

prostate gland Chestnut-sized gland in the male reproductive system which secretes part of the fluid in semen. It is located at the base of the bladder. In elderly men it may become enlarged, and impede urination – a condition known as benign prostate hypertrophy. After lung cancer, prostate cancer is the most common cancer affecting men in Western societies.

psoriasis Skin disease in which skin cells are produced too quickly, causing patches of scaly, itchy skin. It is sometimes coupled with painful swelling of the joints. Sufferers tend to have their first attack between the ages of 10 and 30, and recurrent attacks for the rest of their lives. It is not infectious.

psychiatry The study and treatment of mental illness. Psychiatrists may prescribe drugs, counselling or ▷PSYCHOTHERAPY. Until the middle of the 19th century, no distinction was made between mental illness and mental handicap. Now many psychiatric diseases, for example MANIC DEPRESSION and SCHIZOPHRENIA, can be treated with varying degress of success by medication.

psychosis Serious mental diseases such as SCHIZOPHRENIA and MANIC DEPRESSION in which the sufferer's mood changes or thoughts become disordered. The disorders are often traceable to physical or chemical abnormalities in the brain and sometimes to psychological traumas. Some psychoses run in families. (See HUMAN GENOME PROJECT.)

psychosomatic disorder Condition with physical symptoms caused by psychological factors, such as some cases of ulcers, eczema and IRRITABLE BOWEL SYNDROME.

puberty Physical and psychological changes in adolescence. Boys grow pubic and facial hair, their voices break, their genitalia grow and they start producing sperm. Girls grow pubic hair, begin to menstruate and develop breasts. The development of these secondary sexual characteristics is caused by changes in HORMONE levels. Puberty normally starts between the ages of 10 and 15, but is usually later in boys than in girls.

rabies (hydrophobia) An acute viral disease ENDEMIC among wild animals throughout most of the world, especially dogs, foxes, jackals and, in South America, bats. Rabies is present in the wild animal population of many parts of South Africa. A few human cases are reported each year, usually following the handling of wild animals or after bites from domestic dogs and cats infected by a bite from a wild animal. The virus is carried in the animal's saliva and transmitted to human beings through bites or the licking of an open wound. The virus attacks the NERVOUS SYSTEM and causes paralysis, muscle spasms, foaming at the mouth, fear of water, and hallucinations. The victim must be treated before symptoms appear, otherwise death is almost inevitable. The first vaccine was developed by PASTEUR. Vaccination of pets is compulsory in some parts of South Africa.
❖ About 10 000 people die of rabies every year in India.

radiation sickness Illness following exposure to ▷RADIATION. Effects depend on the amount of radiation and the length of exposure. A victim may start vomiting and have diarrhoea and be dead within hours, days or weeks. But symptoms may not appear for about two weeks, when the IMMUNE SYSTEM has broken down and the body begins to succumb to infection. In this case, a bone marrow transplant may save the victim's life. CANCER may be caused by long-term exposure to low doses of radiation.

radiotherapy Treatment with X-rays and other forms of ▷RADIATION of a disease such as CANCER. The treatment, which attacks abnormally multiplying cells, is based on the fact that abnormal, rapidly growing cancer cells are more susceptible to low levels of radioactivity than most normal, more stable, cells. Nevertheless, radiotherapy may have unpleasant side effects such as hair loss, vomiting and nausea.

reflex Automatic, predictable reaction to a stimulus, for example shivering in response to cold. Simple reflexes such as this are often controlled by the autonomic NERVOUS SYSTEM. They are an important survival mechanism. Babies are born with complex primitive reflexes such as sucking at the nipple and gripping with their hands. They grow out of these after a few months.

repetitive strain injury (RSI) Specific symptoms that affect people such as supermarket checkout staff and keyboard operators, whose work involves the constant repetition of certain movements. Symptoms include aching neck, shoulders and back, tingling fingers and, in advanced cases, an inability to move the fingers and hand without severe pain. Doctors are still unsure why some people are more susceptible than others. The condition can be controversial when there are no physical signs, although some sufferers develop swollen and inflamed tendons.

reproductive system Organs and glands involved in the production of male and female sex cells, fertilization, PREGNANCY and birth. In human males, sperm is produced in the testes; it travels past the seminal vesicles and through the prostate gland, which secretes fluids mixing with the sperm to produce semen. During sexual intercourse semen is ejaculated through the penis into the female vagina. Sperm can survive inside the female for up to five days. In females, the OVARIES release a ripe egg, or in some cases of MULTIPLE PREGNANCY, several eggs. As the egg travels down the Fallopian tubes it is fertilized by a sperm to form a zygote, which implants in the womb and grows into a FOETUS. Hormones, TESTOSTERONE in males, and OESTROGEN and progesterone in females, play a vital role in the production of sex cells and the maintenance of the reproductive system. If a woman is unable to conceive she and her mate may try INFERTILITY TREATMENT.

respiratory system Organs involved in breathing and gas exchange. When the diaphragm flattens and the ribs move upwards and outwards, air is sucked into the body through the nose and mouth. Air travels down the trachea, into the bronchi – the two main channels branching from the trachea into each LUNG. Then it flows along the bronchioles – the airways that branch out from the bronchi – and into the millions of tiny air sacs called alveoli. Here gas exchange takes place in the capillaries which surround each alveolus. Oxygen passes into the BLOOD and carbon dioxide passes into the air which is then forced out of the lungs when the diaphragm moves up.

rheumatic fever Disease that causes inflammation of the joints and can dangerously weaken heart valves. It is now uncommon in most Western countries, but is still a major cause of child mortality in South Africa. It is usually preceded by a streptococcal throat infection and is treated with penicillin.

rheumatism Blanket term for pain of the joints and muscles, most common among the elderly. The term includes many disorders, chiefly ARTHRITIS.

rickets Children's disease in which bones soften, bend and deform. Rickets is caused by vitamin D deficiency, due to poor diet or lack of sunlight. Vitamin D is vital for the absorption of calcium, a major component of bones. In victims of rickets the chest, pelvis and spine may become deformed, long bones bend and certain joints become enlarged. Early treatment with mineral and vitamin supplements can be successful.

ringworm Group of highly contagious fungal skin conditions, characterized by a ring appearing on the skin's surface. This happens because the fungus grows evenly outward while the skin at the centre of the ring recovers. Ringworm infections are usually treated with antifungal agents.

rubella (German measles) Infectious viral disease, usually occurring in children, which causes a body rash and swollen neck glands. If a woman catches it in the first three months of pregnancy, her baby may be born deaf or with a damaged heart. It can be prevented by IMMUNIZATION; many children now receive the MMR vaccine, which prevents MEASLES, MUMPS and rubella.

salivary glands Glands in the mouth that secrete saliva in response to, or in anticipation of, food. The largest are the parotid glands, which swell during MUMPS.

salmonella Bacteria that are a common cause of FOOD POISONING, often through infection of poultry products. The bacteria release a toxin into the intestines, causing diarrhoea, nausea and fever. Adults usually recover from salmonella poisoning in about two to five days, but small children and the aged may be more seriously affected. Many strains of salmonella are resistant to antibiotics and one form of it causes TYPHOID.

❖ Salmonella takes its name from Dr Daniel Salmon (1850-1914), a US veterinary surgeon who identified the bacteria.

scans Painless techniques of viewing the inside of the body. The oldest type of scan is the ▷X-RAY. Computerized Axial Tomography (CT or CAT) scans create a three-dimensional image by taking X-rays from all around the body. Ultrasound, which produces a three-dimensional image by bouncing sound waves off organs, is commonly used to look at babies in the womb. Magnetic Resonance Imaging (MRI) scanners can distinguish between different tissues of the body by comparing their magnetic properties. MRI scans are used to detect diseases such as STROKES, CANCER and SLIPPED DISCS.

❖ The CT scanner was developed by South African-born physicist Allan MacLeod Cormack and British electrical engineer Godfrey Hounsfield, who were jointly awarded the 1979 Nobel prize for this contribution to diagnostic techniques.

ALL-ROUND PICTURE *A patient is moved into a CT scanner which will provide the doctor with a three-dimensional image of his head.*

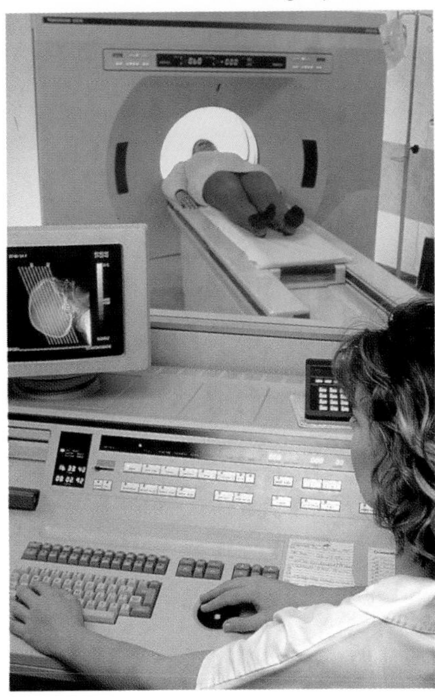

schizophrenia One of the most common psychotic disorders. In South Africa, about 1 person in every 100 is schizophrenic. Treatment with drugs can often be effective. Schizophrenics have a fragmented view of external reality, their understanding of the world being as distorted as a view in a broken mirror. The most common symptoms, unique to schizophrenia, are hearing voices and feeling as if thoughts have been inserted into the mind from somewhere else. Many patients also suffer from PARANOIA. There is some disagreement among psychiatrists about the cause of schizophrenia and its effective treatment. (See R D ▷LAING in 'Human Society'.)

sciatica Pain caused by pressure on the sciatic nerve, which runs from the lower spine to the feet. It is usually caused by a SLIPPED DISC in the spine and results in pain in the buttock and thigh. Milder cases may improve with bed rest and PHYSIOTHERAPY or CHIROPRACTIC treatment ; in more severe cases surgery to remove the disc may be advised.

scurvy The first disease, which was common among seafarers, found to have been caused by vitamin deficiency; in the mid-18th century, it was linked to a lack of vitamin C. With scurvy, wounds fail to heal, teeth become loose and fall out, and bones become weak.
❖ When the cause of scurvy was identified, the British navy began issuing sailors with limes (which, like oranges, are rich in vitamin C) to suck in order to stave off the disease – hence the term Limey, often used in American slang for a Briton.

shingles Re-emergence of the virus that causes chickenpox which may have lain dormant for years. The virus attacks nerve endings, producing a painful rash. This normally disappears after two to three weeks, but the pain may persist for months.

shock Sudden, severe drop in BLOOD PRESSURE which can cause COMA or death if untreated. Circulation slows dramatically, extremities may go grey or blue, body temperature plummets and pupils dilate. Shock is brought on by injury, but may also be caused by an ACUTE illness or ALLERGY. This is the sense in which the term is used by doctors and it is not applied to the effect of a sudden emotional upset.

sick building syndrome Set of flulike symptoms that are apparently produced by working in air-conditioned office buildings. Itchy eyes, headache, fatigue and aching muscles are the commonest complaints. The specific cause has not been identified, but a lack of fresh air and daylight seem to be factors.

sickle-cell anaemia Hereditary BLOOD disease mainly affecting people of West African origin. It causes deformed, crescent-shaped red blood cells to block capillaries, preventing tissues from getting enough oxygen to function efficiently.

skeleton The body's frame is made of bone and CARTILAGE. Human beings have 206 bones, which consist of flexible collagen fibres reinforced with the minerals calcium and phosphorus. A typical long bone, such as the thigh bone, has a compact outer layer surrounding a honeycomb of lighter spongy bone. The central core is occupied by marrow. The red marrow of certain bones produces the body's blood cells.

skin The body's largest organ, which acts as a waterproof covering, keeps out microorganisms and protects the body from the sun's damaging ultraviolet rays. The skin has two layers, which cover subcutaneous fat. The lower layer – the dermis – contains nerve endings which respond to temperature, touch and pain. The dermis also contains SWEAT GLANDS which help to control the body's temperature, and sebaceous glands which produce the oily sebum to prevent the skin from drying out. The thin outer layer – the epidermis – is tough because its cells contain keratin, which is also the main constituent of

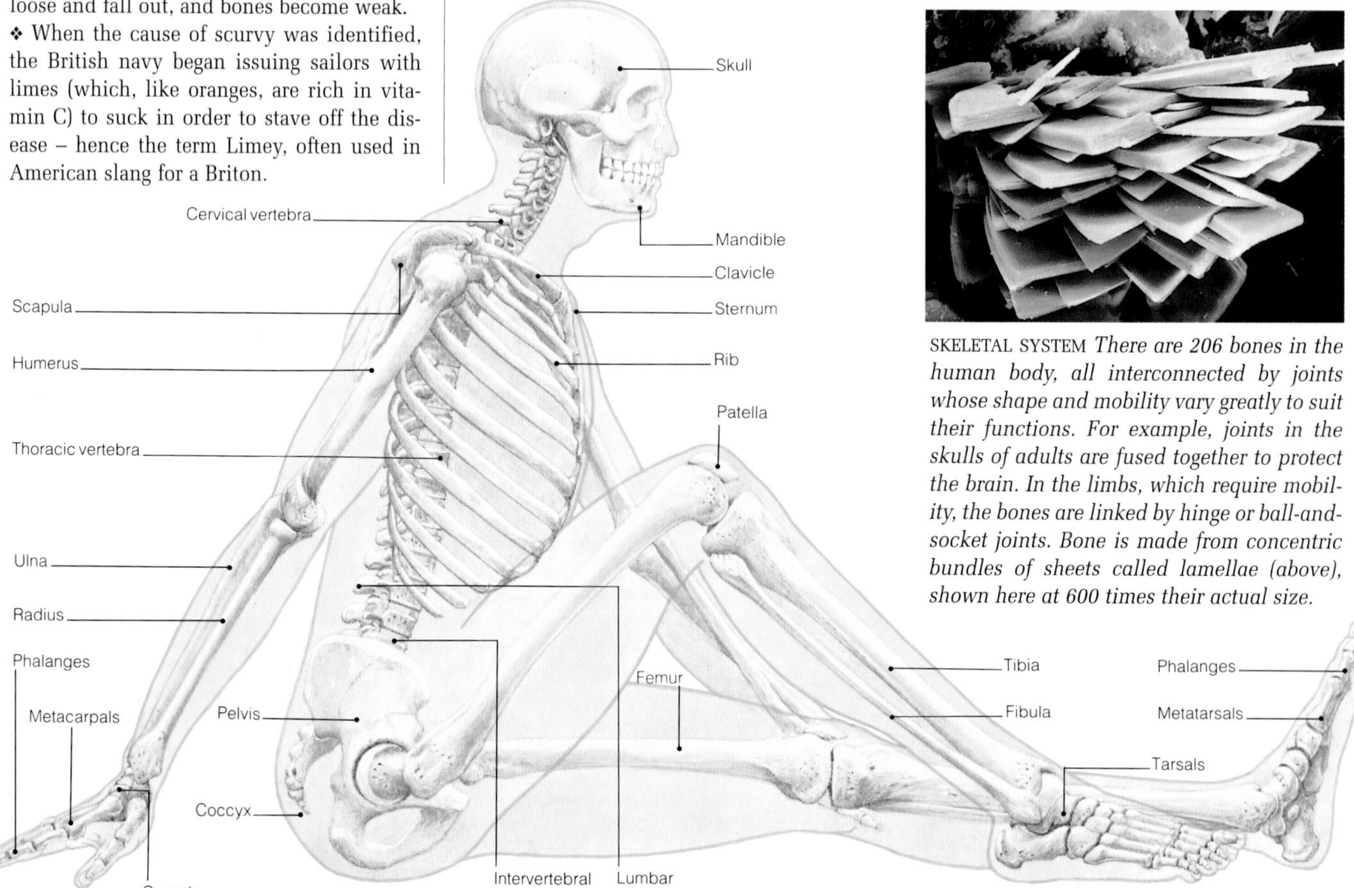

SKELETAL SYSTEM *There are 206 bones in the human body, all interconnected by joints whose shape and mobility vary greatly to suit their functions. For example, joints in the skulls of adults are fused together to protect the brain. In the limbs, which require mobility, the bones are linked by hinge or ball-and-socket joints. Bone is made from concentric bundles of sheets called lamellae (above), shown here at 600 times their actual size.*

hair and nails. The epidermis is constantly shedding dead cells and growing new ones. Skin also contains the pigment MELANIN, which causes suntan, freckles and moles.

skin cancer Common form of CANCER which occurs most frequently in older people who have been exposed to strong sunlight for long periods. There are three main types. Basal cell carcinoma, or rodent ulcer, usually appears as a small lump on the face which grows slowly and which should be removed surgically. This form of cancer rarely spreads to other parts of the body. Squamous cell carcinoma often appears as a slowly spreading ulcer on the hand, lip or ear. Malignant melanoma, the most serious type of skin cancer, often grows from a mole which enlarges, becomes lumpy and starts to bleed. Both of these forms, especially melanoma, can spread to other parts of the body and may prove fatal if not treated promptly by surgical removal of the cancer. Some scientists blame 'holes' in the ▷OZONE layer for the rise in the incidence of skin cancer.

❖ Basal cell carcinoma is one of the two most common cancers among South African men.

sleep Sleep is divided into two types. Most sleep is 'orthodox' – when brain waves and metabolism slow down. This is a phase of deeper sleep which is normally interrupted for a period of about 20 minutes, five times a night – roughly at intervals of about 90 minutes – by rapid eye movement (REM) sleep, in which the eyes move back and forth as if watching a high-speed tennis match. During REM sleep the brain is active and DREAMS occur. Young adults may need eight hours sleep a night, but less as they get older. Babies or invalids may sleep for up to 18 hours a day. Research has shown that people suffer psychologically more from deprivation of the dreaming phase of sleep than of the deeper phase of unconsiousness.

sleeping sickness (encephalitis lethargica) Parasitic disease ENDEMIC in tropical Africa. It is spread by the tsetse fly and affects human beings and wild animals. Early treatment with drugs is required; in advanced cases, victims become totally lethargic and eventually may fall into a coma and die.

slipped disc (prolapsed disc) Painful condition caused by displaced cartilage between the vertebrae of the spine causing pressure on the adjoining nerves of the SPINAL CORD and sometimes producing SCIATICA.

smallpox Highly contagious viral infection eradicated in 1979 by global VACCINATION. It used to be a major cause of death; those who survived the infection were left disfigured by pockmarked skin.

❖ Today the smallpox virus exists in only two laboratories: one in Atlanta, Georgia, and one in Moscow.

smell The only one of the senses that is linked directly to the MEMORY, often prompting a distant recollection. Olfactory receptors located in the roof of the nasal cavity detect odours, and send impulses to the brain which are interpreted as smells. The sense of smell contributes to TASTE.

❖ The average person can differentiate between about 10 000 odours.

snoring People who snore may be overweight or sleep on their backs, but snoring may be caused by excessive alcohol intake or a cold. Snorers may also stop breathing for brief moments during sleep, which is why they then take big, gulping breaths through the mouth; known as sleep apnoea, this can signal a serious blockage of the airways.

spina bifida Congenenital defect in which a part of the spine has not developed, leaving the spinal cord exposed. Surgery in the first few days of life may cure the problem; but the condition can lead to serious disability.

spinal cord Thick string of nerve tissue running down the centre of the spine which acts as the main highway for nerve impulses to and from the brain. Together with the brain it makes up the central NERVOUS SYSTEM. The spinal cord also controls some REFLEX responses without recourse to the brain.

spleen Organ to the left of the stomach which destroys worn-out red blood cells and is a site of white blood cell production. In the foetus, the spleen produces red blood cells. Human beings are able to live without a spleen, but rupture of the spleen can be fatal – usually through loss of blood.

steroid Group of chemicals derived from CHOLESTEROL, some of which help to build proteins: sex hormones and vitamin D are both steroids. Synthetic steroids are used extensively in medical treatment, for example to reduce inflammation.

❖ Synthetic protein-building steroids, usually called anabolic steroids, have been used illegally by some athletes to build up muscle strength, despite dangerous side effects, such as weakening the heart muscle.

stress Tension or distress caused by an emotional or mental state, such as anxiety, or a physical factor, such as injury. Stress can disrupt the body's normal functioning and contribute to certain illnesses such as heart disease. Many complaints, such as ECZEMA, MIGRAINE and ULCERS, may be directly related to mental or emotional stress.

stroke Damage to part of the BRAIN caused by the interruption of its blood supply due to the blockage of a BLOOD VESSEL or bleeding in the brain. Strokes are a major cause of death in the developed world. High blood pressure, often associated with ATHEROSCLEROSIS, increases the risk of a stroke. The effects of a stroke can range from temporary paralysis and slurred speech to permanent brain damage or death. Middle-aged or elderly people are most likely to suffer a stroke.

sweat glands Tiny glands in the skin that release sweat (water, salt and minerals) onto the skin's surface to cool the body – by ▷EVAPORATION – when it is too hot. Sweating is also caused by fear and anxiety.

synapse Gap between the endings of two nerve cells, or neurons, which forms a connection between them. An impulse travels along a nerve cell electrically. At the synapse it stimulates the release of a chemical called a neurotransmitter, which passes across the synapse to the next neuron, causing it to send an impulse along its length.

❖ Amphetamines and narcotics work by acting on the synapses, increasing or limiting the amount of neurotransmitters.

syphilis Disease transmitted by sexual contact or by a mother to her FOETUS. Symptoms include painful sores, called chancres, usually around the genitalia, followed by a rash and more widespread sores. The disease may then lie dormant for as long as 30 years before erupting in its final phase, which can damage the heart, brain and skin. Some victims go insane, experiencing total personality changes and delusions of grandeur. The disease can usually be cured with antibiotics.

❖ Soon after Columbus brought syphilis back from the New World, the French army experienced the first mass outbreak of the disease. It then spread rapidly. Famous people who contracted syphilis include Henry VIII and Franz Schubert.

tapeworm Parasitic worm, up to 9 m long, that lives in the human intestine, where it absorbs food and produces eggs which are expelled in the faeces. Tapeworms are acquired by eating infected meat or fish that has not been properly cooked.

taste Without the sense of SMELL, taste would be crude, able to distinguish only between sweet, salt, sour and bitter. Each of these is

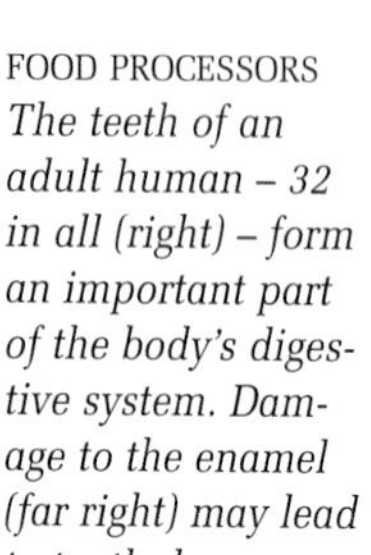

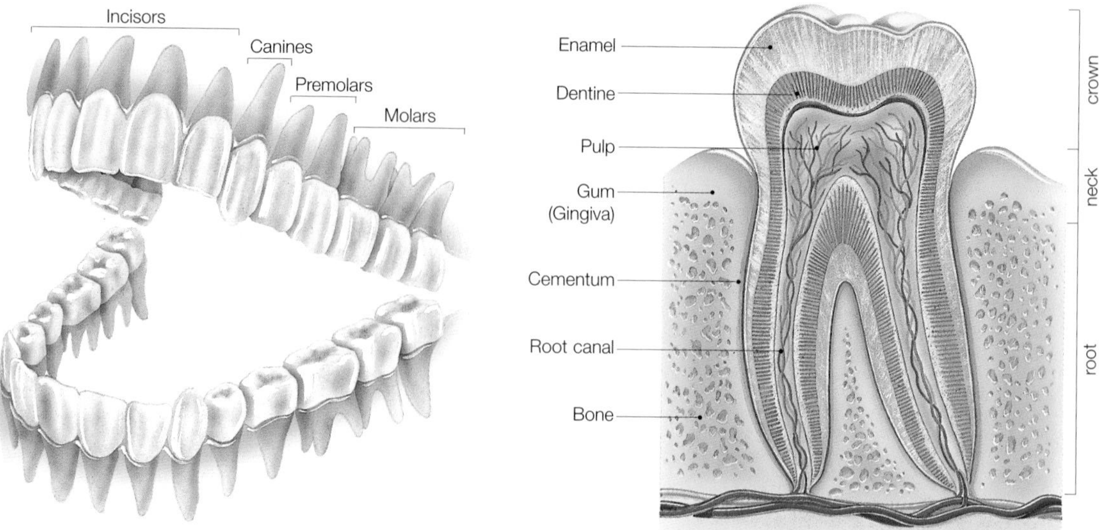

FOOD PROCESSORS
The teeth of an adult human – 32 in all (right) – form an important part of the body's digestive system. Damage to the enamel (far right) may lead to tooth decay.

detected by tastebuds on a different area of the tongue – sweet at the tip, salt and sour at the sides and bitter at the back. What the brain perceives as flavour is a combination of taste and smell.

teeth The crown of a tooth (the part outside the gums) is made mainly of dentine covered with a thin coat of enamel – the hardest substance in the body. The root of the tooth is embedded deeply in the jawbone and held there by a cementlike substance. At the centre of the tooth is the pulp, containing blood vessels and nerves. An adult's full set of 32 teeth gradually replaces the 20 milk teeth from the age of about six. There are eight incisors, used for cutting, four canines for tearing, eight premolars for shearing, and 12 molars for grinding. The hindmost molars, or wisdom teeth, are the last to appear. Tooth decay, or caries, is still widespread in the West because of the high levels of sugar in the diet. Fluoride helps to protect against caries, but plans to fluoridize local water supplies have often met considerable public opposition. Inflammation of the gums, or GINGIVITIS, is a common complaint.

❖ The gums recede naturally with age, leaving more of the tooth exposed – hence the term 'long in the tooth'.

temperature, body The optimal temperature for efficient body functioning is around 37°C, but temperatures vary slightly between individuals, as well as fluctuating during the day. The body uses several techniques to maintain a constant temperature. These include sweating and expansion of the blood vessels in the skin to lose heat, and shivering and contraction of blood vessels in the skin to conserve heat. A high temperature often indicates that the body is fighting an infection, as in a fever. Babies with temperatures over 40°C require immediate medical attention to cool them down. Similarly, temperatures below 35°C, which indicate a person is suffering from HYPOTHERMIA, are potentially dangerous.

tendon Tough band or cord of white tissue that connects muscle to bone. Unlike LIGAMENTS, tendons are not elastic. Rheumatoid ARTHRITIS and age may weaken the tendons. They can also become inflamed if subjected to repeated strain, as in tennis elbow and REPETITIVE STRAIN INJURY.

testosterone Male sex hormone, produced in the testes, that controls the development of male sexual characteristics. After PUBERTY it promotes normal sperm production. Some sportswomen have misused artificial testosterone to build up strength.

tetanus (lockjaw) Acute infectious disease in which the body's voluntary muscles, including those in the jaw, seize up and lock 4-25 days after infection. It is caused by ▷BACTERIA that live in the soil entering the body through a wound, a burn or an animal bite, and releasing a toxin which attacks the central NERVOUS SYSTEM. Owing to mass IMMUNIZATION, the condition is now rare in the West. A routine booster is recommended every ten years.

thalidomide Drug developed in the late 1950s and prescribed as a sedative and sleeping pill. It was withdrawn in 1961 when it was identified as the cause of serious CONGENITAL deformities in more than 5 000 babies of mothers who used it while pregnant.

thrombosis A blood clot. If it occurs in the BLOOD VESSELS supplying the brain, it causes a STROKE. Thrombosis in arteries supplying the heart (coronary thrombosis) is the cause of a HEART ATTACK. Thrombosis often occurs in blood vessels which have been narrowed by ATHEROSCLEROSIS.

thrush (candidiasis) Fungal infection commonly affecting the vagina and sometimes the mouth. Normally, the fungus is kept in check by bacteria. When these are weakened, for example by antibiotics, the fungus can multiply rapidly. Symptoms include a thick, itchy white vaginal discharge. The condition can usually be treated with antifungal drugs and the elimination of certain foods.

thymus Organ in the chest, in front of the heart, which is associated with the LYMPHATIC SYSTEM and plays an important role in building up the body's IMMUNE SYSTEM. The thymus is most active between birth and PUBERTY while the body is building up its immune response.

thyroid gland Important ENDOCRINE gland located in the throat, which secretes hormones that control the body's rate of METABOLISM and growth. Iodine is essential for the formation of the hormones, and deficiency may cause goitre, in which the thyroid gland swells. Underactivity of the thyroid gland – hypothyroidism – is associated with obesity, lethargy and dry skin and hair. Overactivity of the thyroid – hyperthyroidism – leads to rapid pulse, overactivity, weight loss and sometimes bulging eyes.

tickbite fever Disease caused by a bacterium-like organism known as rickettsia. It is transmitted by ticks and commonly affects people living in or visiting bushy areas or veld. Symptoms include a sore at the site of the

HIGH HOPES *Dr Christiaan Barnard, who performed the first heart transplant, gave patient Louis Washkansky, a 55-year-old South African grocer (inset), an 80 per cent chance of survival. After his operation Washkansky said he had never felt better, but 18 days later he died of pneumonia.*

bite, headache, fever and a rash. The disease usually disappears by itself, althrough rare complications may cause death, and treatment is therefore recommended.

tinnitus Ringing, buzzing, whistling or hissing in the ears with no external cause. It is usually a symptom of inflammation or injury, or it may accompany loss of hearing in the higher frequency range in old age. There is often no effective treatment.

tonsils Two pads of lymph tissue at the back of the throat. Like the ADENOIDS, they form part of the LYMPHATIC SYSTEM. Tonsillitis – inflammation of the tonsils due to infection by bacteria or viruses – is a common complaint among children. Today, tonsils are removed only if there are serious complications.

touch Sense that detects temperature, texture and pain. The different types of receptors, in the form of specialized nerve endings, are found throughout the skin, as well as in some of the MUCOUS MEMBRANES. They are particularly concentrated in the face and hands.

toxins Poisonous substances produced from living things. They include animal products such as snake venom, secretions from the skin of some frogs and toads, and alkaloids manufactured by plants. Fungal toxins that kill bacteria are used as ANTIBIOTICS. Human diseases, such as TETANUS, are caused by the toxins produced by bacteria rather than by the bacteria themselves.

transplant surgery Replacement of a damaged or diseased organ or tissue with a healthy one. Blood is the most frequently transplanted tissue, and corneas have also been transplanted since the 1930s. Kidney, heart and liver transplants are now common.
❖ The first human heart transplant was performed in Cape Town by a team of Groote Schuur Hospital staff led by Dr Christiaan Barnard. The patient, Louis Washkansky, received the donor heart on 3 December 1967, but died 18 days later from respiratory failure following an attack of pneumonia. The success rate has improved greatly since then, particularly after the development of more effective antirejection drugs.

trauma Injury to mind or body. In the short term it is often followed by SHOCK; in the longer term it may lead to POST-TRAUMATIC STRESS SYNDROME.

tuberculosis (TB) Infectious bacterial disease that leads to the formation of small nodules, or tubercles, which destroy tissue. It is spread by coughing and sneezing and normally affects the LUNGS, although it can affect the whole body. Victims may cough up blood and suffer from chest pains, weight loss and fever. In the 19th century TB, then known as consumption, was responsible for about a quarter of all deaths. TB still causes some 3 million deaths a year in poorer parts of the world, and despite widespread inoculation programmes, is on the increase in pockets of urban deprivation in cities such as London and New York. It is very common in South Africa, where 70 000 new cases are reported every year, and it is a major cause of illness and death. Treatment is possible, but must be taken for many months; some strains of TB bacteria are now resistant to the ANTIBIOTICS most commonly used.
❖ TB is one of the diseases most frequently identified in AIDS patients in South Africa.

tumour Abnormal tissue growth which may be BENIGN (harmless) or MALIGNANT (cancerous). Malignant tumours may spread to other sites throughout the body (metastases or secondary tumours) and can be fatal if untreated.

typhoid Highly infectious and potentially fatal bacterial disease that spreads through contaminated water supplies. It attacks the intestines, causing abdominal pain and bleeding, as well as high fever, headaches and a state of confusion. Typhoid can be treated with drugs, but IMMUNIZATION is always recommended before travelling anywhere with poor sanitation.

ulcer Inflamed open sore on the skin or on a MUCOUS MEMBRANE such as the inside of the mouth, or the stomach lining. Ulcers may be the result of poor blood supply, inadequate tissue drainage, injury, tumour, infection or general tiredness. Mouth ulcers are the most common, and usually heal without treatment. Gastric and duodenal ulcers are sometimes caused by excessive acidity, often aggravated by smoking, STRESS or alcohol. These ulcers can usually be treated with drugs and alkalis, which counteract the acidity, and sometimes by antibiotics. However, in some instances ulcers may require surgery.

urine Fluid made up of water, urea – the end-product of protein breakdown – and other chemicals surplus to the needs of the body. It

VITAMINS: SOURCES AND USES

Vitamin	Sources	Uses
A (retinol and carotene)	Liver, fish, egg yolk, carrot, greens, dairy products.	Bone growth; skin repair; vision; immune system.
D (calciferol)	Sunlight on human skin; yeast, egg, margarine.	Calcium and phosphorus for healthy bones and teeth.
E (tocopherol)	Vegetable oil, egg, nuts, margarine, whole grain, greens.	Protection of cell membrane, and of vitamins A and C.
B1 (thiamin)	Cereals, white flour, soya flour, yeast, meat, nuts.	Breaks down carbohydrates; healthy nervous system.
B2 (riboflavin)	Yeast, dairy products, egg, cereal, greens.	Processing of energy; forming enzymes; body tissue.
B3 (niacin)	Meat, fish, potato, bread, cereal, wheatgerm, peanuts.	Cell energy; circulation; cholesterol; skin; nervous system.
B5 (pantothenic acid)	Offal, beans, egg, whole grain, wheatgerm, peanuts.	Cell energy; skin and hair; nervous and immune systems.
B6 (pyridoxine)	Yeast, whole grain, fish, nuts, egg, potato, meat, greens.	Processing of protein; nervous system; haemoglobin.
B12 (cobalamin)	Lean meat, liver, kidney, milk, fish, shellfish, egg.	Red blood cells; nervous system; DNA and RNA.
C (ascorbic acid)	Citrus fruit, tomato, capsicum (eg green pepper), berries, potato, greens.	Connective tissues; hormones; general chemical and physical processes; protects vitamin E.
Folic acid	Liver, kidney, raw or lightly cooked greens, brewer's yeast/yeast extract, nuts, citrus fruit.	Production of red blood cells; maintenance of nervous system; formation of DNA and RNA.

is produced in the KIDNEYS by filtering the blood, and passes down two thin tubes called ureters to the bladder. Here it is temporarily stored until it is excreted through the urethra. In men, the urethra is also the passage through which semen is ejaculated during intercourse. Urethritis, or infection of the urinary tract, is a common ailment; some forms are sexually transmitted. A burning sensation during urination is usually the result of inflammation of the urethra, but can also result from acid-producing foods or drinks. Urine tests are often used to aid diagnosis of disease, as well as testing for the presence of alcohol or drugs. Pregnancy tests check urine for hormones from the PLACENTA.

uterus (womb) Hollow, strongly muscled organ in which the foetus is protected and nourished during PREGNANCY and which contracts to expel the baby during CHILDBIRTH. The uterus is located behind the bladder in the lower abdomen. During fertile years, the womb lining is expelled once a month during MENSTRUATION.

vaccination Method of IMMUNIZATION pioneered by Edward Jenner. The term comes from the Latin *vacca*, meaning cow, because the vaccine Jenner used to prevent SMALLPOX was derived from the milder cowpox.

varicose veins Swelling of the veins due to valve malfunctioning. They most often affect the legs. Pregnant women, obese people and those who stand for long periods are likely sufferers. Varicose veins around the anus are known as HAEMORRHOIDS. The veins can usually be shrunk and closed with injections, otherwise they can be removed by surgery.

vasectomy Cutting and tying of the tubes in the male reproductive system which carry sperm from the testes to the urethra. It is used as a form of CONTRACEPTION. The operation, which is relatively simple and is usually reversible, does not result in impotence.

venereal diseases Infections transmitted during sexual contact or intercourse. The best known are SYPHILIS, gonorrhoea, nonspecific urethritis and, more recently, AIDS and HERPES. Doctors now generally refer to them as sexually transmitted diseases (STDs).

vertigo Unpleasant sensation of giddiness, usually due to disorder of the organs of balance in the inner EAR.

viral infections Group of common and sometimes serious diseases, including the common cold, herpes, influenza, rabies, chickenpox, AIDS and Ebola. Viruses operate by taking over the functioning of a cell with its own ▷DNA, and then using it to manufacture more viruses. Healthy cells produce a protein called interferon, which prevents many viral infections from spreading. Unlike ▷BACTERIA, viruses are not affected by antibiotics; however, drugs inhibit some, such as the herpes virus. The main defence is VACCINATION, but for some viruses, such as AIDS, no vaccine has yet been discovered, despite a great deal of research.

vitamins Substances that are essential for normal metabolism and growth, and which the body is unable to manufacture for itself. Vitamins are therefore an essential component of the diet, and their absence leads to a variety of deficiency diseases. Each of the main vitamins has a specific role. (See Vitamins panel.)

wart Small solid growth on the skin, also known as a verruca if it occurs on the sole of the foot. They are caused by a virus and are generally harmless. Hands and feet are the usual sites of warts, but other parts of the body can be affected. Genital warts, transmitted through sexual contact, can be treated with ointments. Medical treatments include freezing or burning them off; they can also be removed by laser.

whooping cough (pertussis) A sometimes severe infectious childhood disease caused by bacterial infection of the air passages. It is marked by violent fits of coughing, followed by a 'whoop' as air is gulped back into the lungs. There may also be fever, loss of appetite and vomiting. In its early stages whooping cough can be treated with antibiotics, but they are not effective in all cases. In South Africa, the incidence of the disease has been greatly reduced by the routine vaccination of babies.

yellow fever Infectious disease prevalent in tropical areas of West Africa and South and Central America and in Asia. It is caused by a virus carried by mosquitoes. Symptoms include fever and yellowing of the skin, which gives the disease its name. In severe cases, the victim may go into a coma and die. Before the discovery of the means of transmission, and the development of an effective vaccine, yellow fever was one of the great plague diseases, spreading from European settlers in affected areas. Many thousands of labourers died from the disease during the construction of the ▷PANAMA CANAL.

SCIENCE, SPACE AND MATHEMATICS

From the tiniest atomic particles to the planets that whirl in space, our Universe functions according to basic laws of physics and chemistry. Scientists armed with the language of mathematics have discovered much about the nature of matter and energy, space and time; but their studies have revealed new mysteries in quarks and quanta, big bangs and black holes.

AERODYNAMIC DESIGN *The body shapes of modern cars are the product of extensive testing for stability and fuel efficiency.*

absolute zero The lowest possible temperature. It is defined as 0 on the KELVIN scale (0 K) and corresponds to -273,15°C. Absolute zero cannot be achieved, but scientists studying the properties of materials at very low temperatures (see CRYOGENICS) have reached within a few millionths of a degree of it. At absolute zero, there would be no heat energy left in a body, and its molecules would cease to vibrate.

acceleration Rate at which the VELOCITY of an object is changing. It is usually measured in metres per second per second (m/s^2). An object that maintains the same speed but changes its direction is also being accelerated. Acceleration is sometimes expressed in terms of the acceleration of a falling body due to the Earth's gravity, *g* (approximately equal to 9,81 m/s^2). Prolonged accelerations above 4*g* are harmful to the human body. (See NEWTON'S LAWS OF MOTION.)

acid Corrosive substance which has a pH below 7 and turns LITMUS PAPER red. When dissolved in water, acids react with metals, alkalis and other BASES to form salts. Technically, acids are compounds capable of producing positive hydrogen IONS in solution. Some acids, such as sulphuric acid (H_2SO_4) and hydrochloric acid (HCl), give up hydrogen ions easily and are highly reactive. Others, such as sulphurous acid (H_2SO_3), give them up less easily and are less reactive. Organic acids – examples include vinegar (acetic acid) and lemon juice (citric acid) – occur widely in nature.

aerodynamics Study of the flow and turbulence of gases, and of the interaction between moving objects and the atmosphere. It is particularly concerned with the principles of flight and with the design of more efficient shapes for aeroplanes and motor vehicles. Wind tunnels are used to test the 'drag' of new car models.

alcohol Compound formed by the fermentation of sugars that occurs nauturally. There are many different types of alcohol, all distinguished by having a hydroxyl group (OH) attached to a HYDROCARBON chain. Ethyl alcohol, or ethanol, the intoxicating component of beers, wines and spirits, has the formula C_2H_5OH. Methyl alcohol, or methanol, has the formula CH_3OH. Alcohols are used in the manufacture of many drugs, solvents, cleaning agents and explosives.

algebra Branch of mathematics in which numbers and numerical relationships are represented by letters and other symbols. It is used to express mathematical relationships in general terms, so that they can be applied to a whole set of numbers. Thus PYTHAGORAS'S THEOREM is expressed algebraically as $a^2 + b^2 = c^2$, which holds good for any right-angled triangle, whereas $3^2 + 4^2 = 5^2$ is true only for a triangle with these precise measurements. Algebra can also be applied to problems in logic (see BOOLEAN ALGEBRA).

alkali Compound, usually a metal hydroxide, which forms a strong BASE when dissolved in water – for example, caustic soda (sodium hydroxide, NaOH). Bases have a pH above 7 and turn LITMUS PAPER blue. Some minerals, such as potash (potassium carbonate, K_2CO_3), are also referred to as alkalis. Alkali solutions feel soapy, and are used in the manufacture of soaps. Alkalis are also often used to neutralize or diminish the strength of acids.

alloy Mixture of two or more metals, or of a metal and another material. Very few metals are now used in their pure state. Examples of alloys include brass, containing copper and zinc, and the many types of steel, made from iron with small amounts of carbon and a variety of other elements. A modern car may contain more than 100 different alloys. The development of lightweight aluminium alloys made the construction of commercial airliners possible.

alternating current (AC) Electric current whose flow alternates rapidly in direction – at 50 cycles per second (50 hertz) in South Africa. AC, unlike DIRECT CURRENT (DC), can be easily stepped up to very high voltages (400 000 volts or more) for long-distance transmission and then stepped down to a safer domestic voltage (220 volts in South Africa), using transformers. Mains current is always AC. (See also ELECTRICITY.)

amp, ampere Unit of electric current or the rate of charge flowing through an electric circuit. It is named after André Marie Ampère (1775-1836), the French mathematician, physicist and philosopher remembered for his important work on electricity and electromagnetism. The intensity of electric shocks depends on amperage. (See also OHM.)

amplitude Height of a crest, or the depth of a trough, of a WAVE, measured from the mid-point of the cycle. Amplitude modulation, or AM, involves altering the amplitude of a wave, usually a radio wave, in such a way that it carries information to the receiver. (See also FREQUENCY.)

anode Positively charged electrode in a battery or in the process of ELECTROLYSIS. (Compare CATHODE.)

antimatter Matter composed of SUBATOMIC PARTICLES in which the electric charge of the normal particle is reversed. The antiparticle corresponding to an ELECTRON is a positron, which has the same mass as an electron but a positive instead of a negative charge. An antiproton has the same mass as a PROTON but a negative instead of a positive charge. Contact between antimatter and matter results in the annihilation of both, with the release of large quantities of energy. Particles of antimatter are sometimes produced naturally by COSMIC RAYS, but they can also be created in PARTICLE ACCELERATORS.

❖ Very little antimatter has been found in our part of the Universe, but it is theoretically possible that other parts of the Universe are composed entirely of antimatter.

Arabic numerals The numbers 1, 2, 3, 4, 5, 6, 7, 8, 9 and 0. This system of notation originated in India and was brought to Europe in the 14th century by the Arabs. Unlike the more cumbersome ROMAN NUMERALS, which they replaced, Arabic numerals were able to represent zero and are much more useful for complex calculations.

Archimedes (*c*287-212 BC) Greek scientist, mathematician and inventor, best remembered for Archimedes' principle. This states that any body partially or totally immersed in a liquid or a gas becomes buoyed by an amount equal to the weight of fluid it displaces: a boat floats and a hot air or helium balloon rises because they weigh less than the water or air they displace. As a mathematician he was important particularly for his discovery of formulae for the volumes and areas of solid and plane figures.

❖ Archimedes is said to have run naked through the streets of Syracuse shouting

UNDER SIEGE *When Syracuse was besieged, Archimedes turned his genius to the design of fortifications and weapons – so successfully that the city held out for three years.*

Eureka! ('I have found it!') after he realized, while bathing, that the volume of an object can be measured by the volume of water it displaces. He used this fact to prove that a supposedly solid gold crown did not have the right DENSITY to be pure gold.

❖ Archimedes also investigated machines, including the lever, and is supposed to have said 'Give me a place to stand and I will move the Earth' – in other words, given a long enough lever and a fulcrum near the object to be moved, it is possible for a single man to move anything, no matter how heavy. The Archimedes screw, which he invented, is still used to raise water for irrigation in Egypt.

Aristotle (384-322 BC) Greek philosopher and scientist regarded as the founder of the European scientific tradition and one of the most important and influential figures in the history of Western thought. Aristotle emphasized the importance of direct observation of nature and believed that all events should have causes, which brought him into conflict with his tutor, ▷PLATO. He laid the foundations for the study of anatomy and embryology and devised a 'ladder of nature' which ranked living things in terms of their complexity – the basis for the science of classification or taxonomy. He also founded the study of ▷LOGIC in which he believed that ▷SYLLOGISM should be the basis of all logical thought. His writings cover a vast range of knowledge. (See also ▷ARISTOTLE in 'Ideas, beliefs and religion'.)

asteroid Small, irregularly shaped lump of frozen rock or metal orbiting the Sun. There are more than 2 000 asteroids in the solar system, mostly in the asteroid belt between Jupiter and Mars. Ceres, the largest, is 940 km in diameter. Asteroids may be fragments of a shattered planet and are also called 'minor planets' or 'planetoids'.

atom The basic building block of matter. The atom is the smallest unit of a chemical ELEMENT that still retains the properties of the element. The concept of the atom was first put forward by the Greek philosophers Leucippus (5th century BC) and Democritus (460-370 BC), but it was not generally accepted until the early 19th century, when scientist John DALTON showed how it explained CHEMICAL REACTIONS and COMPOUNDS. The modern theory of the atom stems from the work of Ernest RUTHERFORD and Niels BOHR in the early 20th century. They demonstrated that the atom is not an indivisible particle of matter, as had previously been thought, but is in fact mainly composed of empty space, with negatively charged ELECTRONS orbiting in distinct 'shells' or 'energy levels' round a positively charged nucleus, which is itself composed of positively charged PROTONS and uncharged NEUTRONS. A large amount of NUCLEAR ENERGY is contained within the atomic nucleus, which is released when nuclei are split or when they fuse together. This is the basis of ▷NUCLEAR REACTORS and ▷NUCLEAR WEAPONS such as the atom bomb.

AT THE HEART OF MATTER *Four electrons circle the four protons and five neutrons, which are themselves made up of triplets of quarks, in the nucleus of a beryllium atom.*

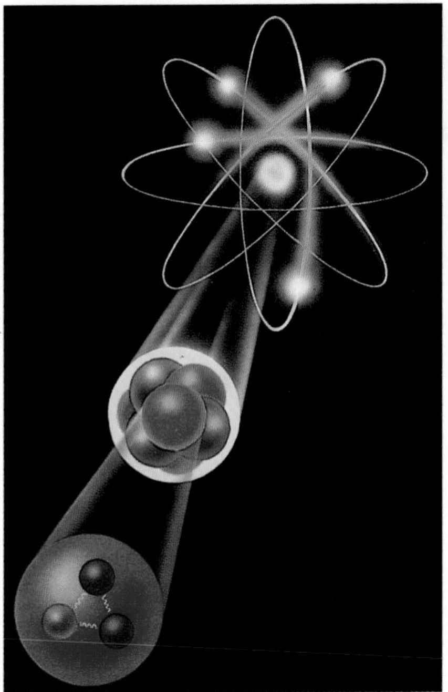

❖ Theoretical physicists dealing with the extreme conditions found in PARTICLE ACCELERATORS or the interior of stars have further divided the atomic nucleus into whole families of SUBATOMIC PARTICLES in their attempts to understand the basic nature of matter and energy (see QUARKS and UNIFIED FIELD THEORIES). The notion of electron shells and orbits has had to be considerably modified to take account of the UNCERTAINTY PRINCIPLE and QUANTUM MECHANICS.

atomic number The number of PROTONS in the nucleus of an atom of a particular chemical ELEMENT. The higher the atomic number, the heavier the atom. The PERIODIC TABLE represents the elements arranged in order of their atomic numbers. (See ATOMIC WEIGHT.)

atomic weight Known more correctly as relative atomic mass, which is the MASS of an atom measured on a scale in which the carbon ISOTOPE C^{12} is taken as 12. Relative atomic masses of the naturally occurring elements range from just over 1 for hydrogen to about 238 for uranium. Since most of the mass of an atom resides in the nucleus, the atomic mass is roughly equivalent to the number of PROTONS and NEUTRONS in the nucleus.

average Figure that is typical or representative of a set of figures, and so allows general conclusions to be drawn about the set as a whole. It generally refers to the mathematical average. (See MEAN, MEDIAN AND MODE.)

axiom In mathematics, a proposition which cannot itself be proved but from which other results are derived. An important axiom in Euclidean geometry (see EUCLID) is that only one line can be drawn through a point that will be parallel to another given line.

axis Straight line about which an object may be rotated (axis of rotation) or divided into symmetrical halves (axis of symmetry). In mathematics, axes are the horizontal and vertical reference lines (the x axis and y axis) used to plot points on a graph. The Earth's axis of rotation runs, by definition, through the North and South poles.

background radiation Any form of radiation, for example light or radioactivity, that is generally present in the surroundings. It often has to be eliminated before scientific experiments can be performed, and it also interferes with such things as radio transmission. It is sometimes referred to as 'noise'. Background radiation due to RADIOACTIVITY comes from cosmic rays and from naturally occurring radioactive isotopes in rocks. (See also COSMIC BACKGROUND RADIATION.)

EATING A STAR *The powerful gravitational force of a black hole pulls gas from a nearby star. What happens to matter in a black hole is a mystery that has given rise to some fantastic theories.*

base Substance which, when it is dissolved in water, reacts with ACIDS to form SALTS. In technical terms, bases form negative IONS in solution (usually hydroxyl ions [OH]) and are capable of accepting a positive hydrogen ion from an acid. ALKALIS form bases when dissolved, as does ammonia (NH_3); the oxides and hydroxides of metals are mostly bases, for example caustic soda (sodium hydroxide, NaOH) and quicklime (calcium oxide, CaO). Bases have a pH of 7 to 14 and turn LITMUS PAPER blue. In ORGANIC CHEMISTRY, bases generally contain nitrogen. The genetic codes contained in ▷DNA are stored as a sequence of organic bases.

benzene Clear liquid HYDROCARBON, the simplest of the group known as 'aromatic' compounds in ORGANIC CHEMISTRY. Benzene has the formula C_6H_6, with six carbon atoms linked in a hexagonal ring. The structure is very stable. Vast numbers of compounds, including phenols and steroids, are formed by substituting other elements or groups of elements for the hydrogen atoms, or by joining several benzene rings together. As a solvent for fats, resins and other substances, it is commonly used as a cleaning agent.

❖ The hexagonal ring structure of benzene was first recognized in 1865 by the German chemist Friedrich August Kekulé von Stradonitz (1829-96) after he had had a dream about a snake biting its own tail.

big bang theory The most widely accepted theory of the birth of the Universe. It states that all matter and energy in the Universe were created in a single colossal explosion between 15 000 and 20 000 million years ago (an estimate which is still the subject of considerable conjecture and dispute). Thereafter, the cosmic soup of dispersed matter became 'lumpy' and began to coalesce to form stars and galaxies. There is evidence for the big bang theory in the RED SHIFT of distant galaxies, which shows that the Universe is still expanding, and in the existence of microwave COSMIC BACKGROUND RADIATION, thought to be the 'echo' of the big bang. (See also STEADY-STATE THEORY.)

❖ Scientists do not know whether the expansion of the Universe will continue forever. The 'oscillating Universe' theory claims that the expansion will stop because of the mutual gravitational attraction of all the matter in the Universe. The Universe will then contract back into a vanishingly small space, another big bang will occur, and a new universe – possibly with different laws – will be born.

binary star Pair of stars which revolve around a common centre of gravity; also known as a double star. About half the stars in the sky are binary or multiple stars. Variable stars, whose brightness seem to wax and wane, are often 'eclipsing binaries', which obscure each other as they revolve.

binary system In mathematics, a system of counting based on the number 2 instead of the number 10 – the basis of the decimal system. Whereas the decimal system uses units (10^0 = 1), tens (10^1 = 10), hundreds (10^2 = 100), thousands (10^3 = 1 000) and so on to represent numbers, the binary system uses units (2^0), twos (2^1), fours (2^2), eights (2^3) and so on. The advantage of the binary system is that any number can be represented by a combination of only two digits, 0 and 1. It can thus be represented by a series of 'ons' and 'offs' in an electronic circuit, and is the basis of the digital ▷COMPUTER.

black hole Object in space that exerts a gravitational pull so strong that nothing, not even light, can escape from it. Black holes millions of times the mass of the Sun may exist in the cores of QUASARS and other galaxies (including our own). Smaller black holes may be what remains after the death of very massive stars in SUPERNOVA explosions. If the surviving core of the star is more than two to three times the mass of the Sun, there will be no force strong enough to prevent complete collapse to a 'singularity', surrounded by a zone from which nothing can escape. Two probable black holes of this type have now been detected in our galaxy.

Bohr, Niels (1885-1962) Danish physicist best known for his work on the structure of the atom, for which he won a Nobel prize in 1922. Bohr's work led to modern QUANTUM MECHANICS. He fled to America during World War II and, despite misgivings, helped to develop the ▷ATOM BOMB.

boiling point Temperature at which a liquid turns to a gas and ceases to increase in temperature. As liquid is heated, the temperature rises and the rate of evaporation increases. However, at the boiling point, all the remaining liquid evaporates with no further increase in temperature. The boiling point of water is defined as 100° on the Celsius scale.

bond, chemical Linkage between atoms that binds them into MOLECULES. Atoms form bonds because they behave as if they were seeking an ideal number of electrons in their outer 'shells'. They will give up or accept electrons from other elements, or in some cases share them, in order to achieve this number, forming bonds as they do so. Most elements are chemically stable when they have eight electrons in their outer shell; hydrogen is an exception, needing only two. Thus oxygen, with six electrons in its outer shell, and hydrogen, with one, can each fill their outer shells if a single oxygen atom shares an electron with each of two hydrogen atoms, forming a molecule of water with the formula H_2O. Bonds in which electrons are shared are called 'covalent' bonds. Chlorine with seven electrons in its outer shell, and sodium with one, will bond if the sodium atom donates its electron to the chlorine atom. The sodium atom acquires a positive charge and the chlorine atom a negative one; the electrical attraction between them forms an 'ionic' bond. (See also VALENCE.)

Boolean algebra The application of mathematical techniques to ▷LOGIC. Developed by the British mathematician George Boole (1815-64), it is fundamental to the design of circuits in modern electronic computers and is also the basis for SET THEORY.

Boyle's law Principle which states that, at a constant temperature, the pressure of a given mass of gas is inversely proportional to its volume. The principle is used in barometers, which monitor changes in ▷ATMOSPHERIC PRESSURE by measuring the expansion and contraction of a fixed mass of gas. The law is named after the British scientist and philosopher Robert Boyle (1627-91), one of the founders of modern chemistry. Boyle also conducted research into acids and alkalis, specific gravity, crystallography and refraction and was the first to prepare phosphorus.

Brahe, Tycho (1546-1601) Danish astronomer who, over a 20-year period, catalogued the position and movements of more than 1 000 stars and planets with great accuracy – a remarkable achievement in the days before telescopes. Brahe believed that the planets revolved around the Sun, but that the Sun itself revolved around a stationary Earth. Ironically, it was Brahe's own data that enabled his assistant, Johannes KEPLER, to prove that the Earth revolves around the Sun – as had been suggested by Nicolaus COPERNICUS.

❖ After losing his nose in a duel when he was 19, Brahe wore a false silver nose.

bubble chamber Device used to observe the tracks of SUBATOMIC PARTICLES created by collisions in a PARTICLE ACCELERATOR. It consists of a pressurized container of liquid hydrogen kept just below its boiling point. When pressure is released, as happens in the wake of a fast-moving particle, the liquid starts to boil, forming strings of bubbles that can be photographed and analysed.

buffer A solution, usually containing a weak ACID and a BASE or SALT, which maintains a constant level of acidity or pH when further acids or bases are added. Buffers are familiar in the form of medicines designed to decrease stomach acidity.

calculus Branch of mathematics that deals with quantities that are continuously changing. Differential calculus studies rates of change at a particular moment, while integral calculus deals with the sum of the changes over a period of time. Differential calculus would be used to work out the acceleration of a car whose speed (or velocity) was changing, while integral calculus would be used to calculate the distance it had travelled. Calculus was developed independently in the 17th century by Sir Isaac NEWTON and Gottfried ▷LEIBNIZ in Germany; there was some dispute over who had prior claim.

calorie The amount of heat required to raise the temperature of one gram of water by one Celsius degree. Since heat is simply a form of energy, it is usually measured in JOULES rather than calories (1 calorie = 4,184 joules). Dieticians, however, still use Calories – with a capital 'C' (also called kilocalories and equal to 1 000 calories with a small 'c') – to measure the energy content of foods, although this is also measured in kilojoules.

capillary Tube with a very small internal diameter, such as the fine blood vessels that supply the individual cells of the body. Capillaries draw up liquids by the action of SURFACE TENSION on the walls of the vessel. Plants absorb and raise water from the soil through capillaries in their roots.

carbon Nonmetallic chemical element which forms the basis of all living tissue (see ORGANIC CHEMISTRY). Pure carbon occurs naturally as diamond, graphite, charcoal and soot. It forms two stable oxides. Carbon monoxide (CO), a constituent of car exhaust, is highly poisonous. Carbon dioxide (CO_2), is found naturally in the atmosphere and is produced by breathing, by decomposition and by burning organic matter, including fossil fuels. Carbon dioxide is a major contributor to the ▷GREENHOUSE EFFECT.

catalyst Substance that initiates, or speeds up, a chemical reaction without itself being changed. Catalysts are used throughout the chemical industry. In living things, ▷ENZYMES act as biological catalysts.

catastrophe theory The mathematical study of sudden or discontinuous change. It is used to analyse situations in which small changes bring about large, catastrophic effects – the collapse of a bridge, for example, or panic on

DANCE OF THE PARTICLES *Showers of subatomic particles, created in the high-energy 'atom smashers' at CERN (below) and Brookhaven (right), trace out intricate arabesques inside the bubble chamber as they are born, decay and die.*

THE HAMMER AND THE FORCE *In order to keep the hammer from flying off at a tangent while he whirls it around, the hammer thrower must exert centripetal force. When he lets go, and the centripetal force is removed, the hammer will hurtle in a straight line to its possibly medal-winning destination.*

the stock market. It has been applied to such situations as diverse as domestic arguments and epidemics. (See also CHAOS THEORY.)

cathode The negatively charged electrode in a battery, or in ELECTROLYSIS, to which positive ions move. (Compare ANODE.)

Celsius Temperature scale, in which water freezes at 0° and boils at 100°, and each degree is one hundredth part of the range between the two. Originally known as centigrade, the scale was renamed Celsius in 1948, after the Swedish astronomer Anders Celsius (1701-44) who devised it. One Celsius degree is equal to 1,8° FAHRENHEIT degrees. To convert Celsius to Fahrenheit, multiply the Celsius figure by nine, divide by five, then add 32; for example, 20°C is 20×9 (= 180) $\div$ 5 (= 36) + 32 = 68°F.

centre of gravity The point in an object through which its entire mass (or weight) can be considered to operate. For an object to stay in an upright position, a line drawn perpendicularly through its centre of gravity must fall within the area of its base. If it falls outside, the object will topple over.

centripetal force Force that keeps revolving objects on a circular path when they would otherwise move in a straight line. Centripetal force appears to be balanced by a corresponding centrifugal force – which is what seems to throw the passengers against the doors when a car goes round a bend. In fact there is no such thing as centrifugal force; the observed effect is merely the result of inertial resistance to the centripetal force.

chaos theory Branch of mathematics dealing with systems that are inherently unstable and unpredictable. Developed with the aid of powerful computers during the 1970s and 1980s, it has considerable implications for much that happens in the real world – the weather, the economy, the flow of traffic or turbulence in liquids, and many other things. In chaotic systems, very small changes may have very large cumulative effects – as if the flapping of a butterfly's wings in Mexico were to produce a tornado off the coast of Indonesia. (See also CATASTROPHE THEORY.)

chemical reaction Process in which the bonds that hold chemical compounds together are rearranged to form new compounds. Chemical reactions are represented by equations, in which the original compounds (known as reagents) are shown on the left, and the products on the right. Thus the equation $C + O_2 \rightarrow CO_2$ represents the combining of a single atom of carbon with two atoms of oxygen to form a molecule of carbon dioxide. Chemical reactions either release or absorb energy, usually in the form of heat. The rate at which a reaction occurs is affected by such factors as temperature, pressure, surface area and the presence or absence of a CATALYST.

chemistry Study of the composition of substances and of the ways in which they interact. Its main branches are ORGANIC CHEMISTRY, which deals with the properties of carbon compounds, inorganic chemistry, which deals with all other elements, and physical chemistry, which deals with such properties as temperature, pressure and volume.

chromatography Method of separating and analysing the components of a mixture of chemical compounds. Chemicals are absorbed to different degrees when passed through absorbent material – just as the dyes in an ink blot will separate when water is dripped onto blotting paper. In gas chromatography, the sample is vaporized and carried by an inert gas through a tube filled with liquid-coated particles. Analysis of the gas as it leaves the tube provides a sensitive means of identifying the components of even complex organic mixtures.

circle Closed curve that is everywhere equally distant from a fixed point known as the centre. Any line that crosses a circle and passes through the centre is known as a diameter, and any line from the centre to the boundary of the circle is known as a radius. The distance round the outside of a circle (its circumference) divided by the diameter is equal to π or PI. The area of a circle is equal to πr^2, where r is the radius, and is greater than the area enclosed by any other figure of equal circumference. This is why a specific number of bricks will build a larger rondavel than a square room.

cold fusion Fusion of hydrogen nuclei to form helium (see NUCLEAR FUSION) at moderate temperatures rather than at millions of degrees Celsius. If it could be achieved, which many scientists doubt, cold fusion would provide almost inexhaustible supplies of clean, safe and cheap power.

colloid Mixture in which fine particles of one substance are dispersed, without being dissolved, in another. Fog, paints and butter are all colloids. (See also EMULSION.)

comet Lump of dust, stones and frozen gas, often referred to as a 'dirty snowball', that follows a highly elliptical orbit round the Sun. As it approaches the Sun, the comet heats up and gives off a bright cloud of dust and gas. The tail of a comet points away from the Sun and is caused by the SOLAR WIND. The best known is HALLEY'S COMET.

❖ The comet Shoemaker-Levy created great interest in 1994 when some of its fragments collided with the planet JUPITER.

compound Substance containing two or more ELEMENTS combined in specific proportions. Compounds are the product of a chemical reaction. Unlike mixtures, they cannot be separated by physical means. Water (H_2O) is a compound of hydrogen and oxygen; common salt (sodium chloride or NaCl) is a compound of the metal sodium and the gas chlorine.

condensation Conversion of a vapour into a liquid, the opposite of EVAPORATION. It is generally the result of cooling, and is most marked where a vapour comes into contact with a cold surface. Dew and fog are both caused by the condensation of water droplets as moisture-laden air cools down.

conduction Transfer of energy through a medium which is itself apparently unchanged. For example, wires conduct electricity, the bottom of a pan conducts heat and optical fibres conduct light. (Compare CONVECTION, RADIATION.)

conic sections Curves formed by slicing through a cone. Depending on the angle of the slice, the curve may be an ellipse, a parabola or a hyperbola. (See panel.)

conservation, laws of Fundamental principles of science. They state that, in a self-contained system, various quantities always remain constant – for example, the amount of energy or matter in a set of chemical reactions, or the total momentum in a system of moving bodies.

constant Number or quantity that never varies or changes. The SPEED OF LIGHT in a vacuum, PLANCK'S CONSTANT and PI are universal constants – they remain the same at all times and in all places.

constellation Group of stars that appear close together in the sky, often represented in pictorial form as an animal or mythological figure formed by drawing lines between the stars. All objects in the sky are assigned to one of 88 constellations for naming and identification. Well-known constellations visible in the southern hemisphere include Orion and the Southern Cross.
❖ In ancient times the names of constellations were applied to astrological signs.

convection Transfer of heat within a fluid (gas or liquid) produced by the movement of the fluid itself. As heat is applied to the fluid, the warmer areas expand, become less dense and rise; cooler fluid takes their place. The ascending fluid loses heat through mixing with cooler fluid and sinks again, causing circular convection currents to develop. Convection currents caused by uneven heating of the Earth's surface drive the circulation of air in the atmosphere, which gives rise to winds and weather. (See CONDUCTION, RADIATION.)

coordinates Set of numbers used to define the position of a point on a surface or in space. Map coordinates and latitude and longitude are familiar examples. Cartesian coordinates are used to define a point in relation to two axes (*x* and *y*) drawn at right angles to each other, and are used for drawing graphs.

CONIC SECTIONS

Conic sections play an important role in several branches of physics, including astronomy. They were first studied in detail by the Greek philosopher Apollonius (*c*262-190 BC).

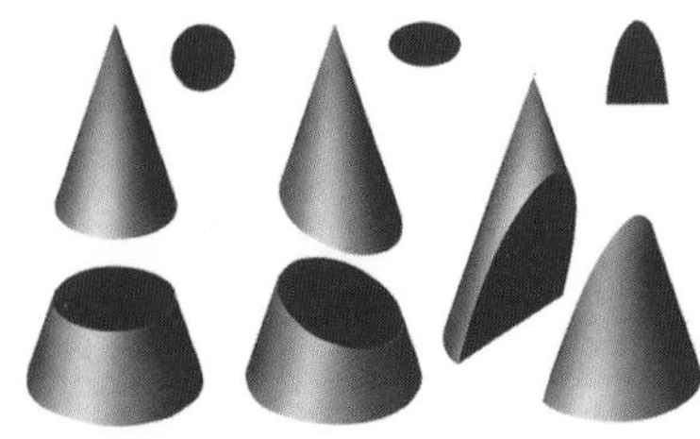

CUTTING THE CONE *As a cone is sliced at increasing angles, the exposed curve changes from a circle to an ellipse and then to a parabola, whose arms can never meet. Eventually, the slice intersects both halves of a double cone, forming a double-branched hyperbola.*

Copernicus, Nicolaus (1473-1543) Polish astronomer who believed that the Sun, not the Earth, was at the centre of the Universe, thus challenging the established orthodoxy that had prevailed since the time of PTOLEMY in the 2nd century AD. However, it was another hundred years before GALILEO and KEPLER provided the theoretical and observational evidence for the theory and established what became known as the Copernican revolution.

cosmic background radiation Weak MICROWAVE radiation in space thought to represent the 'echo' of the BIG BANG. It was discovered in 1965 and appeared to be uniformly distributed throughout space. However, in 1992 the Cosmic Background Explorer satellite (COBE) found 'ripples' in the microwave background, providing evidence for the first time of how the original 'soup' of matter started to become 'lumpy' and how the first seeds of the stars and galaxies may have been formed.

cosmic rays Streams of electrons, protons, x-particles (nuclei of hydrogen and helium atoms) and other atomic fragments, moving close to the speed of light, which continuously 'rain' down on the Earth's upper atmosphere. Here, they interact with further atomic nuclei, producing showers of subatomic particles at the Earth's surface. The origin of cosmic rays is uncertain; some come from the Sun, but others appear to come from SUPERNOVAS or PULSARS.

cryogenics Branch of physics dealing with the behaviour of materials at temperatures close to ABSOLUTE ZERO. It includes such phenomena as superfluidity (the ability of liquid helium to flow up the sides of its container) and SUPERCONDUCTIVITY, in which materials conduct electricity without resistance.
❖ A number of people with incurable illnesses have had themselves deep frozen immediately after death in the hope that it will one day be possible for them to be thawed out and cured. Cryogenic preservation has also been suggested as a possible way of sending astronauts on long space journeys.

crystal Solid in which the atoms are arranged in a rigid geometrical pattern or lattice structure. The regular shapes of crystals reflect their internal structure. Most minerals, including common salt and sand, occur in crystalline form, although the crystals are often microscopically small.

Curie, Marie (1867-1934) French chemist, born Marie Sklodowska, who, with her husband Pierre, discovered the radioactive elements radium and polonium (named in recognition of her Polish origin). The Curies refused to patent their work and tirelessly promoted the use of radium in the treatment of cancer. She herself died of leukaemia caused by her exposure to radioactivity.

MARRIAGE OF MINDS *Pioneering work on radioactivity won fame for the Curies and earned Marie two Nobel prizes.*

❖ Marie Curie remains the only person to have won the Nobel prize in two different sciences – physics and chemistry.

Dalton, John (1766-1844) British chemist and founder of modern atomic theory. He proposed that every ELEMENT was composed of atoms of a distinct type and weight, which combine with atoms of other elements in simple proportions to make COMPOUNDS. In 1803, he published the first table of atomic weights (or relative atomic mass).

dark matter Invisible matter which may make up as much as 99 per cent of the mass of the Universe. Some dark matter consists of planets, dead stars, black holes and general stellar debris, but much of it may consist of hypothetical particles such as axions and gravitons. The fate of the Universe depends on the amount of dark matter it contains. If there is enough of it, the Universe will have sufficient mass for the force of gravity to restrain and then reverse its expansion. (See BIG BANG THEORY.)

Davy, Sir Humphry (1778-1829) English chemist and pioneer of electrochemistry, who also invented the miner's safety lamp. Davy was the first person to isolate barium, calcium, magnesium, potassium, sodium and strontium, using ELECTROLYSIS. He also discovered the anaesthetic effects of laughing gas (nitrous oxide).

decibel Unit of power used to measure the loudness or intensity of sound, usually abbreviated to dB. The faintest audible sound is rated at 0 dB, normal speech is about 50 dB and an aircraft jet engine at close range is some 120 dB.

decimal system A system of counting based on the number 10, with successive digits in a number representing units ($10^0 = 1$), tens ($10^1 = 10$), hundreds ($10^2 = 100$) and so on. (See BINARY SYSTEM.) This is the number system in everyday use. Decimal FRACTIONS are represented as sums of tenths, hundredths, thousandths, and so on. The fractional part of a number is shown to the right of a decimal point (or comma), the whole number part to the left. Thus the number $1^1/_4$ is expressed as 1,25. Many numbers cannot be satisfactorily represented as decimals. For example, π (PI) continues for an infinite number of decimal places and even the simple fraction $^1/_3$ is 0,33333 . . . recurring.

degree In geometry, a unit of measurement of angles, equal to $^1/_{360}$ of a circle. A right angle is 90°, an acute angle is less than 90° and an obtuse angle is between 90° and 180°. A degree is divided into 60 minutes, each of which is further divided into 60 seconds. The geometric degree is used in the measurement of latitude and longitude. A degree is also a unit of temperature (see CELSIUS, FAHRENHEIT and KELVIN). Degrees in both geometry and physics are denoted by the symbol °.

density Measure of the amount of matter in a given volume of a substance, expressed as its mass per unit volume. It is usually measured in kilograms per cubic metre (kg/m³). Density is often expressed as relative density (sometimes known as specific gravity), the density of a substance relative to that of water at 4°C, the temperature at which it is most dense.

Descartes, René (1596-1650) French philosopher and mathematician, known in science for the reformation of algebraic notation and for the development of analytical, or COORDINATE, geometry, a powerful mathematical tool in which algebra and geometry are combined. He also made contributions to the study of light, astronomy and biology. He believed that the material world was ruled entirely by mathematical laws and that science should be subject to the same rigorous standards of proof as mathematics. (See also ▷DESCARTES in 'Ideas, beliefs and religion'.)

diffraction Bending or spreading out of light, sound or other waves as they pass around an obstacle or through an aperture. It means that shadows are not sharp-edged, and waves from different parts of the obstacle or from adjoining apertures may experience INTERFERENCE. In light, this produces 'fringes' of light and dark lines or bands of colour. Diffraction gratings of many fine slits exploit this phenomenon to separate light into its constituent colours. (See SPECTROSCOPY.)

diffusion Spreading of one substance through another by random movement of atoms or molecules. Odours, for example, diffuse through the air, and coloured ink will diffuse through a glass of still water.

direct current (DC) Electric current that flows in one direction only, from positive to negative (compare ALTERNATING CURRENT). Direct current is supplied by ▷BATTERIES, or by dynamos (see ▷ELECTRIC GENERATORS), or can be produced from alternating current by a rectifier, which uses a semiconductor diode or valve to suppress or invert alternate half cycles of the current.

distillation Separation of a liquid mixture into its components by boiling it and then condensing the vapour. The different components condense at different temperatures, allowing them to be separated from each other. Distillation can be used to purify a liquid, as in distilled water, or to separate out the components of a complex mixture, as in the distillation of petroleum from crude oil, or brandy from wine.

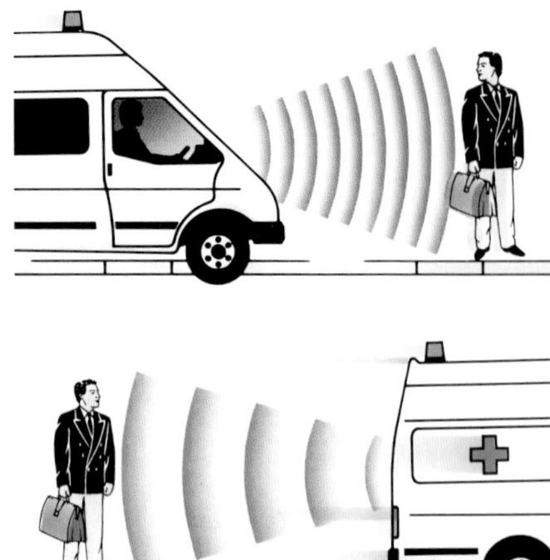

SIREN CALL *The rise and fall in a passing ambulance siren's pitch is due to the Doppler effect; sound waves bunch up as the siren approaches, raising the pitch, and spread out as the siren recedes, lowering the pitch.*

Doppler effect Apparent change in the FREQUENCY of sound, or of electromagnetic radiation such as light, as its source approaches or recedes from an observer. The RED SHIFT in the light from distant galaxies is a form of Doppler effect.

$E = mc^2$ The equation that demonstrated that mass could be converted into energy, and vice versa, and led to the development of the atom bomb and nuclear power. Formulated by Albert EINSTEIN in 1905, it states that the energy content (E) of a particle of matter is equal to its mass (m) multiplied by the square of the speed of light in a vacuum (c^2).

Earth Third planet from the Sun, and the only planet known to have an atmosphere that can support life. It moves in an elliptical orbit at an average of 149,4 million km from the Sun, travelling at about 107 000 km/h and taking 365 days, 5 hours, 48 minutes and 46 seconds to perform a complete orbit. It rotates on its axis once every 23 hours, 56 minutes and 4,1 seconds. The Earth is the fifth largest planet in the SOLAR SYSTEM, as well as the most dense. It has a single MOON. (See also ▷EARTH in 'The Earth and the environment'.)

eclipse Blocking out of light from one celestial object by another. The most familiar are solar and lunar eclipses (see facing page).

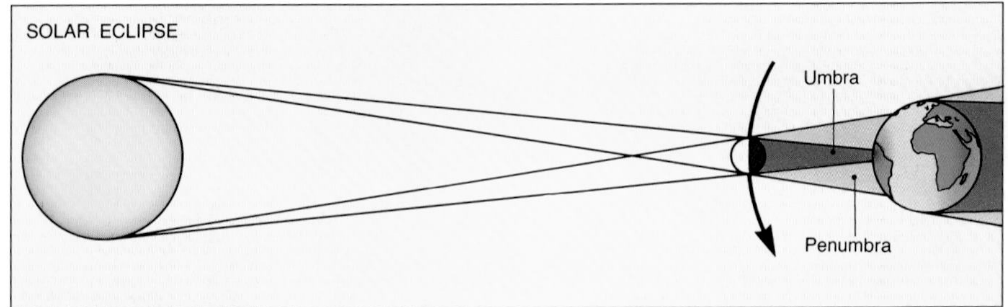

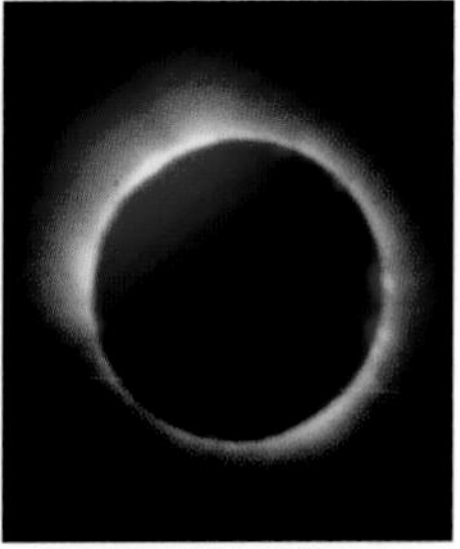

SOLAR ECLIPSE *Eclipses of the Sun are total when seen from within the umbra, allowing a view of the Sun's corona or outer halo, but partial if seen from within the penumbra.*

Einstein, Albert (1879-1955) One of the greatest scientists of all time, born in Germany. In the space of a few years at the beginning of the 20th century, Einstein transformed human understanding of the physical universe. He is known mainly for his theory of RELATIVITY, and for his uncompleted work towards UNIFIED FIELD THEORIES. He also made major contributions to THERMODYNAMICS and to the studies of light that led to QUANTUM MECHANICS. Remarkably, he published his major discoveries while working for the Swiss patent office – having been rejected for a teaching post because he was a Jew. Einstein emigrated to America in 1934 after the Nazis came to power in Germany. In 1940 he was instrumental in persuading President Franklin Roosevelt of the need for America to develop the ▷ATOM BOMB before Hitler. After 1945, he campaigned against the proliferation of the very nuclear weapons which his own work had helped to create.

❖ Einstein said the initital impetus for the development of his theory of relativity came from imagining what it would be like to travel along a beam of light.

FATHER OF MODERN PHYSICS *Einstein's theory of relativity revolutionized 20th-century science and led to the release of atomic energy.*

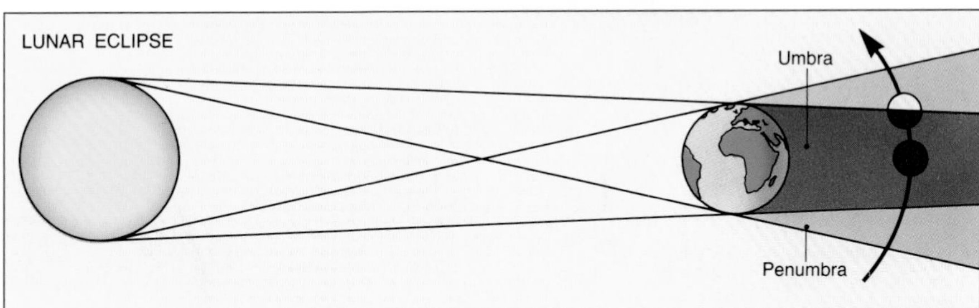

ECLIPSES OF THE MOON *Lunar eclipses can occur only when the Moon is full and the Earth is between the Sun and the Moon. They are visible across half the surface of the Earth.*

electric charge Fundamental property of matter that enables one body to exert a force on another. Two bodies with the same charge – positive or negative – repel each other; those with opposite charges attract each other. All the phenomena associated with electric charge are derived from the interactions of SUBATOMIC PARTICLES – the ELECTRON has a negative charge, the PROTON an equal positive one. An excess or deficiency of electrons gives rise to charged bodies and thus to STATIC ELECTRICITY and electric currents.

electricity Phenomenon associated with an imbalance of ELECTRIC CHARGE in a system. Static charges give rise to STATIC ELECTRICITY, while moving charges, for example electrons flowing down a copper wire in an electric circuit, produce an electric current. The size of the imbalance, which drives the current, is known as the POTENTIAL DIFFERENCE or electromotive force, or more popularly as 'voltage', and is measured in VOLTS; the magnitude of the current is measured in AMPS. Moving electric charges are associated with magnetic fields and ELECTROMAGNETIC RADIATION. Electricity is produced commercially in ▷BATTERIES and ▷ELECTRIC GENERATORS by converting chemical, nuclear or other forms of energy into electrical energy. It is also produced naturally in, for example, muscles and nerves.

electrolysis Splitting of a compound, either in liquid form or in solution, by passing an electric current through it. The IONS in the solution migrate to the electrodes – positive ions to the CATHODE, negative to the ANODE – where they give up or receive electrons to form atoms, which are deposited on the electrode or released as gas. Electrolysis is used to refine metals and in ▷ELECTROPLATING.

electromagnetic induction Production of an electric current in a circuit when placed in a changing magnetic field. It is the basis for the ▷ELECTRIC GENERATOR and for such devices as the transformer.

electromagnetic radiation Form of energy consisting of WAVES of electrical and magnetic fields vibrating at the same frequency at right angles to one another. All electromagnetic waves travel at the speed of light – 299 782 km/s (kilometres per second). But their wavelengths (the distance between peaks or troughs) range from kilometres for low-frequency RADIO WAVES to less than the radius of an atom for high-frequency GAMMA RADIATION; in between these are MICROWAVES, INFRARED RADIATION, LIGHT, ULTRAVIOLET RADIATION and X-RAYS.

electromagnetism Major branch of physics linking ELECTRICITY, MAGNETISM, and LIGHT and other forms of ELECTROMAGNETIC RADIATION in one theoretical framework. Electricity and magnetism were first seen as separate but in the 19th century scientists such as FARADAY and MAXWELL observed their interaction. During the 20th century electro-magnetism was established as one of the fundamental forces in the Universe.

electron Stable SUBATOMIC PARTICLE with a negative charge and a very small mass, a constituent of all matter and the basic unit of ELECTRICITY. Electrons are normally found circling the nucleus of an ATOM, and their number and arrangement determine the chemical properties of an element (see chemical BOND, VALENCE). Although generally thought of as particles, electrons also behave as waves, the description of which is an important aspect of QUANTUM MECHANICS.

element Chemical substance that cannot be broken down into simpler substances. Each chemical element is composed of a specific type of ATOM, and forms COMPOUNDS by combining with other elements. There are 92 elements that occur naturally, of which hydrogen is the simplest and uranium the most complex. A further 17, all of which are radioactive and are known as the transuranic elements, have been produced artificially. (See also PERIODIC TABLE.)

ellipse Curve resembling a flattened circle. An ellipse can be drawn by passing a loop of string round two pins on a board, and then tracing a curve with a pencil held taut against the string. The pins represent the two foci of the ellipse. The orbits of the planets and many comets are ellipses. A CIRCLE is an ellipse with its two foci at the same point. (See also CONIC SECTIONS.)

emulsion Type of COLLOID in which fine droplets of one liquid are dispersed in another. Salad dressing is an emulsion of oil in vinegar. Soaps and detergents contain emulsifying agents which encourage the dispersion of oil in water.

❖ The 'emulsion' on photographic film is not a true emulsion, but consists of silver halide grains dispersed in gelatine.

energy The capacity to do WORK. Every change in the Universe, however small, involves energy. It exists in many different forms, including HEAT, ELECTRICITY, MAGNETISM, chemical energy, as well as LIGHT and other forms of ELECTROMAGNETIC RADIATION. Objects can have energy by virtue of their motion (kinetic energy) or their position (potential energy). The fact that mass can be converted into energy and energy into mass (see $E = MC^2$) is exploited in reactions that release NUCLEAR ENERGY. The standard scientific unit of both energy and work is the JOULE.

entropy Measure of the disorder of any system; the more disordered it is, the higher the entropy. A highly disordered system is one in which molecules move apparently at random in all directions, with many different velocities. The molecules in a crystal, for example, are highly ordered and the entropy is very low, whereas the molecules in a gas are very disordered and the entropy is high. In any spontaneous process, and whenever work is done, entropy always increases and energy is converted into a less usable form – waste heat for example. It has been suggested that the Universe, untold billions of years from now, will become so disordered that no further usable energy will be available – the so-called 'heat death of the Universe' – but many physicists no longer accept this proposition.

equation Mathematical statement of equality, usually used to allow an unknown quantity to be given a value. An equation, for example $5 + x = 9$, can be solved by performing the same operation on each side of the equation (in this case, subtracting 5), to give a value for the unknown x (in this case 4). Simultaneous equations can be used to discover the values of two or more unknowns as long as there are as many equations as there are unknowns.

equilibrium Condition in which a system will remain unless disturbed. In stable equilibrium, as with a ball resting at the bottom of a funnel, the system will return to its initial state when disturbed. In unstable equilibrium, as with a ball on an upturned bowl, a relatively small displacement will give rise to a large movement from the original position.

equinox The moment when the Sun lies directly overhead at the Equator and when day and night are of equal length (the term means 'equal night'). In the southern hemisphere, the spring, or vernal, equinox is around 23 September and the autumn equinox around 23 March. (Compare SOLSTICE.)

Euclid (*c*300 BC) Greek mathematician whose *Elements* remains the basis for much of modern GEOMETRY and, with modifications, was still being used as a school text book in the early 20th century. One of the basic axioms of Euclidean geometry is that, given a line and a point separate from it, only one line can be drawn through the point parallel to the first line. This cannot be proved and attempts to replace it with the axiom that either no lines or many lines can be drawn through the point gave rise to 'non-Euclidean' geometries during the early 19th century, which are now essential to many aspects of modern physics.

evaporation Change of a liquid into a vapour, the opposite of CONDENSATION. In any liquid, there will be some fast-moving molecules with sufficient energy to escape from the surface into the atmosphere. Because of the removal of energy, the remaining liquid cools down. The rate of evaporation increases with temperature. Evaporation of water from the oceans is a major factor in the Earth's climate.

exponential growth Rate of growth which is continuously accelerating. Populations, for example, which depend on the number of people able to breed, would increase exponentially if unchecked.

SPARK OF GENIUS *Michael Faraday, seen in his laboratory at the Royal Institution, pioneered the study of electromagnetism and laid the foundation of the modern electricity industry.*

Fahrenheit Temperature scale on which water freezes at 32° and boils at 212°, devised by Gabriel Fahrenheit, a German instrument-maker, in the 18th century. For most scientific purposes, it has been superseded by the CELSIUS or centigrade scale. To convert Fahrenheit to Celsius, subtract 32, multiply by 5, and divide by 9; for example, 350°F is 350 – 32 (= 318) × 5 (= 1 590) ÷ 9 = 176,66°C.

Faraday, Michael (1791-1867) English physicist and chemist whose discovery of ELECTROMAGNETIC INDUCTION and invention of the dynamo (see ▷ELECTRIC GENERATOR) in 1831 laid the basis for the electricity industry. He also set out Faraday's Laws of ELECTROLYSIS, and demonstrated the effect of magnetism on polarized light. The scientific unit of capacitance – the ability to store electric charge – the farad, is named in his honour.

Fermat's last theorem Celebrated puzzle in mathematics posed by the French mathematician Pierre de Fermat in the 17th century. It has been known since at least the time of the ancient Greeks that $3^2 + 4^2 = 5^2$, but mathematicians wondered whether a similar equation could be written with cubes, fourths or higher powers. Fermat claimed to have proved that this was impossible, but left no record of his proof. A complete proof still eludes scholars after more than 300 years, although it has been shown to be true for many specific cases.

Fermi, Enrico (1901-54) Italian-born physicist who in 1942 completed the world's first ▷NUCLEAR REACTOR – underneath the stands of the football stadium at the University of Chicago – and thus ushered in the nuclear age. He was awarded the 1938 Nobel prize for physics.

Fibonacci sequence Sequence in which each number is the sum of the two preceding numbers. Named after the Italian mathematician Leonardo Fibonacci – who published it in 1202 – the sequence starts: 1, 1, 2, 3, 5, 8, 13, 21 . . . The Fibonacci sequence occurs widely in nature – for example, in the whorls of pine cones and other forms of spiral growth, and in the distances of the planets from the Sun.

fluorescence The ability of certain substances to absorb light (or other forms of ELECTROMAGNETIC RADIATION) and to emit light of a different wavelength or colour. It is similar to phosphorescence, but fluorescence ceases when the incoming radiation stops, whereas phosphorescent materials (as on a television screen) continue to emit light for a short time.

force External agent – a push or a pull – that causes a change in the state of motion of a body, that is, it imparts an ACCELERATION to it. The greater the force the greater the acceleration, and the greater the MASS of the body, the lower the acceleration produced by a given force. (See NEWTON'S LAWS OF MOTION.) Force is measured in newtons. One newton is the force required to give a mass of one kilogram an acceleration of one metre per second per second (1 m/s²). Physicists today describe the four basic forces of nature as gravity, electromagnetism and – operating at the quantum level – the weak and strong force.

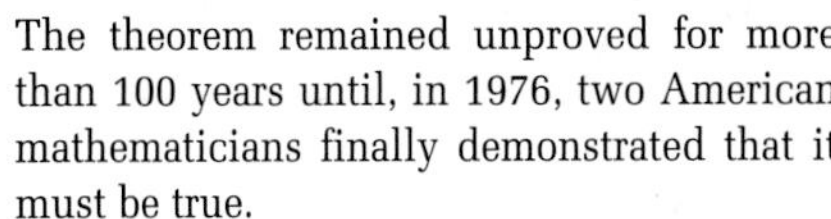

GINGERBREAD MAN *In the fractal shape (above), known as the Mandelbrot set, lurk numerous smaller 'gingerbread men' at every level of magnification.*

formula, chemical Representation of the composition or structure of a MOLECULE using symbols for its constituent ELEMENTS. The formula for water, H_2O, shows that a molecule of water contains two hydrogen atoms and one oxygen atom. Structural formulae also show how the atoms are bonded, so that it is possible to distinguish between different ISOMERS. Thus ethyl alcohol and dimethyl ether have different structural formulae:

```
   H  H              H    H
   |  |              |    |
H—C—C—OH  and  H—C—O—C—H
   |  |              |    |
   H  H              H    H
```

although both can be written as C_2H_6O.

four-colour theorem Proposition that a mapmaker needs only four colours to draw any map, however complicated, so that no two adjoining countries share the same colour. The theorem remained unproved for more than 100 years until, in 1976, two American mathematicians finally demonstrated that it must be true.

fractal Shape or structure which, although it appears to be entirely irregular, nevertheless displays distinct patterns. Fractal shapes are made up of numerous smaller versions of the same shape, each of which in turn is made up of still smaller versions. Fractals occur widely in nature in such features as cloud formations, coastlines, plants and other organic structures. They are also produced on computers, using complex equations similar to those underlying CHAOS THEORY, for example to simulate growth patterns or to create special effects for the cinema or as art.

fraction Part of a whole number. If a number is divided into eight parts, then each part may be represented as $^1/_8$ of the whole. The number above the line is known as the numerator and the number below the line as the denominator. Fractions expressed as ratios of whole numbers are called common or vulgar fractions; those that use the DECIMAL SYSTEM are called decimal fractions.

freezing point Temperature at which a liquid changes into a solid. Under normal conditions, it is the same as the MELTING POINT. Freezing is generally accompanied by a decrease in volume and an increase in density; water is an exception – it expands, which is why ice floats.

frequency The number of complete cycles of a vibration or WAVE motion (such as SOUND, RADIO WAVES or ELECTROMAGNETIC RADIATION) that take place in a given unit of time. It is usually measured in HERTZ (1 Hz = one cycle per second), and can be calculated by dividing the velocity of a wave by its WAVELENGTH – the frequency of a wave increases as its wavelength decreases. (See also AMPLITUDE.)

friction Resistance to the relative motion of two touching surfaces. It is the force that stops a car when the brakes are applied. Friction is usually dissipated as heat, as when meteors burn up in the Earth's atmosphere. Ball bearings reduce friction by allowing surfaces to roll rather than slide, while lubricants make sliding easier.

galaxy Vast grouping of thousands of millions of stars, together with clouds of dust and gas, held together by gravity. Galaxies rotate, tending to take up a spiral shape, with a bright central nucleus of older stars, and spiral arms of younger and newly forming stars. Eventually, the spiral closes in, leaving an elliptical galaxy, which may ultimately collapse into a BLACK HOLE. The Universe contains at least 1 000 million galaxies. The Earth and the Solar System lie in a spiral arm of the MILKY WAY, which is itself part of a cluster of around 20 galaxies known as the Local Group.

Galileo (Galileo Galilei) (1564-1642) Italian astronomer and mathematician who built the first effective telescope and used it to prove that the Earth moves round the Sun. Galileo made many other scientific discoveries. A swinging lamp in Pisa cathedral is said to have made him realize that the rate at which a pendulum swings depends on its length rather than the distance through which it swings, which led to the development of pendulum clocks. He demonstrated that freely falling objects accelerate at the same rate, whatever their mass, and that projectiles follow the path of a PARABOLA. His observations, proving that the Earth moves round the Sun, confirmed the theory put forward by the Polish astronomer Nicolaus COPERNICUS, but conflicted with the teachings of the Church that the Earth was the centre of the Universe and the Sun revolved around the Earth. This brought him to the attention of the ▷INQUISITION and he was forced to recant, under threat of torture. He is said to have muttered, after his public recantation, '*E pur si muove*' ('And yet it moves').

gamma radiation Form of ELECTROMAGNETIC RADIATION with the highest energy, shortest wavelength and highest frequency in the electromagnetic spectrum. Gamma rays are produced by the decay of radioactive nuclei (see RADIOACTIVITY) as well as by PULSARS, QUASARS and other objects in space. They are used in ▷RADIOTHERAPY, particularly in the treatment of cancer, and to sterilize medical equipment.

gas The least dense state of matter. Gases completely fill the vessel in which they are contained. According to the kinetic theory of gases, the molecules of a gas are in constant random motion, and their collisions with the walls of the container give rise to pressure. The relationship between the temperature, pressure and volume of an 'ideal' gas (one in which the molecules have no volume and exert no forces on each other) is given by BOYLE'S LAW. However, real gases usually diverge widely from this, because of the existence of small intermolecular forces.

geometric progression Sequence of numbers in which each number is obtained by multiplying the previous one by a constant factor. For example, in the sequence 1, 2, 4, 8, 16, 32 each number is twice the preceding one. In an arithmetic progression, by contrast, each number is derived by adding a constant number to the previous one, as in 2, 4, 6, 8, 10.

geometry Branch of mathematics that deals with the properties of space and the various different ways of describing it. It is thus concerned with the measurement and relationships of points, lines, angles, surfaces and solids. Standard Euclidean geometry (see EUCLID) is concerned with two and three-dimensional space (planes and solids), while non-Euclidean geometry deals with multiple dimensions. In analytic geometry, algebraic equations are used to represent geometric figures. (See also TOPOLOGY, FRACTAL.)

Gödel's theorem One of the most important mathematical proofs of the 20th century, produced by the Austrian-born mathematician Kurt Gödel in 1931. Until then, many mathematicians (including Bertrand ▷RUSSELL) had believed that the whole of mathematics could be constructed from a few basic axioms. Gödel's theorem showed that this was impossible since any formal axiomatic system must contain a basic proposition that is unprovable and the system's consistency could not be proved without using methods or ideas from outside the system.

graph Visual representation of numerical relationships. It generally takes the form of a series of points, plotted with the use of COORDINATES against two axes set at right angles to each other, and connected by a line or curve. Graphs have many uses in statistics and engineering. In some cases, data may be better presented as a set of vertical or horizontal bars rather than a curve (as in a bar graph or histogram). Another common graphical device is the pie chart, which shows the relation of the parts to the whole by illustrating them as segments of a circle.

gravitation Force of attraction between all forms of matter. It makes objects fall towards the centre of the Earth, holds the planets in orbit round the Sun, and keeps stars and galaxies together. The Law of Universal Gravitation, first laid down by Isaac NEWTON, states that the force of attraction between two bodies is proportional to their masses and inversely proportional to the square of the distance between them. In other words, doubling the mass of one of the bodies doubles the force of attraction, while doubling the distance between them reduces the force to one-quarter. Although the Newtonian system works well enough to land a man on the Moon, it has been supplanted in modern physics by Einstein's general theory of RELATIVITY, which treats gravitation as a distortion of the SPACE-TIME continuum caused by the presence of large masses. Although gravity is

A MATTER OF GRAVITY *Galileo (centre) demonstrated the principles of gravity some 50 years before Newton; contrary to myth, he did so using an inclined plane, not the leaning tower of Pisa.*

OMEN IN THE SKIES *Edmond Halley forecast the return of the comet that bears his name in the 17th century. It was first photographed in 1910 and by the space probe* Giotto *in 1986.*

the weakest of the fundamental forces of nature, it is effective at long range and, on a cosmic scale, it is by far the most important.
❖ A falling apple may well have inspired Newton to conceive his theory of gravitation, since he sometimes sat in the apple orchard in his garden, but there is no evidence that the apple hit him on the head.

half-life The time taken for half the nuclei in a sample of a radioactive ISOTOPE to decay. Because the rate of decay continuously slows down, the half-life remains constant, however many of the nuclei have already decayed. Half-lives of radioactive substances can range from millionths of a second to thousands of millions of years.

Halley's comet Best known of the COMETS, seen most recently in 1986, when it was studied intensively and photographed by the space probe *Giotto*. Its 76-year orbit round the Sun takes it from a point beyond Neptune to within the orbit of Venus. It is named after Edmond Halley (1656-1742), the British astronomer royal who studied it in 1682 and correctly predicted that it would return in 1758. In 1676 he travelled to the island of St Helena to make the first catalogue of stars in the southern hemisphere.

Hawking, Stephen (1942-) British theoretical physicist and author of the best-selling *A Brief History of Time* (1988), in which he presented theories of space, time and the origins of the Universe to a wide readership. Despite severe physical disability caused by a progressive neuromotor disease, he has made substantial contributions to the study of BLACK HOLES, GRAVITATION and UNIFIED FIELD THEORIES (the 'theory of everything').

heat Form of energy that is transferred from a hotter body to a colder one. Heat is transferred in three ways; CONDUCTION, CONVECTION and RADIATION. As the colder body is heated, the atoms and molecules of which it is composed speed up. At the melting and boiling points, heat continues to be supplied without any increase in temperature; the increase in internal energy of the body takes the form of a change in molecular structure rather than an increase in temperature (see LATENT HEAT). Different materials require different amounts of heat to achieve the same rise in temperature. Those with a low heat capacity, such as metals, require a small amount of heat; those with a high heat capacity, such as water, require a large amount. The specific heat of a substance is the amount of heat required to raise 1 kg of the substance through 1°C. Heat is one of the key concepts in THERMODYNAMICS. It is measured in either CALORIES or JOULES.

heavy water (D_2O) Form of water in which hydrogen is replaced by one of its heavier ISOTOPES, deuterium or tritium. Heavy water slows the neutrons given off during NUCLEAR FISSION and is used to control the rate at which fission takes place in some types of ▷NUCLEAR REACTOR.

helium (He) Best known of the NOBLE GASES and the next lightest chemical element after HYDROGEN. It is very unreactive and will not catch fire, which makes it suitable for filling airships and balloons. It becomes a liquid at −268,9°C (close to ABSOLUTE ZERO) and when cooled still further it exhibits superfluidity – it flows with no measurable VISCOSITY.
❖ Helium is one of the most abundant elements in the Universe since it is formed by the NUCLEAR FUSION of hydrogen nuclei, the process from which the Sun and other stars derive their energy.

helix Spiral shape, resembling a spring. Helical structures occur widely in the natural world, the most famous example being the double helix of ▷DNA.

hertz (Hz) The international unit of FREQUENCY: 1 Hz is equal to one cycle (from peak to peak of a wave) per second. It is named after Heinrich Rudolph Hertz (1857-94), the German physicist who was the first to send and receive RADIO WAVES, and who also demonstrated the electromagnetic nature of light.

Hooke's law In physics, the principle that the amount an elastic body stretches out of shape is in direct proportion to the force acting on it. This is why the weight markings on the faces of kitchen scales, which work with a spring, are the same distance apart. The law was first stated in 1678 by Robert Hooke (1635-1703), the English scientist and inventor of the modern microscope.

Hubble, Edwin (1889-1953) American astronomer who demonstrated the existence of galaxies beyond the Milky Way. He also discovered the RED SHIFT in the light from distant stars, which shows that galaxies are receding at a rate that increases in proportion to their distance from us – the foundation of the BIG BANG THEORY. The ratio between the distance of a galaxy and the rate at which it recedes – 15 to 30 kilometres per second per million LIGHT YEARS – is known as Hubble's constant. This gives an age for the Universe of about 10 to 20 thousand million years.
❖ The Hubble Space Telescope (named after Hubble), which orbits the Earth, can 'see' the universe without the blurring of the Earth's atmosphere and without the glow of even the darkest night sky on Earth.

hydrocarbons Organic chemical compounds composed entirely of CARBON and HYDROGEN. They occur mainly in petroleum, coal and natural gas products and are of importance as the starting point for the manufacture of an enormous variety of industrial chemicals.

hydrogen (H) Colourless and odourless gas, the lightest and simplest of the chemical elements. It provides the fuel for NUCLEAR FUSION in the stars and is the most abundant element in the Universe. Hydrogen has a

BUBBLE RAINBOW *Interference between light waves reflected from the front and back of the bubbles' thin, soapy films causes multicoloured fringes.*

single ELECTRON in orbit around a nucleus that contains a single PROTON. It is highly flammable and is sometimes used as a fuel. In combination with oxygen, it forms water. It has two 'heavy' ISOTOPES: deuterium, with a neutron as well as a proton in the nucleus, and tritium, with two neutrons. Both are important in the nuclear power industry.

inertia Tendency of a body to resist any change to its state of rest or uniform motion in a straight line. The larger a body's MASS, the greater its inertia. When a car is brought to a sudden stop, it is the occupants' inertia that causes them to be thrown forward.

infrared radiation Form of ELECTROMAGNETIC RADIATION that has wavelengths longer than those of visible light and shorter than microwaves. The radiant heat from a glowing coal fire, for example, consists of infrared radiation. (See also ▷INFRARED DEVICES.)

PERPETUAL STORM *Jupiter's Great Red Spot, site of a raging storm, is thought to owe its colour to the presence of red phosphorus.*

interference Effect produced by the interaction of two or more different wave motions, for example light, sound or the ripples on a pond. Where the crests or troughs of the waves coincide, they reinforce each other. Where crests coincide with troughs, they cancel each other out. In the case of light, this creates patterns of light and dark, or colour fringes such as those on the surface of a soap bubble; in the case of sound, it creates wavering 'beats', used to tune musical instruments. It also forms the basis of the ▷HOLOGRAM.

ion An ATOM, or group of atoms, that has lost or gained one or more ELECTRONS, and thus carries a positive charge (a cation) or a negative charge (an anion). Many compounds form ions in solution, and atmospheric gases are ionized by incoming solar radiation and by electrical discharges during storms.

isomers Chemical compounds which have MOLECULES made up of the same numbers of the same atoms, but which differ in the arrangement of the atoms. Examples are urea and ammonium cyanate. Isomers are very common in organic chemistry.

isotopes Different forms of the same ELEMENT. The difference lies only in the number of NEUTRONS in the nucleus. They have identical chemical properties, but different relative atomic masses. Nearly all elements occur naturally as a mixture of isotopes. (See also RADIOACTIVITY.)

joule (J) Unit of ENERGY and WORK, defined as the amount of work done by a force of one newton moving through one metre. It is equivalent to the amount of energy dissipated by a power of one watt operating for one second. It is named after the British physicist James Prescott Joule (1818-89), who demonstrated that heat energy and mechanical energy are convertible. Dieticians use kilojoules (one kilojoule = 1 000 joules) or CALORIES to measure the energy content of foods.

Jupiter Largest planet in the SOLAR SYSTEM – with a volume 1 300 times that of Earth – and the fifth farthest from the Sun. It has a 'year' of 11,86 Earth years, but a 'day' of about 9 hours 50 minutes. Its most prominent feature is the Great Red Spot, covering an area twice the diameter of Earth. Jupiter is composed mainly of hydrogen and helium. The atmosphere is mostly hydrogen, methane and ammonia, which forms dense white clouds. It has at least 16 moons.

❖ The collision of the comet Shoemaker-Levy with Jupiter in July 1994 was termed 'the astronomical event of the decade' and was expected to yield valuable information about the planet.

kelvin (K) Standard unit of temperature, based on the CELSIUS scale but with its starting point at ABSOLUTE ZERO (0 K or –273,15°C) rather than the freezing point of water (273,15 K or 0°C). It is named after the British physicist Lord Kelvin (1824-1907), a pioneer in the study of THERMODYNAMICS and ELECTROMAGNETISM.

Kepler, Johannes (1571-1630) German astronomer and mathematician whose laws of planetary motion, based on the observations of Tycho BRAHE, showed for the first time that the planets moved in elliptical orbits around the Sun. Kepler's work provided important support for Nicolaus COPERNICUS's theory that the Sun was at the centre of the Universe, and gave Isaac Newton the raw material for his theory of GRAVITATION.

kilogram (kg) Standard international unit of MASS, equal to 1 000 grams. It is defined as the mass of the International Prototype Kilogram, a platinum-iridium cylinder kept under controlled conditions at the International Bureau of Weights and Measures near Paris. (See also METRIC SYSTEM, SI UNITS.)

kinetic energy Energy possessed by a body by virtue of its motion. It is calculated as $^1/_2mv^2$, where m is the MASS of the body and v its VELOCITY. (See also ENERGY.)

latent heat The heat released or absorbed, without a change of temperature when a substance undergoes a change of state (from solid to liquid, or liquid to gas, or vice versa), such as freezing, boiling, evaporating or condensing. A moistened finger held up to test the wind is colder on the side facing the wind because the moisture draws latent heat from the finger as it evaporates. In the same way, the evaporation of sweat from the skin draws excess heat from the body.

Lavoisier, Antoine (1743-94) French scientist who is regarded as the founder of modern chemistry. He demonstrated that combustion involved a reaction with a constituent of the air which he called oxygen, so finally laying the theory of PHLOGISTON to rest. He also worked out the laws of CONSERVATION of mass, devised the modern method of naming COMPOUNDS and applied chemistry to agriculture. Lavoisier was a tax administrator and although he had worked for the reform of taxation, prisons and hospitals, he was guillotined in the French Revolution.

lens Device for focusing light, consisting of a disc of glass or other transparent material, each face of which is curved like the surface of a sphere. Lenses may be either convex (converging) or concave (diverging). A converging lens magnifies any object placed inside the focal length. Simple lenses are used to correct people's sight defects: concave lenses correct short sight and convex lenses correct long sight. Optical instruments, such as cameras, telescopes and microscopes, often contain compound lenses composed of a combination of concave and convex lenses in order to reduce optical distortion.

light Form of ELECTROMAGNETIC RADIATION that is visible to the naked eye. It has wavelengths between those of infrared and ultraviolet radiation. Light plays a unique part in science: it makes visual observation possible, and the speed of light in a vacuum is one of the fundamental physical constants of the Universe. Scientists have debated whether light is composed of particles or waves since the time of Isaac Newton, who, in 1666, was the first to split ordinary light into its SPECTRUM of component colours. Newton thought of light as a stream of luminous corpuscles, with a different corpuscle for each colour. This explained many properties of light, such as REFLECTION and REFRACTION reasonably effectively. However, it could not explain the phenomenon of INTERFERENCE, which was demonstrated by Thomas Young in 1802 and implied that light must be a wave motion. The wave theory also accounted for DIFFRACTION. Nevertheless, neither theory was explained entirely satisfactory, and it was not until the beginning of the 20th century, when Max Planck proposed that light was emitted as packets of energy called PHOTONS, that the modern view of the nature of light began to emerge. Light is now thought of as both particle and wave – referred to as complementarity – with the wavelike behaviour of photons being explained and described by QUANTUM MECHANICS.

light year Distance covered in a year by light travelling in a vacuum (or 9,46 million million kilometres). It is used as a unit for measuring distances in astronomy, although it has largely been superseded for scientific purposes by the parsec, a unit which is equal to 3,2616 light years.

SIMPLE LENSES *Convex or converging lenses bend parallel beams of light inwards to a single point, the focus. Concave or diverging lenses bend light outwards so that it appears to come from behind the lens. Most optical instruments use combinations of the two.*

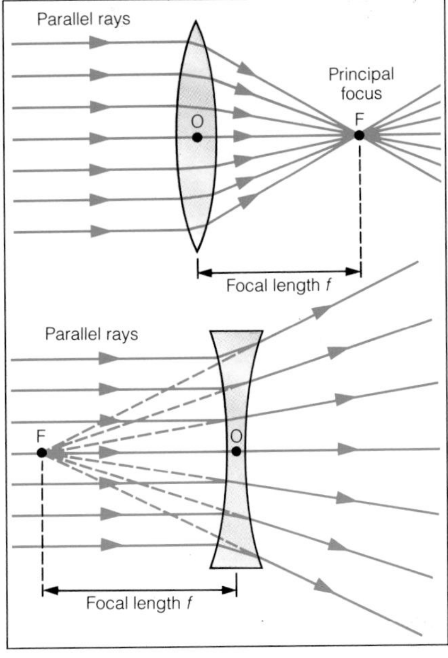

liquid State of matter in which atoms or molecules are held together by mutual attraction so that they cannot move as freely as in a gas, but are not rigidly fixed as in a solid. Liquids take the shape of their container and are relatively incompressible. Pressure in a liquid is transmitted equally in all directions, providing the basis for ▷HYDRAULIC machines.

litmus paper Paper impregnated with litmus, a purple vegetable dye that turns red in ACIDS and blue in ALKALIS, used to determine if a solution is acid or alkaline.

logarithms Mathematical device once used to simplify the multiplication and division of complicated numbers. If two numbers are expressed as the POWERS of the same base number (usually 10), they can be multiplied by adding the powers together and divided by subtracting them. By referring to published tables, complex calculations could be made. ❖ Many natural phenomena are best measured using logarithmic scales, for example sound intensity (decibels), earthquake magnitude (the Richter scale) and acidity (pH). Because numbers on a logarithmic scale present powers of 10, the number 3 is 1 000 times greater than 1, rather than 3 times greater – as it would be on a simple linear scale.

machine Device that converts ENERGY or FORCE into a usable form, that is one that can do WORK. Simple machines include the lever, the pulley, the inclined plane (wedges and screws) and the wheel and axle.

Mach number Speed through the air or other gas expressed as a multiple of the speed of SOUND under the same conditions. An aircraft travelling at the speed of sound is at Mach 1; Concorde flying at more than twice the speed of sound reaches Mach 2,3. The unit is named after the Austrian physicist and philosopher Ernst Mach (1838-1916).

Magellanic clouds Two nearby galaxies visible as faint patches of light close to the MILKY WAY in the southern hemisphere. They are important to astrophysicists because they offer an opportunity to study nearby stars that are not in our own galaxy. They were recorded by Ferdinand ▷MAGELLAN in 1519.

magnetism Property possessed by some materials, notably iron, cobalt and nickel, to attract or repel other similar materials. Magnets may be permanent, retaining their magnetism in all circumstances, or temporary, retaining their magnetism only when in a magnetic field. Every magnet has two poles, a north and a south pole. Similar poles repel each other, while opposite poles attract. Magnetic fields are also created by ELECTROMAGNETIC INDUCTION when a suitable material is surrounded by a fluctuating or moving electric field. Electricity and magnetism are manifestations of the same fundamental force, ELECTROMAGNETISM. (See also ▷MAGNETIC POLES in 'The Earth and the environment'.)

magnitude Measure of the brightness of a star. The scale was devised by the Greek astronomer Hipparchus in about 130 BC. He graded stars from 1, the brightest, to 6, barely visible to the naked eye. Apparent magnitude is less useful to astronomers than 'absolute magnitude', the brightness a star would have if it were a set distance (1 parsec or 3,2616 LIGHT YEARS) away.

Mars Fourth planet from the Sun and nearest to the Earth, also known as the 'red planet' and named after the Roman god of war. Half the size of Earth, Mars has a 'year' of 687 days and two small moons, Phobos and Deimos.
❖ The largest known volcano in the solar system, Olympus Mons, is on Mars. With a height of 27 km, it would collapse if Martian gravity were as strong as Earth's.

MARTIAN LANDSCAPE *Viking spacecraft images, enhanced by computer, reveal high volcanic peaks framing the great Valles marineris canyon, an awesome gash more than 3 000 km long and up to 8 km deep.*

mass Intrinsic property of MATTER. Mass is a measure of the gravitational attraction between one body and another, when it is equivalent to WEIGHT. It is also a measure of a body's INERTIA, or resistance to ACCELERATION. According to the theory of RELATIVITY, a moving object's mass increases with its VELOCITY, becoming greater as the speed of light is approached, with its weight and inertia increasing correspondingly. An observer travelling with the object would not detect any change in these properties. Because mass and energy are interconvertible (see $E = MC^2$), mass is often referred to as mass-energy. (See NEWTON'S LAWS OF MOTION.)

mathematics The universal language of science. The whole complex and diverse structure of mathematics is based on sets of simple AXIOMS. Pure mathematics includes the study of NUMBERS, ALGEBRA, GEOMETRY, CALCULUS and TOPOLOGY. Applied mathematics generally refers to physics (particularly MECHANICS), but mathematical techniques are used in all branches of technology, engineering, computer science, economics and the social sciences. Recent developments in mathematics include CHAOS THEORY, FRACTAL geometry and CATASTROPHE THEORY.

matter Anything that has MASS or that exists in space and time. All matter in the Universe is thought to have been formed in the BIG BANG, when the Universe was created. (See also ANTIMATTER.)

Maxwell, James Clerk (1831-79) Scottish physicist, whose work led to major advances in THERMODYNAMICS and ELECTROMAGNETISM. The four equations that bear his name laid down the fundamental principles of electromagnetic waves and demonstrated the electromagnetic nature of light. They also predicted the existence of other forms of electromagnetic radiation.

mean, median and mode Three different ways of expressing an average for a set of figures. The mean is the same as the arithmetical average and is arrived at by dividing the total for the whole group by the number in the group: the average age of 100 people whose combined ages equal 5 000 is 50. The median is the middle value of the group: half the individual figures fall below the median and half above. If the same group of 100 people is made up mainly of people over the mean age of 50, balanced by a smaller number of very young people, the median age will be over 50. The mode is the most commonly occurring value in the group. For example, if 52 is the commonest age in the group, then 52 is the mode. (See also NORMAL DISTRIBUTION CURVE, STATISTICS.)

mechanics Branch of applied mathematics that lies at the heart of classical physics. It deals with objects in motion as a result of the forces acting on them (termed dynamics), and with stationary objects where the forces are in equilibrium (termed statics). (See NEWTON'S LAWS OF MOTION.)

melting point The temperature at which a solid turns to a liquid. Under normal conditions, it is the same as the freezing point. The

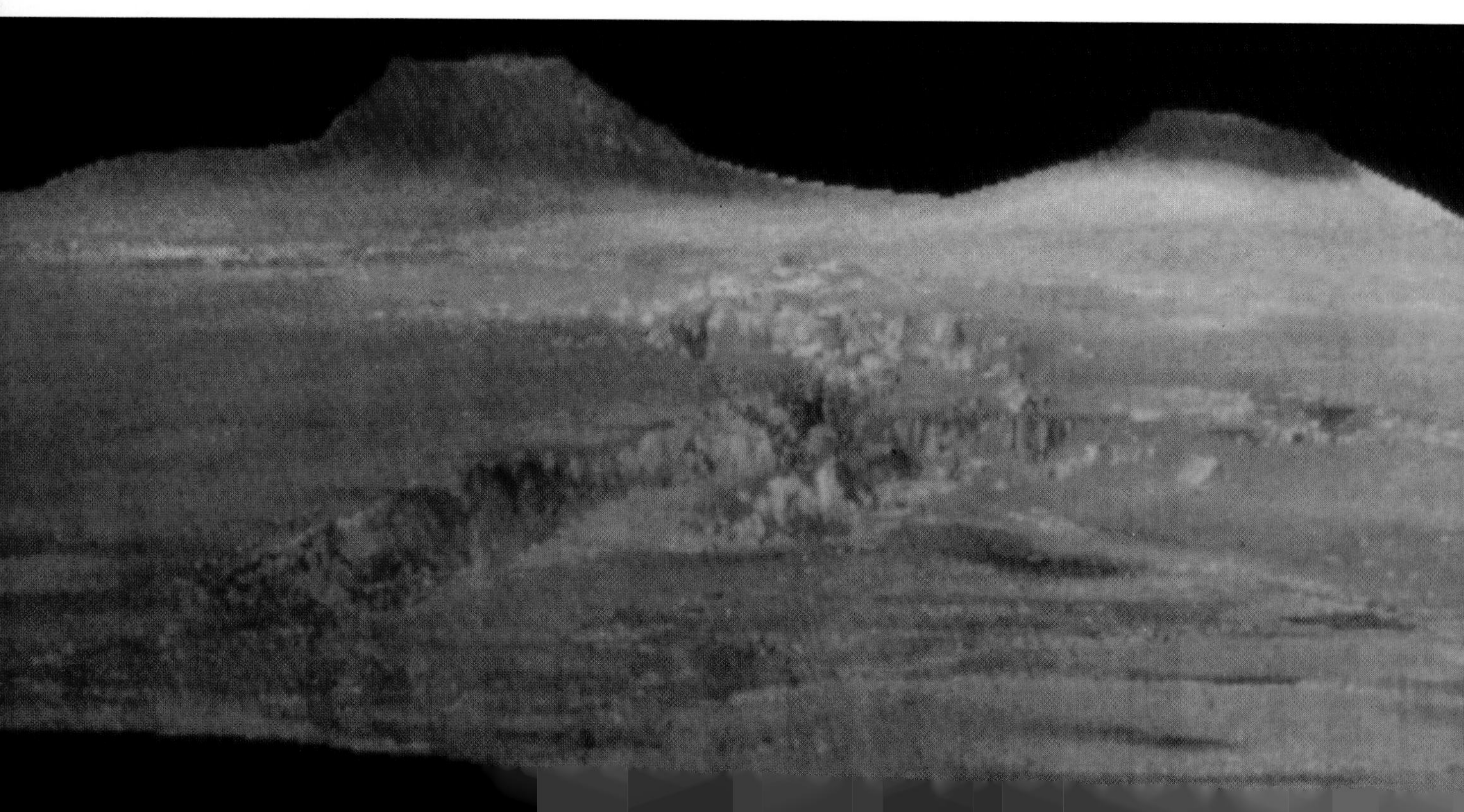

heat required to melt a solid without raising its temperature is known as LATENT HEAT.

Mendeleyev, Dmitri Ivanovich (1834-1907) Russian chemist who devised the modern PERIODIC TABLE in 1869 grouping the elements according to their chemical properties. He also predicted the existence of several hitherto undiscovered elements. The element mendelevium is named after him.

Mercury Planet closest to the Sun, named after the Roman messenger of the gods. It has little or no atmosphere and surface temperatures vary enormously from –160°C to more than 300°C between night and day.

metal Element such as iron, copper or zinc that possesses most or all of the following properties: it is relatively hard, but malleable and can be formed into sheets and wires; it reflects light and has a lustre when polished; and it is a good conductor of heat and electricity. About 75 per cent of elements are metallic. (See PERIODIC TABLE.)

meteor Material from interplanetary space that enters the atmosphere and burns up in a streak of fire, forming a 'shooting star'. Meteors are thought to be particles of debris from COMETS and ASTEROIDS. Normally, about five shooting stars are visible each hour, but when 'meteor showers' occur there may be thousands every hour.

metre (m) International unit of length (see SI UNITS). The French Revolutionaries devised the metric system in 1799, defining the metre as one 10 millionth of the distance from the North Pole to the Equator on the line of longitude which passes through Paris. From 1875, when a world conference established the International Bureau of Weights and Measures, until 1960, the standard was set as the distance between two lines on a platinum bar kept under controlled conditions in Paris. It is now defined as the distance travelled by light in 1/299 792 458 of a second.

metric system System of weights and measures based on the principle that all units are derived from the base unit by multiplying or dividing by multiples of 10. The derived units have standard prefixes:

tera-	1 million million (10^{12})
giga-	1 thousand million (10^{9})
mega-	1 million (10^{6})
kilo-	1 thousand (10^{3})
hecto-	100 (10^{2})
deca-	10 (10^{1})
deci-	1 tenth (10^{-1})
centi-	1 hundredth (10^{-2})
milli-	1 thousandth (10^{-3})
micro-	1 millionth (10^{-6})
nano-	1 thousand millionth (10^{-9})
pico-	1 million millionth (10^{-12})

The metric system was the basis for the system of SI UNITS which was accepted internationally in 1960.

Michelson-Morley experiment Crucial experiment in the history of physics, named after the two American physicists who carried it out in the 1880s. It was designed to detect the presence of the 'ether', the medium through which light was thought to travel in space. It failed in its purpose, but showed instead that light does not require a medium through which to travel, and paved the way for Einstein's proposition that the speed of light is constant, whatever the speed of the observer – the fundamental assumption of the theory of RELATIVITY.

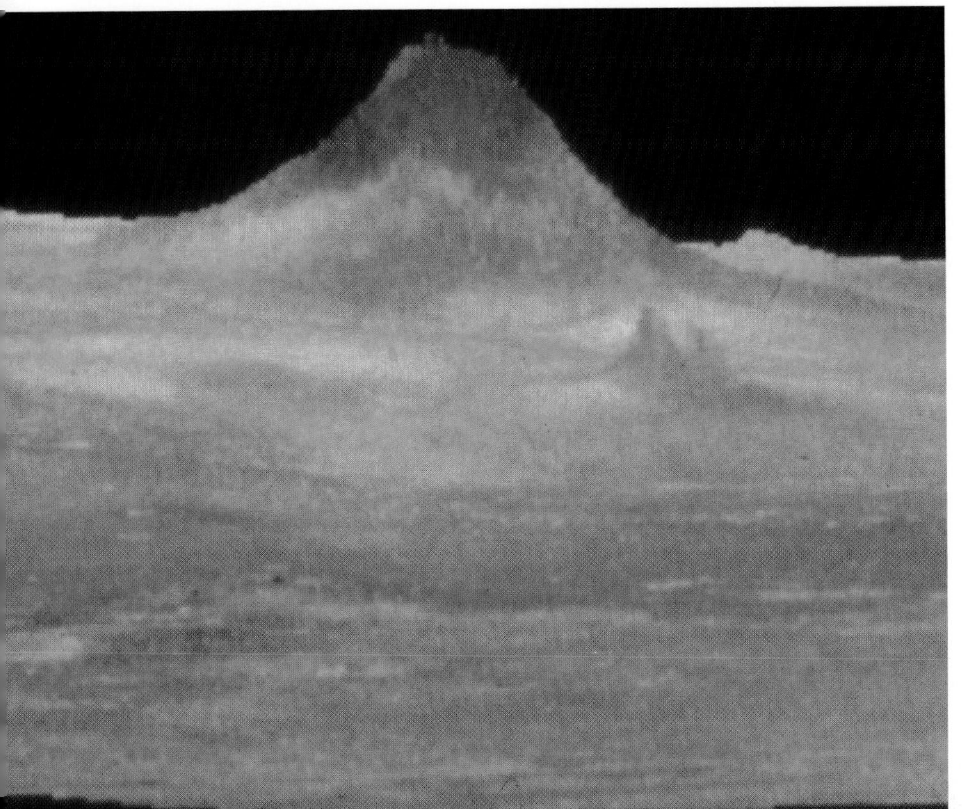

microwaves Type of ELECTROMAGNETIC RADIATION, with wavelengths lying between those of radio waves and infrared radiation. The COSMIC BACKGROUND RADIATION of the Universe is composed of microwaves. They are used in the ▷MICROWAVE OVEN and in telecommunications.

Milky Way Hazy band of light encircling the night sky, composed of thousands of millions of stars in the spiral arms of our own GALAXY.

molecule Group of atoms held together by chemical BONDS, the smallest unit that retains the characteristic properties of a chemical COMPOUND. Molecular mass is the sum of all the relative atomic masses of the atoms in the molecule. It ranges from 2,016 for the lightest molecule, hydrogen (H_2), to 10 000 or more for organic molecules such as ▷PROTEINS, and into the millions for large POLYMERS.

momentum Tendency of a moving body to continue moving. For a body moving in a straight line (linear momentum) it is the product of the body's MASS and its VELOCITY; thus a light fast-moving body may have the same momentum as a heavy, slow-moving one. The principle of conservation of momentum requires that the total momentum of a system remains the same: the recoil of a cannon has the same momentum as the shot it fires, though the shot moves much faster than the cannon. Rotating bodies have 'angular momentum'. Conservation of angular momentum is the basis for the ▷GYROSCOPE.

Moon Earth's only natural satellite, and the only extraterrestrial body on which a human being has set foot (see ▷APOLLO PROJECT). The Moon orbits the Earth about every 28 days at an average distance of 386 000 km; its mass is about one-eightieth that of Earth, and its volume about one-fiftieth. It is about 3 200 km in diameter. It has no atmosphere, and its gravity is only one-sixth that of Earth. It owes its heavily cratered surface to the impact of ▷METEORITES as well as volcanic activity. It is thought that the Earth and the Moon formed some 4 600 million years ago. Several other planets also have moons – 20 or more in the case of SATURN. (See also ECLIPSE, ▷TIDE.)

nebula Cloud of dust and gas in the sky. Some nebulae, such as the Horsehead nebula,

SCIENCE, SPACE AND MATHEMATICS

QUEST FOR THE STARS *Newton's reflecting telescope, built with his own hands, is preserved by the Royal Society. It was one of the many achievements of a genius whose ideas governed science for more than 200 years.*

are dark because they obscure the stars behind them and neither emit nor reflect light themselves. The Orion nebula, however, emits light because of a hot star at its centre, and the Pleiades and Andromeda nebulae shine by reflected light from nearby stars. Nebulae may be the result of a SUPERNOVA, as in the case of the Crab nebula, whose explosion was noted by Chinese astronomers in 1054, and which has a PULSAR at its centre.

Neptune Eighth planet from the Sun and fourth largest in the SOLAR SYSTEM. It is not visible to the naked eye. It has a 'year' of around 185 Earth years. In 1989 the Voyager space probe confirmed that its atmosphere consisted mainly of methane and hydrogen.

neutrino A SUBATOMIC PARTICLE with no mass and no electric charge, but with a characteristic 'spin', produced by COSMIC RAYS and PARTICLE ACCELERATORS. It was predicted as early as 1931, but because it has virtually no effect on other types of matter, its existence was proved only 30 years later.

neutron A SUBATOMIC PARTICLE found in the nucleus of the ATOM. It has much the same mass as a PROTON, but no electric charge. Only the hydrogen atom has no neutrons; heavier elements have more than one proton in the nucleus, which would normally repel each other because of their positive charge. The neutron acts as the 'glue' that holds the nucleus together.

neutron star Small, almost unimaginably dense star, left behind after a large star has reached the end of its life in a SUPERNOVA. The matter in the star collapses under the force of its own gravity, crushing electrons and protons together to form NEUTRONS. A teaspoonful would weigh several thousand million tons. Even larger stars are thought to carry on collapsing indefinitely until they form BLACK HOLES. PULSARS are rapidly rotating neutron stars.

Newton, Sir Isaac (1642-1727) English physicist and mathematician, one of the great figures in the history of science. His most notable achievements were NEWTON'S LAWS OF MOTION, which established the science of MECHANICS, his discovery of the law of GRAVITATION, and CALCULUS, which has been an essential tool of mathematics and physics ever since. Newton made the first reflecting telescope, and was the first to use a prism to split light into the colours of the spectrum. He also studied heat, acoustics and fluids. The newton (N), a unit of FORCE, is named after him.
❖ Newtonian physics offered a model of the Universe as a gigantic machine, in which it seemed that everything was determined by fixed physical laws. In the 20th century, however, Albert Einstein's theories showed that Newton's laws did not apply at speeds approaching that of light (see RELATIVITY), nor with particles the size of an electron (see QUANTUM MECHANICS). Nevertheless, Newton's laws are still valid for most purposes.

Newton's laws of motion Three basic laws that govern the relationships between acceleration of a body and the forces acting on it. They state: 1. Every body continues in a state of rest or uniform motion in a straight line unless acted upon by an external force, such as friction or gravity. (This tendency is called inertia.) 2. The acceleration produced when a force acts on a body is directly proportional to the force applied and inversely proportional to the mass of the body: the stronger the force and the lower the mass, the greater the acceleration. 3. To every action, there is an equal and opposite reaction: for example, a bullet forces a gun to recoil as strongly as the gun forces the bullet forwards. The whole of classical MECHANICS is based on these laws. (See also ACCELERATION, FORCE, INERTIA, MASS, MOMENTUM and VELOCITY.)

nitrogen Colourless, odourless gas which makes up 80 per cent of the atmosphere. Nitrogen compounds can be ACIDS (for example nitric acid HNO_3) or ALKALIS (ammonia NH_3). These compounds are of great importance in nature as essential components of proteins and DNA. Oxides of nitrogen include nitrogen dioxide (NO_2), a pollutant emitted by car exhausts, and nitrous oxide or laughing gas (N_2O). Nitrogen salts (nitrates and nitrites) are widely used in the manufacture of explosives, fertilizers and dyes.

noble gases Group of gases that make up group 0 of the PERIODIC TABLE. They are also known as the inert gases because of their lack of chemical reactivity. The most important is HELIUM; the others are neon, argon, krypton, xenon and radon. They glow in bright colours when an electric discharge is passed through them, and are used for the 'neon' lighting so popular in advertising.

normal distribution curve Important concept in STATISTICS. It is also known as the 'bell' curve because of its shape. Many natural phenomena, such as the height of the population or the weight of a species of animal, have a 'nomal distribution', where most results will fall close to the central mean value; a few will vary by quite a wide margin.

nova Star that suddenly increases in brightness by around 10 000 times, becoming visible to the naked eye; the word *nova* is Latin for 'new'. The star is not destroyed by the eruption, although it loses some of its mass. It gradually fades again over a period of years. Novas (or novae) are thought to occur when an old WHITE DWARF star pulls material from

BELL-SHAPED CURVE *Adult male height is an example of a characteristic that produces a 'normal' distribution curve when plotted on a graph. Statisticians use this curve to evaluate the results of samples and to test theories about such things as the effectiveness of drugs or whether diet affects height.*

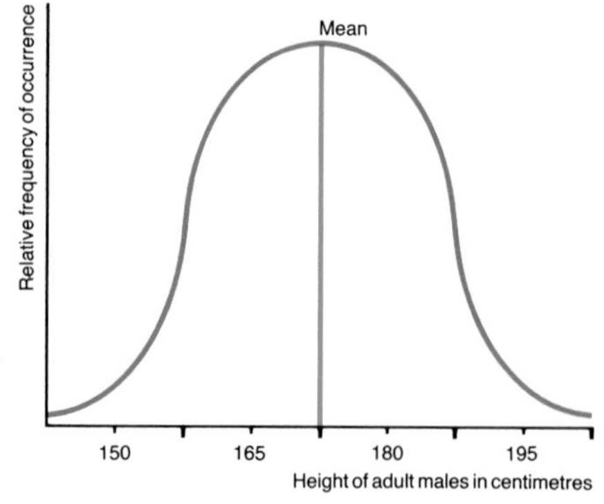

its companion in a BINARY STAR system and starts burning again. (Compare SUPERNOVA.)

nuclear energy Energy released during reactions involving the atomic nucleus. When light atomic nuclei fuse together (NUCLEAR FUSION) or when large nuclei split apart (NUCLEAR FISSION), a small proportion of the mass of the atoms concerned is converted into energy according to Einstein's mass-energy equation $E = MC^2$. Since c (the speed of light) is so great, the conversion of tiny amounts of mass produce huge quantities of energy.

nuclear fission Splitting of heavy atomic nuclei into smaller fragments. In the process, a small amount of mass is converted into a very large amount of nuclear energy. Most ▷NUCLEAR REACTORS use the fission of a uranium isotope, U235, or a plutonium isotope, P238, as their source of power. The reaction is initiated when a NEUTRON strikes the uranium or plutonium nucleus. This splits, releasing three more neutrons, which may then go on to split further nuclei in a 'chain reaction'. Provided there is a sufficient 'critical mass' of fuel present, an uncontrolled chain reaction rapidly builds up to an awesome explosion, as in the atomic bomb. However, if some of the neutrons are absorbed, it is possible to control the reaction and to allow a steady release of energy, which can be used to produce electricity in a nuclear power station. Nuclear fission produces many highly radioactive by-products and ▷NUCLEAR WASTE disposal is a matter of concern. (Compare NUCLEAR FUSION.)

nuclear fusion The combining of light atomic nuclei to form larger ones; in practice, it usually refers to the fusion of two nuclei of deuterium or tritium (ISOTOPES of hydrogen) to form a helium nucleus. The nuclear energy released in the transformation is even greater than that produced by fission. It is the source of the Sun's energy and is used in the hydrogen bomb. Fusion produces very little in the way of radioactive by-products and would offer a clean source of energy for millions of years to come, since deuterium is easily extracted from sea water. However, the reaction is only known to take place at temperatures approaching those in the interior of the Sun, and there is no known material that could act as a container. Nuclear physicists are experimenting with hot PLASMA suspended in strong magnetic fields and have succeeded in sustaining fusion reactions, generating a few megawatts of power for short periods. (See also COLD FUSION.)

numbers The basis of all counting and measuring. The theory of numbers is a major branch of mathematics, and there are various types of number. The most familiar are the integers or whole numbers, and their derivatives, fractions, which together make up the 'rational numbers'. There are 'irrational numbers' which cannot be expressed in terms of integers, for example π (PI) and the square root of 2 ($\sqrt{2}$). And there are 'imaginary numbers', based on the square root of -1 (or i). Imaginary numbers combined with rational or irrational numbers are called 'complex numbers': equations involving these complex numbers are fundamental to CHAOS THEORY and FRACTAL geometry.

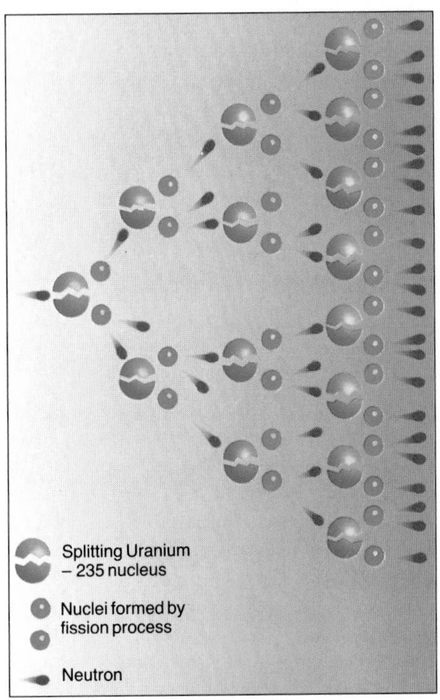

CHAIN REACTION *Once nuclear fission begins, the reaction accelerates, unless checked, culminating in an enormous nuclear explosion.*

octane Liquid HYDROCARBON (C_8H_{18}) found in petroleum. The octane rating of a fuel is a measure of its ability to prevent pre-ignition, or 'knocking' in a motor engine.

ohm Measure of electrical RESISTANCE, named after the German physicist Georg Simon Ohm (1789-1854). Ohm's law states that the current passing through a conductor is proportional to the POTENTIAL DIFFERENCE across it. The law is usually expressed as the formula $v = ir$, where v is the potential difference in VOLTS, i is the current in AMPS and r the resistance in ohms.

orbit Path followed by a celestial object such as a planet or satellite as it revolves around another under the influence of gravity. Orbits are always elliptical. The point at which the orbit approaches closest to the parent body is the 'perigee' (or perihelion in the case of the Sun); the point at which it is the farthest is the 'apogee' (aphelion).

organic chemistry Major branch of chemistry dealing with the compounds of CARBON, which are more numerous than those of all the other elements put together. Organic compounds make up the fabric of living things. They are subdivided into two main groups: 'aliphatic' compounds, in which the carbon atoms are joined in straight or branching chains; and 'aromatic' compounds (so called because they often have a pleasant aroma), based on BENZENE which has a ring structure. Most organic compounds also contain hydrogen. A few very simple carbon compounds, for example the metallic carbonates, are considered inorganic.

❖ Until the early 19th century it was thought that organic compounds could be produced only by living things. But in 1828, the German chemist Friedrich Wöhler succeeded in producing urea, an organic compound, from ammonium cyanate, which is inorganic.

osmosis Tendency of a solvent (usually water) to diffuse through a membrane until the concentrations of the solutions on either side of the membrane are equal. For this to happen, the membrane needs to be semi-permeable as it is in living tissues, particularly cell walls. Osmosis allows the passage of the solvent but not the solute (dissolved substance), such as proteins or sugars. Osmosis can lead to considerable differences in pressure on either side of the membrane. It is osmotic pressure that keeps plant cells rigid; its loss through lack of water leads to wilting.

oxidation Combining of an element with oxygen. Familiar examples are the burning of fossil fuels, in which carbon is oxidized to carbon dioxide, and rusting when iron is oxidized to ferric oxide. All living things derive their energy from oxidation reactions of one sort or another, usually by 'burning' ▷GLUCOSE inside the cell during ▷RESPIRATION. Technically, oxidation involves the removal of electrons from an atom, and is accompanied by its opposite – a REDUCTION reaction.

oxygen Colourless, odourless gas, the most abundant element on Earth. It makes up about 20 per cent of the weight of the atmosphere, about 90 per cent of the water and about 50 per cent of the Earth's crust; uncombined, it normally forms molecules containing two atoms (O_2). However, it combines readily with most other elements to form oxides. Metallic oxides are mostly BASES in solution; nonmetallic oxides are ACIDS. Oxygen

FUNDAMENTAL PHYSICS *The Large Electron-Positron (LEP) collider, 100 m below ground on the French-Swiss border north of Geneva, is Europe's largest particle accelerator or 'atom smasher'.*

is produced by plants during ▷PHOTOSYNTHESIS and is consumed by plants and animals during ▷RESPIRATION.

ozone (O_3) Form of OXYGEN containing three atoms in each molecule rather than the usual two. It has a characteristic pungent odour and is blue in concentrated form. Formed by the action of electrical discharges (such as lightning) or of ultraviolet light on ordinary oxygen, it is a harmful component of photochemical ▷SMOG. In the Earth's atmosphere, the ▷OZONE LAYER filters out ultraviolet radiation from the Sun.

parabola Path traced out by any projectile, such as a golf ball, which is propelled away from the Earth and then drawn back by gravity. Dish aerials are often parabolic in cross-section, as are the mirrors used in reflecting telescopes, since they focus radiation to a point. (See CONIC SECTIONS.)

parallax Apparent shift in the position of an object when viewed from two different places. Viewing close objects first through one eye and then the other provides one example. Parallax techniques are used in astronomy to measure the distance of stars.

particle accelerator Essential tool of modern theoretical physics, also known as an 'atom smasher'. Particle accelerators are used to accelerate SUBATOMIC PARTICLES to speeds approaching that of light so that physicists can study what happens when they collide, and gain greater understanding of the nature of matter and energy. The particles are accelerated by powerful electromagnets either in linear accelerators in a straight line or, in the more common cyclotrons and synchrocyclotrons, in a circular tunnel. The principal particle accelerator in Europe, with a tunnel 27 km long, is at the headquarters of CERN (*Conseil Européen pour Recherches Nucléaires* – the European Council for Nuclear Research) near Geneva.

periodic table Method of arranging the chemical elements in order of their ATOMIC NUMBERS, in such a way that the members of each vertical group show markedly similar properties, and horizontal rows show regular variations in properties going from left to right. Thus the elements in group 1, starting with lithium, sodium and potassium, are all METALS and highly reactive; moving to the right, the elements become less and less metallic and eventually become such typical nonmetals as carbon, sulphur and chlorine. The 'periodic' nature of the table is due to the fact that the number of electrons in the outer shell of an atom determines its chemical properties (see VALENCE); elements in each vertical group have the same number of electrons in their outer shells, while each horizontal period has one more electron shell than the previous one. Some groups of elements have the same numbers of electrons in the outer shell, but different numbers in the penultimate shell. These are the TRANSITION ELEMENTS in groups 1b to 7b and 8. There are also two groups, the lanthanide series or rare earths, and the radioactive actinide series, which are both transition series within the main transition series.

pH A measure of the strength of an ACID or BASE. It is based on the concentration of hydrogen IONS in a solution; the higher the concentration, the lower the pH. Pure water has a pH of 7, acid solutions less than 7, and alkaline ones greater than 7.

phlogiston Substance once thought to be given off during combustion and which, when recombined with ash, would reconstitute the original substance. The phlogiston theory was a basic principle of 18th-century chemistry, until it was discredited by the French chemist Antoine LAVOISIER.

photoelectricity Change in the electrical properties of a material when struck by light or some other form of ELECTROMAGNETIC RADIATION. It generally refers to the photoelectric effect in which light waves release electrons where they strike the material, thus creating a current. The principle is extensively used to motivate devicies in outer space.

photon A 'particle', or quantum, of light or other form of electromagnetic energy. (See PLANCK'S CONSTANT, QUANTUM MECHANICS.)

physics Scientific study of MATTER and ENERGY and the ways in which they interact. It has traditionally been concerned with MECHANICS, ELECTRICITY and MAGNETISM, HEAT and LIGHT. During the 20th century many of the fundamental principles of physics have been challenged. The result has been the development of many new areas of study, among them SUBATOMIC PARTICLES, QUANTUM MECHANICS and RELATIVITY.

pi (π) Symbol for the ratio of the circumference of any circle to its diameter. It is an irrational number – that is, it cannot be written exactly as a fraction or a decimal. It is approximately equal to 3,14 or $^{22}/_{7}$.

Planck's constant Universal constant, of fundamental importance in QUANTUM MECHANICS. It relates the energy E of a quantum of radiation to its frequency v by the formula $E = hv$, where h is Planck's constant. It is named after the German physicist Max Planck (1858-1947), who in 1900 provided the first satisfactory explanation for one of the puzzles of classical physics – why light sometimes behaves like a wave and sometimes like a particle.

planet Any of the nine major bodies orbiting the Sun in the SOLAR SYSTEM. The name comes from the ancient Greek word for 'wanderer'. It is probable that many other stars have planetary systems.

plasma Gas at very high temperatures or pressure in which electrons have been split from their atoms, leaving positively charged IONS and free electrons. Plasma is sometimes referred to as the fourth state of matter. Plasmas are the focus of research into controlled NUCLEAR FUSION. In biology and medicine, plasma refers to the liquid part of blood, minus the red and white blood cells.

Pluto Smallest planet in the SOLAR SYSTEM and usually farthest from the Sun. However, it has a highly elliptical 248-earth-year orbit and for part of the time – between 1979 and 1999, for example – it is closer to the Sun than Neptune. Its discovery in 1930 was predicted by theory to account for observed irregularities in Neptune's orbit.

polarized light Light in which its vibrations, which normally occur in all directions at right angles to its path, have been reduced to a single plane. Much of the light around us is partly polarized by reflection; sunglasses with polarizing lenses filter out this polarized light, thus reducing glare. Two such lenses placed on top of and at right angles to each other block out light entirely.

polymer Very large molecule made up of many repeating subunits, or monomers. Naturally occurring polymers include ▷PROTEINS, ▷CELLULOSE and nucleic acids. Synthetic polymers include ▷PLASTICS and synthetic fibres.

potential difference Electrical 'pressure', analagous to a difference in water levels that causes a current to flow. It is also referred to as the electromotive force (emf). It is measured in VOLTS.

power In mathematics, the indication of the number of times a number must be multiplied by itself. Thus 2^3 or two to the power of three, is $2 \times 2 \times 2$, or 8; similarly 10^6 is $10 \times 10 \times 10 \times 10 \times 10 \times 10$, or 1 million. The number representing the power is called the exponent. Any number to power 0 is, by definition, equal to 1. Different powers of the same number can be multiplied by adding their exponents together, or divided by subtracting one exponent from the other. For example, $2^3 \times 2^3 = 2^6 = 64$; $2^3 - 2^2 = 2^1 = 2$. (See LOGARITHMS.) In physics, power is the rate of doing WORK, generally involving the conversion of energy into a useful form, such as movement, with a loss of heat. It is measured in JOULES per second, or WATTS.

precession Wobbling of the Earth in space. Also the cyclic movement of the axis of rotation of any spinning body, such as a ▷GYROSCOPE or spinning top, when subjected to a TORQUE or turning force. The Earth's axis, for example, traces out a cone every 26 000 years because of the pull of the Sun and Moon on

TABLE OF THE ELEMENTS *The chemical elements were first organized into a periodic table by the Russian chemist Dmitri Mendeleyev in 1869. A modern version, below, shows the elements arranged in horizontal rows in sequence of atomic number and divided into vertical groups of similar elements.*

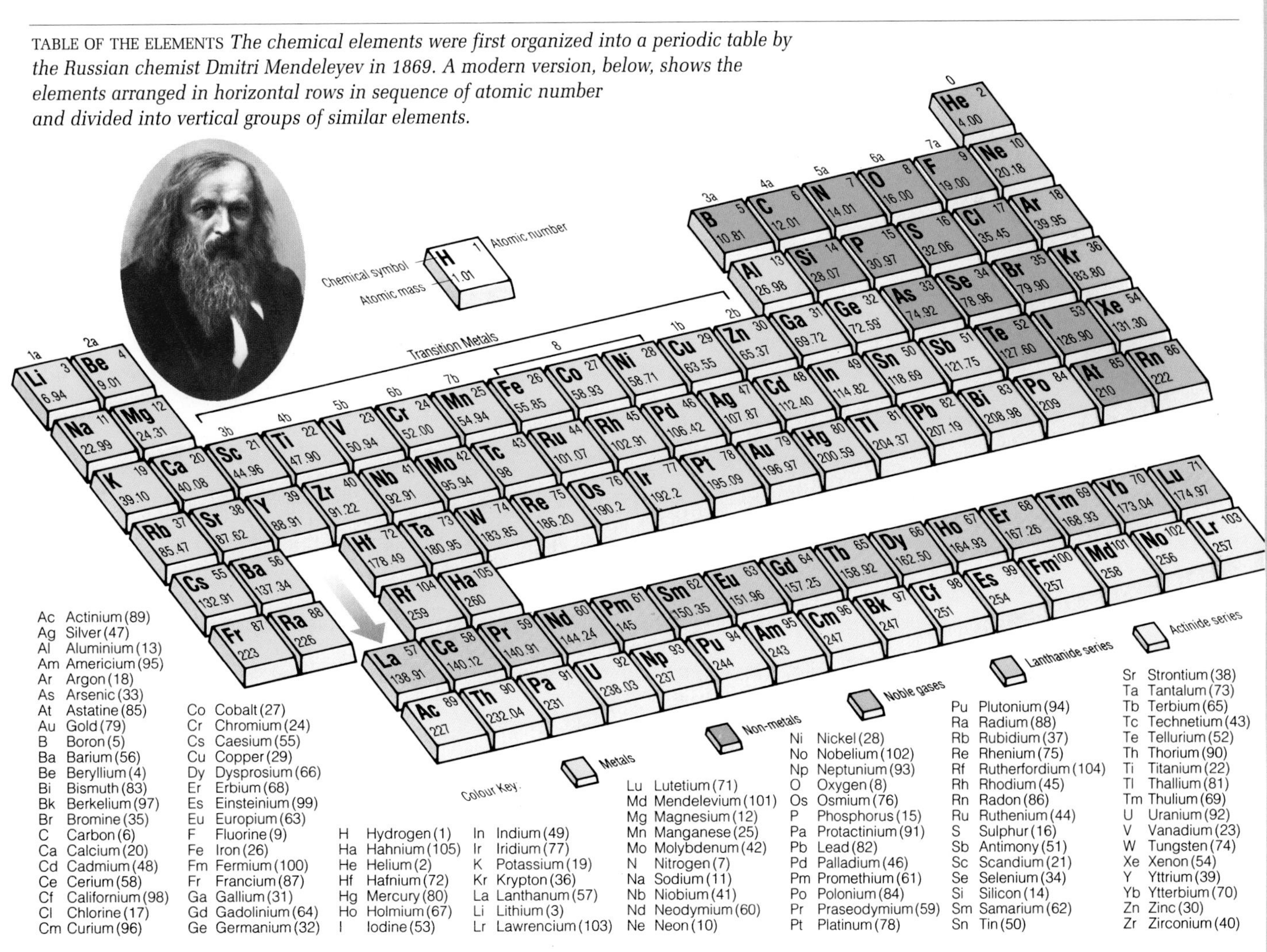

its equatorial bulge. This causes a gradual change in the apparent positions of the stars.

pressure The FORCE per unit area acting on a surface. The standard scientific unit of pressure is the pascal (Pa), named after the French scientist and religious philosopher Blaise Pascal (1623-62). One pascal is equal to a force of one newton (1 N) acting on a surface of one square metre (1 m^2). Pressure is transmitted uniformly in all directions. A force applied to one part of a fluid system can therefore be made to do WORK in another; this is the basis of ▷HYDRAULICS. In a gas, pressure is the result of molecules striking the walls of the container. For a fixed mass of gas, pressure increases with temperature and decreases with increasing volume (see BOYLE'S LAW).

prime number Number larger than 1 that cannot be divided by any whole numbers other than itself and 1. The theory that every even number above 2 is the sum of two primes has never been proved, but no exceptions have ever been found.

probability The chance that a particular event will occur, usually expressed as a number between 0 (no chance at all) and 1 (certainty) or as the ratio between the number of outcomes that give a specific result and the number of possible outcomes. For example, the probability of throwing an even number at dice is $^3/_6$ or 0,5, since a dice has six numbers, three of which are even.

proton A SUBATOMIC PARTICLE found in the nucleus of the atom. It has equal but opposite (positive) charge to the ELECTRON, but about 1 000 times the mass. The number of protons is equal to the ATOMIC NUMBER of an element.

Ptolemy (Claudius Ptolemaeus) (*c*90-168) Alexandrian astronomer and mathematician who synthesized Greek astronomical knowledge in the *Almagest,* producing the so-called Ptolemaic system of the Universe. This system, in which the Sun and planets were held to orbit the Earth, dominated astronomy for 1 500 years, until the Sun-centred system proposed by COPERNICUS gained acceptance. Ptolemy also wrote extensively on astrology, geography and map-making.

pulsar Rapidly rotating NEUTRON STAR which emits a bright beam of radiation as it rotates, like a flashing lighthouse. Pulsars were discovered in 1967 and more than 600 are now known. Pulsar is short for 'pulsating radio star'; most pulsars emit at radio wavelengths, although other wavelengths have been detected. The fastest pulsars emit pulses more than 500 times a second.

Pythagoras's theorem Statement that the square on the hypotenuse (longest side) of a right-angled triangle is equal to the sum of the squares on the other two sides – expressed algebraicially as $a^2 + b^2 = c^2$. It was proved by the Greek philosopher and mathematician Pythagoras in the 6th century BC, but had been applied earlier by Egyptian builders. The simplest example is a triangle with sides of 3, 4 and 5 units. Pythagoras also discovered the mathematical relationships between the intervals of the musical scale.

quantum mechanics Fundamental theory of physics which, together with the theory of RELATIVITY, forms the basis of much of 20th-century science. It states that energy can be released or absorbed only in discrete packets or quanta – the PHOTON, for example, is a quantum of light energy. An electron in orbit round an atom does not move smoothly from one energy level to another, but performs a 'quantum leap', emitting or absorbing a photon as it does so. This simple premise has far-reaching consequences. One of these is the UNCERTAINTY PRINCIPLE, which states that it is impossible to know the position and the MOMENTUM of a particle simultaneously. So the wavelike behaviour of light and electrons represents a 'graph' of the probabilities of a particle or quantum being in a particular place at a particular time. Essentially, the behaviour of matter becomes a question of probabilities. Quantum mechanics accords well with classical physics for large-scale phenomena, but at the subatomic level and at extreme temperatures only quantum mechanics can explain such puzzles as the superfluidity of HELIUM, SUPERCONDUCTIVITY, the behaviour of ▷SEMICONDUCTORS, PHOTOELECTRICITY and the ability of an electron or photon to be in two places at the same time. The modern view of atomic structure and chemical elements is based on quantum theory.
❖ Einstein could not accept the role of chance in this marrying of quantum mechanics with the theory of relativity, saying 'God does not play dice' with the Universe.

quarks Fundamental constituents of matter from which certain heavy SUBATOMIC PARTICLES, notably PROTONS and NEUTRONS, are built. They are endowed with properties that have been given such names as colour, flavour and charm. Some claims have been made for the observation of quarks, which were posited in 1963 by US physicist Murray Gell-Mann and named on a whim from the phrase 'three quarks for Muster Mark' in James Joyce's *Finnegans Wake.*

quasar Intensely brilliant starlike object – the name is short for quasi-stellar object. Quasars appear to be receding from us at close to the speed of light; if so, they would be the brightest and most distant objects in the Universe. They are thought to be the bright centres of galaxies containing huge BLACK HOLES.

radiation Energy sent out in the form of particles or waves. The term is applied to ELECTROMAGNETIC RADIATION as well as SOUND, but it more often refers to RADIOACTIVITY, when it takes three forms: alpha radiation consists of the ejection of two protons and two neutrons – an alpha particle – from a decaying atomic nucleus; beta radiation is composed of high-energy electrons, emitted when a neutron decays into a proton and a corresponding electron; and GAMMA RADIATION is a highly energetic and penetrating form of electromagnetic radiation, which may accompany both alpha and beta radiation.

radioactivity Emission of RADIATION as a result of the spontaneous disintegration of unstable atomic nuclei. Every chemical element has at least one radioactive ISOTOPE (or radioisotope), although only around 50 occur in nature. The others have been produced artificially in PARTICLE ACCELERATORS or as the by-products of NUCLEAR FISSION in power stations and atomic bombs. Radioactivity was discovered in uranium compounds by the French physicist Henri Becquerel in 1896 – the unit of radioactivity, the becquerel (Bq), is named after him. Radioisotopes are of great value in many branches of science, industry and medicine. They can be used to 'label' chemical compounds so that their progress in chemical reactions, or their fate inside the body, can be tracked. They can also be used to kill cancerous tumours. However, radioactivity can also be extremely hazardous to human health, causing birth defects, ▷RADIATION SICKNESS as well as cancer. Because radioisotopes may have a HALF-LIFE of thousands of years, they present considerable problems of disposal.

radio waves Form of ELECTROMAGNETIC RADIATION with the longest wavelengths (between 30 cm and 100 km) and the lowest frequencies in the electromagnetic spectrum. Because they pass through the atmosphere and obstacles such as buildings, they are used for the transmission of radio and television broadcasts. Longer wavelengths are also reflected by the upper layers of the atmosphere, allowing communication around the world.

red giant Large and luminous star which is reaching the end of its life. The Sun will begin to expand once it has exhausted the hydrogen fuel in its core – in about 5 000 million years' time – becoming a red giant

THE COLOURS OF LIGHT *The ability of a prism to split light into its spectrum by refraction was first demonstrated by Isaac Newton.*

100 times larger than it is now, before finally collapsing to form a WHITE DWARF.

red shift Increase in the wavelength of light reaching us from distant stars and galaxies. It is similar to the DOPPLER EFFECT: just as the pitch of a receding police siren falls, so light from a star is shifted towards the red end of the spectrum as it travels away from us. Red shift was discovered by the American astronomer Edwin HUBBLE, and demonstrated that distant galaxies are receding at rates that approach the speed of light. It provides the main evidence for the BIG BANG THEORY.

reduction Removal of oxygen, or a similar element, from a compound. All reduction reactions involve a corresponding OXIDATION reaction and the two are often referred to as a 'redox' reaction.

reflection Bouncing of a ray of light, or other wave, off a surface. From a smooth surface, such as a mirror, the reflected ray makes the same angle to the perpendicular as the arriving, or incident, ray. Reflected sound waves are familiar as echoes.

refraction Bending of a ray of light, or other form of energy wave, when it passes from one transparent medium to another, for example from air to water. Refraction is responsible for the apparent bending of a drinking straw at the point where it enters a glass of water. It is also the mechanism by which a LENS is able to form enlarged or reduced images. The amount by which the light is bent depends on its wavelength; red is refracted least and violet most. Refraction of light by a prism produces the SPECTRUM, just as raindrops split light to form a ▷RAINBOW. Light striking a surface at an angle greater than the 'critical angle' is not refracted but reflected.

relativity, theory of Fundamental theory of physics concerned with the nature of time, space and motion, put forward as the 'special theory of relativity' in 1905 by Albert EINSTEIN. It is based on the startling assumption that the speed of light is constant whatever the speed of the observer – it does not appear to travel faster even if the observer is moving rapidly towards it. Similarly, all other laws of physics will appear to be the same to all observers moving at constant relative velocities with respect to each other. The consequences of these assumptions are far-reaching. The theory predicts that time will move more slowly on a fast-moving object; a moving clock, for example, will run more slowly than a stationary one. Other predictions are that a body's mass will increase with speed while its length will decrease, and that mass and energy are equivalent (see $E = MC^2$). If a body were able to travel at the speed of light (which is impossible), it would have infinite mass, zero length and time on it would come to a standstill. These predictions have been proved over and over again, and it is now accepted that the classical physics expressed by NEWTON'S LAWS OF MOTION, while adequate to explain most earthbound events, does not apply to the Universe as a whole. In 1915, Einstein put forward the 'general theory of relativity', in which he demonstrated that GRAVITATION and ACCELERATION are equivalent – an observer standing in a lift cannot tell whether the force pressing him to the floor is due to gravity or to upward acceleration of the lift. Since a beam of light would appear to be bent as seen by an accelerating observer, so too should it be bent by gravity. This has been confirmed by observation and leads to the conclusion that space itself is curved.

resistance Property of a material that makes it impede the passage of an electric current. It is calculated as the POTENTIAL DIFFERENCE in volts across a circuit, or part of a circuit, divided by the current in AMPS. It is measured in OHMS.

resonance Reinforcement of the natural frequency of vibration of an object when a force is applied with the same frequency. Soldiers break step when crossing a bridge in case their marching rhythm corresponds with the natural frequency of the bridge, which could cause it to vibrate to the point of collapse. Singers can break wine glasses by singing loudly a note with a frequency equal to the natural frequency of the glass.

Roman numerals Numbers represented by combinations of letters, rather than by the more familiar ARABIC NUMERALS. The letter I is equivalent to 1, V to 5, X to 10, L to 50, C to 100, D to 500 and M to 1 000. Intermediate numbers are derived by adding succeeding letters together, except where a smaller letter is followed by a larger one, when the smaller is subtracted from the larger. Thus 8 is written as VIII and 9 as IX. The date 1066 would be written as MLXVI, while 1999 would be written MCMIC.

Rutherford, Ernest (Baron Rutherford of Nelson) (1871-1937) New Zealand-born physicist who, in 1919, was the first to split the atomic nucleus by converting nitrogen into oxygen and hydrogen. His work at the Cavendish Laboratory, Cambridge, provided the groundwork for the modern understanding of RADIOACTIVITY and the structure of the ATOM, and extended the foundations of nuclear physics.

salt Chemical compound formed by the reaction of equivalent quantities of an ACID and a BASE. Common salt or sodium chloride (NaCl) is formed by the reaction of hydrochloric acid (HCl) with sodium hydroxide (NaOH). Most minerals are salts.

SPLITTING THE ATOM *Ernest Rutherford in his laboratory. He achieved the alchemist's dream of transmutation of the elements.*

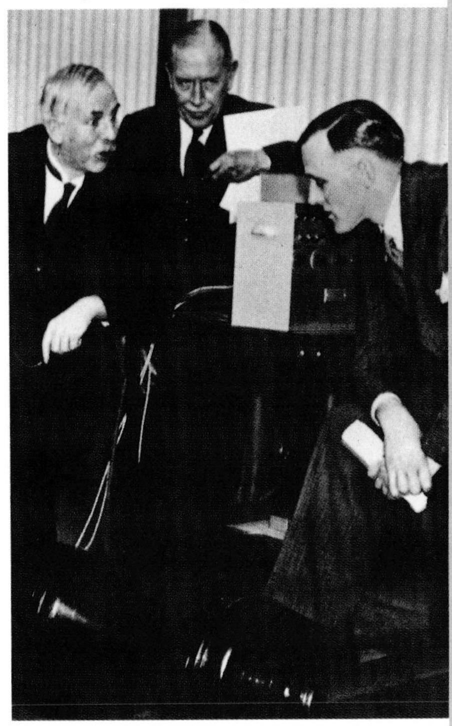

Saturn Sixth planet from the Sun and the most distant visible to the naked eye. It is famous for its rings, which may represent material left over from its formation. It is the second largest planet in the SOLAR SYSTEM, with a mass about 95 times greater than Earth's, but since it is largely composed of hydrogen and helium gases, it is also the least dense. It has a 'year' of 29,46 Earth years and a 'day' of just over 10 hours. It has more than 20 moons, the largest of which, Titan, is about the size of Mercury.

set theory Branch of mathematics that deals with numbers or objects as members of distinct groups or sets. Thus the pupils in a school (the 'universal' set) would contain any number of subsets, for example red-haired pupils, male pupils, female pupils and blue-eyed pupils. In some cases, the sets overlap – some red-haired pupils will also be female and have blue eyes. In other cases they will have no members in common – no female pupils will be male pupils. These relationships can be represented algebraically by BOOLEAN ALGEBRA and visually by VENN DIAGRAMS. Set theory provides the basic language and structure for most branches of modern mathematics. It is also basic to the creation of all computer programs.

silicon Second commonest element (after oxygen), known chiefly for its widespread use as a ▷SEMICONDUCTOR in the electronics industry. It occurs mainly as silica (which includes quartz, one of the chief constituents of sand and glass) and as silicates – some 95 per cent of the Earth's crust is composed of silicate minerals.

❖ It has been suggested that alternative forms of extraterrestrial life might be built on a framework of silicon, just as life on Earth is based on carbon compounds.

SI units Abbreviation for *Système International d'Unités*, the internationally accepted standard for units of measure since 1960. Examples include the METRE (length), the KILOGRAM (mass) and the JOULE (energy).

solar system The SUN and all the celestial objects held by its gravity. These include the nine major PLANETS, including EARTH, and their moons as well as countless ASTEROIDS, COMETS and METEORS.

solar wind Stream of electrically charged SUBATOMIC PARTICLES boiled off from the surface of the Sun. It is responsible for the tails of comets. Gusts of solar wind, caused by solar flares, interact with the Earth's magnetic field and with charged particles in the air, causing auroras and radio interference.

solstice Time of year when the overhead Sun is at its greatest angle to the Equator. At the winter solstice, around 21 June, the Sun is directly overhead at the Tropic of Cancer at noon and the southern hemisphere has its shortest day. At the summer solstice, around 22 December, it is overhead at the Tropic of Capricorn, and the southern hemisphere has its longest day. (See EQUINOX.)

sound Form of WAVE motion which can be detected by the ear. It depends on the physical displacement of a medium, for example air, for transmission and, unlike light and other types of electromagnetic radiation, sound cannot travel in a vacuum. The FREQUENCY of a sound wave determines the pitch of the sound; the AMPLITUDE determines its loudness. The speed of sound through air varies with the conditions, but is about 1 220 km/h at sea level. An aircraft flying close to this speed builds up waves of pressure in front of it, like the bow wave of a boat. When it passes through the sound barrier, the waves are released as a sonic boom.

space-time Concept arising from the theory of RELATIVITY, in which time and the three dimensions of space are treated as a single space-time continuum. It recognizes that both space and time are defined by the SPEED OF LIGHT. Einstein used the idea of the curvature of the space-time continuum to explain the action of gravity.

spectroscopy Analysis of the SPECTRUM of light or other forms of ELECTROMAGNETIC RADIATION emitted or absorbed by a substance in order to investigate its structure. Different atoms and molecules produce distinctive lines in the spectrum. Astronomers examine the light from distant stars to analyse their composition and chemists can analyse complex compounds.

spectrum Bands of colour produced when a beam of white light is passed through a prism and split into its component wavelengths. All forms of ELECTROMAGNETIC RADIATION can be split up into a spectrum. Examination of spectra by SPECTROSCOPY yields valuable information about the structure and composition of substances. (See LIGHT, REFRACTION.)

speed Rate of change of distance with respect to time, calculated on the distance travelled divided by the time elapsed. Unlike VELOCITY, speed is independent of direction.

SUN AND PLANETS *The Sun dominates the solar system, making up more than 99 per cent of its total mass. Its gravitational attraction is strong enough to keep tiny Pluto in orbit, at the extreme edge of the observable solar system, between 4 350 and 7 400 million km away. The solar system is thought to have formed about 4 700 million years ago, when a cloud of gas and dust contracted to create an extremely compact centre which was surrounded by a disc of particles, that very slowly coalesced into Earth and the other major planets.*

speed of light Universal physical constant, approximately equal to 299 792 km/s in a vacuum. (See also LIGHT and RELATIVITY.)

standard deviation In STATISTICS, a measure of how closely an average, or mean, represents the individuals in a population. If most people earn well below or well above average income, for example, the standard deviation is high; if most earn around the mean value, the standard deviation is low. (See MEAN, MEDIAN AND MODE, NORMAL DISTRIBUTION CURVE.)

star Ball of hot, luminous gases fuelled by nuclear reactions at its core. The SUN is a fairly typical medium-sized star. Stars are thought to form when clouds of interstellar dust and gases draw together and start to contract under the influence of their own gravity. Eventually, the compressed core becomes hot enough for NUCLEAR FUSION to begin. This generates sufficient energy to halt the contraction and the star continues to burn for anything from a million to many billions of years, depending on how large it is and how brightly it burns. When all its HYDROGEN has been converted to HELIUM, gravity again contracts the core until it reaches the temperature at which the conversion of helium into CARBON begins. This generates so much heat that the star's outer layers expand considerably. The star becomes a RED GIANT. Finally, when even the helium has gone, there is nothing to stop the star from collapsing to form a WHITE DWARF. For very massive stars, however, the process ends differently. The fusion reactions in the core can become so violent that the star explodes in a SUPERNOVA, throwing off most of its outer layers – when the radiation is so intense that it can briefly outshine a galaxy – and leaving a dense NEUTRON STAR behind. Even this may not be the end for the most massive stars of all. In a star having more than 10 times the mass of the Sun the collapse of the core may be so extreme that the whole mass collapses into a single point – a singularity, or BLACK HOLE. The gravitational field of such a star is so intense that it prevents radiation, or light, from escaping and it can be detected only indirectly by the X-rays given off when matter from a companion star is dragged into it.

static electricity An ELECTRIC CHARGE that has built up on an object, either because rubbing it has dislodged some of its electrons, or because a charge has been induced by an opposite static charge nearby. People sometimes pick up a static charge from the friction of their shoes against certain types of carpet. Static is also responsible for ▷LIGHTNING.

❖ Static electricity was well known to the Greeks, who noticed that a piece of amber rubbed with a cloth would pick up small pieces of fluff.

statistics Branch of mathematics concerned with the collection and analysis of large quantities of data, particularly where the data are of a kind that cannot be predicted with any accuracy. It is of great importance in fundamental physics, economics, the social sciences, market research, drug testing and in the framing of many aspects of public policy. Statistics provides a way of analysing the factors that affect a situation. Many variables affect road safety, for example, but statistics may indicate which ones are most closely correlated with the accident rate and so suggest the most effective preventive measures. It also provides a way of estimating the significance of a set of data, particularly one drawn from a sample, when it differs from the expected or normal result. A high incidence of a disease in a particular area might happen by chance, or there might be environmental factors involved; statistical analysis

will indicate how likely it is that there is an environmental cause, and provides the tools for identifying the factors involved. (See also MEAN, MEDIAN AND MODE, NORMAL DISTRIBUTION CURVE.)

steady-state theory Proposition that the Universe has no beginning and no end, but has always looked much the same in all directions and from all points in space. The Universe is expanding, but new matter is constantly being created to fill the void. This theory, associated with Sir Fred Hoyle, Hermann Bondi and Thomas Gold, has now given way to the BIG BANG THEORY.

stress and strain Internal forces produced in a body by the application of an external force (stress) and the deformations that result (strain). There are four types: bending; shearing; stretching and compression; and torsion (twisting). The response of materials to stress and strain is a crucial aspect of engineering.

subatomic particles The fundamental constituents of matter. Several hundred subatomic, or elementary, particles are known, but scientists believe that they fall into three main groups. One group, known as gauge bosons, is responsible for transmitting the fundamental forces of nature; the PHOTON, for example, carries the electromagnetic force. The second group, the hadrons, includes the heavy baryons, for example the proton and the neutron (thought to be composed of QUARKS), as well as lighter particles called mesons. The third group are the leptons, or light particles, which include various types of ELECTRONS and NEUTRINOS. A major goal of modern physics is to incorporate all elementary particles and the universal forces of nature into a single mathematical framework (see UNIFIED FIELD THEORIES).

Sun Star at the centre of the SOLAR SYSTEM. It is an average star, 1 392 000 km in diameter and with a mass about 1 000 times that of the rest of the solar system combined. Like most stars it is composed mainly of hydrogen, most of the remainder – about 30 per cent – being helium. It derives its energy from NUCLEAR FUSION reactions in the core, where the temperature reaches some 15 000 000°C, converting an estimated 600 million tons of hydrogen into helium every second. The Sun's visible surface, the photosphere, with a temperature of around 5 500°C, is a seething cauldron which sends off jets of very hot gas into the surrounding chromosphere, and where relatively dark patches, or SUNSPOTS, are seen periodically. The outer layer, the corona, is a halo of thinly spread material that has boiled off from the surface. The Sun

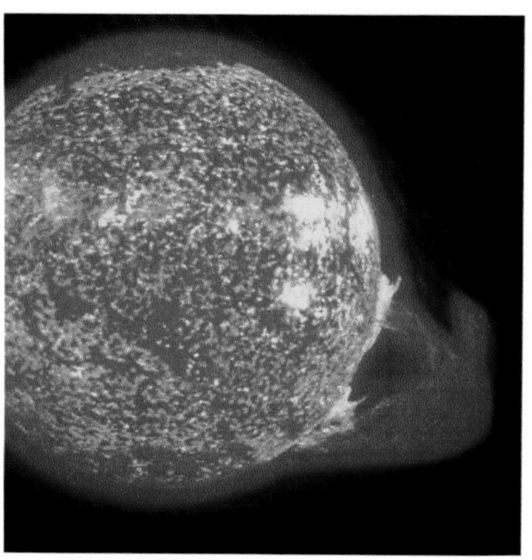

BIG BULGE *A huge prominence on the Sun's surface, etched by lines of magnetic force, was photographed from Skylab in 1973.*

is thought to have formed about 4 700 million years ago. When it has exhausted its nuclear fuel in about 5 000 million years' time, it will expand to become a RED GIANT before finally shrinking to a WHITE DWARF.

sunspot Cooler area on the surface of the Sun, which appears dark by comparison with the surroundings. Sunspots are associated with strong magnetic fields, and with solar flares which send streams of charged particles into the Earth's atmosphere. Here they interact with the Earth's magnetic field, causing auroras and radio blackouts. Sunspots often appear in groups, and their numbers fluctuate in a cycle of about 11 years.

superconductivity Ability of some metals and other materials to conduct electricity with no resistance when cooled to very low temperatures. An electric current in such a material continues to circulate indefinitely. Ceramic materials have been discovered that become superconducting at the relatively high temperature of liquid nitrogen (above –210°C). If these can be incorporated into electrical circuits, superconductors will lead to enormous savings in energy.

❖ Superconductivity was discovered in 1911 by the Dutch physicist Kamerlingh Onnes (1853-1926).

supernova Cosmic explosion of extraordinary violence, in which a massive star (about ten times the mass of the Sun) is destroyed or throws out a substantial part of its mass. The remnant forms a NEUTRON STAR or a BLACK HOLE. For a brief period, the exploding star shines as brightly as 100 million suns and may be clearly visible to the naked eye. A supernova was observed in 1987 in the large MAGELLANIC CLOUD.

surface tension Force of attraction between molecules of a liquid, or between the liquid and its container, which makes the surface behave like a thin elastic skin. It is surface tension that causes water to form small droplets on a polished surface, that draws liquids up CAPILLARY tubes, and that enables pond insects to walk on water.

thermodynamics Branch of physics concerned with the relationships between heat and other forms of energy, including mechanical work. It is important in many industrial and engineering applications, for example in determining the efficiency of vehicle engines or in the design of chemical manufacturing processes. There are three main laws of thermodynamics. The first states that energy can neither be created nor destroyed, merely converted from one form into another; the total energy of an isolated system will remain constant. The second law states that heat will not flow spontaneously from a colder body to a hotter one; the ENTROPY of a self-contained system can never decrease, only increase or remain the same. The third law states the impossibility of achieving the temperature of ABSOLUTE ZERO.

topology Sometimes referred to as 'rubber-sheet' geometry, the study of those properties of figures and shapes that are not changed by stretching and squeezing. The London Underground map, for example, is an example of a topological map. It preserves the connections between lines, and the positions of stations relative to one another, but distorts distance and actual location. Topology is used in a similar way in the design of integrated electronic circuits. In recent years it has developed into an important branch of abstract mathematics, and has played a major role in the development of FRACTAL geometry and CHAOS THEORY.

torque Turning effect of a force on a body able to rotate. Also termed moment of a force, it is measured by multiplying the force by its distance from the centre of rotation. Its unit of measurement is the newton metre (N m). In a car engine, torque is generated by the force the pistons exert on the crankshaft.

transition elements Series of metallic elements that form a separate group within the PERIODIC TABLE. They include many metals that are important in industry, including iron, copper, nickel, zinc, silver and gold. They readily form alloys, and are widely used as CATALYSTS. Their properties are very similar because they have the same number of electrons in their outer shell and differ only in the number of electrons in their inner shells.

triangle Three-sided figure whose internal angles always add up to 180°. A triangle with all its sides and all its angles equal, at 60°, is called an equilateral triangle; one with two sides, or angles, equal is an isosceles triangle; and one with all its sides and angles unequal is a scalene triangle.

trigonometry Branch of geometry that deals with the relationships between the sides and angles of right-angled triangles, and their application in such diverse fields as surveying, navigation and the study of wave forms. If an angle is regarded as being contained within a right-angled triangle, then the ratios between the three sides of the triangle can be calculated. Three main ratios are used: the sine, the cosine and the tangent (usually abbreviated to *sin*, *cos* and *tan*). The sine is particularly important since it is used to analyse such natural wave motions as light and sound.

twin paradox Apparent contradiction predicted by the theory of RELATIVITY. A twin who travels from the Earth at near the speed of light will, when he returns, be younger than his earthbound twin. The effect has been verified using very fast planes and highly accurate atomic clocks.

ultraviolet radiation Form of ELECTROMAGNETIC RADIATION with wavelengths between those of visible light and X-RAYS. It can be detected by its effect on photographic film and by the FLUORESCENCE it produces in certain materials, for example clothes that have been washed in 'whiter than white' detergents. It has powerful effects on living tissues: longer wavelengths produce tanning of the skin and the formation of vitamin D, but shorter wavelengths can be lethal to living tissue and are associated with skin cancer.

❖ Most of the Sun's short-wavelength ultraviolet radiation is filtered out by the ▷OZONE LAYER. Without this protection, most forms of life on Earth would die.

uncertainty principle Statement that it is impossible to measure exactly both the position and the momentum of a particle of matter simultaneously, since the very act of measurement alters the situation at the moment it is being observed. First proposed by the German physicist Werner Heisenberg (1901-76), it became one of the cornerstones of modern QUANTUM MECHANICS. Although the uncertainty is only significant at the subatomic scale, some philosophers have argued that it undermines any attempt to predict the behaviour of the Universe as a whole and that all forms of ▷DETERMINISM are therefore doomed. Recent developments in CHAOS THEORY have given support to this view.

unified field theories Theories that attempt to explain the four different fundamental forces of nature – the strong and weak nuclear forces, electromagnetism and gravity – as aspects of a single natural phenomenon. Current theories interpret forces in terms of the exchange of subatomic particles, although the hypothetical particle that carries the gravitational force – the graviton – has not been found. It is likely that the other three forces can be unified in a 'grand unified theory' (GUT) by treating the particles as 'strings' or 'superstrings' rather than as simple pointlike objects. GUTs are sometimes referred to as 'theories of everything', since they would provide a single theoretical framework for the whole physical Universe.

uranium Radioactive metal, used as a fuel in ▷NUCLEAR REACTORS and the ▷ATOM BOMB. It occurs in the ore pitchblende and has three naturally occurring ISOTOPES. The most stable of the isotopes is U235, with a HALF-LIFE of 710 million years; it undergoes NUCLEAR FISSION when struck by a neutron, and can start a chain reaction. The same process converts U238 to plutonium, which can also be used as a nuclear fuel.

Uranus Seventh planet from the Sun, discovered by the English astronomer William Herschel in 1781; it was the first planet to be discovered by telescope. It is nearly 15 times heavier than Earth, and about four times greater in diameter. It has a 'year' of 84 Earth years, and a 'day' of around 17 hours. Uranus has an ice-coated rocky core, swathed in a thick blanket of hydrogen, helium and methane, which gives the planet a greenish tinge. It was visited by *Voyager 2* in 1986 and revealed to have 15 moons, 10 more than previously thought, and 11 thin rings of rocky debris circling the equator.

vacuum Space that contains no matter. In practice, an absolute vacuum is unachievable since some molecules will always escape from the container's walls. A vacuum is therefore taken to mean a space filled with gas at very low pressure. A vacuum cannot transmit sound, or allow heat to pass by conduction. Vacuum flasks are used to keep liquids hot or cold.

valence Also called valency; the number of chemical BONDS an atom of an element can make when combining with other atoms to form a molecule. Oxygen with a valency of 2 combines with two hydrogen atoms with valencies of 1 to form water, H_2O. Valencies vary according to an element's position in the PERIODIC TABLE, ranging from 1 for the strong metals, such as sodium, and the halogens, such as chlorine, to 4 or higher for such elements as carbon and silicon. Some elements may show more than one valency; nitrogen, for example, may have valencies of 3 or 5.

vector Quantity that is defined in terms of its direction as well as its size. Velocity, acceleration and force are all vector quantities, but speed is not. Two vector quantities, for example the forces of wind and current on a sailing boat, can be combined by drawing a parallelogram whose sides represent the size and magnitude of the forces; the resultant force and its direction are then represented by the diagonal.

velocity Speed in a particular direction; velocity is a VECTOR quantity and, unlike speed, has direction as well as magnitude.

Venn diagram Visual representation of the properties and relationships of sets (see SET THEORY). Each set, for example the set of male pupils or the set of female teachers in a school, is represented by a circle. The circles will overlap when the different sets have members in common; if they have no members in common they will not overlap, as in the case of male pupils and female teachers. The circle representing blue-eyed individuals would, however, overlap with both the other circles, while the set of blue-eyed males would overlap with only one.

Venus Second planet from the Sun, sometimes visible in the east before dawn or in the west at dusk – when it is referred to as the morning or evening star. Venus is similar in size to Earth, but its atmosphere is largely composed of unbreathable carbon dioxide, and the surface is shrouded by thick clouds of corrosive sulphuric acid.

viscosity Friction or drag within a fluid – a liquid or a gas. It determines the speed at which a liquid will flow, and sets limits on the rate at which an object can move through it; a parachutist falls at a speed where the drag of the air is just equal to the force of gravity. When the speed of flow passes a certain point, turbulence sets in – the motion of the particles of gas or liquid becomes chaotic and the viscosity no longer determines the rate of flow.

volt (V) Unit of electrical POTENTIAL DIFFERENCE or electromotive force. It is named after Alessandro Volta (1745-1827), the Italian physicist who invented the first ▷BATTERY. It is defined in such a way that a current of one AMP (1 A) flowing under a potential difference of one volt (1 V) carries a power of one WATT (1 W).

water (H_2O) Colourless, odourless and tasteless liquid, the basis for all the chemical processes of life. In the form of ice and the oceans, it covers about 74 per cent of the Earth's surface. Water owes many of its properties to the strength of the attraction between individual molecules, known as hydrogen bonding. Because of this it is liquid at normal temperatures rather than gaseous, unlike other similar compounds, such as hydrogen sulphide (H_2S). It also reaches maximum density at 4°C and expands when it freezes, so that ice floats on water. It is a good solvent, and conducts electricity fairly well in the presence of dissolved salts. Its capacity to absorb large amounts of heat is one of the main determinants of the Earth's climate.

watt (W) Unit of POWER, equivalent to a rate of energy usage of one JOULE per second (1 J/s). A current of one AMP flowing across a potential difference of one VOLT dissipates one watt of power. The unit is named after the Scottish engineer and steam-engine pioneer James ▷WATT. Power is usually measured in kilowatts (kW) – 1 000 watts – and power consumption is usually measured in kilowatt hours (kWh).

wave Regular disturbance or vibration that travels through a medium or through space and transfers energy but not matter. Light, sound and the ripples on a pond all travel by means of waves. Ripples on water are an example of transverse waves, in which the vibration is at right angles to the direction of travel. A floating cork bobs up and down as a wave passes; it does not travel with the wave. Light and other forms of ELECTROMAGNETIC RADIATION are also transverse waves composed of electrical and magnetic vibrations at right angles to one another. They do not require a medium through which to travel. Sound is an example of a longitudinal wave, in which particles of matter, such as molecules in the air, vibrate from side to side parallel to the direction of travel, forming waves of increasing and decreasing compression. All waves have WAVELENGTH, FREQUENCY and AMPLITUDE. They also show characteristic properties of REFLECTION, REFRACTION, INTERFERENCE and DIFFRACTION. In QUANTUM MECHANICS, the fundamental particles of matter are treated both as particles and as waves. The wavelike behaviour of the electron, for example, makes the electron ▷MICROSCOPE possible.

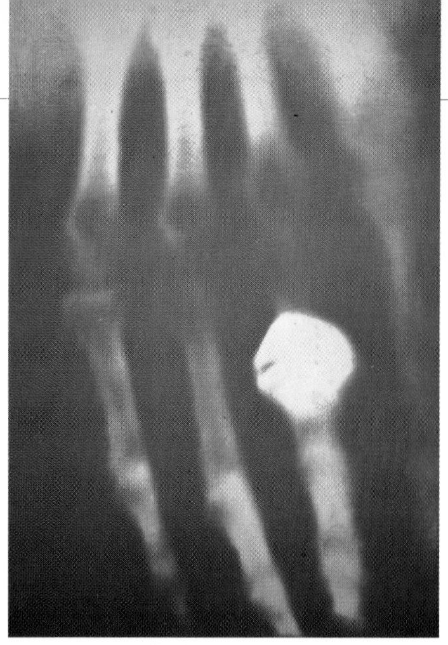

FIRST X-RAY *Wilhelm Roentgen used the radiation he discovered in 1895 to photograph his wife's hand, wedding ring included.*

wavelength Distance between successive peaks or troughs of a wave. As the wavelength increases, the FREQUENCY decreases; the speed of the wave divided by its wavelength is equal to its frequency.

weight The force of gravity acting on an object. It differs from MASS, the amount of matter in a body, in that it varies according to the strength of the gravitational field. An object weighs less at high altitudes or on the Moon, than at the surface of the Earth, although its mass remains constant.

white dwarf Small, hot, dense STAR representing the final stages in the life of a medium-sized star. White dwarfs are now thought to be the contracted cores of RED GIANT stars that have thrown off their expanded outer layers. The material of a white dwarf is so compact that a thimbleful would weigh several tons. White dwarfs cool over billions of years and eventually fade into invisible cinders. They may eventually be formed from stars whose mass is similar to the Sun.

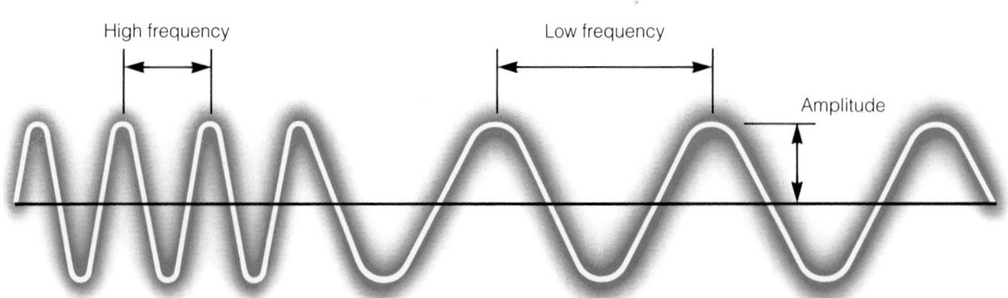

WAVES OF ENERGY *Waves are described in terms of their frequency, wavelength and amplitude. All transmit energy from one place to another. They can also transmit information: both frequency and amplitude can be modulated to carry a coded message to a receiver such as a radio.*

work Application of ENERGY. Like energy, it is measured in JOULES. One joule of work is done when a force of one newton (1 N) acts through a distance of one metre (1 m) in the direction in which the force is being applied. It is also the work done when one WATT of power is expended for one second (1 s).

x-rays Penetrating and highly energetic ELECTROMAGNETIC RADIATION with very short wavelengths. They are capable of passing through considerable thicknesses of material, but are more strongly absorbed by dense materials such as metal or bone than by skin or flesh. This makes them valuable for medical examination, as well as for testing metal structures for cracks or flaws. They are also used in x-ray crystallography, which uses the DIFFRACTION of an intense beam of x-rays to examine the structure of complex biological molecules, such as proteins and DNA.

Zeno's paradoxes A number of statements leading to absurd but apparently inescapable conclusions, which were put forward by the Greek philosopher Zeno of Elea in the 5th century BC. The best known concerns the race between Achilles and a tortoise. Achilles allows the tortoise a 100-m start, and runs ten times as fast as the tortoise; by the time he has reached the tortoise's starting point, the tortoise has gone a further 10 m and by the time he has covered the next 10 m, the tortoise is still a metre ahead; and so on *ad infinitum*. In other words, Achilles can never catch or overtake the tortoise. Similar paradoxes appeared to show that an arrow flying through the air cannot be in motion and that one runner can travel twice as far as another in the same time although they are both running at the same speed. It was not until the 19th century that mathematicians resolved Zeno's paradoxes satisfactorily.

zodiac Band of 12 constellations through which the Sun appears to move during the course of the year: Aries, Taurus, Gemini, Cancer, Leo, Virgo, Libra, Scorpio, Sagittarius, Capricorn, Aquarius and Pisces. The constellations are no longer in the areas covered by their zodiacal signs, because the 'wobbling' of the Earth's axis, causing PRECESSION of the equinoxes, has changed the Sun's apparent path through the stars. (See also ▷ASTROLOGY in 'Myths and legends'.)

TECHNOLOGY AND INVENTION

Early humans became inventors to survive. Their successors helped to create the earliest civilizations, and new tools and technological breakthroughs have followed century by century. In the modern world, faster communications and transport have accelerated innovation worldwide, taking humans into space and increasing the range of their comfort and conveniences on Earth.

MOON WALKER *American astronaut Edwin 'Buzz' Aldrin walks on the Moon where he landed with Neil Armstrong from Apollo 11. Armstrong can be seen reflected in his space helmet visor.*

aerofoil Aeroplane wings, helicopter rotor blades and hydrofoils all have an aerofoil cross-section – curved on top, flat underneath, rounded at the front and tapering to the rear. It is this shape that provides aircraft with enough lift to fly. As the aircraft moves forward, air flows over the wings or blades, and as the air passes over the curved top surface, it speeds up. When air moves faster, its pressure drops. Thus, pressure below the wings or blades exceeds that above it, and the aircraft lifts.

aeroplane The key to aeroplane flight lies in the AEROFOIL cross-section of the wings. Early planes were propelled through the air by propellers, driven by piston engines, but in most modern aircraft, the forward force, or thrust, is provided by JET ENGINES. To climb, descend or turn, the pilot manipulates hinged surfaces at the rear of the wings and tail. To be efficient, aeroplanes must be as light as possible, so they are built from aluminium alloys and, increasingly, from carbon-fibre materials. To keep air resistance (drag) to a minimum, the plane's fuselage is streamlined and the surfaces made as smooth as possible. The shape of aeroplane wings varies. Slow planes, such as the Hercules, which has a cruising speed of 560 km/h, have wings at right angles to the fuselage. Airliners such as the Boeing 767 and the Airbus 320 travel at speeds of up to 900 km/h and have their wings swept back at an angle. The supersonic Anglo-French plane CONCORDE cruises at up to 2 350 km/h and has sharply swept-back wings and a pointed nose to minimize drag. The first aeroplane flight was made by the WRIGHT BROTHERS near Kitty Hawk in North Carolina in 1903.

aerosol can Specialized can, first developed commercially in 1941, which delivers a fine spray. Inside the can, the product – such as hair spray or fire-extinguishing foam – is held under pressure with a propellant gas. When the nozzle is depressed, a valve releases the pressure and allows a mixture of the propellant and contents to spurt out. The propellant evaporates immediately in the air.
❖ Chlorofluorocarbons (▷CFCs) were once common propellants, but were destroying the Earth's ▷OZONE LAYER. They have been largely replaced by isobutanes, believed to be less harmful to the environment.

amplifier Electronic device that takes a weak electric signal and converts it into a stronger one. The amplifier in a stereo system, for example, makes the signal strong enough to power the loudspeakers.

Apollo project American space programme aimed at landing a man on the Moon. The first successful landing took place on 20 July 1969, when Neil ▷ARMSTRONG and Edwin 'Buzz' Aldrin emerged from Apollo 11's lunar module, code-named *Eagle*, to spend 13 hours on the Moon. Michael Collins, the third member of the crew, remained in orbit. Five other successful landings followed, the final mission being Apollo 17 in December 1972. The last three missions took a wheeled 'lunar rover' to transport the astronauts and their equipment over greater distances than earlier missions.
❖ The Apollo missions brought back a total of 383 kg of Moon rock, yielding valuable information about its composition and history. Among the scientific teams chosen to take part in analysing the lunar material was one at the University of Cape Town headed by geochemist Professor Louis Ahrens (1918-90), who received two awards for his work on the samples.

aqualung (scuba [Self-Contained Underwater Breathing Apparatus]) Compact, portable underwater breathing apparatus which allows divers to move freely and to breathe safely at depths of up to 50 m. Compressed air, carried in a cylinder on the diver's back, is delivered to the diver via a device which automatically matches the pressure of the air to that of the surrounding water. It was developed by Jacques Cousteau, a French naval officer and ocean explorer, and Emile Gagnan, an engineer, in 1943. The aqualung enables a diver to stay under water for some 45 minutes, although this depends on depth and breathing rate.

artificial intelligence Branch of computer science concerned with developing ways of imitating by computer aspects of human intelligence, such as learning by experience, solving problems, making decisions, recognizing shapes and understanding language.

AWACS (Airborne Warning And Control System) RADAR equipment, carried in a disclike structure mounted on top of an aircraft's fuselage and used to monitor aircraft movement and to detect missile launches. AWACS planes fly at 9 000 m and can detect targets up to 460 km away.

Babbage, Charles (1792-1871) British mathematician who, in 1834, designed an

TELEVISION PIONEER *John Logie Baird, the Scottish engineer and television inventor, adjusting his wireless vision transmitter.*

'analytical engine' that had many of the features of today's computer. His mechanical device could be programmed, using punched cards, to perform mathematical calculations. The machine was never built, although a small experimental portion was under construction at the time of his death. In 1991 the Science Museum in London built, from Babbage's original plans, a less complex calculating engine – the Difference Engine No 2, designed between 1847 and 1849. The engine works perfectly; it weighs nearly 3 tons.

Baird, John Logie (1888-1946) Scottish inventor and television pioneer. Baird's earliest success came in October 1925, when, using apparatus that included biscuit tins and darning needles, he produced an image of a ventriloquist's dummy on a television screen. Baird's system, based on mechanical scanning, was used in experimental broadcasts by the BBC (British Broadcasting Corporation) from 1929, but was superseded by a superior electronic scanning system when public broadcasting began in 1936. Baird's other inventions included an infrared night-vision device (1926), colour and stereoscopic televisions, demonstrated in 1928, and video recorders, marketed in 1935.

❖ Although television has been one of the world's most influential inventions, Baird made very little money from his discovery.

❖ Baird's South African-born wife, Margaret, a concert pianist, returned to South Africa after his death and taught at the University of Cape Town College of Music.

Bakelite First synthetic PLASTIC, invented in 1909 by Leo Baekeland, a Belgian-born chemist working in the USA. By treating phenol (derived from coal-tar) with formaldehyde, Baekeland obtained a powdered resin which, when heated, could be moulded by pressure into almost any shape. Bakelite, once set, was heat resistant and a good electrical insulator; everything from light switches to kitchenware was made from it. Bakelite's success led to the growth of the modern plastics industry.

bar code Set of vertical lines representing coded information that can be read with an optical scanner and interpreted by a computer. Most product packaging has a bar code that stores information about the item; shops with computerized checkouts use the bar codes to produce itemized receipts and to monitor stock levels.

battery Device that produces ▷ELECTRICITY as a result of chemical reactions between its components. The most common type is the zinc-carbon or dry-cell battery, used for example to power torches. It has a zinc casing containing a moist paste which conducts electricity, and a central carbon rod. When the battery is connected into a circuit, ▷ELECTRONS flow from the battery's negative terminal to the appliance and back to the battery's positive terminal. Eventually the chemicals are used up, and the battery stops working. Car batteries contain a series of lead plates, immersed in sulphuric acid, one of each of the series being coated with lead oxide. Chemical reactions between the plates and acid produce electricity to power the starter motor and ignition system. When the engine is running, electricity from the generator keeps the battery charged. The first battery was developed in 1800 by the Italian physicist Alessandro Volta, after whom the ▷VOLT unit of electric potential is named.

❖ Jars, dating from about 50 BC, with copper rods suspended from wax plugs, were found in Iraq in 1938. The jars once contained acid which, combined with metal rods, would have generated about 2 volts – enough for gold and silver plating.

Bell, Alexander Graham (1847-1922) Scottish-born emigrant to the USA who patented the first TELEPHONE in 1876. Bell experimented on a telephone system while developing his father's work on a method of teaching deaf people to speak, in which symbols represented the position of the lips and tongue. Bell's other developments included the photophone, which transmitted sounds on a beam of light, and a HYDROFOIL which in 1919 attained a speed of 112 km/h.

❖ The first intelligible words transmitted by telephone were: 'Mr Watson, come here, I want to see you!' spoken by Bell to his assistant, Thomas Watson.

❖ The decibel, which is used for measuring the loudness or intensity of sound, is named after Alexander Bell.

bicycle The first bicycle was built in 1839 by Scottish blacksmith Kirkpatrick Macmillan. It had pedals attached to rods which turned the back wheel. In 1861 the French coachbuilders Pierre and Ernest Michaux invented a bicycle which was driven by pedals attached to the front wheel. The so-called

MOVING AHEAD *The penny-farthing gave way to the safety cycle in 1885. Graeme Obree (bottom right) set a record of 4 min 20,894 sec for 4 km in 1993, on a cycle similar to the 1900 Raleigh (right).*

'penny-farthing' first appeared in the 1870s; it had a front wheel as big as 1,5 m across, to make each push of the pedals go farther. The true ancestor of the modern bicycle was the Rover safety cycle, designed by the British engineer John Starley and made in Coventry, England, in 1885. It had wheels of similar size and a chain transferred the drive from the pedals to the rear wheel. After 1888, pneumatic tyres were incorporated into the designs of bicycles by Raleigh and other manufacturers. Today's bicycles have strong but light frames made from aluminium, titanium or fibre-reinforced plastics.

❖ In 1992, Britain's Chris Boardman won an Olympic gold medal riding a bicycle of revolutionary design developed by Lotus, the car makers. It had a one-piece single moulded body made from CARBON FIBRE.

biotechnology The use of living organisms, particularly microorganisms, in industrial processes. Brewing, baking and cheesemaking represent ancient forms of biotechnology, but the industry has been revolutionized in recent years by advances in genetics and GENETIC ENGINEERING. Specially designed microorganisms are now used to produce a wide range of drugs and other chemicals such as ▷ENZYMES to refine ores and to clear up oil slicks and other forms of pollution. Biotechnology has presented a clean and highly energy-efficient alternative to normal industrial processes.

'black box' Popular name for the flight data recorder and cockpit voice recorder carried by aircraft. It records information such as speed, altitude and position, and conversations among the flight crew and between the crew and air-traffic controllers. The 'black box' is carried in the rear of the aircraft and is designed to survive the impact of a crash and any resulting fire, so that the information it contains can be used to assess the cause of the accident.

❖ 'Black boxes' are painted in bright, reflective colours to make them easier to spot in wreckage or at night.

blast furnace Invention that opened the way for the ▷INDUSTRIAL REVOLUTION by making iron much easier to produce. A blast furnace consists of a steel tower, lined with bricks and up to 60 m tall. In it, metal – usually iron – is smelted from its ore. It is so called because hot air is blasted into the furnace to make the raw materials burn more fiercely. In iron smelting, a mixture of iron ore, coke and limestone is heated to temperatures that reach 1 600°C. Molten iron and slag are tapped off at the bottom of the furnace. Iron from a blast furnace is called pig iron; most of it is recast in other furnaces to make STEEL. Smelting of iron from ore probably began about 1500 BC among the Hittites of Anatolia (now in modern Turkey), who built crude furnaces – shallow bowl-shaped hearths lined with clay – and put iron ore and wood in them to burn. The wood became charcoal and the carbon in it combined with the iron ore, making it a spongy mass containing particles of earthy slag. Most of the slag was removed by hammering and fairly pure iron was then left, which could be beaten into shape under heat. In Europe, furnaces capable of producing molten iron developed in the 14th century; these were fuelled by charcoal. In 1709 Abraham Darby (*c*1678-1717), an English ironmaster, introduced a much more efficient coke-fired furnace. In 1856 Henry Bessemer (1813-98), an English engineer, invented a 'converter' to produce steel from molten pig iron cheaply and on a large scale. It is known as the Bessemer process.

Braun, Wernher von (1912-77) German-born rocket engineer and chief architect of the early American space programme. Von Braun led the team that developed the V-2 rocket – V stood for *vergeltungswaffe* ('vengeance weapon') – which bombarded London at the end of World War II. After surrendering to the Allies he went on to design the *Jupiter C* rocket which launched the first American satellite, *Explorer 1*, in 1958, and the *Saturn V* rocket, which was the launch vehicle for the APOLLO PROJECT spacecraft.

Breathalyser The Breathalyser was first used in 1939, when the police in Indianapolis, USA, introduced the 'Drunkometer' developed by an American doctor, Rolla N Harger. In many early Breathalysers, alcohol in the breath was detected by crystals which changed colour. The latest Breathalysers work electronically.

❖ In South Africa, a driver may refuse a Breathalyser test but is obliged to have a blood test if ordered to do so by police. It is an offence for a driver to have a blood-alcohol level of more than 0,08 g in 100 ml of blood. The equivalent Breathalyser reading would be 35 micrograms of alcohol in 100 ml of breath. However, the courts do not accept Breathalyser readings as proof of guilt. The amount of alcoholic drink which would produce the stipulated limit in the blood or breath is highly variable, depending on the person's mass, state of health and the time that has elapsed since taking the drink.

camera The basic principle of the camera is a light-proof chamber with an opening (or aperture), a shutter and ▷LENS at one end, and at the other a piece of film with a light-sensitive coating. The shutter opens briefly to let light in through the aperture, and the lens focuses an inverted image onto the film. Processing the film completes the chemical changes begun by the light striking it. The aperture size and the time the shutter stays open (the shutter speed) can be varied, and the lens can be moved backwards and forwards to focus on subjects at different distances. In many cameras these adjustments are automatic. Compact cameras normally have one built-in lens, and a separate viewfinder. In a single-lens reflex (SLR) camera, the viewfinder allows the photographer to see through the single main lens via a mirror which flips out of the way, in a reflex action, when a picture is taken. In 1839 Louis Daguerre, a French painter, produced a permanent image – the Daguerreotype – on silver-coated copper sheets. It could be reproduced only by being rephotographed. In the same year, the English scientist Henry Fox Talbot developed a negative from which multiple prints could be made. In 1888 George EASTMAN introduced flexible film to replace glass plates; modern colour film was developed by the Kodak company in 1936.

❖ Polaroid cameras develop pictures instantly, using a film pack that contains film, chemicals and printing paper. They were developed by US inventor Edwin Land in 1947, after his daughter's disappointment that his photographs of her would have to be sent away to be processed.

HAPPY SNAPS *The Kodak Brownie camera, developed in 1890 by George Eastman, sold in the US for $1 and turned photography into a pastime for millions of people.*

capacitor (condenser) Device used in electronic circuits to store electric charge. Capacitors typically consist of two metal plates separated by insulation. They are essential components of MICROCHIPS and are used in car distributors to stop electricity jumping between contact breakers (points).

car The pioneers of the motorcar were the German engineers Gottlieb Daimler (1834-1900) and Karl Friedrich Benz (1844-1929). Daimler developed the first lightweight, petrol-powered INTERNAL-COMBUSTION ENGINE

VERSATILE DISC *The coded sound on a compact disc seen at 930 times its actual size (inset). Often used in education, CD-i – interactive CD – lets the viewer control images.*

in 1883, and fitted it first to a bicycle, and then in 1886 to an open carriage. In 1885 Benz developed the first practical car powered by a petrol engine; the three-wheeled vehicle had a top speed of 13 km/h, and was an entirely new vehicle, unlike Daimler's 'horseless carriage'. In 1908 the US manufacturer Henry ▷FORD began mass production of the Model T, and brought car ownership to a far wider public. In the early days of development, electric cars vied with internal-combustion engine models, after improved storage batteries became available in 1881. However their popularity was short-lived because they lagged behind petrol-driven cars in performance and range. Research continues to reduce cars' toxic emissions and the amount of petrol that they use; and to improve performance and safety.

❖ The first car in South Africa was the Benz Voiturette, shown to the public in 1897. Soon afterwards three more models were imported. The first speed limits enforced were often as low as 15 miles per hour (about 25 km/h).

carbon fibre Threads of carbon which reinforce plastic to produce a strong, light material that can withstand high temperatures. Carbon fibre is used in the construction of aircraft and sports equipment.

cat's-eye Road-marking stud that reflects headlights. In 1934 Percy Shaw, a British road contractor, developed an early type made from a glass prism set in a rubber pad. Today cat's-eyes are often plastic prisms set in a tough plastic base.

CD-ROM A COMPACT DISC incorporating a read-only memory – information on the disc can be read but not altered. Text, graphics, photographs and moving pictures can be stored on CDs in the form of a pattern of microscopic pits which are 'read' by a laser beam, as in audio CDs. CD-i – interactive CD – is a CD-ROM that is played through a television set and allows the viewer to control the images. CD-i products are used for recreational and educational purposes: for example, children can 'create' their own planet, and see how animal life is affected by changes in climate.

❖ The entire 12-volume *Oxford English Dictionary* can be stored on a single disc.

cellphone (cellular telephone) Mobile radio telephone system in which the country is divided into areas, or cells, up to 35 km across, although cells are much smaller where heavy cellphone use is expected, for example in cities. Each cell contains a radio transmitter connected via a switching system to the national telephone network. When the phone is switched on, it 'tells' the cellphone system where it is, so that calls made to it can be relayed from the nearest cell transmitter. Calls made from a cellphone are picked up by the nearest cell aerial and routed to the telephone network. When calls are made by people on trains or in cars, for example, the call is handed over from one transmitter to the next without breaking the conversation. By the end of 1994, cells covered areas inhabited by about 70 per cent of South Africa's population.

cinematography The principle underlying the making of films for cinema is that a cine-camera takes a series of still photographs on a roll at the rate of 24 frames (pictures) per second. The film is held stationary for a split second while each frame is exposed, then wound on one frame. The developed film is projected onto the screen at the same speed of 24 frames per second, using a cine-projector which again holds each frame still while it is projected. Persistence of vision – the ability of the human eye to retain an image for a fraction of a second – merges the advancing frames to create the illusion of continuous movement. Motion pictures were first achieved in England by Augustin Le Prince in 1888. The soundtrack is now printed along one side of the film, but in early 'talkies' the soundtrack was played on a separate disc.

clock One of the earliest ways of measuring the passage of time, used by the Egyptians around 2000 BC, was to compare shadows cast by the Sun against a marked scale. Several early civilizations developed water clocks, in which water flowed steadily into or out of a vessel marked with a scale. Mechanical clocks were developed in China in the 8th century AD, and in Europe in the late 13th century. The early European clocks were driven by a system of falling weights. Clocks driven by the energy stored in coiled springs appeared in the 15th century; the mechanism was light enough to be used for portable clocks and watches. In about 1656, the Dutch astronomer Christiaan Huygens designed the pendulum clock, exploiting ▷GALILEO's discovery in 1582 that a pendulum always takes the same time to complete a swing. Long-case, or 'grandfather', clocks became popular in the late 17th century. Clocks powered by electricity were invented in 1840 and became widely used after World War I when mains electricity was installed in many homes. Quartz clocks were invented in 1929; electric current from a battery stimulates constant vibrations in a quartz crystal and the vibrations are converted into one-second 'ticks'. These are cheap and very accurate for everyday use. Atomic clocks – accurate to one second in at least 1 000 years – were first made in the USA in 1948. They work by counting the natural oscillations of atoms.

❖ Atomic clocks are so accurate that time is now defined by them: one second is defined

HEAVENLY TIMEPIECE *Giovanni de'Dondi's astronomical clock of 1350 stands 0,9 m high. This replica is based on his drawings.*

AIR SUPREMACY *The grace and power of Concorde impress even when it is stationary. In the air it is unsurpassed – capable of flying from London to New York in 2 hr 54 min 30 sec.*

as the time taken for an atom of caesium to vibrate 9 192 631 770 times.

compact disc (CD) Small disc, 12 cm across, storing data, especially music, in digital form. To record music on CD, sound signals from the microphone are converted into the 1s and 0s of the ▷BINARY SYSTEM, and stored on the surface of the disc as a pattern of microscopic pits separated by unpitted (flat) areas. The pattern of pits and flats mirrors the pattern of 1s and 0s. During playback, a laser beam 'reads' the pattern of pits and flats and produces signals that represent the signals recorded. When fed to a loudspeaker, they reproduce the original sounds faithfully. The CD was developed by the Philips company in 1972. By the early 1990s it was the established medium for audio recordings. High-quality reproduction is possible using digital recording because the sound is stored as precise digits, not as imprecise waveforms as it is on ordinary tape or disc.

compass Device for determining geographical direction. The magnetic compass relies on a magnetized needle that is free to rotate on a pivot until aligned with the magnetic field of the Earth. The needle points towards the north ▷MAGNETIC POLE, from which true north can be calculated. Gyrocompasses, which work on the principle of the GYROSCOPE, are not affected by the presence of iron, or by the magnetic anomalies of the Earth's magnetic field, and are used in ships and aircraft.

computer Versatile electronic device that stores and processes information, or data, according to a COMPUTER PROGRAM – a series of instructions. The program and other operating instructions are known as the computer's software. The units that physically make up a computer, such as the keyboard, the visual display unit (VDU) or screen and the main systems unit, are the computer's hardware. The main systems unit includes a memory in which programs and data are stored, and a central processing unit (CPU), which controls all computer operations. Items such as printers and MODEMS are known as peripherals. Inside the computer, MICROCHIPS carry the memory needed for processing. Permanent information is stored on removable 'floppy' or 'stiffy' disks, or on 'hard' disks sealed inside the computer. The advent of the microchip in the 1970s led to the development of personal computers (PCs) and portable battery-operated 'lap-tops'. Computers have a memory capacity measured in millions of bytes, or megabytes. A byte is a set of bits (binary digits) representing a piece of data, which can then be used by the computer. A database is a file which stores records, such as, for example, the names and other details of a firm's customers, and enables users to access and update records without affecting its design.

❖ The Internet is a worldwide network of computer networks which communicate via telephone lines. It grew out of the development of the LAN (local area network) and WAN (wide area network). LAN provided facilities for intercommunication between a group of computer users, and WAN connected computers over long distances, usually through the public telephone lines, enabling the provision of an electronic mail service between subscribers. In 1995 as many as 35 million people were linked to the Internet. Anyone with access to a personal computer and a modem can dial in, and, for the cost of a local call, hook up to a network. The USA is the world's largest user. Internet was originally set up in 1969 by Pentagon researchers as a secure communications system in the event of nuclear war.

❖ In 1834, British mathematician Charles BABBAGE designed an 'analytical engine' that had many of the features of the modern computer. The first electronic computer was completed in the USA in 1939.

computer program Set of instructions given to a computer to direct it to carry out certain operations. Programs are usually written in specialised languages such as FORTRAN, COBOL, BASIC and C, which allow the programmer to communicate with the computer in a form of English. The computer translates these 'high level' languages into machine code – the series of ▷BINARY SYSTEM digits by which it operates.

Concorde Supersonic passenger jet developed jointly by Britain and France. The

LIGHT TOUCH *Thomas Alva Edison, the prolific American inventor who patented almost 1 100 inventions, is seen with two electric lamps, products of his fertile imagination. Inset are another lamp in its holder and pages from one of the 3 500 notebooks in which he recorded his ideas.*

British test pilot Brian Trubshaw piloted its maiden flight in March 1969. Concorde cruises at a speed of up to 2 350 km/h – about twice the speed of sound – and at a height of almost 15 000 m.

diode Device that allows electric current to pass in one direction only. Diodes can change ▷ALTERNATING CURRENT into ▷DIRECT CURRENT, for example, in television receiver circuits. Diodes are usually made of SEMICONDUCTOR materials and are essential components in MICROCHIPS.

Dolby system Electronic circuitry used for suppressing background hiss in tape recordings. The system was patented in 1968 by the American electronic engineer Ray M Dolby.

Eastman, George (1854-1932) American pioneer of 'snapshot' photography. In 1888, Eastman introduced the easy-to-use Kodak camera complete with flexible, paper-backed roll film. The film had 100 exposures and the whole camera was returned to the manufacturers for developing. In 1889, Eastman substituted celluloid for the paper in roll film, making processing simpler and cheaper.
❖ Eastman's snappy publicity slogan for the Kodak camera was: 'You press the button, we do the rest.'
❖ Eastman introduced the name 'Kodak' after experimenting with different words beginning and ending with the letter K. He felt it was a 'strong, incisive sort of letter'.

Edison, Thomas Alva (1847-1931) Prolific American inventor who patented nearly 1 100 inventions. Edison's favourite invention was the phonograph of 1877 – the first device that could both record and replay sound. The same year, Edison also improved Alexander Graham BELL's telephone transmitter and made the instrument easier to use by separating the mouthpiece and earpiece. In 1879 he produced a successful light bulb, at the same time as the physicist Joseph Swan was developing a bulb in Britain. Realizing the potential of electric lighting, Edison designed the world's first large-scale power station and in 1882 supplied a district of New York with electricity.
❖ Edison defined genius as '1 per cent inspiration and 99 per cent perspiration'.

electric generator Machine that produces electric current, and works on the principle of ▷ELECTROMAGNETIC INDUCTION first demonstrated by the British scientist Michael ▷FARADAY in 1831. At its simplest a generator consists of a rotating shaft carrying wire coils, surrounded by a magnet. Current is induced in the coils by the rotation of the shaft. There are two basic types of generator: alternators, which produce ▷ALTERNATING CURRENT (AC); and dynamos, which produce ▷DIRECT CURRENT (DC). Power stations produce alternating current for general distribution; the rotating shaft is driven by turbines which are powered by steam (in coal, oil and nuclear power stations) or by water (in hydroelectric power stations).

electric motor Machine that converts electricity into mechanical motion, widely used in factories, transport and in home appliances from washing machines to toothbrushes. The electric motor is constructed like an ELECTRIC GENERATOR, but works in the opposite way. Basically, a wire coil is positioned between the jaws of a magnet; electric current is passed through the coil, creating a magnetic field that interacts with the field of the stationary magnet and forces the coil to turn.

electroplating Process by which a material is coated with a thin layer of metal, by means of ▷ELECTROLYSIS. Electroplating, which began commercially in the 1840s, can be used to protect metals against corrosion and to coat cheaper metals with more valuable ones, such as silver. To coat an object with copper, the object is immersed in a solution of a copper compound such as copper sulphate, along with sheets of pure copper. The object and the copper sheets are connected into an electric circuit, with the copper sheets acting as positive electrodes and the object acting as a negative electrode. When the current is switched on, copper is transferred from the copper sheet to the surface of the object.
❖ Electroplated nickel silver (EPNS) is a product of electroplating.

ergonomics Study of how human beings interact with machines and with their work environment. Its aim is to improve design, especially of machines and the workplace, and so achieve the greatest efficiency and comfort with the minimum of stress.

escalator The first moving staircase, invented by Jesse W Reno, was installed as a novelty ride on the pier at Coney Island, New York, in 1894. Modern escalators are inclined at about 30°, and rise at a rate of up to 36 m per minute. The stairs are carried by a continuous chain that runs around a wheel turned by an electric motor.
❖ The world's longest escalator is in an underground station in St Petersburg, Russia; it has 729 steps and a vertical rise of 59,7 m.

fax Short for facsimile transmission. Method of sending written messages and photographs along telephone lines. In a fax machine, the document or photograph to be transmitted is scanned by a light beam. The pattern of reflected light is converted into electric signals which are fed to a MODEM, which in turn produces signals suitable for transmission along the telephone lines. In the receiving machine, another modem reverses the process, and the signals are fed to a printer where a facsimile of the original image is formed. Colour fax machines scan the image three times, using red, blue and green filters to separate the colour components of the image. At the receiving end, the three images are printed one on top of the other, using three different colour toners. A Scottish clockmaker, Alexander Bain, developed the principle of fax transmission in 1843; his prototype used a sheep's jawbone and springs made from heather. The first fax transmission was a photograph wired from Paris to the 'Daily Mirror' newspaper in London in 1907, using equipment devised five years earlier by Arthur Korn, a German physicist.

Fibreglass Trade name for the tough material made from plastic reinforced with a mesh of fine glass fibres. Fibreglass is used to make a variety of products, including boat hulls, car bodies and fishing rods. Ceiling insulation is made of loose mats of Fibreglass – without plastic reinforcement.

fibre optics Branch of science and engineering concerned with the transmission of light through fine glass fibres. A typical fibre is between 0,005 and 0,1 mm across – less than the width of a human hair. Light introduced into one end of an optical fibre travels down the fibre by bouncing off the sides, with little light escaping. Telephone signals can be sent along optical fibres by coded pulses of LASER light. Optical fibre cables take up far less space than the older copper cables and can carry more information at much higher speeds. In medicine, optical fibres – which can be easily twisted and bent – are used in ▷ENDOSCOPES, which enable doctors to see inside the body and perform microsurgery with tiny instruments or laser beams.

fingerprinting Tiny amounts of sweat on the fingers transfer the fingertip pattern of a person to most smooth surfaces that the fingers touch, and the pattern can be revealed by dusting such a surface with fine powder. The pattern of ridges, whorls and loops on the skin of each person's fingertips is unique to that person, and does not change. Computers can be used to match prints, but final matching is by painstaking visual inspection. William Herschel of the Indian Civil Service used fingerprints in 1877 to check that army pensioners did not draw their pensions more than once. Herschel's technique was improved by the scientist Sir Francis Galton and by Edward Henry – who became Commissioner of the Metropolitan Police in London and opened a fingerprint department at Scotland Yard, the police headquarters, in 1901.

SEEING IS BELIEVING *Industrial fibre-optic cables (right) are used to provide a powerful point of light for precision work in a constricted area, in medicine, for example. A cable contains 10 000 individual fibres and each fibre is about 47 microns thick. The optical fibre strands (below) have been magnified to three times their size.*

firearms The first reliable revolver, in which a revolving chamber moves a fresh bullet into the firing position after one has been fired, was produced by the American inventor Samuel Colt in 1835. In the semiautomatic pistol, the next bullet moves into place automatically, but each shot has to be triggered; automatic weapons, such as submachine guns, continue firing once the trigger is pulled. Rifles have spiral grooves, or 'rifling', running the length of the barrel to improve the accuracy of the bullet's flight. Shotguns, which fire pellets, have a smooth-bore barrel, as no great accuracy can be given to a charge of pellets. Primitive firearms date from the 14th century, but large muskets were not developed until the 16th century. In the flintlocks of the next centrury, the charge was ignited by the spark produced when flint struck roughened steel.

❖ The gas-operated Kalashnikov AK 47 rifle, invented in 1947 by Russian designer Mikhail Kalashnikov, is capable of automatic fire at the rate of 650 rounds per minute.

gears Sets of toothed wheels that mesh together so that one wheel turns the other. Two wheels meshing together turn in opposite directions, which can be used to reverse the direction of motion in a car, for example. Gears also enable an engine to propel a car at different speeds while always working at an efficient number of revolutions (revs) per minute. When one wheel has more teeth than the other, there is a change in speed – the wheel with more teeth rotates more slowly. Bevel gears mesh at right angles and turn the axis of rotation through 90°. Most bicycles are fitted with derailleur gears, which have different sets of chain rings and sprockets that can be combined to give up to 24 gears.

genetic engineering Alteration of the characteristics of an organism by direct manipulation of its ▷GENES. The ▷DNA of different species can be mixed together in the hope that beneficial features of one can be transferred to the other, but increasingly scientists are now able to use the technique of genesplitting to insert individual genes. Pigs, for example, can be genetically altered to have hearts made from human tissues, or to

RECORD FLIGHT *The Russian-born American inventor Igor Sikorsky flying his VS300 helicopter in April 1941. He kept the machine airborne for a world record of 1 hr 15 min 14,5 sec.*

produce human hormones; and plants can be given resistance to disease. Genetic engineering is the basis of the flourishing BIOTECHNOLOGY industry. It was used for the first time to cure a rare hereditary deficiency disease in 1993; and it has become controversial because it could in theory allow scientists to 'design' human beings.

genetic fingerprinting (DNA fingerprinting) Just as every person's fingerprints are different, so too are the precise sequences of genes in their ▷DNA. Techniques developed in 1984 can produce a visual record of this sequence from samples of blood or other tissues. Closely related people have similar sequences of genes. Genetic FINGERPRINTING is frequently used by immigration authorities as well as in paternity suits, to establish fatherhood. It has also been used as proof against suspects in rape and murder cases.

glass The main component of glass is sand. Sand, soda and limestone are heated in a furnace to a temperature of some 1 500°C, at which it turns into a molten mass that cools to form clear glass. Float glass, used for shop windows and mirrors, is made by floating molten glass from the furnace on a bath of molten tin, which ensures the glass remains flat as it cools. Special types of glass include heat-resistant glass, which contains boric oxide, and crystal glass, which contains lead and has a characteristic sparkle when cut. Safety glass is manufactured in such a way that it disintegrates into small fragments rather than shattering into slivers. Laminated glass, used for car windscreens, has plastic sandwiched between two layers of glass; if the glass is shattered, it sticks to the plastic. Glassmaking began in the Middle East in about 3000 BC, and in the 1st century BC the Syrians invented the blowpipe – a hollow tube which when dipped into molten glass could be used to blow it. Mass production began in the 19th century.

gyroscope Device that consists of a rapidly rotating wheel within a supporting frame. Because of its inertia, or resistance to change, the wheel, or rotor, of the gyroscope maintains its orientation in space no matter how the frame is moved. This directional property is used in such devices as the gyrocompass, found in ships and aircraft, and ships' stabilizers. A child's spinning top is an example of a gyroscope.

GHOST PICTURES *A schoolboy marvels at the three-dimensional hologram hovering in mid-air at the museum of La Villette in Paris.*

hacker Someone who, without permission, uses a computer, a MODEM and the telephone network to gain access to other computers. Once connected, the hacker uses trial and error to find the computer's password codes that allow access to its files. Hackers have committed fraud and serious breaches of security, and many countries now have stringent laws against hacking.

helicopter The rotor blades of a helicopter have an AEROFOIL cross-section like that of an aeroplane wing, and when they rotate they develop enough lift to support the helicopter in the air. The rotor can provide propulsion in all directions as the pilot alters the pitch, or angle, of the rotating blades.
❖ ▷LEONARDO DA VINCI sketched an 'air gyroscope' in the 15th century; it would have risen into the air and then dropped. The first practical helicopter, the twin-rotored Fa-61, was built in Germany by Heinrich Focke in 1936. Three years later the Russian-born aeronautical engineer Igor Sikorsky (1889-1972) constructed the first single-rotor machine, the VS-300, in the USA.

hologram Three-dimensional image of an object, made using LASER light. The light is split into two beams. One beam is directed at the object, and is reflected off it and onto a photographic plate. The other beam is shone onto the photographic plate. The two beams coincide to create an ▷INTERFERENCE pattern on the plate, which is then developed. Shining laser light through the pattern produces a realistic-looking, three-dimensional image. Reflection holograms, used on credit cards to make them harder to forge, can be viewed in ordinary light. Holography was invented in 1947 by the Hungarian-born British physicist Denis Gabor, but did not become practical until the development of the laser in 1960.

hovercraft Vehicle that glides over land or water on a 'cushion' of high-pressure air, useful in areas without harbours. The air pressure is sufficient to lift the craft above the surface, reducing friction with the ground. Fans deliver the pressurized air to the cushion, which is often surrounded by a flexible 'skirt' to hold in the air. Air propellers drive the craft forward. The SRN-4 crafts used as ferries across the English Channel can carry 420 passengers and 60 cars at speeds up to 120 km/h. The British electronics engineer Christopher Cockerell (1910-) launched the first full-size hovercraft in 1959.

hydraulics Branch of technology concerned with devices that transmit pressure through fluids. Car brakes work by hydraulic pressure, and consist of fluid-filled pipes connecting the brake pedal to the wheels. When the brake pedal is pressed down, it forces a piston down the master cylinder. The pressure travels through the liquid towards the brake pads, and forces smaller pistons to move and push the pads against the wheels with increased force.

hydrofoil Underwater wing fitted fore and aft to the bottom of a boat to increase its speed. In cross-section the wing has the AEROFOIL shape of an aeroplane wing. As the boat moves forward, water pressure above the wing becomes lower than that below. This forces the foil to rise up, raising the boat's hull out of the water and greatly reducing water resistance. The first hydrofoil was fitted to a boat in 1906 and it came into commercial use in 1956. The Boeing Jetfoil uses water jets to reach speeds of up to 70 km/h.

infrared device Piece of equipment that emits ▷INFRARED RADIATION or detects the infrared radiation that is emitted by all warm objects. The automatic focusing mechanism on many cameras works by bouncing an infrared beam off the subject and measuring the time it takes to return. Infrared detectors are used to look for bodies in smoke-filled buildings and among the debris of earthquakes. In intruder alarm systems, the heat difference between the intruder's body temperature and that of the surroundings triggers the alarm.

internal-combustion engine Type of engine in which combustion of fuel takes place inside an enclosed cylinder. Most cars use a four-stroke petrol engine: the engine produces power with four strokes, or movements, of the pistons, usually contained within four or more cylinders. On the first stroke, the piston moves down the cylinder, sucking in a mixture of petrol and air through an open inlet valve. On the second, the inlet valve closes and the piston moves back up the cylinder, compressing the mixture. When the piston reaches the top, the mixture is ignited by a spark from the spark plug; the burning mixture expands and forces the piston back down the cylinder, forming the third power stroke. On the fourth stroke, the piston moves back up the cylinder, forcing the exhaust gas out of the now open exhaust valves. The pistons turn a crankshaft linked to the wheels of the car via a transmission system. The German inventor Nikolaus August Otto perfected a four-stroke engine, powered by gas, in 1876.

❖ Turbochargers increase an internal combustion engine's power by forcing more air into the engine cylinders with a turbine-driven compressor, or pump. The turbine is driven by the flow of exhaust gases.

irradiation Exposure to radiation, such as ▷GAMMA RADIATION, which in large doses can kill living organisms. Irradiation is used in some countries, including South Africa, to help preserve food; the rays kill off the microorganisms that cause decay. However, there is some concern that irradiation may also destroy vitamins.

jet engine Gas-turbine engine, usually used for aircraft, that produces thrust by jet propulsion – a jet of gases shooting backwards from the rear of the engine. The simplest jet engine is the turbojet. Air is taken in and compressed. Fuel (paraffin) is sprayed into the compressed air and ignited, and the hot gases produced expand and spin the blades of a turbine – which drives the compressor – before escaping as a propulsive jet. British Air Force officer Frank Whittle took out his patent on a jet engine in 1930. Seven years later he tested a practical engine, first used in a plane in 1941.

❖ In Germany during World War II, the engineer Hans von Ohain developed the Messerschmitt Me-262 jet fighter. It was faster than the first British jet fighter, the Gloster Meteor, but was not produced early enough, or in sufficiently large numbers, to influence the course of the war.

laser (Light Amplification by Stimulated Emission of Radiation) Electronic device that produces a concentrated beam of very pure light. In laser light, unlike ordinary light, all the waves have the same length and are exactly in step, with their crests and troughs coinciding. Lasers can be used in a variety of ways – including to drill holes in metal, send telephone signals along optical fibres, carry out delicate surgery and play COMPACT DISCS. The first laser was built by American physicist Theodore H Maiman in 1960.

LCD (Liquid Crystal Display) Method of displaying the numbers in electronic devices such as digital watches and calculators, first used in 1971. The display for each character is usually made up of seven segments, each with liquid crystals built into them. The application of electricity changes the structure of the liquid crystal, twisting the path of light and effectively turning the segment on or off.

LED (Light Emitting Diode) Tiny crystal of SEMICONDUCTOR material that glows when an electric current passes through it. LEDs, invented in 1962, are used in digital displays and for indicating that power is on in electronic devices.

lift The modern safety lift was invented in 1853 by the American engineer Elisha Otis. The passenger car is connected to a counterweight by a steel cable that passes over a pulley at the top of the lift shaft. The counterweight moves down as the lift moves up, and vice versa. In this way only the difference between the weight of the counterweight and the car with its passengers has to be moved – minimizing the load on the motor used to turn the pulley. Otis's safety device was a clamp that automatically gripped a guide rail if the hoist rope broke. His lift

RADIO PIONEER *The young Guglielmo Marconi, photographed soon after his arrival in England in 1896. He had left Italy having failed to gain financial support for the development of radio.*

A MARVEL IN MINIATURE *The intricate circuitry of a microchip, magnified x 60, with (inset) a complete chip on a fingernail x 2 which contains thousands of electronic circuits and components.*

made possible the growth of the skyscraper, the first one being installed in a five-storey shop in New York in 1857. In South Africa, the first electric lift was installed in a Cape Town warehouse in 1896.

❖ Forerunners of the lift were the hoists, used in mines from ancient times until the 19th century. These were operated by hand or a large horizontal rope-drum turned by horses.

lighting Until the 19th century, oil lamps and candles were the principal means of lighting. The earliest lamps, made more than 40 000 years ago, were hollowed-out stones which held burning animal fat. In 1780, the Swiss chemist Ami Argand developed a much more practical oil lamp with a glass chimney and a tubular woven wick; air was drawn up through the centre of the wick, making it burn brighter than earlier lamps. Candles were first made more than 2 000 years ago by dipping strands of cotton or flax into animal fat. Gas lighting – using coal gas – was introduced in the United Kingdom in 1806, but it gave rather low illumination until 1885, when Carl Auer, a Viennese chemist, invented a gas mantle that gave a much brighter light. Electric-powered lamps were invented independently by two men: Joseph Swan in England in 1878, and Thomas EDISON in the United States in 1879. The modern light bulb, a development of their work, contains a filament of fine coiled tungsten wire. When the light is switched on, the wire heats up to as much as 2 500°C and glows white hot. Neon lamps were invented in 1910 when the French chemist Georges Claude passed electric current through neon gas, producing an orange-red light. Other gases produced different colours. In fluorescent lamps, introduced in 1939, gas – usually mercury vapour – gives off invisible ultraviolet light which is absorbed by a fluorescent coating on the inside of the tube, which then gives out visible light. Energy-saving bulbs are small fluorescent tubes. These tubes consume less electricity and last much longer than ordinary (incandescent) light bulbs.

magnetic tape Plastic tape coated with fine magnetic particles – usually of iron oxide or chromium oxide – used in audio, video and data recording. During recording, light and/or sound waves are converted into electric signals which rearrange the magnetic particles into a pattern representing them. When the tape is played back, the pattern is read and used to reconstruct the original sound, pictures or other information. The magnetic recorder was invented by Valdemar Poulsen, a Dane, in 1898. Video tapes were introduced for professional use in 1956, and the Philips company introduced tape cassettes in 1964.

Marconi, Guglielmo (1874-1937) Italian electrical engineer who developed the 'wireless telegraph', the forerunner of the radio. Marconi carried out his first experiments in Italy in 1895, but the following year moved to Britain. In 1897 – by which time wireless telegraphy had a range of 20 km – Marconi founded the Wireless Telegraph and Signal Company, which became GEC-Marconi Electronics Ltd. In 1901, he sent the first trans-Atlantic radio signal from Poldhu in Cornwall to St John's in Newfoundland. Marconi shared the Nobel prize for physics in 1909.

microchip (silicon chip) A very thin sliver of silicon or other SEMICONDUCTOR material, about 7 mm square, that contains thousands of electronic components and circuits. The circuits are built up in a step-by-step process, which involves 'doping' the silicon – adding impurities to alter its electrical properties – and depositing metals to form connections. The first practical integrated circuits were exhibited in 1959. Microprocessors, devised in 1969, are microchips that contain all the circuits needed to enable them to function as the main systems units of COMPUTERS.

microfilm Photographic film often used to store documents and newspapers, reduced to about 1/20th of their original size. The film is read in a viewer that magnifies the text to a readable size.

❖ In the 1850s, English craftsman John Benjamin Dancer produced minute photographic slides. One of them was of Queen Victoria's family mounted in a ring, with a transparent stone as a magnifying glass.

microscope Optical device containing a system of lenses and mirrors which allows objects to be magnified by up to 2 500 times (x 2 500). The object is placed on a platform and illuminated; the objective lens, closest to the object, produces a magnified image of the object, and this image is then viewed and further magnified by a lens in the microscope's eyepiece. Higher magnifications can be obtained with electron microscopes, which use beams of ▷ELECTRONS to project a magnified image onto a screen. Transmission electron microscopes, in which the beam passes through the object, magnify up to a million times. Scanning electron microscopes, working by reflection, give magnifications up to x 200 000; the beam scans the surface of the object allowing three-dimensional images to be built up.

❖ The inventor of the optical microscope is regarded as the Dutchman Anton von Leeuwenhoek (1632-1723). Subsequent discoveries upset many scientific theories. For example, it had been thought that fleas were formed from dust and dirt, but the microscope revealed that they were hatched from minute eggs.

microwave oven Microwaves, a type of ▷ELECTROMAGNETIC RADIATION, cause the water molecules in food to vibrate at about 2,5 billion times a second, generating heat which allows food to be cooked in a very short time. The higher the water content of

Samuel Morse

MORSE CODE

Samuel Morse invented the Morse code in 1844 to make it quicker to send long-distance messages over the electric telegraph that he developed in 1837. Used at sea until 1993, the distress call SOS is rendered . . . _ _ _ . . .

A . _	J . _ _ _	R . _ .
B _ . . .	K _ . _	S . . .
C _ . _ .	L . _ . .	T _
D _ . .	M _ _	U . . _
E .	N _ .	V . . . _
F . . _ .	O _ _ _	W . _ _
G _ _ .	P . _ _ .	X _ . . _
H	Q _ _ . _	Y _ . _ _
I . .		Z _ _ . .

the food, the more quickly the food cooks. Metal containers must not be used in microwave ovens because the radiation is reflected by metal. The first microwave oven was patented in 1953.

missile The first long-range ballistic missile was the German World War II V-2 rocket bomb, developed by Wernher von BRAUN. Intercontinental ballistic missiles (ICBMs), usually launched from silos sunk into the ground, have a range of more than 9 700 km. Advanced missiles are fitted with a guidance system. Some are fitted with infrared homing or heat-seeking devices, which lock onto the hot engines of the target plane. RADAR and LASERS are also used in almost all guidance systems. Cruise missiles are jet-propelled and navigate by means of a map stored in their memories. They are able to hit individual buildings from a range of 2 500 km.

modem (Modulator-Demodulator) Device which enables computer data and FAX messages to be transmitted along telephone lines. When transmitting, the modem takes digital signals from the computer and converts them into sound signals which are suitable for transmission by telephone. When receiving, the modem turns these signals back into digital signals that the fax machine or computer can interpret.

Montgolfier brothers Joseph (1740-1810) and Étienne (1745-99), French papermakers who built the first hot-air balloon to carry human passengers, which it did on 21 November 1783. The French physicist J A C Charles launched a hydrogen-filled balloon which was airborne for two hours.

Morse, Samuel (1791-1872) American pioneer of the electric telegraph and Morse code, which consists of dots and dashes that represent long and short sounds. (See panel.)

napalm Jellified petrol in incendiary bombs and flame-throwers, used widely during the Vietnam War. It was developed by US scientists during World War II at the request of the army. It burns intensely and sticks to its target, human or otherwise.

Nobel, Alfred Bernhard (1833-96) Swedish inventor of dynamite and gelignite. A pacifist, Nobel hoped that the destructive power of his invention would deter warfare. His financial interests in explosives and in Russia's Baku oilfields brought him an immense fortune, the bulk of which he left to found the Nobel prizes. They were to be awarded to those who have 'conferred the greatest benefit on mankind' in physics, chemistry, physiology or medicine, literature and peace. Economics was added in 1969. The prizes were worth more than R3 million each in 1994.

nuclear reactor Unit in which controlled ▷NUCLEAR FISSION takes place to provide energy for nuclear power stations and nuclear-powered ships. The central core of a reactor contains nuclear 'fuel' such as uranium. The rate of fission is controlled by rods that can be pushed into or out of the core. In a power station, the heat produced in the core by fission is extracted by a coolant and is used to boil water into steam, which drives the station's turbines that spin the electricity generators. The whole reactor is enclosed in thick, steel-reinforced concrete. The commonest type of reactor, which is also used at Koeberg in Western Cape, is the pressurized water reactor (PWR), whose core is cooled with water kept under high pressure so that it does not boil, even when heated above boiling point. The water is passed through a heat exchanger, where it gives up its heat to a second, unpressurized, water circuit where the water boils and produces steam. High-level radioactive ▷NUCLEAR WASTE from power stations can be disposed of by storing it as a liquid in steel tanks encased in concrete, or by fusing it into glass cylinders which are then buried deep underground. Major accidents have occurred in nuclear power stations at Three-Mile Island in Pennsylvania, USA, in 1979, and at ▷CHERNOBYL in the Ukraine, in 1986.

HAPPY LANDING *The first manned flight to land safely took place near Paris in 1783. Two volunteers flew 8 km in a hot-air balloon designed by the Montgolfier brothers.*

nuclear weapon Explosive device in which energy is released by ▷NUCLEAR FISSION or ▷NUCLEAR FUSION. Atom bombs use the nuclear fission of uranium or plutonium to bring about a runaway chain reaction which is accompanied by the release of huge amounts of energy as light, heat, blast and deadly radiation. American scientists, led by Robert Oppenheimer, tested the first ▷ATOM BOMB in July 1945, at the Alamogordo Bombing Range in southern New Mexico. Three weeks later, the United States Air Force dropped atom bombs on the Japanese cities of Hiroshima (6 August) and Nagasaki (9 August); more than 220 000 people died. By 1952, scientists had developed the even more powerful hydrogen bomb, in which energy was produced by nuclear fusion. Neutron bombs – small hydrogen bombs – produce high levels of radiation, with only limited heat and blast, and are designed to kill people rather than to destroy buildings.

❖ In 1993, president F W ▷DE KLERK confirmed what had long been suspected by government opponents – from the mid-1970s South Africa had built six nuclear weapons, but they had since been dismantled.

nylon The original wholly synthetic fibre. It was first produced by a team led by Wallace H Carothers in the USA in 1935 and some of its initial uses were for nylon stockings, introduced in 1938, and for underwear, allowing women who had never been able to afford silk to wear silklike clothes. Nylon fibres are made by forcing a molten ▷POLYMER or PLASTIC through tiny holes in a nozzle called a spinneret; the stream from each hole then solidifies into a thread.

oil refining Processing of crude oil (petroleum) into fuels, chemicals and other useful products. Petroleum, recovered from beneath the Earth's surface, is a mixture of hundreds of different compounds called ▷HYDROCARBONS. The first refinery process, called distillation, or fractionation, splits the crude oil into its components or fractions: crude oil is heated, and the resulting hot vapour is passed into a steel tower where the different fractions condense, and are tapped off, at different levels. The major fractions are the fuels petrol, paraffin, diesel oil and heating oil. Further refining can produce more fuels and chemical raw materials such as petrochemicals, which are used to make a range of PLASTICS and other products.

paper Most paper is made from specially grown softwood trees, whose logs are mechanically shredded or chemically treated in order to extract the cellulose fibres and form a pulp. The pulp is then washed, mixed with dyes and other substances, and allowed to flow on a wire-mesh belt. The water drains away, and the damp web of paper is dried and rolled into a continuous sheet. The earliest true paper was made by the Chinese from around AD 105; it reached Europe in the 8th century, and gradually replaced parchment and vellum, which were made from animal skins. Linen and cotton rags were the basic raw materials of paper until 1850, when the use of wood pulp helped to meet the increasing demand. High-quality paper still contains some rag pulp.

photocopier Most photocopiers work on the principle of xerography – dry writing – developed in 1938. Light reflected from the document being copied falls on a rotating drum charged with electricity. Only the parts of the drum that did not receive light – because of writing, or some other image, reflected from the original – remain charged, and attract black 'toner' powder. A sheet of paper then passes over the drum and the toner is transferred to the paper and fixed with heat and pressure. Colour photocopiers repeat the process three times over, using filters to break down the image into its coloured components, and coloured toners to reconstruct it.

plastics Most plastics are made from petrochemicals – obtained during the refining of oil – by a process called polymerization. It involves joining together small molecules, or monomers, to make large molecules, or ▷POLYMERS. The first synthetic plastic, BAKELITE, appeared in 1909. More plastics were developed during the next 40 years, but it was not until the 1950s that plastics started to flood the market. Plastics can be moulded into almost any shape quickly and cheaply and they do not corrode or conduct electricity. However, they may give off poisonous fumes when burnt, and because they do not rot, it is difficult to dispose of them.

power station Electricity is produced in power stations by turbogenerators – ELECTRIC GENERATORS spun by turbines. In most power stations, high-pressure steam spins the turbines. The steam can be produced from water heated in a boiler by burning coal or oil, or by the heat from a NUCLEAR REACTOR. In hydroelectric power stations, the turbines are spun by fast-flowing water. The electricity generated in South African power stations is 25 000 volts AC (▷ALTERNATING CURRENT). At this voltage, much power would be lost during transmission by overhead wires, so the voltage is stepped up to 275 000 or 400 000 volts, using a transformer. The voltage is then reduced again to 220 volts for use in the home. Electricity is distributed by a network of power cables called the national grid.

printing The earliest developments in printing took place in China. In AD 868, a book was printed using a wooden block with the text and illustrations raised in relief. Two centuries later, a Chinese alchemist printed from clay blocks with individual words raised in relief; the blocks could be reused in different combinations. Independently, in about 1450, Johann ▷GUTENBERG developed the same idea of reusable, or movable, type. Gutenberg's printing process was based on small pieces of metal, each bearing a mirror image of one letter raised in relief. Ink was spread over the block of letters and the paper was pressed against them. This method, known as letterpress, has been largely superseded by offset-litho printing. In this method, the printing plate is produced in such a way that the image and the nonimage areas are on the same plane; the plate is treated so that only the image areas – the type and illustrations – will accept the greasy ink. The images are transferred first to a rubber 'blanket' and then to the paper. Another printing process, called gravure, is the reverse of letterpress – the image is etched into the printing surface. Only the recesses in the printing plate retain ink, which is then transferred to paper. In the late 1960s printing and large-scale publishing began to be computerized. With a microcomputer-based or desk-top publishing (DTP) system, text and graphics are combined on a computer screen. Once a page is complete, the entire image is transferred to a phototypesetting device. The phototypesetter projects the image electronically onto photographic film, which is used to prepare printing plates. Modern presses print at high speeds; in the type of press used to print this book, 17 km of paper passes through the press every hour. The text was produced on a DTP system.

❖ In silk-screen printing, used mainly for hand printing of art work, a fine mesh of silk or nylon is treated with an impermeable coating (such as glue) except in the areas where ink is subsequently forced through the mesh onto paper. For multi-colour prints a separate screen is used for each colour of ink.

radar (Radio Detection and Ranging) Method of detecting objects and measuring their distance by bouncing radio waves off them. Radar is used in air traffic control systems to monitor the position of aircraft. Traffic police use radar to check the average speed of vehicles in a given area; the radio wave returns to the radar equipment at a different frequency from the outgoing wave, and the speed can be calculated from this difference. Astronomers use radar to investigate planets; the pattern of radar reflections mirrors the topography of a planet, such as the surface features of cloud-covered Venus. Weather forecasters also use radar – to detect rain; the radio waves are reflected from rain-drops. Radar was developed in Britain in the late 1930s. By the outbreak of World War II radar stations were being used to detect aircraft up to 160 km away.

radio Transmission of signals by the use of ▷RADIO WAVES, as in radio broadcasting. In radio transmission, signals representing sounds are combined with a radio wave that acts as a carrier. The sound signal changes, or modulates, the ▷AMPLITUDE (AM) or ▷FREQUENCY (FM) of the so-called carrier wave. The carrier wave is then broadcast. In the radio receiver, the carrier wave is demodulated and the sound signals retrieved. Guglielmo MARCONI pioneered what came to be called 'wireless telegraphy' in 1895. In 1906 Reginald Fessenden successfully transmitted speech for the first time, at a wireless station he had built in Massachusetts, USA. In South Africa, regular broadcasting officially started at 9 pm on 1 July 1924, when station JB broadcast speeches and a musical programme. The African Broadcasting Corporation – the forerunner of the ▷SABC – was formed in 1927.

recycling The processing of waste products so that they can be used again helps to save materials, and uses less energy than would be needed to make new products from raw materials. Recycling aluminium, for example, uses much less electricity than is used in extracting the metal from bauxite. Other metals that are recycled include the steel from car bodies, which is crushed and returned to steel works, and silver, extracted from used photographic film. Broken glass, separated into different colours, is melted in the furnace with the other ingredients used to make new glass; broken glass of mixed colours can only be used to make green glass. Waste paper is pulped, cleaned and bleached to remove most of the ink and dirt before being reused. The many different types of plastic, mostly made from oil, are cheap to produce so long as oil supplies are plentiful, giving little economic incentive to recycle them.

refrigerator Cold slows down the growth of the microorganisms that cause food to decay. A refrigerator works by circulating a cooling agent, or refrigerant, through pipes inside and outside the cabinet. The cooling agent is a substance that can change from liquid to vapour (a change that absorbs heat) and back from vapour to liquid (a change that releases heat). As it passes through the pipe inside the cabinet, the refrigerant, in liquid form, goes through an expansion valve, then evaporates and absorbs heat from the cabinet, causing the temperature to drop. The refrigerant, now a gas, is pumped into a compressor, and changes back to liquid form, losing heat from pipes at the back of the refrigerator. The liquid refrigerant then passes back to the expansion valve, and the cycle starts again, keeping the temperature of the domestic fridge at 0-5°C. Freon, a ▷CFC, was the most widely used refrigerant, but alternatives are now being introduced because of the damage CFCs cause to the Earth's ozone layer. The first mechanical domestic fridge was developed in 1879 when the German inventor Karl von Linde modified an industrial model he had designed six years earlier.

resistor Component in electronic circuits that resists the passage of electricity. Resistance is measured in ▷OHMS, named after Georg Simon Ohm, a German physicist who made the discovery of Ohm's law.

robot Mechanical device, usually controlled by computer, that simulates human actions. The industrial robots used in car factories are machines with flexible mechanical arms that carry out specific tasks according to a built-in computer program. More advanced robots may be fitted with sensors, such as 'electric eyes', so that they can recognize the shape of objects they handle and perform a wider range of jobs. About 95 per cent of the welding work on most vehicles is done by robots. ❖ The word 'robot' is derived from the Czech word *robota*, meaning slavery.

FLYING EYE *The American space shuttle* Discovery *blasts off in April 1990 carrying the Hubble Space Telescope. The telescope proved to be flawed, but it was repaired in December 1993.*

rocket Device or motor that is propelled by a stream of gases escaping from the rear. The gases are produced by burning fuel in oxygen; space rockets carry their own source of oxygen, and can therefore travel outside the Earth's atmosphere. The rocket's fuel and oxygen provider (oxidizer) are called its propellants. Most rockets use liquid propellants, such as paraffin or liquid hydrogen as fuels, and liquid oxygen as oxidiser. Rockets are the only engines that can develop enough speed to overcome the Earth's gravitational pull, and are used to launch satellites and space stations. Conventional rockets can be used only once, but the SPACE SHUTTLE is partly reusable. The American physicist and engineer Robert Hutchings Goddard launched the first liquid-fuelled rocket in 1926.

satellite Between 400 and 500 working artificial moons, or satellites, orbit the Earth, many of them relaying telephone calls and television signals between ground stations around the world. Most are positioned in geostationary orbit – about 35 900 km above the Earth's equator, the height at which they complete one orbit of the Earth in 24 hours. The satellites therefore appear stationary in the sky, and antennae of ground stations can be permanently locked onto them. *Telstar*, launched in 1962 (although not in geostationary orbit), carried the first live television pictures across the Atlantic. *Early Bird*, launched in 1965, could carry 240 simultaneous telephone conversations; the latest *Intelsat 6* communications satellites can each handle 30 000 telephone calls at a time. Weather satellites give a global view of cloud patterns, supplying information about weather over the oceans. Other satellites carry remote-sensing equipment, which uses different types of ▷ELECTROMAGNETIC RADIATION to collect information about, for example, surface vegetation, rock types and pollution. ❖ The first artificial satellite was the Soviet Union's *Sputnik 1*, launched on 4 October 1957, the 40th anniversary of the ▷RUSSIAN REVOLUTION. It measured 58 cm in diameter.

SEWING THE SEED *Many of the innovations in Isaac Singer's sewing machine of 1865 are still used in today's computerised units.*

semiconductor Material, such as silicon, that only partly conducts electricity, used to make electronic devices such as DIODES, RESISTORS and TRANSISTORS.

sewing machine First labour-saving device used widely in the home. The American inventor Elias Howe produced the forerunner of the modern sewing machine in 1846, but it was Isaac Singer, a mechanic from New York, who made the first machine for domestic use in 1851. Modern domestic machines still use the stitching mechanism of early machines.

smart card Plastic card like a credit card, but incorporating a MICROCHIP. It can carry details of previous transactions, the cardholder's credit balance and other financial details. The cards are also capable of carrying personal data, including photographs and fingerprints, and information that needs to be updated, such as medical records.

solar cell Device that converts solar energy into electricity. Solar cells are made from layers of silicon, specially treated to develop a voltage when sunlight falls on them. They are used to power satellites and pocket calculators, but are too expensive for large-scale generation of electricity.

❖ Solar panels, which are fitted on roofs facing the Sun, consist of liquid-filled pipes set in a dark material to absorb the maximum amount of heat. The heat absorbed by the liquid can then be used for domestic or industrial heating.

sonar (Sound Navigation and Ranging) Method of detection, communication and navigation used at sea, in which pulses of sound are sent out under water by a transmitter and reflected back as 'echos' by any object in their path, such as wrecks or submarines. Sonar is used for locating shoals of fish, mapping the ocean floor and the examination of shipwrecks.

space probe Spacecraft designed to escape the Earth's gravitational pull and explore the solar system. Probes have taken close-up pictures of all the planets except Pluto. The first space probe was the Soviet Union's *Luna 1*, launched in January 1959; after passing some 5 000 km from the Moon, it went into orbit around the Sun. The USA's *Viking* space probes explored Mars in 1976, mapping almost the entire planet; landing craft sent back close-up pictures of the red surface and tested the soil for signs of life – with no success. The US space probes *Voyager 1* and *Voyager 2* were launched in 1977 and have sent back pictures of Jupiter and Saturn. *Voyager 2* visited Uranus and Neptune in 1989 after a journey of seven billion kilometres.

space shuttle Space transport system, with a reusable winged space plane, or orbiter, built to carry astronauts, satellites and scientific equipment into space and back. The US space shuttle consists of the rocket-powered orbiter, which is the size of a medium airliner, riding on a large tank carrying fuel for the orbiter's engines; there are also two rocket boosters to provide extra power at lift-off. The orbiter and rocket boosters are reusable; when the orbiter returns to Earth, it lands on a runway. The shuttle was first launched in April 1981, with the orbiter *Columbia*.

❖ When the second orbiter, *Challenger*, was launched in January 1986, it exploded shortly after lift-off, killing all seven crew.

space station Large spacecraft with living and working space for crew, designed to remain in orbit for an extended period. The first space station was the Soviet Union's *Salyut 1*, launched in 1971. The USA launched the *Skylab* space station in 1973; at 27 m long, it was the largest space station ever launched. In 1986 the Soviet Union's *Mir* space station went into orbit; two Soviet cosmonauts completed a record 366-day stay in *Mir* in 1988. The space station *Freedom*, proposed by the USA's National Aeronautics and Space Administration (NASA), which was to have been a joint project with Europe, Japan and Canada in the mid-1990s, was shelved because of escalating costs.

stealth technology The design of military aircraft to make them 'invisible' to RADAR. An

STEALTHY *Innovative design and materials render the American B2 Stealth bomber invisible to radar. The most successful stealth plane is the Lockheed F-117 (inset).*

aircraft built using stealth technology is made of materials that absorb radio waves and its shape is designed to deflect radio waves, rather than reflect them back to their source. Special paints are also used. The USA's successful stealth plane, the Lockheed F-117 or 'Black Jet', was introduced in April 1990, and saw action in the 1991 ▷GULF WAR.

steam engine The first machine that harnessed the power of expanding steam to drive a piston back and forth in a cylinder was designed by Thomas Newcomen, an English blacksmith, in 1712; it was used to pump water out of mines. The engine was reliable but wasted much heat. James WATT, a Scottish instrument-maker, developed the steam engine, and in 1776 began manufacturing more efficient engines that were the main driving force behind the ▷INDUSTRIAL REVOLUTION. The steam piston engine was superseded by the INTERNAL-COMBUSTION ENGINE and the ELECTRIC MOTOR.

steel Strong, rigid alloy of iron, containing carbon and traces of other metals that is one of the world's major construction materials. Steel is made by refining pig iron from the BLAST FURNACE, often using the basic oxygen process in which a jet of pure oxygen is blasted at supersonic speed into the molten iron. The oxygen burns out impurities, including excess amounts of carbon. Steel was made on a large scale only after 1856, when the inventor Henry Bessemer patented a method of blowing air through molten pig iron in a pear-shaped container known as a Bessemer converter. Stainless steel, which was developed in 1913, usually contains 18 per cent chromium and 8 per cent nickel and is very resistant to corrosion.

❖ South Africa has the world's largest reserves of vanadium, used to harden steel.

RAILWAY PIONEER *George Stephenson perfected the design of the railway steam engine after building the* Rocket *in 1829. He foresaw Britain being crisscrossed by railways.*

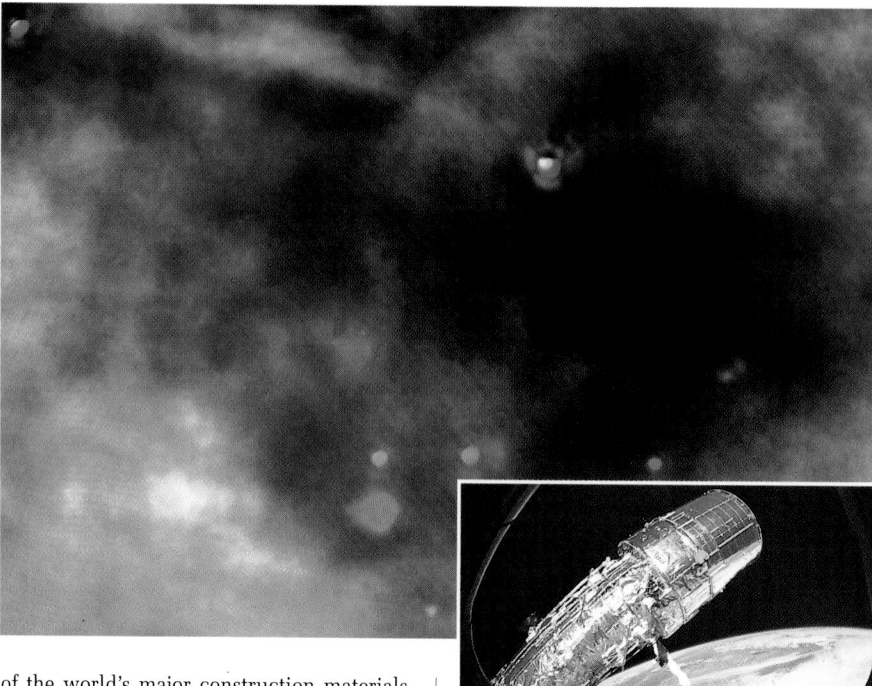

A STAR IS BORN *The birth of a star, upper centre, is the Orion Nebula as seen by the American Hubble Space Telescope. Inset, the telescope being placed in orbit in 1990.*

Stephenson, George (1781-1848) British-born engineer and pioneer of the passenger and freight-carrying steam TRAIN. Stephenson also invented a safety lamp in 1815. (See also George ▷STEPHENSON in 'Architecture and engineering'.)

submarine Underwater vessel that sinks by filling its ballast tanks with water and resurfaces by expelling the water with compressed air. Non-nuclear submarines use battery-powered electric propulsion under water and a diesel engine, which also recharges the batteries, at the surface. The forerunner of the modern submarine was built by an American, John Holland, in 1898. Germany used its first U-boat – *Unterseeboot* – to sink enemy shipping early in World War I, and inflicted heavy losses with U-boats during both world wars.

❖ Nuclear submarines can stay under water indefinitely, but are limited by the supplies they can store. In 1982-3, the British nuclear submarine HMS *Warspite* remained submerged for a record 111 days.

superglue Fast-acting, strongly bonding adhesive based on acrylic resin. In the tube, the resin is liquid and remains so because of the presence of a chemical stabilizer. When the adhesive is applied to a surface, the stabilizer is neutralized by moisture which is present on almost any surface exposed to air. This allows the resin molecules to join together in long chains and set into a plastic film that bonds the surfaces together.

Teflon Trade name for the plastic polytetrafluoroethylene (PTFE). One of the most slippery substances known, PTFE also resists very high temperatures and is affected by few chemicals. It is used for nonstick coatings on pans and other cooking utensils, as well as for coating skis.

❖ One of PTFE's first uses was the heat protection of spacecraft and missiles.

telephone A telephone's mouthpiece contains a microphone whose diaphragm is vibrated by sound waves. These vibrations are converted into electrical signals that travel to the earpiece of the person being called via copper cables, optical cables, communications satellites or CELLPHONE radio links. In the earpiece, the signals pass through the coils of a small electromagnet – causing its magnetism to fluctuate. This makes a diaphragm vibrate and sets up sound waves that are replicas of those that entered the microphone in the mouthpiece. The mouthpiece and earpiece have reverse functions and in modern telephones both are incorporated in a single handset. Alexander Graham BELL patented the telephone in the USA in 1876. The telephone network has developed substantially and now also carries fax messages, computer data and electronic mail, and, on videophones, images.

telescope The two basic types of optical instrument used to produce magnified images of distant objects are refractors, which use lenses to gather and focus light, and reflectors, which use mirrors. The most powerful telescopes are reflectors; on Mauna Kea in Hawaii, the world's biggest telescope, Keck I, has a segmented light-gathering mirror measuring 9,82 m across, so powerful it could detect the light from a candle more than 24 000 km away. The Hubble Space Telescope, which has been in orbit since 1990, is a reflecting telescope controlled remotely from Earth. Hans Lippershey, a Dutch spectaclemaker, built one of the first telescopes, using lenses, in 1608. A year later, the Italian scientist ▷GALILEO built an improved instrument which he used to observe the Moon, Venus and Jupiter. In 1668, Sir Isaac ▷NEWTON built the first reflecting telescope, and its mirror arrangement is still the one most used in amateur instruments today. Radio telescopes use a large metal dish to collect radio waves emitted by stars. Electronic circuits convert incoming signals into a visual image on a display screen.

television The British inventor John Logie BAIRD gave the world's first demonstration of television in 1925, and colour transmission was introduced by RCA in the USA in 1953. Inside the television camera, light is split up into its red, green and blue components, each of which is directed to a separate electron tube. Within each tube is a photoconductive layer which turns the light into tiny electric charges of varying intensities – the brighter the light, the greater the charge. A beam of electrons scans the photoconductive layer in a series of horizontal lines and the result is electrical signals that mirror the pattern of electric charges on the photosensitive layer. The signals are combined with a RADIO carrier wave and transmitted. A TV aerial picks up the carrier wave and feeds it to a television set. The signals are separated from the carrier wave and fed into the television's picture tube – a type of cathode-ray tube – that works like a television camera in reverse. Inside the tube, the red, green and blue picture signals are fed to three electron guns which produce electron beams of varying strength. The beams travel through a perforated mask and hit a phosphor-coated screen, making it glow. The mask ensures that the red signal beam hits phosphor that emits red light, the green signal beam hits phosphor that emits green light, and so on.

thermostat Device to maintain a preset temperature. The thermostat, used in equipment such as central heating systems, refrigerators, room and water heaters, irons and toasters, contains a bimetallic strip. It consists of two metals, which expand at different rates when heated, joined side by side. As the temperature changes the strip bends, and its bending and straightening causes the electric circuit to be turned on or off automatically at the preset temperature.

train From about the 14th century, horse-drawn trucks ran on wooden rails in European mines. The first steam locomotive was built by Richard Trevithick, an English engineer, in 1803, for the Coalbrookdale Ironworks in Shropshire. In 1825 the English engineer George STEPHENSON built the world's first public railway – 16 km of track between Stockton and Darlington – and the steam engine *Locomotion* which travelled on it. With his son Robert, Stephenson built the *Rocket* to run on the Liverpool and Manchester Railway, which opened in 1830. By 1841, some 2 000 km of track had been laid, and in 1851 railways carried 6 million people to London for the Great Exhibition. South Africa's first railway opened in Durban in 1860. The steam engine reached its greatest speed in 1938 when the British locomotive *Mallard* reached 203 km/h. An electric locomotive was first demonstrated in 1879, and it was adopted for underground railways to avoid the problem of smoke and dirt. The first electric underground railway, the 10 km City and South London Railway, was opened in 1890. Diesel locomotives first ran in Germany in 1912. In 1964 Japan introduced the streamlined electric *Shinkansen*, or 'bullet' train, which can travel at 255 km/h. France's electric TGV (*train à grande vitesse*) can cruise at 275 km/h and is the world's fastest passenger train. Experiments have been carried out with magnetic levitation, or maglev, in which the train 'floats' above the track, avoiding friction between wheels and track. In experiments in Germany and Japan, maglev trains have reached speeds of 500 km/h. (See also ▷RAILWAYS in 'Architecture and engineering'.)

❖ The South African Railways and Harbours Administration – forerunner of today's semi-privatized Transnet – was established in 1910 at Union and amalgamated the government railways of the Cape and Natal and the Central South African Railways.

transistor A SEMICONDUCTOR device that can amplify or control electrical signals in electronic circuits or act as a high-speed switch. It consists of a sandwich of three semiconductor materials. By feeding current to the middle of the 'sandwich', current between the outer layers of the transistor can be amplified or switched on or off. Developed in 1948, transistors were responsible for a revolution in electronics: they were far smaller than the thermionic valves that they replaced, required much less power and were more reliable. Transistors have become a major component in the integrated circuits on MICROCHIPS.

❖ The first transistor radios were developed in the USA in 1954, making pocket-sized radios possible for the first time.

Velcro Trade name for a plastic fastener that has become popular for use in clothing. It consists of minute hooks on one strip of material which catch loops on a facing strip. The Swiss engineer Georges de Mestral devised Velcro in 1948.

video recorder Also called videotape recorder (VTR) and videocassette recorder (VCR). Video recorders were first produced in the USA by Ampex in 1956, but home video recorders did not appear until the mid-1970s. Picture signals are recorded on broad MAGNETIC TAPE in much the same way as sounds are recorded in a tape recorder. But in contrast to a tape recorder, where the sound

HOOKED *The nylon hooks and loops of Velcro, magnified 20 times here, was inspired by the way burs cling to fur and clothing.*

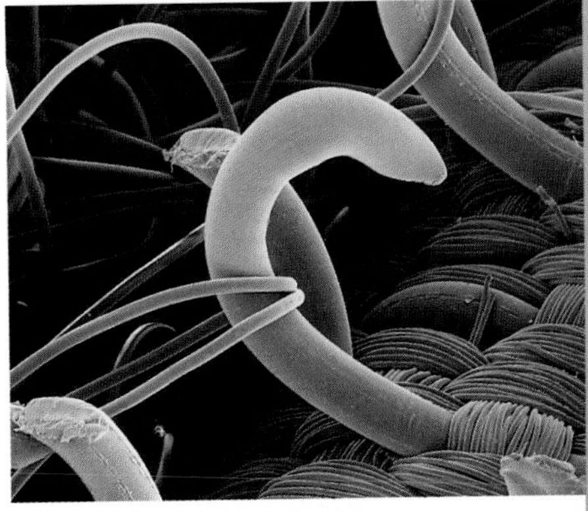

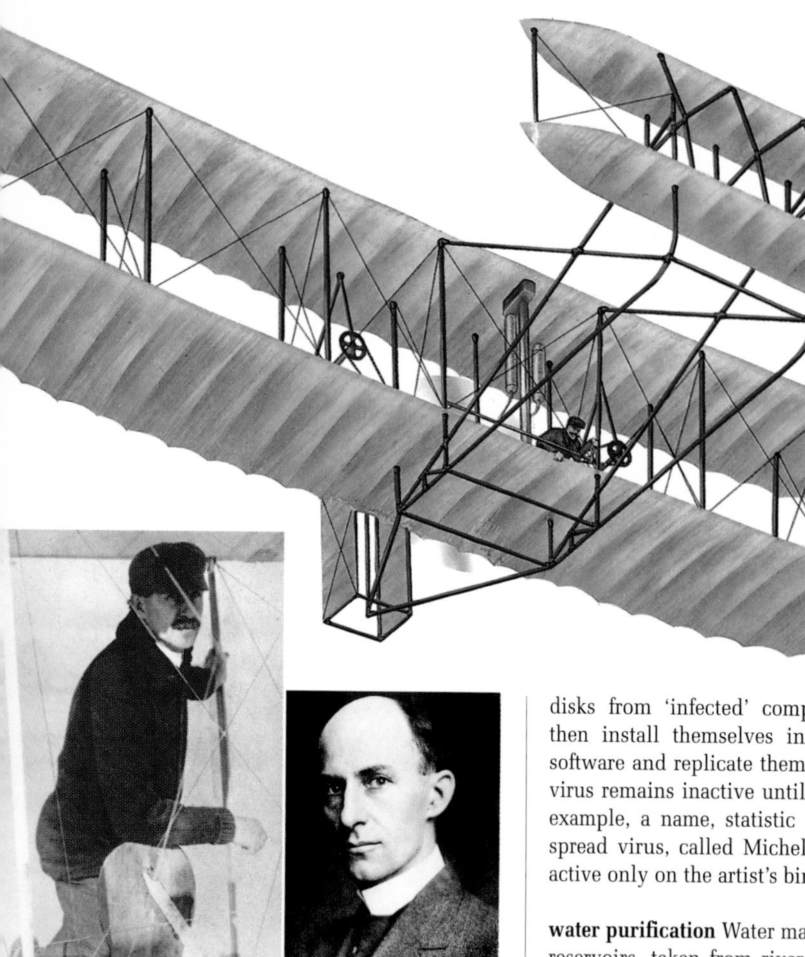

FIRST FLIGHT *Orville Wright (left) pilots the first powered flight by a heavier-than-air machine at Kitty Hawk in North Carolina in 1903. Later the same day Wilbur flew their aeroplane 251,5 m in 59 seconds.*

signals are recorded on lengthwise tracks, the picture signals are recorded as diagonal tracks to fit in more information. Home video camcorders have their own built-in video-recorder unit.

virtual reality Sophisticated simulator system, first developed in 1985, which enables the user to enter an imaginary world created by computer. The user wears special goggles and gloves, and 'moves around' the three-dimensional environment. Architects can walk around buildings which have not yet been built, for example, and cardiac surgeons can enter a simulated heart.

virus, computer Rogue COMPUTER PROGRAM, created intentionally to interfere with a computer's operation, leave cryptic messages or completely wipe out its memory. Viruses spread from computer to computer by way of disks from 'infected' computers; they can then install themselves in the computer's software and replicate themselves. Often the virus remains inactive until triggered by, for example, a name, statistic or date; a widespread virus, called Michelangelo, becomes active only on the artist's birthday, 6 March.

water purification Water may be collected in reservoirs, taken from rivers or pumped up from water-bearing rocks underground. To make it fit for use, it is first allowed to stand so that most suspended matter, such as algae and dirt, settles to the bottom; the water is treated chemically, then removed by filtration. Chlorine is used to kill any surviving microorganisms. Additional treatment sometimes is required to remove metals or nitrates that have entered the water from land used in agricultural production.

Watt, James (1736-1819) Scottish engineer who greatly improved the power and efficiency of the steam engine. In partnership with Matthew Boulton, he began manufacturing steam engines in Soho near Birmingham in 1776. They played a key role in the ▷INDUSTRIAL REVOLUTION. Watt coined the term 'horsepower' and gave his name to the ▷WATT, a unit of power.

wheel One of the most important of human inventions, the wheel was being used by potters by 3500 BC, just before wheeled vehicles were first used in Sumeria and southern Poland. Spoked wheels were fitted to high-speed war chariots in Egypt and Syria by 2000 BC. Toothed gear wheels, pulleys and water wheels to turn stones for grinding corn were all used by the 1st century BC. The flywheel – a heavy wheel or disc that rotates on a shaft and stores energy – was first used in 1781 when James WATT fitted one to his steam engine. Before the mid-19th century, wheels were protected by iron tyres, which damaged roads and were noisy. Pneumatic tyres were invented in 1845 by the Scottish engineer Robert Thomson. His 'aerial wheels' ran for more than 1 900 km, but proved too expensive to be commercially successful. They were further developed by John Boyd Dunlop in 1888, and adopted for bicycles. The French rubber manufacturer Michelin made an important breakthrough fitting pneumatic tyres to a Peugeot motor car in 1895.

word processor COMPUTER system designed to manipulate text and, often, illustrations. Modern word-processing software can produce sophisticated documents in a range of typefaces; it is often also used for sophisticated desk-top publishing (DTP).

Wright brothers Wilbur (1867-1912) and Orville (1871-1948) Wright – American pioneers of flight. The brothers were inspired by Otto Lilienthal's gliding and perfected their piloted glider in 1902. They made the first powered flight on 17 December 1903, at Kill Devil Hill, near Kitty Hawk, North Carolina. On its maiden voyage, their aircraft, *Flyer*, with Orville steering, flew for 12 seconds against a strong wind and covered 37 m. Wilbur later flew 260 m in 59 seconds.

Zeppelin, Count Ferdinand von (1838-1917) German pioneer of the rigid, metal-framed airship. In 1900 Zeppelin, on retiring from the army, built his first cigar-shaped craft – 128 m long, with an aluminium frame covered with cotton. The craft contained huge bags of hydrogen, which is lighter than air, to provide lift. During World War I he went on to supply many 'zeppelins' for military use, some of which made bombing raids over Britain. Zeppelin also helped to pioneer large multi-engine bomber planes.

❖ Travel by airship was fashionable during the 1920s and 1930s, even though 48 people died when Britain's *R101* crashed in 1930. However, in 1937 the *Hindenburg*, the world's largest airship, burst into flames, signalling the end of the airship era.

Zworykin, Vladimir (1889-1982) Russian-born American physicist who in 1923 invented the iconoscope, the first electronic television camera tube. Zworykin's system soon superseded the mechanical system of John Logie BAIRD. He also made important contributions to the development of the electron MICROSCOPE.

Index

The index is arranged letter-by-letter. In a general index of this sort, definitions are often required to distinguish different terms. Definitions are given in brackets and have been ignored when determining the filing sequence [eg Alexandra (*township*) comes before Alexandra Arts Centre]. Surnames are filed before entries of the same word [eg Black, Stephen before *Black Angel*]. Also, a single word followed by a comma is filed before two or more words [eg Agulhas, Cape comes before Agulhas Bank]. Titles such as *Sir* or *Dame* are ignored in the alphabetization.

Abbreviations:
Capt = Captain;
Gen = General;
SA = South Africa;
UK = United Kingdom;
USA = United States of America

Numbers in bold indicate a main entry which may or may not be illustrated. Numbers in *italics* refer to an illustration that does not accompany a main entry.

A

B

C

E

G

H

I

L

M

P

Q

R

S

X

Y

Z

Picture credits

Picture credits for each page read from top to bottom using the top of the picture as the reference point. Where the tops of two or more pictures are on the same level, credits read from left to right.

ABPL – Anthony Bannister Photo Library; BAL – The Bridgeman Art Library; BC – Bruce Coleman Ltd; BN – Bettmann Newsphotos; CA – Cape Archives Depot; HDC – The Hulton Deutsch Collection; IB – The Image Bank; Inpra – International Press Agency; KC – The Kobal Collection; LHM – Local History Museum; MA – Museum Africa; MC – The Mansell Collection; MEPL – Mary Evans Picture Library; MH – Michael Holford; MvA – Mark van Aardt; NPG – National Portrait Gallery, London; RD – Reader's Digest; Rex – Rex Features Limited; RGA – The Ronald Grant Archive; SABC – South African Broadcasting Corporation; SAL – South African Library; SANG – South African National Gallery; SPL – Science Photo Library; SU – Source Unknown; TA – Transvaal Archives

4 (Astaire) KC; (Embryo) SPL/Petit Format/NestlÈ; (Sunflowers) BAL/National Gallery, London/Index; (Aphrodite) MH; (Cetshwayo) LHM; (Table Mountain) MvA; (Kennedy) Camera Press/F. Bachrach; Cry, the Beloved Country by Alan Paton (Longman, Green & Co.) **5** (Violin) Bildarchiv Preussischer Kulturbesitz; (Einstein) SPL/US Library of Congress; (Madonna) MH; (Mandela) Rex; (Rocket) Science Museum, London; (Beryllium) SPL/Michael Gilbert; (Volcano) Explorer/K. Krafft; (Eastwood) British Film Institute; (Pisa) ZEFFA; (Sumo) All-Sport (UK)/Chris Cole **10** MA **14** MEPL; Designed by Julian Rothenstein/from 'Alphabets & Other Signs'; MEPL/Explorer **25** MEPL **28** MEPL **29** EMI Archives **30** ET Archive **32** MA **33** Valerie Rosenberg Collection; *The Star* **34** *Cry the Beloved Country* by Alan Paton (Longman, Green & Co); Video Vision Entertainment **35** Capab Archives **36** *Jock of the Bushveld* by Percy FitzPatrick (Longman, Green & Co) **37** Peter Baasch **38** SU; SAL **39** Nasionale Pers Syndications **40** Bailey's Photo Archives/Bob Gosani **42** Camera Press; MEPL **43** BAL; Inpra/Rex **44** ET Archive; Jakob Skou-Hansen; Royal Library, Copenhagen **45** NPG **46** Novosti; © Glasgow Museum & Art Galleries **47** Popperfoto **48** RGA **49** RD **50** Popperfoto **51** NPG; KC/Columbia Pictures **52** RGA **53** (Background) British Film Institute; NPG; The Penguin Group **54** KC **55** Tromsö Museum; HDC **56** NPG **57** NPG **58** Illustration of 'Rivendell' by J R R Tolkien © George Allen & Unwin (Publishers), 1937. Reproduced courtesy of HarperCollins Publishers **60** Popperfoto; ET Archive **61** BAL/Musée Condé Chantilly **62** The Estate of Edmund Dulac (the publishers have been unable to trace copyright) **63** Popperfoto; From the collections of the Theatre Museum by courtesy of the Trustees of the Victoria & Albert Museum, London **64** HDC **66** Donald Cooper **67** *The Cat in the Hat* by Dr Seuss (Random House, 1957) **68** Courtesy of the Trustees of the Victoria & Albert Museum, London; Pat Hodgson **69** Little Theatre, University of Cape Town **70** Statens Konstmuseer, Stockholm **71** BAL/National Museum of Wales, Cardiff/By permission of Mrs Vivian White; Novosti **72** RGA **73** Inpra/Sygma; Inpra **74** NPG; BAL/Musée D'Orsay, Paris **76** MEPL; MH **77** Bibliothèque Nationale, Paris (Ms. Fr. 343 f. 3) **78** MH **79** Walter Knirr **80** MEPL **81** RD/Sheila Nowers **82** MEPL **84** Popperfoto; MEPL; MC **85** SAL (kha. af. 1700) **86** MC **87** MEPL **88** MEPL **89** MEPL **90** RD **92** *The Argus;* Lucian Niemeyer – LNS Arts **93** BAL **94** BAL/National Gallery, London **95** Permission of the Trustees of the British Museum; Giraudon; Frank Spooner **96** BAL/Bibliothèque Nationale, Paris **97** MH/Prado, Madrid **98** The Israel Museum, Jerusalem; Robert Harding Picture Library/Christina Gascoigne; MEPL **100** Board of General Purposes of the United Grand Lodge of England; BAL/Giraudon **101** Black Star, New York/St Louis Post Dispatch **102** Magnum/Philip Jones Griffiths; MH **104** Magnum/F Mayer **105** Archiv für Kunst und Geschichte, Berlin/Munchen, Bayerische Staatsbibliothek (cod. arab. 1113 fol. 4v) **106** Frank Spooner/Mohamed Lounes **107** SAL; Superstock **108** BAL/Courtauld Institute Galleries; MEPL **109** MH **110** African Images/Mark Tennant **111** The Quaker Tapestry Scheme; Religious Society of Friends **112** MEPL; MEPL/Ida Kar **113** Rex; The Salvation Army **114** Museo del Prado, Madrid **115** Metropolitan Museum of Art/Wolfe Fund, 1931. Catherine Lorillard Wolfe Collection (31.45) **116** MH; SouthLight/David Gilkey **118** Emporio Armani; BAL/By courtesy of the Trustees of theVictoria & Albert Museum, London; Angelo Hornak **119** SANG **120** BAL/Prado, Madrid **121** Cortauld Institute of Art **122** BAL/By courtesy of the Trustees of the Victoria & Albert Museum, London **123** BAL/Metropolitan Museum of Art, New York **124** MH **125** BAL **126** The National Gallery, London **127** RD **128** BAL/Tate Gallery/© David Hockney **129** BAL/© Jasper Johns/DACS, London/VAGA, New York 1995 **130** SANG/Sanlam Collection/© University Museum, Stellenbosch; Archiv für Kunst und Geschichte, Berlin/Erich Lessing/Nationalgalerie, Prague **131** BAL **132** National Trust for Scotland **133** Reunion des Musées Nationaux **134-5** BAL/Vatican Museums & Galleries, Rome **136** Tate Gallery, London **137** BAL; SANG/© 1995 John Muafengejo Trust *Battle of Rorke's Drift* **138** BAL/© The Munch Museum/The Munch-Ellingsen Group/DACS 1995 **139** Cortauld Institute of Art/Hunter Bequest 1982/By permission of Angela Verren-Taunt **140** BAL/Prado, Madrid/© DACS 1995 **141** San Francisco Museum of Modern Art, Albert M Bender Collection, Albert M Bender Bequest Fund Purchase/© ARS, NY and DACS, London 1995; HDC **142** © TMR/ADAGP, Paris 1993, Collection L Treillard; BAL/Kenwood House **143** BAL/John Hay Whitney Collection, New York **144** Studio Des Grands Augustins/Photographer, J F Chavannes; The Cleveland Museum of Art, Gift of the Hanna Fund, 49. 186 **145** BAL/Prado, Madrid; SANG **146** BAL/Art Institute of Chicago, USA; SANG/© Penny Siopis **147** SANG **148** Christie's Colour Library; BAL/By courtesy of the Board of Trustees of the Victoria & Albert Museum, London **149** BAL/National Gallery, London **150** Superstock **151** MvA; BAL/© 1995 Andy Warhol Foundation for the Visual Arts/ARS, New York **152** SANG **154** MH **155** IB/Steve Krongard; RETORIA: Y Futagawa & Associated Photographers **156** Christie's Colour Library; Ullstein; HDC **157** RD **158** BAL/Fitzwilliam Museum, University of Cambridge; Giraudon/Lauros **159** Giraudon/Lauros **160** MvA; IB/Jeff Hunter **161** IB/Joe McNally; Robert Harding Picture Library **162** IB/P & G Bowater; Arcaid/Stephen Couturier; Magnum/René Burri **163** IB/Derik Berwin **164** MvA **165** MvA **166** IB/Robbie Newman **167** IB/Thomas Rampy **168** Arcaid/Scott Frances/Esto; IB/David Gould **170** Colorific/Penny Tweedie **171** Magnum/Eve Arnold **172** Colorific/Dilip Mehta/Contact **173** Topham Picture Library; The Penguin Group **175** Bryan & Cherry Alexander **176** Camera Press; The Freud Museum **177** SouthLight/Brett Eloff **178** SA Communication Services **179** SouthLight/Graeme Williams; Both Shawn Benjamin **180** Camera Press/Karsh of Ottawa; Courtesy of the Trustees of the Victoria & Albert Museum, London **181** UPI/BN **182** The Hutchison Picture Library/John Hatt **183** Magnum/Ernst Haas **185** MvA; SouthLight **188** Walter Knirr; SAL **189** SAL/*Illustrated London News* **190** LHM; MA **191** Mayibuye Centre; Walter Knirr **192** MA; CA/AG15332 **193** William Fehr Collection **194** LHM; Both SA Communication Services **195** TA/TAB31132 **196** LHM **197** SAL; Jürgen Schadeberg **198** Popperfoto; CA/E2151 **199** MA/B123 **200** TA/TAB14577 **201** RD; AAC/De Beers Photographic **202** CA/AG1414; AAC/De Beers Photographic **203** CA/E386; CA/E3309; MA **204** MA; MvA; CA/M247 **205** CA/AG14328 **206** CA/AG12106; MA **207** CA/AG2882 **208** SU **209** SAL; MA **210** CA/AG894; MvA **211** Bailey's Photo Archives; MA **212** *The Star;* LHM; Elite Press Agency **213** MA **214** CA/J1163; *The Star* **215** Robert Botha/Business Day **216** SU **217** Both *The Cape Times* **218** *The Star*/Barnett Collection; MA **220** The Granger Collection **221** Culver Pictures, New York; Popperfoto **222** Scala **224** HDC **225** HDC **226** The Associated Press **227** MEPL **228** Topham Picture Library; HDC **229** Bibliothèque Nationale, Paris **230** Private Collection **232** MC; Ashmolean Museum, Oxford **233** Jean-Loup Charmet **234** HDC **235** Both Rex/© Sipa-Press **236** NPG **237** Lee Boltin Picture Library **239** Camera Press; Camera Press; Camera Press/F. Bachrach **240** Rex **241** Bulloz, Paris **242** 'Execution of Mary Queen of Scots' Scottish National Portrait Gallery; 'Mary Queen of Scots' after Clouet, Scottish National Portrait Gallery **243** Popperfoto **244** Tate Gallery, London **245** Rex **246** ET Archive **247** Scala; Archivi Alinari/Giacomo Brogi **248** HDC; Underwood & Underwood **249** NPG; MC **251** Aspect/Kelly Langley **252** Imperial War Museum; Magnum/Robert Capa **253** Popperfoto; MEPL **254** Magnum/Stuart Franklin; Frank Spooner/Chip Hires **255** Robert Harding Picture Library/F L Kenett **256** The Associated Press/Nguyen Kong (Nick Ut) **257** BAL/by courtesy of the Victoria & Albert Museum, London/Stapleton Collection **258** Private Collection/US Army **260** *The Argus* **261** Rex/Sipa **263** SouthLight/Tim Facey **264** HDC **265** Rex; Topham Picture Library **269** BBC **270** UPI/BN; Frank Spooner/Gamma/Sebah **271** Inpra/© Imapress **272** Rex/Today; Rex/Sipa-Press **273** MC; ET Archive **275** UPI/BNI; Popperfoto **276** Rex/*The Times;* Rex **277** Rex/Sipa-Press **279** Inpra/Rex/David Browne **281** Camera Press; ET Archive; BAL/National Archives Trust, Pennsylvania, USA **282** Sygma/O L Atlan **283** *The Star* **284** *The Argus* **285** SouthLight/Henner Frankenfeld; *The Argus* **286** SouthLight/Gisele Wulfsohn **287** Topham Picture Library; Photo Access/FPG International Corp **288** Sygma/De Keerle/F Grochowiak **290** Armscor **291** Baring Brothers & Co Ltd **292** Both AAC/De Beers Photographic **293** UPI/BN; HDC **294** John Frost Historical Newspaper Service **295** HDC/Bettman; UPI/BN **297** Popperfoto; The Fotomas Index **298** Walter Knirr **299** Lloyd's of London; Magnum/S Franklin **300** HDC **305** Scripophily International Promotions **308** RGA **309** RGA; KC **310** The Joel Finler Collection; Pictorial Press **311** RGA **312** British Film Institute; KC **313** ET Archive/DC Thomson & Co Ltd 'The Beano' & 'The Dandy'/Hulton/News of the World/Beaverbrook **314** KARSH/Camera Press/Inpra; Fotos International/Inpra **315** SABC; British Film Institute **316** SABC; RGA **317** KC **318** KC **319** 1820 Foundation **320** KC **321** Grahamstown Foundation **322** KC; RGA **323** KC **325** Movie Stills Archives **327** SABC **329** KC **330** All KC **331** KC **332** Mimosa Films **333** KC; HDC; KC **334** Pictorial Press **336** Both KC **337** Angermuseum, Erfurt **338** Redferns; Collection Dr H C Bodmer, Beethoven-Archiv **339** Camera Press; KC **340** From the collection of the Theatre Museum by courtesy of the Trustees of the Victoria & Albert Museum, London **341** Inpra/Keith Wiseman **342** Redferns **343** David Kramer **344** Camera Press/Snowdon **345** From the collection of the Theatre Museum by courtesy of the Trustees of the Victoria & Albert Museum, London; NPG **346** Redferns William Gottlieb **347** Redferns Mick Hutson; *The Argus* **348** Pictorial Press; Photo File **349** From the collection of the Theatre Museum by courtesy of the Trustees of the Victoria & Albert Museum, London **350** Popperfoto; Foto File/Alpha; Redferns Michael Linssen **351** Photo File/Sipa-Press; Inpra/Redferns Dave Peabody **352** Internationale Gesellschaft für Musikwissenschaft; Archiv für Kunst und Geschichte, Berlin/Erich Lessing **353** Sygma/M Polak **354** Teatro alla Scala, Milan/Elena Fumagalli **355** Pictorial Press; United States Postal Service **356** Elite/Sue Moore **357** Rex/Guzelian **358** Video Vision Entertainment **359** Capab Archives **360** HDC; ZEFA/K Collignon **361** Elite **362** Inpra/Sygma **364** *Sports Illustrated*/Colorific/Neil Leifer; Topham Picture Library **365** BAL/Marleybone Cricket Club, London **366** (All cards) National Baseball Hall of Fame; Sport and General Press Agency **367** Touchline/Allsport **368** The Press Association Ltd; Express Newspapers; HDC; Topham Picture Library **369** *The Argus* **370** *The Argus* **371** Both Touchline/Allsport **372** MC **373** Touchline/Allsport **374** Touchline/Allsport **375** All-Sport (UK); HDC **376** Permission of the Board of the British Library/News International; Bob Thomas **377** Both Touchline/Allsport **378** Robert Opie; *The Argus* **379** (Greek runners) MH (Discobolos) MC (1936 Olympics) International Olympic Committee (Jesse Owens) HDC **380** Touchline/Allsport; *The Argus* **381** *The Argus* **382** Touchline/Thomas Turck **383** Touchline/Allsport **384** *The Star* **385** All-Sport (UK)/Chris Cole **386** Both Graham Watson **387** Touchline/Allsport **388** *The Argus* **390** MC; MEPL **398** Walter Knirr **399** Walter Knirr **400** Anthony Bannister/ABPL **401** Richard du Toit/ABPL **402** Brendan Ryan/ABPL **403** MvA; Roger de la Harpe/ABPL **404** MvA **405** Walter Knirr; Walter Knirr; Roger de la Harpe/ABPL **406** Anthony Bannister/ABPL **407** Walter Knirr **408** Walter Knirr; Joan Ryder/ABPL **409** Richard du Toit/ABPL; Walter Knirr **410** Walter Knirr; MvA **411** Walter Knirr **412** Phillip Richardson/ABPL **413** Hein von Horsten/ABPL **414** Roger de la Harpe/ABPL **416** NHPA/Anthony Bannister **417** Walter Knirr **419** Walter Knirr **420** Walter Knirr **421** Both Walter Knirr **422** MvA **424** RD **425** IB/J Ramey; Colin Monteath Hedgehog House, NZ **426** RD **427** IB/Paul Slaughter; RD **428** IB/Hans Wolf **430** ZEFA **431** Comstock Photofile Limited **432** Aspect/GeoffCarey; Colorific/Patrick Ward **433** Corific/Snowden/Hoyer/Focus **434** Aspect/Peter Carmichael **435** Andy Williams **436** RD **437** IB/T Williams; Aspect/Michael Hilgert **438** Larry Ulrich Photography **439** IB/Francisco Hidalgo **440** Fotostock **442** Tim Woodcock **443** Aerofilms **444** Photo Access/Visual Communications **445** Superstock **446** Magnum/Inge Morath **447** Photographic Ent/Heaton **448** RD **449** Fotostock **450** ZEFA Streichan **451** ZEFA/Arbril **452** Telegraph Colour Library/VCL; IB/DW Hamilton **453** Aspect/Adrian Greeman **455** RD **456** Colorific/Owen Franklin; ZEFA/Pacific Stock **458** Colorific/Lee Day/Black Star **460** IB/Bernard van Berg **461** Aspect/Horst Gossler **462** Photo Access/Getaway/P Wagner **464** RD; SPL/Pekka Parviainen **465** (Mares' tails) SPL/Gordon Garradd (Altostratus) Thomas Ives (Cumulonimbus) Thomas Ives (Altocumulus) Thomas Ives **466** RD **467** Sygma/Paul X Scott **468** SPL/David Parker; RD **469** SPL/Omikron **470** Thomas Ives **471** RD **472** RD **473** NHPA/George Gainsburgh **474** Larry Ulrich Photography; Auscape/Reg Morrison; Landscape Only/Images Colour Library Limited/Colin Jones; Photo Access/Walter Knirr **475** Explorer/K Kraft **476** Anthony Bannister/ABPL; RD **478** Clem Haagner/ABPL **479** BC/Neville Coleman; Planet Earth Pictures/F C Millington; Planet Earth Pictures/Brian Kenney **480** Oxford Scientific Films/Michael Fogden **481** RD; Rest Oxford Scientific Films **482-3** RD **483** Giraudon **484** SPL/Dr A Lesk, Laboratory of Molecular Biology; SPL/Driscoll, Youngquist & Baldeschwieler, Caltech; BC/John Burton **485** RD **487** RD; SPL **488** Oxford Scientific Films/Breck P Kent/Animals Animals; Oxford Scientific Films/Rudie Kuiter; Oxford Scientific Films/David Wrigglesworth; Rest Oxford Scientific Films/Rudie Kuiter **489** BC/Dr Frieder Sauer; BC/Neill McAllister; Nigel Dennis/ABPL; Hein von Horsten/ABPL **490** RD **491** Anne & Jacques Six **492** RD/Dave Snook **494** The Wellcome Institute Library, London; Impact/Agiajara/Visions **495** SPL/NIBSC **496** Michael Joseph Ltd from 'American Dream' 1993 Copyright Line Drawings © Stephen Wiltshire 1995; Michael Joseph Ltd from 'American Dream' 1993 **497** © Boehringer Ingelheim International GmbH/Photo, Lennart Nilsson, THE INCREDIBLE MACHINE, National Geographic Society **498** RD; Dr Richard Haier, University of California, Psychiatry Dept **499** SPL; RD **500** Both SPL/Adam Hart-Davis **501** SPL/Manfred Kage; RD **502** RD; SPL/Dr G Oran **503** RD **504** All SPL/Petit Format/Nestlé **505** Roger de la Harpe ABPL **506** The Wellcome Institute Library, London **508** The Wellcome Institute Library, London **509** RD; SPL/Prof P Motta/Dept of Anatony, University 'La Sapienza', Rome **511** RD; SPL/CNRI; SPL/Dr Brian Eyden **512** SPL/Don Fawcett; RD **513** Roger-Viollet **515** Photo Access/Visual Communications **516** RD; SPL/Prof P Motta/Dept of Anatomy, University 'La Sapienza', Rome **518** RD/Dave Snook **519** *The Star;* Camera Press; Popperfoto **522** Courtesy of MIRA **523** MC; SPL/Michael Gilbert **524** SPL/Julian Baum **525** SPL/Brookhaven National Laboratory; SPL/Patrice Loeiz, CERN **526** RD; All-Sport (UK)/Gray Mortimore **527** RD; MC **528** RD **529** RD; SPL/Rev Ronald Royer; RD; SPL/US Library of Congress **530** MH **531** SPL/Dr Seth Shostak; SPL/Gregory Sams; SPL/Dr Fred Espenak **532** Scala **533** SPL/European Space Agency; SPL/Harvard College Observatory; SPL/Royal Greenwich Observatory **534** SPL/Peter Aprahamian; SPL/NASA **535** RD **536-7** SPL/US Geological Survey **538** SPL/Royal Greenwich Observatory; NPG; RD **539** RD **540** Both SPL/CERN **541** HDC; RD **543** SPL/David Parker; Topham Picture Library **544-5** RD **546** Photo Access/Telegraph Colour Library **548** SPL; RD **550** SPL/NASA **551** HDC; MEPL; MEPL; All-Sport (UK)/Bruno Bade/Vandystadt **552** RD **553** SPL/Damien Lovegrove; Philips Home Appliances; The Science Museum, London **554** British Airways **555** US Department of the Interior, National Park Service Edison Historical Site; UPI/BN **556** SPL/Adam Hart-Davis; SPL/Martin Dohrn **557** UPI/BN; SPL/Philippe Plailly **558** GEC-Marconi Ltd **559** SPL/Michael W Davidson; SPL/Charles Falco **560** HDC; MEPL **562** SPL; The Science Museum, London **563** Rex/Sipa-Press; Sygma **564** SPL/Space Telescope Science Institute/NASA; SPL/NASA; HDC; The Science Museum, London **565** SPL/Dr Jeremy Burgess **566** RD; HDC; Popperfoto.

Front cover: Scala; IB/Steve Krongard; MH; Anne & Jacques Six; Walter Knirr; Foto File/Sipa-Press; SPL/Dr Jeremy Burgess
Back cover: MEPL; RD; RD; IB/J. Ramey; Topham Picture Library; Courtesy of the Trustees of the Victoria & Albert Museum, London; Angelo Hornak; Rex/Today
Spine: RD

Reproduction by Unifoto (Pty) Ltd, Cape Town
Printed by Toppan Printing Co (S) Pte Ltd, Singapore